# SOCIOLOGY

ROBERT HAGEDORN

# SOCIOLOGY

## FOURTH EDITION

Holt, Rinehart and Winston of Canada, Limited
Toronto

**Canadian Cataloguing in Publication Data**

Main entry under title:
Sociology

4th ed.
Bibliography: p.
Includes index.
ISBN 0-03-922590-9

1. Sociology.   I. Hagedorn, Robert, 1925 –

HM51.S63   1990      301      C89-094267-6

Publisher: Dave Dimmell
Developmental Editor: Sandra Peltier
Publishing Services Manager: Karen Eakin
Editorial Co-ordinator: John Caldarone
Production Editor: Marcel Chiera
Copy Editor: Riça Night
Cover and Interior Design: John Zehethofer
Typesetting and Assembly: Q Composition Inc.
Printing and Binding: John Deyell Company

Printed in Canada

1  2  3  4  5     94  93  92  91  90

# Preface

This book presents in clear and simple prose an overview of the discipline of sociology using the best Canadian data available. Its goals include describing how sociologists view the social world, how they discover what that world is, and what we currently know about that world.

There are two major problems in accomplishing these goals. The first is that sociology, like other physical and social sciences, is faced with growing specialization. As the amount of information in each area of sociology increases, it becomes impossible to know everything about all of them. Increasingly, there is specialization even within single areas — formal organizations, the family, and political sociology, for example. This means that no one person is an expert in "sociology." Some idea of the diversity can be seen in the fact that more than 40 different courses are listed in guides to graduate departments of sociology. Along with these courses and sections there has been a tremendous increase in the number of journals related to subareas.

A simple solution to the problem of specialization is to use specialists to write the various chapters. This is the approach taken here. A question arises as to why such a solution is rarely used in writing introductory sociology textbooks. The answer lies in the problem of presenting writing that is always clear, interesting, and consistent in style. Our solution to this problem was twofold. First, all authors were asked to approach their subareas using three main theoretical perspectives, which helped to tie the chapters together. Second, each chapter was carefully edited for style, clarity, and interest. Whether we have achieved our goals will be determined by you.

Consistent with these goals are the book's organization and features. The text's eighteen chapters are divided into six sections. The sections represent very general but distinct sociological categories that unite the individual chapters. The chapters present an overview of the major sociological areas. Many of these areas (for example, deviance and the family) can be studied in more detail in upper-division and graduate courses. In this sense, each chapter represents an introduction to an area of specialization in sociology.

Features of the book are designed to make learning and remembering easier. These include the use of cross-references between chapters to integrate important ideas and information; pictures to reinforce the written text; boldface type to identify important terms; and boxed readings to illustrate major points. At the end of each chapter you will find a summary of the major points, a glossary that simplifies looking up definitions, and an annotated list of further readings.

The instructor's manual contains test banks of objective questions constructed by the authors, as well as study questions, research projects, and, in many cases, suggestions for films to supplement the text. The test-bank questions are also available on disks for use on microcomputers.

I would like to express a special thanks to the reviewers of the third edition: Ron Hinch, University of Guelph; Charles Hobart, University of Alberta; Hugh Lautard, University of New Brunswick; and Stephen Richer, Carleton University. I would also like to thank all the students who sent in a reply card, and encourage teachers and students to continue letting us know how to improve this text.

ROBERT HAGEDORN
JANUARY 1990

# CONTRIBUTORS

**Reginald W. Bibby**
University of Lethbridge

**James E. Curtis**
University of Waterloo

**Leo Driedger**
University of Manitoba

**Patricia Fitzsimmons-LeCavalier**
Carleton University

**Ellen M. Gee**
Simon Fraser University

**A.R. Gillis**
University of Toronto

**John Hagan**
University of Toronto

**Robert Hagedorn**
University of Victoria

**R. Alan Hedley**
University of Victoria

**Ronald D. Lambert**
University of Waterloo

**Guy LeCavalier**
Concordia University

**Jos. L. Lennards**
Glendon College, York University

**Marlene Mackie**
University of Calgary

**Victor W. Marshall**
University of Toronto

**R. Ogmundson**
University of Victoria

**Harvey Rich**
University of Calgary

**Carolyn J. Rosenthal**
University of Toronto

**Terrence H. White**
Brock University

# Contents

# Detailed Contents

## Social Institutions

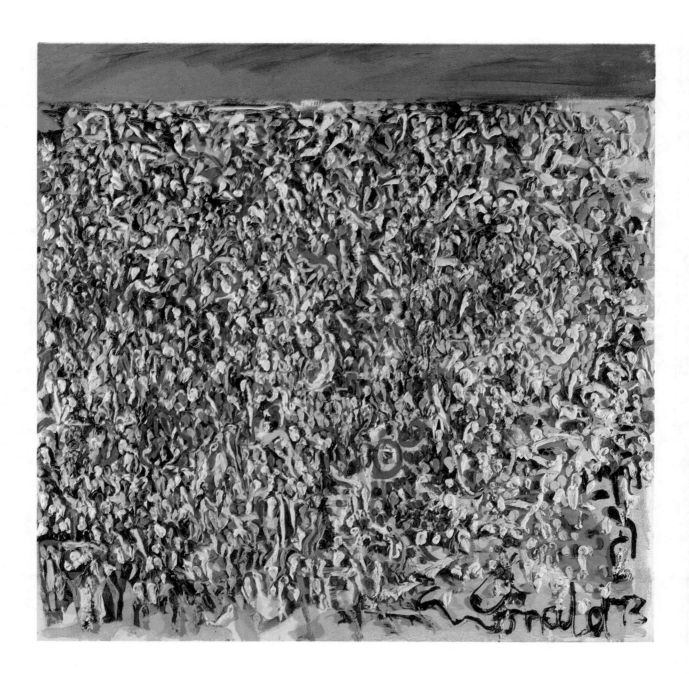

# U N I T   I

# The Field of Sociology

*The first section of this book provides an overview of what is generally called theory. Chapter 1 examines the nature of sociology, paying particular attention to current perspectives in sociology and their historical development. The theoretical perspectives of sociology are the lenses through which sociologists see. The answers you get depend on the questions you ask, and the questions you ask depend on the perspective you use. Perspectives determine what you look at and how you see it. Perspectives, therefore, define sociology.*

*Is a group of people a collection of individuals, or does it have properties of its own? Is society stable, or changing? Do we share basic values, or are we essentially in conflict? The answers to these questions define sociological perspectives, which in turn determine what you will measure, what you will look for, which then determines what you find and what answers you get.*

*In sociology there are three major contemporary perspectives: conflict, structural functionalism, and symbolic interaction. These are discussed in the first chapter and are used throughout the book.*

# C H A P T E R  1

# What Is Sociology?

ROBERT HAGEDORN

Right now you are probably asking yourself, What am I getting into? What is this book about? What is sociology?

To many people, sociology is the most exciting subject on earth — a fresh, lively, coherent, and valuable way of understanding people and the world we live in. For some people, sociology is so compelling that they invest their entire professional careers in learning it, teaching it, and doing it. As Table 1-1 shows, people trained in sociology work in a wide variety of jobs; their knowledge and research influence many decisions that affect our everyday lives.

Sociology is a young science — only about a hundred years old. Like all youngsters, sociology ripples with energy, with promise, with insights, and with the sure sense that what it is doing is important.

Sociology is important because it deals with the stuff of everyday life, but in a new way. What we tend to see as almost boringly familiar, such as the smallest details of human interaction and the largest events of the evening news, take on new meaning and make more sense in the light of the basic sociological insight that our behaviour is affected by social forces beyond our control. Not only do we, as individuals, influence society; society also influences us.

This may surprise you. In this country, individuals are important. So is individual effort. People work hard to get what they want — money, power, a better life for their children, a university education, a flashy car, a house of their own. But most of this individual effort takes place in social groups — in businesses, in classrooms, in organizations. These social groups affect our behaviour and can significantly determine how successful we are in

## Table 1-1. Employment of Sociology Bachelor Graduates by Country

| Vocational Categories | Jobholders in U.S. | Canada | Total |
|---|---|---|---|
| Educational/Academic | 19% | 42% | 37% |
| Business and Commerce | 22 | 21 | 21 |
| Social Services | 31 | 15 | 19 |
| Research, Data Processing, Communications | 5 | 6 | 6 |
| Professions, Professional Assistance | 8 | 5 | 5 |
| Government | 5 | 4 | 4 |
| Other | 10 | 7 | 7 |
| Total | 100% | 100% | 98%[a] |
| Number of Jobholders | (610) | (2366) | (2976) |

[a]The difference between column sums and 100 is the result of rounding error.
SOURCE: R. Alan Hedley and Susan M. Adams. "The job market for bachelor degree holders," *American Sociologist* 17 (1982).

achieving our goals. Look at the students in your class. Most of them have had to work hard all through school for good grades. Some have probably worked at a part-time job to help meet expenses. But hard work is only part of the story. Look again. Are there more women or men? How many native Canadians are in the class? Are these students rich or poor? In fact, studies show that the best indicator of who goes to university is not the individual's ability, but his or her parents' occupations. Social forces influence us and our lives in profound ways, many of which are not at all obvious.

For some of you this may seem trivial. Of course society influences us, you may say to yourself. In many ways the essential insight of sociology, along with many of its discoveries, can seem deceptively like common sense. Common sense tells us that the more severely you punish people, the less likely they are to repeat the forbidden act. Common sense tells us that reading pornography increases the likelihood of sex crimes. Common sense tells us that capital punishment will reduce

crime. Common sense tells us that happy workers are productive workers. Common sense tells us that these statements are obvious. What is not so obvious — but what sociological research has shown — is that each of these statements is false. Far from being trivial, sociological insight, with its emphasis on groups and social interaction, increases human knowledge, extends our awareness of ourselves as human beings, and can expand our power over our own destinies.

Each of the chapters that follows will add to your awareness of the social forces that affect your destiny. In them you will encounter a broad panorama of important social issues — power and the political process, the quality of education, life in the city, the growth of large organizations, crime, discrimination, poverty and wealth, and class conflict, to name only a few. More important, you will see how these issues influence your life. Consider the following questions:

1. Do I have any values?
2. How does a person become a criminal?
3. Can an individual have feminine qualities and masculine qualities at the same time?
4. Why don't more women study math and science?
5. What is the difference between a dirty old man and a sexy senior citizen?
6. When I am too old to work, will society be able to support me?
7. If I work hard, will I get ahead?
8. If I marry, what are the chances my partner and I will be happy?
9. Why do people join religious cults?
10. How did Brian Mulroney defeat John Turner in 1988?
11. Will I get a good job when I graduate?
12. How long can I expect to live, and what will probably kill me?
13. What motivates people to work hard?
14. What would it take to get me out on a picket line?

The answers to some of these questions may surprise you. Sociology can give you important insights into the forces that shape you and your world.

Most sociologists agree on the importance of their work and on the basic sociological insight that groups shape behaviour. But they often dis-

Sociologists of all three major perspectives agree that the social groups to which individuals belong shape their behaviour.

agree among themselves as to precisely what they should study and how they should study it. This is not unusual. Most of the social sciences involve similar internal disagreements and debates. It might be convincingly argued that the interaction of conflicting factions within each discipline has sparked many of the most important discoveries and ideas in the social sciences. Fortunately for a new student of sociology, most of the internal disagreements divide the discipline, more or less, into four perspectives.

There are two major, or general, perspectives — "macrosociology" and "microsociology." Each of these, in turn, includes two approaches. Macrosociologists may take either a *structural-functional* (also known as *consensus*) or a *conflict* viewpoint. Microsociologists generally employ either *symbolic interaction* or *exchange theory* in their work. All four of these approaches are discussed in detail later in this chapter. Each of the first three perspectives (structural functionalism, conflict, and symbolic interaction) has historical roots in the sociological tradition (the approaches are based on the theories of Durkheim, Marx, and Weber,

respectively). The origins of the fourth major approach, exchange theory, are generally considered to be more recent, although some tie it to Georg Simmel (1858–1918).

Before we begin to discuss these four perspectives, and the early theorists whose work underlies the first three, we need a definition of sociology. The usual textbook solution is to give a short definition, with a cautionary note that it is not really sufficient. Here are some examples: sociology is "the scientific study of man's social life" (Horton and Hunt 1972); sociology is "the scientific study of human relationships and their consequences" (Caplow 1971); sociology is "the scientific study of human society and social behaviour" (Robertson 1977).

Our definition of **sociology** is "the description and explanation of social behaviour, social structures, and social interaction in terms of these social structures, and/or in terms of people's perceptions of the social environment." This definition is longer and more complex than those cited above. But we believe it to be more complete and accurate. In the balance of this chapter, you will study the four major sociological perspectives around which this book is organized, the three early theorists whose ideas underlie the first three of these perspectives, and some examples of how the different perspectives contribute to the sociological fund of knowledge. Then we will return to our definition of sociology. At that point it should make more sense to you and give you a more complete and accurate idea of what sociology is all about.

## Three Early Viewpoints

Each of the three theorists to be discussed — Durkheim, Weber, and Marx — is seen by different people as the most important early sociologist. Such assessments indicate that these men were seminal thinkers: profound, original, and influential. They also wrote a great deal, and their ideas changed over time. Sometimes their later work was inconsistent with their own earlier views. But they have strongly influenced what sociology is today. It is no exaggeration to say that very little has been added to their basic perspectives. What follows is a description of how these theorists viewed the sociological world, with emphasis on how each viewpoint has affected current sociology. As you read, remember that we are less concerned with the "rightness" or the "wrongness" of one viewpoint or another than with the established usefulness of all three in shedding light on the social world around us.

## Emile Durkheim, 1858–1917

Durkheim's main concern was to make sociology a separate and unique science. His solution was to define sociology as the scientific study of **social facts** — things that are external to, and constraining upon, the individual.

**Sociology: What We Study.** Most of you would agree with the following statements: Canadians wear clothes in public; rich people are different from poor people; priests behave differently from football players; and large classes are different from small classes. If your reasons or explanations for these statements are "because it is the custom or the law to wear clothes in public" or "because income, occupation, and class size make a difference," you are talking about social facts. For Durkheim, the key characteristics of social facts are that they are *external* to individuals and *constraining* upon them.

These external and coercive facts are seen as a separate and distinct variety of phenomena, "and it is to them the term 'social' is to be applied." Because they represent a new order of phenomena that is distinctly social, Durkheim argued bluntly that they could not be explained psychologically: "Consequently, every time that a social phenomenon is directly explained by a psychological phenomenon, we may be sure that the explanation is false" (Durkheim 1895/1938).

Durkheim's classic analysis of suicide is a good example of his view of sociology. He had observed that certain rates of suicide were stable over time and across countries. He found that rates for married persons were lower than rates for divorced persons, and that Catholics had lower rates of suicide than Protestants. He argued that since the rates were stable — that is, since Protestants everywhere and at different times committed more

Born in France to middle-class Jewish parents, Emile Durkheim spent most of his life as an academic and is considered by many to be the father of modern scientific sociology as well as the originator of the functionalist approach in that field (it had other forerunners in anthropology). He is probably best known for *Suicide* (1897), which is a model of empirical research and statistical/probabilistic reasoning. Durkheim's other major works include his doctoral dissertation, *On the Division of Labor in Society* (1893), *The Rules of Sociological Method* (1895), and *The Elementary Forms of the Religious Life* (1912). One of Durkheim's major goals in life was to establish sociology as a scientific discipline in his country. While he did not succeed during his lifetime (though he held the first professorship in sociology ever to be established in France), his influence on modern Canadian sociology is extensive.

suicides than Catholics — one could not explain the rates by the motivations of individual Protestants and Catholics. Durkheim insisted that one must look to social facts for the explanation of suicide rates. Specifically, one must look to the degree of integration of the groups into society. What explained these rates was the social fact of integration. Married people and Catholics were more integrated into society than divorced people or Protestants. Durkheim's study of suicide was a bold attempt to look at a problem that had been seen as uniquely psychological and to treat it instead as uniquely sociological.

Durkheim's crucial suggestion was that **social structure** — that is, social facts external to the individual — can offer an explanation for social behaviour and other social facts. He isolated what he considered to be unique to sociology, a science that studies social facts independently of individuals. Society is not only more than the sum of its parts, it is coercive or constraining upon the parts.

One example of a social fact would be the position of prime minister in Canada. It exists independently of a specific individual. In a real sense, it is "out there," external to any individual. Further, it is constraining upon any individual elected to the position. Whoever is prime minister is greatly affected by this social fact. Another example of a social fact would be the prestige of a particular department in a university. Certain departments are ranked high in prestige; this is an important social fact that affects future employment.

As with all three men we shall discuss, it is not the correctness of the particular explanation that is crucial, but rather the general approach and the possibilities it suggests. What is important in Durkheim's case, and therefore worth repeating, is the suggestion that social structure, or social facts, can offer an explanation for social behaviour and other social facts.

Durkheim's approach is evident in a contemporary study by Blau and Schoenherr (1971):

*The formal structure of organizations exhibits regularities of its own. Although organizations are made up of people, of course, and what happens to them is the result of decisions of human beings, regularities are observable in their structure that seem to be independent of the personalities and psychological dispositions of individual members. . . . In short . . . organizations are not people.*

**Sociology: How We Study It.** Durkheim believed that social facts could be studied and explained in the same way we study the physical and biological world — that is, scientifically. For Durkheim, the explanation of social facts involved establishing their causes and the functions they fulfill. Durkheim wanted both *causal* explanations and *functional* explanations. He gives this example: "The social reaction that we call 'punishment' is due to [caused by] the intensity of the collective sentiments which the crime offends; but, from another angle, it has the useful function of main-taining these sentiments at the same degree of intensity, for they would soon diminish if offenses against them were not punished" (Durkheim 1895/1938). So for Durkheim, the more intense the collective feelings about a certain crime the more severe the punishment. This is a fairly obvious statement of cause and effect. But he also notes that punishment serves the purpose of maintaining this feeling within the group. This is the *function* of punishment.

It is clear throughout Durkheim's works that he wanted to establish sociology both as a distinct subject (one that could not be explained by other disciplines, especially psychology) and as a science (because social facts could be explained scientifically). Durkheim believed that the scientific study of social facts was a unique field of study, sociology. However, he also believed that science could determine what is best — that is, what goals we should seek. In other words, he argued that science can determine ends as well as means. He asked, Why strive for knowledge if this knowledge cannot be used for the betterment of society? As we will see, Durkheim's question — Why strive for knowledge of society? — is still being asked. But most of those who accept sociology as a science now reject Durkheim's belief that science can determine ends.

## Max Weber, 1864–1920

It is hard to believe that Weber and Durkheim did not know each other's work. However, there is no indication that Weber, a German, was in communication with his French colleague or that they regarded each other as important figures in the development of sociology. This lack of awareness may have been a result of the fundamental differences between their approaches. These differences can be seen by contrasting Durkheim's definition of sociology with Weber's.

**Sociology: What We Study.** Weber (1947) defined sociology as "a science which attempts the interpretive understanding of social action in order thereby to arrive at a causal explanation of its course and effects." *Action* refers to all human behaviour to which an actor attaches subjective meaning. For example, a traveller was at a museum in Spain and wanted to find a particular painting that he thought was in another building. He asked the guard for directions; the guard put his arm out, palm down, and moved his hand up and down. The traveller took this to mean "Go away from me and toward the other building." But as he proceeded to the other building, the guard moved his hand up and down more violently. When he got to the door, he saw that the building was completely dark. He looked back at the guard, who kept his hand wildly moving up and down. Then he remembered that in Spain this motion means not "Go away" but "Come forward." The guard and the traveller had different subjective meanings for the symbols being used for communication. The only way to understand this social action would be to know what these subjective meanings were. As Weber (1947) noted,

*Action is social in so far as, by virtue of the subjective meaning attached to it by the individual (or individuals), it takes account of the behaviour of others and is thereby oriented in its course.*

A **social action** occurs between two individuals when each person takes into account the actions of the other. For Weber, sociology was concerned with the subjective meanings by which people are guided in their social conduct. The purpose of sociology for him, then, was to achieve an objective understanding of how people evaluate, use, create, and destroy their social relationships.

In this view, the individual is the basic unit of analysis. For Weber, sociologists studying a nation should concern themselves with the subjective meaning the nation has for its members, because a nation is only a reality to the extent that it has meaning to its members. Contrast this with Durkheim's view that a nation is a reality in and of itself (a social fact), which therefore cannot be explained by its parts — that is, by the subjective meanings of individuals.

Weber believed that the individual is the sole carrier of meaningful conduct, because only the individual can attach subjective meaning or motives to behaviour. The social scientist can impute motives to individuals and thereby go beyond merely predicting human behaviour to understanding it. This kind of understanding is not part of the physical sciences, where the subjective states of the things investigated are irrelevant. It is im-

Though he suffered from ill health most of his life, the German academic Max Weber exercised a profound influence over European and North American sociology as a consequence of the work he accomplished during productive periods. Often said to have been engaged in a lifelong dialogue with Marx, Weber directed the thrust of many of his major works to the criticism or elaboration of what he regarded as simplistic elements in Marxian thought. He is probably best known for his classic work *The Protestant Ethic and the Spirit of Capitalism* (translated in 1930). But the thesis of this book — the influence of ideology on social structure — is also carried forward in *Ancient Judaism* (translated 1952), *The Religion of China* (translated 1951), and *The Religion of India* (translated 1958). His major work, still incompletely translated into English, is *Wirtschaft und Gesellschaft* (*Economy and Society*, 1922).

portant to note at this point that both Durkheim and Weber were defining sociology by stating what is unique to the field of sociology — that is, what separates it from the other social sciences. Their definitions are diametrically opposed. This opposition is important, because it is still with us.

**Sociology: How We Study It.** Two of Weber's major statements concerning science have had a great impact on contemporary sociology. One concerns the notion of science as **value-free**, or ethically neutral. The second concerns a method for studying social action, that he called *Verstehen* (in German, literally "to understand").

You will recall that for Weber sociology had the advantage of access to subjective aspects of behaviour — the meanings and motives of the individual. Weber would grant that people can be *partly* understood by external manifestations, social facts, or structures, and that for these phenomena, the methods of natural science are applicable for establishing general laws. But structure alone, he would say, is inadequate for a full understanding of people, because it ignores what is unique to humans. Unlike atoms and molecules, humans think, feel, pursue goals, and have motives.

Thus, in Weber's view, general laws explaining human behaviour are possible but inadequate. Just as we can observe natural objects like plants, stars, and chickens, we can also observe from the outside how people behave, and explain the regularities in their behaviour by abstract causal laws. But with humans we can do more than with natural objects. We can impute motives by interpreting actions and words. We can get at the subjective meanings that actors attach to their own behaviour and the behaviour of others. But how do we study motives?

In order to get at what is unique to humans, we need a different approach. This new approach for Weber was **Verstehen**, or the interpretive understanding of social behaviour. Weber suggested that this type of understanding can be achieved in two ways. The first is to reproduce in ourselves the purposive reasoning of the actor. For example, if we see a woman walking with a book under her arm, we might conclude that she is going to read, or that she is returning the book to the library. The second and more important way of understanding, however, is empathy. To achieve empathy, sociologists should put themselves in the place of the actor and understand things as the actor sees them. For example, a sociologist today who wants to study the use of marijuana could begin by determining who smokes it, how often different people smoke it, and the age and social class differences of marijuana smokers to see if there are any trends or empirical generalizations. But this information is inadequate. Our sociologist must also find out what smoking grass means to the people who use it, what motivates them to try it, and what prompts them to continue with it. To do this the sociologist might "associate" with marijuana users, talk to them, observe them, and imaginatively try to experience their situation as they experience it. Only then would the researcher have access to what is uniquely sociological. Weber stated that this approach was scientific.

According to Weber, science by its very nature abhors value judgments. He believed that social scientists can gather information that is not affected by their values. An atheist, for example, can gather accurate data on religious beliefs. He also believed that scientific data and theories, in and of themselves, contain nothing that tells the scientist what *should* be done. There is nothing in the theory of relativity that tells the scientist that it is bad to drop atomic bombs. Good and bad, right and wrong, are beyond science.

To Weber, the physician's only job is to cure the patient. The physician, as a physician, has no right to say whether life is worth living or not. We can ask science, What should we do? But we will get no answer, for on questions of value, science is mute.

## Karl Marx, 1818–1883

Durkheim and Weber were both directly concerned with creating a separate, distinct field of sociology; each consequently took great pains to define what sociology is. Because of this, most of their contributions are directly related to that discipline. Karl Marx is different.

**Sociology: What We Study.** Karl Marx stands alone among the writers we have considered, because of his impact on the world. He wrote many books, articles, and speeches; his theories changed over time; he was both a scientist and a revolutionary. A man of his stature becomes all things to all people. He called himself a philosopher, but some members of every social science claim him as one of their own.

One of the main difficulties in clearly summarizing Marx is that he not only wanted a science of society, he also wanted to change society. Therefore, his theory of society is also a revolutionary program. It is mainly since the 1960s that sociologists have openly paid their debt to Marx.

Born and educated in Germany, Marx went to England after the failure of the 1848 socialist revolution and spent the remainder of his life there, much of it pursuing his studies in the British Museum. He collaborated with Friedrich Engels in writing *The Communist Manifesto* in 1848. The writing of his major work, *Das Kapital*, stretched over the years 1867 to 1894; Engels edited and completed the last two volumes after Marx's death. With V.I. Lenin, Marx is generally considered the father of modern communism.

For a long time, particularly in North America, his work was largely ignored or avoided for political reasons, and for these same reasons some members of every social science disclaim him, sometimes bitterly. But no one ignores him.

Essentially, Marx argued, everything that happens in society is caused by economic relationships. Society is divided into two basic economic classes, each having interests that are fundamentally antagonistic. The class that owns the wealth is the *bourgeoisie*, and the class that produces it is the *proletariat*, or working class. The masses of workers are exploited by a small, privileged elite who manage to control most of the wealth without actually producing it themselves. Society,

therefore, consists of classes of people with unequal power. The inequality of power is the result of the differences in their relationships to the means of production, such as land and factories. The antagonism between these classes is **class conflict**. Periodically, the exploited class revolts and in turn becomes the exploiting class. As Marx put it, "The history of all hitherto existing society is the history of the class struggle" (Feuer 1959). Marx saw revolution as usually necessary for social change, since the "haves" will not voluntarily give up their power. In capitalist societies the haves are the bourgeoisie, the people who own the land and the factories, and therefore the people who employ labourers in exchange for wages. The "have-nots" are the proletarians or working class — who, because they do not own the means of production, are forced to sell their labour in order to survive. In this evolutionary stage, the working class revolts against the bourgeoisie and socializes the means of production. In other words, through the revolution, the workers become the owners of the means of production. Since classes are based on ownership of the means of production — and since, after the revolution, the workers own the means — the result theoretically is a classless society.

Marx also saw the economic system as a major force in determining the other elements that make up the *superstructure* of society. Examples of such elements are law, politics, religion, art, and philosophy. The elements of the superstructure are also to be understood in their relationship to the means of production. However, once developed, the elements can play an independent role and can affect each other. For example, Marx referred to religion as "the opium of the people," because religion urged workers to forgo rewards in this life and strive to build up rewards in an afterlife. Religion, therefore, justifies the current economic system (Bottomore 1964).

Marxist concepts that have influenced present-day sociology include

1. viewing society as constantly changing and change as inevitable (in contrast to those sociologists who stress the stability of society);
2. emphasizing the importance of economic structures as they determine other structures in society, and as they determine an individual's

economic standing, life chances, values, and behaviour; and

**3.** stressing the interrelations among parts of the superstructure, so that any one part, to be understood, must be seen in relation to the others, especially economic institutions.

Furthermore, as an analyst of the class content of historical movements, Marx is unique. He must be seen as one of the major contributors to the study of revolutions. It is remarkable that so few sociologists have concerned themselves with the study of revolutions, given their importance both throughout history and today. In more general terms, Marx has contributed to our understanding of conflict and power as major elements of society.

**Sociology: How We Study It.** Both Durkheim and Weber were directly concerned with defining sociology and describing why sociology could be or was a science. These were not Marx's concerns. Nevertheless, some of his views on science are important in understanding the current state of sociology.

Marx considered himself a scientist and attempted to construct a historical science distinguishable from philosophy. He believed that his theories were based on scientific fact, not just opinion, and that his conclusions were derived from the empirical study of history and society. He also tried to construct a theory of social structure and social change. However, Marx's view of science was pragmatic: he felt that scientists should apply their knowledge in the service of humanity. In this aspect of his thought he was directly opposed to Weber, for whom science was value-free.

A second important difference between Marx and the other two theorists is that Marx believed science to be historically specific. That is, there are no general laws of social change, other than that change will occur. Each problem must be looked at within a historical context. This historical specificity is well illustrated in Marx's reply to a critic who wrote, "According to Marx's philosophical system, Russia, like every other nation, would be obliged to pass through a stage of capitalist development." Marx answered, "Thus we see that events of a striking similarity, but occurring in different historical contexts, produced quite

different results" (Bottomore 1964). Marx's empirical generalizations were always applied to historically specific conditions. For Marx, then, social relations and ideas were grounded in historical periods and were therefore transitory. All historical periods had class struggles, but these struggles differed according to the historical period, and the type of people who participated in class struggles changed over time.

Of these two Marxist views, the first (that scientists should use their knowledge to improve the life of humankind) has had the greatest impact. For certain modern sociologists, however, the second idea (that sociological analysis must be historically specific) has also been important.

In sum, Marx, Durkheim, and Weber all saw themselves as scientists; each believed that a science of society, human behaviour, and history was possible. They meant very different things, however, by the term *science*. On this topic, they posed a number of important questions: Can general laws of social behaviour be established? Can the general methods of natural science be used to study social behaviour and social structure? If they can, are they sufficient? Can and should scientists use their knowledge for the betterment of humanity? Is science value-free? These questions are still with us, and sociologists are still divided in their answers.

## Current Perspectives

Theoretical perspectives are more than attempts to define the subject of sociology. In a sense, a perspective is a pair of glasses for viewing a part of the world. The world is not just there, but is seen and interpreted through the perspective used. A high rate of suicide, for example, can be seen as the result of rainy weather or a chemical imbalance, a product of capitalist society, the result of a lack of integration of the individual into society, or the result of large numbers of people defining their situation as hopeless. Each perspective, by stating what sociology is, is also suggesting what questions to ask, what type of independent variable will be used, and what type of explanation is acceptable.

# Independent and Dependent Variables

A **variable** is a measurable dimension of a concept that can take on two or more values; for example, sex, education, and income are commonly used variables. Two types of variables — independent and dependent — are important. The nature of the independent variable indicates what sociological perspective is being used.

A *dependent variable* is what you are trying to explain or the question you are seeking to answer. For example, if you ask "What causes alcoholism?" alcoholism is the dependent variable. An *independent variable* is the variable that you think explains or causes the differences in the dependent variable. You can think of the independent variable as the cause and the

dependent variable as the effect. Or, you can think that what happens to the dependent variable *depends* on changes in the independent variable.

In order to know what sociological perspective is being used, it is necessary to know what the independent variable is, since in many instances the dependent variable is the same. This is demonstrated in the writings of Durkheim, Marx, and Weber; they were all concerned with explaining the same dependent variable: the changes in society and the changing relation of individuals to society.

Durkheim argued that the independent variable — the cause of these changes — was the division of

labour. The occupational specialization that occurred during industrialization resulted in a new type of social cohesion. For Marx, the independent variable was the relationship of individuals to the means of production. In capitalist societies this would result in the development of two classes and eventually class conflict. The means of production, a macro variable, is seen as affecting the relation of the individual to society, the dependent variable. Weber suggested that the values people have, especially about authority, are the independent variable. Values, being in the minds of individuals, indicate a microsociological perspective.

---

What part of the world you look at and what questions you ask about that part of the world are therefore largely determined by the perspective you use. The **sociological perspectives** discussed so far suggest that certain parts of the world are more important than others. All sociologists would agree that human behaviour is shaped by social groups. But what behaviour is shaped, how it is shaped, and what groups are crucial in the shaping process are viewed very differently, depending on the sociologist's perspective.

The various specific disagreements aside, there is general agreement that the views of Durkheim, Weber, and Marx form the basis of three of the current perspectives in sociology. Consensus theory, or structural functionalism, can be traced to Durkheim; conflict theory to Marx; and symbolic interaction to Weber. In the following sections we examine these current perspectives and classify them as macrosociology or microsociology. A macro perspective studies the large-scale structures and processes of society. A micro perspective studies the small-scale structures and processes of society.

## Macrosociology

Generally, **macrosociology** refers to a set of factors, characteristics, dimensions, or variables that

exist in society independently of individuals and that are believed to constrain individuals to behave and think in particular ways. It is assumed that individuals experiencing the same structure will behave in the same way and that certain parts of the structure affect other parts.

Common to all macro perspectives are the following assumptions:

1. Humans are organized into social systems.
2. Human behaviour and society cannot be understood without attention to the properties that emerge out of social systems.
3. Social change, deviance, and other social processes develop in the context of relationships among parts in systems.

This approach is not unique to sociology. Structural statements are often used by people in their everyday lives. Young people who contend that no one over 30 should be trusted are assuming that, regardless of individual characteristics (such as personality or conviction), there is something about passing this age that constrains people to behave in a certain way. In fact, a structural argument may be used to support this lack of trust. By age 30, most people are well integrated into society. They are out of school and have been working in an occupation for a few years. Most are married, are in or are supporting a family, and have accumulated some material goods. In short, they are closely tied to established society and have something to lose by criticizing it or changing it. They are, moreover, entrenched in a web of relationships that further constrains them to behave in respectable and predictable ways.

Another illustration of a structural statement is found in the question, "What do you do?" The question asks for one's occupation, and the person asking it is imputing to occupation a dominant influence on lifestyle. When we find out a person's occupation, we adjust our behaviour accordingly. We are not likely to tell dirty jokes to a priest, and we may feel uneasy in the presence of a powerful figure like a queen or a prime minister.

Actually, macrosociology may be used in two rather distinct ways that can be stated as basic sociological assumptions. The first assumption is that *a specific structure of society determines its other structural characteristics*. For example, Marx was using a structural approach when he suggested that capitalist countries are likely to experience one economic crisis after another. These countries, he argued, are characterized by the profit motive, and workers receive only a subsistence wage. Profits are plowed back into the corporation and production increases rapidly. But workers, he argued, are not paid enough to buy the products. This situation leads to an economic crisis like financial depression.

The second assumption is that *social structures constrain individual behaviour*. People from cities, for example, behave differently from those in rural areas; and individuals in certain positions, like physicians or lawyers, are likely to wield greater personal power than others, like postal carriers or streetcar conductors. Occupation, the last example, is often used by sociologists as an important determinant of behaviour; in its extreme form, this view may be summed up in such statements as "The office makes the person" and "Bank presidents are conservative." Both consensus and conflict theory are kinds of macrosociology.

**The Consensus, or Structural-Functional, Perspective.** This is one of the four main contemporary perspectives. Certain assumptions are common to most sociologists who take the consensus approach:

1. A society or group is a system of integrated parts.
2. Social systems tend to be relatively stable and persistent, and change is usually gradual.
3. A society or group cannot survive unless its members share at least some common beliefs, norms, and values.
4. Social integration is produced by the consensus of most members of the society on some norms and values.

The consensus, or structural-functional, perspective is directly related to Durkheim, and the concept of social system is central to it.

Think of your body as a system. The system has certain needs or requirements to maintain its existence (for example, a certain temperature range). When the system is maintaining a proper temperature, it is in a state of equilibrium, or balance. When your body gets too hot, the equilibrium is threatened and the system adjusts or adapts by perspiring, which returns it to a state of equilibrium. Perspiring is functional in that it helps the body adjust. In this example, the concept of system is *integral*. In the consensus perspective, the social system is likewise integral.

The **social system** can be defined by four characteristics: boundaries; interdependence of parts; needs or requirements; and equilibrium.

A system must have *boundaries*. This means you can identify what parts are in the system and what parts are outside it. An example would be your university. What it owns, the buildings, and the people who are members are parts of the university system. Nonmembers are not part of the system.

The parts of the university system are interrelated or *interdependent*. What happens to one part in the system affects the other parts. If student membership declines, all parts of the system (number of faculty, number of programs, standards, the budget) are affected.

The university system has *needs or requirements* if it is to survive (for example, no students, no university). The university also needs funds for its programs and salaries for its teachers and other personnel. And the university must have some control over its members to see that they perform at an acceptable level.

When, at a particular time, the university has adequate funds, along with adequate numbers of students, faculty, and staff, it is in a state of **equilibrium**. If this equilibrium is threatened (if, for example, the number of students increases very rapidly), then the university system will be obliged to adapt itself to a new set of circumstances. It is in the use of equilibrium that social systems differ from human systems. In the case of the human body, the only change that takes place is a return to the original state. In our example, 37 degrees Celsius is the equilibrium state; if the body is hot, perspiring will cool it to 37 degrees. Social systems, however, change over time. The university grows. As it grows, a balance or equilibrium — more money, more faculty, more students — is maintained. To describe this condition, the structural functionalist uses the term **dynamic equilibrium**.

It is the concept of social system that makes this analysis structural. What makes it functionalist is the interpretation of the parts in terms of the system. The parts of a system can be functional, dysfunctional, or nonfunctional. Usually, a functional analysis of structures stresses the functional aspects of a part for the system. A part is **functional** if it helps meet the needs of the system, if it helps contribute to the adjustment of the system. A part of the system that is harmful to the rest of the system is **dysfunctional**. A part that is irrelevant to the system is *nonfunctional*. Gans (1972), for example, in his functional analysis of poverty, concluded that poverty persists when it is functional for the rich and dysfunctional for the poor, and that it will persist as long as the elimination of poverty would create dysfunctions for the rich. In the same way, job discrimination against women is dysfunctional for women, but functional for men, and nonfunctional for the retired.

In a functional analysis the system is seen as being in a state of equilibrium, or balance, when the needs of the system are being met. But the social systems that structural functionalism analyzes are made up of individuals. For the system to be integrated and stable, the assumption is usually made that the individuals making up the system are committed to the general values of the system. In other words, the structural functionalist assumes that societies have value systems that are shared by their members. If most of the people in a society did not agree on the values of that society, the society would fall apart. In the structural-functional perspective, consensus on the major values, such as laws, is seen as a requirement of a social system.

Thus, the structural-functional perspective, as a consensus perspective, stresses the order and stability in society. Institutions like the family, education, and religion are analyzed according to how they help meet the needs of society, what role they play in maintaining society's stability. Education, for example, teaches the basic values and skills necessary in an industrial society and fits people into the appropriate societal positions. As you will see in Chapter 14, the educational system accomplishes this latter function by sorting people out on the basis of their achievements and their ability.

In this way individuals are matched with various positions or jobs, and society gets the doctors, lawyers, teachers, machinists, and engineers that it needs. Not everyone can be a doctor, and the educational system identifies those who can and want to be, as well as those who can't and don't have the desire. The general view is, therefore, that modern education serves positive functions for society. The maintenance of social order is one outcome of education. Other social institutions and their functions include the economic system, which operates to produce and distribute necessary goods; the family, which performs the functions of early socialization, sexual regulation and satisfaction, and child-rearing; and the political system, which organizes and legitimates power.

**The Conflict Perspective.** The **conflict perspective** is macrosociological, because it assumes that social structure affects human behaviour. But where structural functionalism emphasizes integration, shared values, and social stability, the conflict perspective stresses conflict, power differences, and social change. While conflict theorists do not necessarily follow Marx's class conflict assumptions, they do follow his general orientation.

The basic elements (adapted from Dahrendorf 1959) in the conflict perspective are as follows:

1. Societies are always changing.
2. Conflict and *dissensus* (lack of general agreement) are always present in every social system.

## Functionalism

For several decades in the social sciences, functionalism has been used by many sociologists (and anthropologists) as a form of explanation of social and psychological phenomena. Emile Durkheim was an early advocate of this approach to explaining social phenomena. More recent sociologists following functionalism include such theorists as Talcott Parsons and Robert K. Merton.

It seems that, particularly because of the last two theorists mentioned, structural functionalism became equated with a consensus theory of society. Parsons stressed shared values as basic to any social system. These shared values were the basis of the social system and were functional for the system. However, sociologists with a conflict perspective can give and have given functional explanations — for example, bureaucracies' "main task is to maintain the status quo" (Mouzelis 1978), or "Racism serves the economic, political, and social interest of the ruling class" (Basran 1983).

Functionalism, then, is a general form of explanation found in biology and psychology as well as in the social sciences. Whatever the system is, the parts are interpreted in terms of what they do for the system — that is, how they meet the needs of the system.

Functionalism, as a general form of explanation, is usually contrasted with causal explanations. It is not surprising that some consensus theorists prefer causal explanations as opposed to functional explanations. They are, however, concerned with structures.

Some sociologists combine structural-functional and psychological-functional orientations by analyzing the functions and dysfunctions for both society and the individual. Bierstedt, for example, attempts to explain the universality of one social institution — the family — by specifying its functions for both units (Bierstedt 1970). For society, the functions of the family are (1) replenishment of the species, (2) sexual regulation, (3) maintenance (providing the physical and economic support to maintain the child for society), (4) cultural transmission, and (5) status ascription. For the individual, the family's functions are (1) life and survival, (2) sexual opportunity, (3) protection and support, (4) socialization, and (5) societal identification. The family, therefore, not only maintains the society in a normal equilibrium state but is also functional for the individual.

**Sources:**

Gurcharn S. Basran, "Canadian immigration policy and theories of racism," in *Racial Minorities in Multicultural Canada*, Peter S. Li and B. Singh Bolaria, eds. (Toronto: Garamond Press, 1983); Robert Bierstedt, *The Social Order*, 3rd edition (New York: McGraw-Hill, 1970); Nicos P. Mouzelis, *Organization and Bureaucracy* (Chicago: Aldine, 1978).

3. There are elements or parts of every social system that contribute to change.
4. Coercion is always present in society; that is, in every society some people have more power than others.

In this perspective, society is seen as ever-changing, as a precarious balance of groups trying to maintain or improve their power positions. Structural functionalists tend to view institutions and groups as integrated and complementary. Conflict theorists, by contrast, suggest that such groups usually work at cross-purposes, that the goals of one group are frequently at odds with the goals of another. Conflict is seen as pervasive, with each group attempting to improve or maintain its position. These continuous power struggles between groups result in a constantly changing society. What stability there is occurs during (usually brief) periods in which there is domination by one group or a balance of power between groups.

Another characteristic of the conflict perspective is that it tends to view values, ideas, and morality as rationalizations for existing power groups. The basic causes for change are thus to be found not in the values of individuals but in the structure of society. By the same token, power is seen not as a result of individual characteristics, but as owing to position in society. The prime minister, for example, has power because of the nature of the office, not because of any individual characteristics. Others are seen as having power because they control resources, such as money or the means of production. This view also stresses that social facts are part of society and are external to and constraining upon the individual.

A conflict theorist studying education would likely view modern mass education in the following manner. First, it teaches the values and skills of the dominant groups in society in the hope that their values will be accepted and that they themselves will not be challenged. Second, it selects individuals so that the power structure of society will be maintained. As we pointed out at the beginning of this chapter, the best predictor of who goes to university is not the individual's ability but the parents' occupation, suggesting that to a certain extent higher education functions to perpetuate the status structure.

In summary, macrosociologists assume the existence of variables that are independent of individuals but that constrain or affect the behaviour of individuals. If a variable ignores particular individuals, and/or extends beyond the life of any one individual, such as parliament or your university, it is a macro, or structural, variable. A basic concern of the conflict perspective is social change; from the consensus, or structural-functional, viewpoint the major concern is with social order. Where change is the focus of study, sociologists tend to stress the tensions, strains, and conflicts in society that produce change. Where the social order is the focus of study, sociologists generally stress those factors that integrate and stabilize a society or group. As an illustration, Durkheim saw the in-

# Challenging Tradition: Recent Perspectives

"Humanists" were the first sociologists to question the traditional sociological perspectives. In response to the question "knowledge for what?", they contended that social scientists should use their knowledge for the betterment of humankind. The values they promoted were "democracy" (Lynd 1946) or, more specifically, "reason" and "freedom" (Mills 1959).

In the 1960s, three groups of sociologists — radicals, feminists, and, in the United States, blacks — continued the criticism of establishment or "mainstream" (O'Brien 1980) sociology. For them, the question was not "knowledge for what?" but "knowledge for whom?" Knowledge, they contended, supports the interests of those producing it, and excludes the interests of the working class, women, and blacks. To best understand this position, we must first examine the general radical, feminist, and black critiques of establishment sociology.

## Criticisms

These criticisms of establishment or mainstream sociology are similar to the humanists' and include the following:

1. Radical, feminist, and black sociologists argue that structural functionalism, specifically Talcott Parsons's version, is based on a theory that supports the status quo: classism, sexism, and racism.

2. Mainstream sociologists maintain that science can only determine what is, not what ought to be. Scientific data cannot determine whether a value judgment is right or wrong. Scientists, moreover, do not have the moral right to dictate policy related to their discoveries. Consequently, mainstream sociologists see the scientist and the citizen as fulfilling distinctly separate roles: a scientist should not take a stand on social issues. As citizens, however, scientists may take a stand on issues and advocate change in society.
  a. Some radical, feminist, and black social scientists agree that science determines only what is, but disagree that the roles of the scientist and the citizen are distinctly separate. They advocate using their knowledge to fight the power structures that maintain the existing classism, sexism, and racism. In this view, "no one is outside society; the question is where each stands within it" (Mills 1959).
  b. Some radical, feminist, and black social scientists assume that values enter into every stage of the research process and cannot be separated from science. Objectivity is impossible, they maintain. How any given sociologist observes behaviour, conceptualizes problems, and interprets data is intimately tied to that individual's values. Therefore, social science is subjective in nature.

3. Radical, feminist, and black sociologists criticize the ahistorical emphasis of mainstream sociology. This ahistorical emphasis most likely stems from the focus on establishing general laws. A common statement supporting the idea of general laws is that sociologists are interested in the general, not the specific: for example, war in general, not a specific war. The argument against this idea is that "we cannot hope to understand any single society without the use of historical material. . . . Any given society is to be understood in terms of the specific period in which it exists" (Mills 1959).

## Solutions

*Radical Sociology.* Radical sociologists use a conflict model based on Marx. Usually, it is a structural model focusing on social class, class conflict, the power structure of society, and the question of who controls what. (In Canada, this includes foreign control of the economy.) They also concentrate on history as a central feature in their analysis of present-day society. As previously stated, they are concerned with using this knowledge to attain a "better" or more "just" society.

*Feminist Sociology.* Granted that social

crease in the division of labour as a new source of social cohesion, whereas Marx saw the increase in the division of labour as increasing alienation from work and creating strain and conflict in society.

## Microsociology

The basic assumption of **microsociology** is that the explanations of social life are to be found at the individual level and/or in social interaction. Like macrosociology, microsociology has two main

subperspectives, symbolic interaction and social exchange theory. A third subperspective, ethnomethodology, is also discussed.

**Symbolic Interaction.** Suppose we are walking down a garden path, turn a corner, and suddenly see a large snake. You might say, "Hey, that snake will be a great addition to my dance act," or "Wow, here comes dinner," or "Poor snake, it might get hurt on this path." The point is that we can both agree that this is a snake — a fact — but our

---

science and sociology have been sexist, what next? Establishment sociologists tend to choose between two approaches: (1) to see sexism as a marginal problem and largely ignore it; or (2) to see it as a valid concern and attempt to resolve the problem by an "add-women-and-stir" approach. This latter response implies that sociological research must be designed to include women, particularly if results are generalized to "all mankind," and that data analysis must use sex as a variable when appropriate. Sociologists must remove any perceived sexist bias before claiming objectivity. Others argue that sexism is a central issue in the social sciences. They consider the first two approaches inadequate and pose the question "What next?"

So far, the major effort seems directed at exposing and correcting biases in language, concepts, questions, and interpretations. The demonstration of a consistent bias in sociological theories and research is in itself a major contribution to sociology. Beyond this, however, lies what has been called a "women-centred" approach, with the emergence of women's studies, feminist studies, or feminology. The world as experienced by women is the subject of the women-centred approach. Some feminist scholars suggest that specific methods are required, and strong disagreement persists among them over the issue of methodology.

One side in the methodology debate argues that quantitative methods are sexist (or, if not sexist, inappropriate) and qualitative methods are preferable.

Others have suggested specific methods such as a "communal approach," simulation, non-hierarchical interviewing, or a historical dialectical method that takes into account the reproductive process. Still others maintain that methods are neutral and consider methodology a non-issue. Most of these arguments are not restricted to feminist social science but are typical of sociology in general.

Methodology in feminist research is analytically separate from the issue of perspective. Again, given that sociologists have yet to agree on any one perspective, it is hardly surprising to find several perspectives suggested. Some feminists take a Marxist approach. Others, frequently referred to as socialist feminists, take a Marxist perspective combined with the recognition of patriarchy as a separate, independent force. Opposed to these essentially structural conflict theorists are feminists who stress a symbolic-interaction perspective, a variation of which is the ethnomethodological approach favoured by Smith (1987). All these approaches are found to some degree in mainstream sociology. However, the approach referred to as the radical feminist perspective is not found in traditional discussions of sociological perspectives. This approach argues that patriarchy (male domination) is the base of sexist social relations: "Women suffer wherever male supremacy exists. It is male supremacy first and foremost, not capitalism, socialism, or industrialization, that exploits women"

(French 1985). Or, as Lerner argues, "the sexual regulation of women underlies the formation of classes and is one of the foundations upon which the state rests" (1986).

So far, three general responses to sexism in social science have been described: ignore it, add-women-and-stir, and women-centred research. Eichler (1987) suggests a fourth and ultimate goal: "non-sexist" research — which, once it is achieved, "will cease to be feminist research and simply become good social science."

---

**Sources:**

Margrit Eichler, "Sexist, Non-sexist, Women-centered and Feminist Research in the Social Sciences," in *Women and Men: Interdisciplinary Readings on Gender*, Greta Hoffman Nemiroff, ed. (Montreal: Fitzhenry and Whiteside, 1987); Marilyn French, *Beyond Power: On Women, Men and Morals* (New York: Summit Books, 1985); Joyce Ladner, ed., *The Death of White Sociology* (New York: Vintage Books, 1973); Gerda Lerner, *The Creation of Patriarchy* (New York: Oxford University Press, 1986); Robert S. Lynd, *Knowledge for What?* (New Jersey: Princeton University Press, 1946); C. Wright Mills, *The Sociological Imagination* (New York: Oxford University Press, 1959); Mary O'Brien, *Politics of Reproduction* (New York: Methuen, 1980); Dorothy E. Smith, *The Everyday World as Problematic: A Feminist Sociology* (Boston: Northeastern University Press, 1987).

responses to it depend on the meaning we attach to it. A snake may mean good luck or bad, may seem beautiful or ugly, may cause joy or fear. **Symbolic interaction** theorists maintain that social facts are relevant only to the extent that people attach meaning and significance to them.

Symbolic interaction is the third of the four main contemporary sociological perspectives. Everyday statements that typify symbolic interaction include "I know how she feels, because I have gone through it"; "I understand his depression, because I too have worked on an assembly line"; and "I once lost my job, so I can understand the feelings of those who are forced to retire." That you can know how other people feel in different situations is implicit in such statements as "People are on relief because they are too lazy to work"; "Anyone who really tries can succeed"; "A good teacher cares about students"; "You're only as old as you feel"; and "He is a good sales rep because he is aggressive." (Contrast this last statement with "He is aggressive because he is a sales rep," which is a structural argument; it implies that there is something about being in sales that makes people aggressive.) These examples express the theme that knowledge of individuals' subjective states is basic to understanding their acts.

A large percentage of sociological research on delinquency, attitudes, company morale, job satisfaction, and social values stems from Weber's notion of social action. (Remember the story of the tourist in Spain.) Herbert Blumer (1962) has explained symbolic interaction in terms that are directly related to Weber's social action theory. Blumer's ideas may be summarized as follows: Symbolic interaction focuses on people. To the symbolic interactionist, social facts are not things that control, coerce, or constrain people; they are little more than the framework for the real subject of sociology. The symbolic interactionist is not inclined to treat society as a set of real structures distinct from people (Blumer 1962).

Humans are feeling, thinking beings who attach meaning to the situations they are in and behave in accordance with that interpretation. In this perspective, people are considered to be far more than passive recipients of society's norms and values: instead, people are viewed as actively *creating* society. Not only are they capable of learn-ing the norms and values of their society, but they also discover, invent, and initiate new norms and values. They create, interpret, plan, and control their environment. People not only react, but act. Blumer (1962) writes,

*The term symbolic interaction refers to, of course, the peculiar and distinctive character of interaction as it takes place between human beings. The peculiarity consists in the fact that human beings interpret or "define" each other's actions instead of merely reacting to each other's actions. Their response is not made directly to the actions of one another but instead is based on the meaning which they attach to such actions. Thus, human interaction is mediated by the use of symbols, by interpretation, or by ascertaining the meaning of one another's actions.*

The similarity between Blumer and Weber should be apparent. Both stress individuals' subjective meanings as the fundamental concern of sociology. A basic difference, however, is the symbolic interactionist's emphasis on symbols: that is, on signs, gestures, and — most importantly — language.

A **symbol** is something that stands for something else. A word, for instance, can stand for a thing. Language, gestures, and flags are symbols. The meanings of symbols are arbitrarily determined by the people who create them. For the symbolic interactionist, it is the use of words, or language, that makes human beings unique among all other forms of life. It is our capacity to symbolically represent ourselves, each other, ideas, and objects that makes us human. To a great degree, humans are free from instincts and must rely on symbols to adapt and survive. Human social organization, therefore, is created, maintained, and changed largely because of our capacity to create symbols.

Because humans can agree on the meanings of symbols and share these meanings, we can communicate effectively. Furthermore, because the meanings of symbols are learned through interaction, symbols are necessarily social. We communicate and interact by interpreting the symbols that others convey. In this process of interaction, humans learn to anticipate each other's responses and to adjust to each other. This ability to anticipate the responses of others, or to imagine the viewpoint of others, Mead (1934) calls **role-taking**, or "taking the role of the other." For symbolic interactionists, role-taking is the basic process by which interaction occurs; we take into account the attitudes, feelings, and subjective intentions of others. In a sense, we can see ourselves from the outside — that is, from the viewpoint of another. Role-taking is the process by which we develop self-awareness and a concept of ourselves. This process is examined at length in Chapter 3.

If the symbolic interactionists are correct, the self-awareness of individuals — whether they see themselves as popular or unpopular, good or bad, bright or dull — depends on their perception of how others think about and treat them. Symbolic interactionists also believe that people are generally correct in their judgment of how they are perceived and treated by others. This development of the self through the process of role-taking is a central concept of the interactionist perspective and shows how our very humanness and distinctiveness as individuals are the result of interaction in society. Closely related to this capacity for self-development is the assumption that we are capable of examining and finding symbolic solutions to future problems — capable, that is, of planning.

Consider W.I. Thomas's (1928) notion of the "definition of the situation." He claimed that if people "define the situation as real, it is real in its consequences." This again stresses the notion of people as active; it is not the structure that determines their behaviour, but their definition of that structure. By interpreting and defining the situation, an individual is making and remaking the environment. This emphasis on the meanings that the situation and interaction have for the individuals involved has led symbolic interactionists to focus on social behaviour in everyday life, to try to understand how people create and define the situations they experience. For example, street gangs, communes, and work groups have been studied using this perspective.

A useful way to summarize the symbolic-interaction perspective is to look at the basic assumptions that most symbolic interactionists accept.

1. Humans at birth are capable of response to others but they are neither social nor anti-social.

2. Humans are acting, thinking, feeling beings who make choices about how to act.

3. Humans respond to others, and their responses to the acts of others depend on the situation in which the acts occur and on the motives that are perceived to underlie the actions.

4. Humans create and use symbols. Human interaction is greatly influenced by the symbols with which people conceptualize the "real world."

5. Through symbolic interaction with others, each of us develops a conception of a self, including a conception of a self that is acceptable in the community. It is the self that selects from the ongoing activity in the environment that to which it will respond.

6. Society is seen as a process in which human beings construct or negotiate social order.

To illustrate these various sociological perspectives, we can ask ourselves how each might be used in studying the students in a classroom. A structural functionalist, focusing on what is common to classrooms, might analyze the functions of tests. A conflict theorist could look at the effects of the power differences between teacher and students. A symbolic interactionist might want to determine how the individual students interpret the class, or the effect of the teacher on the development of their self-images.

**Ethnomethodology.** A fairly new microsociological approach that has much in common with symbolic interaction is called ethnomethodology. **Ethnomethodology** is primarily concerned with understanding how people carry out the ordinary, routine activities of their everyday lives, how they employ language and meanings, and how they construct, interpret, and use rules or norms of conduct.

According to the first point, ethnomethodologists emphasize the direct study of everyday life activities. These activities include interactions and communications — the way people discuss, argue, flirt, teach, leer, question, and order their world into a comprehensible form. Rather than investigating the "products" or "reflections" of activities — such as occupational prestige, formal level of education, or degree of isolation — ethnomethodologists would stress the direct observation of the individual activities involved in prestige, education, or isolation. A person may use a different kind of grammar or initiate new interactions with others, for example, which may be reflected in occupational prestige.

The second point is the emphasis on understanding the language and meanings of the people under consideration. In this regard, ethnomethodology is somewhat similar to social action and symbolic interaction, two other orientations that stress language and communication between individuals. The everyday activities of life, like arguing and questioning, can be viewed as having a grammar or form. The task of the ethnomethodologist is to establish the appropriate categories and rules of such grammar or form. To do so, you need to understand the subtle meanings of language and how people use language in their everyday lives. Ethnomethodologists look unfavourably on the use of questionnaires and interviews, because they believe the subtleties of language are not well enough understood for the formulation of useful questions. For them, consequently, the only valid technique is some form of participant observation, which requires being a member of a group so that the observer can understand what is going on. In this sense, this orientation is somewhat similar to the method of Weber's Verstehen.

Social rules, or **norms**, and the way people use them — the third point — play a prominent part in ethnomethodological investigations. Briefly stated, norms are standards that specify how people should behave. (See Chapter 2 for a more detailed definition.)

The ethnomethodologist considers norms to be general and abstract. They must be interpreted by the individual in an ad hoc manner applied to specific situations. For example, a No Smoking sign in a theatre auditorium really does not apply to the specific situation where, as part of his role, an actor smokes a cigarette. The general norm of no smoking must be interpreted for the specific situation. How people interpret and use norms is a major aspect for ethnomethodological investigation.

**Social Exchange.** In Ann Landers's newspaper advice column, a woman who has been married 18 years asks if her husband is a "gem" or "an emotional cripple." She describes her husband as having a violent temper, but he has never hit her. He has had several affairs, never wanted their children, and reminds her often that "her" kids are "a disappointment."He thinks her family is a bunch of "creeps"; he has never given her a Christmas gift or remembered her birthday; and they have "zero communication." On the "plus side" he is a "good provider," generous with money, neat and clean, well dressed, and "takes wonderful care of the lawn and garden." Most of us would probably agree with Landers that this "appears to be a sad and unrewarding relationship." It seems worthwhile to ask why this relationship has lasted 18 years. It is very likely that the wife has remained "stuck" in the relationship because she has had no acceptable alternative: she is not economically self-supporting, and there is apparently no one else she loves or who will support her. Given the lack of alternatives, one can interpret the plus side as being more rewarding than the negative side is punishing. Or, as social-exchange theorists might put it, the outcome is positive; that is, the rewards are greater than the cost. The **social-exchange perspective** focuses on the benefits and losses people obtain from and contribute to social interaction. The interaction is considered social in that the satisfaction or dissatisfaction that each person in a dyad receives depends on what they both do. The focus is then on the flow of benefits through social interaction.

The past two decades have seen a remarkable increase in the number and complexity of social-exchange theories as well as in empirical research based on these theories (Ekeh 1974; Gergen and Worchel 1980; Emerson 1981). Contributors to these theories come mainly from anthropology, psychology, and sociology. The cross-disciplinary approaches to social exchange and the number of related "theories" make this perspective difficult to describe and at the same time important to understand.

Most social-exchange theorists would subscribe to the following assumptions:

1. People seek others who will satisfy their needs to help them obtain goals. In other words, people act in a way that produces benefits to them.

2. The basic unit of analysis is the form of inter-action between individuals or groups. The basic concepts, then, involve social relations, as opposed to psychological or individual factors.
3. What is exchanged are resources. These resources can be tangible or intangible. Examples of resources commonly studied are love, goods, money, information, and status.
4. All interaction involves costs, which include alternatives forgone.
5. New relations are begun and old ones continue because they are rewarding.
6. People will try to keep their costs equal to or less than their benefits.
7. An important element in any social exchange is power.

Social exchange in sociology and social psychology has been predominantly a microsociological perspective focusing on two individuals interact-ing. There have been recent attempts to extend this theory to the macro level, but it is too early to tell how successful this attempt will be.

## An Overview

These, then, are the major sociological perspectives. Which is right? A better question is, Which of them has been useful in helping us come to an understanding of society? The answer: all of them. They are all based on different assumptions. But so far, each has provided a useful way of viewing part of the social world.

Early in the chapter we defined sociology as "the description and explanation of social behaviour, social structures, and social interaction in terms of these social structures, and/or in terms of people's perceptions of the social environment." This definition is built around three of the

---

## Interpreting Durkheim, Weber, and Marx

Durkheim and Weber were concerned with defining sociology as a separate discipline. For Durkheim, sociology was the scientific study of social facts, which could be explained by both a causal and a functional analysis. He also felt that science could answer the question of what we should or ought to do — that is, that science can determine values. For Weber, sociology was defined as the study of social action using a method Weber called *Verstehen* (the interpretive understanding of social behaviour), which he saw as scientific, value-free, and incapable of answering what should or ought to be. Because neither Durkheim nor Weber was consistent in approach, and because both addressed new and general questions, it is not surprising that different sociologists offer different interpretations of their ideas, interpretations other than those found in this textbook. Durkheim can be seen as a social psychologist and as consistent with a symbolic-interaction approach. Weber's analysis of

bureaucracy is consistent with a macro or structuralist approach (see Chapter 10). Some sociologists see Weber as a conflict theorist (see Chapter 14).

Different interpretations are also put forward regarding Marx's ideas. Marx was not concerned with establishing a new discipline called sociology. His theory operated on a grander scale: it was concerned not only with understanding society and the nature of humankind but also with changing society. And as almost any newspaper will attest, Marx's impact on the world has been great indeed. The complexity of Marx's writing has generated many interpretations — even more than the ideas of Durkheim or Weber have. In discussing the Marxist literature, Jacoby (1981) writes, "A consumer's guide is required to stay abreast of the offerings and the recalls: structural Marxism, semiotic Marxism, feminist Marxism, hermeneutical Marxism, phenomenological Marxism and critical Marxism and so on." Bell (1977) points out "that on no single theme

associated with Marx's name — historical materialism, class, the crisis of capitalism — is there a single unambiguous definition of a concept. Marx never used the phrase 'historical materialism' (it was coined by Engels); Engels never used the phrase 'dialectical materialism' (which was invented by Plekhanov)."

The variety of interpretations should not be surprising; rather, they attest to the importance of these three theorists and to the complexity of their ideas. What is surprising is the insistence of some writers that there is one and only one correct way to interpret Durkheim, Weber, and Marx.

**Sources:**

Daniel Bell, "Review essay: The once and future Marx," *American Journal of Sociology* 83(1977):187–97; Russell Jacoby, *Dialectic of Defeat: Contours of Western Marxism* (Cambridge: Cambridge University Press, 1981).

theoretical perspectives we have just examined. It contains elements of structural functionalism, conflict theory, and symbolic interaction.

Having considered the what and how of sociology (what it is and how we study it) from various points of view, we will now consider the matter of sociology and science.

## Sociology and Science

According to Aristotelian physics, the motion of material objects was governed by motives and goals. Earthly matter sought the centre of the earth as its natural goal; and because heavenly bodies were alleged to be composed of a "quintessence," they were supposed to move only in circular orbits at a uniform speed. These theories led to conclusions that conflicted with observations of falling bodies and the motions of planets.

Slowly, through careful observation, more direct knowledge was gathered about the physical world, first about the stars and much later about human anatomy. Astronomy and physiology became *empirical* — that is, based on observation. "Prove it" became "Show me." As an example, through controlled experiments in which physicists observed balls rolling down planes and objects falling under different conditions, it was suggested that a feather will fall as fast as a rock in a vacuum. Physicists did not actually observe this because they could not then effect the necessary near-perfect vacuum. But using this assumption they could account, for instance, for the rate at which objects do fall under stated conditions, as well as why we do not fly off the earth. Much later, using the theory of gravity, they could predict where a rocket to the moon would land and be correct to within one-third of a metre.

But the social world in Aristotle's time gave rise to pretty much the same sorts of questions that we ask today. Why are some people warlike? Why are some rich and others poor? Why are we civilized while they are barbarians? Why do some people go crazy? Why do some men have many wives and some only one? The answers to these questions — like the answers to questions about the earth's surface, the sun, the functioning of the body, and madness — were based on authority, tradition, revelation, or intuition. All are ways of knowing. It was Auguste Comte who, in the early 1800s, first suggested that sociology should use the scientific method as its way of knowing.

## The Naturalist Position

The naturalist view of social science holds that the scientific method can be applied to the study of social behaviour and that, through the use of the scientific method, causal and law-like statements can be established in sociology. The **naturalist position** is accepted by some members of each of the three main sociological perspectives (consensus theory, conflict theory, and symbolic interaction), and by almost all exchange theorists.

In the naturalist view, **science** is basically a method for collecting and explaining facts. The primary goal of this method when applied to sociology is to discover patterns of social behaviour and to explain these patterns by developing laws. A fact or relationship is explained if it can be subsumed under a **scientific law**. Scientific laws contain predictive statements that certain effects will occur given specified conditions. Scientific laws, then, are statements of relations between two or more variables. These relations have been supported or proved repeatedly by **objective** tests. That we can walk on the earth is explained by the law of gravity. If some of us were to go flying off the face of the earth, this law would have to be modified. Thus the law, in order to be a law, must predict correctly. If it does not — that is, if there are negative cases that do not conform to it — the law must be revised.

In order to make such predictive statements and establish laws, the assumption is made that there is order in the physical and social universes. It is assumed that systematic relations exist that can be observed and formulated into laws. The task for sociologists is to find the order in social phenomena and express it using the scientific method.

**Characteristics of Science.** The goal of the scientific method is to construct scientific laws. But how do we reach this goal? According to the naturalist position, we reach it in three ways:

1. by verifiability;
2. by unbiased observation; and
3. by unbiased interpretation.

*Verifiability.* **Verifiability** means that an observation can be confirmed by independent observers. If we walk out of a movie and you say the heroine had red hair and I say she did not, we have two independent observations that contradict each other. Who is right? We ask twenty friends; nineteen say she had red hair and one says no. But on further questioning we determine that the one who said no is colour-blind and therefore not a competent observer. Then we agree that you are right. Your observation is verified because several other observers made the same observation; we can now say that it is a fact that the heroine had red hair. We say something is a fact when several qualified observers, after careful observation, achieve the same results.

It should be clear that, for science, the final arbiter of knowledge is *observation*. Consequently, science can answer questions only on phenomena that can be directly or indirectly observed. It is important to recognize that observation can be indirect. In many instances, we form concepts about things that we are unable to observe at the time — molecules and atoms, for example. However, these concepts are then employed in science theoretically so that there is an observable outcome. If atoms behave as we think theoretically they do, then when we split them, the bomb should go off. If the bomb detonates as expected, we say that it is useful to accept the existence of atoms as fact. If the observable outcome predicted by our theory does not occur, then we conclude that the theory is not useful.

It follows from this that, while science has proven to be a powerful way of viewing the world, it is restricted to those problems that deal with the observable world. In turn, it should be apparent that some very important problems and concerns cannot be resolved by the scientific method. Thou shalt not kill. We should obey the law. What is beauty? Is there a God? Such questions and statements do not permit an empirical approach. In other words, they cannot be resolved by observation. We may use logic, tradition, authority, common sense, revelation, faith, or intuition to answer these questions, but we cannot answer them by observation. We cannot answer them by science. With science restricted to the realm of the observable, scientists are limited to studying facts. The bomb goes off; crime rates increase; a higher proportion of women were in the labour force in 1980 than in 1960. Such statements are factual; they can be verified by observation. Factual statements are distinguished from statements or questions of preference or values. *Should* the bomb go off? A high crime rate is *bad*. Is it *good* that more women are working outside the home?

Science cannot help us answer such questions. Most Canadians, for example, want capital punishment for certain crimes. Sociologists cannot, as scientists, state that capital punishment is right or wrong. They *can* say that there is no clear relationship between capital punishment and a reduction in the crime rate. They can also state that a poll (Gallup 1981) showed that as many as 74 percent of the Canadians sampled favoured the return of capital punishment for certain crimes. Sociologists can study scientifically what people *do* want, but there is nothing in this method that enables them to tell individuals what they *should* want.

Science, then, is concerned with questions that have observable answers. The colour of the movie heroine's hair can be observed. The colour of a unicorn is not at this time observable and is thus outside the scope of science. It should be noted that the frequently mentioned conflicts between religion and science occur only over questions of fact — that is, questions that pertain to the world of observation. In this perspective, science is objective or unbiased: it is assumed that observations can be made that are unaffected by beliefs, values, or preferences.

*Unbiased observation.* It follows from the idea that science is based on verifiable knowledge that, if the observations are biased — if we see what we want to see, rather than what is — there can be no science. Unbiased observation, the second way we reach our goal of constructing laws, assumes that researchers' values can be controlled adequately in doing social research. For example, if you are a democratic socialist and I am a conservative, is it possible for us to conduct a survey poll without allowing our political biases to affect our results? Can an anti-abortionist conduct an objective (value-free) study of abortion?

Sociologists who accept the naturalist position would say yes, it is possible to control bias. They would also say that the amount of bias can be determined by independent observers. If your poll has the NDP winning and mine has the Progressive Conservatives winning, we do not know who is right. It might be that, just by looking at how the polls were conducted, we could determine who is most likely correct. However, if several other pollsters support your findings, then the evidence suggests either that I did a bad job of polling or that my biases affected my observation.

*Unbiased interpretation.* Besides the problem of unbiased observation, there is also the problem of unbiased interpretation, the third way we reach our goal. If, for example, you do a study that finds higher levels of aggressiveness in salespeople as compared to people in several other occupations, how do you interpret this information? A sociologist with a social-action perspective, who sees motives as important, might argue that because being a salesperson requires a certain amount of aggressive behaviour, people who are aggressive to start out with are attracted to this type of occupation. A sociologist with a structuralist orientation, on the other hand, might suggest that salespeople become aggressive, whether or not they start out that way, because the occupation causes the behaviour and attitude. Most facts or relationships can, like this one, be interpreted in more than one way. Consequently, our biases frequently affect our interpretations.

The naturalist offers a solution to this problem by requiring that interpretations be stated so that they are capable of being tested. In other words, the interpretation becomes a *hypothesis*, a testable statement asserting a relationship between two or more variables. If the structuralist is right, then a study of people before they become salespeople and of people who go into other occupations should show no difference in aggressiveness. A study showing that salespeople become more aggres-

sive over time would also support a structuralist interpretation. Until a study has been conducted, either interpretation is plausible. Before beginning research, it is necessary to state the interpretation in such a way that observations can determine the truth or falsity of the statement. Some interpretations are by definition not testable. If I state that the plague was caused by God's wrath, there seems to be no way that I could test this to determine scientifically whether it is true or false.

A last example of the problems of interpreting facts is dreaming. The question of whether or not people dream is easily answered. We remember our dreams and can relate them. Other behaviour, such as rapid eye movements during sleep, indicates that people dream: it has been found that if we wake sleeping subjects every time we observe rapid eye movements, they will report that they were dreaming. But what if we want to know whether dogs dream? Most people would say yes. We see the dog asleep; we see the creature tremble and make noises; we infer from these observations that the dog is dreaming. But we cannot ask the dog. We have no way of determining — directly or indirectly — whether a dog truly dreams. Consequently, other interpretations of what we observe are possible: for instance, indigestion or some other physical cause. Because none of these interpretations is testable scientifically, we cannot know whether or not dogs dream. At this point you might say, "Science is a waste of time. I know dogs dream." But the knowledge you claim to have is based on intuition, authority, or common sense — something other than science.

The ability to test whether one interpretation or another is correct is a way of controlling for bias in interpreting observations. Another aid is the fact that science is public. There is nothing more sobering and conducive to careful analysis for sociologists than the knowledge that their colleagues will read carefully and criticize what they say. Once research results have been made public, if they are wrong, sooner or later someone will point out the problem. It may take time, and the reasons for the delay are not always clear. Sometimes a given theory fits the biases of most people. So there may be a gap before the error is identified, because most people want to believe the inaccurate interpretation. Sometimes the scientist who makes the erroneous statement is very powerful or has a great deal of prestige in the discipline, and this hinders the discovery of errors in the scientist's work.

An important example of what can happen in the social sciences is the case of the late Sir Cyril Burt, an internationally known and respected British psychologist whose studies of identical twins raised apart were for many years cited frequently as the best evidence that intelligence is hereditary. Burt's publications spanned a period from 1912 to 1969, and he was knighted in 1946 for his service to British education.

Since Burt's death in 1971, however, his findings have been exposed as fraudulent. Evidently his twin studies were fabricated, he invented coauthors, and the other data he presented were fraudulently derived. As Gillie (1979) puts it, "Today there is little doubt that Sir Cyril Burt, apparent guardian of intellectual rigor, hero of educational conservatives, defender of a future to be given over to the genetically pure, was one of the most formidable confidence men British society has produced." Why did Burt's findings go unquestioned for so long? There are probably several reasons: many liked what he was "proving"; he enjoyed considerable prestige; and most scientists believe that other scientists simply do not make up data. Ironically, publication — the cornerstone of Burt's fame when he was alive — later provided the only avenue for detecting his fraud. Public record can be checked and rechecked; if methods or conclusions are unsound, problems will be exposed sooner or later.

In summary, according to the naturalist view, scientists can and must try to keep their values and preferences from affecting what they see and how they interpret what they see. Science is value-free, even though scientists are not. Therefore, by adhering to the rules of science scientists can reduce the effects of values, and by verification and retesting they can determine the extent to which values may have intruded upon their research.

We have just considered some of the qualities of science that make it science, and some of the qualities that sociology must have or acquire to be considered a science. Is sociology now, or can it be, a science? It all depends, as we have seen,

on what is meant by "science." Opinions vary; sociologists differ.

These differences have existed for a long time and seem likely to continue. Like those associated with the other perspectives, these differences are not unique to sociology. Nor are they unhealthy. If you know what stance a given sociologist takes, you should be in a good position to evaluate what is being said and done. There is no one right way to view the world. It is probably true that most sociologists accept a naturalist position as a goal, while realizing that it is extremely difficult in social research to exclude personal values. At the same time, most sociologists are increasingly aware of ethical responsibilities toward the people they study and the results of their study. And in a book such as this, written by many people, it becomes necessary that the reader be aware of these diverse perspectives, since in various chapters you will encounter all of them.

This chapter has presented an overview of the discipline of sociology. Necessarily, much has been omitted and simplified, but the stress has been on the potential value and usefulness of diverse and multiple viewpoints, as opposed to the one right way of seeing society. The chapters to come will provide you with good illustrations of this valuable diversity.

## SUMMARY

1. Durkheim and Weber defined sociology in diametrically opposed ways. For Durkheim, sociology was concerned with social facts, which are external to individuals and which constrain their behaviour. Social behaviour and social facts must themselves be explained by other social facts. Weber, on the other hand, believed that what was uniquely sociological was our ability to understand the subjective states of individuals. The subject of sociology is the individual's subjective meanings, motives, or definitions of the situation.

2. Marx did not define sociology, but his influence has been direct and profound. For Marx, society is seen largely in terms of the relationships people have to the means of production and the class conflict that results. Change and

conflict, in his view, are fundamental characteristics of society.

3. Three of the four major current perspectives are derived from these three classical thinkers: consensus theory, or structural functionalism, is traced to Durkheim; conflict theory stems from Marx; symbolic interaction is clearly related to Weber.

4. The consensus perspective, or structural functionalism, stresses order and stability in society. This perspective emphasizes that a society cannot survive unless its members share some common values, attitudes, and perceptions; that each part of the society contributes to the whole; that the various parts are integrated with each other; and that this interdependence keeps societies relatively stable.

5. The conflict perspective emphasizes that societies are always changing, that conflict and dissensus are always present in society, that parts of every society contribute to change, and that coercion is always present in society because some people have more power than others.

6. Symbolic interaction focuses on people and how they create, use, and communicate with symbols, especially language.

7. Naturalists argue that sociology is based on objective, verifiable data and that science can be value-free.


# GLOSSARY

**Class conflict.** Antagonism between social classes, especially between the class that owns the means of production and the classes that do not.

**Conflict perspective.** A macrosociological view emphasizing that conflict, power, and change are permanent features of society.

**Consensus perspective.** A macrosociological perspective that stresses the integration of society through shared values and norms.

**Dynamic equilibrium.** Parsons's term for the orderly change that constantly occurs among the interrelated parts of a social system.

**Dysfunctional.** Adjective applied to parts of a social system that disrupt or are harmful to the system.

**Equilibrium.** In consensus theory, or structural functionalism, the overall balance that exists among the elements in a system.

**Ethnomethodology.** Sociological perspective concerned with the methods people use to carry out their everyday activities; language and meaning; and the implicit norms that govern behaviour.

**Functional.** Adjective applied to parts of a social system that contribute to the overall stability of the system.

**Macrosociology.** Study of large-scale structures and processes of society.

**Microsociology.** Study of small-scale structures and processes of society.

**Naturalist position.** View that the scientific method, as used in the physical sciences, can be used to study social phenomena. Facts are established by reliable and verifiable observation.

**Norms.** Standards of conduct; statements of how people should and should not behave.

**Objectivity.** Ability to observe and interpret reality in such a way that subjective judgments and biases are eliminated.

**Role-taking.** Process of imaginatively putting yourself in the role of another and seeing the world from that person's perspective.

**Science.** Systematic methods by which reliable, empirical knowledge is obtained. Also refers to the actual body of knowledge obtained by these methods. See also **naturalist position**.

**Scientific law.** A hypothesis that has been repeatedly supported by empirical tests.

**Social action.** Occurs between two individuals when each person takes into account the other's actions.

**Social-exchange perspective.** Set of propositions that relates people's interactions to the level of satisfying outcomes they experience and that specifies the consequences of these outcomes.

**Social facts.** Durkheim's term to indicate things that are external to, and constraining upon, the individual.

**Social structure.** Factors that are persistent over time, are external to the individual, and are assumed to influence behaviour and thought.

**Social system.** Within the consensus, or structural-functionalist, perspective, a series of interrelated parts in a state of equilibrium, with each part contributing to the maintenance of other parts.

**Sociological perspective.** Point of view about society and social behaviour that provides an overall orientation for examining sociological problems.

**Sociology.** The description and explanation of social behaviour, social structures, and social interaction in terms of these social structures, and/or in terms of people's perceptions of the social environment.

**Structural-functional perspective.** A perspective that stresses what parts of the system do for the system. This perspective is usually classified with the consensus perspective.

**Symbol.** Anything that can stand for or represent something else, such as a word or gesture.

**Symbolic interaction.** A macrosociological perspective that emphasizes the interactions between people that take place through symbols, especially language.

**Value-free sociology.** The position, held by naturalists, that personal judgments and biases can and should be excluded from social observations and interpretations.

**Variable.** Measurable characteristic that can take on two or more values (such as age, gender, or violent behaviour).

**Verifiability.** Characteristic of a conclusion or factual statement by which it can be subjected to more than one observation or test.

**Verstehen.** Weber's term for the subjective interpretation of social behaviour and intentions, usually based on empathy (in German, literally "to understand").

## FURTHER READING

**Churchill, Lindsey.** "Ethnomethodology and measurement." *Social Forces* 50(1971):182–91. A clear statement of the basic assumptions of this perspective.

**Gouldner, Alvin W.** "The sociologist as partisan: Sociology and the welfare state." *American Sociologist* 3(1963):103–17. One the the best statements on why science cannot be value free.

**Hagedorn, Robert, and Sanford Labovitz.** *Sociological Orientations*. New York: John Wiley, 1973. A slightly different view of the major perspectives or schools of sociological thought.

**Merton, Robert K.** *Social Theory and Social Structure*. Glencoe, IL: Free Press, 1968. A clear statement of what functionalism is and is not; see especially pp. 19–84.

**Mills, C. Wright.** *The Sociological Imagination*. New York: Oxford University Press, 1967. A classic introduction to sociology from the conflict perspective.

**Ritzer, George.** *Sociology: Multiple Paradigm Science*. Boston: Allyn and Bacon, 1975. A more advanced discussion of theories in sociology, which is compatible with this chapter.

**Rudner, Richard S.** *Philosophy of Social Science*. Englewood Cliffs, NJ: Prentice-Hall, 1966. Chapter 4 is a clear statement on why social science can be value-free.

**Stryker, Sheldon.** *Symbolic Interactions*. Menlo Park, CA: Benjamin/Cummings, 1980. Excellent statement of this approach and the differences among symbolic interactionists.

# UNIT II

# The Individual in Society

*At birth we are colour-coded, blue or pink. We are tagged with names, usually according to gender. We are fed the types of food that society deems best. Sooner or later we are toilet-trained, introduced to eating schedules, and taught the proper way to eat. We learn to be polite. We learn whom and what to love, and whom and what to fear. Thus we are born into, and adapt to, a social and (more or less) orderly world.*

*Our world is ordered by the beliefs, norms, and values of the group into which we are born. Every society has rules governing who is responsible for taking care of children, who is an eligible marriage partner, how to behave when one's father dies, what to eat and how often. Chapter 2 discusses culture: the variations and uniformities in these rules and values.*

*Implied here is the notion that human beings are systematically taught how to behave, feel, and think. This process of learning to become a member of society continues throughout life. What we learn is part of our culture; how we learn it is called* socialization, *and is discussed in Chapter 3.*

*Chapter 4 talks about gender: how sex has been used to categorize people, what this means, what the consequences of gender roles are, and how gender roles are changing.*

*Chapter 5 examines age and aging. All societies expect different behaviours from the young, mature, and old. As with gender roles, the expectations may vary greatly from society to society, but within each society the expectations are usually very clear. While people in different societies have very different life expectancies, everyone gets older and nobody gets out alive.*

*Every society has deviants. These are people who are different — people who break the rules. Lawbreakers are deviants, but so are people who break unwritten rules. The question of what is deviant, the puzzle of who becomes a deviant, and the attempts of various sociological perspectives to explain deviance are the topics of Chapter 6.*

# CHAPTER 2

# Culture

JAMES E. CURTIS
RONALD D. LAMBERT

In ordinary language, we may describe people as cultured, meaning that they speak a second language, are well versed in history and philosophy, and appreciate literature and art. It is in this sense that universities are sometimes thought of as places where one goes to "get culture." There is also the related distinction between "high" and "low" cultures, with the implication that the former is superior to the latter.

Sociologists do not ordinarily use the concept of culture in this value-laden fashion. As far as sociologists are concerned, everybody possesses culture as a member of society. To be human is to be cultured. **Culture** refers to shared symbols and their meanings prevailing in any society or part of society. These symbols and their meanings include ideas about facts, ideas about desirable goals, and ideas about how people should or should not act.

The effects of culture can be witnessed in the most mundane situations. Imagine people waiting for a bus, for example. They stand close together but do not speak, apparently oblivious of one another's existence. As the bus approaches, a woman steps back to permit an obviously elderly person to board first. This act is just one indication that the people have, in fact, taken account of each other while waiting. In stepping back, the woman has acknowledged the unwritten rule that one should defer to the elderly in such circumstances. By contrast, an apparently less generous person chooses to protect her position in the queue, adhering to the rule of "first come, first served." She has decided that this rule supersedes rules having to do with age. These rules — indeed, all rules of behaviour — are part of culture.

Social interaction is typically patterned and ordered because people share in a culture. Take automobile traffic on city streets, for example. Drivers know what to expect of other drivers, as well as of pedestrians, on the basis of commonly understood rules of the road. Drivers can make reasonably accurate predictions about others' behaviour on the basis of what others *should* do. As drivers and pedestrians, we routinely stake our lives on the assumption that other people's behaviour is governed by rules.

Activities as simple as boarding a bus or driving a car, or as complex as sending a rocket to the moon, are possible because people can depend on others to behave in more or less predictable ways. Without this dependability, of course, society would be impossible. No wonder, then, that people have devised rules to ensure that we act and interact in a predictable and acceptable manner. The sociologist's task is to identify the origins, characteristics, and consequences of these rules, and of people's understandings of them.

Having people do what is expected is only possible when the individuals involved possess reciprocal, or shared, understandings, with each person knowledgeable about and motivated to abide by the same rules. All regularly occurring or repetitive social relationships involve shared understandings. Spouses respond to each other in more or less regular ways over time because of shared understandings. The same is true of the relationships between customers and sales clerks, between parents and children, between the police and criminals, between ministers and members of the congregation, and between people waiting in a queue. These shared understandings of how to behave are not always to our liking. We sometimes violate them; but when we do, we often experience feelings of guilt and remorse, or make efforts to keep the violations secret. These responses testify to the power these understandings hold for us, even when we oppose or violate them.

## Defining Culture

### Shared Symbols and Meanings

Culture, then, involves *shared meanings*. In other words, what is important is the *idea* content of culture. In contrast, some social scientists — especially some anthropologists — emphasize that culture also possesses a *material* side. **Material culture** consists of all manner of material objects that people create and use, ranging from simple tools to advanced machinery (such as a computer) to works of art. For anthropologists studying past cultures, of course, material artifacts often contain the only remaining evidence of past cultures.

To fully describe a culture, however, requires more than examining some of the material objects left by its people. This task demands that we draw on the meanings attached to objects by their producers and users; that is, it requires looking at objects as symbols. Crossed sticks may mean firewood in one culture and Christ's crucifixion in another. Automobiles, part of our material culture, may be taken as a symbol of social standing, as a practical or impractical means of transportation, as a social problem involving energy depletion, or as some combination of these three definitions, depending on the social group doing the defining. Material artifacts embody a culture and communicate their meanings to those versed in that culture, but they do not in themselves constitute the whole of culture.

Let's consider symbols and meanings in more detail. As defined in Chapter 1, a **symbol** is anything taken by people, as a matter of convention, to stand for something else. It may be any object, sound, word, gesture, or action useful for communicating with others. In other words, symbols achieve much of their significance because they are the means of communication. Any society or group within a society is a community of interaction — that is, of communication — within which culture is affirmed and modified in varying degrees.

One such community of interaction is sociologists (thought of as a professional group). It is the purpose of a textbook such as this, or of a course in sociology, to introduce the student to the culture of sociologists — that is, to the shared symbols that have meaning for sociologists.

Most of the symbols presented here, as you will see, are common to speakers in the larger society, although the meanings attached to them by sociologists are more circumscribed and precise. Other symbols are more or less peculiar to sociologists, who have fashioned words to refer to specific meanings for which the existing language did not seem adequate. To the unsympathetic outsider or to the novice, these words have the appearance of jargon. As you become familiar with them and begin to share their meanings with sociologists, however, you will see these symbols as useful tools for communicating sociological ideas.

It should be emphasized that a symbol, while referring to something else, is not itself the thing that is symbolized. A flag bearing a maple leaf symbolizes the nation, but it is not the nation itself. The word *freedom* symbolizes a certain type of relationship between humans; it is not the relationship itself.

It follows, then, that the same object or concept may mean different things in different contexts. In one context a red light is a symbol for stopping traffic; in another it may stand for the availability of sexual services. In other words, when we respond to symbols, we react to the meaning commonly attached to them in particular situations.

The meanings assigned to symbols, at least originally, are often quite arbitrary. Shakespeare's poetic lines "a rose / By any other name would smell as sweet" suggest the arbitrary way we attach words to things. The difference between defining a distance, or the speed of a car, in miles and defining it in kilometres is another example of this. It is historically arbitrary. Having agreed which definition of distance we will use, however, we respond and think in those terms.

We have indicated that the symbols and meanings making up culture are shared. Some aspects

## A Subtle Meaning of "the Umbrella"? *or* Are "Real Men" All Wet?

*The meaning of symbols may vary greatly across social groups, even within the same society. Strange as it may seem, something as simple as the umbrella illustrates this. On first consideration this object would seem to have a common meaning for all North Americans — it is something with which to protect oneself in a rainstorm. The following newspaper story, however, tells us that for some people an umbrella symbolizes something about its bearer's manliness. It appeared under the title "Real Men May Use Umbrellas in Navy."*

WASHINGTON — After almost two decades of debate, the Navy has decided that its men may carry umbrellas while in uniform.

The decision by Adm. Carlisle A.H. Trost, the Chief of Naval Operations, might not appear to be the stuff of controversy. But his authorization makes the Navy the second military service to allow its men to carry umbrellas. The decision also defies an old military sentiment that a military man protecting himself from the rain with an umbrella looks too effete.

Comdr. Tom Jurkowsky, a spokesman, said Monday that Admiral Trost recently received a recommendation from the Navy's Uniform Board to make the change and decided to authorize the move "as a common-sense approach to the climatic conditions that Navy men have to face."

Previously, only the Air Force allowed its men to carry umbrellas. All four services have allowed women to carry umbrellas for years.

The Navy's Uniform Board and top brass have debated the issue off and on since 1969, always rejecting the change with such explanations as the contention that it would hamper saluting.

Two years ago, when the Army's Uniform Board recommended the same step, Army Secretary John O. Marsh and Gen. John A. Wickham Jr., then the Army Chief of Staff, blocked the recommendation and vowed that no soldier would ever carry an umbrella while they were still in office.

General Wickham has since retired, but Mr. Marsh remains in his post.

A source said at the time that Mr. Marsh and General Wickham considered umbrellas an "artificial affection" that was "intrinsically unmilitary."

Admiral Trost, while finally breaking with such arguments for the Navy, is issuing some ground rules just to be safe.

Commander Jurkowsky says the Navy is requiring that umbrellas be plain black, that they cannot be carried in formations, that they must not be used as walking sticks and that they must be carried in the left hand to leave the right hand free for saluting.

Admiral Trost's decision does not affect the Marine Corps, a branch of the Navy.

A Marine officer who asked not to be named said he expected his service to continue resisting the move along with the Army.

**Source:**

*New York Times*, November 11, 1987.

of culture are shared by almost all members of a society. Examples from Canadian society include ideas about the monetary value of different coins and paper bills; the rules of traffic governing drivers and pedestrians; and the meaning of parents, police, and teachers. No individual knows or needs all the culture of a society, however. Some aspects of culture — such as the specialized knowledge of medicine, engineering, or law — are shared by only a few people. Culture is like an idea bank on which all members of the society draw, though different groups may use different sections of the bank more than other groups. How much sharing takes place, by which groups and for what aspects of culture, is a research question of special interest to the sociologist.

## Loyalty to Culture

If culture is as important and as pervasive as our discussion has implied, then we should expect people to develop intense loyalties to it. And, indeed, they do: witness the loyalty many Canadians feel for the Imperial system of weights and measures, and their hostility toward metrication. Culture is external to individuals, in the sense that they learn about it, but it is also internal — it becomes part of them and bestows meaning on their lives. So people's loyalty to their culture is an intensely personal matter.

Since we tend to have such an emotional investment in our own culture, we are often skeptical about the worth of ideas and practices in other groups and societies. Would it not be best for everybody, we may think, if others' beliefs and values corresponded to our own? Anglophones, for example, may believe that francophones would be better off if they simply abandoned their language and adopted a more vital and progressive language — that is, English. This kind of loyalty to one's own culture and belittling of others' cultures is called **ethnocentrism**.

Ethnocentrism reveals itself in judgments about all kinds of beliefs and practices. We may wonder, for instance, how any culture could think that filed teeth are attractive, or how another group could possibly find country music interesting and enjoyable. Until recently many Westerners questioned the "misguided" notion that acupuncture

Some aspects of culture are shared by almost all members of a society, while other components of culture are adopted by a smaller group.

has significant medical benefits, since our own doctors did not practice it. We can detect similar processes between townspeople and students in university communities, between civilians and members of the military, between young and old, between religious groups, between sociologists and psychologists, and so on. Ethnocentrism is involved, then, in our judgments of other cultures, or of other subcultures within our own society. Some social scientists regard this very human tendency as the seed from which most intergroup prejudice grows (LeVine and Campbell 1972).

William Sumner (1960), writing in 1906, was one of the first social scientists to emphasize the pervasiveness of ethnocentric thinking. He argued that it seemed to be a universal phenomenon that people see the world in terms of "us versus them," and disapprove of the ways "they" see and do things.

Why do people think ethnocentrically? There are a number of reasons, including the previously mentioned preference for predictability. Confronting significantly different ideas about how to do things implicitly challenges the judgments inherent in one's own culture. It is easier to simply reject differences out-of-hand than to systematically and repeatedly embark on a major re-evaluation of one's beliefs.

In addition, families, schools, churches, peer groups, and so on, do more than simply teach specific beliefs and values. The culture they transmit is linked to self-images so that acting in culturally approved ways affirms people's self-worth. Acting in culturally disapproved ways, on the other hand, arouses feelings of shame and guilt. Much of what is transmitted is further justified by invidious comparisons that are made with "outgroups" and their cultures. Consider, for example, how religious culture is transmitted in some groups in our society. Beliefs having to do with sin, damnation, and salvation may be taught as catechism and as sacred duty to young children well before they can exercise critical and independent judgment. Children learn to judge their own worth, as well as the worth of people outside the faith, in terms of these emotionally charged beliefs.

The personal disorientation experienced when one is immersed in a foreign culture has been labelled *culture shock*. The experience is shocking in the sense that the things one has taken for granted are profoundly challenged. This happens, for example, when people travel to, or through, other countries for the first time. It may even occur within our own society — for instance, when moving from English to French Canada, from a farm to a large city, from high school to university. The point is less dramatically made when we interact with people from different cultures on our home turf. These contacts may prove awkward, even if they do not produce shock. Hall (1962) offers the following example of a situation where different cultural assumptions about interpersonal space are seen to collide:

*A conversation I once observed between a Latin and a North American began at one end of a 40-foot [12-metre] hall. I watched the two conversationalists until they finally reached the other end of the hall. This maneuver had been effected by a continual series of small backward steps on the part of the North American as he unconsciously retreated, searching for a comfortable talking distance. Each time, there was an accompanying closing of the gap as his Latin friend attempted to re-establish his own accustomed conversation distance.*

Many sociologists have cultivated an approach of **cultural relativism** to counteract ethnocentrism when their work involves contact with different cultures. Under this approach sociologists should only describe and explain the workings of a culture; they should not judge it against the morality of their own culture. It is proper to assess the internal consistency of a culture or how successfully it deals with a society's problems, but it is inadmissible to moralize about the culture's goodness or badness. A behaviour that is condemned as immoral in one society may be acceptable in another society. However, in the absence of absolute standards of judgment, it is said to be arbitrary and unscientific to evaluate the moral worth of the behaviour. All cultures are valid when judged on their own terms. In other words, according to cultural relativists, the only way to judge a culture is according to its own standards. To do otherwise is ethnocentric.

The idea that culture is relative to societies is reinforced in the results of cross-cultural studies. Research comparing activities defined as immoral in different societies, past and present, has shown few rules that are universal across all societies. There is evidence that all societies oppose incest and violence within the community, although the specific types of behaviour prohibited (what specific sex-partners are taboo, for example) vary markedly across cultures. Beyond this there are few moral universals. However, ideas about what is moral are present in all societies. Despite the differences among societies in what is thought to be good or bad, all have some ideas about good and bad behaviour. Cultures differ only in their detailed contents.

## Culture and Social Behaviour

We have noted that people's behaviour is oriented to their culture and its rules. However, there is no mechanical one-to-one relationship between the culture associated with a particular situation and the behaviour of a set of individuals in the situation. Therefore, we cannot predict all behaviour from knowing the culture of the group.

What we are warning against is a *blueprint theory* of culture, which supposes that culture is always closely followed or that it is overwhelming and absolute in its impact on individuals' actions. We prefer to say that culture frames people's behaviour, rather than rigidly determining it. By *framing*, we mean that people draw on cultural meanings to define the choices available to them and to make sense of their experiences.

Sometimes culture is a poor predictor of people's behaviour simply because the rules have been poorly communicated, or because they are uninformed. It is difficult to abide by rules of which you are ignorant, even if you are otherwise disposed to do so. At other times there is inconsistency in the culture communicated — for instance, when following the rules taught in one situation means contradicting what has been learned in other situations. Conflicting expectations about premarital sex may exist in a person's peer group and in his or her family, for example. Where the different rules learned are not absolutely situation-specific, then following the rules of one group can mean acting contrary to the rules of another group. The ideas and rules taught within a given situation may even be inconsistent among themselves.

Rules also vary in the vigour with which infractions are monitored and sanctions administered. This affects the likelihood that the rules will be obeyed. In a given situation, different activities may be required, preferred, permitted, tolerated, disapproved, or prohibited. For behaviours in the middle of this continuum, predictions based on the rules may be less clear than for behaviours near the ends. Other things being equal, behaviour can be more confidently predicted from strongly enforced rules.

## Concepts for Describing Culture

### Components of Culture

We have emphasized in our definition that symbols and their meanings are essential elements of culture. These provide the basis for three types of shared ideas that warrant our attention: beliefs, norms, and values.

**Beliefs**. We can distinguish two broad categories of beliefs: descriptive and normative beliefs. **Descriptive beliefs** are ideas or claims about what is, was, or will be, including opinions about cause-and-effect relations. All of the following are descriptive beliefs: politicians are dishonest; God created the universe; cigarette smoking causes cancer; Soviets are superior hockey players. Descriptive beliefs may be mistaken and inaccurate, as judged by scientific rules of proof. But even factually incorrect beliefs can shape the perceptions and behaviour of people who hold them. To a considerable extent our thoughts and actions are shaped by what we are convinced does, will, or did exist. An example is Christians' belief in the existence and meanings of God and Jesus, and the ways these meanings shape and justify the believers' actions.

A November 1987 survey of a national sample of 1500 Canadians conducted for *Maclean's* magazine provides other good examples of descriptive beliefs. This poll showed what people in this country believe about themselves compared to Americans. As Table 2-1 indicates, Canadians believe they are less violent and competitive, but more hard-working, informed, and honest, and more likely to be concerned about the poor and the environment than Americans are (Phillips and Barrett 1988).

### Table 2-1. Canadians' Beliefs About Themselves Compared to Americans

| Compared to Americans, Canadians are | Percentage Who Said | | |
| --- | --- | --- | --- |
| | "More" | "Less" | "The Same" |
| Violent | 8 | 67 | 24 |
| Competitive | 19 | 53 | 27 |
| Hard-working | 33 | 14 | 52 |
| Informed/sophisticated | 34 | 26 | 39 |
| Honest and fair | 42 | 6 | 52 |
| Concerned about the poor | 56 | 10 | 33 |
| Environmentally concerned | 69 | 11 | 20 |

SOURCE: Adapted from Andrew Phillips and Cindy Barrett, "Defining Identity," *Maclean's*, January 4, 1988, p. 45.

# Canadians' Beliefs about the Federal Government and Politicians

The 1984 National Election Survey asked a representative sample of more than 3300 adult Canadians various questions about their political beliefs (see, for example, Lambert, Curtis, Brown and Kay 1986). The accompanying table presents some of the questions and responses as illustrations of descriptive beliefs. The responses of English Canadians and French Canadians are presented separately. Contrary to what might be expected from the political conflict between Quebec and the federal government in recent decades (and the rise to power of the Parti Québécois), the French-Canadian respondents did *not* report a more negative view of the federal government than the English Canadians. French Canadians were more likely to see the federal government as difficult to influence, but English Canadians were more likely to believe that the government wastes money and less likely to see federal politicians as smart. It is interesting, too, that fully three-quarters of the respondents in both language groups believed that politicians lose touch with the people. And 60 percent or more of each language group saw government as not caring much about people, too complicated to understand, difficult to influence, and wasteful of tax monies.

**Source:**

Ronald D. Lambert, Steven D. Brown, Barry J. Kay, James E. Curtis, and John M. Wilson, *The 1984 Canadian Election Study Codebook* (Waterloo, ON: 1986).

## Descriptive Beliefs on Politics By Language Group

| | Percentage Who Agree | | |
| --- | --- | --- | --- |
| | English N = 2190 | French N = 776 | Total N = 2966 |
| Generally, those elected to Parliament soon lose touch with the people | 74 | 76 | 75 |
| I don't think the federal government cares much about what people like me think | 60 | 64 | 61 |
| Sometimes, federal politics and government seem so complicated that a person like me can't really understand what's going on | 66 | 62 | 63 |
| People like me don't have any say about what the government in Ottawa does | 59 | 69 | 62 |
| So many other people vote in federal elections that it doesn't matter very much whether I vote or not | 17 | 22 | 18 |
| Many people in the federal government are dishonest | 39 | 36 | 39 |
| People in the federal government waste a lot of money we pay in taxes | 87 | 70 | 83 |
| Most of the time we can trust people in the federal government to do what is right | 59 | 57 | 58 |
| Most of the people running the federal government are smart people who usually know what they are doing | 60 | 73 | 63 |

Descriptive beliefs can change markedly over time, as people come to believe new and different things. Examples abound in medicine and science: for instance, it was once thought that draining blood from whose who were will — using leeches and such — would cure many diseases. Another interesting example is emphasized in the recent work of Nancy Theberge (1989). She describes how people have come to revise their belief in women's "frailty." She points out that women's increased participation — and success — in such endurance sports as marathons has helped break down the frailty image. In the past, "a vicious circle of illogic and discrimination" existed, in which "women were excluded from sport and their exclusion was interpreted as evidence of their weakness" (Theberge 1989).

**Normative beliefs** are beliefs about what should or ought to be. They refer to the goodness or badness of things, actions, or events; to their virtuousness or wickedness; or to their propriety or impropriety.

We have referred to several examples having to do with rules governing queues. Other examples are the convictions of some Mennonites that they are morally obliged to wear dark clothing in public and to use the horse and buggy as transportation. Religious doctrines generally involve normative beliefs designed to guide behaviour in various situations. Many economic and political beliefs are of this sort. Some people think that Canada should have a more equitable distribution of income and wealth than exists now; they argue that we should pursue policies aimed at greatly improving the incomes of our poorest citizens, while containing, through more taxes, the incomes of the highest earners. Others think the status quo should be preserved and defended at all costs. Some believe that the traditional family is the cornerstone of society and that divorce and the erosion of family ties should be resisted. Still others believe that family life can effectively take many forms — and, indeed, that it should.

**Norms.** The rules regulating people's behaviour in particular situations are called **norms**. Norms may or may not correspond to our normative beliefs. People may prefer that there be different rules in a given situation (their normative beliefs), but they may nonetheless choose to honour the prevailing norms, at least for the moment.

Norms are said to be *institutionalized* when they are supported by people's normative beliefs. Sociologists, therefore, have an interest in assessing the degree of correspondence between normative beliefs and established norms. An example of a norm that is not well institutionalized is the current prohibition against capital punishment in Canada. Judging from public opinion polls, there is little support for the legislation. For example, a 1982 Gallup poll showed that 72 percent of the adult population favoured capital punishment for people who killed a prison guard or police officer, and 69 percent favoured it for killers of any other innocent persons (*Toronto Star*, February 13, 1982). Yet the prohibition legislation persists, governing the behaviour of judges and jurors in our courtrooms. These people follow the rules prohibiting capital punishment despite the public's views — and sometimes despite their own conflicting views.

Sociologists also attempt to explain how normative beliefs may contribute in time to the modification of norms — and, conversely, how the existence of norms may lead people to adopt new normative beliefs. In the former case, for example, the use of a referendum on capital punishment would be one avenue by which people's wishes might be translated into legal norms. As this example suggests, whether normative preferences become norms or not is broadly speaking a political process. In the latter case, human rights codes are premised on the idea that rules forbidding certain kinds of discrimination will lead people to think differently about appropriate and inappropriate behaviour. This is also the subject matter of socialization, the process by which people learn and acquire respect for group norms (see Chapter 3).

Norms are situation-specific. Behaviour prohibited in one situation may be permitted, even required, in another situation. While norms of modesty generally forbid nudity, it is permitted in such specific situations as bedrooms, medical examination rooms, nudist camps, and striptease joints. The general prohibition against taking human life also has a number of well-understood exceptions, including warfare and self-defence. The significance of these distinctions is conveyed in our choice of words: murder, execution, abortion, suicide, assassination, self-defence. The word chosen conveys something about the situation involved, the people in it, and the permissibility of the act.

Norms are of different types. Some norms take the form of written rules, as in the Highway Traffic Act, while others are merely conveyed informally, as when a parent instructs a child how to behave in a restaurant. Some norms, such as rules of etiquette, are advisory in nature, compared to norms against theft and homicide, which are more punitive in their intent. Norms differ in their enforcement, too, some depending on community opinion and others on designated officers of the law. Furthermore, the origins of some norms can be traced, while the history of other norms is a mystery.

These are the kinds of distinctions that Sumner (1960) sought to capture in his well-known classification of folkways, mores, and laws. **Folkways** are rules about customary ways of behaving. Their

# Canadians' Beliefs about Racial and Religious Intermarriage

Normative beliefs are illustrated in a study by Lambert and Curtis (1984). Using results from interview surveys of four different national samples of adults, they inquired into the beliefs of Canadians regarding racial and religious intermarriages. The surveys were conducted over a fifteen-year period in 1968, 1973, 1978, and 1983. Each survey asked respondents the following questions: "In general, do you approve or disapprove of marriages between Catholics and Protestants? What about marriages between Jews and non-Jews? and whites and blacks?"

As the accompanying table shows, there was a marked decline from 1968 to 1983 in the proportions of people who opposed the three kinds of intergroup marriages, among both English-Canadian and French-Canadian interviewees. Among English Canadians, for example, those disapproving of marriages between whites and blacks dropped from 60 percent to 24 percent in 1983; the comparable figures for French Canadians were 38 percent and 10 percent. Although there were higher levels of disapproval of interracial marriages among English Canadians than among French Canadians in each survey, this was not the case for reactions to religiously mixed marriages. In this case, there was a similarly low level of disapproval for both the English and French Canadians, especially over the last two surveys.

Lambert and Curtis speculated about some of the factors that may have lowered popular opposition to intergroup marriages. One of the theories has to do with the possible impact of television. By the 1960s, television had become a pervasive force in Canadians' lives. It would seem that something this widespread in its impact

| | Percentage Disapproving of Marriages Between | | |
| | Catholics and Protestants | Jews and Non-Jews | Whites and Blacks |
| --- | --- | --- | --- |
| *1968* | | | |
| French | 27% | 24% | 38% |
| English | 29 | 30 | 60 |
| *1973* | | | |
| French | 19 | 18 | 20 |
| English | 13 | 13 | 38 |
| *1978* | | | |
| French | 11 | 11 | 16 |
| English | 8 | 9 | 25 |
| *1983* | | | |
| French | 11 | 11 | 11 |
| English | 8 | 8 | 24 |

on Canadians must have been involved in producing the change in beliefs on intermarriage, because of the magnitude of the change. While television often, but not always, portrays minority groups in a negative way, it has probably also stimulated a generation or more of viewers to imagine the possibility of interacting across a variety of intergroup barriers, including racial and religious boundaries. It can do this in different ways. First, it can portray favourable or neutral evaluations of intermarriage, which viewers may then accept. Second, when it simply portrays people from other racial and religious backgrounds, viewers probably experience a rehearsal of positive attitudes toward these people. Whenever viewers engage in role-taking with "personalities" from other groups, there is the potential for developing more positive beliefs about those groups. Also, portrayals of people from minority groups on television are often mundane. This probably helps establish the belief in their ordinariness, their similarity to the viewer. However, given that television is more or less a constant across the households of English Canadians and French Canadians, we would have to look for still other explanations of why — despite the overall trend toward more approval of intermarriage — there is less approval of interracial marriages among English Canadians than among French Canadians.

**Source:**

Ronald D. Lambert and James E. Curtis, "Québécois and English-Canadian opposition to racial and religious intermarriage, 1968–1983," *Canadian Ethnic Studies* 16(1984):30–46.

beginnings lie in tradition, so their precise point of origin is often unknown. The violation of folkways usually results in only minor inconvenience. Since folkways deal with matters of little consequence, members of a society do not have strong feelings about them and their enforcement is informal. Table etiquette is an example of folkways in our society. Eating food with the wrong fork is greeted by little more than stares and the occasional comment from nearby diners.

**Mores** are "must" rules, referring to "must behaviours" or "must not behaviours," that are strictly enforced. The norms here are thought to touch on things held dear or sacred. Like folkways, mores are also traditional in origin. An example would be norms against showing contempt for the symbols of one's country, such as booing the national anthem. Some other examples of mores from political life were offered by the Supreme Court of Canada in its historic ruling on the Canadian Constitution in 1981. The Court observed that "many Canadians would be surprised to learn that important parts of the Constitution of Canada . . . are nowhere to be found in the law of the Constitution" and that "being based on custom and precedent, constitutional conventions are usually unwritten rules" (Supreme Court 1981). Thus, the Court noted, the requirement that the government resign if the opposition wins a majority in a general election is a matter of convention and not of law. The sanctions supporting such conventions are political rather than judicial in nature.

---

# Two Kinds of Values: Instrumental and Terminal

*Social psychologist Milton Rokeach has developed two classifications of values based on cross-cultural research, some of which was conducted in Canada while he taught at the University of Western Ontario. He has argued that values can take the form of* terminal values, *which are goals, and* instrumental values, *which are standards for judging the means to achieve goals. In his research, people are given a descriptive statement for each value and are asked to rank the terminal values in terms of their personal importance. They are then asked to rank the instrumental values in terms of their importance. Rokeach's two lists of values are presented here.*

**Terminal Values**

A comfortable life
  (a prosperous life)
An exciting life
  (a stimulating, active life)
A sense of accomplishment
  (lasting contribution)
A world at peace
  (free of war and conflict)
A world of beauty
  (beauty of nature, arts)
Equality
  (brotherhood, equal opportunity for all)
Family security
  (taking care of loved ones)
Freedom
  (independence, free choice)
Happiness
  (contentedness)
Inner harmony
  (freedom from inner conflict)
Mature love
  (sexual and spiritual intimacy)
National security
  (protection from attack)
Pleasure
  (enjoyable, leisurely life)
Salvation
  (saved, eternal life)
Self-respect
  (self-esteem)
Social recognition
  (respect, admiration)
True friendship
  (close companionship)
Wisdom
  (mature understanding of life)

**Instrumental Values**

Ambitious
  (hard-working, aspiring)
Broadminded
  (open-minded)
Capable
  (competent, effective)
Cheerful
  (lighthearted, joyful)
Clean
  (neat, tidy)
Courageous
  (standing up for your beliefs)
Forgiving
  (willing to pardon others)
Helpful
  (working for the welfare of others)
Honest
  (sincere, truthful)
Imaginative
  (daring, creative)
Independent
  (self-reliant, self-sufficient)
Intellectual
  (intelligent, reflective)
Logical
  (consistent, rational)
Loving
  (affectionate, tender)
Obedient
  (dutiful, respectful)
Polite
  (courteous, well-mannered)
Responsible
  (dependable, reliable)
Self-controlled
  (restrained, self-disciplined)

---

**Source:**

Adapted from Milton Rokeach, "Some reflections about the place of values in Canadian social science," in *Perspectives on the Social Sciences in Canada*, T.N. Guinsburg and G.L. Reuber, eds. (Toronto: University of Toronto Press, 1974), p. 180.

**Laws** take two forms — common and enacted. *Common law* is based on custom and precedent, reflecting the past practice of the courts. *Enacted laws* are formally codified and enacted by legislative bodies. Both types of laws are sustained by police and court actions. They are, of course, laws about which people feel strongly, such as those against treason, and others about which they feel mildly or indifferently, such as some traffic laws. The degree of feeling is generally reflected in the severity of the penalty for violations.

**Values.** In every culture there are general conceptions of the desirable goals, or ends, that people should strive to attain and criteria by which actions should be evaluated. Rokeach (1974) calls these two types of **values** "terminal" and "instrumental," respectively (see the adjacent boxed insert). Values are more general in their application than either norms or normative beliefs. They constitute standards by which people evaluate goals and actions. For this reason, people attach a great deal of emotional importance to them.

Sociologists study the basis for values within a culture, as well as the kinds of trade-offs worked among values in specific situations. We consider the former matter in the second half of this chapter. As far as the latter question is concerned, we should anticipate complex interactions among values because there will generally be at least several values relevant to any given situation. Canadians, for example, are said to value efficiency, meaning that they wish to economize on the use of time, money, and other resources in their activities. They also place a high value on democratic decision-making, with the result that values of democracy and efficiency periodically collide. In some situations, democratic decision-making may prove to be expensive in both time and money, while in other situations what is efficient may lose the support of the people affected. *Value analysis* involves identifying and explaining the kinds of trade-offs among values that cultures tolerate or require.

## Complexes of Culture

The concepts to which we turn next are built on the distinctions just described, but are more complex (in the sense that they combine the cultural elements already defined). We can therefore label them *cultural complexes.*

**Status. Status** defines a position in society according to its rights and obligations. *Status rights* consist of ideas about what you may properly expect from others when you occupy a particular status. *Status obligations* are ideas about what others have a right to expect from you when you are in a given status. Statuses locate people in groups, organizations, and, more generally, in society at large. Certain statuses are relative to the relationships contained in particular groups or organizations. Other statuses, however, such as those based on age, gender, and race, are not specific to any particular group or organization. Nonetheless, they presuppose or imply interaction; men are defined relative to women, and so on.

The most important consequence of statuses is their effect in shaping interactions among people. The shared understandings of rights and obligations among individuals in different statuses make for predictable and ordered social behaviour. Statuses are generally highly interrelated in the sense that their rights and obligations are defined in terms of one another. A mother, for example, cannot have that status unless and until she has a child. There are no wives without husbands, no teachers without students, no leaders without followers, no bosses without subordinates.

Statuses can be *ascribed* or *achieved*. Entry into an achieved status depends on a person's satisfactory performance of some relevant requirement. Movement into or out of an achieved status, in other words, is based on personal accomplishment or failure. The relevant accomplishments are typically prescribed by the rules of the situation. An example is passing bar examinations and being called to the bar in order to practise law. An ascribed status, by contrast, is assigned to an individual regardless of personal merit. This assignment typically occurs at birth. Examples of ascribed statuses in our society include racial and ethnic status, gender status, and age status. Occasionally, normally ascribed statuses may be changed, as when a person undergoes a sex change operation or when a member of a racial minority passes as a member of the racially dominant group. But these are rare instances.

In a complex society such as Canada, each person possesses several statuses simultaneously by virtue of membership in various social categories, groups, and organizations, and the statuses defining participation in each. All of a person's statuses taken together, at any given time in her or his life, are called a *status set*. The existence of status sets makes for the possibility of *status conflict*, a situation in which fulfilling the obligations associated with one status interferes with the fulfillment of obligations associated with another status. For example, a working mother with young children is often placed in a situation of status conflict. She assumes the status of worker and must perform her duties as, say, an accountant. She must put in long hours at her place of work, thus intruding on her other obligations as mother (and possibly as wife, too). Another example is provided by the status of lead hand in a factory. This person is caught between management and workers, with competing obligations toward each. And young people often find themselves having to reconcile conflicting demands from their parents and from their peer group.

**Ideology.** Sociologists define **ideologies** as emotionally charged sets of descriptive and normative beliefs and values that explain and justify how society is or should be organized (Mannheim 1936; Parkin 1972; Lambert and Curtis 1979).

Three types of ideologies can be identified. *Reformist* and *radical ideologies* rally the forces of change, while *conservative ideologies* support existing social arrangements. Reformist ideologies seek changes without challenging the basic rules and regulations — as when medicare, welfare, and unemployment insurance are established without eliminating either the unequal distribution of wealth between workers and the owners of capital, or the principle of private property that underlies our economic order. Radical ideologies call for a fundamental restructuring of society or of one of its institutions, as the Co-operative Commonwealth Federation (predecessor of today's New Democratic Party) did at the time of its founding in the 1930s. The independence movement in Quebec also seeks to restructure the Canadian state. But reformist and radical ideologies may also call for a restoration of former ways of doing things in society. An example would be a proposal to eliminate social welfare measures on the grounds that welfare programs are too costly for taxpayers

and that people should take care of themselves as they (allegedly) once did.

Conservative ideologies are sometimes called **dominant ideologies** to emphasize their prevailing and ruling character. Private property and capitalism currently prevail in our society. In the context of a socialist state, however, the dominant or "conservative" ideology would be socialist. Reformist and radical ideologies in any society are called **counter-ideologies** to emphasize their competing, but not prevailing, character (Parkin 1972).

According to Marchak (1975), "ideologies are screens through which we perceive the world. . . . They are seldom taught explicitly and systematically. They are rather transmitted through example, conversation, and casual observation." The following example suggests how a dominant economic ideology is conveyed in an otherwise innocent exchange between parent and child:

*The child asks the parent "Why is that family poorer than us?" and receives an answer such as "Because their father is unemployed." The accumulation of such responses provides a ready index to the organization of the society in occupational terms, and with reference to age and gender roles. The child is informed by such responses that some occupations provide higher material rewards than others, that an occupation is essential, and that fathers, not mothers, earn family incomes. The child is not provided with an explanation for the differential between postmen and sales managers, between the employed and unemployed, between families in one income group and families in the other, but some children think to ask. There are, then, additional responses such as "If you work hard at school, you can go to the top," or "Sales managers are more important than postmen," or "Well, if people don't work, they can't expect to get along in the world." (Marchak 1975)*

Counter-ideologies challenge the assumptions and beliefs of dominant ideologies. For example, one might ask (Marchak 1975), Why is education related to occupations? What is meant by "the top," and why should people strive for it? Why is status associated with material wealth? What do sales managers do that makes them important, and to whom is their work important? Why would anyone not work when the penalties for unemployment are so severe? It is the point of counter-

**Some subcultures distinguish themselves from the wider culture by distinctive dress and lifestyle.**

ideology to expose ideological inconsistencies and hypocrisies and to offer an alternative vision.

**Subcultures.** In a large and differentiated society such as our own, there is considerable cultural variation among the groups that make it up. Any group that has a great deal of interaction within itself and whose experiences set it apart from the rest of society will tend to develop local cultures, or what sociologists call **subcultures**. These are distinctive sets of beliefs, norms, and values that are possessed by particular groups in society and that set these groups off from others. While a subculture contains culture common to members of the wider society, it also has elements more or less unique to it.

Limited interaction with outsiders makes the development of unique beliefs, norms, and values both possible and probable. Occupational groups, such as medical doctors; ethnic populations, such as Italian Canadians; religious groups, such as Orthodox Jews; people living in small, isolated communities like those in the Canadian North: all such groups will develop sets of beliefs, norms,

and values that make sense especially to them. Such differences guarantee that none of us acquires all the culture of a society. There are too many groups for us to be able to learn everything. And none of us can experience all groups; for example, very few of us are Jewish, Lutheran, and Catholic — only three of many religious statuses possible in Canada — within a lifetime.

One thing that often helps to maintain subcultural groups are the ways they distinguish themselves to outsiders through characteristic dress, lifestyles, and vocabularies. These distinctions sometimes create barriers to interaction between outsiders and group members. At the same time, they make participants in a subculture aware of their discreteness, thus providing a basis for group loyalty. The specialized vocabulary of a group is a particularly obvious badge of subcultural group membership.

The Hutterites provide an example of a religious subculture. They are an Anabaptist sect closely related to the Amish and Mennonites who live on farms in the western regions of Canada and the United States. They are the largest family-type communal grouping in the Western world, with over 20 000 members living in approximately 200 settlements (Hostetler and Huntington 1967). Among their beliefs is the idea that communal living is necessary for people to be trained in proper obedience to God. No private property is allowed; no member of the group may individually own so much as a pair of shoes. The Hutterites are set off from the wider society by a distinctive mode of dress — dark clothing for males and long patterned dresses for females, whether adults or children. Social interaction with outsiders is further restricted by the belief that formal education beyond the primary level should not be pursued; religious services are conducted in German. The Hutterites do not attempt to achieve full social isolation from the wider society and its culture, though. They are successful farmers who trade with people in the surrounding area, and they buy modern farm machinery from outsiders. They also read newspapers, use telephones, and patronize non-Hutterite professionals (such as physicians and attorneys).

As suggested by the other examples of subcultures in this section, we do not have to go so far afield as the Hutterites to find subcultures. Most do not involve the degree of geographical and social isolation of the Hutterites. The poor, for example, have a presence in almost any city, town, or rural region, if not in all neighbourhoods. The "subculture of poverty" is said to be characterized by a lack of skills for occupational and income attainment and by strong feelings of deprivation, helplessness, inferiority, dependency, and social marginality (Lewis 1966; Clark 1978). These feelings result from the economic and work experiences of the poor and the dominant ideology of the wider society. The ideology places a high value on having wealth and a good job, and blames poverty on personal inadequacy. Many of the poor accept these ideas. There is nothing inevitable or permanent about the views of the poor, however; they have been known to change, as in cases of revolution.

*By creating basic structural changes in society, by redistributing wealth, by organizing the poor and giving them a sense of belonging, of power and of leadership, revolutions frequently succeed in abolishing some of the basic characteristics of the culture of poverty even when they do not succeed in ceasing poverty itself.* (Lewis 1966)

## Explaining Cultural Persistence and Change

Having labelled and defined the contents of culture, we are now prepared to consider some of the ways culture is maintained and changed. The related question of how culture is transmitted to new members of society — the problems of socialization — is dealt with in Chapter 3.

Our discussion illustrates the major explanations of how culture develops. These explanations convey the kind of processes thought to be operating in the creation and change of symbolic meaning within society. We have also grouped these ideas according to three broad sociological perspectives from which they are drawn: symbolic interaction, structural functionalism, and conflict.

### The Symbolic-Interaction Perspective

The symbolic-interaction approach focuses on the facts that the use of symbols by people, and the shared meanings of symbols, are basic to a clear understanding of social life. Symbolic-interaction

---

## The Road Hustler's Vocabulary

*Sociologists are not the only group that possesses its own specialized vocabulary or jargon. So do hockey and football fans, politicians, police officers, and so on. Here is a partial list of the specialized vocabulary of the road hustler, "a confidence man whose specialty is the manipulation of card and dice games."*

*Amateurs (cheats)* naive cheating; edge-taking by persons not into the hustling subculture

*Amateurs (hustlers)* rough hustlers, nonprofessionals

*Bird-dogs* tipsters, persons providing information on parties or action people

*Booster* one who steals on a regular basis, a career thief

*Bottoms (cards)* dealing off the bottom of the deck

*Clocking (money)* keeping tabs on the money circulating in a game

*Coolers (cold decks)* prearranged decks switched in for the game deck

*Cooling out (suckers)* pacifying one who has been beaten for his money

*Contacts man* a hustling crew role, a person with access to action spots

*Crack out* busting out persons, quickly relieving them of their money

*Crews* mobs, gangs, a group of usually three or four persons hustling a unit

*Crimp (cards)* marking a deck of cards by slightly bending or folding certain cards

*Daub* a waxy substance used for marking cards

*Deadhead* an unpromising target, one who provides little or no action

*Double duke (cards)* prearranging a deck so that two persons receive good hands

*Double steer* a double-cross involving a target who believes he is taking advantage of another

*Fade* covering a bet

*False cut (cards)* a simulated cut designed to maintain the present ordering of the deck

*False shuffle (cards)* a simulated shuffle designed to maintain the present ordering of the deck

*Flats* percentage dice, dice that have been sanded down on one or more sides to promote those numbers

*Front man* sponsor, one who establishes credibility for another

*Hedge* to vacillate or waver on one's involvements; to decrease one's risk taking

ideas have guided our definition and descriptions of culture.

When we turn to the matter of how the symbolic interactionists view culture's change and persistence, it is important to emphasize that culture is the product of interaction between people in their everyday social relationships. In these relationships, the culture from the larger society is adapted to daily life, and sometimes new ways of doing things are developed. Culture is fluid rather than static; it is always open to revision. It is especially situated in specific relationships and occasions for interpersonal interaction (Lauer and Handel 1977).

One of the types of shared meanings emphasized in the symbolic-interaction approach is the definition of the situation; it is this that guides the course of interaction in social relationships. A **definition of the situation** is contained in a package of norms governing and regulating a recognizable situation, such as a classroom, a hockey game, or a bathroom; it includes norms defining the appropriate reasons for people's participation in the situation and the goals they may properly pursue within it. It also spells out how these goals may be achieved, as well as regulating the relationships among the various participants. Because definitions are shared, they permit people to co-ordinate their actions in pursuing their goals. Seen this way, a definition of a situation is a source of meaning for participants and observers alike, because it permits them to make sense of the situation.

Culture is seen by symbolic interactionists as the product of interpersonal negotiations. Negotiations may be formal and explicit (for example, when a contract is drafted between a union and an employer). However, most agreements are less dramatic and tangible, as people informally and tacitly communicate with each other about the situations in which they find themselves. Communication is often verbal, of course, but it may also consist of gestures, body language, and people's attire. One way people communicate involves the impressions they create, sometimes intentionally and other times unintentionally, when they first encounter each other. Wearing a clerical collar, highly polished shoes, jeans, or one's hair in a bun, or introducing oneself as "Doctor" — all have consequences for how people regard one

---

*High roller* big better

*Holding out* the act of keeping one or more cards out of the game for use in establishing a better hand

*Hop (cards)* pass, a move which restores a cut deck to its original order

*Hustler* one who regularly capitalizes on less than legitimate opportunities

*Illegits (dice)* any bogus dice

*Laying the note* shortchanging cashiers

*Legits (dice)* game dice

*Little front man* referring to a bona-fide patron as means of establishing credibility

*Managing (a game)* operating a confidence game

*Mark* the target, sucker

*Mechanic* one who manipulates cards or dice

*Muscle* muscle man; someone providing protection for crew members

*Nut (the)* expenses

*Nuts (nut, the)* in cards, having a "nut hand" or "the nuts" refers to having the best hand or what should be the best hand in the game

*Padding a roll* a technique of controlling the outcome of legitimate dice

*Percentage dice* dice favoring certain outcomes

*Public relations (man)* person promoting a hustle, a shoot-up man

*Raking the game* charging the players a fee or percentage for the privilege of gaming

*Read paper* being able to identify the face value of marked cards

*Rolling (hotels, restaurants)* avoiding paying for one's accommodations

*Run up (cards)* stacking a deck to give one player a good hand

*Seconds* dealing the second card from the top

*Shade* distractions designed to assist a mechanic or operator

*Shooting up (the pot)* promoting more extensive betting

*Shoot-up man* public relations man, one who promotes a game and game involvements

*Shortcake* getting less than equal share of the profits

*Spreading a game* starting a game

*Still games* regularized card games (e.g., a weekly game involving six regular participants)

*Sting* beating someone for his money

*Stonewall Jackson* a very cautious player, one who usually "waits for the nuts" before betting; an extremely knowledgeable poker player

*Taking an edge* gaining an advantage proscribed by "game rules"

*Tops (tops and bottoms, buster, tees)* dice not having all the numbers on them (i.e., some numbers are duplicated, etc.)

*Weights* percentage dice, dice in which lead weights have been inserted to promote certain outcomes

---

**Source:**

Robert Prus and C.R.D. Sharper, *Road Hustler* (Toronto: Gage, 1979), p. 169.

# Basic Assumptions of the Symbolic-Interaction Perspective

*Assumption 1.* People live in a symbolic environment as well as a physical environment and can be stimulated to act by symbols as well as by physical stimuli.

Example: Watching a movie or reading a book can bring laughter, tears, anger, or joy. The words used in these are only symbols, but they have the capacity to provoke reactions in readers or viewers.

*Assumption 2.* Through symbols, people have the capacity to stimulate others.

Example: Frowns, smiles, body posture, fists, or changes in the tone of voice are stimuli to other people; express anger, love, or pleasure; and cause a reaction by others.

*Assumption 3.* Through communication of symbols, people can learn huge numbers of meanings and values — and hence ways of acting — from other people.

Example: It is unnecessary for each generation to reinvent the wheel, or to re-establish social order or most patterns of social life, such as families, churches, or schools.

*Assumption 4.* Through the learning of culture and sub-cultures, people are able to predict each other's behaviour most of the time and gauge their own behaviour to the predicted behaviour of others.

Example: When driving a car, drivers expect that other drivers will stop for a red light and proceed on a green. If such behaviour could not be predicted, auto traffic would cause enormous problems for drivers and pedestrians.

*Assumption 5.* The symbols — and the meanings to which they refer — occur not only in isolated bits, but often in clusters, sometimes large and complex.

Example: None of the symbols of space-age travel would have meaning to our seventeenth-century ancestors or to pre-industrial peoples; only when we understand the entire complex of modern technical language does any of these symbols make sense.

*Assumption 6.* Thinking is the process by which possible symbolic solutions and other future courses of action are examined and assessed for their relative advantages and disadvantages in terms of the values of the individual, and by which one of them is chosen for action.

Example: Decisions about which course of study to take or which word to use in conversation, as well as how to act in class, with a date, or at a game, involve the use of symbols.

**Source:**

Adapted from Arnold M. Rose, "A systematic summary of symbolic interaction theory," in *Human Behavior and Social Processes: An Interactionist Approach*, Arnold M. Rose, ed. (Boston: Houghton Mifflin, 1962), pp. 3–19.

---

another. Impression management and first impressions foster understandings about the meaning people attach to their relationships, their goals, and what actions are acceptable and unacceptable to them. In the words of Erving Goffman (1959),

*[When] an individual projects a definition of the situation and thereby makes an implicit or explicit claim to be a person of a particular kind, he automatically exerts a moral demand upon . . . others, obliging them to value and treat him in the manner that persons of his kind have a right to expect. He also implicitly forgoes all claims to be things he does not appear to be and hence forgoes the treatment that would be appropriate for such individuals.*

People have many motives governing how they present themselves and the kinds of interpretations they invite. They may or may not be conscious of these motives, and they may or may not be sensitive to the cues they convey to others. For this reason, counsellors advise job applicants to dress carefully for interviews with potential employers, lest they create the wrong impression. On the other hand, members of the clergy are often mindful of the stultifying effects their clerical attire has on conversation and on the jokes people tell at parties.

To say that culture for symbolic interactionists is fluid and dynamic does not mean that it is unlicensed, except for the whims of the people involved. Situations physically and socially constrain what can reasonably be done in them and therefore limit the kinds of definitions that are effectively available. It is difficult to play ice hockey, for example, where there is no ice. And what we do in the classroom is surely constrained by the facts of organizational life outside the classroom. Sexual harassment policies, for instance, remind

**Symbolic interactionists see culture as the product of interpersonal negotiation, through which agreement as to the definition of the situation is reached.**

those who are forgetful that the larger community has a continuing interest in what transpires within the classroom, as well as the workplace.

A definition of the situation constrains interaction, but it is not rigid. Relationships between fellow workers or between customers and clerks sometimes turn into romantic relationships, which is to say that the relationships have been redefined. Symbolic interactionists are therefore interested in the subterranean tactics used to reconstruct relationships. Seduction, for example, refers to a class of interpersonal manoeuvres, impressively labelled "realigning actions" by Goffman (1959), that bring about a redefinition of the relationship between a man and a woman. The possibility of realignment underscores the fact that people are actively involved in exploiting and modifying culture, and are not merely its puppets.

The structural-functional and conflict perspectives, to which we turn next, do not necessarily contradict the symbolic-interaction approach. For one thing, much of the cultural content talked about by symbolic interactionists is not at all unique or original to a relationship. Much of it has its origins in the larger culture and is simply reworked for the more immediate requirements of

a relationship. We can also easily imagine interpersonal negotiations being studied by sociologists working within the structural-functional and conflict perspectives, even though this would not be a priority for them. Structural functionalists might analyze what is functional in such negotiations, while conflict theorists might consider the different forms of conflict in such negotiations. The structural-functional and conflict viewpoints emphasize, though, that there are important shared meanings beyond those found in small groups. In addition, these meanings are seen as less transitory and localized than the symbolic-interaction view might lead us to expect.

## The Structural-Functional Perspective

Strictly speaking, the structural-functional perspective does not explain why some feature of culture, such as a particular norm, is created (Johnson 1960). Rather, structural functionalism deals more with the reasons for the persistence of cultural elements in a society or group once they are available. This persistence is explained by the *functions* — the positive consequences — of these elements for the society or group. A norm, or some other element of culture, is said to persist because it "works" or is "useful," in some sense. This approach is applied by structural functionalists both to the culture as a whole and to subcultures. For example, structural functionalists may study the persistence of dress codes among motorcycle gangs and their consequences for gangs. A related concern of the structural functionalist is **cultural diffusion**, the way elements of culture are often borrowed by one society (and culture) from another society (and culture) when individuals and groups from the two societies interact. Here, too, the emphasis is on the fact that the borrowed element is adopted because it is useful to people in the borrowing society.

We will first describe four explanations that structural functionalists have offered for the persistence of cultural elements within a society or group. Then we will make some observations on cultural borrowing. It should be noted that these structural-functional explanations, in spite of their different emphases, are complementary rather than contradictory. The processes they describe can each — simultaneously or at different times — affect cultural persistence and change. We reiterate, though, that even if a specific norm, value, or the like is functional for a society or group, this is not necessarily the reason it was originally established.

**Culture Mirrors Society.** The first (and the most all-inclusive) structural-functional explanation emphasizes that value systems mirror the economic, political, and social organization of the societies in which they appear. As the structure changes, so will its values. This is said to occur because similarities of values and social organization are functional for the smooth working of the society. There are different versions of this view, but we have selected Inglehart's (1977, 1981) for purposes of illustration. In his opinion, ours is a post-industrial society, increasingly characterized by "post-materialist" concerns and values. Post-materialist values are largely intellectual, aesthetic, and social in nature. In surveys conducted in ten nations, Inglehart measured these values by people's support for freedom of speech and the importance of ideas in society, as well as their desire for a greater say on the job and in government, for a less impersonal society, and for more beautiful cities. He concluded that these values are becoming important and that materialist values, with their emphasis on social control and economic matters, are losing ground. What Inglehart (1977) calls a "silent revolution" has brought about a "shift from overwhelming emphasis on material consumption and security toward greater concern with the quality of life."

The major transformation in values described by Inglehart is the product of a number of profound changes in the way society is organized that are occurring simultaneously. These social changes include major technological innovations, such as computer-chip technology and miniaturization; changes in the occupational structure, most notably the growth of the service sector of the economy at the expense of manufacturing; the rise in real income since World War II; the immense expansion of higher education and the rising levels of education among the population; the wiring of the world by sophisticated mass communications into what has been called a "global village"; and the appearance of a fortunate generation that has personally known neither total war nor widespread economic depression. Inglehart believes, following psychologist Abraham Maslow (1970), that people's mental and spiritual needs become important once their more basic physical needs have been satisfied. Given these psychological assumptions, he expects and finds that the same factors that produce differences between societies also engender differences within societies (Inglehart 1977, 1981). Post-materialist values are most prevalent among those groups in society, such as the young and the well educated, that have benefited most from the social changes taking place.

Of course, history is more complex than any theory admits. Inglehart's description of modern societies sounds strangely dated now, not a decade later. Maybe he anticipated the economic and military malaise of the 1980s when he wrote of possible counter-trends. However, he believed that "the principal evolutionary drift . . . is unlikely to be changed unless there are major alterations in the very nature of these societies" (Inglehart 1977).

**Cultural Adaptations to Technological Change.** New tools increase people's capacity to exploit their environment, with far-reaching consequences for their relationships with each other and thus for the meanings with which they invest their lives.

Three different patterns can be discerned in the effects of technology on culture and social behaviour (Ogburn and Nimkoff 1964). The first is a *dispersion* or *multiple-effects pattern*. The invention of the birth control pill, for example, might have had the following effects, some of them cultural in nature: new ideas about independence on the part of women; a sense that the arrival of children can be effectively planned and can be weighed against alternative investments; smaller families; new notions about the nature of sexual morality.

The second way technology shapes culture involves a *succession of effects* or *derivative effects*, where one effect leads to another, and so on. For example, we have probably not seen the end of the stream of effects produced by the invention of the computer. The ability to process large amounts of information in very short periods of time leads to computer networks and information sharing. This, in time, provokes questions about the privacy of individual citizens, national sovereignty, and the need for laws to regulate access to information.

In the case of *convergence*, the third pattern, the effects of a number of technological innovations come together and produce a common effect. The development of birth control technology, new techniques for building high-density housing with limited space per living unit, and the proliferation of innovations in mass communication (especially satellite transmissions) jointly threaten the survival of minority language groups, such as francophones in Canada.

**Cultural Adaptations to Social Invention.** Technological inventions are visible and tangible, but we are apt to lose sight of the significance, for cultural change, of *social inventions*. Included here are new forms of social organization, new roles, new practices, and new procedures (Whyte 1982). Consider some of the social inventions that many now take for granted: the forty-hour work week, flextime, labour unions, the limited company, Crown corporations, daycare centres, rape crisis centres, halfway houses, franchise operations, indoor soccer, family allowances, medicare, sociology, public opinion polls, fast-food restaurants, the novel, compulsory school attendance, community colleges, multiple-choice exams, federal/provincial conferences, legal-aid clinics, lotteries, jogging. Each of these refers to a way of organizing human activity and incorporates a significant cultural component. Accordingly, sociologists are interested in explaining the appearance of these inventions, as well as identifying their effects.

Why is that person running along the darkened street? Need we fear him? Is he running away from something or after somebody? Not to worry: his attire suggests that he is a jogger, thus "explaining" his otherwise bizarre behaviour. There is something new under the sun as concern for health and doing something about it have spawned a visible and easily recognizable phenomenon. Not only do joggers have repercussions for the economy, (manufacturers hire workers to supply the growing demand for running shoes, jogging outfits, and so on), but they also nourish our values and beliefs about physical fitness.

Think of the multiple-choice exam and the intelligence test, and what they have come to symbolize in our society. They have surely reinforced certain conceptions about the nature of knowledge and intelligence and the purposes of education. Students' success or failure has been premised on the idea that there are certifiably correct and incorrect answers to questions of knowledge, and that the purpose of their education is to find out what these predetermined answers are. Success in the job market often depends on the belief that people can be graded, like eggs, and that some particular level of intelligence is necessary for employment.

Or think of the limited company — the modern corporation. Marchak (1979) quotes the definition from the Canada Business Corporations Act: "A Corporation has the capacity, and subject to this Act, the rights, powers, and privileges of a natural person." This legal fiction places companies on the same footing as you and me. So we can talk about corporations in moral terms, in much the same way we talk about individual humans. Although there may be no afterlife where companies are concerned, they can fire us, cheat us, lie to us, and pollute our environment. We can discuss whether my claims to rights infringe on the rights of a corporation. Socialists have to contend, for instance, with the sentiment held by many people that the rights of corporations to own property are sacrosanct in the same way that the rights of individuals are. In other words, corporations are cultural and social inventions that have cultural repercussions in terms of how we think about the economy and our place in it.

As a final example of a social invention (a much older one), consider the Gregorian calendar, around which we organize our lives, and which we take very much for granted. It is no exaggeration to say that the calendar is one of the chief pillars of Western culture. The failure of France's Revolutionary metric calendar, introduced in 1793, to win people's loyalty over a period of twelve years, attests to the close relationship between the previous calendar and culture. "It is hard to overemphasize the extent to which the reformers obliterated the existing system of units of time as well as the existing time-reckoning and dating framework," Zerubavel has written. "The scope of the . . . calendrical reform was almost total, since its architects strived to bring about a total symbolic transformation of the existing calendrical system" (Zerubavel 1981). Thirty-day months, ten-day weeks, decimal minutes, and decimal seconds, along with nonreligious labels for the days and months, were intended to establish time on a firmly secular, quantitative, scientific, naturalistic, and patriotic basis. An important factor in the system's final abandonment by Napoleon in

1805 was the fact that its inventors underestimated the contribution of the Gregorian calendar to French culture and the hold of religious symbolism on the French people.

**The Cultural Marketplace and Culture Production.** According to another interpretation, an important source of a society's culture lies in the strength and autonomy of its **cultural infrastructure**. This term refers to groups and organizations having a specific interest, often economic, in the creation and conservation of culture. It also includes the groundrules or laws governing the activities of these groups and organizations. The institutions of religion, politics, and education, of course, play an important role in creating and

---

# The French Revolutionary Calendar, 1793–1805

*The French Revolution produced an interesting social invention that is by now little more than a curious historical footnote. According to Eviatar Zerubavel, a metric calendar was introduced in post-Revolutionary France in an effort to establish time on clearly scientific grounds, and to strip away all the religious and qualitative connotations of the old system. Although metrication was accepted for weights and distances by the French population and the international community, it was never accepted as a measure of time. It offended the religious sensibilities of the French by seeking to undo their Christian traditions; and it effectively isolated France internationally, because few nations were prepared to concede that time should be reckoned from the founding of the French Republic. The following excerpt describes the Revolutionary or metric calendar.*

1. The establishment of a *new chronological dating framework*. The traditional Christian Era was replaced by the Republican Era, which began on September 22, 1792, the day on which the French Republic was founded.
2. The establishment of a *new annual cycle*. The traditional January 1 was replaced by September 22 as New Year's Day. Not only did the year on which the Republic was founded become a standard reference point for the new chronological dating framework, the day on which it was founded became a standard reference point for the new annual cycle.
3. The *uniformization of the months*. Unlike the traditional Gregorian year, which consists of 31-day, 30-day and 28- (or 29-) day months, the Republican year consisted of 12 isochronal 30-day months. The five complementary days (Sansculottides) were grouped together at the end of the year, as in the ancient Egyptian calendar. A sixth intercalary day was added on leap years (sextiles), which still fell every four years, although on the third — rather than the fourth — year of every group of four years (Franciade); that is, on years III, VII and XI, rather than on years IV, VIII and XII.
4. The *abolition of the seven-day week and Sunday*. Each 30-day month was divided into three ten-day cycles called "décades." Sunday was replaced by "Décadi," which was celebrated only every ten days, as the official rest day.
5. The *decimal subdivision of the day*. Days were divided into ten hours, hours into 100 "decimal minutes" and decimal minutes into 100 "decimal seconds."
6. The introduction of an entirely *new nomenclature*. Aside from introducing new concepts such as *Franciade, Sansculottides, décades*, decimal minutes and decimal seconds, the reformers renamed each day and month within the new calendar. The day of the décades were named in accordance with their numerical order as follows: *Primidi, Duodi, Tridi, Quartidi, Quintidi, Sextidi, Septidi, Octidi, Nonidi, Décadi*. The five *Sansculottides* were named after Virtue, Genius, Labor, Opinion and Rewards. The Catholic saints' days were abolished, and the days of the year were renamed after trees, plants, seeds, roots, flowers, fruits, farming implements and domestic animals. The new months were named after seasonal aspects of nature in the following manner: *Vendémiaire* (vintage), *Brumaire* (mist), *Frimaire* (frost), *Nivôse* (snow), *Pluviôse* (rain), *Ventôse* (wind), *Germinal* (seeds), *Floréal* (blossom), *Prairial* (meadows), *Messidor* (harvest), *Thermidor* (heat) and *Fructidor* (fruits).

---

**Source:**

Eviatar Zerubavel, "The French Republican Calendar: A case study in the sociology of time." *American Sociological Review* 42(1977):870.

disseminating symbols. But beyond these institutions, we have in mind the various business enterprises, especially in the mass and specialized media, whose economic interests entail some amount of culture production. At various times, the federal and some of the provincial governments have concluded that the private sector needed encouragement or direction in meeting its cultural obligations (see, for example, Crean 1976; Ostry 1978). In the absence of an effective indigenous cultural infrastructure, we know that we will be served by the American infrastructure. We also know that one of the effects of this kind of dependency will be that the culture we consume reflects American preoccupations rather than our own.

It is a useful exercise to think about what aspects of life in Canada would escape our attention were we to depend on other societies to tell us about ourselves. Many of the symbols and shared meanings that make up our culture would be borrowed from other people's experiences and would only accidentally reflect our own. On the other hand, creating an economic base for Canadian literature, from writing through publication to sales, means that our thinking about French–English relations, for example, is enriched. In a similar fashion, Canadian nationalists argued for a long time that there was a relationship between producing Canadian doctorate-holders and hiring them in Canadian universities, on the one hand, and producing new knowledge about Canadian society, on the other. These observations extend no less to the production of scientific and technological knowledge, for these are dynamic ingredients of contemporary culture (see, for example, the Gray Report 1972; Britton and Gilmour 1978).

The Canadian infrastructure includes

- *government bodies* (for example, the Canadian Radio-television and Telecommunications Commission; the Canada Council; the Social Sciences and Humanities Research Council of Canada; and Telefilm Canada);

- *publishers* (for example, Holt, Rinehart and Winston, a Canadian subsidiary of an American publisher; and James Lorimer, a wholly owned Canadian publisher);

- *periodicals and newspapers* (for example, *Maclean's* magazine and *The Globe and Mail*);

- *electronic media* (that is, privately owned television and radio stations and networks);

- *Crown corporations* (such as the Canadian Broadcasting Corporation); and

- *regulations* (for example, the Canadian-content rules for TV programming and for popular music on radio, the Canadian-quota rule in the Canadian Football League, and preferential hiring of Canadian faculty in our universities).

The usefulness of this idea for explaining national differences in culture is shown in a study by Griswold (cited in Peterson 1979). She wished to explain the apparent differences in literary taste between British and American novelists writing in the nineteenth century. Americans wrote about "isolated male protagonists combatting nature, the supernatural, or an evil society," while the British wrote about "love, marriage, and domestic bourgeois life" (Peterson 1979). One might try to explain these differences in literary culture in terms of national character and civilization, but Griswold preferred a much more direct explanation. Before 1891, the United States was not a party to the prevailing international conventions respecting copyright. It was cheaper for American publishers to pirate British novels on love and marriage than to pay their own authors. This compelled American authors to turn to topics that were relatively neglected by British authors — hence the peculiar division of literary labour between the two nations. Griswold reports that these national divisions eroded after 1891, when the United States decided to respect literary property rights.

**Cultural Diffusion.** While the new technology or social inventions that are added to a particular culture sometimes originate from within it, most elements of modern culture appear not to be of this sort. Most of the contents of modern cultures have been gained through diffusion from other cultures, past and present. As noted earlier, cultural diffusion refers to the borrowing of cultural elements from another society in contrast to their independent development within the society. The borrowing takes place, structural functionalists emphasize, because individuals or groups from

## Cultures Are Heavily Borrowed: An Illustration

*Probably no culture is purely indigenous. Each culture involves elements taken over from other cultures from the current period and from earlier times. Indeed, most modern cultures are, like Canada's, largely composed of borrowed elements. In a classic study, the anthropologist Ralph Linton provided a good illustration of this point by caricaturing the beginning of the day for a typical North American male.*

Our . . . citizen awakens in a bed built on a pattern which originated in the Near East but which was modified in Northern Europe before it was transmitted to America. He throws back the covers made from cotton, domesticated in India, or linen, domesticated in the Near East, or silk, the use of which was discovered in China. All of these materials have been spun and woven by processes invented in the Near East. He slips into his moccasins, invented by the Indians of the Eastern woodlands, and goes to the bathroom, whose fixtures are a mixture of European and American inventions, both of recent date. He takes off his pajamas, a garment invented in India, and washes with soap, invented by the ancient Gauls. He then shaves, a masochistic rite which seems to have been derived from either Sumer or ancient Egypt.

Returning to the bedroom, he removes his clothes from a chair of southern European type and proceeds to dress. He puts on garments whose form originally derived from the skin clothing of the nomads of the Asiatic steppes, puts on shoes made from skins tanned by a process invented in ancient Egypt and cut to a pattern derived from the classical civilization of the Mediterranean, and ties around his neck a strip of bright-colored cloth which is a vestigial survival of the shoulder shawls worn by the seventeenth century Croatians. Before going out for breakfast he glances through the window, made of glass invented in Egypt, and if it is raining, puts on overshoes made of rubber discovered by the Central American Indians and takes an umbrella, invented in southeastern Asia. . . .

On his way to breakfast he stops to buy a paper, paying for it with coins, an ancient Lydian invention. At the restaurant a whole new series of borrowed elements confronts him. His plate is made of a form of pottery invented in China. His knife is of steel, an alloy first made in southern India, his fork a medieval Italian invention, and his spoon a derivative of a Roman original. He begins his breakfast with an orange, from the eastern Mediterranean, a cantaloupe from Persia, or perhaps a piece of African watermelon. With this he has coffee, an Abyssinian plant, with cream and sugar. Both the domestication of cows and the idea of milking them originated in the Near East, while sugar was first made in India. After his fruit and first coffee, he goes on to waffles, cakes made by a Scandinavian technique from wheat domesticated in Asia Minor. Over these he pours maple syrup, invented by the Indians of the Eastern woodlands. As a side dish he may have the eggs of a species of bird domesticated in Indo-China, or thin strips of flesh of an animal domesticated in Eastern Asia which have been salted and smoked by a process developed in northern Europe.

**Source:**

Ralph Linton, *The Study of Man* (New York: Appleton-Century, 1936), pp. 326–27.

one society see a way of doing things that seems to work well in another society and they adopt this practice for their own situation. Then the borrowed way is transmitted from generation to generation within the borrowing society.

Cultural borrowing has been a common occurrence for Canadian society. We can easily take for granted our society's cultural borrowing because much of it occurred before our lifetimes and without our direct knowledge. For the same reason, few of us know the exact origins of many of the cultural elements that we employ. Indeed, experts on culture can often only guess at the origin of a word, a type of food, or an item of etiquette. Their roots are lost in antiquity.

When a new item of culture is borrowed from another society, it is useful to distinguish between the separate effects on the borrowing society of two things: the new item of culture and the relationship between the societies that provided for the borrowing. Each can have its own consequences. An example of this difference is provided by Ray's (1974) study of the introduction of new hunting technology into the native Indian societies of colonial Canada. He showed, on the one hand, that these societies gained an improved capacity to exploit the environment after the cultural borrowing. Guns were clearly more efficient and deadly than arrows, and horses increased hunters' territories. On the other hand, the Indians' trading relationships with Europeans created new economic and political dependencies. Both sets of factors exerted an influence on the composition of native culture. A more contemporary example is Canada's well-known reliance on the United States for much of its technological innovation. This means that technology and economic dependency are intertwined in their cumulative impact on Canadian culture.

## The Conflict Perspective

All the structural-functional explanations share the idea that some factor, A (perhaps technological change), leads to Z, a change in some feature of culture. Conflict interpretations, on the other hand, are more complicated. They posit a conflict relationship between at least two factors, A and B, and hold that Z arises from this relationship. Sometimes the A–B relationship is referred to as *dialectical*, implying that there is a productive tension between the two.

The conflict perspective has a certain kinship to the symbolic-interaction approach. Both assume that interaction between A and B leads to Z. They differ in that A and B are individuals in the case of symbolic interaction, but subgroups in society or different societies in the case of conflict theory. A second difference is that interactionists do not start from the assumption that A and B are in conflict; in fact, they generally assume co-operation between people to find a working consensus. Conflict theorists, alternatively, start from the assumption that A's and B's interests are opposed rather than mutual. Then, out of the clash between their respective ambitions, culture is produced.

The conflict perspective assumes, as do the structural-functional and the symbolic-interaction perspectives, that a minimum level of shared culture exists in a society, even between parties in conflict. That is, there is some mutual understanding between conflicting parties on the character of their differing interests and the fact that their relationship is a conflictual one. Often, conflicting groups share more than this — for in-

stance, a common language and similar goals.

Conflict theorists, however, are more likely to emphasize the cultural differences than the similarities between groups. They also tend to focus on the relationship between the groups: how it is defined; and to what degree, why, and with what consequences it is conflictual. As we will show, the conflict approach also emphasizes how cultural elements emerge from conflict and how they may even come to be shared across the groups involved. What is important to recognize is that conflict, too, is a form of interaction. And it is from interaction, both conflictual and nonconflictual, that culture emerges.

We will discuss three conflict-oriented explanations in this section. In all of them, cultures are created or embellished as adaptive responses to conflicts. Culture can be seen as an accommodation to conflict, as when groups learn to live symbolically with the ruptures that have occurred in their society and with the resulting unequal distribution of power. As ideology, culture is a weapon used by either side to buttress its position and perhaps even to alter the relationship to its advantage, in time. In the latter case, ideology is a way of asserting the symbolic superiority of one group.

**Cultural Accommodations to Historical Conflicts.** This explanation can probably be illustrated in the history of most societies. From the Canadian case, we will draw on two examples: the cultural accommodations that English and French Canadians have made to the battle of the Plains of Abraham and those that English Canadians have made to the American War of Independence. Although the specifics would differ, the logic of what we have to say can be illustrated equally well by the cultural adaptations of the native Indians to the European settlers in Canada (see Patterson 1972).

We will begin with the example of the conquest and its consequences for French–English differences in culture. A number of writers have reported on the cultural differences, historically, between English Canadians and the French-speaking people of Quebec (for example, Hughes 1943; Taylor 1964). English Canadians have been depicted as more individualistic, materialistic, and achievement-oriented in their outlook. The Québécois have been described as more oriented to the family and the kinship system as well as to religious and spiritual values (but see Baer and Curtis 1984 for evidence that such differences are now small, if they obtain at all). French Canadians have also been described as more authoritarian in their relationships and more xenophobic — that is, negative toward immigrants and foreign influences (Curtis and Lambert 1975, 1976; Lambert and Curtis 1982, 1983). The picture of French Quebec that has emerged is of a "folk society," compared to the modern, cosmopolitan society of English Canada.

We can distinguish between two broad views on these differences (Lambert 1981). According to the first view, the historical dominance of English Canadians in business was the result of their interest in worldly success. The Québécois were scarce in business pursuits, because of their loyalties to religious and family-oriented values. If the Roman Catholic Church was prominent in Quebec life, this reflected the wishes of the people. In short, culture determined the shape of society in Quebec and in English Canada.

In more recent years, these cultural differences have been interpreted as cultural responses to more fundamental changes in the organization of Quebec society brought about by the conquest of 1759–62. In this view, Quebec was effectively "decapitated" by the conquest, because much of its secular elite returned to France. One consequence of this decapitation was to leave the leadership of Quebec society by default in the hands of the Church. Then, with the economy firmly tied into the British system of colonial trade, and with English established as the language of commerce, the Québécois were compelled to look elsewhere for national fulfillment. The emergent French-Canadian culture was one of the accommodations made by the Québécois to their new economic, political, and social circumstances. This perspective also leads us to expect that the cultural preoccupations of the Québécois will continue to change, reflecting contemporary shifts in their economic and political power.

The choice between these two points of view is a matter of some political as well as scholarly significance. If the behavioural differences between the two language groups are attributable simply to differences in cultural values, then it is tempting to conclude that people simply get what they want. If, however, cultural differences are themselves the product of who won or lost a war and the ways in which the winners have organized society, then we are more likely to question social justice and the redress of historical grievances.

Another example of how historical conflicts are thought to shape culture is found in the emergence of cultural differences between English Canadians and Americans. One view traces these differences to the (quite different) reactions of Americans and English Canadians to the American Revolution, while another focuses on the ideological content of the institutions that were transplanted at particular periods in European history to North American soil.

Lipset (1963, 1965, 1985), an American sociologist, best exemplifies the first line of thought. The American Revolution was a traumatic event that left its imprint not only on the victorious Americans, but also on the defeated British Americans — who, with the French, went on to create Canada. Traces of our ancestors' rejection of the American Revolution may be found even today in the institutions, culture, and perhaps even the character of Canadians. Thus, according to Lipset, Canadians show greater deference to authority and are more likely to put the welfare of the community ahead of their personal interests. It was these values that the losing side, the Tory United Empire Loyalists, carried to the Canadian colonies. Once established in Canada, these values were reinforced by our British, monarchical, and religious traditions. Americans place a greater value on achievement in their relationships with and evaluations of other people.

It was obviously impossible for Lipset to test the specific link between reactions to the American Revolution and contemporary culture. His approach, therefore, was to test the claim that the two countries differ in their values in the predicted direction. This he did using statistics on divorce, crime rates, levels of educational attainment, and government spending patterns. If Canadians put the common good ahead of self-interest, then they should be less likely to divorce; if they were more deferential to authority and more attached to the common good, they should be less likely to commit a variety of criminal offences; if they placed less value on achievement, they should spend less money on higher education; and so on. In general, the data tended to support Lipset's picture of Canada as a more conservative nation — and, by inference, his historical hypothesis.

Lipset's interpretations of his findings have been criticized on a number of grounds. For example, divorce rates reflect more than people's values and their readiness to say "I quit." Divorce laws affect how easy it is to obtain a divorce, making it difficult to say how much of the differences between the two countries was owing to values and how much to legal hurdles. To correct for this ambiguity, a number of studies (for example, Crawford and Curtis 1979) have asked respondents directly about their opinions on a variety of issues. Their answers have then been used to measure value orientations. Suffice it to say that the results of these studies are equivocal in their support of Lipset's predictions. While finding differences in the responses of contemporary Canadians and Americans in the predicted direction would not be sufficient to demonstrate their connection with specific historical events, the failure to find these differences must nonetheless be seen as damaging.

The second version of this explanation is called the Hartzian thesis, after its originator, Louis Hartz (1964). Its basic premise is that ideologies develop out of conflict waged by their respective proponents. Compared to the variety of contending ideologies to be found in Europe, however, the debate in North America has been exceedingly truncated. According to Hartz, immigrants to the new North American societies did not carry with them the full spectrum of ideological opinion that prevailed in the countries from which they had come. Only parts of the spectrum made the journey, with the result that these parts were free to flourish unchecked by the ideological adversaries they had known at home. The institutions founded in the new societies, therefore, bore the ideological imprint of their founders. This historical hypothesis requires that we know something about the ideological origins of our society. In the case of the United States and English Canada, the English-speaking peoples carried with them the assumptions of liberal individualism. The assumptions of conservatism and socialism were missing or underrepresented among the English-speaking settlers of North America, thus permitting liberalism to develop virtually without impediment. But Quebec was another matter, because this society was founded prior to the French Revolution and represented a corporatist and authoritarian extrusion from France.

The general view presented here was later revised by Horowitz (1968) to allow for significant cultural differences between Canada and the United States. While the United States can fairly be described as a liberal society, Horowitz argued, the appearance of a "Tory touch" complicates the Canadian case. The United Empire Loyalists and our British traditions introduced distinctly non-liberal elements into English-Canadian culture. This Tory presence meant that Canadian conservatism would not be like its American cousin, and it provided the fertile ideological soil out of which an indigenous Canadian social democratic party would emerge.

**Structural Contradictions and Cultural Change.** Next, we turn to the continued strain toward cultural change produced by contemporary points of conflict within society. We can illustrate this by referring to Hershel Hardin's description of culture as a product of structural contradictions. The contradictions or points of conflict are French Canada against English Canada, the regions against the centre, and Canada against the United States: "To get at the Canadian circumstance . . . is above all to see the country in terms of its contradictions — the contending forces that underlie the character of the people" (Hardin 1974). So long as one remains in this country, he argues, it is impossible to escape these sources of creative tension, for they are "the forcing ground of our identity" (Hardin 1974). Canadians interacting with one another around these points of division produce symbols, norms, ideology, and other elements of culture as a means of coming to terms with their society and with each other. Hardin (1974) offers the following illuminating example of the immpact of one such Canadian contradiction on a new Canadian:

*One poignant case sticks in my mind, because it illustrates the leading Canadian contradiction at work on a man whose identity as a Canadian was still in the process of formation. It was during the St.*

*Leonard controversy over whether all schools should be French-language, or whether there should be English-language instruction available as well. An ethnic spokesman caught in the crossfire protested with quiet emotion to CBC radio that his group was an innocent victim . . . because they had no ingrained hostility against French-Canadians. "We're not against the French-Canadians," he said. "And we're not against the English-Canadians. We just want to be Canadian." It never occurred to him that having to explore this linguistic conflict and cope with it, and in intensely passionate, practical circumstances, would give him more insight into what it meant to be a Canadian than most Canadians would gather from a lifetime. Even while he was protesting, he probably had already realized there was no total escape from the contradiction other than by leaving the country. Wasn't that why he was protesting in the first place? And after going through that experience, would he ever agree that being a Canadian and an American involved more or less the same thing?*

The origins of this society's culture in conflict, as sketched by Hardin, are vastly more complex than the Lipset and Hartzian theses would have us believe. The central historical conflicts were not settled centuries ago but have persisted through the generations and into the present. Paradoxically, the forces on either side of each contradiction have strengthened their opposites while flexing their own muscles.

The "thick continuity" (Hardin's expression) of our history has created a people for those with the eyes and the patience to see. It is a commonplace for visitors from Britain or the United States to miss what is Canadian, because their sensibilities have been shaped elsewhere. Closer to home, sociology textbooks that treat Canada as a cultural extension of the United States, Hardin would ar-

---

# "Culture Carriers" in Canada and the U.S.

Bell and Tepperman (1979) have characterized the native-born proportion of Canada's population as its "tradition carriers." By this they mean that Canada's cultural traditions are more likely to be learned and known by native-born people, who have gone through the school system and who have had long-term contact with the Canadian media and fellow Canadians.

Looked at in this way, Canada has had fewer culture carriers than the United States in recent decades. The proportions native-born have been considerably lower in Canada. The accompanying table shows the relevant figures for selected census years since 1881. If Bell and Tepperman's characterization of the role of the native-born is correct, we should expect to find less consensus on beliefs and values in Canada, a culture that is less "set" than that of the United States.

In the 1984 Canadian National Election Survey referred to earlier, respondents were also asked if they had native-born parents. Of those surveyed, 63 percent were native-born and had

## Foreign-born Persons as a Percentage of the Total Population in Canada and the United States

| | Percentage Foreign-born | |
|---|---|---|
| Year | Canada | U.S. |
| 1981 | 16.1 | 6.2 |
| 1961 | 15.6 | 4.0 |
| 1941 | 17.5 | 8.8 |
| 1921 | 22.3 | 13.2 |
| 1901 | 13.0 | 13.6 |
| 1881 | 13.9 | 13.3 |

two parents who were native-born. This figure varied markedly by province, decreasing from east to west, from a high of 97 percent in Newfoundland to a low of only 34 percent in British Columbia. This range is to be expected, given the differences in recruitment of immigrants to Canada's regions over the years. However, these findings suggest that differing proportions of native-born Canadians may affect patterns of beliefs and values across regions.

**Source:**

Adapted from D.V.J. Bell and Lorne Tepperman, *The Roots of Disunity* (Toronto: McClelland and Stewart, 1979), p. 92.

gue, display this same insensitivity. Nor is it un-common for Canadians to miss what is Canadian, because their ideology is American and bor-rowed. This is especially the case, he believes, when Canadians persist in seeing Canada as a free-enterprise economy, either forgetting or blind to the fact that this country has a history rich in public enterprise.

**Dominant Ideology and the Preservation of the Status Quo.** Another conflict-oriented use of the concept of culture emphasizes that there are dom-inant social classes or groups in society, a topic to be discussed more fully in Chapter 8. These classes develop ideologies that are self-justifying and hence help unify the dominant groups themselves. There is great debate among sociologists about how ex-tensively dominant ideology is disseminated in society and how important it is in maintaining the status quo. If people in the subordinate classes are not persuaded by dominant ideology, it may nonetheless intimidate them and impede their de-velopment of counter-ideologies (Abercrombie, Hill, and Turner 1980).

If dominant ideology is disseminated, then it makes sense to look at the institutions assigned this task — as conflict theorists have done. Edu-cation, religion, and the mass media have been the subject of much research and speculation in this thesis. We will limit our comments to some studies of education.

A good example of research testing the domi-nant ideology thesis is a study by McDonald (1978) on the establishment of the Ontario public school system by Egerton Ryerson in the nineteenth cen-tury. Ryerson believed that the educational sys-tem should be firmly under government control, rather than locally controlled. It should be highly regulated and uniform throughout the province, staffed by local and professional teachers, and open to all children. Its mission was to produce loyal citizens who would reject the ideas of republican democracy emanating from the United States. Properly indoctrinated citizens would never again participate in a rebellion like the one crushed in Upper Canada in 1837. The schools should also promote harmony among the social classes. This meant persuading the working classes that "their interests were also those of the middle and upper classes, and that, as a collectivity, there was a

'common' or 'public good' towards which all must work" (McDonald 1978).

The relationship between people's level of edu-cation and their belief in dominant ideology among Canadians interviewed in 1977 was tested by Baer and Lambert (1982). Dominant ideology was sig-nified by support for the kind of economic ine-quality that prevails in Canadian society and rejection of the idea that government has a re-sponsibility for creating employment. Support for dominant ideology was greatest among the most educated respondents. Belief in dominant ideol-ogy was also greatest among people who felt that their income matched their qualifications. Doubts were most frequently expressed by the less ed-ucated and by those who felt underpaid (see also Curtis and Lambert 1976).

The findings of the Baer and Lambert study, however, suggest that the aspirations of the foun-ders of our educational system to indoctrinate children from all social classes have not been fully realized. If the point of dominant ideology is so-cial control, then its effects seem to be limited to the most educated members of society. Mann (1970) has claimed that this is all that is really necessary, for there are other ways of controlling people with less education. For one thing, the prominence given to dominant ideology in our mass media and in the educational system may simply undermine the emergence of counter-ideologies. In other words, they disorient more than they persuade. Cynicism bred by our political system, the ab-sence of significant political options, and the control exercised by work and the fear of unem-ployment may lead to a sense of resignation on the part of citizens. It is less a matter of belief in the status quo, Mann argues, than a matter of "pragmatic acquiescence" on the part of subor-dinate groups in society to what appears inevitable.

## Toward a Unified Perspective

Our treatment of the three perspectives and the explanations generated from them has implied that they are mutually exclusive. This may be a useful device for purposes of exposition, but so-cial reality is not so simply constructed. In fact, the sensitive observer can probably detect all three processes intertwined in the creation of most cultural phenomena. We pointed out earlier that interpersonal interactions are subsumed by the two macro perspectives, structural functionalism and conflict. The problem is with these two perspectives, because they have often been defended as though they were theoretically irreconcilable.

We can find evidence for both processes at work in specific cases, although their mix may well differ among cases. The development of regional and provincial cultures in Canada is a case in point. On the one hand, provincially based economies and cultural infrastructures operate to produce provincial or regional cultures. On the latter point, the British North America Act and its successors, the Constitution Acts, assign to the provinces clear responsibilities in such fields as education. This means that some of the factors that shape culture, as discussed above in connection with the structural-functional perspective, have a provincial presence. On the other hand, there are enduring rivalries and conflicts between regions and between the provinces and the federal government, as Hardin (1974) has emphasized, and these contribute to cultural variations across the country. In fact, political scientist Alan Cairns (1977) has argued that key instruments in the development of the "societies [and cultures] of Canadian federalism" are the governments of Canada themselves. In asserting this proposition, Cairns objects to the traditional view that sees politics and government as mere products of society; once created, they react on society, changing it in the process. Who would deny, for example, the significance of the struggle between the Ottawa and Quebec governments in producing the stuff of culture in this country?

## SUMMARY

1. The most useful view of culture is that it is a shared set of symbols and their meanings. The effects of these shared meanings can be seen in people's actions and their relationships with one another, as well as in their manufactured world.
2. Beliefs, norms, and values are the building blocks for more complex components of culture — statuses, ideologies, and subcultures.
3. The fact that culture is defined in terms of some minimum level of sharing or consensus is common across the three basic theoretical perspectives in sociology. However, the three approaches differ in whether they emphasize the functional or conflicting origins and consequences of culture, as well as micro- versus macro-level interests.
4. The symbolic-interaction approach locates culture in specific relationships and situations. Culture is seen as fluid and dynamic rather than static. The principal cultural concept is the definition of the situation, which is a product of people's negotiations with each other. Symbolic interactionists emphasize the initiative and activity of individual actors in the process.
5. According to the structural-functional perspective, culture mirrors the society as a whole or some part of society; culture is also exchanged between societies, in cultural diffusion.
6. The conflict perspective is represented by three explanations. Culture can be interpreted as an accommodation to historical conflict, as a product of social contradictions, or as a weapon used by dominant groups to justify their privileged status and to unify themselves.
7. Each of these three perspectives is sensitive to particular themes in the creation, maintenance, and change of culture. Because the relationship between society and culture is multifaceted, it should be theoretically possible to adopt a unified approach.
8. Although some sociologists emphasize either culture or the organization of society in their explanations of social life, it should not be necessary to choose one over the other. Social process and social change within a society are best understood as products of the interplay between a society's structure and its culture. The sociologist's task is to make sense of this interplay for the research question at hand.

## GLOSSARY

**Counter-ideologies.** Reformist and radical ideologies that call for changes in the status quo.
**Cultural diffusion.** The process whereby cultural elements are borrowed by one society from another (as opposed to independent development of these elements in each society).

**Cultural infrastructure.** Specialized groups with an interest, often economic, in the production and preservation of cultural symbols and the supporting groundrules.

**Cultural relativism.** The view that all cultures are equally valid and valuable and that each culture must be judged by its own standards.

**Culture.** Shared set of symbols and their definitions or meanings prevailing in a society.

**Definition of the situation.** Beliefs and norms about an interaction setting.

**Descriptive beliefs.** Statements or claims about what is, was, or will be, including ideas about cause and effect.

**Dominant ideologies.** Ruling ideologies that explain and justify the existing ways of doing things.

**Ethnocentrism.** Tendency to use one's own culture as the only valid standard for evaluating other cultures, societies, and peoples.

**Folkways.** Traditional rules about customary ways of behaving that are informally enforced and of mild concern to society members.

**Ideologies.** Emotionally charged sets of descriptive and normative beliefs and values that either explain and justify the status quo or, in the case of counter-ideologies, call for and justify alternative arrangements.

**Laws.** Norms that have been formally promulgated by a legislative body and are enforced by an executive body of government.

**Material culture.** Physical artifacts or products of a society embodying cultural meanings.

**Mores.** Traditional rules about how the individual must or must not behave, invested with strong feelings and informally enforced.

**Normative beliefs.** Ideas about what should or should not be, referring especially to goodness, virtuousness, or propriety.

**Norms.** Formal or informal rules stating how categories of people are expected to act in particular situations, violations of which are subject to sanction.

**Status.** Culturally defined position in society, consisting of ideas about rights and obligations.

**Subcultures.** More or less distinctive beliefs, norms, symbols, values, and ideologies shared by groups within a larger population.

**Symbol.** Anything, such as a word, gesture, or object, taken by people as a matter of convention to stand for something else, to have a meaning.

**Values.** Cultural conceptions about what are desirable goals and what are appropriate standards for judging actions.

## FURTHER READING

**Audley, Paul.** *Canada's Cultural Industries: Broadcasting, Publishing, Records and Films.* Toronto: CIEP/Lorimer, 1983. A study of Canada's cultural infrastructure — performances, problems, prospects, and policies.

**Bell, D.V.J., and L. Tepperman.** *The Roots of Disunity.* Toronto: McClelland and Stewart, 1979. Describes the contours of Canada's culture and shows the differences across regions, social classes, and linguistic groups.

**Christian, W., and C. Campbell.** *Political Parties and Ideologies in Canada.* Toronto: McGraw-Hill Ryerson, 1974. Although organized in terms of political parties, contains extensive treatments of the ideologies of liberalism, conservatism, socialism, and nationalism in this country.

**Crean, S.M.** *Who's Afraid of Canadian Culture?* Don Mills, ON.: General Publishing, 1976. A detailed description and interpretation of the personnel, groups, practices, policies, and "facts of life" affecting the arts in Canada.

**Hardin, H.** *A Nation Unaware: The Canadian Economic Culture.* Vancouver: J.J. Douglas, 1974. This book argues that Canada has a history of public enterprise that Canadians fail to appreciate when they perceive it through the ideological categories of American business.

**Hiller, Harry H.** *Canadian Society: A Macro Analysis.* Scarborough, ON.: Prentice-Hall, 1986. Discusses Canadian culture and society from the point of view of seven research questions. Chapter 7, "The Question of Identity," is especially relevant.

**Lakoff, G., and M. Johnson.** *Metaphors We Live By.* Chicago: University of Chicago Press, 1980. Metaphors are sources of meaning. Metaphors taken from areas of life that we understand are applied to areas that we cannot understand on their own terms. Differences in cultures can be found in their prevalent metaphors.

# CHAPTER 3

# Socialization

MARLENE MACKIE

Human beings must eat to stay alive. For babies, the matter is quite straightforward. They experience abdominal discomfort; they cry; a parent responds; they suck. Adult satisfaction of this basic physiological need is more complicated. Canadians consider some things proper food (steak, hamburgers), but gag at the thought of eating equally nutritious alternatives (caterpillars, horsemeat). Food preferences also mark ethnic group boundaries (Anderson and Alleyne 1979). Italian Canadians are often partial to pasta, German Canadians to sauerkraut, and Jewish Canadians to bagels and lox. Eating is surrounded by rules (Goffman 1963a). Even when people are ravenous, they are not supposed to attack the apple pie before the spinach. Adults who jam food into their mouths until their cheeks bulge seem disgusting, especially if they try to talk while they stuff. Plucking an interesting item from a neighbour's plate will result in raised eyebrows. So will scratching one's tonsils with a fork.

How, then, does the carefree infant become transformed into the disciplined adult? There is a one-word answer to this question — socialization. The whole story, of course, is not quite that simple.

**Socialization** is the complex learning process through which individuals develop selfhood and acquire the knowledge, skills, and motivations required for participation in social life. This process is the link between individual and society and may be viewed from each of these two perspectives.

From the point of view of the individual, interaction with other people is the means by which human potentialities are actualized. The newborn infant is almost completely helpless. Although more is happening in infant heads than scientists previously guessed, the newborn's abilities are limited to crying, sucking, eliminating wastes, yawning, and a few other reflexes. It has no self-awareness. Though it has the potential for becoming human, it is not yet human. The physical care, emotional response, and training provided by the family transform this noisy, wet, demanding bundle of matter into a functioning member of society. It learns language, impulse control, and skills. It develops a self. Knowledge is acquired of both the physical world and the social world. The child becomes capable of taking on social roles with some commitment. It learns whether it is female or male. It internalizes, or accepts as its own, the norms and values of, first, the family and, later, the wider society.

Effective socialization is as essential for the society as it is for the individual. Untrained members disturb the social order. For example, physically handicapped people report that children often stare and ask blunt questions about their conditions (Goffman 1963b). Furthermore, Canadian society could not continue to exist unless the thousands of new members born each year eventually learned to think, believe, and behave as Canadians. Each new generation must learn the society's culture. Social order demands self-discipline and impulse control. The continuity of our society requires that children come to embrace societal values as their own. Citizens must adhere to cultural norms because they themselves view those norms as right and proper. Cultural breakdown occurs when the socialization process no longer provides the new generation with valid reasons to be enthusiastic about becoming members of that society (Flacks 1979). However, individuals may redefine social roles and obligations, as well as accepting them as they stand. Social change thus occurs over time (Bush and Simmons 1981).

The heterogeneous nature of Canadian society complicates the socialization process. Although many values and norms are shared by all Canadians, differences are found by language, by region, by ethnicity, by religion, by social class, by urban/rural residence. These variations in social environment bring with them variations in the content of socialization. The perpetuation of these distinctive Canadian groups depends on children learning the relevant subcultural norms and values. For example, the Danish-Canadian community cannot continue in any meaningful fashion unless children of this ethnic background learn to view themselves as Danish Canadians, and learn the traditions and perhaps the language of that group. Similarly, the continuation of the unique features of the Maritime region requires that Canadians who live there acquire, by means of specialized socialization, the identity of Maritimers and the special norms, values, and history of that region.

Historical events — such as the Great Depression, World War II, and the protest era of the late 1960s — mean that successive generations of Canadians have different socialization experiences (Mannheim 1953). For example, people who grew up during the "Dirty Thirties" often learned what it meant to go hungry, to give up career plans, to delay marriage. We would expect their perspective on life to contrast sharply with that of earlier and later generations (Elder 1974).

The socialization process explains how commitment to the social order is maintained. Paradoxically, most people find their own fulfillment as individuals while simultaneously becoming social beings. However, it is important to note that socialization for deviance also occurs. Some folks learn to forge cheques, to crack safes, and to snort cocaine.

## Types of Socialization

We have defined socialization as the lifelong learning process through which individuals develop selfhood and acquire the knowledge, skills, and motivations required to participate in social life. Incidentally, these various socialization lessons are intertwined. Before we go on, we should make some further definitional distinctions.

**Primary socialization** is the basic socialization that occurs in childhood. It involves developing language and individual identity, learning cognitive skills and self-control, internalizing moral standards and appropriate attitudes and motivations, and gaining some understanding of societal roles.

**Adult socialization** occurs beyond the childhood years. Although primary socialization lays the foundation for later learning, it cannot completely prepare people for adulthood. For one thing, our age-graded society confronts individuals with new role expectations as they move through life. Moving beyond the family or day-care centre into the neighbourhood, entering school, becoming an adolescent, choosing an occupation, marrying, bearing children, encountering middle age, retiring, and dying all involve new lessons to be learned.

Also, society changes, and people must therefore equip themselves to cope with new situations — for example, technological job obsolescence brought about by computers, and changes in sexual norms produced by the threat of AIDS.

Finally, some individuals must deal with specialized situations. Geographical and social mobility, marital breakdown, physical handicaps, and so on all require further socialization (Brim 1966).

**Anticipatory socialization** occurs in advance of the actual playing of roles. This rehearsal for the future involves learning something about role requirements, both behaviours and attitudes, and visualizing oneself in the role. Children begin to practise being pupils before they ever enter school. Law students mentally try on the role of practising lawyer. We think about being married, being parents, being divorced, before we actually assume these statuses.

**Resocialization** occurs when a new role or a new situation requires a person to replace established patterns of behaviour and thought with new patterns (Campbell 1975). Old behaviour must be unlearned because it is incompatible in some way with new role demands. Usually, resocialization is more difficult than the original socialization; the established habits interfere with new learning. Fortunately, though, human beings retain the capacity for change across the entire lifespan. Indeed, thousands of organizations, from Alcoholics Anonymous to Zen, are designed to help individuals change (Brim and Kagan 1980).

Resocialization is more characteristic of adult socialization than of primary socialization. However, as youngsters mature, they too are expected to discard former behaviour. Block printing is fine for a first-grade pupil, but a fourth-grade pupil must learn to write. A two-year-old boy can cry when he is frightened, but a twelve-year-old boy who climbs into his mother's lap and whimpers may be considered odd.

Resocialization necessarily confronts the individual with contradictions between old and new behaviour that are sometimes confusing and sometimes painful. A new immigrant to Canada describes learning about this country's food: "If they gave me hot dog, I wouldn't eat it! I thought it was a dog meat! Well, I translated, you see, hot dog. You know, if no one tells you. . . . " (Disman 1983). The fact that the nonresponsible, submissive, asexual child must become the dominant, sexually active adult (Mortimer and Simmons 1978) illustrates one contradiction between childhood and adulthood. The resocialization involved in new situations also entails contradictions for adults. For example, the women's liberation movement has resulted in redefinitions of the ways men and women relate to each other. Can either sex initiate a date? Should husbands help with the housework or sit back and watch their wives do it? More dramatic discontinuities between old and new selves are experienced by individuals who get caught up in extreme instances of resocialization such as brainwashing, religious conversion, and "therapeutic" programs in prisons and mental hospitals.

## The Lifelong Process

We have noted that socialization is a lifelong process. Despite some anticipatory socialization during childhood, primary socialization simply cannot prepare people for roles and situations that either are unforeseeable at the moment, or lie far ahead in the future.

Adult socialization is particularly necessary in complex, changing societies such as Canada. Here, a comparison may be made with the Hutterities, a culture that has remained very much the same for 450 years. Hutterites live out their lives in small rural colonies in western Canada. Everybody knows everybody else. There are few secrets;

therefore nearly all adult roles are open for the Hutterite children's inspection (Mackie 1975). Eventually, the children will inherit those very roles they see enacted before them. In cases such as these, adult socialization is less extensive than in Canadian society generally.

Although socialization continues throughout life, the social science literature has emphasized childhood socialization. The main reason for this somewhat distorted focus is that primary socialization provides the groundwork for all later learning. The major structures of personality are formed in childhood. In addition, the lessons learned during this impressionable period are the first lessons, and learning comes easily. We have already pointed out that resocialization is difficult because old behaviour must be unlearned before new behaviour can be acquired. Finally, it should be noted that, even when new expectations do not conflict with previous expectations, primary socialization channels and sets limits for adult socialization. For example, a person who emerges from childhood without a strong motivation to achieve is unlikely to excel in medical school.

A number of fundamental differences exist between primary socialization and adult socialization (Brim 1966), in addition to those just considered.

1. With some exceptions, adult socialization concentrates on overt behaviour, rather than on values and motives. Society assumes that adults already hold the values appropriate for a given role and that they are motivated to pursue that role. All that remains is to teach the incumbents how to behave. Universities, for example, do not attempt to convince students of the value of higher education or to motivate them to work hard at their studies. Prisons, on the other hand, are resocialization agencies, but their high rates of recidivism (individuals relapsing into crime after release from imprisonment) illustrate the impracticality of wholesale attempts to alter basic values and motives.

2. While primary socialization tends to be idealistic, adult socialization tends to be realistic. Children are taught how society ideally operates and how people ideally behave. They are shielded from knowledge of how society actually operates and how people actually be-

have. At the same time that parents exhort children to be honest, they protect children from awareness of corruption in government and their own "fudging" of the truth. Part of growing up, then, involves the substitution of sophistication for naiveté.

3. The content of adult socialization is more specific than the content of primary socialization. Although there are exceptions, children learn general knowledge, skills, and behaviour relevant to many roles. Adults, on the other hand, acquire information specific to particular roles. For example, children learn to read and to write. This knowledge is useful in a wide range of roles and situations. By contrast, adults learn to diaper a baby or to wire a circuit board. Such information pertains to the parent and the electronic-technician roles, respectively, and not elsewhere.

4. As a general rule, adults are socialized by formal organizations (schools, corporations), while children are socialized in informal contexts (the family, babysitters, peer groups). This distinction, however, reflects a general tendency rather than a rule. Although the school, for example, is a formal organization, it is an important primary socialization agency. Also, the actual socializing of adults within organizations is often done through primary relationships. For example, the impact of the inmate subculture on prisoners' experience of being incarcerated and on their responses to treatment programs is well documented (Ekstedt and Griffiths 1984). Throughout life, people remain sensitive to the opinions and examples of their family and friends.

5. The nature of the relationships between socializer and socializee differs in primary and adult socialization. The family is the major socializer of the child. Familial relationships are marked by high levels of both feeling and power. Because of the emotionally charged familial context and the power of the parents to mete out rewards and punishments, parents have a tremendous impact on children. In contrast, the relationship between adult socializer and socializee is usually more emotionally neutral and more equal in terms of power. However, this does not mean that the adult socialization experience is devoid of emotion. For example,

McMaster medical students are plagued by anxiety and uncertainty (Haas, Marshall, and Shaffir 1981). Moreover, the adult socializee is often in that position voluntarily: one *chooses* to be an apprentice welder or a college student. The volunteer has rights that the conscript lacks in defining what will be learned and how the learning will occur. The youngest child in the Jones family, however, did not choose his or her fate.

## Nature Versus Nurture

Since the beginning of this century, social scientists have been preoccupied with the relative contributions of biology and environment to human development. Those who have emphasized the role of biology in this nature/nurture debate argued that the individual's psychological characteristics and social behaviour result from the unfolding of inherited factors, such as instincts. On the other hand, sociologists on the nurture side of the argument believed that environmental influences are all-important.

Recent discoveries in biology and genetics have resulted in the problem becoming increasingly complex. Although the nature/nurture debate has not yet been resolved, modern scientists have abandoned the simplistic approach of nature versus nurture. Biology and environment interact to transform the infant into a functioning member of society. (See Chapter 4 for a discussion of the nature/nurture issue as it applies to gender patterns.)

Socialization provides the link between biology and culture. Biology gives human beings the capacity to learn and the ability to use language. In addition, the human infant's relatively long period of helplessness (compared with that of the lower animals) enforces dependence on adult caretakers. The resulting emotional bonds forged between parents and children are necessary for normal childhood development. This deep emotional attachment gives parents the power needed to socialize children. In other words, children are responsive to parental influence partly because they are dependent on the parents' love and approval.

## Effects of Social Deprivation

What happens when parental love and approval are not forthcoming? Two specific cases impressively demonstrate the importance of socialization. Both illustrate clearly that the infant's biological potential cannot be actualized without close emotional attachments to at least one adult. The first case concerns two American children who were deliberately reared in isolation (Davis 1940, 1947). The second case involves experiments by Harlow and his colleagues on the effects of isolation on rhesus monkeys (Harlow 1959; Harlow and Harlow 1962).

### Children Reared in Isolation

Anna was an illegitimate child born in 1921. At the insistence of her grandfather, she was hidden away in an attic-like room until she was nearly six years old. During this period, her mother had given her only enough care to keep her alive. When Anna was discovered, her clothing and bedding were filthy. She was extremely emaciated; her stomach was bloated. There were no signs of intelligence; she was unable to talk, walk, feed herself, or respond to people. At first, it was believed that she was blind and deaf. Four years later, she finally began to develop speech. By the time of her death (a year later), she was operating at the level of the normal child aged two-and-a-half. Although the possibility that Anna was born mentally deficient cannot be ruled out, Davis thinks that "Anna might have had a normal or near-normal capacity, genetically speaking."

Isabelle was also an illegitimate child kept in seclusion. She and Anna were discovered at about the same time, at about the same age. Isabelle had lived with her deaf-mute mother in a dark room shut off from the rest of her mother's family. As a result, she had had no chance to develop speech. Instead, she made only a strange croaking noise. An inadequate diet and lack of sunshine had produced a severe case of rickets. When Isabelle was confronted with strangers, especially men, she behaved like a frightened wild animal. The child appeared to be hopelessly feeble-minded. However, her caretakers began a long, systematic training program. Isabelle went very rapidly through the usual stages of learning characteristic of the years one to six. Within a week, she made her first attempt at vocalization. In less than a year, she could identify written words, and could also write and add. By the time she was eight-and-a-half years old, she had reached a normal level. Davis reported that she was a bright, cheerful, energetic little girl.

Isabelle had two advantages that Anna did not. She received prolonged, expert attention. Also, she had had the constant companionship of her deaf-mute mother. The story of these neglected children points up the primary importance of contact with reasonably intelligent, articulate people in the early years of child development.

## Monkeys Reared in Isolation

Monkeys need this early contact too. The experiments by Harlow and his associates on the effects of isolation on rhesus monkeys show that the animals' infantile social experience has crucial effects on their behaviour in later life.

In one of this series of studies (Harlow and Harlow 1962), young monkeys were separated from their mothers a few hours after birth. They were caged in such a way that each little monkey could see and hear other monkeys, although it could make no direct physical contact with them. These socially deprived infants matured into emotionally disturbed adults. The monkeys sat in their cages and stared fixedly into space or clasped their heads in their arms and rocked for hours. They developed compulsive habits, such as chewing and tearing at their own bodies until they bled. They did not know how to relate to other monkeys, and were either passive and withdrawn or extremely aggressive. Harlow's work showed that there was a critical period of development during which social experience was absolutely necessary. Isolation for the first six months of life rendered animals permanently inadequate. The effects of shorter periods of isolation (60 to 90 days) were, however, reversible.

Another phase of Harlow's (1959) research involved comparing the importance of the act of nursing with the importance of bodily contact in engendering the infant monkey's attachment to its mother. Two surrogate "mother" monkeys were constructed. Both were wire cylinders surmounted by wooden heads. One was bare. The wire of the other was cushioned by a terry-cloth sheath. Each "mother" had the nipple of a feeding bottle protruding from its "breast." Eight newborn monkeys were separated from their natural mothers and placed in individual cages. Each was given access to both types of surrogate "mothers." Four monkeys were fed from the wire "mother" and four from the cloth-covered "mother." All the infants developed a strong attachment to the cloth-covered "mother" and little or none to the wire "mother," regardless of which one provided the milk. Both groups spent much more time clinging to the cloth-covered "mothers" than to the wire "mothers." Moreover, the soft "mother" was sought out for security. Experimenters confronted the monkey infants with a mechanical teddy bear, which moved toward them beating a drum. When frightened by this device, the infants sought comfort from the cloth-covered "mother," whether they had nursed from a wire mother or from a cloth-covered one. These results showed the importance of bodily contact in developing the infant/mother affectional bond.

The cloth-covered surrogate "mother" provided tactile comfort; however, it could not supply communication or training. Therefore, the social development of all the infant monkeys was severely and permanently impaired. Both the rhesus monkey experiments and the case histories of Anna and Isabelle show the fundamental need for childhood social experience. In addition, both show us how futile the nature/nurture controversy really is when nature and nurture are viewed as mutually exclusive alternatives.

## Socialization Theories

Although socialization — learning norms, attitudes, values, knowledge, skills, and self-concepts — occurs throughout life, the learning that takes place during the formative years of childhood has been of special concern to psychologists and sociologists. The family, which bears the major responsibility here, has therefore received considerable attention from these social scientists. This section considers the principal ideas involved in four theoretical approaches to childhood socialization: learning theory, Piaget's cognitive developmental approach to moral thought, Freud's psychoanalytic theory, and symbolic-interaction views on development of the self. These theoretical perspectives vary in their emphases on how learning occurs and what socialization comprises, but for the most part, they are complementary rather than opposed sets of ideas. All of them can contribute to our understanding of childhood socialization.

## Learning Theory

Very little human behaviour is directly determined by the individual's genetic makeup. For this reason, the precise mechanisms involved in learning are well worth knowing.

**Three Main Types of Learning.** We are concerned here with three main types of learning: classical conditioning, operant conditioning, and observation. In the first two types, learning occurs as a result of practice or the repetition of association (Yussen and Santrock 1978). However, since much of what children learn is through observation rather than extensive practice, the last type is the most important for socialization.

**Classical conditioning** was first discovered by Russian physiologist Ivan Pavlov in his famous experiments with a salivating dog. The basic idea is quite simple (Deutsch and Krauss 1965). Meat powder, an "unconditioned stimulus" (UCS), is placed in a dog's mouth, automatically eliciting salivation, an "unconditioned response" (UCR). A neutral stimulus, that does not elicit salivation, such as the sound of a bell, is presented just before the presentation of the food. The neutral stimulus is called a "conditioned stimulus" (CS). Soon the CS by itself elicits the flow of saliva without the meat or UCS. This learned response to the bell is the "conditioned response" (CR).

The classical conditioning paradigm explains some learning children do that is unintended by their parents. For example, a child may munch cookies while watching "Sesame Street." Before long, television becomes a signal to eat. This type of learning also represents one established source of phobias, or irrational fears. Many social attitudes are acquired in exactly the same fashion. If, for example, a little boy has an unpleasant experience with a red-haired girl, he may (unlike Charlie Brown) go through life disliking red-haired girls.

**Operant conditioning**, a second type of learning, is associated with American psychologists E.L. Thorndike (1898, 1913) and B.F. Skinner (1953). In this case, the organism must first make a specific response. If that response is followed by a reward or a punishment, it then becomes a conditioned, or learned, response. In a typical experiment, a hungry pigeon is placed in a cage equipped with four differently coloured keys. It goes through a trial-and-error procedure of pecking at the keys, eventually pecking the red key. The red key, when depressed, releases food. Because this particular response was rewarded, the pigeon will, after a few trials, go directly to the red key when hungry. In avoidance learning, an animal would be exposed to a noxious stimulus, such as an electric shock. In that case, it would learn to prevent punishment by pressing a certain key. In general, though, punishment is not a very reliable way of shaping future behaviour. It stops unwanted behaviour for the moment, but for various reasons its effects on future behaviour tend to be somewhat uncertain.

Children learn many of their socialization lessons through operant conditioning. Parents positively reinforce desired verbal responses, such as "please" and "thank you." Parents punish unwanted behaviour, such as rude talk, selfishness, or taking candy from stores without paying for it.

One sociologist (Cahill 1987) observed what happens when a small boy attempts to recycle a wad of gum:

*While a woman is inspecting cans on a supermarket shelf, an approximately four-year-old boy leaves her side, walks over to a shelf on the opposite side of the aisle, picks up a piece of previously used chewing gum, and starts to put it in his mouth. The woman glances over her shoulder and loudly commands the boy to "STOP." Still holding the gum in his hand, the boy points to the shelf from which he removed the gum and objects that "it was there." The woman responds: "I don't care where you found it. It's been in someone else's mouth."*

Although children do learn by operant conditioning, complications inevitably arise whenever results from pigeon and rat experiments are extrapolated to human beings. For one thing, experimenters consciously decide what they want the animals to learn; much human learning, however, is accidental. In addition, human beings find a much broader range of responses rewarding or punishing than do animals. Imagine this scene. A mother and her three-year-old daughter are in the kitchen. The child is bored and wants attention. Because the mother is busy, she is ignoring the child's chatter. Eventually, the little girl repeats the word she heard her father say that morning when he cut himself shaving. The mother, shocked by the profanity, scolds the child — unwittingly reinforcing the vulgar response by giving the bored child attention. Guess what the little girl learns that day?

**Observational learning**, the third type of learning, was discovered through research on the social behaviour of human beings. Bandura and Walters (1963) have shown that children can learn novel response patterns through observing another's behaviour. No reinforcement or reward is required for such learning to occur. Observational learning does not involve the gradual building up of responses required by operant conditioning.

Language appears to be learned mainly through observation. If children had to learn speech through operant conditioning, they would be senior citizens before they mastered their native language. Each sound, syllable, word, and sentence would have to be uttered spontaneously, then systematically reinforced by the caretakers. Instead, children copy the language behaviour of their adult models (and learn the meaning behind the language forms), just as they imitate other forms of behaviour. Children are especially likely to imitate adult models who are warm, nurturant, and powerful. In families that are functioning effectively, the child's parents provide extremely influential models. Models are also provided when trial-and-error learning is likely to have dangerous consequences; parents *show* their children how to cross streets and how to drive automobiles. During adolescence, the peer group is influential as a model in the use of verbal expressions, hairstyles, clothing, and entertainment preferences (Muuss 1988).

Unintentional learning often occurs through observation, as well as through classical and operant conditioning. Although a father may deliberately demonstrate to his son the movements involved in tying shoelaces, he does not set out to teach the boy his vocal inflections or facial expressions. Similarly, parents often tell children one thing and model quite another. For example, parents may preach that reading books is worthwhile but never read books themselves. Their child is more likely to copy parental deeds than parental words.

## Piaget's Cognitive Developmental Approach to Moral Thought

The career of Swiss psychologist Jean Piaget began early. At age ten, he published an article on a rare albino sparrow in a natural history journal. Four years later, he was considered for a position as a curator in a Geneva museum. When this creative child's age was discovered, the offer was hastily withdrawn (Hetherington and Parke 1979).

Piaget's general theory (1928) considers how children think, reason, and remember. The development of moral thought — a sense of right and wrong, an understanding of societal values — is a particularly important dimension of his theory (Piaget 1932). Piaget observed children playing marbles and asked them to explain the game to him. He in turn talked to them about such ethical concepts as stealing, cheating, and justice. In many respects, childhood games are small-scale analogs of society. When children learn about the rules of the game, they are learning, at their level, about the norms of society. Similarly, when they learn to play game roles, they are also learning something about playing societal roles.

From his observations and discussions, Piaget concluded that two stages of moral thought exist. Children from four to seven years old display the more primitive level of morality, **moral realism**. The second stage, **moral autonomy**, develops around the age of eight. Several characteristics are associated with each stage.

The moral realist judges wrongdoing in terms of the outcome of the act. Extenuating circumstances and the intentions of the wrongdoer are disregarded. For example, Piaget told his subjects stories about two boys, John and Henry, and asked them to decide which boy deserved the more severe punishment. John was summoned to the dinner table. He came immediately. As he entered the dining room, he knocked over a teacart that, unknown to him, had been left behind the door. John's collision with the teacart resulted in fifteen

## The First Hockey Game

*Games teach youngsters about social life. When they learn the rules of the game, they are also learning something about the rules of society. Here, a father describes taking his five-year-old son to see his first hockey game.*

"After the face-off both teams skated hard, the lead changed back and forth, and — well, it turned out to be a pretty good game . . . , with no ugly stuff and, as pro hockey goes, relatively few penalties. I think this must have been a disappointment for my son, for, aside from eating, the aspect of hockey that seemed to appeal to him most was the penalty box. I decided that it must answer powerfully to something basic in a five-year-old's ideal of justice: immediate, *brief* punishment, and then return to one's peers without shame or guilt. Anyway, he leaned forward expectantly each time the ref blew his whistle, and whenever a player was sent off he appeared to take a stern, Calvinist pleasure in making certain that the offender didn't attempt to return to the ice an instant before his sentence had expired."

**Source:**

"The Talk of the Town," *The New Yorker*, December 27, 1982.

broken cups. The other boy, Henry, had been forbidden by his mother to eat jam. When his mother left the room, Henry climbed up to the cupboard in search of the jam and knocked a cup to the floor.

Children under seven years, in the moral realism stage, believed that John should be punished more severely. After all, John had broken fifteen cups while Henry had broken only one. However, the older children, the moral autonomists, were more concerned with the fictitious boys' *reasons* for acting than with the consequences of the acts. These older children felt that Henry deserved the greater punishment, because his offence had been committed while disobeying his mother's order. John's offence, on the other hand, had been accidental.

The moral realist believes that all rules are sacred and unchangeable absolutes. Rules are handed down by adult authority, and not the slightest deviation from them should be tolerated. The moral autonomist, in contrast, views rules as somewhat arbitrary social conventions. Older children involved in a game agree that certain rules are appropriate or inappropriate to that particular game situation. When the players consent to change, new rules can be adopted.

For example, the moral realist would agree that the child able to knock the most marbles out of a circle drawn in the dirt should have the first turn. Asked why, the moral realist would answer, "That's the rule. That's the way things are done." The moral autonomist would also agree that turns are decided by this preliminary trial. However, the older child would explain the procedure this way: "Well, the first turn has to be decided somehow. There are probably other ways to do it, but we decided to do it this way, and it works fine."

Piaget believes that maturation of cognitive capacities is the primary determinant of moral thought. This cognitive development results from the interaction of genetic capacities and social experiences. According to Piaget, it is the child's interaction with peers, rather than with parents, that provides the social experiences crucial for the development of morality. For one thing, freewheeling games with other children show that rules are conventional products that arise out of co-operation. Parents, on the other hand, are often reluctant to debate the reasons for their rules and regulations. This authoritarian stance promotes the younger child's view of rules as arbitrary and immutable. That, briefly, is Piaget's approach. Many studies have borne him out, showing that children from different cultures and social class backgrounds do go through a stage of moral realism before they reach moral autonomy.

Lawrence Kohlberg (1976) continued to study moral development in the Piaget tradition. In his procedure, those being interviewed were asked to respond to moral dilemmas such as the following:

*In Europe, a woman was near death from cancer. One drug might save her, a form of radium that a druggist in the same town had recently discovered.*

*The druggist was charging $2,000, ten times what the drug cost him to make. The sick woman's husband, Heinz, went to everyone he knew to borrow the money, but he could only get together about half of what it cost. He told the druggist that his wife was dying and asked him to sell it cheaper or let him pay later. But the druggist said, "No." The husband got desperate and broke into the man's store to steal the drug for his wife. Should the husband have done that?* (Kohlberg, 1969)

From his analysis of boys' responses to these dilemmas, Kohlberg concluded that moral thought develops through six stages rather than the two hypothesized by Piaget.

Gilligan (1982) discovered that both Piaget and Kohlberg had based their ideas about moral development on research conducted almost exclusively with male samples. From her own observations of people of both sexes, Gilligan maintains that females and males speak with different "moral voices." The male **justice orientation** is concerned with preserving rights, upholding principles, and obeying rules, while the female **care orientation** speaks of concern for, connectedness with, and sensitivity to other people. For example, 11-year-old Jake was clear that Heinz should steal the drug. Jake saw the moral dilemma as "sort of a math problem with humans." He reasoned that while laws are necessary to maintain social order, a judge would give Heinz the lightest possible sentence. By contrast, Amy, also a sixth-grader, argued that Heinz should not steal the drug. Her reasoning was grounded not in law but rather on the effect that the theft would have on the relationship between Heinz and his wife.

*If he stole the drug, he might save his wife then, but if he did, he might have to go to jail, and then his wife might get sicker again, and he couldn't get more of the drug. . . . So, they should really just talk it out and find some other way to make the money.* (Gilligan 1982)

## Psychoanalytic Theory

Psychoanalytic theory, as formulated by the Viennese physician Sigmund Freud (1856–1939), is both a theory of personality and a system of therapy (see Brill 1938). In practice, Freud was not an orthodox Freudian. He insisted that his psychoanalytic disciples be passive listeners and never respond emotionally to their patients. However, Freud himself gossiped, cracked jokes, offered advice, and often surprised his patients by handing them photographs of himself (*Time*, March 8, 1982).

Freud's theory views socialization as society's attempt to tame the child's inborn animal-like nature. He believed that the roots of human behaviour lie in the mind's irrational, unconscious dimensions. He assumed that the adult personality is the product of the child's early experiences within the family.

Freud saw the personality as composed of three energy systems: the Id, the Ego, and the Super-ego. The **Id** is the biological basis of personality, the **Ego** is the psychological basis of personality, and the **Super-ego** is the social basis of personality (Shaw and Costanzo 1970).

The Id is the reservoir of inborn, biological instincts. This "seething cauldron of sex and hostility" is wholly unconscious. It seeks immediate gratification: it operates according to the *pleasure principle*. The selfish, impulsive Id is not in contact with the reality of the external world.

Unlike the Id, the Ego develops out of the child's learning experiences with the environment. If all the Id's desires were gratified, the Ego would never emerge. The Ego encompasses the cognitive functions of thinking, perceiving, and memory. It also contains the defence mechanisms (such as rationalization, repression, projection) that have emerged from the Ego's previous encounters with reality. Part of the Ego is conscious and part is unconscious. The Ego's primary purpose is to direct the personality toward realistic goals: it is oriented toward the *reality principle*. Therefore, the Ego mediates among the demands of the Id, the Super-ego, and the external world.

The Super-ego, or conscience, emerges as a result of the child's identification with her or his parents. Through reward, punishment, and example, the parents communicate society's rules to the child. When these social values and behavioural standards have been "introjected" (adopted as the child's own standards), the Super-ego censors the Id's impulses. This internal authority also guides the Ego's activities.

Freud held that every child goes through a series of personality development stages, each stage marked by sexual preoccupation with a different part of the body — the mouth, the anus, the genital area. Personality development, according to psychoanalytic theory, is essentially complete by five years of age.

**Erikson's Revisions.** Freud's ideas have been revised by his many disciples, especially Erik Erikson. Though Erikson entered Freud's Viennese circle as a 25-year-old itinerant artist, with no university degree at all, he emerged as a prominent child psychoanalyst. As well, he contributed the term "identity crisis" to our everyday language (Ewen 1980).

Erikson's (1963, 1968) ideas about socialization differ from Freud's in four ways:

1. Erikson is convinced that the rational Ego has an important independent role in personality development. The irrational Id is played down in his thinking.
2. One function of the autonomous Ego, according to Erikson, is to preserve a sense of identity and to avoid identity confusion. While patients in Freud's time suffered from sexual inhibitions, contemporary patients are plagued with questions of who they are or what they should believe in.
3. Freud's biological theory holds that "anatomy is destiny." By contrast, Erikson's theory emphasizes society's role in molding personality. What is really involved here is a matter of degree.
4. According to Erikson, personality development continues throughout the life cycle, from infancy to old age. It does not stop at five years of age. Adolescents have the problem of establishing their identity. Young adults must establish intimacy with others in deep friendships and marriage, without sacrificing this sense of identity. Middle-aged adults are preoccupied with productivity and generativity (providing guidance for the next generation). Mature adults are concerned with ego integrity, a conviction that the life they have lived has meaning (Ewen 1980). Growth continues through all of these developmental crises.

Other writers besides Erikson disagree with Freud's belief that personality development ends with childhood. Such phrases as "life crisis," "critical transitions" (Levinson 1978), "turning points," and "passages" (Sheehy 1974) have all entered popular culture. Research is needed, however, to establish whether life transitions are biologically linked, invariant, or necessarily traumatic (Bush and Simmons 1981). In other words, must everyone go through painful transitions, such as mid-life crises, because they were born human? Moreover, the self-contained individual postulated in these lifespan approaches must be placed in a social context (Dannefer 1984). Discussion of these ideas does emphasize that socialization occurs over the life cycle.

## Symbolic-Interaction Views

Symbolic interaction, as a theoretical perspective on primary socialization, is more sociological than any of the approaches discussed so far. Like learning theory, it emphasizes the environmental influences that impinge on the child, rather than the unfolding of the child's biological capacities. (Both Piaget and Freud stressed the latter.) However, symbolic interaction directs particular attention to the impact of the social environment. The term "interaction" emphasizes the importance of group influences. These theorists also take issue with the Freudian position that a fundamental conflict exists between individual and society. Symbolic interactionists view the individual and society as two sides of the same coin. One cannot exist without the other.

Interactionists and learning theorists differ on two other major assumptions. Interactionists believe that human behaviour is qualitatively different from animal behaviour, because humans use much more complex language. This assumption is the reason for the word "symbolic" in these theorists' title. A *symbol* is something that stands for something else. A red light means stop. A five-dollar bill symbolizes buying power. Although there is some physical reality "out there," people respond not directly to this "objective reality," but to a symbolic interpretation of it (Charon 1979). These interpretations are called *definitions of the situation*. Definitions of the situation may be personal (idiosyncratic) or cultural (standard meanings embedded in a community's culture and learned through socialization) (Stebbins 1967). Symbolic interactionists are especially interested

## You and Your Self

*The acquisition of personal identity, or a sense of self, is one of the major goals of socialization. Therefore, researchers often have occasion to measure this concept. Despite its centrality, the "self" remains elusive. One of the most frequently used measures of the self-concept is Kuhn and McPartland's (1954) Twenty Statements Test.*

Before you complete this test, remember these three things.

First, the self is difficult to define. Although we know intuitively what we mean when we say we have a self, this label implies a number of related components. It can refer to the stream of consciousness, the self as experiencer of thoughts, emotions, physical sensations. As well, it implies the conviction of continuity over time. (This self who thinks, experiences, and acts today is essentially the same self as the one who thought, experienced, and acted five and ten years ago.) Sometimes, the "self" means the director of action, the planner, and the doer. Sometimes, it means the cognitive picture of who I am, the self-concept. In addition, the sense of self encompasses an ideal self, the self that I wish I were. Related to the latter component is self-esteem, or my evaluation of myself. Finally, the material self, which includes my body and, perhaps, my possessions, seems to be involved.

The first task of researchers is to specify exactly which component of the self they wish to measure. Below, we will focus on the self-concept (Mead's "Me"), and define it as a "set of attitudes toward the self."

Second, techniques to measure the self are often vulnerable to the "social desirability effect," which is the tendency for research subjects to present a flattering view of themselves. For example, people who really regard themselves as neurotic and overweight may not care to reveal these thoughts to a researcher.

Third, measures of the self are sometimes affected by the context in which they are administered. If you complete the measure described below at university, those aspects of your self-concept related to being a student will probably be uppermost in your mind. If you complete it at home, however, family identities may supersede the student dimension of your self-concept.

### The Twenty Statements Test

1. Write the numbers one to twenty on a page. The standard instructions for the test read as follows: "There are 20 numbered blanks on the page below. Please write 20 answers to the simple question 'Who Am I?' in the blanks. Just give 20 different answers to the question. Answer as if you were giving the answers to yourself, not to somebody else. Write the answers in the order that they occur to you. Don't worry about logic or importance. Go along fairly quickly, for time is limited. Give yourself about 10 minutes to complete the answers."

in how human beings attach meanings to the actions of other people as they attempt to make sense of both themselves and their social worlds.

Finally, symbolic interactionists emphasize the importance of the child's active involvement in role-learning processes, such as role-taking (discussed under "Genesis of the Self," below) and altercasting, as opposed to the more passive processes of modelling or conditioning. **Altercasting** involves casting the other person in a role we choose for him or her in order to manipulate the situation (Charon 1979). For instance, a child may say, "Toby, you're supposed to let me use your bike, because friends are supposed to share" (Weinstein 1969).

Although the symbolic interactionists are interested in many facets of socialization, we will concentrate here on the question of how the child acquires a self. We will consider the pertinent work of two pioneer theorists — Charles H. Cooley and George Herbert Mead.

**Cooley's Looking-Glass Self.** Cooley was an American sociologist who derived many of his ideas about socialization from observing and recording the behaviour of his own children. He used the metaphor of the looking glass to illustrate his point that children acquire a self through adopting other people's attitudes toward them. The self is social in that it emerges out of interaction with primary group members. Its content reflects the child's interpretation of others' appraisals of what kind of person that child is.

The **looking-glass self** has three elements: "the imagination of our appearance to the other person, the imagination of his judgment of that appearance, and some sort of self-feeling, such as pride or mortification" (Cooley 1902).

2. Next, the researcher classifies each of the 20 answers as either "consensual" or "nonconsensual" references. By "consensual references," Kuhn and McPartland meant groups and classes whose limits and conditions of membership are matters of common knowledge (for example, student, male, wife, Baptist, youngest child). By "nonconsensual references," they meant groups, classes, attributes, or traits that require interpretation by the individual. These statements are either ones without positional reference (happy, tall) or consensual references whose meaning is obscured by ambiguous modifiers (good student, ungrateful daughter).

   Go through your 20 answers and write "consensual" or nonconsensual" beside each of them.

3. The final step is to compute your "locus score." The "locus score" is the total number of consensual references made. The TST was designed to measure Mead's "Me," the self as a social entity. The locus score is intended to provide an indicator of the social anchorage of the self, because it measures citations of social positions.

## Some Comparative TST Results

You might find it interesting to compare your own TST results with some of its developers' findings. Differences do not mean that you are abnormal in any way.

1. Most people tend to exhaust all the consensual responses first, before going on to nonconsensual responses. For example, a person might describe himself as "male," "a university student," "a son," "22 years old," and then as "athletic," "skinny," and so on. However, the actual locus score may vary from none to twenty. Kuhn and McPartland argued that the self-descriptions given early are the most important ones. Therefore, they felt that the fact that the consensual responses come first provided evidence for the social nature of the self.

2. The locus score increases with age as people acquire an increasing number of social statuses. The average locus score for 7-year-olds is 5.8, and for 24-year-olds, 11.0.

3. Females mention their gender earlier than do males. Of those university undergraduates mentioning

gender at all, the mean rank for females was 1.7, and for males, 2.5.

4. Respondents 19 to 22 years old mention their age in average rank order of 5.6.

5. Most TST responses fall into five general categories: social groups and classifications (such as age, gender, occupation, marital status, kinship relations, ethnicity); ideological beliefs (statements of a religious, philosophical, or moral nature); interests; ambitions; self-evaluations. The fifth category can be analyzed as an indicator of self-esteem.

---

**Sources:**

Manford H. Kuhn, "Self-attitudes by age, sex and professional training," *Sociological Quarterly* 9(1960):39–55; Manford H. Kuhn and Thomas S. McPartland, "An empirical investigation of self-attitudes," *American Sociological Review* 19(1954):68–76; Marlene Mackie, "The domestication of self: Gender comparisons of self-imagery and self-esteem," *Social Psychology Quarterly* 46(1983):343–350.

---

Notice that what is important here is the child's *interpretation* of other people's attitudes. This interpretation may or may not be accurate. A little boy may pick up messages from his parents that they think he is short, fat, and clumsy, and that they think being short, fat, and clumsy is deplorable. If the assessment of his extremely authoritative parents is not countered by other sources of opinion, the boy has little choice but to define himself as short, fat, and clumsy. In all likelihood, therefore, he will feel ashamed of himself. Cooley was arguing, as we would put it today, that both self-imagery and self-esteem are social products.

**Mead's Theory of the Self.** In formulating his ideas about the child's acquisition of a self, Mead elaborated on many of the insights of Cooley, his symbolic-interaction contemporary. Mead's ideas on the subject are, however, much more sophis-

ticated than Cooley's. Mead's major work on the self is contained in *Mind, Self, and Society* (1934), a series of social philosophy lectures given at the University of Chicago, assembled after Mead's death. Although in his own lifetime Mead's impact was through ideas presented in lectures rather than through published works, he was not a charismatic teacher. In fact, he was boring. Schellenberg (1978) tells us that "his lectures were not very dramatic occasions. He seldom looked at his students, and he spoke with little expression. Looking at the ceiling or out a window, he sat and calmly lectured on the subject of the day."

The word "self" has rather mystical connotations. In order to specify what he meant by the "self," Mead made three fundamental assumptions:

1. The newborn infant does not come equipped with a self. Although the infant is born with

the physiological potential to reach this goal eventually, the self is acquired, not innate.

2. Mead defined "self" as that which is an object to oneself. At first glance, this definition does not seem very enlightening. However, Mead meant that the self is reflexive. To have a self is to have the ability to think about oneself and to act socially toward oneself. For most of us, the self is the most fascinating object in the world. We devote considerable time to self-contemplation. When we congratulate ourselves for an honest act or chastise ourselves for a piece of stupidity, we are acting toward ourselves.

3. The self is a communicative process, not a "thing." The self is analogous to a verb rather than a noun; it consists of the processes of thinking and acting toward oneself. The self is not a substantive entity that dwells behind the eyes or under the heart.

**Genesis of the Self.**  Mead's complex explanation of how the child acquires a self can be summarized in a small number of central ideas.

*The development of the self depends on development of the capacity to use language.* According to Mead, language and self develop concurrently. As a first step in developing self-awareness, the child must differentiate himself or herself as a separate "thing" from the myriad other "things" in the environment. Through language, the child learns the names of things. This object is called a "chair"; that one is called "Mommy." The child learns his or her name along with other object names: there is an object called "George." The child also learns the characteristics of objects. Fire is hot and dangerous. Chairs have four legs and are intended for sitting. Similarly, George learns what sort of object he is — a boy, little, someone who likes cookies. (See Chapter 4 for an application of this theory to gender socialization in particular.)

*Both language and the development of the self require "taking the role of the other."* In order to communicate with another person, it is necessary to take the role of the other — that is, to adopt the other's point of view about what is being said. Suppose you greet me Monday morning by asking, "How are you?" Before I can properly reply, I have to put myself in your shoes and decide whether you really want to hear all about my physical and psy-

chological wellbeing or whether you are merely being polite. In the first case, I will tell you at great length how I am feeling. In the second, I will answer, "Fine, thank you."

The development of the self requires this ability to take the role of the other, which is a fundamental aspect of language use. Because the self is social, the child must be able to adopt the perspective of other people toward himself or herself. Having a self means viewing yourself through the eyes of other people.

**Stages of Development of the Self.**  According to Mead, the ability to role-play and the consequent genesis of the self occur through the two main stages (Meltzer 1978) described below.

1. During the *play stage*, the child begins role-playing. The little girl pretends she is a mother or a doctor or a store clerk. What is important here is that the child is demonstrating the ability to adopt, for example, the mother's role, and to act back on herself from the perspective of this role. In pretending that she is the mother scolding her imaginary child for lying, the little girl is placing herself in her own mother's shoes and reacting to her own behaviour. This type of play indicates that the self is forming. However, the self at this stage is fragmentary because the child is taking the role of only one person at a time. The self lacks unity because the reflected view of the self is a series of fragmented views, not a coherent whole.

2. A coherent self develops during the *game stage*, when the child becomes capable of taking a number of roles simultaneously. Mead used the game of baseball to explain this process. Playing baseball requires the ability to adopt several different roles at the same time. Being a catcher involves understanding the roles of pitcher, shortstop, umpire, opposing team member up to bat, and so on. The events in a particular game must be understood from all of these various perspectives. The child manages this task by forming a composite role out of all the particularized roles. Mead called this generalized standpoint from which the child views himself or herself the **generalized other**. He called the corresponding standpoint involved in the earlier play stage the **significant other**. During

the play stage, the child might think, "Dad says I'm bad when I tell lies." During the game stage, the child would instead think, "*They* say lying is wrong." Behaviour thus comes increasingly to be guided by an abstract moral code rather than the opinion of one individual. Because parents (and other central caretakers) interpret the social order for the child, significant others are the source of the generalized other (Acock 1984).

Mead's ideas imply that self-development does not stop in childhood. As the person adopts new roles and encounters new situations, the self will continue to evolve (Bush and Simmons 1981).

**The "I" and the "Me."** Mead's formulation of the self makes room for both a socially defined aspect of the self (which was stressed above) and a spontaneous, creative aspect of the self. The **Me** represents the self-concept, especially internalized societal attitudes and expectations. The **I**, on the other hand, is the acting, unique, unfettered self.

Unlike the Freudian Id, Ego, and Super-ego, the "I" and the "Me" collaborate. The "I" provides individuality and initiative for behaviour, while the "Me" provides direction for that behaviour according to the dictates of society. Remember, though, that the self is a process and that the "I" and "Me" are phases of that process, not concrete entities.

## Theoretical Overview

The ideas of the learning theorists and of Piaget, Freud, and the symbolic interactionists all contribute to our understanding of childhood socialization. The learning theorists focus on the specific mechanisms involved in socialization. They tell us *how* the child learns the lessons of socialization. Piaget's work, on the other hand, analyzes the development of morality. Both Freud and Mead are also concerned with the question of how society's notions about proper behaviour are internalized by the child. However, their theories also address other questions. Freud emphasizes emotions, sexuality, and the unconscious. In addition, his theory provides many ideas concerning the role played by specific family members in socializing the child. Finally, Mead and Cooley empha-

size the social context of child development. The link they isolated between the emergence of self-awareness and the acquisition of language is extremely insightful. The work of these people, then, should be seen as complementary rather than competing systems of thought.

## Socialization: The Contemporary Context

What does it mean to grow up in the 1990s? As mentioned above, individuals who were born about the same time and who have similar experiences during their formative years share characteristics throughout their lives that distinguish them from other generations. In other words, the larger society provides a complex and changing socialization context. In this section, we discuss major factors affecting the experiences of Canadians currently 5 to 20 years old.

Each generation is somewhat distinctly influenced by *demographic*, or population, characteristics. (See Chapter 7.) Take generation size. There is more room for this generation — in classrooms, for example — than there was for the "baby-boomers," the "most massive glut of people ever to compete for the same space" (Ford 1983). The trends of decreased fertility, later marriages, and postponed births (Statistics Canada 1987) mean youngsters have fewer siblings or none at all. Previously viewed as "jealous, egotistical, selfish, spoiled little brats who grew into lonely, neurotic adults" (Pappert 1983), only children have now become commonplace and, hence, respectable. Also, because parents have fewer children, the potential exists for their relationships with the children they do have to increase in intensity. Finally, later marriages and postponed births means that this generation of young people has slightly older parents, whose greater experience with living and more comfortable economic position will translate into socialization advantages for at least some children.

Declining death rates also involve changes in socialization. The probability of a child's being orphaned or growing up without grandparents has diminished (Sullivan 1983). Since Canada is an "aging society," children will be increasingly familiar with the elderly. However, death is no longer the commonplace family event it was through most of history. Living in a low-mortality society that isolates the dying in hospitals and nursing homes leaves young people inadequately prepared to cope with death when it does touch their lives.

Population migration into Canada represents an important contextual aspect of socialization. In the 1960s and 1970s, large numbers of people arrived from Asian, Latin American, and Caribbean countries. These newcomers face the dual challenges of conveying something of their culture of origin to their children while they and their offspring learn to fit into their new society. Often, the new immigrant family protects its members from stress by developing a "creative schizophrenia" that allows its members to be "modern" at work and "traditional" at home (Berger and Berger 1984).

National economic circumstances during the past 15 years or so — inflation, recession, regional disparities in employment levels — have also affected the socialization experiences of Canadians. Many wives and mothers have sought employment outside the home. Many families have migrated across the country in search of jobs. For example, Barnett Richling, a professor at Mount Saint Vincent University, studied migration between Newfoundland and the mainland. One individual, who had recently returned to Newfoundland, observed that

*up there [Toronto] it's hard to save money since you owe so much in rent and all. At least here a house is reasonable enough. . . . With a regular job you could save money. You could hardly find three Newfoundlanders up there who wouldn't go back home, but what's the good of it to return without jobs?* (Richling 1985)

Economic trends have an especially severe impact on adolescents. As economic opportunities for young adults have become scarce, many older children, instead of becoming independent, are returning to the parental home (Schnaiberg and Goldenberg 1986). This "crowded nest" phenomenon produces difficulties for both generations. Also, because the work ethic has long been a central motivation in Canadians' lives (Burstein et al. 1984), youth unemployment and the prospect of permanent unavailability of preferred jobs represent serious concerns to both adults and young people.

Technological developments also affect socialization. Children are experiencing computerized learning and computerized play. In this high-tech era, "for the first time, many youngsters know more than their elders and are . . . teaching their elders in ways that parents have traditionally encultured children" (Williams 1983). Young people spend hours in the space-age atmosphere of video arcades. They cocoon themselves in portable stereo headsets. At home, they live in a constant bombardment of noise from radios, stereos, and rock videos. Listening to music, especially rock music, is Canadian adolescents' top leisure activity (Bibby and Posterski 1985). Many parents find rock music's "knee-jerk misogyny" (Harding and Nett 1984) and rebellious messages worrisome, and the antireligious, satanic content of the heavy-metal subculture particularly offensive. Parents also worry about the physical and mental passivity of younger children slumped in front of the television set. While children of the past may have been preoccupied with the "knife, compass, 36 cents, a marble, and a rabbit's foot" in their pockets (Winn 1983), today's children turn to electronic amusements.

As Chapter 11 points out, the Canadian family today is no longer the "classical family of Western nostalgia" (Goode 1963). Many of these changes have serious implications for socialization. Divorce produces inevitable social and economic changes in children's lives. For example, many learn that when marriages break up, "money is tight for winter coats, babysitters, running shoes and penicillin" (Maynard 1984). Moves to new neighbourhoods or communities, which often occur in the wake of a divorce, mean the loss of friendships and the challenge of establishing new ones. Relations with both custodial and noncustodial parents deviate from traditional nuclear-family scripts. Children are likely to find these changes stressful, at least initially. One beloved parent may now be labelled a villain and enemy by the other. A small proportion of fathers become *Mr. Moms* in custodial-father households. Many more join the legion of indulgent "Uncle Dads" (C.W. Smith 1985), playing limited meaningful roles in their children's lives beyond visiting privileges.

# Children Live in Darkness

*Childhood is a time of hunger, poverty, disease, and danger for millions of youngsters growing up on the streets of many developing nations. United Nations children's rights advocates argue that unless the world wakes up to the urgency of this sad problem, these abused children will become undereducated, underemployed street adults who threaten the social order.*

Kham Suk is 13 years old. She is a small child, with a delicate face. When she giggles, she sounds like any little child at play. But Kham Suk doesn't have much time for fun. Three months ago, her mother walked her across the border from Burma into Thailand and sold her to a brothel for $80.

Kham Suk's family desperately needed the money. Kham Suk is still paying the price: $4 a customer.

Jafar Ibrahimi was only 10 years old when Iranian soldiers took him away from his village in northern Iran and put him on the front line of the Iran-Iraq war. He was sent into battle as a human minesweeper. "In front of me, children were being killed," he remembers. "I can't say how many, but too many." Miraculously, he survived two or three days in the mine fields before Iraqi soldiers captured him.

For more than five years now, Jafar has been living in a prisoner-of-war camp in Iraq.

Sunil Dutt left his home in Pakistan when he was five years old. His stepfather was so cruel to him that he got on a bus one day and never went home. Today, the 12-year-old works as a waiter in New Delhi, in a grimy dhaba, a teahouse in an alley behind the Times of India building. Sunil sleeps in the street. He gets up every morning about 4 or 5 o'clock and works without a break until 9 p.m. Sunday is his day off. He earns about $11.72 a month.

These are children who live in darkness, the darkness of poverty, ignorance, greed — and indifference. There are tens of millions of children like them in the world today. They are the pawns, the possessions, and the products of an adult world that all too often exploits childhood for its own ends.

A few — a very few — of these children are being rescued from society's shadows by small grassroots programs around the world. But the increased awareness of the needs and rights of children that was triggered in 1979 by the United Nations' International Year of the Child is being overwhelmed by sheer numbers.

Children under 15 years old represent as much as 40 per cent of the total population in some developing countries. Their numbers are growing steadily, especially among the poor. And a constant flood of poor peasants into packed cities means that millions more children will be on the streets — living in conditions where the poor have a hard time getting clean water, let alone sending their children to school or breaking out of the relentless cycles of poverty that make children especially vulnerable to exploitation.

"These children are bearing the responsibility of adults," says Jennifer Schirmer, an anthropologist at Wellesley College in Massachusetts, who has worked with exploited children in Latin America. "The kinds of burdens they bear are a type of daily violence — the daily, grinding violence of poverty."

Experts say that children are at risk in virtually every country in the world (sexual abuse of children in Western families is one often-cited example). And they argue that children invariably wind up at the bottom of almost all national agendas for political and social action. Yet, within this sphere of universal indifference, the problem of exploitation is most pressing in the developing world.

**Source:**

Sara Terry, *Calgary Herald*, June 30, 1987.

---

Many noncustodial parents eventually disappear altogether. Parents' boyfriends or girlfriends may come and go, exercising temporary authority over children of divorce.

Despite all this, it is important to acknowledge that divorce frequently involves positive consequences for children. Many youngsters benefit by escaping the stressful family environment produced by a conflict-ridden marriage, and by establishing closer relations with their custodial parent. Though divorce can make children cynical about marriage, they do develop a broader vision of "normal" social arrangements (Whitehurst 1984). Children's responses depend on such considerations as their age at the time of divorce, and the level of pre-existing conflict in the home.

As a result of divorce and births to never-married mothers who keep their offspring, many Canadian children are growing up in one-parent families. Single parenthood typically means single motherhood. Families headed by women often experience poverty (Ambert 1985). The custodial parent is frequently overwhelmed with responsibility for earning a living, child care, and housework (Michelson 1985). In such homes, the single parent may treat the child as a pseudo-adult equal, loading the child with many of the responsibilities of the missing parent: for example, serving as a listening post for the parent, discussing sex, cooking, cleaning, and caring for younger siblings (Schlesinger 1983).

In addition, many children are growing up in "blended families," with stepparents and siblings unrelated to them by blood. Sociologists are just beginning to understand the nature of socialization in such reconstituted families. Discipline frequently becomes a thorny issue. For example, during courtship of the children's mother, the stepfather often tries to be popular with the youngsters, an "easygoing pal." With marriage, his perceptions of his role tend to change. Now he strives to exercise firm control, as well as love, over the children. The children are apt to resent this discipline, especially if it differs from that of their mother or biological father (Spanier and Furstenberg 1987).

By 1985, more than half the mothers of preschoolers were in the labour force (Labour Canada 1987). As a result, a majority of Canadian children are now cared for by someone other than a parent (Eichler 1983). Children are increasingly involved with peers, television, and secondary socialization agencies such as schools, daycare centres, or YMCA and YWCA groups. Although it is now more common to see fathers pushing baby strollers, many studies, such as those carried out by Lupri and Mills (1987) in Calgary and Michelson (1985) in Toronto, conclude that when wives go out to work, husbands do *not* substantially increase their share of child care.

Finally, the dark side of the family must also be acknowledged. Family members often treat one another with love, support, and warmth. Paradoxically, "the most likely place for a person to be murdered or seriously assaulted is at home, by family members" (Van Stolk 1983).

Novelist Sylvia Fraser (1987) has written poignantly about her own childhood experience of incest: "Thus for me the usual childhood reality was reversed. Inside my own house, among people I knew, was where danger lay. The familiar had proven to be treacherous, whereas the unfamiliar, the public, the unknown, the foreign, still contained the seeds of hope." Obviously, the social-

ization of battered and sexually abused children, for whom home is not a safe place, is seriously affected (Guberman and Wolfe 1985).

## Agents of Socialization

The socialization process involves many different types of influences that impinge on people throughout their lives. This part of our discussion will concentrate on four major socialization agents: the family, the peer group, the school, and the mass media. The agents singled out here are important because they affect almost every Canadian. In addition, they all exert a powerful influence during the impressionable childhood years.

Society has charged two of these agents, the family and the school, with the socialization of children. Although much of the impact they have on children is unintentional, both the family and the school also deliberately set out to equip children with the knowledge required to fit into adult society. The influence of the peer group and the media is frequently unintentional.

### Family

Although the contemporary family now shares aspects of its function with other agents, the family's impact on the child transcends that of all other agents of socialization. In Clausen's words (1968), "the 'widening world of childhood' spirals out from the parental home." Learning occurs rapidly during these crucial years of early childhood when the family has almost exclusive control and no relearning or contradictory lessons are involved. Moreover, learning takes place in the context of close emotional bonds. The family touches every sphere of the child's existence. The early immersion of the child within the family guarantees that this institution lays the foundation for the later and lesser influences of the other socialization agents, which are considerably more segmented. Chapter 11 offers more details about the nature and content of socialization by the family.

There is a second reason that sociologists assign primacy to the family. Various family characteristics orient the child to specific configurations of

# Canada's Child Care Problem

*In 1984, the federal government appointed a Task Force on Child Care to study the issue and make recommendations. Although some steps were taken by the government in response to the Task Force, providing quality child care and adequate leave policies for parents continues to be a major challenge in the 1990s.*

It is clear . . . that child care and parental leave programs in Canada today do not constitute a system in any sense of that term. They are, rather, a miscellaneous collection of measures that fail to adequately meet the needs of children and their parents, or to support the quality of family life. . . . The present state of child care in Canada is on a par with the state of education in this country in the late 1800s and health care in the 1930s. In a global perspective, Canada's child care and parental leave programs lag far behind systems operating in most western industrialized countries.

Our investigation revealed that, while child care licensing and training systems do exist in most areas of the country, so few licensed child care services are available that only a small minority of children who receive child care on a regular basis benefit in any way from these systems. In 1984, for example, just 172 000 licensed child care spaces were available in the country, sufficient to serve only nine per cent of the children whose parents worked or studied 20 hours or more each week. The remaining children — and estimated 494 000 on a full-day basis, 1 284 000 on a daily basis before and after school, and an additional 2 739 000 on a part-time or intermittent basis — are left in unlicensed care arrangements, which, by definition, are not subject to even minimal standards, or to any system of quality control. This should be a matter of concern to us all, for although individual unlicensed care arrangements can be very good, many are not, and some are actually dangerous for children.

While the uncertain quality of unlicensed child care has always been a problem for families, many more families are now affected, and the effects are becoming more acute. Whereas in the 1960s or even the 1970s, there was a ready supply of energetic young mothers as well as capable middle-aged women available to provide child care on an informal basis, today a majority of both groups are, themselves, in the labour force. As a result, good informal child care arrangements are becoming more and more difficult for parents to find. Children are left in inadequate arrangements, many of them are shifted frequently from one arrangement to another, and perhaps as many as one million Canadian children are left alone before or after school. Parents who wrote to the Task Force described their anxiety and frustration as they search time and again for good care for their children. As the participation in the labour force of mothers with young children continues to rise over the next decade — causing, simultaneously, the demand for child care to rise and the supply of good informal arrangements to fall — the child care crisis can only grow more acute in the years to come.

**Source:**

Dr. Katie Cook, Chairperson, *Report of the Task Force on Child Care* (Ottawa: Supply and Services, 1986).

experiences, values, and opportunities. Growing up in a one-parent or blended family is different from growing up in an "intact" family. Also, by being born into a particular family, the child automatically becomes part of a larger family — grandparents, aunts, uncles, cousins. Moreover, the family's social class position means that the child will learn one set of values, rather than another. The opportunities of a child born into an upper-middle-class family are considerably different from those of a child born into the working class. Social class, as we will see below, is the most studied demographic variation in socialization (Wright and Wright 1976). The family's ethnic background is another important determinant of the content of socialization.

Finally, the family's geographical location is also the child's. Growing up in Toronto and growing up in Newfoundland (Firestone 1978) are quite different experiences.

**Child as Socializer of the Parents.** The socialization that occurs within the family is a two-way process (Rheingold 1969). The child is not just a passive recipient of parental influence. Just as the parents socialize the child, the child also socializes the parents. This mutual influence extends from infancy, where the effect of an infant's cry on the mother is "all out of proportion to his age, size, and accomplishments" (Rheingold 1966), through adolescence (Peters 1982) and into adulthood.

In infancy, the child's demands and responses

serve to teach the mother and father how to behave as parents. A newly married couple have, of course, many abstract ideas of what parenthood entails, which they have gleaned from observation, reading, and so on. Nevertheless, many young adults are very ignorant about babies. (A brand-new mother wrote a newspaper medical columnist to ask whether it was true that her baby could split the seam of its head open by crying.) Interaction with their first-born, however, teaches them the actual behaviours involved in the role of parents. For example, it is one thing to know that parents are responsible for their children when they are ill, and quite another to cope with a sick baby who cannot breathe properly at two in the morning.

Once past infancy, children may unintentionally shape their fathers' and mothers' performance as parents by administering reinforcements. A three-year-old may say, "You're a bad Mommy!" or "You're a nice Daddy." When four-year-old Joshua approves of his parents' behaviour that day, he wordlessly leaves smooth pebbles beside their dinner plates. In short, children's relationships with their caregivers are characterized by two-way interactions.

As the child matures from infancy through adolescence to adulthood, the parents become aware of new facets of mothering and fathering. Although theorists tend to emphasize the early childhood years, it is also important to remember that the mutual parent/child influence often continues until the death of the parents.

**Social Class.** Canadian society, like all other large societies, is socially stratified. (For a detailed discussion of the nature of stratification in Canada, see Chapter 8.) When sociologists talk about *social stratification*, they are referring to the arrangement of a "group or society into a hierarchy of positions that are unequal with regard to power, property, social evaluation, and/or psychic gratification" (Tumin 1967). The occupations of the parents provide the best indicator of the Canadian family's social class position, and this position influences the child's socialization experiences and consequent opportunities.

Growing up in a lower-class (as opposed to a middle-class) home means less money. Satisfaction of such basic needs as housing, diet, medical and dental care, clothing, and so on is relatively

**Family members socialize children while being socialized into new family roles themselves.**

less adequate. For example, poor people are more likely to grow up in overcrowded homes. The experience of overcrowding is associated with poor physical and mental health, poor child care, and poor social relations in the home (Gove, Hughes, and Galle 1979). The amount of income at the family's disposal also determines less tangible aspects of socialization. Opportunities to read a wide variety of books, to visit museums, to travel, to attend camp, and so forth all widen the growing child's intellectual horizons, and all tend to narrow the parental purse. If the parents in a lower-class home are vulnerable to job layoffs and unemployment, their feelings of powerlessness and insecurity will be communicated to their children. Moreover, social class is a key factor affecting socialization in single-parent families (Ambert 1985). As noted earlier, single parenthood typically means single motherhood. The end of marriage frequently spells downward economic mobility, even poverty, for the women involved (Boyd 1977). Single mothers from lower socioeconomic levels are especially vulnerable.

Members of different social classes, by virtue of experiencing different conditions of life, come

# In the Playgrounds of Canada, Poverty is the Hidden Bully

*Sociologists writing about primary socialization sometimes unwittingly convey the impression that all Canadian children experience the protection and physical comfort enjoyed by middle-class children. Toronto journalist June Callwood reminds us that this is not so.*

Go where children are and watch them. Five minutes will suffice, if the watcher has more important matters that clamor for attention.

Children are small, hopeful, intense. Every day is the only day of their life that matters. Their feelings spill out every which way, rash and unexamined. Since they apparently cannot dissemble, their natures seem transparent. A watcher cannot but enjoy how spontaneous and exuberant they are.

The spectator is being bluffed: though most children in this country appear well-dressed and well-fed, child poverty is flourishing in Canada, and with it child hunger, child alienation and child despair. The laughing children conceal great pain, and every teacher and public-health nurse knows it.

Among the children seen romping in the playgrounds of the nation are 1.2 million who live below the poverty line. Their position in the economic order is a disaster for them. Most children of the poor leave school early, before some of them can read or write with assurance. Their illnesses are more frequent and more prolonged, their deaths sooner. Bitterness is their lot. Poor children are excluded from the world of glossy-haired people seen on television in cars eternally new.

Until about the age of 8, children born to someone poor do not believe that the bad times will last. They wait confidently for deliverance. Ten-year-olds already are wiser and know that being poor will be endless. They protest unbecomingly, some with rage, some with cunning, some by withdrawing. Their personalities are trapped and twisted by economic distortion. In repose, their faces are sullen and sad.

Watch children play. They offer a rewarding sight, and one that would give even greater pleasure if the spectator could be certain that every child in sight was getting a fair break.

**Source:**

June Callwood, *Globe and Mail,*
September 16, 1987.

to see the world differently and develop different conceptions of social reality (Gecas 1976; Kohn 1977). Prince Charles's royal upbringing provides an extreme example. In public, he walks behind the Queen and never refers to her as "my mother," let alone "Mummy" (Heald 1982). Distinctive occupational backgrounds are related to parental values. According to a Hamilton, Ontario, study (Pineo and Looker 1983), white-collar families consider their children's self-direction to be more important and obedience to parents to be less important than do blue-collar families.

The class origins of a child remain important throughout his or her life. They are a significant influence on the occupation that a child will eventually choose (Porter, Porter, and Blishen 1982; Boyd et al. 1985). Indeed, the evidence suggests that children have a high probability of achieving a class position very similar to that of their parents (Pike 1975). Lower-class children are relatively less successful in school, leave school earlier, and have lower occupational aspirations. Middle-class parents are more likely to socialize their children to internalize the values of individualism, high mo-

tivation, and deferred gratification required for success in school (Pike 1975). However, the impact of social origin on educational attainment has declined through the century. Although social origin now plays a decreasingly important role in high school completion, it still affects the probability of attaining some university experience (Guppy, Mikicich, and Pendakur 1984).

**Ethnicity.** Because Canada is not a "melting pot" that culturally homogenizes its people, ethnicity exerts a major influence on many families. Although most Canadians share a common core of experiences and values, their socialization may also reflect ethnic differences in values, norms, and identity. The matter is further complicated by the fact that ethnic background and social class position are frequently related. For example, as we will see in Chapter 9, in comparison with most other ethnic groups, the British are overrepresented in the higher-status occupations.

The role of ethnicity in primary socialization varies enormously. The experiences of the non–English-speaking recent immigrant from Vietnam differ from those of the fourth-generation Ukrainian Canadian raised in this country. Ethnicity means something different to the visible-minority child from Jamaica than to the child from Germany, who is physically indistinguishable from Caucasian Canadians. It matters whether a child's mother and father come from the same or from different ethnic backgrounds (Elkin 1983). Ethnicity is a different proposition for aboriginal Canadians — Indians and Inuit — than for more recent arrivals (Peters 1984). Clearly, then, the term "the Canadian family" represents an abstract oversimplification (Ishwaran 1976).

Despite Canada's official policy of multiculturalism within a bilingual framework, it is difficult for ethnic groups to maintain their ethnic identity in the face of powerful pressures for assimilation to the Anglo-dominant culture (Zureik and Pike 1975). As Elkin (1983) notes, "Unless a child learns and experiences his basic ethnic identity within his family and other early primary groups, it seems unlikely that he will ever strongly feel it thereafter." A study of immigrant Indian and Pakistani children in a western Canadian city (Wakil, Siddique, and Wakil 1981) makes the point that primary socialization is especially difficult for new Canadians. While parents were willing to tolerate their children's enthusiasm for Western food, music, and festivals such as Christmas and Halloween, the generations clashed over critical matters such as dating and arranged marriage. These immigrant parents perceived that Canadian practices such as dating and courtship weakened their authority and threatened basic values of their ethnic group.

**Socialization by Siblings.**   Brothers and sisters play an important role in socializing one another. An older sibling can provide a role model. The learning theorists tell us that children learn many of their socialization lessons through imitation. Also, a younger sibling gives the older child the opportunity to try out some portion of the parental role. Guiding and protecting a younger brother or sister helps the child internalize his or her parents' perspective. Much of the older child's influence is, of course, quite unintentional.

Sibling interaction provides practice in co-operation and competition. As Freud observed, sibling rivalry is one of the more emotional experiences encountered in growing up. Humorist Erma Bombeck wonders why a child will "eat yellow snow" but won't drink from his brother's glass (Blount 1984). Sibling comparisons have an impact on the child's developing self-image (Yussen and Santrock 1978). All children are concerned about how smart, how big, how worthwhile they are. Children with siblings close to their own age arrive at some of these answers by comparing themselves with brothers or sisters. One dimension in this rivalry is sibling concern for equally fair treatment by parents. But at times, brothers and sisters also provide useful allies against parents. Siblings appear to organize themselves into twosomes, bound together by love or hate; these sibling pairs result from such situations as being close in age or sharing a bedroom (Bank and Kahn 1982). The fact that the Canadian birth rate has dropped to 1.7 births per woman (Statistics Canada 1987) means that many youngsters now grow up without siblings. The more adult-oriented only child benefits from the exclusive attention of the parents but, lacking siblings, may be somewhat unskilled in social relations with peers.

## Peers

After the family, peers (other children approximately the same age) constitute the second most potent socialization agent. The importance of peer relations in not confined to human beings. Harlow and Harlow (1962) found that interaction with other infant monkeys compensated for most of the negative effects of the maternal deprivation undergone by the experimental groups of monkeys. The age-grading of Canadian society increases the impact of peer socialization; people in similar age categories tend to be segregated in schools, neighbourhoods, and various recreational settings. Propinquity (simply being in the same place at the same time) tends to facilitate friendship.

Although children do not consciously set out to socialize one another, their need for companionship and approval results in mutual learning of a variety of information. Interaction with friends provides the first major social experiences outside the family circle. Peer relations allow children to begin to separate themselves from the family's influence and to develop other facets of their iden-

Peer socialization operates on a more egalitarian plane than family or school socialization.

tity. One of the goals of socialization, remember, is the eventual ability to function independently of the family. Another point worth stressing is that peers share relatively equal power. This equality contrasts sharply with the power position of the child vis-à-vis the parents and other caretakers. Some things can be learned only from equal-status peers. However, peer and family influences are not necessarily in opposition. Peers sometimes reinforce family socialization.

**Peer Influence Throughout Life.** From early childhood through to old age, people attach a great deal of importance to peer relationships (Matthews 1986). Even young infants stare at each other with fascination. By the age of two, children play alongside each other. By three or four years old, this parallel play becomes shared play. Most parents know that companionship with other children is a necessity, not a luxury. They take pains to find little companions for their children, and worry if their offspring do not seem to make friends. Within a few years, children are able to relate to groups of children. (Recall the emphasis both Piaget and Mead placed on games for the child's social development.) By eight or nine years, most children are concerned with having one spe-

cial friend. Many of us may remember being rejected by a best friend as one of the poignant tragedies of childhood.

Adolescence marks the peak of peer-group influence. The teenager's orientation to the companionship, opinions, and tastes of age-mates helps to bridge the gulf between childish dependence on the family and adulthood. Peer relations continue to matter a great deal to people in the middle adult years and on into old age. Although adults have more inner resources than children, they remain sensitive to the opinions of their friends.

**Content of Peer Socialization.** What do children learn from one another? Smith (1979) reminisces about belonging to a club in childhood:

*It was a pitiful wreck of a tarpaper hut, and in it I learned the difference between boys and girls, I learned that all fathers did that, I learned to swear, to play with myself, to sleep in the afternoon, I learned that some people were Catholics and some people were Protestants and some people were Jews, that people came from different places. I learned that other kids wondered, too, who they would have been if their fathers had not married their mothers, wondered if you could dig a hole right to the center of the earth, wondered if you could kill yourself by holding your breath.*

Although a complete inventory of the contents of peer socialization would fill volumes, it is possible to isolate at least some of the more notable types of learning. (The actual mechanisms of learning are, of course, those emphasized by the learning theorists — namely, modelling, and positive and negative reinforcement.)

Contact with peers provides opportunities to practice social roles and to develop interaction skills. For example, children gain experience in leader and follower roles. During Mead's game stage, they learn the meaning of all the interdependent roles involved in games, such as baseball. They learn to co-operate and to compete.

As symbolic interactionist Gecas (1981) notes, egalitarian peer relations provide frequent opportunities for role-making, as opposed to role-taking. *Role-taking* involves adapting to roles that are explicitly predefined in the culture. In such cases, there is little opportunity for the idiosyncratic needs of the particular role-taker. Role-taking is especially likely in hierarchical social relationships, such as business or the military. By contrast, *role-making* refers to situations where roles can be either created or substantially modified to the actors' own specifications through interaction (Turner 1962). The role of clown or wit in a friendship group provides a good illustration of role-making.

Children's comparison of their appearance and abilities with those of their peers influences their attitudes toward themselves (Kagan 1984). For example, to a sixth-grade boy, his classmates' clothing or relative ability in skateboarding may be critical information in assessing his own worth. In other words, the looking-glass self mentioned earlier reflects the child's interpretation of peer, as well as familial, judgments.

Peers are a source of information. Children interpret the world for one another in a manner adults cannot possibly duplicate. Adults are ignorant of many aspects of reality that matter greatly to their children, like the latest fads. Moreover, some sensitive topics are more easily discussed with peers than with adults, such as how babies are born or the etiquette of dating. Finally, that much of this peer information might be the wildest misinformation is beside the point and in no way minimizes its importance to the young people in question.

Peers influence one another's values and attitudes. The concern of parents to protect their offspring from bad influences reveals their recognition that children influence one another's values. Is religion nonsense? How important is school? Should people be judged by the clothes they wear and the amount of money they have? Piaget was well aware of the impact of peer experiences on moral development. Such ethical abstractions as rules, fair play, and honesty become meaningful in the give-and-take of peer interaction. Similarly, children teach each other attitudes toward such diverse subjects as TV programs, homosexuality, and drugs.

## School

Industrialized nations such as Canada assign to the school a major role in preparing children for adulthood. The knowledge and skills required to function effectively in urbanized, industrialized societies are too extensive and too complex for

parents to convey to their offspring. The educational system performs two major functions for society (Parsons 1959). The *socialization function* involves the internalization of commitment both to broad societal values and to doing the tasks that the society requires done. The *allocation function* refers to the channelling of people through programs of occupational preparation into positions in the socioeconomic structure. (See Chapter 14 for details about how these functions are carried out.)

Most children are eager to begin school. For the majority, enrolling in school is their first encounter with a formal institution. This significant step beyond the family or daycare centre represents "being grown up." In school, the child is treated not as a unique individual but as a member of a cohort (see Chapter 5). If Suzy is feeling grumpy and does not want to go out to play, her mother may abandon her plan to have a quiet house all to herself. At recess, however, regardless of her mood, Suzy will march out to the school playground with the other pupils. As a lone child at home, she gets her own way. But at school Suzy is "processed" as one of a "batch." Experiences like this prepare children for adulthood, where the demands of organizations often take priority over the individual's own wishes.

Some of the content of socialization is consciously planned; some is incidental to the school's stated goals. In addition, no two children have precisely the same school experiences. A variety of factors — such as the child's ability and temperament, the parents' social class position and their attitudes toward academic success, the teachers, and relations with the peer group — all influence what happens there. For example, to children from some ethnic minorities or from very poor environments, the school may be an alien place ( a resocialization context) that devalues what they have learned in their families (Gecas 1981). Nonetheless, it is possible to offer some generalizations about the content of school socialization:

1. *Formal Knowledge.* The most obvious purpose of the school is to provide students with some of the information and skills required to function in society.
2. *Values.* Educational systems attempt to transmit to their charges some appreciation of the sentiments and goals considered important in our

Through socialization, children are taught basic skills and acquire knowledge as they learn how to interact with others.

society (for example, motivation to achieve, individual responsibility, respect for other people's rights). In addition, the school plays a vital role in orienting the child to Canadian society as such, a function particularly important in a society like ours, which fosters strong regional and ethnic identities and consumes American mass media.

The school also transmits values concerning ethnic groups within our society. The selection of school names serves as an interesting indicator of these values (Goldstein 1981). Between 1880 and 1979 in Winnipeg, 79 percent of the schools were named after noteworthy Anglo-Saxons, 15 percent after persons of French origin, and only 6 percent after persons from other ethnic groups. Overall, this school-naming supports the pre-eminence of English culture. However, the decline in Anglo-Saxon names to 56 percent in the 1970s suggests a decline in the popularity of Anglo-conformity.

3. *Interpersonal Skills*. Because elementary school represents most children's first experience in coping with the demands of a formal organization, new social skills are developed. Young pupils are confronted with impersonal rules for behaviour — waiting their turn, being on time, co-operating — that are not rooted in parental or peer authority.

4. *Self-Evaluation*. Throughout childhood and adolescence, interaction at school provides reflections for the looking-glass self. The child needs to know what sort of person she or he is, relative to others of the same age. Educational authorities attempt to judge all children according to universal criteria.

Although it is possible to comment in general terms on the school as socialization agent, Canadian schools provide young people with a wide variety of socialization experiences. In addition to the public schools attended by the majority of children, many youngsters attend denominational schools, which teach religion. Others go to private schools or military colleges. In any case, we should remember that school is an abstraction and children are really socialized by teachers, textbooks, and other pupils.

**Teachers.** When we think back to our days in elementary and junior high school, many of our thoughts revolve around particular teachers. Some are remembered as heroes or heroines and some as villains. Sometimes, we liked a particular subject, or school in general, because we had a warm, talented teacher that year. In contrast, perhaps our attitude toward school was soured by contact with an unpleasant teacher.

Teachers (and teacher-administrators) are powerful socialization agents because they are the human point of contact between pupils and the formal organization of the school (Martin and Macdonnell 1978). These people constitute young children's first exposure to adult authority outside the family. Although the teacher/student relationship is not devoid of emotion, the tie is considerably more impersonal than that between parent and child.

The teacher exercises influence on the child in several ways. He or she acts as the major vehicle for transmitting the school curriculum and associated values. The teacher interprets the wider society. As principal agents of socialization of the young, Quebec's teachers play a key role in that province's struggle between francophones and anglophones (Murphy 1981). In addition, the teacher sets up the rules of expected behaviour and metes out punishment when these are broken. Finally, the teacher is a potential role model. Richer (1979) observed that the female teacher of an Ontario kindergarten class was a powerful role model for the girls, but not the boys. The girls initiated physical contact with the teacher — handholding, caressing, leg-hugging. Often, one of the girls would sit on the piano stool (the teacher's territory), book in hand, and pretend to read to the class. This surrogate teacher particularly enjoyed punishing "deviance" in her pupils.

**Textbooks.** Schools also socialize through textbooks, as well as computers, films, and videotapes. The content of such materials augments the information conveyed by teachers and, as pupils advance through the educational system, an increasing proportion of their new knowledge is obtained through this more impersonal source.

Sociologists have been very interested in how texts affect students' attitudes toward, for example, racial groups (Pratt 1984) and gender roles. This concern for the attitudinal content of texts has its source partly in the nature of young readers. Particularly in the formative elementary school years, textbooks make up the bulk of reading material for many children. In addition, this assigned reading carries the cachet of authority because it is "official" school reading. For better or worse, therefore, texts have considerable potential for conveying social attitudes along with factual material. A related concern has been to provide children with Canadian, not American, texts. Extreme nationalism is, of course, a dangerous sentiment; however, parents are rightfully disturbed when their children are more familiar with the president of the United States, the Fourth of July, and "The Star-Spangled Banner" than with their Canadian counterparts.

**School Peers.** The age-graded school system puts children into contact with a large number and variety of children their own age. Peer-group influence, noted above, is greatly accelerated once children enter school.

Some of this influence takes the form of peer reinforcement of school-related behaviour, as when the children themselves adopt performance in academic work and semi-official activities such as sports as criteria for judgment of one another.

However, school provides a context for the operation of youth subculture. Here, the socialization lessons may be irrelevant to school-sponsored values or may even contradict them.

Being accepted by one's peers is a serious matter. Research shows that children (as well as adults) sometimes judge one another by standards that seem rather odd. For example, McDavid and Harari (1966) measured grade-school children's liking for particular first names, and another group of children's liking for classmates who bore these names. A high relationship was found between liking of names and liking of children. Probably the reason is that, other things being equal, people like what is familiar to them. A boy named "Peter" or "David" has a distinct peer acceptance advantage over one named "Horatio" or "Marion."

From an early age, children also respond to the physical appearances of other children. Nursery school children whom adults judged as being physically unattractive were not as well liked by their classmates as were more attractive children (Dion and Berscheid 1972). Part of the reason children (as well as adults) like attractive children is that they extrapolate from appearance to assume that "beautiful is good" and "ugly is nasty." In other words, other desirable characteristics are assumed to go along with being good-looking. Conversely, unattractive children are assumed to possess undesirable traits. Peers, teachers, and other adults expect a nice-looking child to be intelligent, well behaved, and popular. Ugly children are expected to be bratty and stupid. In view of the looking-glass self notion, it is not surprising that attractive children score relatively high in self-esteem (Maruyama and Miller 1975).

Both educational authorities and parents have been especially interested in the high school peer group and competition between its values and official school values. Considerable homophily characterizes this group. *Homophily* is the tendency to similarity in various attributes among persons who affiliate (Lazarsfeld and Merton 1954). For example, adolescents whose friends use illegal drugs are more likely to use drugs themselves. The homophily stems both from a selection process in which individuals choose friends who already resemble themselves and from a socialization process in which individuals, irrespective of prior similarity, influence one another (Kandel 1978). A national study of Canadian teenagers (Bibby and Posterski 1985) found that "many teenagers tend to find high levels of gratification from friends rather than from their mothers and fathers. They consequently place more value on friendship than they do on family life." However, other researchers (Davies and Kandel 1981) conclude that when the issues concern teenagers' life goals and educational aspirations, rather than current lifestyle matters such as fashions and music, parents are a more important influence than peers.

## Mass Media

The mass media — television, videotapes, radio, newspapers, magazines, books, movies, records — are impersonal communication sources, and they reach large audiences. If you try to imagine what a week in Canada spent without any of these media would be like, you will gain some idea of the important part they play in the lives of most Canadians.

The media act as direct agents of socialization. Television, the "universal curriculum" (Gerbner and Gross 1976), is a major transmitter of culture and information. For this reason, psychologist Gregory Fouts (1980) regards the deliberate elimination of television from the home as a "misinformed and unwitting example of [parental] irresponsibility."

The media reflect nearly every aspect of society, but these reflections are, of course, not necessarily accurate. Children see or hear world news. Their country is presented visually, along with its political leaders, diverse cultures, arts, and sports. Situation comedies ("sitcoms") picture what happens in other people's families. "Cops and robbers" programs present children with an astonishing number of violent crimes each evening. Media advertisements show children all the paraphernalia supposedly required for them to be happy, healthy, and accepted by their peers.

In providing children with common interests and experiences, the media also function as indirect socialization agents. Being part of this "community of discourse" (Tuchman 1979) constitutes a vital dimension of peer socialization. From coast to coast, Canadian youngsters recognize this chant: "Alligator pie, alligator pie / If I don't get some I think I'm gonna die" (Lee 1974). From his records and concerts, they are familiar

with Raffi's folk music for children. They know the words of "Baby Beluga" and "Gonna Shake My Sillies Out."

Television and rock music are especially critical components of young people's subculture. Being television-wise brings prestige on the playground (Ellis 1983). Children discuss what they have seen on television and enact the roles of TV characters in their fantasy play (Fouts 1980).

Who produces the media content that feeds into the youth subculture? Television, radio, and books are packaged by adults in the mainstream of society. However, "much of the music youth listen to is created by individuals close to their own age who stand apart [from] and may be at odds with adult society" (Larson and Kubey 1983).

Child development experts have been particularly concerned about television as a socialization agent. Television has been called the "plug-in drug" (Winn 1977), the Phantom Babysitter, and the Great Leveller, "mowing down all the bright young minds to the same stunted level" (Landsberg 1982). Many children are zombie viewers, who watch anything and everything, "silent, immobile, mesmerized" (Goldsen 1979). Television has also been labelled the Total Disclosure Medium because information and imagery intended for adults are readily accessible to children. Youngsters tune in to "incest, promiscuity, homosexuality, sadomasochism, terminal illness, and other secrets of adult life" (Postman 1982).

Television reaches 87 percent of all Canadian children aged two through eleven. These children watch an average of 21 hours of TV each week (Singer 1986). Television "crowds out" other uses of time (Condry and Keith 1983). Sleeping is the only activity that commands more of children's time. Television time is replacing hours of playtime — and, as we have seen, children learn both social norms and social skills through their games. Because of its relatively easy availability, television slows down the acquisition of reading skills. Its provision of ready-made ideas dampens creative thinking:

*People who grow up with unlimited access to television may construct the maxim "when bored, watch TV," whereas people who grow up with limited or no access may develop many solutions, for example, "when bored, make something, take something apart*

# Video Games

*Sherry Turkle, a professor in the Massachusetts Institute of Technology's Program in Science, Technology, and Society, describes the impact of computers on children's play and on their relationships with their parents.*

The girl is playing Asteroids. A spaceship under her control is being bombarded by an asteroids shower. There are separate control buttons for steering, accelerating, and decelerating the spaceship and for firing its rocket guns against threatening asteroids and enemy ships. The player must keep up a steady stream of missiles as she maneuvers the ship. The finger on the "Fire" button must maintain a rapid staccato, an action that is tense and tiring.

The girl is hunched over the console. When the tension momentarily lets up, she looks up and says,

"I hate this game." And when the game is over she wrings her hands, complaining that her fingers hurt. For all of this, she plays every day "to keep up my strength."She neither claims nor manifests enjoyment in any simple sense. One is inclined to say she is more "possessed" by the game than playing it.

There has been controversy about video games from the days of Space Invaders and Asteroids, from the time that the games' holding power provoked people who saw it as a sign of addiction to become alarmed. The controversy intensified as it became clear that more than a "games craze" was involved. This was not the Hula-Hoop of the 1980s. By 1982 people spent more money, quarter by quarter, on video games than they spent on movies and records combined. And although the peak of excitement about the games may have passed with their novelty, video games have become part of the cultural landscape.

Not all of the arguments against video games can be taken at face

value, for the debate is charged with feelings about a lot more than the games themselves. Protest against video games carries a message about how people feel about computers in general. In the past decade, and without people having had anything to do or say about it, computers have entered almost every aspect of daily life. By 1983 the computer had become so much and so active a part of the everyday that *Time* magazine chose it to fill the role usually given to a Man or Woman of the Year. Only one other gift of science has been so universally recognized as marking a new era of human life. That was atomic energy.

It is an understatement to say that people are ambivalent about the growing computer presence: we like new conveniences (automated bank tellers, faster supermarket lines), but on the eve of a new era we, by definition, do not know where we are. The changes have been rapid and disquieting. We are ill at ease even with our children, who are so much at ease with a technology that many of

---

to see how it works, imagine what the clouds are, flood your backyard and skate (and perhaps daydream while skating), read, hit a tennis ball against a wall, play a board game, sell lemonade," and so on. (Williams 1986)

What happens to the development of children's cognitive processes when their concentration on the program they are watching is interrupted every 12 minutes by irrelevant material — that is, commercials (Tavris 1988)?

By age eighteen, children will have spent more time in front of the television than anywhere else, including school. However, schools also make extensive use of television and other media as teaching aids. Indeed, the activities of all the other socialization agents — school, family, peer groups — are affected by media. For example, teachers complain that their pupils, accustomed to the short sequences of television, become impatient with extended lectures or discussions (Singer and Singer 1988).

Considerable attention is being given to the significance of television advertising for children. On a Saturday morning, the typical Canadian child is exposed to approximately 75 commercials. Research shows that although children as young as four can distinguish commercials from programming (through cues such as the use of jingles, faster pacing of material, and adult voiceovers), the majority of first-graders cannot explain the selling intent of commercials (Singer 1986). The situation is confused further by children's programming designed "to shuffle kids straight from the TV set into the toy store" (*Time*, November 30, 1987). In late 1987, 25 TV shows were being aired that featured toys — such as Smurfs, Transformers, and Pound Puppies — as their main characters.

The ability of television to influence children has become an extremely important issue. If children are acquiring stereotyped images of women, old people, and ethnic groups; if they regard fictional TV families as more significant than their

us approach at arm's length. They take it for granted. To them it is not a new technology but a fact of life. They come home from school and casually report that they are "learning programming." The comment evokes mixed feelings. Parents want their children to have every advantage, but this new expertise estranges them. It seems to threaten a new kind of generation gap that feels deep and difficult to bridge. And so, for many people, the video game debate is a place to express a more general ambivalence: the first time anybody asked their opinion about computers was when a new games arcade applied for a license in their community or when the owner of a small neighbourhood business wanted to put a game or two into a store. It is a chance to say,"No, let's wait. Let's look at this whole thing more closely." It feels like a chance to buy time against more than a video game. It feels like a chance to buy time against a new way of life.

Video games are a window onto a new kind of intimacy with machines that is characteristic of the nascent computer culture. The special relationship that players form with video games has elements that are common to interactions with other kinds of computers. The holding power of video games, their almost hypnotic fascination, is computer holding power. The experiences of video game players help us to understand this holding power and something else as well. At the heart of the computer culture is the idea of constructed "rule-governed" worlds.

Those who fear the games often compare them to television. Game players almost never make this analogy. When they try to describe the games in terms of other things, the comparison is more likely to be with sports, sex, or meditation. Television is something you watch. Video games are something you do, something you do to your head, a world that you enter, and, to a certain extent, they are something you "become." The widespread analogy with television is understandable. But analogies between the two screens ignore the most important element behind the games' seduction: video games are interactive computer microworlds.

Using analogies with television or with drugs, the popular debate about video games is filled with images of game players caught in a "mindless addiction." Half of this description is certainly wrong. There is nothing mindless about mastering a video game. The games demand skills that are complex and differentiated. Some of them begin to constitute a socialization into the computer culture: you interact with a program, you learn how to learn what it can do, you get used to assimilating large amounts of information about structure and strategy by interacting with a dynamic screen display. And when one game is mastered, there is thinking about how to generalize strategies to other games. There is learning how to learn.

**Source:**

Sherry Turkle, *The Second Self: Computers and the Human Spirit* (New York: Simon and Schuster, 1984).

own extended families; if they pressure parents to buy heavily advertised toys and breakfast cereals; and, worse, if they learn to solve problems through violent means from watching crime shows, then this medium constitutes a socialization agent whose power is almost beyond imagination.

Unfortunately, tracing the direct effects of the media is a very difficult research task. When the media operate in the natural environment, their influence is one among many other factors. For example, if Peter behaves aggressively, is the cause the type of television programs he watches, or his family, or his nasty temperament? On the other hand, experimental studies that attempt to control for variables besides media content become so artificial that their conclusions may not hold beyond the experimental situation. However, persuasive data from natural experiments are becoming available. For example, University of British Columbia researchers had an unusual opportunity to study the effects of television when they heard about a town whose location in a valley had prevented it from receiving television until the mid-1970s. By studying this community before and two years after television arrived, they learned a great deal about the impact of TV on children's aggressive behaviour, creativity, leisure activities, and gender attitudes (Williams, 1986). More important than any single piece of research, however, are an accumulation of consensual findings from many studies employing a variety of research methods.

In general, research on specific media effects shows that children are indeed influenced by their media consumption. Before we review some of this evidence in more detail, a major factor that reduces this influence must be emphasized. Children are exposed to media content in a social context. What they see and hear is monitored, at least to some extent, by parents. Similarly, their interpretation of media content is molded by the opinions of parents, teachers, and friends. Parents may forbid watching violent television series or may recommend an educational series. They often offer their own opinions on fighting as a way of solving differences of opinion, or the advisability of spending the contents of one's piggy bank on a heavily advertised toy. "When parents encourage their youngsters to think about and evaluate content and to consider alternative actions, the impact of negative or antisocial contents [is] considerably reduced" (Fouts 1980). In other contexts, children are exposed to the points of view of the other socialization agents. These may or may not agree with the media's perspectives. In short, the media have an impact on children, but this impact is just one of the influences that shape a child's attitudes and behaviour.

We now turn to more specific considerations of the media as an agent of socialization.

**Violence and the Media.** Canadian history contains many violent incidents — for example, the 1935 Regina riot and the 1970 FLQ crisis. A few subcultural pockets of Canadians, such as prison populations and hockey spectators, approve of violent tactics. Nevertheless, in comparison with other nations like the U.S., the incidence of violence here is relatively low. Indeed, Canada takes great pride in being "the peaceable kingdom" that disapproves of violence (Torrance 1986).

Despite this cultural injunction, it has been well established that violence is a staple in the television diet available to Canadian children. Researchers in Canada and elsewhere have been very concerned with the possible negative effects on children of exposure to media violence. (For a discussion of the influence on children of the mass media's portrayal of gender roles, see Chapter 4.) What messages, for example, do children take away from their Saturday morning cartoon sessions? Week after week, they see cartoon characters like the coyote in "Road Runner" being smashed with giant mallets, blown up with dynamite, and crushed by trains.

Two different positions exist regarding the effect of media violence. The observational-learning position holds that the media do encourage children to solve their problems by violent means. Constant exposure to media content normalizes violence; children come to believe that society is violent, and that is the way things are. The opposite position maintains that violence in the media provides a catharsis — that is, the individual's frustrations are relieved or purged through vi-

carious participation in media violence. Alfred Hitchcock's defence (quoted in Schellenberg 1974) of his own television program illustrates the catharsis position: "One of television's great contributions is that it brought murder back into the home where it belongs. Seeing a murder on television can be good therapy. It can help work off one's antagonisms. If you haven't any antagonisms, the commercials will give you some."

Three decades of experimental studies and naturalistic field research clearly support the observational-learning position rather than the catharsis position. Despite an occasional apparently negative finding, the bulk of the evidence leads to the conclusion that there is indeed a causal relationship between heavy television viewing and overt aggressive behaviour in children and adolescents (Liebert and Sprafkin 1988; Singer and Singer 1988).

Social scientists conclude that although other variables — for example, parent/child relations, socioeconomic status — are certainly involved, televised violence is a significant factor in the production and maintenance of violence in our society (Roberts and Maccoby 1985). Put another way, TV is *a* cause, not *the* cause, of aggressiveness and criminality (Liebert and Sprafkin 1988). Televised violence does make young people more tolerant of aggression in other children and less emotionally responsive to violence in themselves. In the words of an 11-year-old interviewed by *Newsweek* (Water 1977), "You see so much violence that it's meaningless. If I saw someone really get killed, it wouldn't be a big deal. I guess I'm turning into a hardrock" (quoted in Greenfield 1984). When the modelling effect, personality, and circumstances collide, the results are tragic: "Friends and family of 18-year-old Gary White, who gunned down a Toronto police officer before being shot to death himself, told a coroner's inquest that the youth had become obsessed with the Rambo character, watching *First Blood* constantly on videocasettes" *Calgary Herald*, September 17, 1985).

**Television's Beneficial Effects.** Researchers have also been interested in assessing the mass media's positive socialization functions for children. For example, television has been studied as an agent of anticipatory socialization for work roles. The main conclusion is that "television's representation of occupational roles . . . is both a wider perspective than everyday experience and a caricature of the actual world of work" (Peterson and Peters 1983). While television exposes young people to career models beyond their own experiences, the portrayal of occupations has definite limitations. High-prestige professional occupations occur much more frequently and low-prestige occupations much less frequently than in the actual job market. Moreover, DeFleur and DeFleur (1967) found that the information television provides children about occupations tends to be superficial and misleading; stereotypes portray clever, unethical lawyers; temperamental, eccentric artists; burly, aggressive truck drivers, and so on.

The discussion of television's contribution to occupational socialization illustrates its unintentional influence on children: children go to television to be entertained but, while being entertained, they absorb much incidental information about their society. Attempts have been made to deliberately harness television's potential to benefit children. Because educators recognize the importance of youngsters' preschool experiences for their later educational development, programs such as "Sesame Street" have been developed to provide preschool experiences at home. Assessment research (Bogatz and Ball 1972) has shown that frequent "Sesame Street" viewers had improved skills, such as alphabet recitation and reading skills, and were rated by teachers as better prepared for school than infrequent viewers. Although it was hoped that "Sesame Street" would narrow the gap between economically advantaged and disadvantaged children, it turns out that children from advantaged homes are more likely to watch "Sesame Street." Therefore, any cultural or intellectual gap could be widened (Cook et al. 1975).

Attempts have been made to positively influence children's attitudes and behaviour, as well as their skills. For example, a 30-second TV spot tried to show children that there are nonaggressive alternatives for solving problems:

*In one spot . . . two children are running toward the one empty swing in a playground. They arrive at the same time, and each child grabs an end of the swing. Impasse. The kids must either fight or find some other way to resolve the situation. Finally they decide to take turns. Both kids are winners, nobody loses.* (Liebert, Sprafkin, and Davidson 1982)

**Children learn a great deal about the world from television characters, such as these Muppets.**

The award-winning CBC series "Degrassi Junior High" deals with problems teenagers face, such as pregnancy, alcoholic parents, smoking, and sexual harassment. Sitcoms such as "The Cosby Show" and "Family Ties" teach children that family members love and respect one another. We can hypothesize that TV programs featuring single-parent or blended families, adopted children, or youngsters with physical handicaps may help children with similar experiences feel comfortable with their situation.

Although the evidence clearly shows that television has great potential power to socialize, the actual socialization process is complex. For example, studies show that, although pro-social episodes in TV programs have pro-social effects, their influence is limited to situations that are quite similar to those presented in the program. In addition, while a single exposure to a pro-social episode has immediate effects, these specific effects do not last, even for a day. And of course the majority of children simply do not see such programming, which is usually made for educational television. Finally, critics raise the questions "Should television entertainment be consciously designed to socialize the young?" and "Does such programming amount to subtle brainwashing?" (Liebert, Sprafkin, and Davidson 1982).

## An Overview

This section has dealt with the influence of major socialization agents: the family, the peer group, the schools, the mass media. Children are, of course, also socialized by babysitters and daycare workers; by such institutions as Sunday school and the church; or by community organizations such as the YWCA and the YMCA, with their athletic and camping activities.

As children mature into adults, they encounter an increasing diversity of socialization agents that help them to learn relatively more specialized roles. For example, a considerable amount of occupational socialization occurs on the job. Young interns learn how to be effective doctors partly by attending medical school (Chappell and Colwill 1981) and partly by practicing on hospitalized patients. Newly divorced adults are often socialized into the single role through self-help groups such as Parents without Partners. Many universities offer noncredit courses on topics such as effective parenting, coping with divorce and widowhood, and re-entry into the labour market by women who have been full-time homemakers for many years. On the whole, adult socialization agents tend to be impersonal — formal organizations such as universities, technical colleges, corporations, social welfare agencies, and the like. Nonetheless, family and peers continue to be important influences throughout life.

## Oversocialization

Throughout this chapter, we have contended that the socialization process serves both society and the individual. Societal order and continuity depend on members learning to share values, norms, and language. Interaction and role-playing rest on these common understandings. On the other hand, socialization allows individuals to realize their potential as human beings.

Because socialization is such a powerful process, there is a danger that those who read about it may end up with what Wrong (1961) called the "oversocialized conception of man." By this phrase, Wrong meant the erroneous idea that people are completely molded by the norms and values of their society. Such thoroughgoing indoctrination would, of course, destroy individuality and render nonsensical free will and responsibility for one's actions.

But this does not happen. It is quite true that people brought up in a particular society speak the same language, value much the same things, and behave in a similar fashion. Fortunately, however, they are not all identical products turned out by an omnipotent socialization factory. There are many reasons why absolute conformity just does not occur.

To begin with, each person is biologically unique. The raw material of temperament and inborn aptitudes leaves considerable room for individuality. In addition, human beings possess the ability to question norms and values and to innovate. Socialization theorists have also allowed for some measure of independence. Mead acknowledged the spontaneous, creative "I," as well as the socialized "Me." Similarly, Freud's personality-structure theory contained the impulsive, selfish Id, as well as the conventionalized Super-ego. Individuals make roles as well as take roles, by modifying situations to suit themselves.

Furthermore, although nearly everyone is socialized within the family, the actual content of children's socialization varies from family to family. Even brothers and sisters brought up in the same home experience growing up somewhat differently. Also, the fact that parents and children represent two different generations ensures two different perspectives on the lessons of socialization (Yoels and Karp 1978). And though we can speak of societal norms and values, these are really abstractions that must be interpreted by specific agents of socialization; the people responsible for teaching the child to fit into society have differing interpretations of these norms and values. Finally, because socialization is carried out by multiple agents, the person being socialized is exposed to diverse perspectives.

All of this means that although we can speak about Canadians in general, and in so doing distinguish them from Japanese or Brazilians, we are talking about characteristics that make Canadians similar, not identical. The existence of at least some deviant behaviour within every society, including our own, testifies to the fact that no system of socialization is perfectly efficient.

## SUMMARY

1. Through socialization, individuals develop selfhood and acquire the knowledge, skills, and motivations required for them to participate in social life. This symbiotic learning process is functional for both the individual and the society. From the individual's point of view, intense interaction with adult caretakers allows the infant to realize its human potentialities. Later socialization equips the person to handle societal roles. In addition, socialization ensures that commitment to the social order is maintained over time.

2. Sociologists have distinguished four types of socialization. ''Primary socialization'' refers to the learning that occurs in childhood. It lays the foundation for all later learning. ''Adult socialization'' describes the socialization that takes place beyond the childhood years. ''Anticipatory socialization'' is the role-learning that occurs in advance of the actual playing of roles. ''Resocialization'' occurs when a new role or situation requires that a person replace established patterns of behaviour with new patterns.

3. Since the turn of the century, social scientists have been perplexed about the relative contributions of biology and environment to human development. More recently, however, evidence that both factors interact to transform the infant into a functioning member of society has resulted in the abandonment of the overly simplistic nature/nurture debate.

4. There are four major theoretical approaches to childhood socialization: learning theory, the cognitive developmental approach, psychoanalytic theory, and symbolic interaction. Learning theory explains the precise mechanisms involved in socialization. Piaget's work focuses on the development of morality. The psychoanalytic approach analyzes the development of personality structure. The symbolic interac-

tionists emphasize the child's acquisition of language and self. These approaches are complementary, rather than competing, systems of thought.

5. There are four major agents of childhood socialization: the family, the school, the peer group, and the mass media. Because society has given the family and the school a mandate to socialize youngsters, both these agents deliberately attempt to equip their charges with the knowledge and values required to fit into adult society. The influence of the peer group and the media is, for the most part, unintentional.

6. Socialization is a lifelong process. Primary socialization cannot possibly equip individuals for all the roles and situations they will encounter throughout their lives. Compared to primary socialization, adult socialization tends to concentrate on overt behaviour (as opposed to values and motives). It tends to be realistic, rather than idealistic; to be more specific in content; and to occur in formal organizations, rather than informal contexts. In addition, the relationship between socializer and socializee in the adult situation is marked by lower levels of feeling and power than in the childhood situation.

7. The ''oversocialized conception of human beings'' is a viewpoint that exaggerates the effectiveness of the socialization process. Socialization does not mold members of society into identical products. Fortunately, there is considerable room for spontaneity and individuality.

## GLOSSARY

**Adult socialization.** Socialization that takes place after childhood to prepare people for adult roles (for example, husband, mother, computer technician).
**Altercasting.** Casting the other person in a role we choose for him or her in order to manipulate the situation.
**Anticipatory socialization.** Role-learning that occurs in advance of the actual playing of roles.
**Care orientation.** Gilligan's feminine orientation to morality, which emphasizes concern for and connectedness with others.
**Classical conditioning.** Type of learning that involves the near-simultaneous presentation of an unconditioned stimulus (UCS) and a conditioned stimulus (CS) to an organism in a drive state (that is, a state during which needs such as hunger or thirst require satisfaction). After several trials, the previously neutral stim-

ulus (CS) alone produces the response normally associated with the UCS.

**Ego.** The director of the Freudian personality. The Ego attempts to mediate among the demands of the Id, the Super-ego, and the external world. The Ego, which encompasses the cognitive functions and the defence mechanisms, is governed by the reality principle.

**Generalized other.** Mead's "organized community or social group [that] gives to the individual his unity of self." Although the equivalence of terms is not exact, "reference group" is the more modern way of referring to this notion of the organized attitudes of social groups.

**I.** The dimension of Mead's notion of self that is active, spontaneous, creative, and unpredictable. The "I" is a component of a process, not a concrete entity.

**Id.** The reservoir of inborn, biological propensities in the Freudian personality structure. The selfish, impulsive Id operates according to the pleasure principle.

**Justice orientation.** Gilligan's masculine orientation to morality, which emphasizes preserving rights and upholding principles.

**Looking-glass self.** Cooley's formulation of the self as the interpreted reflection of others' attitudes. It consists of "the imagination of our appearance to the other person, the imagination of his judgment of that appearance, and some sort of self-feeling, such as pride or mortification."

**Me.** The dimension of Mead's notion of self that represents internalized societal attitudes and expectations. The "Me" is an aspect of a process, not a concrete entity.

**Moral autonomy.** Piaget's later stage of moral thought, in which children over age eight judge wrongdoing in terms of intentions and extenuating circumstances, as well as consequences, and view rules as social conventions that can be changed.

**Moral realism.** Piaget's early stage of moral development, in which children from four to seven years old judge wrongdoing strictly in terms of its consequences, and believe all rules are immutable absolutes.

**Observational learning.** No reinforcement or reward is required for the initial learning to occur. However, reinforcements do influence where and when learned responses that are in the individual's repertoire (for example, swearing) will be performed.

**Operant conditioning.** Type of learning whereby the organism gives a number of trial-and-error responses. Those responses followed by reward (positive reinforcement) tend to be repeated on future occasions. Those responses followed by negative reinforcement, or by no reinforcement, tend to be extinguished.

**Primary socialization.** Socialization that occurs during childhood.

**Resocialization.** Replacement of established attitudes and behaviour patterns.

**Significant other.** The particular individuals whose standpoint the child adopts in responding to himself or herself during Mead's play stage.

**Socialization.** Complex learning process through which individuals develop selfhood and acquire the knowledge, skills, and motivations required to participate in social life.

**Super-ego.** The Freudian conscience, or internalization of societal values and behavioural standards.

# FURTHER READING

**Bibby, Reginald W., and Donald C. Posterski.** *The Emerging Generation: An Inside Look at Canada's Teenagers.* Toronto: Irwin, 1985. A survey of the attitudes and values of 3000 young Canadians.

**Brim, Orville G., Jr., and Jerome Kagan (eds.).** *Constancy and Change in Human Development.* Cambridge, MA: Harvard University Press, 1980. An analysis of the extent to which childhood experiences constrain adult behaviour.

**Elkin, Frederick, and Gerald Handel.** *The Child and Society: The Process of Socialization.* 4th edition. New York: Random House, 1984. A compact overview of the subject of socialization.

**Lancaster, Jane B., et al. (eds.).** *Parenting Across the Life Span: Biosocial Dimensions.* New York: Aldine De Gruyter, 1987. Examines parenthood as a lifelong commitment.

**Kaye, Kenneth.** *The Mental and Social Life of Babies.* Chicago: University of Chicago Press, 1982. Research on how the newborn organism becomes transformed into a two-year-old person.

**Matthews, Sarah H.** *Friendships Through the Life Course.* Beverly Hills: Sage Publications, 1986. A study of elderly people's views on friendship from the symbolic-interactionist theoretical perspective.

**Turkle, Sherry.** *The Second Self: Computers and the Human Spirit.* New York: Simon and Schuster, 1984. A sociologist and philosopher considers how computers are affecting psychological development and social life.

**Williams, Tannis MacBeth (ed.).** *The Impact of Television: A Natural Experiment in Three Communities.* Orlando, FL: Academic Press, 1986. A before-and-after study of what happens to Canadians in towns where television is first introduced in the mid-1970s.

**Winn, Marie.** *Children Without Childhood.* Markham, ON: Penguin Books, 1983. Argues that adults have abandoned their traditional role as protectors of childhood innocence — and, moreover, have encouraged early involvement in adult concerns.

# CHAPTER 4

# Gender Relations

MARLENE MACKIE

Female. Male. The difference that makes a difference. She menstruates, gestates, lactates. He ejaculates and impregnates (Armstrong and Armstrong 1978). She can identify 25 colours, including taupe and magenta. He can identify 25 cars (Aston Martin, Lamborghini). Except for anger, she expresses more feelings: women convey their moods and sentiments more clearly than men (Rosenthal and DePaulo 1979). He thinks sexual humour is funny (Brodzinsky, Burnet, and Aiello 1981); she relishes jokes that satirize the status quo between the sexes.

Consider courtship. It is women who show primary (though not exclusive) interest in makeup, cosmetic surgery for wrinkles and jowls, Weight Watchers' meetings, and fashion shows. Men, on the other hand, take responsibility for initiating contact with women (and the risk of rejection). Surprisingly, males are more romantic, more likely to believe "that true romantic love comes once and lasts forever, conquers all barriers and social customs, is essentially strange and incomprehensible, and must be basic to marriage." Females are more pragmatic. They are convinced that "they can be in love many times, that it may not last, that it inevitably fades into some disillusionment when the honeymoon ends" (Alcock et al. 1988).

As far as marriage is concerned, both sexes are ambivalent. In addition to some common goals, each seeks somewhat different benefits from legal unions: women look to marriage for security, while men seek intimacy and emotional support (Greenglass 1985). The burdens of marriage also differ. Whether or not they work outside the home, women still assume primary responsibility for meals, housecleaning, and children (Armstrong 1987). On the other hand, the responsibility for economic support of the family is carried disproportionately by men, whose jobs are better paid.

Gender also affects education and economic position. From elementary school to college, teachers interact more with boys and give boys more attention (Houston 1987). Females now constitute 52 percent of the total undergraduate enrolment in Canadian universities (Labour Canada 1987). Nevertheless, because many women accept marriage and the family as their major commitment, they continue to enrol in educational programs that lead to the traditionally lower-paid women's occupations (Turrittin, Anisef, and MacKinnon 1983). Despite increasing numbers entering traditionally masculine trades and professions, most Canadian women are still segregated in relatively few, mostly low-skilled, poorly paid jobs (Armstrong and Armstrong 1984a). Women's lower-paid work makes them economically dependent on men. When relationships break down through death, separation, or divorce, many women suddenly find themselves plunged into poverty (Luxton 1987).

Old age is not easy for either sex. Compared to older men, older women are more likely to be poor and widowed, to be living alone, or to be institutionalized (Gee and Kimball 1987). Elderly men, on the other hand, generally lack the occupational prestige, income, physical strength, and sexual prowess that are considered prerequisites of masculinity in our society (Abu-Laban 1980).

Men and women experience physical and mental health differently. "Women get sick and men die" (Nathanson 1977). Though women are ill more often than men, their illnesses are less serious. The average woman outlives the average man by seven years (Statistics Canada 1987). Women are more prone to depression and to phobias; men to personality disorders, such as alcoholism and drug addiction, and psychophysiological disorders, such as ulcers, heart disease, and respiratory illnesses (Al-Issa 1982). Although females attempt suicide more often, males are two to three times more "successful" at it, depending on age (Barnes 1985). Typically, men use violent methods such as firearms, explosives, and cutting instruments, while women prefer pills or gas (Greenglass 1982).

Men command a disproportionate share of power, prestige, and resources. As a result, the sexes are socialized differently, play different roles, and have different thoughts and experiences (Bernard 1981). They live out their lives in social worlds that are separate at some points and overlapping at others. "Men and women march to different drummers"; in some respects, "they are not even in the same parade" (Bernard 1975).

## Sociology of Gender Relations

This chapter explores femininity and masculinity in contemporary Canadian society. Human social life always and everywhere has been built around the relationships between the sexes. Changes in these relationships thus affect the entire social structure.

The sociology of gender relations developed in the early 1970s in response to the feminist movement. Until then, with a few exceptions (Hacker 1951; Komarovsky 1946), the social behaviour of females had been ignored by sociologists (Daniels 1975). Sociology was a science of male society (Bernard 1973) that emphasized those social institutions and settings in which males predominate, such as the occupational, political, and legal systems. Where women were noticed at all, as in the sociology of the family (Parsons and Bales 1955), it was their connection with men that counted. Matters of interest to women were often neglected. For example, urban sociology ignored the behaviour of mothers and children in parks, women at beauty parlours, widows in coffee shops (Lofland 1975). Indeed, labelling the suburbs as "bedroom communities," because the *men* leave during the day, conveys the message that what women and children do doesn't matter very much (Richardson 1981). There was also a tendency to assume that the results of studies of male behaviour automatically applied to women (for example, that people respond to leaders generally as they respond to male leadership). On other occasions, it was assumed that what was true of men could simply be reversed for a description of women (Fuller 1978). Ambitiousness and competitiveness, for example, were seen as masculine, not feminine, traits. More generally, exclusion of the feminine intellectual perspective meant that pre-1970s sociology suffered from major deficiencies (Dorothy Smith 1974, 1975). The pioneering

**Prime Minister Benazir Bhutto of Pakistan reviews the guards with eyes cast down; Moslem tradition forbids women to make eye contact with men.**

most influenced by gender (for example, husband, wife) are reciprocal roles. Moreover, the role of power in the perpetuation of gender makes it essential that both sexes be studied.

Although the bulk of the social science literature has been written by men on topics of interest to men, consideration of the implications of cultural beliefs about maleness per se is a recent phenomenon. The literature of the 1970s that attempted to bring masculinity into focus concentrated on the restrictions and penalties attached to being born male. The "essential feminist insight that the overall relationship between men and women is one involving domination or oppression" (Carrigan, Connell, and Lee 1985) was evaded. In books such as Goldberg's *The Hazards of Being Male: Surviving the Myth of Masculine Privilege* (1976), the source of the "masculine dilemma" was seen as primarily psychological. In contrast, several recent discussions of gender from the masculine perspective (for example, Pleck 1981; Kimmel 1987) have appreciated its basis in the social structure. An important influence in this regard has been gay liberation politics, which have called into question traditional definitions of masculinity and femininity.

## Some Definitions

Before proceeding further, let us define *gender* and distinguish it from the closely related word *sex*. According to the "Humpty Dumpty Theorem," this definition, like all definitions, is a matter of conventional usage:

*Humpty Dumpty: When I use a word it means just what I choose it to mean, neither more nor less.*
*Alice: The question is whether you can make words mean so many different things.*
*Humpty Dumpty: The question is, who is to be master, that's all.* (Carroll 1986)

**Sex** refers to the physiological differences between males and females. In other words, the term *sex* indicates sexual anatomy and sexual behaviour — that is, behaviour that "produces arousal and increases the chance of orgasm" (Hyde 1979). **Gender**, on the other hand, is what is socially

work of feminist sociologists (for example, Henschel [Ambert] 1973; Stephenson 1973; Millman and Kanter 1975) "made it clear that there were feminist questions that had not yet been imagined and that the answers would demand a fundamental transformation of the social sciences" (Ferree and Hess 1987).

The sociology of gender relations attempts both to remedy the discipline's previous exclusion of the feminine perspective and to encompass the masculine side of the equation (Lipman-Blumen and Tickamyer 1975). Note that the term *gender relations* is not a code-word for women. The women's movement stimulated remedial sociology to analyze previously ignored female behaviour, but sociologists soon realized the futility of attempting to study one sex in isolation from the other. Masculinity and femininity derive their meaning from the relation of one to the other. The roles

recognized as femininity or masculinity (Gould and Kern-Daniels 1977). The cultural norms of a particular society at a particular point in time identify some ways of behaving, feeling, and thinking as appropriate for females, and other ways of behaving, feeling, and thinking as appropriate for males. Below we differentiate biologically based and culturally based role behaviours vis-à-vis offspring (Gould and Kern-Daniels 1977).

|       | *Sex Role*   | *Gender Role* |
|-------|--------------|---------------|
| Women | Childbearer  | Mother        |
| Men   | Sperm Donor  | Father        |

Gender is socially constructed and socially alterable. That is, gender is a set of social attitudes that vary greatly from culture to culture and that change over time. Gender is *not* an attribute of the individual, always there, like a nose (Thorne 1983). In other words, gender is a quality of social interaction that matters more in some social situations than in others. For example, gender would be irrelevant for university students concentrating on a chemistry lecture. However, a sociology lecture that focuses on men's and women's contrasting labour-force experience would make gender highly salient for the students. Similarly, gender would be more salient for students on a date than those at home studying.

## The Importance of Gender

Our argument for the importance of gender rests on two major points. First, in Canadian society, as in all human societies, the genders are *differentiated*. A great fuss is made over the biological distinctions between female and male. Elaborate sets of meanings are built on them. The impact of gender on the individual begins at the moment of birth and continues until the moment of death. The parents of a newborn infant ask, "Is it a boy or a girl?" Although at this stage the infant is little more than a bundle of tissue with potentiality, members of society immediately begin to react to it in terms of its gender. It will likely be wrapped in a pink or blue blanket. It will usually be given a name that signals its sex. This initial gender assignment is the beginning of a process that sorts people into different socialization streams (Goffman 1977).

Sex-typing begins even before birth. Lewis (1972) reported that pregnant women responded to the activity of fetuses in a sex-differentiated fashion. If the fetus kicked and moved a great deal, this behaviour was often interpreted as a sign that the baby was male. There is a great deal of folk wisdom on this subject. For example, a child's prenatal position supposedly indicates its sex, boys being carried high and girls low.

Parents' perceptions of their infants after birth continue to be sex-typed. Aberle and Naegele (1952) reported that fathers expected their daughters to be pretty, fragile, sweet, and delicate, and their sons to be athletic and aggressive. Rubin, Provenzano, and Luria (1974) interviewed thirty pairs of parents at a Boston hospital within twenty-four hours of the birth of their first child. Fifteen of the couples had daughters and fifteen had sons. Infant girls were described by the parents as "softer," "finer-featured," "littler," and "prettier," boys as "bigger," "stronger," "firmer," and "more alert." Although males are generally slightly longer and heavier at birth (Barfield 1976), the hospital records showed that these particular male and female infants did not differ in birth length, weight, or health.

Gender permeates every social relationship and every sphere of human activity throughout life. There are girls' games and boys' games, women's work and men's work. Being a male university student is not the same as being a female university student. Being a wife, mother, divorcée, widow, or elderly woman is not the same as being a husband, father, divorced male, widower, or elderly man. The male/female distinction serves as a basic organizing principle for every human society (Bem 1981). Family, work, religion, politics, and sports have traditionally employed divisions of labour that cleave along gender lines.

A second reason for gender's importance is that society values men's characteristics and activities more than women's (Lipman-Blumen 1984). The sexes are ranked. As a category, males have more status, power, influence, and resources than females. Our society has not shared Maurice Chevalier's sentiment of "Vive la différence!"

Richer's (1983) study of Ottawa kindergarten children found evidence of early understanding of gender inequality. The children maintained that their school was rife with "girl germs," which threatened boys who came into physical contact with girls. The only way for a boy to ward off girl germs was to enact the purification ritual of crossing his fingers as soon as possible after touching the girl.

*The fact that the expression "boy germs" was never used and that, in general, the girls made no effort to challenge the girl germs label is indicative of the very early acceptance by both sexes of a hierarchical division between males and females.* (Richer 1983)

When parents ask the doctors which sex their newborn infant is, in all likelihood they are hoping for a particular answer. If the baby is their first child or intended to be their only child, research shows that parents tend to prefer a boy (Williamson 1976). Which sex would you yourself prefer to be? Chances are that if you are female, you sometimes wish you were male and, if you are male, you are quite satisfied to remain that way. Why do people condone — even admire — masculine behaviour in a 12-year-old girl and abhor feminine behaviour in a 12-year-old boy? Even the labels for these children, "tomboy" and "sissy," communicate societal sentiments. The answer to this question, and many more just like it, is clear: society values males more highly than females.

## Female/Male Similarities and Differences

Our society emphasizes both sex and gender. People tend to view these physiological distinctions and the cultural elaborations on them as equally natural. It makes sense to determine just what these differences really are. Possible origins of such differences are explored in later sections.

### Misleading Female/Male Comparisons

Because so much emotion and mystery surround male/female relations, it is not surprising that many notions about sex differences have been biased (Tresemer 1975). We dwell on the differences between males and females and ignore their simi-

larities. Men and women are seen as *either* this *or* that, not both. We are fascinated with anatomical differences and reproductive capacities. However, we tend to overlook the fact that males and females really share much the same body blueprint. Psychological traits provide another example. Deaux (1984) analyzed a decade's research on gender in the field of psychology and concluded that sex differences are "surprisingly small." We assume — correctly, as it happens (Maccoby and Jacklin 1974) — that males are more aggressive than females. However, this does not mean that *all* males are aggressive, while *all* females are passive. Research shows that this gender difference, as well as others, can be represented as a pair of overlapping normal curves, as in Figure 4-1. The trait appears to be distributed normally within each category, but the two group means differ. Both males and females range from highly aggressive to very unaggressive. The group average for males is somewhat higher, but a substantial number of females will be as aggressive as, or more aggressive than, a substantial number of males.

**Figure 4-1. Overlapping Normal Curves of Aggressiveness**

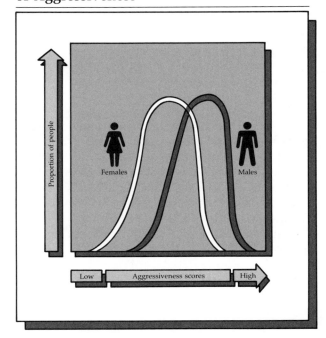

The following classroom exercise makes the point that females and males are not diametrically opposite beings. Ask a number of males and females to answer "yes" to the following questions by raising their hands: Do you have blue eyes? Are you 172 cm or taller? Ever consider growing a beard? Do you like mathematics? Do you know the meaning of "sauté," "puce," and "placket"? Have you cried at least once this month? Ever had a fist fight? Do you support the New Democratic Party? Do you like kittens? If people answer honestly — social desirability might influence some responses — you would probably find no gender difference on some questions (eye colour, political party); overlapping, but gender-related, responses on others (height, mathematics); and completely dichotomous responses on still others (beard, definition of words).

## Gender Differences and Their Sources

"What," asks the nursery rhyme, "are little girls made of? / What are little boys made of?" The answer given by scientists do not mention sugar and spice or snips and snails and puppy-dog tails. Instead, they tell us that, physiologically, females carry two X chromosomes and males an X and a Y chromosome. Female endocrine glands secrete estrogen into the bloodstream, while the primary male sex hormone is testosterone. A female is equipped with ovaries, a clitoris, and a vagina, and a male with testes, a penis, and a scrotum.

In addition, a number of secondary sex characteristics exist; these become more pronounced with puberty. On the average, males are taller, heavier, and have a greater percentage of total body weight in muscle and a smaller proportion of fat. Females have lighter skeletons, different shoulder/pelvis proportions, different pelvic bone shapes, and different socket shapes at the hip and shoulder. These differences contribute to women having less strength, less endurance for heavy labour, more difficulty in overarm throwing, and a better ability to float.

With regard to psychological characteristics, "the sexes are more alike than different" (Maccoby 1980). To date, research has established that females have superior verbal ability, while males have superior mathematical ability and visual/spatial skills. These cognitive differences are, however, slight and the performance of both sexes can be significantly al-

tered by training (Deaux 1985). As mentioned earlier, males tend to be more aggressive than females (Maccoby and Jacklin 1974, 1980). Finally, some evidence suggests that females are more likely than males to conform to group pressure (Eagly and Carli 1981).

Researchers' inventory of female/male distinctions grows longer when consideration is given to fashion (trousers and hair length are no longer reliable guides); etiquette and demeanour (who drives the car on dates? who lights cigarettes for whom?); language (which gender is more often likened to food — a dish, tomato, peach, cookie, honey, cheesecake? [Eakins and Eakins 1978]); nonverbal communication (women gaze at men [Lamb 1981] and are touched by men [Henley 1975] more than vice versa); moral thinking (Gilligan 1982); social roles (nurses versus soldiers, mothers versus fathers); spheres of existence (the domestic world of women versus the public world of men).

Up to this point, we have concentrated on enumerating gender differences rather than explaining them. The sections that follow will consider the causes of these differences.

# Biological Explanations of Gender

To what extent are men masculine and women feminine because they were born that way? In particular, is women's social subordination a reflection of their biological inferiority? These questions have concerned practitioners of many academic disciplines.

## Animal Research

Studies have been made of our evolutionary cousins the monkeys and apes in an attempt to determine whether human sex differences are innate or learned (Tavris and Wade 1984). The logic here rests on the assumption that primates are like human beings, but do not undergo the intensive social learning that we do. Primate sex differences that parallel human sex differences therefore constitute evidence for biological causation of human sex differences.

This type of argument-by-analogy (Tavris and Wade 1984) presents at least three problems. First, the conclusion reached depends greatly on the particular species chosen (Rosenberg 1976). The male baboon is much more aggressive than the female baboon; both male and female gibbons are highly aggressive (Lancaster 1976). As far as human differences are concerned, do baboons support biological causation and gibbons social learning? Second, extrapolation from lower-animal behaviour to human behaviour is risky "for the simple reason that humans are not non-humans" (Weisstein 1971). As the evolutionary ladder is ascended, the effects of physiology on behaviour become less dramatic and the role of learning more important (Frieze et al. 1978). Third, even when the same label is used for human and animal behaviour, the behaviours may not be at all comparable. Take, for instance, sex differences in aggression. The animal findings refer to such measures as threat displays, the latency of initial attack, and the outcome of fights, whereas the human studies refer to quite different measures, such as verbal aggression, teachers' ratings of assertiveness, questionnaire responses, and so on (Archer 1976).

Do criticisms like these mean that animal studies are worthless to students of human sex differences? Not at all. But research into animal differences is best viewed as a source of hypotheses, rather than definitive answers concerning sex differences in *Homo sapiens*.

## The Anthropological Approach

Anthropologists have provided yet another perspective on the question "To what extent do gender differences stem from essential human nature?" Put another way, are the division of labour and male superiority that characterize contemporary Western societies biologically based? See Rosaldo and Lamphere (1974); Friedl (1975); Martin and Voorhies (1975); Ortner and Whitehead (1981); Sanday (1981); Leacock (1983); and Liebowitz (1983).

The presence or absence of **cultural universals** in the anthropological record is taken to be evidence for or against a biological explanation. If a certain type of behaviour is found in many cultures, despite other variations in cultural patterns, that behaviour is assumed to be biologically determined, or at least linked in some way to physiology. According to this conservative position, existing gender arrangements being "essentially 'natural,' they *should* stay about what they

are: major change would be unsuccessful, or would exact too high a price in emotional strain" (Friedl 1975). If, however, cultural comparisons show inconsistency, if social arrangements are sometimes this way and sometimes that, this cross-cultural inconsistency is interpreted as evidence that gender differences are socially caused.

Debate has centred on two interrelated and apparently universal aspects of the anthropological record: male dominance and the division of labour between the sexes. The first cultural universal refers to the fact that although women sometimes have a good deal of informal influence, "societies in which women are consistently dominant do not exist and have never existed" (Friedl 1978).

The second cultural universal summarizes anthropological evidence that all societies distinguish between tasks usually performed by men and tasks usually performed by women. These arrangements appear to have had their original source in women's reproductive capacities, the long helplessness of the human infant, and the generally greater size and strength of men. Since women were tied down with pregnancy and breastfeeding, their activities were restricted to a home base. They were responsible for feeding and nurturing family members of all ages, and for gathering food available near home. Men, by necessity, filled the more public roles of hunter, political leader, soldier, and religious official (Rosaldo 1974).

Most feminist anthropologists acknowledge the near-universality of male dominance and sexually based divisions of labour. However, they challenge the biological inevitability of these gender arrangements. According to them, the cultural meanings given these "natural" facts merit special attention. They point out that considerable cross-cultural variability exists in which sex performs which tasks. Feminist anthropologists argue that women's status and the way work is organized have a lot do with a society's level of technology (Friedl 1975). In hunting and gathering societies, which prevailed for 98 percent of human history, the sexes are generally full economic partners. In horticultural societies, in which food is cultivated by hoe, relations between the sexes tend to be relatively egalitarian (Basow 1986). Since neither sex controls the food supply, there is considerable flexibility in gender roles. Such was the case in the New Guinea tribes studied by Margaret Mead (1935).

# Sex and Temperament in Three Primitive Societies

*More than fifty years ago, anthropologist Margaret Mead set off to New Guinea to discover whether North American sex differences in temperament were innate or learned. Her analysis of three New Guinea societies is a classic argument for cultural conditioning of sex differences. Mead visited three primitive tribes located within a 160-km area on the island of New Guinea: the gentle, mountain-dwelling Arapesh; the fierce, cannibalistic Mundugumor; and the headhunters of Tchambuli.*

Arapesh men and women alike displayed an unaggressive, maternal personality that would seem feminine in our society. The mild-mannered Arapesh "see all life as an adventure in growing things, growing children, growing pigs, growing yams and taros and coconuts and sago, faithfully, carefully, observing all the rules that make things grow." An Arapesh boy "grew" his wife. The girl was betrothed when she was seven or eight to a boy about six years older. Although the marriage was not consummated until both reached sexual maturity, the Arapesh male's greatest claim on his wife was that he contributed the food that became the flesh and bone of her body. Later, both parents participated in childbirth. Conception was believed to require repeated sexual union in order to feed and shape the child in the mother's womb. Both parents lay down to bear the child and observed the birth taboos and rituals. Mead said that "if one comments upon a middle-aged man as good-looking, the people answer: 'Good-looking, Y-e-s? But you should have seen him before he bore all those children.' "

Aggressiveness was eschewed by both sexes. The ideal Arapesh male never provoked a fight, and rape was unknown. Males considered leadership to be an onerous duty.

Mead found that the Mundugumor tribe offered a striking contrast to the Arapesh. Whereas the Arapesh standardized the personality of both men and women in a mold that, out of traditional bias, we would describe as womanly and maternal, the Mundugumor went to the opposite extreme. Again, ignoring sex as the basis for establishing sex differences, they standardized the behaviour of both men and women as actively (almost pathologicaly) masculine. Both sexes were expected to be violent, aggressive, jealous, competitive, and active.

The structure of the Mundugumor family system appeared to be the source of these insecure, aggressive personalities. Here, the social organization was based on a "theory" of natural hostility among members of the same sex. Because father and daughters formed one rival group (called a "rope") and mother and sons another, neither parent welcomed pregnancy. The resulting offspring could abet the forces of the opposing group. The infant, regardless of sex, was not cherished by its mother. For example, weaning consisted of slapping the child. Hostility existed among siblings. All this unpleasantness was intensified by the fact that polygyny (a man having more than one wife at a time) was the ideal. Although wives brought wealth, additional marriages fuelled hostility and jealousy. Sex took the form of a rough-and-tumble athletic tryst in the bushes. The delights of these bush encounters could be enhanced by copulating in other people's gardens, an act that would spoil their yam crops. The fact that this society was rich was the reason it managed to exist at all, with so little of its structure based on genuine co-operation.

Among the lake-dwelling Tchambuli, Mead found that the gender roles and the accompanying temperament reversed Western notions of normalcy. The woman was the "dominant, impersonal, managing partner, the man the less responsible and the emotionally dependent person." The Tchambuli derived their greatest satisfaction from art. Economic affairs were relegated to the women, while the men devoted themselves to art and ceremony. The women worked together in amiable groups and enjoyed the theatricals the men put on, and "whereas the lives of men [were] one mass of petty bickering, misunderstanding, reconciliation, avowals, disclaimers, and protestations accompanied by gifts, the lives of the women [were] singularly unclouded with personalities or with quarrelling."

The Tchmabuli women were described as "solid, preoccupied, powerful, with shaved unadorned heads" and the men as having "delicately arranged curls," "handsome pubic coverings of flying-fox skin highly ornamented with shells," and "mincing steps and self-conscious mien." The women were more "urgently sexed" than the men. And from early childhood, males continued to be emotionally dependent on the women.

From her observations of the three New Guinea tribes, Mead arrived at this conclusion: "The material suggests that we may say that many, if not all, of the personality traits which we have called masculine or feminine are as lightly linked to sex as are the clothing, the manners, and the forms of head dress that a society at a given period assigns to either sex . . . . [The] evidence is overwhelmingly in favor of the strength of social conditioning." Nevertheless, Mead's conclusion has not gone unchallenged.

**Source:**

Margaret Mead, *Sex and Temperament in Three Primitive Societies* (New York: William Morrow, 1935; repr. Mentor Books, 1950).

With the rise of agrarian societies some five to six thousand years ago, women's status declined. Sociologist Rae Blumberg (1978) warns: If you believe in reincarnation, hope that you will never come back as a woman in a traditional agrarian society! Because plow cultivation requires fewer workers at sites farther from the home base, men dominate the economy. As land became property to be owned, defended, and inherited, concern for paternity increased men's desire to control women's sexuality. When class societies developed and goods were produced for exchange, rather than for sharing, women's child-care responsibilities rendered them economically dependent on men (Sayers 1982).

Every one of today's industrialized societies emerged from an agrarian base (Basow 1986). Women's status worsened with the Industrial Revolution, which began in England and northwest Europe in the 1800s. Tasks formerly performed in the home were transferred to the factory and taken over by men. Women from the poorer classes also worked in the factories. However, their presence in the workplace was defined as merely temporary diversion from females' primary responsibility to children and home. These women entered the labour force either when factories were especially short of workers or when extra wages were badly needed at home. The dead-end, poorly paid, low-level jobs they filled did little to improve women's status. At the same time, women in the higher social classes were discouraged from working outside the home. As a result of these developments, men increasingly assumed dominance in the public sphere. Men's public activities gave them privileged access to resources and symbo.s that enhanced their power and provided disproportionate rewards. As dominant groups usually do, males propagated definitions of the situation that aggrandized themselves and their work. There is considerable pressure on subordinate groups, such as women, to accept the dominant groups' definitions.

The real issue then is cultural meanings, not reproductive capabilities. As human products, ideas are subject to revision (Richardson 1981). The notion of male superiority is therefore open to question; moreover, "technology permits humans to transcend biology — people can fly although no one was born with wings" (Huber 1976).

Technology has made it possible for the average woman in industrialized nations to be pregnant only a few months of her life. Inventions such as bottle feeding and daycare centres have made the child-bearing function separable from the child-rearing function. The allocation of domestic tasks to women and public tasks to men can no longer be justified on biological grounds. In short, male dominance is universal but not inevitable (Richardson 1981).

## Psychosexual Deviations

**Gender identity** (a person's conviction of being male or female) and genitals usually match. Children born with penises believe themselves to be males and display masculine personalities and behaviour. Similarly, children born with vaginas develop female gender identities and feminine characteristics. Occasionally ambiguous genitals occur through birth defects or accidents. People with psychosexual abnormalities function, to a certain extent, as natural experiments that provide some insight into the question of the relative weight of biological and social causation in the development of gender. Evidence on both sides has been reported. However, the case described below suggests that **gender assignment** is socially caused.

In the 1960s, the parents of perfectly normal seven-month-old twin boys took their children to a hospital to be circumcized.

*The physician elected to use an electric cauterizing needle instead of a scalpel to remove the foreskin of the one who chanced to be brought to the operating room first. When this baby's foreskin didn't give on the first try, or on the second, the doctor stepped up the current. On the third try, the surge of heat from the electricity literally cooked the baby's penis.*
*Unable to heal, the penis dried up, and in a few days sloughed off completely, like the stub of an umbilical cord.* (Money and Tucker 1975)

Doctors recommended that the boy's sex be reassigned and that female external genitals be surgically constructed. The child's name, clothes, and hairstyle were feminized as the parents made every effort to rear twins — one male and one female. As the following anecdotes concerning the twins at age four-and-a-half shows, both parents and children successfully developed gender-appropriate attitudes and behaviour. The mother, talking about the boy, reported, "In the summer time, one time I caught him — he went out and took a leak in my flower garden in the front yard, you know. He was quite happy with himself. And I just didn't say anything. I just couldn't. I started laughing and I told daddy about it." The corresponding comments about the girl went this way: "I've never had a problem with her. She did once when she was little, she took off her panties and threw them over the fence. And she didn't have no panties on. But I just gave her a little swat on the rear, and I told her that nice little girls didn't do that, and she should keep her pants on" (Money and Ehrhardt 1972). For Christmas, the girl wanted dolls, a doll house, and a doll carriage. The boy wanted a toy garage with cars, gas pumps, and tools. We are told that the feminized twin grew up to be a healthy young "woman" (Schulz 1984).

This case and others suggest that sex by assignment outweighs biological factors in determining gender identity. For example, of forty-four cases of individuals with female XX chromosomes, ovaries, excessive male hormones, and ambiguous external genitals, thirty-nine were assigned as female at birth. Thirty-seven of them developed a female identity. In contrast, all five assigned and reared as males developed male gender identity (Green 1974). However, gender reassignment is usually unsuccessful after the age of 18 months (Money and Ehrhardt 1972). By then, the child has the ability to understand verbal labels for gender and to view the world from a "female" or "male" perspective. Finally, we must point out that the conclusions of psychosexual abnormality research have been criticized because gender reassignment has been supplemented by appropriate surgery and hormone treatment. That is, the individual's biology has been modified to correspond to the assigned gender (Hyde 1979).

## Brain Lateralization

Recent efforts to explain the slight gender differences in language fluency and visual/spatial abil-

## Siamese Twins and Gender Identity

*The surgical separation of Siamese Twins Lin and Win involves an interesting story of gender reassignment. According to North American research, gender reassignment is usually unsuccessful after the age of 18 months. However, the fact that Lin and Win will grow up in the traditional Burmese culture makes prediction difficult in this particular case.*

In July 1984, Siamese twins, Lin and Win Htut were flown from Burma and separated at Toronto's Hospital for Sick Children. The seventeen-hour operation required a surgical team of forty-three members. For two-and-a-half years, the twins had shared the lower half of a body, including liver, intestines, and genitals. Joined at the pelvis in a Y-shape, they would never have walked. Indeed, they lived a "see saw" existence. When one twin wanted to sit up, the other had to lie down.

The twins were genetically male but had only one penis between them. The doctors had to decide which one would retain a complete set of genitals. How to divide up the twins' body-in-common was a decision to challenge Solomon. "You wonder what happens when they grow up and say, 'How come you got that and I didn't?' " muses surgeon-in-chief Dr. Robert Filler. After consultation by telephone with the parents at home in Burma, the doctors agreed that Lin, the livelier and more aggressive (albeit smaller) of the two, should keep the male genitals. His sexuality is expected to be fully functional. During the surgery, the team constructed a vagina for Win from a tubelike section of the colon. Though she will take female hormones when she reaches puberty, she will not be able to have children or, probably, a full sexual response. [Recent photographs show the "female" twin, now six years old, outfitted in dresses and hairbows. Commentary focuses on her adjustment to her new artificial limb, rather than her altered gender identity.]

**Source:**

*Life Magazine* (October 1984).

ities have focused on apparent differences in the way male and female brains function (Goleman 1978; Bryden 1979; McGlone 1980). This research has attempted to tie the slight gender differences in language fluency and visual/spatial abilities to innate sex differences in the brain. The assumption is made that the brain is programmed before birth by sex hormones. Although so far, the scientific verdict on this research is "case not proven" (Nicholson 1984), popular magazines and books have picked up this interesting topic (Durdin-Smith and DeSimone 1983; Maynard 1984).

The cerebral cortex is divided by a deep groove down the middle into two hemispheres that specialize in different intellectual functions. In about 95 percent of the population, the left hemisphere is primarily responsible for verbal skills, such as understanding other people's speech, learning and remembering verbal material, and reasoning verbally, while the right hemisphere executes visual/spatial skills, such as sensing direction and locating objects in space (Nicholson 1984). **Lateralization** is the term used to label the specialized functioning of each brain hemisphere.

Apparent differences in the brain damage suffered by male and female victims of strokes, accidents, and tumours stimulated the brain lateralization controversy in gender relations. According to this research (McGlone and Kertesz 1973; Inglis and Lawson 1982), a male who experiences damage to his left brain hemisphere suffers impaired verbal skills. He may no longer be able to say what he wants to say in a logical order or understand the meaning of certain words (Doyle 1985). However, if the damage occurs to his right hemisphere, he is apt to experience loss of visual/spatial abilities, such as his sense of direction. On the other hand, females who suffer damage to either right or left hemisphere experience less severe loss of either verbal or spatial abilities than their male counterparts. Moreover, women (but not men) are reported to have lost some verbal ability through damage to the right hemisphere.

The above findings led some scientists to speculate that female brains are less specialized than male brains, their left and right hemispheres being involved in the performance of both verbal and visual/spatial functions (Levy 1976). They hypothesize that superior female verbal proclivities stem from their location in two hemispheres. Female spatial abilities are thought to be reduced somewhat because part of the right hemisphere's capacity is taken up with verbal tasks (Nicholson 1984).

In general, the research so far has been inconclusive. Whether brain specialization is related to sex hormones, whether the alleged differentiation occurs in childhood or puberty — or, indeed, whether gender differences in brain specialization exist at all — remain highly speculative matters. A significant flaw in the brain lateralization theory is the difficulty in establishing the direction of causality that plagues brain studies. Even if sex differences in brain functioning were unequivocally documented, such brain differences might be the result, rather than the cause, of distinctive (and socially caused) experiences of males and females (Lowe 1983). Two final points are worth considering. First, female and male brains are more alike than different. Second, even if some differences in specialization do occur, the environment enhances or diminishes these potentialities, depending on the sociocultural definitions of femininity and masculinity.

## Conclusions

Every approach to the problem of the biological foundation of female/male differences raises more questions than it answers. Biology may be directly involved in cognitive differences and aggressiveness, and indirectly involved in the gender division of labour. The secondary sex characteristics of male size and strength may also contribute indirectly to gender differences. In a culture such as ours, which values "sheer bigness," the generally greater male body size may translate into status (Garn 1966). The gender-role implications of strength are more obvious. Superior male strength is an ingredient in the traditional gender division of labour. More important, however, is the implicit or actual physical threat that males present to females. As Goffman (1977) points out, "Selective mating ensures that with almost no exceptions husbands are bigger than wives and boyfriends are bigger than girlfriends."

The biological differences between females and males are really very slight in comparison with the immense gender differences erected on this substructure. However, to search for either biological *or* environmental causation of gender patterns, to pose the issue as nature versus nurture, is a misleading and simplistic formulation of a complex question. In gender patterns, as in social behaviour in general (remember the discussion in Chapter 3), both biology and environment are implicated. Biochemical and genetic factors set the stage, but culture and history provide the script for social life (Kunkel 1977). The fact that socialization often emphasizes "natural" sex differences further complicates the situation. For example, our society provides more athletic facilities and opportunities for the physically stronger males. However, because most of the psychosocial differences between the sexes involve learning in one way or another, let us look at socialization as an explanation of gender.

## Socialization Explanations of Gender

Chapter 3 defined *socialization* as the lifelong learning process through which individuals develop selfhood and acquire the knowledge, skills, and motivations required for participation in social life. **Gender socialization** involves the particular processes through which people learn to be masculine and feminine according to the expectations current in their society. As we have already seen, there are a number of theoretical approaches to socialization: the learning, Freudian, cognitive developmental, and symbolic-interaction perspectives. Symbolic interaction will be emphasized here.

Each society has its scripts (Laws 1979) for femininity and masculinity. The emotions, thoughts, and behaviour of children are shaped in approximate conformity with these **gender scripts**. However, the content of gender socialization for all Canadians is not uniform. Gender scripts are differently interpreted in different social classes, ethnic groups, and regions of the country. In addition,

these scripts are age-graded — that is, the gender norms that pertain to given individuals change as they move through the life cycle. Gender stereotypes and occupational sex-typing tell us something about our society's scripts for gender socialization.

## Gender Stereotypes

Imagine yourself talking with a friend who describes two people whom you have never met. One person is said to be independent, adventurous, and dominant, while the other is described as sentimental, submissive, emotional, and affectionate. Would it be easier to picture one of these persons as male and the other as female? If you visualize the first person as male and the second as female, you have demonstrated your knowledge of gender stereotypes. What is more, you could be Canadian, American, Peruvian, Nigerian, Pakistani, or Japanese. Cross-cultural research shows that citizens of 30 nations share similar general beliefs about the sexes (Williams and Best 1982).

A **stereotype** refers to those folk beliefs about the attributes characterizing a social category on which there is substantial agreement (Mackie 1973). The term refers to consensual beliefs about the traits people choose to describe categories of people, such as ethnic groups, old people, or university students. In themselves, stereotypes are not good or bad; they simply are. Some stereotype traits are false — for example, that women are illogical. Other traits may be generally fitting but, like all generalizations, fail to take into account individual differences within the sexes or the degree of overlap between the sexes (Williams and Best 1982). For example, the male stereotype contains the trait aggressiveness. Our previous discussion noted both the accuracy of this sex difference and the female/male overlap. In short, "stereotypes both represent and distort reality" (Eagly and Steffen 1984).

Gender stereotypes capture folk beliefs about the nature of females and males generally. Many studies show that, despite the activities of the women's movement, gender stereotypes are "widely held, persistent, and highly traditional in content" (Ward and Balswick 1978). When researchers (Broverman et al. 1972) ask respondents to describe the average man and the average woman, the gender traits fall into a feminine *warmth/expressiveness cluster* and a masculine *competency cluster*. The latter cluster includes such characteristics as being independent, active, competitive, and ambitious. A relative absence of these traits supposedly characterizes women. In other words, relative to men, women are seen to be dependent, passive, noncompetitive, and not ambitious. The warmth/expressiveness cluster, on the other hand, consists of such attributes as being gentle, quiet, and sensitive to the feelings of others. Relative to women, men are perceived as lacking these traits. Gender-stereotype studies (Broverman et al. 1972) also report that many more of the characteristics valued in Western societies are seen as masculine rather than feminine traits.

Gender stereotypes embody our societal script's edicts regarding appropriate major time and energy investments for women and men. According to this "ideal" division of labour, men are expected to work outside the home, marry, and support their families, while women are expected to marry, carry the major responsibility for child-rearing, and rely on men for financial support and social status. Although a woman may also work outside the home, attracting a suitable mate and looking after his interests (and eventually those of their children) take priority over serious occupational commitment. The two clusters of traits reflect this division of labour.

It appears that beliefs about gender develop, at least in part, from people's observations of women and men playing these traditional social roles. For example, children are more likely to encounter women taking care of babies and men wielding authority in the workplace than the other way around, and come to believe that the characteristics thought to be necessary for child care (nurturance, warmth) and for success in the labour force (dominance, objectivity) are typical of women and men, respectively. It is likely that fundamental changes in the "pictures in people's heads" (Lippmann 1922) about men and women must await social change. In other words, "Gender stereotypes . . . will not disappear until people divide social roles equally, that is, until child care

**The relative who gives most care to young children whose mothers work for pay is most likely to be the children's father.**

and household responsibilities are shared equally by women and men and the responsibility to be employed outside the home is borne equally" (Eagly and Steffen 1984).

The gender stereotypes themselves, since they function as self-fulfilling prophecies, constitute an important impediment to social change. If women are assumed to be less competent, their performance may be judged less successful than it actually is. In addition, if women are assumed to be less competent, they may be given fewer opportunities to assert themselves.

## Occupational Sex-Typing

The sex-typing of occupations is a central element of the societal script for masculinity and femininity that children learn. In many occupations workers are primarily of one sex or the other. For example, most nurses are women and most law-yers are men. As you will learn, this sex-segre-gated occupational structure is partly responsible for the large differences between Canadian men and women with respect to income, job security, and opportunities for advancement (Boyd 1984).

**Occupational sex-typing** refers to the tendency to regard sex-segregated occupations as more appropriate for one sex or the other. Kindergarten teaching has traditionally been regarded as women's work, university teaching as men's work. Beliefs that men are better suited for certain occupations and women for others are buttressed by gender stereotypes. Women may be considered suited to nursing "because they are nurturant" and men to law "because they are logical" (Williams and Best 1982).

A study of elementary school children in Saskatchewan and Quebec (Labour Canada 1986) suggests that these traditional ideas are undergoing some change. A high proportion of the children believed that most occupations could be undertaken by both sexes. However, there is a stronger expectation that traditionally masculine occupations will attract both men and women than that traditionally feminine occupations will attract men. As the study points out, attempts have been made to attract girls into science-based careers such as engineering. Comparable efforts have not been made to interest boys in becoming secretaries or nurses. Of course, the lower salaries paid in predominantly female occupations militates against attracting men into them.

When the children were asked "What do you want to be when you grow up?" their own occupational aspirations showed both persistence and change in traditional notions. Ninety-three percent of the boys chose a traditionally male occupation. Only one percent chose traditionally feminine careers. No boy wanted to be a dental assistant, librarian, nurse, or hairdresser. Forty-three percent of the girls also chose traditionally masculine occupations. The jobs they had in mind were professional ones requiring a high level of education, such as dentistry or medicine. Some boys (but no girls) mentioned mathematician, stockbroker, astronomer, or air traffic controller.

Many of the girls seemed to believe that equality of the sexes does not apply to them personally. "Many of them seemed to be saying, 'Yes, women

can become doctors, but I expect to be a nurse,' [or] 'Bank managers can be women as well as men, but I am going to be a teller' " (Labour Canada 1986).

## French-Canadian/English-Canadian Comparisons

French-Canadian gender attitudes seem to have become increasingly egalitarian over time. Lambert (1971) found French-Canadian parents to be more traditional than English-Canadian parents. French-Canadian children, however, had less differentiated views of appropriate gender behaviour than did English-Canadian children. Lambert suggests that the parental difference might be due in part to the higher average educational level of his English-speaking sample. This interpretation agrees with his finding of greater traditionalism in the working class.

Somewhat later studies show that, although some changes were occurring, French Canadians remained quite traditional about those aspects of gender relations concerning the family. For instance, Boyd's (1975) analysis of Gallup poll results shows that French Canadians supported equality between the sexes, but only when the Gallup questions did not evoke maternal or wifely imagery. When answering questions about these roles, French Canadians were more traditional in their attitudes toward women.

More recently, Ponting's (1986a) national study found that francophones' gender attitudes were generally more egalitarian than those of anglophones. For example, 80 percent of the francophones and 72 percent of the anglophones agreed with this statement: "There should be more laws to get rid of differences in the way women are treated, compared to men." And 87 percent of the francophones (versus 73 percent of the anglophones) agreed that "In the business world more women should be promoted into senior management positions." In contrast to Boyd's (1975) findings, discussed above, Ponting reported no francophone/anglophone differences in responses to items relating to the domestic sphere. For instance, 62 percent of the francophones and 63 percent of the anglophones agreed with the statement "When children are young, a mother's place is in the home."

## The Role of the Mass Media in Gender Socialization

The mass media are impersonal communication sources that reach large audiences. As such, they function as symbolic socialization agents. The media have been described as the cement of modern social life and the co-ordinator of other societal institutions (Tuchman 1978). Calling them "a community of discourse" captures their real impact on society: many individuals — regardless of age, social class, religion, or political predilection — can talk about the hosts of TV talk shows (Phil Donahue, Oprah Winfrey), newspaper advice columnists (Ann Landers), or comic-strip characters (Calvin and Hobbes, Adam). A community of discourse is comparable to a language. It integrates and controls; it provides common elements for strangers to use when they meet and limits what can be noticed or said (Tuchman 1979).

Concerns about the effects on children of violence depicted in the mass media led to the studies described in Chapter 3. Since the advent of the women's movement, a parallel concern has been voiced over the impact of the media on the development of gender attitudes and behaviour. The Royal Commission on the Status of Women in Canada (1970) accused the media of perpetuating stereotypes of both sexes. It was especially critical of the "degrading, moronic" depiction of women in advertisements and argued that, although men as well as women are stereotyped, "the results may be more damaging for women since advertising encourages feminine dependency by urging women not to act but to be passive, not to really achieve but to live out their aspirations in the imagination and in dreams."

More than a decade later, the Canadian Radio-television and Telecommunications Commission (1982) voiced similar concerns about gender stereotyping both in commercials and in programming. Its recommendations included the following:

- Broadcasting should include a wide variety of images reflecting the diversity of women in our culture. This includes women of all ages, women of differing ethnic groups, and women of differing physical appearance.

- Broadcasting should present women engaged in a wide variety of activities, including athletics.

- Women should not be used as sexual stimuli or lures, or as attention-getting, but otherwise irrelevant, objects.

- When families are presented, the diversity of lifestyles that exist today should be reflected (for example, single parents and extended families).

- Women should be more adequately represented as news readers, reporters, and hosts.

- A balance of female and male perspectives should be represented in stories, issues, topics, and images, as well as in writing, editing, directing, and producing.

The gender-related content of television has certainly changed since the Royal Commission on the Status of Women (1970) brought the matter to the attention of Canadians. Feminist issues, such as the provision of daycare, are aired on educational panels and dramas. There are now significant, if not representative, numbers of female newscasters, business commentators, and disc jockeys. The gender scripts portrayed in TV sitcoms show both persistence and change. Mrs. Huxtable on "The Cosby Show" is a lawyer; Mrs. Keaton on "Family Ties" is an architect; Alexis on "Dynasty" and the three "Golden Girls" challenge the notion that only young women belong on television.

Nevertheless, systematic analysis of television's content demonstrates that traditional patterns linger. Most areas of TV entertainment feature twice as many males as females. The stars are more likely to be males. Despite such departures from stereotypical depiction as those mentioned above, the males are still apt to be autonomous and aggressive, while the females remain nurturant, dominated by others, and defined by their relationship to males (Durkin 1986). Even when women hold professional jobs, their first concern is their family and home. (Although both characters have an amazing amount of time to spend at home, we do see Dr. Huxtable in his medical office much more often than Mrs. Huxtable in her law office.) Females are still typically young and attractive, but middle-aged and older males are commonplace. Moreover, Joan Collins and the "Golden Girls" are expensively groomed, attractive women, not everyday figures.

Advertising continues to sell stereotyped messages about the sexes along with products (Singer 1986). Men predominate as voices of authority. Ads trivialize and infantilize women. Males remain rugged individualists, dressed for success (Wernick 1987). Although both sexes are portrayed as consumer-oriented, women especially appear "born to shop." Males as well as females are now being sexually exploited (Posner 1987). As ads such as the Calvin Klein "Obsession" campaign demonstrate, the emphasis is now on sexuality under the guise of liberalism. Even the Miss Mew cat food commercial features "a buxom feline complete with false eyelashes and sultry voice being lusted after by a variety of toms" (Posner 1987).

In the late 1980s, two matters particularly concern people who are worried about the role the media play in gender stereotyping. First, how is the Canadian Radio-television and Telecommunications Commission to enforce the recommendations outlined above? Second, how is the issue of sexually explicit and violent portrayal of females in pornographic videotapes and magazines to be handled?

## The Symbolic-Interaction Perspective on Gender Socialization

Symbolic interactionists, such as Cooley and Mead, view "reality" as a matter of social definition. Socialization involves the acquisition of a self, which is also socially defined. The "looking-glass self" notion described in Chapter 3 holds that children learn who they are by adopting other people's attitudes toward themselves. The roles played by language and significant others in the socialization process are emphasized in this perspective. In this section, we want to apply some of these themes to gender socialization. Because gender consists of social constructions built on female/male physiological differences, symbolic interac-

tion seems a particularly appropriate theoretical approach to the questions we have been asking in this chapter (Mackie 1987).

**Development of Gender Identity.** As a first step to self-awareness, the child differentiates herself or himself from other objects in the environment. As you learned in Chapter 3, Mead hypothesizes that the capacity to use language allows the child to learn the meaning of many things, including himself or herself. Names form a basis, then, for the development of the self. A given name individualizes the infant and usually classifies it by gender. That is, baptizing a child "Barbara" simultaneously separates this infant from other infants and signifies its femaleness. This gender classification influences caregivers to treat the infant as a boy or as a girl. For example, for the first six months or so, male infants are touched more, while female infants are talked to more (Lewis 1972). Later, the male toddler is tossed into the air ("How's my big boy?"), while the female child is tickled under the chin ("How's my sweet little girl?") (Richmond-Abbott 1983). In other words, when we attach gender-designating labels we invite gender-specific interactional experiences (Cahill 1980).

Although the adults who socialize a child place it in a gender class at birth, some time must pass before the child responds to its own self in terms of gender. After eighteen months, gender reassignment becomes less successful, perhaps because the child labels itself "male" or "female." By the age of three, a child can accurately and consistently answer the question "Are you a girl or a boy?" At the same age, children show preferences for either "girl" or "boy" toys and activities (Kessler and McKenna 1978). This self-categorization as male or female becomes a major axis of identity. However, young children do not necessarily interpret gender in the same way that adults do. For instance, they may use hair length and clothing, not genitals, as gender cues. Lindesmith, Strauss, and Denzin (1977) tell the story of a five-year-old acquaintance of theirs who attended a party at which children of both sexes bathed in the nude. When asked how many boys and how many girls were at the party, she answered, "I couldn't tell because they all had their clothes off." This misconception is understandable in a society such as ours, where the naked body is usually covered.

Socialization agents — such as the family, peers, mass media, and schools — teach children what sorts of traits and behaviours go along with the female/male distinction. Parents admonish that "Boys don't cry" and "Girls don't sit with their legs apart." Especially in the past, children's storybooks were sex-typed. Pyke's (1975) survey of 150 Canadian children's books found few women in jobs outside the home. Women's trademark was the "perennial apron," worn "even by female squirrels." Storybook characters who had interesting adventures were most often male.

Richer's (1979) observational study of Ontario kindergarten classrooms shows how the teacher provided cues to enable children to "properly" classify the two sexes. The teacher found gender to be a practical means of organizing the children. For example, children lined up by gender to move from one activity to another — trips to the library or the gymnasium, retrieving food from their lockers, preparing to go home. Gender was also used to motivate the children: "The girls are ready, the boys are not," or "Who can do it the fastest, the boys or the girls?" During co-ordination exercises, commands were given by gender: "Boys, put your fingers on your nose; girls, put your hands in your laps; boys, touch your toes." When someone slipped up here, the teacher's admonishment sometimes took this form: "Are you a girl? I thought all along you were a boy." Richer (1979) tells us that such situations left the child squirming with embarrassment. Probably part of the reason was the loss of status associated with his "demotion" from boy to girl. Be that as it may, the various socialization agents teach children both gender identity — awareness of being a member of one gender or the other — and the different social value accorded females and males. Let us turn now to some examples of how language reinforces the ranking of the sexes.

**Language and the Ranking of the Sexes.** The English language (among others) denigrates women, while it asserts male superiority. Therefore, children unwittingly imbibe sexism along with language.

The "problem of the generic masculine" describes the way in which the English language fails to speak clearly and fairly of both sexes (Martyna 1980). Our language excludes and subsumes women by using generic masculine terms to refer to people in general: "he," "mankind," "man, the social animal," "men of good will" — even "Man, being a mammal, breast-feeds his young" (Martyna 1980). Some grammarians argue that the generic masculine implies "woman," "she," "her," — that "man" embraces "woman"; feminists claim that the generic masculine is both ambiguous and discriminatory. For instance, Ritchie's (1975) survey of 200 years of Canadian law concluded that the ambiguity of the generic masculine allowed judges to interpret statutes and regulations as including or excluding women, depending on the climate of the times or their own personal biases (Martyna 1980).

Another way language treats the sexes differently is by regarding the female as a sex object (Eakins and Eakins 1978). The impression is thereby conveyed that women's sexuality completely defines them, while sexuality is only part of men's identity as well-rounded human beings. A male professional is assumed to be a doctor or lawyer. A women "professional" is assumed to be a prostitute. Research on sexual terms produced 10 times as many for females as for males. Women are labelled "nympho," "hooker," "tramp," "whore," and "slut." Similar terms for men carry more positive associations and reflect, perhaps, the morality of machismo and the social double standard — "Casanova," "Don Juan," "letch," "stud" (Eakins and Eakins 1978).

There is also reverse devaluation. Here, what is admirable in one sex is disdained in the other. Men may fare worse in this trade-off. Labelling a woman "mannish" is considered by some to be less insulting than labelling a man "womanish" or "sissy." Indeed some males think it a compliment to tell a female that she "runs, talks, or most especially, *thinks* 'like a man'" (Eakins and Eakins 1978).

Then there are "praise him/blame her" pairs of words. He is a "bachelor" (romantic, eligible, free), while she is an "old maid" (poor thing). He is a "chef"; she is merely a "cook." He is "master of all he surveys"; she is a "mistress" cohabiting without marriage. She "chattered"; he "discussed." She "nagged"; he "reminded." She "bitched"; he "complained." She is "scatterbrained"; he is "forgetful." She has "wrinkles"; he has "character lines" (Eakins and Eakins 1978).

Finally, occupational titles also establish males as primary, females as secondary. The majority of the titles for occupations are male (policeman, fisherman), and it is assumed that males occupy them. A few titles (prostitute, charwoman, maid) seem to belong to females. When either sex moves beyond its traditional sphere, special markers are needed — woman pilot, male nurse; these often carry negative connotations. (On the other hand, there is the story of the children who were disappointed to discover that the "dog doctor" was only a human being [Miller and Swift 1977].)

The point to be emphasized is that as girls and boys learn their language, they also learn something about women's place and men's place (Spender 1985).

**Parents as Significant Others.** The provocative ideas of David Lynn (1959, 1969) emphasize the significance of parents in gender socialization. Lynn postulates that, because of the greater availability of the mother and the relative absence of the father during early childhood, little girls easily develop their gender identity through imitation and positive reinforcement. However, little boys must shift from their initial identification with the mother to identification with the father. Because male models are scarce, they have greater difficulty than females in achieving gender identity. According to Lynn, males must learn through abstractly piecing together the intellectual problem of what it means to be male. Some of this learning comes from peers and from media presentations of gender stereotypes. Some results from punishment for displays of feminine behaviour. Masculine behaviour is rarely defined positively as something the boy *should* do. One reason is that the male gender role is "so strongly defined in terms of work and sexuality, both of which are usually hidden from the eyes of children" (Colwill 1982). Instead, undesirable feminine behaviour is indicated negatively as something he should *not* do (Harley 1959). Consequently, males remain anxious about gender. Females freely imitate males (in fashion, for example), but not vice versa. As adults, men

are more hostile than women toward both the opposite sex and homosexuals. Nevertheless, the boy learns to prefer the masculine role to the feminine because being male implies countless privileges.

During childhood, the male role is the more inflexible. More pressure is placed on boys to act like boys than on girls to act like girls. Girls' problems start with adolescence:

*Since girls are less likely to masturbate, run away from home, or bite and draw blood, their lives are relatively free from crisis until puberty. Before that, girls do not have to conform to threatening new criteria of acceptability to anywhere near the extent that boys do.* (Bardwick and Douvan 1971)

As children of both sexes reach the teenage years, they are exposed to more complex and more precisely defined norms of gender-appropriate behaviour. Girls' socialization makes connectedness to others all-important to females throughout the life cycle; ruptured relationships, power, and aggression all deeply threaten them. Males, on the other hand, see the world in terms of autonomy, hierarchy, and conflict; it is intimacy that threatens them (Gilligan 1982).

**Peers as Significant Others.** Children's experience with age-mates is also important in learning masculine or feminine behaviour. Boys and girls have different friendship patterns and different forms of play. Consequently, they acquire different sorts of social skills that may well have implications for their later adult behaviour. Peer activities also reinforce the notion that males are more important than females.

Engaging in what sociologist Fine (1986) has labelled "dirty play" seems important in the gender socialization of little boys. Pre-adolescent pranks such as "mooning" cars (pulling down one's trousers while facing away from the traffic), "egging" cars, and ringing doorbells and running away are thoroughly disapproved of by adults. However, these activities serve as anticipatory socialization for manhood. Males are supposed to be tough, cool, and aggressive. "There is risk involved in throwing eggs at houses or at moving cars; one could get caught, beaten, grounded, or even arrested" (Fine 1986). Boys gain status within their peer group for behaviour adults regard as troublesome. Boys' identity as males is enhanced by engaging in "dirty play," partly because it is "dirty" play (that is, it defies adult authority), and partly because it is *not* girls' play.

After formal schooling begins, children's play becomes increasingly sex-segregated. The rare cross-sex play that does occur tends to be courtship activity at an unsophisticated level. According to one study (Richer 1984), the most common type is a chasing game, in which girls chase boys and kiss them when they are caught. When boys do bother to chase girls, they pull their hair or push them. Both courtship games (where the desirable males are chased) and the general tendency of both sexes to evaluate boys' activities and boys more positively than girls' activities and girls tend to perpetuate traditional gender arrangements (Richer 1984).

A gender difference exists in the size of children's sex-segregated play groups (Eder and Hallinan 1978). Girls tend to play in small groups, especially dyads (two-person groups). Boys prefer to congregate in larger groups. Thus girls tend to learn the type of interpersonal skills required by small, intimate groups, such as sensitivity to others' feelings, the ability to disclose information about themselves, and the ability to show affection. Boys learn other sorts of skills; in general they learn something about group leadership and decision-making. In addition, girls protect their exclusive groups against the advances of newcomers, while boys tend to welcome new members. Little girls probably blame themselves for the greater trouble they have in making friends.

The type of play preferred by boys versus that enjoyed by girls partly explains the size difference of their friendship groups (Lever 1978). Although such differences seem to be diminishing somewhat, boys tend to play competitive games requiring teams of interdependent players with definite roles. Such games are played according to specific rules. (Hockey is a good example.) In comparison, girls prefer to converse or to engage in physically undemanding activities in an indoor setting that require few participants. Playing dolls or board games does not demand the co-ordination of effort that hockey or baseball does. One result is the learning of different types of skills — and, again, these very likely carry over into adulthood.

Boys acquire the ability to co-ordinate their actions, to cope with impersonal rules, to work for collective as well as individual goals, to deal with competition and criticism. Girls learn to be imaginative, to converse, and to be empathetic. All these social experiences would be valuable for both sexes. While there is some evidence that sex differences in play are lessening (many girls now play ringette, soccer, and softball), the data suggest that the impression of the sex hierarchy conveyed by peer socialization is still very strong (Best 1983; Richer 1984).

**Conclusions.** Symbolic interactionists view gender as a matter of social definition and social behaviour learned through interaction during the socialization process. Other theoretical viewpoints on gender socialization are also useful. For example, Lynn's (1959, 1969) ideas incorporate psychoanalytic and learning notions, as well as symbolic interaction. Learning by imitation (Chapter 3) merits special emphasis. Children growing up in a home organized according to traditional gender patterns regard this organization as perfectly normal and readily accept gender stereotypes (Lambert 1971).

Many social scientists are convinced that the traditional gender stereotypes are arbitrary and even damaging gender scripts for socialization. During the 1970s, some became intrigued with the possibility of making androgyny rather than sex-typing the goal of socialization. The term **androgyny** combines the Greek words for male (*andro*) and female (*gyne*), and refers to the presence of both feminine and masculine elements within individuals of both sexes (Laws 1979). Allowing people to have both instrumental and expressive capabilities within their repertoires may help to free the human personality from the restricting prison of stereotyping (Bem 1976). An androgynous person might characterize himself or herself as understanding and compassionate, *and* assertive, self-reliant, and ambitious. A sex-typed person, on the other hand, might use either the first two *or* the last three traits in self-description. In recent years, the ideal of androgyny has been criticized on the grounds that it does not eliminate gender stereotypes; it just combines them in new ways (Lott 1981). The current ideal of **gender transcendence** looks to a state where femininity and masculinity are superseded as ways of labelling and experiencing psychological traits (Garnets and Pleck 1979). In a utopian society where gender has been transcended, each child would be taught that the distinctions girl/boy and female/male are exclusively biological. The multitude of sociocultural elaborations on sex would disappear. Personality traits, interests, hobbies, toys, clothing, occupations, domestic division of labour — none would any longer be a function of sex (Bem 1983).

# Social-Structural Explanations of Gender

A structural explanation of gender involves seeing what can be learned about gender by assuming that people's behaviour is influenced by external social factors or patterns of social relationships, such as norms, roles, statuses, social classes, institutions. According to this perspective, gender is the result of societal, not individual, characteristics. The structural-functional and conflict perspectives on gender are reviewed below.

## The Structural-Functional Explanation of Gender

Structural-functional theorists like Parsons and Bales (1955) ask how societal arrangements, such as gender differences, contribute to the stability and survival of the social system. The family, as a social institution, is seen as functional for the society because it performs such crucial tasks as satisfaction of sexual needs, procreation, child care, and socialization.

Role specialization of adult family members enhances the ability of the family to perform these functions. The father/husband assumes the instrumental role, meaning that he connects the family to the wider society. In our society, this implies bringing home income from an outside job. The mother/wife, on the other hand, assumes the expressive role. She looks after the relationships within the family.

According to Parsons and Bales (1955), these structural patterns developed from a biological base. The female bears and nurses children. Pregnancy, lactation, and the human child's long period of helplessness restrict women's activities outside the home. Therefore, it is convenient for women to carry out the family's expressive functions. Men perform the instrumental tasks almost by default. Someone has to perform the instrumental role, and men's biology does not restrict their movements in the outside world.

As noted above, feminist anthropologists (Rosaldo 1974, 1980) agree that the structural functionalists' distinction between women's domestic orientation and men's public orientation is an extremely important point. Moreover, that distinction goes a long way toward explaining female subordination. Women's dependence on men for food and physical protection makes men seem their natural superiors. Men's public activities (work in the labour market, hunting, military activities, religion) have traditionally given them privileged access to resources and symbols that enhance their power and provide disproportionate rewards. The corollary, according to Rosaldo, is that women would gain power either by entering the men's public world or by encouraging male participation in domestic life. Her solution assumes that males would lack sufficient interest in the domestic sphere to usurp women's authority there.

However, structural functionalists have been severely criticized for putting forth scientific arguments that serve to justify the traditional view that women's place is in the home. Although it is not entirely the fault of structural-functional theorists, "the function is" translates too easily into "the function should be" (Friedan 1963). Just because it is functional for women to stay home does not mean that women *must* stay home. Arrangements that were convenient in preliterate societies do not necessarily make sense in modern societies. For one thing, women need no longer be constantly pregnant to ensure survival of the species. For another, social inventions, such as daycare facilities, free women from these biological imperatives. And male physical strength matters much less in our society than it did in earlier societies. Anyone can "man" a computer. Moreover, newer research shows that the role segregation hypothesized by the structural functionalists is not a universal feature of family life. Aronoff and Crano (1975) examined how work was distributed among women and men in 862 societies and concluded that both sexes often share the instrumental function. Finally, the labels "instrumental" and "expressive" sometimes get applied on ideological rather than empirical grounds. Who says the household activities of chauffeuring, cheque-writing, financial management, and shopping are expressive? Who says male executives' wining and dining of clients is really instrumental (Richardson 1981)?

## The Conflict Perspective

The analysis of the inequality of the sexes in *The Origins of the Family, Private Property, and the State (1884)*, by Karl Marx's associate Friedrich Engels, provides the starting-point for a conflict theory of gender (Smith 1977; Fox 1982). The main idea here is that females and males are tied to the economic structure in different ways, and this difference explains why males are the more powerful gender (Nielsen 1978).

In capitalist societies, men and women constitute two separate classes. The reason: classes are defined by their relation to the means of production, and the sexes have different relations to these means. The difference flows from the distinction in capitalist societies between **commodity production** (products created for exchange in the marketplace) and the **production of use-values** (all things produced in the home). In a society based on commodity production, such as our own, household labour, including child care, is not considered real work because it lies outside the marketplace. Men have primary responsibility for commodity production, women for the production of use-values. Herein lies women's inferior status.

*In a society in which money determines value, women are a group who work outside the money economy. Their work is not worth money, is therefore valueless, is therefore not even real work.* (Benston 1969)

Women's unpaid work in the home, however, does serve the capitalist system. To pay women for their work would mean a massive redistribution of wealth.

Women who are employed outside the home also have a different relation to the economic structure than do men. For one thing, women's position in the family facilitates the use of women as a **reserve army of labour** (Morton 1972). They are called into the labour force when they are needed (during wartime, for example) and sent home when the need disappears. The cultural prescription that women belong in the home assures that the women will return to the home (Glazer 1977).

Women's primary allegiance to the family is used by the capitalist system as an excuse for deploying them in menial, underpaid jobs. A large pool of unqualified women in competition for jobs depresses wages. Women are untrained, unreliable workers because their families come first. They require less money than men because they are secondary workers anyway. Or so the argument goes.

Women's unpaid labour directly and indirectly subsidizes men's paid labour (Eichler 1978). Women entertain husbands' business acquaintances, type, help with husbands' small businesses and farms, all without compensation. All these services cost money when someone outside the family performs them. This sort of work allows husbands to devote their efforts to full-time paid work.

In general, the conflict perspective explains the inequality of Canadian women in these structural terms:

*A glance at the Canadian social structure indicates that it is men who own and control the essential resources . . . Ownership of the most important resource, the means of production, is mainly in the hands of a few men who have power over almost all women as well as other men. . . . Men also have control of the next most important resource, access to the occupational structure and control of policy making in the major areas of social life.* (Connelly and Christiansen-Ruffman 1977).

The concept of **patriarchy** emphasizes that this domination of women by men is a pervasive feature of the social organization of all kinds of societies (Smith 1983). Women are consistently located in strata below men of their own social group (Lipman-Blumen 1984). Men predominate in the highest strata of every social institution — the economic system, the political and legal systems, the family, the military, the educational and religious systems.

Nevertheless, men's power over women is not the only power differential at issue. Pleck (1981) argues that "patriarchy is a *dual* system, a system in which men oppress women, and in which men oppress themselves and each other." According to this view, the nature of men's relationships with women must be understood contextually as only a part of this more significant masculine "game." Men create hierarchies among themselves, according to such criteria of masculinity as physical strength, athletic capabilities, ability to make money. From the male perspective, females have various uses in their competition — for example, beautiful women have traditionally been used as symbols of success.

The division between homosexual and heterosexual men is a critical aspect of male/male ranking. According to Pleck (1981), "our society uses the male heterosexual-homosexual dichotomy as a central symbol for *all* the rankings of masculinity, for the division on any grounds between males who are 'real men' and have power and males who are not. Any kind of powerlessness or refusal to compete becomes imbued with the imagery of homosexuality."

Despite the foregoing, it would be a mistake to assume that women do not wield any significant social power (Duffy 1986). For one thing, women often manage to resist or subvert masculine power. The distinction between *macromanipulation* and *micromanipulation* is useful here. "When the dominant group controls the major institutions of a society, it relies on macromanipulation through law, social policy, and military might, when necessary, to impose its will and ensure its rule. The less powerful become adept at micromanipulation, using intelligence, canniness, intuition, interpersonal skill, charm, sexuality, deception, and avoidance to offset the control of the powerful" (Lipman-Blumen 1984). Moreover, some women do have access to power beyond personal, face-to-face situations. For example, upper-class women have exercised considerable power on the boards of cultural and social welfare organizations, and social reform groups (Duffy 1986).

Finally, a major point registered by conflict theorists is that traditional gender arrangements are extremely useful to the capitalist system. For example, the ideological position that women really belong in the home, that they are only temporarily in the labour force as secondary earners, obviates payment of fair wages to female workers. Similarly, the ideology that links the breadwinner role to masculinity motivates many men to devote their lives to the performance of intrinsically unsatisfying jobs in order to take care of their families. "By training men to accept payment for their work in feelings of masculinity rather than in feelings of satisfaction, men will not demand that their jobs be made more meaningful" (Pleck 1981).

This section completes the trilogy of theoretical perspectives on gender: the biological, social-psychological (or socialization), and structural explanations. These should be regarded as complementary approaches. Focusing on all three increases our understanding of the phenomenon beyond what it would be through appreciation of any one alone. Nevertheless, the various theories of gender remain incomplete. Like any new sub-discipline, the sociology of gender relations must be given time to develop fully.

# Gender Relations in Canadian Institutions

This section presents a brief overview of some of the ways in which female and male experiences differ in selected Canadian social institutions.

## The Family

Marriage and the family affect men and women differently. Indeed, Bernard (1971) argues that each family unit actually contains two families — his and hers. What evidence supports this allegation?

**His and Her Priorities.** Females are expected to give priority to the family and males to their occupation. Through a recent cultural innovation, women may now combine the wife/mother and career roles (Gee 1980). However, the woman still has the cultural mandate to give priority to the family. Even when she works outside the home, she is expected to be committed to her family first, her work second (Coser and Rokoff 1971).

This cultural mandate means that in early adulthood, locating and marrying a suitable man takes precedence over investment of time and money in extensive job training. Baker (1985), who conducted a national study of the aspirations of Canadian teenagers, concludes that many young women hold unrealistic notions about the future. A 17-year-old Toronto girl had this to say:

*(At age twenty-two) "I'll be owning or managing a clothing store." (At age thirty) "At 6:00 I'll get up and get breakfast for my husband and two kids. One is a baby and one is school-age. I'll drive one kid to school, feed the baby, and play with it. Then I'll put the baby to bed and watch the soaps. . . ." (Later in the interview) "What happened to your store?" "Oh! I forgot about it. I guess someone is looking after it."*

Baker observes that "in the eyes of many of these adolescents, there is no unemployment in their future, no divorce, no poverty. Only interesting jobs, adequate incomes, loving husbands, trouble-free children, home ownership, and international travel were on their horizons" (1985).

The fact that women marry 2.3 years earlier than men (Statistics Canada 1987) is one indication of this cultural mandate. Looking ahead, the young woman's decision is not between family and work, but between family and *demanding* work. After marriage, her husband and his work are what counts. If his job requires geographic mobility, she gives up her job and goes with him. Her work is disrupted by pregnancy, child-rearing, and family emergencies. But these disruptions really don't matter, because her low-status work doesn't matter.

The cultural mandate has directed men to focus much of their energy on fulfilling the breadwinner role in the nuclear family: "As the chief breadwinner, a man's success and ultimately his definition of masculinity has been primarily judged by himself and many others by how well he provides for his family's needs and wants" (Doyle 1983). Studies of the male life cycle (Levinson 1978) report priority shifts over time. Men in their twenties and thirties, during the early years of marriage and family formation, remain "largely passive spectators in the home setting." In mid-life, there tends to be a shift from this high centrality of work to a greater investment in family (Rossi 1980). This life-cycle change happens because of some combination of age, stress, and perceived failure in work. At the same time, the full-time housewife/mother in mid-life often becomes interested in achievement outside the home (Rubin 1979).

**Division of Labour.** Familial priorities are closely related to familial division of labour. In the traditional marriage, husbands and wives have distinctive responsibilities labelled by the structural functionalists as instrumental and expressive roles.

Sociologists have shown considerable interest in who does the work around the home. If life is to proceed smoothly, someone has to prowl supermarket aisles in search of food, someone has to cook dinner, someone has to scrub toilet bowls, someone has to wipe children's runny noses. That someone is usually the wife. Regardless of individual variation in talent and inclination, society consigns "a large segment of the population to the role of homemaker solely on the basis of sex" (Bem and Bem 1971). Outside work does not let women "off the hook": they carry two jobs. Recent studies (Michelson 1985; Lupri and Mills 1987) conclude that when wives go out to work, husbands do *not* substantially increase their share of the housework. The weight of child-rearing responsibility falls on the mother's shoulders. A Flin Flon, Manitoba, mother has this to say:

*I know that when my children are small they need me. But sometimes I think I'll go nuts if I don't get out of this house and meet some grown-ups. I find I'm starting to talk like a three-year old all the time now. (Luxton 1980)*

One consequence of the familial division of labour is asymmetry in conjugal power. Because our society values and rewards occupational achievement, the husband's status in the outside world typically spills over into the family in the form of enhanced power. In contrast, the bargaining position of the dependent wife, especially one encumbered with young children, is weakened. The relative powerlessness of the women, in conjunction with the fact that they are usually physically smaller and weaker, partially explains why in 1985 an estimated 33 000 Canadian women were physically, psychologically, and sexually abused by their partners (MacLeod 1987).

**Marital Dissolution.** No consistent differences exist in global ratings of husbands' and wives' satisfaction with marriage (Peplau and Gordon 1985). However, when marriages are dissolved, separation and divorce affect men and women somewhat differently. First, custom but not the law favours women in the area of child custody. The mother is the custodial parent of over 75 percent of the children involved in divorce (Eichler 1987).

The economic implications of marriages ending are often different for husband and wife. Divorce often spells downward economic mobility, even poverty, for the women involved (Boyd 1977). There are a number of reasons for this situation. Women generally earn less than men. Moreover, divorced and separated women suffer from the widespread assumption that men are the chief breadwinners and women merely secondary earners. Also, women returning to the labour market after years of full-time homemaking are unlikely to be well trained. Often, the woman is supporting children and must pay for child care while she works. Husbands often renege on child-support payments. A further reason for women's economic disadvantage was the failure of the law, until recently, to recognize the financial contribution to the marriage of the wife who chose to be a full-time homemaker or to work in a family business.

Divorced women are less likely to remarry than divorced men. Four-fifths of divorced men versus two-thirds of divorced women remarry (Ambert 1980). The double standard of aging is the major factor involved here, with women's age being a greater barrier to their remarriage than dependent children. Older women have less chance of remarriage, because custom says they must marry someone at least their own age. In comparison, even much younger women are considered suitable marriage partners for divorced men. Of course, many divorced people of both sexes prefer not to remarry.

Death still ends most marriages, and widowhood has different consequences for men and women. First of all, there are many more widows than widowers. Because women marry men who are, on the average, two years older than themselves, and because men die earlier than women, most men die while married, while most women die *not* married. For instance, 62 percent of all men who died in 1984 were married, as compared to 32 percent of the women who died. This means that most men have a spouse who looks after them until death, while most women do not (Eichler 1987). Elderly women are more likely to be poor, as well as alone. Earlier generations of women devoted their lives to their families without pay; in other words, they obeyed the cultural mandate mentioned earlier.

## Work Outside the Home

Our discussion of women's cultural mandate to give the family priority and of conflict theorists' ideas about women as a "reserve army of labour" would lead us to expect that the labour-force experiences of women and men will differ.

**Labour-Force Participation.** Although there are more men than women who work for pay — 77 percent versus 54 percent in 1985 (Labour Canada 1987) — the participation of women in the labour force has risen dramatically since World War II. This is especially so for married women and mothers of young children. For example, between 1975 and 1985, the labour-force participation of women with children under three years of age rose from 31 percent to 54 percent (Lindsay and McKie 1986). One of the most significant changes in the labour force in the last decade has been the growth of part-time employment. In 1985, 73 percent of all part-time employees were women. More than one in every four employed women worked part-time, compared with 8 percent of employed men (Burke 1986).

How is this rising labour-force participation to be explained? Women's increasing education, and consequent higher earning capabilities, is one reason (Gunderson 1976). For example, in 1985, 77 percent of women with a university degree were in the labour force, compared with only 25 percent of those with a grade-school education (Labour Canada 1987). Also, though marriage and chil-

# Inequities Show It's Still a Man's World

*Labour-force participation and household work are high-priority issues for the women's movement. Women throughout the world tend to do more than their share of the work for less than their share of the rewards.*

GENEVA (REUTER): Whether in offices, factories or down on the farm, in industrial countries or poor agrarian states, most women work outside the home. They find that it is still a man's world.

Be they New York executives, European computer clerks or drudges in the fields of the Third World, women, according to a Maoist adage, "hold up half the sky" — for about two-thirds of what men get for holding up the other half, says the International Labor Organization.

That is the global average. In communist Eastern Europe, men earn 20 to 30 percent more for the same jobs. In the Third World and Japan, males can earn twice as much.

Data gathered by the ILO, a United Nations agency, indicates that women are more likely to get fired than men. The ILO says this is often because women have traditionally performed the tasks most easily taken over by word processors and other new technology.

Or the reason may simply be male chauvinism, or the fact that women take time off to have babies.

China, following Mao, has a law that all women should work. There is no such thing as Occupation: Housewife.

But the All-China Federation of Trade Unions reports that when economic reforms authorized managers to dismiss workers to boost productivity, women were the first to go.

Neither in China, where newspapers say educated women are arbitrarily denied jobs, nor in the Soviet Union does ideological stress on equality always translate into practice.

And in Japan, "no fundamental change has taken place," says sociologist Yoriko Meguro. Despite a 1986 Equal Opportunity Law, Japan stresses women's roles in the home.

"Women take care of the family and bring up children, letting men concentrate completely on work, to the extent that they become workaholics," says government adviser Mariko Bando.

Elsewhere in the world, where the norm is for a woman to both have a job and be a mother, progress towards making this easier has been slow.

The ILO says day-care needs are far from being met. Often, where laws say a company must open a nursery if it hires a specific number of women, few women get hired.

Particularly in the West, mothers opt for part-time jobs. But part-time pay and benefits are often inferior, the ILO notes.

In the Third World, poverty is especially hard on women.

In the villages of India, where 80 percent of the country's 780 million people live, girls of seven or eight begin lives of unremitting 18-hour-a-day toil. They do everything except plow — a male preserve.

"They are malnourished, they are social inferiors, they are illiterate," says a senior government official. "They do not see anything outside their own village."

In Indian cities, women are pushed into unskilled, low-paid work, according to a 1985 government study.

The ILO says roughly two-thirds of Third World women workers are engaged in agriculture. Their plight has deteriorated because of increasing landlessness — particularly in Latin America — and migration of men to seek work in cities.

Third World women who leave the land tend to find only low-paid and precarious jobs, the ILO's 1987 World Labor Report says. Many young women in Asia work up to 60 hours a week making electronic goods.

**Source:**

Ronald Farquhar, *Calgary Herald*, March 17, 1988.

dren still reduce women's labour-force participation, they are weaker deterrents now than in the past (Bruce 1978), and women are having fewer children. The economic circumstances of the past decade — first inflation and then recession — have compelled many women to enter the labour force. Also, more clerical and service jobs have become available in the post–World War II economy, and women have qualified for these jobs. Finally, many women are lone parents who carry some or all of the financial responsibility for their children. Of course, paid work is a real choice for those women who have developed challenging careers or who prefer an outside job to the isolation of the household. However, most women have little alternative to paid work (Armstrong and Armstrong 1987).

**Sex Segregation of Work.** Although the female participation rate in the Canadian labour force has risen sharply, corresponding changes have not occurred in the nature of women's work.

*The segregation of women in specific industries and occupations characterized by low pay, low skill*

*requirements, low productivity, and low prospects
for advancement has shown remarkable stability
throughout the century.* (Armstrong and
Armstrong 1984a)

**Occupational segregation** by sex means that one
sex or the other predominates among the incumbents of the occupation. For example, 99 percent
of stenographers and typists and 95 percent of
nurses are women, while 92 percent of dentists
and 85 percent of lawyers and notaries are men
(Armstrong and Armstrong 1984a). Women are
considerably more occupationally segregated than
men. Women tend to work in a relatively few
traditionally "female" jobs (for example, clerical,
health, teaching, and service occupations). Since
women hold about 75 percent of all clerical jobs,
the office is a "female job ghetto" (Lowe 1980).
Although considerable publicity is given to female
physicians, lawyers, dentists, and pharmacists,
in 1981 each of these professions involved one-
tenth of one percent (or less) of all female workers
(Armstrong and Armstrong 1984a). The concept
of occupational sex-typing, which was discussed
earlier, reflects societal ideas that sex-segregated
jobs are quite properly women's work or men's
work.

**Income.** The money women derive from their
work represents a key indicator of progress toward equality. The facts are unequivocal: employed women earn considerably less money than
their male counterparts. In 1985, Canadian women
who were employed full-time earned, on the average, sixty percent of men's average earnings,
a slight decrease from 1984. Forty-eight percent
of men, and only sixteen percent of women, earned
$25 000 or more in 1985. Married women earn
about forty-seven percent as much as married men,
but single, divorced, or widowed women earn
about eighty-eight percent as much as unmarried
men (Labour Canada 1987). These differences are
accounted for by women's cultural mandate to
give their families priority, by their consequent
greater involvement in part-time work and career
interruptions, by discrimination, and by lower-
paying jobs available to them.

**Additional Characteristics of Women's
Work.** Women's work is more unstable than men's
work. The female unemployment rate is slightly

**Although some are now in professional jobs, most
employed women work in clerical and service
occupations.**

higher than the male unemployment rate. In 1985,
for example, the unemployment rate for women
25–44 years was 10.3 percent versus 8.9 percent
for men of the same age (Lindsay and McKie 1986).
Men, more than women, are benefiting from the
microchip revolution. Computer technology is increasing employment opportunities in the occupations where women are least represented, and
is decreasing employment opportunities in the
clerical occupations, where women are most represented (Menzies 1984). Also, because women
have lower labour-force participation and earning
levels than men, they receive fewer employment
benefits, such as pensions (Labour Canada 1987).

Women's work in the labour force parallels their
work at home (Armstrong and Armstrong 1978).
In both contexts, they nurture others, cook and
serve food, take care of the sick, sew clothes, clean
rooms, wash hair. In addition, women's work typically offers few opportunities for advancement.
Because they have fewer chances than men to
move up a career ladder (Rosenfeld 1979), Canadian women frequently end their working lives
where they began.

Women are much less likely than men to occupy
positions of authority at work (Symons 1986). As

University of Alberta sociologists Lowe and Krahn (1984) point out, "True enough, we can now point to some 'high profile' women in corporate and government organizations and in male-dominated occupations and professions, but they are usually the exception." Although women's lack of qualifications is an explanatory factor, just as important are discriminatory employer policies based on the assumption that women are unfit to supervise others (Wolf and Eligstein 1979).

Fewer Canadian female workers are unionized: 32 percent versus 42 percent of Canadian male workers in 1984 (Labour Canada 1986). The main reasons are that white-collar workers and part-time workers are difficult for unions to organize (Marchak 1975). Also, unions have not given women's issues high priority (Baker and Robeson 1986). However, "women have dominated union membership growth in recent years . . ., almost doubling their share of organized workers over the last two decades" (Armstrong and Armstrong 1983).

## Religion

Church organization has traditionally assigned different roles to women and men. With few exceptions, men are the authority figures: deacons, priests, clergymen, bishops, cardinals, popes. Ceremonial ties with the deity are maintained by men. When women are permitted a role beyond member of the congregation, it is usually a service position. For example, nuns in in the Roman Catholic Church teach and nurse, while priests celebrate mass, perform marriage ceremonies, and ordain other priests.

Iona Campagnolo, former Canadian Minister of Amateur Sport, discussing her childhood ambitions, was quoted in *Today* magazine as saying, "I always thought I'd be a missionary of some kind. Because I was a female, I never thought of becoming a minister." Although some of the large Protestant denominations, such as the United Church, have agreed after much deliberation to ordain women, the numbers involved are very small. Often, these female clergy are deflected from ministerial roles into teaching (Roberts 1984).

Women's marginal position in the churches has serious implications for gender socialization. Ruether (1974) claims, perhaps extravagantly, that religion is "undoubtedly the single most impor-

tant shaper and enforcer of the image and role of women." While children might encounter female Sunday School teachers, they again see the important roles as a male prerogative and experience only males making ceremonial contact with God. Other consequences are more indirect. As long as women remain outside the church's inner circle, the female point of view is missing on matters of considerable concern to them, such as abortion and birth control (Ambert 1976).

The religious doctrine presented to children is also male-oriented. For instance, the male image of God — in his traditional presentation as father, judge, shepherd, king — serves to indirectly buttress male supremacy on earth. If God is male, how can females be made in the divine image?

All of this is quite ironic in view of the fact that on a variety of measures, such as church attendance and commitment to religious beliefs, women tend to be more religious than men (de Vaus and McAllister 1987).

Only a handful of studies have attempted to measure the effects of religious socialization on gender attitudes. A recent study of Canadian and American university students (Brinkerhoff and Mackie 1985) reported that the greater the religiosity, the more traditional the gender attitudes. Mormons and Fundamentalist Christians hold the most traditional gender attitudes, followed by mainline Protestants, and then Roman Catholics. People with no religious affiliation are the least conservative of all. Although this particular study reports correlations and cannot therefore establish the causality of religious experiences, it seems, in general, that religious socialization augments and reinforces other sources of gender socialization.

## The School

Although most Canadian classrooms are not segregated by sex, school does not seem to be the same psychological or social environment for girls as for boys. Elementary school is a place where women teachers rule. Seemingly, many approve of the girl students who identify with them and scold boy students for being rambunctious. An observational study of elementary school pupils (Best 1983) noted that when the boys eagerly ran outside to play, the girls fought among themselves for the "privilege" of staying indoors and helping the teacher. Considerable evidence supports the hypothesis that students of both sexes are exposed to a feminizing process in school (Schneider and Coutts 1979). As a consequence, young boys escape into the macho world of their peers (Best 1983).

During the early years of school, girls are more successful academically than boys. Girls beginning school are, on the average, two years more advanced developmentally than boys. They begin to speak, read, and count before boys do. This developmental advantage is reflected in girls' academic achievement. In the early grades, girls are at least equal with boys in mathematical skill (Fink and Kosecoff 1977). Two to three times as many boys as girls have reading problems. Boys also seem to have a more difficult time adjusting to elementary school classroom demands for obedience, order, and neatness. "Feminine" behaviour seems more appropriate to school. Girls may have already learned at home to be obedient and quiet, while boys have been reinforced for "bouncing about, questioning, being curious or aggressive" (Howe 1974). Finally, the female authority figure in the elementary grades makes it easier for girls to identify with their teacher, and hence with general academic values (Richer 1979).

In the 1984–85 academic year, women earned 51.1 percent of Bachelor's and first professional degrees. Greater opportunities have opened for women in some areas. For example, women received 42 percent of the law and 38 percent of the medical degrees (compared with 9 percent and 15 percent, respectively, in 1970–71). However, higher education continues to have a segregated structure. In 1984–85, women received 97 percent of the degrees in nursing and 81 percent of the degrees in social work. However, only 11 percent of the graduates in engineering and 27 percent of those in the physical sciences were females (Guppy, Balson, and Vellutini 1987). As women's overall participation in post-secondary education has grown, degrees and diplomas have lost economic value.

Many girls have confused images of the future and are unable to formulate realistic plans for their lives (Press 1985). Although she has been exposed to an ideal of both occupational achievement and her eventual destiny in marriage and family roles, the girl is apt to hold her future in abeyance until the right young man comes along. Though males' job plans are not sabotaged by dreams of settling down with Mrs. Right and producing babies, they also encounter life-course obstacles. The majority of young Canadian men abandon earlier hopes for university education or technical training (Bibby and Posterski 1985), presumably for economic reasons.

The term "reversal of success" has been used to label the fact that females, the sex most comfortable in school, end up doing less well in the occupational structure. As we saw earlier, most Canadian women who work outside the home are concentrated in a small number of low-skilled, poorly paid jobs. Research tells us that gender contributes a more formidable barrier to women's occupational achievement than does lack of resources, such as academic ability or socioeconomic background (Marini and Greenberger 1978). Girls "receive less family encouragement to pursue higher education than do boys, but such encouragement, it turns out, is especially critical for girls" (Turrittin, Anisef, and MacKinnon 1983). Girls from poor families, from Indian or Inuit families, and from remote regions of the country, will be even more disadvantaged.

Why are women's educational ambitions so modest? Possibly men's occupational ambitions are greater than women's because work is a major ingredient of masculine self-esteem, and because they expect to spend a lifetime in the labour market. As they reach adolescence, males take school, the avenue to the breadwinner role, more seriously.

The school is only one of many agents that encourage gender stereotypes and depress women's ambitions. However, the school reflects the values of the surrounding society, and consequently its teachers, curricula (official and hidden), textbooks, and guidance counsellors are engaged in the business of gender socialization. Things are changing, albeit slowly. Under the auspices of the women's movement and the exigencies of the economic climate, women's lives are less determined by the family cycle. Concomitant with the recent trends toward later marriage, later initiation of child-bearing, reduced family-size expectation, and the rising number of female-headed families is women's growing occupational commitment (Garrison 1979).

## Women's and Men's Liberation Movements

The 1960s were marked by protest and by demands for just treatment by native peoples, blacks, the poor, university students, and, eventually, women. In 1967, the Royal Commission on the Status of Women was set up to enquire into the situation of Canadian women and "to recommend what steps might be taken by the federal government to ensure for women equal opportunities with men in all aspects of Canadian society" (Royal Commission on the Status of Women in Canada 1970). The federal government's decision to establish the commission was the first official recognition of the feminist movement in Canada (Morris 1980). Prior to this, women's situation was not widely regarded as a social problem. Three years later, the commission tabled its report, which contained 167 recommendations involving the economy, education, the family, taxation, poverty, public life, immigration and citizenship, and criminal law.

Legal discrimination against women has decreased over the years. However, informal or customary injustices continue. Therefore, feminist groups across Canada are organized around such issues as ensuring women's reproductive freedom and control over their own bodies; protesting misogynistic presentations of women in rock videos and advertising; battling pornography and violence against women; providing affordable daycare; securing pensions for women; and achieving

---

## A Ukrainian Girlhood

*Helen Potrebenko's autobiographical statement illustrates how gender, ethnic background, and social class position can often interact to place many Canadians in "triple jeopardy."*

It's strange to be an ethnic after all the years of just being poor. The main difference seems to be that now I get to explain instead of apologizing. But since the whole time I was growing up Ukrainian I thought I was growing up poor, the explanations are all hindsight and probably untrue.

I was born and brought up in a farming community in northern Alberta. Ukrainians lived east of town, Germans to the west. In Woking itself the small businesses were run by English people. The teachers in the school were invariably English (i.e., non-Ukrainian). It was a small village and in the way of modern Canadian farming communities, has grown even smaller since I knew it.

The world I knew then was divided into various groupings. There were children and adults; our people and the English; males and females. At home, I learned more or less the following about the sexes: Men were good and strong and capable of earning money. Women were not very good, had the wrong kind of strength and couldn't earn enough money to support their children.

Just in case any of us missed the more subtle socialization, we were trained by the boys. It was expected and accepted that older boys should brutalize the girls and the sissies among the boys. We could not complain to anyone; adults condoned the violence. The abuse we took was considered evidence of our unworthiness. We could not defend ourselves — the boys were older and travelled in groups. . . .

At school I learned that everything about Ukrainian society was bad and that everything English was good and the exact opposite of Ukrainian. So if Ukrainian men were chauvinists, English men were not. This led to a great many misunderstandings. I also thought that since English society was free and democratic, unlike the autocratic paternalism of Ukrainians, one did not have to follow the rules. By the time I learned the truth, I was a long way from home. . . .

I stumbled around the world trying and failing to be feminine, to be Canadian, to be accepted, to be worthy. I was not successful; my differentness was like a brand in the middle of my forehead. It was as they said — I never got married, was never happy, never had children, could not get a good job. I thought it was all my own personal fault. Never once did I think my failure was a consequence of class, size, ethnicity, or the definition of failure. Like all other women, I thought it was my own personal failure. It wasn't until I met up with Women's Liberation that I ceased to be paralyzed by my own sense of inadequacy.

---

**Source:**

Abridged from Helen Potrebenko, "Ethnicity and femininity as determinants of life experience," *Canadian Ethnic Studies* 13(1981):39–41.

equality in religious organizations. In addition, women have organized around the more general issues of nuclear disarmament and environmental concerns. Finally, structural changes have involved setting up special institutions for women, parallel to those in mainstream society. Examples include self-help medical clinics, rape crisis centres, and co-operative daycare schemes.

The potential social base for a significant men's movement simply does not exist. Males experience psychological oppression from their gender socialization. Nevertheless, "they have not been economically or politically discriminated against because they are *men*" (Richardson 1981). The contemporary gender-stratification system favours men as a group. Not many men would willingly forfeit the power, privileges, and resources that accrue to those at the top of the gender hierarchy. Unfortunately, many males are caught in a "double bind" (Baker and Bakker 1980). Masculinity exacts high costs, as well as the rewards mentioned above. For example, the traditional linkage between masculinity and work fails to satisfy the needs of many men. "Each day men sell little pieces of themselves in order to try to buy them back each night and weekend with the coin of 'fun' " (Mills 1951). Insistence that males achieve, be aggressive and competitive, and resist emotional expression has been described as the "lethal aspect" of the male role (Jourard 1964). The higher male suicide rates and earlier death rates appear to be consequences of the masculine role.

Despite the foregoing, social definitions of masculinity are changing. Gay liberation politics continue to call into question the conventional understanding of maleness (Carrigan, Connell, and Lee 1987). In the 1980s, small numbers belong to groups seeking equality for men who have lost custody of their children, self-help for their own violent behaviour, or intellectual understanding of "the new man." The flavour of these groups has been therapeutic or concerned with self-improvement. Some, such as the fathers' rights groups, have been antifeminist. Certainly, there has been a deepening of tensions around male/female relationships. Nonetheless, "a good many feel themselves to be involved in some kind of change having to do with gender, with sexual identity, with what it is to be a man" (Carrigan, Connell, and Lee 1987).

The political and religious conservatism of the 1980s threatens attempts to establish healthier definitions of femininity and masculinity. For example, REAL Women, an antifeminist organization based in Toronto, champions traditional roles for the sexes and opposes equal pay for work of equal value, affirmative action programs, easier divorce, universal daycare, abortion, and homosexuality (Riley 1985). Traditional gender arrangements continue because they are based on power differences. The ideology that sustains these arrangements is instilled through the socialization process and buttressed by most of our social institutions.

## SUMMARY

1. The sociology of gender relations examines masculinity and femininity across cultures and historical periods. This subdiscipline, which was inspired by the feminist movement, attempts to remedy sociology's previous exclusion of women.

2. Human social life is built around the relationships between the sexes. The sexes are both differentiated and ranked.

3. According to the study of animals, the anthropological record, and psychosexual abnormalities, and research on hormones and genes, biology seems to be directly involved in cognitive gender differences and aggressiveness and indirectly involved in the female/male division of labour. However, both nature *and* nurture are involved.

4. Theories based on biology, socialization, and social structure provide complementary explanations of gender.

5. The socialization process teaches children society's gender scripts, which include gender stereotypes and occupational sex-typing. As well, children acquire their gender identity through this process.

6. The social-structural approach assumes that gender results from external social factors, not individual characteristics. The structural-functional and conflict perspectives are examples of these macrosociological theories.

7. To a great extent, women and men inhabit their own social worlds. Therefore, they have somewhat different experiences in societal institu-

tions, such as the family, work, education, and religious institutions.

8. The women's and men's liberation movements have pressed for more egalitarian social arrangements and healthier definitions of gender.

## GLOSSARY

**Androgyny.** Presence of both masculine and feminine characteristics within individuals of both sexes.

**Commodity production.** Goods and services created for exchange in the marketplace.

**Cultural universals.** Behaviour patterns found in many cultures.

**Gender.** Societal definition of appropriate female and male traits and behaviours.

**Gender assignment.** The designation of a person as female or male.

**Gender identity.** The individual's conviction of being male or female.

**Gender script.** The details of a society's ideas about masculinity and femininity contained, for example, in gender stereotypes and gender attitudes.

**Gender socialization.** The lifelong processes through which people learn to be feminine or masculine according to the expectations current in their society.

**Gender transcendence.** Ideal socialization goal in which masculinity and femininity are superseded as ways of labelling and experiencing psychological traits. Boy/girl and male/female would then refer exclusively to biological distinctions.

**Lateralization.** Functional specialization of left and right hemispheres of the brain.

**Occupational segregation.** The concentration of one sex in a relatively few occupations in which they greatly outnumber the other sex.

**Occupational sex-typing.** The societal view that certain occupations are more appropriate work for one sex than the other.

**Patriarchy.** A society oriented toward and dominated by males.

**Production of use-values.** Goods and services produced in the home.

**Reserve army of labour.** According to conflict theorists, women constitute a flexible labour supply, drawn into the labour market when needed, and sent home when the need is past.

**Sex.** The physiological differences between females and males.

**Stereotype.** Folk beliefs about the attributes characterizing a social category (the genders, ethnic groups) on which there is substantial agreement.

## FURTHER READING

**Armstrong, Pat, and Hugh Armstrong.** *The Double Ghetto: Canadian Women and Their Segregated Work.* Revised edition. Toronto: McClelland and Stewart, 1984. An analysis of gender and work based on census data and the conflict perspective.

**Emecheta, Buchi.** *The Joys of Motherhood.* New York: George Braziller, 1979. A poignant novel about the changing family in Nigeria.

**Fausto-Sterling, Anne.** *Myths of Gender: Biological Theories About Women and Men.* New York: Basic Books, 1985. A distinguished biologist reviews the evidence concerning the question "Do women and men think, feel, and behave differently due to something innate in their biology?"

**Gaskell, Jane, and Arlene McLaren (eds.).** *Women and Education: A Canadian Perspective.* Calgary: Detselig Enterprises, 1987. An overview of the relationship between gendered education and the society in which it exists.

**Kaufman, Michael (ed.).** *Beyond Patriarchy.* Toronto: Oxford University Press, 1987. A collection of articles exploring the links between masculinity and social structure.

**Mackie, Marlene.** *Constructing Women and Men: Gender Socialization.* Toronto: Holt, Rinehart and Winston, 1987. Application of symbolic interaction and the sociology of knowledge to gender across the life course.

**Tomm, Winnifred, and Gordon Hamilton (eds.).** *Gender Bias in Scholarship.* Calgary Institute for the Humanities. Waterloo: Wilfrid Laurier University Press, 1988. A multidisciplinary discussion of women as subjects of research and as researchers.

# CHAPTER 5

# Aging and Later Life

VICTOR W. MARSHALL
CAROLYN J. ROSENTHAL

From the early years of sociology, scholars have been interested in the ways aging affects social life. Today, unlike earlier times, almost every Canadian can expect to grow old and, because of the aging of the "baby-boomers," an ever-increasing number will do so (see Chapter 7). Even in Third World societies, for the first time, large proportions of the population can expect to live into their later years.

Mannheim suggested a mental experiment that involves trying to imagine "what the social life of man would be like if one generation lived forever and none followed to replace it" (1952). Mannheim's experiment, like much contemporary science fiction, directs attention to the ways in which the organization of society has taken into account human aging and mortality. Moore (1966) has described the paradox that human beings are mortal while, in a sense, societies are immortal. To him, as to Mannheim, aging is a key aspect of society as well as an opportunity for social change to occur.

The growing proportion and number of older Canadians, along with the decreasing proportion and number of young people, affects every aspect of social life. Because of population aging, changes have been and will continue to be made in the way we allocate work and leisure at various points of the life course. On the whole, young adults enter the labour force at a later age than they did 85 years ago. Retirement, now a taken-for-granted stage of life, was quite rare at the beginning of this century. Our ideas about education are less tied to the early years than they once were, and now include the concepts of "lifelong learning" and "continuing education." Family life is also changing, as people find their parents and grandparents reaching ages thought highly unlikely by Canadians at the time of Confederation. With increasing numbers and proportions of older people in our society, new concerns are arising about the ability of social welfare and health-care systems to meet the needs of this growing segment of our population.

The sociology of aging is the scientific study of how age is relevant or "makes a difference" in social life and social structure. Age and changes in age make a difference for both individual life and social organization. Our approach therefore encompasses both the experiences of aging individuals and the effects of age structure on the dynamics of social institutions. The sociology of aging is therefore not just about "the aged" — it is about the entire society.

## Population Aging

Let us start with a basic reference point at the beginning of this century. In 1901, of about 5.5 million Canadians, just 5.2 percent were aged 65 or more. In 1986, over 10 percent of our 25 million people were aged 65 or over. The percentage is expected to rise in the coming years, with the size of increase depending on the fertility rate. (The proportion of the population that is aged is affected by the numbers already born and the rate at which they die, which change little, and by the numbers yet to be born, which can change significantly over time with changes in the fertility rate.) According to one projection, if Canadian fertility rates increase to 2.1 from their current

### Table 5-1. Population Projections for Selected Age Groups, Canada (Thousands)

| Year | 0–17 | | 18–64 | | 65 + | | Total |
|------|------|------|-------|------|------|------|-------|
| 1984 | 6 611 | 26.3 | 15 956 | 63.5 | 2 556 | 10.2 | 25 123 |
| 1991 | 6 622 | 24.7 | 16 986 | 63.4 | 3 173 | 11.9 | 26 781 |
| 2001 | 6 464 | 22.7 | 18 181 | 63.7 | 3 884 | 13.6 | 28 529 |
| 2011 | 5 927 | 20.1 | 19 055 | 64.5 | 4 544 | 15.4 | 29 526 |
| 2021 | 5 780 | 19.2 | 18 374 | 61.2 | 5 871 | 19.6 | 30 025 |
| 2031 | 5 537 | 18.6 | 17 114 | 57.5 | 7 128 | 23.9 | 29 779 |

NOTE: Projection 3 assumes a fertility rate of 1.66 children per woman, net immigration of 50 000, and life expectancy at birth to increase to 74.9 for males and 81.6 for females by the year 1996.
SOURCE: Hans Messinger and Brian J. Powell, "The implications of Canada's aging society on social expenditures," in *Aging in Canada: Social Persectives*, 2nd edition, Victor W. Marshall, ed. (Toronto: Fitzhenry and Whiteside, 1987), pp. 569–585.

level of 1.7, then the percentage of the population aged 65 and older will be 12.8 by 2001 and 19.5 by 2051. However, if fertility rates decline to 1.4, a level close to that currently experienced in some European countries, the percentage of the population aged 65 and older would rise to 13.6 by 2001 and 29.1 by 2051 (Denton, Feaver, and Spencer 1987).

All population projections rely on assumptions about fertility, mortality, immigration, and emigration (see Chapter 7). Table 5-1 is based on a continuance of the low fertility and immigration rates that now characterize Canadian society, but allows for modest increases in life expectancy. If these suppositions hold, the percentage increases, together with increases in the total size of the population, translate into very large increases in the *number* of old people. In the 25 years prior to 1986, the increase in the percentage of the population aged 65 or older from 7.6 to 10.4 percent meant a 143-percent increase in the actual number of older Canadians (Dumas 1987). Assuming continued low fertility, the number of older Canadians is projected to double by 2016 and to reach 7.1 million by 2031, compared to about 2.5 million now (Messinger and Powell 1987). Of these, a large proportion will be very old people in their late seventies and eighties, because of increases in life expectancy at later ages (Dumas 1987). Over the same period the numbers of people aged less than 18, after an initial rise, actually declines to a point below the current level.

The age structure of the population is characterized not only by the numbers and proportions in different age groups but also by the median age. The current median age of the Canadian population is about 31; it is projected to increase to 42 by the year 2051 (Foot 1982).

Changes in the age structure of the population vary greatly by gender. Women live about seven years longer than men and currently outnumber men in every age category after age 50–59 (Gee and Kimball 1987). While there are today about 138 women aged 65 and older for every 100 men, by the year 2031 there will be 148 women for every 100 men in that age category. By that year, in the aged 80 and older category, there are projected to be 229 women for every 100 men, compared to a ratio of 192/100 today (Denton, Feaver, and Spencer 1987). Not only is the gap in life expectancy

between men and women large, it is widening. For example, life expectancy in the past fifteen years has increased by about two years for women but only about a quarter of a year for men.

## Income, Health, and Gender Differentiation among the Aged

Just as the lives of young Canadians differ greatly depending on factors such as their class of origin and their gender, the same factors differentiate people in the later years. In the later years, as well, health becomes an important differentiating feature among people.

### Income Differences

Probably the most critical personal dilemma facing the aging individual is difficulty in maintaining an adequate income. At the same time, the provision of income security is an important policy issue facing society as a whole. In our society, the basic sources of income for most people are tied to their participation in the labour force or to their connection to a labour-force participant. The problem for older people stems from their almost total exclusion from the labour market by the social institution of retirement. As recently as half a century ago, about half of Canadian males over the age of 65 were still in the labour force. Today, most people retire before age 65. In addition, the majority of older women have been prevented by social custom and gender discrimination in the workplace from regular, consistent labour-force participation. This diminishes their ability to secure pension entitlements for their later years.

Public transfer payments are the major source of income in retirement. Canada has a three-tiered retirement income system (Powell and Martin 1980). The first tier consists of the federal Old Age Security (OAS) program. All people aged 65 or older who meet residence requirements receive OAS payments (about $315 per month in 1988), regardless of their work history. Also in the first tier are the Guaranteed Income Supplement (GIS) and the Spouse's Allowance program. In 1988, GIS provided maximum payments of about $375 per

**The major source of income for retired Canadians is through public transfer payments.**

month for a single person and $245 for a married person (these levels are adjusted to inflation). The Spouse's Allowance is income-tested and provides benefits to people aged 60–64 who are spouses of old age pensioners. Various provinces add additional support, some of it income-tested. Currently, about one-third of the total income received by Canada's older population comes from the first tier (Messinger and Powell 1987).

The second tier consists of the Canada Pension Plan (CPP) or, in Quebec, the Quebec Pension Plan (QPP). These plans cover almost everyone in the labour force. Employees and employers both contribute to these plans, which are portable (that is, accrued benefits carry over from job to job). About 9 percent of total old age income stems from the second tier.

The third tier in Canada's income security system for the aged, accounting for about 58 percent of the total income received by the elderly (Messinger and Powell 1987), is private income — from wages and salaries, investments, private pension plans, life insurance, and other sources.

The proportion of income the aged receive from all three tiers varies by gender and marital status. Unattached women receive relatively more from the first tier and less from the third tier than do unattached men. The income from private sources of married couples is similar to that of unattached men (Gee and Kimball 1987).

About half of all old age pensioners received at least partial GIS benefits in 1989. GIS benefits are received if income from the second and third tiers is insufficient to bring an aged person to a point near the poverty level.

Even if an employee is enrolled in a private pension plan, there is no guarantee that he or she will collect anything from it (Ascah 1984; Messinger and Powell 1987). In most private pension plans, employees who leave a company with less than 10 years of service or before age 45 receive only their personal contributions. Insofar as the company's contribution is viewed as deferred wages, this represents a loss to the employee. Most Canadians change jobs frequently, and women especially have irregular work histories; yet there is very poor portability of pensions. Employees who change jobs must start afresh with a new pension plan, losing the accrued benefits of their previous plans.

The scope and significance of private pension plans is evident from the following: the assets of trustee pension plans in Canada rose from $21.2 billion in 1975 to $82.7 billion by 1983. During the same period, life insurance company assets, which also relate to the provision of later-life income security, rose from $23.6 billion to $63.4 billion. Registered Retirement Saving Plan (RRSP) savings rose from $14.5 billion to $27.5 billion over the period 1980–83 (Messinger and Powell 1987).

The private pension industry — together with the other components of the third tier, the private income security system — is clearly massive in scope and in its implications for the control and direction of the Canadian economy. Nonetheless, many observers charge that it has failed almost completely to meet the income security needs of older Canadians. Among recommended changes to the private pension system are better pensions for women, earlier "vesting" (that is, the employee assuming legal ownership of pension credits, so that they are not lost with a change of employment), pensions that continue to be paid to a surviving spouse after widowhood, and splitting of pensions on marital breakdown.

Adequate understanding of the economic position of the aged also requires an appreciation of their assets. Almost 70 percent of older Canadians own their homes, a figure slightly larger than that for younger Canadians. Moreover, they are very likely to own their homes completely — unlike younger people, who usually carry mortgages. Housing is thus a significant asset for the aged, but their houses are generally older; have a lower market value; and are more expensive to repair, keep up, and heat (Collins 1978). Other assets, such as investments, do not play a large part in providing economic security for the aged.

The economic situation of older Canadians should improve in the future, for a number of reasons. The CPP/QPP tier was initiated only in 1966 and was not fully effective until 1976. Some very old people had ceased working before the full introduction of the plans. Rising labour-force participation rates for women, a steady increase in the proportion of the labour force covered by private pension plans, and reform in the plans should enhance their ability to provide economic security. However, the impact of these improvements is likely to be limited — particularly for women, who frequently work in industrial sectors with poor or nonexistent private pension arrangements.

## Poverty in Later Life

The result of these financial arrangements is that the majority of older Canadians are poor. Great differences in degree of economic security occur among the older population, and many of the most wealthy people in the world are old. However, in 1982, 11.7 percent of families whose heads were aged 65 and older, and 58 percent of individuals aged 65 and older, had incomes that fell below the official Statistics Canada poverty line. Women fared somewhat worse than men. For example, the incomes of fully 60 percent of unattached elderly women, compared to 49 percent of unattached elderly men, fell below the poverty line. The Statistics Canada poverty line varies by region and family size, but is based on the assumption that 58.5 percent of income is required for the basic necessities of life (food, clothing, shelter). Gee and Kimball (1987) estimate that about 78 percent of elderly unattached women and about 68 percent of elderly unattached men are either poor or near-poor. However, there are fewer un-

**Older, unattached women are especially prone to poverty.**

attached elderly men than women, because women are more likely to be widowed.

While most old people are poor, we should not lose sight of the fact that many young people are also poor. To put the inadequacy of income security in perspective, Eichler (1983) has contrasted the situation of single parents in Ontario with the elderly. In January 1981, according to Eichler, an elderly couple was guaranteed $853 per month, while a welfare family consisting of a mother, father, and three children was guaranteed only $650. Eichler sees political support for children diminishing, while that for the elderly is growing, and she sees a danger that the young and the old might be played off politically against each other.

## Health

A second major difference among older people is health. Contrary to commonly held beliefs, most people over the age of 65 are quite healthy. However, aging leads to an increased likelihood of a person experiencing chronic health problems — such as heart and circulatory diseases, cancer, athritis, rheumatism, or diabetes — and experiencing greater severity in the effects of acute health problems (Marshall 1987a). For example, an older person may take longer to recover from a simple ailment. Older people are also more likely than younger people to have multiple or compounded health problems (Chappel, Strain, and Blandford 1986).

From a sociological point of view, one important way to describe how healthy people are involves ascertaining whether they need help with such everyday activities as preparing meals. These are referred to as activities of daily living (ADL). One study (Tilquin et al. 1980) asked if respondents in Quebec required help with the following five activities: rising and going to bed, daily personal hygiene, walking around inside the house, bathing, and shopping in summer. The proportion reporting no disability was 84 percent for those aged 65 to 69 but just 67 percent for those aged 75 and over. The results of various Canadian community studies are remarkably similar (for example, Cape and Henschke 1980: Gutman 1980; Marshall 1987a). These suggest that most older people remain quite healthy until their late seventies or their eighties.

Gender differences in health are apparent in the mortality and life expectancy data noted above and in Chapter 7, but appear as well in the ADL data from community studies. There is a significant upward shift in the proportion of people requiring assistance with the activities of daily living at the mid- to late seventies for men, and about the late seventies to mid-eighties for women (Marshall, Rosenthal, and Synge 1983). In this — and in other areas, such as economic status — it is imperative to consider older men and older women separately.

Most older people live in their own homes. About 7 to 8 percent (there is debate about the precise figure) of Canadians aged 65 and over live in institutions such as nursing homes and homes for the aged (*Fact Book on Aging* 1983). Even in the 80-and-over age category, the proportion is only about 40 percent (Large 1981). Most of the institutionalized aged are women.

Major factors leading to institutionalization of the aged are advanced age itself, decreasing health, and the nonavailability of a spouse to provide help with such things as medication, bathing,

**Contrary to popular belief, most people over the age of 65 are quite healthy.**

preparation of meals, shopping, and housekeeping (Shapiro and Roos 1987). U.S. studies (Brody 1978; Tobin and Kulys 1980) indicate that between 70 and 80 percent of such care is provided informally, mostly by daughters or sons (there are as yet no comparable Canadian studies).

Despite comprising only about 10 percent of the population, older people account for almost half of all hospital-bed occupancy in Canada (Auer 1987). Ontario data show that older people account for 17 percent of the services of general practitioners, 23 percent of general surgeons' and internists' services, and even higher proportions of the services provided by some other specialists (Ontario Council of Health 1978).

A careful study of health-care costs projected into the future (Denton, Li, and Spencer 1987) leads to the conclusion that a quality of health care comparable to that currently provided can be realized without a major shift in the allocation of societal resources. Nonetheless, health-care costs are rising. Major changes in the costs of health care do not result from the changing age structure of the population, but rather from changes in the organization of health-care delivery and in the decisions made about the level of care we wish to provide. For example, in a study for the Economic Council of Canada, Auer (1987) notes that increased costs for hospital care in Canada associated with the increase in the proportion of the aged have been offset by cost reductions due to declines in the birth rate. Auer argues that "most of the growth in per capita hospital expenditures did not come from higher hospital admission rates but from higher costs per admission. It is therefore necessary to look at utilization-based factors to determine why the cost per hospital admission (or per patient) increased so much." As but one example, it is currently estimated that in Canada over 10 percent of acute-care hospital beds are occupied by inappropriately placed older patients. Most of them could be discharged to more appropriate care settings such as chronic-care hospitals or nursing homes (Aronson, Marshall, and Sulman 1987; Marshall 1987b). So despite frequent allegations to the contrary, particularly in the popular press, we must realize that increased health-care costs cannot be blamed on population aging alone — and, indeed, are not attributable to population aging to any great extent.

For the sociologist of aging, health is as essential a factor to consider in examining social life as social class. Like class, health is important both in the experience of the individual and in the working out of social structure.

## Gender

It should be apparent that many concerns about aging and the aged are concerns about women and gender-role differentiation. Not only are most older people female, but the older female is much more likely to be economically deprived than the older male.

The health of older people, as it varies by gender, has profound implications for their day-to-day experiences of physical limitation, dependency on other people, and the discomfort and pain of illness. In addition, as we will describe below in discussing family life, the all-important tasks of providing nursing care and daily assistance to the elderly who become ill fall mainly to wives and daughters.

Gender is a major differentiator of social status across the life course. In our society, the status of women is, on the whole, lower than that of men. Woman are in general more likely to be identified with child-rearing statuses — which, judged by the economic rewards associated with them, are not highly valued. Status emanating from occupation is higher for men than women for several reasons. Older men are more likely than older women to have been in the paid labour force. This situation is changing, with over half of women currently of working age in the paid labour force. However, as pointed out in Chapter 4 women continue to be located primarily in jobs of lower status and lower income than those of men. This decreases women's accumulated economic worth, as we discussed above, and in addition deprives them of the deference and prestige that are so important in a society such as ours in which social worth is closely tied to occupation.

Being old and female places a person in what has been referred to as "double jeopardy" (Chappell and Havens 1980). Our culture values youthful, feminine beauty (Posner 1980; Abu-Laban 1981). The low economic status and financial dependency of the older woman may be a more important cause of her low social status than her loss of youthful attractiveness. However, these cultural standards should not be underestimated as a factor influencing the self-esteem of older women, many of whom were strongly socialized to define their worth in these terms. Their male age-peers may also adhere strongly to these standards.

Having considered the demographic aspects of population aging, along with three important bases of social differentiation among the aged — income, health, and gender — it is important to acknowledge that certain other factors significantly affect the aging experience. In the Canadian context, ethnicity represents an additional factor of great influence (Bienvenue and Havens 1986; Dreidger and Chappell 1987; Ujimoto 1987). While less important than frequently thought (Cape 1987), the rural/urban context has been found to be related to such factors as social network intensity among the aged (Corin 1987). Space limitations preclude discussing these additional dimensions in detail. We turn now to an examination of some theoretical approaches that aid our understanding of aging.

## Macro-level Theories of Aging

Macro-level theories of aging deal with the way in which aging individuals are tied to the society and the social status of deference accorded them. We find it useful to view these theories in relation to one very important strand of thought, which can be referred to conveniently as the **modernization thesis** of aging.

### The Modernization Thesis

One of the founders of the sociology of aging, Ernest Burgess, argues that as a result of "modern economic trends" the aged "lost their former favored position in the extended family." In addition to a move from the extended to the nuclear family, he lists urbanization, industrialization, bureaucratization, increased leisure time, and enhanced life expectancy as factors that combine to leave the aged with little of any consequence to do in and for their society (Burgess 1960).

This argument assumes that older people once had a more important place in society and in the family than they currently occupy. These arguments rest on a structural-functional view of society as consisting of a number of status positions to which role expectations are attached, all of which contribute in some way to the maintenance and survival of the society.

Cowgill and Holmes (1972) developed a systematic theory of how modernization led to a decline in the status of the aged, illustrated in Figure 5-1. The theory describes four dimensions of modernization. First, modern economic technology creates new urban occupations and leaves older occupations to become obsolete. Since obsolete occupations are predominantly held by older people, their status declines relative to that of younger people in the newer, high-technology occupations. Second, urbanization leads the young to establish new families geographically distant from their parents. This creates both residential and social segregation of the old from the young. Third, the progressively higher educational attainment of younger people provides them with more societally relevant knowledge than the old have. Because such knowledge is itself a valued commodity, it enhances the status of the young relative to the old; in addition, educational differences segregate the generations both intellectually and morally. Fourth, advances in health technology increase life expectancy. People are able to remain in the labour force for longer periods of time. This blocks the upward career mobility of younger generations, leading to increased intergenerational conflict. The social institution of retirement, in this theoretical framework, may be seen as an attempt to resolve such conflict at a macro-social level.

The theory is much more complicated than we have described. As originally formulated (Cowgill and Holmes 1972), it included 22 propositions. One of these, for example, states that "the status of the aged is highest when they constitute a low proportion of the population and tends to decline as their numbers and proportions increase." This claim rests on a notion of scarcity based on supply-and-demand thinking from economics. The refined version on the theory relies on chains of linked hypotheses that you can create by following the diagram in Figure 5-1.

Sociologists argue vehemently about the best ways to describe modernization and how to describe the status of the elderly. For a start, modernization does not progress uniformly across all four dimensions (economic technology, urbanization, educational attainment, health technology) in any particular society. For example, many societies that today are not well developed technologically have large urban population concentrations. Nor can it be assumed that any society will progress uniformly along a single dimension from "nonmodernized" to "modernized," or that modernization is an indigenous process.

A second set of problems stems from the conceptualization of social status. If social status is taken to be accurately measured by the proportion of the Gross National Product (GNP) allocated to the aged for health care and pensions, then the status of the elderly has never been higher. Apparently, then, how one views the relationship between modernization and the social status of the aged depends on just what is considered an indicator of modernization or of social status.

# Figure 5-1. Aging and Modernization

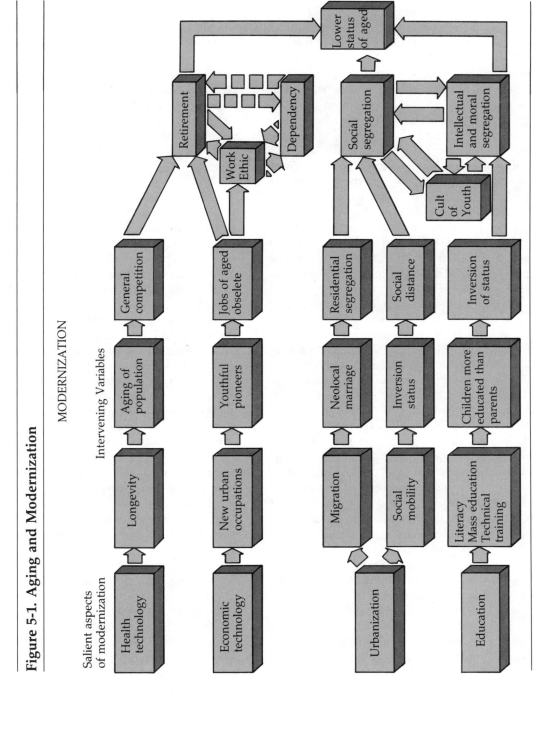

MODERNIZATION

Salient aspects of modernization          Intervening Variables

SOURCE: Donald O. Cowgill, "Aging and modernization: A revision of the theory," in *Late Life,* Jaber Gubrium, ed. (Springfield, IL: Charles C. Thomas, 1975).

A third set of problems with the modernization thesis stems from the relative timing of changes in modernization and changes in the social status of the elderly. For example, Cowgill and Holmes, as can be seen from the model in Figure 5-1, argued that retirement follows modernization and contributes to devaluing the status of the aged. However, Quadagno (1980) has shown that "in England and Wales, a substantial portion of the population was retired prior to any demographic aging of the population and well before the application of modern health technology." This finding directly contradicts two of the four major postulated links between modernization and the status of the aged (see Figure 5-1).

A fourth set of problems concerns the modernization theorists' assumption that the status of the aged was high in early historical periods. Recent criticism (Dowd 1980; Hendricks 1981; Marshall 1981a) has suggested that the modernization thesis rests on a somewhat romanticized vision of the past. Laslett (1976, 1977) has shown that, in England at least, the family and household status of the old was probably never very high and that older people were not as highly integrated into their families as is often assumed in contemporary aging research and in general studies in the sociology of the family.

Finally, the modernization theorists can be faulted for a uniform or undifferentiated view of the past. In contrast, Synge (1980) has shown great rural/urban differences in the pattern of familial care for the aged in Ontario at the beginning of this century, and Dowd (1980) has pointed to the importance of class differences in the status of the aged in the past and the present. In other words, a person's social status has always been determined by many factors in addition to age.

In a recent work, Cowgill (1986) addresses these criticisms. He acknowledges that the status of the aged in the past has sometimes been idealized, and he recognizes the need for greater differentiation of the theory as it applies to the status of older people who vary in gender and social class. Cowgill now argues that the social status of the aged may have a complex relationship to modernization. He suggests that the aged have low status in hunting-and-gathering societies, a higher status in agricultural societies, and a declining status with industrialization — and that they may

have enjoyed recent gains in status with the development of post-industrial society (Cowgill 1986; see also Palmore and Manton 1974).

Despite its shortcomings, the modernization thesis especially as expanded and articulated by Cowgill and his associates, has been valuable. By clearly enunciating the theoretical propositions implied by the theory, these theorists have provided a major reference point for scholars in developing theory in the sociology of aging.

## The Age-Stratification Perspective

A second major theoretical approach also rests on the structural-functional perspective. This is the age-stratification perspective developed by Riley and a number of associates (Riley, Johnson, and Foner 1972; Foner 1974; Riley 1976, 1980).

To understand this perspective, it is necessary to understand two concepts: cohort and age stratum (Marshall 1983). A **cohort** consists of individuals born at approximately the same time, who move through the life course together. The definition of the boundaries of cohorts is arbitrary and based on practical decisions made by researchers rather than on theoretical considerations. For example, a researcher may compare the cohort of all people born in Canada between 1900 and 1905 with that of people born between 1950 and 1955.

By **age stratum**, we mean "an aggregate of individuals (or of groups) who are of similar age at a particular time" (Riley, Johnson, and Foner 1972). Any population, examined at one point in time, can be seen as consisting of a set of such strata, organized as an age-stratification system. The important point that distinguishes a cohort from an age stratum is that an individual or group assumes cohort membership at birth and retains it throughout life. With aging, a cohort passes through successive age strata.

Every society makes at least some distinctions between individuals on the basis of age or of age-related events. Our society uses both a finely differentiated system of age strata based on single years of age, and a more loosely defined set of age strata based on biological, familial, and more general social phenomena. The arbitrariness underlying age grades or age strata is apparent in the recent changes in legal ages for drinking, voting, and eligibility to marry without parental

**People in different age cohorts experience different social worlds.**

consent — changes that refer to the social differentiation of adulthood from youth.

Canadian society, then, may be thought of as differentiated not only by social class and gender, but also by age stratification. Age strata have associated with them different rights, responsibilities, obligations, and access to rewards. Aging in this perspective is a process by which successive cohorts pass through the age-stratification system. The **age-stratification perspective** in the sociology of aging brings together the notion of cohort with that of age stratum in a dynamic system. The model focuses on the flow of successive cohorts through the age strata of the society.

Cohorts will vary in a number of their social characteristics. For example, in Canadian society, almost every successive birth cohort has entered the age stratum of old age (say, at age 65) with a higher level of income, education, and health status. Simultaneously, the age-stratification system is changing. Expectations for behaviour of age-stratum members, as well as opportunities to behave in certain ways, change from one historical period to another. The school system that the 1900–1910 cohort passed through was far different from that encountered by the 1950–1960 cohort. Some cohorts encounter adulthood during a period of economic prosperity and have an easy time entering the labour market; others reach the initial working years in a time of economic recession or depression. Such accidents of birth are fateful for individuals and for whole cohorts and may affect the life chances, political attitudes, and values of the various cohorts in different ways.

Focusing on cohort differences poses an alternative explanation to one based on age. Are people of a certain age politically conservative because aging leads to conservatism or because their formative years were lived during a general societal climate of conservatism? In this view, age differences are hypothesized to result not so much from the aging or maturation of the individuals as from the different experiences that individuals have as a result of their cohort membership.

Waring (1976) uses the term *cohort flow* to describe the "movement of successive cohorts through an age-graded sequence of roles" and argues that in the normal case "a mutually accomodative situation obtains between the people in the cohort and the roles available to the age structure." However, these accomodations constitute social change and are at times characterized by conflict.

One example of such conflict, given by Foner and Kertzer (1978), concerns the timing of transitions. Because progression through the age strata of a society is normally associated with increasing access to power and rewards (with the occasional exception of transitions at the very end of the life course, such as retirement), cohorts occupying higher age strata may seek to delay the transitions of younger cohorts, while younger cohorts may wish to accelerate their passage into a higher age stratum. Younger cohorts may wish to lower the age of legal drinking or voting. In the case of the progression into retirement, which decreases power and rewards, older workers may seek to elevate the age of retirement. However, the potential for conflict surrounding processes of cohort flow is reduced by the relative flexibility of the age-stratification system in our society and by such adaptive mechanisms as skipping grades in elementary school, early or mature entry into university, and flexible retirement.

When the supply of people provided by an age cohort is either too small or too large in relation to the number of available role positions, then we have a situation of *disordered cohort flow*. The societal response to this is often to change age-related role expectations and the timing of the transitions between age strata. In response to the increasing size of cohorts entering the retirement years, and because of concern about providing economic security to this large cohort in retire-

ment, suggestions have been made to raise the age of retirement. As another example, one reaction to the large "baby-boom" cohort was to expand the post-secondary educational system. This led in Canada to massive expansion of the university system during the 1970s, thereby delaying entry of many baby-boom cohort members into the labour force. As Waring (1976) points out, many nations have sought to rectify disorders of cohort flow by relying on large-scale immigration or emigration. She argues, however, that, as immigration policies become more restrictive, attempts to maintain an orderly flow of cohorts rely increasingly on adjusting the age-stratification system — for instance, by modifying the age of retirement.

The age-stratification perspective, together with the modernization thesis discussed earlier, constitute the major focuses of research interest in the macrosociology of aging. It is noteworthy that both approaches exemplify the structural-functional perspective. While both attempt to deal with fundamental processes of social change, in their different ways they view such change as orderly or smooth and as functional for the society. The age-stratification approach has generated a reaction based primarily on the conflict perspective. Tindale and Marshall (1980; see also Marshall 1983; Tindale 1987) have attempted to go beyond the age-stratification approach by using the concept of generation. In contrast to a cohort, a generation's boundaries are not arbitrary, but depend on characteristics and social experiences shared by cohort members. A **generation** is a cohort, large proportions of whose members have experienced significant socio-historical changes, such as depressions or wars.

Not all single-year birth cohorts will experience such profound historical and social events in the same way. A difference of a year or two, for example, may mean being too old or too young to serve in the armed forces during a major war. Generational experiences, as indicated above, are usually thought of as cataclysmic and shaped by such major changes as depressions or wars. However, as Ryder (1965) has pointed out, "Cohorts can also be pulled apart gradually by the slow grind of evolutionary change." Similarly, not all members of any generation will necessarily respond to significant historical events in the same way. For example, some young people in Canada, Germany, and the United States responded to the Vietnam War by becoming "doves," while others became "hawks" (Levitt 1984).

Generational consciousness developed early in life may persist, although probably with some modification, throughout life (Dowd 1986). The politically active, antiwar generation of young people formed from those born on the leading edge of the baby-boom cohort still retains its generational membership as its members pass into their mid-thirties, while its age-group relationship changes.

Class differences influence the encounter of cohort members with important historical events and therefore influence generational experiences. For example, the children of the upper class who reach prime military service age during a major war are less likely to see active service or die in it than are the children of the lower class, despite shared cohort membership. Similar class differentiation occurs in response to fluctuations in the economy and the job market (Tindale 1987).

As noted earlier, Cowgill's theory of aging and modernization argued that growing proportions of older people in the population lead to increased age-group conflict over job scarcity (Cowgill 1986). This conflict may be affected to some degree by differences based on the shared historical experiences of a generation. However, the potential for conflict is probably even greater because of age-group differences in the present. Just as a group of people may form a distinctive consciousness of themselves as different from others on the basis of generational experiences, they may also form such a distinctive consciousness based on age itself. This takes us to the matter of subculture or minority-group formation among the aged, or indeed among groups of any age.

## The Aged as a Minority Group versus the Age-Irrelevance Perspective

Two contrasting approaches have been taken to the question of age-group formation in later life. Some scholars argue that the aged are increasingly taking on the characteristics of a group. Others contend that age is of decreasing importance as a basis for group formation. Rose (1965) argues that the aged are increasingly coming to constitute a subculture, because of their large numbers, increased vigour and health, collective concerns in fighting for adequate health care, and growing geographic segregation in such areas as small towns or age-segregated housing. He also stresses the exclusion of older people from integration with the society through employment, but he feels that the good health and economic security of most older people would facilitate their interaction, and thereby allow them to develop a shared consciousness of themselves as older people. Older people are discriminated against in the labour markets (Nishio and Lank 1987) and treated legally as a distinct category for many purposes, such as pensions. The extent to which these factors lead to a shared consciousness based on age is, however, open to dispute.

Abu-Laban and Abu-Laban (1980) argue that minority status should be viewed as multidimensional and as a matter of degree, rather than as a uniform attribute of the older person. Different individuals of the same age may vary greatly in their physical characteristics, in the extent of their active participation in the society, in the esteem they are accorded by others, in their power and privileges, and in their ability to resist or be exempt from the disadvantages of age.

At macro levels, the arguments against the formation of an aged minority group or subculture have been clearly articulated by Neugarten (1970). In her view, each successive cohort entering the later years is more like young and middle-aged cohorts with regard to health, educational attainment, income security, and shared social values. Therefore the objective basis for conflict between age groups should diminish.

From the age-stratification perspective, Foner (1974) adds additional support to Neugarten's thesis. Foner argues that the potential for age-based consciousness is diminished by generational consciousness. In other words, because each successive cohort entering the old-age stratum brings with it its unique encounter with history, its values and interests will be different from those of previous cohorts already in the old-age stratum, thereby weakening the unanimity or consensus of shared values. Foner also suggests that membership in associations that are not age-graded provides opportunities for a better understanding and greater tolerance of opposing views. Recognition by the young that they will eventually grow older, together with tolerance by the old of the frustrations of the young, combine to reduce the potential for age-based conflict. Finally, Foner also argues that material disputes tend to cut across generational and cohort boundaries. For example, class interests might unite workers of all ages (see Kernaghan 1982).

On the other hand, it is clear that the past decade or so has seen a tremendous increase in concerns about age. The rise of interest in aging is itself an indication of the growing importance of age, as is the increase in volume of political rhetoric and public policy discussion concerning pensions, health care for the aged, and related issues. American political scientist Neil Cutler (1981) has in fact argued that age consciousness is itself a generational cohort phenomenon.

## The Political Sociology of Aging

Other developments in the macrosociology of aging that draw on the conflict perspective focus on the political and economic impact of population aging on the old and on the entire society. Guillemard (1977, 1980) offers yet another reason why the apparent strains toward conflict between age groups and generations have not led to much open conflict. She argues that the state actively fosters an ideology that discourages older people from recognizing their common interests and their distinctive and disadvantaged position in society. She describes the promulgation of a positive view of retirement in which retirement is seen as a time for leisure and self-expression. Failure to attain satisfaction in retirement is attributed to inadequate preparation for it by the individual. Such an individualistic ideology directs the attention of many older people away from the structural foundations of age-related poverty and leads them instead to blame themselves for their misfortune. As with many other deprived groups, an ideology is provided that contributes to their pacification by "blaming the victim" (Ryan 1971).

Orbach (1981) has shown that policy initiatives directed toward the elimination of mandatory retirement in the United States and Canada are ideological mechanisms — that is, they are meant to pacify. He goes so far as to suggest that abolishing mandatory retirement at age 65 might mean "that

the poor elderly would have to keep on working, while the well-to-do could afford to retire" (1981). In Orbach's view, the debate over mandatory retirement is a symbolic issue, and the real issue is over the continuation into retirement of lifelong class inequities.

Estes (1979) calls attention to the ways in which old age has been defined as a social problem of crisis proportions. Drawing on the symbolic-interaction approach and on conflict sociology, she argues that

*to define old age as a social problem of crisis proportions is politically useful, because such a crisis may be portrayed as not the fault of prior social inaction or economic policy, but [rather] the result of increased longevity, retirement, declining birth rates, and so forth. In addition, the aging crisis label serves to advance the interests of those seeking expansion of government resources to deal with the crisis.*

The real issue of debates over income security and pension policy, according to Myles (1980, 1984), concerns control over massive pools of capital. As he says, "Pension policy . . . is not primarily an issue of individual welfare, but rather an issue of power, power to control and allocate the capital generated through the savings put aside by workers for their old age" (1980).

Many policy issues relating to aging and the aged cannot, therefore, be attributed to demographic causes. McDaniel (1987) argues that attributing such problems as maintaining adequate pensions to demographic pressures can lead to political inaction, because of a belief that population structure cannot be manipulated by policy thrusts.

Although the preceding material in this chapter has focused on social-structural and macro-social theoretical and practical issues, the great bulk of research in the sociology of aging until very recently has been social-psychological. Most of this research has fallen within the structural-functional perspective. More recently, a number of sociologists, including many Canadians, have worked within the symbolic-interaction perspective. Most of them view conflict as inherent both in the interaction among individuals and in the character of macro-social relations. Many feel that the conflict and symbolic-interaction approaches provide compatible theoretical perspectives that enable the sociologist to take this broader view — considering the aging individual in an aging society (Marshall 1987c).

## The Focus on Individual Adjustment and Life Satisfaction

From the beginning, the sociology of aging has focused unduly on the adjustment of the aging individual to his or her fate in the society. This emphasis on individual adjustment reflects the overall individualistic bias of North American sociology.

Underlying this preoccupation with happiness in later life, there appears to be an assumption by social scientists that this time of life is a problem for those who pass through it, a time when people find it difficult to be happy or satisfied with life.

Three variants of structural-functional role theory have been concerned with attempts to predict morale. These are *activity theory, disengagement theory*, and *continuity theory*. While these theories guided voluminous work in the earlier stages of the sociology of aging, their findings can be briefly summarized. The factors that most strongly predict morale or life satisfaction are (in order of importance) health, income security, and — a distant third — levels of social activity or role involvement.

Theoretical debate among these approaches focused on a structural-functional concern with the integration of the individual in society. Individuals were considered to be tied to their society through role occupancy. **Activity theory** hypothesized that the adaptation of the individual to society was threatened by age-related declines in role occupancy. Activity theorists argued that, in order to be happy in later life, people should remain as active in their role relationships as possible (Palmore 1969; Maddox 1970; Palmore and Luikart 1972). This theoretical approach is consistent with both Durkheim's structural functionalism and a symbolic-interaction approach. As we saw in Chapter 1, Durkheim argues that having few social ties leads to anomie and sometimes to suicide. According to Lemon, Bengtson, and Peterson (1972), the major argument of activity

theory "is that there is a positive relationship between activity and life satisfaction and that the greater the role loss, the lower the life satisfaction." Interaction, in symbolic-interaction terms, is capable of maintaining stable self-concepts or identities — and these, Lemon, Bengtson, and Peterson argue, represent the link to self-esteem and, ultimately, life satisfaction. High morale results from activity through the intermediate variable of confirming feedback from others.

Disengagement theory was explicitly formulated in structural-functional terms (Cumming and Henry 1961; Hochschild 1975) and argued against activity theory. **Disengagement theory** viewed the decline of activity as an inevitable and natural severing of the ties between the individual and the society that was functional to both. The society "granted permission" to the individual to disengage from active participation in social roles. This was seen as functional to the society because it allowed a smooth passing of people through the positions that make up the society, maintaining society as a *dynamic equilibrium*. (See Chapter 1 for a discussion of dynamic equilibrium.)

Disengagement was also viewed as functional for the aging individual who needed to conserve energy because of failing health. Moreover, the process of disengagement from the individual's point of view was thought to be initiated by a heightened recognition of mortality. Reduction of activity allowed more time for the individual to prepare for death.

The debate between activity and disengagement theorists dominated the sociology of aging for many years. For the most part, disengagement theory was discredited. Major withdrawals from role relationships, such as widowhood and retirement, are not voluntary (Shanas et al. 1968). In general, as noted above, higher levels of activity do lead to higher life satisfaction, though this is not a strong relationship. Psychologists (for example, Riechard, Livson, and Peterson 1962; Neugarten, Crotty, and Tobin 1964) found that psychological and sociological disengagement did not always occur simultaneously as postulated by the theory, and they stressed that there were many different styles of successful aging, depending on personality characteristics.

Translated into sociological terms, the idea that there are many different successful ways of aging led to the **continuity theory** (Atchley 1977). Sociologists such as Atchley (1971) and Rosow (1973, 1974, 1976) argued, with the aid of supporting data, that not the actual level of, but rather changes in, role involvement or activity constitute the important determinants of adaptation in later life. Some people, in other words, are lifelong loners and happy to be so; others have always been happy only when busy and active with other people. Change in either direction can lead to low morale in later life.

These three approaches have produced a wealth of empirical studies. It should be noted, however, that these approaches are more similar to than dissimilar from one another. Unlike the approaches reviewed in the following sections, they share structural-functional assumptions of dynamic equilibrium and the conception of role as the major link between the individual and the society.

Related to this general attitude is the assumption that middle-aged people have to be socialized to old age (Riley et al. 1969). Rosow (1974) views socialization as important but inadequate in the later years because of low motivation to learn the devalued role of older person. Symbolic interactionists, focusing on the individual as the active creator of roles, question both the existence of a role of aged person and the importance of this problem (Marshall 1980b). They would argue that there are other, more important, aspects of aging that are completely ignored by these theoretical approaches. The issues discussed in the next section, for example, stand in vivid contrast to structural functionalism and its stress on life satisfaction and adjustment.

## Identity and Identity Management

Age is a somewhat ambiguous identity marker in our society. Physical appearance usually gives only a very rough clue to a person's age – and in any case, we are not terribly clear as to how expected behaviour should differ by age.

Anthropologist Christine Fry (1976; see also Keith 1982) asked a sample of adult Americans to sort into piles a deck of cards depicting people in typical life situations "based on their decisions regarding the appropriate age or similarity in age bracket" of the people depicted. Respondents could create as many piles as they wished to describe appropriate ages or age brackets. The average number of categories identified was five or six, depending on age, gender, marital status, education, and other variables. Some respondents identified as many as fifteen age categories, but others identified only two; and more than 100 different terms were used to describe the categories.

Such lack of agreement as to the age categories used in our society creates some of the flexibility, but also some of the points of tension that we discussed in relation to age-stratification theory. Our society does not in fact have a single system of age categories that encompasses all spheres of life and receives wide agreement (Waring 1976). To the extent that such agreement is lacking, age-stratification theory — which suggests that there is considerable agreement on a system of age strata — may be considered somewhat unrealistic as a way of understanding the importance of age in our society.

People are not entirely sure just what it means to be old, but they have a vague feeling that it is not such a good thing. It is commonly acknowledged that ours is an "ageist" society — that is, one in which people share negative stereotypes of the old and are likely to discriminate against them in various ways. A number of studies suggest that negative stereotypes about later life are held by young, middle-aged, and even old people; a careful review is found in McTavish (1982). However, such studies also identify some positive stereotypes about the aged.

Reviewing the research on attitudes toward old age, Kalish (1982) concludes,

*Older people consistently view themselves much more optimistically than they are viewed by the non-elderly. However, when older people are asked about "older people in general" they use very much the same stereotypes that the non-elderly use. Once again, we have evidence of the syndrome "I'm fine, but look at those poor old people over there."*

We should expect that, to the extent that stereotypes about old age are negative, people will seek to exempt themselves from the status of being old. This tendency for people to view themselves

# Kuypers and Bengtson Model

*Maintaining Positive Identity in Later Life: The Social Breakdown Model*

Kuypers and Bengtson (1973) and Bengtson (1973) have applied Zusman's (1966) concept of social breakdown to examine identity change [in] the aged. They see the elderly as susceptible to stigmatizing labeling because of role loss, normative ambiguity, and a lack of confirmatory feedback from others. Such vulnerability creates a dependence on [such] negative external portrayals as useless and obsolete. Learning to be old under such conditions of vulnerability induces people to surrender their independence and to self-identify as sick or inadequate. Each point in this cycle can become a place of formal or informal intervention to enhance the self-reliance, coping skills, and self-esteem of the individual. D'Arcy (1980) has presented a similar model to describe psychiatric institutionalization of the aged in Saskatchewan.

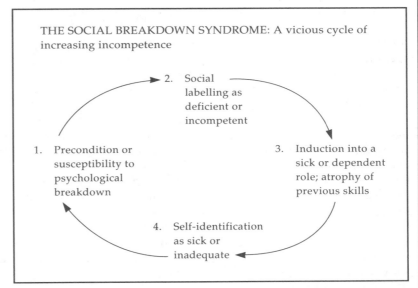

THE SOCIAL BREAKDOWN SYNDROME: A vicious cycle of increasing incompetence

1. Precondition or susceptibility to psychological breakdown
2. Social labelling as deficient or incompetent
3. Induction into a sick or dependent role; atrophy of previous skills
4. Self-identification as sick or inadequate

**Source:**

V.L. Bengtson, *The Social Psychology of Aging* (Indianapolis, IN: Bobbs-Merril, 1977).

---

as young for their age, or as younger than others might think them, is frequently found in studies on this topic. Yet many people do not appear to disassociate themselves from the status of being old; nor do all older people, or younger people, view old age in highly negative terms. This suggests a more situational interpretation of the relationship between socially shared attitudes and self-identity. That is, people are free to draw from a number of different, and often conflicting, values and meanings in order to make sense of age-related phenomena in any specific situation.

## Stigma and Identity Management among the Aged

People of the same chronological age may be more likely to see themselves as old in some kinds of situations than in others. For example, they may be more aware of being "old" when receiving a pension cheque in the mail than when receiving a love letter. They may be less aware of their age when attending a symphony concert with their children than when attending a rock concert with their grandchildren. The extent to which people think about age as a description of themselves, and even the value they place on this description, is therefore variable and situational (Matthews 1979).

A number of studies describe the situational variation of the stigma of being old. According to Tindale (1980), old, poor men in Hamilton, Ontario, do not feel stigmatized when among themselves but, when dealing with outsiders, they feel stigmatized and go to great lengths in attempting to manage their stigma. One method of stigma management used in encounters with strangers is information control:

*The men are slow to reveal aspects of their past or personal elements in their present life except when they want to do so. The subject of family relations is the most prominent area where information is controlled. . . . When dealing with mission staff [in a hostel where they receive meals] . . . there is an implicit notion that the men are inferior and that they should improve the moral tenor of their lives. The men sometimes feign information, but are able to laugh behind their humble smiles, i.e., they go to church only if a meal is served in return.*

In fact, Tindale says, the men maintain differentiation among themselves. They stigmatize as "mission stiffs" those of their peers they see as adopting without reservation the identity imputed to them by the public.

Similar internal differentiation to maintain self-esteem is described by Hochschild (1973) as occurring among older widows living in an apartment building. When they compared themselves to people in the outside world, they saw themselves as united, but among themselves they made distinctions: "She who had good health won honor. She who lost the fewest loved ones through death won honor, and she who was close to her children won honor. Those who fell short on any of these criteria were often referred to as 'poor dears.' "

Whether or not a person accepts the label "old" will determine the extent to which old people become a reference group, a source of comparison, a scale against which the person measures his or her own abilities, wellbeing, and indeed all aspects of personal identity (see Keith 1982). Evaluations of old people and of the self are most likely interdependent in the later years and serve self-protective purposes. As Keith (1982) says, "Old people . . . think more highly of themselves than they do of old people on the whole. The old, in other words, share many stereotypes of old age, and feel good as individuals because they don't fit them."

Another adaptive strategy in the face of the stigma of old age is what Keith calls "community creation." While many younger people bemoan the increase in geographic age segregation exemplified by senior citizens' housing and retirement communities, Keith argues that such living arrangements protect the older person from an external status system that devalues the aged, while providing enhanced opportunities for social support. In addition, people living together who face common problems, such as impending death or economic problems, can invent ways to deal with them.

Similarly, Marshall (1975a, 1975b) and Hochschild (1973) have shown how older people living congregatively have creatively fashioned ways to deal with impending death, and Rosow (1967) has found

that many older people prefer congregate living because it enhances their ability to form new friendships — a finding that no doubt applies to people at many stages of the life course (for example, students in residence, members of housing co-ops, tenants in adult-only apartment complexes).

All these ways of managing identity are also employed by the older women studied by Matthews (1979). In addition, Matthews characterizes many old people as adopting a strategic approach to organizing everyday activities so as to avoid situations that threaten their identity. This may affect such things as the timing of shopping excursions and the choice of restaurants and other public places in order to avoid contact with young people, from whom they fear disrespect.

## Exchange and Dependency

One of the greatest fears of older people is that they might become dependent on others. In Chapter 1, you were introduced to **exchange theory**. Some sociologists of aging draw on exchange-theory principles to explain identity management and the social interaction patterns of the aged. Exchange theory views the individual as strategic and voluntaristic; Dowd (1980) and Mutran and Reitzes (1984) explicitly link the exchange-theory approach to the symbolic-interaction perspective.

In exchange-theory terms, people are assumed to interact with others in order to obtain rewards, and stable social relationships develop if both parties receive roughly equal rewards in return for roughly equal costs, or if the balance of rewards and costs is roughly equal. Dowd (1980) argues that decreased interaction with increasing age is a result of a decline in the resources that can be brought to such encounters: material possessions, positions of authority, access to power resources, and strength and beauty (as socially defined). Also, as friends and family die, they cannot be drawn on as resources and they are lost as sources of respect.

If a person is not able to offer resources or rewards to another, but needs resources that the other has, she or he may become dependent on the other. But human beings seek to maintain independence, autonomy, and control over their situations (Marshall 1980b); therefore, they seek to avoid dependent situations or relationships. In an Australian study (Kendig 1986), rates of depression among widows and widowers were found to be associated with autonomy in living arrangements. For those living alone, physical-health status was not associated with depression, but for those living with a child and family, decreased physical health was associated with higher rates of depression. This suggests that dependency can lead to demoralization.

The exchange-theory perspective should be viewed as one of the most promising social-psychological approaches to understanding aging (Wellman and Hall 1987). What might otherwise appear to be confusing, irrational behaviour by individuals may be interpreted in exchange-theory terms as rational or strategic behaviour designed to protect autonomy or independence. Some of the older women studied by Matthews (1979) withdrew their participation in a seniors' centre. Matthews argues that this was a calculated decision taken to avoid the costs of having to interact with the centre's middle-aged staff, who viewed the women as old and therefore dependent. Withdrawal was a way for these older women to eliminate the psychological costs of dependency. Examining social exchange within the networks of older residents of East York, Ontario, Wellman and Hall (1987) describe efforts to maintain reciprocity at the network level: "Network members do unto others as they would have their networks do unto them."

## Life-Course Transitions

In recent years, a number of sociologists, together with demographers, historians, psychologists, and other scholars, have systematically sought to characterize aging in terms of a sequence of life-course transitions (see, for example, Ryff 1986; Gee 1987; Norris 1987) This work draws on the structural-functional approach and relates closely to work on age stratification. However, it also draws heavily on symbolic interactionism (Marshall 1986a). The life course, according to Rossi (1980), may be defined as "the pathways through the age-differentiated structure in the major role domains of life."

Hughes's concept of career (1971) and the derivative notion of status passage (Glaser and Strauss 1971) are helpful in understanding life-course transitions. Hughes distinguished between *objec-*

*tive career* (a series of social statuses and clearly defined offices) and *subjective career* ("the moving perspective in which the person sees his life as a whole and interprets the meaning of his various attributes, actions, and the things which happen to him"). Marshall (1980a, 1987b) has applied the career perspective to aging "to point to a person negotiating a passage from one age-linked status to another, and then to others, finally coming to the end of the passage through life at death" (1980a).

### Objective Careers

A number of investigators have noted that the events marking the early stages of objective careers in our society have become more compressed in time and more predictable (Hogan 1981; Hagestad 1982). For example, the average timing of school completion fell significantly during the first half of this century, while variability around the average age of completing school decreased. In statistical terms, the mean age decreased and the dispersion around the mean also decreased (see "Measures of Central Tendency" in Chapter 18). Similar patterns showing a greater standardization of life events, and a earlier timing of such events, have been observed for age of entry into the labour force, age of first marriage, birth of first child, birth of last child, and marriage of last child. In a similar way, the timing of widowhood has also become more predictable but has moved to a point later in the life course (Gee 1987; Gee and Kimball 1987; Martin Matthews 1987). Some of these patterns are visible in Table 5-2.

It is only in this century that the "empty-nest" stage — the period of life from the departure of the youngest child until the first parent dies — of the family life course has emerged. Gee (1987) estimates that, among female cohorts born between 1831 and 1840, 90 percent of the years lived after marriage were spent rearing dependent children. In contrast, cohorts born between 1951 and 1960 are expected to spend only 40 percent of the years following marriage in child-rearing.

Family life factors such as age at marriage and the timing of child-bearing are consequential for intergenerational relations and for the social character of later life. They affect the average number of children, grandchildren, siblings, and other relatives who will be available to the individual in old age.

## Table 5-2. Median Ages at Family-Life-Course Events

| | | Approximate Birth Cohorts | | | | | | | | | | | |
|---|---|---|---|---|---|---|---|---|---|---|---|---|---|
| | | 1831–1840 | 1841–1850 | 1851–1860 | 1861–1870 | 1881–1890 | 1891–1900 | 1901–1910 | 1911–1920 | 1921–1930 | 1931–1940 | 1941–1950 | 1951–1960 |
| **Females** | | | | | | | | | | | | | |
| | *Median Age at:* First Marriage | 25.1 | 26.0 | 24.9 | 24.3 | 25.1 | 23.4 | 23.3 | 23.0 | 22.0 | 21.1 | 21.3 | 22.5 |
| | First Birth | 27.1 | 28.0 | 26.9 | 26.3 | 27.1 | 25.4 | 25.0 | 25.4 | 23.5 | 22.9 | 23.3 | 24.5 |
| | Last Birth | 41.0 | 40.0 | 38.2 | 36.2 | 36.2 | 33.9 | 29.1 | 28.8 | 29.5 | 29.1 | 26.7 | 26.3 |
| | Empty Nest* | 61.0 | 60.1 | 58.2 | 56.2 | 56.2 | 53.9 | 49.1 | 48.8 | 49.5 | 49.1 | 46.7 | 46.3 |
| | Widowhood | 58.2 | 59.5 | 58.9 | 58.3 | 60.1 | 59.4 | 61.3 | 63.0 | 67.0 | 67.2 | 68.8 | 69.9 |
| **Males** | | | | | | | | | | | | | |
| | *Median Age at* First Marriage | 27.9 | 29.1 | 29.2 | 28.0 | 28.5 | 28.4 | 27.0 | 26.3 | 24.3 | 24.0 | 23.5 | 24.6 |
| | First Birth | 29.9 | 31.3 | 31.2 | 30.0 | 30.5 | 30.4 | 28.7 | 28.7 | 25.8 | 25.8 | 25.5 | 26.6 |
| | Last Birth | 43.8 | 43.1 | 42.5 | 39.9 | 39.6 | 38.9 | 32.8 | 32.1 | 31.8 | 32.0 | 28.9 | 28.4 |
| | Empty Nest* | 63.8 | 63.1 | 62.5 | 59.9 | 59.6 | 58.9 | 52.8 | 52.1 | 51.8 | 52.0 | 48.9 | 48.4 |

\* Age at which last child is 20 years old.
SOURCE: Ellen M. Gee, "Historical change in the family life course of men and women," in *Aging in Canada: Social Perspectives*, 2nd edition, Victor W. Marshall, ed. (Toronto: Fitzhenry and Whiteside, 1987), p. 278.

## Subjective Careers

People have their own ideas about the appropriate timing and sequence of life-course transitions. This sense has been called the **social clock** (Hagestad and Neugarten 1985). In relation to these social clocks, people see themselves as "on time" or "off time" — early, late, or "just right" — in getting married, bearing a child, obtaining a promotion, becoming a grandparent, or retiring. Very little research has actually been done on the extent to which conceptions of life-course timing, or social clocks, are associated with sanctioning in order to keep people roughly "on time" in the life course (Hagestad 1982), but most of us have experienced or will soon experience pressures (sometimes not so subtle) in this regard.

One study of cohort differences in the preferred timing of female life events (Fallo-Mitchell and Ryff 1982; Ryff 1986) found that young adult women preferred later ages for family-career events (such as having their first child), but earlier ages for general events (such as settling on a career choice), than did middle-aged or older women. But the different cohorts attributed their own timing preferences to women of the other cohorts. Such differences in actual preferences, coupled with misperception, create grounds for potential conflict among different generations in families.

An aspect of subjective careers that has been quite neglected in the sociology of aging is the increasing awareness of impending death as age increases. That is, as people grow older, and typically when they see themselves as having about 10 years to live, the fact that they are mortal becomes very important to them (Marshall 1980a, 1986b). This recognition is heightened by self-perceived changes in health and by the death of parents, siblings, and friends (Marshall and Rosenthal 1982). Awareness of impending death normally leads individuals to focus on their past experiences in order to make sense of any past life events that lack meaning or coherence. In addition, highly aware individuals frequently focus on the meaning of death and engage in concrete preparations for it, such as making a will and making peace in their personal relationships.

Two life-course transitions have been of particular interest to sociologists of aging: widowhood and retirement. Too frequently, these have been viewed as the problems of the elderly female and elderly male, respectively. It is important to bear in mind that large numbers of both men and women experience each of these transitions, though in somewhat different ways. In addition, people of both sexes are affected by the transitions faced by those close to them — a spouse or a sibling, for example.

## From Working to Retirement

In an earlier section, we discussed retirement as a socioeconomic institution. Our concern here is with the retirement experiences of individuals. Retirement occurs within the context of age discrimination in employment that can either accelerate departure from the labour force or make retirement more palatable for the worker. With increasing age, men and women in the work force frequently encounter pressure from younger employees who feel that their older co-workers are blocking advancement opportunities (Stryckman 1987). Contrary to popular belief, for almost all tasks, skill at industrial work increases with age and older workers are generally as competent as — and often more accurate, punctual, and com-

mitted to the employer than — younger workers (Koyl 1977).

To some extent, seniority provisions provide job security for older workers, giving them advantages over the young (Stryckman 1987; Tindale 1987). Nonetheless, older workers are more harmed by plant shutdowns and layoffs than are younger workers. A shutdown places young and old on the labour market, and the older worker is disadvantaged in that market. A hypothesis of "selective retention" suggests that those older workers who are able to remain in the labour force despite economic pressures affecting employment opportunities are more highly skilled and educated (Nishio and Lank 1987).

Many Canadians retire before reaching a formal, compulsory retirement age. McDonald and Wanner (1984) report that, by age 63, 75 percent of Canadian women and 30 percent of Canadian men are retired. Those taking early retirement are disproportionately from higher socioeconomic levels. While the reasons for and implications of retirement in Canada are a major unresearched area, American data suggest that a large proportion of early retirees leave the work force for health reasons (Chirikos and Nestel 1981). Earlier studies that noted a correlation between being retired and being in poor health had led to the view that retirement is a crisis that adversely affects health. However, more recent research suggests that in most instances the direction of causation is the reverse: poor health is a cause rather than a consequence of retirement, and retirement may even produce health benefits (Adams and Lefevre 1980; Foner and Schwab 1981).

Contrary to popular belief, retirement does not appear to be a major crisis for most people. In a sample of 300 recently retired men and women in Southern Ontario, Martin Matthews and associates asked respondents to indicate the extent to which 34 life events had affected them. Experiencing the death of a spouse was rated as having the strongest effects, followed by birth of children and marriage. Retirement ranked twenty-seventh. There was some evidence to suggest that retirement was more consequential for men than for women, but the differences were not great (Martin Matthews et al. 1982). In some respects, on the other hand, retirement may be a more consequential life-course transition for women than for men. In many instances, women have had to struggle harder to fashion any stable career in paid employment, and they may therefore value it more (Connidis 1982).

There is no retirement from domestic labour — that form of unpaid work that is essential to the maintenance of our socioeconomic order and still largely the domain of women, even if they are also in paid employment (Luxton 1980). Whether or not a married woman has also been in paid employment, her husband's retirement might produce a profound and, at times, adverse life transition for her. Her home is no longer her castle, and she may find new difficulties with her husband around the house not quite knowing what to do with himself. Her loss of autonomy may, however, be offset by other aspects of the relationship, such as increased opportunity to express nurturance (Keating and Cole 1980) and to enjoy leisure time with her husband (McPherson and Guppy 1979). Sometimes women and men retire together. For example, farm couples in Alberta were found to plan ahead together for their retirement, a gradual and mutually supportive experience in most instances (Keating and Marshall 1980).

Not enough attention has been paid to the ways in which retirement is affected by social class and type of occupation (McDonald and Wanner 1982). As with most aspects of aging, income security and good health are the critical factors influencing retirees' morale and satisfaction with life. Seeing retirement as a negative experience rests on the assumption that work is a positive experience. This assumption is clearly untrue for many individuals and may reflect the middle-class bias of many researchers.

## From Marriage to Widowhood

Until quite recently, little was known about the experience of widowhood. Most men have the bad fortune not to experience this life-course transition, because most men predecease their wives: the alleged disadvantages of widowhood for women should be weighed against this alternative. Widowhood is both a social status and a process. The process involves changes in identity and in feelings toward both the self and the de-

**The experience of retirement varies widely by social class.**

ceased spouse. This process is affected by the social characteristics of the deceased and the survivor, by the nature of the death, and by the social relations that the widowed person maintains.

Many deaths of older people can be thought of as appropriately timed according to the life-course social clock. There is time for the dying person and the spouse to prepare for the death. In general, grief is more intense in the case of a younger death and when death is relatively unexpected (Vachon et al. 1976; Vachon 1979; Marshall 1980a).

There is increased mortality among the recently bereaved. Because about three-quarters of the increased death rate among the bereaved is a result of various types of heart disease, the term *broken-heart syndrome* has been applied to this phenomenon (Parkes, Benjamin, and Fitzgerald 1969). Although the dynamics of this syndrome are not clearly understood, they undoubtedly go beyond the stress implied in the folk dictum "she (or he) died of a broken heart" to include the stresses probably experienced by the remaining spouse in caring for the other during the process of dying.

Canadian research (McFarlane et al. 1980; Martin Matthews et al. 1982; Martin Matthews 1987) shows that widowhood is the single most disruptive transition of the life course. The potential severity of the stress of bereavement may be indicated by Norris's (1980) finding that some elderly women remained committed to the role of wife for as long as 10 years following their husband's death.

Women, as noted earlier, are much more likely to occupy the social status of widowhood than are men. Remarriage is likely to take place (if at all) after a longer period of widowhood than is the case for men (Northcott 1984). Studying a Quebec sample of widowed people, Stryckman (1981) found that half the males had remarried within a year and a half of bereavement, while four and a half years passed before half the females had remarried. Although men are more likely than women to remarry, Berardo (1970) has suggested that the transition to widowhood may be more serious for men than for women, partly because it is "off time" in relation to social clocks. However, a Canadian study (Wister and Strain 1986) found no difference in the wellbeing of elderly widows and widowers.

Much research on widowhood focuses on social support. Lopata (1979) concludes that children are by far the most prominent category of kin providing support to elderly female widows. A Canadian study conducted in Guelph, Ontario, also found children to be important sources of support. But siblings, especially sisters, were also actively involved in the widow's support system. Half of these widows named a sister as one of the three people to whom they felt closest. Moreover, two-thirds of the widows listed an extended-kin member — sibling-in-law, cousin, and/or niece — as part of their emotional support system (Martin Matthews 1982, 1987). Wister and Strain (1986) found that widows were more strongly embedded than widowers in interaction patterns with family and neighbours.

Martin Matthews, applying a symbolic-interaction perspective, stresses the active part that widows play in reconstructing their lives and identities and in attributing meaning to widowhood. For example, she notes that diminished social ties in widowhood may mean rejection to one widow, loneliness to another, but independence to a third (Martin Matthews 1982, 1987). Like retirement and other life-course transitions, widowhood brings changes in identity and in social relationships. Like these other transitions, it is no

doubt influenced by social class, cohort, and other bases of social differentiation.

The ramifications of widowhood extend beyond the widow to other family members. If a widow is receiving support from a sibling or from a child, then we should also look at the child who is providing such support. Considerations such as these lead us to a general discussion of the intergenerational family.

## Family and Intergenerational Relations

One of our society's most persistent myths about the family is that the elderly are isolated from and abandoned by their children. This is related to a view that our family system consists of self-sufficient nuclear family units composed of parents and young, dependent children isolated from one another geographically, socially, and emotionally. When children mature and leave home, they are thought to sever ties with their parents. If this characterization were entirely accurate, the elderly would be cut off from intergenerational family life. Sociologists have therefore been very interested in investigating the family relationships of older people. Three decades of research have led sociologists to suggest that we have a *modified extended-family system* consisting of many nuclear family units maintaining separate households but bound together in ongoing relationships (see Chapter 11).

### The Changing Structure of the Family

Changes in mortality and fertility have made the multigenerational family more common. In one Canadian study (Rosenthal 1987a), 78 percent of a random sample of community-dwelling respondents aged 70 and older were members of three- or four-generation families — a figure comparable to national American data (Shanas, with Heinemann, 1982). We may expect a substantial increase in the number of four- and five-generation families between now and the end of this century. Adults now have greatly increased opportunities to have ongoing relationships with their parents and grandparents, and with their adult children and grandchildren. At the same time, families are more and more likely to have some members who are old and frail, placing burdens of responsibility for care on other family members, especially those in the younger generations.

While families now have more generations alive than they did in the past, declines in fertility mean that there are fewer people within each generational level. Despite great cohort variability in fertility, there has been an overall trend toward fewer children. This also means that people have fewer brothers and sisters. Thus we can conceive of the contemporary family structure as being long and thin; it is also somewhat fragile, in the sense that death or geographic mobility may have greater impact than in multigenerational families with more members.

Much research on the family life of older people has focused on their relationships with adult children. To describe this research, the following discussion is organized around certain dimensions of family life.

## The Proximity and Availability of Kin

On the whole, most people at age 65 have a spouse. The percentage declines as the years go by — very sharply for women. About four out of five people over 65 have at least one child and at least one sibling. Further, about three-quarters of older people have grandchildren and one-third have great-grandchildren. These figures are based on large American studies (Harris et al. 1975; Shanas, with Heinemann, 1982) but smaller Canadian investigations suggest the pattern is similar in Canada (Rosenthal 1987a).

Clearly, most older people have kin. However, a very small but important minority have no living spouse, child, or sibling (Rosenthal 1987a). These people find it extremely difficult to remain in the community should they suffer health losses in later life; indeed, in the United States, about half of them are institutionalized (compared with only 4.5 percent of the American older population as a whole). Canada has a higher overall rate of institutionalization of older people (Schwenger and Gross 1980), but here, as in the United States, people without kin are more vulnerable to being institutionalized than others their age who have kin (Shapiro and Roos 1987).

Like people of all ages, married old people usu-

ally live with their spouses, and those who are widowed or never married are likely to live alone (Connidis and Rempel 1983; Stone and Fletcher 1987). In the Hamilton study, of women aged 70 and over, 23 percent lived with a spouse and a further 60 percent lived alone. Most older people prefer this living arrangement, striving to remain autonomous from their children (Connidis 1983; Wister 1985; Béland 1987), in a relationship that has been called "intimacy at a distance" (Rosenmayr 1977). For people over the age of 80, living with a son or daughter is somewhat more common, partly because of age-related health problems. It should be noted that intergenerational residency patterns may be caused by the parent living in the home of a child or the child living in the home of a parent (Rosenthal 1986).

Although most older people do not live with a child, they usually live near at least one of their children. We may assume this is related to the concern of children to keep a watchful eye on their parents' condition (Marshall, Rosenthal, and Synge 1983; Rosenthal 1987a) and to the health-care needs of aging parents. American and Danish data (Marshall and Bengtson 1983) suggest that in the majority of cases, community-dwelling people aged 80 and over either lived in the same household as a child or within 10 minutes of a child, with the child assuming primary responsibility as caregiver.

## Interaction, Exchange, and Helping Patterns

Contrary to popular belief, most older people interact frequently with their children. For example, studies in the United States, England, Denmark, and Canada of people who have children suggest that about four out of five older parents see a child at least once a week. About half of these older people have daily telephone contact with a child and the vast majority have at least weekly contact (Marshall and Bengtson 1983; Rosenthal 1987a). One of the reasons for such contact is that it allows the exchange of help.

A variety of studies point to high levels of exchange between generations of a broad range of goods and services, including assistance with home repairs, child care, grocery shopping, transportation, and health care, as well as financial assistance and support (Chappell 1983; Marshall and Bengtson 1983; Rosenthal 1987a). Contrary to popular images of older people as dependent, these studies suggest a more appropriate image of interdependence. Help flows across the generations in both directions, with older people both giving and receiving. Certainly, the amount and type of help given and received varies by the socioeconomic status of the parent and child, but, except for the extremely poor, most elderly people are more likely to give financial help to their children than they are to receive it (Cheal 1983; Rosenthal 1987a).

The familial provision of health care is becoming increasingly prevalent as parents live into very old age and experience health losses. If a spouse is present, he or she is generally the primary caregiver (Aronson 1985). If there is no spouse, caregiving responsibilities generally fall to people in the second-oldest generational level in a family, who may themselves be getting on in years. The second-oldest generation in families, especially women, experience added familial concerns and burdens in mid-life, leading scholars to refer to them as the "caught generation" (Brody 1981; Rosenthal 1982).

## Familial Norms and Consensus between the Generations

The extent to which older people and their adult children feel that the latter should be obligated to provide assistance to their aged parents is a matter of some policy concern. Most people feel some obligation to provide emotional support to other family members and to assist them financially and in times of health crises. However, there are great differences in the strength of adherence to what are referred to as *norms of filial obligation*. In a Prince Edward Island study, younger people expressed stronger adherence to such norms than did elderly people (Storm, Storm, and Strike-Schurman 1985). In the Hamilton study, few age differences were found. When respondents aged 70 and older were asked to report on their expectations for the help their children should provide to them, their answers were not related to the parental reports of assistance actually received. This lack of relationship is due in part to the abstract nature of the normative statements put to respondents. In symbolic-interaction terms, filial expectations and their fulfillment are highly "situated": they are realized in concrete circumstances of parental need,

familial bonds, and resources (Marshall, Rosenthal, and Daciuk 1987).

Disagreement between parents and children concerning norms of filial obligation or other issues creates the potential for intergenerational conflict. Some research (Bengtson and Kuypers 1971; Marshall and Bengtson 1983) suggests that both parents and children think they are in greater agreement on a number of issues than they really are. Bengtson and Kuypers found that the parents of college students saw themselves as closer in political ideology to their children than the children considered to be the case. The researchers interpreted this as an example of the *developmental stake* that parents invest in the parent/child relationship. Parents devote many years to building this relationship and want it to be close and successful.

Children, too, want this kind of relationship, but they also have a stake in developing their own autonomy and independence. These differential investments of two generations contribute to somewhat different perceptions of the characteristics of the relationship. The *developmental* in developmental stake refers to changing perceptions and motivations of both child and parent as they proceed through the life course.

## Affective Bonds

A number of investigations focus on such qualitative aspects of intergenerational relationships as closeness, warmth, trust, concern.

Research in the Netherlands (Knipscheer and Bevers 1985) inquired of older people and their adult children whether the parent/child relationship had become better or worse compared to the past. Parents viewed the relationship as stable and thought their children would agree, but children were more likely to see changes for the better. In contrast to the discussion in the previous section, here the developmental stake principle seems to be weighted toward the younger generation taking the more positive view of the relationship. This may be a reflection of the aging parents' desire to deny growing dependency, and of the satisfaction gained by the child in contributing more to the parents' welfare as a representation of increasing equality.

In the Hamilton study (Marshall 1987a), adult children showed a high level of concern about health and health changes in their parents.

Daughters, in keeping with traditional gender-role stereotyping, showed more concern than did sons; and fathers were worried about by their children more than were mothers. Greater concern was evident among adult children who were providing more care to parents.

## Maintaining the Family

Family relationships do not develop inexorably because of functional requirements of the society. Instead, they are an achievement worked out by family members in response to social and histor-

## Age and Friendship

*We have emphasized the family and especially the parent/child relationship as an important context in which the aging individual receives social support. However, about one in five older people have no children. For them, and perhaps especially for widowed, never-married, separated, or divorced older people, friendship may be very important. The joint effects of lower fertility and higher divorce and separation rates for successive cohorts may make friendship even more important to older people in the future. Yet little is known about friendship — and, indeed, it is hard to define. Friendship may be less intense for older men than for older women, and men may be more passive and less intimate than women in later-life friendships (Abu-Laban, 1980). B. Bradford Brown has systematically reviewed the literature on friendship over the life course. The following brief excerpt suggests some important features of friendship that merit future research.*

There is an ageless quality to friendship. We can make friends at virtually any age, keep them for as many years as we like, and disavow them whenever it seems necessary or convenient. Friends differ from parents, children, siblings and other kinfolk, whom we inherit at birth (ours or theirs). They aren't like a spouse, for whom we have to wait two decades and then must promise to love and live with for the rest of our life. Nor are they like neighbors and co-workers, who "come with the territory" or the job, and who, by definition, are lost as soon as we move to a new home, a new position. Unlike the other close associations of one's life, friendship is a relationship for all seasons—or for none, as we so choose.

It is perhaps this "agelessness" that has induced most researchers to ignore age as a crucial variable in friendship. To many investigators, friendship is friendship, regardless of when it occurs or how long it lasts. Yet, there are three ways in which age enters into the fabric of friendship. It is, first of all, a relational characteristic of the partners, representing the difference in age between oneself and one's friend. Although we commonly conceive of friends as age mates, there is nothing in the definition of friendship (at least as I define it in this essay) that requires them to be so. But as relational age expands, the inherent similarity between individuals diminishes. It seems likely that individuals who share the same life stage and who have lived through the same historical events would forge a

different relationship than two people from separate generations.

Age can also be viewed as a temporal characteristic of the relationship. That is, friendships are formed, deepened and sustained across time. One cannot expect two individuals who have been friends for decades to relate in the same fashion as they did during the first months of their acquaintance, just as one cannot expect the "honeymoon phase" to be maintained over the entire course of marriage.

Beyond this, of course, is the individual age of each partner. As people progress across the life course, they witness changes in their abilities, experiences and developmental needs, as well as in the expectations and opportunities they have for close interpersonal attachments. Both the form and function of friendships must adjust to these developmental changes.

Each of these age-related characteristics adds to the complexity of friendship. Each, in a sense, undermines its "agelessness."

**Source:**

B. Bradford Brown, "A life-span approach to friendship: Age-related dimensions of an ageless relationship," in *Research in the Interweave of Social Roles: Friendship*, Helena Z. Lopata and David Maines, eds. (Toronto: JAI Press, 1981).

ical conditions. Among these conditions are the demographic changes affecting the family context of older people and their middle-aged children.

On the various dimensions of family life that we have discussed, most families may be aptly characterized as having high cohesion. Not only does this refute myths of the abandonment of the elderly, but it occurs despite pressures on contemporary families. Economic constraints, geographic mobility, and demographic changes pose threats to the family. Additional tensions arise out of the normal course of intergenerational life. The quest for autonomy and independence by both young and old represents one such source of tension. New members must be absorbed into families. Family relations are disrupted by death. Family members work at maintaining the family through a variety of accommodations and negotiations, including mutual tolerance, self-deception, and role segregation (Marshall and Bengtson 1983; Rosenthal 1987b).

There are also changes in the organization of the extended family that are related to the family life course transitions of its members. Recent research on "kinkeeping" indicates that many families have one person who takes on the task of keeping the family together and that this is considered especially important in times of family crisis such as the death of a parent (Rosenthal 1985). Most families have a person who is considered to be the "head of the family" (Rosenthal and Marshall 1986). Such people provide leadership and advice for the extended family. When one "head" dies, another usually takes his or her place (Rosenthal 1987b). Yet another family position is the "comforter" (Rosenthal 1987c), the person to whom other family members turn for emotional support. The presence in most families of such specialized roles suggests that the family is valued and that, because it is valued, its members work to preserve it (Marshall and Rosenthal 1982; Rosenthal 1987a).

In summary, the ramifications of population aging at the level of the family have not demonstrated a failure of the family or the end of the family; rather, these ramifications have shown that people have transformed the family to meet new challenges.

## SUMMARY

1. The sociology of aging deals with the changes experienced over the life course, with the social relationships of older people, and with the implications, both micro and macro, of individual and population aging for the entire society.

2. Canada has experienced, and will continue to experience, a significant increase in the number and proportion of older people and in the average age of the population. The great majority of very old people are women.

3. It is essential to differentiate among the aged by health status, economic characteristics, gender, age itself, and other social characteristics such as ethnicity.

4. Political and social concern about population aging results in large measure from increased societal allocation of resources toward health care and income security for the aged; but economic and service-delivery problems are often incorrectly blamed on the aging of the population.

5. Modernization has been associated with a decline in the status of the aged. However, it cannot be assumed that old people had high status in premodern societies, nor that age is a more important criterion for assigning status than other factors.

6. Society is differentiated by age, with each age having rights, obligations, and rewards. The age-stratification system itself changes as cohorts with varying social characteristics flow through it.

7. A number of factors, including cross-cutting allegiances and differences within generations, decrease the potential for conflict based on age, while the growth of the proportion of aged people in the population and the economic implications of population aging increase the likelihood of age-group conflict.

8. Much of the sociology of aging has focused on happiness. The major predictors of happiness in later life are good health, income security, and — to a lesser but still important extent — supportive interaction with other people.

9. Being old carries mild stigmas. As a result, many people resist identifying themselves as old and adopt various interaction strategies, such as information control and selective interaction, that protect their self-esteem.

10. Old age is associated with a decrease in the resources people can exchange in interaction. This may partially explain the decreased role involvements of older people and the kinds of involvements they have.

11. Over the past century, major life-course transitions have become more predictable. Retirement is less a crisis than is usually thought, while widowhood is undoubtedly the most significant transition of later life. Also, people develop subjective views of the timing of their own transitions over the life course. Disagreements and misperceptions about the social clock can create tension between generational and age groups.

12. Relationships between older people and their adult children are characterized by high levels of interaction, exchange, and solidarity.

13. Structural-functional sociology has dominated the sociology of aging at both macro and micro levels. It provides the theoretical foundations for both the modernization and the age-stratification theories, as well as for the activity, disengagement, and role theories of later-life adjustment.

14. Conflict theorists have developed a political economy of aging. They emphasize that the economic issues underlying provisions for income security for old people are primarily resolved in relation to decisions about the balance between public and private sectors over the control of capital. Other conflict theorists have examined the ways in which age and historical generations have become bases for conflict.

15. Symbolic interactionists have rejected the equilibrium assumptions of the sociology of later-life happiness, and have stressed the strategic interaction of older people as they seek to maximize personal autonomy and self-esteem.

## GLOSSARY

**Activities of daily living (ADL).** Everyday activities, such as rising and going to bed, personal hygiene, and shopping.

**Activity theory.** A theory that emphasizes that continuing activity through social roles is required in order to attain high life satisfaction in the later years.

**Age strata.** Socially recognized divisions ordered over the life course, with which are associated rights, responsibilities, obligations, and access to rewards.

**Age-stratification perspective.** A theoretical approach that focuses on the progression of birth cohorts through the age strata of a society and, in addition, views the age-stratification system as changing in response to cohort characteristics and other social phenomena.

**Cohort.** A set of individuals born at approximately the same time, who move through the life course together.

**Continuity theory.** A loosely defined theoretical approach that argues that life satisfaction in the later years is enhanced by a continuation of lifelong patterns of activity and role involvement, whether high or low.

**Disengagement theory.** A theory that argues that successful aging involves a mutual withdrawal of the aging individual and society. This is seen as functional for the society and beneficial for the individual. Such disengagement is viewed as normal and, ideally, voluntary on the part of the individual.

**Exchange theory.** A view of social interaction as an exchange of rewards. Individuals are assumed to seek to maximize rewards and minimize costs.

**Generation.** When used in other than the kinship or family sense, the term refers to a cohort, large proportions of whose members have experienced significant socio-historical experiences. Such generational experiences frequently lead to the development of shared generational consciousness.

**Modernization thesis.** An argument that maintains that as societies modernize, aspects of modernization — such as industrialization, urbanization, increased emphasis on technology, and improved health and longevity — contribute to a decline in the social status of the aged.

**Social clock.** Socially shared expectations about the normal or appropriate timing and sequence of events over the life course. For example, people may see themselves as making slow or rapid career progress compared to general expectations, or they may see themselves as "delaying" marriage or parenthood.

## FURTHER READING

**Canadian Journal on Aging.** A quarterly journal of scholarly, research-based papers on aging. Many articles reflect a sociology and social science perspective.

**Connidis, Ingrid A.** *Family Ties and Aging.* Toronto: Butterworths, 1989. An exploration of the family life of the aged, including parent/child and sibling ties, and the situations of single, divorced, widowed, remarried, and childless older people. Family and aging policy is also considered.

**Driedger, Leo, and Neena L. Chappell.** *Aging and Ethnicity: Toward an Interface.* Toronto: Butterworths, 1987. A critical review of the research and policy literature on aging and ethnicity in Canada, by two sociologists.

**Gee, Ellen M., and Meredith M. Kimball.** *Women and Aging.* Toronto: Butterworths, 1987. An exploration of aging as a women's issue, by a sociologist and psychologist.

**Marshall, Victor W. (ed.).** *Aging in Canada: Social Perspectives.* 2nd edition. Markham, ON: Fitzhenry and Whiteside, 1987. Thirty chapters by leading Canadian sociologists of aging, and other social and health scientists, presenting demographic data and information about aging in relation to work and retirement, the family, the health-care system, and other social institutions.

**Marshall, Victor W. (ed.).** *Aging and Later Life: The Social Psychology of Aging.* Beverly Hills, CA: Sage, 1986. Ten chapters focusing on theory in the symbolic-interaction and interpretive perspectives, as applied to aging and later life.

**Novak, Mark.** *Aging and Society: A Canadian Perspective.* Scarborough, ON: Nelson Canada, 1988. This introductory-level textbook is written by a sociologist but provides a comprehensive review of aging from the social science perspective.

**Rathbone-McCuan, Eloise, and Betty Havens (eds.).** *North American Elders: United States and Canadian Perspectives.* New York: Greenwood Press, 1988. Contains chapters by a number of Canadian sociologists of aging exploring social policy, the demography of aging, long-term care, the family, rural aging, and multicultural issues.

# CHAPTER 6

# Crime and Deviance

JOHN HAGAN

Deviance involves variation from a norm. In other words, to be different is to be deviant. But there is more to deviance than this. If there were not, our topic would be considerably less interesting than it is; we would simply be talking about the human diversity that surrounds us. What makes deviance a matter of great interest and importance is the reaction it provokes. Through the reactions of others, diverse human beings may be singled out as both different *and* disreputable.

## Kinds of Crime and Deviance

**Deviance**, then, is variation from a norm and the societal reaction involved. With this definition in mind, let us begin to identify several character- istics that help distinguish among kinds of devi- ance (Hagan 1977). Table 6-1 illustrates these characteristics for easy comparison.

The first of these characteristics is the *severity of the societal response*. Historically, we have re- sponded to our most serious deviants, including first-degree murderers, by making them liable to capital punishment. We may do so again. At the other end of the spectrum, some deviants, par- ticularly those who are badly disturbed or dis- abled, are simply ignored. If they are slightly more disturbing, they are ostracized. Between the two ends of this societal-response continuum, there are other types of institutional and community responses, including imprisonment, mental hos- pitalization, probation, fines, and outpatient treatment. The point is that these many societal

## Table 6-1. Kinds of Deviance

| Kind of Deviance | Severity of Societal Response | Peceived Harmfulness | Degree of Agreement | Examples | |
|---|---|---|---|---|---|
| Consensus Crimes | Severe | Extremely Harmful | Consensus | Premediated Murder | |
| Conflict Crimes | Punitive | Somewhat Harmful | Conflict | Victimless Crimes (e.g., prostitution, narcotics | |
| Social Deviations | Indeterminate | Potentially Harmful | Uncertainty | Mental Illness, Juvenile Delinquency | |
| Social Diversions | Mild | Relatively Harmless | Apathy | Fads and Fashions | |

responses vary in the degree to which they limit a citizen's freedom. Generally speaking, the more seriously the act of deviance is regarded, the more the freedom of the alleged deviant will be curtailed.

A second characteristic of deviance is the *perceived harmfulness* of the behaviour in question. Some deviant behaviours, like aggravated assault and aggravated sexual assault, are regarded as serious because of the harm they are perceived to cause. Other forms of deviance, including some sexual predilections of consenting adults, are regarded as inconsequential because they are perceived as causing little or no harm. Between the extremely harmful and the relatively harmless are a number of behavioural deviations from the norm that are thought to be only mildly harmful or whose degree of harm is uncertain. Included here are activities like marijuana use. Governments have spent millions of dollars assessing the presumed

harmfulness of this drug, while the public has seemed to grow steadily less interested in, even skeptical of, government findings.

In general, however, where a form of deviant behaviour is perceived to be more harmful, it will be seen as more serious. The key word here is *perceived*: the point is not so much what harm these deviant acts do, but what harm they are perceived to do. As Shakespeare observed, "There is nothing either good or bad, but thinking makes it so."

A third characteristic of deviance is the *degree of agreement* among the public about whether an act should be considered deviant. Across nations and generations there is a high degree of consensus that some forms of behaviour are indeed seriously deviant (for example, armed robbery, aggravated sexual assault, and premeditated homicide). Yet there are also many forms of behaviour about which there is considerable disagreement. Included among these debated subjects, called **conflict crimes** because of conflicting opinions regarding them, are most types of drug use and many forms of sexual activity. Finally, there are those forms of behaviour about which most of us are disinterested. Among the more intriguing subjects of our apathy are many fads and fashions. As bizarre as these styles can become, most of us have no strong interest in calling them deviant.

We have briefly considered three related characteristics of deviance: the severity of the societal response to the deviant activity, the perceived harmfulness of the behaviour, and the degree of agreement among the public that the acts involved should be considered deviant. Taken together, these characteristics provide a measure of how seriously a particular form of deviance is taken. In other words, the most serious forms provoke a severe societal response, are perceived as extremely harmful, and are defined as deviant with a high degree of consensus. Less serious forms of deviance result in more moderate or indeterminate forms of societal response, are perceived as less harmful, and may be the subjects of uncertainty or conflict. Finally, the least serious forms of deviance call forth only mild responses, are perceived as relatively harmless, and are subjects of widespread apathy.

## Consensus Crimes

With these points in mind, we can now attach names to the kinds of deviance we have begun to identify. The first of these categories comprises the **consensus crimes** (Toby 1974); these acts are defined by law as crimes. The Criminal Code of Canada specifies a large number of criminal acts, yet only a few are widely regarded as extremely harmful, are severely punished, and are consensually identified as deviant. One such act is premeditated murder. In many nations and for many centuries, laws of a similar form have designated this type of behaviour as a crime. The consistency of these statutes has led some legal philosophers to call such acts *mala en se*, or "bad in themselves." A quick examination of our criminal codes, however, will convince most readers that the number of *mala en se* criminal and deviant acts is few. His-

tory and anthropology demonstrate that most conceptions of crime and deviance are subject to change. What is called criminal in one time or place is frequently seen quite differently in another. This being so, many people find the notion of inherent and universal evil somewhat dubious. This changeable character of crime and deviance is a salient feature of the kind of deviance we consider next.

## Conflict Crimes

Our second category of deviance is what we earlier defined as conflict crimes. Although people convicted of conflict crimes may receive punitive treatment from the courts, acts of this type are usually regarded as only marginally harmful and, at that, are typically subjects of conflict and debate. Legal philosophers refer to such crimes as *mala prohibita*, or "wrong by definition." It is significant that many conflict crimes were once consensus crimes, and that some of what were once conflict crimes have now achieved considerable consensus. Into the former category fall many of the victimless crimes, including prostitution, drug use, and many sexual acts between consenting adults. For example, during much of this century marijuana use was regarded as a serious form of narcotics abuse requiring strict legal control (Bonnie and Whitebread 1974). Today marijuana use is subject to much milder penalties. Significantly, however, this change did not begin until marijuana use became a part of middle- and upper-class youth cultures in the 1960s. What was once a consensus crime is now a subject of some conflict.

In contrast to marijuana use, sexual assault seems to be a crime whose roots involved conflict; its legal definition has only recently become a focus of debate. It can be argued that historically, rape laws emerged out of men's efforts to protect women — not because these women were women, but because these women were "theirs." From this viewpoint, rape consisted of one man taking the property of another. Consistent with this view is the fact that, prior to 1982, a husband could not be charged with raping his wife. Indeed, Lorenne Clark (1976) demonstrated that rape usually resulted in sentences quite similar to those handed down for robbery (a crime that involves taking property). For most of our Canadian experience these facts have been the subject of apparent consensus, and only recently has the conflict underlying this law become a topic of public concern.

## Social Deviations

Our next category consists of **social deviations**. Many of the behaviours included in this category are not criminal but are nonetheless subject to official control. Some are dealt with under statutes defining mental illness, others under juvenile delinquency legislation, and still others under numerous civil laws that attempt to control various forms of business and professional activities (for example, those laws dealing with securities and stock transactions). A common feature of these official measures is the vagueness with which they define their subject. In the case of business and professional activities, this vagueness may reflect an attempt to protect the powerful from public harassment; in the cases of juvenile delinquency and mental illness, however, it may be that we simply do not have clear notions of what these official categories include.

The concern in all of this is that while business and professional people may escape official control of their social deviations under such statutes, people with fewer resources may not. Furthermore, those defined as delinquent or mentally ill may be designated as such on the basis of their perceived potential for harm, rather than on the basis of actual harm done. Finally, their assigned treatments may be of indeterminate duration, rather than for a fixed term of punishment. All of this comes from the announced desire to help rather than penalize people who commit social deviations. But such help is all too often perceived by those on the receiving end as punishment and usually constitutes some form of offical control. The troubled history of official and unofficial responses to homosexuality is an unhappy example of the latter point.

## Social Diversions

Our last deviance category is made up of **social diversions**. All of us personally or vicariously experience these. They are the lifestyle variations that help make our lives more interesting and at times exciting: the fads and fashions of speech, appearance, and play. Constant among these di-

**Social diversion is a form of deviance that is relatively harmless.**

versions is the pursuit of pleasure, though there is, of course, extreme variation in what is regarded as pleasurable. Joggers brave exhaustion and sub-zero temperatures in search of the "runner's high," while surfers circle the world and endure the ravages of weather and water in their quest for "the perfect wave." As odd as some of these activities seem to many of us, however, we typically react with no more than a mixture of amusement and apathy to the time, energy, and resources expended by their enthusiasts. Other societies would regard our tolerance of the diverse and the bizarre as indulgent, and indeed it is. We do not consider the behaviours involved good or bad, but simply different, diverse, and, to their participants, enjoyable.

So far we have given an extended definition of deviance, seeking to answer the question "What is it?" Let us now turn our attention to the question "Where do we find it?"

Using several alternative approaches (considered later in the chapter) to measuring crime and deviance, sociologists have attempted to collect valid and reliable information about how these behaviours are socially distributed. One way of beginning this task involves comparing the official statistics of crime and deviance with those gathered through one or more alternative methods. Where the findings generated by alternative methods agree with the official measures, we can have some confidence in our conclusions. Where disagreement occurs, we can examine possible explanations for the disparities. Often these alternative explanations can tell us a good deal, not only about the social distribution of deviance, but also about the official agencies that control deviance. In the next section, we use the strategy just described to consider the distribution of crime and deviant behaviour by gender and social class in Canada.

# Social Distribution of Crime and Deviance

Are criminal and noncriminal forms of deviant behaviour randomly distributed in Canadian society? Or do these behaviours occur at different rates among identifiable social groups in our society? Accurately identifying the social distribution of crime and deviance is an important first step toward explaining these behaviours.

## Gender Distribution of Crime and Deviance

It is clear that criminal and noncriminal forms of deviant behaviour are not distributed randomly by gender. Regardless of the mode of measurement, men are significantly more likely to be alcoholic (Cahalan 1970), addicted to illegal drugs (Terry and Pellens 1970), and involved in the more serious forms of crime (Hindelang 1979). This does not mean, however, that men in all ways or at all times are necessarily more deviant than women. We know that women tend to take more legally prescribed psychoactive drugs than men (Manheimer et al. 1969) and that they report higher rates of mental illness (Gove and Tudor 1973). It is in criminal forms of deviance that males clearly exceed females. But the relationship between gender and crime is not a simple one. The disparity between the sexes fluctuates with the type of crime, the time, and the social setting. For example, while it has been estimated from official statistics in North America that males exceed females in crimes against the person on the order of more than eight to one, males exceed females on the order of four to one for crimes against property (Nettler 1973).

The most fascinating aspect of this deviance-by-gender situation is the possibility that it may be changing, along with attitudes toward gender roles. It has been argued that women are increasing their involvement in all types of offences, and more specifically that a new breed of violent, aggressive, female offenders may be arising (Adler 1975). On the other hand, it has also been suggested that the new female criminal is more a social myth than an empirical reality (Steffensmeir 1978). Both these arguments could have some validity. For example, it may be that the new female criminal is to be found in some areas of crime more frequently than in others. In other words, some convincing evidence suggests that certain areas of crime may be changing faster than others.

For example, a recent review (Smith and Visher 1980) of official data and **self-report surveys** (anonymously answered by adolescents and adults) on crime and deviance indicates that behavioural differences between the sexes are diminishing (see also Hagan, Gillis, and Simpson 1985, 1987). Interestingly, the gap is narrowing faster for minor deviant acts than for more serious crimes. Equal gender representation in the area of serious criminal behaviour has not yet occurred. Similarly, while the relationship of gender to deviance is declining for both youths and adults, the data indicate that this trend is stronger for youths. This latter finding is particularly interesting, because it is consistent with the expected effects of changing gender roles. That is, it seems likely that current shifts in gender roles would have a greater effect on the behaviour of younger women, and this is exactly what the data indicate. These patterns of change deserve to be closely watched in the future.

## Class Distribution of Crime and Deviance

The relationship between deviant behaviour and class position is a matter of considerable controversy. At the centre of the debate sits a pair of assumptions that are often viewed as incompatible. The first holds that being a member of the lower class implies a denial of opportunities and a harshness of circumstances to which deviant behaviour is a predictable response. The second maintains that the prejudice and discrimination of official control agents and agencies result in members of the lower class being disproportionately targeted for control. These contrasting assumptions are not necessarily mutually exclusive; the argument will be made in this and in a later section that both assumptions are correct.

The official statistics of crime and delinquency make one point rather clearly: persons *prosecuted* for criminal and delinquent offences are disproportionately members of the lower class (Braithwaite 1981). The issue is whether this official sampling of criminals and delinquents is representative of the population from which it is drawn, or whether it is biased by, for example, selection from one class more than another. The answer to this question seems to depend in part on the type of deviance we are considering.

Self-report data have often been compared with official records to examine the class distribution of crime and delinquency. The most serious forms of crime and delinquency are seldom encountered in self-reports, however, and these comparisons therefore tend to concentrate on the less serious and most frequent types of deviant activity (Hindelang et al. 1981). Self-report studies show a wide range of results. In some, the relationship between self-reported deviant behaviours and class position is weak (Braithwaite 1981); in some, inconsistent (Tittle, Villemez, and Smith 1978); and in some — depending on the measure of class — even positive (Hagan, Gillis, and Simpson 1985). Braithwaite (1981) summarizes 47 of these studies, 25 of which found some evidence that lower-class people more often report deviant behaviours, and 22 of which found no relationship at all between reports of deviant behaviour and class position. Official statistics have traditionally shown such a relationship. Comparisons with self-report data imply that some class bias exists in the official reports of the most frequent forms of crime and delinquency. One recent Canadian study (Hagan, Gillis, and Chan 1978) reinforces this conclusion, noting that the police in particular tend to believe that the densely populated lower-class areas of the city most need police patrols. Because more telephone complaints come from these areas, for example, the police may develop an exaggerated idea of such areas' relative incidence of crime and delinquency. Therefore more police resources are allocated to patrol these areas, resulting in higher rates of crime and delinquency being recorded, since more police are looking for and finding deviance.

Recently more serious forms of crime have been studied by surveying victims. In the United States, victimization surveys have been used nationwide to examine racial involvement in personal crimes of the common law (crimes against persons that have long been considered serious). These studies reveal a substantially greater involvement of blacks in the crimes of rape, robbery, and assault (Hindelang 1978). There is also some evidence of police bias in this research, but evidence of bias is far outweighed by evidence of real behavioural differences. Insofar as race and class are strongly related in the United States, this American research suggests that there is a relationship between social class and criminal behaviour for serious forms of crime.

It bears repeating, however, that our conception of what constitutes a serious form of deviance is subject to change. We saw this earlier with regard to marijuana use. Within one generation, marijuana use has changed, in the assessment of many, from allegedly causing "reefer madness" to symbolizing radical-chic status. Self-report surveys have sometimes reflected this change, documenting higher levels of marijuana use in the middle and upper classes than in the lower (Suchman 1968; Barter, Mizner, and Werme 1970). More recently, there have been significant class changes in the use of cocaine. Changes in the use of hard drugs like heroin, however, have been less substantial (Berg 1970). Self-report and official statistics are in agreement that these hard drugs have been and continue to be used more extensively in the lower class, and their use is still generally regarded as a serious matter.

Official and alternative types of statistics have also been compared in the areas of alcohol abuse and mental illness. Official statistics in these areas, as in others, show a higher representation in the lower class. Self-report studies parallel these findings. For example, household surveys have contained the following question: "Have you or any member of your household ever had difficulty because of too much drinking?" Many of these studies report both higher incidence and higher

**Secondary deviance follows the societal response to behaviour and imposes a deviant role on the individual.**

prevalence of such problems in the lower class than in other classes (for example, Bailey, Haberman, and Alksne 1965; Cahalan 1970). Similar conclusions are found in the area of mental illness. Dohrenwend and Dohrenwend (1969) report that "the highest overall rates of psychiatric disorder have been found in the lowest social class in 28 out of 33 studies that report data according to indicators of social class."

We can thus draw some conclusions. Serious crimes, hard-drug use, alcohol abuse, and mental illness are more prevalent in the lower class, while less serious and more common forms of crime, delinquency, and drug use are more evenly distributed across the social classes. It is in the latter areas that official statistics appear most dubious, because members of the lower class are here disproportionately selected for official attention. To some extent, doubt or confidence in a given de-

viance statistic depends on how such deviance is measured. Let us turn then from our consideration of the social distribution of deviance to a consideration of how to measure it.

## Measuring Crime and Deviance

Because many forms of deviance are controlled officially, they are also counted officially. These enumerations constitute the official statistics of deviance found in the reports of police, of criminal and civil courts, of correctional institutions, of mental-health centres, and of various agencies dealing with alcohol and drug abuse. A myriad of statistics exist, therefore; if these were as credible as they are accessible, the sociologist's task would be an easier one. Unfortunately, the same biases that can affect the legislation of crime and deviance (considered below) can also affect the counting of criminal and deviant behaviours. That is, organizations involved in controlling these behaviours may not be strictly impartial, and may instead follow their own interests in the types and amounts of crime and deviance they count.

Giffen (1966), for example, suggests that one latent function of processing skid-road alcoholics in a "revolving-door" fashion is that it makes the criminal justice system look both busy and efficient: and the budgets of control agencies often depend heavily on how busy and efficient these agencies appear. Thus, some statistics produced by official control agencies may tell us more about the agencies themselves than about the persons and events counted. The challenge for scholars, then, is to make sociological sense of the statistics official agencies collect.

Analysts of deviance have responded to this challenge by developing alternatives to the use of official records, such as collecting data from non-official agencies: insurance companies dealing with theft; hospitals, private physicians, and public-health agencies, whose records reflect much alcoholism and drug abuse; and business accounting and consulting firms, which encounter much internal theft and fraud.

A second alternative is to collect and record first-person accounts generated through anonymous self-report surveys of adolescents and adults and personal face-to-face interviews with subjects in their natural settings. The self-report approach, as seen earlier, has been used to study crime, delinquency, alcohol and drug abuse, and the symptoms of mental illness. Personal interviews are most often used to study *career deviants*, those individuals who persist in deviant lifestyles.

A third approach involves surveys of the victims of crime. Done by telephone or in a door-to-door census-like fashion, victimization surveys provide a unique measure of deviant behaviour that includes crimes committed against people and property.

A fourth and final approach involves actual observations of deviant behaviour (in which the observer may or may not be a participant). Consensus crimes such as homicide do not, of course, readily lend themselves to being studied in this way. So this method has been used primarily in the study of conflict crimes and other controversial forms of deviance, like homosexuality and marijuana use.

These, then, are four alternatives to reliance on official statistics, which may reflect official control and official preoccupation with certain kinds of deviance.

But why are some forms of difference and diversity subject to official control while others are not? Scholars have been particularly concerned that this discrepancy reflects part of the activities of certain self-interested groups and individuals, who may lobby for the official control of some types of deviant behaviour. Let us therefore turn our attention to the issue of crime and deviance legislation.

## Legislation Against Crime and Deviance

*Moral entrepreneurs* is the term Becker (1963) uses for those individuals most active in striving for official control of deviance. These are the people whose initiative and enterprise are essential in getting the legal rules passed that are necessary to "do something" about a particular type of deviant behaviour. Often these individuals seem to be undertaking a moral crusade — they perceive some activity as an evil in need of legal reform, and they pursue this task with missionary zeal (Gusfield 1963). Moral entrepreneurs and crusaders assume that enforcement of the wished-for legal rules will improve the lives of those who are ruled. We will see that this is often a very dubious assumption as we consider two moral crusades that brought legal control of two different types of deviant behaviour in North America.

### Narcotics and Alcohol

The moral entrepreneur most responsible for the passage of Canada's first narcotics laws was none other than Mackenzie King (Cook 1969). King became aware of Canada's "opium problem" when he discovered — by accident — that opium could be bought over the counter in Vancouver. As Deputy Minister of Labour, he had been sent to Vancouver to supervise the payment of compensation to Chinese and Japanese businessmen who had suffered losses during the anti-Asiatic riots of 1907. Two of the compensation claims came from Chinese opium-manufacturing merchants. Shocked by his inadvertent discovery, King prepared a report to the government — and his report led in a short time to the Opium Act of 1908.

Along the route to becoming prime minister, King made a modest career out of this particular moral crusade. He was selected as part of a five-person British delegation to attend the Shanghai Opium Commission in 1909. In 1911, as a member of Laurier's Cabinet, he introduced a more stringent Opium and Drug Act. By 1920, calls for still more stringent legislation were coming in the form of sensational articles in such periodicals as *Maclean's* magazine. Several of these articles were written by Emily Murphy (1920, 1922), an Edmonton juvenile court judge who ultimately went on to expand her views in a book titled *The Black Candle*. The background of these efforts tells us much about the way in which moral crusades can be generated.

During the period leading up to our first narcotics legislation, Canadian doctors were probably just as responsible for addiction as the Chinese opium merchants. Medications containing opiates were indiscriminately prescribed by physicians and used by patients of all classes. In fact, syrups containing opiates, particularly paregoric, were frequently used by mothers for their infants. So it was not only fear of the drug itself, but also hostility toward Asian immigrants, that stimulated much of the narcotics legislation. Many Asian labourers had immigrated to this country, arousing antagonism among whites, who probably feared that their own jobs would be threatened. Much of the parliamentary debate that had preceded passing the first Opium Act had involved a proposed trade treaty with Japan that was to allow Japanese immigration.

A dramatic example of how the logically separate and distinct issues of opium and Asian immigration could be tied together occurred in the 1922 narcotics debates, when the following remarks by the secretary of the Anti-Asiatic Exclusion League were read:

*Here we have a disease, one of many directly traceable to the Asiatic. Do away with the Asiatic and you have more than saved the souls and bodies of thousands of young men and women who are yearly being sent to a living hell and to the grave through their presence in Canada.* (House of Commons Debate 1922; quoted in Cook 1969)

Others, like Murphy (1922), spoke of "Chinese peddlers" bringing about the "downfall of the white race."

The point here is that hostile attitudes toward a minority group were an important part of the crusading efforts that resulted in Canada's first narcotics legislation.

The moral entrepreneur best known for his role in the passage of American narcotics legislation is H.J. Anslinger, the first Director of the U.S. Federal Bureau of Narcotics (Lindesmith 1947; Becker 1963). Anslinger used his office to arouse American public and congressional concern about what he regarded as a growing "drug menace." For example, in 1937 Anslinger published a widely circulated magazine article, "Marihuana: Assassin of Youth." As in Canada, much of this attention combined hostile attitudes toward minority groups with discussions of the drug problem (Musto 1973). In media accounts, for example, the Chinese were associated with opium (Reasons 1974), southern blacks with cocaine (Musto 1973), and Mexicans with marijuana (Bonnie and Whitebread 1974). The fear was fostered that drug use by minorities posed a particularly dangerous threat to American society.

It made little difference that in Canada and the United States, Duster (1970) reports, most narcotics addicts were upper and middle class well into the second decade of this century. Not until after the passage of America's first narcotics legislation, the Harrison Act of 1914, did this picture seem to change. By 1920, medical journals were referring to the "overwhelming majority [of drug addicts who came] from the 'unrespectable parts' of society" (Duster 1970). The technique used is called guilt by association; by persuading the public to associate narcotics use with disenfranchised minorities, moral entrepreneurs were able to lay

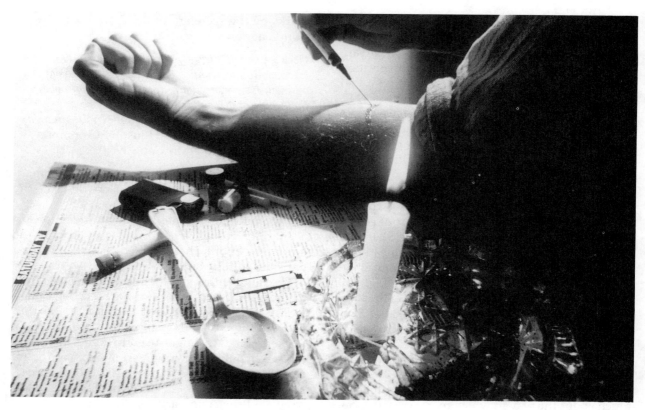

**The incidence of deviance is difficult to measure when it is hidden.**

a foundation for legislation prohibiting the nonmedical use of drugs.

The prohibition against alcohol offers an interesting comparison with drug legislation because, while the latter endured, the former failed. Alcohol prohibition in the United States was a result of the well-organized lobbying activities of the Women's Christian Temperance Union and the Anti-Saloon League. These efforts constituted a moral crusade reflecting an apparent effort to protect an established way of life that was perceived as threatened during the early part of this century by the immigration of new Americans into the nation's cities. Gusfield (1963) argues that alcohol prohibition was a response to the fears of American-born, middle-class Protestants that their established positions in American life, and this style of life itself, were endangered by the alcohol use they saw as increasing among the urban immi-

grants around them. As with drugs, a concerted effort was made to link alcohol with poverty, minorities, crime, and insanity.

Alcohol prohibition was only partly successful, however. Early resistance to it emerged in the ranks of organized labour. When alcohol prohibition attempted to criminalize the mass of the poor, it ran into the opposition of unions and urban political machines.

Timberlake (1963) observes that, although wage earners were unable to thwart the enactment of temperance legislation, they were strong enough to ensure its ultimate failure. He notes that many workers opposed prohibition because it smacked of paternalism and class exploitation. To them it was a hypocritical and insulting attempt to control their personal lives in order to exact greater profits for their employers. The employers themselves had no intention of abstaining. Indeed, it is es-

# Cannabis Criminals

*The law is an imperfect social invention. Indeed, the law produces many social embarrassments that most of us successfully ignore. One of these embarrassments is the role our laws have played in creating what Patricia Erickson (1980) calls "cannabis criminals." Erickson has documented the details of this embarrassment in terms it may no longer be possible to ignore.*

Did you know that by 1976 more than 100 000 Canadians had been designated "criminal" for simple possession of cannabis? While many of us assume that our attitudes, and therefore our laws, dealing with cannabis are changing, to date changes have not occurred. Erickson reports that the great majority of "cannabis criminals" receive absolute or conditional discharges or fines. Many citizens may wonder why we bother, and Erickson's findings should raise this feeling from curiosity to dismay.

Adopting the sensible standard of the Le Dain Commission, Erickson examines how the costs of criminalizing cannabis offenders compare with the presumed beneficial deterrent effects of cannabis prohibition. To this end, 95 Canadians sentenced for possession of cannabis were interviewed and their responses analyzed.

The implication of Erickson's findings is a stark indictment of the logic of our cannabis laws. What she finds is that being criminalized for cannabis possession has negative consequences for other aspects of the individuals' lives, but no demonstrable deterrent effect in the individuals' cannabis use. Why, then, have these laws been enforced with such apparent enthusiasm?

Erickson's argument here is provocative, providing a more general and important insight into how good legislative intentions can produce bad law enforcement. The problem is that in Canada special police powers of search, the widespread availability of cannabis to users, rewards to police for generating large numbers of arrests, and few restrictions on the admissibility of illegally obtained evidence in court all seem to encourage an aggressive seeking out of cannabis offenders. Unfortunately, the burden of the evidence reported in Erickson's research is that more problems have been created than solved by this type of law and its enforcement.

**Source:**

John Hagan, from Preface to Patricia Erickson, *Cannabis Criminals: The Social Effects of Punishment of Drug Users* (Toronto: ARF Books, 1980).

---

timated that as much as 81 percent of the American Federation of Labor was "wet," a figure consistent with Samuel Gompers's claim that the great majority of AFL members opposed prohibition. In sum, alcohol prohibition seems to have failed because it attempted to define as criminal what too large and well-organized a part of the poor, as well as the rich, were doing. By contrast, narcotics legislation focused more narrowly, and more successfully, on minorities among the poor — who, as such, could be more easily defined as criminal without arousing organized opposition.

## Juvenile Delinquency

The work of moral entrepreneurs is often associated with the growth of professional organizations that have their own bureaucratic interests to develop and protect. One example of this is the development of juvenile delinquency legislation and a resulting juvenile court bureaucracy staffed in large part by probation officers trained in the emerging profession of social work. The efforts that led to the separate designation of juvenile delinquency and to the development of the juvenile courts were often called "child-saving" (Platt 1969). Parker (1976) points out that, contrary to common-sense understanding,

*the history of child-saving in the twentieth century is not the history of improving the general conditions of child-life (because most of the battles have been won), or the history of juvenile institutions (which changed very little after the initial efforts of the founders of the House of Refuge and their imitators). It is not even the history of the juvenile court itself, because it provided, as legal institutions tend to do, a purely symbolic quality to child work. The real history of the period is a history of probation.*

Probation was a new idea at the beginning of this century. Its attraction was the prospect of keeping young offenders in their homes and out of institutions. The emphasis on probation within the juvenile court movement reflected a concern for the family that pervaded the early part of this century. Known as the Progressive Era, this was a time of extensive social, political, and legal reform work. From this ferment emerged a system of social control that was intended to be less formal and less coercive than institutionalization. The use of probation actually extended the range of control efforts, however, and this new control was imposed largely on the families of the urban poor, often outside the courts (thus limiting or eliminating the possibility of appealing decisions through the legal system). The results of these activities can be seen in Canada and the United States.

J.J. Kelso, for instance, was a moral entrepreneur who guided the passage of Canada's first juvenile court legislation. This legislation allowed the development of an entire bureaucracy, staffed primarily by probation officers (Hagan and Leon 1977).

Kelso began as a crusading Toronto newspaper reporter and went on to serve as Ontario's first Superintendent of Neglected and Dependent Children. Possibly the most important step toward juvenile delinquency legislation in Canada came in 1893, when Kelso and others convinced the Ontario legislature to enact a comprehensive Children's Protection Act that gave explicit recognition and authority to the Children's Aid Society (CAS). It became the duty of the court to notify the CAS before initiating proceedings against a boy under 12 or a girl under 13; a CAS officer would then investigate the charges, enquire into the child's family environment, and report back to the court. These procedures were extended the following year to federal law, and a federal Juvenile Delinquents Act was passed in 1908, incorporating and expanding upon the earlier procedures for juveniles. Kelso was prominent in all these efforts; he promoted his beliefs frequently and well.

It is widely believed that the juvenile court movement just described represented an effort to get children out of criminal courts and prisons. Although this effort does seem to have been one of the purposes of juvenile delinquency legislation, it was in fact less than successful. Juveniles continued to be sent to institutions. The most dramatic consequence of the new legislation was a rapid expansion of the number of probation officers and of the number of juveniles with whom they dealt. In this sense, control over juvenile behaviour was actually increased by the new legislation. Moreover, in 1924 the federal Juvenile Delinquents Act was amended to include control over adolescents "guilty of sexual immorality or any similar form of vice" — effectively making most of the fun of adolescence illegal! The suspicion inevitably arises that one purpose behind much of this moral-reform effort was to increase the "need" for probation officers and spur the growth of this bureaucracy.

A diminished reliance on institutions combined with increased control (particularly through probation personnel) is apparent in other fragmentary data. The prominent reformer Frederic Almy (1902) wrote from Buffalo that "the . . . Juvenile Court has not quite completed its first year, and no definite records have been compiled, but two results are already notable — the decrease in the number of commitments to the truant school and to reformatories, and the increase in the number of children arrested." Between 1913 and 1914 in Chicago, the number of delinquents referred to court rose from 1956 to 2916, an increase of nearly 50 percent in the delinquency rate for Cook County. Haller (1970) notes that the reason for this was that 23 additional probation officers were hired in 1914. Similar points have been made by Schlossman (1977) regarding the development of the juvenile court in Milwaukee.

A general picture begins to emerge from these reports. The Progressive Era was characterized by a widely shared view that rehabilitation should be family-centred. Advocates of legal reform therefore focused on the offender's home as the locus of treatment and on the probation officer as the key remedial agent. Among the most vigourous proponents were members of women's groups and those who eventually became the "professionals" charged with responsibility for probation. Again, one suspects that a purpose of much of this moral-reform effort was to increase both the need for probation officers and the growth of this bureaucracy.

To say that the legislation of deviance is influenced by individual and group interests, however, is not to say that legislation of this kind is unnecessary. But not all such laws can be taken at face value: individual and group interests can determine the form various laws take. The line that separates those forms of deviance that are socially controlled from those that are controlled officially and by legislation is a fine one.

## Theories of Crime and Deviance

We have discussed what deviance is, where it is found, how it is measured, and how and why legislation is introduced against it. Our chief remaining question is, How do we account for the actual phenomenon? How do we explain deviance? We will now turn to theoretical explanations of the class differences in criminal and deviant behaviour discussed above. We will examine these explanations according to the three basic sociological perspectives: structural-functionalism, symbolic interaction, and conflict.

### Structural Functionalism and Deviance

Structural-functional theories regard deviant behaviour as the consequence of a strain or breakdown in the social processes that produce conformity. The focus here is on agents (such as the family and school) that socialize individuals to conform to the values of the existing society, and on the ways in which this process can go wrong. This approach assumes wide agreement, or consensus, about what the prime values of our society are. Structural-functional theories try to explain why some individuals, through their deviant behaviour, come to challenge this consensus. In other words, why do individuals violate the conforming values that nearly all of us are assumed to hold in common?

**Anomie.** The roots of functional theory can be found in Durkheim's notion of *anomie* (1956, originally published 1897). To Durkheim, this term meant an absence of social regulation, or normlessness. Merton (1938, 1957) revived the concept to describe the consequences of a faulty relationship between goals and the legitimate means of attaining them. Merton emphasized two features of social and cultural structure: culturally defined goals (such as monetary success) and the acceptable means (such as education) to their achievement. The problem for Merton was that in our society success goals are widely shared, while the means of attaining them are not.

Merton's theory is intended to explain not only why people deviate but also why some types of people deviate more than others. Members of the lower class are most affected by the disparity between shared success goals and the scarcity of means to attain them. The result of this structural inconsistency is a high rate of deviant behaviour.

Merton outlined a number of ways individuals can adapt when faced with inadequate means of attaining their goals. These methods of adapting include *innovation*, comprising various forms of economically motivated crimes; *ritualism*, involving various forms of overconformity; *retreatism*, consisting of escapist activities such as drug abuse; and *rebellion*, involving revolutionary efforts to change the structural system of goals and means. The common feature of these separate patterns is that they all represent adaptations to failure, a failure to achieve goals through legitimate means.

**Delinquent Subculture.** The adaptations to failure described above occur for groups as well as for individuals. One form of social adaptation is represented by the **delinquent subculture**. Cohen (1955) suggests that members of the lower class, and potential members of a delinquent subculture, first experience a failure to achieve when they enter school. When assessed against a "middle-class measuring rod," working-class children are often found lacking. The result for these students is a growing sense of "status frustration." Working-class children are simply not prepared by their earliest experiences to satisfy middle-class expectations. The delinquent subculture therefore emerges as an alternative set of criteria, or values, that working-class adolescents *can* meet.

Subcultural values represent a complete repudiation of middle-class standards; the delinquent subculture expresses contempt for a middle-class lifestyle by making its opposite a criterion of prestige, as if to say, "We're everything you say we are and worse." The result, according to Cohen (1955), is a delinquent subculture that is "nonutilitarian, malicious, and negativistic" — an inversion of middle-class values. Yet this is only one possible type of subcultural reaction to the frustration of failure. The theories we consider next suggest three other potential responses to the denial of opportunity.

**Differential Opportunity.** When legitimate opportunities are denied, illegitimate opportunities may be the only game in town. Cloward and Ohlin (1960) argue that to understand the different forms that criminal and delinquent behaviour can take, we must consider the different types of illegitimate opportunities available to those who are seeking a way out of the working class. Different types of community settings produce different subcultural responses. Cloward and Ohlin suggest that three types of responses predominate: a stable criminal subculture, a conflict subculture, and a retreatist subculture.

The **stable criminal subculture** is, as its name suggests, the best organized of the three. According to Cloward and Ohlin, this subculture can emerge only when there is some co-ordination between those in legitimate and in illegitimate roles — for example, between politicians or police and the underworld. One pictures the old-style political machine, with protection provided for preferred types of illegal enterprise. Only in such circumstances can stable patterns be established allowing opportunities for advancement from lower to upper levels of the criminal underworld. The legitimate and illegitimate opportunity structures are linked in this way, the streets become safe *for* crime, and reliable upward-mobility routes can emerge for criminals. Interesting relationships are observable among opportunity structures, crime, and ethnicity.

Violence and conflict, on the other hand, are disruptive of both legitimate and illegitimate enterprise. When both types of enterprise co-exist, violence is restrained. In the "disorganized slum," however, where these spheres of activity are not linked, violence can reign uncontrolled. Cloward and Ohlin see these types of communities as producing a **conflict subculture**. A result of this disorganization is the prevalence of street gangs and

## Crime and Ethnicity: An Example of the Structural-Functional Approach

Some of the most interesting applications of structural-functional theories of deviance have dealt with the topic of crime and ethnicity. For example, Ianni (1972) has noted that over several generations a series of different ethnic groups has been associated with organized crime in North America. Ianni proposes the concept of *ethnic succession* to explain the changing ethnic participation in organized crime activities. Ethnic succession refers to the process by which successive ethnic groups have come to North America in search of a better life, but without the ready means to achieve it — education and job skills. They responded to this disparity through involvement in organized crime. Ianni notes that in the United States, first the Irish, then the Jews, later the Italians, and most recently black Americans have been prominently involved in organized

crime. As they gained access to legitimate means of attaining success, and consequently moved up the social ladder, their involvement in organized crime declined.

Ianni illustrates his argument most convincingly in a discussion of Italian involvement in organized crime. This discussion begins with a historical analysis of organized crime in Italy. Here Ianni notes that the roots of organized crime can be found in a collection of secret societies, of which the Mafia is only one. Furthermore, the word Mafia has been used in two ways: first as an adjective to describe the type of man who is known and respected because he gets things done, and second as a noun to refer to criminal organizations and societies. These meanings are often confused and may be a source of the exaggerated claims made for the existence of a single, all-powerful

criminal organization. In contrast to this image of unity and omnipotence, Ianni notes that the Mafia began as a collection of local organizations in Sicily in the early nineteenth century. The emergence of the Mafia coincided with the breakdown of feudalism. In effect, the Mafia served as a middleman, paying landowners who had fled to the cities lump-sum rents for their rural estates, and then re-renting them to peasants. In other words, the Mafia filled a vacuum between the social strata in Sicily and became a source of order within the Sicilian social system. The Mafia continued to be prominent until Mussolini. Thus, the Mafia was not a single organization that could have emigrated en masse to North America.

Nonetheless, the cultural attitudes that surrounded the term "Mafia" as an adjective did begin to have an impact in North America in the 1920s,

violent crime, making the streets unsafe for profitable crime.

The final type of subculture posited by Cloward and Ohlin, the **retreatist subculture**, comprises those individuals who fail in their efforts in both the legitimate and illegitimate opportunity structures. These "double failures" are destined for drug abuse and other forms of escape.

So far we have focused on a strain between goals and means as the source of deviant behaviour in structural-functional theory. It is this strain that theoretically produces the subcultural responses we have discussed. Before moving on, however, we should note a final form of structural-functional theory that also takes into account those individuals who are relatively unimpressed by the goals, values, or commitments that our society emphasizes.

**Control and Commitment.** To have goals and means is to be committed to conformity and to be controlled by this commitment; to have neither

goals nor means, however, is to be uncommitted and thus *un*controlled. Hirschi (1969) has argued that the absence of control is really all that is required to explain much deviant behaviour. There are other types of controls (besides *commitment to conformity*) that may also operate: *involvement*, in school and other activities; *attachments*, to friends and family; and *belief*, in various types of values and principles. Hirschi argues that deviant behaviour is inversely related to the presence of these controls. Alternatively, as these controls accumulate, so too does conformity. Again, Hirschi's point is that no special strain between goals and means is necessarily required to produce deviant behaviour; all that is required is the elimination of constraint.

In all the approaches we have considered, values or beliefs play some role in the causation of deviance. The presence of success goals or values without means to obtain them can produce deviant behaviour, as can the absence of these goals or values in the first place. It is an emphasis on these values, and the role of the school and family

---

notably because of Prohibition, one result of which was to create an illegal industry well suited to a large new immigrant group whose other opportunities were minimal. Many Italians, who had traditionally produced their own wine at home, began turning their household wineries into home stills, and central organizations emerged to collect this new source of illegal profits. Later, with the coming of the Depression and the repeal of Prohibition, it became necessary for these organizations, or crime families, to enter new fields of illegitimate enterprises, particularly drugs and prostitution. By this time, however, second-generation members of organized crime families were taking over, and the Italian-American involvement in organized crime was becoming more North American than Italian in character. Ianni notes that today the process of ethnic succession is working toward its logical conclusion, with declining involvement of Italians in organized crime.

Clairmont (1974) has given a parallel structural-functional explanation of the development of a "deviance service centre" in the Nova Scotian community of Africville. Until its displacement for industrial and harbour development in the mid-1960s, Africville was a predominantly black community located close to Halifax. This community was settled by descendants of blacks who fled from slavery in the United States during the War of 1812. Few economic opportunities were available to the residents of Africville. At the same time, the community was given the "functional autonomy" by the City of Halifax to develop in almost any way it wished: "that is, not sharing fairly in society's wealth, they . . . [were] allowed by authorities a range of behavior that would not be countenanced elsewhere" (Clairmont 1974). A result was that during World War I a growing bootlegging trade developed, and eventually a full-scale deviance service centre consisting of several vice industries emerged.

Clairmont (1974) summarizes the situation in this way: "Minority group members, if oppressed and discriminated against, often find a mode of adjusting to their situation by performing less desirable and sometimes illegitimate services for the majority group." Vice industries have served this function for many generations. Lacking the legalization of all forms of vice, or the availability of economic opportunities to all who seek them, organized crime is likely to continue to serve this function for some time to come.

**Sources:**

Francis A. Ianni, *A Family Business: Kinship and Social Control in Organized Crime* (New York: Sage, 1972); Donald Clairmont, "The development of a deviance service centre," in *Decency and Deviance*, Jack Haas and Bill Shaffir, eds. (Toronto: McClelland and Stewart, 1974).

in transmitting them, that ties the structural-functional theories together.

## Symbolic Interaction and Deviance

The symbolic-interaction theories of deviance are concerned less with values than with the way that social meanings and definitions help produce deviant behaviour. The assumption, of course, is that these meanings and definitions, these symbolic variations, affect behaviour. Early versions of symbolic-interaction theory focused on how these meanings and definitions were *acquired* by individuals *from* others; more recently, theorists

have focused on the role of official control agencies in *imposing* these meanings and definitions *on* individuals. The significance of this difference in focus will become apparent as we consider the development of the symbolic-interaction approach.

**Differential Association.** One of the fathers of North American criminology was Edwin Sutherland (1924). Sutherland anticipated an emphasis of the symbolic-interaction perspective with his early use of the concept of **differential association**. This concept referred not only to associations among people but also, and even more importantly, to associations among ideas. Suth-

---

# Crime as Work: An Example of the Interaction Approach

The symbolic-interaction theories of deviance place a heavy emphasis on the role of meanings and definitions in the explanation of deviant behaviour. Even when these theories have been applied in the study of very different kinds of behaviour, it has been emphasized that these meanings and definitions can play a quite similar role. Letkemann has illustrated this point in a unique Canadian study of career criminals. His thesis is that crime can be a form of work, incorporating all the elements of a profession. But to understand this contention we must see the world of crime in the same terms — that is, with the same meanings and definitions — as the persons who participate in it. To do this, Letkemann conducted detailed interviews with a sample of skilled and experienced property offenders.

One of the most striking results of these interviews is the awareness of how different the official and criminal classification of offenders can be. The problem is that legal categorizations of offenders according to criminal-code designations often constitute distorted descriptions of offenders' career patterns. For example, while safe-cracking has been a lively and venerable criminal career in Canada, it is not a term found in the Criminal Code. Instead, offenders involved in

this form of criminal work are often convicted of breaking and entering. This example illustrates the need to appreciate the meanings and definitions offenders attach to their own activities.

Pursuing this theme, Letkemann found that his subjects define not only their own activities, but those of their colleagues in crime, in terms of several important distinctions. The first of these distinctions is between a group referred to as "rounders" and a larger group referred to as "alkies," "dope fiends," and "normals." The first of these groups, the rounders, is distinguished by its commitment to an illegitimate lifestyle, a commitment that is demonstrated in a consistent and reliable, albeit criminal, pattern of behaviour. The sense here is of a concern for "honesty among thieves," in which the emphasis is on a record of consistency and integrity among peers. In sum, the rounder seems to hold and apply work standards that are not so different from those of the more orthodox professions. James Caan, the safe-cracker par excellence in the movie *Thief*, was a man's man and a rounder's rounder.

In contrast, the second group is characterized by its use of psychoactive chemicals and involvement in small-scale illegal activities, primarily theft. The alkies,

dope fiends, and normals share the dedication of the rounder, but in this case their dedication is to their drug, rather than to their own illegal activities. Property crime for these offenders is a "means to an end" (drugs, alcohol), rather than an end in itself. The importance of this difference is that the dependence of the members of this group on drugs and alcohol makes them unreliable partners in criminal undertakings.

Another important distinction that Letkemann's respondents made is between "amateur" and "experienced" criminals. One identifying feature of amateur criminals is that they are primarily concerned with avoiding detection, while more experienced criminals concentrate on avoiding conviction. The point here is that experienced criminals have technical skills that make them rather easily identifiable by police. Their concern, then, is less with being detected as the culprits than with making certain that they leave no evidence. Without evidence, of course, there can be no conviction.

Skilled and experienced property offenders also distinguish among themselves according to the specializations they pursue. These offenders speak of "having a line" — that is, a generalized work preference and a related repertoire of skills. We

erland argued that people behave criminally only when they define such behaviour as acceptable. The connection postulated between people and their ideas (that is, definitions) is as follows:

*The hypothesis of differential association is that criminal behavior is learned in association with those who define such behavior favorably and in isolation from those who define it unfavorably, and that a person in an appropriate situation engages in such criminal behavior if, and only if, the weight of the favorable definitions exceeds the weight of the unfavorable definitions.* (Sutherland 1949)

Sutherland (1949) applied his hypothesis in a famous study of white-collar crime, arguing that individuals become white-collar criminals because they are immersed with their colleagues in a business ideology that defines illegal business practices as acceptable.

A student of Sutherland's, Donald Cressey (1971), applied a form of this hypothesis to the specific crime of embezzlement. Cressey interviewed more than 100 imprisoned embezzlers and concluded that they had committed their crimes after they had rationalized, or redefined, these activities using statements like these:

"Some of our most respectable citizens got their start in life by using other people's money temporarily."

"All people steal when they get in a tight spot."

---

will come back to this point in a moment; for now, let us simply note again that the defining features of a criminal occupation are seen to parallel the more conventional world of work.

A final distinction is drawn in terms of prison experience. This distinction gives new meaning to the common concern shared by labelling theorists that "prisons are schools for crime." Letkemann points out that prison experience can operate much like college or university experience: as a prerequisite to status. Furthermore, some prisons are known for the specialized contacts they allow. For example, since provincial institutions in Canada can hold an offender for no more than two years less one day, they offer little exposure to more experienced criminals. Thus, to obtain full standing as a rounder may require experience in a federal penitentiary, where the more seasoned professionals are often to be found.

Letkemann goes on to describe two kinds of skills that characterize two very different criminal career paths. This description is central to his main argument that crime *is* work, often of a highly skilled form. Therefore, the argument is concerned with defining features that make it explainable, using the same principles applied to understanding legitimate behaviour. The first of these career paths involves surreptitious crimes; the second, overt crimes.

Surreptitious crimes include burglary, and, more specifically, safe-cracking. These crimes emphasize mechanical skills and victim-avoidance. Persons involved in this kind of criminal work must develop a set of technical skills: working with explosives and learning how to use them to blow a safe. At the same time, they must acquire a set of techniques for gaining entry to sites where safes are used and for minimizing the chances of being observed in the course of their work. While this set of activities may be defined by law as anti-social, its more interesting feature in sociological terms is that it is so *non-social*: the emphasis here is on avoiding others while engaging in criminal activity.

By contrast, overt crimes, like bank robbery, can involve a highly developed set of social, as opposed to mechanical, skills. In overt crimes, the victims are confronted and skill must be applied to handle this social event in a way that does not lead to violence. While it may often be thought that because a weapon is used an armed robbery involves no skills, the skill required is to avoid the use of a weapon. The film *Dog Day Afternoon* illustrated, at times comically, how in inexperienced hands this type of situation can escalate beyond control. As well, very basic decisions must be made. Does the getaway driver stay in the car or enter the bank? The problem is whether the waiting driver will actually wait, or panic and take off prematurely. Also, who should lead the exit from the bank? While on the one hand it might be wise for the most experienced person to lead the way, the first one out may also be the person most likely to get shot. These and other factors must be taken into account, and decisions must be made. The point is that a successful robbery is a complex accomplishment, demanding considerable social and planning skills. To the extent that these skills are conscientiously developed and applied, the criminal career will have much in common with other more conventional careers.

Symbolic interactionists remind us that criminals, like the rest of us, define their worlds and act accordingly. Often, these meanings and definitions are developed with skill and experience. The importance of this different but sophisticated world-view is well summarized by Letkemann: "The model of a criminal as one who takes a craftsman's pride in his work, and who applies his skills in the most profitable way he thinks possible, is very different from the model of the criminal as one who gets kicks out of beating the system and doing evil."

**Source:**

Peter Letkemann, *Crime as Work* (Englewood Cliffs, NJ: Prentice-Hall, 1973).

"My interest was only to use this money temporarily, so I was 'borrowing' it, not 'stealing.' "

"I have been trying to live an honest life, but I have had nothing but trouble so 'to hell with it.' "

**Techniques of Neutralization.** Symbolic-interaction theory is not exclusively concerned with lower-class deviance; it gives considerable attention to crimes of the upper and middle classes as well. But when attention is turned to the underworld, the explanatory framework remains essentially the same. The key to this consistency is Sykes and Matza's (1957) observation that lower-class delinquents, like white-collar criminals, usually exhibit guilt or shame when detected violating the law. Thus the delinquent, like the white-collar criminal, is regarded as an "apologetic failure," who drifts into a deviant lifestyle through a subtle process of justification. "We call these justifications of deviant behavior techniques of neutralization," write Sykes and Matza, "and we believe these techniques make up a crucial component of Sutherland's definitions favorable to the violation of the law" (1957).

Sykes and Matza list four of these **neutralization techniques:** *denial of responsibility* (for example, blaming a bad upbringing), *denial of injury* (for example, claiming that the victim deserved it), *condemnation of the condemners* (for example, calling their condemnation discriminatory), and *an appeal to higher loyalties* (for example, citing loyalty to friends or family as the cause of the behaviour). Sykes and Matza's point is that crime in the underworld, like crime in society at large, is facilitated by this type of thinking. A question remains, however: Why are underworld crimes more frequently made the subjects of official condemnation?

**Dramatization of Evil.** The beginning of an answer to this question appears in the early work of Franklin Tannenbaum (1938). Tannenbaum points out that some forms of juvenile delinquency are a normal part of adolescent street life — aspects of the play, adventure, and excitement that many nostalgically identify later as an important part of this period. But others see such activities as a nuisance or as threatening, so they summon the police.

Tannenbaum's concern is that police intervention begins a process of change in the way the individuals and their activities are perceived. He suggests that there is a gradual shift from defining specific *acts* as evil to defining the *individual* as evil. Tannenbaum sees the individual's first contact with the law as the most consequential, referring to this event as a "dramatization of evil" that separates the child from his or her peers for specialized treatment. Tannenbaum goes on to argue that this "dramatization" may play a greater role in creating the criminal than any other experience. The problem is that individuals thus singled out may begin to think of themselves as the type of people who do such things — that is, as delinquents. From this viewpoint, efforts to reform or deter deviant behaviour create more problems than they solve. "The way out," Tannenbaum argues, "is through a refusal to dramatize the evil." He suggests instead that the less said about it the better.

**Primary and Secondary Deviance.** Sociologists have expanded on Tannenbaum's version of the interactionist perspective. For example, Lemert (1967) suggests the terms primary and secondary deviance to distinguish between acts that occur before and after the societal response. Acts of **primary deviance** are those that precede a social or legal response. They may be incidental or even random aspects of an individual's general behaviour. The important point is that these initial acts have little impact on the individual's self-concept. **Secondary deviance**, on the other hand, follows the societal response and involves a transformation of the individual's self-concept, "altering the psychic structure, producing specialized organization of social roles and self-regarding attitudes" (Lemert 1967). From this point on, the individual takes on more and more of the "deviant" aspects of his or her new role. The societal response has, from this point of view, succeeded only in confirming the individual in a deviant role (Becker 1963, 1964).

**The Labelling Process.** As we have developed our discussion of the interaction perspective, we have focused more and more on the official societal reactions to deviant behaviour — that is, on what many analysts of deviance call "the labelling process." Attention to societal labelling and its effects has involved examinations of not only the conventional topics — crime, delinquency, and drugs — but also the much-neglected topic of mental illness. Scheff (1966), for example, has suggested that our society uses the concept of "mental illness" in much the same way as other societies use the concepts of "witchcraft" and "spirit possession." That is, this label provides a catch-all category wherein we can place a variety of forms of **residual rule-breaking** for which our society provides no other explicit labels.

Scheff (1966) observes that in childhood we all learn the stereotyped role behaviour that is labelled insanity. On the basis of this knowledge, Scheff (1966) suggests that

*when societal agents and persons around the deviant react to him uniformly in terms of the traditional stereotypes of insanity, his amorphous and unstructured rule-breaking tends to crystallize in conformity to these expectations, thus becoming similar to the behavior of other deviants classified as mentally ill, and stable over time.*

In other words, the process of labelling mental illness may help create secondary deviance — deviance indistinguishable from the sort that the control agents are attempting to cure.

In the end, symbolic interactionists do not insist that all, or even most, deviant behaviour is caused by officially imposed labels. Official labels are thought, rather, to create special problems for the individuals to whom they are applied, often increasing the chances that additional deviant behaviour will follow. The point is that not only the actor but also the reactors participate in creating the meanings and definitions that generate deviant behaviour. The symbolic interactionists note that the poor are more likely than the rich to get caught up in this process. This point is further emphasized in conflict theory, the approach we consider next.

## Conflict Theory and Deviance

The most distinctive feature of the **conflict theories of deviance** is their focus on the role of dominant societal groups in imposing legal labels on members of subordinate societal groups. The issues are how and why this happens. We will see that attention to these issues focuses as much or more on the groups imposing labels as on the individuals receiving them.

**Crime as Status.** For conflict theorists, crime is a status that is imposed by one group on the behaviour of another. Turk (1969) suggests that "criminality is not a biological, psychological, or even behavioral phenomenon, but a social status defined by the way in which an individual is perceived, evaluated, and treated by legal authorities." The task, then, is to identify the group or groups involved in creating and applying this status.

Turk (1969) responds by observing that there are two types of people in society: "There are those . . . who constitute the dominant, decision-making category — the authorities — and those who make up the subordinate category, who are affected by but scarcely affect law — the subjects." In short, authorities make laws that in turn make criminals out of subjects. The difference is a matter of relative power. Authorities have sufficient power to define some subjects' behaviour as criminal. Because the poor have the least power, we can expect the poor to have the highest rate of "criminalization." The process by which groups are differentially criminalized is the subject of much of the following discussion.

**Legal Bureaucracy.** Determining which groups in society will be more criminal than others is largely a matter of determining which laws will be enforced. Chambliss and Seidman (1971) observe that in modern, complex, stratified societies such as our own, we assign the task of resolving such issues to bureaucratically structured agencies. The result is to mobilize what we call "the primary principle of legal bureaucracy." According to this principle, laws will be enforced when enforcement serves the interests of social control agencies and their officials; laws will not be enforced when enforcement is likely to cause organizational strain. In other words, the primary principle of legal bureaucracy involves maximizing organizational gains while minimizing organizational strains.

Chambliss and Seidman (1971) conclude that a consequence of this principle is to bring into operation a "rule of law," whereby "discretion at every level . . . will be so exercised as to bring mainly those who are politically powerless (i.e., the poor) into the purview of the law." Because the poor are least likely to have the power and resources necessary to create organizational strains, they become the most rewarding targets for organizational activities. In sum, according to the conflict theorists, the poor appear disproportionately in our crime statistics more because of class bias in our society and the realities of our bureaucratic legal system than because of their actual behaviour.

**A New Criminology.** Arguments such as those expounded in the preceding paragraphs culminated in a call — first sounded in the early 1970s — by a group of British researchers for a "New" or "Critical Criminology" (Taylor, Walton, and Young 1973, 1975). This group argues that the roots of modern crime problems are intertwined with those of Western capitalism. Capitalist ideology, they suggest, has conditioned the very way we conceive of crime.

For example, the New Criminologists observe that we think about crime largely in terms of "an ethic of individualism." This ethic holds individuals responsible for their acts, thus diverting attention from the social and political structure in which these acts take place. Moreover, this individualist ethic focuses primarily on one group

of individuals — the poor — making them the chief targets of criminal law and penal sanctions. In contrast, the New Criminologists argue that employers and other advantaged persons will be bound only by a civil law that seeks to regulate their competition with one another. The New Criminologists maintain that such an arrangement creates two kinds of citizenship and responsibility, the more advantaged of which tends to be "beyond incrimination" and therefore above the law (see also Hagan, Nagel, and Albonetti 1980).

**A Marxian Theory of Crime and Deviance.** The New Criminology represents the re-emergence of a Marxian theory of crime and deviance. Until recently, early forms of this theory (Bonger 1916; Rusche and Kirchheimer 1939) were neglected, and the theory consequently remained underdeveloped. Spitzer (1975) is among those who have helped revive and expand it.

Spitzer begins by arguing that we must account for criminal and deviant acts as well as for the status of those labelled as deviants. Thus, "we must not only ask why specific members of the

## Suite Crime: An Example of the Conflict Approach

The conflict and critical (that is, New Criminology) theories are particularly important in emphasizing the role of powerful interest groups in defining what gets treated as criminal. Goff and Reasons (1978) illustrate this point in the distinction they draw between "suite" and "street" crimes. While we are all familiar with the common-sense meaning of the latter, the former refers to "the illegal behavior which occurs in the business suites of the corporate, professional, and civic elites of society. . . . These types of offenses are largely carried out by persons representing an organization and are committed for individual and/or collective benefits." Examples of suite crimes include misrepresentation in advertising, price-fixing, fraudulent financial manipulations, illegal rebates, misappropriation of public funds, fee-splitting, fraudulent damage claims, failure to maintain safety standards,

and the violation of human rights. Goff and Reasons focus on anti-combines legislation to provide one example of how one type of suite crime has been defined and presumably controlled in Canada.

Canada's first anti-combines legislation was sponsored by small businesses who, in the midst of Sir John A. Macdonald's emerging National Policy, felt their firms were at the mercy of big businesses then in the process of entering into powerful combines. Macdonald's Conservative government supported a much-amended version of this legislation, possibly to divert attention from the National Policy, and certainly to show at least symbolically that it was concerned about alleviating the economic conditions brought on by the combines. The resulting legislation was passed in 1889. The ineffectiveness of this, Canada's first

combines legislation, is evidenced by the legislators' failure to establish a permanent enforcement agency at the federal level to administer the law. As well, the wording of the Act left even its potential for enforcement dubious. It was not until the turn of the century that any active enforcement of anti-combines legislation began to take place.

Later governments were also slow to pursue seriously the enforcement of laws against combines. As prime minister, Mackenzie King displayed a reluctance to follow even the very tentative policies of American governments, showing particular antipathy for American attempts to enforce the Sherman Anti-Trust Laws. King noted that "we have tried to avoid the error which the United States have experienced in going too far" (cited in Goff and Reasons). More recent governments may have gone

underclass are selected for official processing, but also why they behave as they do." Spitzer's answer draws on the structural characteristics of capitalism. More specifically, Spitzer suggests that what he calls "problem populations" (such as "social junk" and "social dynamite," discussed below) in capitalist societies consist of those whose behaviours threaten the social relations of production. These threats may take various forms as they disturb, hinder, or call into question any of five key components of capitalist society:

1. capitalist modes of appropriating the product of human labour (for example, when the poor "steal" from the rich)
2. the social conditions under which capitalist production takes place (for example, those who refuse or are unable to perform wage labour)
3. patterns of distribution and consumption in capitalist society (for example, those who use drugs for escape and transcendence rather than for sociability and adjustment)
4. the process of socialization for productive and nonproductive roles (for example, youths who refuse to be schooled or people who deny the validity of "family life," such as gays)
5. the ideology that supports the functioning of capitalist society (for example, proponents of alternative forms of social organization).

All such threats are thought to derive from one of two sources: directly, from fundamental contradictions in the capitalist mode of production; and indirectly, from disturbances in the system of class rule. An example of the first source involves the emergence of "surplus populations" — what Marx called the class of the chronically unemployed — and the problems of unemployment. An example of the second source involves the critical attitudes that educational institutions may produce, resulting in school dropouts and sometimes in student radicals.

Spitzer goes on to suggest that the processes he outlines create two distinct kinds of problem populations. On the one hand, there is *social junk*, which, for the dominant class, represents a costly but relatively harmless burden to society. Examples of this category include the officially admin-

---

further than King in drafting and enforcing anti-combines legislation, but the record is not impressive.

For example, Goff and Reasons note that, between 1952 and 1972, a total of 157 decisions were made against 50 corporations in Canada. These decisions were predominantly against small- and medium-sized businesses, rather than against the larger corporations, and attempts to pursue larger enterprises are actually decreasing. Nonetheless, more than half of Canada's largest corporations have been recidivists (that is, convicted more than once), with an average of 3.2 decisions registered against them.

Most interestingly, however, Goff and Reasons report that no individual has ever been jailed for illegal activities under the Combines Act. Instead, the government has usually issued Order of Prohibition penalties, rather than fining the offender or issuing other penalties, such as lowering the tariff duties on foreign products to compensate the Canadian consumer by way of increasing competition. Finally, Goff and Reasons note that since 1923, when mergers were brought under the control of the new combines legislation, only 0.003 percent of the total number of mergers have been charged as constituting violations of combines laws. During this same time period, the courts have found only 0.0005 percent of the mergers to be illegal.

Goff and Reasons note that these findings are the logical consequences of the allocation of government priorities and resources. They observe that federal authorities spend much more money to control street crimes than suite crimes. Presumably, one reason for this differential is that on a per-case basis it would cost the government far more money to vigorously prosecute these complicated suite crimes than everyday street crimes. Given bureaucratic demands for productivity, this type of investment is unlikely to be made. Beyond this, conflict theory asserts that in capitalist societies the state is controlled by economic and business interests, and that we should therefore not expect the state to interfere legally in the operations of these interests. C. Wright Mills summarizes the societal implications of this interpretation: "It is better, so the image runs, to take one dime from each of ten million people at the point of a corporation than $100,000 from each of ten banks at the point of a gun. It is also safer" (cited by Goff and Reasons).

---

**Source:**

Colin Goff and Charles Reasons, *Corporate Crime in Canada* (Scarborough, ON: Prentice-Hall, 1978).

istered aged, handicapped, mentally ill, and retarded, as well as some kinds of alcohol and drug offenders. In contrast to "social junk," there is also a category described as *social dynamite*. The distinctive feature of people in this category is their "potential actively to call into question established relationships, especially relations of production and domination" (Spitzer 1975). Correspondingly, Spitzer notes that "social dynamite" tends to be more alienated and politically volatile than "social junk." Listed by Spitzer as among the groups with the potential to become "social dynamite" are the welfare poor, homosexuals, and "problem children."

Finally, Spitzer suggests that two basic strategies are used by capitalist societies in controlling criminals and deviants. The first strategy is referred to as *integrative*, the second as *segregative*. The first approach involves control measures applied in the community, such as probation and parole, while the second relies more on the use of institutions. Spitzer notes that integrative controls are becoming increasingly common in capitalist societies, as we embrace diversion, decarceration, and deinstitutionalization programs designed to divert or remove designated deviants from prisons and other places of official detainment. Spitzer and others (for example, Scull 1977) have argued that this trend arose due to the spiralling costs of institutionalization, and that this treatment is reserved for "social junk." This perspective may well prompt us to think critically about what has usually been considered a humane set of developments, including proposals for halfway houses, group homes, and so on. Scull writes that deviants are increasingly dealt with "as if they are industrial wastes which can without risk be left to decompose in some well-contained dump" (Scull 1977). This is quite a different picture of the movement to keep deviants out of institutions than has previously been common.

## The Processing of Crime and Deviance

One of the most important consequences of the emergence of the symbolic-interaction and conflict theories of crime and deviance has been a heightened awareness of the role official agencies play in determining who or what we label criminal or deviant. This increased awareness has stimulated research that focuses on decision-making in official agencies — for example, decisions made about mental-hospital admissions, police arrests, plea bargaining, and judicial sentencing. The often-provocative results have been suggestive of biases in official decision-making.

### Processing Mental Illness

Doubting the accuracy with which psychiatrists distinguish the sane from the insane, Rosenhan (1973) designed a unique study to test the diagnostic skills of those who control mental-hospital admission and release. In this study, Rosenhan himself and eight other individuals with histories free from mental disorders sought admission to twelve different psychiatric hospitals. Each person complained of fictional symptoms (hearing voices saying "empty, hollow, thud") resembling no known form of mental illness. Despite the fictitious symptoms, all the pseudopatients were diagnosed as schizophrenics. Immediately following admission, the pseudopatients ceased to report symptoms and resumed what they regarded as a normal pattern of behaviour. After an average period of more than two weeks, all the pseudopatients were released as "schizophrenics in remission." None of the individuals, in other words, was discovered *sane*. These results do not indicate, of course, that there are no differences between the sane and the insane; but they do suggest that mental-hospital personnel may often overlook or mistake these differences.

It is important to note that in the above experiment the pseudopatients were seeking admission voluntarily. Gove (1975) has observed that most people who receive psychiatric treatment do so voluntarily and that concerned friends and relatives do not frivolously seek hospitalization for others. Indeed, there is evidence (Smith, Pumphrey, and Hall 1963) that the typical psychiatric patient performs three or more "critical acts," each of which might justify hospitalization, before commitment procedures are initiated. Hospitalization is sought earlier for economically more important family members than for those less consequential to family life (Hammer 1963–64).

Beyond this, Gove (1975) reviews a variety of studies leading to the observation that "officials do not assume illness but, in fact, proceed rather cautiously, screening out a substantial number of persons." Significantly, this results in a situation where (for disorders of equivalent severity) hospitalization is more readily obtained by members of the upper class (Gove 1975). One explanation for this situation, as it relates to courts, is offered by Rock (1968): "The more important problem today is not the filing of petitions [for institutionalization] that are without cause, but rather finding a person willing to petition." Apparently, there are class differences in the willingness to assume the role of petitioner for another person. A second explanation is that some forms of treatment for mental illness may be preferable to other possible fates, particularly when the other forms of response carry the stigma of criminal disrepute. This point will become clear as we turn next to the problems of alcoholism.

## Processing Alcoholism

The treatment of alcoholism is perhaps the area where the connection between class background and societal response is most apparent. The descending social rank of the persons typically receiving treatment in private sanitaria, from Alcoholics Anonymous, and from the Salvation Army will be obvious to anyone who has passed through the doors of each. The underlying issue: how do members of various classes find their way into these widely divergent treatment situations?

One approach to this problem involves studying the admission and treatment practices of an institution that deliberately tries to attend to people of varying class backgrounds. This type of study seeks to determine whether patterns within such an organization can suggest more general principles for alcoholism treatment.

Schmidt, Smart, and Moss (1968) carried out a study of this sort in the Toronto clinic of the Alcoholism and Drug Addiction Research Foundation. Although this study deals entirely with voluntary admissions, it carries important implications for our concern with the courts. One of its major findings is that lower-class alcoholics in the Toronto clinic were more likely to receive treatment involving drugs administered by phy-

sicians, while upper-class alcoholics were more likely to receive "talk" therapies from psychiatrists. These apparently class-related treatment differences could not be traced to differences in diagnosis or age. Differences in verbal skills (also usually related to class) prove to be an intermediate explanatory variable.

Even more interesting than these treatment differences, however, are variations by social class in the sources of referrals to the clinic. Upper-class patients are more likely to find their way to the clinic through the intermediary services of private physicians, middle-class persons by way of Alcoholics Anonymous, and lower-class persons through general hospital and welfare agency referrals. Schmidt, Smart, and Moss conclude that these class patterns are attributable largely to differences among given social settings in tolerating behaviours that result from alcohol excess and to differences in the modal drinking patterns of the classes. Here we are interested in the role the courts play in responding to these class differences.

To understand the role of the courts in the societal response to alcoholism we can use the findings of voluntary-clinic studies as indications of what may be happening in the whole range of agencies, especially in the involuntary sector. Lowe and Hodges (1972) took this route in studying the treatment of black alcoholics in the southern United States. They began by studying a single voluntary clinic, but soon found that "any variation in amount of services given to patients within the clinic was insignificant beside the overwhelming fact that so few black alcoholics entered into service at all." Eventually they observed that black alcoholics are less likely to view admission to the clinic as offering treatment and are therefore unlikely to admit themselves voluntarily into any program. Black alcoholics thus frequently find themselves the involuntary subjects of law-enforcement operations that start with the police, take further form in the courts, and end up in prison. Lowe and Hodges note that the courts rarely attempt to reverse this pattern by making referrals to alternative treatment programs. This pattern also holds for native peoples in Canada.

Hagan (1947b) followed up the treatment received by native and white offenders in Alberta following incarceration. On the basis of either judicial recommendation or inmate request, offenders in Alberta are considered for transfer to an open institutional setting offering a program particularly designed for alcoholic offenders. However, Hagan found that although the target population of problem drinkers is almost twice as large (proportionately) among native offenders as among whites, more whites than native offenders received treatment in the open institutional setting. Thus, although only a minority of alcoholic offenders from either ethnic group experienced the open institution, white offenders were more than twice as likely as native offenders to find their way to this treatment setting. There are three plausible explanations for this situation. First, judges may recommend referrals of native offenders to the open institution less often. Second, native offenders may seek and accept such referrals less frequently. Third, correctional personnel may consent to the transfer of native offenders less often. It is important to note, however, that the three possibilities described are certainly not mutually exclusive — and in fact are likely to be mutually supportive. In other words, there may be general agreement that in its present form the open institutional setting is less beneficial for native than for white offenders.

## Policing Crime and Delinquency

Winding up in a correctional institution can be seen as the end result in a series of decisions whose effect has been likened to using a sieve or a leaky funnel. Most of those whose cases enter the first stages of a criminal or juvenile justice system are eventually diverted or deflected from the stream that leads to institutionalization. For example, an offence may go undetected or unsolved in the first place. If an offender is identified, the police may decide against arrest. If an arrest occurs, the prosecutor may decide to dismiss the charges. If a case results in conviction, the judge may decide to suspend sentence. That is, any number of things may happen along the way to prevent the offender from being institutionalized. The issue is the extent to which these outcomes are random, legally determined, or socially biased.

Starting with police decisions made early in this process, some of the most important research has been done by Black and Reiss (1970; Reiss 1971).

Black and Reiss distinguish between two basic ways in which police can be mobilized. *Reactive mobilizations* are citizen-initiated (for example, by a telephoned complaint), while *proactive mobilizations* are police-initiated (for example, in response to an observed incident). In the Black and Reiss research, 87 percent of the mobilizations were reactive. This figure implies that the police usually do not seek out deviant behaviour, but rather respond to citizens' complaints about such behaviour. As Black and Reiss note, when a complainant in search of justice makes demands, police officers may feel compelled to comply. Differences in the number of complaints received — between, for example, different neighbourhoods — may therefore help explain differential rates of arrest.

However, Ericson (1982), studying a suburban Toronto jurisdiction, raises some important questions about the applicability of these findings in Canada. Of 1323 encounters observed between citizens and police officers in Ericson's study, 47.4 percent were characterized as proactive mobilizations, and only 52.6 percent as reactive mobilizations. "On the surface," Ericson (1982) notes, "our data reveal that patrol officers are much more assertive in producing encounters with citizens than the figures provided by Reiss, Black, and others would lead us to believe." Still, when considering only "major incidents," Ericson reports that more than 82 percent result from reactive mobilizations. In serious cases, complainants may still loom large in the decision-making process.

Another study — this one by Smith (1982), who examined 742 contacts between suspects and officers in 24 American police departments — confirms the influence of complainants but also points to the impact of suspect characteristics. According to this study, antagonistic suspects are much more likely to be taken into custody than suspects who display deference (see also Piliavin and Briar 1964). Futhermore, black suspects are more likely to be arrested. Smith suggests that this difference can partly be accounted for by the fact that black suspects are significantly more likely to act toward the police in a hostile or antagonistic manner. Nonetheless, even taking suspect behaviour and victim demands into account, black suspects remain somewhat more likely to be arrested than white suspects.

## Prosecuting Crime and Delinquency

Once an individual has been arrested and charged, the media image of the court process is that of a trial by jury, with prosecution and defence attorneys assuming adversarial roles in a battle for justice. In fact, however, few criminal cases follow this adversarial pattern. The typical sequence, followed in up to 90 percent of the cases in some jurisdictions, is for the defendant to plead guilty and forfeit trial. Grossman (1969) observes, on the basis of interviews with prosecutors in York County, Ontario, that guilty pleas are an important way of avoiding the time, expense, and uncertainty of trials. Plea bargaining is seen as an effective way of increasing court efficiency (Blumberg 1967). It is important, therefore, to take a close look at plea bargaining.

Sudnow (1965) has attempted to spell out in sociological terms the procedures involved in bargaining for reduced charges (see also Hagan 1974a; Wynne and Hartnagel 1975a, 1975b). Sudnow notes first that the reduction of charges focuses on two types of offences: "necessarily included" offences and "situationally included" offences. Necessarily included offences are those that occur together by legal definition; for example, "homicide" cannot occur without "intent to commit a murder." In contrast, situationally included offences are those that occur together by convention; "public drunkenness" usually, but not necessarily, occurs in association with "creating a public disturbance." Plea bargaining involves reducing the initial charge to a lesser charge — either a necessarily or situationally included offence.

As Sudnow points out, however, the procedural rules followed in deciding what sort of reduction is appropriate are not entirely defined by law. Rather, lawyers and prosecutors develop working conceptions of what they regard as "normal crimes": "the typical manner in which offenses of given classes are committed, the social characteristics of the persons who regularly commit them, the features of the settings in which they occur, the types of victims often involved, and the like" (Sudnow 1965). According to Sudnow, these conceptions of "normal crimes" are used to create an initial legal categorization; attention is then directed to determining which (necessarily or situationally included) lesser offence

may constitute the appropriate reduction. As an example, Sudnow notes that in the jurisdiction he studied, a burglary charge is routinely reduced to petty theft; however, "the propriety of proposing petty theft as a reduction does not derive from its . . . existence in the present case, but is warranted . . . instead by the relation of the present burglary to 'burglaries,' [as] normally conceived." Finally, Sudnow notes that a balance must be established between the sentence the defendant might have received for the original charge, and the probable sentencing outcome for the lesser charge. This brings us to the issue of sentencing.

## Judging Crime and Delinquency

Legislation outlining the sentencing responsibilities of the criminal courts in Canada entrusts presiding judges with extensive freedom to determine minimum sentences. A wide range of discretion is also allowed in determining maximum penalties. The problem, however, extends beyond the simple absence of statutory guides to minimum and maximum sentences. There is also confusion as to what basic principles should be used in determining sentences. Decore (1964) notes that even the use of precedents in sentencing is a matter full of contradictions and doubt. Consequently, the criminal justice system relies heavily on the discretion of the sentencing judge, and variation and disparity predictably follow. An important attempt to explain variation in criminal sentences is found in the research of Hogarth (1971).

Hogarth begins by noting that judges in the lower provincial courts in Canada have broader jurisdiction (that is, 94 percent of all indictable cases are tried in these courts) and wider sentencing powers (for example, to life imprisonment) than any comparable set of courts in the Western world. Hogarth then provides data suggesting that Canada in the mid-1960s also had one of the highest rates of imprisonment in the Western world (see also Cousineau and Veevers 1972; Matthews 1972). However, Hogarth also presents evidence of a recent shift in this pattern, with the heavy reliance on prison sentences giving way to an increasing reliance on fines.

The most recent evidence on Canada's use of imprisonment is provided in an exceptionally careful analysis by Waller and Chan (1975). This analysis indicates that Canada's overall imprisonment rate is no higher than that of the United States and several other countries, with only the Yukon and the Northwest Territories remaining high in comparison to most American states. Waller and Chan are careful to emphasize the difficulties of drawing any final inferences from the data they present, and to their cautions we will add several additional comments. First, it is not surprising to find that Canada's imprisonment rate per 100 000 population is low relative to some other countries, particularly the United States, for Canada's serious crime rate is also relatively low. Considering ratios of incarcerations to occurrences and convictions would allow more useful comparisons. Waller and Chan appropriately point out the complications in accurately computing these ratios using current official data. Second, it should be noted that, where imprisonment rates are highest in Canada (that is, in the north), native people are most likely to be experiencing the consequences. Finally, we can observe that while efforts to avoid incarceration through the increasing use of fines may be successful on the whole in Canada, economic and ethnic minorities unable to pay these fines remain at a disadvantage. These comments should discourage any sense of complacency about the conditions in our courts, a complacency that Waller and Chan clearly disavow (see also Waller 1974).

The research by Hogarth (1971) described above, probably because it concentrated primarily on the large urban areas of Ontario, paid little attention to the social consequences of sentencing for ethnic and economic minorities, particularly native people. Yet native people are present in Canadian court and prison populations far beyond their representation in the general population. To understand the influence of race and other offender characteristics on judicial sentencing, we will need to consider briefly a large body of American research.

A variety of American studies focus on the effects of the offender's race, gender, age, and socioeconomic status on sentencing decisions (for example, Bullock 1961; Green 1961; Nagel 1969; Wolfgang and Riedel 1973). A review of such studies concludes that generally there *is* a small relationship between the extralegal attributes of offenders and sentencing decisions (Hagan 1974a; see also Hagan and Bumiller 1983). However, because the authors of many of these studies have failed to take into account either the seriousness of offences or the prior records of offenders, it is sometimes difficult to know whether the reported relationships can be taken as evidence of discrimination. For example, do blacks in the United States receive longer sentences because they are discriminated against, or because they commit more serious offences and more frequently have prior convictions?

When these factors *are* controlled for, relationships reported between extralegal offender characteristics and sentences are sometimes reduced or eliminated (for example, Chiricos and Waldo 1975). However, there continues to be compelling evidence that in certain areas — such as sexual assault (see, for example, LaFree 1980) and white-collar crime (Hagan, Nagel, and Albonetti 1980; Hagan and Parker 1985) — race and class position can make a difference in the severity of sentence received. To this extent the symbolic-interaction and conflict theorists are clearly correct: there is more to criminal and delinquent labels than the behaviours presumed to have provoked them. There is evidence (Hagan and Albonetti 1982) that public perceptions mirror this reality.

Interestingly, judges in Canada are frequently accused of being differentially lenient, as well as punitive, with native offenders. The apparent leniency may reflect an attempt on the part of some Canadian judges to take cultural differences into account when sentencing native offenders. However, recent evidence on this issue suggests that most judges do sentence primarily on the basis of offence seriousness and prior conviction records. Hagan (1975) divided a sample of Albertan judges into two groups according to whether they scored high or low on a "law and order" scale. He predicted that judges who scored high would sentence native offenders punitively, while those who scored low would sentence leniently. Perhaps surprisingly, the results showed that "law and order" judges sentence almost exclusively on offence seriousness, while judges less concerned about such issues provided native persons only minimal leniency. More generally, this study suggests that most judges sentence most offenders mechanically, without taking the time to consider their social backgrounds. This is particularly the case, and becomes particularly problematic, with people charged with minor offences.

We noted earlier that the police typically apprehend native offenders for minor alcohol-related charges. In turn, judges typically sentence such offenders to "so many dollars or so many days." The outcome of this approach is predictable, given the economically disadvantaged position of many native people: Hagan (1974b) reports that nearly 66 percent of all native people who go to jail are incarcerated in default of fine payments. This is nearly twice the rate for whites. One result is that in Hagan's Albertan sample, native people are represented in the prison population four times more frequently than in the general population.

One final point is worth noting: there is evidence that corporate entities are playing an increasingly important role as complainants in Canadian courts — for example, in cases of shoplifting. A recent study in a suburban Ontario jurisdiction (Hagan 1982) revealed that nearly two-thirds of the victims in cases where an offender was charged were corporations (mostly retail stores). The corporations in this study were better able than individuals to get convictions against the accused. The implication, again, is that the courts may serve some interests better than they do others in our society.

## Crime, Race, and Violence in Canada and the United States

We turn now to a topic most Canadians at some time think about, but less often discuss: crime, race, and violence in Canada and the United States. There is no doubt that officially recorded rates of violent crime and many other kinds of deviance are higher in the United States than in Canada. In fact, the disparity between the rates of violent crime in the two countries is clearly growing.

There are differences in kind as well as in the amount of criminal violence in the two countries. In the United States, for example, about half of all homicides involve handguns, while in Canada

the figure is approximately 10 percent. Friedland (1981) illustrates this point with some graphic comparisons:

*In 1971 there were fewer than 60 homicides committed with handguns in all of Canada. Metropolitan Toronto, with more than 2 000 000 persons, had only four handgun homicides that year. In contrast, in 1979, handguns were used in almost 900 killings in New York City, and 300 in Metropolitan Detroit, and 75 in Metropolitan Boston. . . . The six New England states had over 200 handgun homicides in 1979; the four Canadian Maritime provinces did not have a single handgun homicide in 1979. There were over 10 000 handgun homicides in the U.S. in 1979, almost 20 times the Canadian per capita rate.*

The racial character of American criminal violence also differentiates the two national experiences. While blacks constitute about 12 percent of the American population, they have accounted for over half the arrests for murder for most of the last two decades (Nettler 1978). While there is some evidence that native people in Canada and the United States also have high rates of assault and alcohol-related crimes (Jensen, Strauss, and Harris 1977; Hagan 1985), there is no indication that the connection between race/ethnicity and serious crimes of violence is nearly as strong in Canada as it is, particularly for blacks, in the United States. There do seem to be real differences between the countries and by race, at least for serious crimes of violence, that are not the exclusive product of the kind of deficiencies in official data discussed earlier in this chapter.

Why, then, are patterns of criminal violence so different in the United States and Canada? And how are these differences connected to issues of race? With regard to violence generally, these national differences are widely thought to have a base in the way the American and Canadian West were settled. Quinney (1970) observes that on the American frontier, local authorities were free to develop their own law-enforcement policies or to ignore the problem of crime altogether. Similarly, Inciardi (1975) observes that "the American frontier was Elizabethan in its quality, simple, childlike, and savage. . . . It was a land of riches where swift and easy fortunes were sought by the crude, the lawless, and the aggressive, and where written law lacked form and cohesion." Put simply, the American frontier was also a violent frontier — a model in some ways for the city life that followed (Bell 1953).

Canada intended to be different. This is one of the reasons Canada chose to have a federal criminal code, with John A. Macdonald arguing in the Confederation debates that "this is one of the most marked instances in which we take advantage of the experience derived from our observations of the defects in the constitution of the neighbouring Republic" (cited in Friedland 1981). The Canadian approach initially involved firmer, but necessarily more strategically focused, control (McNaught 1975). MacLeod (1976) notes that, by the 1870s, the American government was spending over $20 million a year just fighting the Plains Indians. At the same time, the total Canadian budget (of which defence was only a part) was just over $19 million. Accord-

ing to MacLeod (1976), "it is not an exaggeration to say . . . that the only possible Canadian west was a peaceful one." The North West Mounted Police (NWMP), with powers unparalleled by any other police force in a democratic country, were given responsibility for establishing "peace and order." Kelly and Kelly (1976) contend that the RCMP of the 1890s "attended to the health and welfare problems of Indians and Eskimoes," while Brown and Brown (1973) write that "the NWMP were established as a semimilitary force designed to keep order on the prairies and to facilitate the transfer of most of the territory of the region from the Indian tribes to the federal government with a minimum of expense and bloodshed."

Whichever of the above accounts of the role of the NWMP is the more accurate, it is clear that Canada's native peoples were treated in a significantly different way than were native peoples in the United States. America's treatment of both its

---

## A Tale of Two Countries: Crime in Canada and the United States

By a variety of crime measures, Canada is only a moderately violent nation, at least as compared to the United States. As noted earlier in this chapter, much violent crime is consensual crime: that is, it involves infrequent and severely sanctioned violations of widely shared, and strongly held, values. Although some differences exist in the collection and categorization of offences in Canada and the United States, the findings suggest an interesting, enduring pattern: over the past 10 to 20 years, even with population differences taken into account, violent offences have remained much more frequent in the United States than in Canada.

For example, in 1985 the incidence of the most serious types of violent crime (for example, homicide, attempted murder, rape and aggravated sexual assault, wounding and aggravated assault) was more than five times higher in the United States than in Canada. There were more than 500 such crimes per 100 000 population

the United States in 1985, compared with little more than 100 in Canada. Furthermore, rates of serious violent crimes have been moving in opposite directions in the two countries in recent years. The rate of serious violent crime fell 10 percent between 1983 and 1985 in Canada, while it rose 3 percent in the United States.

A more specific comparison can be made between the two countries in terms of homicide rates. Since bodies are difficult to hide and because homicides are more likely to be reported and solved, homicide statistics are among the most reliable and valid crime statistics. For many years (see the accompanying figure), Canada's homicide rate has been between one-third and one-quarter of that in the United States. For example, in 1986 the homicide rate in Canada was 2.2, compared to 8.6 in the United States. Compared to other countries, we seem to occupy something of a middle ground. In 1985, the Canadian homicide rate was more than two and

a half times higher than in Scotland (1.1) or England and Wales (1.2), but lower than in Italy (4.4) and France (4.6).

One of the most dramatic reflections of national differences in crime and its control in the United States and Canada involves the use of imprisonment. The number of people in prison has increased dramatically in recent years in the United States, while the Canadian prison population has alternated between periods of slow growth and decline. For example, between 1982 and 1985, during a period in which the Canadian prison population remained largely unchanged in size, the sentenced prison population in the United States grew by 22 percent. One result is that in 1985 about 201 of every 100 000 Americans was in prison, compared to about 95 of every 100 000 Canadians. Another result is that in some U.S. jurisdictions the overcrowding of prison facilities has reached crisis proportions, while in Canada there are

black and native minorities was extraordinarily violent. Canada treated its native peoples — and may still treat them — badly, both socially and economically, but with not nearly as much actual violence. It seems unlikely that this difference in the form of mistreatment would not have had behavioural consequences — for example, in rates of violent crime (on the assumption that violence begets violence).

A more general point can be made before we end this necessarily speculative discussion of national differences. Once again, this point involves the very different policies the two countries have adopted to accomplish quite similar goals. These alternative policies are reflected in what have been called the "due process" and "crime control" models of law enforcement (Packer 1964). Societies vary in their commitment to these models, and it can be argued that, *at least in symbolic terms*, Americans give considerable deference to the due

process model, while Canadians have a more explicit commitment to a crime control model.

The **due process model** has its roots in the British Enlightenment and in English philosopher John Locke's notion that the law can be used effectively in the defence of "natural" and "inalienable" rights. Accordingly, the due process model is greatly concerned with procedural safeguards thought useful in protecting accused persons from unjust applications of criminal penalties. Because errors can always be made in law enforcement, advocates of the due process model would prefer to see a guilty person go free before an innocent person is punished.

In contrast, the **crime control model** received its philosophical support from the conservative reaction to Enlightenment thought and from the arguments of Englishman Edmund Burke that civil liberties can have meaning only in orderly societies. Thus, the crime control model places heavy

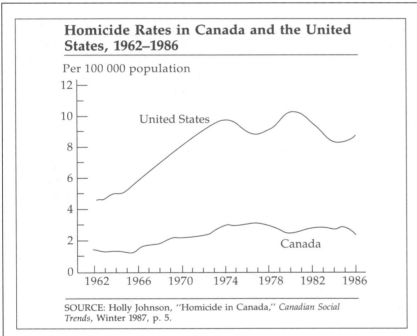

### Homicide Rates in Canada and the United States, 1962–1986

Per 100 000 population

SOURCE: Holly Johnson, "Homicide in Canada," *Canadian Social Trends*, Winter 1987, p. 5.

compared to about $8100 in the United States. The difference seems to derive from differences in policy as well as scale. While U.S. prisons often house 3000 to 4000 inmates, the largest Canadian institution houses 500; U.S. prisons commonly house inmates two to a cell, while Canadian inmates are usually housed individually; and Canadian institutions have higher staff-to-inmate ratios. These two countries experience and respond to crime in quite different ways.

**Sources:**

Craig McKie, "Canada's prison population," *Canadian Social Trends*, Summer 1987, pp. 2–7; Holly Johnson, "Homicide in Canada," *Canadian Social Trends*, Winter 1987, pp. 2–6; Holly Johnson, "Violent Crime," *Canadian Social Trends*, Summer 1988, pp. 24–29; Robert Cormier, "Corrections Costs," *Impact: Costs of Criminal Justice*, 2 (1984):23–35.

few reports of overcrowding. Perhaps partly because of resulting differences in economies of scale, Canada continues to spend more per capita on crime control than the United States, and there are signs that this difference is also growing.

For example, it is estimated in Canada that the average cost per inmate for 1980–81 was about $45 000,

emphasis on the repression of criminal conduct, holding that only by ensuring order can society guarantee individuals' personal freedom. For this reason, advocates of crime control are less anxious than the proponents of due process to presume the innocence of accused persons and to protect such persons against sometimes-dubious findings of guilt. It is not that the crime control model favours the unfair treatment of individuals, but rather that it is willing to tolerate a certain amount of mistreatment when the measures involved are seen as generally necessary, at least symbolically, for the maintenance of social order. Under this model, authorities are granted a good deal of discretion as to how they protect individual "rights."

The distinction between the Lockean due process and the Burkean crime control models is clear, but the difference in intent is one of degree. Both have as their goal the creation and maintenance of legal order. With this in mind, one Canadian social scientist notes that the "approach which is truest to our experience and most in keeping with our capabilities is that of Edmund Burke, not John Locke. Canadians . . . are [not] creatures of the Enlightenment" (Russell 1975). Some might argue that Canada's new Charter of Rights and Freedoms will dramatically change our approach. By constitutionally enshrining Lockean-style "fundamental freedoms" for individuals, and limiting the power vested in authorities, the Charter could reduce or remove the national differences between Canada and the United States. But the roots of these differences are deeply embedded in our social and historical fabric, so we remain doubtful. Meanwhile, as Margaret Atwood (1972) notes, "Canada must be the only country in the world where a policeman is used as a national symbol."

A final example, involving national differences in the control of guns, may help to bring our discussion together. Canada has long had tighter and more effective gun-control legislation than the United States. This distinction, too, reflects the different attitude maintained toward the rights of individuals in the two countries. We have already noted the contrasting records of handgun homicide found in the United States and Canada. We have also noted the historical dissimilarities in treatment of racial and ethnic minorities in the two countries. The United States violently suppressed its black and native minorities within a

society that makes handguns — a rather democratic instrument of violence — freely available. Canada socially and economically suppressed its native peoples, but much less violently, and makes access to instruments of violence — particularly handguns — rather difficult. These divergent national experiences could be expected to produce different behavioural effects. For example, Canada's native peoples might be less violent in their criminal behaviour than are native peoples in the United States. Research into such matters may hold a key to a deeper understanding of the dramatic differences in crime rates that characterize the United States and Canada.

Meanwhile, it is interesting to speculate more generally about the consequences that may follow from Canadian and American strategies for dealing with crime and deviance. The consequences for the socially advantaged of both countries are much the same: both nations possess a legal order that allows the relatively safe and stable conduct of social and economic affairs. The consequences for the socially disadvantaged in each country are, however, somewhat different. Overall, violent crime rates are significantly higher in the United States than in Canada, with evidence that this gap is widening. Because it is the poor who are far more likely to be arrested and convicted in both countries, it is the poor who are most affected by this difference (see Hagan and Albonetti 1982).

The American situation allows some freedom to deviate, but there is also a heightened likelihood of criminalization for members of subordinate groups. The Canadian situation discourages deviation at all levels; this in turn reduces the likelihood that subordinates will be criminalized. Thus, the poor are likelier to become a part of crime and deviance statistics in the United States than they are in Canada. This difference may reflect an important part of what is unique about the Canadian experience.

## SUMMARY

1. Deviation consists of variation from a norm and is made socially significant through the reactions of others.
2. There are several kinds of deviance — consensus crimes, conflict crimes, social devia-

tions, and social diversions. These can be distinguished according to their socially determined seriousness.

3. Whether or not different kinds of deviant behaviour come under official control is influenced by the activities of moral entrepreneurs and various interest groups.

4. There are a variety of means used to count deviant behaviour, including data gathered by official agencies and nonofficial agencies, through first-person accounts, through surveys of crime victims, and through observations of deviant behaviour. Comparison of these measures leads to the conclusion that serious crimes, hard-drug use, alcohol abuse, and mental illness are found more frequently in the working class, while less serious and more frequent forms of crime, delinquency, and drug use are more evenly distributed across the social classes.

5. The structural-functional theories of deviance argue that the presence of success goals or values without the means to attain them can produce deviant behaviour, as can the absence of these goals or values in the first place.

6. The symbolic-interaction theories of deviance are concerned with the role of social meanings and definitions in the production of deviant behaviour.

7. The conflict theories of deviance have focused on the role of dominant societal groups in imposing legal labels on members of subordinate societal groups.

8. Consideration of the processing of various kinds of crime and deviance indicates that social as well as legal factors influence when, where, and on whom deviant labels are imposed.

9. Two societal strategies for maintaining legal order are the due process and crime control models of law enforcement. Although the differences involved are often a matter of ideology and emphasis, at a formal and symbolic level Canada tends more toward a crime control model than does the United States.

10. Serious forms of crime and deviance are more common in the United States than in Canada. The social and historical roots of this difference may reflect an important part of what is unique about the Canadian experience.

## GLOSSARY

**Anomie.** Term originally used by Durkheim to refer to an absence of social regulation, or normlessness. Merton revived the concept to refer to the consequences of a faulty relationship between goals and the legitimate means of attaining them.

**Conflict crimes.** Acts that are defined by law as criminal and are often severely punished, but are usually regarded as only marginally harmful; typically they are subjects of conflict and debate.

**Conflict subculture.** Illegal group activity that is prone to violence and is common in settings (for example, "disorganized slums") where legitimate and illegitimate spheres are not integrated.

**Conflict theories of deviance.** Theories that focus particularly on the way dominant societal groups impose their legal controls on members of subordinate societal groups.

**Consensus crimes.** Acts defined by law as criminal that are widely regarded as extremely harmful, are severely punished, and are consensually identified as deviant.

**Crime control model.** Model of law enforcement that places heavy emphasis on the repression of criminal conduct, because ensuring order is seen as the only way to guarantee individual freedom.

**Delinquent subculture.** Collective response of working-class adolescents to their failure to satisfy middle-class expectations; the result is an inversion of middle-class values.

**Deviance.** Variation from a norm, made socially significant through the reaction of others.

**Differential association.** Process by which criminal behaviour is learned in conjunction with people who define such behaviour favourably and in isolation from those who define it unfavourably.

**Due process model.** Model of law enforcement that emphasizes procedural safeguards thought useful in protecting accused persons from unjust applications of criminal penalties.

**Neutralization techniques.** Linguistic expressions that, through a subtle process of justification, allow individuals to drift into deviant lifestyles.

**Primary deviance.** Deviant behaviours that precede a societal or legal response and have little impact on the individual's self-concept.

**Residual rule-breaking.** Category conventionally called "mental illness" that includes forms of rule-breaking for which society has no specific labels.

**Retreatist subculture.** Group-supported forms of escapist behaviour, particularly drug abuse, that result from failure in both legitimate and illegitimate spheres of activity.

**Secondary deviance.** Deviant behaviours that follow a societal or legal response and involve a transformation of the individual's self-concept.

**Self-report survey.** Paper-and-pencil questionnaires used with adolescents and adults to obtain first-person accounts of amounts and types of deviant behaviour.

**Social deviation.** Noncriminal variation from social

norms that is nonetheless subject to frequent official control.

**Social diversion.** Variations of lifestyle, including fads and fashions of appearance and behaviour.

**Stable criminal subculture.** Illegal group enterprises made more persistent by the protection they receive from persons in legitimate social roles (for example, politicians and police).

terns of official action — referred to as "structural deviance" — such as arresting, charging, harassing, and warning, which can have organizational roots.

## FURTHER READING

**Black, Donald.** *The Behavior of Law*. New York: Academic Press, 1976. One of the most widely read of recent theoretical works on the way criminal and other kinds of law actually operate in real legal settings.

**Boydell, Craig L., and Ingrid Arnet Connidis.** *The Canadian Criminal Justice System*. Toronto: Holt, Rinehart and Winston, 1982. An up-to-date and comprehensive collection of readings.

**Brannigan, Augustine.** *Crimes, Courts and Corrections: An Introduction to Crime and Social Control in Canada*. Toronto: Holt, Rinehart and Winston, 1984. This book focuses on the criminal justice system, giving particular attention to the police, courts, and corrections. New perspectives on these institutions are offered, while common assumptions of the past are questioned.

**Chambliss, William, and Robert Seidman.** *Law, Order and Power*. Reading, MA: Addison Wesley, 1982. A conflict perspective on criminal law and its enforcement. This book deals with all aspects of the criminal justice system and with the development of criminal law.

**Durkheim, Emile.** *Suicide*. John A. Spalding and George Simpson (trans.). Glencoe, IL: Free Press, 1964. The classic work on this form of deviant behaviour. Durkheim anticipated much of what is thought modern in sociological theorizing about crime and deviance, including anomie theory and the labelling perspective.

**Ericson, Richard.** *Reproducing Order: A Study of Police Patrol Work*. Toronto: University of Toronto Press, 1982. This volume presents the results of the most comprehensive field study of policing done in Canada.

**Griffiths, Curt T., John F. Klein, and Simon N. Verdun-Jones.** *Criminal Justice in Canada*. Vancouver: Butterworths, 1980. This volume provides a concise yet comprehensive introduction to the Canadian criminal justice system, with particular attention to the police, courts, and correctional subsystems.

**Hagan, John.** *The Disreputable Pleasures: Crime and Deviance in Canada*. 2nd edition. Toronto: McGraw-Hill Ryerson, 1984. An integrated textbook treatment of crime and deviance with a twist: it is argued that crime and deviance can be pleasurable, albeit disreputable, pursuits.

**Shearing, Clifford.** *Organizational Police Deviance*. Toronto: Butterworths, 1982. This book brings together a collection of articles that broadens the subject of police misbehaviour from simple corruption, which can be dismissed as a private moral failing, to pervasive pat-

ANDRÉ LAPINE A.R.C.A.

# UNIT III

# The Social Base

*The fabric of life in every society is largely determined by its social base. For example, a society where people usually live to age 40 is very different from one where they usually live to age 80.*

*Major factors are working to shape society. The density and distribution of population, the ways in which society is stratified or divided into levels, the size and distribution of various ethnic groups, and the number and nature of formal organizations all play an important part.*

*Consider the fact that Canada is larger than the United States but has roughly the population of California. Or this: The world's population is expected to double in approximately 40 years — to more than 9 billion people in the early years of the next century. Chapter 7 examines the causes and consequences of the population characteristics of societies.*

*Every society is stratified, or ranked, in some way: leaders and followers, rich children and poor children, vice presidents and junior clerks. The ways in which societies are stratified and the degree of mobility between levels are the concerns of Chapter 8.*

*The interaction of various ethnic groups is important in most societies, and this is particularly true in Canada, where we are committed to maintaining the identities of different ethnic groups. Chapter 9 discusses the concepts of ethnicity and race, and their importance for understanding Canadian society.*

*Modern societies increasingly are arranged into large, formal organizations. Today, most of us are born and educated, work and die in formal organizations. Chapter 10 examines some of the causes and consequences of this type of social organization.*

# CHAPTER 7

# Population

ELLEN M. GEE

Population is a fundamental element of society; its characteristics are important determinants of social, economic, and political structure. In turn, the social organization affects the characteristics of a population.

The interrelationship between population and social factors can be seen by noting one "population fact" about Canadian society: compared to many non-Western societies, women in Canada produce few babies. Why? The answer lies not in biology or instinct, but in the social setting in which women, and couples, find themselves. Canada is primarily an urban society, and children are more expensive and less economically useful to parents in an urban society than in a rural one. Approximately half the married women in Canada work outside the home, a fact that is itself related to our urban economic structure. In other words, our society provides for women an alternative that competes with the traditional child-rearing role. Also, in Canada contraception is generally accessible and acceptable. Our acceptance of contraception reflects our social beliefs that such behaviour is not immoral, that marriage exists for reasons other than just procreation, and that we can and should control our fates as individuals.

Not only is the rate of child production subject to social causes, but it has social consequences as well. One consequence of the low production of children in Canada is that our population is becoming "old." That is, we have proportionately more older people and fewer younger people than societies producing more babies per woman. An "old" population poses a number of social challenges, such as housing, income maintenance, and health care for a large number of elderly people who no longer make a direct economic contribution to the wider society. Since one of the social factors that helps create an "old" population is a decreased emphasis on families, we may not be able to expect the family to be a major source of aid to our increasing elderly population, although current evidence suggests that the family continues to play an important role in this regard.

**Demography**, a subfield of sociology, is the scientific study of population. Demographers describe and explain the characteristics of population and the processes underlying those characteristics. The study of both the characteristics and the processes of population encompasses an examination of social variables. Neither the society nor the population can be understood apart from the other.

There are three major characteristics of population: size, composition, and distribution. **Population size** refers to the number of people in a given area. **Population composition** concerns the characteristics of the people in the population, particularly age and sex. When we say that women represent approximately 51 percent of the Canadian population and that nearly 11 percent of our population is aged 65 and over, we are talking about the composition of our population. **Population distribution** refers to the geographic location of people in a population. For example, approximately 9 percent of the Canadian population lives in Alberta; about one-quarter of the Canadian population lives in rural areas. These are facts concerning population distribution in Canada.

These population characteristics are, in turn, determined by the three demographic processes of fertility, mortality, and migration. **Fertility** refers to actual child-bearing in a population. **Mortality** refers to the deaths that occur in a population. **Migration** is the movement of persons from one geographic location to another.

Perhaps most importantly, these three processes together affect change in population size. Is the population increasing or decreasing? At what pace? Why? An examination of fertility, mortality, and migration will help us answer these questions, particularly the "why" of population change. Given that "population bomb" and "population explosion" are household words, it is important

to know the mechanisms underlying population change. We will therefore turn our attention first to the issue of population growth.

## Population Growth

We tend to think of population change in terms of increase, but it is important to keep in mind that populations can also decrease, and certainly some have done so. Populations can grow quickly or slowly. A glance at Figure 7-1 shows that world population increased relatively slowly until about 1650, and that rapid population growth is unique to the twentieth century. In 1650, the total population of the world was approximately 500 million; by 1987, it was over 5 billion.

Underlying the huge increase in the world's population is a changing growth rate. **Growth rate** refers to the number of people added to (or subtracted from) a population in a given time period for every 100 or 1000 people in the population. Often, growth is expressed as an annual rate per 1000 population.

**Figure 7-1. A Schematic Representation of the Increase in the Human Species**

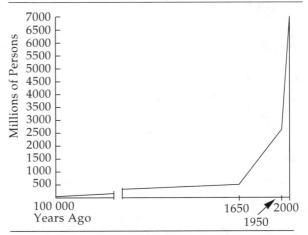

SOURCE: W. Peterson, *Population*, 3rd edition (New York: Macmillan, 1975), 9.

The history of world population growth is one in which growth rates increase markedly over time. For the period from 8000 B.C. to 1750, world population grew by approximately half a person per 1000 population per year. In comparison, world population is currently growing by about 17 persons per 1000 population per year. This growth rate, the highest in the history of humankind, cannot continue indefinitely. If it did, the human population would outweigh the earth it stands on in less than 1200 years from now (Coale 1974). The present era of growth is, by necessity, a transitory phenomenon. Indeed, it is expected that the annual growth rate will slow down; the United Nations projected rate for the end of this century is 15.1.

The growth rate plays the important role of determining how fast a population will change in size. Demographers often measure the pace of population increase in terms of doubling time. **Doubling time** is the number of years it will take for a population to double in numbers, assuming that the current growth rate remains unchanged. If the annual growth rate for 1987 (17 per 1000 population) were to remain unchanged, the world's population would double in approximately 40 years. In that event, the world would contain more than 10 billion people in 2027.

## Variations in Growth

So far, we have looked at population growth in terms of the world as a whole. The world's population has increased dramatically, particularly in the twentieth century, due to rising rates of growth. Against this background of general increase, however, different parts of the world have experienced different rates of growth, both in the past and in the present.

From 1600 to 1950, Europe (including the USSR) and the areas of European settlement (for example, the United States, Canada, Australia, and New Zealand) experienced large-scale population growth. In contrast, non-Western populations grew very slowly.

But the present situation is radically different. In today's world, non-Western or "developing" nations are growing at a much faster pace than Western populations. The annual growth rate in the developing nations is around 21 per 1000 population; in the developed world, it averages 5.

Projections concerning future growth suggest a continuation of the present pattern. The United Nations estimates that at the end of this century the growth rate in the developing regions of the world will be approximately 19. Africa, particularly, is singled out for predicted large-scale future growth, with a growth rate of over 30 expected for the end of the century. Such a figure implies a doubling time of around 23 years. The projected growth rate for the developed regions is, by contrast, approximately 5 (United Nations 1984), implying a doubling time of approximately 140 years.

## Components of Growth

To understand the causes of growth for the world population and for the different societies that make it up, we have to look at the components of growth: the three demographic processes of fertility, mortality, and migration.

For the world, population increase is a direct result of the extent to which births (fertility) outnumber deaths (mortality). The excess of births over deaths is termed **natural increase**. (If deaths exceed births, the term *natural decrease* is used.) A population can also change in size as a result of migratory movement. **Net migration** refers to the difference between the number of *in-migrants* (people moving into an area) and the number of *out-migrants* (people moving away). Net migration is positive when the number of in-migrants exceeds the number of out-migrants and negative when out-migrants outnumber in-migrants.

When we are talking about the world as a whole, only natural increase is involved in population growth: no one, at least so far, has been able to leave the earth's surface for any appreciable length of time and no "people" originating elsewhere have moved in. In some parts of the world, however, including Canada, net migration does play a role in population growth.

**Rate of Natural Increase.** The rate of natural increase, arrived at by subtracting what is termed the **crude death rate** from the **crude birth rate**, is usually measured in terms of a single-year interval and is expressed as a figure per 1000 population. The formula for the computation of the rate of natural increase is

RNI = CBR - CDR,
where
RNI = rate of natural increase in a given year per 1000 population

CBR = crude birth rate,
or
$$\frac{\text{Number of births in a given year}}{\text{Mid-year population}} \times 1000$$

CDR = crude death rate,
or
$$\frac{\text{Number of deaths in a given year}}{\text{Mid-year population}} \times 1000$$

High positive values indicate that the population is growing substantially due to natural increase. Negative values indicate natural decrease. A rate of zero means that the birth rate and the death rate are identical, with no change in population size due to natural increase.

Table 7-1 presents 1987 data on rates of natural increase, and on birth and death rates, for major areas of the world and for selected countries. The highest rates of natural increase occur in Africa and Latin America. The lowest rates occur in Europe, and some European countries (for example, West Germany) are currently experiencing natural decrease. The "new" societies with a European heritage — like Canada, the United States, and Australia — have low rates as well, although somewhat higher than those of Europe.

Different amounts of societal variation exist in the two variables that make up the rate of natural increase: the crude birth rate and the crude death rate. Birth rates vary considerably from society to society. In 1987, the highest level was recorded in Malawi and Rwanda: 53 births per 1000 population. The lowest rate, 10, was registered in West Germany and Italy. In general, the level of the crude birth rate is related to the level of economic development. That is, developed societies experience low birth rates, while Third World societies have much higher birth rates. Variations in the crude death rate, however, bear no such clear-cut relationship to the level of economic develop-

## Table 7-1. Rates of Natural Increase, Crude Birth Rates, and Crude Death Rates, 1987

| | Rate of Natural Increase (per 1000) | Crude Birth Rate (per 1000) | Crude Death Rate (per 1000) |
|---|---|---|---|
| *World* | 17 | 28 | 10 |
| *Africa* | 28 | 44 | 16 |
| Egypt | 26 | 37 | 11 |
| Niger | 29 | 51 | 22 |
| Ethiopia | 23 | 46 | 23 |
| *Asia* | 19 | 28 | 10 |
| Bangladesh | 27 | 44 | 17 |
| India | 21 | 33 | 12 |
| Japan | 6 | 12 | 6 |
| China (People's Republic) | 13 | 21 | 8 |
| *North America* | 7 | 15 | 9 |
| Canada | 8 | 15 | 7 |
| United States | 7 | 16 | 9 |
| *Latin America* | 22 | 30 | 8 |
| Mexico | 25 | 31 | 7 |
| Venezuela | 27 | 32 | 6 |
| Argentina | 16 | 24 | 8 |
| *Europe* | 3 | 13 | 10 |
| United Kingdom | 2 | 13 | 12 |
| France | 4 | 14 | 10 |
| Spain | 5 | 13 | 8 |
| West Germany | −2 | 10 | 12 |
| Poland | 8 | 18 | 10 |
| *Oceania* | 12 | 20 | 8 |
| Australia | 8 | 16 | 8 |
| *USSR* | 9 | 19 | 11 |

SOURCE: *World Population Data Sheet* (Washington, DC: Population Reference Bureau, 1987).

ment. Many nations in the developing world have very low death rates. On the other hand, western European societies, all highly industrialized, do not experience particularly low death rates. For example, Sweden's 1987 death rate, 11, was more than double that of Singapore. That is partly a reflection of differences in the age composition of the two countries. Sweden has an older population than Singapore, and therefore has more deaths relative to its population size than does Singapore.

## Natural Increase and Net Migration: The Canadian Case

For most populations, natural increase plays a much more important role than net migration in affecting population growth. For the world as a whole, only natural increase is involved; for the different societies in the world, the migration component plays a greater or lesser role depending on a number of factors, such as political stability, economic conditions, and the like.

Canada is one society in which migration has played an important role in population growth. Because Canada is usually perceived as an immigrant-receiving country, we would expect that positive net migration has played a major part in bringing our population to its current size. Let us see if the data confirm this expectation. Table

7-2 provides information concerning the roles played by natural increase and net migration in Canada's population growth from 1851 (the time of the first regular census) to 1986. While the historical factors accounting for Canadian population growth are complex and vary over time, natural increase has clearly played the major role in Canada's growth since 1851.

The trend of the growth rate in Canada has had an uneven history. Growth has been substantial at some points in history and quite small at others. The early decades of this century, particularly 1901 to 1911, and the decade of the 1950s can be singled out as times of rapid growth. On the other hand, the latter part of the nineteenth century, the 1970s, and the early 1980s are characterized by low growth rates. What accounts for these fluctuations in the trend of population growth? The answer lies in

### Table 7-2. Natural Increase and Net Migration in Canada,[a] 1851–1986

| Census Year | Population (in thousands) | Average Annual Growth Rate (per 1000) | Rate of Natural Increase (per 1000) | Rate of Net Migration (per 1000) |
|---|---|---|---|---|
| 1851 | 2 436 | — | — | — |
| 1861 | 3 230 | 29 | 22 | 6 |
| 1871 | 3 698 | 13 | 18 | −4 |
| 1881 | 4 325 | 16 | 17 | −1 |
| 1891 | 4 833 | 11 | 14 | −3 |
| 1901 | 5 371 | 11 | 13 | −2 |
| 1911 | 7 207 | 30 | 16 | 13 |
| 1921 | 8 788 | 20 | 16 | 4 |
| 1931 | 10 377 | 17 | 14 | 2 |
| 1941 | 11 507 | 10 | 11 | −1 |
| 1951 | 14 009 | 17 | 15 | 1 |
| 1956 | 16 081 | 28 | 20 | 8 |
| 1961 | 18 238 | 25 | 20 | 6 |
| 1966 | 20 015 | 19 | 16 | 3 |
| 1971 | 21 568 | 15 | 10 | 4 |
| 1976 | 22 993 | 13 | 9 | 3 |
| 1981 | 24 343 | 12 | 8 | 4 |
| 1982 | 24 632 | 12 | 8 | 4 |
| 1983 | 24 885 | 10 | 8 | 2 |
| 1984 | 25 124 | 10 | 8 | 2 |
| 1985 | 25 360 | 9 | 8 | 1 |
| 1986 | 25 591 | 9 | 8 | 1 |

[a] Excludes Newfoundland prior to 1951.

SOURCES: Adapted from Roderic P. Beaujot, "Canada's Population: Growth and Dualism," *Population Bulletin* 33(2):6 (Washington, DC: Population Reference Bureau, 1978); David K. Foot, *Canada's Population Outlook* (Toronto: James Lorimer/Canadian Institute for Economic Policy, 1982), p. 4; Minister of Supply and Services, *Current Demographic Analysis: Report on the Demographic Situation in Canada in 1986*, Cat. 91–209E.

different combinations of rates of natural increase and net migration.

Let us focus first on the two periods of rapid growth. The high growth rate for 1901 to 1911 can be largely accounted for by a large increase in the rate of positive net migration. The level of positive net migration that occurred in this decade is the highest recorded for any decade since 1851. This large excess of immigrants, relative to emigrants, reflects a change in immigration laws that took place at the time. It was the goal of the Laurier government to populate the western, rural part of the country, the prairies, with people who had a background in agricultural skills. To achieve that goal, immigration restrictions were liberalized, and Europeans from countries previously defined as "nonpreferred" (for example, the countries of eastern Europe) were allowed relatively easy entrance into Canada. Their movement into Canada, occurring as a wave, helped bolster the rate of net migration. Even with this unprecedented rate of in-migration, however, natural increase still accounted for more than half the total population growth in the decade.

In the second period of rapid growth, the 1950s, a very different picture emerges. This was not a time of unusually high positive net migration; the rate does not approach that of 1901 to 1911, for instance. Even if the rate of net migration had been zero, the 1950s would have experienced a growth rate higher than that occurring in earlier or later decades. It was a high rate of natural increase, not positive net migration, that was largely responsible for the high growth rate. As we will see later, the phenomenon known as the "baby boom," a period of high crude birth rates, was concentrated in this decade. As a result, the rate of natural increase, affected as it is by the level of the crude birth rate, was high.

The two periods characterized by low population growth rates also resulted from differential combinations of natural increase and net migration. In the latter decades of the nineteenth century, negative net migration rates operated to deflate the growth rate. Why was net migration negative for the 40-year period from 1861 to 1901? How does an immigrant-receiving country like Canada end up with negative rates of net migration, especially for such a long period of time? It was not the case that no immigrants entered Canada. In fact, it is estimated that between one and

two million people came to Canada from other countries in the period from 1861 to 1901 (Kalbach and McVey 1979). However, greater numbers of people left Canada than entered during this time. In large part, the out-migrants — who consisted of both the Canadian-born and people who had immigrated to Canada at an earlier time in their lives — went to the United States, attracted to the possibilities offered by a rapidly expanding American economy.

The current period of relatively small growth is not similarly a function of negative net migration, although positive net migration is not large. Rather, a historical low point has been reached in the rate of natural incrase, the result of our currently low birth rate.

Growth in the Canadian population, then, has resulted from the combined factors of natural increase and net migration. Of these, natural increase has played a dominant role. For most decades, the contribution of natural increase to population growth has far exceeded that of net migration. The role played by migration has varied over time; migration has functioned to increase our size at some points and to lessen it at others. As a result, the pattern of migration accounts for much of the unevenness in the trend of Canadian population growth, although fluctuations in fertility have been important as well.

While natural increase has played the major role in Canada's growth to date, projections concerning the future growth of our population present a very different picture. If we assume that fertility remains at its current low levels and that annual net migration averages 50 000 (in 1986, net migration was 37 500), then, after the turn of the century, net migration will make a larger contribution to population growth than natural increase. Indeed, given these assumptions, after 2015, net migration will be the only contribution to our growth, and after 2021, the annual net migration of 50 000 will be exceeded by natural decrease, and the total Canadian population will begin to decline in size (Employment and Immigration Canada 1984).

## Malthusian Theory

One of the earliest and most influential statements regarding population growth was that of Thomas Malthus, an English clergyman and economist (for summaries, see Thompson and Lewis 1965; Bogue 1969; Overbeek 1974). Malthus wrote a series of essays expanding on his theory concerning the growth of population in relation to human welfare. Reacting against the optimism in eighteenth-century Europe, Malthus came to be viewed as a "prophet of doom" because he saw the human condition as inevitably worsening due to the working of the "principle of population."

Malthus's principle of population is that unchecked population grows at a rate that surpasses the ability of the means of subsistence (food) to support it. The means of subsistence, if they do increase, can increase only in *arithmetic* progression (1, 2, 3, 4, 5); population increases in *geometric* progression (1, 2, 4, 8, 16). Figure 7-2 graphs the growth curves for population and for food that result from these laws of increase, and shows the ever-widening gap Malthus saw as inevitable if populations were to grow unchecked.

The tendency to reproduce at a rate exceeding the supply of food has, of course, disastrous consequences. Something must counteract unlimited population growth. For Malthus, the checks on population are of two types: preventive and positive.

The *preventive checks* result from human action that operates to lower the number of births. For Malthus, the postponement of marriage is the major preventive check, since a late marrying age implies that fewer children can be born to a woman before she "ages out" of her reproductive years. Another type of preventive check is possible: the prevention of births within marriage by some voluntary means other than abstinence. Reflecting the times in which he lived, however, Malthus felt such action to be immoral and did not view it as a permissible preventive check.

The *positive checks*, on the other hand, result from either humans or natural forces operating chiefly to increase the number of deaths. War is an example of a positive check stemming from action on the part of people. Famines, plagues, and natural disasters are examples of positive checks not caused by human hands. Malthus also puts forth "vice" as a positive check on population growth. For example, Malthus saw prostitution as a "vice," and claimed that such activity has a dampening effect on the birth rate.

Any of these checks can prevent population from growing at its maximum rate, but Malthus

### Figure 7-2. The Malthusian Curves

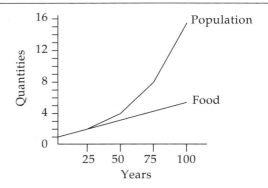

| Period | | 1 | 2 | 3 | 4 | 5 | 6 | 7 | 8 |
|---|---|---|---|---|---|---|---|---|---|
| Year | | 1 | 25 | 50 | 75 | 100 | 125 | 150 | 175 |
| Growth of Population | 1 | 2 | 4 | 8 | 16 | 32 | 64 | 128 |
| Growth of Food | 1 | 2 | 3 | 4 | 5 | 6 | 7 | 8 |

SOURCE: J. Overbeek, *History of Population Theories* (Rotterdam: Rotterdam University Press, 1974), p. 43.

did not think that the preventive checks were effective or powerful enough to do the job alone. Sooner or later, the more drastic positive checks would come into play. Therefore the fate of humanity was inevitable, governed by the laws of nature: humans were bound to over-reproduce themselves relative to the means of subsistence; their numbers, however, would necessarily be diminished, in the end, by an increased death rate.

The Malthusian position implies an acceptance of the way things are. Improvements in people's living conditions are self-defeating, for "good times" lead to a lifting of the preventive checks, and the consequent population growth, following the law of geometric progression, would surpass the ability of the means of subsistence to support it.

## Marx's Perspective

Although Karl Marx's writing on the subject of population was secondary to his general social and economic theory (for summaries, see Bogue 1969; Overbeek 1974), his arguments are a direct, negative reaction to Malthusian theory and to Malthus.

Marx objected to the Malthusian idea that there is one principle of population that applies to all types of societies. Marx argued that each "mode of production" in history is characterized by its own particular law of population. Feudal society, for example, and later capitalist society, operated in terms of a law of population peculiar to each, and Marx's envisioned communist society would likewise forge a unique law.

According to Marx, the "law of relative surplus population" is characteristic of capitalist society. Capitalism, he believed, creates overpopulation — that is, a surplus of people relative to jobs, leading to high unemployment and increasing poverty. It is the nature of capitalist society to produce this end, he felt, given that the bourgeoisie, in their own economic interest, will continue to introduce labour-saving machinery and equipment, thus making workers obsolete. Capitalists who do not, or cannot, follow suit will be unable to meet their automated competition; their bankruptcies will lead to further unemployment among workers. However, according to Marx, capitalism not only creates unemployment, it *requires* unemployment in order to ensure a docile, low-paid class of labourers. The capitalist system, then, as Marx saw it, is one fraught with unemployment and underemployment, regardless of the rate of growth of the population (or labour force). Furthermore, for Marx, unemployment and poverty themselves lead to a high rate of population growth as a result of the high fertility of the poor, thus compounding human misery.

Overpopulation would, according to Marx, be overcome in a communist society. He did not specify the nature of the law of population corresponding to a communist society, however, so it is difficult to know precisely how this population control would be achieved. Probably Marx believed that a new social and economic order based on communist principles could ensure full employment, regardless of the rate of population growth.

Partly as a result of the lack of detail in his writing concerning population, Marx's impact on demography has been less than on most other areas within sociology discussed in this textbook. His focus on the employment aspect of population is narrow, neglecting other dimensions of importance. In fact, it has been argued that Marx, while attempting to outline a theory of population, actually formulated a theory of employment

(Overbeek 1974). Nevertheless, his overall point — that population growth and overpopulation are products of the wider social and economic structure — is indisputable. Marx understood that social factors play an influential role in population; Malthus generally lacked that insight.

## Demographic Transition Theory

Much contemporary writing on population growth stems from **demographic transition theory**, formulated on the basis of observed changes in population growth in western European societies (for summaries, see Stolnitz 1964; Coale 1973). It provides both a description and an explanation of historical change in population growth.

According to demographic transition theory, a population goes through three major stages in its "transition" to a modern pattern. *Stage One* is the stage of pretransition. The population is characterized by high fertility and high mortality. Birth rates are constantly high, whereas death rates fluctuate around an "average" high level in response to external conditions, such as the presence or absence of famines, epidemics, and so forth. Because both rates are high, population grows slowly, if at all.

*Stage Two*, the stage of transitional growth, consists of two phases or substages. In the first substage, the death rate declines, but the birth rate remains at the high level characteristic of Stage One. As a result, the population grows rapidly. In the second substage, the birth rate begins to decline while the death rate continues to decrease. Because mortality decline has had a head start, the death rate remains lower than the birth rate. A high rate of population growth characterizes this substage as well.

In *Stage Three*, the transition to low birth and death rates is complete. The rate of population growth, then, slows in comparison with Stage Two. The completion of "transition" implies zero population growth, or what demographers call a stationary population, at least in the long run. The rates of population growth in Stage Three and Stage One are therefore similar but are achieved differently.

In Stage Three, death rates do not fluctuate; they are constantly low because the means exist to control short-term mortality crises such as

**All Western populations have experienced fluctuating and declining fertility, making large families a thing of the past.**

epidemics. Birth rates, however, fluctuate in accordance with wider trends in society, such as economic recessions and booms. The low but fluctuating fertility level of this stage is accomplished through deliberate control of child-bearing.

As a population moves out of Stage One into Stage Two and later into Stage Three, there is no turning back to an earlier stage of demographic development, according to transition theory. Societies may differ in the pace of transition, in the time gap between death-rate decline and the commencement of birth-rate decline, or in the factors precipitating transition; but the process, once begun, is irreversible.

Demographic transition theory (outlined in Figure 7-3) explains this course of demographic events in terms of changes in the wider social and economic environment, particularly industrialization and urbanization. The demographic characteristics of Stage One result from the inability of pre-industrial society to control mortality. Given a deadly environment, the predictable response is to maximize fertility. However, high fertility represents more than a reaction to high mortality. In a pre-industrial society, children are economically advantageous because they contribute to agricultural productivity at young ages and function as a source of security for aging parents. The costs of child-rearing, on the other hand, are small. The economic utility of children is buttressed by a system of social beliefs that reinforces the value of children.

Technological advance results in improvements in the production and distribution of food, in sanitation, and in medicine. A society is quick to accept these improvements, given their life-sus-

## Figure 7-3. Model of Demographic Transition

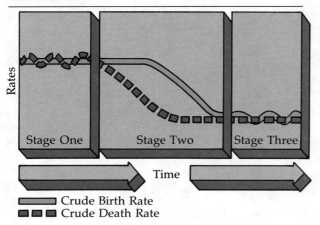

Rates

Stage One    Stage Two    Stage Three

Time

▭ Crude Birth Rate
▬▬▬ Crude Death Rate

taining effects. As a result, death rates decline, and the first phase of transition begins.

Fertility, however, responds more slowly to modernization; declines in fertility are more difficult to bring about than declines in mortality. The high fertility of pretransitional societies is upheld by social beliefs and values that run counter to the behavioural changes needed to reduce fertility.

Nevertheless, modernization eventually operates to lower fertility. Declining mortality, for example, acts as a damper on the birth rate, since one of the first groups to benefit from mortality reduction is young children; when more infants begin to survive past early childhood, "insurance" births become less necessary. Furthermore, urbanization, one facet of modernization, lessens the productive utility of children. At the same time, the cost of child-rearing rises in an urban setting, as education costs increase; big families thus come to be seen as liabilities.

Demographic transition theory is not without critics (for example, Okediji 1974). One major criticism is that the theory, both as description and as explanation, has been modelled after the Western experience and may not be applicable to today's Third World countries.

Indeed, there is one crucial difference between the demographic transition as it was experienced in the Western world and the transition in today's developing countries. In the West, mortality decline was relatively slow, generally paralleling the course of economic modernization. Today's Third World countries, in contrast, have experienced very rapid declines in death rates, in most cases achieved since World War II. Also, the rapid mortality decline in the Third World has occurred, in many instances, as a result of borrowing Western mortality-reducing technology rather than through the more difficult and lengthy process of economic development.

## Malthus and Marx: Sociological Theory in Demography

In demography, the major perspectives are Malthusian theory, Marxist theory, and the theory of demographic transition. Each concerns population growth and the mechanisms determining it. They vary in terms of detail, the types of variables that are viewed as important, and the degree to which they are accepted by contemporary demographers. Demographic transition theory is the perspective that currently dominates the study of population.

Only one of the three major theoretical perspectives mentioned in Chapter 1 — the Marxist or conflict model — is found within the history of academic demographic thought. The other sociological perspectives lack representation for at least two reasons. First, early recognition of the importance of population, and early attempts to explain population change and population processes, came from economics rather than sociology. Malthus was an economist; the early statements of demographic transition theory were formulated, in the main, by economists; even Marx's orientation to population was largely economic, with a focus on the variable of employment. As a result, the study of population lacks a history of theoretical contribution from either structural functionalism or symbolic interaction.

A second reason, closely related to the first one, is that demography is somewhat peripheral to mainstream sociology. While demographic variables are common within sociology, they are largely used as explanatory or independent variables. Demographers alone have sought to explain population variables — that is, formulated demographic variables as dependent variables. As a consequence, demography has developed theoretical perspectives that have no parallels in other branches of sociology.

# Fertility

Natural increase — the excess of births over deaths — is a major component of population growth. For the world as a whole, it is the only component. For most societies, including Canada, it is the largest component. Since the demographic process of fertility is one of the elements of natural increase, let us now turn our attention to that process and examine it in more detail.

Demographers use the term *fertility* to refer to the actual child-bearing of a woman or group of women. It is distinguished from **fecundity**, which refers to the potential child-bearing of a woman or group of women. Fertility is always lower than fecundity. No society has ever produced babies at a rate approaching women's physiological capacity to do so. The production of babies at a rate lower than the biological maximum is the consequence of either, or both, of two mechanisms.

First, fertility can be consciously limited by individuals. Some action is taken with the deliberate aim of preventing the occurrence of a conception or a birth. The contraceptive pill, intrauterine devices, diaphragms, spermicidal foam, sterilization, and condoms are all methods that help prevent pregnancy. Abstinence and coitus interruptus ("withdrawal") can also be viewed in this light. Abortion, on the other hand, is an act aimed at preventing a birth after conception has occurred.

Deliberate fertility-control measures such as those just listed may be used at different times during an individual's reproductive years. They may be used to postpone the beginning of family formation, to space children at desired intervals, or to prevent births altogether. The conscious limitation of fertility, through any of these techniques and for any of these purposes, depends on people's attitudes (is fertility control viewed as desirable? as morally acceptable?), their knowledge of effective means to control fertility, and the availability and proper use of those means.

The second fertility-limiting mechanism involves actions intended to achieve other ends. French demographer Louis Henry (1961) introduced the term **natural fertility** for the less-than-biological-maximum fertility occurring in a population due to behaviour that, although not aimed specifically at modifying the number of children born, nevertheless has that effect. A number of practices can be identified as having fertility-limiting effects without having fertility-limiting intentions. Prolonged lactation (breastfeeding) temporarily diminishes a woman's capacity to conceive another child. Also, some societies are characterized by long post-partum ("following the birth") bans on sexual intercourse. Similarly, the practice of marriage postponement can effectively limit fertility, provided that the society does not have a high occurrence of births outside wedlock.

These, then, are the two major types of fertility control: voluntary or deliberate control, and unintentional control. To the degree that any control occurs, fertility falls short of the maximum possible.

Another factor affects fertility. Some portion of any population is involuntarily childless. People incapable, for physiological reasons, of producing children are termed **infecund**. Also, some portion of any population is subfecund. The **subfecund** are people who are biologically capable of producing children but, even in the absence of any fertility-limiting measures, have difficulty doing so.

## Fertility Measurement

Two types of fertility measurement exist: period and cohort. **Period measures** of fertility, of which the crude birth rate is one example, assess the number of births that occur in a population in one time period, usually a year. **Cohort measures**, on the other hand, assess the number of births that occur to a particular group of women (a cohort) over a longer period of time. With cohort measurement, we can assess the total number of births that a cohort of women has over the reproductive span — that is, their "completed family size." For example, ever-married women aged 45 to 49 in 1981 (the 1932–1936 cohort) had a completed family size of 3.3 children per woman.

**Period Measures.** The crude birth rate is a period measure of fertility; it assesses the number of births that occur in one year in relationship to the total population. For purposes of assessing the extent to which births contribute to natural increase and hence to population growth, the crude birth rate is an adequate measure of fertility. For other purposes, however, more refined rates are required.

The crude birth rate is a "crude" or unrefined measure in the sense that its denominator, the total population, includes people (like males of all ages, children, and the female aged) who do not bear children. A more refined measure (called a **refined rate**) limits the denominator to those directly exposed to the risk of child-bearing — that is, women in their child-bearing years. A hypothetical example will show us the limitations in using crude measurement. Suppose there are two populations, A and B. Both have a population of 1000 and both produced 25 babies last year. The crude birth rate in both cases is 25, and we would be tempted to conclude an equivalency in fertility. However, let us say that population A comprised 500 people who could give birth (that is, women aged 15 to 49) and population B comprised only 350. Then one in twenty women had a baby last year in population A, whereas in population B the ratio is one woman in fourteen. Looked at in this way, the women in population B had a higher fertility level than the women in population A, but that fact is masked when we relate number of births to the total population.

There are several kinds of period fertility measures that are more refined than the crude birth rate. We will now look very briefly at the ones most commonly in use.

The **general fertility rate** represents a refinement over the crude birth rate in that it restricts the denominator to women in the prime reproductive ages. In Canada in 1985, the general fertility rate was 55.1 births per 1000 women aged 15 to 49.

**Age-specific birth rates** are a third widely used type of period fertility measure. Age-specific birth rates for any year are obtained by dividing the number of births to mothers of a certain age by the number of women of that age in the population. These rates are useful because the rate of child-bearing in any population is not uniform throughout the reproductive ages. By studying these rates, we can see the particular pattern of child-bearing in a population, how it compares with other populations, and how it has changed over time.

**Cohort Fertility Analysis.** With period measures of fertility, the frequency of births in a given year is assessed. With cohort fertility analysis, the frequency of births occurring to a cohort of women over a longer period of time is measured. A **cohort** is a group of individuals who experience a "demographic event" at the same time. That is, all people born in 1960 constitute a cohort: a birth cohort. All people married in 1980 also constitute a cohort: a marriage cohort.

In cohort fertility analysis, the child-bearing of a birth cohort of women (or a marriage cohort of women) is traced throughout their reproductive years. It is then possible to assess the actual total number of children that different cohorts of women bear over the course of their reproductive span (completed family size) and to compare the timing of those births throughout that span.

We can see that cohort and period rates measure fertility from different perspectives. It is important *not* to place a cohort interpretation on period rates. For example, if we observe a trend of declining general fertility rates in a population, we cannot automatically conclude that the number of children born to women over the course of their reproductive years is declining. It is possible that a declining trend in general fertility occurs because women are delaying child-bearing at present, perhaps because of an economic recession. They could go on to have as many children as did women of an earlier time — or even more children than those women did. Similarly, a trend of increasing general fertility rates may reflect, rather than an increment in completed family size, a trend toward child-bearing at earlier ages in the reproductive span. Given that period rates are subject to these timing differences, demographers usually consider cohort measurement a more accurate representation if they are more interested in the actual reproductive behaviour of the women in a population during their total child-bearing years than in the reproductive performance of a population in a particular year.

## Fertility Change in Twentieth-Century Canada

Over the course of this century, the level of period fertility in Canada has declined. The trend, however, was not smooth. Fertility rates fell to low levels during the Depression of the 1930s, peaked for a 15-year period following the end of World War II, and declined during the 1960s, reaching unprecedentedly low levels in the 1980s. The period of post-war peak fertility is commonly termed the "baby boom"; the present low levels have been referred to as the "baby bust" (Grindstaff 1975).

This twentieth-century trend is not unique to Canada; all Western populations have experienced a pattern of declining, but fluctuating, period fertility levels. Canada is nevertheless distinctive in the sense that its baby boom lasted for a longer time and was larger than in other Western populations. However, the boom was not equally big in all parts of Canada. For example, Quebec experienced a smaller baby boom than did other provinces.

The baby-boom era is responsible for the major deviation from the trend of overall declining fertility that would be expected from demographic transition theory. What factors account for this unevenness in trend? Specifically, why did the baby boom occur?

One important variable is the timing of child-bearing. Significant changes have occurred in Canada over this century in terms of when women have their children. During the baby-boom era, women had their children at younger ages compared to women before or after them.

A trend toward child-bearing at a younger age gives rise to increasing period fertility rates. Similarly, a trend toward an older age at child-bearing results in decreasing fertility rates. A change in child-bearing timing affects the level of fertility because there are more younger women than older women in a population. If proportionately more women bear children at younger ages, more babies will be produced for the simple reason that there are more younger women. The high fertility of the baby-boom period reflected a shift toward younger child-bearing; the present trend of low fertility reflects, in part, a shift back to older child-bearing.

The timing of child-bearing in a population is itself the result of a complex of factors. One important variable is age at first marriage. If women marry at young ages, the possibility exists that they will have children relatively early in life. On the other hand, an older age at marriage tends to be associated with older child-bearing.

Throughout the course of the twentieth century in Canada, the average age at marriage has undergone significant changes. For both sexes, age at marriage is younger now than in the past. For example, the mean age at first marriage for women in the twentieth century before World War II was over 25. By 1951, the median had declined to approximately 22, and in 1961 it had dropped further, to just over 21. It rose again slightly, but in 1985, the median age remained under 23.

The essence of the baby boom, then, was a change in the timing of events in the lifespan of women. The baby-boom mothers married earlier than women before them and had their children in a short span after marriage. They did not go on to have significantly more children than earlier cohorts of women. Canadian census data for 1981 reveal that ever-married women born between 1927 and 1931, women whose chief child-bearing years occurred in the baby-boom era, bore 3.4 children on average. This figure is not much higher than the completed family size of ever-married women of earlier cohorts. For example, ever-married women born between 1907 and 1911 and between 1912 and 1916, women whose chief child-bearing years occurred prior to the baby boom, bore 3.3 and 3.1 children on average, respectively. Figure 7-4 shows general fertility rates in Canada from 1921 through 1985.

The heightened period fertility of the baby boom did not signify an increase in completed family size in Canada so much as a change in child-

## Figure 7-4. General Fertility Rates, Canada, 1921–1985

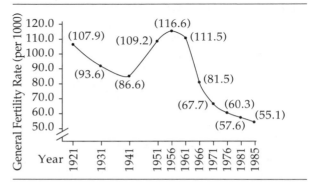

SOURCE: *Vital Statistics, 1976*, Volume 1, Statistics Canada, Cat. 84-206, Table 6; and *Vital Statistics, 1981* and *1985*, Volume 1, Statistics Canada, Cat. 84-204, Table 5.

bearing pattern. The low fertility of the baby bust similarly reflects a change in the age patterning of child-bearing to some degree. Today's young women are marrying and having children at older ages than their mothers. This is a generation of "postponers," whose behaviour reflects normative change, an economic recession, and the availability of effective contraceptive technology. We cannot assume that their completed family size will be as low as present period fertility levels suggest, although it is a certainty that they will have smaller families than earlier cohorts of Canadian women.

The fertility experience of Canada in the twentieth century points to the importance of distinguishing between period and cohort measures of fertility. Period rates indicate a substantial increase in fertility occurring in the 15 years following World War II (the baby boom), but cohort measures show us that the magnitude of the fertility increase was more influenced by changes in the timing of child-bearing than by actual changes in the size of completed families.

## Factors Affecting Fertility

Fertility levels vary across societies, within societies, and over time in some societies (Canada, for one). Some part of fertility variation is due to physiological variables, such as the incidence of infecundity. However, most of the variation is the result of differences in the degree to which fertility is consciously limited. The degree of deliberate fertility limitation is a product of the wider social environment within which the population exists. Fertility is a social fact and, as such, a complex phenomenon. Its level is determined by a number of factors interacting together. Four factors are particularly important: demographic, cultural, socioeconomic, and governmental. We will look at each factor separately, but it is important to keep in mind that they are highly interrelated.

**Demographic Factors.** Two population-related variables play an important role in affecting the fertility level: infant mortality and marriage pattern.

Infant mortality, usually measured by the **infant mortality rate**, refers to the incidence of death among children under the age of one in a population. For the world as a whole in 1987, the infant mortality rate was 81. In other words, more than 8 percent of all children born in 1987 died in the first year of life. Rates varied from a high of 183 (in East Timor, in Southeast Asia) to a low of 5.7 (in Iceland). The level in Canada was 7.9.

When the level of infant mortality is high, the level of fertility is high. A high incidence of infant death fosters a situation in which women produce many babies in order to ensure some surviving children. Insurance births result; that is, extra babies are produced "just in case." High infant mortality does not cause high fertility. However, the social and economic factors that affect high infant mortality affect high fertility as well.

The marriage pattern in a population also affects fertility level. Marriage pattern consists of two aspects: the average age at marriage and the proportion of people in a population who eventually marry. These two aspects tend to be related: where marriage occurs at young ages, most of the population marries. Conversely, old age at marriage and a high proportion of never-marrying tend to occur together.

The significance of marriage pattern for fertility level lies in its effect on the exposure of women to the risk of child-bearing. When virtually all women marry, and at young ages, there is greater exposure to the risk of producing children. This is so not only because more women are married for a longer period of time, but also because more are married at the time of peak child-bearing — that is, at ages under 30.

A second aspect of the effect of marriage pattern on fertility level concerns the structure of opportunities for women. If women marry at young ages, there are few alternatives for them outside the home. The focal point of their existence is their domestic role; and children justify that existence.

**Cultural Factors.** The cultural environment that people live in plays an important role in determining fertility behaviour. Culture affects the motivational structure of reproductive behaviour largely through the institutionalization of values that guide people in their actions regarding the number of children they have. These values bear directly on the acceptance (or rejection) of deliberate fertility-limiting practices. Two dimensions of culture are particularly important in this regard (Okediji 1974):

1. cultural definitions of the nature of human relations; and
2. cultural definitions of the "human condition."

Societies differ in the emphasis they place on the importance of the individual in relation to the wider group — that is, kin, or community. Where the wider group is viewed as taking precedence over the individual, children are highly valued since they increase the membership of the wider group. Consequently, child-bearing is highly rewarded. Societies that value the wider group, and hence the production of children, are termed *familistic*. In contrast are societies like ours, in which cultural values emphasize the individual over and above the wider group. The rewards for child-bearing are smaller; therefore, the motivation to produce children is less.

A related aspect of the cultural view of human relations concerns definitions of appropriate gender-role behaviour. If a man is considered a "real man" only if he fathers children, and if manliness is culturally gauged in direct proportion to the number of children he fathers, then the motivation for children is so great that their production in large numbers is virtually assured. If the cultural environment further stipulates that only male children "count," fertility will be high in order to ensure that the requisite number of sons are born (and survive). A cultural setting that assesses "maleness" in terms of the number of sons a man fathers is one that typically affords a low status to women. Because women lack economic and political power, the only avenue open for them to enhance their status is to produce children, preferably sons. Therefore, if culture defines expected gender-role behaviour in terms of reproductive performance, both men and women are strongly motivated to produce children and highly rewarded for so doing.

Keep in mind that all societies reward people for producing children. We can see that our society does by observing the degree of negative sentiment attached to homosexuality, voluntary childlessness, and any act or relationship that,

even symbolically, challenges parenthood. However, variations do exist in the degree to which reproduction is rewarded, resulting from differences in gender-role definitions and the extent of familism.

The second cultural factor that bears directly on fertility is the way the culture views the human condition. Cultures vary in attitude concerning the degree to which the environment can be controlled. At one end of the continuum are cultural settings characterized by what is termed *fatalism*. Fatalism entails an acceptance of the way things are: "What will be will be." Often intermeshed with religious ideology and convictions, it results in the production of as many children as is "God's will." Interference with God's will — that is, deliberate fertility control — is viewed as unnatural, immoral, or just plain impossible. More often than not, the idea of interfering does not even arise. At the other end of the continuum are social settings like ours, where it is culturally defined as proper and possible that individuals exercise control over their own lives. In such an environment, deliberate fertility limitation is viewed as acceptable behaviour.

Within a society, the impact of cultural factors on fertility is often assessed by examining ethnic and religious differentials in child-bearing. In Canada, women of French origin have traditionally had substantially larger families than women of British origin. Catholic women tend to have the largest families and Jewish women, the smallest. Such cultural differences, however, are diminishing in Canada. For example, the fertility differential between French-Canadian women and British-Canadian women has virtually disappeared, especially for younger women.

Convergence in fertility behaviour illustrates that the influence of culture on child-bearing can change. It appears that the cultural environment influences the degree of initial resistance to fertility-limiting practices. Once initial resistance is overcome (a shift that typically occurs in conjunction with wider social and economic changes), a cultural group with a high fertility level can decrease its fertility very rapidly. In Canada, the province of Quebec underwent decline last, but accomplished fertility transition in the shortest period of time.

**Socioeconomic Factors.** We have already seen that economic development is closely associated with fertility level. The developed countries all have low levels of fertility; the developing countries experience much higher levels. We have seen that demographic transition theory views economic modernization as a significant variable affecting fertility decline. Also, within societies there is an inverse relationship between socioeconomic status and fertility — that is, groups of high socioeconomic status are characterized by low fertility, and vice versa. Here, we will focus on the interrelated social and economic factors that are important determinants of fertility behaviour:

1. *Type of economic production.* In an agrarian society, children are economic assets. They contribute to agricultural production at young ages and provide economic support for aged parents. At the same time, children in an agrarian setting are not expensive to rear. In other words, the economic benefits of children outweigh their costs.

   In an industrial society, on the other hand, children are economic liabilities. The structure and content of jobs in an urban, industrial setting exclude the participation of children. Labour-force participation depends on acquiring skills through education. Children are no longer "workers"; they are "students." As such, they are expensive: they do not contribute to family earnings, and their education is costly.

2. *Female labour-force participation.* While women in all societies work, the location of their work varies according to the level and type of economic production. Women in urban environments are more likely to work outside the home than women in rural settings. Also, the higher the level of economic development of the society as a whole, the greater the likelihood of female outside-the-home employment.

   At the societal level, an inverse relationship exists between the percentage of women employed outside the home and the fertility level. In other words, societies with a high rate of female labour-force participation have low fertility levels, and vice versa. Also, at the individual level, women who work outside the home have fewer children than women who stay home. However, it is not clear whether employment in the labour force helps bring about

lowered fertility, or whether women with few children are more likely to work outside the home. Probably the relationship is two-way, with female labour-force participation and fertility influencing one another.

One reason for the fertility-deflating influence of female labour-force involvement concerns the conflict between the worker role and the traditional female child-bearing/child-rearing role. Since both are demanding roles, one strategy to accommodate the conflict is to minimize the number of children born. In contrast, when women's work occurs within the confines of the household, it is easier to co-ordinate that work with child-rearing tasks.

3. *Mobility opportunities.* The perception of opportunities for social and economic advancement affects fertility behaviour. If people perceive that they have a chance to "get ahead," one response aimed at realizing that possibility may be to minimize fertility. Family resources can then be mobilized toward the goal of social and economic betterment, a goal that can more easily be attained with a small family.

   The perception that opportunities exist will likely have some basis in fact. Ordinarily, people will not perceive that a better life is possible if it is actually not possible at all. The real opportunities that exist for people in a society are not equally distributed; people with higher socioeconomic status have more opportunities open to them than people of lower socioeconomic status. These differential opportunities may explain the inverse relationship between fertility and social rank.

4. *Educational attainment.* One very important factor determining fertility behaviour is level of educational attainment, particularly among women. High levels of educational attainment are associated with low levels of fertility. This relationship is found both across societies and within societies.

   There are several factors underlying the inverse relationship between fertility and education. With increasing education, people come to define themselves and their world in a different way. Education enhances the individual's sense of self. Also, education facilitates the viewpoint that the environment can be controlled by the individual. Education not only creates people who are willing to exercise control over their lives, but also provides the tool for that control — knowledge. In terms of fertility behaviour, increased educational attainment breaks down traditional barriers to fertility-limitation practices, making fertility control an acceptable behaviour. At the same time, the increased knowledge gained through education can be applied directly to reproduction, enhancing the likelihood of the effective use of contraception.

**Governmental Factors.** Governments intentionally (and sometimes unintentionally) act in ways that can affect fertility level. Attempts are often made to alter the birth rate in accordance with governmental aims and intentions. Sometimes governments are successful in this attempt, sometimes not.

Historically in the West, government attempts to influence fertility have been aimed at increasing the number of births. This pronatalist stance, which mirrors a "bigger is better" mentality, is reflected in a number of strategies that have been employed regarding reproduction. The strategies implemented fall into two major categories: negative measures and positive measures. Negative measures include outlawing birth control, criminalizing abortion, and imposing stringent legal restrictions on divorce. Canada used all three types of negative measures until fairly recently.

Canadian law reveals a history of restricting birth control. Legislation concerning contraception was enacted in 1892, under the part of the Criminal Code that deals with Offences Against Morality. The law did not make the use of contraception illegal; rather, the sale, distribution, and advertisement of contraceptive products became illegal acts. As such, Canadian law did not differ from that of Great Britain (the Indecent Advertisements Act of 1889) and the United States (the Comstock Laws of 1873). In Canada, the law banning birth control remained on the books until 1969. At that time, the acts of selling, distributing, and advertising nonabortive contraceptive products and literature were removed from the Criminal Code. Also, therapeutic abortion was decriminalized. Canadian law reveals a similarly restrictive history regarding divorce. Not until 1968 was divorce made relatively accessible.

Positive measures representing pronatalism include family allowances and tax exemptions to larger families. Canada implemented a family allowance program after World War II; the program is still in existence. In 1967, the province of Quebec instituted its own baby bonus scheme, whereby graduated allowances were paid for additional children. And tax benefits accrue to larger families across the country.

Despite these government measures, Canada's birth rate has fallen throughout the twentieth century, with the exception of the baby-boom era. The Canadian case, then, illustrates one government's failure to influence the birth rate. Indeed, all Western governments have proven incapable of altering the course of fertility decline. If people are highly motivated to limit their fertility, they will do so, regardless of how difficult the attainment of that goal is made for them.

While the history of Western societies reveals a number of government attempts to increase fertility, the situation in today's Third World countries is radically different. There, for the most part, governments seek to limit fertility. We would be in error, however, if we assumed that the Western failure to increase fertility indicates that government attempts to lower fertility in the Third World are doomed. Rather, success can be expected as long as government attempts to lower fertility are coupled with social and economic structural change that reduces the motivation to produce children. Government measures are usually not enough in themselves, but if they occur in conjunction with social and economic change, they can significantly help to lower fertility.

The strategies for limiting fertility are as varied as the measures that have been employed to increase fertility. However, fertility-limiting measures are of two basic varieties: family-planning programs and legal measures. Family-planning programs represent an organized effort to educate people concerning the available techniques of contraception, to disseminate contraceptive products, and to extol the benefits of small families. Evidence suggests that family-planning programs are working in many Third World countries; fertility is being reduced at a faster rate than would be expected as a result of modernization gains alone (Tsui and Bogue 1978).

Legal measures to reduce fertility include legalizing contraceptive devices, abortion, and sterilization, and enacting legal restrictions concerning age at marriage. In the People's Republic of China,

---

# Romania: Permanent Struggle Against Falling Birth Rates

*Events occurring in Romania illustrate government attempts to influence the birth rate — in this case, negative measures aimed at raising fertility.*

Following the lead of the USSR and other Eastern European countries, Romania legalized abortion on request in September 1957. By 1965 the abortion ratio had soared to about 4,000 per 1,000 live births and the birth rate had dropped to 14.6 per 1,000 population.

To reverse these trends, legal abortion was suddenly and drastically restricted and the import of contraceptives curtailed in October 1966. Abortion was authorized only for victims of rape or incest, for women over 45 or with four living children, where there was a chance that the child would be handicapped, and under a few other special mental and physical conditions.

The following year, in 1967, abortions dropped to about the 1958 level and the birth rate surged to 27.4. However, the trends reversed again and by 1983 the birth rate had dropped to 14.3 and abortions were up to 1,300 per 1,000 births — most of them provided on "mental health" grounds. In March 1984, President Nicolae Ceausescu announced dramatic new pronatalist measures:

• Doctors who perform abortions other than under the strict terms of the 1966 law (only for women over 45 or with four living children and for medical reasons) are subject to 25 years' imprisonment or even death.

• The minimum age at marriage for women was lowered to 15.
• Childless couples will be taxed an extra 5 percent on top of a surcharge already levied.
• All women aged 20–30 must regularly undergo a pregnancy test, followed by a monthly checkup in the event of pregnancy.

The official target is a fertility rise to four children per woman. This number is now held up as "the most sublime duty toward the nation and its people." Women who do not meet the target risk their careers.

**Source:**

Dirk van de Kaa, "Europe's second demographic transition," *Population Bulletin* 42(1) (Washington, DC: Population Reference Bureau, 1987).

---

for instance, all these legal strategies have been employed in recognition of the negative consequences of too-rapid population growth. The evidence that we have available to us indicates that these legal strategies are facilitating fertility decline (Aird 1978).

## Mortality

Mortality, as noted earlier, refers to the occurrence of deaths in a population (as opposed to **morbidity**, which refers to the occurrence of illness in a population). There is some relationship between mortality level and morbidity level; that is, high mortality and high morbidity tend to occur together. The relationship is not one-to-one, however, since of course some illnesses are not fatal and some deaths are not due to illness.

Fertility and mortality are the two components of natural increase: fertility determines how many people will be "added" to a population and mortality determines how many people will be "sub-

tracted" from it. Fertility and mortality differ in the extent to which human intervention is possible. While human beings have considerable choice about child-bearing and can choose to bear no children, they have much less choice about dying and cannot indefinitely postpone it. Nevertheless, social and economic factors are still important in determining the probabilities of mortality within populations. Also, the social consequences of mortality level and change are significant. As the model of demographic transition shows us, mortality decline (and the subsequent gap between fertility and mortality level) is *the* factor that accounts for the rapid population growth rate that is currently being experienced in the world. It is therefore important to know how mortality is measured.

### Mortality Measurement

At the simplest level, mortality is measured by the crude death rate. For many parts of the world, data are so limited that it is not possible to measure mortality in a more sophisticated way. The crude measurement of death is, however, like the "crude" measurement of births, subject to limitations. Since the denominator of the crude death rate is the total population, this type of mortality measure does not take into account population composition differences. For example, Population A may have a higher percentage of people with high death-risk characteristics than Population B. Even if the two populations were characterized by identical levels of mortality for different types of people, Population A would have a higher crude death rate because it has more people of the type likely to die than Population B.

Age is one significant variable affecting mortality risk. Two age groups are particularly susceptible to dying: young children (particularly those under the age of one) and old people. Therefore, if a population has a high proportion of people in these high-risk ages, its crude death rate will be proportionately inflated. This effect of age composition on the death rate explains why crude death rates in certain Western populations are higher than those in some less developed countries: the Western populations have a much higher percentage of old people.

Another important variable affecting the risk of dying is sex; in most populations, males die off more quickly than females. The effect of the sex differential in mortality on the crude death rate is, however, much smaller than the effect of age differences, because societies vary less in sex composition than they do in age composition.

The **life table** is a mathematical model for estimating the average number of years that people of a given age and a given sex can expect to live, assuming that mortality rates continue at current levels. The most commonly used statistic arising from life-table construction is the estimation of **life expectancy at birth**. Correctly interpreted, this is a particularly meaningful statistic. It tells us the average number of years that newborn babies can expect to live under current mortality conditions. We already know that babies are a high-death-risk group. If babies survive the high-risk young ages, however, their expectation of living is greater than the average for their cohort at birth. For example, if the males in a population have a life expectancy at birth of 71.9 years (as was the case in Canada in 1980–82), a male who has survived to the age of 40 can expect to live longer than 31.9

more years. How much longer depends on the particular age schedule of mortality in the male population of which he is a part. In Canada, the 40-year-old male could expect to live 34.7 more years.

## Mortality Variation

While contemporary death rates are not as variable as birth rates, substantial differences continue to exist, globally, in terms of life expectancy at birth. (See Table 7-3.) For the world as a whole in 1987, the average life expectancy was 63 years.

### Table 7-3. Life Expectancy at Birth, 1987

| Country | Life Expectancy (in years) |
|---|---|
| *World* | 63 |
| *Africa* | 51 |
| Egypt | 59 |
| Niger | 44 |
| Ethiopia | 41 |
| *Asia* | 61 |
| Bangladesh | 50 |
| India | 55 |
| Japan | 77 |
| China (People's Republic) | 66 |
| *North America* | 75 |
| Canada | 76 |
| United States | 75 |
| *Latin America* | 66 |
| Mexico | 67 |
| Venezuela | 69 |
| Argentina | 70 |
| *Europe* | 74 |
| United Kingdom | 74 |
| France | 75 |
| Spain | 76 |
| West Germany | 74 |
| Poland | 71 |
| *Oceania* | 72 |
| Australia | 76 |
| *USSR* | 69 |

SOURCE: *World Population Data Sheet* (Washington, DC: Population Reference Bureau, 1987).

The range extended from 36 years (in Gambia) to 77 years (in Iceland, Sweden, and Japan).

In past centuries, all populations existed under mortality conditions that resulted in short life expectancy. Only in the twentieth century has mortality been controlled to a degree that allows world life expectancy at birth to average 63 years. In the past, mortality was high for three main reasons: acute and chronic food shortage; epidemic disease; and poor public-health standards (Thomlinson 1965).

Recent increases in life expectancy have resulted from the partial control we have achieved over these traditional killers. Other factors that have contributed to overall mortality decline include the development and acceptance of germ theory, the development of immunology, and improvements in agricultural techniques. This last is important because, although famines took their toll on human life, continued undernourishment has probably been just as significant in human history, since it weakens people to such a degree that they succumb to even mild infections.

As a population undergoes mortality reduction, the causes of death change. In a population with high mortality levels, communicable or infectious diseases are the prime cause of death. The mortality declines that have occurred are largely the result of the control of communicable diseases. With the control or eradication of such diseases, new ones emerge as the chief takers of life — in particular, cardiovascular diseases and cancer. These new killers gain in prominence, at least in part, because the avoidance of communicable disease allows people to live to older ages, when the risks of heart disease and cancer are greater.

The two leading causes of death in Canada are diseases of the heart and cancer. This pattern is in keeping with a low-mortality regime, where deaths are concentrated at old ages. However, some differences between the sexes can be observed. (See Table 7-4.) While the leading causes of death for men and women (all ages combined) are identical, men exhibit higher death rates. Also, cerebrovascular disease is the third most likely cause of death for females, but the fifth for men. To some degree, this difference reflects the fact that women survive longer than men. Since women live to older ages, they are more likely to die of diseases of old age like strokes.

## Table 7-4. Death Rates, Canada, 1985

| Cause of Death | Death Rate (per 100 000) |
|---|---|
| *Males* | |
| 1. Diseases of the heart | 263.3 |
| 2. Cancer | 205.4 |
| 3. Respiratory diseases | 68.3 |
| 4. Accidents | 49.6 |
| 5. Cerebrovascular diseases | 47.3 |
| All causes | 801.1 |
| | |
| *Females* | |
| 1. Diseases of the heart | 202.2 |
| 2. Cancer | 164.1 |
| 3. Cerebrovascular diseases | 62.0 |
| 4. Respiratory diseases | 42.8 |
| 5. Accidents | 23.3 |
| All causes | 630.8 |

SOURCE: *Vital Statistics, 1985*, Statistics Canada, Cat. No. 84–206, Table 5.

## Mortality Differentials

Almost universally, women outlive men. The gap in life expectancy favouring women is greater in developed societies than in developing societies. Also, in the developed world, the gap has increased over time. For example, in Canada fifty years ago, female life expectancy at birth exceeded that of males by approximately two years; at present, the gap is about seven years.

The male/female gap in mortality in developed countries is not equal at all ages. The difference is particularly large for people in their twenties, when the death rate for males is about three times that for females. One major factor involved is death by accident. In 1985, the death rate for males aged 20 to 24 due to accidents was 72.6 (per 100 000); the comparable figure for females was 17.3. One reason for this large difference may be that men seem to find or put themselves in riskier situations. Men are more likely to work at jobs where the risk of accidental death is high; the traditional male gender role and "give 'em hell" attitude (David and Brannon 1976) place men in situations where the risk of death is high.

Married people have a better chance of surviving than single people. And single people, in turn, have somewhat lower death rates than the widowed and divorced. The reasons for the mortality advantage of marriage are not well established, but two factors are likely involved. One is marital selectivity. It is possible that marriage selects healthier people — that is, the unhealthy and disabled are less likely to get married. Thus, the married and the single populations are systematically different in a way that affects survival chances.

Another explanation centres on the advantages of married life. Behaviour patterns are more stable; each spouse is available to care for the other in the event of illness; a more cautious lifestyle may be followed in recognition of other people's dependence. In other words, marriage provides a more secure and stable type of existence. On the other side of the coin, a couple-orientated society may cause certain psychological stresses for those not tied to another person, making them more susceptible to illness and death.

Within any given society, different levels of mortality are often found among various ethnic and racial groups. It is difficult, however, to interpret such differentials. Probably a combination of factors is involved: heredity; inequalities in the availability of medical services and facilities; differences in socioeconomic status; and differences in socialization that affect the motivation to achieve good health.

In Canada, one group has a particularly high mortality level and short life expectancy at birth: native peoples. Their life expectancy at birth is approximately nine years less than that of the overall population. Similarly, in the United States, a consistent differential in mortality exists between the black population and the white population, a differential that favours whites.

Native peoples in Canada and blacks in the United States have one thing in common, aside from mortality higher than the national average. They are both minority groups — that is, groups that have been excluded from full participation in the social and economic life of the wider society. We can say that one of the "rewards" that is unequally distributed in a society is life itself.

## Migration

Migration that crosses national boundaries is termed *international migration*. If the movement, on the other hand, occurs within the confines of a society, the migration is said to be *internal*. For both varieties of migration, there are two kinds of movers: people moving into a given geographic area (in-migrants) and people moving out (out-migrants). In the case of international migration, these two types of movers are termed *immigrants* and *emigrants*, respectively.

Net migration refers to the difference between the number of in-migrants and the number of out-migrants. As we have seen, net migration is one of the important components of population growth, and may be either positive (where the number of in-migrants exceeds the number of out-migrants) or negative (where the number of out-migrants is larger than the number of in-migrants). Net migration is used in reference to both international and internal migration.

### International Migration in Canada

Four periods can be identified when considering the volume and types of immigrants entering Canada. Initially, Canada was settled by the French. The bulk of French immigration occurred in connection with the colony of New France, spanning the years 1608 to 1760. The total volume of French immigration was quite small, probably less than 10 000 (Beaujot 1978).

The second period of immigration brought a new group to Canada — the British — and was much larger in scale. Initial in-migration of the British to Canada took place mainly via two distinct routes: from the United States, United Empire Loyalists entered Canada during the time of the American Revolution; from Great Britain, direct immigration in significant numbers occurred in the early years of the nineteenth century. The British-origin population in Canada was further augmented by an influx of Irish people escaping famine in the 1840s. Also in the nineteenth century, other western European groups, particularly Germans, immigrated to Canada. The total volume of immigrants in this period is uncertain; for the period from 1851 to 1901, estimates range from 1.3 million to 2.3 million (Kalbach and McVey 1979).

The third period encompasses the first three decades of the twentieth century, during which a historically unprecedented number of immigrants entered Canada. Estimates range from 3.7 million to 4.6 million for the period from 1901 to 1931 (Kalbach and McVey 1979). For the first time in Canadian history, groups other than western Europeans entered Canada in significant numbers. This was the period of large-scale immigration of eastern Europeans, particularly Ukrainians.

The fourth period is the post–World War II years. From 1946 to 1984, more than 5 million immigrants entered Canada. During this period, in-migration from non-European countries steadily increased. In the earlier part of the period, the ten leading source countries for immigrants to Canada were all European countries (predominantly western European), and the United States. For example, in 1951, the ten leading countries, in order, were Britain, Germany, Italy, the Netherlands, Poland, France, the United States, Belgium, Yugoslavia, and Denmark. In 1984, the situation was quite different. (See Table 7-5.) Seven of the ten leading sources were Third World countries. However, Britain and the United States remain leading source countries.

Changes in the overall numbers of immigrants entering Canada reflect differences in the attractiveness of Canada to immigrants, particularly in comparison with the United States. Throughout most of our history, Canada has welcomed immigrants, viewing them as important for economic development, as long as they were of the "right" variety. Recently, there has been a change

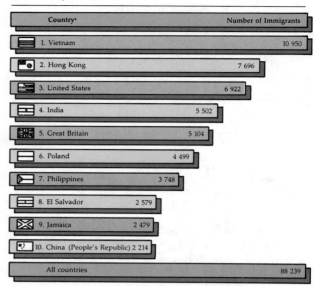

**Table 7-5. Source Countries of Immigrants, Canada, 1984**

| Country[a] | Number of Immigrants |
|---|---|
| 1. Vietnam | 10 950 |
| 2. Hong Kong | 7 696 |
| 3. United States | 6 922 |
| 4. India | 5 502 |
| 5. Great Britain | 5 104 |
| 6. Poland | 4 499 |
| 7. Philippines | 3 748 |
| 8. El Salvador | 2 579 |
| 9. Jamaica | 2 479 |
| 10. China (People's Republic) | 2 214 |
| All countries | 88 239 |

[a]Country of last permanent residence.
SOURCE: *Immigration Statistics,* Table 1M7 (Ottawa: Employment and Immigration Canada, 1984).

in attitude toward the volume of immigration; the shift is reflected in the establishment of quotas on the total number of immigrants allowed entry into Canada. However, this policy is currently under review by the federal government, due to fears concerning future population decline.

Changes in the ethnic origin of immigrants in Canada, on the other hand, reflect alterations in Canadian immigration policy over time. Until 1962, Canadian immigration policy was largely based on ethnic criteria. There were "preferred" immigrants and, therefore, "nonpreferred" immigrants. The "preferred" immigrants were those of western European origin, people viewed as highly suitable for assimilation into Canadian society.

One of the most blatant examples of racism in Canadian immigration history was the Oriental Exclusion Act, in existence from 1923 to 1947. No Asians were allowed entry to Canada during those years, because they were viewed as a group that could never assimilate into Canadian society. Further, throughout most of the first half of this century, Asian-Canadian citizens were required by law to pay a head tax to re-enter Canada if they left for any reason, however temporarily.

**When conditions in their own country deteriorate, desperate immigrants enter Canada as refugees.**

Beginning in the early 1960s, changes in Canadian immigration policy have been designed to remove race and ethnicity as grounds for admission. As a result, the percentage of non-western Europeans and non-Europeans entering Canada has increased. Also, until 1987, Canada had one of the most generous policies concerning refugees. The Canadian government is now taking a much harder line toward refugees, based on its interpretation of such incidents as the boat with 174 Sikhs arriving in Nova Scotia.

When we look at emigration, we find that the major receiver of Canadians (both foreign-born and Canadian-born) has been the United States. As we have already seen, emigration from Canada was very high in the period from 1861 to 1901 — a major concern of the authorities at the time, since the number of emigrants exceeded the number of immigrants. This situation reversed itself

in the early decades of this century, due to changes in Canadian immigration policy together with economic expansion. However, emigration from Canada to the United States occurred in greater numbers than immigration to Canada from the United States until relatively recently. For example, in every year from 1950 to 1970, Canada lost numbers in Canadian/American migration exchanges (Beaujot 1978). Perhaps more importantly, Canada was losing trained people to the United States and not receiving comparable numbers of skilled, well-educated people from the United States. This phenomenon has been termed the "brain drain." But although, on the whole, a brain drain did occur, for certain occupational categories the reverse was the case. One example is university professors. More American professors entered Canada, encouraged by short-term exemption from paying federal income tax, than Canadian professors left to go to the States. In recent years, Canadian immigration policy has favoured the admission of skilled, educated persons. As a result, a "reverse brain drain" has occurred, with Canada receiving highly educated and skilled people, especially from the developing countries.

Not all people are equally likely to move the distance required for international migration; some people are likelier than others to be international migrants. One important variable is age. People in the younger working ages are more likely to migrate. Age selectivity in migration exists for two reasons. It is younger people who are most likely to be desirous of moving into a new environment. Also, it is young people who are most likely to be allowed admission into a new country like Canada, given their potential labour-force contribution.

Sex is another variable involved in international migration, but its effect has changed over time in countries like Canada. Historically, men have been more prone to international migration, although there has lately been a reversal of this traditional pattern. In recent years, Canada has received approximately 86 male immigrants for every 100 female immigrants.

A third international migration variable is marital status. Historically, single people have been more likely to migrate than married people. However, there has also been a recent change in this pattern, with the married outnumbering the single among female immigrants. This fact may help explain why more females than males are currently entering Canada. Married women may be immigrating to Canada to join their husbands, who had immigrated earlier.

## Internal Migration in Canada

Historically, two aspects of internal migration within Canada stand out as particularly important. One is the fact of western expansion. In 1901, approximately 88 percent of the Canadian population resided in the Maritime provinces (excluding Newfoundland), Ontario, and Quebec; the western part of the country comprised less than 12 percent of the population. By 1981, the western provinces (the prairies and British Columbia) had increased their share of the total population to nearly 29 percent. The western expansion of the Canadian population has been encouraged by Canadian authorities. The "peopling of the prairies"

---

# Canadian Backlash on Refugees

A political storm over refugees is brewing in Canada, one of the world's last significant destinations for immigrants and refugees.

In 1980, the number of aliens asking for Canadian asylum was only 1,800. By 1986, some 17,000 aliens claiming refugee status were admitted, and 30,000 are expected in 1987. At the same time, some 115,000 immigrants were admitted in 1986, giving Canada an immigration rate of 4 per 1,000 — considerably more than the U.S.'s 2.6.

The controversy over immigration comes at a time when Canada is conducting a major three-year review of the effects of demographic change upon its society.

In August, Conservative Prime Minister Brian Mulroney asked for

Parliament to be called into special session to draft legislation that would tighten immigration laws. Under the proposal, refugees with no credible claim could be expelled (rather than allowed to remain for years during the lengthy course of the appeals process). Criminal penalties for those who smuggle in illegals would also be made harsher.

Critics say such proposals would also bar entry of legitimate refugees. But public opinion has reportedly turned against political immigrants and refugees because of incidents like the landing last July of a boatload of 174 Sikh immigrants from India on a lonely Nova Scotia beach — incidents that were depicted in near-invasion terms by some Canadian media.

The captain of the ship carrying the Sikhs pleaded guilty to violating immigration laws and was sentenced to one year in prison.

Some Canadians argue that the country needs the immigrants for economic and social well-being. They cite the country's low total fertility rate (an average of 1.7 lifetime children per woman, slightly lower than the U.S's 1.8) as argument that the country's population is aging and could benefit from an infusion of skilled labor.

**Source:**

*Population Today* 15(10), 1987.

was one of the motivations underlying the admittance of previously "nonpreferred" people into Canada in the early decades of this century.

The second significant aspect of internal migration in Canada is the trend of urbanization — that is, the movement of population from rural areas to urban areas. Urbanization, reflecting wider economic transformation, is a major aspect of social change within Canadian society in the twentieth century. In 1901, only 34.9 percent of the population resided in urban centres; by the 1980s, the proportion of urban-dwellers had reached approximately 75 percent. This urbanization has largely taken place along the southern rim of Canada; few cities in Canada are located any great distance from the American border.

The growth of urban Canada is only partly a function of internal migration — of people moving from rural areas within Canada to urban centres. International migration has also played a role in the urbanization of Canada. When immigrants enter Canada, they are more likely to move to cities than to settle in rural areas. Until now, the Canadian government has made only a minimal attempt to control the location of immigrants in Canada, by giving some preference to immigrants who "intend" to settle in specified areas — for example, areas where labour-force needs are greater.

## Consequences of Fertility, Mortality, and Migration

The levels of fertility, mortality, and net migration in a population have important effects on the characteristics of that population. We have already seen that these three demographic processes operate together to determine growth rate. There are other, equally important, effects.

### Age Structure

The fertility level in a population is the major determinant of **age structure** — that is, the proportion of people in each category in a population. Age structure, or age composition, is usually rep-

resented in a graph known as a **population pyramid** (two examples of which are shown in Figure 7-5).

Demographers have identified three major types of population pyramids:

1. The *expansive* type, which has a very broad base. This type of pyramid reflects a population that has a high proportion of children, the result of high past and present fertility levels. A population with an expansive pyramid is termed a "young" population.
2. The *constrictive* type, which has a base that is somewhat narrower than the middle of the pyramid. This type of pyramid occurs with rapidly declining fertility levels.
3. The *stationary* type, which has a narrower base and approximately equal percentages of people in each age group, with a tapering off at older ages. Stationary pyramids occur when a population has had low fertility levels for a considerable length of time and the number of births equals the number of deaths. A population with a stationary pyramid is referred to as an "old" population.

While fertility level is the most significant demographic variable affecting age structure, migration can play a role as well, although generally a minor one. Given the age-selectivity of migration, a population that receives in-migrants will display a pyramid that has a bulge in the young working ages. Conversely, a population that loses people through out-migration will have an indentation at the age groups that are most likely to migrate out.

Figure 7-5 shows age-sex pyramids of the Canadian population in 1881 and 1986. The pyramid for 1881 is expansive, as a result of the high fertility of the nineteenth century. On the other hand, the pyramid for 1986 is constrictive. The declining fertility of the 1970s and 1980s resulted in a relatively small proportion of children in 1986. The bulge in the ages from 20 to 39 is a direct result of the baby boom. That bulge will continue to show up in population pyramids of the Canadian population until the large cohort of the baby-boom era eventually dies out. When that happens, and assuming that fertility has reached the level of mortality and does not increase substantially in

## Figure 7-5. Population Pyramids, Canada, 1881 and 1986

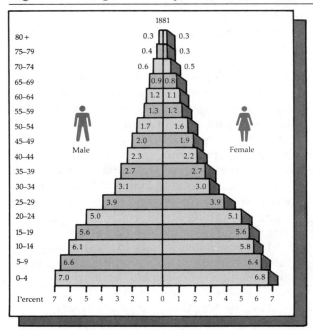

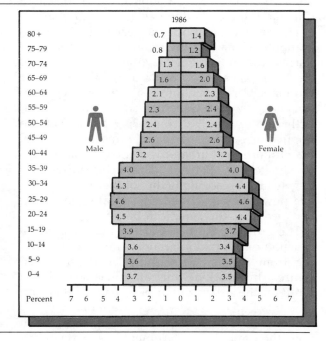

NOTE: The exact percentages appear in the boxes.
SOURCE: For 1881, Dominion Bureau of Statistics, *1921 Census of Canada*, Vol. 2, table 4; for 1986, Statistcs Canada, *1986 Census of Canada*, Cat. No. 93–101, Table 3.

the future, the population pyramid for Canada will gradually become that of a stationary population with zero growth.

The social and economic significance of age structure lies in what is termed the **dependency ratio**, or *dependency burden*. This is the ratio of the number of people in the economically dependent age groups to the number of people in the productive ages. Usually, the economically dependent ages are arbitrarily taken to be the ages under 15 and the ages of 65 and over — in other words, children and the elderly. The higher the dependency ratio, the more people in a population that must be economically supported relative to the number of supporters.

As a population undergoes a fertility transition — moving from an expansive pyramid to a constrictive one, then later to a stationary one — its dependency ratio changes. First, a high dependency ratio occurs with an expansive pyramid; high fertility creates a large population in the economically dependent young ages. For example, the dependency ratio in Canada in 1881 was 74.8;

that is, there were approximately 75 economically dependent persons for every 100 persons in the productive ages. Most of these economically dependent persons were children. Nearly 40 percent of the population was under 15; only 4 percent was 65 and over. The dependency ratio lessens with a constrictive pyramid. In Canada in 1986, the dependency burden was 47 — substantially smaller than in 1881. The dependency burden at the young ages was much smaller, since only about 21 percent of the population was under the age of 15 in 1986. At the same time, the percentage of older people had increased. In 1986, nearly 11 percent of the Canadian population was aged 65 and over.

Dependency burden plays an important role in economic and social development. Other things being equal, the lower the dependency ratio, the easier the economic and social modernization. A population with a lower dependency ratio will have a higher per capita output, a better standard of living, greater savings, and more investment capital for development. Also, a lower depen-

**A society's economic and social development are affected by the dependency ratio of its population.**

dency burden implies that less will be spent per capita on education (especially primary education) and housing.

The societies most in need of economic and social development are, however, the same societies that have expansive pyramids and high dependency burdens. Their age structures represent one stumbling block to development, since the needs of the young can be met only at the expense of production.

What will decrease the dependency ratio in Third World societies? Lowered fertility. What will lower fertility? Economic and social modernization. What will facilitate modernization? Lowered fertility and the resulting lessened dependency burden. This is the vicious circle existing in many developing countries. In order to lower fertility, they must modernize; in order to modernize, they must lower fertility.

Age structure has a second important implication, apart from dictating dependency burden: age structure plays an important role in determining the future growth of a population.

For example, a population that has an expansive pyramid has, *built into it*, the potential for substantial future growth. The large numbers of children will age into the child-bearing years, resulting in large numbers of potential parents. Even if they have small families, the population will grow because there are so many parents. Therefore, even if Third World countries reduce their fertility levels substantially, their populations will continue to grow — the legacy of their current age structures. These populations have what is termed **demographic momentum** built into them.

The current Canadian structure also has a demographic momentum built into it. A large percentage of our population — the bulge in our pyramid resulting from the baby boom — is now in the early child-bearing ages. As a consequence, the number of babies born is increasing somewhat, not because we are returning to large families, but because there are many people in the child-bearing ages. The percentage of our population aged 0–4 has increased slightly since 1981, reflecting this fact.

## Sex Structure

The sex structure in a society is a direct result of the action of demographic processes, particularly mortality and migration. Sex structure is usually measured in terms of the **sex ratio** — that is, the number of males per 100 females.

In Western populations, the sex ratio at birth is typically 105. Slightly more male babies are born than female babies. After birth, however, males lose this advantage. By the older ages, women outnumber men by a substantial margin. For example, in Canada the sex ratio at ages 65 and over is approximately 72 (72 males per 100 females). The major factor accounting for this changing sex ratio is mortality. As we have already seen, the life expectancy at birth for males is less than that for females.

Sex ratios, particularly in the young working ages, are influenced not only by mortality but also by migratory movement. In the past, receiver societies like Canada experienced an excess of males to females; sender societies wound up with an excess of females. On the other hand, internal migration, particularly rural-to-urban migration, has tended to be female-dominated. As a result, cities tend to have sex ratios below 100, with women outnumbering men, and rural areas tend to have sex ratios over 100.

Sex ratio distortion (values of the sex ratio deviating significantly from 100) can have many effects on the wider society. One obvious effect concerns marriage chances. If there is a large excess of one sex relative to the other sex, the marriage opportunities for the numerically greater sex will be correspondingly lessened. Some people will have to forgo marriage because of a lack of available mates.

Other effects of sex ratio distortion will vary from society to society, depending on the roles of men and women in the wider social environment. For example, in a society in which productive work is concentrated in the hands of men, a sex ratio favouring males would, other things being equal, facilitate production. There are, however, societies in which productive work is not defined as a wholly male activity. In such societies, sex ratio distortion would have different effects.

## What the Future Holds

We have already seen that in terms of demographic characteristics the contemporary world can be divided into two camps: the developed societies and the developing societies. Partly as a result of the existing differences, the respective camps face different demographic prospects and issues in the near future.

### Developing Societies

The developing societies are growing very rapidly as a result of high rates of natural increase. While some authors, most notably American economist Julian Simon (1981), argue that high growth is nonproblematic and can even be considered positive, most serious demographers recognize that rapid population growth can interfere with development goals. To lower the rate of population growth, three possibilities exist:

1. heightened mortality;
2. increased emigration; and
3. lowered fertility.

The first possibility is, of course, morally reprehensible as a course of action. That is, one does not simply kill surplus people. The second possibility is not likely. Where will the emigrants go? In recent years, most developed societies have increased restrictions on immigration. The third possibility, reduced fertility, is the only option available.

How is reduced fertility to be achieved? While this is a crucial question for the future of all of us, attempts to answer it have caused a deep split in both scientific and political circles. The split concerns the relative importance of demographic measures versus economic development in dealing with the problems the Third World faces.

On the one side is the "Neo-Malthusian" school of thought. Proponents of this view argue that family-planning programs should be implemented where they do not exist and intensified where they do exist. In other words, the problem facing the Third World is defined as a demographic one: too-rapid population growth as a result of too-high fertility levels. On the other side is the "development first" school of thought. Supporters of this idea argue that economic development of the Third World should be a first priority. Their slogan at the 1974 United Nations World Population Meetings was "Take care of the people, and the population will take care of itself."

As is often the case in disagreements of this nature, neither side is totally wrong or right. The Third World faces the twin problems of rapid population growth and economic underdevelopment. Each reinforces the other, and each makes the other more difficult to solve. Both fertility reduction and economic development must therefore occur in the developing societies. One cannot occur without the other. Fertility is lowered with economic development; economic modernization is facilitated by fertility decline, which lessens the dependency burden. Attempts to lower fertility in the absence of economic modernization are

# Vatican on Misuse of Statistics

*The fact that demographic issues have political and ideological implications can be observed in the following passage. The Vatican, for its own purposes, is suggesting that the dissemination of demographic information be subject to state control, and presumably, censure.*

Laying down guidelines for sex education, the Vatican's Congregation for Catholic Education last December issued a document [entitled] "Educational Guidance in Human Love."

The document reaffirmed the church's teachings on sexuality as a fundamental component of personality and of communication, and of expression of love.

Paragraph 65 of the document, however, deserves some amplification for demographers, because it notes: "It is the task of the state to safeguard its citizens against injustices and moral disorders such as the abuse of minors and every form of sexual violence, degrading dress, permissiveness and pornography, and the improper use of demographic information."

While seeming to lump demographic analysis with more tawdry practices, the purpose of this paragraph is more plain. The 1980 Synod of Bishops on the Family had decried "improper" use of demographic statistics to cause "hysteria" or other emotional reactions of despair. This new warning against employing "improper" demographics was based on the same concern, and — like the 1980 statement — was aimed square at governments. "Misuse" of demographics wound up on the list, not because it's like pornography, but because preventing it is, according to the guidelines, a government responsibility.

**Source:**

*Population Today* 12(February 1984): 5.

---

probably doomed to fail. At the same time, attempts to modernize with the current high rates of population growth are self-defeating. Therefore, the answer to the question posed earlier — How is reduced fertility to be achieved? — is two-fold: through intense family-planning efforts *and* through economic development.

## Developed Societies

The demographic situation in the developed world is entirely different from that in the Third World. Our fertility levels have decreased substantially over the past century. As a result, our future holds stationary growth and an "old" age structure. Stationary growth, or zero population growth, will not occur in Canada for some time yet because of demographic momentum, the continuation of birth rates that are somewhat higher than death rates, and positive net migration. Nevertheless, stationary growth is, in the long run, inevitable.

Stationary growth is not unique to the future of the developed world. All societies will eventually reach no-growth conditions. Similarly, all societies, before demographic transition, experienced little population growth or none. This situation was caused by high birth and death rates rather than low birth and death rates, but the result was the same. In contrast, stationary growth in conjunction with an "old" age structure is historically unprecedented. There are no lessons to be learned from the past; the impact of our future demographic regime is somewhat uncertain and subject to speculation.

Here, in this chapter's final section, we will indulge in a little such speculation, focusing on some of the economic and social effects that are likely with an "old," no-growth population (Day 1972; McDaniel 1986). It is important to keep in mind, however, that the characteristics of developed societies in the future only partly depend on demography. The way in which societies *respond* to new demographic situations is as important as the demographic situations themselves. In other words, our future demography will have an impact on the wider social and economic environment, but will not absolutely determine that environment.

One set of effects concerns the larger percentage of people in the older age groups. On the one hand, that larger percentage implies a greater societal need for, and a greater economic expenditure on, health-care facilities. But on the other hand, there is no necessary one-to-one relationship between an increasing elderly population and increasing requirements for health-care facilities.

Much will depend on our health habits and our system of health-care delivery. Also, societal definitions and attitudes toward age and aging may change. Because age is, at least partly, socially defined, the behaviour of old people could significantly change if our expectations and their life conditions were transformed. Attitudinal change in the wider society may make an increasing percentage of old people less of a burden than we might at first glance suppose. In fact, an "old" age structure may lead to a lessened emphasis on age-grading as a defining principle of social organization.

An older population implies an older labour force. As a consequence, opportunities for social advancement may be less than they are now. At least initially, this will probably be defined as a "social problem." Possible ways to deal with it include altering retirement practices and reappraising our competitive and success-oriented values. One likely demographic consequence of reduced opportunities for social advancement is a lower rate of internal migration. If there are no "better jobs" drawing people to new geographic locations, people will be less likely to move. As a result, the neighbourhood and community may become, as in former times, more important aspects of people's lives.

Our future demographic situation may also influence the status of women in our society. Again, it is not possible to predict the demographic impact with any certainty, since much depends on our social and cultural responses, but it does seem that developed societies like Canada face a future where a higher percentage of women will experience fewer and shorter obligations, or none, concerning child care. Some lessening of child-care obligations has already occurred, and the female response has been to take on other roles, particularly the role of worker outside the home. A continuation and intensification of female labour-force participation therefore seems likely; and as the female gender role changes, so will the male gender role, at least in the long run. Therefore, we might expect a narrowing of the gulf between men and women in terms of prestige and power as their roles become more similar. This is, of course, no foregone conclusion and will depend to a large degree on changes in our value structure.

One issue that is often raised concerns the effect of stationary population growth — that is, zero growth — on the wider economy. Does stationary population growth imply stationary economic growth? Not necessarily. Economic growth, stagnation, and decline are all possible with a stationary population. The type of economic situation that arises will depend more on the soundness of our economic policies than on any specific demographic characteristics (Espenshade 1978).

In the last few years, increasing concern has been raised about the possibility of population decline in Canada. Once zero growth is achieved, there is no automatic mechanism that will keep fertility at just the right level to ensure an equal number of births and deaths. As pointed out earlier, if fertility remains at its current level and annual net migration approximates 50 000, the Canadian population will begin to decline in size around 2021.

## SUMMARY

1. The study of population, or demography, is intimately related to the study of society. Within demography, the important areas of study are the three demographic processes of fertility, mortality, and migration. Together, these determine population growth. Singly or in combination, they determine population composition and distribution.

2. The components of growth are natural increase and net migration.

3. Population growth in Canada reveals a history of unevenness. Natural increase has been the major component of our growth, with net migration playing a variable role over time.

4. There are three major theories of population growth. Dominant at present is demographic transition theory. Based on the historical experience of the West, it provides a three-stage model of population change, with rapid growth occurring in the second stage.

5. Fertility is an important element of population growth; it affects the rate of natural increase. Fertility is assessed by two types of measurement: period and cohort.

6. Fertility in Canada has declined over the course of this century, with the exception of the period known as the "baby boom." Variations in fertility level result from the combined action

of four types of factors: demographic factors; cultural factors; socioeconomic factors; and governmental factors.

7. Mortality acts jointly with fertility in determining rate of natural increase.
8. As a population undergoes mortality reduction, the causes of death change, from infectious diseases to degenerative-type diseases.
9. Within societies, differentials in mortality exist. Women outlive men; married people have higher life expectancies than persons in other marital statuses; minority groups experience higher mortality than the national average.
10. Migration is the movement of people from one geographic location to another. Migration is of two types: internal and international.
11. Four periods of immigration in Canada can be identified, each differing in volume and type of immigrants. Emigration from Canada, for the most part, has been to the United States.
12. Fertility level is the major determinant of age structure. The three types of age structures, graphically represented in population pyramids, are expansive, constrictive, and stationary.
13. Age structure dictates dependency ratio or dependency burden, which plays an important role in economic development.
14. In the near future, developing and developed societies face different population issues and prospects. The developing societies face the twin problems of economic underdevelopment and rapid population growth. In the developed societies, the future holds stationary, and perhaps declining, growth in conjunction with an "old" age structure.

## GLOSSARY

**Age-specific birth rate.** Incidence of births in a given year per 1000 women of a given age group. The rates are calculated for five-year age groups. For example, the age-specific birth rate for women aged 20 to 24 would be calculated as follows:

$$\text{Age-specific birth rate} = \frac{\text{Number of births to women aged 20 to 24 in a given year}}{\text{Mid-year population of women aged 20 to 24}} \times 1000$$

**Age structure.** When pertaining to population, the proportion of people in each age category.

**Cohort.** Group of people in a population sharing a common demographic event (for example, year of birth, or year of marriage).

**Cohort measures.** Measures of the frequency of a given event characteristic of a cohort.

**Crude rate.** Frequency of an event per unit of the total population, usually 1000. Applied especially to deaths and births.

**Demographic momentum.** Tendency for future population growth due to a concentration of people in the young ages.

**Demographic transition theory.** Description and explanation of the three-stage transition or "shift" from high birth and death rates to low birth and death rates as societies become industrialized and urbanized.

**Demography.** Scientific study of population.

**Dependency ratio.** Ratio of the economically dependent population (under 15, 65 and over) to the productive population (15 to 64). Calculated as follows:

$$\text{Dependency ratio} = \frac{\text{Population under 15 + population aged 65 and over}}{\text{Population aged 15 to 64}} \times 100$$

**Doubling time.** Number of years it would take for a population to double its present size, given the current rate of population growth. Calculated as follows:

$$\text{Doubling time} = \frac{693}{\text{Annual rate of growth}}$$

**Fecundity.** Physiological capacity of a woman or group of women to produce children.

**Fertility.** Actual child-bearing performance of a woman or group of women; an important component of population change.

**General fertility rate.** The incidence of births in a given year per 1000 women between the ages of 15 and 49. Calculated as follows:

$$\text{GFR} = \frac{\text{Number of births in a given year}}{\text{Mid-year population of women aged 15 to 49}} \times 1000$$

**Growth rate.** Number of people added to or subtracted from a population in a given period for every 100 or 1000 total population.

**Infant mortality rate.** Incidence of death among children under the age of one in a population.

$$\text{IMR} = \frac{\text{Number of deaths of children under the age of 1 in a given year}}{\text{Number of live births in a given year}} \times 1000$$

**Infecund.** Term applied to people incapable of producing children.

**Life expectancy at birth.** Statistic indicating the average number of years that newborn babies can expect to live.

**Life table.** Mathematical model used to estimate the average number of years that people of a given age and a given sex can expect to live.

**Migration.** Movement of people from one geographic locale to another; can be either internal or international.

**Morbidity.** Occurrence of illness in a population.

**Mortality.** Occurrence of deaths in a population; an important component of population change.

**Natural fertility.** Fertility that is lower than the biological maximum level and results from behaviour not aimed deliberately at reducing child-bearing.

**Natural increase.** Excess of births over deaths in a population in a given time period.

**Net migration.** Difference between the number of in-migrants and the number of out-migrants.

**Period measures.** Measures of the frequency of a given event at one point in time.

**Population composition.** The characteristics of people within a population, particularly age and sex. Also included are marital status, religion, ethnicity, and other characteristics.

**Population distribution.** The geographic location of people within a population.

**Population pyramid.** Graphic representation of the age and sex composition of a population.

**Population size.** The number of people in a given area.

**Refined rate.** Frequency of an event per unit of population, usually 1000, that are exposed to the risk of experiencing that event.

**Sex ratio.** Number of males per 100 females in a population.

**Subfecund.** Term applied to people who are biologically able to produce children but, even without using birth-control measures, have difficulty doing so.

**Kalbach, Warren E., and Wayne W. McVey.** *The Demographic Bases of Canadian Society.* 2nd edition. Toronto: McGraw-Hill Ryerson, 1979. Describes major demographic characteristics of Canadian society with chapters on ethnicity, religion, education, labour force, family, and housing.

**McDaniel, Susan A.** *Canada's Aging Population.* Toronto: Butterworths, 1986. A highly readable discussion of the social causes and consequences of Canada's changing age structure.

**Menard, Scott W., and Elizabeth W. Moen, (eds.).** *Perspectives on Population: An Introduction to Concepts and Issues.* New York: Oxford University Press, 1987. A book that provides classic and interesting readings on such topics as population growth and decline, population theory, mortality, fertility, migration, population structure, and others. Focuses on controversies in population change.

**Overbeek, Johannes.** *Population and Canadian Society.* Toronto: Butterworths, 1980. A short book on Canadian population, describing our major demographic characteristics.

**Romaniuc, Anatole.** *Fertility in Canada: From Baby Boom to Baby Bust.* Statistics Canada Catalogue No. 91–524E. Ottawa: Supply and Services, 1984. An interesting discussion of the underlying causes of declining fertility, the future of Canadian fertility, and the implications of low fertility.

**Weeks, John R.** *Population: An Introduction to Concepts and Issues.* 3rd edition. Belmont, CA: Wadsworth, 1986. A particularly well-written basic introductory textbook on population.

## FURTHER READING

**Beaujot, Roderic, and Kevin McQuillan.** *Growth and Dualism: The Demographic Development of Canadian Society.* Toronto: Gage, 1982. An excellent introduction to population issues in Canada, with separate chapters on regionalism and linguistic balance.

**Foot, David K.** *Canada's Population Outlook: Demographic Futures and Economic Challenges.* Toronto: James Lorimer/Canadian Institute for Economic Policy, 1982. A recent book on Canadian demography, focusing on future demographic characteristics and their relationship to economic and policy issues.

**Grindstaff, Carl F.** *Population and Society: A Sociological Perspective.* West Hanover, MA: Christopher Publishing, 1981. A book about the Canadian population that places population variables in the context of the wider society.

# CHAPTER 8

# Social Inequality

R. OGMUNDSON

Many of the readings you are asked to do at university deal with topics that are of interest to a very limited number of people. This is definitely not the case with the topics discussed here. While you are reading this chapter, it is likely that somebody somewhere is being killed because his or her opinions about social inequality happen to differ from those of someone else. During your lifetime, riots and revolutions have taken place partly because the protagonists seriously disagreed about the topics we will discuss on the following pages. If there is a World War III, a leading cause of that war will almost certainly be ideological disputes between capitalists and communists about what causes **social inequality** and what can be done about it.

Inequality is apparently a universal characteristic of social life. It takes many forms: economic (some people have more money than others); social (some people are more popular than others); political (some people are more able to have their own way than others); and physical (some people are taller, stronger, or prettier than others). The potential list of examples is almost endless.

One way to imagine the impact of these inequalities is to look around you during a typical introductory sociology class in Canada. Some students in that class will probably be suffering from the effects of excessive consumption of food, alcohol, or some other substance. Several will probably be wearing clothes or jewelry worth hundreds of dollars. A few will likely be complaining about the difficulty of finding a parking spot for their car, while others will be outlining plans for their next trip to Florida or Hawaii. During that class, approximately 3000 people will starve to death somewhere else in the world.

At this point, you might well be tempted to ask "Why is this so?" Students of society have been asking this question for thousands of years, but they have yet to agree why inequality is an apparently universal characteristic of human societies and what, if anything, can be done about it. Their disagreement stems from three sources: value judgments, interests, and scientific beliefs.

Moral and ethical opinions (that is, **value judgments**) about inequality differ. Some people feel that there is nothing seriously wrong with the inequality they observe around them; consequently, they see no particular need for change. Others disagree. They feel that the inequality they see around them is thoroughly unfair; consequently, they favour changes. Those who oppose inequality disagree among themselves regarding how far inequality should be reduced. Some would be satisfied with a moderate reduction of some types of inequality (for example, providing everyone with a free university education). Others would be satisfied only if we were all the same in as many respects as possible (for example, all wearing the same clothes and hairstyles, such as was done in Maoist China).

So people disagree about inequality partly because they make different value judgments about what is right and what is wrong. They also disagree because they all usually want to benefit from the situation (that is, they have various — and often differing — **interests** to pursue). Those who are well off usually think that the situation is fine just the way it is. Those who think they would benefit from changes tend to argue that major changes would be a good idea. The type of change favoured by an individual or group tends to correspond with the interests of that individual or group. For example, your sociology instructors might think it is a fine idea to decrease the salaries of business executives and to increase those of factory workers. It is unlikely, however, that they would favour a reduction of their own salaries so that the salaries of their secretaries could be increased.

Yet another basis of disagreement has to do with different empirically based judgments (that is, **scientific beliefs**) about the causes of social inequality, and what, if anything, can be done about it. This is where the sociologist comes in. Remember that in Chapter 1 we learned that the expertise of sociologists does *not* qualify them to make value judgments concerning inequality that are any better than those of anyone else. Likewise, sociology professors have no more right to advance their own interests than you do. Nevertheless, the sociologist *can* tell us what the major schools of thought on social inequality have been. And the sociologist can also tell us some of the facts about inequality in Canada.

## Theoretical Perspectives

Theories about social inequality are similar to those about society generally. Indeed, much general sociological theory began with an attempt to explain the specific phenomenon of inequality. We learned in Chapter 1 that there are three major sociological theories — structural functionalism, symbolic interaction, and conflict theory. In the case of social inequality, symbolic-interaction theory is rarely used. Hence we will focus on the other theories.

It is convenient to divide the macro theoretical perspectives on social inequality into two major schools — the radical and the conservative (Lenski 1966). Briefly, the **radical perspective** is opposed to inequality; the **conservative perspective** supports it. These views go back a long way. A clear example of the conservative view can be found in Hindu texts from around the year 800 B.C., in which Manu, a great lawgiver, proclaimed that social inequality was ordained by God for the good of the people. An example of the radical view can be found in the Old Testament account from around the year 200 B.C. describing the Hebrew prophets Amos, Micah, and Isaiah denouncing wealth and privilege in the society of their time. These two basic views can be traced from those dates to the present day (Lenski 1966).

Contemporary radical and conservative theories are similar to those preceding them in that they are largely **normative** in their content — that is, they concern themselves chiefly with making value judgments about how things *should* be. As noted in Chapter 1, differing views such as these survive because they each illuminate some aspect

help us to develop inductive theories based on what we know.

**Sorokin.** Pitirim Sorokin took an empirical approach to the study of inequality. A Russian-born Harvard sociologist, he examined the data made available by history (Sorokin 1927). He found that all known human societies had been characterized by inequality. This was true even in experimental societies like communes, which were developed precisely for the purpose of building egalitarian communities. Furthermore, he found that none of the egalitarian revolutions throughout history, which go back as far as ancient Egypt and China, had produced an egalitarian society that lasted for any length of time. Indeed, extreme attempts to equalize had often resulted in economic catastrophes, famine, and disease, proving a curse to the very people who were supposed to benefit.

Sorokin also found, however, that unusually great amounts of inequality seemed to attract what he called "levelling" forces (for example, invasion, revolution, reform, taxation, or robbery), which had the effect of reducing inequality to something like a "normal" level. He concluded that there seemed to be both upper and lower limits to the amount of inequality that characterized human societies. If a society became too equal, it was forced to change in the direction of inequality. Conversely, if a society became too unequal, it would somehow be forced to change in the direction of greater equality. Looking at history as a whole, Sorokin discovered a pattern of apparently trendless fluctuation in the amount of inequality.

Sorokin's findings are conservative in one way: they suggest that inequality cannot be completely eliminated. Yet they are also radical: they suggest that the amount of inequality in a given society can usually be reduced to some degree. His findings thus give minimal satisfaction to both conservatives and radicals, just as one would expect a genuine synthesis to do.

**Lenski.** Contemporary American sociologist Gerhard Lenski (1966) has made the most self-conscious attempt to synthesize the traditional viewpoints. In an attempt to provide an empirically based theory of inequality, Lenski, like So-

rokin, studied historical experience. His survey of the data indicated that the degree of inequality in human societies varies considerably depending on the level of technological development (that is, on what Marxists call the forces of production). Within the limits set by technological level, he found that there seemed to be a predictable range of inequality with an apparent central tendency as well as upper and lower limits. (This latter finding is similar to Sorokin's.) Figure 8-1 diagrams social inequality in different types of societies.

Lenski attributed the apparent central tendency to certain presumably universal or constant aspects of the human situation — for example, human nature. Likewise, he attributed the tendency toward variation to factors that differ from one society to another — such as environmental conditions, or the degree of external threat. He found that the ideology of the dominant group (that is, radical or conservative) had only a minor influence on the amount of inequality in a given society.

Lenski's theory, like Sorokin's, gives little comfort to either conservatives or radicals. The substantial variation in the degree of inequality across contemporary societies clearly indicates that some reduction in the degree of inequality is possible in most situations. This aspect of the theory displeases conservatives. On the other hand, Len-

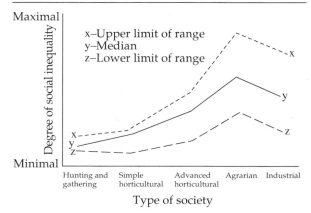

**Figure 8-1. Degree of Social Inequality by Type of Society**

x–Upper limit of range
y–Median
z–Lower limit of range

*Type of society*

SOURCE: Gerhard Lenski, *Power and Privilege* (New York: McGraw-Hill, 1966).

ski's study indicates that many of the factors influencing the degree of inequality are as yet impossible to change. This aspect of the theory displeases radicals.

**Connor.** Contemporary American sociologist Walter Connor (1979) has attempted to compare inequality in the capitalist democracies of western Europe and in the state socialist societies of eastern Europe. This empirical comparison helps us understand how much difference the presence of capitalism or socialism makes to the degree of inequality in an advanced industrial society. Connor found that some types of inequality are less in eastern Europe than in western Europe, and vice versa. However, he also found that the overall degree of inequality was not dramatically different between the two types of societies. Once again, the empirical reality gives little comfort to either traditional viewpoint.

This concludes our discussion of major theoretical orientations to the problem of inequality. In the next sections of the chapter, we will examine some of the facts regarding inequality in Canada. Our treatment of these facts will be divided into two major parts — a discussion of *inequality of condition* and a discussion of *inequality of opportunity*.

## Inequality of Condition

Canadians enjoy one of the highest standards of living in the world. How much wealth we possess is one question; how we distribute that wealth is another. **Inequality of condition** (or, as it is often called, *inequality of results*) refers to the overall distribution of rewards in a society. It involves questions like these: What is the average income? What

## Territorial Inequality

Probably the single most important determinant of your life chances is the territory within which you are born and spend your life. International inequality is very great indeed. As Table A shows, the Canadian position is a highly affluent one.

Our affluence, however, has been created and sustained by the sale of nonrenewable resources to the rest of the world. Unfortunately, a good case can be made for the argument that we have often sold our resources far too cheaply. And the experience of other countries whose affluence also stemmed from selling their resources indicates that our present affluence is probably temporary. This situation could conceivably have a direct impact on your life. As one influential report stated in 1972,

*before the children of today can reach middle age, most of the resources may be gone, leaving Canada with a resource-based economy and no resources.* (Bourgeault 1972)

Indeed, the position of Canada relative to countries in western Europe, East

**Table A. Gross National Product per Capita (U.S. Dollars) in 20 Countries, 1985**

| | |
|---|---|
| United Arab Emirates | 19 270 |
| United States | 16 690 |
| Switzerland | 16 370 |
| Canada | 13 680 |
| Japan | 11 300 |
| France | 9 540 |
| Saudi Arabia | 8 850 |
| United Kingdom | 8 460 |
| Singapore | 7 420 |
| New Zealand | 7 010 |
| Hong Kong | 6 230 |
| Trinidad | 6 020 |
| Israel | 4 990 |
| Greece | 3 550 |
| Algeria | 2 550 |
| Mexico | 2 080 |
| Poland | 2 050 |
| Malaysia | 2 000 |
| Hungary | 1 950 |
| Brazil | 1 650 |
| Botswana | 840 |
| Indonesia | 530 |
| China | 310 |
| India | 270 |
| Ethiopia | 110 |

SOURCE: The World Bank, *World Development Report 1987* (New York: Oxford University Press, 1987); pp. 202–203.

Asia, and the Middle East has declined in recent years.

Table B demonstrates that regional inequality within Canada is also very substantial. As a Canadian, your life chances are strongly influenced by where you live.

**Table B. Median Incomes for Families and Unattached Individuals by Province, 1982**

| | |
|---|---|
| Canada | $24 041 |
| Alberta | 27 154 |
| Ontario | 25 578 |
| British Columbia | 25 130 |
| Newfoundland | 22 438 |
| Saskatchewan | 22 368 |
| Quebec | 22 254 |
| Manitoba | 21 205 |
| Nova Scotia | 20 143 |
| New Brunswick | 19 738 |
| Prince Edward Island | 19 595 |

SOURCE: Adapted from Statistics Canada, 1982, *Income Distribution by Size in Canada* Cat. No. 13-207, Table 2. Reproduced with permission of the Minister of Supply and Services Canada.

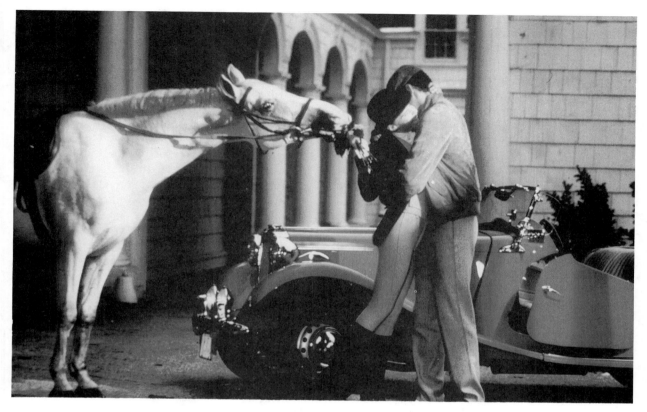

**In Canada the top 20 percent of the population receives over 40 percent of the national income.**

is the range between the richest and the poorest people? What is the overall distribution of rewards? How equal or unequal is this distribution?

## Material Dimensions

One useful way to examine inequality of condition involves looking at income distribution. The standard way to do this is to divide the national population into fifths, or quintiles, and determine how much of the national income each quintile receives in a given year. Table 8-1 shows what happens when we treat Canadian income this way. It is interesting to note that the top 20 percent of the population consistently receives over 40 percent of the the national income, while the bottom 20 percent regularly receives about 4 percent of the national income. (It should be noted that this measure also captures life-cycle effects; so the bottom quintile includes old age pensioners and students like yourself.)

How should we evaluate these facts? Should we be impressed by how *equal*, or by how *unequal*, Canadian income distribution is? In order to evaluate these figures scientifically, we must put them into historical and international perspective.

The historical trend appears to be one of little or no change in the distribution of income (Gunderson 1983). In other words, there is no trend toward greater equality or inequality. The present distribution of income is similar to that which existed in the past.

The results of an international comparison indicate that, compared to most other countries in the world today, Canada's income distribution is relatively equal (Jackman 1975; Stack 1980). But the international findings also indicate that Canada is relatively unequal compared to many other industrial societies.

It should also be noted that these income figures refer to income before taxation. In many affluent industrialized countries like Canada, the taxation system redistributes money from those with more money to those with less money. The Canadian taxation system fails to do this (Hunter 1986). Consequently, the degree of inequality of income distribution after taxes in Canada is significantly greater than in some other industrialized countries (Osberg 1981).

One other way to assess inequality of condition is to consider inequalities in the distribution of accumulated wealth. This measure indicates much greater inequality. It would appear that the bottom half of the population control only about five percent of the total wealth, while the top one percent control about twenty percent of the total wealth (Hunter 1986). While this concentration of wealth appears to be less than that in the United Kingdom, it has probably been increasing over the past two decades (Coyne 1988). Unlike most affluent industrialized countries, Canada does not have a tax on overall wealth and also generally does not have a tax on inheritances. This facilitates the development of greater inequality in the distribution of wealth.

## Subjective Dimensions

Inequality of condition can also be studied in terms of its subjective aspects. In this section, we will discuss Canadian findings on class consciousness, occupational prestige, and ethnic standing.

**Class Consciousness.** Those who are interested in equality are often concerned about the degree of consciousness of inequality among the popu-

---

# The Question of Poverty

There are two basic definitions of poverty — an absolute definition and a relative definition. An absolute definition of poverty concerns whether or not people have enough money to obtain necessities (such as food, clothing, shelter, and medical care). This definition corresponds with the popular understanding of the term. To measure poverty this way, we must ascertain exactly how much money is currently needed to meet "minimum" standards. But first we must decide exactly what the "minimum" standards are. For example, should false teeth be considered a "necessity" or a "luxury"? Such questions necessarily involve value judgments. Conservatives usually favour an absolute definition of poverty.

The other basic definition of poverty is the relative definition. According to this view, poverty is best defined in relation to the living standards of a given contemporary society, and not in relation to minimal physical needs, historical living standards, or living standards in other countries. In effect, this definition of poverty involves value judgments about how much inequality can be justified. Arguments for reducing poverty using this definition are really arguments for reducing inequality. Radicals usually favour this definition.

To measure poverty according to this view requires deciding how unequal an individual's or family's position must be before they can be pronounced "poor." (In other words, we must make a value judgment concerning how equal income distribution should be: When has a satisfactory level of equality been achieved?) The proportion of the population considered poor by this definition depends on where the "poverty line" is drawn. This, in itself, is an arbitrary decision based very much on the values and interests of the decision-makers.

It is worth noting that the two definitions have some interesting arithmetical properties. If the standard of living in Canada miraculously doubled overnight, and if everyone in Canada had exactly twice as much money tomorrow, the amount of poverty in Canada would be exactly the same by a relative definition. By an absolute definition, the amount of poverty would be reduced by doubling the standard of living. Conversely, if we were hit by a ruinous depression, and if everyone in Canada had exactly half as much money tomorrow, the amount of poverty in Canada would still be exactly the same by the relative

definition. Since we would all be in the same boat, we would not feel any more poor relative to others than we did before. But by an absolute definition of poverty, the amount of poverty would be substantially increased by a depression.

How much poverty is there in Canada? By historical and international standards, almost none. By an absolute definition, probably 5 to 10 percent. By relative definitions, anywhere between 15 and 30 percent of the Canadian population is poor. You must decide for yourself which of these measures is most meaningful to you.

Official Statistics Canada figures combine the absolute and relative approaches. In 1985, people in Canada were considered to be below the poverty line if more than 58.5 percent of their income was spent on the necessities of food, clothing, and shelter. By this definition, 17 percent of Canadians were considered "poor" in 1985 (Hunter 1986).

---

**Source:**

A. Hunter, *Class Tells: On Social Inequality in Canada*, 2nd edition (Toronto: Butterworths, 1986).

### Table 8-1. Income Distribution by Quintile, Canada, 1951–1981

| All Units (both families and unattached individuals) | | | | |
|---|---|---|---|---|
| | 1951[a] | 1961[a] | 1971 | 1981 |
| Richest Quintile | 42.8 | 41.4 | 43.3 | 41.8 |
| Fourth Quintile | 23.3 | 24.5 | 24.9 | 25.2 |
| Third Quintile | 18.3 | 18.3 | 17.6 | 17.6 |
| Second Quintile | 11.2 | 11.9 | 10.6 | 10.9 |
| Poorest Quintile | 4.4 | 4.2 | 3.6 | 4.6 |

[a]Excludes families with one or more farmers.
SOURCE: Statistics Canada, Cat. No. 13–207, Table 74. Reproduced with permission of the Minister of Supply and Services Canada.

lation. One way to measure this is to study *class consciousness* — that is, the degree to which individuals identify themselves in terms of a class position.

It turns out that Canadians do not often think of themselves as members of a social class. In national surveys, less than half the respondents indicate an awareness of membership in a social class. If Canadians are simply asked to classify themselves in terms of a class position without further guidance from an interviewer, an overwhelming majority of those who respond consider themselves "middle class." If an interviewer provides respondents with a list of class positions from which to choose, about 60 percent of the Canadian population views itself as "upper middle" or "middle" class, while about 30 percent views itself as "working class" (Goyder and Pineo 1979).

**Occupational Prestige.** One of the most commonly used measures of social inequality is occupational prestige. Those who use it argue that this approach does more than simply provide a direct measure of a subjective dimension of inequality. They argue that it also provides an indirect measure of the material and political rewards that go with an occupational role. Furthermore, they maintain that occupation is a central deter-

### Table 8-2. Prestige Rankings of Selected Sources of Income, Canada

| Occupation | Score |
|---|---|
| Provincial premier | 90 |
| Physician | 87 |
| University professor | 85 |
| County court judge | 83 |
| Lawyer | 82 |
| Catholic priest | 73 |
| Civil engineer | 73 |
| Bank manager | 71 |
| Owner of a manufacturing plant | 69 |
| Registered nurse | 65 |
| Economist | 62 |
| Public school teacher | 60 |
| Social worker | 55 |
| Computer programmer | 54 |
| Policeman | 52 |
| Electrician | 50 |
| Bookkeeper | 49 |
| Ballet dancer | 49 |
| Someone who lives on inherited wealth | 46 |
| Farm owner and operator | 44 |
| Machinist | 44 |
| Plumber | 43 |
| Bank teller | 42 |
| Typist | 42 |
| Barber | 39 |
| Carpenter | 39 |
| Automobile repairman | 38 |
| Bus driver | 36 |
| Trailer truck driver | 33 |
| Used car salesman | 31 |
| Restaurant cook | 30 |
| Private in the army | 28 |
| Assembly-line worker | 28 |
| Clerk in a store | 27 |
| Logger | 25 |
| Cod fisherman | 23 |
| Waitress | 20 |
| Bartender | 20 |
| Janitor | 17 |
| Someone who lives on relief | 7 |

SOURCE: Peter C. Pineo and J. Porter, "Occupational Prestige in Canada," *Canadian Review of Sociology and Anthopology* 4(1967): pp. 36–40.

## Table 8-3. Prestige Ranking of Religious, Ethnic, and Racial Categories in English and French Canada

### Hierarchy of Ethnic and Racial Groups in English and French Canada

| English Canada (N = 300) | # | French Canada (N = 93) |
|---|---|---|
| English Canadians (83.1) | 83 | |
| English (82.4) | 82 | |
| British (81.2) | 81 | |
| | 80 | |
| | 79 | |
| | 78 | |
| | 77 | French Canadians, |
| | 76 | English Canadians, Catholics (77.6) |
| Protestants (75.3), Scots (75.2) | 75 | |
| My own ethnic background (74.4) | 74 | My own ethnic background (73.7) |
| | 73 | |
| | 72 | French (72.4) |
| | 71 | English (71.0) |
| Catholics (70.1) | 70 | |
| Irish (69.5) | 69 | |
| | 68 | |
| | 67 | |
| | 66 | British (66.0) |
| | 65 | |
| | 64 | |
| | 63 | |
| | 62 | |
| | 61 | |
| French (60.1) | 60 | |
| | 59 | |
| Dutch (58.4) | 58 | Scots (58.5) |
| French Canadians (56.1), Swiss (55.7) | 57 | |
| | 56 | |
| Norwegians (55.3) | 55 | Irish (55.2), Protestants (54.8) |
| | 54 | |
| | 53 | |
| Danes (52.4) | 52 | |
| | 51 | Italians (51.3) |
| People of foreign ancestry (50.1), Austrians (49.6) | 50 | Dutch (49.7) |
| Belgians (49.1), Germans (48.7) | 49 | |

| English Canada (N = 300) | # | French Canada (N = 93) |
|---|---|---|
| Finns (47.6) | 48 | |
| | 47 | |
| Jews (46.1), Icelanders (45.6) | 46 | |
| | 45 | Belgians (45.3), Swedes (44.8) |
| Ukrainians (44.3) | 44 | Swiss (44.4) |
| Italians (43.1), Hungarians (42.6) | 43 | Jews (43.1) |
| Poles (42.0), Romanians (42.1) | 42 | |
| Lithuanians (41.4), Czecho-Slovaks (41.2) | 41 | |
| Greeks (39.9) | 40 | Germans (40.5), Ukrainians (40.0) |
| | 39 | People of foreign ancestry (38.9) |
| | 38 | Hungarians (38.4), Poles (38.0) |
| | 37 | Norwegians (38.0), Austrians (37.5) |
| Russians (35.8) | 36 | |
| Japanese (34.7) | 35 | |
| | 34 | Romanians (33.9) |
| Chinese (33.1) | 33 | Greeks (33.5), Russians (33.2), Icelanders (32.9) |
| | 32 | Canadian Indians (32.5), Czecho-Slovaks (32.4), Finns (32.3), Danes (32.2) |
| | 31 | |
| | 30 | |
| | 29 | Lithuanians (29.1) |
| Canadian Indians (28.3) | 28 | Japanese (27.8) |
| | 27 | |
| Coloureds (26.3) | 26 | Coloureds (26.5) |
| Negroes (25.4) | 25 | Chinese (24.9) |
| | 24 | |
| | 23 | Negroes (23.5) |

SOURCE: Peter C. Pineo, "The social standing of ethnic and racial groupings," *Canadian Review of Sociology and Anthropology* 14(May 1977):154. Reprinted by permission.

minant of the overall position of an individual or family unit in the entire social structure. Hence, in their view, studying occupational prestige is a convenient way to look into the heart of a society's social inequality.

Studies of the prestige accorded various sources of income in Canada indicate that white-collar workers have more prestige than blue-collar workers, and that higher educational status tends to be associated with higher occupational prestige. At the top of the scale, political leaders and professionals have more prestige than business owners and managers. However, both managers and professionals have substantially more prestige than clerical workers, farmers, and manual labourers. Interestingly enough, police officers and ballet dancers have higher prestige than those who live on inherited wealth. Clerical workers have slightly more prestige than farmers; farmers have slightly more prestige than manual workers. At the very bottom, we find those who live on welfare. Table 8-2 shows prestige rankings for a selected group of occupations.

The structure of occupational prestige appears to be very similar in almost all countries and all time periods for which we have information (Treiman 1978; Haller and Bills 1979). Thus the degree of inequality by occupational prestige in Canada appears to be about the same as that found everywhere else.

**Ethnic, Religious, and Racial Prestige.** Another indicator of social inequality is the prestige that various categories of people experience because of an ascribed status such as race, religion, or ethnicity.

A study of racial prestige in Canada indicates that Caucasians have greater prestige than non-Caucasians. Visible minorities enjoy the least prestige. Where religion is concerned, the same study indicates that anglophone Canadians rank Protestants slightly higher than Catholics, and that they rank either type of Christian well above the Jews. Conversely, francophone Canadians rank Catholics much higher than either Protestants or Jews. Studies of ethnic prestige indicate that the English and the French are ranked above other ethnic groups (Pineo 1980). Table 8-3 shows the full hierarchy of prestige rankings that Pineo's study generated.

Once again, let us put these findings into historical and international perspective. The order of ethnic ranking in Canada appears to be similar to that in the United States. However, the degree of inequality of ethnic prestige is much greater in English Canada than in the United States (Pineo 1980). Although our present degree of inequality of ethnic prestige may be considerable, other evidence indicates that it is probably less than it used to be (Darroch 1980). In other words, there has probably been a historical trend toward the reduction of this type of inequality.

## The Political Dimension

Inequality of condition can also be studied in terms of its political aspects. We will discuss first the distribution of *authority* (the recognized right to make binding decisions) and then the distribution of *power* (the ability to control the behaviour of others whether such ability is considered legitimate or not).

**Authority.** Perhaps the most notable finding concerning the distribution of authority in Canada is that it is largely, perhaps even mainly, located outside the country. Almost half the businesses, two-fifths of the unions, and about two-thirds of the media to which Canadians are exposed are externally controlled (Watkins 1973; Clement 1975; Ogmundson 1980a). The military is highly integrated with that of another country (Warnock 1970). The economic policy and foreign policy of the Canadian government are substantially limited by agreements with foreign powers (Levitt 1970). The major churches (excepting the United Church) have their headquarters elsewhere. Thus, a substantial portion of final authority in almost every realm of Canadian life is located outside the country. The degree to which Canada is externally dominated appears to be unusually great in an international perspective.

Of the authority that remains in Canada, a great deal appears to be concentrated in relatively few hands. In every institutional sphere (except perhaps education), it is possible to locate a small group of people at the heads of formal organizations who have the authority to make binding decisions for that part of our society (Porter 1965; Clement 1975; Olsen 1977). In this sense, it is widely agreed that authority is distributed in a highly unequal manner in our society. If we put the Canadian authority structure in international perspective, it would appear that our situation parallels that of other capitalist democracies. If we compare Canada to the advanced state socialist countries, it would appear that the distribution of authority is more equal in Canada than in those countries.

But the distribution of authority is one issue, while the distribution of power is another. Two questions arise: Who or what has power? Who or what influences or determines the decisions these elite groups make? And on these matters, sociologists have been unable to agree.

**Power.** Some theories about the distribution of power in countries like Canada give the impression that the distribution of power is highly democratic (for example, Downs 1957); others give the impression that power is moderately well distributed (for example, Dahl 1961); still others give the impression that it is distributed in a highly unequal manner (for example, Miliband 1969). However, while there has been considerable theorizing on these topics, there has been a thoroughly insufficient amount of research. In short, it cannot be honestly stated that Canadian sociologists agree on who has power in our society. And even when relevant data are available, they are subject to varying interpretations. Let us look at two examples.

Earlier research clearly indicated that decision-making in Canada tended to be dominated by an atypical group of well-educated males of British, Protestant, upper- or upper-middle-class origins (Porter 1965). An international perspective tells us that this situation — the overrepresentation of dominant groups in positions of power — is found virtually everywhere, even in state socialist countries (Putnam 1976).

The trend in Canada, however, is apparently toward an "opening up" of the elites to non-British, non–upper-class groups. In particular, French Canadians, Jewish Canadians, and those of middle-class origins are found more and more in the upper levels of our society. One recent study found that people who are of neither British nor French ancestry are actually *over*represented among individuals who control $100 million or more (Hunter 1986). Likewise, our civil service elite is one of the most socially representative in the world (Campbell and Szablowski 1979).

Scholars differ in their interpretation of these data. When the early data showed very substantial British upper-class dominance of elite groups, radicals argued that this indicated a "ruling class" or "capitalist class" dominance of elite decision-making in our society (Clement 1975). Conservatives replied that the data were not especially meaningful, because people in such roles perform about the same regardless of their origin and background. Now that the data are changing, the two sides are switching their favoured modes of interpretation. Conservatives view the opening up of the elite structure as proof that "democracy works." Radicals (for example, Olsen 1977) now tend to argue that elite social background is unimportant.

A second example of differing interpretations of the same information involves the fact that a great deal of data indicate an often minimal correlation between public opinion and elite decisions, even in the state system. For example, a majority of Canadians favour capital punishment, but our political elites have thus far refused to reinstate the death penalty. Some (for example, Ogmundson 1976) feel that such facts make one point reasonably clear: public opinion is of minimal importance as a determinant of elite decision-making. However, this view has also been subjected to a vigorous critique (Ogmundson 1980b; Schreiber 1980), and no discernible consensus on the matter appears to have developed among sociologists in Canada.

## Correlates of Inequality

As you read the various chapters of this book, you will find that almost all the behaviour and attitudes discussed — life expectancy, crime, divorce, child-rearing, religious and political behaviour — are related to socioeconomic status in some way. Interestingly, many of these differences appear to be independent of income. Construction workers, for example, typically drink beer, while many underemployed intellectuals insist on drinking wine. This suggests that how much money you make is one issue, while how you spend it — that is, what lifestyle you adopt — is another. For whatever reason, people in similar income categories often adopt different consumption habits.

In most countries, unequal positioning in society shows some clear relationship to political behaviour. People who have less usually attempt to use the political process in order to get more, while those who are privileged attempt to defend their privilege. Canadians are unusual from an international perspective, because we show very few signs of behaving this way. In particular, those who are less well off — the "working classes" — fail to vote the way most sociologists would expect. Consequently, political parties that have no commitment to redistributing wealth continue to govern the country. This phenomenon has been the subject of continuing debate among sociologists.

## Inequality of Opportunity

In the previous section we outlined the unequal distribution of rewards. The next questions are obvious: How do we decide who gets what? Who said he could be a general when I am a private? Couldn't I be a doctor instead of a nurse? Why should I enjoy the privilege of being a university student? To answer these questions, we must talk about **inequality of opportunity** — that is, the unequal chances available to members of society for obtaining valued resources such as money, status, or power. Also involved is **social mobility**, the upward or downward movement of individuals or groups into different positions in the social hierarchy.

Some people make the value judgment that equality of condition is much more important than equality of opportunity. To them it is more important that the pay differential between managers and workers be reduced than that everyone have a fair chance to be manager. Hence, they tend to study the topics discussed in the previous section.

Others take a different value position. They consider it fair that surgeons are paid a lot more than secretaries. What concerns them most is that people should be placed in these positions on the basis of merit and not on ascribed bases like age, gender, race, language, religion, ethnicity, or social background. People who take this value position tend to devote themselves to the study of inequality of opportunity.

Views on equality of opportunity are also influenced by individual and collective interests. Those with confidence in their ability to do well are likely to be concerned mainly with keeping the competition fair. They look forward to receiving substantial rewards, which they feel will be richly deserved. Those with less confidence in their abilities, or in the possibility of reasonably equal opportunity, are likely to be more concerned about equalizing rewards.

## Amount of Opportunity

How much opportunity exists in this country? Recently reported research on mobility in Canada has indicated that we have more upward mobility than downward mobility. This study found that 57.5 percent of males aged 25 to 64 had experienced upward occupational mobility, while only 18.8 percent had experienced mobility downward from their father's position. The rest (23.7 percent), had approximately the same occupational level as their father. For females in the same age group, the figures were even more remarkable — 68.2 percent had experienced upward mobility, but only 17.2 percent had experienced downward mobility (Pineo 1983).

An international perspective indicates that chances for upward mobility in Canada have apparently been among the highest in the world (Tyree et al. 1979). However, these findings seem to be largely a result of the extraordinary economic growth and consequent changes in the occupational structure experienced during the past 50 years. It is not clear that your generation will be as fortunate as the previous one.

## Distribution of Opportunity

As we have just seen, Canadians have enjoyed a high level of opportunity. However, how much opportunity we possess is one question; how we distribute opportunities is another. Students of social mobility have traditionally been interested in the degree to which access to opportunities is influenced by such factors as class origin, ethnicity, race, immigrant status, language, and gender.

**Socioeconomic Origins.** A central interest for those who study inequality of opportunity has been the effect of socioeconomic status. To what degree are your chances in life determined by the class position of your parents? One study found that about 15 percent of the variance in the occupational status of typical Canadian males could be explained by their socioeconomic origins. When the children of farmers were removed from the analysis, it was found that only about 10 percent of the variance in the occupational status of males who were not born on farms could be explained by socioeconomic origin. As might be expected, this relationship declines even further when one looks at status transmission over three generations (that is, grandfather to grandson). When one compares the status of great-grandfathers to great-grandsons, there is no statistically significant relationship at all (Goyder and Curtis 1979). Analysts of a more recent national survey have concluded that "mobility and status attainment are largely the result of individual effort and motivation rather than a return on privileged status" (Boyd et al. 1985). In sum, it appears that if you are a Canadian male, your socioeconomic origins will be a significant but nevertheless relatively minor determinant of your life chances. Other data indicate that your status inheritance will probably be even less if you are female (Pineo 1983).

Furthermore, the findings indicate that privileged parents are best able to transmit their status by ensuring that their children obtain a high level of education. If their children are unwilling or unable to obtain schooling, the influence of high socioeconomic origin is even more limited. Finally, data from other countries indicate that the effects of initial social origin diminish even further as you move through the life cycle. As you grow older, class origin becomes less and less important as a determinant of your position (Matras 1980).

As always, it is useful to put these data into international and historical perspective. The degree of status transmission in Canada is generally similar to that found in the United States and in western European countries (Goyder and Curtis 1979). At least one study (Rich 1976) has indicated that opportunities for working-class children to go to university in Canada are unusually good relative to those in other countries (see Table 8-4). There has been some suggestion that status inheritance at the higher levels of Canadian society is greater than that found in other countries (Porter 1965; Clement 1975). Other studies indicate that some Canadian elite groups are probably less exclusive than those in other countries (Rich 1976; Grayson and Grayson 1978; Campbell and Szablowski 1979).

The historical evidence indicates some decrease in the degree of status inheritance at the mass level in Canada (Boyd et al. 1985). This means that opportunity for the average person, relative

### Table 8-4. Percentage of University Students of Working-Class Origin in Nine Countries

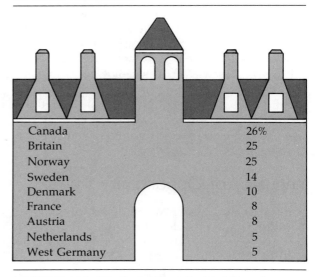

| Canada | 26% |
| Britain | 25 |
| Norway | 25 |
| Sweden | 14 |
| Denmark | 10 |
| France | 8 |
| Austria | 8 |
| Netherlands | 5 |
| West Germany | 5 |

SOURCE: H. Rich, "The Vertical Mosaic Revisited: Towards a Macrosociology of Canada," *Journal of Canadian Studies* 1976:14–31.

to the privileged, is improving. At the elite level, the findings are mixed. In the cases of the business elite (Niosi 1981; Newman 1982), the state elites (Olsen 1977), the civil service elite (Campbell and Szablowski 1979), and the Toronto elite (Kelner 1970), opportunities are apparently becoming more equal. In the case of the media elite, opportunities are evidently becoming less equal (Clement 1975).

**Ethnicity.** Ever since the publication of John Porter's book *The Vertical Mosaic* in 1965, it has been widely believed in sociological circles that ethnicity is a major determinant of individual life chances in Canada. It has also been widely believed that the role of ethnicity in Canada is unusually great (Porter 1965; Forcese 1980). More recent work, however, has indicated that the relationship between ethnicity and occupational status is steadily decreasing (Boyd et al. 1985) and that the relationship was never particularly strong in the first place (Darroch 1980). Pineo (1976) concluded that "no more than 2 percent of the current occupational status of the Canadian male labour force can be said to derive from ethnic origin," and Darroch (1980) has shown that the role of ethnicity in Canada is not much greater than in the United States. Thus, while it may be that ethnicity continues to play some role (Lautard and Loree 1984), it now appears likely that ethnic background will

**The standard of living among Canada's native people is typically very low and has not improved in recent years.**

probably have little or no influence on the life chances of young Canadians like you.

**Native Peoples.** It appears that one's life chances are strongly, and negatively, influenced by being born a native person. The standard of living among Canada's native Indians and Inuit is very low. Data indicate that the relative position of our native people has not been improving significantly (Darroch 1980) and that they still "have the lowest incomes, the poorest health, and the highest rates of unemployment of any single group in the country" (Valentine 1980).

This situation is of special normative concern because, unlike the rest of us, native peoples made no choice to take their chances and immigrate to this country. Furthermore, they have been wards of the federal government (that is, of the people of Canada) during most of our history. Comparative data indicate that our treatment of native peoples has been much less enlightened than that of some other countries (Hobart and Brant 1966). Hence, as Canadians, we must accept some responsibility for the miserable conditions they face — conditions far worse than those of American blacks.

**Visible Minorities.** Given the recent immigration policies of the Canadian government, our population has begun to include an increasing proportion of "visible minorities" other than our native peoples. This naturally raises interest in how non-Caucasian racial characteristics influence life chances in Canada. Many recently immigrated visible minorities do experience very low socioeconomic status (Rosenberg and Weinfeld 1983) and are subject to significant discrimination (Henry and Ginzberg 1988). But many visible minorities, especially those of Asiatic origin, do very well in the economic system. Indeed, Asian Canadians were, as a group, earning the second highest average income compared with all ethnic groups as early as 1971. (Those of British origin were the sixth highest). All categories of non-Caucasian Canadians, except the Indochinese, outranked Canadians of Greek ancestry in 1981. The trend appears to be toward reduced inequality, with non-Caucasian Canadians experiencing upward mobility while other categories have been experiencing downward mobility. Existing data seem to suggest that the visible minority with the greatest claim to special concern, aside from native peoples, is Canadian-born blacks, especially those born in Nova Scotia (Winn 1988).

**Immigrants.** In this context, it is interesting to look at the position of immigrants in Canadian society. In most countries, it is anticipated that immigrants will come in at the lower levels of society and work their way up. It is considered sufficient that they be treated fairly in this process. In Canada, however, the socioeconomic position of male immigrants is about the same as that of males born in Canada (Boyd 1985). In fact, immigrants — largely as a consequence of our immigration policy — control a significant proportion of the highest occupational positions in the country. So immigrant status has minimal impact on one's life chances in Canada.

**Language.** The differing life chances of anglophones and francophones have also been the subject of considerable study. Early research clearly indicated that francophones received a considerably lower income than anglophones, especially in Quebec. Dissemination of this knowledge helped to convert many Québécois to the separatist cause.

**In Canada, the effect of government policy has been that many recent immigrants are highly skilled and employable.**

Subsequent research, however, has tended to modify the initial impression of wholesale discrimination given by earlier work. On the one hand, it has become clear that francophones contributed in part to their position through their attitudes toward mobility and through their failure to obtain appropriate educational qualifications (Tepperman 1975). One study suggested that a full 60 percent of anglophone/francophone differences could be explained by education alone (Manzer 1974). This, in turn, could be attributed largely to the Quebec educational system — which, until the 1960s, discouraged attendance beyond elementary school (Porter 1965).

Recent research indicates that the situation in the 1970s and 1980s had substantially improved relative to the 1950s and 1960s, when most of the earlier studies were done. By the mid-1970s evidence suggested that francophone/anglophone differences were decreasing (Cuneo and Curtis 1975; McRoberts et al. 1976). Indeed, one study of engineers and middle-level managers even showed patterns of discrimination in *favour* of francophone Canadians (Armstrong 1970). A more recent study (Boulet et al. 1983) showed that a substantial decline in anglophone/francophone income differentials did indeed occur during the 1970s. A subsequent study (McRoberts 1985) has confirmed this trend. Significant differences still remain, especially in Montreal. But if present trends continue, anglophone/francophone income differentials could well become insignificant before too long.

**Gender.** The topic of gender has received considerable attention in other chapters of this book (see especially Chapter 4). This section can only outline a few key points regarding inequalities based on gender. Perhaps the most important determinant of life chances in Canada is gender. Males were at one time much more likely to participate in the work force than were females. But today in Canada, differences between the genders in work-force participation have diminished considerably (among those in the age group that is eligible for work-force participation — that is, those aged 16 to 65 — the proportions currently participating are 75 percent for males; 50 percent for females). Substantial occupational segregation remains the norm, however: females continue to dominate occupations that are extensions of their traditional roles. The relative life chances of males and females are also influenced by the fact that females still generally perform traditional domestic work with little help from males, and by the fact that females earn considerably less than males when their work is done for pay. In 1981, the average income of females was 59 percent of that for males. Some of this differential is due to such factors as variations in hours worked and work experience, but it seems clear that discrimination also plays a part. Recently reported data indicate that women who stay single earn 90 percent as much as men, but females who marry earn much less. Apparently, then, marriage and the unequal division of domestic labour represent part of the explanation for these income disparities (Kingston 1989).

The historical trend is toward greater female labour-force participation, and a slight decline in occupational segregation. The gap in average income differentials has apparently decreased a little: females now earn 65 percent as much as males (Kingston 1989). And substantial increases have also occurred in female attainment of educational qualifications, in political participation, and in appointment to such roles as Supreme Court justice (in three out of nine possible positions) and Governor General. This indicates a trend toward reduction of inequality.

## Inequality and Social Change

What the future holds is not at all clear. At the least, it is fair to say that there is no consensus among sociologists. Nor do they agree about what kind of social policy we should be pursuing. On this complex issue, some points can usefully be made.

First, there is no doubt that inequalities of most kinds can be reduced to some degree. Granted, there is some question as to the exact degree by which particular forms of inequality can be reduced, but at present there seems little need to be concerned about whether we are approaching those limits. For example, one study (Hewitt 1977) ranks Canada fifteenth among seventeen industrialized Western democracies in attempts to redistribute income. Sweden, which was the most unequal of the seventeen countries in 1934, had become the most equal by 1954. Clearly Canadians could reduce some kinds of inequality to some degree, if we had the political will to do so.

Moreover, there is no shortage of ideas for policies intended to reduce inequality. Entire books have been filled with them. For example, it has been suggested that educational opportunity could be somewhat equalized by such reforms as reduced tuition, increased scholarships, and subsidized housing. Similarly, it might be possible to reduce inequality of condition by revising our taxation system and reducing regional wage differentials. And other such ideas abound. There are, however, scientific differences of opinion about exactly which reforms are likely to be most effective. On these matters, the experts very clearly disagree.

Another set of problems involves conflicting values. Do we want to reduce inequality? What kind of equality do we want? How much equality do we want? How much are we willing to sacrifice in order to achieve it? Probably all of us have different ideas about these issues.

Moving toward equality could indeed mean sacrificing other values we consider important. For instance, it is often argued that certain equalizing programs reduce freedom. Suppose we insisted that all university students wear uniforms. This would make them more equal in appearance but would certainly impinge on their freedom. Would you prefer the equality of uniforms or the freedom of personal clothing choice?

Similarly, reducing one kind of inequality could conceivably increase other kinds of inequality: for example, centralized union negotiations might reduce regional economic inequality but increase regional political inequality. Would you be willing to equalize wages across Canada at the cost of

**Poverty often coexists in close proximity to wealth and power.**

## A Final Comment

As you have seen, scholars who have devoted their lives to these issues have been unable to agree. As a student and as a citizen you must make up your own mind about such matters. Here's some advice: First, remember how little you know. Perhaps you should read more. Be sure to expose yourself to a variety of viewpoints. Second, remember that professors and authors have their limitations. Do not blindly accept anyone's lead. Third, remember that you have the right to take whatever value position you prefer, and that sociology instructors are no more qualified than you are to say what is right or wrong. Finally, remember that your views, too, are likely to be biased by your own interests. What you think is best for the world may be, in fact, what you secretly believe is best for yourself.

concentrating further power in Ottawa? This is the kind of value choice that must be faced.

A final group of problems concerns the differing interests of various segments of our society. Those who think they would benefit from reforms tend to support them. They adopt positions (for example, the radical perspective) meant to legitimate their claim for more of society's resources. Those who think they would not benefit from such policies tend to oppose them. They, too, adopt positions (for example, the conservative perspective) that help them defend their interests. Such concerns usually make it difficult to assess policy options in a clear-headed way.

It is worth noting, in this context, that sociologists and sociology students have a material interest in the expansion of some forms of aid to the underprivileged because this provides a market for our services. But government programs to help a needy group will not necessarily help that group if the programs are poorly designed. Ironically, it has occasionally been shown that most of the money spent on a specific progam went to pay the salaries of those who helped design it. Those who are truly concerned about the underprivileged will take great pains to see that such citizens actually receive benefits from money spent in an attempt to help them.

## SUMMARY

1. Disagreements about the issue of social inequality stem from three sources: values, interests, and scientific beliefs. Our values influence the amount of inequality we judge right or wrong. Interests involve the question of who stands to benefit or to lose by a change. Scientific beliefs underpin viewpoints on what causes social inequality, how much social inequality actually exists, and what can be done about it at what cost. Sociologists are qualified to speak only about scientific matters.

2. Sociological theories on inequality can be usefully divided into three types — the radical perspective, the conservative perspective, and attempts at scientific synthesis. Radical theories emphasize the injustice of inequality. Conservative theories emphasize the inevitability of inequality. The synthesis approach attempts to use the best ideas of both traditional approaches, and to base conclusions on known facts.

3. Canadians enjoy a very high standard of living by international standards. There is, however, significant regional inequality in Canada.

4. Income distribution in Canada is relatively equal by world standards, but relatively unequal when

compared to some other industrialized democracies. There appears to be no trend toward greater equality or greater inequality. There is considerable debate about how much "poverty" we have. Views differ depending on the definition of poverty one adopts.

5. Less than half the Canadian population reports awareness of belonging to a social class. However, Canadians identify themselves as middle class (60 percent) or working class (30 percent) if asked to do so.

6. The structure of occupational prestige in Canada parallels that found in other developed countries. Different religious, ethnic, and racial groups in Canada have different levels of social prestige. The range of such differences is greater here than in the United States.

7. There is substantial inequality in the distribution of authority in Canada. A very large portion of our authority structure is controlled by foreign interests. Little is known for certain about the distribution of power in Canada.

8. The amount of occupational mobility in Canada appears to be substantial and unusually high in an international perspective. Class origins appear to be a significant but nevertheless relatively minor determinant of occupational opportunity in Canada. Ethnic background and immigrant status appear to have a minimal influence on life chances. Language is a significant, but declining, determinant of life chances. Gender is a major determinant of life chances. There is evidence that native peoples and blacks born in Nova Scotia are subject to considerable discrimination.

9. It is evident that Canadians could reduce most kinds of inequality to some degree if they had the political will to do so.

## GLOSSARY

**Biosociology.** The branch of sociology that studies the interaction and mutual influences between the social order and the biological makeup of its members.
**Conservative perspective on social inequality.** Normative theory holding that inequality is necessary, inevitable, and basically just.
**Inequality of condition.** Inequality in the overall distribution of rewards (for example, money or prestige) in a society.
**Inequality of opportunity.** Inequality in the chances

available to various members of a society for obtaining resources such as money, prestige, or power.
**Interests.** A basis for individual or group profit, benefit, or advancement.
**Marxism.** A conflict theory that emphasizes the economic basis of social inequality.
**Normative theory.** Any theory concerned mainly with moral evaluation and the question of justice. Can be contrasted with scientific theory.
**Radical perspective on social inequality.** Normative theory holding that inequality is unnecessary and unjust.
**Scientific beliefs.** Thoughts about what actually exists (or could exist) that are felt to be consistent with what is known about empirical reality. Can be contrasted with value judgments and normative theories.
**Social democracy.** Normative theory of inequality holding that ownership consists of a divisible bundle of rights and that satisfactory progress toward equality can be achieved through nonviolent, gradual reform within the political institutions of democratic capitalist societies.
**Social inequality.** Situation in which various members of a society have unequal amounts of socially valued resources (for example, money or power) and unequal opportunities to obtain them.
**Social mobility.** Upward or downward movement of individuals or groups into different positions in the social hierarchy.
**Synthesis.** A theoretical approach to the study of social inequality that attempts to use insights from both the radical and the conservative perspectives and attempts to be scientific in its methodology.
**Value judgments.** Moral or ethical opinions about what is right or wrong, good or bad, desirable or undesirable. Can be contrasted with scientific judgments about what actually exists or could exist.

## FURTHER READING

**Berger, Peter.** *The Capitalist Revolution.* New York: Basic Books, 1986. Compares the development of capitalist and noncapitalist countries.
**Boyd, Monica, et al.** *Ascription and Achievement.* Ottawa: Carleton University Press, 1985. The best source on opportunity and mobility in Canada.
**Connor, Walter.** *Socialism, Politics and Equality.* New York: Columbia University Press, 1979. Informative comparison of inequality in advanced capitalist and Marxist countries.
**Curtis, James, et al.** *Social Inequality in Canada.* Scarborough, ON: Prentice-Hall, 1988. A recent collection of readings about the Canadian case.
**Grabb, Edward G.** *Theories of Social Inequality: Classical and Contemporary Perspectives.* 2nd edition. Toronto: Holt, Rinehart and Winston, 1990. A lucid introduction to the major theoretical perspectives on inequality.
**Hunter, A.** *Class Tells: On Social Inequality in Canada.* 2nd edition. Toronto: Butterworths, 1986. An informative and recent Canadian text.

# CHAPTER 9

# Ethnic and Minority Relations

LEO DRIEDGER

"Ethnic" comes from the Greek word *ethnos*, meaning a group bound together and identified by ties and traits of nationality, culture, and race. French Canadians, for example, promote a national and cultural ethos that originated in France. Native Indians, too, have subcultural and racial ties and traits. Canadians whose origin was British identify with their heritage as well. Each of these three groups constitutes *ethnos*.

An **ethnic group**, according to Shibutani and Kwan (1965), "consists of those who perceive . . . themselves as being alike by virtue of their common ancestry, real or fictitious, and who are so regarded by others." An ethnic group includes a sense of belonging and particular ways of acting, thinking, and feeling.

Gordon's (1964) definition differs somewhat in emphasis from Shibutani and Kwan's: "An ethnic group is a group of individuals with a shared sense of peoplehood based on presumed shared sociocultural experiences and/or similar characteristics." This sense of sharing includes all dimensions of language, nationality, culture, religion, and race. This is the group's **ethnic identity**. Ethnicity is thus a very broad term, which recognizes that all people have basic historical origins, but that the form and importance of this heritage may vary from group to group. Their sense of belonging and loyalty may also vary.

When people of many different nations, cultures, religions, and races come into contact with each other, some are bound to be more numerous, or influential, or both. Thus, minority/majority relations are inevitable. A group can be considered a minority if it either has fewer members than another group or has less influence than another group. In Canada, the Hutterites are considered a minority on both these counts: their numbers are relatively few, and they also lack political power. The Jews are also considered a minority group, but largely because their numbers are relatively small; they have more influence than their numbers might suggest. French Canadians are a minority, too — everywhere except in the province of Quebec, where they are the numerical and political majority. While Canadians of British origin constitute the majority in the Atlantic provinces and Ontario, they constitute a minority in Quebec, due solely to their relatively small numbers in that province. However, this small English minority is very influential economically in Quebec (Porter 1965). In Canada, much of the economic — as well as political — power is concentrated in the hands of British Canadians.

Wagley and Harris (1958) summarize five important characteristics of minorities:

1. Minorities are subordinate segments of complex societies.
2. They have special physical or cultural traits which are [usually] held in low esteem by the dominant society.
3. They are self-conscious units bound together by special traits.
4. Membership is transmitted by descent, capable of affiliating succeeding generations.
5. By choice or necessity members [usually] marry within the group.

According to these general characteristics, Hutterites, native Indians, blacks, and Jews will almost always be seen as minorities in Canada. Germans, Ukrainians, Scandinavians, and Italians will also constitute minorities most of the time. The basic difference between an ethnic group and a minority group is that each of us belongs to an ethnic group or groups, while not everyone belongs to a **minority group**. Minority status has to do with either the size or the lack of power of a group.

## Immigration

To understand the patterns of ethnic relations in Canada, we must first analyze the demographic and ecological macrostructures. (The term *ecological* is used here in the sociologists' sense of having to do with the spacing of people and institutions, and their resulting interdependency.) When did the many peoples first come to the land we now call Canada, and where have they settled? Did Canadians of various racial, ethnic, cultural, and religious origins cluster more in one region than another? If so, why? What are the implications of such varied enclaves and patterns for ethnic relations?

## A Demographic History

To document the coming of *Homo sapiens* to Canada, we begin with the earliest native Indians and Inuit. They were followed much later by the French and British, who traded in and settled this vast territory. Later still, many other Europeans came — and, more recently, Third World immigrants. A short history will help us gain some perspective on who came when and to whom Canada belongs.

**The Earliest Inhabitants.** Anthropologists tell us that the earliest *Homo sapiens* came to the two American continents at least 12 000 years ago, probably via the Bering Strait. (The Indians were here, therefore, when the Europeans were still barbarians roaming the European continent.) Some Indians remained food gatherers, but others turned to agriculture; and when the Spaniards came (in the early 1500s), they found the great civilizations of the Maya, the Aztec, and the Inca in Central and South America.

The French and the British did not find equivalent civilizations among the native Indians of what is now Canada. Indians of the central plains and northlands were food gatherers. The Hurons and Iroquois had begun farming (Trigger 1969), however, and the natives of the west coast were engaged in large-scale fishing (Rohner and Rohner 1970).

Canadians tend to see a very small part of the great variety of Indian groupings who live throughout the two Americas. We also often forget that the native peoples have lived in what is now Canada 25 times longer than any Europeans. This fact gives rise to interesting questions: Whose land is Canada, and what are the land rights of native peoples who have not yet signed treaties with white immigrants?

**The first immigrants came to Canada at least 12 000 years ago, probably via the Bering Strait.**

**The Charter Europeans.** In 1608, the French established the first European settlement in Canada, at what is now Montreal. Some 150 years later, the British settled permanently in this country. Those first European settlers in Canada are considered by Porter (1965) as Canada's two **charter groups**.

In 1871, when the first census after Confederation was taken, almost all (92 percent) of the 3.5 million people who lived in Canada were either of British (61 percent) or French (31 percent) origin. Except for a small number of Germans (6 percent), early eastern Canada was two-thirds British and one-third French. Table 9-1 lists immigrants to Canada by nationality. The 1871 census did not include the estimated half million or more native Indians scattered over the northern territories, because the census included only the four original provinces of the east — only a fraction of the territory that is now Canada.

The British North America Act, 1867, legalized the claims of the two original European immigrant groups for such historically established privileges as the perpetuation of their separate languages and cultures. The Royal Commission on Bilingualism and Biculturalism (1965) continued to support and encourage the charter-group status of the French — even though, by 1981, immigrants of other ethnic origins composed one-third of the Canadian population.

Since so much of the history of Canada has been dominated by the presence of these two charter (European-origin) groups, Canadian literature in every field tends to reflect French/English relations. Both Britain and France explored various regions of North America, and numerous skirmishes and wars were fought: the most famous in 1759, when Canada became British. However, the Acadians had already lived in the St. Lawrence region for 150 years; their roots and tradi-

## Table 9-1. Country of Origin of the Canadian Population[a], 1871–1981

| Ethnic Group | 1871[b] | 1901 | 1921 | 1941 | 1961 | 1981 |
|---|---|---|---|---|---|---|
| *Total[c]* | 3486 | 5371 | 8788 | 11 507 | 18 238 | 24 084 |
| *Charter Europeans* | | | | | | |
| British | 2111 | 3063 | 4869 | 5 716 | 7 997 | 9 674 |
| French | 1083 | 1649 | 2453 | 3 483 | 5 540 | 6 439 |
| *Other Europeans* | 240 | 458 | 1247 | 2 044 | 4 117 | 4 625 |
| Austrian, n.o.s. | — | 11 | 108 | 38 | 107 | 41 |
| Belgian | — | 3 | 20 | 30 | 61 | 43 |
| Czech & Slovak | — | — | 9 | 43 | 93 | 68 |
| Finnish[d] | — | 3 | 21 | 42 | 59 | 52 |
| German | 203 | 311 | 295 | 465 | 1 050 | 1 142 |
| Greek | — | — | 6 | 12 | 56 | 154 |
| Hungarian[e] | — | 2 | 13 | 55 | 126 | 116 |
| Italian | 1 | 11 | 67 | 113 | 450 | 748 |
| Jewish | — | 16 | 126 | 170 | 173 | 264 |
| Dutch | 30 | 34 | 118 | 213 | 430 | 408 |
| Polish | — | 6 | 53 | 167 | 324 | 254 |
| Portuguese | — | — | — | — | — | 188 |
| Russian | 1 | 20 | 100 | 84 | 119 | 49 |
| Scandinavian | 2 | 31 | 167 | 245 | 387 | 283 |
| Ukrainian | — | 6 | 107 | 306 | 473 | 530 |
| Other European | 4 | 5 | 37 | 61 | 102 | 285 |
| *Asiatics* | — | 24 | 66 | 74 | 122 | 742 |
| Chinese | — | 17 | 40 | 35 | 58 | 289 |
| Indo-Pakistani | — | — | — | — | — | 121 |
| Indochinese | — | — | — | — | — | 44 |
| Japanese | — | 5 | 16 | 23 | 29 | 41 |
| Other | — | 2 | 10 | 16 | 34 | 247 |
| *American Aboriginals* | — | — | — | — | — | 632 |
| Indian | — | 93 | 110 | 117 | 208 | 413 |
| Inuit | — | — | — | 9 | 12 | 23 |
| Métis | — | — | — | — | — | 78 |
| Hispanic American | — | — | — | — | — | 118 |
| *Multiple Origins* | — | — | — | — | — | 1761 |
| *Other* | 52 | 84 | 53 | 64 | 242 | 191 |

[a]Numbers rounded to the nearest 1000.
[b]Four original provinces only.
[c]Excludes Newfoundland prior to 1941.
[d]Includes Estonia prior to 1941.
[e]Includes Lithuania and Moravia in 1901.

SOURCE: Dominion Bureau of Statistics, *1961 Census of Canada*, Bulletin 7:1–6, 1966, Table 1; Statistics Canada, *1971 Census of Canada*, Bulletin 1:3–2, 1973, Table 1; D. Kubat and D. Thornton, *A Statistical Profile of Canadian Society* (Toronto: McGraw-Hill Ryerson, 1974), Table 1-10.

tions were well entrenched. So it was necessary to recognize distinctive English and French regions of influence on the Canadian upper and lower shores of the St. Lawrence River. Since then, the francophones in Quebec and the anglophones in the rest of Canada have tended to see each other across the Ottawa and St. Lawrence rivers

as distinctive cultural and linguistic solitudes. Some scholars have called these solitudes "two nations" residing in one (Crean and Rioux 1983; Elliott 1983).

Much research has evolved dealing with English/French relations. Breton, Reitz, and Valentine (1980) address the problem of cultural boundaries and how this affects the cohesion of

Canada; Richmond and Kalbach (1980) are concerned with the proportions of populations and their adjustments; deVries and Vallee (1980) focus on languages; Crean and Rioux (1983) are interested in politics and power relations; Berry, Kalin, and Taylor (1977) studied the attitudes of Canadians with respect to this duality and the potential for pluralism. Although the history of Canada has been influenced mostly by these two charter groups, a shift is taking place that will modify the original dominance of the early Europeans.

**The Multi-European Entrance.** Although European settlers other than the French and British represented only about 7 percent of the Canadian population in 1871, many more have since immigrated to join the two charter groups. Table 9-2 shows that in 1901 the charter groups constituted a great majority; but by 1981 this majority had

dwindled, and the 8 million others represented one-third of the Canadian population. While the French-origin population held fairly steady at 27 percent, the proportion of British origin had dropped to 40 percent. The British and French ranked first and second, followed by the Germans, Italians, and Ukrainians.

Most of these other European groups entered Canada well after the charter groups. Many of the Germans came to Ontario as early as 150 years ago, but the majority of the others arrived in a country where the charter groups had already established the political and economic patterns. In other words, the rules were made and the terms of admission were set down. Some of the earlier European immigrants, such as the Germans, Scandinavians, and Jews, had a relatively high status and have been upwardly mobile, but more recent immigrants, with some notable exceptions,

**Table 9-2. Composition of the Population of Canada by Ethnic Origin, 1901 and 1981 (Percentages)**

| Ethnic Origin | Total | BC | Alta. | Sask. | Man. | Ont. | Que. | NB | NS | PEI | Nfld. |
|---|---|---|---|---|---|---|---|---|---|---|---|
| *1901* | | | | | | | | | | | |
| British | 57.0 | 59.6 | 47.8 | 43.9 | 64.4 | 79.3 | 17.6 | 71.1 | 78.1 | 85.1 | |
| French | 30.7 | 2.6 | 6.2 | 2.9 | 6.3 | 7.3 | 80.2 | 24.2 | 9.8 | 13.4 | |
| Other | 12.3 | 37.9 | 46.0 | 53.2 | 29.4 | 13.4 | 2.2 | 4.1 | 12.0 | 1.5 | |
| Total | 100.0 | 100.0 | 100.0 | 100.0 | 100.0 | 100.0 | 100.0 | 100.0 | 100.0 | 100.0 | |
| *1981* | | | | | | | | | | | |
| British | 40.1 | 51.0 | 43.5 | 38.3 | 36.9 | 52.6 | 7.8 | 53.5 | 72.5 | 77.0 | 92.2 |
| French | 27.1 | 3.4 | 5.1 | 4.9 | 7.3 | 7.7 | 80.2 | 36.4 | 8.5 | 12.2 | 2.7 |
| Other | 32.2 | 45.6 | 51.4 | 56.8 | 55.8 | 39.7 | 12.2 | 10.1 | 19.0 | 10.8 | 5.1 |
| Total | 100.0 | 100.0 | 100.0 | 100.0 | 100.0 | 100.0 | 100.0 | 100.0 | 100.0 | 100.0 | 100.0 |

SOURCE: Dominion Bureau of Statistics, *1921 Census of Canada*, Vol. 1, 1924, Table 23; Statistics Canada, *1981 Census of Canada*, Ethnicity Update, April 1983.

have remained largely in the lower strata of Canadian society.

**Recent Third World Immigrants.** Table 9-3 shows that in 1951, shortly after World War II, the leading immigrant source countries were predominantly northern European; in 1984, a prominent number of the ten leading source countries were Third World countries. This change in immigration trends to some extent reflects the change in Canadian immigration procedure from the discriminatory system described in Chapter 7 to a point system, which was introduced to provide immigrants of all countries with a more equitable chance to enter Canada.

The new regulations for selection of immigrants, established in 1967 and modified from time to time, set forth nine criteria for entrance. "Independent" applicants are assessed by and awarded points according to these nine criteria; those able to score 50 or more points out of 100 are given permission to enter Canada, from any part of the world. Canadian citizens may also sponsor close relatives by agreeing to support them if necessary for the first year. "Sponsored" close relatives do not need to meet the requirements of the point system. The "nominated" applicant (intermediate between "independent" and "sponsored") is subject to the point system, but can gain extra points by means of short-term arrangements with relatives. This new policy is designed to facilitate entry of next-of-kin, but it gives more non-Europeans a chance to compete for immigration as well. Thus, in the last 15 years many more immigrants from non-European countries have entered Canada than previously, adding more racial, religious, and ethnic heterogeneity to our population.

## Regional Ethnic Mosaic

Our discussion so far of population patterns over time illustrates that the native Indians inhabited the land first, followed by the French, the British, other European groups, and Third World immigrants. Table 9-1 shows that the various groups increased at different times. Table 9-2 indicates that the many groups were unevenly distributed throughout Canada. It is obvious that the various Canadian regions are very different ethnically, and we need to examine these differences.

**Table 9-3. The Leading Source Countries of Immigrants, Selected Years**

| 1951 | 1960 | 1968 | 1976 | 1984 |
|------|------|------|------|------|
| Britain | Italy | Britain | Britain | Vietnam |
| Germany | Britain | United States | United States | Hong Kong |
| Italy | United States | Italy | Hong Kong | United States |
| Netherlands | Germany | Germany | Jamaica | India |
| Poland | Netherlands | Hong Kong | Lebanon | Britain |
| France | Portugal | France | India | Poland |
| United States | Greece | Austria | Philippines | Philippines |
| Belgium | France | Greece | Portugal | El Salvador |
| Yugoslavia | Poland | Portugal | Italy | Jamaica |
| Denmark | Austria | Yugoslavia | Guyana | China |

SOURCE: Department of Manpower and Immigration, *The Immigration Program*, Vol. 2, *A Report of the Canadian Immigration and Population Study* (Ottawa: Informaton Canada, 1974) p. 84; *1976 Immigration Statistics*, Table 3; and Employment and Immigration Canada, *Annual Report to Parliament on Future Immigration Levels*, 1985. Ottawa: Minister of Supply and Services Canada, 1985. Statistical Appendix.

**In the last 15 years, many more immigrants from non-European countries have entered Canada than previously, adding more racial, religious, and ethnic heterogeneity to our population.**

Culturally and linguistically, Canada can be regarded as six regions: the northlands, the west, Upper Canada, Lower Canada, New Brunswick, and the Atlantic region. Today, the regions vary from multicultural and multilingual in the northwest to unicultural and monolingual in the east. High concentrations of native people in the north, other ethnic groups in the west, French Canadians in Quebec, and British in the east constitute an interesting mix of cultural values and social organizations.

**The Northlands.** The northlands include all of the Yukon, the Northwest Territories, Labrador, and roughly the upper three-quarters of the six western and central provinces (British Columbia, Alberta, Saskatchewan, Manitoba, Ontario, and Quebec). This area constitutes about 80 percent of the Canadian land mass, though it includes a relatively small proportion of the Canadian population. Demographically, it is the area where 69 percent of the population is of native origin, and 56 percent uses its native tongue at home. Vallee and deVries (1975) illustrate that these northern

Indian and Inuit peoples perpetuate multilingual and multicultural societies, where European influences are increasing but not yet dominant.

The native residents lived here first, and they occupy the majority of our land area. However, they constitute a very small percentage of our population, and are, economically and politically, virtually powerless. The trend, however, seems to be for native people to come south, into more urban settings. There is strong evidence that, having moved, they quickly adopt either English or (in Quebec) French; only 33 percent of native people in urban areas use their mother tongues (Vallee and deVries 1975). The northlands are multicultural and multilingual.

**The West.** The west, which includes the southern portions of British Columbia, Alberta, Saskatchewan, and Manitoba, was the domain of food-gathering peoples, and was settled most recently by immigrants of many European origins. The region is highly rural and agricultural; it includes a multitude of substantial British, German, Ukrainian, French, and smaller ethnic settlements. A diversity of European ethnic groups settled the region and established social institutions.

Native peoples constitute a significant proportion of the population on the prairies. Asiatics represent an important part of British Columbia's population. Although many western ethnic groups seek to retain their language, the language used at home by the majority – 85 percent – is English. The west is multicultural and anglophone.

**Upper Canada.** Until recently, Upper Canada, now southern Ontario, was English linguistically and British culturally. It was the stronghold of the British, a charter group whose large population promoted urban industrial growth while maintaining a strong economic and financial base.

But lately this urban industrial area has attracted many newcomers to its labour market, especially immigrants to Toronto. These immigrants represent many cultures from northern and southern Europe, as well as the Third World. Therefore, the urban areas of Ontario are changing from being very British to being highly multicultural and multilingual. These new immigrants, however, are competing for jobs, and are therefore learning English. So, although British culture and the English language are not threatened in Upper Canada, multiculturalism is on the rise.

Some 75 percent of Ontarians use English at home (Vallee and deVries 1975). Only about 5 percent speak French at home. Although Ontario has made some efforts to become bilingual (French and English), it appears that English is dominant, and other languages subordinate. This region could best be described as anglophone with strong multicultural trends.

Although the linguistic and cultural conditions of the west and Upper Canada may seem similar, they are very different historically. The west has been strongly multicultural and multilingual throughout its short history. But since it is less industrialized, new immigrants do not seem to be streaming into the area in large numbers. Consequently, it is not as culturally diverse as southern Ontario.

**Lower Canada.** In Lower Canada, now the southern portion of Quebec, 82 percent of the population speak French at home (Statistics Canada 1981). Speaking English in the home is declining, from 13 percent in 1971 to 10 percent in 1981. One reason for the persistence of English in Quebec is that the economic elite tended to be English and were influential because of their industrial connections with the rest of North America. Toronto is now Canada's dominant financial and industrial base, which means that business headquarters and offices are slowly shifting to Ontario. Therefore, the power of the English business elite in Quebec will decline, and the use of French will increase.

A second reason for greater French linguistic and cultural influence in Quebec involves provincial legislation favouring that language. The influence of the Québécois nationalists resulted in some English interests leaving Quebec, redoubling the emphasis on French language and culture.

The more than five million French Canadians living in Quebec constitute the largest regional ethnic block in Canada. With their long Canadian history, their new drive for French identity, federal efforts to promote French in Canada, and provincial legislation to protect French language and culture, it is likely that southern Quebec will remain the strongest single ethnic region. Lower Canada is francophone and francocultural.

**New Brunswick.** In New Brunswick, about 25 percent of the residents speak French at home; about 66 percent speak English at home. Other languages are spoken in the home by fewer than 10 percent of the population. This area supports only 2 or 3 percent of Canada's population. According to Joy (1972), the French in New Brunswick will in all likelihood retain their language, because they are part of the bilingual belt adjacent to francophone Quebec. French/English bilingualism is therefore both a current fact and the pattern for the future. Cultures other than French and English are not represented in large numbers in New Brunswick. New Brunswick is Canada's only bilingual and bicultural region.

**The Atlantic Region.** The most easterly Atlantic region (Nova Scotia, Prince Edward Island, and the island of Newfoundland) is unilingual and unicultural. Of the residents in this area, 95 percent speak English at home (Vallee and deVries 1975). Their long history is largely British, and demographically they are British. Very few immigrants enter these provinces. This area supports only 6 or 7 percent of the Canadian population, and it is highly unlikely that residents of this region will push for heterogeneity. Their native population is very small, their black population is anglophone and small, and other ethnic groups are hardly represented.

This discussion of our country's cultural and linguistic composition suggests that Canada is indeed a **regional mosaic**. The differences between the multicultural and multilingual northwest and the unicultural and unilingual east are great. Indeed, New Brunswick is the only region that approaches a bilingual and bicultural condition, and it is a very small part of Canada. The recommendations of the Royal Commission on Bilingualism and Biculturalism (1965), whose first report advocated a bilingual and bicultural nation, have been promoted by the federal government of Canada. The more recent Task Force on Canadian Unity (1978), however, appears to stress regionalism and diversity. This latter emphasis seems to be more in line with the cultural, linguistic, demographic, and ecological realities of the nation. Canada is a mosaic of many ethnic cultures and languages. Such diversity is a source of problems

— but a source, too, of opportunities for expanding our personal and national horizons, by experiencing and appreciating the rich variety that is the hallmark of Canadian society.

## Ethnic Stratification

A regional mosaic indicates the ecological distribution of ethnic groups. A "vertical mosaic" (Porter 1965) indicates strata of status and prestige. Some ethnic groups are heavily represented in the upper strata of the power elite; other groups are heavily represented in the lower strata. Let us start our examination of **ethnic stratification** with a discussion of the legal status of three ethnic categories — *charter groups*, *entrance groups*, and *treaty status groups* — and follow this with a discussion of the social class groupings of ethnic categories by education, income, and occupation.

### Legal Ethnic Status

**Charter Groups.** We noted earlier that the British North America Act, 1867 (now officially known as the Constitution Act, 1867), gave the British and French charter-group status. Though the Canadian charter-group status of the French is legally secure, the French have always been "junior partners" with the British, and they have had difficulty matching the numerical, economic, and political strength of the British. The French came to rely on regional segregation and on institutional and cultural development as a means of counteracting British dominance (Crean and Rioux 1983).

The collective dominance of the charter groups has never been seriously challenged, because of the high levels of British immigration and the high rate of natural increase in the French population that were experienced in the past (the latter rate is now among the lowest in Canada). Also, the ethnic structure of a country, in terms of its charter and noncharter groups, is determined early and tends to be self-perpetuating. The French have held at about 30 percent of the Canadian population (although that has declined recently); the

British have always been the largest ethnic group (although their proportion, too, has been dropping steadily).

At the time of Confederation, the British and French in Upper and Lower Canada and the Atlantic Region (other than Newfoundland) formed a bilingual and bicultural nation, with few representatives from other countries. It is these other immigrants who are in the process of slowly changing Canada from a bicultural to a multicultural and plural society, and it is to them and their statuses that we now turn.

**Entrance Groups.** Many ethnic groups are not founders of the country; they enter as immigrants and are called **entrance groups**. Porter (1965) calls the position to which ethnic groups are admitted and at which they are (at least initially) allowed to function in the power structure of a society *entrance status*. For most entrance groups in Canada this position is characterized by low-status occupational roles and a subjection to processes of assimilation laid down by the charter groups. This situation held and holds for immigrants generally. Less "preferred" immigrants, moreover, although allowed to enter Canada, were channelled into even lower-status jobs than the norm. Because of their later entrance, they were often left with marginally productive farmlands.

Some immigrants of German, Dutch, Jewish, Chinese, and Scandinavian origin entered Canada earlier than many of the others; they can be considered older entrance-status groups. Many Germans, such as the ones who settled in the Berlin (now Kitchener-Waterloo) area, have been here more than 150 years; in Manitoba many have been here for more than a century. Many of these older immigrants have moved out of entrance status into higher educational, financial, and occupational statuses. The Jews, for example, placed great value on education, and have entered higher-status occupations — higher, on the average, than those of any other groups, including the charter groups.

Immigrants from eastern Europe, however, came in large numbers in the early twentieth century; southern Europeans came later still. Ukrainians, for example, were left with relatively less fertile rural areas to settle, and urban Italians, many of them unskilled, were left with the relatively more

**The early policy of acquiring land for Europeans' use by isolating native Indians led to land claims, many of which remain unresolved.**

menial jobs. Third World immigrants who arrived during the 1970s were better educated and more highly skilled than were the eastern Europeans, and often entered the higher occupational strata; but since many were different by race, culture, and religion, they often found competition difficult.

**Treaty Status Groups.** According to Frideres (1974),

*Until 1755 the English followed a policy of expediency. At first they chose to ignore the Indians, but when this was no longer feasible (because of westward expansion), they chose to isolate them (through the reserve system), or to annihilate them (as in the case of the Beothuk Indians of Newfoundland).*

By 1830, Indian Affairs, initially a branch of the military, had become a part of the public service (Surtees 1969). The Indian Act was first passed in

1876, and has been revised a number of times since then. The general policy at first was to isolate Indians on segregated reserves, thus freeing most of the land for use by Europeans.

The first treaties were made in 1850: these included the Douglas Treaty in British Columbia, and the Robinson Superior and Huron Treaties in Ontario. As Europeans increasingly moved westward, Treaties 1 to 11 were begun in southern Manitoba in 1871, a year after Manitoba became the first western province. By the terms of these agreements, native Indians ceded most of their land to the Europeans, and received in return reserved land claims; annuities of $3 per person; and various gifts of clothing, medals, and equipment. Thus the **treaty status** groups were created.

At present there are about 240 000 treaty Indians (also called "status Indians"), who belong to 592 bands located on more than 2200 reserves west of the province of Quebec (Canadian Almanac 1988). Treaties with Indians have generally not been made in the five easterly provinces, most of British Columbia, large parts of the Yukon, and the Northwest Territories. There may be as many non-treaty Indians as there are Indians under treaty; in addition, there are large numbers of Métis (offspring of unions involving non-Indians and Indians).

Although native peoples were the original inhabitants of the land Canada now occupies, treaty Indians are currently designated "wards" of the federal government. This lowly legal status was originally intended to restrict them to small groups, so that white Europeans could more freely occupy the land. This legal **segregation** has had the additional effect of creating many islands of inertia and poverty, with little hope of improvement. Many Indians and non-Indians are very unhappy about the subordinate legal status of Indians. Some of them question whether any of the treaties, made between literate Europeans and illiterate food gatherers, are valid. To return to our initial question: Whose land is Canada, especially the vast areas where no treaties have been signed as yet?

## Socioeconomic Status

There are forms of status other than legal. The amount of income people earn, the years of education they have obtained, and the occupation in which they are engaged are all indicators of socioeconomic status. Most Canadians desire more money; those who attain it thereby gain prestige. Similarly, education is often seen as a means of obtaining well-paying occupations; education is therefore also valued by many. Blishen (1967) used the combined indicators of income and education to develop a socioeconomic occupational index that ranks occupations. Pineo and Porter (1967) also ranked occupations, by asking respondents to order the occupations according to prestige. Thus, various populations can be ranked by socioeconomic status, or strictly by occupational prestige. Ethnic groups can be ranked in this way as well.

Canada's Jewish population, for example, is very heavily represented in the higher-prestige occupations such as the managerial and professional categories, while sparsely represented in the lower,

blue-collar categories. Thus, a group that is not legally one of the advantaged charter groups ranks highest on the socioeconomic occupational index. The British, one of the two charter groups, rank second highest, suggesting that occupational prestige and socioeconomic status reinforce charter status to some degree; the British, in addition to being most numerous in Canada, rank high socioeconomically (Darroch 1979).

The ranking of ethnic groups by occupations also shows that the French have not fared as well socioeconomically as their charter status might suggest (Goyder 1983). They rank in the middle, below the Jews, the British, and the Germans, but above the Ukrainians, Italians, and native peoples. Various scholars — Hughes (1943) in his study of Cantonville, Rioux (1971) in his research about Quebec society — show that even in Quebec, where francophones are a large majority, the British tend to have a disproportionate socioeconomic influence. Much of the industrial capital is in the hands of non-francophone entrepreneurs, who dominate the higher managerial occupations. The Québécois have been working hard at gaining more control over their economic destiny so that they can perpetuate the French language and culture without fear of assimilation. Thus, and to emphasize a point made earlier, the legal charter status of the French remains very much a "junior partner" status in Confederation (especially since it is not backed by strong socioeconomic status), and it is the effects of this junior status that the Québécois seek to counter.

The most recent occupational data also show that immigrants, such as the Italians, are very heavily represented in the lower occupational strata, such as construction trades, manufacturing, and service. Native Indians are especially heavily represented in the lower-status occupations, and many are unemployed. Many native peoples have emerged only recently from the food-gathering state, and their special status as wards of the federal government has made it very difficult for them to compete socioeconomically. The middle-class curriculum in schools has not served many natives well, and they have been reluctant to enter unfamiliar industrial occupations. Thus, Canadian Indians find themselves in the lowest socioeconomic stratum. Some writers, such as Cardinal (1969), have referred to them as the "niggers'' of Canada, the disadvantaged targets of discrimination by Canadian whites.

## Racial Differentiations

If this were a chapter in an American sociology text, race would likely be the central theme. A full 11 percent of the American population is black; America has as many blacks as Canada has people, plus some 6 million Chicanos. By comparison, Canada is predominantly Caucasian; only about 5 percent of Canadians are nonwhite. Canadian Indians (1.7 percent) and Asiatics (1.2 percent) represent the largest of the nonwhite groups. Some might therefore contend that race is not a significant factor in Canada, and does not need special treatment. They would be wrong.

There are at least three important reasons for including race as an influential factor in Canadian stratification. First, Canadian Indians, although less than 2 percent of our population, were the first inhabitants, have special legal status, and are perceived by many as belonging to another race. Second, new immigration laws now permit many more immigrants from the Third World to enter Canada than previously, and many of these are neither of European racial stock nor of Judeo-Christian religious background. Third, Canadians are greatly influenced by their neighbour to the south, and the preoccupation of Americans with racial questions also tends to affect Canadian attitudes and thinking. A brief discussion of race is therefore necessary (Ramcharan 1982; Li and Bolaria 1983).

Anthropologists tell us that **race** is an arbitrary biological grouping; estimates of the racial component of large populations are still based on subjective opinions (Hughes and Kallen 1974). Physical features, genetics (including blood types), and theories about racial origins have given rise to various classifications. Although there are many such classifications, ''Caucasoid,'' ''Mongoloid,'' and ''Negroid'' are the most common. Head form; face form; nose form; eye, lip, and ear form; hair, skin, and eye colour; hair texture and amount of hair on the body; and stature and body build have all been used as criteria for racial classifications. Skin colour (Caucasians, white; Mongoloids, yellow; Negroids, black) is the most common crite-

rion. However, large groupings of the world's people, such as the native Indians of the Americas, the East Indians, and the Pacific Polynesians, do not fit any of these three categories. Many scholars, especially in the United States, also find that differences between races (such as intelligence levels) tend to disappear in controlled situations. Then why have whites of European origin made so much of race, and of skin colour especially?

Although we cannot delve deeply into the origins of racial differentiation here, it would appear that European explorers found that most of the people they encountered were of darker skin colour, and were also less technologically advanced, than the Europeans themselves were. ''Technologically advanced'' and ''superior'' tended to be equivalent in the European mind. Europeans thus developed an image of ''white superiority.''

Northern Europeans in particular, the dominant population in Canada, tend to be very conscious of skin colour and often classify people accordingly. Certainly, native Indians — who are segregated on reserves, and who are also racially classified as Mongoloid — are accorded low status in Canada. There is already evidence that, as more Third World immigrants, racially classified Negroid and Mongoloid, enter our larger cities, racial incidents tend to erupt more frequently.

Porter (1965) suggests that the idea of an ethnic mosaic, as opposed to a **melting pot**, impedes the process of social mobility: ''The melting pot with its radical breakdown of national ties and old forms of stratification would have endangered the conservative tradition of Canadian life, a tradition which gives ideological support to the continued high status of the British charter group.'' As you saw in Chapter 8, however, this situation seems to be changing; many entrance groups are gaining status educationally, occupationally, and economically, but are retaining many of their ethnic characteristics. The Jews are an excellent example of high upward mobility coupled with high maintenance of ethnic identity.

Any theory of Canadian ethnic relations must make provision for these multidimensional regional, economic, and political status structures in order to account for the factors that influence the composition of the Canadian mosaic, and also the identity of individual ethnic and racial groups.

# Theories of Ethnic Change and Persistence

What happens to the multitudes who enter Canada? How do they adjust to their new environment (Richmond and Kalbach 1980)? Do some immigrants fare better in one region than in another? Do they simply wish to retain a separate identity, or are they determined to maintain geographic/ethnic boundaries that will keep them separate? Various theories have been developed to explain what will happen to ethnic groups in an industrial/technological society. The first two theories, *assimilation* and *amalgamation*, assume that the urban industrial forces of technology will result in vanishing ethnicity. The third and fourth theories, *multivariate assimilation* and *modified pluralism*, admit that the technological forces will change the ethnic minority, but predict that groups will retain ethnic characteristics in part, or in a changed form. The remaining two theories, *ethnic conflict* and *pluralism*, posit the maintenance of ethnic identity in both rural and urban environments. A discussion of the six theories follows.

## Assimilation: Anglo-Conformity

The theory of assimilation has influenced North American thinking greatly since the 1920s. It is the product of an evolutionary perspective, which assumes that ethnic groups are constantly becoming more like the majority culture, represented in Canada and the United States by the British. This theory tends to be deterministic; **assimilation** assumes that the power of the majority will be too much for any minority group to resist, and therefore the group will assimilate into the majority.

A chief advocate of this concept was Robert Park, who contended that immigrants, when they came into contact with the new American society, either followed the course of least resistance (contact, accommodation, assimilation) or took a more circuitous route (contact, conflict, competition, accommodation, fusion) (Hughes et al. 1950). (These two possibilities are designated Route A and Route B, respectively, in Figure 9-1.) Whereas the latter route would take longer and entail considerable resistance on the part of the immigrant,

the end results would be the same: assimilation and a consequent loss of distinctive ethnic identity.

Enough minorities did assimilate as Park predicted to keep American researchers occupied with documenting this process. For 50 years these scholars tended to ignore groups that retained a separate identity and tended to regard their separateness as a relatively insignificant and temporary factor in the total pattern of minority/majority relations. The assimilation theory was so influential, combined with the evolutionary thinking of the day, that evidence to the contrary often made little headway.

The theory of assimilation was and is attractive because it is dynamic. It takes into account the distinctiveness and enormous technological changes visible in North American societies. Fur-

## Figure 9-1. Parkean Assimilation Alternative

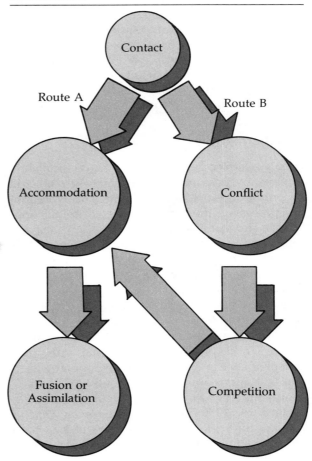

thermore, numerous studies show that many northern European groups, such as the Dutch, the Scandinavians, and the Germans, do lose many of their distinguishing cultural traits, such as original-language use, fairly quickly. However, in the eyes of some, assimilation theory is too deterministic. That is, as a macro theory it may explain a general process for some groups, but it does not take into account the many aspects of cultural change that may not all be moving in the same direction. Further, it does not sufficiently account for the possibility of nonassimilation by some groups. Finally, it does not address the idea that when assimilation is complete, the end result may not resemble the majority culture (that is, Anglo-Saxons), but may turn out to be something quite different.

We learn from Canadian history that many British leaders had the Anglo model in mind for native peoples, the French, and everyone else. Lord Durham, for example, assumed that others would assimilate into the dominant British legal, political, economic, and cultural system (Stanley 1960). And many seem to have hoped that somehow even the French would finally so assimilate, although via Park's more circuitous route of conflict and competition. These leaders assumed the preeminent desirability of British social institutions.

## Amalgamation: Melting Pot

**Amalgamation** theories differ from assimilation theories by positing that immigrant groups will be synthesized into a new group. The evolutionary process is the same as that of assimilation, but the end result is a melting pot — an amalgam, different from any of the groups involved. This concept is frequently taken by Americans to be typical of their society. They broke free of British dominance 200 years ago and created a nation ostensibly dominated by no one group. All contributed to the American dream, with its new constitution, a multitude of cultures from many parts of the world, and a system of free enterprise. Independence and freedom were popular watchwords. It was a new nation, a new culture, a new continent, a pot to which all might contribute.

Herberg (1955) contends, however, that in America the Protestants, Catholics, and Jews have never "melted." Nor have they in Canada. People of minority races — well represented in Canada

by the native peoples and in America by 25 million blacks — seem not to be melting very noticeably either. To what extent other ethnic groups, such as the French, Chinese, and Italians, are melting is the subject of much research, and it is perhaps somewhat early to tell. But certainly the French in Quebec remain a bulwark against amalgamation. The prophesied synthesis is slow in coming in Canada, and even in the United States, where the melting-pot theory is often applied, more and more scholars are having doubts about its usefulness (Kallen 1924; Herberg 1955; Newman 1973).

Canada's relatively open immigration policy has provided the potential opportunity for many peoples to contribute to a melting pot. At the time of Confederation, however, the two founding peoples represented most of the population, and as we have seen, their historical influence has been much stronger than any of the other groups that followed. Early British and French influences have tended to dominate early Canadian history and the lives of more recent immigrants. The two charter groups have fought hard not to amalgamate either culturally or linguistically, so that from the beginning our pot has contained ingredients that do not melt.

The synthesis of British, French, Germans, Ukrainians, Italians, Canadian Indians, and others into a recognizable national character has been a long time coming. Perhaps it is this "melting" process, more than any other, that is needed to develop a spirited Canadian nationalism. The Americans, on the other hand, have stressed amalgamation more and have evolved a stronger feeling of nationalism than Canadians have been able to manage. Could this be why Canada was at one time seriously discussing the possibility of Quebec's separation? Perhaps too many Canadians feel that some parts of Canada are not really so much a part of them. Speculation aside, amalgamation seems not to explain the Canadian scene as well as some other theoretical perspectives. Perhaps in the future amalgamation may apply to a greater extent than it does now.

## Pluralism: Ethnic Mosaic

The metaphor of the mosaic to describe the plural Canadian society is useful in answering such questions as the following: How are the tiles in the mosaic distributed? Are the tiles equal, or can some be seen as more important than others because of their size or the way in which they cluster in the total design? What would be missing if particular tiles no longer remained distinctive? The first question corresponds to the regional and spatial distribution of various ethnic groups in Canada; the second, to the status and power of the various ethnic groups within the total society; and the third, to the cultural and institutional contributions of the groups.

Cultural **pluralism** suggests that over time different ethnic groups maintain their unique identities. Cultural pluralism is often viewed as an arrangement whereby distinct groups live side by side in relative harmony. One proponent of this view was Horace Kallen, who did so for three main reasons (Newman 1973). He argued that, first, while there are many kinds of social relationships and identities that can be chosen voluntarily, people cannot choose their ancestry. Second, each of the minority groups has something of value to contribute to a country. And third, the American constitution carried with it an assumption that all were created equal, even though there might be many distinct differences. Kallen wished to refute the reigning notions of assimilation and the melting pot.

Assimilationists and amalgamationists emphasize the overwhelming influence of social phenomena like technology and urbanization as constituting the master trend that would sweep all forms of ethnic differentiation before it. Cultural pluralism, on the other hand, tends to focus on countervailing ideological forces, such as democracy and human justice, fundamental to which are the beliefs that all people are of equal worth and all may live as they choose, provided that they respect the rights of others. Whereas the preceding theories call for the disappearance of immigrant and racial groups, pluralism holds that there may be greater resistance to assimilation and amalgamation than had formerly been thought, and that the trend toward permissive differentiation already seems to be set. In Canada, we have accepted pluralist religious expressions and a diversity of political parties and ideologies. **Multiculturalism** in Canada is now also increasingly promoted — although not without some resistance, as Burnet's (1978) review clearly shows.

In 1971, the government of Canada announced a policy of multiculturalism within the bilingual framework. The government sought to encourage and assist Canadian cultural groups who so desired to continue to develop their cultural heritage, while seeking also to acquire one of the two official languages and thus increase their integration into the Canadian society. Berry, Kalin, and Taylor (1977) show in their national study that people in Quebec — predominantly French Canadians — and the Atlantic provinces — predominantly British — are not sold on multiculturalism, while people in Ontario and the west, where more of the noncharter groups reside, are more in favour of multiculturalism.

Our large French-Canadian population has always made up a very substantial, very distinct tile in the mosaic. Pluralists would say, too, that native Indians and the Inuit of Canada's northlands represent several more, quite durable tiles in the mosaic, and that, to a lesser extent, so do Canada's blacks, Jews, Hutterites, Doukhobors, Italians, Asiatics, and many other groups (such as the Ukrainians, and Germans in block settlements on the prairies). Canada's original natives, dominant charter groups, and relatively open immigration policy seem to have contributed toward the creation of a differentiated country, more like Belgium or Switzerland than like either of our most influential allies, Britain and the United States.

## Multivariate Assimilation

The central theme of Milton Gordon's (1964) *Assimilation in American Life* is **multivariate assimilation**, the theory that assimilation is not a single social process but a number of subprocesses, which he classifies under the headings "cultural" and "structural." Cultural assimilation includes acceptance by the incoming group of the modes of dress, language, and other cultural characteristics of the host society. Structural assimilation concerns the degree to which immigrants enter the social institutions of the society and the degree to which they are accepted into these institutions by the majority. Gordon suggests that assimilation may occur more in the economic, political, and educational institutions, while it may be resisted more in the areas of religion, family, and recreation. It would seem, therefore, that the opposing processes of assimilation and pluralism may occur simultaneously, depending on the dimension of ethnic activity examined. But as Newman (1973) points out, "Gordon contends [that] once structural assimilation is far advanced, all other types of assimilation will naturally follow."

Gordon's multivariate approach forced scholars out of their unilinear rut. But each of the seven stages or types of assimilation he established (listed in Table 9-4) tended to be oriented toward either an assimilation or an amalgamation target.

Gordon's major contribution is his complex, multilinear, multidimensional view of the assimilation process. It has been seen as a considerable improvement on Park's assimilation cycle. Although Gordon was mainly concerned with assimilation as such, and did not dwell on pluralism, he did not negate plural expressions in the areas of religion, the family, and recreation. The Hutterites emphasize religion, for example, and the Jews the family.

## Modified Pluralism

Glazer and Moynihan (1963) are able to distinguish four major events in New York history that they think structured a series of ethnic patterns in that city. The first was the shaping of the Jewish community under the impact of the Nazi persecution of Jews in Europe and the establishment of the state of Israel. The second was a parallel, if less marked, shaping of a Catholic community by the re-emergence of the Catholic school controversy. The third was the migration of southern blacks to New York following World War I and continuing through the 1950s. The fourth was the influx of Puerto Ricans during the 15 years following World War II.

Their implicit point is that the melting pot did not function in New York. They claim further that throughout America's history the merging of the various streams of population that remained differentiated from one another by origin, religion, and outlook seemed always to lie just ahead, but the looked-for commingling was always deferred.

Glazer and Moynihan suggest that the blacks are often discriminated against, and their assimilation is not tolerated by the majority. The Jews, with their distinct religion, do not wish to assimilate, but rather are proud of their identity. The Puerto Ricans and Irish Catholics represent combinations of these variations: over time they change, but they remain distinct ethnic groups.

### Table 9-4. Gordon's Seven Assimilation Variables

| Subprocess or Condition | Types or Stages of Assimilation |
| --- | --- |
| Change of cultural patterns to those of host society | Cultural or behavioural assimilation |
| Large-scale entrance into cliques, clubs, and institutions of host society, on primary group level | Structural assimilation |
| Large-scale intermarriage | Marital assimilation |
| Development of sense of peoplehood based exclusively on host society | Identificational assimilation |
| Absence of prejudice | Attitude receptional assimilation |
| Absence of discrimination | Behaviour receptional assimilation |
| Absence of value and power conflict | Civic assimilation |

SOURCE: Milton M. Gordon, *Assimilation in American Life* (New York: Oxford University Press, 1964).

Perhaps the Hutterites best represent pluralism without much change. Most other groups, however, change a great deal more over time, yet many retain a distinctive identity. This would seem to suggest **modified pluralism**. The francophones in Quebec are a good example of change from a predominantly rural, religious population, to an increasingly urban, industrial one. But this enormous shift in value orientations seems not to have affected their determination to survive as a distinct people in North America. Modified pluralism takes account of change, as do the assimilation and amalgamation theories, but it also provides for the degrees of pluralism often demonstrated in Canadian groups such as native Indians, Italians, French Canadians, Jews, Asiatics, and many others.

Glazer and Moynihan hold that all groups change, but those able to shift from traditional cultural identities to new interest foci may maintain their identities in a modified form. This view recognizes change, maintains that identification can be shifted, suggests that some groups may change more than others, and implies that the outcome may be a pluralist mixture with a non–Anglo-conformity target. Indeed, Glazer and Moynihan contend that traumatic experiences, such as conflict, encourage the development of a sense of identity among minorities. And that brings us to our sixth and last theory of ethnic change and persistence: conflict.

## Conflict: Dialectic of Incompatibles

The theories of assimilation and amalgamation posit an ordered society, one for the most part in a state of equilibrium, within which social change and group conflict are but temporary dislocations. In contrast, the theories of pluralism, multivariate assimilation, and modified pluralism allow for a greater measure of inherent conflict in the social system. But Georg Simmel (1950a) contends that conflict is the crux of the matter, and that both conflict and consensus are ever-present in society. His general assumption is that all social phenomena reflect a combination of opposed tendencies.

The conflict focus, although concerned with structure and institutions, emphasizes the processes of ethnic group relations. Since conflict implies the meeting of people with dissimilar or opposite values and norms, it includes processes of competition, confrontation, and argumentation. Following Dahrendorf (1959), we will define *social conflict* as "all relations between sets of individuals that involve an incompatible difference of objectives (with regard to positions, resources, or values)."

One way to view conflict is as Marx did in *The Communist Manifesto*: "The history of all hitherto existing society is the history of class struggles." As was described in Chapter 1 and elaborated on in Chapter 8, Marx saw the relationship between the bourgeoisie and the proletariat as a class struggle between opposites, as a macro power struggle for control over the economic and political institutions of a society, and as pervasive conflict that would inevitably lead to revolution.

Marx viewed this struggle as much more serious than ethnic territorial squabbles (Bottomore and Rubel 1963). Most ethnic groups in Canada do not aspire to such an extensive power struggle, although the FLQ movement in Quebec might be a good example of one that did. And the Parti Québécois can be seen as a milder form of conflict institution, since it would seek to gain sovereign control of Quebec's economic, political, and social institutions.

While conflict may occasionally take the form of revolution and secession, it is also present in lesser forms. When many subgroups and a multitude of cultures exist side by side they will maintain distinct identities, thus providing a potential for conflict of values, territorial interests, and power relationships. Jackson (1975) studied French/English relations in the Windsor, Ontario, area and found considerable competition and conflict, which he viewed as a normal outcome of the processes of power-position and boundary maintenance by these groups. By the same token, Quebec's "Quiet Revolution," the native peoples' quest for equal rights, and the relations between adjacent ethnic prairie communities all demonstrate a constant potential for dissension. Hutterite expansion into more of the Alberta farmlands (and subsequent restrictive legislation); the conflict of French and other ethnic groups over language rights and education during the Manitoba Schools Question; and Bill 22 and the conflicts of Italians and recent immigrants with the Quebec government over English education in Montreal are all examples of such ethnic counter-cultural conflicts (Hostetler and Huntington 1967; Richmond 1972).

These theories — assimilation, amalgamation, and the rest — have been introduced to illustrate attempts by various scholars in a variety of situations to explain how immigrants in our society change, adjust, and persist in their ethnic identities. While the first three may be important ideal descriptions, few, if any, societies conform to any of them. And while ideal, general theories are useful, they are much too broad and sweeping to explain the many specific changes undergone by scores of particular ethnic groups in a variety of definite regions in Canada. The more precise multivariate, modified pluralist, and conflict versions are therefore needed to account for many more changes and to explain in much more detail the enormous diversity of our country.

## Ethnic Identity

In our discussion of Canadian ethnicity we noted that the two charter groups, the British and the

French, are by far the two largest ethnic groups in Canada.

The British have from the outset been dominant demographically; English-language use is dominant outside Quebec; and British economic, political, and legal influence on the nation is strong. The French are highly segregated. In the province of Quebec they can maintain some of their linguistic, cultural, and legal distinctiveness by provincial government control. So much we have already determined.

The Anglo-dominant industrial and political environment acts as a magnet on ethnic minorities. Access to jobs, economic enterprise, and influence are appealing. But how do the Hutterites, the Jews, the native Indians, the French, and others retain a separate identity when they wish neither to assimilate nor to amalgamate? On the other hand, are there racial and ethnic groups who may wish to assimilate into Canadian society, but who are not permitted to compete equally? In this section, we will explore ethnic identity maintenance, and in the next section, ethnic prejudice and discrimination. These are the two sides of the identity coin: voluntary and involuntary maintenance of ethnic identity.

In our discussion of ethnic identity in this section, we will consider *group identification*. To what extent do various ethnic groups in Canada adhere to distinctive cultures that differentiate them from the rest? Dashefsky (1976) defines group identification as

*a personal attachment to the group and a positive orientation toward being a member of the group. Ethnic identification takes place when the group in question is one with whom the individual believes he has a common ancestry based on shared individual characteristics and/or shared sociocultural experiences.*

Dashefsky (1976) has reviewed some of the literature on identity and identification, which illustrates the many dimensions attributed to this concept:

*Rosen [1965] has . . . argued that an individual may identify . . . with others on three levels: First, one may identify oneself with some important person in one's life, e.g., parent or a friend (i.e., significant other). Second, one may identify oneself with a group from which one draws one's values, e.g., family or*

## Louis Riel: Traitor or Hero?

*Métis leader Louis Riel vividly illustrates this chapter's sociological emphases. As European immigrants invaded the native Indian lands, they disrupted a food-gathering way of life. Rich farmlands for the immigrants meant eviction for the natives. Conflict was inevitable and continued until the Europeans prevailed. The Indians were herded into reserves, and to this day they remain in the lower strata of Canadian society. Many lost their former identity, and only a few are now beginning to*

*make a new life. Prejudice and discrimination against Indians and Métis are common. People of Indian ancestry are shunted to the margins of Canadian society. Very few know what to do about it, and still fewer care.*

Brilliant, eloquent, compelling, moody, sensitive, argumentative — all these words applied to Louis Riel. He was born in St. Boniface, where his French father owned a flour mill, but he was educated in Montreal, where he first studied for the priesthood, then, after his father died, turned to law. When Marie-Julie Guernon's father refused Riel's request to marry his daughter, Riel packed his bags and set out for

the United States . . . Chicago . . . Minnesota . . . finally back to the Red River settlement — places he had last seen when he was just a boy.

By 1868, more easterners were entering the area — settlers from Ontario and the Maritimes who wanted farmland; Americans selling union with the United States; members of the Canadian Party plugging union with Canada. Sir John A. Macdonald wanted farmland. The Métis were apprehensive.

The next year Macdonald bought the Métis homeland from the Hudson's Bay Company and appointed William McDougall governor of the vast new territory. Riel was enraged. When McDougall tried to reach Fort Garry, he was turned back by the Métis. Riel took over Fort Garry, set up a provisional government, took several

*coworkers (i.e., reference group). Last, one may identify oneself with a broad category of persons, e.g., an ethnic group or occupational group (i.e., a social category). It is on the third level that ethnic identification occurs.*

That, very briefly, is what constitutes identification. We turn now to the various kinds. In our discussion of ethnic identification we shall touch on six identification factors: ecological territory, ethnic institutions, ethnic culture, historical symbols, ideology, and charismatic leadership. These factors are some of the basic components of an ethnic community, and taken together they constitute what Gordon (1964) refers to as a group of individuals with "a shared sense of peoplehood."

## Territory

Maintaining a separate language and culture is difficult and unlikely without a sufficiently large ethnic concentration in a given area. Minorities need territory that is within their control — territory within which their offspring may then perpetuate their heritage. This can be best done in a tightly knit community. Community space thus becomes an arena in which ethnic activities occur and are shared.

Joy (1972) demonstrates how, in Quebec, French Canadians retain control of the provincial territory, where they perpetuate their language and culture through religious, educational, and political institutions. French scholars such as Rioux (1971) have shown how, historically, the French were the first Europeans to settle along the St. Lawrence River, where they set up a seigneurial (manorial) system, with the long, narrow tracts of land still in evidence today. Miner (1939) describes beautifully the community life of the 1930s in St-Denis, a typical rural French-Catholic parish: everyone spoke French, attended Roman Catholic churches, and generally lived as depicted in the 1971 Claude Jutra film *Mon Oncle Antoine*. Gold (1975), who studied St-Pascal, the adjacent community, describes how the modern rural French-Canadian parish has changed, but how territory remains very important in maintaining rural Quebec culture.

The Hutterites constitute a good example of a rural ethnic community characterized by extensive boundary maintenance and controlled exposure to outsiders. Indian reserves also dem-

---

prisoners (including a man named Thomas Scott), and demanded a Bill of Rights for his people. His provisional government persisted, and Manitoba became Canada's fifth province in 1870.

Riel's fatal error was executing Thomas Scott. Scott had escaped and made a vain attempt to liberate Fort Garry with his supporters. Scott was a troublesome, defiant Ontario Orangeman. He was tried by Métis court-martial, found guilty of insubordination, and executed. As news of his death spread, Ontario Orangemen demanded quick revenge. Riel was forced to flee to the United States.

Fifteen years later, in 1885, Riel was invited by the Métis in Batoche, Saskatchewan, to plead their cause with the federal government. The buffalo were now gone. Big Bear and his Cree, who had refused to sign Treaty 6 in 1876, were becoming

increasingly restless. Poundmaker, one of the foremost chiefs to sign the treaty, had become bitter. In the south there was Piapot; in Alberta, Crowfoot, chief of the Blackfoot. There was rebellion in the air.

The final drama unfolded in Batoche in 1885, when Riel and his Métis fought against the Second Army sent from eastern Canada. The Métis were greatly outnumbered, as well as short on ammunition and supplies, and the hoped-for native Indian allies did not join the final battle. It was Riel's last fight, and it was all over in a few days.

On September 18, 1885, in a crowded Regina courtroom, six English-speaking jurors pronounced Louis Riel guilty of treason. Two months later he was hanged.

Less than 100 years later, commemorative monuments to Louis Riel stood on the legislative grounds in both Regina and Winnipeg. Hindsight

had led to second thoughts. More and more the Regina execution seemed unjust, and Manitobans increasingly consider Riel the father of their province. His grave occupies a place of honour in front of the oldest Roman Catholic basilica in the west, located in St. Boniface, which is now part of metropolitan Winnipeg. It is surrounded by the La Verendrye monument, the French St. Boniface college, the French Catholic archdiocese, the museum and first Grey Nuns hospital, the CBC French radio and television station, and the recently built French cultural centre. Louis Riel's grave is the hub of an important Franco-Manitoba centre.

The CBC film *Riel* documents the sequence of events in this western drama. Rudy Wiebe's novel *The Scorched-Wood People* (McClelland and Stewart, 1977) portrays the life and aspirations of the Métis on the South Saskatchewan River.

onstrate ethnic territorial segregation. China-towns are urban examples. Most minorities cannot maintain such exclusive control over a territory; it is a goal, however, to which many minority groups seem to aspire.

Ethnic block settlements are common, especially in the west. The Germans are heavily concentrated in the Kitchener-Waterloo area of Ontario; and the Ukrainians settled in the Aspen Belt, which stretches from Manitoba's Inter-Lake region to Edmonton. Rural hinterlands often supplied migrants to the city who tended to perpetuate the "urban villager" way of life — as illustrated by the north end of Winnipeg, until recently the stronghold of Ukrainians, Poles, and Jews (Driedger and Church 1974). Richmond (1972) also found extensive residential segregation in Toronto. Kalbach (1980) found historical Jewish and Italian settlement patterns in Toronto and traced how they shifted over time.

Individuals, then, can identify with a territory; it is the bounded area within which ethnic activity can take place. Territory is essential.

**The maintenance of an ethnic culture is supported when the community occupies a recognizable territory.**

## Ethnic Institutions

Forces of attraction are generated by the social organization of ethnic communities within their established social boundaries. Integration into one's own ethnic community, supported by the "institutional completeness" of the group, reinforces solidarity (Breton 1964).

The importance of institutional completeness is that the extent to which a minority can develop its own social system, with control over its own institutions, is the extent to which the group's social actions will take place within the system. Religious, educational, and welfare institutions are therefore crucial. Driedger and Church (1974) found that in Winnipeg, for example, the French and the Jews maintained the most complete set of religious, educational, and welfare institutions of all ethnic groups. These two groups were also the most segregated — in St. Boniface and the north end, respectively, where they had established their institutions. The French and the Jews identified with both territory and ethnic institutions. Residential segregation and institutional completeness thus tend to reinforce each other.

## Ethnic Culture

Kurt Lewin (1948) proposed that the individual needs to achieve a firm, clear sense of identification with the heritage and culture of the group in order to find a secure ground for a sense of wellbeing. The territory becomes a crucible within which solid ethnic institutions can be built and within which ethnic culture can be protected.

Ethnic cultural identification factors have been studied by numerous scholars (Breton, Reitz, and Valentine 1980; Ishwaran 1980). Driedger (1975), for example, found at least six factors that tended to influence group adherence to culture: language use, endogamy (marriage within the group); choice of friends; and participation in religion, parochial schools, and voluntary organizations. The French and the Jews in Winnipeg, who were more residentially segregated and who maintained their ethnic institutions to a greater degree than some other comparable ethnic groups, also ranked high on attendance at parochial schools (79 and 74 percent, respectively), endogamy (65 and 91 percent), and choice of in-group friends (49 and 63 percent). Use of the French language at home was significantly widespread (61 percent), as was church attendance (54 percent). Research on the importance of language is quite extensive — as shown by deVries and Vallee's (1980) work, as well as many Statistics Canada (1985b) studies. Other ethnic groups (such as Canadians of German, Ukrainian, Polish, Scandinavian, and British origin) supported their in-group cultures less actively.

Examination of territorial, institutional, and cultural identification factors suggests that they tend to reinforce each other; when individuals of a given ethnic group identify with their group along these lines, they then tend to remain relatively more ethnically distinct and proportionately less prone to assimilation. Such maintenance of distinctive ethnic features is necessary to the integrity of the Canadian ethnic mosaic.

## Historical Symbols

Villagers may perpetuate their ethnic social structure and community as an end in itself, without much reference to their past or future. Among ethnic urbanites, however, a knowledge of their origins and pride in their heritage would seem to be essential for a sense of purpose and direction. Without such pride and knowledge, the desire to perpetuate tradition rapidly diminishes. The Jews expose their children to a ritualized ethnic history expressed in the form of symbols: special days, fasts, candles, food habits, and other commemorative observances. Such historical symbols can create a sense of belonging, of purpose, and of continuing tradition that is important and worth perpetuating.

A comparison of identity among seven ethnic groups in Winnipeg indicated strong in-group affirmation and low in-group denial among the French and the Jews (Driedger 1976). Jewish students and French students were proud of their in-groups, felt strongly bound to them, wished to remember them, and contributed to them. The French indicated particularly low in-group denial; they did not try to hide, nor did they feel inferior about, their ethnicity; they seldom felt annoyed or restricted by their identity. The Ukrainians, Polish, and Germans felt less positively about themselves as ethnic groups, and at the same time were

more inclined to deny their ethnicity. Ethnic heritage can therefore be a strong or weak, positive or negative, influence on personal identity.

## Ideology

For certain individuals, a religious or political ideology can relegate cultural and institutional values to second place. For many in the younger generation, territory, culture, and ethnic institutions seem less intrinsically valuable than for their elders. As urban ethnic youth become more sophisticated, they tend to value their ethnicity less. A political or religious ideology, however, supplies purpose and impetus; it promotes values considered more important than cultural and institutional ones.

Often, there is a very strong correlation between religion and ethnicity. Almost all French Canadians are Roman Catholic, and the parish system in rural Quebec has been studied thoroughly (Miner 1939; Gold 1975). Of course, Catholics have also founded many essentially ethnic urban parishes: in Quebec City, in Montreal, and in Winnipeg. Similarly, most Canadians of Polish origin are Roman Catholic, and, consequently, urban Polish parishes abound.

By the same token, Jewish religion and culture are so interdependent as to seem identical; they are so unified that the distinction between "religious" and "ethnic" tends to blur. Indeed, Zionism has been and is so strong that Jews from all over the world have migrated to Israel. Closer to home, Mennonites and Hutterites also integrate and thus mutually strengthen their cultures and religious ideologies.

Ideology can help unite a people, but it can also divide them. The Ukrainians are a good example of divided loyalties. The Ukrainian Catholic and the Greek Orthodox faiths are and have long been opposed. This opposition has led to conflict among Ukrainians themselves, illustrating both the importance of ideology and its potentially divisive power.

Identification with religious beliefs or a political philosophy adds force and point to the question "What is the meaning of this territory, these institutions, and this ethnic culture, and why should it be perpetuated or changed?"

## Charismatic Leadership

Charismatic leaders have played important roles in a variety of minority movements: Martin Luther King and Malcolm X among American blacks; and Harold Cardinal among Alberta Indians, to name a few. Individuals with a sense of mission often adapt an ideology to a current situation, linking it symbolically with the past, and using the media effectively to transform the present into a vision of the future.

Such charismatic leaders ordinarily use social-psychological means to gain a following. Designed to create trust, these methods forge a cohesive loyalty to both leader and in-group. The leader's commitment is passed on to the followers, resulting in new potential for change. In the beginning, the group may not be particularly oriented to territory, institutions, culture, and heritage. But slowly, as the movement ages, such structural features become more important.

Although there may be many more ethnic dimensions with which minorities identify, we have noted that territory, institutions, culture, heritage, ideology, and charismatic leaders are crucial. Different ethnic groups identify more with some of these dimensions than with others, and some groups are more successful than other groups in maintaining a distinct community. The Hutterites have successfully survived in a rural setting, for example, and the Jews have for centuries done so effectively in the city. Any study of ethnic identity needs to explore such dimensions and foci of ethnic identification.

In many ways this discussion of ethnic identity can be capped by introducing the concept of ethnocentrism. Identity and ethnocentrism are closely linked. As you learned in Chapter 2, Sumner (1906) coined the term **ethnocentrism** to describe the tendency of ethnic groups to view other people and groups in such a way that "one's own group is the center of everything and all others are scaled and rated with reference to it. . . . Each group nourishes its own pride and vanity, boasts itself superior, exalts its own divinities, and looks with contempt on outsiders." Although Sumner seems to emphasize the negative aspects of ethnocentrism, the concept does have its positive side. Murdock (1931) thought that "positive ethnocentrism" would include a belief in the unique value of the in-group; satisfaction, solidarity, loyalty, and co-operation with it; and preferences for association with members of it. Positive ethnocentrism is akin to positive ethnic identity. Murdock also recognized negative ethnocentrism: believing in the superiority of one's own group and judging others strictly by that group's standards; ignorance of, and lack of interest in, other groups; and potential hostility toward out-groups. Ethnic identity and ethnocentrism can provide security and support for minority individuals and groups. However, if taken too far, these loyalties can also create problems of hostility toward out-groups, including prejudice and discrimination. It is to these negative features that we turn next.

# Prejudice and Discrimination

In our discussion of ethnic identity we illustrated positive features of ethnicity. There can also be many negative variations, including social distance, stereotypes, prejudice, and discrimination.

## Social Distance

When Simmel (1950a) introduced the concept of **social distance**, he posited, among other relationships, the existence of an inversely varying association between in-group solidarity and social distance from out-groups. The closer you feel to the group, the further you feel from others. Simmel's discussion of "the stranger" shows both social nearness and social distance. Consider these minority Canadians: immigrants coming as strangers to a new land; French Canadians visiting other parts of Canada and feeling like strangers; native Indians segregated in reserves away from the urban industrial mainstream; Jewish Canadians who feel they are practicing their religion among a strange and seemingly alien majority. How can these strangers, who strongly identify with their in-group culture and tradition, retain their own social world — or "ground of identification," as Lewin (1948) would put it — and at the same time relate securely to others? We would expect minority strangers entering the environment of others to be secure only if grounded in an ethnic reference group, or if socially and psychologically motivated by the norms of such an in-group. Hence "distance" and "security" are linked concepts.

Levine, Carter, and Miller Gorman (1976) contend that "Simmel's utilization of the metaphor 'distance' was by no means restricted to his pages on the 'stranger,' [but] constitutes a pervasive and distinctive feature of his sociology as a whole." They summarize the meanings Simmel attached to distance as follows:

1. ecological attachment and mobility;
2. emotional involvement and detachment; and
3. the extent to which persons share similar qualities and sentiments.

Simmel himself also thought that distance could be expressed many ways. While recent work has attempted to sort out these meanings, Bogardus (1959), famous for his "social distance scale," chose to use "the degree of sympathetic understanding that functions between person and person, between person and group, and between group and group" as his measure of social distance. The Bogardus scale has been widely used, although not extensively in Canada.

Driedger and Mezoff (1980) studied a random sample of 2520 high school students to determine students' feelings about different degrees of closeness in their contacts with members of various ethnic groups. Students were asked about people they would be willing to marry, have as a close friend, have as a neighbour, work with, or be acquainted with. They were also asked whether they would be willing to ban members of these ethnic groups from Canada, or to impose "visitor only" status on them — that is, not allow them as immigrants. The students (almost all of whom were Caucasian) were much more willing to marry those of European origin than those of non-European origin (for the most part these latter were non-Caucasian). Willingness to marry, which Bogardus considered a measure of "nearness," seems therefore to indicate less nearness toward non-Europeans. The study also showed that as students identified more strongly with their in-group, they tended also to prefer more distance from others, possibly in order to maintain their identities. Although many of the high school students indicated a willingness to be close friends with most non-Europeans, most suggested an unwillingness to marry a non-European. This does seem to indicate a desire for identity maintenance. Relatively few students wished to bar these groups from Canada or to receive them only as visitors,

although 11 percent preferred such a distance from the Jews. Such extreme desire for distance is in this instance most likely evidence of prejudice.

## Stereotypes

A **stereotype** is an exaggerated belief associated with a category. Allport (1954) says it differs from a category in that it is a fixed idea that accompanies a category and carries additional judgments or "pictures" about a category or group. A stereotype may be either positive or negative and is often used to justify behaviour toward a specific group. Negative stereotypes of racial and ethnic groups have been and are widespread. Jews are supposed to be shrewd and ambitious, Italians heavily involved in crime, Irish men drunkards, native Indians lazy and undependable, Germans aggressive and boorish: all stereotypes, all negative. Positive stereotypes are also numerous: Asiatics are supposed to stress family loyalty, Hutterites to be very religious, the British to be efficient.

Mackie (1974) found that her group of 590 adults selected from organizations in Edmonton had an overwhelmingly negative image of Canadian Indians as sharing neither the work nor the success values of the surrounding society. The stereotype of Hutterites was mostly positive (clean-living, religious, hard-working, thrifty, rural, law-abiding, pacifistic, sexually moral, sober) but also contained negative elements (exclusive, opposed to higher education, old-fashioned, disliked). Mackie's sample also reported a flattering image of Ukrainians. On the other hand, Berry, Kalin, and Taylor (1977) found that in Quebec images of Ukrainians were not nearly as positive as in Edmonton, which illustrates how stereotypes may vary by region. Mackie, of course, tried to determine how far these stereotypes conformed to fact and to what extent they did not. She found some correlations and some exaggerations.

## Prejudice

The word "prejudice" derives from the Latin *praejudicium*, which means precedent, a judgment based on previous decisions and experiences (Allport 1954). Words change over time, and **prejudice** has come to mean thinking ill of others without sufficient warrant. One dictionary defines it as "a feeling favorable or unfavorable toward a person or thing, prior to, or not based on, actual experience." These definitions suggest that prejudice is unfounded judgment and that emotions are heavily involved. While biases can be both positive and negative, we tend to think of ethnic prejudice today as mostly negative, although Allport suggests that such prejudgments constitute prejudice only if they are not reversible in the light of new facts.

Allport further suggests that prejudgment is normal and necessary, because the human mind can think only with the aid of categories or generalizations. A human being is continuously bombarded with millions of stimuli, and it is impossible to react to them all. As a result, we tend to select for attention and memory only a relative few of the many experiences available to us. Our minds form clusters of previous experiences for guiding daily adjustments. As we have new experiences, we tend to assimilate them as much as possible within the clusters already formed. This enables us to identify related objects quickly.

These categories are also more or less emotional, depending on what the experiences of a particular individual may have been. Thus, a person may feel more negative about some experiences (and the people related to those experiences) than about others. Some categories are more rational than others, but the clustering process permits human beings to slip easily into ethnic prejudice. Erroneous generalizations can be made, with the result that some categories of people may evoke not merely feelings of dislike, but feelings of actual hostility.

Such tendencies toward bias are present in the media, books, and everyday conversations that mold our impressions. Depending on prejudicial

## Democracy Betrayed

*In 1988 Prime Minister Brian Mulroney and Art Miki of the National Association of Japanese Canadians signed a historic redress agreement in which Canada acknowledged having treated the Japanese unjustly and agreed to make symbolic redress payments to Japanese individuals and the community. The following is from a submission by the National Association of Japanese Canadians to the federal government.*

In February 1942, the government of Canada ordered the expulsion of all Canadians of Japanese ethnic origin from the West Coast of British Columbia. By its action, the government perpetrated the view that ethnicity and not individual merit was the basis of citizenship. The seven years that followed witnessed the violation of human and civil rights on a scale that is without precedent in Canadian history (Sunahara 1981).

Armed with the unlimited powers of the War Measures Act, RCMP officers entered homes without warrant, day and night, giving people only hours to move. Fishing boats, automobiles, and radios were confiscated. A dawn-to-dusk curfew was imposed on "every person of the Japanese race" (Adachi 1976). Husbands and wives were forcibly separated, the men interned in road camps in such places as Rainbow, Jasper, and Yellowhead. Those who refused to abandon their families were sent to prisoner-of-war camps at Petawawa and Angler in Ontario.

The government's first measure, which was to intern only "male enemy aliens," rapidly escalated to the removal and incarceration of each and every Japanese Canadian. Families were ejected from their homes and placed in animal pens in Hastings Park, Vancouver, which became the clearing house for removal to the interior of British Columbia. On March 28, 1942, the British Columbia Security Commission, the civilian body established to carry out the uprooting, announced the sugar beet program.

Families were allowed to stay together on the condition that they leave British Columbia to work in the beet fields of Alberta and Manitoba, where there was an acute labour shortage. The first to go were families from Steveston and Fraser Valley. On arrival, they were inspected and chosen for labour like slaves at a public auction (*A Dream of Riches*, 1978).

Having been branded "enemy aliens" by the highest authority in the land, Japanese Canadians were met with suspicion and distrust in their forced migrations. Alberta accepted them only on the condition that the federal government guarantee their removal after the war was over. They were prohibited from buying or leasing land and could not grow crops except by special permission from the minister of justice; businesses and residential leases were strictly controlled; and municipalities such as Chatham, St. Catharines, and Toronto banned Japanese Canadians from their city limits.

The Security Commission began its work on March 4, 1942, and, by October, its mandate had been accomplished: 21 000 people of

bias, young people can be referred to as "youthful" or "immature"; people who are cautious may be regarded as "discreet" or "cowardly"; someone who is bold may be considered "courageous" or "foolhardy."

While social distance from others may be the result of a desire to maintain a separate ethnic identity, it can also, as we have observed, stem from negative attitudes. Berry, Kalin, and Taylor (1977) found that those who favoured multiculturalism in Canada also tended to have more positive attitudes toward others. Canadians of British and French origin, however, although they tended to have fairly positive attitudes toward each other, wished to identify less with others. Those who were more ethnocentric still, such as Quebec francophones and British Maritimers, tended to be more negative toward new immigrants and multiculturalism. Similarly, Cardinal (1969) claims that

prejudice against Canadian Indians is common and occasionally reflected in the media.

Tienhaara (1974) found in her analysis of postwar Canadian Gallup polls that historical situations created varied responses. Polls taken in 1943, during the war, showed that a majority of Canadians thought that Japanese people living in Canada should be sent back to Japan, although the respondents made distinctions between those Japanese who were Canadian citizens, and those who were not. After the war, Canadians became more tolerant, but many still favoured deportation. In fact, most Japanese people living on the Pacific Coast of Canada during World War II were sent inland involuntarily.

A 1955 poll taken in Canada showed that more than one-third of the respondents did not wish to have "a few families from Europe come to [their] neighbourhood to live" for a variety of reasons.

---

Japanese ethnic origin had been displaced from their homes and torn from their livelihood without recourse to legal appeal. Yet these deprivations merely presaged what was to come.

Once Japanese Canadians were uprooted from their communities on the west coast, the Custodian of Enemy Property, who was solemnly charged with holding homes, businesses, and property *in trust*, proceeded to liquidate these belongings *without the owners' consent*. Possessions that had taken lifetimes to accumulate were disposed of in fleeting moments. Furniture, appliances, sewing machines, pianos, and household goods were snapped up at fire-sale prices by the general public. Unopened and unvalued boxes and trunks of china, silver, clothing, and irreplaceable family heirlooms were auctioned off for $2 per bid. Homes and businesses were sold by public tender to eager buyers. In the Fraser Valley alone, 769 farms comprising 13 000 acres [5260 ha] of the finest agricultural land in British Columbia were disposed of for $64.00 per acre (Berger 1981; Sunahara 1981). The 1200 fishing boats impounded on December 8, 1941, were disposed of under Orders-in-Council P.C. 288 and P.C. 251, which were passed on

January 13, 1942. Any capital from property sales was wiped out by realtors' and auctioneers' fees, storage and handling charges, and deductions for welfare while interned. Japanese Canadians, unlike prisoners of war or enemy nationals under the Geneva Convention, were forced to pay for their own internment.

In August, 1944, Prime Minister William Lyon Mackenzie King declared, "It is a fact no person of Japanese race born in Canada has been charged with any act of sabotage or disloyalty during the years of war" (King 1944). Nevertheless, in 1945, when World War II was clearly over, the government once again invoked the spurious issue of loyalty to deal with the "problem" of Japanese Canadians still remaining in British Columbia.

A "loyalty survey" was conducted throughout the detention camps of British Columbia during April and May of 1945. Proof of loyalty consisted of "volunteering" to remove oneself east of the Rocky Mountains. Those unwilling or unable to make such a move were to be classified as disloyal, divested of citizenship and nationality, and banished to Japan. The original orders authorized the deportation of 10 000 Japanese Canadians. A

groundswell of public opinion, reinforced by a declaration from the United Nations that the act of deporting citizens was a crime, stopped this action by the government, but not before 4000 Japanese Canadians, half of whom were Canadian-born, had departed for Japan. Those who escaped exile to Japan were forced to disperse across Canada.

Once outside British Columbia, however, restrictions continued. In 1944, the House of Commons passed a special order to ensure that Japanese Canadians expelled from British Columbia would be unable to vote in federal elections; lack of franchise in British Columbia had prevented Japanese Canadians from voting in federal elections as long as they remained in British Columbia.

---

**Source:**

Adapted from National Association of Japanese Canadians, *Democracy Betrayed: The Case for Redress* (a submission to the government of Canada on the violation of rights and freedoms of Japanese Canadians during and after World War II), 1984.

A national poll in 1961 showed that over half the Canadians questioned thought we should continue to restrict nonwhites. A poll in 1963 showed that almost two-thirds would not move if "coloured people" came into their neighbourhood, but over one-third — 38 percent — said they would or might (Tienhaara 1974). These polls seem to indicate that, depending on historical situations and social events, there are latent or potential attitudes of prejudice among many Canadians.

## Discrimination

Prejudice is an attitude; **discrimination** is action that is usually based on prejudiced attitudes. Allport (1954) argues that "discrimination comes about only when we deny to individuals or groups of people the equality of treatment which they wish." Hagan (1977) suggests that in this connection four distinctions are important: differential treatment, prejudicial treatment, denial of desire, and disadvantaging treatment. Obviously, we cannot treat everyone equally; distinctions must be made. This constitutes *differential treatment*. Although this may not be discrimination as such, it can be a predisposition to discrimination. *Prejudicial treatment* will likely lead to unfair treatment. *Denial of desire* involves placing restrictions on the aspirations of some members of society, such as their desire to live in any part of the city, or their desire to belong to any club, if they can afford it. (In some cities of the United States, for example, despite widespread official desegregation, blacks still cannot buy houses in strictly white neighbourhoods. Jews often claim that they are denied membership in select clubs.) *Disadvantageous treatment* is a clear form of discrimination that may take a variety of forms.

Allport (1954) outlines several forms of disadvantageous treatment. *Anti-locution* (verbal expressions such as jokes and name-calling) would be the mildest form. *Avoidance* is more severe: prejudiced people restrict their own movements so that they do not come into contact with undesirables. *Discrimination* is still more intense in that now acts of inequality, of disadvantage, extend to the ethnic or minority victim, including disadvantages in citizenship, employment, education, housing, or public accommodation. It gets worse. *Physical attack* (ejection from a community,

lynchings, massacres, and genocide) would be the severest form. Until recently blacks were still lynched in the United States; massacres of native Indians occurred in Canada; and the Jewish holocaust is still fresh in our memories, as Glickman and Bardicoff (1982) clearly show. Religious and political persecution remain constants in Northern Ireland, the Middle East, and elsewhere.

Driedger and Mezoff (1980), in their sample of 2520 high school students in Winnipeg, found that perception of discrimination varied among ethnic groups. (See Table 9-5.) About one-third of the students reported discrimination. Jews, Italians, and Poles perceived the greatest discrimination in the classroom and in textbooks. The Jews, especially, reported discrimination in clubs, and denial of access that was free to others. While verbal abuse was reported most often, the Jews reported vandalism and physical attack as well. Blacks and Asians often report discrimination — and such reports seem to be growing more frequent every week, especially in large urban centres like Toronto.

One of the things sociologists do is study the way society is structured for discrimination. Canadian immigration laws permit quotas and restrictions on immigrants considered undesirable. Agencies and institutions restrict the opportunities of treaty Indians, non-treaty Indians, and Métis. The cycle of poverty is too often nourished rather than eliminated. During World War II, as noted earlier, the Canadian government forcibly evacuated Japanese Canadians from the west coast and sent them inland because of a perceived threat to national security. (Not until 1988 did the Canadian government make restitution for these wrongdoings by agreeing to make payments to survivors — and to the Japanese-Canadian community — and by issuing a formal apology for the unjust treatment they received from the government 40 years previously.) The Chinese were legally restricted from voting and denied access to public places, especially in British Columbia. Laws were passed in Alberta to restrict the expansion of Hutterite colonies. While English and French languages were once legally used in Manitoba, and other ethnic groups were permitted to educate their children in their own mother tongues, these rights were later changed and English alone was forced on minorities. Racism is increasingly

**Table 9-5. Type of Discrimination Reported by High School Students, by Ethnic Groups (Percentages)**

| Type of Discrimination | Discrimination reported by | | | | | | | | |
|---|---|---|---|---|---|---|---|---|---|
| | Jews (N = 290) | Poles (227) | Italians (65) | French (396) | Ukrainians (517) | Germans (333) | Scandina-vians (78) | British (502) | Total (N = 2408) |
| Total[a] | 68 | 51 | 46 | 45 | 36 | 33 | 19 | 18 | 35.5 (856) |
| Ethnic jokes | 50 | 45 | 37 | 33 | 30 | 23 | 9 | 8 | 27.5 (662) |
| Verbal abuse | 53 | 17 | 19 | 21 | 13 | 19 | 8 | 4 | 18.3 (440) |
| Language ridicule | 27 | 15 | 30 | 29 | 13 | 13 | 4 | 8 | 15.7 (377) |
| Hate literature | 19 | 2 | 6 | 4 | 3 | 5 | 0 | 2 | 5.0 (121) |
| Physical attack | 21 | 2 | 3 | 4 | 3 | 3 | 1 | 2 | 4.7 (114) |
| Vandalism | 13 | 1 | 2 | 1 | 2 | 3 | 1 | 0 | 2.7 (64) |

[a]The percentages in this row represent the proportion of students in each category who reported at least one type of discrimination or reported discrimination in a given place.
SOURCE: Leo Driedger and Richard Mezoff, "Ethnic prejudice and discrimination in Winnipeg high schools," *Canadian Journal of Sociology* 6 (1980):13.

raising its head in urban centres such as Toronto and Montreal. Nova Scotia has discriminated against blacks. In most societies, including Canada, there are powerful attempts to control and sometimes repress minorities. Those who control the political and economic institutions often use such power to their own advantage, forgetting about the rights and aspirations of the weak. This frequently leads to conflict, because many minorities feel that Canada is theirs as well — it does not belong only to those who have power.

Although studies of discrimination in Canada are few, discrimination clearly does exist, as native Indians, Jews, and non-Caucasian immigrants can well attest.

## Whose Land Is Canada?

Whose land is Canada? The answer depends on perspective. Some lay claim to this land because they came here first; others claim it on grounds of numbers and power; still others, who have come recently, claim a right to it by virtue of a right to human freedom and dignity. What Canada will become depends on the goals Canadians have for the future. If homogeneity is desired, then the dominant British may wield their power increasingly to select and protect Anglo-conformity. Others who desire homogeneity among themselves, like the French Canadians, may leave to form a separate nation. But can this nation be culturally heterogeneous and still move forward with purpose? Some think it can. Some fear that this will lead only to differences, discrimination, and conflict. Others believe that such pluralism is inevitable in modern industrial society. Increasingly, freedoms have been extended to include choices in religion and politics; must these also be extended to a diversity of ethnic identities? So it would seem. That is the great Canadian experiment.

Whose land is Canada? Ours.

# SUMMARY

1. An ethnic group is a group of people with shared sociocultural experience and/or similar characteristics. Its members perceive themselves as alike by virtue of their common ancestry. An ethnic group that is subordinate to any other group is called a minority group.

2. Canada is a land of immigrants. The native Indians arrived first, followed much later by the Europeans. The French originally settled in what is now Quebec, followed by the British, and other northern, eastern, and southern Europeans. Today, the British constitute the largest ethnic group (40 percent), followed by the French (27 percent).

3. Only New Brunswick approximates a bilingual and bicultural area. The rest of Canada is highly diversified ethnically and marked regionally by the various native, French, British, and other European cultures. Thus, multiculturalism in a bilingual framework seems to reflect the demographic and regional facts of Canadian life.

4. Most urban industrial societies are highly stratified, and in Canada the ethnic groups are differentially located in the various strata. The British and the French, the two charter groups, have special language status legally enshrined in the Canadian Constitution. This legal advantage, together with their early arrival and large populations, make them the two most powerful groups. But the French have always been junior partners. The treaty status groups, the native Indians, were relegated to reserves by treaties that made and kept them subordinate. The entrance groups came later.

5. With the increase of the Canadian Indian population, as well as a large influx of new immigrants, Canada has increasingly been faced with ethnic diversity. Various changes have occurred, and conflicts have arisen. Whose land is Canada? The question is on the minds of many. Official bilingualism and multiculturalism are hotly debated. No one theory seems best to explain Canadian ethnic change, though many — such as assimilation, amalgamation, pluralism, multivariate assimilation, modified pluralism, and conflict — have been suggested and studied.

6. Early in Canadian history many groups actively sought to maintain their ethnic identities by territorial segregation in rural communities; others were forced into reserves and ghettos. Some believe that language is the most important means of preserving ethnic identity; others value religion most highly; still others seek to foster heritage, endogamy, and choice of in-group friends. Ethnic identity can be maintained through identification with an ecological territory, with ethnic institutions, with an ethnic culture, with historical symbols, with an ideology, or with charismatic leadership.

7. Amidst the Canadian ethnic diversity, some groups are valued more highly than others. In many cases, distances between groups simply maintain identity, but sometimes they emerge as either prejudice (a prejudgment, usually negative and not based on actual experience, of a group of people) or discrimination (an action toward a group of people based on prejudiced attitudes).

# GLOSSARY

**Amalgamation.** Process by which groups are blended into a melting pot where none remains distinctive.

**Assimilation.** Process by which a group becomes like the dominant group, and no longer remains distinctive. Also referred to in North America as "Anglo-conformity."

**Charter groups.** The two original European migration groups (British and French) whose legalized claims for such historically established privileges as the perpetuation of their separate languages and cultures are enshrined in the Canadian Constitution.

**Discrimination.** Process by which a person is deprived of equal access to privileges and opportunities available to others.

**Entrance group.** Ethnic group that is not a founder of the country and whose members enter as immigrants after the national framework has been established.

**Ethnic group.** Group of individuals with a shared sense of peoplehood based on presumed shared sociocultural experiences and/or similar characteristics. They perceive themselves as alike by virtue of their common ancestry.

**Ethnic identity.** Attitude of being united in spirit, outlook, or principle with an ethnic heritage. An attachment and positive orientation toward a group with whom individuals believe they have a common ancestry and interest.

**Ethnic stratification.** Order in which ethnic groups form a hierarchy of dominance and socioeconomic status in a society.

**Ethnocentrism.** Tendency to see one's in-group as being in the centre of everything and to judge other ways of life by the standards of one's own group.

**Melting pot.** Situation in which the amalgamation and blending of groups have left none distinctive.

**Minority group.** Ethnic group that is subordinate to another group.

**Modified pluralism.** Glazer's and Moynihan's modification of pluralism theory, describing a situation in which numerous groups maintain distinctly different cultures, ideologies, or interests; although they will be changed and modified somewhat, they will not be transformed entirely.

**Multicultural.** Relating to or designed for a combination of several distinct cultures.

**Multivariate assimilation.** Gordon's modification of assimilation theory, which maintains that assimilation is not a single social process but a number of cultural, structural, marital, identificational, attitudinal, behavioural, and civic subprocesses.

**Pluralism.** Social situation in which numerous ethnic, racial, religious, and/or social groups maintain distinctly different cultures, ideologies, or interests.

**Prejudice.** A feeling (usually negative) toward a person, group, or thing prior to, or not based on, actual experience. Prejudging others without sufficient warrant.

**Race.** Arbitrary biological grouping of people on the basis of physical traits.

**Regional mosaic.** Distinctive ethnic patterns formed by the various regions of a country that have different combinations of linguistic and cultural groups.

**Segregation.** Separation or isolation of a race, class, or ethnic group by forced or voluntary residence.

**Social distance.** In contrast to social nearness, Simmel defines social distance as ecological, emotional, and social detachment from others.

**Stereotype.** Opinions and judgments of others that create an exaggerated view of a type of person or group.

**Treaty status.** Certain privileges and obligations passed on to native Indians from their ancestors, who signed treaties with the Canadian government.

contributions on ethnic relations, change, attitudes, inequalities, and conflict.

**Bolaria, B. Singh, and Peter S. Li.** *Racial Oppression in Canada.* 2nd edition. Toronto: Garamond Press, 1988. This volume deals with race and racism toward Indians, Chinese, Japanese, East Indians, and blacks in Canada.

**Driedger, Leo.** *Ethnic Canada: Identities and Inequalities.* Toronto: Copp, Clark, Pitman, 1987. A collection of 22 readings on ethnic theory, demography, ecology, identity, conflict, and the need for human rights and social equality.

**Driedger, Leo.** *The Ethnic Factor: Identity in Diversity.* Toronto: McGraw-Hill Ryerson, 1989. This is an integrated volume on ethnic relations in Canada dealing with the effects of industrialization on ethnic identity, stratification, and human rights.

**Elliott, Jean Leonard (ed.).** *Two Nations, Many Cultures: Ethnic Groups in Canada.* Scarborough, ON: Prentice-Hall, 1983. 2nd edition. An edited volume of 30 contributions on the native peoples, the French, and other ethnic groups in Canada.

**Frideres, James S.** *Native People in Canada: Contemporary Conflicts.* Scarborough, ON: Prentice-Hall, 1983. 2nd edition. A comprehensive sociological study of Indians in Canada.

**Herberg, Edward N.** *Ethnic Groups in Canada: Adaptations and Transitions.* Toronto: Nelson, 1989. Herberg reviews ethnic groups in Canada, considering immigration, changing cultures, new adaptations, and changing transitions.

**Kallen, Evelyn.** *Ethnicity and Human Rights in Canada.* Toronto: Gage, 1982. A discussion of Canadian human rights and the 1981 Charter and new Constitution.

**Li, Peter S.** *The Chinese in Canada.* Toronto: Oxford, 1988. Li reviews the development of institutional racism, the exclusion of the Chinese in early Canada, and the post-war Chinese community (covering new immigration, mobility, and human rights).

**Samuda, Ronald J., John W. Berry, and Michel Laferrière (eds.).** *Multiculturalism in Canada.* Toronto: Allyn and Bacon, 1984. A collection of writings on multicultural policies, attitudes, and adaptation.

## FURTHER READING

**Berger, Thomas R.** *Fragile Freedoms: Human Rights and Dissent in Canada.* Toronto: Clarke, Irwin, 1981. Berger deals with the loss of freedoms by the Acadians, the Métis, Japanese Canadians, and religious and Indian minorities.

**Bienvenue, Rita M., and Jay E. Goldstein (eds.).** *Ethnicity and Ethnic Relations in Canada.* 2nd edition. Toronto: Butterworths, 1985. An edited volume of 20

# CHAPTER 10

# Formal Organizations

TERRENCE H. WHITE

In developed societies, organizations are everywhere. Governments, stores, hospitals, schools, universities, churches, restaurants, railways, airlines, funeral parlours, and massage parlours are but a few pieces in the vast organizational mosaic of Canadian society.

Ask a group of people what *organization* means, and you will receive a wide array of answers. For some, the term is synonymous with bureaucracy. For others, it suggests the dull routine of work, or the fun of membership in a ski club. Or it may have more sinister connotations, evoking thoughts of organized crime and the Mafia. Ask sociologists for their views on the subject, and they are likely to respond guardedly: "Well, that depends. Are you talking about voluntary associations, or formal organizations, or complex organizations, or institutions, or what?"

Such a wide range of responses is understandable because *organization* is a very general term with many possible meanings. So it is necessary to narrow the focus on the term. This chapter examines the nature of organizations and their effects on our lives. Our main attention will be on formal organizations. But lest we narrow our focus too quickly, let us begin by looking at the role of organizations in the broader social spectrum.

## Social Organization

Organizations are a universal attribute and a natural consequence of the social behaviour of human beings. People are *social* in that they do not live in isolation from other people. There are, of course, always a few people who do live most of their adult lives in isolation — hermits, for example. But even they find themselves in social settings from time to time in order to get essential supplies, emergency health treatment, perhaps a bath, or whatever. Generally, no functioning human is ever totally asocial — or not for long.

The reasons for this social tendency in human beings are many. At the most basic level, the biological necessities of human procreation require social behaviour if the species is to survive. Human sexual intercourse, the usual prerequisite activity to children — test-tube babies notwithstanding — presupposes co-operative social action. And offspring are dependent on adults for many years. In the absence of provisions for reproduction and child care, the species would disappear. At the most fundamental level, therefore, human social behaviour is necessary to ensure human survival.

Furthermore, when people interact with others, they may find themselves developing dependencies other than those associated with mere survival. If, for example, I am a farmer and you are a blacksmith, I may find that plowing is easier and more effective using a metal plow that you have made. In return for the plow, I provide you with fresh vegetables and grain for your family. And later, if my horse needs shoeing, I bring that work to you. And so it goes.

What happens is that, in the process of our social interaction with each other, certain mutual dependencies develop. You need the food I grow, and I need your blacksmithing skills. Unable to do everything for ourselves, we divide most of the work so that we tend to do those things at which we are good or for which we have special facilities. As a consequence, we come to rely on others for additional skills, goods, or services. A basic division of labour results. **Division of labour** refers to the tendency for general tasks and roles to become increasingly specialized.

These three concepts — social behaviours, division of labour, and dependencies on others — are interrelated. (See Figure 10-1.) Human intelligence, skills, and abilities are not evenly distributed, so social behaviour eventually results in a very rudimentary division of labour. This division may be along gender and age lines, as in primitive

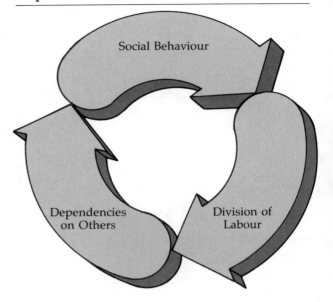

**Figure 10-1. Relationships among Social Behaviour, Division of Labour, and Dependencies on Others**

tribes where the males are usually the hunters and women and the elderly tend to family and household duties. Or it may be more of an occupational division of labour, as in our example of the farmer and the blacksmith.

The division of labour, no matter how simple or basic, leads to increasing dependencies among people that, in turn, reinforce social behaviour. As industrialization or development advances in a society, the cycle of interrelationships among these three components (gender, age, and occupation) becomes even more intense, with greater specialization in work resulting in a more complex division of labour, and so on. As a consequence, most people become bound into a web of dependency; they need others in order to survive or at least to live in the manner to which they are accustomed. The intricacy of these developments creates an expanding need for co-ordination and control of the various elements in society. As this cycle of relationships develops and intensifies, the necessity for organization increases.

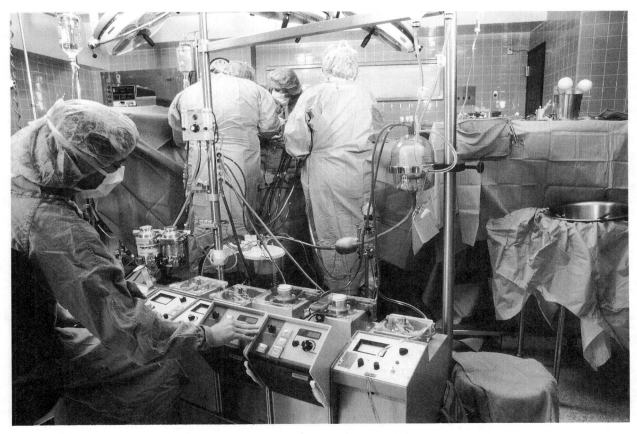

**As specialization of tasks increases, interdependency develops, requiring co-ordination and control.**

## Durkheim and the Division of Labour

An early scholar who pointed to the link between the division of labour and the necessity for social organization was Durkheim. He was interested in the impact on societies of the increasing division of labour. In *The Division of Labor in Society* (1964a, originally published in 1893), he focused on the question of *social solidarity* — what is it that binds people together in larger social networks? — and the mechanisms that create social solidarity. He identified two types of social solidarity: mechanical and organic.

In primitive societies, Durkheim suggested that the links between people take the form of **mechanical solidarity**. Based on strong systems of common beliefs, the division of labour is rudimentary, with people engaged in similar tasks and having relatively high degrees of self-sufficiency.

Because people are able to supply most of their own basic needs, their dependencies on others through the division of labour are not great. As a result, their social bonds are kinship and neighbourliness. Outside the basic family unit, they get together with other people because they want to, rather than because they have to in order to survive.

But as societies evolve and become more complex, the division of labour increases, and specialization results in greater differentiation among people. No longer is everyone doing relatively similar tasks. Consequently, individual self-sufficiency decreases and greater dependencies on others develop. Greater dependency means that people must maintain social relations in order to survive at a desired standard. This basis for solidarity Durkheim termed **organic solidarity**.

The state of the division of labour is a critical element in Durkheim's analysis. Social behaviour mediated through the division of labour, as we saw above, determines the development of organization. As societies evolve from mechanical to organic solidarity, the specialization in the division of labour and the complex interdependencies generate needs for co-ordination and control. That is, they generate the need for organization.

Durkheim's focus on society as a system and his analysis of the impacts on human behaviour as an aspect of societal structure are good examples of the elements in the structural-functional approach.

## Organization Defined

*Organization* is a general term encompassing many interrelated elements. In order to identify the basics of organization, let us employ an imagined set of circumstances. You are driving in the country when you happen upon a farm where the barn is burning. Wanting to help, you join the farmer and a group of neighbours standing before the blaze. The necessity for action is obvious if damage to the barn is to be contained and the fire's spread to adjacent buildings averted. Fortunately, there is a water well in the yard, some buckets are lying around, and a ladder sits close at hand.

Given these particulars, you can easily imagine the next step. Those at the fire start a bucket brigade, moving water from the well to the barn and up the ladder onto the fire. Each individual performs a specific task, and probably some attempt is made to match people to appropriate tasks. The heavy chore of drawing water from the well, for instance, is assigned to a well-muscled individual, and people afraid of heights are on the ground rather than at the top of the ladder, facing the blaze.

Let us step back for a moment and analyze some of the components of this situation — for example, the group's goals. The burning barn presents a very clear challenge or goal for the people on the site: to put out the fire. And as it happens, a necessary prerequisite for an organization is a goal or series of goals whose achievement serves as a motivation for concerted action.

In our imaginary farmyard, the means for achieving the goal are clear: to move the water from the well onto the fire. The men and women could each fill their own buckets and run with them individually to the fire. These disorganized and independent actions may be successful if the fire is small and our firefighters are all fairly strong and hardy. On the other hand, such unrelated individual actions may result in failure if the fire is big. Imagine people crowded at the well waiting to fill their buckets, people bumping into each other and spilling their water en route to the fire, and so on. Clearly, the bucket brigade organization is much more likely to realize the group's goals.

Our bucket brigade illustrates some important concepts besides the achievement of goals. First, it exemplifies the use of a technology in goal achievement. **Technology** is the application of a body of knowledge through the use of tools and processes in the production of goods and/or services. In this case, the technology is based on the knowledge that water can be used to extinguish certain types of fires. The tools in this instance are simply the buckets and the ladder, while the process involves filling the buckets and passing them along a human chain to the fire. Certain additional resources are required if the technology is to function; here they are the supply of water and people to fill the various roles or jobs in doing the work. Thus, in our elementary organization, the bucket brigade, the resources of water and volunteers are utilized in a division of labour employing a simple technology to achieve the goal of putting out the fire.

Back to the scene of the blaze. Good progress is being made in getting water to the fire, but a problem has developed, one requiring co-ordination: the buckets, once emptied on the fire, are not being returned to the well so that the process can be repeated. Several uninvolved children are commissioned to return the empty buckets regularly to the well, thus completing the circuit.

An observer of the scene would be impressed not only with the need to solve problems in pursuit of the goal but also with the communication between members of the organization as suggestions pass among them and as they give each other encouragement or reprimands for ups and downs in performance. In addition, one person has emerged as a leader, whose concern it is to co-ordinate the activities of the group, as well as take the lead in identifying and resolving problems. The reader will be relieved to learn the happy ending of this scene: the fire is speedily doused and only minor damage to the barn has resulted.

To sum up, our organization, the bucket brigade, although not as complex as a metropolitan fire department or a large business, does contain the basic elements of an organization:

1. goal(s)
2. resources (for example, water, buckets)
3. technology
4. division of labour
5. co-ordination
6. communication
7. leadership

An **organization**, therefore, is an entity in which people and resources are co-ordinated through a division of labour in the use of a technology to achieve a goal. Co-ordination, control, and problem-solving are facilitated through communication and leadership.

## Spontaneous Organization

Our bucket brigade has disbanded; all the stalwart men, women, and children are enjoying a well-deserved rest. While it was in operation, though, the brigade constituted a good example of an organization. Furthermore, it was an example of a **spontaneous organization**. The fire was a one-time event. The people who were at the scene of the fire linked themselves in a co-ordinated activity to achieve a specific goal at a particular time. The goal achieved, the organization resolved itself into individuals, who went their separate ways.

Spontaneous organizations are often generated in crisis or emergency situations. For instance, volunteers may band together to fill sandbags and build dikes during a flood. Or the first people to arrive at a car accident may organize to extricate victims, provide first aid, and direct traffic. Once people and other regular service personnel arrive, this temporary organization scatters.

Spontaneous organizations do not always occur, however, even though a worthwhile goal or goals may be clear. One reason for nonoccurrence is that the technology to achieve the goals is not known or readily available. Consider the events one evening in a mountain campground overflowing with campers and their children. In the middle of the site was a large container full of compacted garbage. After supper, a black bear and her two cubs strolled through the campground to the container, and the mother climbed inside and began throwing out leftovers for her hungry cubs.

Everyone in camp pressed forward to watch the proceedings; oblivious to the onlookers, the three bears ripped open garbage bags and consumed practically everything but the cans. One of the cubs climbed up and into the high-walled container to join the mother. After a while, the mother clambered out and waited for her cub to join her. But the cub could not get out. The mother's concern mounted and she began bellowing and tentatively charging the crowd. The longer this behaviour went on, the more it became a threat, especially in view of the many children nearby.

Adults in the crowd began to look for some solution to the problem of getting the cub out of the garbage container. But no ready solutions were apparent. In this instance, participants in a possible organized action to achieve a goal were unable to proceed because no suitable technology was known to them; the situation was compounded further by their fear.

A bit later, a park warden drove up in his truck, surveyed the scene, and left. He quickly returned with a fence post, drove alongside the container, rolled down his window, and leaned the post against the inside wall of the container so that the cub could climb out. Mother and cubs reunited and scrambled into the bush, while the campers glanced sheepishly at one another with why-didn't-we-think-of-that looks.

So spontaneous organizations may not form because the appropriate technology is either unknown or unavailable to those at the scene. Also, of course, the goal may not be clear, as in unfamiliar circumstances such as an earthquake or tornado. Another possibility is that people on the scene are not prepared to make a commitment to co-operative action for reasons of fear. For example, bystanders may watch motionless on a dock while someone is drowning or ignore the pleas for help from an assault or mugging victim. Such people do not want to get involved.

## Formal Organization

Many organizations are more enduring than the spontaneous ones we have considered so far. Earlier we referred to the circular nature of the interrelationships among social behaviour, division of labour, and social dependencies. We observed that as these links intensify, societies move, in Durkheim's phrasing, from mechanical to organic solidarity. Along with these developments, we suggested that people tend increasingly to be enmeshed in a dependency web whereby the specialized division of labour makes them more reliant on others for survival at a desired standard of living. To manage the complexity of these links, societies come to be increasingly formalized. **Formalization** is a process by which the informality of relationships in earlier social situations is gradually replaced by varying degrees of rules, codes of conduct, laws, and other means of regulation.

Formalization is a way of guiding and regularizing human interactions; it is an attempt to avoid the chaos that would result if every human contact was completely spontaneous. Most cities, for instance, have a network of stoplights to regulate, guide, and control traffic flow in areas of congestion.

The intent of formalization is to achieve social order and a degree of stability through the patterned conduct of individuals and social units. As a co-ordination mechanism, formalization is an attempt to anticipate possible variations and to reduce them to an acceptable range of desired behaviour through the use of guidelines, rules, and regulations. Formalization begets formalization, and in time the resulting volume necessitates that the rules be codified in written form to ensure that they are consistent and enduring.

Few areas of Canadians' lives are not subject to the incursions of formalization. Governments have laws and bylaws governing everything from traffic to trash. They certify our births and deaths and collect taxes in between. We sign contracts, arrange mortgages and loans, and make wills for our heirs. Our clubs and associations require commitments and dues from members; students raise their hands in class, asking the teacher's permission to go to the washroom. Social contact relies on varying degrees of formalization to provide acceptable conduct and to ensure stability and continuity. Formalization may also be a co-ordination and control technique in organizations.

In our earlier example of the bucket brigade, a spontaneous organization developed in response to particular circumstances of the moment and disbanded when the task was completed. Others elsewhere may decide that fire protection is not something that can be left to the chance that each time people will happen to appear at the fire scene and successfully organize to battle the blaze. Instead, they elect to have in place a continuing capability to answer fire alarms and to provide a ready-made organization to deal with emergencies. Fire departments, volunteer or full-time, are examples of formal organizations.

Unlike the spontaneous organization — our bucket brigade — the fire department is an organization of relatively enduring character that normally outlives individual members.

You may recall from earlier chapters that a role is the behaviour expected of the incumbent of a particular position. In a formal organization, the roles necessary in its division of labour are specified in its documents, and the requirements of each role are written out in job descriptions. When the fire chief retires, the department usually does not disintegrate; instead, a new individual is recruited to fill the vacant role and the department continues to meet its goals.

Continuity and formalized procedures are the main characteristics that distinguish a formal organization from a spontaneous organization. We are now in a position to complete our definition. A **formal organization** is a relatively enduring or continuing social entity in which roles and resources are co-ordinated through a division of labour in the use of a technology to achieve a goal or goals. Co-ordination, control, and problem-solving are facilitated through communication and leadership and are formalized through written rules and procedures.

Spontaneous organization is encountered at different times throughout our lives, but formal organizations have more profound and frequent effects on us. These will be our focus for the remainder of the chapter. One of the first scholars to stress the importance of formalization was Max Weber.

# Bureaucracy

There are many possible ways of structuring and administering an organization. From societies to universities, one of the great problems in survival and success is how to co-ordinate social behaviour so that a reasonable degree of social order is maintained and desired communal goals are attained. Central to any consideration of social order are the means of control. How does a society or organization get people to co-operate? What power does it have over its members to ensure conformity to established norms? Who is to wield this power?

Weber was much intrigued by questions of social order and power. Why, he wondered, do people obey commands from persons in authority? Is it because the person issuing the command has *power* and is able to achieve his or her objectives in spite of resistance? Or is it a question of *discipline* — that is, is it because people, as a condition of their membership in the group, are expected to obey?

His further analyses led him to conclude that one factor people assess before deciding whether or not to obey is the legitimacy of the authority issuing the command. From this perspective, Weber argued that there are three major bases of legitimate authority: traditional, charismatic, and legal-rational. Table 10-1 outlines these three types of authority and some of their characteristics.

## Traditional Authority

**Traditional authority** rests on "an established belief in the sanctity of immemorial traditions and the legitimacy of the status of those exercising authority under them" (Weber 1947). In monarchies, for example, people may believe in the divine right of their king or queen to rule. People accept the authority as legitimate because they

The authority Canadian society bestows on police officers is an example of legal-rational authority.

believe that it is a God-given right transferred down through eligible descendants and delegated under certain conditions to members of the official court. Likewise, people may accept that, in families, the parents exercise authority over their children by virtue of the early dependence of children on them for survival.

Traditional authority is something we see in a limited way in Canada with the monarch and his or her representatives, the Governor General and the various provincial lieutenant-governors.

## Charismatic Authority

**Charismatic authority**, by contrast, depends "on devotion to the specific and exceptional sanctity, heroism or exemplary character of an individual person, and of the normative patterns of order revealed or ordained by him" (Weber 1947). The authority of charismatic figures derives from the belief that they are special, that they possess some exceptional ability or magic that inspires the loyalty of their followers. Such is the pervasive character of leaders of various religious cults, such as the "Moonies" or the Doukhobors. (This effect is discussed further in Chapter 9.) Political charisma has been attributed to Churchill in Great Britain, Gandhi and Nehru in India, Chairman Mao in China, Nkrumah in Ghana, John F. Kennedy in the United States, Pierre Trudeau in Canada, and Khomeini in Iran.

## Legal-Rational Authority, or Bureaucracy

We occasionally witness charismatic leadership, but by far the most frequent authority pattern we experience is Weber's third type. **Legal-rational authority** is based ''on a belief in the 'legality' of patterns of normative rules and the right of those elevated to authority under such rules to issue commands'' (Weber 1947).

The underlying process of this type of authority is formalization. As a result, legal-rational authority tends to be more systematic and impersonal than either traditional or charismatic authority. Weber argued not only that this was the case but that organizations based on rational authority tend to have similarities. In its pure form, he called this authority pattern **bureaucracy**.

Weber was curious about the relationships between an increasingly complex division of labour in a society and the nature of the organizations in which that work was done. As we have already noted, his research indicated that as work and the

## Table 10-1. Characteristics of Ideal Types of Authority

|  | Rational | Traditional | Charismatic |
|---|---|---|---|
| **Source of leadership** | Leader has special training or expertise to occupy the position | Leader traces origin to a traditional status or was born into the position | Leader has special personal qualities: e.g., magical powers, exemplary character, heroism, etc. |
| **Name of rank and file** | Members, citizens | Subjects, comrades | Followers, disciples |
| **Grounds for obedience** | Owed to a set of rules, laws, and precedents, to an office rather than the individual who fills the office | Owed to leader out of personal loyalty because of leader's personal wisdom | Owed out of duty to recognize a charismatic quality and act accordingly |
| **Form of administration** | Highly trained personnel who are appointed and dismissed, whose task it is to keep written records and implement leader's policy | Personal retainers of the leader chosen on basis of social privilege or the favouritism in which leader holds them | Persons who are called to serve on the basis of the charismatic qualities they themselves possess |
| **Relationship to property** | Strict legal separation between property of leaders and community | Leader often legally possesses all property in the realm and others own only what leader gives them | Leaders are not expected to own much but are supported through the devotion of their followers |
| **Form of opposition** | Directed against the system | Directed against the person of the leader | If leader does not continue to show charismatic qualities, he or she loses authority and followers leave |

SOURCE: Max Weber, *The Theory of Social and Economic Organization* (New York: Free Press, 1964), pp. 324–406. Table compiled by Kathryn M. Kopinak.

division of labour become more complicated, there is a tendency for the organizational form in which the work is undertaken to resemble what he referred to, in its pure form, as bureaucracy.

Weber identified certain common features of bureaucratic organizations.

1. A bureaucracy is governed by a set of fixed and official rules and regulations. They outline the jurisdictions and responsibilities of each unit and usually each position in the organization. In a large hospital, for instance, the housekeeping department is charged with maintenance and upkeep of the facility, as opposed to the nursing departments, which are charged with patient care. Within the housekeeping department, the tasks of laundry personnel are specified and are quite distinct from those of dishwashers in the kitchen area. Thus we can see that a bureaucracy has a set of comprehensive rules that govern the division of labour in the organization and clearly fix the duties and jurisdictional areas of each department and each person within it.

2. A bureaucracy has a *pyramid of authority*. That is, there are various levels of authority, and the lower offices are supervised by the higher ones. With so many rules and regulations instructing everyone as to the expected practices and outcomes of their offices, an extensive chain of command is necessary to monitor and oversee operations. A function of the hierarchy is to make certain that people and departments actually do what they are supposed to do, and in the proper manner. A characteristic of bureaucratic authority pyramids is that each supervisor has a limited sphere of authority. His or her span of control is confined to particular subordinates, and, in turn, subordinates are expected to acknowledge and respond to the authority vested in their immediate supervisor.

3. The management of the organization is based on written documents. "Get it in writing" is the key to successful bureaucratic management. These written documents — whether memos, reports, letters, or computer printouts — are all preserved in the files for future reference, guidance, or clarification.

4. The written rules and procedures in a bureaucracy ensure that clients are treated in a con-

Among the common features of bureaucracy identified by Weber is that the management of organizations is based on written documents.

sistent fashion without regard to personal considerations. This impersonality of relationships applies not only to client contacts but also to contacts among members of the bureaucracy.

5. Because the rules that govern the operation of a bureaucracy are so specific as to the duties and responsibilities of each unit and position, there tends to be a relatively high degree of specialization in tasks. This high division of labour often means that a prerequisite for assuming a position in the organization is some degree of specialized training.

6. The presence of extensive operating rules and the impersonal nature of many of the interactions in a bureaucracy are means of ensuring that people are recruited into the organization and promoted within it on the basis of their performance, competence, knowledge, and ability. Such advancement is based on achievement criteria; that is to say, people in a bureaucracy move ahead because they are best qualified to fill the requirements of the position

**Bureaucratic organization is efficient when people perform in a predictable and consistent manner.**

as outlined in the operating rules and duties of the bureaucracy. Recruitment and advancement involving favouritism or particularism — where the basis is who you know or being someone's son or daughter or other reasons unrelated to the demands of the job — are regarded as inconsistent with the underlying principles of bureaucracy.

These six components of bureaucracy are seen to be minimum essentials if the organization is to operate efficiently and endure. Highly bureaucratized organizations are most likely to develop in situations in which the tasks essential to the organization's technology are, by nature, routine and repetitive. It is also the view of many observers that, as organizations grow, the necessity for control and co-ordination increases and, therefore, so does the tendency toward bureaucrati-

zation. We shall explore this observation more fully later.

Bureaucracies are more likely to persist when their environments are relatively stable. As we shall see, organizations seek to avoid or reduce uncertainty. A bureaucracy, through its formalized rules and authority structures, attempts to anticipate requirements and demands so that it can operate predictably and consistently. Another consequence is to ensure with the greatest probability possible that its members will perform in a predictable and consistent fashion.

**Department-Store Bureaucracy: An Example.** We have all experienced the standardizing qualities of bureaucracies. Most people who shop at a department store pay for their purchases with cash or a credit card. These are the normal procedures, and customers who follow them are speedily processed through the cashier's line and are on their way.

If you have ever varied from the norm and used a personal cheque as payment, then you have created a special circumstance. The smooth flow of customers grinds to a halt as you write your cheque (often having to enquire as to the date, the exact amount of the purchase, and other necessary bookkeeping details). Furthermore, accepting a cheque is usually outside the specified jurisdiction of cashiers. Therefore, your variation from the norm calls into action a series of carefully orchestrated alternative procedures. The cashier rings a bell and waits for the supervisor, who may take some time to appear. The supervisor verifies the details of the cheque and asks, "Do you have a valid driver's licence and major credit card?" These documents are carefully scrutinized and appropriate notations made on the cheque. Some stores have additional procedures, such as further clearance with a central registry and so on. Regardless of the specific details, every reader will recognize the basic scenario.

In order to avoid bad cheques (and encourage use of their charge cards), stores and other businesses have highly formalized rules and procedures and clearly specified jurisdictions of responsibilities for dealing with customers paying by cheque. The rules and hierarchy of authority combine to provide a consistent and reliable means of dealing with this variation from the standard expectation. One is treated the same throughout the store, regardless of the clerk or the department.

The rules were made in an attempt to anticipate variations from the norm, and if there are unanticipated difficulties, such as a man offering a live pig as payment, they can be referred up the hierarchy to responsible authorities for a decision. Students in colleges and universities usually become familiar with bureaucratic problem-solving as they attempt to drop or add courses, transfer from one program to another, or cope with student aid procedures.

The more variations an organization regularly experiences, the more difficult it is to anticipate and cover them in the regulations. In other words, in highly changeable and uncertain circumstances, it becomes impossible to incorporate all the exceptions in the rules. If there are too many exceptions, the hierarchy will eventually get bogged down in providing interpretations and directions. So, as we indicated earlier, a bureaucratic form of organization performs best in situations involving a routine technology in a relatively stable environment.

At about the same time Weber was studying bureaucracy, certain developments were occurring in North America that were to have a profound influence on the study and operation of organizations.

# The Organization

In the 1860s and 1870s, industrialization was well advanced in the United States and was slowly picking up momentum in Canada. With industrialization had come concentrations of workers in plants and factories and the rise of large-scale industrial organizations. In this context came the development of a movement in North America to see how organizations might be made more efficient and productive.

An industrial engineer, Frederick Winslow Taylor, believed that the full potential of industrial organization was not being realized because of inefficiency and that the answer to this problem lay in more systematic management. He viewed organizations as large mechanical systems and suspected that much of their inefficiency was a result of a natural tendency of workers to take it easy and not to produce at their optimal capacity.

## Scientific Management

Taylor's strategy was to make every worker a specialist responsible for a single, narrowly defined task. The key, he argued, was to find the one best way to do each and every task. The means to achieve this desired perfection in productivity was through what he modestly called **scientific management**.

For Taylor, individual workers were simply instruments of production to be employed by management in the same way as the machines of the plant. The responsibility for finding the one best way of doing a job rested with management because, Taylor explained, "the science which underlies each workman's act is so great and amounts to so much that the workman is incapable (either through lack of education or through insufficient mental capacity) of understanding this science" (1947, originally published 1911).

As the first time-and-motion specialists, proponents of scientific management sought to improve organizational productivity through more efficient procedures. To find the one best way of completing a task, they would observe workers who were thought by their supervisors to be the most capable at that job. The work patterns of these superior employees would be analyzed and broken down into their basic components, then rearranged to make them more efficient. The workers were subsequently retrained in the job, doing it in the prescribed best way, and put on an incentive pay scheme so as to encourage continued use of the desired procedures.

Taylor's method became widely used because it increased productivity and workers generally made more money than they had before. His approach was to focus on individual roles in organizations because he believed groups tended to constrain individual productivity.

Scientific management, although successful in many organizations, was not without its critics. The methods were seen to be too employer-oriented; unions felt that the greater efficiency derived would result in fewer jobs. On humanitarian grounds, speeding up work routines was believed to be potentially damaging to health. Highly specialized work was thought to deprive people of meaning in their work. The rapid pace and income geared to exceeding a production minimum put older workers at a considerable disadvantage.

Although Taylor and other scientific management advocates were practically oriented, they tended to have a view of organizations quite similar to Weber's. They saw the organization as an instrument for the co-ordination of human action in the achievement of specified objectives. With the organization viewed as a machine-like instrument, the clear objective of scientific management became to fine-tune the efficiency of highly specialized roles by determining the one best way for each.

The Weberian and scientific management conceptions of organizations tend to be rather narrow and limited; they are concerned mainly with an impersonal focus on internal organizational structure and process. Even though these perceptions came early in the development of our knowledge about organizations, they continue to have a profound influence over many practitioners today. Structure is still an important factor in the study of organizations.

## Structure

In our definition of formal organization, we suggested that co-ordination, control, and problem-solving in the organization are facilitated through communication, leadership, and varying degrees of written rules and procedures. Indeed, written rules and regulations are a mechanism of formalization that Weber demonstrated to be a major component of bureaucracy. As we have seen, one function of these formalized regulations is to define the relationships among the various positions that the division of labour comprises and to establish a hierarchy of authority. That is, the rules describe the organizational structure.

The relationships among various roles in a division of labour may be left to chance, as with our bucket brigade. But formalization is a characteristic of formal organizations that ensures a deliberate patterning of behaviour so that good achievement is not left to chance. Instead, the requirements in relationships for the optimal division of labour are specified in advance and serve as a model for the organization's operations.

You may recall from Chapter 2 that a position in a social network is designated as a status. President, vice-president, treasurer, and secretary are common statuses in organizations. What the occupant of a particular status is required to do is known as a role. A university department may have an unfilled status — for instance, an assistant professor. The people in charge of hiring will be looking for someone to take on the status; his or her likely role will be to teach some junior-level courses, conduct research, and assist with minimal administrative responsibilities.

Formalization usually states how an organization's various statuses are to be arranged into some sort of a structure. **Organizational structure** is the pattern of relationships among the organization's component statuses. The rationale for the particular structure is usually the complementary or interdependent nature of various roles for the completion of specific tasks important to the organization.

As the example in Figure 10-2 shows, a radio station may elect to group its personnel according to specialties, with the advertising and sales people in a department separate from the broadcasters. Furthermore, it may place one person in charge of each of the groups with a title such as "assistant manager — sales" or "assistant manager — broadcasting." At the top of the hierarchy will be a station manager. This structure not only specifies the links among various statuses based on role specializations but also provides for a basic authority hierarchy.

The structure of an organization may be relatively *simple*, such as that of the radio station, or it may be very *complex*, with numerous statuses of various levels in a myriad of specialized departments or units, as in a multibranch bank. Figure 10-3 illustrates several types of complex structures. An organizational structure may specify an authority hierarchy, such as a **centralized structure**, in which subordinates report directly to a supervisor. Or it may be a **decentralized structure**, in which no supervisor is specified. An organizational structure that specifies many levels of hierarchy is referred to as *tall*. Alternatively, the structure may be relatively *flat*, with few levels in the hierarchy. These six terms — simple/complex, centralized/decentralized, and tall/flat — are some of the more common descriptions of organizational structures. They refer to patterns or configurations of the statuses observed.

Organizational structure has remained a key variable for researchers since Weber's pioneering work, and later in this chapter we shall review some of the influential structural impacts or constraints. But at this stage in our analysis, there are two key points: that the formal structure of an organization refers to the expected patterns of relationship among its various statuses, and that the formal structure was of primary concern for early organization researchers and theorists.

On a more practical level, organizational structure has been and remains a key concern for managers and employees. For instance, when Chrysler took over American Motors recently, restructuring was deemed necessary to incorporate the newly acquired plants and employees. Most of these units could be used in the expanded corporation, but a few were found redundant or unnecessary and were shut down. (One of the unfortunate casualties in this restructuring was the engine-block foundry in Sarnia, Ontario.)

Early understandings of organizations tended, as we have noted, to focus heavily on structure. A broader and more personalized view did not begin to develop until some chance findings at a large electrical manufacturing plant — the Western Electric or Hawthorne research.

## The Hawthorne Studies

Between 1924 and 1932, a series of important studies were conducted at the Hawthorne Works of the Western Electric Company (Mayo 1945; Roethlisberger and Dickson 1947). The original research was undertaken, in the scientific management tra-

## Figure 10-2. Structure of a Radio Station

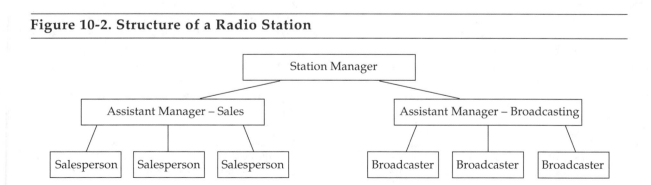

## Figure 10-3. Structures of Organizationsm

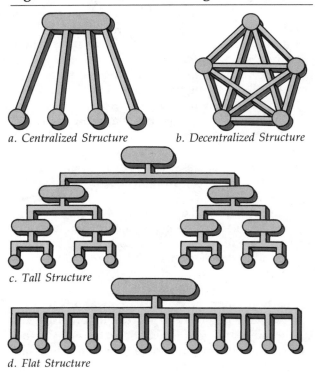

a. Centralized Structure

b. Decentralized Structure

c. Tall Structure

d. Flat Structure

dition, to test the relationship between the quality of the lighting under which people worked and its effects, if any, on their production. The initial results were inconclusive, and the research continued with a total of seven studies exploring a range of physical conditions of work. Of the seven, four are well known: the Relay Assembly Test Room Experiment, the Second Relay Assembly Group Experiment, the Mica Splitting Test Room Experiment, and the Bank Wiring Room Observation Study (Parsons 1974). The last study is of particular relevance to our considerations.

The work habits of the 14 men in the Bank Wiring Room were observed over time. These three soldermen, nine wiremen, and two inspectors were engaged in complicated wiring and soldering of banks of wires making up telephone exchanges. The men were paid on a piecework basis, which the company intended as an incentive for groups to produce at a maximum pace. The more they produced, the more they would be paid.

The experimenters found that in this particular group, however, the financial incentives of piecework did not urge workers to ever-increasing levels of production. Instead, the group had informally decided that wiring two exchanges a day was a reasonable output. This constituted for them "a fair day's work," and they produced steadily at that pace with little concern for the piecework incentive.

Not only did the informal work group keep an eye on how much members produced, but they actively sought to bring everyone into line with group norms. If a man worked above the accepted level, he was labelled a "slave" or "speed king," and if he consistently worked below standard, he was known as a "chiseller" (because he was making others in the group carry him). If sarcasm was ineffectual in enforcing the informal group norm, other group members would give violators a sharp punch on the shoulder in what was called "binging."

These actions were seen as means for workers' groups to control changes in plant routines. It was the workers' belief that if some of them consistently produced at higher levels, the company would expect that of everyone. Also, they had become comfortable in their relationships with other group members and were convinced that changes in rates of production caused by rate busters might put others out of work and lead to the breakup of groups.

Group norms on productivity in the Bank Wiring Room served to neutralize the effects of the company's piecework system. The group held its members in check and produced at a steady two units per day. Another observation was that, in spite of the rules, soldermen and wiremen rotated their jobs from time to time in order to provide some variety in their tasks and to reduce the tedium and boredom of repetitive jobs.

These findings were totally unexpected and provided new and valuable insights into the internal operations of organizations. The Hawthorne studies diverted researchers from the machine-like view of organizations consistent with the perspectives of Weber and Taylor. Instead, researchers discovered that individuals and groups within an organization may act in ways not predicted by formalized rules and structures. This recognition or discovery of informal organization represented a significant advance toward a more adequate and balanced understanding of organizations and their operations.

As indicated earlier, the formal structure of an organization refers to the expected or desired patterns of relationships and behaviours. The Bank Wiring Room Study demonstrated that organizational structure has an important additional dimension — the *social* dimension.

The discovery of the social dimension of organizations led to a rash of studies of so-called informal organization. Many of them confirmed the Hawthorne findings that organized work groups tend to slow production down (Mathewson 1931; Anderson 1944; Roy 1952). A number of researchers detailed how people in organizations cope with the working conditions created by various structural and technological arrangements. Roy (1954), for example, described his participant-observer experiences as a machine operator doing very simple and repetitive work. (See Chapter 18 for a discussion of participant observation as a research method.) Roy and his immediate group of workers spent long hours over a six-day week performing the following role:

*Standing all day in one spot beside three old codgers in a dingy room looking out through barred windows at the bare walls of a brick warehouse, leg movements largely restricted to the shifting of body weight from one foot to the other; hand and arm movements confined, for the most part, to a simple repetitive sequence of place the die, punch the clicker, place the die, punch the clicker; and intellectual activity reduced to computing the hours to quitting time.*

How did the machine operators cope with the tedium and meaninglessness of their jobs? Roy and his work group played little games to pass the time and made the most of social contacts. They also employed trivial rituals to break the routine. For example, each day one of the workers brought a couple of peaches and shared them with the others during a morning break; this was "peach time." The same person also brought a banana in his lunch bucket; each day, one of his co-workers would sneak into the bucket, consume the banana with much flourish, and announce "banana time!" There would be a ritual protest that the banana had been stolen, and so on. But the next day, the worker would bring another banana, and "banana time" would be repeated to the delight of the entire group. "Peach time" and "banana time" were followed throughout the day by "window time," "pickup time," "fish time," and "Coke time." These little devices, not predicted by the structure or rules of the organization, helped these organizational participants to cope with their daily regimen.

The Bank Wiring Room Study and subsequent research kindled an interest in the human side of organizations. They underscored the point that organizations are not merely structures for producing goods or services; they also contain human beings who are capable of acting and reacting. Human relations in organizations, as a result, became a major preoccupation of organization researchers. The organization became a context in which to view people at work. From this changed perspective, subsequent research drew on a number of social/psychological theoretical resources, including those of symbolic interactionists, to explore such questions as worker alienation, job satisfaction, group cohesiveness, and decision-making and change, to name but a few.

Before looking at some of these issues, it is important to stress that although this shift in emphasis from a machine-like view of organizations to a concern with what was happening to people in organizations was a major one, it did not result in the demise of scientific management or concern for organizational efficiency and productivity. That strongly entrenched emphasis continued, and improvements in technology, advancements in automation, and so forth served to keep organizations competitive. But with the addition of the human relations perspective, the study of organizations was broadened. It had become apparent that, in addition to the technical system of an organization, there is a social system; a broadened sociotechnical perspective is essential to a fuller understanding of organizations (Trist and Bamforth 1951).

Roy's study illustrates some of the ways people devise for coping with the specific conditions of their work within an organization. It also provides a good example of alienation, which we shall explore next.

# Alienation

**Karl Marx.** In the Hawthorne research and in Roy's accounts, we were introduced to the effects that organizations have on their members. This aspect of industrialization and the development of large-scale work organizations had many years earlier interested Marx. It was his view that people distinguish themselves from animals the moment they begin to produce their means of subsistence. Production of goods in order to assist oneself to stay alive was, for Marx, a basic social fact.

Marx believed that people can find self-fulfillment only through productive, or creative, labour. Work is a central feature of people's identities and allows them to develop to their fullest potential. As the industrialization process occurs and a capitalist system develops, however, the process of self-realization for individuals becomes frustrated and **alienation** results. That is, people begin to lose control of their destinies because they no longer possess the major means of production. Instead, they work in organizations on someone else's machines. Expanding on this concept of alienation, Marx (quoted in Bottomore and Rubel 1956) asked,

*In what does this alienation consist? First that the work is* external *to the worker, that it is not a part of his nature, that consequently he does not fulfill himself in his work but denies himself, has a feeling of misery, not of well-being, does not develop freely a physical and mental energy, but is physically exhausted and mentally debased. The worker, therefore, feels himself at home only during his leisure, whereas at work he feels homeless. His work is not voluntary but imposed,* forced labor. *It is not the satisfaction of a need, but only a* means *for satisfying other needs.*

For Marx, individuals experience alienation as a result of shifts in ownership patterns, changes in technology, and the rise of industrial organization. Alienation, according to Rinehart (1987), "refers to a condition in which individuals have little or no control over (a) the purposes and products of the labor process, (b) the overall organization of the workplace, and (c) the immediate work process itself." We are reminded of Roy and his co-workers looking through barred windows at a brick wall while they placed the die, punched the clicker, placed the die, and punched the clicker.

**Technology.** Robert Blauner (1964) was interested in the impact that technology has on workers — how what someone does in his or her work (the technology) affects that person. In the early 1960s, he performed a secondary analysis on data involving workers in a number of industries in an attempt to answer the following question: Under what conditions are the alienating tendencies of work organizations the strongest, and under what conditions are they the weakest or least noticeable?

Blauner argued that technology is a key factor in an organization's distinctive character. In view of this position, it is not surprising that he turned to differences in technology to see if they might explain differences in alienation levels. As a preliminary step, he identified four basic technologies in the industries he studied: assembly-line, machine-tending, continuous-process, and craft technologies.

The work processes on an *assembly line* are highly particularized, so that each worker has a very small number of routine, specialized tasks to complete. Each worker generally has a fixed work station, and the pace of the line determines the speed at which people work. The manufacture of automobiles was Blauner's example of this type of technology.

In *machine-tending technologies*, work processes are highly routine, and workers' tasks consist of watching or tending to the needs of machines. Blauner saw textile manufacturing as representing this type of technology. In the production of textiles, large machines spin the fibres, and automated looms weave materials. The worker's role is paced by the machines; when the machines run out of materials, the worker replaces the spools of fibre, and so on. Simple tasks are completed according to the needs of the machines.

*Continuous process* is a very advanced form of technology in which a raw material, such as petroleum, enters one end of the operation and undergoes a number of automated conversion steps; finished products are derived at various stages along the way. Blauner used oil refining and chemical production as examples. The complexity of this kind of technology requires workers to be highly knowledgeable about the processes, so that they can monitor operations and make spur-of-the-moment decisions when necessary to ensure continuous operation.

*Craft technology* is characterized by a considerable amount of handwork. It also tends to be relatively unstandardized because it is difficult to establish routines in a technology in which the products vary considerably. In Blauner's sample, craft technology was represented by printers. Because of the skill involved, printers must use judgment and flexibility in organizing and executing their work.

Blauner arranged these four technologies according to the level of control, meaning, and self-expression they afforded the worker. Assembly-line work provided very little of these features for individual workers, while machine tending contained slightly more of each. Continuous-process technology, he found, provided workers with greater control, more responsibility, and more meaning in their work than did the previous two. The highest levels of control were found in craft technology.

Worker alienation — that is, feelings of powerlessness, meaninglessness, self-estrangement, and social isolation — was highest, he found, for assembly-line workers, and diminished as technologies afforded more control, meaning, and self-expression. For his sample, therefore, alienation was lowest among printers. Blauner's findings are summarized in Table 10-2; similar results were found by Fullan (1970) in a Canadian study.

Whenever individuals, groups, or organizations interrelate, there is, of course, the potential for conflict. Within organizations, labour and management may have differing objectives or views that lead to conflict. The organization may, from time to time, find some of its elements conflicting with each other. Research on alienation also serves to remind us that factors within the organization, such as its technology, may stimulate conflict. The perspective of conflict theory increases our sensitivity to such possibilities in organizational analysis.

Technology remains a major focus of interest for researchers who examine alienation-producing conditions in organizations. Alienation is likely to be lowest in organizational settings in which members have control, meaning, and opportunities for self-fulfillment in their roles. We saw earlier that Roy and his group of machine-tenders coped with the alienating tendencies of their organizational roles through informal social activity. Many researchers have attempted to explore the dynamics of groups in the social structure of organizations and the impact they have on individuals and the successful attainment of organization goals.

## Group Dynamics

We have been considering some of the ways in which the organization acts to influence the in-

## Table 10-2. Blauner's Findings on the Relationship Between Technology and Alienation

| Industry | Technology | Control over Work | Meaning in Work | Self-Expression | Alienation |
|----------|-----------|-------------------|-----------------|-----------------|------------|
| Printing | Craft | Very high | Very high | Very high | Very low |
| Oil refining | Continuous process | High | High | High | Low |
| Textiles | Machine tending | Low | Low | Low | High |
| Automobile assembly | Assembly line | Very low | Very low | Very low | Very high |

SOURCE: Robert Blauner, *Alienation and Freedom* (Chicago: University of Chicago Press, 1964).

teraction of its members. People in organizations find themselves in a variety of circumstances. Some people, for instance, work in isolation, while others work in groups of varying sizes. People working in groups may be dependent on one another to complete a joint task, or they may do their jobs independently but be in close proximity to one another. We have already seen how groups may act to influence the production standards or levels of their members. But, of course, all groups do not influence their members to the same extent.

In attempting to account for these differences, the concept of **cohesiveness** has proven useful.

Groups differ according to how much individuals perceive themselves as members, how much interest they have in belonging to the group, and how highly they regard other members of the group. Where individuals identify themselves as members of the group, where group members want the group to remain together, and where group members have a high regard for each other, there will be a group with high cohesiveness.

## The Team Concept

*Research has shown that highly cohesive work groups frequently provide positive gains in the psychological welfare of members and in performance improvements for the organization. One such application of this concept is in the form of self-regulating work groups.*

*For most energy production companies, the design of work at production plants has evolved out of requirements of the technology. The typical site design develops out of a business plan that combines, in turn, a production plan and an engineering plan. The distribution of work, in terms of jobs and organizations, is based on principles of engineering design and economics of scale.*

*Planning for the human operations of new facilities has normally been regarded as a management task. Midway through the engineering design effort, a management representative is asked to develop a plan describing*

*required personnel levels, skill requirements for the operation, work systems, and organization. This is reviewed at successive levels of management. Shortly before the plant is ready for startup, the work force is brought on board and oriented. The organization turns to the tasks of equipment testing and commissioning. Startup commences on the completion of construction, although it typically takes some time before the facility moves into full swing.*

*In the Everdell plant, management took a different approach to operational planning. As before, a manager prepared a preliminary operations plan and reviewed the plan with his management. However, over a nine-month period prior to startup, this plan was further developed and modified by plant management and a joint team of operators destined to work in the new plant. This design team used the original plan to create a design for the organization of*

*plant work. Rather than building from pre-established personnel levels and skill requirements, their principles of operations planning were based on an explicit philosophy of work aimed at maximizing the quality of work life. The work environment they produced was shaped out of a set of business goals that included both productivity demands and employee work-life concerns.*

The managers responsible for Everdell decided to fashion the work design around a team concept that emphasized the development of a cooperative, multi-skilled work force. In contrast to the increasing specialization of work found in most plants, operators and maintenance personnel would be expected to work as a single team, carrying responsibility on a shift basis for the whole facility.

Most of the energy behind the team concept came from the manager responsible for a number of production facilities in central Alberta. His image of an effective operation was rooted in his early experiences where conditions and less sophisticated technology had forced cooperation among workers and their

Groups vary in the degree to which these characteristics are present, and researchers have investigated what difference, if any, this makes. In other words, they have considered what variations in behaviour and attitudes may normally be expected when a person belongs to a highly cohesive group as opposed to a group with low cohesion.

Seashore (1954) looked at this matter in a study of 228 work groups of different sizes comprising 5871 individuals working in a machinery factory.

He saw group cohesiveness as "an attraction of group members to the group in terms of the strength of forces on the individual member to remain in the group and to resist leaving the group." Seashore's major findings are summarized here:

1. Members of highly cohesive groups exhibit less anxiety than members of less cohesive groups.
2. Highly cohesive groups have less variation in productivity among members than do less co-

---

learning a variety of skills. This experience led him to believe that a multi-skilled work force would enhance both productivity and employee satisfaction. He pointed out: "We've had some weak spots over the past years. When I ask myself why, the answer is always that we haven't developed the people enough."

Operations management had a number of particular expectations for Everdell. One was that the multi-skilled team would reduce the need for slack resources, particularly in maintenance. Small plants like Everdell have a limited number of mechanical and instrumentation maintenance staff on site. This required that the operating group have the skills to provide effective back-up.

Management also hoped that the team concept would improve the quality of operator decision-making.

A third, and related, expectation was that the team concept would reduce traditional conflicts among field and plant operators and between operators and maintenance staff. Lack of cooperation within and among these groups was frequent in larger production plants; in a small plant, it could be disastrous. By cross-training, and by giving a single shift group full responsibility for both plant and field, it was hoped that the negative effects of territoriality could be reduced.

Finally, staff retention was a concern. Plant effectiveness depended on a skilled and experienced work force. Management believed that the increasingly well-educated and mobile work force in Alberta would find traditional operations jobs boring and routine. Compensation limits placed

on these jobs would also add to the likelihood of attrition. Multi-skilling was seen as a vehicle for increasing job variety and employee potential for advancement.

To the group operations manager, trying the team concept was worth the relatively low risk: "The plant is going to run either way. It's a new project and, if it doesn't work, it can always default to the traditional organization."

Management was clear that Everdell's success depended on a willingness of both plant management and workers to make it work. This meant assembling a work force that would be open to a philosophy of increased responsibility and getting plant management to commit themselves to open the decision-making process.

Hiring began with the plant foreman and crew leader. Both were selected on the basis of competence and support for the team concept. They believed that individual operators were underutilized in traditional work designs, and they saw Everdell as an opportunity to practice a more participative management philosophy. As the crew leader observed:

I've lived under supervisors who didn't tell you anything. They didn't have a clue what was happening so anything you did was wrong. I've lived under supervisors who told you how to do everything and that was the only way you did it. I've lived under supervisors who had everything bolted down shut and, even if you wanted to do something, you couldn't because you couldn't get to the tools.

I figure that if a person is hired and he is given the job then he should be responsible and trusted enough to do the job. There shouldn't be any doors with locks. If you give people jobs to do and let them use their own initiative, many times they will come up with better ways of doing it, ways you never even thought of.

Management also pushed for the early selection of operations and maintenance staff, for planning and training purposes. Field training of plant operators was essential in order to begin functioning without the traditional barriers of separate plant and field operations. Most of the Everdell employees were recruited from other production facilities in Esso Resources, and all were aware they would transfer to Everdell on a full-time basis before start-up. During the months of Everdell design following their selection, these employees were seconded on training assignments and were brought in regularly to assist in the design effort.

---

**Source:**

B. Dresner and J.C. Younger, "Designing Everdell," in *Quality of Working Life: Contemporary Cases*, J.B. Cunningham and T.H. White, eds. (Ottawa: Labour Canada, 1984), pp. 77–105.

hesive groups. Highly cohesive groups, such as the group in the Bank Wiring Room, establish and enforce a group standard that is usually missing in less cohesive groups.

3. Highly cohesive groups differ more frequently and significantly from the plant norm of productivity than less cohesive groups. Highly cohesive groups tend to have productivity levels either noticeably above or noticeably below the plant norm.

4. Whether the productivity of a highly cohesive group is above or below the plant norm is a function of the degree to which its supervisor is perceived by group members to be knowledgeable about the work and to provide a supportive setting for the group. If members of a highly cohesive group feel secure in their setting (feel that the group will be able to continue to exist), they are more likely to have productivity above the plant norm than members of a highly cohesive group in which the organizational setting is not as supportive of the group.

5. Similarities in members' ages and educational levels are not related to the degree of cohesiveness in a group. Instead, group cohesiveness is positively related to opportunities for interaction by members. Such opportunities are most likely to occur in smaller groups of relatively stable composition.

Seashore's findings on group cohesiveness are entirely consistent with expectations based on some of the studies we have already reviewed. Roy's cohesive group, for instance, provided relief from the alienating tendencies of the members' work through such social diversions as "peach time" and "banana time." White (1977) showed that individuals' opportunities for belonging to cohesive groups and other social networks were factors more important than organization size in explaining workers' attitudes about their jobs. And, of course, we recall the impacts of group standards on productivity as evidenced in the Bank Wiring Room Study.

More recently, Ouchi's (1981) study of the reasons for Japan's success in international trade detailed the way that organizational culture in that country is based on the effective use of teams in production. Many more North American organizations are now emphasizing team-building and empowering teams to undertake increased responsibility in production and quality control, so

as to derive the benefits attributed to highly cohesive groups.

Alienation — along with its positive counterpart, job satisfaction — and cohesiveness are examples of the types of research interests that have been pursued since the Hawthorne studies. The organization is a setting in which to view and seek improved understandings of human behaviour and the social system. One important final example, which we shall now consider, relates to opportunities for organization members at the lower levels to be involved in decision-making.

## Decision-Making in Organizations

Decision-making is a central component in the operation of organizations. Decisions involving the purposes of an organization and the means for their pursuit are a constant matter of concern for organization members. These policy matters are often long-term, but in almost every instance of an organization's activity, there are problems to be solved and decisions of the moment to be made. As we have seen, organizations are structured with an authority hierarchy that is usually charged with assuming the dominant role in decision-making. As a matter of fact, in many organizations this decision-making role becomes an exclusive and jealously guarded right of management.

We are also reminded that the technology a person works with may afford very little opportunity for flexibility and decision-making. This was the case for Blauner's assembly-line and machine-tending workers, in contrast to those in continuous-process and craft technologies. There have been many research efforts since the Hawthorne studies to examine the possibly good effects that a more broadly based decision-making structure and process have on participants. But before considering these, we should return to the Hawthorne studies and the Relay Assembly Test Room Experiment.

**Relay Assembly Test Room Experiment.** The Relay Assembly Test Room Experiment took place at the Hawthorne Works of the Western Electric Company from 1927 to 1932. It involved the study of a small group of women (several members of the group changed at one point) making relay assemblies for telephones. In the tradition of scientific management and industrial psychology, the researchers were attempting to see if changes in conditions affecting worker fatigue would result in increased productivity and morale. The assembly of a telephone relay was completed by a single worker and required about a minute's time. Since each worker produced a large number of relays each day, it was relatively easy to observe the effect on productivity of any changes introduced.

Before the start of the experiment, the women's normal work week was 48 hours long and included Saturday mornings; the only break provided during the day was a brief lunch period. The changes introduced in the Relay Assembly Test Room Experiment centred largely on rest pauses and the length of the work day and work week. One of the first changes introduced was the introduction of two five-minute rest breaks during the day; after five weeks, this schedule was changed to two ten-minute rest breaks; then after four weeks, six five-minute breaks, and so on.

As these minor changes were introduced, any effects on the women's behaviour and attitudes were noted. During the majority of the changes introduced, the workers' attitudes and morale remained good, their productivity increased, and their absenteeism decreased (Parsons 1974).

Most observers tended to attribute the positive outcomes of the Relay Assembly Test Room Experiment to the cohesive work group. Before the experiment, the women were part of a 100-member department. This large size precluded the opportunities to form cohesive groups that were available in the smaller setting during the test.

Much later, analysts re-examined the data from these experiments and argued that although the cohesive nature of the work group was an important factor, equally important was the fact that the women in the experiment had an opportunity to participate in decisions about matters that affected them, an opportunity that they had not had before in their work. Blumberg (1968) comments on this factor (emphasis is added):

*I believe that a* major, *although of course not the exclusive, explanation for the remarkable increases in productivity and morale lay in the crucial role which the test room workers played in determining the conditions under which they worked. The operatives, from the very beginning of the experiment, were* *drawn into the decision-making process and achieved a large measure of direct and active control over their tasks, and working conditions. In other words, a small but* genuine *dose of workers' participation was introduced into the test room.*

It is important to note that the women's participation in decision-making was not contrived or irrelevant to their work; rather, it was, as Blumberg has described, genuine. In addition to cohesiveness, the lesson to be learned from the Relay Assembly Test Room Experiment is put most succinctly by Kahn (1975): "Real participation has real effects. When people take a significant and influential part in decisions that they value, the quality of decisions is likely to be improved and their implementation is almost certain to be improved."

Many organization studies have examined the amount of control individuals have in their work, and, as in Blauner's (1964) study on technology and alienation, there has been remarkable consistency in reporting positive association with job satisfaction. Where control and relevant participation in decision-making are present in organizations, individuals are more likely to have higher job satisfaction and lower alienation. There are fewer studies of the effects of control on productivity, and those that have been undertaken have yielded less clear-cut results. That is, control and participatory decision-making may or may not have direct positive relationships with individual performance levels.

Just as the Hawthorne studies shifted the focus of organization research more than 50 years ago, so did a more recent view of organizations as open systems effect a considerable change.

## Organizations as Open Systems and Their Task Environments

Most of the materials we have reviewed so far have tended to reflect a very simple view of organizations as **closed systems**. According to this concept, organizations are relatively self-contained units with particular structural arrangements and individual behaviour patterns that can be accounted for by factors internal to the organization. Max Weber, as we have seen, viewed organizations or bureaucracies as mechanisms for control of participants, and his overriding interest was internal mechanisms and operations of bureaucracies. Similarly, the human relations researchers we considered were interested in organizations only insofar as they provided a context within which to assess attitudes and to view groups and individual behaviour. Adherents of these essentially closed-system approaches conceive of organizations as autonomous social entities; the analytical approach is largely one of short-range observation and deduction because of a belief that "all consequences of action are contained within the system and all causes of actions stem from within it" (Thompson 1967).

There has been a gradual tendency to regard this closed-system view of organizations as too narrow because organizations are also part of a larger social system (Barnard 1938; Selznick 1949; Clark 1956; Parsons 1960; Scott 1987). Organizations do not operate in a vacuum; instead, they are located in a multifaceted environment. They are affected by governments and their legislation, by customers and suppliers, by competitors, and by numerous other external bodies and groups. An organization may attempt to insulate its internal operations as much as possible, but its environment will ultimately affect even these. Figure 10-4 depicts, in simplified form, an organization as an **open system**: in this model, the organization is dependent for its viability in part on external inputs and outputs.

An automobile plant, for instance, buys steel, electronics, glass, and component parts from suppliers and hires its workers from the community. These inputs from the outside are necessary for the organization's operation. The organization's internal procedures combine these resources so that vehicles roll off the assembly line. But, once again, without sales of the cars and trucks to outside customers, the organization is unlikely to survive. Information about the success of its products or the availability of various input resources, for instance, provides feedback for the organization that is important in determining its future moves. John Donne's admonition "No man is an island, entire of itself" applies equally well to organizations.

## Task Environment

When we regard an organization as an open system, we take a more realistic view of it; in order to comprehend its operation, we must not only understand its internal workings, but also identify those elements in its environment that significantly influence it. We must determine not only how an organization reacts to its environment but also how it acts to influence and control its environment.

Furthermore, if we become concerned with an organization's environment, we are confronted with the problems of exactly defining the boundaries of that environment. Is an organization's environment everything external to it? Technically, this is the case, but practically speaking there are some elements in the environment that are more important than other elements to a given organization. A manufacturer of air conditioners, for instance, is likely to be especially concerned with climate, since more air-conditioning customers live in warmer regions than in colder ones. Dill (1958) suggests that in analyzing organizational environments, it is useful to think of a **task environment**, or those elements in an organization's environment that "are relevant or potentially relevant to goal setting and goal attainment."

Figure 10-5 depicts a typical manufacturing organization's task environment. In Canadian society, organizations are influenced by a wide range of government legislation at the federal, provincial, and municipal levels. Legislation governs, among other things, hours of work, pollution and

## Figure 10-4. Organizations as Open Systems

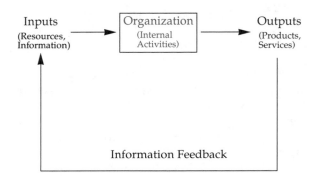

Inputs
(Resources,
Information)

Organization
(Internal
Activities)

Outputs
(Products,
Services)

Information Feedback

**Figure 10-5. Some Elements in a Typical Task Environment**

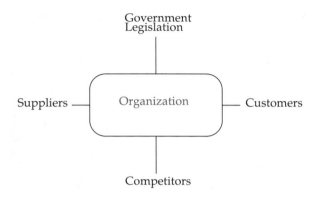

noise limits, safety, union activity, health standards for products or services, taxation, competition practices, exports, imports, and building codes. A comprehensive list would be so long that it would save considerable space to list those areas of an organization's existence *not* affected by government legislation.

O'Toole (1981) provides a chilling example of how legislation and court interpretations in the extreme can pull internal organizational operations away from a reasonable standard of common sense: "A Brooklyn College professor is suing his college on the grounds that he was fired because he is an alcoholic, and the government is arguing that it is illegal for colleges to prefer sober professors to alcoholics because alcoholics are considered handicapped persons under the 1973 [U.S.] Rehabilitation Act."

In most task environments, suppliers and customers are equally important; related to them are an organization's competitors. But to determine accurately the components of a task environment, we should also consider four significant subareas: the political, the physical, the economic, and the sociocultural.

**Political Environment.** The political component of a task environment, through government legislation and regulation, affects in some way or other virtually all of an organization's activity. Or-

ganizations, of course, may and usually do lobby to influence developments or changes in government legislation. **Lobbying** consists of activities by various interest groups wishing to state their cases to politicians in the hope of influencing the course of legislation.

**Physical Environment.** The physical component of an organization's task environment is often a major consideration. The weather in Canada is frequently a factor in organizational planning. It may affect the location of organizations, such as fruit or vegetable growers, who need warm summers, water, and moderate winters. It may also affect the scheduling of activities; in oil drilling and logging, for instance, access to isolated locations makes winter months the most desirable period for operations. The most visible and negative feature of the interrelationship between organizations and their physical environments is pollution.

**Economic Environment.** The impact on organizations of the current unsettled economic environment underscores its importance. The bulk of organizational theory and models was generated during the economic boom years after World War II. Continuous growth was, therefore, an underlying assumption. Not surprisingly, managers have generally proven ill-equipped to deal with the consequences of prolonged economic downturns or uncertainties. These circumstances have created opportunities for mergers and takeovers that, in Canada, are leading to increasing concentrations of corporate ownership in a small number of huge conglomerates.

**Sociocultural Environment.** The sociocultural features of an organization's task environment are increasingly important. The significance of issues relating to language for organizations in Quebec, for instance, is a matter of historical record. Lucas (1971) and Perry (1971) give excellent accounts of the relationship between organizations and their host communities. Of particular interest are the large number of Canadian communities that are dominated by a single industry or company.

Figure 10-6 depicts some of the important elements in these four subareas of the task environment of an organization. The examples given are by no means complete, and their relevance for

## Figure 10-6. The Task Environment

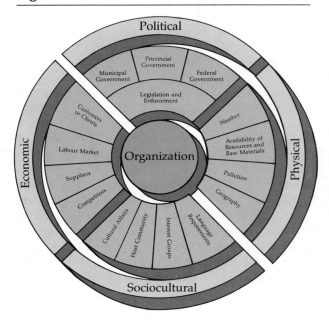

any specific organization varies. Also, it is important to realize that, although we have dealt with each of the four task environments separately, what happens in one area may have consequences in another. If, for instance, public opinion (a sociocultural element) becomes persuasive about a particular state of pollution (a physical element), then politicians (a political element) may be moved to provide pressure or legislation or even funds to force or encourage organizations to take desired action on the matter. Finally, it is worth reemphasizing that organizations and environments are in a state of dynamic tension: the organization's role may be proactive or reactive or both.

## Complexity and Change in Task Environments

We have identified four major subareas within task environments. Dill (1958) characterizes task environments further as being homogeneous or heterogeneous, and stable or rapidly shifting. Ho-

mogeneous or heterogeneous refers to the relative complexity in the task environment. Does the organization produce a single product for a single customer? Its task environment would be highly homogeneous. The production of a single product for multiple customers would be less homogeneous. The production of multiple products for multiple customers would create a highly heterogeneous task environment.

The stable or shifting characterization refers to the amount of change in the task environment. Making a single product for the same customer every time would be a very stable task environment in comparison to that of providing a single product for a different customer each time.

Researchers have considered the effects of various task environments on organizations. Lawrence and Lorsch (1967), for example, were interested in combinations of the two characteristics. They concluded that the shifting/heterogeneous task environment contained the greatest degree of uncertainty, and the stable/homogeneous, the least. They wanted to determine those organizational characteristics that are required to deal effectively with different levels of uncertainty. "Such a question," said Lawrence and Lorsch, "is quite different from the central theme of most organizational studies, which have tended to focus on the question of what is the one best way to organize, irrespective of the external environmental conditions facing the business."

These researchers selected three industries to represent various points along a continuum of task-environment uncertainty. The plastics industry was the most uncertain, the standardized-container industry the least uncertain, and the packaged-food industry was roughly in the middle. Lawrence and Lorsch found that, as a result of the changing complexity of task environments, organizations in the plastics industry created many specialized roles to deal with various dimensions of their environments. This role differentiation led to problems of integration; control and co-ordination of the more diverse roles required continual mechanisms of conflict resolution and problem-solving. As a result, the uncertainty generated by the task environment necessitated structures and processes where "the lower and middle echelons of management had to be involved in reaching joint departmental decisions; these managers were centrally involved in the resolution of conflict. In resolving conflict all the managers relied heavily on open confrontation." In order to be responsive to change, organizations in the plastics industry created specialized roles to deal with specific characteristics of their task environments, and control and co-ordination mechanisms were brought down to the lower level of the organization.

Conflict resolution in a changing environment needs to be based on familiarity with the current situation and to be relatively speedy so as to ensure appropriate solutions. When the ship is sinking, fast action is required. You cannot wait for a response to the captain's request for action from the general manager at head office, who in turn

# Organizational Dynamism

*Although organizations are the focus of much study, their dynamic qualities are often overlooked or ignored. Organizations are social inventions. They exist, at least in part, because of the benefits of co-ordination that they provide. In the absence of organizations, individuals would not have the means at their disposal to create the interdependencies necessary for the accomplishment of numerous sets of tasks. Organizations provide the social mechanism necessary to realize the benefits that can be gained by co-ordinating the activities of a large number of people toward some common end. Organizations, however, are hardly mechanical devices. They are owned, designed, and managed by people. As such, they possess most of the limitations and potentials that people have. Organizations are fluid and dynamic: they move in time and in space; they act and react.*

Of the ten most profitable companies on a Forbes magazine list 15 years ago, three no longer exist, one is involved in bankruptcy proceedings, and four have meagre returns on equity.

Edward Priestner, president and chief executive officer of Westinghouse Canada Inc., uses that list to indicate how important it is for companies to manage change.

Since the early 1980s he has overseen Westinghouse Canada's shift away from a highly centralized structure, which had existed since the early 1900s. In the process, the company has shed 2,000 of its 8,000 employees and nine of 14 divisions.

It hasn't been easy, Mr. Priestner warned a Conference Board of Canada meeting on management in Toronto. "It is a long, tough, continuous process which consumes much management energy." What Westinghouse has tried to do is use strategic management to enhance its competitive advantages. He admits the job has just begun.

There are three intertwined aspects to strategic management, Mr. Priestner said. A company must determine where it is currently, where it wants to be and what tactics it will use to get there. Knowing where a company should be is perhaps the most important function of the CEO, he added.

Once that vision is developed, it must be communicated to all levels of the organization. It is the "principal energy source" to bring about change.

This communication may be one of the most underestimated ingredients in successful strategic change, he said.

Another key is having a set of values to which all employees can relate. At Hamilton-based Westinghouse, there are two: customer satisfaction and improvement of quality.

The notion of customer satisfaction is extended to include "internal customers" — the next person in the work process — so that each employee knows and can satisfy the needs of his "customers."

"The value we're trying to instill is that quality is everyone's job, not something that gets inspected in at the end of the line or fixed in the next office."

Mr. Priestner said some of the most promising advances so far have been made through self-regulating work groups, while some of the toughest obstacles have been supervisors and managers.

In the work groups, teams of employees are totally responsible for their own scheduling, budgets and work methods. With this concept, traditional supervision is nonexistent.

Supervisors' roles are changing drastically – from controlling, scheduling and disciplining, to clearing obstacles, finding resources and communicating. "It's a big change and our supervisors don't always welcome it."

Meanwhile, managers find that overcoming inertia and turning the "ship" around requires a great amount of their energy and time. Some are eager; others find it easier to do things the way they have always been done.

**Source:**

Margot Gibb-Clark, "Managing change a long, tough road but a key to survival, executive warns," *Globe and Mail*, April 30, 1987.

contacts the vice-president of operations, who must clear his directives with the president. A steep hierarchy is not conducive to fast response time — something that is required in uncertain environments such as that of the plastics industry.

By contrast, the low uncertainty in the task environment of the standardized-container industry meant that events could be anticipated in advance in much the same way as we earlier described for bureaucracies. As a result, specialized roles for dealing with the environment were not required, and the formal hierarchy of the organization was suited to the resolution of problems. Middle managers did have some influence, but the real power rested with those at the top.

The packaged-food industry was structured and acted in a manner closer to that of the plastics industry than to standardized-container operations. Because organizations in packaged foods experienced a fair degree of uncertainty, they had different roles for their environmental contacts and decentralized decision-making. But "the major difference between them was that the plastics organization appeared to be devoting more of its managerial manpower to devices that facilitated the resolution of conflict," according to Lawrence and Lorsch.

The comparative results of Lawrence and Lorsch's research are summarized in Table 10-3. This study is an important one because it clearly shows that successful organizations adopt structures and procedures appropriate to the conditions of their task environments.

Lawrence and Lorsch provided some insights into the dynamics of management required under situations of varying uncertainty. A more explicit statement of the suitability of particular management styles to varying environmental contingencies was contained in an earlier study by Burns and Stalker (1961), who sampled 20 firms in the British electronics industry. In their interviews with managers, Burns and Stalker observed two polarized and idealized styles of management: the mechanistic and the organic.

**Mechanistic management** is typically bureaucratic in style. Everyone's duties and responsibilities are precisely defined. Communication is filtered upward through a formalized hierarchy of authority and in this way is maintained by those at the top. "This command hierarchy is maintained by the implicit assumption that all knowledge about the situation of the firm and its tasks is, or should be, available only to the head of the firm" (Lawrence and Lorsch 1967).

By contrast, the **organic management** style is much less formalized. Reliance on the formalized hierarchy is less evident. Instead, decisions are based on knowledgeable suggestions, whether they come from the top or bottom of the hierarchy. As a result, communication patterns are much more open and tend to be lateral as well as vertical. Commands give way to consultation, and status

### Table 10-3. Uncertainty in the Task Environment and Consequent Structures and Procedures

|  | Plastics Industry | Packaged-Foods Industry | Standardized-Containers Industry |
|---|---|---|---|
| Environmental uncertainty | High | Medium | Low |
| Role differentiation | High | Considerable | Low |
| Decentralized decision-making | High | Considerable | Low |
| Conflict resolution | Heavy management involvement across levels | Some management involvement across levels | Heavy reliance on bureaucratic hierarchy |

SOURCE: Paul R. Lawrence and Jay W. Lorsch, *Organization and Environment: Managing Differentiation and Integration* (Cambridge, MA: Harvard University Press, 1967).

differentials are of minor import. Duties and responsibilities are not clearly defined and are subject to change as conditions warrant.

You may have guessed under which conditions each management style was most prevalent. Burns and Stalker observed that the organic style was usual among electronics firms in particularly uncertain or unstable task environments, where new problems seeking new solutions are the norm. The mechanistic style typified managers in electronics firms in relatively stable, unchanging task environments.

In our review of the open-system model of organizations, we noted the importance of task environments to organizations and their operations, and we saw how organizations adapt to the particular demands of their environments by altering their structures and processes. We also argued that organizations are not merely reactive but that they adopt proactive strategies through which they attempt to influence or change parts of their task environments.

In addition, we noted that government legislation provides not only constraints on organization behaviour but opportunities as well. In the next section we shall explore this more fully when considering incorporation processes and the corporations that result.

## Corporations

Canadian federal and provincial governments have large volumes of legislation that relate to organizations within their jurisdictions. This legislation may regulate labour practices, pollution controls, product standards, and a host of other organizational subjects. One segment of these statutes is, however, particularly relevant to organizations as such: it is concerned with corporations. These laws in particular provide both constraints on organizations and some unique opportunities. It is little wonder then that the dominant business mode in Canada is the corporation.

The simplest way to conduct business, however, is as a **sole proprietor**. A person purchases the necessary local business operating permits and sets up shop. Little video-rental stores or small word-processing services will likely be sole proprietorships. These owners use their own resources to establish and develop the businesses. They reap the profits of their efforts, but if they get into financial difficulty, they are in a legal position of unlimited liability. That is, not only may the assets of the business have to be sold to satisfy creditors, but "the owner's personal assets such as house, furniture, car, and stocks, may be seized, if necessary, to pay the outstanding debts of his business. Thus a person's life savings could be wiped out by a business failure" (Amirault and Archer 1976).

Sometimes individuals wish to collaborate in a business venture and establish a **partnership**. A partnership operates in much the same way as a sole proprietorship, but there are additional people and sources of money on which to base the venture. Unlimited liability is generally also a feature of partnerships, and one has to be very careful about selecting partners because all are responsible for partnership debts. If, for instance, one partner cannot meet his or her fair share of the debts, the other partners must assume it. The sole proprietorship and partnership are easy and convenient to start, but the situation of unlimited liability is a risk that could be very costly for participants.

A **corporation**, on the other hand, is a legal entity that interested persons may create if certain criteria are met. The founders incorporate their joint venture with a province or the federal government. Operating capital is provided by the sale of shares, and the affairs of the corporation and the rights of the shareholders are overseen by a board of directors. The major advantage of the corporation is that it affords the shareholders limited liability, in that they stand to lose only to the extent of their investment in the corporation; other personal effects are not liable to claims by creditors. Other advantages for this legal entity, the corporation, include separation of ownership and management, possibly lower income taxes, and enduring existence (Amirault and Archer 1976; Smyth and Soberman 1976).

These advantages have made the corporation the dominant organizational form in developed societies, and most of the organizations we have studied throughout this chapter are corporations. Two questions that have been of considerable interest to organization researchers in Canada concern the sources of power and control in Canadian corporations and the patterns of existence for these corporations.

In his classic work *The Vertical Mosaic*, Porter (1965) examines the locus of power in various sectors of Canadian society. Of particular interest to us is his study of what he refers to as "economic power" — that is, who controls big business. Porter was concerned with how large corporations are administered and how they form links with other corporations. Because many of Canada's biggest corporations are largely or wholly owned subsidiaries of large American, British, or other foreign corporations, the power probably rests with the board of directors of the parent companies.

In Chapter 8, you learned that economic authority in Canada is concentrated in relatively few hands. That information comes from Porter, who discovered that there is a frequent tendency for a director of one large corporation to sit on the boards of others. This situation of two or more corporate boards having a common director or directors creates an interlock between these boards and their corporations. There are striking patterns of interlocking directorships, and key individuals in these networks hold large numbers of such posts. This is particularly true of bank directors.

The central figures identified in this interlocking directorship matrix constitute Porter's "economic elite." In assessing their backgrounds, he found that in many respects they are a very homogeneous group. They attended similar private schools and universities; intermarry; belong to similar clubs, organizations, and churches; and maintain close ties in their social and political activities.

Clement (1975) provides a followup analysis and finds similar trends. His picture of the economic elite shows it tending to be even more exclusive than previously, with little evidence of penetration by persons of lower social origins. In another study, Clement extends his view of the corporate elite because "it is no longer possible to provide an adequate understanding of the power structure of Canadian corporations without expanding the horizons of study outside into the United States and, to a limited extent, beyond" (1977).

The works of Porter and Clement, as well as Carroll's (1986) recent study, provide valuable data and insights for readers on the nature of power in large corporations and the extent to which it is controlled by a relatively small elite group.

White (1978) examined a range of variously sized corporations with different patterns of ownership — Canadian versus foreign, private versus public — to determine the locus of control within them. He finds that the size of the corporation is not as important a factor as ownership in explaining the activity of corporate boards of directors. For example, boards of independent or parent corporations are more active in control than those of subsidiaries. The suggestion is not that subsidiary corporations are not closely monitored but that the mechanisms are somewhat different:

*Control of subsidiaries by parents is considerable, but it usually tends to be exercised through management links rather than by the subsidiary's directorate. In subsidiary corporations in our sample there is at least one senior manager in the parent who is responsible for subsidiary operations. The chain of command from the parent to the subsidiary is through this responsible authority in the parent to his [or her] subordinate who heads the subsidiary. This link is the control coupling for the parent, a bypass around the subsidiary's board which in most instances is little more than a legally prescribed structural adornment.* (White 1978)

The composition of the board, says White, is a second important factor related to board of director control or lack thereof. If the board is made up of some directors who are outsiders, not employees of the corporation, then the board is more active than if it consists solely of inside directors.

Corporations and foreign ownership remain dominant factors in Canadian life, and organization researchers have only begun to systematically explore their impacts.

## SUMMARY

1. The need for organization is consistent with the social nature of humans. Basic divisions of labour result in increasing interdependencies, and, in order to maintain some degree of social or-

der, preliminary forms of organization are generated.

2. The establishment of an organization centres on goal attainment. Its establishment may be spontaneous, left to chance or circumstance, or it may be established and maintained in a more formalized manner.

3. Early theorists and researchers regarded organizations as closed systems and were mainly concerned with their formal structures and processes. The technical system tended to be a primary focus. Only with the accidental discoveries of the Hawthorne studies did there develop a more balanced view that included the social system as well.

4. In the scientific management perspective of organizations, individual workers are regarded as instruments of production to be employed by management in the same way as machines. Efficiency is achieved by finding the one best way to do each and every task.

5. Technological or organizational arrangements that fail to give people reasonable control over important aspects of their work and that deprive them of social contacts and meaning in their tasks are likely to result in worker alienation.

6. Every organization interacts with other organizations. Those elements outside the organization that affect its operations or directions constitute its environment.

7. Corporations are legally created entities that allow people to establish organizations while minimizing their personal liabilities. Most organizations in business and industry are corporations.

## GLOSSARY

**Alienation.** Individuals' feelings that, as workers, they are small, meaningless parts of an insensitive production system over which they have little control.

**Bureaucracy.** A formal organization based on the application of legal-rational principles.

**Centralized structure.** Structure of an organization in which authority and decision-making are concentrated in a few people at senior levels.

**Charismatic authority.** Authority that is based on the belief that the individual leader is special and possesses some exceptional ability or magic, which inspires loyalty in the followers.

**Closed system.** Theoretical perspective of organizations as relatively self-contained units in which particular structural arrangements and individual behaviour patterns can be accounted for by factors internal to the organization.

**Cohesiveness.** Conditions whereby individuals identify themselves as members of the group, members want the group to remain together, and group members have a high regard for each other.

**Corporation.** Legal entity created for purposes of conducting business; it has an existence separate from that of its members while providing them with limited liability.

**Decentralized structure.** Structure of an organization in which authority and decision-making are widely distributed among people at various levels.

**Division of labour.** Process whereby general tasks and roles become increasingly specialized.

**Formal organization.** Relatively enduring or continuing social collectivity in which roles and resources are co-ordinated through a division of labour in the use of a technology to achieve a goal or goals. Co-ordination, control, and problem-solving are facilitated through communication, leadership, and varying degrees of written rules and procedures.

**Formalization.** Process by which the informality of relationships is gradually replaced by varying degrees of rules, codes of conduct, laws, and other means of regulation.

**Legal-rational authority.** Authority based on belief in the legality of formally specified rules and relationships.

**Lobbying.** Activities by special interest groups aimed at influencing government legislation.

**Mechanical solidarity.** Feeling of people in primitive societies that they are held together by kinship, neighbourliness, and friendliness.

**Mechanistic management.** Management style in which duties and responsibilities are precisely defined, communication is filtered upward through a formalized hierarchy of authority, and control is maintained at the top.

**Open system.** Theoretical perspective of organizations whereby particular structural arrangements and individual behaviour patterns can be accounted for by a combination of factors internal to the organization and its external environment.

**Organic management.** Management style in which decisions are based on knowledgeable suggestions, communication patterns tend to be lateral as well as horizontal, duties and responsibilities are not rigidly defined, and status differentials are of minor importance.

**Organic solidarity.** Dependencies among people in developed societies created as a result of a more specific division of labour.

**Organization.** A collectivity in which people and resources are co-ordinated through a division of labour in the use of a technology to achieve a goal. Co-ordination, control, and problem-solving are facilitated through communication and leadership.

**Organizational structure.** Patterns of relationships among organization statuses.

**Partnership.** Joint business venture in which normally all partners experience unlimited liability equally.

**Scientific management.** Taylor's term for achieving perfection in productivity by finding the one best way to do each and every task.

**Sole proprietorship.** Simplest manner in which to establish a business; the sole owner experiences unlimited liability.

**Spontaneous organization.** Temporary co-ordination of individuals and resources that disbands when its task or mission has been completed.

**Task environment.** Those elements in an organization's environment that are relevant or potentially relevant to setting goals and attaining them.

**Technology.** Application of a body of knowledge through the use of tools and processes in the production of goods and/or services.

**Traditional authority.** Authority that is based on followers' belief that the monarch has a divine right to rule that is transferred down through eligible descendants.

**Zald, Mayer N. (ed.).** *Power in Organizations.* Nashville: Vanderbilt University Press, 1970. A collection of articles exploring the nature of power structures and relationships in a variety of organizational settings.

## FURTHER READING

**Coleman, James S.** *Power and the Structure of Society.* New York: W.W. Norton, 1974. Traces the development of corporations as unique legal creations for the transaction of business affairs.

**Kiesler, Sara B.,** *Interpersonal Processes in Groups and Organizations*; **MacKenzie, Kenneth D.,** *Organizational Structures*; **Pfeffer, Jeffrey,** *Organizational Design*; **Tuggle, Francis D.,** *Organizational Processes.* Arlington Heights, IL: AHM Publishing Corporation, 1978. A series of books that examines contemporary directions in the study of organizations.

**March, James C., and Herbert A. Simon.** *Organizations.* New York: John Wiley, 1958. A good description of the many facets of organizational structure and operation.

**Ouchi, William.** *Theory Z.* Reading, MA: Addison-Wesley, 1981. Describes the adaptations Japanese organizations have made of conventional organizational designs for their particular needs and culture.

**Perrow, Charles.** *Complex Organizations: A Critical Essay.* Glenview, IL: Scott, Foresman and Company, 1972. A critical view of major theoretical perspectives on organizations.

**Peters, Thomas J., and Robert H. Waterman, Jr.** *In Search of Excellence.* New York: Harper and Row, 1982. Examines the internal structure and processes of those corporations most successful in adapting to today's environmental uncertainties.

**Thompson, James D.** *Organizations in Action.* New York: McGraw-Hill, 1967. Discusses approaches to the study of organizations and development of a framework for their analysis.

# UNIT IV

# Social Institutions

*Institutions are defined as relatively stable sets of norms, values, and beliefs developed to resolve the recurring problems faced by all societies. Institutions are a central part of social structure and are major factors defining society.*

*Family, religion, polity, and education are the social institutions considered in this section of the book. They are found in every society. The emphasis here is on Canadian institutions, but each chapter also deals with these institutions as they appear in other societies and discusses how the various sociological perspectives have been used to analyze them.*

*Marriage and the family are the concerns of Chapter 11. How we are socialized into family roles and the ethnic differences among Canadian families are discussed. Other topics included in this chapter are getting married, staying married, divorce, and family violence.*

*Every society defines which religious beliefs are proper, the correct way to honour god(s), and the acceptable procedures involved in becoming a priest or minister. Chapter 12 defines what religion is, and why it is important to the individual and society. How do we explain the universality of and the differences in religion, and what is religion's future in Canada? This chapter explores such questions.*

*How do people govern themselves and maintain order in society? Chapter 13 examines the political process, including the role of the individual, pressure groups, political parties, and the state. Explanations of these processes, along with the future of Canadian polity, are discussed.*

*Every society has some systematic way of educating its members. In our society this task is accomplished largely in schools. What is the purpose of schools? What differences do they make? How are they organized? Is there equal opportunity for all to be educated? How is the educational system changing in Canada? These are some of the issues explored in Chapter 14.*

# CHAPTER 11

# The Family

ELLEN M. GEE

The family is considered the most basic social institution. Although the form the family takes varies considerably from society to society and changes over time in many societies (such as Canada), it always and everywhere plays a pivotal role in meeting basic societal needs. These needs include reproducing and socializing new members of society, producing and/or distributing goods and services, transmitting wealth, and ensuring social order. At the same time, the family plays an important role in the lives of most individuals: it is the social setting in which we forge a self-identity; it provides us with a sense of belonging; and it is an arena in which a large portion of everyday social interaction occurs.

The importance of the family as a social institution can be illustrated by its relationship to other topics covered in this book. For example, a major part of socialization occurs within the family setting; gender roles are both learned and played out in families; fertility level, an important determinant of population growth, results from decisions and actions made within families; families play an integral role in the lives of elderly persons, often providing needed care and support; the particular structure of inequality in a society is experienced at the family level; and female labour-force participation both affects and is affected by family organization.

In other words, understanding the family is fundamental to understanding society. By studying families, we can better grasp the workings of society. But we must also examine the wider society as it influences the family. A useful way of thinking about our task in this chapter is that we will address both *the family in society* and *society in the family*. In the first case, we are concerned with the roles families play in meeting social and individual goals. When families change, the society and the lives of individuals change. In the second case, we are concerned with how characteristics of the wider society influence the structure, organization, and functioning of families. When society changes, the family is affected.

Given its pivotal and interdependent role vis-à-vis society, the study of the family represents an important part of the sociological enterprise. But when we try to analyze the family from a sociological viewpoint, we encounter a number of difficulties. One problem is that most of us live, or have lived, in family settings; therefore we feel we are experts on this aspect of social life. Yet knowledge about the workings of our own family does not help; it may even hinder us from gaining a wider understanding of families. In other words, our "insider" status as family members can blind us to a comprehensive, analytical perspective on families and family diversity. A second difficulty is that in many societies — Canada among them — family life is played out in an essentially private arena. Sociologists cannot observe family behaviour as easily as more public types of behaviour — the kind that occurs in the workplace, in schools, or in clubs, for example. And since many aspects of family life are "sensitive" or are considered to be "nobody else's business," interview and questionnaire data may be invalid to some degree.

A third problem for those interested in the Canadian case is that foreign (mainly U.S.) media portrayal of families and reports of research findings present an image of families and family life that we may assume holds for us but that, in many aspects, does not. These incorrect assumptions can lead us to ask research questions that are irrelevant to families in Canada, and to miss issues that are important.

A final difficulty surrounds defining the family. We will turn to this issue in the next section. After considering the definition of family, we will turn to a comparative examination of families in different cultures, focusing on several dimensions, including family structure, types of marriage, descent, and authority. We will then look at how the family is viewed by the three major sociological perspectives, as well as introduce a fourth theoretical approach — the family life course perspective. This will be followed by a section providing a broad historical overview of selected dimensions of family change in Canada. The final part of the chapter examines a number of aspects of contemporary Canadian families, along with recent changes in family patterns and family life, using Canadian-based research findings and data.

## What Is the Family?

It is ironic that the family, often considered to be an "obvious" concept, is very difficult to define. In everyday life, we use the term in a variety of ways. Consider the following statements:

*"My family came to Canada at the turn of the century."*
*"I grew up in a small family."*
*"My family is close-knit."*
*"My husband would like to start a family."*
*"I want a son to carry on the family name."*

In each of these statements (adapted from Hayford 1987), the term "family" is used in a different way, but we have no difficulty understanding what is meant. We use this word to refer to many different relationships, interactions, and identities.

For sociologists, a definition of the family that takes into account its possible different meanings within a society as well as having universal applicability has proven elusive. Consider these two often-used definitions of the family:

*[The family] finds its origin in marriage; it consists of husband, wife, and children born in their wedlock, though other relatives may find their place close to this nuclear group, and the group is united by moral, legal, economic, religious and social rights and obligations.* (Coser 1974)

*[The family is] a social arrangement based on marriage and the marriage contract, including recognition of the rights and duties of parenthood, common residence for husband, wife and children, and reciprocal economic obligations between husband and wife.* (Stephens 1963)

Both these definitions stress the biological role of the family (that is, the production of children), and emphasize that family members are tied together by a system of rights and duties. However, these definitions fail (as perhaps any definition will) to take account of the various forms the family may take, both in our society and cross-culturally. In the case of Canadian families, these definitions do not include families based on a common-law union; situations where a single adult lives with her (or his) children; situations where a remarried person sees his or her children on a regular basis, but the children live with a former spouse; and families in which one spouse commutes between two households, for example. Also, both definitions imply that a childless couple is not "really" a family. In addition, the Stephens definition does not take into account families that include members beyond the nuclear unit of husband, wife, and children. This is an important omission for members of certain ethnic groups in Canadian society. It is obvious, then, that these standard definitions of the family exclude too much of the variety of family life in our society.

Eichler (1983) argues that the problem with defining the family lies not so much in the "family" part as in the "the" part. When we assume that there is such a thing as "the" family, we automatically, and arbitrarily, make other groupings nonfamilies. She suggests that we would be better off looking at how families vary along certain key dimensions:

1. *The procreative dimension.* Families are social units responsible for the production of children. Variation along this dimension for a given couple ranges from having children with each other, to rearing various combinations of children from other unions, to having no children at all. Children may also be raised by one adult who has never, or who is no longer, married.

2. *The socialization dimension.* Families act as one of the primary agents in the socialization of children (although other agents are involved as well, as we saw in Chapter 3). Within the family setting, parents may be the major socializers, or other family members may have a crucial role; in some societies, for instance, the mother's brother plays a role much like that often played by fathers in our society. In Canada, both parents may be involved in the socialization of children; only one parent may be involved, as is the case with deserting fathers; one parent may be primarily involved and the

other parent have visitation rights; or neither parent may be involved — as, for example, when a child is given up for adoption. And of course, in countries like Canada, other family members (grandparents, aunts and uncles, cousins, and so on) may also play a significant role in socialization. But their role here is more voluntary, less obligatory, and less clearly defined than in many other societies.

3. *The sexual dimension.* Persons married to one another form a unit in which sexual intimacy is permitted and expected. Here, the variations for a married couple could include having sex with each other only; having sex with other persons (either along with each other or not); or being celibate. In Canada, extramarital sexual intimacy is frowned upon, but premarital sexual activity has become increasingly acceptable (Hobart 1979). In a good number of other societies, extramarital sex is permitted (Stephens 1963). However, sexual relations within marriage have a distinct characteristic in all societies — they carry obligations with them. As Stephens (1963) puts it, sex within marriage is never "free."

4. *The residential dimension.* Families form the basis of the residential distribution of persons. At one end of the spectrum, all family members (however the society defines family membership) reside together. At the other end, at least theoretically, all live in separate residences. In societies like Canada's, it is expected that a married couple and all their dependent children will share a common residence — although, as we will see later, there are many deviations from this expectation. As we will see in the next section of this chapter, the rules of residence in other societies are often quite different. For example, a married couple may be expected to live with the siblings and parents of one of the spouses. Or the husband/father may reside in a separate location from the wife/mother and the children. In still other societies, it is common practice for older boys to live away from their families.

5. *The economic dimension.* Family members are tied together economically, in terms of obligations as well as in the actual provision of economic support. One family member may be held responsible for supporting all other members. At the opposite end of this continuum, all family

The discrepancy between ideal and actual family organization and behaviour is often overlooked.

members could be totally independent. But neither of these theoretical extremes ever occurs in actuality. While it may sometimes appear that one member is totally responsible, the contributions of other people make that "breadwinner" role possible. And total independence would require complete economic equality, which is impossible for children and extremely difficult for women. In other words, family members exist in relationships of economic interdependence. This interdependence may occur within the husband/wife/children unit, or it may extend beyond that unit to encompass other kin.

6. *The emotional dimension.* Since families are important primary groups, family members are emotionally involved with one another. The quality of emotional relationships within fam-

ilies ranges from the highly positive to the highly negative, although detachment is also possible. There is cross-societal variation concerning which particular family relationships are most emotionally laden. In Canada, we place a strong emotional emphasis on the husband/wife relationship (although the parent/child bond is also stressed, particularly when children are young); in other countries, like traditional China, the father/son relationship (termed *filial piety*) is most important emotionally.

So we can say that families are units within society whose members interact along the above six dimensions in a variety of different ways. This variation, which exists both within a society and across societies, occurs for both *ideal* and *actual* family behaviour. Societies vary in terms of what is considered the "best" (or the normative) way to organize family life. And societies also differ in the actual ways that family members live out their lives. We will look at some of this cross-cultural variation in ideal and actual family organization in the next section. But all societies are similar in one respect: no society has ever been able to avoid a discrepancy between the ideal and the actual in family matters. To use the Canadian case as an example, ideal family organization involves a heterosexual man and woman who marry and, in terms of the key dimensions outlined above, (i) have children, (ii) both raise the children into adulthood, (iii) are sexually intimate with each other and no one else, (iv) reside together with their own children, and no one else's, until, and only until, those children reach maturity, (v) co-operate together economically until one of them dies (although there is an unwritten rule that economic contribution will not be quite equal), and (vi) have a mutually satisfying emotional relationship. We only have to look around us to see that this socially defined ideal family situation does not correspond to the reality of family life for very many Canadians. Later in this chapter, we will look at empirical data concerning actual families in Canada. For the time being, the important point is that inevitable gaps between ideal and actual family life highlight the problem of defining "the" family.

Let us consider the variety of arrangements created by different societies to deal with matters related to the family. We cannot place family arrangements in our own society into any useful perspective unless we have comparative information to draw upon.

# Cross-Cultural Variation in Family Patterns

In all societies, families consist of persons tied together by marriage (*affinial relations*) and by blood (*consanguine relations*). The marriage tie need not be a legal, contractual arrangement; and the blood tie may be fictive (as in adoption), partial (as in the case of half-siblings), or nonexistent (as with childless couples). Nevertheless, marriage and blood ties form the basis of kinship and of family units. Although biology (being related by blood) represents an integral component of the family as an institution, different societies have developed a tremendous variety of ways to organize families and family life. This illustrates the predominance of social over biological determinants of human behaviour. Let us now look at these variations in more detail. Much of the cross-cultural information that follows is derived from Murdoch's (1957) sample of 554 societies.

## Family Types

The most basic family type is the **nuclear family**, consisting of a married couple and their unmarried children who live apart from other relatives. (Childless couples and lone-parent families are also considered nuclear families.) This is the family type most familiar to Canadians. The nuclear family must be distinguished from the **extended family**, which consists of two or more nuclear families joined together through blood ties — that is, through a parent/child relationship. The classic example consists of a man and his wife, their unmarried children, their married sons, and the wives and children of the married sons. The members of this three-generation unit may reside in one dwelling or in a cluster of adjacent dwellings. One subtype of the extended family is important to note in the Canadian case, as we will see later in this chapter. The **stem family** is a three-generational family in which only one son, upon marriage, remains in the parental home (along with his wife and children). All other sons move away when they marry, as do all daughters.

There is a wide range of possibilities between the nuclear family and the extended family. (Indeed, the stem family may be viewed as an intermediate type.) Sociologists are somewhat divided as to how to classify family arrangements that do not represent "pure" types. The present tendency is to classify all families that are not strictly nuclear as extended (see, for example, Beaujot 1982). For example, a family that consists of a married couple, their children, and the wife's sister would be classified as an extended family. However, for the purposes of this chapter, an extended family must consist of three generations linked by blood ties.

Nuclear families may also be joined through marriage ties. Plural marriage produces **polygamous families**. This leads us to our next topic, types of marriage.

## Types of Marriage

The variations in family forms reflect variety in what constitutes marriage in different societies. **Marriage**, in the broadest sense, constitutes a commitment or exchange that is recognized by the society in which it takes place. There are four basic types of marriage: monogamy, polygyny, polyandry, and group marriage. **Monogamy** involves the marriage of one man and one woman, and is the only type of marriage permissible in Canada. In societies that practise **polygyny**, one man is allowed to have more than one wife. Most societies prefer polygyny; in Murdoch's sample, polygyny was considered the ideal marriage type in approximately three-quarters of societies. The Arab countries represent a major example of societies favouring polygyny: the Koran, the Islamic sacred text, stipulates that four wives per man is ideal. However, no society actualizes its polygynous ideal; most marriages in polygynous societies are monogamous. This is so for various reasons. Polygynous marriages are an expensive proposition for a man. The cost of supporting several wives and the numerous children they can bear means that polygyny is reserved for the social and economic elite in these societies. Also, if the practice of polygyny were widespread, it would create a high proportion of single men, an imbalance that often creates social control problems (such men may, for example, in the absence of adult family responsibilities, be unmotivated to work and more inclined to "wild" behaviour).

In polyandrous marriage, one woman has more than one husband. Unlike polygyny, **polyandry** is rare as an ideal, as well as in practice. There are only four known polyandrous societies — three in the general area of the Indian subcontinent (Toda, Nayar, and Tibet) and one in Polynesia (Marquesas) — although a handful of societies allow polyandry as a variant marriage type. Also in contrast with polygyny, polyandry is associated with economic adversity. However, we cannot say that adverse economic conditions cause polyandry, since many societies existing at or below the subsistence level never adopt polyandry. In **group marriage**, more than one man is married to more than one woman. An extremely rare marriage type, it tends to co-occur with polyandry.

## Marriage Rules

Societies also have rules about other aspects of marriage. One set of rules concerns whom one is eligible to marry. There are two basic norms in this regard: exogamy and endogamy. With **endogamy**, marriage must occur within a defined social group. An often-cited example of endogamy is the marriage practices among the Hindus in India; one must marry within one's own caste. In the case of **exogamy**, marriage must occur outside a defined social group. A classic example is that of China. A traditional Chinese saying illustrates the rule of exogamy. When Chinese parents are teaching their children to use chopsticks, they employ this rule to encourage the children to follow proper etiquette by holding their chopsticks as close as possible to the ends away from the bowl. Loosely translated, the parents' advice is this: "The higher up you hold your chopsticks, the farther away (from this village) will your future spouse be from." The idea is the farther away, the better.

The rule of exogamy may be viewed as an extension of the **incest taboo**. All societies have incest taboos (which prohibit close relatives from marrying and/or having intimate sexual relations), although they vary in stipulating who is "off limits" to whom.

Another set of rules concerns who decides whom one will marry. Marriages may be arranged or self-selected. In the case of **arranged marriage**, one's spouse is chosen by one's parents and/or family elders. With arranged marriage, financial negotiations between the two sets of families usually play an important role in the selection process. With **self-selected marriage** individuals choose for themselves whom they will marry.

## Residence, Descent, and Authority

Most societies have stipulations, conventions, or rules regarding where, once married, a couple will live. One such rule stipulates that the couple will move away from both sets of parents. While this is the general rule in Canada (with occasional exceptions), it is the preferred practice in a minority of societies — about 10 percent of Murdoch's sample. The most common convention involves the couple moving in with the husband's parents; this arrangement is preferred in approximately 60 percent of societies. Considerably rarer is a rule requiring the couple to reside with the wife's parents. Among societies stipulating that the married couple lives with either spouse's parents, there is variation in the degree of nearness to parents deemed desirable. Take, for example, societies in which residence is determined by the husband's parents. Such a rule may mean in one society that the couple lives in the same household as the parents; in another society, that they live in the same cluster of houses or huts; and in yet another society, that they live in the same village or general area.

There are many other rules of residence that have been adopted at one time or another by smaller numbers of societies. For example, the couple may be expected to reside with the husband's mother's brothers; or the couple may live with the wife's parents for a few years, then move in with the husband's parents. Once again, we can see that a substantial degree of diversity is involved in matters relating to the family.

Closely related to the various rules of residence just outlined are the rules societies use to determine how kinship is reckoned. Descent can be traced through both the male and female lines — that is, one may be considered related to both one's mother's and one's father's relatives (*bilateral descent*). This is the rule here in Canada, although children usually take their father's surname. In Spain, children take the surnames of both parents, a custom that is clearly more bilateral than ours. Descent may also be traced along the male line only: in this case, one is considered related only to one's father's relatives (*patrilineal descent*). Chinese kinship terminology reflects this system of descent. For example, one's paternal grandmother (one's father's mother) is called by a name that reflects the exact kinship relationship; in contrast, one's maternal grandmother (one's mother's mother) is called by a respectful term that is used to refer to all older women. This symbolizes that only the relatives on one's father's side "count." Alternatively, where descent follows only the female line, one is considered related only to one's mother's relatives (*matrilineal descent*). As noted above, most families in Canada trace descent through both male and female lines. But within many minority groups in Canada, descent follows one line only; and most native Indian tribal traditions trace descent through either the father's or the mother's line.

Family organization also varies in terms of power structure. In **patriarchal families**, authority resides with males and is meted out autocratically. The power men wield in this type of arrangement extends beyond the family setting and characterizes the wider society as well. Patriarchal family arrangements have been very common throughout human history, occurring most frequently in pre-industrial, autocratic states such as pre-industrial Japan, China, India, and the Middle East (Stephens 1963). Such arrangements do not, by the strictest definition, occur in Western democracies, although it has become quite fashionable in recent years to refer to our society as "patriarchal." There is no question that we live in a male-dominated society; but the degree of gender inequality is less than in a "true" patriarchy, we do not have a patrilineal kinship system, and we do not have patrilocal residence rules.

In **matriarchal families**, authority is vested in females. However, the power women hold within the family setting does not extend to the wider society. In **egalitarian families** (also called "democratic"), authority is shared equally by men and women. While this is an ideal that is realized only sometimes, it is the normative foundation of Canadian families.

This section has provided a brief overview of the wide range of family arrangements that exist cross-culturally. It is very important to note that type of family pattern has a significant relationship with the wider society and has a major impact on the lives of individuals. To give one example, if descent in a society is traced along the father's line only, then kin groups (called *clans*) will be a basic element of its social organization. These kin groups usually form the basis of economic, political, and religious organization. The society will likely be patriarchal as well, which affects the nature of the relations between men and women and the power structure in general. Kin-group membership will determine the individual's rights and obligations, will dictate his or her behaviour vis-à-vis other people, and will provide his or her major sense of "belongingness."

We have now placed contemporary Canadian families within a comparative perspective. Although there are ethnic variations, our families are typically nuclear units based on self-selected monogamous marriage in which descent is traced through both the male and female lines. Couples live away from both parents, and have something approaching egalitarian authority relations. Historically and cross-culturally, this is quite a rare way of arranging family matters. It has been termed the **conjugal family** pattern because of its emphasis on the husband/wife tie and its relative de-emphasis on the wider kin network.

As we end this section, it must be emphasized that although family organization varies substantially cross-culturally, families everywhere manage to accomplish essentially the same tasks. These tasks relate to the six dimensions we examined in the preceding section — procreation, the socialization of children, sexual regulation, the location of persons in residential units, economic co-operation, and the provision of emotional support.

## Theoretical Perspectives

As you already know, there is no one "correct" theoretical perspective within sociology; the different perspectives represent different ways of looking at the same phenomena. Within the sociology of the family, there are four major theoretical approaches: structural functionalism, the conflict perspective, symbolic interaction (and other related micro theories such as exchange theory), and the family life course perspective.

### The Structural-Functional Perspective

Structural functionalism has dominated the sociological study of the family, particularly in the United States. In terms of the family, structural functionalism has focused on two major issues: the functions the family fulfills for society (that is, the contribution the family makes to maintain-

ing societal equilibrium) and the functions of the subsystems within the family.

A major structural-functional tenet holds that the family has lost some important social functions with industrialization and modernization. In the past the family performed numerous functions and, indeed, was the fundamental social unit — the social institution around which all other aspects of society revolved. With industrialization, new social institutions — such as schools — developed, each taking over at least some of the tasks that families used to perform (Ogburn 1933). Also, industrialization required the separation of the home and the workplace; hence, according to the structural-functional point of view, the family ceased to be a unit of production and became a mere unit of consumption. As a result, family functions have been reduced to three — the replacement of individuals (that is, reproduction), the socialization of new members of society, and the provision of emotional support. This last function is highlighted whenever the family is referred to as "a haven in a heartless world" (Lasch 1977). Accompanying this loss of functions has been a change in family structure: industrialization led to the demise of the extended family and the emergence of the nuclear family (Goode 1970). Parsons (1949) wrote about the "isolated conjugal family," which he felt was the type of family best suited to meet the economic and social needs of industrial society.

When focusing on the functions of the subsystems within the family, structural functionalists have emphasized the division of labour between the sexes. In industrialized societies, the roles of husband and wife are differentiated: the husband performs the *instrumental* tasks — that is, the "breadwinner" role — and the wife performs the *expressive* tasks — that is, providing emotional support and nurturance to other family members (Parsons 1955). According to the structural-functional perspective, this gender-based division of labour is necessary for the integration and stability of families and of modern industrial societies.

Given the dominance of the structural-functional perspective within the sociology of the family, it has come under close scrutiny. Major challenges have come from two fronts: historical demography and feminist sociology. Empirical research done by historical demographers (for example, Anderson 1971; Laslett and Wall 1972) has demonstrated that the nuclear form of the family predominated in European-based societies long before industrialization. Canadian researchers concluded that the same was true of pre-industrial Canada (Nett 1981). Indeed, Levy (1965) has shown that the nuclear family has existed as the dominant family form throughout all of human history, because high mortality levels made family extension impossible even in those societies that highly idealized it.

Feminist sociologists have challenged a number of aspects of structural-functional theory as it applies to families. They have been highly critical of the postulate that the family has lost its productive functions and become only a unit of consumption (Cowan 1986). In their view, this way of looking at the family ignores the contributions that women make as wives and mothers. They are also critical of the idea that the family functions as an emotional refuge (see, for example, Bernard 1973; Barrett 1980). Instead, they argue that while family life is structured for the emotional benefit of men, it operates to the emotional detriment of women. In a related view, feminist sociology has been critical of the Parsonian idea that the conjugal family "fits" well with the needs of modern industrial society, suggesting instead that our family system creates tensions and strains that work against wider social stability.

## The Conflict Perspective

Marx and Engels (1942) were influential proponents of a conflict perspective regarding the family. A fundamental proposition of the Marxist perspective is that the family in capitalist society is an exploitive social institution. In fact, according to this approach, it is the family that is most responsible for women's oppression. This is in direct contrast to the structural-functional view of the desirability of a gender-based division of familial labour.

The conflict perspective focuses on family change and the economic determinants of that change. Like the structural-functional perspective, it views industrialization, and particularly the separation of home and work, as a major cause of family change. However, the conflict perspective assesses the consequences of capitalist industrialization differently, holding that the creation of a work/family dichotomy led to the removal of women from the public arena of life and a subsequent downgrading in their status. This perspective also points out that certain (that is, bourgeois) class interests are served by a family system that oppresses women and downplays their economic contribution both to families and to society.

The conflict perspective takes a more complex view of the relationship between economic change and family change than the structural-functional perspective. Structural functionalists believe that industrialization causes the family to change in certain virtually inevitable ways. (However, some structural functionalists, such as Goode [1970], have suggested that the family may change prior to industrialization in ways that make the society more receptive to economic change.) In contrast, the conflict model considers the relationship between economic change and family change to be a dialectical one. That is, inherent tensions and contradictions in the mode of production lead to changes in the structure of economic organization; these in turn affect family life and family arrangements, creating tensions and conflicts within the family arena that have implications for the wider economy.

The idea of conflict as inherent in family life directly contradicts the notions of family harmony implicit in such structural-functional concepts as the division of labour based on gender roles. Within the conflict perspective, the relationships between husbands and wives and between parents and children are characterized as confrontational on an ongoing basis because each has different interests. Thus the conflict perspective has led to a concern with such phenomena as wife abuse, battered children, and family violence in general.

Although the conflict model provides a useful way of looking at families, in actual fact very little research or writing on the family exists within traditional Marxist analysis. This is so because domestic labour does not produce "surplus value"; therefore, it does not fit into the standard Marxian conceptualization of economic relations (Porter 1987). Only in the last 10 or 15 years has the conflict perspective been applied to the study of the family, with its adoption by feminist scholars focusing on women's inequality in both the family and the economy.

Although different in many ways, both the structural-functional and the conflict perspectives represent macro approaches to the study of the family. That is, they focus on the family as an institution in society and its relationship with other aspects of society. In contrast, the symbolic-interaction perspective is a micro approach; it addresses the dynamics of social relationships within family settings.

## The Symbolic-Interaction Perspective

In the examination of family life, symbolic interaction turns our attention to the subjective aspects of family relations — particularly shared meanings and shared expectations in marital and family interaction. A number of concepts related to the major sociological concept of *role* are important in this perspective. In family interaction, individuals are constantly involved in role-taking (see Chapter 3), which involves imagining oneself in the role of the other person (the *counter-role*) and then perceiving and judging one's acts from that standpoint. This interpretive process occurs in husband/wife interaction, and the give-and-take that inevitably results is necessary for marital stability. Role-taking is particularly important in the socialization process. As children, we observe the roles played by family members and incorporate these roles into our own personality structure. Through interactions in the family setting, we come to define the acts of others and, in that way, become aware of our own actions. In other words, we learn everyone else's roles first and then learn to react to ourselves in terms of these other roles. One may be said to have a self only in relationship to other people; the self emerges out of a social — that is, familial — context. Thus the most important process in socialization is learning how to perceive one's acts from the standpoint of other people; much of this learning occurs within family interaction. Note, then, the different approach taken to socialization within this micro perspective as compared to macro approaches. Whereas structural functionalism, for example, looks at socialization in relation to the wider society (that is, as a family function), symbolic interaction focuses on *how* individuals are socialized, on the interactive social process involved in learning to be a functioning member of society.

Role-taking is closely linked to the set of expectations that guides role performance and the evaluation of role performance. In families, there must be a degree of consensus about what is involved in the roles that each family member plays. If a husband and wife have different expectations about their respective roles, marital stability is threatened. And any family member who feels unable to meet role expectations will experience discomfort, or *role strain*. The classic example is the woman who is overwhelmed by parental, wifely, and career duties. Note, however, that this perspective focuses on the subjective experience of discomfort. People in positions that look exactly the same from an objective point of view may actually perceive things quite differently: one person's negatively experienced "stress" may be the next one's positively experienced "exciting challenge."

The symbolic-interaction approach to the family, then, is concerned with the internal workings of families, with the interactive context in which family roles and relationships are subjectively defined, redefined, and played out. Emphasis is placed on the subjective element of familial interaction and the dynamics of the interactive process. An emphasis on interactive dynamics also occurs in other microsociological theories — for instance, social exchange theory, which explains familial behaviour in terms of incentives and disincentives, negotiation, and bargaining (see, for example, Edwards 1969; Nye 1982; Scanzoni 1982).

The fourth approach to the family — the family life course perspective — combines elements of macro- and microsociology. It may be viewed as an attempt to link or integrate the two levels in the understanding of family life.

## The Family Life Course Perspective

An emerging perspective within the sociology of the family focuses on family change in conjunction with wider social change and individual change (Elder 1978; Hareven 1978; Demos 1986). At the macro level of analysis, this approach examines structural changes in the family in relation to historical factors and wider societal development. At the micro level, it looks at changes in individual families as they move through time, going through various stages.

According to the family life course perspective, two types of time exist: *social time* and *family time*.

# "Corners of the Yards"

Once, when my children were little, my father said to me, "You know those years you were growing up — well, that's all just a kind of blur to me. I can't sort out one year from another." I was offended. I remembered each separate year with pain and clarity. I could have told how old I was when I went to look at the evening dresses in the window of Benbow's Ladies' Wear. Every week through the winter a new dress, spotlit — the sequins and tulle, the rose and lilac, sapphire, daffodil — and me a cold worshipper on the slushy sidewalk. I could have told how old I was when I forged my mother's signature on a bad report card, when I had measles, when we papered the front room. But the years when Judith and Nichola were little, when I lived with their father — yes, blur is the word for it. I remember hanging out diapers, bringing in and folding diapers; I can recall the kitchen counters of two houses and where the clothesbasket sat. I remember the television programs — *Popeye the Sailor, The Three Stooges, Funorama*. When *Funorama* came on it was time to turn on the lights and cook supper. But I couldn't tell the years apart. We lived outside Vancouver in a dormitory suburb: Dormir, Dormer, Dormouse — something like that. I was sleepy all the time then; pregnancy made me sleepy, and the night feedings, and the West Coast rain falling. Dark dripping cedars, shiny dripping laurel; wives yawning, napping, visiting, drinking coffee, and folding diapers; husbands coming home at night from the city across the water. Every night I kissed my homecoming husband in his wet Burberry and hoped he might wake me up; I served up meat and potatoes and one of the four vegetables he permitted. He ate with a violent appetite, then fell asleep on the living-room sofa. We had become a cartoon couple, more middle-aged in our twenties that we would be in middle age.

Those bumbling years are the years our children will remember all their lives. Corners of the yards I never visited will stay in their heads.

---

**Source:**

From Alice Munro, "The Moons of Jupiter," in her short-story collection *The Moons of Jupiter* (Markham, ON: Penguin Books, 1983).

---

**Family time** refers to changes that occur within a family as it develops over time. For example, a childless couple becomes a family with young children, then reaches the "empty-nest" phase, and eventually widowhood. Of course, not all families go through all family life course transitions, and some families may have very complex patterns due to divorce, death, and remarriage. And some individuals may experience no family life course transitions. **Social time** refers to changes occurring in the wider society that influence the family life course. For example, mortality levels will determine the likelihood of living long enough to experience family life stages (Uhlenberg 1980); changes in the level of female labour-force participation will influence the way the family life course is experienced; and changes in the legal and ideological environment will influence the degree of variation in the family life course (for instance, whether divorce is a likely event).

The family life course perspective takes into account the individual's location in historical time, as well. For example, people born in the Depression have tended to experience a different family life course from that undergone by those born during the "baby boom." The first group faced a very favourable economic situation due to its small cohort size (less competition for jobs) and an expanding economy when it reached young adulthood. As a result, its family life course was speeded up. People born in the Depression years married young, had their children young, and experienced the "empty nest" at relatively young ages. In contrast, the "baby-boomers" faced a very different situation. This large cohort's size created a high degree of job competition — which, coupled with a stagnating economy, has meant that family life course events have occurred at later ages.

A related issue concerns the normative timing of life events. As pointed out by Elder (1978), a "social timetable" exists, dictating the preferred ages for experiencing family (and other) life course events such as getting married, having one's first child, and so on. Depending on the degree to which this social timetable has been internalized, being "off time" can produce distress for the individual.

The family life course perspective provides the missing link in our understanding of the relationships among individual, familial, and social change

(Hareven 1987). It points out the development dynamic that is characteristic of family change in the context of wider social and historical factors.

## Historical Overview of Canadian Families

Canadian families have changed in many ways over the last 300 years, and continue to change. In this section, we will briefly consider selected aspects of familial change, wielding a broad historical brush. In the next section, we examine more recent information about families and family change.

### Family Size and Structure

It is often assumed that Canadian families in the past consisted of large extended-family units. This assumption often carries an element of nostalgia — we tend to think family life was better in the "good old days." Whether or not family life was better (according to what criteria? by whose standards?) is probably impossible to ascertain, but we do know that the image of extended families is false, part of what has been called the "world we have lost syndrome" (Laslett 1983).

Families in anglophone Canada were generally of the nuclear type — the two-generational unit. This pattern prevailed for at least two reasons: mortality levels in the past were so high that the likelihood of three generations of a family being alive at the same time was quite low; and English-Canadian families drew upon a cultural background that preferred the nuclear-family form (Laslett and Wall 1972). Similarly, in francophone Canada, the majority of families lived in nuclear units. However, the situation in Quebec was more complex than in anglophone Canada. It seems that although most French-Canadian families lived in nuclear units, a significant proportion lived in stem families, which are considered the "traditional" French-Canadian type. Again, mortality levels would have precluded a preponderance of stem families. It is worth noting, however, that in the past English and French Canada had different concepts regarding the "ideal" family structure. Recent research (Verdon 1980) also indicates

that even those French-Canadian families who were able to actualize the stem ideal did not operate as patriarchal arrangements. Therefore, both French- and English-Canadian families were similar in familial authority structure.

Very little information is available about the family structure of Canada's native peoples prior to European settlement. Extended families were probably the ideal. But whatever family extension may have existed in practice, the ideal was rendered impossible to achieve by the extremely high mortality suffered by native people after initial European contact. Later, the extended-family ideal could not be realized due to a combination of factors — government policies, Western technology, and economic imperialism (Peters 1984).

While most Canadian families in the past lived in nuclear units, as is the case today, household structure did differ in one way. Households (not families) in the past were far more likely to contain both relatives and nonrelated persons like lodgers, apprentices, and servants (Katz 1975; Gaffield 1979). And it may well be that nuclear families were tied together more closely in the past; they probably had more social interaction and more economic links with one another. However, we can overstate the degree to which contemporary Canadian families are isolated nuclear units. There is evidence pointing to strong links between and among nuclear families today. Some researchers argue that contemporary kin relations can be characterized as a "modified extended family" pattern (Litwak 1965).

Family size has declined dramatically, particularly since the mid-nineteenth century. The major factor involved in this change is a decrease in the number of children the average woman bears, a topic discussed in Chapter 7. Women born in the earlier part of the 1800s bore approximately 6.6 children each on average; women today have about 1.7 children. Declining fertility results from a complex combination of factors in the wider society; it also has major consequences for the wider society, such as significantly altering the age structure (that is, causing population aging).

### Timing of Family Life Events

As Table 11-1 shows, considerable change has occurred in the timing of significant family life events. With regard to age at first marriage, the traditional

Canadian pattern was to marry at quite late ages. These data are in keeping with the western European experience or what has been termed the "European marriage pattern" (Hajnal 1965) — a pattern of late marriage related to cultural and economic factors. The pattern changed among persons born between 1920 and 1950, with people marrying earlier. Age at first marriage is now increasing — for example, the most recent (1985) data from *Vital Statistics* reveal that the median age at first marriage is 25.6 for men and 23.7 for women. The important point here, however, is that the traditional Canadian pattern was one of late marrying age.

Age at first birth has declined over time, generally paralleling trends in age at first marriage. Age at last birth had decreased dramatically. People born in the middle of the last century tended to be in their early forties when their last child was born. In contrast, those born in the middle of this century had their last child during their middle to late twenties. As a result of this change,

the "empty-nest" phase now occurs when people are in their mid-forties, whereas in the past, the last child left home when the parents were approximately 60. This represents a fundamental change in the family life course of Canadians, particularly Canadian women. For women born in the early part of the last century, 90 percent of the years lived after marriage were spent rearing dependent children; the comparable figure for women born in the 1950s is 40 percent (Gee 1986). It has been argued that the decreased time women now devote to child-bearing and child-rearing has been an important determining factor in the feminist movement and in changing gender roles (Davis and van den Oever 1982).

Another important change in the family life course results from the decline in age at first birth combined with longer life expectancies: it concerns the relative timing of the "empty nest" stage and widowhood. In the past, the average Canadian woman would be widowed before her last child left home; now, a couple can expect to have

## Table 11-1. Median Age at Family Life Course Events and Years Spent in Family Stages, by Sex and Year of Birth, Canada

| | Men Year of Birth | | | | Women Year of Birth | | | |
|---|---|---|---|---|---|---|---|---|
| | 1841–50 | 1901–10 | 1931–40 | 1951–60 | 1841–50 | 1901–10 | 1931–40 | 1951–60 |
| **Median age at** | | | | | | | | |
| first marriage | 29.1 | 27.0 | 24.0 | 24.6 | 26.0 | 23.3 | 21.1 | 22.5 |
| first birth | 31.1 | 28.7 | 25.8 | 26.6 | 28.0 | 25.0 | 22.9 | 24.5 |
| last birth | 43.1 | 32.8 | 32.0 | 28.4 | 40.0 | 29.1 | 29.1 | 26.3 |
| empty nest[a] | 63.1 | 52.8 | 52.0 | 48.4 | 60.1 | 49.1 | 49.1 | 46.3 |
| widowhood[b] | — | — | — | — | 59.5 | 61.3 | 67.2 | 69.9 |
| **Years spent between** | | | | | | | | |
| marriage and first birth | 2.0 | 1.7 | 1.8 | 2.0 | 2.0 | 1.7 | 1.8 | 2.0 |
| raising dependent children | 32.0 | 24.1 | 26.2 | 21.8 | 32.1 | 24.1 | 26.2 | 21.8 |
| married, with no dependent children | −1.1 | 14.2 | 17.5 | 23.2 | −0.6 | 12.2 | 18.1 | 23.6 |
| in widowhood | — | — | — | — | 4.8 | 6.0 | 12.2 | 12.3 |

[a]Assumed to occur when youngest child is 20 years old.
[b]Assumed that all wives outlive their husbands.
SOURCE: Adapted from Ellen M. Gee, "Historical change in the family life course of Canadian men and women," in *Aging in Canada: Social Perspectives*, 2nd edition, Victor W. Marshall, ed. (Markham, ON: Fitzhenry and Whiteside, 1987), pp. 265–287.

nearly a quarter of a century together (if no divorce occurs) without children in the home. Thus, a new stage of family life has developed over time.

## Families, Privacy, and Intimacy

Over the years, families have become increasingly private units in society. According to Laslett (1972), the Western family has changed from a public institution to a private one. Using a symbolic-interaction framework, this means that there has been a decline in the number of potential observers of family behaviour and of family role-playing. In the past, home and work were often located in the same place; family members were therefore subject to the watchful eyes of nonfamily members. Also, households were more likely to contain nonfamily members such as boarders and apprentices, who also observed family members in their interactions with one another. In addition, family members were more likely to spend more time in public places such as parks, streets, and churches. In response to widespread economic and social changes, the family has turned "inward." For most of us, family and workplace are separate; households do not contain nonfamily members; and much entertainment is likely to occur inside the home, thanks to the TV, the VCR and the CD player. As a result, there is less informal social control over family members. This trend has mixed consequences: on the one hand, it means that individuals are free to break away from the constraints and rigidities of prescribed family roles; on the other hand, it opens the door for socially unacceptable behaviour (it is easier to beat your spouse or child if no one else is looking).

Paralleling this trend toward privacy in family interaction, increased emphasis is being placed on intimacy and companionship in family interactions and family life. In the past, people sought emotional gratification from a variety of sources, including religion and the wider community. With secularization and the development of "mass society," these traditional emotional anchors crumbled away. In their place, the (nuclear) family emerged as the centre of emotional gratification, nurturance, and affection. It can be said that we now ask a lot from the nuclear family; if it sometimes fails us, it is because we expect so much of it. This, then, is a very different way of viewing contemporary families than the "death of the family" image the media frequently portray.

## Families in Contemporary Canadian Society

In this final section, we examine aspects of family structure, organization, and functioning in contemporary Canada.

## Mate Selection

In Canada, as in all societies, the majority of people marry at least once. By ages 40–49, 92.0 percent of men and 93.4 percent of women in Canada have been married (Burch 1985). What are the norms and processes that govern how we choose whom we marry? First and foremost, we are guided by a norm that stipulates that we should marry "for love." Such a norm is rather rare from a cross-cultural perspective: most societies do not leave something as important as who marries whom to the capriciousness of an ill-defined emotion. The norm corresponds to the development of the intimacy dimension of family life discussed in the previous section. However, despite our norm, marriages do not occur randomly; clear patterns are observable. This is illustrated by the operation of **homogamy**, or "like marries like." Homogamy occurs along two dimensions: personal and social. *Personal homogamy* means that people with similar personality characteristics and similar levels of physical attractiveness tend to marry one another. *Social homogamy* means that people with similar social characteristics tend to marry. For example, people usually select spouses with the same racial origin, ethnic origin, religion, and level of schooling. Homogamy involving ascribed criteria, particularly religion, has decreased in recent years. For example, in 1981, 44 percent of marriages in Canada involved couples of different religious denominations; the comparable figure 20 years ago was 30 percent (Nagnur and Adams 1987). However, among Roman Catholics in 1981, only 32 percent of marriages involved persons of a different religious denomination. (Among unique ethnic/religious groups in Canada, **exogamy** —

**The principle that "opposites attract" may work for magnets but not for people in choosing their mates: Canadians tend to be both personally and socially homogamous.**

also called *out-marriage* — is very rare. For example, among the Hutterites less than one percent of marriages are to non-Hutterites [Peter 1988], although Hutterites are expected to marry outside their own colony.) So generally we can say that the principle "opposites attract" may work for magnets but not for people in choosing their mates.

There is one nonhomogamous element in Canadian marriage practices — age at marriage. Wives are about two years younger than their husbands in first marriages in Canada. While this may not seem like a large difference (and indeed it was bigger in the past), it has an important social consequence. It sets up the process by which an economic disadvantage increases over time. The younger person (the wife) begins the marriage with fewer social assets — less schooling, less job experience, a lower income. This disadvantage cumulates over the years: the husband's job will usually be given priority because it is more important to the overall economic situation of the family. For example, the husband's job may dictate that the family must move; the wife, if working outside the home, will have to start over whenever they relocate. The wife will usually be the one who quits her paying job to care for small children (unless her income is sufficiently high to make working outside the home "pay off" given the high costs of daycare). Over time, the initially small economic difference between husband and wife becomes a substantial gap.

Due to the operation of the principle of homogamy, spouses choose one another from within a socially delimited range of acceptable "possibilities." This choice-making occurs within the context of the dating process, which functions, at the same time, as a mechanism for us to "practise" for our eventual role as husband or wife. Research on dating interaction, and particularly on the process involved in moving from "just" dating to "serious" courtship, has revealed the importance of such variables as physical attraction, shared values, and role compatibility (Adams 1980). Virtually all the research on dating has been concerned with young, single heterosexuals. At the present time, we do not know how dating may differ among the previously married and among homosexuals.

## Marriage and Marital Relationships

We already know that the majority of Canadians marry. In addition, a high percentage of adult Canadians live in a husband/wife relationship. As can be seen in Table 11-2, more than three-quarters of our population aged 25 to 64 live in a marital unit. (The low percentage for women aged 65 and over reflects high rates of widowhood, a topic we will explore later in this section.) These facts alone make marriage an important subject for sociological study. Let us now look at what marriages in Canada are like.

**Division of Family Labour.** Since female labour-force participation has increased dramatically over the last decades, one would expect that the division of labour within the domestic unit would change as well — that is, that husbands would take on more domestic chores. However, both Canadian and international studies do not show this to be the case. In Canada, Meissner et al. (1975) found that the husband's share of housework tasks is small and does not vary with his wife's labour-force status. Other Canadian studies have come to the same conclusion (see, for example, Clark and Harvey 1976; Luxton 1981; Mich-

### Table 11-2. Family Living Arrangements of Population[a] Aged 15 and Over, by Sex: Canada, 1986

| Age and Sex | Living Arrangement | | | | | | | |
| --- | --- | --- | --- | --- | --- | --- | --- | --- |
| | Husband or Wife[b] | | Child[c] | | Living Alone | | Other Arrangements[d] | |
| | No. | % | No. | % | No. | % | No. | % |
| **15–24** | | | | | | | | |
| Males | 222 200 | 10.8 | 1 519 370 | 73.7 | 76 850 | 3.7 | 242 260 | 11.8 |
| Females | 444 805 | 21.9 | 1 250 610 | 61.6 | 76 785 | 3.8 | 258 615 | 12.7 |
| **25–44** | | | | | | | | |
| Males | 2 246 020 | 78.5 | 119 810 | 4.2 | 248 170 | 8.7 | 247 895 | 8.7 |
| Females | 2 177 250 | 75.1 | 69 525 | 2.4 | 172 760 | 6.0 | 478 620 | 16.5 |
| **45–64** | | | | | | | | |
| Males | 1 953 160 | 82.8 | 26 640 | 1.1 | 197 495 | 8.4 | 181 055 | 7.7 |
| Females | 1 813 050 | 74.3 | 20 710 | 0.8 | 267 705 | 11.0 | 339 915 | 18.8 |
| **65 +** | | | | | | | | |
| Males | 844 650 | 79.7 | 1 115 | 0.1 | 153 895 | 14.5 | 80 095 | 7.5 |
| Females | 582 580 | 41.7 | 1 405 | 0.1 | 525 275 | 37.7 | 287 680 | 20.6 |

[a]Excludes institutionalized population.
[b]Includes common-law unions.
[c]Child lives with parent(s).
[d]Includes living with non-relatives, lone parents, etc.
SOURCE: *1986 Census of Canada*, Statistics Canada Cat. No. 93–106.

elson 1985; Statistics Canada 1985). Lest we think that Canada is an aberration in this regard, an international study of 12 countries (Lupri and Symons 1982) reports that women, regardless of their marital and labour-force status, carry the major responsibility for domestic labour. Whether or not we accept his ideological underpinnings and structural-functional evaluation, it appears that Parsons was correctly describing modern families when he claimed they involved a high level of role differentiation.

This situation carries with it the potential for conflict between the spouses as well as within the wife — who is, in popular media terms, "overloaded" in her attempts to be "superwoman." The study of conflicts between home and work is a complex one (see Armstrong and Armstrong 1987), but it is worth noting here that Canadian research has shown housework chores to be a major area of dispute between spouses (cited in Kome 1982). It is also important to note that the women facing the most psychological distress (anxiety, depres-

sion, and so on) are not the overloaded career women so commonly presented in the media (who can afford housecleaning services and restaurant meals) but rather are working-class working women and working-class homemakers (who work long, arduous hours in socially isolated conditions and who receive very few social rewards), particularly those with young children in the home.

**Marital Power.** Marital relationships vary in their power arrangements. Although in certain other societies, the man is legally and in practice the owner of the wife (this is called an *owner/property* arrangement), this extreme imbalance in **marital power** no longer occurs in Canada, because it runs counter to the intimacy and expressive quality we have built into our expectations about marriage. In another arrangement — more common, but still not predominant, in Canada — the husband is the family decision-maker, but the wife's wishes are taken into account (The *head/complement* arrangement). Typically, the husband acts as "breadwinner" and the wife takes care of the domestic front. Probably about 40 percent of marriages in Canada today fit into this category. A marital arrangement in which the husband and wife operate as unequal partners (the *senior-partner/junior-partner* arrangement) exhibits a little more equality in the husband/wife relationship than does the previous type. However, the husband clearly remains the "boss" in decision-making, and any housework contribution he makes is perceived as "helping" rather than "sharing." About 55 percent of Canadian marriages are of this type. Arrangements in which the spouses contribute equally to family income and domestic tasks (that is, *equal-partner/equal-partner* arrangements) are still quite rare in Canada; and, when they do occur, they tend to involve couples who have no children.

We might expect that a woman with a paid job would have more power in her marriage than would a homemaker. Social exchange theory, introduced in Chapter 1, would predict as much, since an employed woman brings more bargaining resources with her into the marriage. However, a Canadian study (Brinkerhoff and Lupri 1978) does not support this hypothesis; it was found that wives with jobs have slightly *less* marital power than homemakers. Further research is needed to ascertain whether this finding will hold up in other samples. If it does, the explanation may lie in the symbolic-interaction concept of role expectations. If a wife who works outside the home cannot, because of time constraints, fulfill the duties expected of a "proper" wife, she may lose bargaining resources from her husband's point of view or she may "give away" some of her bargaining power due to guilt feelings. In both cases, the loss of power is the direct result of internalized role expectations. If these expectations change, we would expect wives with jobs to gain relative power in the marital relationship.

There are social class differences in marital power that operate in an interesting way. In middle-class marriages, the husband often believes in equality, but in actual fact has a large amount of power relative to his wife. In working-class marriages, the husband is often less ideologically committed to marital equality, but in practice has power closer to that possessed by his wife than he would in a middle-class marriage. In other words, working-

Much of the domestic work done by husbands and fathers is perceived as "helping" rather than "sharing."

class marriages are more likely to approximate an egalitarian power relationship in everyday family activities and decision-making.

**Marital Satisfaction.** Satisfaction with marriage varies by sex and by stage of the family life course (Lupri and Frideres 1981), but not by employment status of the wife (Drake S. Smith 1985). Men are more satisfied with their marriages than are women. This is perhaps not surprising, given the above discussion of inequalities in domestic-labour contribution and marital power. Both husbands and wives are most satisfied in the beginning years of marriage. Satisfaction declines quite substantially, particularly among women, when the couple has preschoolers in the home, and declines even further until all children leave home. After that, there is a marked increase in marital satisfaction. The low levels of satisfaction with marriage during the child-rearing years can be viewed, from a symbolic-interaction perspective, as due to role strain. The apparent increase in marital satisfaction in later life must be accepted cautiously. These are the marriages that have "made it": most highly unsatisfactory marriages would have been dissolved before this stage of life, and would not be included in study samples. This leads us to our next topic — marital dissolution.

**Marital Dissolution.** Marriages break up as a result of either divorce or death. Over the years the percentage of marriages that end in divorce has increased; the percentage dissolving due to death has decreased. Even so, more marriages now end because of the death of one of the spouses than because of divorce in any given year (Robinson and McVey 1985).

*Divorce.* The divorce rate has increased markedly in Canada — particularly since the late 1960s, when divorce laws were liberalized. However, there has been a trend of decline in refined divorce rates in the 1980s.

Figure 11-1 illustrates trends in the Canadian divorce rate, measured both crudely (divorces per 100 000 total population) and in a more refined manner (divorces per 100 000 married women aged 15 and over). The more refined measure is preferable, since it limits the denominator to the population that can divorce. Considerable controversy exists among Canadian researchers about what our current rates of divorce mean — specifically, what percentage of marriages will eventually end in divorce? Some have argued that about 40 percent of marriages will result in divorce (McKie, Prentice, and Reed 1983). However, Basavarajappa's (1979) estimate of 30 percent is generally considered to be more accurate. Note that this estimate, while high, is still considerably lower than the 50 percent figure that is estimated for the United States.

Divorce has increased as a result of a combination of factors operating in the wider society: declining religious influence; increasing female labour-force participation, which has lessened women's economic dependence; decreasing mortality, which has meant that unhappy marriages are less likely to dissolve due to death; changing divorce laws, which have made it considerably

**Figure 11-1. Crude Divorce Rates per 100 000 Population and Divorce Rates per 100 000 Married Women 15 Years and Over: Canada, 1952–85.**

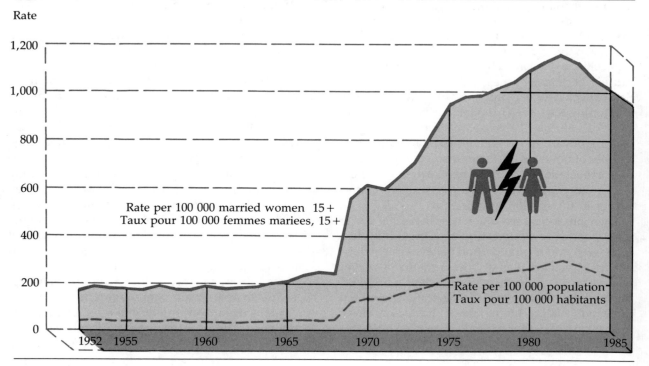

SOURCE: *Vital Statistics*, 1985. Statistics Canada Cat. No. 84–203.

easier for people to divorce; and changing views about what marriage should be like — that is, an increased focus on intimacy, expressiveness, and mutual gratification. Some researchers suggest that increasing "narcissistic" and "hedonistic" trends are causal factors (for example, Ambert and Baker 1984). Of the above factors, increasing female labour-force participation has received the most research attention. The relationship between divorce and women's employment outside the home has caught the eye of structural functionalists (who use it to show the importance of maintaining traditional spousal role differentiation for marital stability) and of conflict theorists (who use it to illustrate the dialectic between changes in the mode of economic organization and family change).

Which marriages are most at risk of divorce? The best single predictor of divorce is marrying young. A recent Canadian study shows that the probability of divorce is more than three times greater for people who marry before the age of 20 than for those who marry after 25 (Balakrishnan et al. 1987). Other important factors include premarital conception (leading to a "shotgun" wedding) or birth; having no religion; living in an urban setting; experiencing an economic crisis such as unemployment; and a lack of marriage homogamy — that is, the existence of social class, education, or racial differences between spouses (Balakrishnan et al. 1987; Peters 1987).

So far, we have looked at the hard facts about divorce, but divorce has another important side. As a legal and interpersonal process, divorce is never easy for the couple involved, not to mention their children (nearly half the divorces in Canada involve dependent children) and other family members. Peters (1987), using a symbolic-interaction perspective, shows how the process of separation and divorce proceeds through stages, with changing definitions of marital roles, of other family roles, and of self-identity. These reformulations occur in an interactive social context of interpersonal conflict and negotiation.

*Widowhood.* Widowhood is largely a women's issue. Of the 1 250 395 widowed persons in Canada in 1986, 83 percent were women. Among the population aged 65 and over, nearly half the women are widows, whereas only 14 percent of men are widowers. A woman is more likely to experience the life-course transition into widowhood for two reasons: she tends to be younger than her husband, and women live longer than men. It is generally agreed that widowhood is the most stressful family role transition that women experience (Martin Matthews 1987). Along with bereavement and adjustment to loss, the widow generally faces a sharp drop in income: about 60 percent of widows live at or below the poverty line, and more than 75 percent are poor or "near-poor" (Gee and Kimball 1987). Widowhood also carries with it the potential for social isolation, but research findings indicate that most widows, health permitting, are quite involved with age peers or what is often called the "culture of widows." It has often been assumed that men who are widowed are more likely to be lonely and socially isolated because they lack a peer group of widowers to draw upon. However, a recent Canadian study found no differences between widows and widowers in measures of wellbeing. Its authors (Wister and Strain 1986) suggest that this finding may be due to gender differences in definitions of minimal social support; that is, as a result of their earlier socialization, widowed men may expect — and settle for — less. It is also possible that men who remain widowers (that is, those who do not remarry) represent a special group comprising people who are quite satisfied with their marital status. This leads us to our next topic — remarriage.

**Remarriage.** Canada's relatively high divorce rate should not be taken to mean that people in Canada reject marriage. Individuals may reject a particular marriage, but they do not give up on the institution itself. Three-quarters of divorced men and two-thirds of divorced women in Canada remarry (Ambert and Baker 1984). At present, approximately 20 percent of marriages — for both men and women — are second or later marriages (Nagnur and Adams 1987), a figure that has increased markedly since 1970 (see Table 3).

There are several differences between people who are marrying for the first time and those who are remarrying after a divorce. One major difference concerns the presence of children (although some people who are marrying for the first time also have children). Remarriages that involve children are called **blended** (or *reconstituted*) **families**. Establishing a workable relationship with stepchildren (who may or not reside with the remarrying couple) presents a challenge to remarriages. The difficulty is heightened by the fact that we,

## Table 11-3. Percentage Distribution of Brides and Grooms by First or Later Order Marriage, 1955–1985

| | 1955 | 1965 | 1975 | 1985 |
|---|---|---|---|---|
| | | % | | |
| *Brides* | | | | |
| First marriage | 91.5 | 91.1 | 85.4 | 79.7 |
| Second or later marriage | 8.5 | 8.9 | 14.6 | 20.3 |
| Total | 100.0 | 100.0 | 100.0 | 100.0 |
| | | | | |
| *Grooms* | | | | |
| First marriage | 91.7 | 91.5 | 84.5 | 78.2 |
| Second or later marriage | 8.3 | 8.5 | 15.5 | 21.8 |
| Total | 100.0 | 100.0 | 100.0 | 100.0 |
| | | | | |
| *Total number of marriages* | 127 777 | 145 519 | 197 585 | 184 096 |

SOURCE: D. Nagnur and O. Adams, "Tying the knot: An overview of marriage rates in Canada," *Canadian Social Trends* (Autumn 1987), Statistics Canada Cat. No. 11–008E.

as a society, have not worked out a set of norms and expectations to guide these relationships: Should the stepparent act as a friend or as a parent? Should the child call the stepparent by a kinship name or by his or her given name — should it be "Dad" or "Brian"? The social interaction setting of blended families calls for much definition, redefinition, and negotiation of role performances.

Another difference is that the age gap between spouses in remarriages tends to be greater than

the two years typical among those marrying for the first time. Also, remarriages involve less homogamy in social class and ethnicity (Peters 1987). The interactive difficulties that are posed in remarriages (in the absence of guiding rules), together with the lower degree of marital homogamy, may account for the fact that remarriages are more prone to divorce than are first marriages.

Remarriage following widowhood has received considerably less research attention than remarriage following divorce. However, we do know that widowers are much more likely to remarry than widows: Canadian data indicate that, for all age groups, widowers are four and a half times more likely to remarry; among the population aged 70 and over, widowers are nine times more likely to remarry (Northcott 1984). This wide discrepancy is a direct result of the shortage of men relative to women at older ages — that is, older women have only a small pool of men from which to draw prospective marriage partners, whereas older men have an excess number of women to choose from.

**Common-Law Unions.** Common-law unions (also called cohabitation arrangements, consensual unions, and "living together" unions) have become increasingly common in Canada. As of 1984, approximately 17 percent of women and 15 percent of men reported ever having lived in a common-law arrangement (Burch 1985). Living common-law is more prevalent among younger people (27 percent of women and 20 percent of men aged 18 to 29 have ever been in a "living together" union) and occurs more often in Quebec, Alberta, and British Columbia than in other provinces (see Figure 11-2).

**Figure 11-2. Percentage of the Unmarried Population Living in Common-law Unions, by Province, 1981**

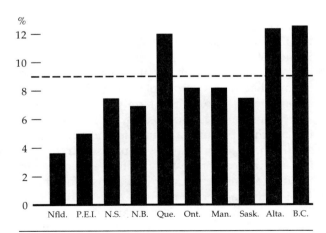

SOURCE: C. McKie, "Common-law: Living together as husband and wife without marriage," *Canadian Social Trends* (Autumn 1986), Statistics Canada Cat. No. 11–08E.

"Living together" is usually a one-time experience: less than two percent of Canadians have ever lived in more than one common-law union. About two-thirds of first common-law unions result in marriage. These data suggest that most common-law unions are not casual relationships; such an arrangement typically represents a prelude to marriage, rather than a substitute for it (Burch 1985). A new family life course stage is apparently emerging, at least among some portion of the Canadian population.

The common-law union has become more prevalent and more socially acceptable in recent years. Not so long ago, such arrangements were rarer, and were disparagingly labelled "living in sin" or "shacking up." So we do not know a lot about them in the Canadian context. Why, for instance, are growing numbers of people choosing this option? It is generally agreed that factors operative in the wider society — for example, improved methods of birth control; increased availability of abortion; more permissive attitudes toward premarital sexual activity; economic insecurity; and higher divorce rates — have functioned together to facilitate the growing popularity of common-law unions (Hobart 1983).

Interest in the consequences of common-law unions fuels another area of investigation. Researchers have considered, for instance, the relationship between premarital cohabitation and marital stability: Are people with premarital cohabitation experience more or less likely to have marriages that end in divorce? It is often assumed that living together before marriage gives marriage a "trial run," resulting in increased stability in marriage. Research findings do not tend to support this everyday belief. DeMaris and Leslie (1984) report no differences in marital success between marriages preceded by a common-law union and those not so preceded. Balakrishnan et al. (1987) found cohabitation before marriage to be significantly related to marital dissolution in Canada, and suggest that people willing to enter a common-law union before marriage may be more likely to end a marriage if it is not going well. In contrast, White (1987) reports that cohabitors have a lower probability of divorce than noncohabitors in Canada. Clearly common-law unions require much more research before we understand their nature and significance in Canadian family life and for society in general.

## Parenting and Parent/Child Relationships

In this section, we move away from focusing on the marital unit and turn our attention to parents and children. Of course, such a distinction is quite arbitrary, since family life for most Canadians involves a complex combination of relationships among spouses, parents, and children. Nevertheless, for analytic purposes, it is useful to separate our topics.

**Child-rearing.** Although the number of children being born to women in Canada is at an all-time low (see Chapter 7 for a discussion of declining fertility), it is still the case that the majority of Canadians have children. (Childlessness will be considered later in this section.) The transition to parenthood represents a major change in an individual's life — particularly for women, who continue to assume most of the duties involved in rearing children. We have already seen that marital satisfaction declines during the child-rearing years. LeMasters (1977) has articulated the difficulties of the parent role in modern society:

1. The role is poorly defined and ambiguous. Uncertainties abound — for example, what are the rights of parents? How much punishment is "too much"? How much TV should one allow one's children to watch?
2. There is no margin for error. When one has only a few children, they *have* to turn out "right."
3. Parents cannot quit. While most other roles can be given up if one does not like them, the role of parent cannot be relinquished except with considerable social disgrace.
4. Parents have responsibility without authority. They are responsible for their children both on a daily basis and in the long run — that is, for how they "turn out" — but authority has been usurped by other social institutions, such as schools, medicine, and the law, and by the informal adolescent peer group.
5. Parents are judged by professionals (such as psychiatrists, social workers, and teachers) rather than by their peers.
6. Parents do not have a child-rearing model to follow, and consequently rely on a series of fads and fashions based on whatever the "experts" of the day are writing and saying.
7. Parents are expected to raise children who are not only different than they are, but also better than they are.
8. Most parents have no training for this extremely difficult role.

In other words, due largely to changes in the wider society, the role of parent — never an easy one — has become even more difficult than ever before. As a result of this (along with other factors), people have fewer children — which in turn affects the economy, the age structure, and so on.

**Leaving Home and the "Empty Nest."** In the normal and normative course of events, children leave their parental home and establish their own independent residence. This transition is considered part of becoming an adult in contemporary Canadian society. In the past, leaving home often co-occurred with getting married; now, it tends to occur before marriage (although many ethnic minority groups in Canada, particularly those from Asia, do not approve of a period of independent living before marriage). The median age of leaving home is the early twenties, with females leaving home at slightly younger ages than males (Burch 1985). The young person's age at leaving home is unrelated to the mother's employment status, but is related to whether or not the child is a stepchild. Stepchildren leave home at significantly younger ages than natural children (Burch 1985).

The "empty-nest" stage of the family life course occurs when all children have left home. This stage has emerged quite recently in Canadian families, as Table 11-1 indicates. In earlier times, people did not live long enough to see all their children leave home. With increased longevity, decreased fertility, and a decline in the age at which child-bearing is completed, the empty-nest stage has become an important part of the family life course. Research has tended to focus on whether the exit of the last child presents a trauma for mothers. Many studies have found that the empty-nest transition is a neutral or somewhat positive experience (a "relief") for most women; it is a crisis for only a small percentage of women (Gee and Kimball 1987). This finding is perhaps not surprising, given our earlier discussion of the difficulties inherent in the parent role — and given the fact that more women now participate in the labour force, so that their lives are not focused *solely* on the rearing of children — but it was nevertheless assumed until very recently that the empty-nest transition was a very difficult one for women.

**Adult-Child/Parent Relationships.** Relationships between adult children and their parents are diverse, depending on a number of variables such as personality factors, geographical location, sex of child, and ethnicity. Overall, however, these relationships are quite important in people's lives; it is simply not true that children abandon their parents in old age. (Indeed, the existence of this widely held myth is hard to explain. We expect the parent/child relationship to be intimate and emotionally close when the children are young. Why do we think people would be willing or able to turn off the "emotional tap" later in life?) Research by Chappell, Strain, and Blandford (1986) reveals that about 80 percent of the care and support that older people in Canada receive comes from informal sources, particularly family members. Daughters and daughters-in-law are the family members most likely to provide caregiving. Findings such as this deal a severe blow to the structural-functional idea of the modern family as an isolated nuclear unit. (It has also been found that sibling relationships are very important in the lives of older people [Gold 1987]).

However, older parents are not likely to live with their children or children-in-law. They prefer "intimacy at a distance," although there are ethnic differences along this dimension (Thomas and Wister 1984). Even widows prefer to live independently, which accounts for the high incidence of living alone among the female population aged 65 and over, as shown in Table 11-2.

**Lone Parents.** According to the 1986 census, there are over 850 000 lone-parent families in Canada, accounting for 13 percent of all families and including about 1.2 million children under the age of 25. In the past 20 years, there has been a large increase in lone-parent families relatlive to husband/wife families. From 1966 to 1986, the number of lone-parent families increased by 130 percent; the comparable figure for husband/wife families was 42 percent (Moore 1987). However, the percentage of lone-parent families in 1986 is *lower* than the 1931 level, as shown in Figure 11-3. Canada has always had a considerable minority of families headed by a lone parent. What is different

### Figure 11-3. Lone-Parent Families as a Percentage of All Families, 1931–1986

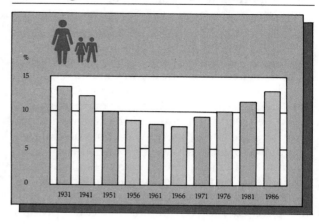

now is the way such families come into existence. In the past, high mortality levels were the major cause of lone-parent families; now, though mortality levels are lower, divorce has "taken up the slack" and now represents the dominant reason.

Most lone-parent families — approximately 82 percent — are headed by women. Of the 53 000 lone-parent families with a head aged 15 to 24, 94 percent were female-headed. More than half (57 percent) of the women who become lone parents do so because of separation or divorce. Approximately 28 percent are widows, and the remaining 15 percent have never been married (Moore 1987). Women vastly outnumber men as lone parents due to a combination of factors: mothers are more likely to get custody of children following divorce; men are more likely to remarry; and women are more likely to be widowed.

The recent increase in female-headed lone-parent families has important economic consequences. The average family income of lone-parent families headed by women was around $20 000 in 1985, considerably less than half the income of husband/wife families with children. Even more telling is the following statistic: in 1985, 60 percent of lone-parent families headed by women had incomes below the poverty line, compared to 11 percent of husband/wife families with children (Moore 1987). This is so despite the fact that female lone parents have a high rate of labour-force participation. While the economic situation of female-headed lone-parent families is very bleak, and obviously requires serious policy attention, it is important to note that research indicates that children in these families are at no special risk (other than economic) because one parent is absent (Schlesinger 1978).

**Childlessness.** Historically in Canada, childlessness has not been rare. For example, approximately 12 to 15 percent of ever-married women born between the middle of the nineteenth century and the end of World War I bore no children. A number of factors helped produce this relatively high rate of childlessness: many people used abstinence rather than the less reliable forms of birth control then available; infertility rates were higher; people died younger (before they could produce children); and, because of the difficulty of obtaining a divorce (not to mention the stigma attached to it), many marriages existed "in name only," with minimal or no sexual contact between the spouses. The percentage declined dramatically among the women who produced the "baby boom"; only about 7 percent of ever-married women born in the 1930s were childless (Gee 1986). Childlessness is now on the increase, but it is difficult to predict whether today's young women will have a childlessness level surpassing that of earlier generations, although it does look as if their levels will exceed 20 percent.

Childlessness may be either voluntary or involuntary. Research conducted on the voluntarily childless in Canada shows that while one-third of these couples decide prior to marriage that they will not have children, the other two-thirds go through a series of stages in making this decision (Veevers 1980). The first stage involves postponement for a definite period of time — for example, until they have saved a certain amount of money or until they have travelled to Europe. In the second stage, having a baby is postponed for an indefinite time. A shift takes place toward more vagueness: rather than wanting to wait until they have a fixed sum of money in the bank, the couple speak of waiting until they "can afford it," for example. The third stage involves weighing the pros and cons of parenthood, and openly acknowledging the possibility that there may be no baby. Veevers points out that this is a very critical stage: just considering the advantages and disadvantages of having children is so "morally deviant" that couples who reach this stage have an increased likelihood of remaining permanently childless. In the fourth stage, the couple arrives at a definite decision not to have children. This decision is usually not a direct one; rather, after a number of years of postponing, the couple becomes aware that they have made an implicit decision to not have children. At this point, sterilization is often considered as a way to ensure their childless state. These couples must work out strategies to deal with the stigma of childlessness and with pressures from parents, physicians, and so on. The voluntarily childless share a number of social characteristics. They are more likely to have no religious preference; have been raised in a Protestant home; have fewer siblings; be of middle-class origin; marry at a later age; and have higher levels of education.

Involuntary childlessness (that is, sterility) has taken on increasing importance in recent years. It is generally agreed that between 10 and 15 percent of couples today are involuntarily childless (see, for example, Pfeffer and Woollett 1983; Miall 1986). So infertility rates have risen quite dramatically (recall that only about 7 percent of ever-married women born in the 1930s ended their reproductive years childless, whether voluntarily or involuntarily). Possible reasons for this shift include infertility associated with waiting too long to begin trying to have children; side effects of contraceptives (for example, pelvic inflammatory disease related to IUD use); and decreased sperm counts resulting from pesticides. Whatever the reasons, the social and psychological consequences are significant. Adoption is now very difficult. There is an acute shortage of adoptable babies, because unmarried women who bear children are now more likely to keep them, and because decreases in mortality levels have reduced the likelihood of being orphaned. Consequently, many couples find that they must redefine themselves and their relationship in making the transition to (possibly permanent) nonparenthood (Martin Matthews and Matthews 1986). Many have sought relief among the new reproductive technologies. But "solutions" such as surrogate motherhood are producing confusion and debate at the wider society level. Each fresh development seems to raise a whole series of questions with important legal and moral implications: What is the nature of parenthood? What should be the role of med-

# Childlessness: The Consequences of Being Different

Becoming and being a parent are experiences that people share. They are matters of common concern. The childless recognize that they cannot always escape enquiries about their parental status and that difficult questions may sometimes be asked. Their response depends upon the question, how it is asked, by whom and under what circumstances.

*Joan Ellison:* People will say to you, "Do you have a family?" And I say, "No", and they sort of raise their eyebrows and I haven't said anything up until now . . . but I think I will soon. In fact I met somebody on Friday night and she was, you know, trying to get into it a bit and she got round and she was talking about her own family . . . I said I had no children and was about to launch off to see what her attitude would be but decided that it might launch into a sort of argument if I said I just don't want to have children or I don't see what difference it is going to make to my life to have children. She might get all het up about it and it might upset her. So I just thought, "Don't say anything".

*Brenda Oliver:* I met this woman on a bus and I got talking to her. I know her very vaguely but not particularly — she's not even a friend of my mother as such but I know her to speak to — I've known her for a long time in that sense. This was only about two years after we were married, she said to me, "Oh, have you any family yet?" I said, "No". She said, "Oh, what's the matter with you?" I don't think I had an answer to that, I was dumbfounded.

*Martin Todd:* The worst thing about not having children is being considered some kind of weird freak by the vast majority of the population.

*Patricia Campbell:* Many people . . . a neighbour next door thinks I'm weird — I overheard a conversation and there was a girl at work who asked, "Is she alright?" — because I didn't have a baby.

*Charles Quin:* I don't consider it is anybody's business, including parents . . . my parents certainly haven't mentioned it, they haven't said "Come on, where's the grandchild?", sort of thing. And I would tell them it wasn't any of their business if they did because I don't consider it is.

*Claire MacDonald:* I'm really very close to my parents . . . And I know they would like a grandchild. Mummy, she'd never say it to me and make me feel terrible. In fact she's never said it but I know she would. And father used to say, "I wouldn't mind being a grandfather" — jokingly.

*Carol Blair:* With some other [friends] I would say they couldn't really understand why I didn't want children, they thought I was compensating by going to the university, you know, doing something new and that sort of thing . . . And also we had a dog at the time — I baby substituted!

*Edwina McCausland:* Women who were not as intelligent as I could overnight after having a baby immediately adopt a totally superior attitude because they had had a baby and if I hadn't had a baby then I knew nothing about nothing.

**Source:**

Excerpted from Elaine Campbell, *The Childless Marriage: An Exploratory Study of Couples Who Do Not Want Children* (London: Tavistock Publications, 1985).

---

icine in contemporary society? Can (and should) we reverse the trend of increasing medical intervention in people's lives?

## Family Violence

Given that family life is played out in a private arena (and thus comes under minimal external social control), that we expect family relationships to be emotionally laden (and emotions can always have a negative side), and that family relationships involve power inequalities, it is perhaps not surprising that the family can be a violent environment. In fact, Western culture has traditionally approved and sanctioned violence in the family (Drakich and Guberman 1987). An old English saying — "Horses, wives, and chestnut trees; the harder you beat them, the better they be" — illustrates our longstanding cultural acceptance of violence in the family setting.

We do not know whether familial violence has increased in recent years. However, we are certainly more aware of it and less willing to view it as socially acceptable. Perpetrators of family violence are almost always men; victims are wives, children, and old people. In other words, the strongest and most powerful tend to victimize the weakest and least powerful (Finkelhor 1983). This pattern does not arise by accident; it is a direct reflection of male gender-role socialization and gender-related social inequalities both in the family and in the wider society.

## SUMMARY

1. Defining family is very difficult; there is no such thing as "the" family. Families may be looked at in terms of six key dimensions: procreation; socialization; sexual intimacy; residential location; economic interdependence; and emotional involvement.
2. There is always a discrepancy between ideal and actual family organization and behaviour.
3. Substantial cross-cultural variation exists in both family structure and family organization.
4. The two basic family types are nuclear and extended.
5. There are four types of marriage: monogamy; polygyny; polyandry; and group marriage. Polygyny is the preferred marriage type in three out of four societies.
6. All societies have rules about who is eligible to be a marital partner and how a spouse may be chosen, as well as rules concerning residence, descent, and authority.
7. Structural-functional theory concerning the family has focused on the loss of family functions brought about by industrialization and on internal role differentiation. The conflict perspective is concerned with the dialectical relationship between economic change and family change. The symbolic-interaction perspective looks at subjective aspects of the interactive setting of family life. The family life course perspective attempts to integrate macro and micro dimensions of family change.
8. In Canada, family size has declined substantially, but family structure has always been of the nuclear type.
9. Significant changes have occurred in the timing of family life events, and a new stage — the "empty nest" — has emerged.
10. Family life has become more private and intimate.
11. Most Canadians marry at least once. Most marriages are characterized by homogamy and by inequality in domestic labour and marital power. Marital satisfaction varies over the family life course.
12. In conjunction with changes in the wider society, the divorce rate has increased markedly since the late 1960s. The best single predictor of divorce is young age at marriage. The majority of people who divorce remarry.
13. There are many difficulties associated with the parenting role in modern society.
14. Adult children do not abandon their parents in old age; however, older parents prefer not to live with their children.
15. About 13 percent of families are headed by a lone parent. Female-headed lone-parent families have a high incidence of poverty.
16. Family violence is not a new phenomenon; Western society has a cultural tradition of approving violence in the family setting. Family violence reflects male gender-role socialization and socially structured power inequalities that are gender-related.

## GLOSSARY

**Arranged marriage.** Marriage in which the spouses are chosen by parents or other family elders.

**Blended family.** Type of nuclear family that is based on remarriage and includes children from previous marriages; also known as a *reconstituted* family.

**Conjugal family.** Type of nuclear family pattern characterized by an emphasis on the husband/wife tie and a relative de-emphasis on the wider kin network.

**Egalitarian families.** Families in which the spouses share equally in power and authority.

**Endogamy.** Marriage rule stipulating that marriages must occur within a defined social group.

**Exogamy.** Marriage rule stipulating that marriages must occur outside a defined social group. This rule may be seen as an extension of the incest taboo.

**Extended family.** Family type consisting of two or more nuclear families joined through blood ties — that is, through a parent/child relationship.

**Family time.** Changes that occur within a family as it develops over time.

**Group marriage.** The marriage of more than one man and more than one woman.

**Homogamy.** Persons with similar characteristics choosing one another for marriage partners. Occurs along two dimensions: personal and social.

**Incest taboo.** Rule that prohibits close relatives from marrying and/or having intimate sexual relations.

**Marital power arrangements.** Varying arrangements of power between the husband and wife in a marriage. These arrangements include *owner/property* (the husband is legally and in practice the owner of his wife); *head/complement* (the husband is the decision-maker); *senior-partner/junior-partner* (the husband and wife are unequal partners with the husband having more power);

and *equal-partner/equal partner* (husband and wife contribute equally to income and tasks).

**Marriage.** A commitment or exchange, recognized either legally, contractually, or socially, in which reciprocal rights and obligations (both instrumental and expressive) are carried out.

**Matriarchal families.** Families in which power (authority) is vested in females.

**Monogamous marriage.** The marriage of one man and one woman.

**Nuclear family.** Family type consisting of a married couple and their unmarried children who live apart from other relatives.

**Patriarchal families.** Families in which power (authority) resides with males and is meted out autocratically.

**Polyandry.** The marriage of one woman and two or more men.

**Polygamous families.** Occur when nuclear families are joined together through marriage ties.

**Polygyny.** The marriage of one man and two or more women.

**Self-selected marriage.** Marriage in which individuals choose for themselves who they will marry.

**Social time.** Changes occurring in the wider society that have an influence on the family life course.

**Stem family.** A three-generational family in which one son, upon marriage, remains in the parental home, along with his wife and children.

## FURTHER READING

**Anderson, Karen L., et al. (eds.).** *Family Matters: Sociology and Contemporary Canadian Families.* Toronto: Methuen, 1987. An excellent set of articles about Canadian families, combining theoretical issues and empirical data.

**Baker, Maureen (ed.).** *The Family: Changing Trends in Canada.* Toronto: McGraw-Hill Ryerson, 1984. A recent book of readings on Canadian families that focuses on contemporary issues such as divorce, family violence, social policy, and nontraditional living arrangements.

**Eichler, Margrit.** *Families in Canada Today: Recent Changes and Their Policy Implications.* Toronto: Gage, 1983. This book represents a feminist approach to family issues in the framework of social policy concerns.

**Goode, William J.** *World Revolution and Family Patterns.* 2nd edition. New York: Free Press, 1970. An analysis of the relationship between industrialization and family change by a leading structural functionalist.

**Ishwaran, K. (ed.).** *Marriage and Divorce in Canada.* Toronto: Methuen, 1983. A collection of 14 articles dealing with the processes and dynamics of marriage, interethnic marriages, and marital conflict and divorce.

**Mandell, Nancy, and Ann Duffy (eds.).** *Reconstructing the Canadian Family: Feminist Perspectives.* Toronto: Butterworths, 1988. Eight articles on the family written by leading Canadian feminist scholars.

**Scanzoni, John.** *Shaping Tomorrow's Families.* Beverly Hills: Sage, 1983. An examination of family change by a leading American sociologist of the family.

**Stephens, William N.** *The Family in Cross-Cultural Perspective.* New York: Holt, Rinehart and Winston, 1963. A classic book, written in a very readable style, presenting a summary of anthropological findings on family organization.

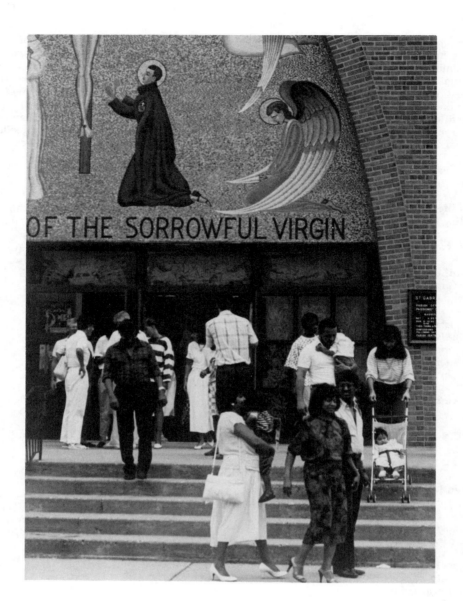

# CHAPTER 12

# Religion

REGINALD W. BIBBY

Religion has been present in virtually every society since the beginning of time. To be sure, its influence has varied from culture to culture and from century to century. In different places and in different eras, religion has known both its dark and golden ages. Moreover, changes such as the rise of rationalism and the advent of modern science and technology have led many observers to predict its demise. Yet religion lives on into the present, embraced by at least a minority in all cultures. Social scientists have consequently given it considerable attention.

## Sociology and Religion

Sociology, as discussed in Chapters 1 and 18, uses the scientific method of investigation to study social life. In doing so, it seeks to understand reality by relying on what we receive through our senses, on perceptions that are empirical and can be verified. Sociologists can thus discover patterns of behaviour and develop theories to explain these patterns. Religion, on the other hand, has traditionally asserted that the world we know through the senses is just part of a greater reality, which — because of the limitations of perception — can be known only through faith. Historian Arnold Toynbee (quoted in Cogley 1968) puts it this way:

*[The world] is not limited to that part of it which is accessible to the human senses and which can therefore be studied scientifically. . . . The key to a full understanding of this part [may] lie in that other part of [the world] which is not accessible.*

Science and religion, therefore, represent two different approaches to knowledge. In their pure form they are compatible. Science deals with the perceivable, religion with the nonperceivable. Science and sociology are unable to make statements about issues of religious faith — for example, claims that there is a God or that God is the source of events or ideas. These are supernatural issues and therefore cannot be resolved by science. Conversely, as Durkheim (1965) pointed out, religion "can affirm nothing that [science] denies, deny nothing that it affirms." Conflict between the two arises only when they invade each other's territory, such as when people who believe in a literal Biblical account of creation want equal time in the science classroom with the proponents of evolution.

Sociology focuses on the social component of religion. People hold beliefs, worship together, display attitudes, relate to others, vary in their mental health, and enjoy a wide variety of lifestyles and social characteristics. While sociology cannot pass judgment on the truth of religious claims, it can explore the social aspects of those claims — who believes what, the relationship between individual commitment and group support, the personal and societal factors that influence the inclination to be religious, and the impact of religious commitment on attitudes and behaviour. As Weber (1964) put it, "The essence of religion is not even our concern, as we make it our task to study the conditions and effects of a particular type of social behaviour."

What is important for our purposes is not whether religious beliefs *are* true, but rather that they are *believed* to be true, and therefore have potential consequences for individual and social life.

## Theoretical Traditions

The sociology of religion has been strongly influenced by three individuals: Karl Marx, Emile Durkheim, and Max Weber.

## The Voice of God or Human?

*Social scientists cannot address the issue of whether or not God exists. However, they can explore the sources of the claims people make "in God's name." Sometimes human claims attributed to God are contradictory, suggesting that social rather than supernatural factors are involved. An example is the conflicting arguments of the archbishop of Toronto and Dr. Henry Morgentaler concerning abortion.*

TORONTO (CP) — The archbishop of Toronto has urged his congregation of more than 1.1 million Roman Catholics to fight laws that "do not sufficiently protect the unborn."

Without referring specifically to the recent acquittal of Dr. Henry Morgentaler and two associates on abortion-related charges, Gerald Emmett Cardinal Carter declared, "Even where partial protection is afforded, the law is being flouted."

Carter's statement was in a letter read or distributed Sunday in the archdiocese's 196 parishes.

"This is not just a church matter," the letter said. "This is the killing of innocents.

"As citizens, as well as believers in God's law, we cannot stand idly by. Our position is without equivocation.

"I urge all Catholics, all Christians and all who respect human life to work together to curb and, if possible, eliminate this abomination."

EDMONTON (CP) — Dr. Henry Morgentaler said Thursday he has come to the conclusion that "God is guiding my hand" during abortion procedures.

"God told me to help women," Morgentaler told a wildly cheering crowd of about 700 at a fund-raising speech in Edmonton Thursday night. Gerard Liston, 25, an anti-abortionist, had asked him why he did not give up performing abortions.

"God is all-powerful," Morgentaler replied. "If He wanted to, He would have stopped me. I have come to the conclusion that God is guiding my hand."

The crowd howled with derision when one anti-abortionist asked, "How do you know you haven't aborted a Messiah?"

**Source:**

Canadian Press, November 25, 1984 (Carter) and January 17, 1985 (Morgentaler).

## "So much for . . . Christianity"

The social principles of Christianity justified the slavery of Antiquity, glorified the serfdom of the Middle Ages and equally know, when necessary, how to defend the oppression of the proletariat, although they make a pitiful face over it.

The social principles of Christianity preach the necessity of a ruling and oppressed class, and all they have for the latter is the pious wish the former will be charitable.

The social principles of Christianity transfer . . . all infamies to heaven and thus justify the further existence of those infamies on earth.

The social principles of Christianity declare all vile acts of the oppressors against the oppressed to be either the just punishment of original sin and other sins or trials that the Lord in his infinite wisdom imposes on those redeemed.

So much for the social principles of Christianity.

**Source:**
Karl Marx and Friedrich Engels, *On Religion* (New York: Schocken Books, 1964), p. 83.

## Marx and Conflict

Marx (1970) asserted that "man makes religion; religion does not make man," and argued that man has "found only his own reflection in the fantastic reality of heaven, where he sought a supernatural being." This human creation, Marx felt, compensated the deprived and represented "the self-consciousness and self-esteem of a man who has either not yet gained himself or has lost himself again."

Central to Marx's thought on religion is the belief that religion serves to hold in check the explosive tensions of a society. Aligned with the interests of the dominant few, religion soothes the exploited majority like an anesthetic — "the opium of the people" (1970) — blinding them to the inequalities at hand and bottling up their creative energies. Consequently, the dominant few encourage religious belief among the masses as a subtle tool in the process of economic exploitation. So intertwined are society and religion, wrote Marx, that attacks on religion are often attacks on society. Attacks on feudalism were above all attacks on the church; revolutionary social and political doctrines were simultaneously theological heresies (Marx 1964).

Marx saw religion as an inadequate salve for a sick society. When the sickness is remedied, there will be no need for the salve. Accordingly, his criticism of religion was an attempt to expose the chain that was binding people so that it could be broken. To criticize religion was to enable individuals to think, act, and fashion their reality with illusions lost and reason regained.

## Durkheim and Collectivity

Durkheim inherited nineteenth-century positivism, which held that the scientific study of society — in contrast to a preoccupation with religious or philosophical speculation — would produce an understanding of social life to rival the achievements of the natural sciences. Though he was the son of a Jewish rabbi and was raised in a Catholic educational tradition, Durkheim ended as an atheist and an anticleric. (His work is covered in more detail in Chapter 1.)

In *The Elementary Forms of the Religious Life* (1965), Durkheim argued that religion has a social origin. Through living in community, people come to share common sentiments, and thus a **collective conscience** is formed. It is experienced by each member, yet is greater than the sum of the individual consciences. When individuals have the religious feeling of standing before a higher power, they *are* in fact in the presence of a greater reality. But this reality is not a supernatural being; it is instead the collective conscience of society. Thus humans create ideas of "God" out of their experience of society; yet in actuality, God is no more than a symbol for society.

Having experienced this apparently supernatural force, humans proceed to classify all things into two groups — either **profane or sacred**. In Christianity, for example, sacred objects have included the cross, the Bible, and holy water. Religious beliefs articulate the nature of the sacred and its symbols, while religious rites develop as rules of conduct prescribing how men and women should act in the presence of the sacred.

**Religious beliefs identify particular objects as sacred.**

In all societies, the need to uphold and reaffirm collective sentiments brings societal members together to form a church. According to Durkheim, "The idea of religion is inseparable from that of the Church" since it is "an eminently collective thing" (1965). Even when religion seems to be entirely a matter of individual conscience, society is still the source that nourishes it. Besides meeting needs at the individual level, claimed Durkheim, religion creates and reinforces social solidarity. Collective life is thus seen as both the source and the product of religion. Accordingly, Durkheim defined religion as "a unified system of beliefs and practices relative to sacred things . . . which unite into one single moral community, called a Church, all those who adhere to them" (1965).

Durkheim saw religious thought and scientific thought as closely related. Religion, like science, tries to take the realities of nature, humanity, and society and translate them into intelligible language. Yet while both pursue the same end, scientific thought is a more perfect form than religious thought.

In 1922, Durkheim observed that the times were characterized by "moral mediocrity." He readily acknowledged the decline of traditional Christianity. Unlike his teacher, Auguste Comte, who saw religion as disappearing, Durkheim did not predict the end of religion. Although the forms of expression might change, the social impetus that gives rise to religion will remain, he predicted, and hence religion itself. Likewise, Durkheim contended that there will always be a place for religious explanations. Science is fragmentary and incomplete, he wrote, advancing too slowly for impatient people. Religion will therefore continue to have an important explanatory role.

## Weber and Ideas

Weber was trained in law and economics. As we saw in Chapter 1, his interest in the origin and nature of modern capitalism led him into extensive debate with Marx, and stimulated much of his work in the sociology of religion. Weber did not concern himself with the question of whether religion is true or false. Rather, he recognized that it has a social dimension whose nature and relationship to the rest of life can be studied. Weber maintained that despite its supernatural emphasis, religion is largely oriented toward *this* world. Therefore, he argued, religious behaviour and thought must not be set apart from everyday conduct.

In *The Protestant Ethic and the Spirit of Capitalism* (1958b), for example, Weber examined the possibility that the moral tone that characterizes capitalism in the Western world — particularly the attitudes toward work embodied in the **Protestant Ethic** — can be traced back to the influence of the Protestant Reformation. He hoped that this study might "in a modest way form a contribution to the understanding of the manner in which ideas become effective forces in history."

Like early University of Chicago symbolic interactionists such as W.I. Thomas and George Herbert Mead, Weber maintained that ideas, regardless of whether they are objectively true or false, define an individual's reality. Consequently, they have the potential to influence behaviour.

Thomas explained this concept in a famous phrase: "If we define things as real, they are real in their consequences." Accordingly, Weber emphasized the need to interpret action by understanding the motives of the actor ("Verstehen"). Such an awareness is to be sought, he said, through placing ourselves in the roles of those we study.

Weber took religion seriously as a force that can influence the rest of life. This is not to say that he saw religious ideas as completely independent causal factors. Behaviour is produced by the highly complex interaction of many factors; religion is just one of them. Yet in analyzing the sources of behaviour, Weber insisted that we do need to consider religious ideas.

Weber became aware early on that we must study societies other than our own in order to know how culture affects the influence of religion (Parsons in Weber 1963). After *The Protestant Ethic* in 1905, he embarked on a number of comparative studies of religion, which unfortunately were left incomplete at his death. In *Sociology of Religion* (1963), which was compiled and translated after Weber's death, he noted that people's concepts of deity are strongly related to the economic, social, and political conditions under which people live. The birth of the gods of light and warmth, rain and earth have been closely related to practical economic needs; heavenly gods who rule the celestial order have been related to people asking questions about death and fate. After political conquest the gods of the conquered are fused with the gods of the conqueror, reappearing with revised characteristics. The growth of *monotheism* (belief in one god) tends to be related to goals of political unification.

In addition to examining the social sources of the gods, Weber dealt with such themes as religious organization and the relationship between religion and social class. He discussed the function of priests and prophets, and described *routinization* (the important process whereby a personal following is transformed into a permanent congregation). Weber further noted that different groups within society vary in their inclination to be religious: the peasants are religious when they are threatened; the nobility find religion beneath their honour; the bureaucrats view religion with personal contempt, while regarding it as a manipulative tool; the solid middle class see it in ethical terms and largely accept it; the artisans freely adopt religion; and the working class supplant it with other ideologies.

In its lack of concern with the truth or falsity of religious beliefs, Weber's work represents a major step forward in the scientific study of religion.

## Religion: Its Nature

In defining religion for sociological study, we might begin by noting that humans everywhere develop systems of meaning to interpret the world. As Glock and Stark (1965) point out, some such systems — commonly called "religions," and including Christianity, Judaism, and Islam — have a supernatural referent. Others, such as a science-based system ("scientism") and political "isms," do not. These latter systems could be viewed as human-centred or **humanist perspectives**. The two types of system differ on one critical point: religion has a concern for life's meaning, while humanist perspectives have a concern for making life meaningful. Humanist Bertrand Russell illuminated this difference well when he stated, "I do not think that life in general has any purpose. It just happened. But individual human beings have purposes" (quoted in Cogley 1968).

Religious perspectives suggest that our existence has meaning beyond that which we as humans decide to give it. In contrast, humanist perspectives play down the search for the meaning of existence in favour of a concern for making existence meaningful. If life does have meaning beyond what we assign to it, then that meaning lies with some supernatural or transempirical reality; if we dismiss the transempirical referent then we ask a different set of questions.

We shall define **religions** as systems with supernatural referents that are used to address the meaning of life. Humanist perspectives, on the other hand, are empirically based systems used to make life meaningful. This chapter focuses on the former.

## Personal Religiosity

Individuals vary in their levels of religious commitment — that is, in their religiosity. A major issue in the scientific study of religion is how to define and measure **personal religiosity**. This hurdle is a most important one, for until we can specify what constitutes religiousness, we cannot proceed to examine the characteristics of religious people — namely, the sources and the consequences of their commitment. Suppose you set out to learn something about the "religious" people in your sociology class — say, to determine whether they generally adhere to the same faith as their parents. How would you first go about deciding which of your classmates *are*, in fact, "religious"?

Most of the early empirical work in the field used one of three basic indicators to determine religiosity: group identification, church membership, and service attendance. So, for instance, you might do a survey of your entire class, asking such questions as "What is your religion?"; "Do you belong to a congregation?"; and "How often do you attend religious services?" You might then decide to define as "religious" all those who answered "once a week" or more to the last question. Now you can proceed to analyze these

---

# Lenin a Deity in the Soviet Union

*Humanist systems of meaning differ from religions in not having a supernatural referent. In the Soviet Union, Lenin remains a symbol of salvation in this life.*

MOSCOW — Every day of the year Muscovites and tourists from around the USSR queue in their thousands in a serpentine line around and inside the Kremlin wall. Each one will briefly peer at the embalmed Lenin in his tomb.

For them, Vladimir Illyich Ulianov (Lenin's proper name) is more than their long-dead leader in his permanent Kremlin shrine.

Lenin, who died in 1924, has become a sixty-year ikon to be seen, honored, even worshipped as were the religious ikons of a sombre Russian history.

Lenin's name proliferates throughout Soviet public life in a way that suffocates the visiting Westerner. Streets, often called "prospekts" in Russia, many city and town squares, a library in Moscow as large as the Library of Congress, all are named for Lenin.

Lenin in death is more than a secular ikon and Leninism more than the ideology of the Soviet state. In a country which proclaims itself as godless and atheistic, Lenin is the deity and Leninism is the state religion.

Moreover Lenin, unlike Stalin, his towering contemporary who died in 1953, also is the USSR's father-figure. Lenin did not live long enough to take part in or be blamed for the many mistakes made since the mid-1920s by his Marxist-Leninist state. These included failures on the land, badly planned industrial development and an inability to prepare for the German invasion in 1941.

The tall flickering tapers and woeful saints' ikons of the Uspensky Cathedral (also part of the Kremlin pile), paraded in the long-gone coronations of the Czars, once reminded the faithful of the glories awaiting them in the life to come.

Leninism, by comparison, promises "salvation" in this life — as dogmatic as any fundamentalist sect of Christendom. Why one must conform is a constant message in such propaganda vehicles as the daily newspaper, *Pravda* (Truth), the official organ of the Communist Party.

Not to conform can be punishable through loss of privileges, internal banishment or declaration of non-person status.

How can the Soviet citizen express himself and remain loyal to his country?

Perhaps such expression reveals itself in the Soviet fascination with medals and badges — harmless forms of self-identification and indications of personal achievement pinned on civilian suits and military tunics. Uniforms of the Soviet soldiers and officers of both senior and junior rank are replete with medals or ribbons. Many of these merely commemorate a battle's anniversary.

Civilians wear badges which represent their city, state, cultural or labor organization.

To our considerable confusion in the west, paradoxes persist.

How can the many peoples and races of such a huge nation be kept in place by a political orthodoxy that is seventy years old and yet continue to be so intensely nationalistic?

Forty years ago, Briton Sir Bernard Pares, the great and sympathetic Russian scholar, wrote: "the attempt to take away religion from those who choose to have it is entirely un-Russian."

Lenin, perpetuated as an ikon through almost seven decades of Communism, meets a deep-set Slavic need.

**Source:**

John D. Harbron, Thompson News Service, January 25, 1985.

**A religion is defined as a system of meaning with a supernatural referent that is developed to interpret the world.**

people's characteristics, and compare them with those you have defined as nonreligious.

Unfortunately, this approach leaves many problems unresolved. For example, one analysis of the consequences of religious commitment (Lenski 1961) explored differences in areas like economic and educational attainment between "Protestants," "Catholics," and "Jews." Unfortunately, the fact that an individual answers "Protestant" when asked "What is your religion?" tells us very little about that person's actual commitment to the Christian faith. Even affiliation with such religious cultural groups as the Mennonites or Hutterites does not guarantee that a given individual is highly religious. Likewise, church members may be active or inactive, committed or uncommitted. And church attendance, while indicative of participation in a religious group, has the disadvan-

tage of excluding people who could — by our definition — be very devout yet not be active in religious organizations.

In recent years, most social scientists have viewed religious commitment as multidimensional. Glock and Stark's proposed dimensions (1965) may still offer the best scheme for analyzing religiosity without introducing a church involvement or Christian theological bias. Briefly, they contend that while the religions of the world vary greatly in the details of their expression, considerable consensus exists among them as to the more general ways in which their adherents manifest religiosity. Glock and Stark cite four such manifestations: belief, practice, experience, and knowledge. They refer to these as the core **dimensions of religiosity**. The religiously committed, Glock and Stark maintain, typically hold certain beliefs (concerning the supernatural and life after death, for example), engage in specific practices (for example, prayer and worship), experience the supernatural, and possess a basic knowledge of the content of their faith.

In Canada, the ongoing *Project Canada* national surveys, which originated in 1975, have provided pioneering, comprehensive data on personal religiosity in this country. The surveys have found that Canadians exhibit relatively high levels of belief, practice, experience, and knowledge (see Table 12-1). Indeed, only 4 percent maintain that they do not believe in God, just 13 percent dismiss altogether the possibility of life after death, and only 23 percent claim they never pray. On the surface, late-twentieth-century Canadians seem to be a highly religious people. However, important questions can be raised concerning the depth

## Table 12-1. Religious Commitment, Along Four Dimensions, Canada

| Dimension | | Percentage |
|---|---|---|
| *BELIEF* | | |
| God | "I know God exists, and I have no doubts about it" | 46 |
| | "While I have doubts, I feel that I do believe in God" | 20 |
| | "I don't believe in a personal God, but I do believe in a higher power of some kind" | 16 |
| | "I don't believe in God" | 4 |
| | Other[a] | 14 |
| Jesus | "Jesus is the Divine Son of God, and I have no doubts about it" | 46 |
| | "While I have some doubts, I basically feel that Jesus is Divine" | 22 |
| | "I think Jesus was only a man, although an extraordinary one" | 16 |
| | Other[b] | 16 |
| Life after death | "There is life after death, with rewards for some people and punishment for others" | 19 |
| | "There must be something ... but I have no idea what it may be like" | 40 |
| | "I am unsure whether or not there is life after death" | 16 |
| | "Reincarnation expresses my view" | 7 |
| | "I don't believe there is life after death" | 13 |
| | Other[c] | 5 |
| *PRACTICE* | | |
| Private prayer | "Regularly, once a day or more" | 28 |
| | "Regularly, many times a week" | 9 |
| | "Sometimes"/"Only on special occasions" | 40 |
| | "Never or hardly ever" | 23 |
| *EXPERIENCE* | | |
| God | "Yes, I'm sure I have" | 20 |
| | "Yes, I think I have" | 23 |
| | "No" | 57 |
| *KNOWLEDGE* | | |
| Who denied Jesus? | "Peter" | 54 |
| | "Judas" | 19 |
| | "I don't know" | 20 |
| | Other wrong answers | 7 |

a"I find myself believing in God some of the time, but not at other times"; "I don't know whether there is a God, and I don't believe there is any way to find out"; and a write-in option.
b"I feel that Jesus was a great man and very holy, but I don't feel him to be the Son of God"; "Frankly, I'm not entirely sure there really was such a person as Jesus"; and a write-in option.
c"There is life after death, but no punishment" and a write-in option.
SOURCE: Data derived from Reginald W. Bibby, "Project Can80: A Second Look at Deviance, Diversity, and Devotion in Canada," codebook (Lethbridge, Alta.: University of Lethbridge, 1982).

of this apparent religiosity. The surveys have found that just over 40 percent of Canadians claim to be committed to Christianity (42 percent) or to another religion (1 percent), with fewer than half of these demonstrating the belief, practice, experience, and knowledge characteristics deemed central to commitment by Glock and Stark. Among the other 57 percent of Canadians, some 40 percent indicate that they are interested in but not committed to any religion, while the remaining 20 percent simply say that they are not religious (Bibby 1987).

In short, isolated religious beliefs and practices abound, but it appears that a majority of Canadians make neither a traditional nor a nontraditional commitment to religion.

## Collective Religiosity

It is frequently argued that one can be religious without having anything to do with such religious organizations as churches or synagogues. Most social scientists, however, would maintain that personal religiosity is highly dependent upon **collective religiosity** — that is, on group support of some kind. Such dependence is not unique to religion but rather stems from a basic fact of life: most of the ideas we hold come from our interaction with other people. However creative we are personally, the fact is that most of the notions we have about life and about ourselves can fairly easily be traced back to the people with whom we have been in communication — family, friends, teachers, authors. We come to hold few ideas, religious or otherwise, in isolation from other people. Moreover, if we are to retain ideas, they must be continually endorsed by those around us — not necessarily by a lot of people, but at least by a few who think as we do.

The point is not that we as individuals are incapable of creativity, but rather that our ideas are for the most part socially imparted and socially sustained. In this light, Durkheim (1965) contended that

*it is the Church of which he is a member which teaches the individual what these personal gods are, what their function is, and how he should enter into relations with them. . . . The idea of religion is inseparable from that of the Church.*

In modern societies, where religious orientations compete with nonreligious ones, the existence of social groupings that can transmit and sustain religious ideas is essential to the maintenance of those ideas. Over the centuries, religion has not lacked for such support.

**The Church–Sect Typology.** Those who have examined religious groups in predominantly Christian settings have historically dealt with two major kinds of organizations. On the one hand there have been numerically dominant groups — for example, the Roman Catholic Church in medieval Europe, the Church of England, or the so-called "mainline" denominations in Canada and the United States (Episcopalian, Anglican, Methodist, Presbyterian, and United Church). On the other hand, smaller groups that have broken from the dominant bodies have also been common. These smaller groups have ranged from the Waldensians of the twelfth century through the "protest-ants" four centuries later to the Baptist and Pentecostal splinter groups found in virtually every major North American city today. So sociologists studying religious groups have developed a conceptual scheme that features these two major organizational forms. This framework, known as the **church–sect typology**, describes the central characteristics of the two types, and accounts for the origin and development of sects.

In perhaps the typology's earliest formulation, Weber differentiated between churches and sects primarily on the basis of each group's theology (churches emphasize works, while sects stress faith) and relationship to society (for churches, accommodation; for sects, separation). Weber noted the irony in the sect's development: while initially a spin-off from an established church, the sect gradually evolves into a church itself (Gerth and Mills 1958). The sect movement is at first characterized by spontaneity and enthusiasm; in time, however, these traits give way to institutionalization and routinization. Thus Weber saw the sect in dynamic terms, as moving along the church-sect continuum. Niebuhr (1929) used the dynamic relationship between church and sect as a way of explaining the appearance and ultimate absorption of new religious groups in Europe and the United States.

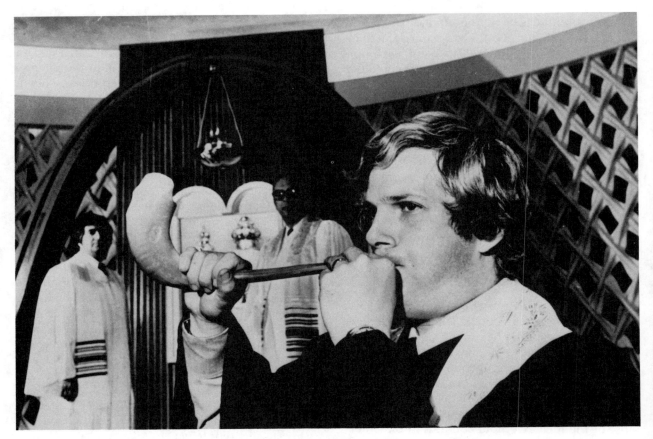

**Rituals are developed as codes of conduct to prescribe how people should act in the presence of the sacred.**

The church–sect typology has been extensively employed in the sociology of religion. It has been the central framework in a number of key studies, both American (for example, Niebuhr 1929; Pope 1942; Demerath 1965) and Canadian (for example, Clark 1948; Mann 1962). The terms *church* and *sect* or *church-like* and *sect-like* have been much-used in the discipline.

Over the years the typology has been modified many times, as analysts have sought ways to deal adequately with diverse forms of religious organization. Becker (1950) and Yinger (1971) both expanded the simple church–sect dichotomy. Yinger, for example, using the three criteria of inclusiveness of membership, accommodation to society, and extent of bureaucratization, suggested six

major types of organizations: the *universal church*; the *ecclesia*; the *denomination*; the *established sect*; the *sect*; and the *cult*. Examples of these six types would include, respectively, the Roman Catholic Church in thirteenth-century Europe; a state church such as the Church of England; the United Church of Canada; the Quakers; the Jehovah's Witnesses; and Scientology.

In recent years, the church–sect typology has been discarded by many sociologists because of its apparent limitations as an analytical tool. Its legacy can still be seen, however, in the ongoing use of organizational types. Stark and Bainbridge (1985), for example, in their important research on new religious movements, have defined sects as deviant religious movements within nondeviant religious traditions; in contrast, they view cults as deviant religious movements within deviant religious traditions.

**Organizational Approaches.** The result of the increasing dissatisfaction with church–sect typology has been a growing tendency to study religious groups within the framework provided by the sociology of organizations (see Chapter 10). The obvious advantage to this approach is that sociologists of religion can draw upon the extensive organizational literature available and have access to well-developed concepts and analytic frameworks.

From an organizational point of view, major groups might be seen as similar to companies — the Roman Catholic Church as "a multinational corporation," or the United Church as a company that is "Canadian owned and operated" (Bibby 1987). An individual congregation might be examined along a number of dimensions:

1. the nature and the sources of its members;
2. its formal and informal goals;
3. the norms and roles established to accomplish the group's purpose;
4. the controls used to ensure that norms are followed and roles are correctly played;
5. the success that the group experiences in pursuing its goals.

Studies of this kind include Harrison's (1959) pioneering examination of the American Baptist Convention and Westhues's (1973, 1978) analyses of the Roman Catholic Church, in which he viewed that organization as a type of nation-state. Although such case-study types of research are still relatively few, they can provide considerable insight into the nature of religious groups.

Looking, for example, at Protestant churches, we notice that members are typically the offspring of previous members, and that geographical mobility is the prime factor in the determination of group sizes. That is, there is a fairly stable pool of church members who merely move between churches as they (the members) change geographical locations; and this mobility serves as the primary source of "new" members for any given church. After following 20 theologically conservative groups in Calgary over 15 years, Bibby and

Brinkerhoff (1973, 1983) found that some 70 percent of new members had come from other conservative churches, while approximately 20 percent were the children of members. Only about 10 percent of the new members had come from outside these conservative groups; even these people had commonly been fairly active in other, more theologically liberal, churches (for example, the United Church).

Because new members come primarily from an existing pool, churches are in considerable competition with one another. One area of competition is quality of leadership: in this respect, smaller, lower-status congregations are usually at a severe disadvantage compared to larger and more prestigious groups. In an analysis of eight American denominations, one researcher found that ministers have standards comparable to those of secular executives when it comes to interchurch movement (Mitchell 1966). Comfort and success loom large. As a result, "attractive" churches in all denominations can be more selective in choosing their ministers and can hold them longer than those churches that are deemed less attractive. Similarly, a study of over 500 Southern Baptist ministers revealed that the dominant pattern of ministerial movement is from smaller to larger congregations (Wimberley 1971).

Such competition is not confined to ministers and other church workers. Physical attributes and range of services are also perceived by the churches as significant in winning new members and holding old ones, with the result that churches tend to build structures as lavish as their resources will permit. In 1985, for example, the (Pentecostal) Queensway Cathedral opened its new building in Toronto. The structure has seating for 4500 people, is serviced by 10 ministers, and has an annual budget of over $3 million. Churches, like secular businesses, expand their services and personnel in keeping with their economic means. And in this pursuit of members — who have been observed (Berger 1961) to pick their churches as carefully as they pick their golf clubs — congregations run the risk of compromising their "product" in order to attract the "consumer." Indeed, competition among churches may often be resolved not in favour of the most religious but in favour of the least religious (Demerath and Hammond 1969).

The conscious and unconscious goals of Protestant churches vary both across congregations and from member to member within any given congregation. As with those of other social groupings, these goals commonly appear to be in conflict with one another. "Formal goals" (for example, spiritual growth), which derive from religious doctrine frequently exist in tension with "survival goals" (for example, numerical growth), which reflect the need to keep the congregation alive (Metz 1967). Glock and his associates (1967) have suggested that churches have difficulty reconciling the *pastoral* (or "comfort") function with the *prophetical* (or "challenge") function. One clergyman quipped that he couldn't decide whether his church building was a locker room or a hospital!

Other observers (Herberg 1960; Hoge 1976) have noted that North American Protestantism has historically experienced tension between emphasizing individual versus social redemption. Driedger (1974), for example, in a study involving 130 Winnipeg Protestant clergy, found theologically conservative ministers to be far less inclined to favour social change than their theologically liberal counterparts.

Despite this apparent divergence in what people expect their religious groups to be doing, there is good reason to believe that churches survive and even thrive precisely because different goals are realized. A rather extreme but informative example is the "skid road" mission (Bibby and Mauss 1974). The mission operators, skid roaders, and suburban supporters all appear to have different informal goals. The operators need employment, the skid roaders need food and lodging, and the suburbanites need an outlet for their talents. And the mission functions in a way that allows these varied goals to be attained. Thus, somewhat ironically, the skid road mission survives, even though it largely fails to accomplish what it officially claims to do — namely, rehabilitate homeless derelicts rather than simply lodge and feed them.

If groups are to achieve their official or formal goals, they must establish norms for thought and action, and roles for members to play. These norms and roles are facilitated by communication, which co-ordinates the interaction, and by the use of social controls in the form of rewards and punishments.

Many Protestant groups, reliant as they are on volunteers, have considerable difficulty executing goals in this norms/roles/communication/social-control pattern of efficient organizations (Brannon 1971). Congregations compete for volunteer members and depend on them for attendance, financial support, and general participation. Thus, while they can establish norms concerning belief and behaviour, and assign organizational roles for members to perform, churches have few and weak methods of social control in such a "buyer's market." In short, churches are painfully vulnerable organizations. The clergy receive no exemption from such organizational fragility. On the contrary, they too are highly dependent on these volunteer parishioners. This has important implications for what the clergy can do and how they can do it.

The overall result is that many congregations are primarily "paper organizations." That is, the formal organizational structure of many congregations — what their internal hierarchy looks like on paper or in theory — is a far cry from the way they are run in practice. So the informal structure of churches bears watching. One study of small churches found that individuals without formal leadership roles have considerable influence: longstanding members were observed to have influence beyond their official roles; people who gave the most money were consulted on key decisions; relatives of official leaders had unofficial input (Chalfant, Beckley, and Palmer 1986). Another study of churches both large and small has documented the presence of "inner circles" — groups that largely control the affairs of local congregations (Houghland and Wood 1979). While the researchers concluded that such groups often arise because of the absence of strong ministerial leadership, it seems equally plausible that inner circles also function to restrict the influence of such leadership.

Westhues (1978) has offered a stimulating organizational analysis of the Roman Catholic Church. He points out that the Catholic Church is a multinational religious body that both predates nation-states and, like them, has a high degree of organization. As a result, relations between the Church and nation-states like Canada and the United States are essentially relations between equals. But not all host countries will so recognize the Church, a fact that frequently forces it to make adaptations.

In the United States, the Catholic Church was denied special recognition in the founding of the country; it was relegated to a common category with other religious bodies, all of which are given no official public authority. Tax monies could not be used to build churches, pay clergy, or support schools. The Church responded by trying to create a self-contained Catholic world, a subsociety within American life that included such institutions as schools, hospitals, welfare agencies, and senior citizens' homes. Nevertheless, the "Catholic Church in America remains today what it was defined to be two centuries ago, the voluntary construction of that minority of American citizens whose active commitment permits it to continue to exist" (Westhues 1978).

In Canada, wrote Westhues, there was no rigid principle of church-state separation. Rather, the creation and evolution of the country has seen the Catholic Church partially institutionalized in Quebec. In that province, the Church has historically had the right to use tax money to support itself and its related educational and social service institutions. In general, says Westhues, the "opposition between civil society and the Catholic church has never been so pointed in Canada as in the United States, fundamentally because the two are less distinct" (Westhues 1978). Yet in Canada, region, language, ethnicity, and legal status have so divided Catholics that the national Church is scarcely more integrated than the nation itself. Westhues summarizes the differences between the Catholic Church in Canada and in the United States as follows:

1. The Church is integrated to a partial but significant degree into the legal and constitutional structure of Canada, but not of the U.S.
2. The Catholic population has high geographical concentration in Canada, but not in the U.S.
3. Catholics account for a larger proportion of the Canadian than of the American population.
4. The extent of structural assimilation is greater for American than for Canadian Catholics.
5. A major issue for the Church in the U.S. has been the extent to which it should "Americanize"; "Canadianizing" has never arisen as an issue.
6. The communication links across the Canadian Church seem weaker than those in the U.S., and the vertical links with the Vatican stronger.
7. The Canadian Church enjoys marginally higher prestige within international Catholicism than does the American Church. (Westhues 1978)

**The Canadian Situation.** Affiliation with religious groups has been widespread in Canada since the founding of this country. Close ties have always been apparent between Canadians of British descent and the Church of England, Methodism, and Presbyterianism; between French Canadians and the Roman Catholic Church; and between other ethnic groups and the churches of their homelands. Such general affiliation continues to be very common in Canada. Indeed, as of the 1981 census, less than 8 percent of Canadians indicated that they had no religious preference (see Table 12-2). Although group preferences clearly differ in various parts of the country, on a national basis Roman Catholics comprise 47 percent of the population and Protestants 41 percent. The remaining 4 percent consist of Jews (1 percent) and those with other religious preferences (3 percent).

Thus it is an exaggeration to think of Canada as a diversified religious mosaic. The reality is that almost 90 percent of Canadians identify themselves as Christians. The next largest category consists of those with no preference — but as we will see shortly, many of these are only temporarily removed from Christian group identification. Only a small minority (about 4 percent) of Canadians feel ties with non-Christian religions. While there is obviously diversity in the way people across the country express Christianity, "a Christian monopoly" clearly does exist in Canada.

When asked about church *membership*, as opposed to mere affiliation, more Canadians — over 50 percent — claim to belong to a church than to any other single voluntary group. According to various polls, approximately one in three say they attend services weekly, and roughly the same proportion of people with school-age children expose those children to church schools that convene outside the regular school day. At the same time, however, there has been a considerable decline

## Table 12-2. Religious Preference, Canada, 1981 (in rounded percentages)

| Denomination | Canada | NWT | Yukon | BC | Alta. | Sask. | Man. | Ont. | Que. | NB | NS | PEI | Nfld. |
|---|---|---|---|---|---|---|---|---|---|---|---|---|---|
| Anglican | 10% | 33% | 20% | 14% | 9% | 8% | 10% | 14% | 2% | 9% | 16% | 6% | 27% |
| Baptist | 3 | 2 | 4 | 3 | 3 | 2 | 2 | 3 | — | 13 | 12 | 5 | — |
| Greek Orthodox | — | — | — | — | 2 | 2 | 2 | 2 | — | — | — | — | — |
| Jehovah's Witnesses | — | — | — | 1 | — | 1 | — | — | — | — | — | — | — |
| Jewish | 1 | — | — | — | — | — | 2 | 2 | 2 | — | — | — | — |
| Lutheran | 3 | 1 | 4 | 5 | 7 | 9 | 6 | 3 | — | — | 1 | — | — |
| Mennonite | — | — | — | 1 | 1 | 3 | 6 | — | — | — | — | — | — |
| Pentecostal | 1 | 3 | 2 | 2 | 2 | 2 | 2 | 1 | — | 3 | 1 | 1 | 7 |
| Presbyterian | 3 | 1 | 3 | 3 | 3 | 2 | 2 | 6 | — | 2 | 5 | 10 | — |
| Roman Catholic | 47 | 40 | 24 | 19 | 26 | 29 | 27 | 35 | 88 | 54 | 37 | 47 | 36 |
| Salvation Army | — | — | — | — | — | — | — | 1 | 1 | — | 1 | — | 8 |
| Ukranian Catholic | 1 | — | — | — | — | — | 1 | 5 | 3 | 2 | — | 1 | — |
| United Church | 16 | 8 | 14 | 20 | 24 | 28 | 24 | 19 | 2 | 13 | 20 | 24 | 19 |
| Other | 7 | 6 | 8 | 11 | 9 | 5 | 4 | 6 | 3 | 3 | 3 | 4 | 3 |
| No Religon | 7 | 6 | 20 | 21 | 12 | 6 | 8 | 7 | 2 | 3 | 4 | 3 | — |
| TOTALS | 100 | 100 | 100 | 100 | 100 | 100 | 100 | 100 | 100 | 100 | 100 | 100 | 100 |

SOURCE: Computed from Statistics Canada, 1981 Census, Cat. 92–912.

in church attendance in recent years, as indicated by the Gallup poll findings presented in Table 12-3. Since approximately the end of World War II, Protestant attendance has dropped drastically, from around 60 percent to under 30 percent, levelling off in the last few years. Among Roman Catholics the decline appears to have started around 1965, with attendance moving from roughly 85 percent to 45 percent during the 1980s.

This drop in attendance is further documented by the *Project Canada* national surveys. While only one in three Canadians now claims to attend service weekly, two in three maintain that they attended weekly when they were growing up (Bibby 1985). Survey findings do not support the possibility that many people are substituting television

"electronic churches" for service attendance. Only 4 percent of Canadians say that they regularly watch religious services on TV or listen to them on the radio — a decline from 29 percent reported in a Gallup poll for 1957 (Bibby 1987). Some 68 percent of those who regularly draw on religious programs are weekly church attenders, suggesting that the programs are largely a supplement rather than a substitute for those already affiliated with a church.

Given the already noted dependence of personal religiosity on collective religiosity, this significant decrease in service attendance has probably been accompanied by a decline in the national level of personal religious commitment. Belief and practice fragments persist. But there has undoubt-

**Table 12-3. Church Attendance for Roman Catholics and Protestants, Canada, Selected Years**

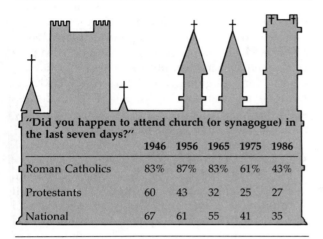

| "Did you happen to attend church (or synagogue) in the last seven days?" | 1946 | 1956 | 1965 | 1975 | 1986 |
|---|---|---|---|---|---|
| Roman Catholics | 83% | 87% | 83% | 61% | 43% |
| Protestants | 60 | 43 | 32 | 25 | 27 |
| National | 67 | 61 | 55 | 41 | 35 |

SOURCE: Canadian Institute of Public Opinion.

edly been an erosion in the proportion of Canadians who are committed to religion as a system that gives meaning to their lives.

This downward trend, of course, may change. Indeed, some observers contend that it is changing, that there is a renewed interest in religion. Critical to discerning such shifts is an understanding of the individual and societal factors that influence the prevalence of religious commitment. We will now turn to this important issue, the sources of commitment.

## Religion: Its Sources

Much important early work in the scientific study of religion focused on primitive or simple cultures, in which religion was pervasive. Everyone seemed religious. So, not surprisingly, observers sought to understand the origin of religion itself, rather than the sources of individual variations in commitment. However, individual differences in religiosity in modern societies have called for theories that can explain why some people are religious and others are not. To date, these explanations have tended to focus either on individuals or on the social structure.

## Individual-Centred Explanations

At least three dominant "person-centred" explanations of religious commitment have emerged. In essence, the proposed explanatory factors are probably as old as the major religions themselves.

**Reflection.** The desire to comprehend reality is widespread among humans. Geertz (1968) noted that

*it does appear to be a fact that at least some men — in all probability, most men — are unable . . . just to look at the stranger features of the world's landscape in dumb astonishment or bland apathy without trying to develop . . . some notions as to how such features might be reconciled with the more ordinary deliverances of experience.*

In the course of reflecting on the meaning of existence, people have commonly concluded that life has a supernatural or transempirical dimension. As Weber (1963) put it, religion is the product of an "inner compulsion to understand the world as a meaningful cosmos and take up a position toward it." For some, religion appears to be the result of considering one's place in the universe, as the psalmist does in the following passage:

*When I consider thy heavens, the work of thy fingers, the moon and the stars, which thou hast ordained; What is man, that thou art mindful of him? (Psalms 8:3–4)*

Canadians who say they often think about questions pertaining to origin, purpose, happiness, suffering, and death are generally somewhat more likely than others to exhibit religious commitment (Bibby 1983). Yet the tendency is very slight. Fewer than one in three of the people in Canada who often raise these so-called "ultimate questions" give evidence of being religiously committed. At the same time, some of the committed do not give evidence of raising such questions. Indeed, some ten percent of Canadians who exhibit traditional Christian commitment say that they have never thought about life's origin and purpose. This latter group appears to learn the "answers" (by uncritically accepting religious teachings) before they consciously ask the questions.

**Socialization.** A second person-centred explanation of religious commitment sees religiosity as the product of learning. As noted earlier, ideas are for the most part socially instilled through individuals and institutions. People who are exposed to social environments that are positive toward religion — whether an entire society, a community, an institution, or a reference group — would therefore be expected to be religious. As Freud (1962) put it, many apparently learn religion just as they learn the multiplication table.

Primary family and friendship groups, so central to socialization generally, are particularly important to religious socialization, along with religious institutions. Involvement in religious organizations has been commonly attributed to two types of factors: *association* and *accommodation*.

The inclination for association has often found expression in religious group participation. In Canada and the United States, for example, churches and synagogues have played an important role in the social life of both native-born and immigrant people in communities of all sizes. Involvement has undoubtedly fulfilled a variety of functions — among them, helping satisfy an individual's desire for identity, providing social status, and enhancing group solidarity. Not surprisingly, participation has been observed to follow class and ethnic lines. Hiller (1976), for example, comments that the churches of Canadian immigrants have played a vital role by helping to provide an ethnic anchor in an alien society.

Accommodation to social pressures, notably the pressures of a primary group, seems to be another source of religious group involvement. For example, one marital partner may become more active in response to the hopes and expectations of the other, friends in response to friends (see, for example, Gerlach and Hine 1968), and parents in response to school-age children (Nash and Berger 1962). In some tightly knit rural communities, as well as in larger communities where religion is pervasive, accommodation will probably act as an important source of religious involvement.

The *Project Canada* analyses have documented a noteworthy relationship between the commitment of respondents and that of their parents (Bibby 1987). Some 90 percent of Canadians with Protestant parents are Protestants themselves today. The same level of identification is found for people with Roman Catholic parents (Bibby 1987). Further, close to one in two Canadians who perceive their fathers or mothers as being (or having been) "very religious" are themselves weekly attenders, as compared to one in five of the respondents with parents who were not very religious (see Table 12-4). Those with devout parents are also more likely than others to view themselves as "very religious."

On the other hand, the relationship between childhood religious service attendance and adult commitment is weaker. Weekly attendance as a child does not necessarily lead to a similar level of participation in adulthood. Only 35 percent of Canadians who attended services weekly as children are still doing so as adults. Conversely, 20 percent of those who were *not* weekly attenders as young people are involved on a weekly basis now. Childhood attendance is also tenuously related to a religious self-image.

The religious socialization of children thus appears to be important in the generation of commitment, but with the family rather than the church exerting the greater influence. Such findings are consistent with those of Hunsberger (1980, 1984), whose analyses of students at Wilfrid Laurier University and the University of Manitoba have led him to conclude that a family emphasis on religion in childhood is positively associated with later religiosity.

Table 12-4 also confirms that the commitment level of one's spouse is strongly related to personal commitment, while association with religious friends also has a noteworthy effect. The presence of school-age children is not, in and of itself, tied to commitment for Canadian parents generally. As would be expected given the previously discussed dependence of personal religiosity on organized religion, a strong positive relationship exists between regular church attendance and defining oneself as religious. The relationship, however, is far from perfect. Less than half the weekly attenders (44 percent) see them-

## Table 12-4. Religious Socialization and Commitment, Selected Category Findings

| | Weekly Atten- dance | See Self as "Very Religious" |
|---|---|---|
| **IN CHILDHOOD** | | |
| *Father's Commitment* | | |
| "Very Religious" | 45% | 43% |
| "Not Very Religious" | 20 | 5 |
| *Mother's Commitment* | | |
| "Very Religous" | 41 | 36 |
| "Not Very Religous" | 18 | 4 |
| *Childhood Attendance* | | |
| Weekly | 35 | 19 |
| Less than Weekly | 20 | 12 |
| **IN ADULTHOOD** | | |
| *Parnter's Commitment* | | |
| "Very Religous" | 79 | 82 |
| "Not Very Religious" | 10 | 3 |
| *Religious Friends* | | |
| Yes | 83 | 35 |
| No | 25 | 15 |
| *School-Age Children* | | |
| Yes | 32 | 17 |
| No | 29 | 18 |
| *Service Attendance* | | |
| Weekly | — | 44 |
| Less than Weekly | — | 5 |

NOTE: Responses scored positively on belief, practice, experience, and knowledge.
SOURCE: Date derived from Reginald W. Bibby, "Project Canada: A Study of Deviance, Diversity, and Devotion in Canada," codebook (Lethbridge, Alta.: University of Lethbridge, 1976).

selves as "very religious." On the other hand, only 5 percent of those who attend services less often than weekly regard themselves as devout. In adulthood, then, two factors — the commitment level of one's spouse and friends, and one's own church attendance — appear to be strongly associated with involvement and commitment.

**Deprivation.** A third person-centred explanation, which has long been popular with both scholar and layperson, is that the religious are drawn primarily from society's deprived or disadvantaged. Such people, it is often thought, turn to religion as a means of compensating for their deprivation. This idea has received considerable Judeo-Christian support (for example, "Blessed are the poor in spirit. . . . Blessed are the meek") and has characterized the thinking of such influential social scientists as Marx and Freud. Glock and Stark (1965) contended that five types of deprivation are predominant in the rise and development of religious and secular movements: economic; social; organismic (that is, physical or mental); psychic; and ethical. The first three are self-explanatory; psychic deprivation refers to the lack of a meaningful system of values, and ethical deprivation to having one's values conflict with those of society.

Yet if we use such so-called objective indicators as income, health, and social relationships (to probe for economic, organismic, and social deprivation, respectively), deprivation is neither consistently nor strongly related to religious commitment in either the United States (see Roof and Hoge 1980) or Canada (Hobart 1974; Bibby 1980). This is not to say that deprivation is never a significant factor for some individuals and some religious groups, but rather that, generally speaking, the religiously committed in North America are not any more or less disadvantaged than others.

## Structure-Centred Explanations

So far we have examined what we might call "kinds of people" explanations of religious commitment. What these explanations have in common is their emphasis on individuals, who are said to turn to religion out of reflection, socialization, or deprivation. An adequate understanding of commitment, however, must also take into account the

# Where the Crazy Fish Swims . . .

*In one of the most astounding exhibitions of religious fanaticism in recent history, some 900 followers of the Reverend Jim Jones's People's Temple commune in Guyana committed mass suicide in November 1978. Their commitment, along with that of other sect and cult members, has commonly been explained in terms of deprivation.*

Today's cults are seeking the simple ways of life, an escape from social turbulence. Dr. Robert Lifton, a Yale University psychiatrist and authority on brainwashing, says, "There's some kind of historical phenomenon here. When people are facing dislocations of rapid social change and the present looks frightening, there is often a cry for a return to absolute simplicity in the rules of living. People seek to return to a past of perfect harmony that never was. When they find their fundamentalist principles threatened by the outside world believers have many times chosen suicide as a way of immortalizing their purpose."

Certainly mass suicide, though mercifully rare, is not an unheard-of phenomenon. A few years after the death of Christ, 960 Jews killed themselves in the besieged fortress of Masada rather than yield to Roman soldiers, while in 1944, when the Americans took the Japanese island of Saipan, hundreds of men, women and children leaped off a cliff into the ocean rather than surrender. As Dr. Edwin Shneidman, a leading suicide expert at the University of California, says, "In the altruistic suicide the pressure of the group can be so powerful that suicide may not be the individual choice but it is nonetheless demanded. If you're in the Marine Corps and the sergeant says it's time to go, you can't just say, 'Gee, Sarge, I prefer not to.' "

But in the case of a cult there is another factor involved — the leader — and Manhattan psychiatrist Richard Rabkin draws a disturbing analogy about him. Says Rabkin, "A school of fish has no real leader. If one fish strays he comes back into the school. But if you brain-damage that fish and he goes on ahead, the others will follow him. He becomes the leader not because of anything he has, like charisma, but because of what he's lacking."

**Source:**

*Maclean's,* December 4, 1978, p. 36.

---

societal context in which people find themselves, and its influence on religious inclination. Individual religiosity is not formulated in a vacuum: it is highly dependent on the larger social environment in which individuals and their reference groups are located. Clark (1948), for example, has argued that in Canada's past the tendency of sect-like religious groups to emerge was tied directly to the existence of unstable conditions produced by factors such as immigration and economic depression. With industrialization, increased prosperity, and stability, sects tended to evolve into denominations, a process referred to as **denominationalism.**

The climate provided by modern industrial societies for religion is a subject of considerable controversy. On the one hand there are those who claim that religion is experiencing a decline in pervasiveness and influence that parallels the rise of industrialization. Such a **secularization argument** dates back at least to Comte, Marx, Freud, and Durkheim. On the other hand, there are a number of observers who claim that religion — traditional or otherwise — is making a comeback and that it persists in part because people experience dissatisfaction with modern industrial living and its emphases on rationalism and materialism. The actual influence of modern cultures on the tendency of people to be religious or otherwise is not at all clear. Considerable cross-cultural research is necessary to clarify the picture.

The *Project Canada* findings make it possible to explore how some of the correlates of change in Canada — for example, urbanization, higher education, work-force participation, and exposure to the mass media, along with the sheer passage of time — are related to religious commitment. However, if the secularization argument is correct, then social characteristics such as community size and education should have increasingly less effect on differences between the committed and others. In time, people who live in rural areas should come to resemble their urban counterparts in being nonreligious; the same should be true of high school dropouts and college graduates, and of retired people and those under the age of 30. This lack of differentiation would automatically result once the culture has become so secularized that no sector of the population remains untouched.

What do the findings actually show? Differences related to the general era of birth continue to exist among Canadians. But as community size, education, work-force participation, and media exposure increase, commitment tends to decrease only slightly (see Table 12-5). These data suggest that Canada is already a highly secularized society. Interestingly, there is a tendency for the industrialization/secularization pattern to be reflected regionally: the (least industrialized) Atlantic re-

gion has the highest levels of commitment. It appears that much of the drop-off in Roman Catholic attendance between 1965 and 1980 was primarily related not to the changes resulting from Vatican II, but rather to the accelerated industrialization and hence secularization of Quebec.

## An Assessment

In modern societies, religion frequently finds itself competing with the world of here and now. Emphases on science, technology, and human progress are accompanied by the expectation that a person's attention, capabilities, and energies will be directed toward successfully living out everyday life. This **industrial world-view** is perpetuated quite unconsciously by virtually every major institution, and is assimilated with equal unawareness by the average person.

To the extent that people in a highly industrialized country like Canada are religiously committed, the key sources of their commitment are neither such institutions as the media, education, or the work world nor the desire for compensation in the face of deprivation. Rather, the people in this country who are religiously committed tend to be those so socialized. Religion, like so many other things, is transmitted through relationships; it is primarily learned from and supported by family and close friends, with the assistance of the church.

But with the industrialization and "post-industrialization" of Canada, two important developments have occurred that have seriously affected the social transmission of religion. First, the above-noted influence of family, friends, and church has been reduced by the advent of other decisive socializing agents, including secular peer groups, the mass media, and the modern educational system. These agents are typically concerned with everyday life; thus, however inadvertently, they function to instil the industrial world-view with its empiricism/materialism emphases.

Second, in addition to the decreasing effectiveness of religious socialization, as personal religious commitment declines, socialization of a religious nature is simply not as common as it once was. In other words, there is less commitment to transmit. Some 15 percent of the men in the 1975 *Project Canada* national survey viewed

## Table 12-5. Industrialization Correlates and Commitment, Selected Category Findings

| | Weekly Attendance | See Self as "Committed" Christian |
|---|---|---|
| ERA *(date of birth)* | | |
| 1931 & Earlier | 43% | 61% |
| 1931–1950 | 25 | 44 |
| 1951–1967 | 14 | 33 |
| | | |
| EDUCATION | | |
| High School or Less | 24 | 46 |
| Some High School | 25 | 43 |
| Degree or More | 26 | 44 |
| | | |
| WORK-FORCE PARTICIPATION | | |
| Not Employed Outside the Home | 38 | 54 |
| Employed Outside the Home | 20 | 40 |
| | | |
| MEDIA EXPOSURE | | |
| Watch TV: | | |
| "Seldom" or "Never" | 24 | 46 |
| "Very Often" or "Sometimes" | 25 | 38 |
| | | |
| REGION | | |
| Atlantic | 42 | 66 |
| Quebec | 27 | 38 |
| Ontario | 23 | 45 |
| Prairies | 23 | 47 |
| British Columbia | 19 | 31 |

SOURCE: Data derived from Reginald W. Bibby, "Project Can85: A Third Look at Deviance, Diversity, and Devotion in Canada," codebook (Lethbridge, Alta.: University of Lethbridge, 1986).

themselves as "very religious," while 25 percent so designated their fathers. The women indicated a similar decline in commitment, from 45 percent for their mothers to 19 percent for themselves. Further, while two in three adults actively attended religious services when they were growing up, only one in three school-age children are currently receiving the same level of religious exposure.

In short, religious socialization is the key determinant of commitment. But socialization efforts — when they are made — are often neutralized by a strongly secular culture. The result is a decrease in the number of people who are even attempting to religiously socialize their children. The implications for the continuing decline in commitment are obvious.

## Religion: Its Consequences

From the standpoint of social scientist and layperson alike, one of the most significant questions about religion is its consequences. Does religion have an impact on the way individuals live their lives, or is it largely irrelevant? If such an influence exists, does religion contribute to individual and societal wellbeing, or is it inclined to produce anxiety and guilt, social indifference, and bigotry? And if religion does have an impact, whether positive or negative, to what extent is this impact unique to religion, and to what extent is it common to other institutions?

Religious people, of course, would claim that faith does have consequences for individuals and hence for societies. Christians, for example, are likely to tell us that mature followers of their faith do find that it influences both their personal lives and their relations with others. Specifically, Christians maintain that the committed experience joy, satisfaction, peace, and hope. Moreover, they would point out that according to their tradition, committed, mature Christians will exhibit only love in their relationships with others ("Love thy neighbour as thyself") and that this love will be manifested in such qualities as concern for others,

acceptance, benevolence, forgiveness, self-control, honesty, and respect. In living in accordance with this norm of love, Christians are expected to follow such ethical guidelines as the Ten Commandments, the Sermon on the Mount, and the teachings of the Apostle Paul. At the same time, religious groups certainly differ on specific norms. If an issue such as abortion is perceived as "religiously relevant," one would expect that the attitudes of the committed would be influenced; if not, their attitudes would simply vary according to other factors such as age and education.

Social scientists exploring the consequences of Christianity, then, give their attention to two main areas: personal characteristics and relations with others. However, they do not limit themselves to studying only the kinds of effects officially claimed by religion. Rather, they also freely explore the possible latent or unintended consequences of commitment. One religious counsellor tells of dealing with a distraught young woman who exclaimed, "My troubles began the day I became a Christian!" (Southard 1961). The sociologist keeps an open mind to such a possibility. Similarly, the ideal of Christian love does not stop the researcher from probing the incidence of Christian hostility.

### Individual Consequences

Both Marx and Freud essentially conceded that religion does contribute to positive personal characteristics such as happiness, satisfaction, and hope. Their adverse criticism rested in their belief that such qualities were based on people believing in an illusory reality proposed by religion. However, their concessions to religion were more speculative than soundly documented.

Actual research on the consequences of individual commitment is surprisingly limited; moreover, it suffers — as do consequence studies generally — from serious methodological flaws. *Time-order* is often vague, so that one does not know whether religion is the cause, the effect, or simply correlated with something like happiness; the *strength of relationships* is not always specified; and *controls* for other explanatory factors are commonly inadequate (Bouma 1970; Wuthnow 1973; Bibby 1979).

Apart from methodological shortcomings, the research findings on religion and what we might refer to generally as "mental health" are contradictory. Rokeach (1965), summing up a number of his studies, wrote that he had

*found that people with formal religious affiliation are more anxious [than others]. Believers, compared with non-believers, complain more often of working under great tension, sleeping fitfully, and similar symptoms.*

Yet researchers have consistently found a negative relationship between religious commitment and *anomie* (Lee and Clyde 1974) — a characteristic of valuelessness and rootlessness that Srole (1956) sees as related to anxiety. Further, as early as the work of Beynon (1938), Boisen (1939), and Holt (1940), involvement in such groups as sects and cults was seen as providing improved self-image and hope in the face of economic and social deprivation — a theme echoed by Frazier (1964) for American blacks, Whyte (1966) for Canadian rural-to-urban immigrants, and Hill (1971) for West Indian immigrants to Britain. Lindenthal and his associates (1970) found in a New Haven, Connecticut, study of some 1000 adults that church affiliation and mental health were positively related, a finding corroborated by Stark (1971) using a California sample.

Analyses to date suggest that Canadians who exhibit religious commitment are slightly more inclined than others to claim a high level of happiness; to find life exciting; to express a high level of satisfaction with family, friends, and leisure activities; and to view death with hope rather than as mysterious or even fearful (Bibby 1987). However, when controls are introduced and the impact of other variables such as age, education, and community size is taken into account, the apparent modest influence of commitment is found to dissolve. This pattern holds true both on a national level and among Roman Catholic, United, Anglican, and Conservative Protestant church members.

In short, religious commitment, by itself, appears to have a very limited influence on valued personal characteristics. Moreover, it is often less important than such variables as age, education, or employment in predicting personal wellbeing, even among active church members.

## Interpersonal Consequences

One of the first empirical attempts to examine the relationship between religious commitment and compassion was carried out by Kirkpatrick in 1949. Using a Minnesota sample of students and other adults, Kirkpatrick found that religiously committed people were actually somewhat *less* humanitarian in their outlook than others.

Some twenty years later, two important studies gave support to Kirkpatrick's findings. Stark and Glock (1968), in their classic examination of American religiosity, contended that traditional Christian commitment (which they termed "orthodoxy") was negatively associated with social concern (or "ethicalism"). They did note, however, that this was true for Protestants but not for Catholics, where the relationship was slightly positive. In an attempt to explain this difference, they suggested that Protestants are more inclined than Catholics to see the best solution to social problems as involving God's changing of individuals. Catholics — and more theologically liberal Protestant groups — assume that humans are limited and therefore attempt "to offer moral guidance for the conduct of man-to-man relationships" (Stark and Glock 1968).

Rokeach (1969), drawing on a representative American sample of some 1400 adults, similarly observed that, overall, religious commitment was negatively related to social compassion. In the particular case of Roman Catholics, however, he found that no relationship (either positive or negative) existed. Rokeach (1969) concluded that "the results seem compatible with the hypothesis that religious values serve more as standards for condemning others . . . than as standards to judge oneself by or to guide one's own conduct."

These findings, however, have not gone unchallenged. Some research conducted on specific religious groups — on Mennonite students, by Rushby and Thrush (1973) — and in certain localities — in a southwestern American city, by Nelson and Dynes (1976) — has found a positive relationship between commitment and compassion.

## "Do you Have Love in Your Heart?"

*Christian commitment has historically been associated with humanitarian ideals and practice. Yet like other religions, it has also on occasion known socially undesirable consequences. Following is one such bizarre manifestation of commitment, taken not from the middle ages in Europe, but from the middle 1970s in the state of Washington.*

YAKIMA, WASH. (AP) — In three years of life, David Weilbacher knew brutality, pain, and humility — forced upon him by the people who made up his world. But those three years never gave David enough time to understand or fight back.

The blond and dimpled child was too young to know why the people he trusted to provide security would beat him repeatedly with sticks and tell him he did not have love in his heart.

He could not comprehend what "the devil" was, much less understand why they felt it had to be driven from his body.

The five people who made up David's world are in the Yakima county jail, across town from where the three-year-old is buried.

They can't see the small stone grave marker, which says "David Weilbacker." The name is misspelled — an ironic finality for the people to whom David, in his last months of life, was not David at all.

David's mother, Debra Marie Weilbacher, was 19 when she and her son moved to the yellow house, used as a church by those who lived there, in a neighborhood of crumbling streets and poverty on Yakima's southeast side.

Debra's four-year marriage to David's father had ended, and she looked to members of the religious household to help her overcome the emptiness. Edward Leon Cunningham, 51, told her God was his master, and he was God's messenger.

Also living in the house were Cunningham's wife, Velma, their daughter Carolyn, 27, and Lorraine Edwards, a former schoolmaster of Debra's. All are awaiting sentencing on manslaughter and assault convictions in David's death. . . .

Cunningham began to point out things about David to the family . . . wetting his pants, smearing his waste on the bathroom wall. The child

---

Considerable research has also been carried out on another facet of interpersonal relations — racial prejudice. Gorsuch and Aleshire (1974) reviewed all the published empirical studies on the topic through the mid-1970s; they concluded that the key to understanding conflicting findings is how religious commitment is measured. If church membership is used as the measurement, members are more prejudiced than those who have never joined a church. If beliefs are used, the theologically conservative are more prejudiced than others. And if church attendance is the measure of commitment, then marginal church members show more prejudice than either the nonactive or the most active members. Gorsuch and Aleshire (1974) conclude that

*the results of the present review are clear: the average church member is more prejudiced than the average nonmember because the casual, nontheologically motivated member is prejudiced. The highly committed religious person is — along with the nonreligious person — one of the least prejudiced members of our society.*

These researchers point out, however, that the precise role organized religion plays in influencing prejudice is unclear. Sophisticated studies that measure the impact of churches on individuals over time have not yet been done.

An analysis of *Project Canada* data has disclosed that the religiously committed in this country do not differ significantly from others in their attitudes toward interpersonal relationships (Bibby 1987). They hold a similar view of people, claim a comparable level of compassion, and appear to be no more or less tolerant of deviants, minority groups, and people of other religious faiths than nonreligious Canadians. Further, in contrast to the findings of Rokeach (1969) and Stark and Glock (1968), no noteworthy differences appear in the interpersonal attitudes held by Roman Catholics and by Protestants.

At this point, it is important for us to pause and ask ourselves whether we should expect religion to make a real contribution in such areas as happiness and compassion at this stage in Canadian history. In highly specialized industrialized societies, religion becomes only one source of inter-

smelled wicked, too, for some unknown reason. Once he put glass chips in his shoes and wore them.

David acted as if he would rather be an adult than a child, although he had a laugh, a foolish laugh, that seemed to be neither young nor old. In the end, it was clear, particularly to Cunningham, that David was possessed by the devil.

The spankings began in April, the family says. Cunningham had pointed to something in the Bible which he believed was the answer: "Withhold not correction from the child; for if thou beatest him with a rod he shall not die. Thou shalt deliver his soul from hell."

Twice a day for four months, the paddles — lath sticks 46 cm [18 in.] long, sanded and rounded — were passed around to each family member. Each took his turn swatting David a few times or many times, on his legs, his rear, his back, his arms — almost everywhere except the genitals and the kidney area.

"Do you have love in your heart?" Cunningham would say to David.

"Yes," David would say.

"Then show it," Cunningham would say.

David would hug and kiss Cunningham, who didn't think the three-year-old was being honest. So he would pass the stick to the next family member to use on David.

On the morning of July 22, Debra remembers picking David off the floor after an extra-long spanking. A tiny splotch of blood appeared on his lips, and the family saw little David raise his fists and growl. Then he stopped breathing.

They put David in a sealed room in the back of the house and waited for God to resurrect him.

On September 1, Sgt. Robert Langdale went to the house, acting on a tip from Mrs. Cunningham, who began to suspect her husband after an Anti-Christ prophesy didn't come true. Langdale went to the back bedroom, to the door where deodorant had been sprayed to stop the smell. He burst through the door into the fly- and maggot-infested room and got the shock of his life.

With his gas mask on, Langdale looked under the sheet on a cot and saw something that was bloated, beaten black, one metre long, and three years old.

A pathologist later would say there was no way he could tell how David died. But he had a guess, and he guessed David was beaten to death.

"That's the way it goes," Carolyn Cunningham said after the convictions were announced.

---

**Source:**

Associated Press, November 24, 1976.

---

personal norms. Valued relational characteristics such as compassion, integrity, and co-operativeness are emphasized by virtually everyone — the family, the school, youth groups, voluntary associations, the mass media. Norms specific to work and play, on the other hand, are largely created and disseminated within the business and social contexts in which they are used. The predictable result, in Berger's (1961) words, is that we can expect the religious to "hold the same values as everybody else, but with more emphatic solemnity." There are many paths to valued interpersonal traits, as well as to valued personal characteristics; religion is at best only one such path, and it is used by what seems to be a decreasing number of people.

At the same time, there is one area where the Christian religion still speaks with a fairly loud, if not unique, voice — the area of personal morality, notably sexuality. Here Christian churches, with varying degrees of explicitness, tend to function as opponents of "moral innovation." Examples include opposition to the changing of sexual standards, to the increased availability of legal abortion, to the legalized distribution of pornographic material, and to the legalization of currently prohibited drugs. In recent years, churches have been supported in such campaigns by Jerry Falwell's high-profile "Moral Majority" movement and its Canadian counterpart, Ken Campbell's "Renaissance" movement.

Table 12-6 reports findings that support the "opposition to moral innovation" argument. Religiously committed Canadians are more inclined than others to hold negative attitudes toward nonmarital sexuality, homosexuality, abortion, pornography, and the use of marijuana. A national study of Canadian Mennonites has similarly found that commitment has consequences for the moral rather than for the social sphere (Driedger, Currie, and Linden 1982).

Yet even here, the influence of religion both nationally and across religious groups, while important, is generally no more significant than the year of one's birth (Bibby 1979). What this means is that the era in which a person was born is just as important in determining opposition to moral innovation as is religious commitment; and in

## Table 12-6. Commitment and Moral Attitudes, Expressed as Percentage Opposed

| Religious Self-Image | Premarital Sex | Extra-marital Sex | Homo-sexuality | Abortion: Rape | Abortion: Child Unwanted | Pornog-raphy | Marijuana |
|---|---|---|---|---|---|---|---|
| A Committed Christian | 39 | 91 | 84 | 22 | 72 | 52 | 82 |
| Other | 10 | 73 | 60 | 6 | 41 | 28 | 60 |

SOURCE: Derived from Reginald W. Bibby, "Project Can85," 1986 and "Project Teen Canada," 1985.

Canada's past, resistance to moral change was greater than in recent years or today.

Religious commitment in Canada, then, appears to have relatively little influence in the areas of personal characteristics or interpersonal relations, where secular influences abound; it has its greatest influence in the sphere of personal morality.

## Societal Consequences

The influence of religion can be examined not only in terms of individuals and of social inter-action but also with reference to society as a whole. From at least the time of Marx and Durkheim, observers have argued that religion contributes to social solidarity. Marx was particularly critical of what he saw as the fusion of religion with the interests of the powerful, to the point where political and theological heresies become synonymous. Similarly, Durkheim viewed the supernatural both as reflecting the nature of a society and as functioning to unite it.

Certainly religion can also be socially disruptive. Efforts on the part of Protestant leaders to bring about social change (Crysdale 1961; Allen

## Pope Liked But Ignored

*Two public opinion polls, one taken before Pope John Paul II's 1984 visit to Canada, and the other after his departure, point to the selective use of Roman Catholicism by Canadian Catholics. While the Pope himself is respected, what he says is not necessarily taken seriously.*

September 8, 1984

OTTAWA — A major pastoral goal of Pope John Paul's visit is doomed even before he sets foot in Quebec City Sunday, according to a national opinion poll commissioned by Southam News.

The survey strongly suggests the Pope will be cheered as a media superstar, respected for his goodness, applauded for his engaging personality but ignored as irrelevant when he preaches on individual and public morality.

Preaching to the public on morality and humanity is one main goal of a papal visit, according to Vatican officials. The other is to strengthen the resolve of local bishops and priests.

Yet more than half the 1011 adults interviewed for the poll reject the pope's social thinking as "out of touch" and object to any religious figure taking strong stands on political and economic issues.

Barely one in seven — rising to nearly one in five among Catholics only — consider John Paul's social thinking in line with Canadian society. Only a third of those interviewed even like the idea of religious leaders speaking out on politics and economics.

Such widespread opposition means the Pope will be preaching mostly to people with closed minds, whether restating his traditional views on contraception and abortion or outlining his progressive ideas on social justice and human work.

"He gets it from both sides," agreed a leading Catholic theologian who requested anonymity. "Liberals object to his moral traditionalism and the conservatives balk at his ideas for political and economic reform."

While Canadians may turn off the preaching, they will give a joyous and warm welcome to the "Pope for all Christians" on his 12-day visit.

Three out of every four interviewed this July said the papal visit was a good idea, rising to 88 per cent

1971) have challenged the Canadian status quo. At the provincial level, Roman Catholicism in Quebec can be seen as having contributed to a considerable ethnic and regional cohesion. But at a national level, this contribution to such a solidarity can be seen as disruptive to Canadian unity. In the United States, Falwell's "Moral Majority" became a vocal "Christian Right" that was committed to altering the nature of American life through influencing the country's major institutions. The disruptive effects of religion can also be seen in the Protestant/Catholic strife in Northern Ireland; in the Islamic resurgence in Iran; in the Hindu/Sikh conflict in India; and in the call of the Roman Catholic clergy for political and economic change in Poland and Latin America. The Canadian Council of Roman Catholic Bishops has been especially vocal recently in criticizing the profit orientation of the country's economy, and in opposing attempts to stymie workers' efforts to organize — even going so far as to indict Eaton's stores. Disruption is also a consequence of the activities of other religious groups, for example Canadian Doukhobors and youth-oriented cults. Conflict also occasionally arises over the

opposition of Christian Scientists and Jehovah's Witnesses regarding blood transfusions, and over the pacifist stance of Quakers and Mennonites.

Nevertheless, Berger's (1961) observation still seems generally valid: while an adequate sociological theory of religion must be able to account for the possibility of dysfunctions, Durkheim's assertion that religion integrates societies aptly describes religion in America. Religion, at least the mainline segment of organized Christianity that embraces the largest number of affiliates, appears for the most part to endorse culture rather than to challenge it, to reinforce North American society as we know it rather than to call for its reformation. As Hiller (1976) has put it, "There are times then when religion can be a vital force in social change. . . . But as a general principal, we can say that in Canada organized religion has generally been a conservative force supporting the solidarity of the society." Historically the Protestant churches have reflected the British position of legitimizing authority through supporting government — by, for example, offering prayers for government success in securing order and justice (Fallding 1978). Significantly, America's new

---

approval among Roman Catholics. Only eight per cent of Canadians think the visit is a bad idea, largely because of the expense, estimated from $50 million upward. Another seven per cent say the visit is a good idea so long as taxpayers don't wind up with a big bill.

January 31, 1985
OTTAWA (CP) — More than three-quarters of Canadians of all denominations approved of Pope John Paul's September visit, but they remember the man more than his message, a Gallup poll released today indicates.

The poll, commissioned by the Canadian Conference of Catholic Bishops, found 77 per cent of respondents approved of the visit for a number of reasons, including the spirituality of the event and its unifying effect.

Of the 15 per cent who disapproved of the Pope's presence, 82 per cent cited the cost of the visit as the reason.

Residents of Atlantic Canada and Quebec showed more interest and support for the visit than did the rest of the country, says the survey, conducted in October, a month after the Pope's departure.

The survey estimated 10 per cent of Canadian adults, fewer than two million, attended a papal event or watched motorcades. That number is far lower than was originally planned for by church and security officials.

But 63 per cent of those surveyed said they followed the papal visit through television, newspapers or radio.

Father William Ryan, a general secretary for the conference, said the poll confirms that the visit "helped Canadians to take time out to think about important issues while at the

same time enjoying an historic and spiritually renewing event."

It now is up to the church to foster this interest, Ryan said in a statement. "The long-range effects (of the visit) are harder to estimate."

Sources:

Peter Calamai, September 8, 1984, and January 31, 1985.

## Protestants and Catholics at War

*The potential for religion to contribute to conflict has been dramatically illustrated in modern Northern Ireland. During a 1984 visit to Toronto, the Ulster Protestant leader Rev. Ian Paisley had this to say.*

TORONTO (CP) — Even if Irish Roman Catholics "wash their bullets in holy water," Rev. Ian Paisley says it won't stop him in his fight to keep Northern Ireland a part of the United Kingdom.

In an uncompromising address Sunday to a church delegation in Toronto, the hardline Ulster Protestant leader denounced the Irish Republican Army, which he said "is very busy carrying out a campaign of terror" in his homeland.

Paisley's visit to Toronto differs sharply from his last trip here in September, 1983, when he was part of a multi-party delegation that came to persuade Canadian businessmen to invest in the troubled Irish province.

During the visit, the outspoken head of the Democratic Unionist party deliberately avoided the strident tone and epithets for which he is known.

But on Sunday, unencumbered by economic commitments, Paisley was his usual self as he delivered a fiery sermon to the predominately Irish congregation of the Toronto Free Presbyterian Church.

The church is one of three Canadian fundamentalist congregations with close links to Northern Ireland. Paisley was instrumental in establishing the Free Presbyterian Church of Ulster in the 1950s.

Paisley said he hopes British Prime Minister Margaret Thatcher "will take the same stand in Ulster that she took in the Falklands and see to it that we are delivered from those that would bring us under the heels of a Roman Catholic-dominated state."

A member of both the British Parliament and the Northern Irish Assembly, Paisley acknowledged he is often accused of being a bigot.

But he defended himself by saying, "I'm a Protestant non-apologetic. . . . I believe that, as a Protestant, I'm entitled to make my protest against the system of Roman Catholicism."

He praised the recent action of members of the Toronto church, who passed out pamphlets during the Pope's visit to Canada which railed against the public having to pay costs of the pontiff's trip.

"I'm glad the church was able to make its protests in an uncompromising way," he said.

After the church service, Paisley refused to answer questions from reporters, saying, "I never give interviews on the Lord's Day."

---

"Christian Right" is calling not for revolution but for a return to "the values that made America great."

The primary reason for this pattern of religion reflecting culture is clear from our examination of the individual and interpersonal consequences of commitment. Culture seems to inform religion more than religion informs culture. The result, in the words of one Canadian theologian, is that religion has difficulty saying something to the culture that the culture is not already saying to itself (Hordern 1966). Rather than standing apart from culture, religion is typically coloured by culture — it represents culture's product rather than its source.

This pattern can be seen in the association between religion and social class. Since at least the time of Weber, social scientists have drawn attention to the relationship between class characteristics and religious ideas and practices. Niebuhr emphasized that the church-sect cycle is largely a response to economic deprivation and the ensuing social mobility. The religiously neglected poor, he said, fashion a new type of Christianity that meets their own distinctive needs, proceed to climb the economic ladder through the influence of religious discipline, and then "in the midst of a freshly acquired cultural respectability, neglect the new poor succeeding them" (Niebuhr 1929). His examples included the Quakers, the Methodists, and the Salvation Army. Observing religion in Alberta in the first half of this century, Mann (1962) noted that people living in the prairies preferred an informal and emotional expression of religion, in contrast to the structured and less personal style of eastern Canadians. New groups consequently arose in response to this need.

In like manner, Protestant, Catholic, and Jewish congregations have to the present day commonly displayed considerable class homogeneity. However alarming this may be to those who hold that churches should know the presence of people from all classes, it is nevertheless not surprising. As we saw in Chapter 2, when people interact, they tend to gravitate toward those who share a common lifestyle. We socialize with similar people, we date and marry those who are like us. We believe that common interests are of central importance in interpersonal relationships. Accordingly, when people meet to share their faith, they are most comfortable with people of a similar class (and often a similar ethnic) background.

One of the results of such a pattern is that supernatural imagery (our "mental pictures" of, say, God, Jesus, heaven, and hell), along with worship forms (hymns, prayers, sermons) come to be shaped along distinctive class lines. The "Lord Jesus" and "mansion over the hilltop" of the lower middle class are relatively foreign to the "Christ our Saviour" and "life eternal" of the upper middle class. In Berger's (1961) words, "Their ethics and aesthetics, not to speak of their politics, faithfully mirror [their] class prejudices and tastes."

The point here is that religion mirrors culture. To the extent that it does so, it gives supernatural endorsement to culture, and functions as social cement. But when certain segments of society develop ideas that challenge and oppose the dominant societal norms and attribute those ideas to a supernatural source, religion can be potentially divisive. There is good reason to believe that the dominant religious groups exercise considerable social control over the legitimation of ideas proposed by less powerful groups (such as the gay religious community's assertion that "God loves gay people too").

More than a few observers decry this inability of religion to rise above culture. Theologian Paul Tillich (1966) has written that religion "cannot allow itself to become a special area within culture, or to take a position beside culture." In describing the social roots of denominationalism, Niebuhr (1929) called such division "an unacknowledged hypocrisy, a reflection of the inability of churches to transcend the social conditions." Herberg (1960) stated that religion in America seems to possess little capacity for rising above national consciousness. "The God of judgment," he said, "has died." Berger (1961) has claimed that American religion is not unlike a nation-serving imperial cult, an unconsciously affirmed state religion.

Nevertheless, religion's inclination to mirror culture rather than to stand apart from it may be inevitable. If humans, however unintentionally, create religion in their own image, it is not at all surprising that religion leans toward personal and societal endorsement rather than toward personal and societal judgment.

## Religion: Its Future

Since social scientists first turned their attention to religion, they have been divided on the question of its future. Comte asserted that the world was experiencing an ever-increasing level of rationalism, with religious ideas progressively giving way to metaphysical and then to scientific modes of thought. Marx and Freud also thought religion was being replaced by reason, a movement that would usher in a superior quality of life.

Durkheim, on the other hand, was among those who believed that religion would persist. Religious explanations, he said, may be forced to retreat, reformulate, and relinquish ground in the face of the steady advance of science. Yet religion will survive, both because of its social sources and because of the social functions it serves (for an important discussion of the applicability of Durkheim's predictions to current new religious movements, see Westley 1978). This secularization/persistence debate has not diminished in recent years.

### The Secularization Argument

According to the proponents of the secularization argument, traditional religion has experienced a decline that parallels industrialization. The increase in specialized activities has led to a reduction in the number of areas of life over which religion has authority, including meaning. Such a trend can be seen in the church's loss of influence in Europe since the medieval period, or in the similar loss of authority experienced by the Roman Catholic Church in Quebec since approximately 1960.

Secularization further involves adopting an empirical/material outlook (the industrial world-view), whereby the individual's focus and commitment are given to the reality perceived through the senses. The correlates of social change (such as urbanization, urban growth, higher education, technological development, work-force participation, an emphasis on consumption, and the advent of mass media) are seen as factors that contribute to this secularization of consciousness.

## The Persistence Argument

Other observers, however, have questioned the reality of this posited decline of religion, arguing instead for its viability. There are various forms of the **persistence argument.** Davis (1949) has contended that because of the functions religion performs, its future is not in question. Although there is a limit to the extent to which a society can operate guided by illusion, says Davis, there is also a limit to the extent to which it can be guided by sheer rationality. He therefore argues that while religion will certainly experience change, including the birth of new sects, it is unlikely to be replaced by science and technology.

Similarly, Bell (1977) has argued that a return to the sacred is imminent. After three centuries of emphasis on the rational and the material, we are beginning to experience the limits of modernism and of alternatives to religion. "We are now groping for a new vocabulary whose keyword seems to be limits," says Bell. New religions, Bell predicts, will arise in response to our ongoing concern with the core questions of existence — death, tragedy, obligation, love.

Parsons (1964) notes that Christianity continues to flourish in the modern Western world, "most conspicuously in the United States." Specialization, he says, need not be equated with a loss of significance for religion. On the contrary, religious values have now pervaded society and religion is currently being sustained with unprecedented efficiency, precisely because religious organizations can concentrate on religion. He further sees "the individualistic principle inherent in Christianity" as contributing to religious autonomy. Individuals are responsible for deciding what to believe and with whom to associate in socially expressing and reinforcing commitment. Far from being in a state of demise, then, Christianity is for Parsons characterized by *institutionalization* and **privatization**.

For Greeley (especially 1972), secularization is a myth. Contemporary religion does indeed face secular pressures and is certainly unimportant for some people. But Greeley contends that such pressures and variations in commitment are not unique to our time, and expresses confidence in religion's future.

More recently, Stark and Bainbridge (1985) have argued that humans persist in having intense desires that require supernatural solutions. Because we want, for instance, to live forever, and because we can see all around us the immutable fact that we will one day die physically, we resort to ideas about God, heaven, and everlasting life as a way to "solve" the problem. Consequently, secularization is countered by sect-inspired revival and cult-initiated innovation. The result is not the end of religion but rather the replacement of some faiths and groups with new ones. Religion constitutes an ever-changing "marketplace." Rather than destroying religion, said Stark and Bainbridge, secularization stimulates it.

On the one hand, then, there are a number of social scientists who see industrialization and its specialization and empirical/material features as having a negative effect, largely irreversible, on religious commitment. On the other hand, there are observers who deny such a relationship. How industrialization actually influences religious commitment is still very much in question.

## The Preliminary Evidence

The debate over modern industrialization's relationship to religion clearly needs to be informed by cross-cultural data if industrialization's effect on religion is to be understood apart from specific societal idiosyncrasies.

**International Data.** In a significant summary of international Gallup poll data, Sigelman (1977) reports that religious commitment varies significantly between countries. Religious beliefs (and their importance to those who hold them) are highest in the developing Third World countries, and lowest in the highly industrialized western European countries such as Scandinavia, West Germany, France, and Britain, along with Japan (see Table 12-7). Consistent with the industrialization/secularization hypothesis, the commitment level of an increasingly industrialized Canada lies between these two extremes.

## Table 12-7. Religious Beliefs and Their Importance for Selected Countries and Areas

| | Beliefs: Very Important | God | Life After Death |
|---|---|---|---|
| India | 81% | 98% | 72% |
| Africa | 73 | 96 | 69 |
| Far East | 71 | 87 | 62 |
| Latin America | 62 | 95 | 54 |
| United States | 56 | 94 | 69 |
| Canada | 36 | 89 | 54 |
| Italy | 36 | 88 | 46 |
| Britain | 23 | 76 | 43 |
| France | 22 | 72 | 39 |
| West Germany | 17 | 72 | 33 |
| Scandinavia | 17 | 65 | 35 |
| Japan | 12 | 38 | 18 |

SOURCE: Compiled from Lee Sigelman, "Multi-nation surveys of religious beliefs," *Journal for the Scientific Study of Religion* 16(1977):290.

Stark and Bainbridge (1985), however, having carried out extensive research in the United States, Canada, and Europe, provide data confirming their hypothesis that cults will abound where conventional churches are weakest. Yet their evidence for cult viability is based almost exclusively on the presence of cult headquarters and centres, rather than on data indicating that these groups are making noteworthy numerical inroads into national populations. Until such new movements have embraced the nonreligious, the secularization thesis has not been seriously challenged. While these international findings do not exclude the possibility of a return to religion, as envisioned by Davis and Bell, at this point, the data appear to support the secularization thesis. Certainly no clear-cut, contrasting return to religion is currently visible.

There is one important exception to this general relationship between societal industrialization and religion — the United States. In that country commitment levels remain high. Yet according to such writers as Herberg (1960), Berger (1961), and Luckmann (1967), the United States may not be exempt from the effects of industrialization. While outwardly still alive and well, American religion does give considerable evidence of being secularized not only from without but also from within.

These observers argue that religious organizations are being increasingly infiltrated by American culture, with the result that secularization does not stop at the church steps.

But this process works both ways. Religion has historically been strongly embedded in American ideology and continues to play a significant role in powerful nationalistic tendencies — a phenomenon that Bellah (1967) and others have referred to as **American Civil Religion**. As Herberg (1960) has put it,

*Americans, by and large, do have their "common religion" and that "religion" is the system familiarly known as the American Way of Life. . . . By every realistic criterion the American Way of Life is the operative faith of the American people.*

As a result, says Herberg, "To be a Protestant, a Catholic, or a Jew are today the alternative ways of being an American." More recently, Mauss and Rokeach (1977) have argued that

*any comparisons between the United States and other countries in religious matters must take into account the unique part that religion has played in the history of the United States. . . . In America, a declaration of belief in some kind of deity is little more than an affirmation of the national heritage. [This is why] belief in deity can easily coexist, as it always has in America, with continuing increases in educational levels and in scientific advancements.*

However, even in the United States, mainline denominations have suffered considerable membership losses since the 1960s. Some observers have argued that prior to that time institutional religion in America prospered because the values expounded by Protestants, Catholics, and Jews were consistent with conservative political and family values (Nelsen and Potvin 1980). With the post-1960s shift in values, religion is no longer experiencing its previous level of "establishment." Instead, an increasing level of "disestablishment" has been found, especially among the affluent young. This shift has so far had the greatest impact on the affluent, educated, culture-affirming mainline denominations. But the trend will eventually spread to the more theologically conservative denominations as well (Hoge and Roozen 1979). In sum, relative to other countries, religion in the United States continues to flourish, though it does give evidence of experiencing the secularizing tendencies of modern industrialization.

**The Canadian Situation.** We have already observed that to varying degrees Canadians assert belief in God, claim to pray and to experience God, believe in the divinity of Jesus, and maintain that there is life after death. The *Project Canada* surveys have further documented widespread interest in supernatural phenomena more generally. For example, almost one in three Canadians find astrological claims to be credible, some 60 percent think ESP exists, 63 percent believe some people have special psychic powers, 58 percent think they themselves have experienced premonition, 51 percent claim they have experienced telepathy, and only one in three rules out the possibility that we can communicate with the dead (Bibby 1987). Supernatural beliefs and practices are alive and well in Canada.

Yet as noted earlier, when asked point-blank, only about 40 percent of Canadians say that they are committed Christians, with just half of these people exhibiting the conventional belief/practice/experience/knowledge kind of commitment conceptualized by Glock and Stark. The precise content of the religion of the other half is unclear. A mere 2 percent claim to be committed to religions other than Christianity. The remaining 60 percent of the population consists of the uncommitted (40 percent) and the nonreligious (20 percent). You will recall that on a given weekend only one in three people across the country can be found in churches or synagogues.

It appears on the surface that commitment to established religion is not high, and that the religious situation in Canada represents fairly open territory for new competitors. Thus it is that Hexham, Currie, and Townsend (1985) have written that "a market exists for new religious movements in Canada to fulfill needs which many people do not see traditional churches meeting." But looks can be deceiving. Invariably, the question asked is, "Where are the dropouts going?" Some observers have thought that the dropouts are joining new religions. However, only about one percent of Canadians claim to be strongly interested in such activities and groups as Transcendental Meditation, Hare Krishna, the "Moonies," Eck-

ankar, and Scientology. And less than half of those who express strong interest are actually participating in any groups. The possibility that interest and involvement are transitory is suggested by the finding that almost another three percent of Canadians say that they were at one time (but are no longer) strongly interested in one or more of the new religions. A recent related study of new-religion participation in Montreal found that, although participation is high, adherents typically establish peripheral ties with groups and then drop out (Bird and Reimer 1982). Toronto psychiatrist Saul Levine (1979) suggests that the large cult dropout rate may in part indicate that cult values that initially seem to present attractive alternatives to mainstream cultural values — for example, group identification versus individualism, sharing versus competition, and spiritualism versus materialism — are found to be impractical in the long run.

A recent examination of the claims of Stark and Bainbridge has also uncovered little support for their suggestion that cults have made significant inroads (Bibby and Weaver 1985). The analysis focused on people who come from homes where their parents claimed no religious affiliation. It found that, over their lifetime, about one in three has adopted a religious tie. This affiliation, however, has typically been with mainstream Catholic or Protestant groups, rather than with a cult. In addition, panel data involving "religious nones" (Sociologists' term for those who answer "none" when asked "What is your religion?" in a survey or census) followed from 1975 to 1980 found that one-third had relinguished their unaffiliated status by 1980 but, as with the parental "nones," were now claiming Catholic or Protestant — rather than cult — ties.

The numbers of adherents to new religions are small, and are expected to remain so in the foreseeable future. Hexham, Currie, and Townsend (1985) acknowledge that as of the mid-1980s this country of 25 million had only about 700 full-time Scientologists, 450 Hare Krishna members, 350 to 600 "Moonies," and 250 Children of God.

Other observers have argued that such conservative Protestant groups as Baptists, Pentecostals, and Nazarenes — commonly referred to as "evangelicals" — are picking up large numbers of the newly "unchurched" (or "unaffiliated").

There is little evidence to support such an assertion. Nationally, conservative Protestant groups currently comprise about seven percent of the population; in 1871, that figure stood at eight percent.

Still others, like Parsons, maintain that religion is now taking a less visible, privatized form. The problem with this assertion is that such personal expressions of religion are very difficult to locate. Perhaps more seriously, with the possible exception of the 20 percent who exhibit nontraditional commitment to Christianity, at least 60 percent of Canadians claim no commitment whatsoever — private or otherwise.

If not the new religions, the evangelicals, or private forms, then the choice of the religiously inactive, some say, must be the obvious remaining option — no religion. At first glance, support for this assertion does appear to exist. In 1971, only about four percent of Canadians told the census-takers that they had no religious preference. By 1981, that figure had risen to seven percent. However, the analysis of "religious nones" mentioned earlier found that most are single and young. As these people marry and have children, many of them leave the "none" category and adopt a Catholic or Protestant affiliation. That affiliation, very significantly, is usually the same one as their parents'. Most appear to reaffiliate not out of spiritual urgency but out of the need for rites of passage pertaining to marriage, the baptism of children, and death. The newly reaffiliated tend to be nominal in their beliefs and practices. The result is that within a short number of years, more than one in three "religious nones" join the 90 percent of Canadians who claim Protestant or Catholic ties.

In short, the search for religious dropouts in Canada yields an intriguing result: few have actually strayed far from their roots. Indeed, as noted earlier, almost 90 percent of Canadians with Catholic parents remain Catholics, as do some 90 percent of those with Protestant parents. Denomination by denomination, there is remarkable stability between generations — about 75 percent for United Church affiliates, 70 percent for Anglicans, and 65 percent for Protestants (conservative and otherwise). The figure for non-Christian religious groups is about 80 percent. Even in the "no religion" category, some 65 per-

cent of offspring remain, like their parents, unaffiliated (Bibby 1987).

Clearly, religious group identification is valued in this country. But it is equally clear that Canadians differ considerably in the role they want religion to play in their lives. Some embrace it wholeheartedly, seemingly as a system of meaning that informs much of their lives. Others want some beliefs, some practices, some specialized services. Still others — a small minority — want nothing from religion or religious organizations.

It may well be that the significant religious development associated with the industrialization of Canada has not been the abandonment of religion. Instead, perhaps, it has been a tendency for Canadians to reject Christianity as an authoritative system of meaning, in favour of drawing on Christian "fragments" — selected beliefs, practices, and organizational offerings — in a highly specialized, consumer-like fashion. In a similar manner, Canadians select fragments of other non-naturalistic systems — astrology, ESP, and so on — without adopting the entire system. In the words of Stark and Bainbridge, these systems become "consumer cults."

While the churches might decry such selective consumption, over time they have in fact responded to this consumer mentality. In the face of consumer demand, Canada's main established groups — the Roman Catholics, the United Church, Anglicans, and conservative Protestants — have been offering increasingly varied "religious menus." The charismatic movement, which provides people with a pentecostal style of faith (that is, one that emphasizes spiritual gifts like healing and speaking in tongues), embraces more than one in ten Protestants and three percent of Roman Catholics and Anglicans (Bibby 1987). The United Church Renewal Fellowship, organized nationwide, represents an effort to change the church spiritually from within, and is particularly attractive to those who are evangelically minded. The social activists in the major denominations have not lacked for interest groups encouraged by the church; groups have focused on such issues as nuclear disarmament, human rights, poverty, and equality of the sexes. Churches have even been patient with the individual who wants minimal involvement. They seldom withhold basic rites of passage from such people, deny them occasional admission to services, or remove them from membership rolls.

Thus it is that today's Catholic, Anglican, United Church member, or conservative Protestant in Canada typically has the option of being detached or involved, agnostic or evangelical, unemotional or charismatic. Switching, even to the "none" category, rarely takes place, because it has become increasingly unnecessary. One can find what one wants — in whatever quantity, ranging from a lot to a little to virtually nothing — in the familiar confines of the tradition in which one was reared. Contrary to the assertion made by Stark and Bainbridge, the Canadian "religion market" actually appears to be very tight. The diversifying of functions by Canada's religious establishment has in fact made it extremely difficult for new rivals to penetrate the country's "religion market."

The stability of the religious scene in Canada, along with its prevalent "fragment" style, has been further documented by a national survey of teenagers aged 15 to 19 (Bibby and Posterski 1985). This survey has found that the country's "emerging generation" differs negligibly from adults when it comes to religion. Approximately 90 percent of teenagers claim the same group affiliation as their parents, with only about 2 percent indicating any strong interest in the new religions (see Table 12-8). Belief, practice, experience, and knowledge levels are similar to those of adults. Interest in other supernatural phenomena is also very high.

Yet when it comes to commitment, almost the same proportion of teens as adults — some 60 percent — claim not to be religiously committed. Only about one in four attends religious services regularly, with less than 10 percent of Canadian teens saying that they receive a great deal of enjoyment from church or synagogue life (including only 25 percent of the regular attenders). At the age of 15, 30 percent are going to services frequently; by the time they are 19, that figure drops to about 15 percent, a level of attendance similar to that characterizing adults 18 to 29 years old.

Like their parents, however, young people are not angry with the churches. A two-thirds majority indicate that they have a high level of confidence in church leaders, similar to the degree of confidence they accord educational, scientific, and judicial leaders. Moreover, they infrequently make religion a target of humour. The dominant ten-

## Table 12-8. Religiosity of Canadian Teens and Adults

| Dimension | Teenagers | Adults |
|---|---|---|
| **BELIEF** | | |
| God | 85% | 83% |
| Divinity of Jesus | 85 | 79 |
| Life after death | 80 | 65 |
| Communication with dead | 36 | 22 |
| Some have psychic powers | 69 | 63 |
| Astrology claims are true | 37 | 35 |
| **PRACTICE** | | |
| Pray privately | 46 | 53 |
| Read the Bible | 17 | 25 |
| Attend religious services | 23 | 25 |
| Watch religious programs | 8 | 20 |
| Read horoscope | 54 | 39 |
| **EXPERIENCE** | | |
| God | 44 | 42 |
| **KNOWLEDGE** | | |
| Peter denied Jesus | 41 | 46 |
| **SELF-IMAGE** | | |
| Religiously committed | 39 | 45 |

SOURCE: Derived from Reginald W. Bibby, "Project Can85," 1986 and "Project Teen Canada," 1985.

dency is to draw selectively from religion, rather than allow it to become an all-embracing system of meaning. Churches, whether they like it or not, are faced with a reality that involves not suffering wholesale membership dropouts but rather serving as identification groups for large numbers of Canadians who want to choose selectively from what they have to offer.

It may well be that the structural and cultural changes associated with the industrialization of Canada have made meaning systems that encompass all of an individual's life incongruent with the varied roles people must play. Expressed another way, fragments are perhaps more functional than all-encompassing religions in a society that requires people to compartmentalize their experience in order to play a number of diverse roles. Religious systems may also frequently seem at odds with dominant cultural values such as rationalism, consumption, and enjoyment.

So people do not choose belief, practice, and service fragments over systems because there are no appropriate systems. Rather, we choose fragments because they are more conducive to present-day life. As Wilson (1975) put it, modern societies offer "a supermarket of faiths: received, jazzed-up, homespun, restored, imported and exotic. But all of them co-exist because the wider society is so secular, because they are relatively unimportant consumer items."

If this theory is correct, the "fragment" pattern should not be unique to Canada, but should instead be typical of other highly industrialized countries that have known the historical dominance of one or more major religions. Indeed, this appears to be the position of British sociologists Roy Wallis and Steve Bruce (1984) as they view Europe and beyond. They write that people both inside and outside religious groups "synthesize various selections to suit their own tastes. New ideas are simply added to the sum total of legitimate ideas; there is no possibility of producing a neat, coherent set of dogmas" (Wallis and Bruce 1984).

As in Canada, it seems likely that the future of other highly industrialized societies will not lack for the presence of religious fragments. Whether fragments will become meaning systems, religious and otherwise, will depend largely on major changes in the structural and cultural makeup of those societies.

## SUMMARY

1. Sociology uses the scientific method to study religion, in contrast to religion itself, which explores reality beyond what can be known empirically.
2. The sociology of religion has been strongly influenced by the theoretical contributions of Marx, who stressed the compensatory role of religion in the face of economic deprivation; Durkheim, who emphasized both the social

origin of religion and its important social cohesive function; and Weber, who gave considerable attention to the relationship between ideas and behaviour.
3. Religion can be defined as a system of meaning that uses a supernatural referent to interpret the world. Humanist perspectives make no such use of the supernatural realm, attempting instead to make life meaningful.
4. Personal religious commitment has increasingly come to be seen as having many facets or dimensions, with four being commonly noted: belief, practice, experience, and knowledge.
5. Collective religiosity instils and sustains personal commitment. The theologically centred church-sect typology has been increasingly abandoned in favour of organizational analyses that examine religious collectivities in the same manner as other groups. In Canada, organized religion has experienced a considerable decline in participation in recent years, a trend that has critical implications for commitment at the individual level.
6. The variation in levels of individual commitment characteristic of complex societies has led to explanations that emphasize individual and structural factors. Reflection, socialization, and deprivation have been prominent among the individual explanations, while the dominant structural assertion has been the secularization argument.
7. The key source of religious commitment that emerges in an industrializing Canada is socialization. Due to the highly secular milieu in which religious socialization efforts must take place, such efforts are decreasing in both incidence and impact.
8. Religion appears to be at best one of many paths leading to valued characteristics such as personal happiness and compassion.
9. While religion sometimes has a disruptive impact, it more commonly seems to contribute to social solidarity, frequently mirroring the characteristics of groups and societies.
10. Historically, observers of religion have been divided on its future, asserting both secularization and persistence hypotheses. Internationally, the secularization argument appears to have substantial support.

11. The search for alleged religious dropouts in Canada reveals that few have turned to new religions, conservative Protestant groups, privatized expressions, or the "religious none" category. Most still identify with established groups.

12. The apparent paradox of widespread beliefs and practices existing alongside relatively low commitment suggests that many people in Canada find it functional to draw selectively on religion, rather than to embrace it as an all-encompassing system of meaning. Such a pattern is to be anticipated in highly industrialized societies more generally.

## GLOSSARY

**American Civil Religion.** Tendency for nationalistic emphases in the United States to have many characteristics similar to religions; established Judeo-Christian tradition is drawn upon selectively.

**Church–sect typology.** Framework, dating back to Weber and historian Ernst Troeltsch (1931), that examines religious organizations in terms of ideal-type, church, and sect characteristics.

**Collective conscience.** Durkheim's term for the awareness that the group is more than the sum of its individual members; norms, for example, appear to exist on a level beyond the consciences of individual group members.

**Collective religiosity.** Religious commitment as manifested in and through religious groups; key to the creation and sustenance of personal religiosity.

**Denominationalism.** Tendency for a wide variety of Protestant religious groups to come into being, seemingly reflecting variations not only in theology but also — and perhaps primarily — in social characteristics.

**Dimensions of religiosity.** Various facets of religious commitment; Glock and Stark, for example, identify four — belief, experience, practice, and knowledge.

**Humanist perspectives.** Systems of meaning used to interpret the world without a supernatural referent (for example, communism, scientism).

**Industrial world-view.** Outlook associated with industrialization and characterized by empiricism (the limiting of reality to what can be known through the senses) and materialism (the commitment of one's life to the pursuit of empirical reality).

**Persistence argument.** Assertion that religion will continue to have a significant place in the modern world, arguing either that it has never actually declined, or that people can absorb only so much rationality and materialism.

**Personal religiosity.** Religious commitment at the level of the individual.

**Privatization.** Parsons's term for people's alleged tendency to work out their own religious beliefs and associations in an individualistic, autonomous manner.

**Profane and the sacred.** Two categories into which Durkheim claimed all things are classified by human beings; the sacred represents those things viewed as warranting profound respect, the profane encompasses everything else.

**Protestant Ethic.** Term (associated with Weber) that refers to the emphasis placed by Calvin, Luther, and other leaders of the Protestant Reformation on the importance of work performed well as an indication of living one's life "to the glory of God"; key characteristics include diligence, frugality, and rational use of time.

**Religions.** Systems of meaning used to interpret the world that have a supernatural referent (for example, Christianity, Hinduism, astrology).

**Secularization argument.** Assertion that religion as it has been traditionally known is declining continuously and irreversibly.

## FURTHER READING

**Bibby, Reginald W.** *Fragmented Gods: The Poverty and Potential of Religion in Canada.* Toronto: Irwin Publishing, 1987. This book pulls together the work of the author and of others and offers an interpretation of the nature and role of religion in Canada.

**Chalfant, H. Paul, Robert E. Beckley, and C. Eddie Palmer.** *Religion in Contemporary Society.* 2nd edition. Palo Alto, CA: Mayfield Publishing, 1986. A sociology of religion textbook that covers the field in a comprehensive and readable manner.

**Clark, S.D.** *Church and Sect in Canada.* Toronto: University of Toronto Press, 1948. A Canadian classic that examines the social factors contributing to the rise of different types of religious groups in this country.

**Crysdale, Stewart, and Les Wheatcroft (eds.).** *Religion in Canadian Society.* Toronto: Macmillan, 1976. One of the few available works dealing with the social scientific study of religion in Canada; contains articles by leading scholars in sociology, anthropology, and history.

**Niebuhr, H. Richard.** *The Social Sources of Denominationalism.* New York: Henry Holt and Company, 1929. A classic attempt to probe the role of social factors (for example, economics, nationality, race, region) in creating denominationalism in Europe and America.

**Westhues, Kenneth (guest ed.).** *Canadian Journal of Sociology* 3 (Spring), 1978. A valuable collection of articles by leading academics, comparing organized religion in Canada and the United States. Groups include mainline and conservative Protestants, Roman Catholics, Jews, Mennonites, and Mormons.

# CHAPTER 13

# Polity

HARVEY RICH

It is election day in Canada. As night falls, ballots are counted across the country. From east to west the polls are closing, in one time zone after another. Depending on how closely matched the major parties are in terms of number of seats won, that evening or early the next morning television and radio newscasters will relay the election results: the government has lost power, is barely clinging to power, or has retained power. If another party has received a mandate to govern, we will be told that the transfer of power will be taking place in the coming weeks. The outgoing prime minister uses the opportunity to remind the nation that popular sovereignty means that power ultimately rests with the people. Taking defeat philosophically, he or she congratulates the successor and says "The people are always right" or words to that effect.

## Power in State and Society

Political sociologists are highly skeptical of two assumptions about power that are found in the foregoing scenario. The first is that power resides completely in the government or state. The second is that the government gets all its power from the people, who may take it back at the next election. Political sociology arose in the nineteenth century as a reaction against such a state-centred view of power. While power is the core concept in political sociology, the government is not the only power centre, nor even necessarily the most important one.

**Government is only one of a number of power centres in modern societies.**

There are countries on every continent in which the military uses its control of the instruments of violence to overthrow governments not to its liking. In communist countries, it is not the incumbents of the office of prime minister and the council of ministers who wield the most power. Instead, it is the Communist Party's general secretary and supporters on the politburo and central committee who make the big decisions and get them implemented by their control of the party apparatus. In Third World countries, it is often the large landowners who can dictate the terms of their co-operation, without which governments founder. In the industrially advanced capitalist societies, those who own and/or control the very large corporations have a privileged position (Lindblom 1977).

Business, particularly big business, expects to be consulted over decisions that will affect business operations. Big business can retaliate with a slowdown on investments if policies detrimental to its interests are advanced. This would result in higher rates of unemployment, lower consumer spending, and an economic recession. The governing party would then face a bleak future at the next election.

## The Two Revolutions

We live in the shadow of two great revolutions — the democratic revolution and the **industrial revolution** (Giddens 1987). They have shaped the modern world. The democratic revolution received concrete expression in the late eighteenth century in the French and American revolutions. The leaders of both revolutions testified to the fundamental equality of all mankind in contrast to the inequalities in the hierarchy of ranks based on birth that had existed in much of Europe for centuries and had been partially transplanted to the British North American colonies.

On the other hand, the industrial revolution generated new inequalities based on a new economic system: **industrial capitalism**. Factories and large cities were built where none existed before. These cities contained an overwhelming majority of wage workers, most of whom were impoverished and lived in overcrowded, filthy slums.

Over the past century, it has been the tension between the pull toward equality of the democratic revolution and the push toward inequality associated with industrial capitalism that has been the source of conflict and compromise in Canada and other societies with similar politico/economic systems.

## Four Perspectives

Except for short intervals, conflict theory has dominated political sociology since its inception in the nineteenth century. Over the past two decades, it has become the leading intellectual influence among Canadian political sociologists. Karl Marx (1818–1883) and Max Weber (1864–1920) are the intellectual giants among conflict theorists. [This chapter follows Collins (1985) in viewing Weber as a contributor to the conflict tradition in sociology. — ED.] They are also considered the founders of the field of political sociology. Rather than choosing between them, we will compare the ideas of one with those of the other after a brief examination of two other perspectives.

### Structural Functionalism

The functional model (described in Chapter 1) has been applied to politics. It views society as a system of interdependent parts. One such part, politics, is interrelated with other aspects of society, such as its economy and its system of social stratification. According to this perspective, the polity fulfils certain functions for society. The polity can be seen as an aspect of the division of labour through which the various parts of the social sys-

tem exchange specialized services. In Parsons's model of the social system, the polity's task is the goal-attainment function (Parsons and Smelser 1956). This is echoed in Porter's (1965) assertions that the political system is the means through which the collective goals of a society can be achieved.

Individuals are integrated into the polity by internalizing the values and norms of the political culture. Functionalists have focused on the process of political socialization to explore the ways in which political loyalty to the **status quo** is created in individuals and groups. Political deviance is a result of imperfect political socialization, according to this view, and may be the source of political change. Political change is to be understood in relation to changes in other parts of the social system: Political structure is generally a dependent variable. For example, a certain level of economic development is seen as a prerequisite of democracy (Lipset 1960). Collins (1968) concludes that structural-functional theory does not treat politics as a source of change. Structural-functional theory applied to political studies first became popular in the 1950s and 1960s. Its appeal can be related to the following factors:

1. The conceptual scheme associated with Talcott Parsons (1951), a structural-functional theorist at Harvard University, brought the promise of a truly scientific status for sociology, including political sociology. S.M. Lipset (1963) employed Parsons's pattern variables to systematically analyze central value differences between Canada and the United States. The results were the subject of intense controversy for two decades and ensured that structural-functional theory became well known in Canadian political sociology (Brym 1986). (See Chapter 2 for details of this controversy.)

2. During the late 1950s and 1960s, the study of non-Western societies mushroomed. The study of the political systems of the newly independent nations of Africa and Asia became a high priority of government agencies, and of foundations offering research grants, particularly in the United States. The emphasis on functions in the structural-functional perspective was considered to be of great value in studying so-

cieties with less differentiated institutions. For example, the absence of a separate institution for dealing with conflict does not mean that the adjudication function (centred in the courts in Western societies) does not exist. It is to be found elsewhere, for example in the role of the patriarch within kinship groups. Almond and Coleman (1960) signalled to political scientists that structural-functional theory was "where the action is."

3. The bias in structural functionalism in favour of equilibrium and stability fitted in with the optimism prevalent in the 1950s and early 1960s: many North Americans believed that we had already achieved the "good society." The continually rising standard of living, high educational attainment levels, and increasing life expectancy led to a widespread sentiment that we need more of the same, that change is risky, that it would be better not to "rock the boat." Many of the architects of post-war political sociology had become Marxists during the Great Depression of the 1930s, when it seemed that capitalism was indeed in an incurable crisis,

just as Marx had predicted. They were later disillusioned when it became apparent that the communist regimes in the Soviet Union and its eastern European satellites were as oppressive as the anticommunist Western press had portrayed them. For many political sociologists, this disillusionment manifested itself in a swing toward conservatism and the adoption of functional theory in place of Marxism.

## Symbolic Interaction

The symbolic-interaction perspective is opposed to the emphasis on macro systems at the level of whole polities. Instead, the emphasis is on process and on the interaction of individuals and groups of political actors (Charon 1979). In symbolic-interaction theory, power is viewed as control over the actions of others in order to achieve one's goals. The instruments of power include naked force, the manipulation of symbols and information, and persuasion. Authority is based on a shared commitment to collective goals and on a knowledgeable consent by members of the col-

---

## Put Out More Flags

*This article, which appeared in a British publication, shows how national symbols can be used to unite or divide a polity.*

If you happen to live in an industrial area there is one thing to be said for the slump; it's a lot quieter at night. As more and more factories, foundries, and mills close or go onto short time, the great clangings, bangings, and hisses that used to emanate from them and resound through the surrounding terraced streets until all hours exist now only in the memory.

   Walking through one such district the other night the only sound I could hear was a low chattering. I asked a passerby what it was. "Sewing machines," he replied. "But I thought the textile trade was worse off than

most," I said. "Certainly, every dress shop and gents' outfitters I pass seems to be having a closing down sale." "Too true," he answered, "but that place is making flags for the Royal wedding in July."

   A few inquiries quickly showed that this was no isolated case. Right across the country the flag makers are working at full belt. From large firms with contracts to decorate The Mall and Constitution Hall, down to back street workshops turning out tiny tatters of red, white, and blue for tiny tots to wave at village fetes, the trade has not been so good since the British Empire was wound up in the fifties and sixties.

   Then they shared with the fireworks manufacturers in the great bonanza of orders that poured in from Tanzania and Togoland, Ceylon and the Seychelles. The present boom will

inevitably be shorter but it promises to be nearly as sweet.

   Oddly enough flags, like fireworks, seem to have originated in China. There are records showing that the founder of the Chou dynasty (1122 B.C.) had a white flag carried in front of him wherever he went. Further, a low relief sculpture on the tomb of one Wou Leang T'sue of the Han dynasty, who died around 200 B.C., depicts cavalrymen with small flags on their lances. From China the use of flags seems to have travelled to India and the Middle East. Mohammed's followers carried black banners and it is generally assumed that the Crusaders who went to fight for the Holy Land copied the idea from the Saracens. This would seem to explain why the motif on most early European flags was a cross in one form or another.

lectivity to the orders given by office-holders. The processes of power and authority include bargaining and negotiating, control of information flows, and symbolic mobilization of support (Hall 1972).

The symbolic interactionists are in opposition to structural functionalism and to the Marxist perspective on conflict theory. But there is some similarity between the Weberian orientation to conflict theory and symbolic interaction. Both share a rejection of the concept of society as a system. Instead, the emphasis is on individuals, groups, and concrete political units, such as organizations, struggling with and against each other.

## Conflict Theory (I and II)

In the 1960s and 1970s, the pendulum swung away from the celebration of the status quo toward a desire for social and political change. University students played a leading role in what came to be known as the **"new left" movement**. Intellectually, the opening to alternative futures was reflected in a turn toward conflict theory, which remains the dominant theory in political sociology. There are two major forms of conflict theory, one associated with Karl Marx and one with Max Weber. Each will be described separately and then compared to the other.

**Conflict Theory I: Karl Marx.** It was the genius of Marx to see through the outward appearance of legal equality in democracies like Canada's and to reveal, with painstaking clarity, the underlying inequalities generated by the new economic order, industrial capitalism. Briefly stated, Marx exposed the seamy side of the democratic revolution. Unlike serfs, wage workers were free to change jobs or refuse to work altogether. But freedom to starve is not real freedom. Anatole France, the great French satirist, caught the gap between formal legal equality and the underlying economic inequality when he noted that "under the majestic laws of France the rich as well as the poor are forbidden to sleep under the public bridges or to beg in the streets."

Having toppled the feudal lords and freed the serfs, the capitalists gave an enormous impetus

---

From the Middle Ages on, the significance of flags grew and their making and meaning developed into a vast complex of lore and laws inextricably bound up with chivalry and heraldry. Firm rules governed their design, display, and even their size. Henry VIII laid it down that a king was entitled to eight yards, a duke seven, an earl six, and a baron five. The flag of a knight bachelor was a pennon which had swallow tails. To mark a deed of valour on the battlefield the kind could, if he chose, cut off the swallow tails, converting it into a square banner and promoting its owner into a Knight Banneret or, as we have it nowadays, a baronet. A similar association between flag and rank lies behind the term ensign. It was originally applied to a British junior officer whose duty it was to carry the ensign or flag. It is obsolete here now, but the American navy still uses it.

Civilians can sometimes be as fascinated by flags as soldiers and sailors. They are called Vexillologists, a term coined from the Latin vesillum, a military standard, by Mr. Whitney Smith, formerly professor of political economy at Boston University and believed to be the only full-time professional vexillologist in the world.

There are Flag Institutes in America, Britain, and many other countries, including Czechoslovakia, and Mr. Smith keeps them in touch with one another through a quarterly magazine, the Flag Bulletin, which he edits from the Flag Research Centre in Massachusetts. He explains this worldwide interest by pointing out that more than half the independent nations have designed and adopted their national flags since the last war. Not only that, but they keep changing them. Syria changed its flag four times in 13 years, while Zanzibar had as many in only 18 months.

For most civilians, however, interest in flags tends to wane between periods of national crisis or celebration. Flags seem only to get into the news when some drunken holiday-maker unwittingly insults the symbol of his host country, when planning authorities object to some over-enthusiastic display of them, or when controversies break out in conservative newspapers about when, where, and how they should be displayed on public buildings. And I would be surprised if a whole new controversy is not even now brewing up about the expense in the present hard times of those now being feverishly sewn together in readiness for July 29. As so often happens a device intended to unite people ends up dividing them.

**Source:**

Harry Whewell, *Manchester Guardian,* April 12, 1981.

to the system of production. But this great achievement rested on the exploitation of wage workers. These workers were crowded into factories. Their labour as appendages of machines was dehumanizing. The increasingly severe contradictions of capitalism, the waste involved in production for profit not for use, and the deadening work that so many have had to endure have led Marxists to assert that it has long been time to ring down the curtain on capitalism. Capitalism has been diagnosed as being on its death-bed on many occasions. Ruling classes, Marx argued, always outlive their usefulness. Having completed their historical role of raising the level of the **forces of production** to new heights, the capitalists wish to maintain the now obsolete property system on which their wealth and power rests.

Yet in the advanced capitalist societies the process of technological innovation continues. Economic growth, especially after World War II, has brought a rising standard of living to the working class. Marxists have tried to account for the survival of capitalist society by focusing on the expanding role of the state in stabilizing the economy and on the role of the schools, the mass media, and advertising in disseminating the bourgeois ideology that keeps the working class confused about its real interests (see Chapter 8).

The Marxist theory of social change asserts that when a ruling class has outlived its usefulness, a revolutionary movement will arise that will banish it to the history books and open the way to epoch-making changes. The contrast between the world the bourgeoisie made and the feudal society it vanquished is enormous. But *historical materialism* (the formal term for the Marxist theory of social change just described) promises even greater changes — changes that will dwarf the accomplishments of the bourgeoisie. Under communism, there will no longer be private ownership of the means of production. This will signal the end of exploitation for all time. Instead of alienation, there will be autonomy. Instead of decisions based on the interests of the rich and powerful, there will be consensual authority based on reason. After a short transition period, classes will cease to exist. No new social conflicts will replace class struggle.

The end of class conflict will make it possible for the first time to base decisions on the public interest rather than on the interests of one class. The removal of a property system that limits the development of the forces of production will quickly result in an unprecedented rise in the standard of living. Necessary labour time will be so drastically reduced that the entire population will devote much of each day to what they wish to do, not to what they must do to earn a living. The Marxist vision of a communist society has inspired many millions of people to participate in struggles to turn the vision into reality.

**Conflict Theory II: Max Weber.** Compared to this radiant scenario, Weber's expectations for the future are rather gloomy, although not totally without hope. He saw the liberal values that he held dear, especially freedom of the individual, as imperilled, and his concern was to safeguard, at least for a few, the autonomy intrinsic to the heroic age of the bourgeoisie. The spread of bureaucracy (see Chapter 10), which threatened to enslave the population in deadening routines, could not be stopped. But its negative consequences could be checked, Weber believed, by strengthening the power of elected politicians over appointed officials. Maintaining a separation between the polity and the economy would prevent a "dictatorship of bureaucrats."

In the political sphere, Weber urged institutional changes that would encourage people of ability, energy, and ambition to go into politics. In competition with other aspirants to political office, those who pass the test of charismatic leadership (see Chapter 10) by a successful conquest of the masses on the "electoral battlefield" will master the bureaucracy and effect changes in accordance with their political vision. In small groups and among outstanding individuals, the flame of freedom will continue to burn.

Whatever injustices and inequalities people endure, Weber contended, cannot be attributed to capitalism. They are the price we must pay for a high standard of living for the masses. Weber argued that to collapse the two power centres — the state and the economy — into one, as Marx suggested would result in a new and unprecedented despotism. Weber saw politics as the struggle to influence the distribution of power in a society. The existing configuration of power is the temporary product of an ongoing conflict among contending organizations and groups, of which the state is but one.

**Marx and Weber: A Comparison.** Marxists can argue that the kind of radical social change Marx had in mind has not yet occurred anywhere. Never mind that Marx expected a successful proletarian revolution (which never came) several times in his own lifetime. Marxists consult a different calendar. It is divided into epochs, which sometimes last for many centuries. A single century is not especially significant on this time scale.

Moreover, according to Marxists, the Marxist regimes that currently claim to be building socialism in various parts of the world are misusing the term. They are backward societies — economically, politically, and culturally. In this way the theory is safeguarded and the vision of achieving "true" socialism sometime in the future is preserved.

Weber and Marx both considered that the democracy attainable in capitalist society fell far short of the claims made for it. However, their reasons for thinking so were very different. For Marx, the capitalists as a ruling class use the state, democratic or otherwise, to preserve their property rights and, more generally, to serve as a conservative force in support of their vested interests in safeguarding corporate capitalism. But the end of capitalism and the abolition of classes would mean that socialist societies would constitute the first genuine democracies. Rule by a political elite would give way to mass participation. This is the Marxist view.

Weber did not see any hope at all for genuine democracy — that is, government by the people — in modern societies. Going even further, he enunciated "the principle of the small number" (Weber 1968). The mass, Weber claimed, is always disorganized, ignorant of the issues, and lacking in communication skills. But just the opposite is true of the few who comprise the political elite. Marxists disagree, arguing that this pessimistic view turns what is only a stage in history into a timeless and universal condition. Weber's pessimism has some foundation in the epoch of capitalism and class struggles.

Weber described ideal types of authority, pure cases that are aids to the study of political systems (see Chapter 10). In practice, all existing authority structures are mixed cases. In modern mass democracies, important elements of both *charismatic* and *legal-rational* authority are found. We can see the innovative force of charisma in the work of the politician who has a following, controls the party machine, and through demagogic appeal, wins over the masses in an election. Elections for Weber are votes of confidence. Their function is to provide a superior method of selecting leaders and of replacing those who have made serious mistakes. They serve to legitimate and thereby strengthen the power of the leader. We can see the legal-rational element in the civil service bureaucracy, which provides the continuous administration of government business according to established rules and procedures.

The disappointing outcome of revolutions led by Marxist parties that have culminated in totalitarian dictatorships, has compelled Marxists to rethink their theory. To argue that Marx would have rejected much that is done in his name by Marxist regimes misses the point. Did Marx provide adequate intellectual tools and moral scruples with which to struggle against such outcomes as Stalin's tyranny in the Soviet Union? The answer to this question, sadly, is no.

Similarly, the victory of the Nazis in Germany compels us to reassess Weber's political theory. The Nazis got more votes than any other party in the 1932 elections (Hamilton 1982). Hitler's effectiveness as a charismatic leader (see Chapter 10) while he ruled Germany from 1933 to 1945 is not in doubt. He was genuinely popular. Hitler boasted, and many Germans agreed, that his was both a legal and a national revolution. He never actually abolished the **Weimar constitution**, which in 1919 had established a republic with guarantees of civil liberties. Instead, he simply circumvented it by using "emergency powers." Weber died in 1920. Hitler became Chancellor of Germany in 1933. There can be little doubt that Weber would have found Hitler's regime repugnant, despite his charismatic leadership, his use of plebiscites to give the German people the opportunity to renew their confidence in him, and his restoration of Germany to the status of a great power. Weber was a liberal; constitutional government and due process of law were for him fundamental values. Did he compromise these values in his consuming concern for effective leadership? The answer to this question, sadly, is yes. As one commentator has written, "When [Weber] argued that it is the charismatic qualification of leaders which matters whereas the democratic institutions are a mere functional machinery in their hands, he overstated his own case and came dangerously close to the *Fuehrerprinzip*, the Fascist leadership principle" (Mommsen (1974).

So neither Marx nor Weber, the two founders of political sociology, left us adequate guidelines for strengthening and extending our democratic institutions. Since they view our polities as necessarily limited to **bourgeois democracy** — that is, democracy that serves the capitalists — Marxists have questioned whether there is anything worth preserving in our political institutions. Weber, half a century after Marx, saw democracy as limited to a device used by charismatic leaders to legitimate their rule.

Lipset (1961), the leading American political sociologist, and Porter (1965), the leading Canadian political sociologist, adopted Weber's conception of democracy as entailing the formation of a political elite in competition for the votes of a largely passive electorate. Bachrach (1967) coined the term **democratic elitism** for this view of mass democracy.

# The State and Violence

## Defining the State

In Weber's famous definition, the state is an association that successfully claims a monopoly on the legitimate use of force within a given territory (Gerth and Mills 1958). The threat of force is usually sufficient to secure the lawful conduct of most citizens. The use of force occurs more frequently in societies where loyalty to the state is fragile. Secession attempts on the part of an ethnolinguistic, religious, or racial minority that is concentrated in one region can seriously threaten the territorial inviolability of the state. Military rule is widespread in countries in which the army is frequently called upon to restore order, and the subordination of military chiefs to civilian rulers is not firmly established. There is a longstanding tradition in a number of Latin American countries for senior military officers to push aside civilian rulers in a *coup d'état*, which, they claim, is their patriotic duty to avert a state of anarchy. There have been similar political overthrows in some post-colonial African and Asian countries where internal unity has been fragile.

## Violence and Democracy

A democratic society faces a dilemma when a group uses violence to achieve its goals. The October 1970 crisis in Canada is a case in point. The Front de libération du Québec (FLQ) advocated the use of violence to achieve the goal of independence. One FLQ cell kidnapped James Cross, the British Trade Commissioner; subsequently, another cell kidnapped (and later murdered) Pierre Laporte, the provincial Minister of Labour for Quebec. Small in number, and convinced that independence for Quebec would not come without the use of violence, these people acted from a deep ideological commitment that was born of desperation. (The FLQ members were also inspired by the struggles for independence, often involving violence, of national liberation movements in Africa and Asia.) The federal government invoked the War Measures Act, which gave police and army units virtually unlimited power to remove people from their homes and imprison them without laying any charges. These emergency powers suspended many of the civil liberties that we cherish as our birthright. Ostensibly, they were invoked because of what the law would define as "an apprehended insurrection." That should mean that there was a conspiracy to topple the legitimate government of Quebec and seize the reins of power. Neither at the time nor since has any evidence been made public that any such conspiracy actually existed. This was the first use in peacetime of the sweeping powers granted by the War Measures Act. Most of the people rounded up in the early morning hours and hustled to the nearest jail were released days or weeks later without any charges ever being laid. A democracy cannot afford repetitions of this kind of overreaction without endangering public trust or rendering citizens too intimidated to exercise their rights of freedom of speech, assembly, and association.

## Quebec: Ballots Instead of Bullets

Threats to the sovereignty of the state are not always settled through the use of force. The largest of the independence movements in Quebec, the Parti Québécois, won the provincial election in 1976. In keeping with its election campaign pledge, it conducted a referendum in 1980, asking for a mandate to negotiate with the federal government for *sovereignty association*: that is, a sovereign Quebec in economic association with the rest of Canada. That mandate was rejected by a vote of 60 percent to 40 percent. It is uncommon in human history for matters involving the territorial integrity of a nation-state to be settled by ballots instead of bullets. Jane Jacobs (1980) provides another rare example, the separation of Norway from Sweden in the early twentieth century.

# The Canadian Polity

## Plural Elites or Ruling Class?

The most influential work in Canadian political sociology is John Porter's *The Vertical Mosaic: An Analysis of Class and Power in Canada* (1965). Porter's basic conceptual approach bears many similarities to Weber's. It is critical of Marxism. Porter states that the capitalism that Marx studied no longer exists. The working class is fragmented. Instead of class struggle, we have a power conflict among **elite** groups that form the top decision-makers in the main institutional orders in society. Bureaucratic organization facilitates decision-making by a small group. Given the extent of institutional specialization, (as in the state and corporate administrative elites) these elites are not interchangeable. This means each elite has some autonomy from the others. They are in competition with each other for opportunities to acquire more power. They also co-operate with one another to deal with situations that affect them all. This type of power structure corresponds to the model of **plural elites**.

Porter contrasted the pluralist society, in which elites compete for power, with the **totalitarian so-**ciety, in which power is concentrated in a single elite. In a totalitarian society, the various institutional elites are unified by the dictatorship exercised by top leaders of the ruling party. No other parties are permitted. Examples are Nazi Germany (1933–45) and Soviet Russia, particularly during Stalin's tyranny (1929–53).

Marxists use the concept of the **ruling class** to explain the connection between economic power and the political power that inevitably goes with it. In a capitalist society, the ruling class is the capitalist class, those who own and control productive property. The requirements of a capitalist economic system set limits on what the government of the day can do, regardless of which party gets a mandate to govern. That is why Marxists (and other radicals) are so insistent on the need to *change* the capitalist system and so impatient with "mere reforms" that leave the foundations of capitalism intact.

Porter's elite studies were mostly conducted in the 1950s and early 1960s. He concluded that the **corporate elite** in Canada was more powerful than the political, labour, bureaucratic, or ideological elites. However, Porter held to a different interpretation from the Marxist one: the political elite, he argued, *could* be the most powerful, using its power as a resource for achieving national goals. According to Porter, it was by default and not by necessity that the corporate elite extended its power into other institutional spheres. Only when the political elite is sufficiently powerful to have its will prevail can we speak of a democratic society, for it is the only elite that is accountable to the citizens in periodic elections.

In his emphasis on the independent role of the political system, Porter tied his theoretical perspective to Weber rather than to Marx. Weber held very strongly to the view that politics is not subordinate to economics. Since the political elite is the only elite that requires a popular mandate, its decisions have greater legitimacy than those of the other elites. Porter's emphasis on the importance of "creative politics" that would change Canadian society echoes Weber's vision of the politician whose goals for the nation transcend the economic interests of any class.

Porter's own vision for Canadian society is stated clearly: "If power and decision-making must always rest with elite groups, there can at least be open recruitment from all classes into the elites" (1965). Elsewhere Porter considered the possibility of a more radical vision of participatory democracy (1961), but he did not give it more than a passing reference in *The Vertical Mosaic*.

In his study of each elite group, Porter focused on the class origins of elite members. First, he set out to determine whether Canada provides equality of opportunity to reach the top without being helped or hindered by social background. He claimed that the extent to which such equality of opportunity exists indicates the extent to which talent is being used in the society studied. He further maintained that the extent of social homogeneity within the elites would alert us to the extent of ideological bias common to the various elite groups.

Porter concluded that membership in the elites (with the exception of the labour elite) was largely limited to those from upper- and upper-middle-class backgrounds. The likelihood of coming from an upper-class background was greatest within the corporate elite. Some sociologists have criticized Porter's methodology for exaggerating the extent of inequality of opportunity (Brym 1986); others point out that researchers using a similar methodology have arrived at different conclusions regarding the structure of power in Canada.

For example, Clement's (1975) data on the corporate elite are similar to Porter's, but his interpretation of the data differs in important respects. Clement interpreted the data to support the Marxist theory of the ruling class. He concluded that the corporate elite dominates decision-making in the economic system and shapes the dissemination of ideas through ownership of the mass media. The interests of corporate capitalism take precedence in the relations between government and business. A similar conclusion is reached by Olsen (1980) in a study focusing on the state elite (the political, bureaucratic, and judicial elites combined) in Canada. But Porter rejected the Marxist theory of the ruling class. He emphasized the creative role of politics and of political institutions as a means of achieving the major goals of society. The implications of accepting one or the other theory are great. The Marxist theory of the ruling class subordinates politics to economics. The interests of the economically dominant class prevail in the political arena as well as in the marketplace. Elections are mostly important for keeping the populace in the dark about where power really lies.

Are elections mere charades in which nothing substantial will change, regardless of which party gets a mandate to govern? According to Marxist theory, even if a left-wing but non-Marxist party like the New Democratic Party should become the government, it would not threaten the dominant position of the capitalist class. On the other hand, according to Porter's theory of plural elites (1965, 1970, 1979), elections can result in significant social change. The political elite, receiving a mandate for change from the electorate, can introduce sweeping reforms in spite of opposition from entrenched economic interests.

## Bureaucracy

An outstanding contribution to understanding modern society was made by Weber in his classic essays on bureaucracy. Writing in the early twentieth century, Weber was the first to understand the implications of the irreversible growth of bureaucracy in government, the economy, and other institutions in modern societies. The common features of bureaucratic organizations are presented in Chapter 10. Our concerns here limit us to the state bureaucracy.

The belief that elected politicians make policy decisions and civil servants carry them out remains deeply ingrained in our conception of democratic government. It is crucial to the survival of democratic government that competing teams of politicians, leading their respective parties, appeal to the electorate at regular intervals for a mandate to govern. To enable such a change in government to take place without disrupting government services, career civil servants stay at their posts and continue to operate the bureaucratic machinery. And we continue to give lip service to the supposed neutrality and anonymity of civil servants and to the principle of **ministerial responsibility**. But more and more senior civil servants are willing to admit (anonymously of course) that there exists a widening gap between rhetoric and practice. Occasionally, politicians also speak openly of this problem. In support of a major reorganization of the Ontario government to relieve some ministers of departmental responsibilities, one cabinet minister concluded that "the majority of ministers . . . [were] turning into mere approvers" of policies that emanated from the civil service (Ontario Legislature 1972).

## Sources and Limits of Bureaucratic Power

Weber's praise for the technical superiority of bureaucratic organization over all other types of organization was fulsome. He was filled with scorn for those who would do away with bureaucracy and replace it with direct democracy. The standard of living of citizens in modern society, he asserted, depended on the reliable provision of expert services of all kinds. Weber was fully aware of the difficulties involved in keeping the bureaucracy subordinate to elected government leaders: "Under normal conditions, the power position of a fully developed bureaucracy is always overpowering. The 'political master' finds himself in the position of the 'dilettante' . . . facing the trained official who stands within the management of administration" (Weber 1958).

In his general sociology, Weber stressed the inevitable growth of bureaucracy in the modern state. But in his political writings, Weber stressed the distinction between the elected politician and the appointed official. Weber's contribution to the sociology of organizations addresses the issue of efficiency. In his political sociology, he addresses the issue of bureaucratic power. Here we must emphasize that Weber was not committed to the democratic values of political equality or popular participation. The notions of any significant dispersion of power to the masses or control over policy by the people seemed illusory in the extreme in the "Age of Bureaucracy." Weber was a "liberal in despair" (Mommsen 1974). He believed in limited government and due process of law, at the same time insisting that strong leadership is essential if politics is to remain an autonomous sphere, especially in the face of powerful economic interests.

Toward the end of a lifetime of studying politics in his homeland (Germany) as well as elsewhere (Britain, Russia, the U.S.), Weber concluded that the real choice in modern complex societies was between *leadership* democracy and *leaderless* democracy. Charismatic politicians win over the masses on the strength of personal qualities; once granted a mandate to govern they must demonstrate that they deserve the public's confidence or face defeat at the next election. This type of leadership democracy would give leaders the strength to control the career officials and to resist surrendering to powerful interest groups. The voters-at-large are not expected to understand policy issues and should keep quiet between elections. All that is required of or permitted to them is the act of voting every four or five years for the political leader with the greatest personal appeal (Beetham 1974; Mommsen 1974). Leaderless democracy refers to a state of affairs in which there is uninspired rule by officialdom in the absence of effective political leadership. Weber saw this as the case in his homeland, Germany, and criticized the situation relentlessly until his death in 1920.

## Bureaucracy and Social Change

Other perspectives on the tendency of bureaucrats to value administration over politics give a more important role to elections than Weber did. Lipset (1968) has concluded that serious tension between cabinet ministers and their senior officials is more likely to occur when a party proposing major reforms first receives a mandate to govern. This is what happened in Saskatchewan in 1944 (Lipset 1968). The Co-operative Commonwealth Federation (CCF), a democratic socialist party, won a resounding mandate at the polls to introduce sweeping reforms. This was the first victory of a socialist party in North America above the municipal level. Most of the cabinet ministers had no administrative experience in a large organization. When the "political bosses" were told by their deputy ministers (the nonelected career officials) that a proposed policy could not be implemented because it was impractical, they felt no recourse but to withdraw it. There were complaints at party conventions about the interminable delay in realizing some of the policies for which the party had campaigned. In response to these complaints, some deputy ministers were transferred out of politically sensitive positions.

## "Would the minister not agree?"

The Employment Development Fund is one of the mechanisms by which the Ontario government attempts to create a favourable economic climate for investment by industry and to keep unemployment rates low. But some have asked whether industry has taken unfair advantage of governments' willingness to subsidize it by playing individual governments off against each other, and by locating in the jurisdiction of the highest bidder.

For example, on May 24, 1979, the Ontario government announced that it would provide TRW Canada Limited, which manufactures parts for automobile steering systems, with a grant of $420,000 through its Employment Development Fund to expand its plants in St. Catharines and Tillsonburg. At the time, Mr. Bradley, MPP for St. Catharines, replied that "helping healthy companies is not a credit to you. . . . They've expanded already." When given an opportunity to pose a question at Queen's Park a few days later, Bradley had this to say:

*In view of the fact that I attended a sod-breaking ceremony in St. Catharines on April 6, four days before the announcement of the Employment Development Fund in the provincial budget on April 10, and in view of the fact it was known in business*

*circles months before the budget was brought down that TRW was to establish a plant outside of St. Catharines, would the minister not agree the expansion is taking place as a result of favourable markets being taken advantage of by a capable management and a competent work force? Would the minister not agree that . . . the $420,000 really represents a windfall to TRW?*

This was one of several grants given to what were considered well-established industries in Ontario in the spring of 1979. Political journalist Hugh Winsor was the first critic to call this bribery:

*Of course, there is nothing illegal in giving away taxpayers' money in this fashion. Indeed, there is some suggestion that Mr. Grossman is doing a good job of it, if you are convinced that that is the only way companies are going to be persuaded to do what it is in their interest to do anyway. There is an important question of policy involved here and Ontario is in a genuine dilemma because it is competing with other jurisdictions that have also been drawn into the auction.*

Those who support the government funding of private industry would say that the policy question is whether or not governments should allow companies to go to other jurisdictions,

while those against this practice would say that the question is whether or not the government should take money from the have-nots, through taxation, and give it to the haves.

A survey conducted by the *London Free Press* in 1981 to follow up on the results of this grant found that instead of creating new jobs, the money was invested in capital expenditures, such as equipment, which later sat idle because of the downturn in the economy. The results of the newspaper's survey showed that "of five Southwestern Ontario companies which shared more than $1 million in direct grants from the Ontario Employment Development Fund, none was able to report the government aid had increased employment."

**Source:**

Legislature of Ontario Debates, No. 52, Third Session, Thirty-first Parliament, pp. 2121–2122; Legislature of Ontario Debates, No. 58, Third Session, Thirty-first Parliament, p. 2375; Hugh Winsor, "Sweet deals questioned," *Globe and Mail*, May 29, 1979; Gordon Sanderson, "Ontario's job creation program a dismal flop," *London Free Press*, March 7, 1981.

Others were demoted. A few were dismissed. In the end, some positions in government agencies were classified as exempt from civil service appointment procedures. Political values compatible with those of the government became a condition of appointment, together with the usual qualifications of education and experience.

## The Electoral System and Political Parties

North American political sociology achieved recognition as a distinct academic field only after

World War II. It accomplished this by focusing on the social aspects of politics and leaving the study of formal government institutions to the political scientists. By the early 1960s, the two orientations were cross-fertilizing each other. Political science underwent what has been termed a "behavioural revolution," after which it focused more on the actions of individuals and groups in various political arenas and less on formal government institutions. At about the same time, political sociologists such as Lipset (1963) acknowledged that the electoral system itself can affect voting patterns just as socioeconomic status and other sociological variables affect party formation and voting behaviour.

Canada has what amounts to a two-and-a-half-party system. The two major parties, Liberal and

Progressive Conservative, are the only ones that have ever formed a government at the national level. A number of **third parties** have also been represented in Parliament, but have never formed a government. In 1921, the Progressive party won 65 seats, the largest number ever for a third party. The Social Credit party held the balance of power in the minority government of 1962–63. The longest-lasting third party, the New Democratic Party (NDP) — along with its predecessor, the CCF — has had elected members in the Canadian House of Commons since 1935, and held the balance of power in the minority government of 1972–74.

## The Single-Member Plurality System

A critical factor in voting patterns is the nature of the electoral system. A **single-member plurality system**, in which the candidate with the most votes (not necessarily a majority) wins the seat, tends to result in a two-party system. This is the type of electoral system we have in Canada, both federally and provincially. Since it is "winner-take-all" in each constituency, the party that can muster a significant edge in the popular vote overall will usually win more seats than the opposition parties combined, even though it gets considerably less than a majority of the votes cast. In federal elections, the party with the largest share of the votes cast has rarely gotten a majority of the popular vote. But it does usually win a majority of the seats in the House of Commons. For example, in the 1988 federal election the Progressive Conservative party obtained a substantial majority of the seats with only 43 percent of the popular vote. The advantages of this type of electoral system are twofold. The usual outcome of elections is a majority government; this is seen as contributing to political stability. And the election of a member of parliament for each geographically demarcated constituency promotes two-way communications between citizens and a specific lawmaker, the MP who represents them. So goes the conventional wisdom. Critics point out that a minority government does not necessarily spell political instability. They point to the two successive minority governments that presided from 1963 to 1968, and note that some very important legislation was passed during this period — for example, the Health Care Insurance Plan (the scheme that supports provincial health insurance plans

**Party discipline in our parliamentary system means that most of the time MPs vote the party line.**

through transfer payments; popularly known as medicare), the Canada Pension Plan, and the Canada Assistance Plan (which served to promote greater equality in welfare payments across the provinces). It was also during this period that the lawmakers finally agreed on a distinctive Canadian flag. The critics also note that party discipline in our parliamentary system means that most of the time, MPs vote the "party line" regardless of what their constituents' — or, for that matter, their own — views might be. They also note that greater ease of communication and the development of regional offices for many agencies spell the decreasing importance of the MP as the link between the citizen and government.

## Proportional Representation

**Proportional representation**, in which each party gets seats in proportion to the overall percentage of the popular vote it obtains, tends to result in a multi-party system and coalition governments. The advantage of this type of electoral system is that the representation of political parties in parliament reflects the support of each party among the electorate. There are no "wasted votes" such as occur in the single-member plurality system. Since the establishment of the State of Israel in 1948, elections of the *Knesset* (the country's parliament) have been based on proportional representation. It is as if the entire country is one constituency. Each government formed after an election has been a coalition government. This has resulted in small parties gaining a far greater influence on government than their support among voters would suggest, since the withdrawal from the coalition of some of the small parties can bring down the government.

## Third Parties

The two major political parties in Canada (the Liberals and the Progressive Conservatives) have not received as much attention in academic studies as have various third parties. Particular interest has been shown in third parties that originate as social movements, a phenomenon that has occurred most frequently at the provincial level. With the important exception of Quebec, victorious third parties are concentrated in Western Canada. Agrarian social movements seeking to redress the grievances of farmers successfully contested elections in Alberta, Manitoba, and Ontario within a year or two of 1920. The movements were short-lived in Ontario, but established a long-lasting tradition of third-party government in Alberta and Manitoba.

The Great Depression saw the birth of the CCF, which in 1961 became the NDP. Although its influence remained relatively small at the federal level, a provincial wing won a stunning electoral victory in Saskatchewan in 1944. Over two decades of government, the party set the pace for social reform, spurring both the federal government and the other provinces to institute changes. In Quebec, the Union Nationale party governed from 1936 to 1939 and from 1944 to 1960 on a platform of provincial autonomy, in alliance with traditional elites such as the Catholic Church. More recently, the Parti Québécois — close to the NDP on socioeconomic reform issues, but also strongly committed to independence for Quebec — governed from 1976 to 1985. The Social Credit party has governed British Columbia from 1952 through 1971, and since 1975.

In the Canadian federal system, the entrenched powers of the provinces provide an opportunity for political parties that lack the broad support to be serious contenders for electoral victory nationwide, to form the government in a province. This has been the source of much of the dynamism in Canadian politics, particularly since these third parties frequently arise out of movements for social change. Even when third parties fail to get a mandate to govern, elected governments will often try to placate voters by introducing legislation that cuts into the potential electoral strength of a third party. In Canada, Liberal governments have time and again cut into the electoral appeal of the left-wing New Democratic Party (and its CCF predecessor) with new social welfare legislation when public opinion polls have shown support for such moves. There is more than a grain of truth in the observation by former Prime Minister Louis St. Laurent that the CCF were "Liberals in a hurry."

## Canada in Comparative Perspective

How does the Canadian political system compare to American and British politics? The Canadian system is similar to the British parliamentary system in that the governing party must retain the confidence of parliament to remain in office. Party discipline in both nations is strictly enforced on pain of expulsion from the party caucus, losing whatever office(s) one holds, and possibly not receiving party funds in the next election campaign. Legislators are released from these constraints only in specific cases in which they are permitted to "vote their conscience." Examples in recent times are the debates regarding capital punishment and new abortion legislation.

But Britain has a unitary political system. Sovereignty resides fully in the British Parliament. Canada has a **federal system**, with powers divided between the national and provincial governments. Britain is a more homogeneous society. Scottish and Welsh nationalist movements have not had anything like the political impact that ethnolinguistic and regional conflicts have had in Canada. The attempt to impose the British parliamentary system in Canada, on a population that is highly dispersed geographically and that has differing and often opposing economic interests from region to region, has resulted in much

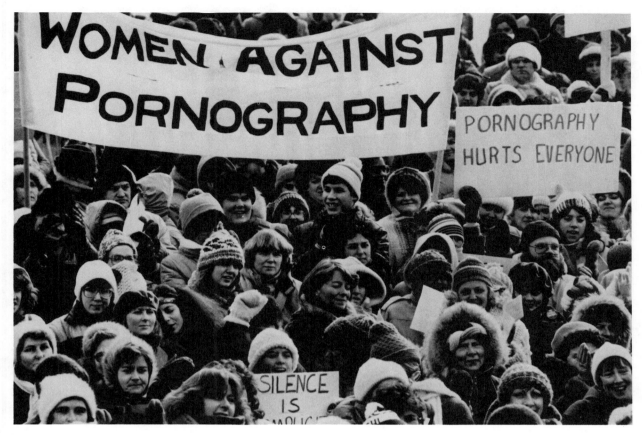

**Interest groups are groups that have a specific social or political cause.**

friction and deadlock. Consider the fact that it took the federal and provincial governments 55 years and endless conferences to reach sufficient agreement to patriate the British North America (BNA) Act — since renamed the Constitution Act — in 1982, and to come up with an amending formula and the Charter of Rights and Freedoms. This historic move inaugurated a new chapter in Canadian independence. Prior to 1982, it was required that a bill be introduced in the British Parliament to change our own constitution!

The American federal system handles national and state government entrenched powers quite differently, using built-in checks to limit the concentration of power in any one branch of government. The American Constitution was specifically designed to curb tendencies toward despotism on the part of the chief executive. It originated as a

response to the British interferences with self-government in the 13 colonies that had precipitated the War of Independence (1776–83). Congress, as the legislative branch, has jealously guarded its prerogatives ever since. Although the president can veto legislation, Congress can override the veto by a vote of at least two-thirds in both chambers. Membership in the House of Representatives is based on population. The Senate has two seats for each state. This means, for example, that a state with scarcely half a million residents has the same representation as California, which has a population more than 50 times that size.

In Canada, by contrast, the executive and legislative functions are combined in the leadership of the victorious party, so long as it retains the confidence of the House of Commons. Unlike the United States Senate, ours is based on unequal

**It took the federal and provincial governments 55 years and many conferences to reach sufficient agreement to patriate the BNA Act in 1982.**

representation; that is, provinces with bigger populations have more senators. Moreover, senators are appointed by the government of the day. Because Liberals have governed for much of the past 25 years, there are currently more Liberals in the Senate than there are Progressive Conservatives. However, the Senate's powers are largely limited to delaying the endorsement of legislation passed by the House. In this respect, it resembles the British House of Lords more closely than it does the American senate.

Provinces with smaller populations are alienated from the political system by the fact that one or both of the largest provinces, Ontario and Quebec, can decide elections. For example, each riding in Alberta elected only Progressive Conservative candidates in five successive federal elections from 1972 through August 1984. But with the exception of the nine-month Progressive Conservative minority government in 1979–80, all the

Alberta MPs sat on the opposition benches. The number of Alberta MPs is less than the number of MPs from the Toronto area alone. It is not surprising, then, that there is strong support in Alberta for a revitalized Senate with representation arrangements resembling those in the U.S. — that is, on a provincial rather than on a population basis. This would bring it closer to the U.S. senate.

## Voting

Much of the post-war development of political sociology has taken the form of voting studies. In part, this is due to the availability of election outcomes and public opinion surveys in quantitative form, which facilitates the testing of hypotheses. It is also related to the fact that elections are an important aspect of the political system in liberal democratic societies.

Voting studies have been inspired, in part, by Marxian hypotheses regarding the links between class and party support. As this connection manifests itself in the industrially advanced capitalist democracies, it has been referred to as "the democratic class struggle" (Lipset 1960). Generalizing from voter preference surveys in many countries, Lipset concluded that lower-income voters in manual and service occupations disproportionately support parties on the left, while higher-income voters in white-collar occupations disproportionately support parties on the right. Left-wing parties promote the further development of welfare services, financial assistance to enable the children of low-income families to attend university, and subsidized housing. They also favour high income-tax rates for the rich and for corporations. Right-wing parties promote the market as the most efficient and fairest system to determine economic outcomes. Interference with the market, they maintain, should be avoided unless there are compelling reasons for such interference. They argue that providing a favourable economic environment for investment will result in strong economic growth, which means more jobs and a higher standard of living. This is known as the "trickle-down theory." A favourable environment for investment may initially benefit the rich, but it will eventually benefit nearly everyone.

Some of the western European voting surveys showed a strong relationship between class and party preference. Britain provided one of the classic examples of this pattern until recent times, when class-based voting has begun to decline.

When survey research was undertaken in the early 1960s, it was concluded that there was very little class-based voting in Canada (Alford 1963). Subsequent studies have led to a reconsideration, based on a critical analysis of the early studies (Brym 1986):

1. The position of Canadian political parties on class issues was incorrectly determined. The Liberals and the NDP were both classified as leftist. The Progressive Conservatives were classified as rightist. Subsequent studies revealed flaws in this placement from several points of view. The main change was to move the Liberals to a rightist position.

2. The class position of individuals was wrongly determined. The manual/nonmanual distinction is misleading for an advanced capitalist society such as Canada. Rather, the principal cleavage is between blue-collar and routine white-collar workers on the one hand and those in intermediate and higher white-collar occupations (including the professions) on the other.

3. The *subjective class vote* (voting for the party one perceives to be in favour of one's class interests, regardless of what the party's record actually shows) in Canada is significantly greater than the *objective class vote* (Ogmundson 1975).

4. The determination of where an occupation belongs in the social stratification hierarchy is an important decision that can significantly affect the perceived level of class-based voting. Some cases are ambiguous and require careful consideration.

With appropriate revisions based on the above factors, the relationship between class origin and voting behaviour in Canada is similar to that found in the United States. Compared to many other advanced capitalist societies it is weak. But this discovery has been helpful. We no longer need to account for the Canadian case as *the* anomaly, the only case where politics and class are not closely connected, among the industrialized societies. Instead, we can focus research on North American "exceptionalism" (Myles 1979). Why is class a less important influence on politics in Canada and the United States compared to most western European countries? The short answer is that there are less rigid class barriers in Canada and the United States. Neither country experienced the rigidities of status associated with the feudal system, which existed in many European countries for centuries and left a lasting legacy of inequality of opportunity well into the twentieth century (Chapter 8).

## SUMMARY

1. Government is only one of a number of power centres in modern societies.

2. In industrially advanced capitalist societies, business occupies a privileged position. Business leaders make decisions that are as im-

portant for the wellbeing of society as the decisions made by government.

3. The democratic revolution initiated a movement toward equality in modern societies. The capitalist economic system that arose out of the industrial revolution has generated long-lasting inequalities. The wide-ranging consequences of both revolutions persist. Thus, they provide checks on each other's effects.

4. The dominant perspective in political sociology is conflict theory. The ideas of Marx and Weber continue to influence the development of conflict theory, albeit in different directions.

5. Structural functionalism is not as dominant as it was in the two post-war decades (1945–65). This perspective figured prominently in John Porter's *The Vertical Mosaic*, the most influential book in Canadian political sociology.

6. Symbolic interaction has not as yet had a significant impact on studies of the Canadian polity. But the use of symbols in a variety of forms, including the mass media, is of great importance in the political process. So the neglect of symbolic interaction relative to other perspectives is likely to be only temporary.

7. The Canadian polity has been studied from the vantage point of the Marxist theory of the ruling class as well as the neo-Weberian emphasis on plural elites. Since these perspectives are opposed to each other, further research is urgently needed if we are to move beyond ideological polemics.

8. While elected politicians do govern, the role of higher civil servants in the decision-making process is undeniable. Bureaucratic power is here to stay. The only question is whether it can be kept within reasonable limits.

9. Electoral systems are as important as social and economic variables in shaping election outcomes. Canada's single-member plurality system has resulted in two major parties, one of which has formed the government after each election since Confederation.

10. Voting studies have revealed that the relationship between class background and voting behaviour is weak in Canada compared to many western European countries, including Britain. Canada is similar to the United States in this regard.

## GLOSSARY

**Bourgeois democracy.** The view held by Marxists that government policies in a capitalist society necessarily favour the bourgeoisie — that is, the capitalist class. This is so even in polities with universal voting rights.

**Corporate elite.** Those who sit on the boards of directors of the largest corporations and financial institutions.

**Democratic elitism.** Idea that the most important function of mass participation in politics is the formation of a political elite, the members of which compete for the votes of a largely passive electorate.

**Elite.** A relatively small number of persons who occupy the key decision-making positions in an institutional sphere.

**Federal system.** Political system in which entrenched powers are divided between a central government and subcentral governments. In Canada, the latter are called provinces.

**Forces of production.** A Marxist term for the resources, both natural and human, and for the technology typical of a particular economic system.

**Industrial capitalism.** Economic system in which productive property (for example, factories) is privately owned and goods and services are produced for profit.

**Industrial revolution.** The changeover, occurring first in Britain, to an economic system marked by widespread use of high-energy technology and inanimate sources of energy.

**Ministerial responsibility.** Principle that cabinet ministers in a parliamentary system are held accountable for the actions of civil service officials in the departments over which the ministers preside.

**"New left" movement.** A largely student-centred movement in many Western societies in the 1960s and early 1970s that emphasized participatory democracy (in contrast to the state-centred views of what adherents called the "old left"). In both cases, a socialist society was the goal.

**Plural elites.** Situation in which the elites in each of the major institutional spheres remain sufficiently autonomous to enable them to check each other's power and compete for additional power resources.

**Proportional representation.** Electoral system in which each party is allotted seats according to the percentage of the popular vote it receives.

**Ruling class concept.** Idea that the economically dominant class has the overriding influence on government policies; a central tenet of Marxist theory.

**Single-member plurality system.** Electoral system in which the candidate with the most votes wins the seat in each constituency, and the number of seats won by each political party is determined on a constituency-by-constituency basis.

**Status quo.** The existing state of affairs.

**Third parties.** In Canada, any party contesting an election other than one of the two major parties that have formed the government and the official opposition, changing places from time to time, since Confederation.

**Totalitarian society.** A one-party state that exercises control over all institutional spheres and mobilizes mass participation in the building of a new social order.

**Weimar constitution.** Document drawn up in Germany following World War I that abolished the monarchy and established in its place a republic with a popularly elected president and a two-chamber parliament.

## FURTHER READING

**Dahl, Robert A.** *A Preface to Economic Democracy*. Berkeley: University of California Press, 1985. A critique of the insulation of the economy from processes of democratization that have taken place in the polity in industrial societies.

**Lindblom, Charles E.** *Politics and Markets*. New York: Basic Books, 1977. A lucid account of the privileged position of business in capitalist democracies.

**Niosi, Jorge.** *Canadian Capitalism: A Study of Power in the Canadian Business Establishment*. Toronto: James Lorimer, 1981. A neo-Marxist analysis that challenges some of the conclusions reached by radical sociologists regarding the changes in Canadian capitalism since World War II.

**Panitch, Leo (ed.).** *The Canadian State: Political Economy and Political Power*. Toronto: University of Toronto Press, 1977. A collection of essays on the Canadian power structure by Marxist social scientists.

**Porter, John.** *The Vertical Mosaic: An Analysis of Class and Power in Canada*. Toronto: University of Toronto Press, 1965. Part II, "The Structure of Power," provides insights into distinctive features of the Canadian polity from a sociological perspective.

**Wrong, Dennis.** *Power: Its Forms, Bases and Uses*. Oxford: Basil Blackwell, 1979. A conceptual analysis of power; includes some of the controversial issues in contemporary political sociology.

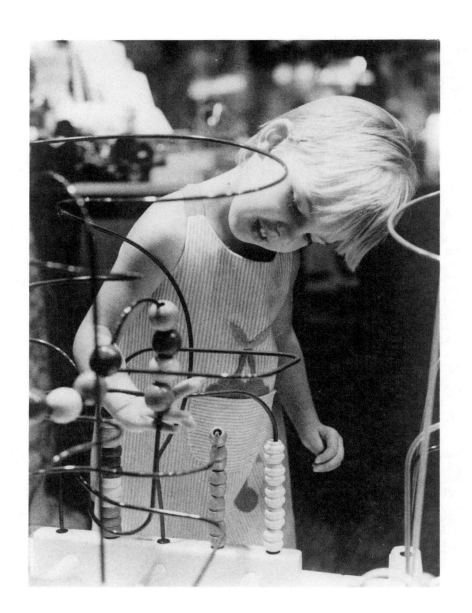

# CHAPTER 14

# Education

JOS. L. LENNARDS

Education is an institution that affects us all. By law we are compelled to attend school for at least ten years, but the great majority of young people in Canada spend more than this required minimum in school. From kindergarten to high school graduation, the average young Canadian currently spends about 17 000 hours in school. In addition to this, a substantial segment of the young population pursues further full-time education at the post-secondary level. Going to school is such a regular part of growing up that it seems difficult to imagine how the socialization process could take place without it. Recall from Chapter 3 that education is an important agent in the socialization process. For the greater part of human history, however, young people were prepared to assume adult responsibilities without the benefits of a system of universal schooling.

Universal public education is a modern invention dating from the nineteenth century. One of the main promoters in Canada of a state-supported system of mass schooling was Egerton Ryerson. As superintendent of education in Upper Canada from 1844 to 1876, Ryerson played a major role in formulating and implementing a series of legislative acts that, by 1871, had resulted in the establishment of a provincially controlled system of free and compulsory schooling for all young people. The main features of the Ontario system of education were subsequently adopted by the Atlantic and western provinces.

The situation of education today is historically unique. To gain some perspective on it, it might be useful to contrast it with earlier practices. Education in the early nineteenth century consisted of a patchwork of formal and informal arrangements. Children of "common" people learned much of what they needed to know either at home or in apprenticeship training at the workplace. Formal training at an elementary level was offered: for a fee in private schools (organized by individuals or churches); in the local, government-aided common schools; and, at no cost to the poor, in large schools run by charitable organizations. The majority of children received some schooling, but attendance was seasonal and brief. Still, Ontario data indicate that this combination of formal and informal, of publicly supported and privately financed, instruction did produce basic literacy for the greater part of the population (Graff 1975).

The introduction of a state-supported system of compulsory schooling in 1871 constituted a sharp break with previous practices. It meant, first of all, that education had achieved a new social significance. Schools were turned into government-supported organizations because they were perceived as performing important public functions. This new view made voluntary participation no longer acceptable; students were now compelled to attend. Education had become too important to be left to the discretion of parents. Henceforth

the family would have to delegate part of its responsibility for the socialization process to the schools.

This shift in the role of the school — from an agency serving private purposes to an instrument for the attainment of public ends — was accompanied by changes in the organization of education. The educational system was transformed into a bureaucracy, with regulatory power centralized at the top. Authority over such important areas as teacher certification, curricula, and school texts was transferred to the state. Diversity was replaced by uniformity; schools were required to operate within common guidelines formulated and enforced by a central, state-controlled administration.

In this chapter we focus mainly on one aspect of education — its social significance. Why has education become an important social institution? What role exactly does it play in our society? What determines the ebb and flow of support for education? How effectively does it discharge its public responsibilities? Has educational expansion delivered on its promises? Have its benefits been equally distributed? What are some of the main factors producing unequal educational outcomes? These

## Growing Up In School

One of the crucial stages in a young person's transition toward adulthood is adolescence. The psychological task at this first stage is the development of a firm identity, a sense of what you are and what you want to become. It involves a search for purpose in life: "Where am I going?" and "What do I want to commit myself to?" The resolution of this identity crisis is the general developmental task of adolescence.

Prolonged education has made the school into the central social setting within which adolescents confront the problem of identity formation. But do schools provide students with an appropriate maturational environment? Are they good places in which to grow up and discover one's identity? Is it a good thing that the task of preparing

young people for adult life has been delegated to such a great extent to the educational system? A number of scholars have argued that the school setting provides an incomplete basis for the attainment of many important maturational objectives (Coleman et al. 1974).

Schools are oriented to developing self-centred skills that expand a person's instrumental resources, especially in the economic area. But schools do less well in developing other sets of skills — those that are crucial to the process of identity formation. They provide, for instance, little opportunity for developing a sense of self-direction and responsibility. Students occupy a subordinate position in the school system. The student role does not

allow for much initiative and self-management. Students are given assignments rather than responsibilities. The ends to which their activities are directed are determined by the school; their "job" is restricted to carrying out their duties and requires little decision-making or discretionary judgment. Because little responsibility for managing their own affairs is given, little training for self-direction takes place. Responsibility cannot be taught where freedom of choice is absent.

The student role has a second characteristic that reduces the school's ability to generate a sense of self-involvement and, hence, responsibility. In school, knowledge is taught, rather than acquired through experience. Schools are information-are the topics to be discussed in this chapter. They are more than just theoretical issues, part of the ongoing debate between structural functionalists and conflict theorists. They are also of immediate importance to you. What is happening to the educational system is also happening to you.

Before we proceed, however, let us clarify what we mean by education. In this chapter the word carries a specific meaning. It is not interchangeable with either socialization or learning. Although education involves both, not all socialization or learning takes the form of education. Here, **education** means the deliberate, organized transmission of values, knowledge, and skills. It implies the notion of a set of actors — teachers and students — meeting at a designated time to systematically pursue a defined learning objective in a setting deemed appropriate for the purpose at hand. Schools are therefore educational organizations, but educational activities also take place outside schools, in such forms as apprenticeship training, English-language courses for immigrants, lecture series, and religious instruction in Sunday schools. Because of their central importance, we concentrate here on schools and universities only. The passage to adulthood for young people in our society leads through these organizations.

## The Functions of Education

The most widely recognized aim of the educational system is to facilitate the transition from participating in the primary relationships of the family to involvement in the affairs of the larger society. What social positions are considered so essential that preparation for them has been brought within the province of the educational system? Participating in society involves membership in four key areas: the economy, the social stratification system, the polity, and the culture of the society. The educational system fulfills a specific function with regard to each of these areas.

### The Economy

In any society, the socialization process is bound to be tied to the economy. Preparation for adulthood always involves training in the practical skills

---

rich, but action-poor. The realities of the outside world are presented in an abstract fashion. Students are made aware of the choices they face, but they are given little opportunity to learn from experience what choosing a particular course of action entails. Schools teach cognitive understanding without providing students with the experience on which to base this understanding. Separated from the world of experienced reality, students find it difficult to establish the personal relevance of what they are learning.

Schools provide an incomplete environment for the socialization of the young. They do not offer a sufficiently wide range of maturity-promoting experiences. Schools are not the right places in which to face the most pressing of adolescent concerns: the formation of a secure identity. The task of moving toward adulthood needs to be facilitated in such a way that young people are no longer shielded from responsibility and meaningful experience. Several proposals have been advanced in this regard; two are briefly outlined below.

1. *The introduction of a voucher system for youth.* Vouchers — equivalent in value to the average cost of, say, three years of college education — would be given to young people at age 16, to be used at their discretion for schooling or other forms of skill training. Such a system would have the advantage of placing the resources required for further schooling directly into the hands of young people, thereby giving them a chance to take responsibility for managing their own education. Under these conditions, a much higher degree of self-involvement could be expected.

2. *Alternation of school and work.* One way of providing young people with opportunities for obtaining experience is to encourage movement between school and workplace. Students could spend part of their time in a work setting related to the educational studies they are pursuing. This would help them establish the personal relevance of what they are learning, while at the same time presenting them with a realistic opportunity for testing the strength of their interest and commitment to their chosen line of study.

---

**Source:**

James S. Coleman et al., *Youth: Transition to Adulthood* (Chicago: University of Chicago Press, 1974).

required to become a productive member of society. In the past, except for the most specialized occupations, much of this training took place on the job. Today, the school has come to occupy a central role in the occupational training process at all levels of the occupational hierarchy.

Apprenticeship programs and other forms of on-the-job training still exist, but their contribution to the total occupational training process has been greatly reduced. The basic vocational training for the overwhelming majority of jobs in our society takes place within the educational system. Training and apprenticeship programs build on the foundation laid by the school. Education has become the major agency of **occupational socialization**, the students' preparation for entering the job market. The economy depends for its operation on an adequate supply of efficient and motivated workers. One of the tasks of the educational system is to maintain this flow.

## Social Stratification

As we saw in Chapter 8, social inequality or social stratification is a pervasive aspect of social life. Everyone is born into a particular class (*class of origin*), and as an adult everyone occupies a position in the social stratification hierarchy (*class of destination*). These two positions can be, but are not necessarily, the same.

Inequality is a potential source of conflict in all societies; it makes the smooth assimilation of people into the social structure problematic. As long as occupations carry unequal benefits in income and prestige, we can fairly assume that people will try to "better themselves"; that is, they will tend to avoid the less rewarded positions in favour of the more attractive ones. Social stratification, then, introduces an element of status competition. To deal with this problem, societies have developed strategies for regulating the process of status acquisition.

Two basic strategies can be distinguished, each based on a different type of eligibility criterion. The crucial distinction here is between ascriptive and achievement criteria. Allocating people to positions on the basis of *ascriptive criteria* leads to a system of closed competition, in which the range of positions for which new cohorts can compete

is determined at birth. That is, the class of destination is determined by the class of origin. When *achievement criteria* are recognized as the basis for status allocation, the competition is open, not closed. Future position is a function not of initial placement, but of an individual's effort and ability.

In the closed system, your final position is identical with your starting position; but in the open system, social position at birth is only a temporary status that does not restrict how far you are allowed to move. Instead of ending up where you started, you arrive at the position you have earned.

In their pure forms, these two strategies for status allocation hardly ever exist. Completely open and completely closed competition represent two extremes. Still, this typology gives us a useful tool of analysis, because most societies gravitate toward one side or the other. According to their central tendency, then, societies can be characterized as either open or closed. Like other advanced industrial societies, Canada subscribes to the principle of open competition for status allocation. This has important ramifications for the role of education.

In a *closed society*, education fulfills a mainly passive role. Its function is not to change students' class positions, but to confirm them after the fact by teaching students the skills and values appropriate to their class of origin. In a closed society, the purpose of university education, for example, is to put the icing on the cake: gentlemen attend in order to become cultivated. Education is largely a consequence, rather than a determinant, of social class position, and it serves to stabilize social class positions across generations (see Figure 14-1). In an *open society*, education has a different mandate. Its task is to play an active role in the process of allocation. Rather than simply being a transmitter of the stratification system, education becomes an independent "assignment office for social chances" (Schelsky 1961). Instead of accepting class of origin as a determinant of future status, the school functions as society's testing agency, screening claims to future status on the basis of standards presumed to be relevant and objective. Its tasks are to provide everyone with an equal chance to compete and to assess a student's class of destination on the basis of talent and ability. In an open society, the school functions as the arena in which the status passage from class of origin to class of destination is publicly negotiated (see Figure 14-2).

As a social selection agency, the school has the job of identifying, allocating and certifying talent. The educational system in our society is supposed to operate as an independent review board, giving people a fair hearing before making its decision on what their social stratification credentials are. Consequently, schools are places where students are tested, where their academic achievement is evaluated and compared to that of their peers, and where, based on a comparative assessment of their performances, they are channelled in appropriate directions. Students emerge from this process with a diploma, certificate, or degree that qualifies them for entrance to a particular level of the social stratification hierarchy.

It is not enough, however, to have a system for assessing status claims. What happens when someone is not happy with the assessment? A way to ensure that people respond favourably to status allocation is also necessary. Given the existence of social stratification, a favourable reaction of the members of a society to their class of destination cannot be taken for granted. Allocative decisions may give rise to serious discontent, especially among those facing limited prospects. The process of status induction therefore also includes a second, subjective, component. People need to be taught two things concurrently: what their place is, and that they should accept that place. As the major social selection agency, the school not only is involved in the screening process but also functions as an instrument of status socialization. The task of the educational system

## Figure 14-1. Closed Society: Education as an Institution of Social Inheritance

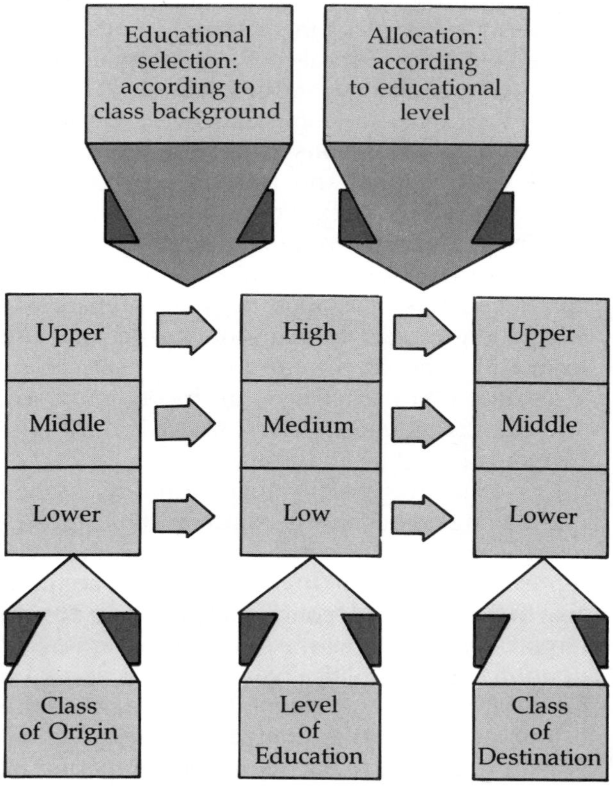

## Figure 14-2. Open Society: Education as an Institution of Social Mobility

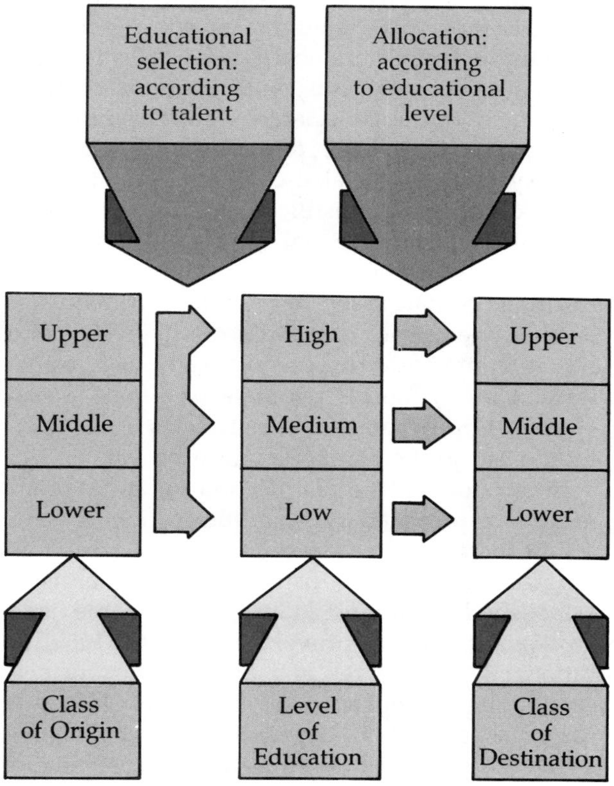

is twofold: to select fairly, and to generate compliance with the outcome of the selection process.

How is compliance generated? What exactly does status socialization entail?

First, **status socialization** implies regulation of ambition. This means that students' aspirations need to be brought into line with the school's estimation of their abilities. Bright students are encouraged to have high aspirations, while students who are weak but ambitious need to be "cooled out" (Clark 1960). The main problem associated with the processing of ambition is that students' aspiration levels are strongly influenced by their social class. The educational system is expected to neutralize the impact of this powerful factor by either raising or lowering class-based ambition levels, depending on its independent assessment of talent. Therefore, schools not only evaluate performance, but also offer guidance counselling.

Second, status socialization implies legitimation. Allocation means that people have different levels of access to privileged positions. In order for people to accept the allocation process — particularly those people who receive fewer benefits — they not only must learn to be realistic about their mobility prospects, but also must come to believe in the appropriateness of the pinciples governing the allocation process. As Marx pointed out, systems of social inequality generate their own ideologies of justification. Once this happens, the existing system of privileges becomes more firmly entrenched, since notions of justice can now be harnessed in its defence. Inequality is no longer a fact of existence with which one has to come to terms pragmatically; it is transformed into a normative state of affairs. Social stratification becomes a social reality that rightfully exists and commands our approval.

In our society, the justification for social stratification is provided by a meritocratic ideology. In a **meritocracy**, social inequality is warranted as long as privileges are distributed on the basis of established merit, and as long as all people have an equal chance to prove themselves. The educational system serves as a major agency for disseminating meritocratic ideology. Schools try to convince students of the importance of their selective criteria, so that educational achievement comes to be seen as the standard by which social merit is to be assessed. Schools also attempt to create confidence in the fairness and accuracy of their assessment procedures, so that educational success or failure is accepted by students as a true manifestation of their ability.

The school, then, is expected to function both as an agency promoting social mobility according to talent and as an agency promoting acceptance of social stratification. The same processes that make the school a place of opportunity also transform it into an instrument of social control for the stratification system. The provision of equality of opportunity implies the notion of status training. Social selection and status socialization are complementary activities. They define, from different angles, the social stratification mandate of the school in the open society.

## The Political Order

Learning to participate in social life includes, as a third component, preparation for membership in the political order. Your initial encounter with authority takes place in the family, and you receive your first political training at home. Learning to be a child involves learning to be a subordinate and to follow directives, learning to anticipate that violations of the rules will call forth negative sanctions, and learning to accept that parental authority exists for your own good. However, authority in the family is personal and takes a variety of forms from one unit to another; so your early socialization does not prepare you adequately for the formally organized and uniform authority structure of the larger society. As a resident of a particular municipality, province, and country, you must also learn to deal with the demands of public authority.

In Canadian society, public authority is organized along democratic lines. Democratic government is based on the consent of the governed and represents an attempt to make authority accountable to the people. Accountability requires a counterpart: responsiveness. As citizens we are called upon to become politically involved, to speak up for our interests, and to monitor the performance of our elected representatives. The educational system has been given the task of preparing us for these types of active participation in the affairs of society. Part of the school's effort, therefore, is directed toward **democratic citizenship training**; courses in history and civics are included in the school curriculum for this reason.

## Culture

All the functions of education identified so far have one element in common — all aim at preparing students for life in a socially differentiated society in which each person will occupy a particular niche in the division of labour. But participating in society implies an additional dimension — learning to be members of the same community. One of the central aims of the educational system, from its inception, has been to create a common cultural identity as discussed in Chapter 2. The common school was meant to serve as an agency of social integration, bringing together people from different classes, ethnic backgrounds, and religions, and connecting the local community to the larger society. In its cultural function, the educational system attempts to foster a sense of collective identity and purpose. We learn in school that we are a people bound together by common traditions. We are taught about the components of our common cultural heritage and about the distinctive qualities and achievements we collectively value. But schools do not only inform us; they also appeal to our sentiments. They attempt to capture our commitment and loyalty, so that what we have in common becomes a source of self-identification and pride.

## Human Enlightenment

In the preceding discussion we have highlighted the role of the school as a preparatory agency easing our entrance into the existing social order. The importance of the educational system as an instrument for role socialization should not be underestimated, but it would be one-sided to define its teaching mandate solely in these terms. The task of the educational system is not just to fulfill the demands of society and to mold our personalities accordingly. One important function of education is personality development as a value in its own right. Official curriculum guidelines frequently include statements to the effect that education should lead to "the full development of each child's potential" and that it should develop "the moral and aesthetic sensitivity necessary for a complete and responsible life" (Ministry of Education, Ontario 1975).

Universities are not far behind in expressing a commitment to liberal education as a nonutilitarian search for self-enrichment. From the ancient Greeks, who believed that the educated person should live "the examined life," we inherited the notion of education as worth pursuing for its own sake. From this perspective, the school's function is to enhance the capabilities of the individual, particularly the ability to reason, and to lay the basis for self-realization and autonomy.

A final function of education also derives from our cultural commitment to knowledge as an end in itself. The school is expected to do more than preserve and pass on the collective wisdom of the past. The educational system also functions as a source of innovation. At the higher levels in particular, centres of learning are involved in both transmitting and creating knowledge. They are places where new scientific ideas are born and developed, where new interpretations of our cultural traditions are undertaken, and where our existing stock of knowledge is subjected to critical examination and modification in the light of changing circumstances.

## The Basic Reference Points

These, then, are the major functions of education:

1. to be the major agent of occupational socialization;
2. to identify, allocate, and certify talent, and to function as an instrument of status socialization;
3. to train students for democratic citizenship;
4. to create a common cultural identity; and
5. to develop the student's personality and human potential and to function as a source of innovation.

Having identified the major functions of education, we now have a framework within which we can analyze the interaction between education and the larger society in more detail.

Before proceeding with this analysis we should clarify one point: these are not the only interconnections that can be made between education and other areas of social life. Schools also have latent functions, which produce side effects that, in an unintentional and/or unrecognized way, sustain certain social phenomena. One latent function of high schools and post-secondary institutions, for example, is to provide a dating and marriage market. Schools also fulfill a custodial function, providing the daycare that enables both parents to participate in the labour market. At the same time, schools prevent youngsters from entering the work force, thereby alleviating unemployment and the social dissatisfaction it creates.

In the following analysis, we focus mainly on the five manifest functions enumerated above. These represent the publicly recognized contributions of education in its societal context.

One good starting point for a macrosociological analysis of education is to ask how much weight is attached to each of its manifest functions. Not all of them receive equal emphasis, and systems of education differ in assigning priorities. What, in our society, are the functions that receive high and low priority? What are the areas of performance on which public concern is mainly focused? If the school is criticized for not doing a good job, what types of complaints receive widespread public attention, and what types of criticism fail to arouse much general interest? The answers to these questions provide important clues about the nature of the power field within which the educational system is located.

The list of manifest functions serves a second useful analytical purpose. It allows us to identify more precisely the nature of the contradictions and controversies that accompany the operation of education in our society. Tensions and debates can be reduced to three causes.

First, while a particular function is generally considered to be important, there might exist disagreement about how to define it more specifically. In fact, the greater the importance attached to a particular function, the more likely it is that such differences of opinion will occur. A good example in Canada is the historical conflict about the cultural role of the school. What does creating a common cultural identity entail? Whose culture should the school promote? Should the goal be assimilation or cultural pluralism — the melting pot or the mosaic?

Second, tension results from the fact that a particular function might involve contradictory demands. For example, we have seen that our society subscribes to the principle of open status competition. As a result, the educational system is expected, on the one hand, to extend and equalize educational opportunities and, on the other hand, to sort the more able from the less able students. In other words, the school is supposed to create and raise the aspirations of students while, at the same time, blocking the educational opportunities of the less talented pupils, thereby limiting their stratification prospects. How realistic is it to expect that these two tasks can be accomplished simultaneously? Can each be achieved only at the expense of the other?

Third, in addition to these two internal contradictions, there also exist external contradictions among the various functions. One controversy concerns the conflicting demands of human enlightenment versus role-training. The pendulum of educational reform seems to swing back and forth between these poles. At the elementary and secondary levels of the educational system, it is expressed as a conflict between "child-centred" education and a concern for the basics. An increased emphasis on the former inevitably produces, in reaction, a demand for a renewed emphasis on "the three Rs." At the university level, a similar, seemingly perpetual tug-of-war is conducted between those who support a more humanistic and general type of education and those who are in favour of a more specialized and professionally oriented curriculum.

Another, much less widely debated, contradiction exists between the political and the cultural socialization functions of the school. In its cultural role, the school is engaged in nation-building. It tries to increase people's identification with their society and to instill feelings of solidarity and national pride. But political citizenship in a democracy requires an attitude not of blind loyalty but of critical involvement, of conditional approval. Actually, we often see that democratic citizenship training is sacrificed for or confused with nation-building and that docile patriotism, rather than informed consent, is the desired result.

# Expansion

Education in Canada has undergone several profound and fundamental changes in recent decades. In this section we describe these changes and then relate them to the underlying shift in perspective on the functional significance of education.

## From Elite Preparatory to Mass Terminal

In 1951, only 46 percent of people in Canada aged 14 to 17 were enrolled on a full-time basis at the senior high school level of education (grades nine and up). Ten years later that figure had increased to 72 percent; in 1971 it had reached 98 percent (Statistics Canada 1978). Beginning in the 1960s, Canadian education moved decisively and rapidly into a new phase — from an **elite preparatory** system, it has been transformed into a **mass terminal** system (Trow 1961). The third phase of development, *mass preparatory* (where most students continue through post-secondary education), is beginning to emerge in the United States.

Until the 1950s, the main function of the high school in Canada was to prepare an elite — a relatively small group of students — for advanced studies. The demands of the universities largely determined the curriculum and the philosophy of secondary education, especially at the senior level. During the 1960s, there was a rapid expansion in the number of students who continued through to matriculation — from 49.8 percent in 1961 to 80 percent in 1971 (Statistics Canada 1973). This shift changed the educational system in a fundamental way.

Mass terminal education produced a new set of organizational demands. The secondary school system had to accommodate itself to a much wider range of educational interests. No longer could it orient itself solely toward the needs of the university. And the post-secondary sector, having lost control over the direction and nature of secondary education, had to deal with a more heterogeneous and much larger student population. In this section, we will concentrate on the quantitative dimension of this transformation and on its external social causes and consequences.

Table 14-1 shows the startling speed with which Canadian education moved into its new phase. Between 1951 and 1971, the total student population more than doubled — it increased by a factor of 2.33. This increase was partly a product of the post-war ''baby boom.'' The eligible student population (that is, people aged 5 to 24) grew in the same period by a factor of 1.83. But the greatest share of the growth resulted from increased participation levels. The most rapid increase in student enrolment occurred at the senior secondary (grade nine and up) and the post-secondary levels, where attendance is a matter of choice. Between 1951 and 1971, the senior secondary sector grew by a factor of 4.38, the non-university sector by a factor of 6.39, and the university sector by a factor of 5.09.

Part-time university enrolment expanded at an even faster rate. Between 1962 and 1971, the number of part-time students grew from 43 990 to 185 387, increasing by a factor of 4.21 (Statistics Canada 1978). Full-time university enrolment during the same period increased by a factor of 2.29 (Statistics Canada 1978).

To teach this vastly expanded student population, a great number of additional instructors were recruited. Between 1950 and 1971, the number of full-time teachers in elementary and secondary schools almost tripled (1:2.93), increasing from 89 682 to 263 126. At the university level, the full-time faculty body grew from 5 339 to 27 557, a factor of 5.16 (Statistics Canada 1978). Because graduate programs at Canadian universities had just started to expand, many of the university instructors recruited during this period were of foreign origin and/or had received their graduate training abroad, particularly in the United States. So successful was the recruitment effort that, despite the rapid growth of the student population, the teacher/pupil ratio actually declined. In the elementary–secondary sector it dropped from 25.5 in 1961 to 21.4 in 1971; in universities, it decreased from 14.7 to 8.4 during the same ten-year period.

In 1971, Canada had 68 universities, 16 of which were affiliated with another Canadian university. Only 44 of these institutions had been in existence 10 years earlier. Many of the new universities had roots in the religious sector. Additionally, a whole new set of post-secondary institutions had been created as an alternative to university. In most provinces, the only fields of study available at the post-secondary level outside the university had been nursing and teacher training. The 1960s saw the emergence of a comprehensive new branch of post-secondary education: the community college. In 1960, only 29 institutions of this kind existed; by the end of the decade their number had increased to 133.

The community college sector still constitutes the most rapidly growing part of post-secondary education. The names and functions of these colleges differ according to province. In the west, they are sometimes called junior colleges; in On-

tario, colleges of applied arts and technology (CAATs); in Quebec, collèges d'enseignement général et professionnel (CEGEPs). In British Columbia, Alberta, and Quebec, the colleges offer both vocational training and two years of university-level studies from which a student can transfer to a university. In the other provinces, the colleges form a separate stream; their specific objective is to provide a comprehensive career alternative to university education. Teacher training has largely been transferred to the university, while nursing programs have been incorporated into the community colleges.

The simultaneous and rapid expansion of the secondary and post-secondary sectors had a tremendous impact on expenditures. In 1950, only 2.4 percent of the Gross National Product was allocated to educational spending. By 1961 this figure had risen to 4.9 percent; in 1971 it reached 8.8. In recent years the percentage has hovered around 7.5.

The greatest proportion of the increase in expenditures occurred at the post-secondary level.

**Table 14-1. Trends in Full-Time Enrolment, By Level, Canada 1951–1985**

|  | 1951 | 1961 | 1971 | 1981 | 1985 |
|---|---|---|---|---|---|
| *Elementary–Secondary* | | | | | |
| Kindergarten–Grade 8 | 2 230 300 | 3 514 900 | 4 096 100 | 3 461 300 | 3 411 200 |
| Grade 9 and up | 394 500 | 894 900 | 1 726 500 | 1 565 700 | 1 513 900 |
| Subtotal | 2 624 800 | 4 409 800 | 5 822 600 | 5 027 000 | 4 925 100 |
| *Post-secondary* | | | | | |
| Non-university | 27 200 | 53 400 | 173 800 | 273 400 | 322 500 |
| University | 63 500 | 128 600 | 323 000 | 401 900 | 467 300 |
| Subtotal | 90 700 | 182 000 | 496 800 | 675 300 | 789 800 |
| TOTAL | 2 715 500 | 4 591 800 | 6 319 400 | 5 702 300 | 5 714 900 |
| Post-secondary enrolment as percentage of 18–24 age group | 6.0 | 10.6 | 18.5 | 20.5 | 24.5 |

SOURCE: Adapted from Statistics Canada, *Historical Compendium of Education Statistics from Confederation to 1975* (Ottawa, 1976), pp. 16–17; Statistics Canada, *Education in Canada, 1986* (Ottawa, 1987), pp. 67, 119.

**Canada's educational systems have moved from elite preparatory systems to mass terminal systems.**

University expenditures, for example, increased at an annual rate of 15 percent between 1950 and 1971 (Statistics Canada 1978). The burden of these expenditures was increasingly borne by the government. In 1950, tuition fees accounted for 26 percent of university income, and private financing accounted for an additional 15 percent, so that only three-fifths of the total expenditures came from public sources. In 1961, the combined share of tuition and private support had dropped to 30 percent; in 1971, to 18 percent (Statistics Canada 1978). More than four-fifths of all university revenues are now derived from government sources.

## The Impetus to Expansion

In 1975, a group of foreign experts — who had been commissioned to review educational policy in Canada — characterized the development we have just noted in this way:

*Until the late 1940s, Canada could be counted as one of the less developed (educationally) of the great democracies. Today, it is numbered clearly among the educational leaders. . . . It is hardly an exaggeration to talk about a second great Canadian pioneering achievement.* (OECD 1976)

What was behind education's sudden leap into a position of institutional prominence? Obviously a profound change in the functional importance attached to education must have taken place. What was the nature of this change?

The impetus for the enormous expansion of the Canadian educational system came from two sources. One was the growing belief in the central significance of higher education as a source of national strength. The other was the desire to create a more just society.

**Productivity.** The recognition that higher education could be a source of national strength dates from the 1940s. Before World War II, universities were seen as regional institutions important chiefly to the province in which they were located. The war effort created a great demand for scientific research and highly trained personnel; with this came the realization of how much the nation's survival and development depended on the university sector. In the immediate post-war period, the federal government for the first time started to give direct financial support to universities to assist them in meeting the expenses created by the influx of veterans — who, supported by government grants, were enrolling in large numbers.

When the veteran program and the accompanying subsidies were about to expire, a royal commission was appointed to study the federal role in the arts, letters, and sciences. The Royal Commission on National Development in the Arts, Letters, and Sciences, headed by Vincent Massey, took special note of the state of higher education, documented the precarious financial situation the universities — especially the humanities departments — faced, and recommended that the federal government embark on a program of annual grants to the universities to help them meet operating costs. The recommendation was accepted; beginning in 1951, the federal government became involved in the financial support of the post-secondary sector on a regular basis. The commission's report — known as the Massey Report (1951) — had based its recommendations on the idea that universities are national institutions vital to the preservation and growth of Canada's cultural identity. This cultural argument carried some weight, but the real push for expansion came from a different direction.

In the wake of economic fluctuation during the 1950s, the Canadian government set stable economic growth and the reduction of unemployment as two of its national priorities. It realized that the weakness of the Canadian economy had a structural source, and that the goal of sustained economic development could only be attained by shifting the economic base of Canadian society

from resources to industry. The society taken as a model of how to achieve industrial strength was the United States. According to the economic theories then in vogue in the U.S., economic growth in an advanced industrial society depended foremost on human capital.

The core postulate of the **human capital theory** was that knowledge had replaced muscle and physical capital as the principal factor in production. It was the fusion of science with industry, theorists believed, that made possible the great increases in productivity on which economic prosperity depended. Advanced industrial societies were "knowledge societies," and organized technological rationality was the key to their economic success. If knowledge was the strategic resource of an advanced industrial society, then the educational system was its key institution, for it could produce the scientific ideas on which innovation depended and the skilled workers required to operate the system. In an "expert society" (Clark 1962), education as a means for mobilizing human capital had become a crucial investment.

If education was a key component of economic growth, then the level of schooling in the Canadian labour force compared to that in the United States was a matter of concern. In 1961, among the male labour force in the 25 to 34 age group, 14.7 percent of American workers had university degrees, compared to 6 percent of Canadian workers; 57.2 percent of the same group in the United States had completed four years of high school, compared to only 28.2 percent in Canada.

Even more striking was the fact that the differences in educational attainment were highest for the youngest age group. For the 55 to 64 age group, the gap between the educational levels of the two countries' male labour forces was not so wide (Porter 1967). The conclusion was obvious. If Canada wanted to catch up with its industrial neighbour, the education gap between the two countries needed to be closed. This required a drastic expansion and reform of the existing educational system. For too long Canada had relied on immigration to supply highly skilled personnel. From now on, our own educational system had to be equipped to undertake the crucial task of meeting industrial society's ever-increasing demand for expertise. This was the opinion expressed in the

1960s by the influential Economic Council of Canada in its first and second annual reviews (1964, 1965) and by sociologist John Porter in his pioneering study *The Vertical Mosaic* (1965).

**Social Justice.** The second major force behind educational expansion was the desire to create a more just society. As Clark (1976) noted, the postwar period was a time of social ferment. Barriers to social and geographical mobility were breaking down, and new groups were trying to enter the mainstream of social life. A revolution of rising expectations was taking place, especially among the middle class. The steady increase in the proportion of students opting for university education, for example, dates from the early 1950s and was well under way before the government became involved financially. Everyone, it seemed, wanted a bigger share of the pie. To accommodate these pressures, an active policy of promoting opportunities through improved access to educational institutions was adopted by Canadian governments during the 1960s. Social justice demanded that all people, regardless of gender, region, or social class, be given an equal opportunity to develop their talents.

The appeal of this policy rested on more than social grounds alone. It also served important economic functions. Both social justice and efficiency demanded the mobilization of talent, and education could satisfy these two objectives simultaneously. It was this match between social and economic objectives that provided such a powerful justification for the expansion of education.

In addition to being economically attractive, the policy of relying primarily on the educational sector to bring about a more just society had important political advantages as well. It provided a way of meeting rising social aspirations without having to undertake more radical reforms.

The policy of equality through education was based on a narrow definition of what constitutes social justice. The concern was to open up opportunities for individual advancement: to provide equal chances to become unequal. The system of social inequality as such, the shape of income distribution, was not under attack. What was offered was fairness of selection procedures *(equality of opportunity)*, not fairness of results *(equality of*

*condition)*. (See Chapter 8 for a detailed discussion of these two different types of social equality.)

## Mobility Strategies

In pursuing this goal of equal opportunity for all, Canadian education underwent a distinct shift in social orientation. The nature of this change can best be described in terms of the typology developed by the American sociologist Ralph Turner (1961). The basic assumption behind Turner's typology is that because schools are important social selection agencies, their organization will be determined by the prevailing ideas about how social mobility ought to proceed. Turner distinguishes two modes of upward mobility: sponsored mobility and contest mobility. Turner (1961) characterized **sponsored mobility** this way:

*Elite recruits are chosen by the established elite or their agents, and elite status is given on the basis of some criterion of supposed merit and cannot be taken by any amount of effort or strategy. Upward mobility is like entry into a private club where each candidate must be sponsored by one or more of its members. Ultimately, the members grant or deny upward mobility on the basis of whether they judge the candidate to have the qualities they wish to see in fellow members.*

In contrast to this, Turner defined **contest mobility** as

*a system in which elite status is the prize of an open contest and is taken by the aspirants' own efforts. While the "contest" is governed by some rules of fair play, the contestants have wide latitude in the strategies they may employ. Since the "prize" of successful upward mobility is not in the hands of the established elite to give out, the latter are not in a position to determine who shall obtain it and who not. (1961)*

This difference in mobility is related to the nature of the stratification system, particularly the elite structure, of a particular society. Sponsored mobility will be found in societies where one particular group has been able to establish cultural control, so that only the attributes it values will form the basis for elite selection. Contest mobility emerges in societies where no status group has been able to establish a monopoly over elite credentials. Historically, England and continental Europe belong in the former category, the United States in the latter. This has been reflected in the organization of their respective educational systems.

**Contest Mobility.** In the United States, the educational system is organized to encourage students to stay in the competition as long as possible and to teach them whatever skills are useful in attaining high rewards. Within the American educational system, contest mobility is characterized by

1. lack of early selection or allocation of students to different "streams" (for example, all students attend the same comprehensive high school);
2. relative ease of transfer between types of programs and institutions; and
3. relative openness of the curriculum.

Because no elite has monopolized elite credentials, the school system has no legitimate criteria for excluding particular subjects as inappropriate. American schools and universities offer a curriculum that ranges from traditional arts and science subjects to home economics, and financial support is offered to both scholars and football players. Any skill that is in demand is considered legitimate and worthy of inclusion in the curriculum. The educational system is structured in such a way that selection is postponed as long as is practicable, to permit a fair race. Junior colleges offer second chances to students who were not successful in their first attempt to qualify for university entrance. The onus is on the educational system to prove a student's ineptitude for elite positions, not on the student to prove special worth. The problem of creating an open contest is met by creating diversified curricula in a unitary structure within which transfer chances are optimized.

**Sponsored Mobility.** The purpose of education in a sponsored-mobility system is to identify and select those with elite potential as early as possible

in order to ensure control over their training. This purpose is articulated into

1. early selection and segregation of students into different streams;
2. prescribed curricula aimed at the cultivation of qualities deemed necessary by the established elite; and
3. restriction of transfer possibilities from nonelite to elite training institutions.

If students do not make it into the university stream at an early age, their chances of ever getting there are slim. The desire to control the content of the selection process leads to the creation of prescribed curricula in a binary or tripartite structure precluding transfer.

In Canada, education has historically tended to follow a sponsored-mobility tradition, although in the western provinces the American model has been influential. The prevailing belief was that higher education was the privilege of a carefully screened intellectual elite, rather than the right of as many people as possible. With the post-war emphasis on educational accessibility, however, this has changed, and in recent decades the Canadian educational system as a whole has moved in the direction of contest mobility, particularly at the secondary level. Abolishing departmental exams, loosening university entrance requirements, breaking down the rigid structure of the curriculum by introducing a credit system, abolishing Latin (the traditional symbol of elite status) as a required subject: all these curriculum changes were clearly motivated by a desire to loosen control over elite credentials and to encourage students to stay in the race as long as possible.

But these sentiments were not as evident in post-secondary education policy. We noted earlier that in the majority of provinces community colleges were established as a separate system, not intended to be systematically associated with the university sector. Even though the idea of mass education was generally accepted at the secondary level, support for such a policy at the post-secondary level was much more guarded. Here remnants of sponsored mobility can still be seen.

# Can We Be Excellent and Equal Too?

A reservation frequently expressed in conservative circles is that equalizing educational opportunities inevitably entails lowering academic standards. High quality, so the argument goes, can only be maintained in an elitist system. *More* necessarily means *worse*. Inequality is the price we have to pay for excellence. The progress of bright students will be endangered when they are mixed with students of average ability.

Are excellence of academic standards and equality of access irreconcilable objectives? One answer to this question can be found in the studies conducted by the International Association for the Evaluation of Academic Achievement. These studies contain information about the performance of students in at least 12 different countries on internationally devised math and science tests (Husén 1967; Comber and Keeves, 1973). The secondary school systems in the countries selected range from very selective (Germany, France) to comprehensive (United States).

Which systems provide more equality of educational opportunities? Upper-class students are over-represented and lower-class students are underrepresented in all countries, but the rate of underrepresentation of lower-class students is significantly higher in the more selective school systems. The more selective the school system, the greater the social bias.

Is the lack of equality in selective systems compensated for by their excellence in academic achievement? The legitimation of elitism rests on its supposedly superior results. How do the graduates of the academic programs in the selective and comprehensive systems compare on math or science test scores? The average math and science scores among United States high school graduates who recently took courses in these subjects is far below, for instance, that of their West German counterparts. But this should come as no surprise. The West Germans who were studying these subjects in their graduating year represent a small group of academic survivors — only 4 to 5 percent of the relevant age group; in the United States about 18 percent of the graduates' age group were studying math or science in their final year. If we compare the top 4 percent with the top 18 percent, the results are predictable. So the two systems cannot be compared on the basis of the average score for the whole student population. The question has to be refined.

Is it possible within a comprehensive system to produce an elite comparable in size and quality to the one produced by the selective system? Let us compare the average math or science score of the top 4 percent of the U.S. students with the average score of the top 4 percent of students in other countries. In such a comparison, the average score of the top 4 percent in the U.S. is about the same as that in most of the selective European countries. In the whole study, none of the comprehensive systems ranks among the five countries at the bottom. So more does *not* mean worse. Nor is there evidence that less means better. The selective systems do not all rank at the top. They do not produce an elite superior to the elite cultivated in the comprehensive system.

What can we conclude from this? The price to be paid by selective systems in lack of equality cannot be justified. On the grounds of both justice and efficiency of performance, comprehensive systems seem preferable to selective systems. They are more egalitarian, produce as good and as big a crop of top students, and bring more of the student population along further.

**Source:**

Torsten Husén, ed., *International Study of Achievement in Mathematics: A Comparison of Twelve Countries*, 2 vols. (Stockholm: Almqvist and Wiksell, 1967); C. Comber and John P. Keeves, *Science Education in Nineteen Countries: An Empirical Study* (New York: John Wiley and Sons, 1973).

**The Case of Quebec.** Among all the provinces, it was in Quebec that the economic and social ideas we have just outlined had their greatest educational impact. The Liberal government of Jean Lesage, which came to power in 1960, committed itself to a policy of *rattrapage* — that is, of catching up with social and economic development elsewhere. Education became one of the main targets of this modernization drive.

Before the 1960s, the provincial government had had little control over the educational system. Public education was divided into two sectors: one Catholic and largely French, and the other Protestant and largely English. In addition to the public French–Catholic sector, there was also an extensive network of private educational institutions operated by the Catholic church. Each sector was autonomous in matters related to organization, curriculum, examinations, and teacher cert-ification. Power resided in a Catholic committee and a Protestant committee. Together these com-mittees formed the Council of Public Instruction. It is indicative of the lack of co-ordination between these two sectors that from 1908 to 1960 the coun-cil never once met as a body.

The English–Protestant school system in Que-bec had evolved much like its counterparts in other provinces. It offered a wide selection of courses, ranging from vocational and commercial courses to university preparation, through an interlocking network of public elementary and secondary schools. The French–Catholic system was orga-nized in quite a different manner. Free public edu-cation was available at the elementary level, but secondary and higher education were provided by private institutions controlled by the Catholic church. Francophone Catholic students could ob-tain secondary education leading to university study, for a fee, at the classical colleges, which were sponsored and supported by various reli-gious orders. These colleges, all affiliated with the arts faculties of one of the three private franco-phone universities (Laval, Montréal, Sher-brooke), offered an eight-year program comprising both high school and undergraduate liberal arts education. On graduation, students received a BA from the parent university.

The education offered at the classical colleges and these three universities was high in quality, but it had a limited intellectual range. Both types of institution were oriented toward the humani-ties and the traditional professions (law and med-icine) and placed low priority on scientific and technological subjects. Francophone Catholic stu-dents who wanted to enter a faculty of science could do so only after completing 15 years of schooling, while an English–Protestant student could start science studies after matriculation from grade 11.

French–Catholic education in Quebec before the 1960s provided the purest example in Canada of a sponsored-mobility system. The elite and the masses were separated at an early age. Because cultural control was in the hands of one group, elite training was restricted to the cultivation of the qualities favoured by the Catholic church.

In the early 1960s, all this changed. The so-called Quiet Revolution initiated by the Lesage government represented a shift in ideological ori-entation away from the past and toward the pres-ent. Modernization was to be embraced rather than feared, and government power would be the major instrument through which the desirable changes would be introduced. The Lesage gov-ernment recognized from the outset that a reform of the educational system was crucial, and ap-pointed a Royal Commission of Inquiry on Edu-cation (the Parent Commission), to undertake a complete examination of all aspects of the Quebec educational system.

One of the Parent Commission's first recom-mendations was that a provincial Ministry of Edu-cation be created. This recommendation was implemented in 1964. The effect of the new Min-istry was to secularize the control structure and to sharply reduce the role of the Catholic and Protestant committees. Henceforth, the commit-tees would have power to regulate only in moral and religious matters. In all other areas, full au-thority for education rested in the hands of the provincial government. This done, the govern-ment was able to act on the other recommenda-tions made in the five volumes of the *Parent Commission Report*. The francophone educational system was upgraded by the introduction of free public secondary schools. Secondary education in Quebec now lasts for five years and is patterned on the contest-mobility model of the comprehen-sive high school, *l'école polyvalente*. Secondary schools now serve all categories of students, sep-arate programs have been abolished in favour of a credit system with various levels, and the cur-riculum now includes all subject areas.

At the post-secondary level in Quebec, the CEGEP offers both a two-year university program and advanced technical training of two or three years' duration. Unlike those in other provinces, this college education is free and is not organized on a binary basis. All students at the post-sec-ondary level, whether they are headed for the university or for the labour market, receive their education in the same institution. In its commit-ment to accessibility, comprehensiveness, and ease of transfer, then, Quebec has moved farther than any other province in the direction of contest mobility.

# Disillusionment

The 1970s witnessed a change in public support for education. All governments began to curtail their educational spending. Clearly, the boom period in education is over. Education has entered an era of institutional retrenchment.

This shift was to be expected. Enrolment swells and contracts in response to the demographic factors outlined in Chapter 7. As shown in Table 14-2, the school population reached its peak in 1971; since then the size of the student population at the primary and junior high school levels has decreased. The repercussions of this decline will continue to be felt, particularly at the secondary level.

But economic and demographic factors alone cannot explain the reduced support for education. As Table 14-2 also indicates, the participation rate in post-secondary education has continued to grow, but the desirability of this trend is now being questioned. Many believe that the policy of educational expansion has failed to deliver the promised economic and social benefits.

## The Economic Failure

Students now realize that post-secondary education does not automatically give them access to a well-paid job. The educational requirements of the job market have been steadily rising, and the purchasing power of a degree has declined accordingly. Three decades ago, a BA put a graduate into competition for a high-status position; in today's job market one needs a more advanced degree to obtain the same competitive advantage. Both Canadian and American studies (Harvey 1974; Freeman 1976) have convincingly demonstrated that the personal rate of return on education has been falling in recent years.

However disappointing these might be, they do not by themselves justify the conclusion that

**Table 14-2. Full-Time Post-Secondary Enrolment as a Percentage of the Relevant Age Group, by Level and Gender, Canada, Selected Years.**

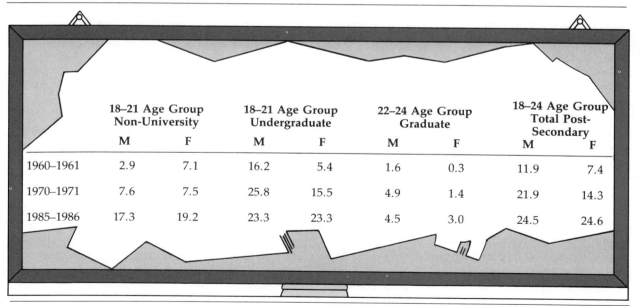

|  | 18–21 Age Group Non-University | | 18–21 Age Group Undergraduate | | 22–24 Age Group Graduate | | 18–24 Age Group Total Post-Secondary | |
|---|---|---|---|---|---|---|---|---|
|  | M | F | M | F | M | F | M | F |
| 1960–1961 | 2.9 | 7.1 | 16.2 | 5.4 | 1.6 | 0.3 | 11.9 | 7.4 |
| 1970–1971 | 7.6 | 7.5 | 25.8 | 15.5 | 4.9 | 1.4 | 21.9 | 14.3 |
| 1985–1986 | 17.3 | 19.2 | 23.3 | 23.3 | 4.5 | 3.0 | 24.5 | 24.6 |

SOURCE: Adapted from Statistics Canada, *Education in Canada 1972* (Ottawa, 1973), Table 35, pp. 150–151; Statistics Canada, *Education in Canada 1986* (Ottawa, 1987), Table 19, pp. 119–131.

post-secondary education has failed to deliver the goods. Rather, it can be argued that our expectations about the mobility benefits that post-secondary education should bring have not adjusted to changing circumstances. Only in an elitist system can students expect that an attractive position will be available to them after graduation. In a contest-mobility system, such a guarantee does not exist. Contest-mobility systems do not try to protect the social value of a degree by restricting the number of competitors. But the social expectations appropriate to the previous elitist system, having survived its demise, now create disappointment when students discover that their education does not give them the social stratification advantages that tradition has led them to expect. A more realistic way of assessing the value of post-secondary education as a mobility strategy is to determine whether it confers more of an advantage than other forms of education.

As far as protection against unemployment is concerned, the answer is clear — unemployment tends to be lower among those with more education. In June 1984, Canada's unemployment rate stood at 10.7 percent overall, and at 17 percent among those aged 15 to 24. A study conducted at that time on the work experience of 1982 post-secondary graduates two years after graduation found that their unemployment rate was lower than the Canadian average for all ages and much lower than the overall average for their age group. It stood at 10 percent for community college graduates and holders of Bachelor's degrees, 8 percent for those with Master's degrees and 7 percent for those with doctorates. Among those who had found full-time employment, annual earnings varied directly with educational qualifications. The median annual salary for community college graduates was $6 000 below that of university graduates: $18 000 versus $24 000. Among university graduates, the highest median annual salary was earned by holders of doctorates ($34 000), followed by those with an MA ($32 000) and those with a BA ($23 000) (Clark, Laing, and Rechnitzer 1986). The absolute purchasing power of post-secondary education may have declined, but it still confers a competitive advantage in the job market. So this argument in favour of educational expansion is not necessarily invalid.

The expansionist policy *is* challenged, however, if we can demonstrate that the price of upward mobility has been rising because of an artificial inflation of "educational currency." And it seems that we can. In a book cleverly entitled *Education and Jobs: The Great Training Robbery*, Berg (1970) presents evidence that the escalation in educational requirements is not justified by the growing complexity of jobs. The educational credentials needed for many jobs have outstripped the actual skill levels required.

The relationship between education and the economy, then, seems to be more complex than the human capital theory suggests. The educational level of the labour force in an advanced industrial society is high, but not necessarily because expertise has become a functional necessity for an increasing number of jobs. While it cannot be denied that some jobs are highly specialized and require extensive educational preparation, it is also clear that other occupations have educational entrance requirements that cannot be justified on strictly technical grounds. Contrary to the human capital argument, rising educational requirements are not just a reflection of the increasing complexity of the occupational structure. To a large extent, education functions as a purely formal credential, as a screening device unrelated to the knowledge requirements of the job.

## The Social Failure

If educational expansion has not produced the expected economic benefits, what about the other reasons for its support? Has the belief in the importance of education as promoter of social justice been justified? Here, too, disappointment has set in. In spite of the attempt to make education more accessible, the underlying inequalities of gender and social class have not been overcome. Expansion has resulted in increased educational participation rates for all groups, but true reduction of inequality would involve relative gains. The crucial question is whether group disparities in educational achievement have been significantly narrowed.

**Gender Disparities.** Gender has been a traditional basis of social and educational inequality.

To what extent has expansion succeeded in making education more equally accessible to both males and females?

First, gender inequalities have been reduced at the secondary level; girls are now as likely as boys to finish high school. Also, equal proportions of boys and girls are enrolled in academic programs leading to university studies. But within academic programs boys are more likely to take science and mathematics, while girls tend to concentrate on the arts and the social sciences (Synge 1977).

Second, this relative equality at the secondary level is only partly matched at the post-secondary level. As the last column in Table 14-2 indicates, the overall group disparities in gender participation rates among full-time post-secondary students have disappeared. The gains, however, are unevenly distributed. In general, the lower the level of education, the greater the gender equality. Females have made the greatest relative gains at the undergraduate level. In 1985, 51.9 percent of the recipients of Bachelor's degrees were female; but female students received only 42.0 percent of the Master's degrees, and only 26.4 percent of the doctorates (Statistics Canada 1986).

Third, although females have increased their proportionate representation at the undergraduate level, the increase is distributed unequally among different types of programs. The overall full-time female undergraduate enrolment rate in 1985 was 48.9 percent; but it was only 12.3 in engineering and 45.7 in law, as compared to 59.8 in fine arts and 66.0 in education (Statistics Canada 1986).

These research findings indicate that progress has been made toward bridging gender disparities, but equality has not yet been achieved.

**Class Disparities.** Of all the barriers to equality, none has received more political attention than class of origin (see Chapter 8). No other topic has been investigated more fully than the relationship between education and social stratification. It remains difficult, however, to arrive at exact conclusions regarding the extent to which expansion has improved educational opportunities for lower-class students. Social class has been measured in so many different ways that it is not always possible to relate research findings directly to one

another or to develop comparisons over time. But we can identify a general pattern, even though we cannot be precise (OECD 1975; for Canada, see Guppy 1984).

First, despite all efforts, students from the lower classes remain less likely to be enrolled in academic programs on the secondary level, even when they possess the academic ability for university study. In 1971 in Ontario, for instance, almost all (96 percent) of the bright grade-12 students from the upper class were enrolled in the academic program; only 77 percent of the bright students from the lower class were in the program of study that matched their talent (Porter, Porter, and Blishen 1973). Canada-wide data collected in 1965 showed a similar pattern (Harvey and Lennards 1973).

There is a correlate to this finding: low-ability students from the upper class are enrolled disproportionately in academic programs. The school system seems to have great difficulty in "warming up" the aspirations of bright lower-class students and "cooling out" the aspirations of less bright upper-class students: 72 percent of upper-class students whose scores on a mental ability test placed them among the bottom third of all students were in the academic program, as compared to 38 percent of lower-class students of similarly low ability. Low ability at the upper end of the class scale has a much less inhibiting effect on educational plans than at the lower end.

Second, lower-class students are less likely to continue their formal education at the post-secondary level. This holds true regardless of talent. The proportion of bright students in grade 12 expecting to go to work after graduation from high school was found to be twice as high in the lower class as for students at other class levels (Porter, Porter, and Blishen 1973).

Third, lower-class students who do decide to continue their education at the post-secondary level are more likely than upper- or middle-class students to enrol in a community college (Guppy 1984).

Fourth, in addition to class inequalities in access to higher education, there are also class inequalities within higher education. Among the different faculties, law and medicine have the highest enrolment ratios of upper-class students, while education has the lowest. Upper-class students are also more likely to continue their education at the graduate level (Harvey and Lennards 1973).

Fifth, both Canadian and international data indicate that educational expansion has not succeeded in reducing existing social class differentials in university attendance. Proportionately, lower-class students have not improved their representation; as a group they are still as heavily under-represented as before. The major beneficiaries of expansion at the university level have been middle-class students (for U.S. see Carnoy and Levin 1976; for Canada see Guppy 1984).

One general conclusion emerges clearly from this: while expansion has led to a democratization of educational opportunities for individuals from previously disadvantaged sectors, it has been less successful in reducing existing group inequalities. The number of lower-class students receiving higher education has increased, but so has the size of the upper- and middle-class student population. In relative terms, no major victories have been won. It can even be argued that expansion has had detrimental effects in certain areas. In a number of ways, it has reinforced, rather than weakened, the existing structure of inequalities.

**Decreasing Equality.** As noted above, the massive increase in the supply of university graduates has resulted in a decrease in the value of educational credentials — a kind of inflation of educational currency. To the extent that upgraded educational requirements are artificial and bear no relationship to the actual job skills required, educational achievement has turned into a new form of job discrimination. Qualified people are denied access to jobs on the basis of irrelevant criteria. Career lines previously open to people without extensive training are now closed, and job ceilings based on education have reduced the possibility of working one's way up through the ranks.

The price of educational expansion has been lost job opportunities. This price is paid largely by those whose educational investment has not kept up with the rate of inflation. The social composition of this group will be obvious from the preceding discussion.

The escalation of educational job requirements has produced a second unfortunate effect: it has substantially reduced the relative gains to be achieved by attaining additional years of schooling. This has made entry into the mainstream of society more difficulty for groups that, as late-comers to the social mobility process, start from a low position. Native peoples, for example, labour under this special handicap. Educational expansion improves mobility prospects only as long as it confers a competitive advantage. In the past, when educational entrance requirements for access to middle-level jobs were not high, it was possible to improve one's opportunities considerably by spending a few more years in school. But the educational entrance fee to middle positions has risen sharply. To achieve the same relative improvement, a much greater educational investment is required. In fact, as long as the inflation affecting educational credentials continues unchecked, disadvantaged groups will have to run harder simply to avoid falling behind.

Under these conditions, how fair is it to expect that education will give these groups an equally good chance to catch up with the main pack? The problems faced by latecomers in the race are different. When we collectively refuse to admit this and continue to insist that education is the major avenue of social advancement, these groups are put at a considerable disadvantage. At the same time, their failure is rationalized: it must be deserved. ("Other groups have done it in the past. Why can't they?")

We have just identified two ways in which educational expansion has made matters worse for the groups with the least educational attainment. There is a related question: Who has profited most from it? The benefits of increased educational opportunities have accrued to groups that were well placed at the start of the race. As a result of educational inflation, the competition for good jobs has now moved up to a higher level and requires more years of education. The cultural and motivational advantages possessed by middle- and upper-class students enable them to meet these demands and to maintain or even increase their relative position. Our discussion of inequalities within higher education is of particular relevance in this regard.

The high hopes that spurred the rapid development of the Canadian educational system have been shaken. Educational expansion has brought about an escalation of educational prerequisites. As a result of this development, the economic and social underpinnings of an expansionist policy for education have been undermined. Opening up access to higher education is of little social benefit when, in response to a greater supply of university graduates, educational requirements for employment are raised by a similar amount. The economic basis for expanding education is also undermined, because the artificial upgrading process does not guarantee a high return on educational investment, on either the societal or the personal level. Neither justice nor efficiency is automatically assured by the expansion of the educational system.

The present skepticism about the policy of educational expansion provides us with a good sociological opportunity for assessing the nature of the support base for education. Increased opportunities for schooling can be defended on a number of grounds. Studies of the effects of higher education on attitudes have demonstrated, for instance, that university education makes an important contribution to the goal of democratic citizenship training. Support for civil rights, degree of tolerance, willingness to participate in political activities, level of political awareness: all these qualities, which are arguably relevant to the operation of a democratic society, increase with education (Harvey and Lennards 1973). And as the Massey Report (1951) pointed out, education is also vital to the cultural life of a society. Universities are important instruments of nation-building; on the individual level, they are sources of personal self-enrichment. These possible rationales for educational expansion have not been invalidated by recent developments; however, they are seldom mentioned in the public debate about the benefits to be derived from schooling.

At present, the argument in favour of education tends to be cast mainly in economic terms. In order to protect our standard of living, we need to be able to compete successfully in international markets. Education is a crucial strategic resource in the tough world of high-tech development. The human capital or educational investment view popular in the 1960s is still being promoted, with a couple of refinements. First, Japan has replaced the U.S. as the nation to catch up with. Second, proponents of this view no longer consider eco-nomic efficiency to be closely linked to mass education and educational expansion. Academic excellence and tougher standards have now become the catchwords. Some observers have argued that this increased concern with selectivity is not unrelated to the fact that the number of qualified students has increased faster than the supply of jobs. The educational system, they hold, should now be called upon to reduce the number of competitors and to bring social aspirations more firmly into line with economic realities.

So far we have described the facts of the recent history of educational expansion in Canada. In the next two sections, we will review the attempts undertaken by sociologists to make theoretical sense of these facts and to come up with explanations for them.

## The Theoretical Perspectives

Until recently, the dominant framework for analyzing the role of education in modern society has been provided by the human capital theory. As Collins (1971, 1979) has noted, if we translate human capital theory into sociological terms, it becomes a version of the structural-functional theory of social stratification (discussed in Chapters 1 and 8). When discussing education, a combination of these theories creates the idea of technological functionalism.

### Technological Functionalism

The basic premises of **technological functionalism** include the following:

1. The skill requirements of occupations in our society are constantly increasing.
2. Talented people need to be recruited to fill the more highly skilled jobs.
3. The educational system is the place where the selection and training of talent occur.
4. Rising skill requirements for occupations therefore require an expansion of the educational system.

It is assumed that educational requirements reflect the functional needs of the occupational structure. Employers assess the skill level required for particular jobs and set the educational entrance requirements accordingly. That is, the relationship between education and the labour market is technically determined. But in this chapter we have presented data that cast serious doubts on the accuracy of this view of the role of education in modern society. The function of education cannot be explained in these purely instrumental terms. We saw earlier that educational requirements for employment often bear little relationship to the actual knowledge demands of the job. The disappointing results of the policy of educational expansion might therefore be related to the weakness of its theoretical base. Indeed, the functional view of the relationship between education and the labour market has been challenged from two quarters, both of which approach education from a conflict perspective and both of which stress the nontechnical relevance of educational certification.

## The Weberian Challenge

Like Marx, Weber saw society as a constellation of conflicting interest groups (Bendix 1962). But unlike Marx, Weber believed that the struggle for social advantages takes place on more than one front.

In addition to economic power there is *status power*. Status power depends on one's position in the cultural order. It is acquired by monopolizing the possession of particular cultural attributes and using these attributes as a basis for establishing social superiority. Status power is obtained by the formation of status groups; those who advance the same claim start associating with each other and act out their claim to deference by creating a distinctive way of life (through taste, manners, opinions, or leisure activities). This serves to differentiate them from others and becomes a mark of social distance and exclusiveness (Gerth and Mills 1958).

To the extent that a status group's claim to cultural superiority is accepted by other groups, its demands are treated with deference and its power is legitimized. Thus, status power based on deference is an important social resource, and status group needs to be recognized, according to Weber, along with social class as a basic unit of organization within the social stratification system.

Drawing on these Weberian ideas about the importance of status groups, Collins (1971, 1979) has advanced a conflict interpretation of the role of education in our society. The link between educational certification and jobs is based largely on the desire to impress others, and has little or nothing to do with technical competence. Advanced education functions as a *status attribute*, a mark of social distinction that enables its possessors to convince others of the importance of their work.

Impression management plays a central role in the occupational world. For many jobs the degree of competence required is difficult to assess. The expertise of mechanical engineers can be evaluated readily; they help make tangible products. As long as their bridges do not collapse, their competence is accepted. The work speaks for itself and claims for higher income can be staked on this basis. But what about the work of teachers, civil servants, bank managers, doctors? Here the product is not clearly visible, and the criteria for adequate performance are not all obvious. For example, what exactly does a bank manager contribute, and what is required to be a good one? Since the product does not speak for itself, such occupations face a credibility problem. They are confronted with the task of creating trust in the importance and competence of their services. It is here that education comes in.

According to Collins, educational certification operates as a trust-generating device in our society. Educational credentials are widely recognized and generally accepted symbols of competence. By making them a condition for entrance, some occupations and organizations secure for themselves the confidence and awe they need from the public. If it is difficult to enter, the occupation must be important and demanding; because the practitioners form a select group, their competence can be taken for granted. Exclusiveness breeds prestige. It makes you look better. Prestige so obtained can in turn be converted into claims for higher income. One basic strategy followed by occupational groups in search of advancement has been to raise the educational requirements and then to command a salary commensurate with the supposedly "increased importance and difficulty" of the job. Collins maintains that the upgrading of educational requirements is largely artificial. Educational credentials are social weapons used by occupations and organizations in the struggle for social advantages.

This explanation of the link between education and jobs constitutes only one of Collins's theoretical concerns. His second major objective is to demonstrate how a theory of status group competition explains why, as we noted earlier, educational requirements have been steadily rising. An increased supply of educated people reduces the prestige value of education. What was previously a mark of distinction (a Bachelor's degree, for example) becomes merely a mark of average respectability. In response to this devaluation of education, educational entrance requirements will be raised in order to restore the lost prestige value: an MA may now be required for a job that used to call for a BA. This, in turn, will trigger a further round of educational inflation. Unless we take the drastic step of making it illegal to set formal education requirements for employment, Collins sees no end to this spiral (Collins 1979).

## The Marxist Challenge

The second challenge to the functional interpretation of the role of schooling in modern society comes from Marxism. In *Schooling in Capitalist America*, Bowles and Gintis (1976) present a radical critique of the notion that education promotes social justice. They view schools not as instruments of social and economic progress that serve the needs of a technological and meritocratic society, but as agencies of social control and repression that serve the interests of the economic elite. As such, the main task of the schools is to produce workers who will accept their positions within the capitalist system.

The key to the analysis of the educational system, claim Bowles and Gintis, is the structure and functioning of the capitalist economy. Under capitalism the social relations of production are characterized by alienation and domination. Workers are treated as commodities: they exchange their labour for wages in a workplace based on a hierarchical division of labour. Schools prepare individuals for alienated and stratified work relationships. In effect they "reproduce" labour power.

Like Collins, Bowles and Gintis reject the view that the relationship between education and the labour market has a strictly technical base. Education is important primarily for reasons that have nothing to do with knowledge. It fosters the type of worker consciousness required by the very nature of the capitalist work situation. Workers must be psychologically prepared to accept their positions in the productive system. This psychological preparation is accomplished by the creation of a correspondence between the social relations of production and the social relations of education, a correspondence between workplace and classroom.

Schools are organized like factories, and the educational process is analogous to commodity production. Students have little control over the content of their work, and they are spurred on by grades and other external rewards. Schools, in other words, teach students to accept meaningless, alienating work for the sake of future external rewards (the paycheque). The authority relations between teachers and students replicate the hierarchical division of labour. Students are permitted limited freedom and autonomy and are taught to be docile and passive: "Students are rewarded for exhibiting discipline, subordinacy, intellectually as opposed to emotionally oriented behaviour, and hard work independent from intrinsic task motivation" (Bowles and Gintis 1976).

The way in which particular schools reproduce the values and personality characteristics necessary to a capitalist society varies depending on the level of the occupational structure toward which their graduates are headed. The social organization of instruction for future manual workers is not the same as that for future managerial personnel, because their work situations will differ.

Lower-level workers perform tasks requiring little discretion and responsibility, and their work is closely supervised. Consequently, discipline among vocational students tends to be strict and emphasis is placed on punctuality and unquestioned rule-following. Higher-level workers must be flexible and innovative and must work autonomously without direct supervision. Their efficiency depends on how thoroughly they have internalized the work ethic.

This flexibility is reflected in the social atmosphere of the college-oriented program. The emphasis is on "soft socialization" rather than on behavioural control. Students are permitted more choice in their activities and the interaction between teachers and students is more relaxed. Instead of demanding blind obedience, the program encourages students to be co-operative, to be involved, and to choose voluntarily what is good for them. This is merely another version of social control — internal, rather than external, compliance. It does not change the objective of schooling. The function of education is to teach the appropriate type of worker discipline. The social organization of schools is shaped by the demands of the capitalist production process.

Because the capitalist order is based on inequality, it is unrealistic, warn Bowles and Gintis, to expect that education can produce a more egalitarian society. Schools try to convince people that their selection process is meritocratic, but they are essential props for the reproduction and legitimation of existing inequalities. Educational expansion has not been more successful in promoting justice because the policy has been based on the wrong assumptions about the relationship between schooling and society. Schools are dependent institutions serving the interests of the capitalist elite. As long as capitalism persists, schools will never be instruments of social liberation.

We will shortly turn to an assessment of the theories discussed in this section. But first let us consider how structural functionalists and conflict theorists differ in their approach to another important topic.

## The Sources of Inequality

The difficulty encountered by the schools in extending equal opportunities to all has spawned a vast research literature. A major preoccupation within the sociology of education has been to locate empirically the social factor or factors that determine educational success. The research has proven informative in two ways: it identifies fairly precisely the nature of the obstacles experienced by lower-class students; and it illustrates how each of the two major theoretical perspectives — the structural-functional perspective and the conflict perspective — studies the problem of inequality in a different way.

## Defining the Problem

The major contribution of empirical research has been to demonstrate that social class functions not only as a barrier to **equality of access** to education, but also as a barrier to performance in education. Scholarships, the regional spread of post-secondary educational institutions, the equalization of teachers' salaries and of school resources in general: these remove certain external barriers to equal participation in education. But equality of access is not enough. The strategy of equalizing educational resources makes a politically convenient assumption: that the problem can be solved by administrative changes. This strategy, however, is based on too narrow a view of the nature of the handicaps experienced by students from underprivileged groups. It assumes that, once there is equal access, there will be no further differences between the social classes in their ability to profit equally from the opportunities available to them. This is not accurate. It is not enough to provide equal entrance to the race when not all social classes are equally able to participate in the competition.

Consequently, the task of the educational system is to equalize starting positions by providing **equality of nurture;** attention and resources must be distributed according to students' needs. This definition of the role of the school has important policy implications. The educational system is now entrusted with the new responsibility of ensuring that all students participate in the race under equal conditions. Instead of just making learning opportunities available — with the result that those who are well equipped by their social class background to take advantage are favoured — the school is called upon to play an active, interventionist role and to compensate for milieu disadvantages. The initiative for overcoming inequalities has shifted from the student to the educational system.

## Home Environment

Sociologists have located social determinants of unequal school performance in both the home and the school environments. What are some of the salient intellectual and motivational factors that have been singled out as blocking the potential

**Along with teaching knowledge and skills, the mandate of Canadian school systems is to identify students' abilities and potential.**

of lower-class students? Let us turn to the home environment first.

**Achievement Motivation.** Researchers have consistently found that school performance is related to aspirations for educational success. Lower-class children do worse in school, it is argued, because they do not receive enough encouragement at home. Their parents visit school less frequently and tend to have lower ambitions for them. But the conclusion that lower-class children and their parents have less desire to succeed must be critically examined, because it appears to result partly from the way ambition has been measured.

Often, ambition levels are inferred by asking parents and students about their specific aspirations. Aspirations for university education, for instance, are viewed as an index of a strong desire to succeed. This measurement assumes that the goal of higher education is equidistant for individuals from all social classes. But the desire to attend university may or may not signify a high level of ambition. As a measure of the actual distance to be travelled, it indicates a very high degree of ambition for lower-class students and only a moderate degree for upper-class students. To avoid the problem that occurs when striving for a specific goal is taken as an index for level of ambition, Breton (1972), in his study of Canadian high school students, measured ambition in terms of a general desire to succeed. His findings reveal that lower-class boys and girls tend to be more ambitious than is generally assumed: 44 percent of lower-class boys (and 38 percent of girls) expressed a high ambition to succeed, as compared to 42 percent of middle-class and 36 percent of upper-class boys (28 and 24 percent of girls respectively).

**Language Use.** Starting with the work of Bernstein (1973, 1974, 1976), sociologists have tried to relate social class differences in educational achievement to social class differences in language use. According to Bernstein, lower- and middle-class people use different "language codes" — identified, respectively, as a restricted and an elaborated code. The **restricted language code** is characterized by its use of implicit, context-bound meanings, while the **elaborated language code** meanings are explicit and universal.

An example can best illustrate the difference. A group of middle-class and lower-class five-year-olds were asked to tell a story in response to a series of pictures: some boys playing football, the ball going through a window, a man making a threatening gesture, a woman looking out of the window, and the boys moving away. A middle-class child told the following story:

*Three boys are playing football and one boy kicks the ball and it goes through the window the ball breaks the window and the boys are looking at it and a man comes out and shouts at them because they had broken the window so they run away and then that lady looks out of her window and she tells the boys off. (Bernstein 1970)*

Based on the same pictures, a lower-class child told this story:

*They're playing football and he kicks it and it goes through there it breaks the window and they're looking at it and he comes out and he shouts at them because they'd broken it so they run away and then she looks out and she tells them off. (Bernstein 1970)*

The first story can be understood without reference to the pictures; the second one cannot. Children in middle-class families are encouraged in their speech and writing to elaborate their meanings, to be explicit and specific, so that their language is understandable to all, including outsiders. Lower-class language is more particular: it is the language of insiders, and it is accessible only to those who have knowledge of the context within which it is generated.

What is the educational significance of these language codes? How do these different ways of communicating affect school performance? One interpretation of the different language codes Bernstein found is that they reflect differences in cognitive skills. The restricted code is viewed as an "inferior" form of speech. Students who have been taught to communicate in this mode understandably fail to perform well in school; after all, they suffer from a cognitive deficit. They have been raised in an unstimulating, "culturally deprived" environment that has stunted their verbal and, hence, their analytical ability. Whether it is accurate to use the language differences that Bernstein noted as a basis for a deficit theory will be considered shortly. For now, let us move out of the home and into the school.

## School Environment

Several characteristics of the school environment are sources of inequality of nurture for lower-class children.

**Influence Structure.** Inequalities in educational performance derive from inequalities in the normative support available to students in their immediate school environment. One major source of influence is teacher expectations. The best-known study of teacher expectations and their possible self-fulfilling effect was conducted by Rosenthal and Jacobson (1968). In this study, students in an elementary school were given a general achievement test at the end of the 1963–64 academic year. Teacher expectations were created by claiming that the test had been developed to identify intellectual "late bloomers," children who could be expected to show unusually large achievement gains during the coming academic year. In the fall, a few children in each classroom were identified to their teachers as late bloomers. These students had been randomly selected; absolutely no factual basis existed for the expectations induced in the teachers. In the spring, when all the students were retested, the data showed some evidence that the children who had been identified as late bloomers did indeed make more intellectual gains than the others. Rosenthal and Jacobson concluded that it was the favourable expectations they had created that caused these gains. Teacher expectations have a self-fulfilling effect on students.

The Rosenthal and Jacobson (1968) study has been criticized for its methodological weakness, and attempts to replicate it have not produced consistent findings. Studies using a naturalistic, rather than an experimental approach have yielded less ambiguous results (Brophy and Good 1974). Instead of manipulating or creating teacher expectations, these naturalistic studies take as their point of departure the teacher's own expectations of students, as they actually exist. Such teacher expectations have proven not to be automatically self-fulfilling. As yet, not enough is known about how the process actually operates at the classroom level.

With regard to lower-class students, there is some evidence that some teachers make judgments about a student's academic potential on the basis of such factors as neatness of dress, general deportment, and home background (Silberman 1970). A certain number of teachers probably form stereotyped opinions about what can be expected from certain categories of students, but there is little systematic information on how widespread stereotyping is and who is most adversely affected by it. For this information, sociologists will have to undertake more detailed analyses of classroom behaviour.

A second source of influence on academic achievement is the student body. Several researchers have established that aspirations are affected by the social class composition of the student population. Lower-class boys in predominantly middle-class schools have been found to possess higher aspirations than lower-class boys in working-class schools (Wilson 1959). Because schools recruit their students from the areas in which they are located, residential segregation is a built-in source of inequality in our school system. In the United States, busing has been introduced partly as a means of equalizing peer-group support for aspirations.

**Selection Procedures.** To the extent that school rely on IQ tests to assess a student's academic ability, lower-class students are put at a disadvantage. Intelligence consists of two components: an innate, genetically determined potential; and a learned, environmental element that determines how far that potential will be fulfilled. The more favourably it is nurtured, the more a person's natural ability will flourish. No test can measure innate potential; we can only establish nurtured ability. IQ tests therefore favour those who have received good intellectual nurturing and systematically underestimate the reservoir of talent existing among lower-class students.

In addition, IQ tests are often culture-bound. Lower-class children score less well simply because they have not had exposure to the types of situations emphasized in the tests. A final consideration to keep in mind is that test-taking is a performance. It is a challenge of a particular kind. Only students possessed of a truly competitive intellectual spirit will be able to generate the motivation required for answering questions that have little intrinsic relevance. Lower-class students generally are less well prepared to perform in this fashion. When they are given special training in taking IQ tests, however, their scores improve dramatically (Boocock 1972).

**The Missing Dimension: Cultural Transmission.** We have identified the range of variables generally included in a structural-functional analysis of educational inequality. Before introducing the contribution of conflict sociologists, let us pause for a moment and consider what this selection of variables implies about the way the relationship between schooling and inequality is conceived. School performance is seen as a product of ability and motivation. Because of deficiencies in nurture in both home and school environments, these educational resources are not equally distributed among lower-class students and students from families of higher status. Two kinds of remedial action are typically undertaken in an attempt to equalize nurturing conditions.

To remedy the deficiencies of the home environment, preschool compensatory programs are introduced to help bridge the distance between the culturally deprived child and the school. Even though the roots of unequal performance lie in the interaction between the home and school environments, policy intervention is directed primarily at the former. Preschool enrichment programs such as Head Start try to cultivate in their charges the characteristics required for adaptation to school. The problem is defined largely as stemming from cultural deprivation in the home, rather than from cultural unreceptiveness in the school. As Bernstein (1970) rightfully claims, the concept of compensatory education "serves to direct attention away from the internal organization and the educational content of the school and focus our attention onto families and children." The cultural standards of the school are not questioned; rather, children's inability to live up to them is seen as evidence of a deficiency in the home environment. In this context, Bernstein's research on the existence of different language codes is often applied in a particular way.

Because the restricted code deviates from the accepted middle-class norm, it comes to be seen as an index of linguistic deprivation, rather than merely a mark of linguistic difference. The unequal school performance of lower-class children is seen in that light. There is, however, a much simpler and more accurate explanation of the relationship between restricted-code use and school failure. Lower-class children are handicapped in school not because they lack verbal and cognitive ability, but because their normal mode of communication is not accepted as an appropriate form of discourse. Forced to suddenly switch to an unfamiliar language code, these children perform poorly. Their performance is then *interpreted* as lack of general ability. It is this inability of the school to adjust its cultural standards that creates the problem for the lower-class child.

The analysis of how the school affects inequality of opportunity displays a similar blindness to its culture-bound operation. Where it is recognized that attributes of the school environment might also provide unequal conditions for nurture, corrective policies have been aimed primarily at improving the organization and techniques of instruction: increasing per-student expenditures, abolishing rigid selection procedures and IQ tests, developing attractive teaching materials. In other words, the school-related sources of inequality are taken to involve the delivery of education, not its content. What is being taught, that is, the curriculum, the very nature of the school as an agent of cultural transmission, is not seen as a possible cause of inequality.

From a social stratification point of view, this neglect of the role of the school in cultural transmission appears to represent serious oversight. Schools are not neutral institutions. They teach certain values, they select certain subjects for inclusion in the curriculum, they call upon particular skills: in so doing, they give cultural recognition — and social stratification advantages — to certain groups over others.

Bourdieu (1974) has coined the term "cultural capital" to refer to the role of the school curriculum in maintaining social inequality. According to him, schools present upper-class culture as an objective measurement of merit. Because of this orientation, upper-class parents are able to provide their children with the type of cultural resources required for educational success. Privileges are still passed on from one generation to another; only the form of inheritance has changed. What counts now is not economic but cultural capital.

That we must study the school as a medium of cultural transmission has been forcefully asserted in recent years by conflict sociologists. According to Bernstein (1971), schools define what counts as knowledge (curriculum), how knowledge is to be transmitted (pedagogy), and what counts as a valid realization of it (assessment procedures). What determines the schools' decisions in each of these areas? Who loses and who gains as a result of each particular selection? Raising these questions enlarges our awareness of the way the school is involved in the social stratification process.

## Theories: A Comparison

We have presented the relationship between education and society from both a technological-functional and from a conflict perspective. By way of summary, let us systematically identify the major

# A Fable — The Animal School

Once upon a time, the animals decided they must do something heroic to meet the problems of a new world. So they organized a school.

They adopted an activity curriculum consisting of running, climbing, swimming, and flying. To make it easier to administer the curriculum, all the animals took all the subjects.

The duck was excellent in swimming, in fact, better than his instructor. But, he only made passing grades in flying and was very poor in running. Because he was slow in running, he had to drop swimming and stay after school to practice running. This was kept up until his web feet were badly worn, and he was only average in swimming. But average was quite acceptable in school, so nobody worried about that — except the duck.

The rabbit started at the top of his class in running, but had a nervous breakdown because of so much make-up work in swimming. The squirrel was excellent in climbing, but he developed frustrations in flying class because his teacher made him start from the ground up instead of from the tree-top down. He developed charlie horses from overexertion and then got C in the climbing and D in running.

The eagle was a problem child and was severely disciplined. In climbing classes he beat all the others to the top of the tree, but insisted on using his own way to get there.

At the end of the year an abnormal eel who could swim exceedingly well, and could also run, climb and fly a little, had the highest marks and was class valedictorian.

The prairie dogs stayed out of school and fought the tax levy, because the administration would not add digging and burrowing to the curriculum. They apprenticed their child to a badger and later joined the ground hogs and gophers to start an independent school.

**Source:**

George H. Reavis *Phi Delta Kappa* (n.d.).

---

points of difference between these two approaches. Under the conflict perspective we include both the Weberian (Collins) analysis and the Marxist (Bowles and Gintis) analysis. Let us start with the four major points of difference:

1. *Societal Determinants of Education.* Technological functionalists see education as an instrument for the fulfillment of societal needs. Both the size of the educational system and the curriculum are thought to be determined by the technological requirements of talent production in an expert society.

   Conflict theorists, on the other hand, see education as an instrument of domination: they hold that group interests, not functional needs, determine the nature and shape of education.

2. *Stratification Role of Education.* For technological functionalists, education operates as an instrument of social mobility in a meritocratic society. Educational selection takes place according to objective criteria and is universalistic.

   The conflict perspective sees education as an instrument of social class reproduction. Schools teach students to accept their future class position and legitimize the process by which students arrive at this destination. Because the criteria of educational selection favour the cultural capital of the privileged groups, schools also perpetuate the inheritance of social advantages for those groups.

3. *Relevance of Educational Credentials.* Educational requirements reflect the technological needs of the labour market, according to technological functionalists. Education is used as a screening device for assessing technical competence.

   Both versions of the conflict perspective argue that education is used as a nontechnical attribute. Collins claims that education is a resource in the competition for social status. In order to maintain the prestige on which their privilege rests, elite occupations will increase educational requirements in response to an increased supply of more highly educated people. For Bowles and Gintis, education is relevant because it produces appropriately socialized workers. It is an instrument of social control. Educational requirements rise in response to changes in the nature of the production process. Monopoly capitalism, with its attendant bureaucratization, has produced a need for dependable workers who have internalized labour discipline — hence the increased demand for graduates from the higher levels of the educational system.

4. *Sources of Unequal Academic Achievement.* Technological functionalists are well aware of the discrepancy between the ideal and the real meritocratic society and are concerned about increasing equality of educational opportunity. They believe that the obstacles to equality are in principle removable and that the determinants of inequality in school performance are located either in the home environment or in the delivery system of the school.

Conflict theorists, however, claim that inequality of educational opportunity is inevitable. Discrimination is embedded in the cultural operation of the school system. Education is not a neutral institution that stands outside the social stratification system; it is a constituent part of that system. Schools decide the basis on which social stratification entitlements are to be granted. Only certain skills and values are taught in the schools and receive cultural recognition. Inevitably, therefore, certain groups and individuals will be favoured over others.

The conflict perspective on education emerged in the 1970s in opposition to the conventional wisdom about education embodied in the technological-functional view. Because of the polemical thrust of the argument, little attempt has been made to explore possible areas of agreement. For example, functionalists would have no trouble accepting that the school functions as an instrument of both mobility and social control. Social selection according to talent and status socialization into the meritocratic ideology are complementary rather than alternative ways of defining the social stratification function of education in our society.

Similarly, with regard to the relevance of education as a credential, Collins (1971) admits that "at appropriate points" the technical-skill argument must be considered. Although status competition provides the principal dynamic behind the rise in educational requirements, changes in the technical requirements of jobs have also contributed to the process (Collins 1971). The exact role of both these factors needs to be investigated further.

Despite disagreements on many substantive issues, technological functionalism and some Marxist versions of conflict theory (Bowles and Gintis, for example) hold similar views on the relationship between education and society. Both see schools as merely reflecting the demands of the wider society. What happens in schools is substantially determined either by the technological requirements of society or by the economic needs of the capitalist elite. We may call this the **empty box view of education**. Schools as organizations do not seem to possess a life of their own; they merely act as passive transmitters for outside influences.

However, there is a danger of oversimplification inherent in such an approach. As an example of this danger, let us take Bowles and Gintis's (1976) analysis of the correspondence between the social relations of the classroom and of the marketplace. The authors postulate that the correspondence between classroom and marketplace is not accidental. Schools are bureaucratically organized and teach passivity and docility, they claim, because such behaviour is functional from the point of view of the capitalist elite. But this ignores alternative explanations.

A system of mass public education faces unique problems of organizational control generated from within. Unlike other organizations, public schools have no say in the selection of clients. They are not allowed to follow selective admission procedures; they must accept every student in their area, regardless of motivation or ability. Unlike other organizations, schools cannot get rid of their failures. Students are legally obliged to attend until age 16. Faced with a captive student population, what steps can schools take to create positive commitment? Here again, the options are limited. For many students, learning is boring and generates little intrinsic interest. The only universal incentive the school can offer is an external one: grades. Grades are promises of future rewards; they are pieces of investment in a career. But grades work only as an incentive to those who are ambitious and are doing well. To a failing or low-achieving student, school has few rewards to offer. Disciplinary practices in the school can be seen as attempts to deal with the constraints imposed by the need to motivate and control a captive clientele. An emphasis on strict rule-following will probably be found in the lower streams of all schools, regardless of the nature of the economic order, because the discipline problem is most severe where the school has the fewest tangible benefits to offer.

Similarly, classroom management will present fewer problems among students who can see that their education is going to pay off. "Soft" socialization practices can replace emphasis on rule-following among college-oriented students. All this socialization may turn out to be functional for the workplace, but it is fallacious to infer that workplace requirements have a direct casual impact on school organization. Such an inference ignores the fact that these organizational tendencies are found in all types of societies once mass public education is introduced.

So school organization produces pressures of its own; it is not merely acted upon. Moreover, teachers and students also have some control over the way they respond to pressures, whether generated from within the school system or from the wider society. Both technological-functional and conflict explanations of schooling too readily assume that life in school involves a mechanistic response to outside demands. But teachers do not always behave the way the system wants, and students do not always follow what teachers say. Teachers have a high degree of classroom autonomy. As you know from your own experience, within the same educational institution you can find considerable variation in teaching style and emphasis. Teacher autonomy is one of the reasons it has proven so difficult to change the educational system. Similarly, students have their own ways of dealing with the demands of the school system. They develop many responses, ranging from challenging the authority of the teacher (Hargreaves 1967) to attempts to control their workload so that they can "make it" (Becker, Geer, and Hughes 1960).

Life in school represents a negotiated, rather than a unilaterally imposed, social order. Teacher and students are neither free to conduct the education process as they see fit nor completely constrained by the system. What happens in individual classrooms represents the combined product of societal pressures, organizational conditions, and the type of coping strategies teachers and students manage to develop in response. A full analysis of the educational system must do justice to all these factors. In recent years, researchers working within the conflict tradition have started to move in this direction.

## The Future of Education

The story is told of an old man who returned to his birthplace after a long absence. Many things had changed, but there was one place where he felt immediately at home: his former school. This is not surprising; the basic social pattern of education has changed little since the beginning of this century. Schooling remains to a large degree, as it was then, an age-specific enterprise pursued in the early stages of a person's life before entering the world of work. It takes place in isolation from the rest of the community, within the walls of a building or group of buildings. Schooling is based on group instruction. Students are differentiated according to their age into grade levels; within each grade they take courses. Advancement proceeds from one grade level to the next. The entire process is teacher-directed. Classes are run by teachers, who are considered the experts in charge of the educational process. But familiar as this social framework might be, it is unlikely to survive your lifetime.

One major trend already under way is the change from education as an age-specific process to education as a lifelong endeavour. In the future, education will probably extend from cradle to grave. The growth of the double-income family, along with other related changes (discussed in Chapter 11), is already creating strong pressures for the provision of daycare centres for the very young. In time, many hope to see these facilities made available on the same basis as public schooling — as a right for all. If this happens, we can expect that regulations will be tightened, and that the amateur will be replaced by the certified expert. Daycare will be turned into early childhood education.

At the other end, education will not be completed for most of us once we enter the world of work. Given the rapidity of scientific and technological change, the stock of knowledge and skill we acquire between the ages of five and twenty-four will no longer suffice for a lifetime. We will probably return to education for professional up-

**Adult education is often pursued for occupational socialization.**

grading and new career training. But for many people, lifelong learning will not be motivated only by instrumental considerations. Education will also be pursued for intrinsic reasons: as a means of self-enrichment and self-realization. The cultural motive of self-fulfillment is gaining strength in our society; it is fed by, among other things, the increase in the number of highly educated people. Education tends to create its own demand.

The opening up of new markets for education will almost certainly be accompanied by a weakening, particularly at the post-primary level, of the monopoly now held by the school system. Financial and technical considerations would bring about this shift. Education is a labour-intensive rather than a capital-intensive enterprise. That is, we use people, rather than machines, to produce educational outcomes. Salaries for the teaching staff constitute the largest item in education budgets. Expanding education further will therefore be costly, unless we can find alternatives to the traditional, labour-intensive teaching methods. The microcomputer and the video disk make such a change in instructional technology possible. For many subjects, attractive, high-quality educational materials will become available at reason-

able cost. This will lead, some predict, to the creation of a decentralized, geographically dispersed network of learning opportunities that people will be able to plug into from anywhere — home, school, or work. Schools would constitute only one part of our educational system. So that they would undergo a common socialization experience, children would still be required to attend school, but they could also study at home. Also, instruction and promotion could be more individualized. Teachers would no longer simply dispense knowledge; they would manage and facilitate a student-centred learning process.

These are some of the directions education is likely to take in the future. The speed and exact scope of these changes is difficult to predict. They will not be universally welcomed; some groups whose interests will be affected will no doubt oppose them. For sociologists, all this will guarantee that education will continue to be an area worthy of investigation.

## SUMMARY

1. Universal, state-supported schooling is a modern invention that dates from the nineteenth century.
2. The functions of education are occupational socialization; social selection and status socialization; democratic citizenship training, creation of a common cultural identity; development of personality and human potential; and innovation.
3. Education is likely to be surrounded by controversy. First, not all the functions of education receive equal public support. Evidence has been presented to show that the economic and the social stratification functions have received the strongest emphasis. Second, some of the functions of education contain internal and external contradictions, and disagreement about specific objectives is not uncommon.
4. The impetus for the massive expansion of the educational system in Canada since the 1950s has come from two sources: a concern for economic productivity and a concern for social justice. Human capital theory provided the

economic rationale for educational expansion. Social justice without major revision of the social stratification system provided the social rationale.

5. In terms of social orientation, Canadian education has shifted from sponsored mobility to contest mobility. The Quebec educational system is an example of this trend.

6. One of the main effects of educational expansion has been an escalation of educational requirements. This has undermined both its economic and social rationales. Although some absolute gains have been made in the area of social justice, existing gender and class inequalities, in relative terms, have not been resolved.

7. The sociological counterpart to human capital theory is technological functionalism, a perspective that sees the school as a neutral instrument for satisfying a society's technological needs. There are two alternatives, both involving conflict interpretations of the role of education: Collins has presented a Weberian-inspired and Bowles and Gintis a Marxist-inspired theory of education. Both stress the role of the school as an instrument of social domination.

8. Two strategies for improving educational opportunities can be distinguished: equality of access and equality of nurture. Each implies different responsibilities for the school system.

9. Two home-based and three school-related sources of unequal nurture have been identified. The home-based sources are achievement motivation and language use; the school-related sources are the influence structure of the school, its selection procedures, and the cultural transmission role it performs. Structural functionalists (here represented by technological functionalists) and conflict theorists differ in the emphasis they place on these factors.

10. The functional and conflict perspectives have been compared along four dimensions: societal determinants of education, the stratification role of education, the relevance of education as a credential, and sources of unequal academic achievement. Some of the differences are more apparent than real and represent only differences in emphasis. Others are more substantive. Both perspectives have been criticized for ignoring the study of school life as a variable in its own right.

11. Education in the future will probably be lifelong, with schools becoming just part of a larger network of educational facilities. Instructional technology, many predict, will make available more individualized and decentralized forms of learning.

## GLOSSARY

**Contest mobility.** Open competition for elite status.

**Democratic citizenship training.** Preparation for political participation in the affairs of a democratic society.

**Education.** Deliberate, organized transmission of values, knowledge, and skills.

**Elaborated language code.** Form of communication that makes meanings explicit and universal.

**Elite preparatory.** Stage of educational development in a society: the majority of students do not finish high school, and the function of the high school is restricted to preparing a select group of students for university education.

**Empty box view of education.** View that schools are passive transmitters for outside influences, with no life of their own.

**Equality of access.** Removal of external barriers to educational participation.

**Equality of nurture.** Removal of barriers to educational performance.

**Human capital theory.** Economic theory holding that the skill level of the labour force is the prime determinant of economic growth.

**Mass terminal.** Stage of educational development in a society: secondary education has become universal, but post-secondary education is pursued by a minority only.

**Meritocracy.** Society in which merit constitutes the basis for social stratification and in which all people have an equal chance to display their talents and to be evaluated fairly.

**Occupational socialization.** Preparation for entering the job market.

**Restricted language code.** Form of communication that leaves meanings implicit.

**Sponsored mobility.** Competition for elite status on the basis of criteria set by the existing elite.

**Status socialization.** Process of teaching people to accept their position in the social stratification system. Includes two components: *ambition regulation* and *legitimation*.

**Technological functionalism.** A perspective that sees rising educational requirements as a reflection of the increased complexity of the occupational structure.

# FURTHER READING

**Husén, Torsten.** *The School in Question: A Comparative Study of the School and Its Future in Western Societies.* Oxford: Oxford University Press, 1979. A wide-ranging international assessment of some central problems confronting mass education.

**Illich, Ivan.** *Deschooling Society.* New York: Harper and Row, 1972. A fundamental attack on the whole concept of schooling. Controversial and stimulating.

**Livingstone, D.W.** *Social Crisis and Schooling.* Toronto: Garamond Press, 1985. A neo-Marxist analysis of the state of education in Canada.

**Murphy, Raymond.** *Sociological Theories of Education.* Toronto: McGraw-Hill Ryerson, 1979. A solid and even-handed discussion of major sociological approaches. Provides a thorough assessment of Canadian contributions to the field.

**Prentice, Alison.** *The School Promoters: Education and Social Class in Mid-Nineteenth-Century Upper Canada.* Toronto: McClelland and Stewart, 1977. Examines a formative period in the history of anglophone Canadian education. The ideas and actions of Egerton Ryerson are analyzed from a conflict perspective.

**Wotherspoon, Terry.** *The Political Economy of Canadian Schooling.* Toronto: Methuen, 1987. A selection of articles analyzing the ways in which Canadian education contributes to the reproduction of class, gender, and racial inequalities.

# UNIT V

# Social Change

*For thousands and thousands of years, human beings or their ancestors walked, or rode horses, or sailed ships. In 1926, the rocket was invented, and in 1934, the jet engine. In 1969, astronauts walked on the moon. The world is changing, and the rate of change itself is accelerating.*

*It took more than a million years for the world's human population to reach about a quarter billion, in A.D. 1. It took an additional 1650 years for the population to double, to about half a billion. But it took only 200 years for it to double again; it reached one billion in 1850. Less than 100 years later, it was two billion. Then it doubled again in 36 years, reaching four billion by 1976. By the year 2000, it is expected to double again to eight billion. What will your world be like in a decade or two?*

*For a very long time the role a person played in youth was not much different from that played in later life: a farmer was a farmer; a parent was a parent. Today roles change constantly. For example, sociologists estimate that 10 years from today, half the jobs now available to high school graduates will have faded out of existence. They will have been replaced by jobs that do not exist today.*

*Social change is an essential ingredient of our society. Most of the earlier chapters include some discussion of social change in particular areas, such as the family and education. Two fundamental changes that occurred in the Western world were the industrial revolution and urbanization.*

*It is no accident that sociology developed during the industrial revolution. The changes that this revolution brought about in society were a major concern to Durkheim, Weber, and Marx. Chapter 15 discusses what these changes were and how they were interpreted by the three thinkers. Changes in work and occupations and what future changes we can expect are also discussed.*

*Chapter 16 discusses one of the major social changes of modern times, the population shift from rural to urban. This chapter examines the extent, the causes, and the consequences of urbanization, emphasizing urban life in Canada.*

*Chapter 17 is a more general and theoretical treatment of social change, giving special attention to groups that promote or resist change. The focus is the role of such social movements in Canada.*

*Whether through organized groups or individual effort, whether conscious or unconscious, rational or intuitive, sane or crazy, social change is one constant on which we can depend.*

# Industrialization and Work

R. ALAN HEDLEY

"What do you do?" This question isn't specific, yet we all know what it means: "What *work* do you do?" This important question is almost always asked within a few minutes of strangers' meeting. Work is such an integral part of our lives that the answer reveals much more about a person than simply what he or she does for a living. It also allows us to estimate the individual's educational level, probable income, prestige, and lifestyle. In other words, because work is so central in our society, it is a major source of personal and social identity.

Work is the driving force of society. It is primarily a means to other ends, although for some people it becomes an end in itself. Work permits us to exist, and the type of work we do determines in large part the quality of that existence. **Work** is any activity that permits individuals a livelihood; it includes conventional paid employment within the labour force, as well as illegal employment outside it and homemaking. (Those people — usually women, because of certain accepted domestic divisions of labour — who take care of home and family are also workers, even though they are not directly paid for their labour. Their homemaking activity permits others in the family to concentrate their energies more fully on paid employment. However, some homemakers also enter the labour force; their responsibilities for maintaining the household do not diminish, as the chapters on gender relations [Chapter 4] and the family [Chapter 11] indicate.) In this chapter, we examine how the institution of work affects us and how we in turn view the world of work.

# The Industrial Revolution

The history of modern work can be traced to the **industrial revolution** at the end of the eighteenth century (see Lenski and Lenski 1982). As a result of a number of technological changes, the whole structure of British and European societies was thrown into radical social change. Beginning in the textile and agricultural-equipment industries, large factories utilizing mechanical power and employing hundreds of workers were built to produce a hitherto unimagined volume of goods. These goods, because they were made more cheaply than was possible by traditional methods, were distributed widely throughout society; thus, their production provided a great stimulus to the European economy.

The new agricultural equipment was responsible for increasing yields per hectare, thereby raising per capita income and freeing people who had worked on the land to serve the new industrial enterprise. It was now possible to produce more food with less labour.

The industrial revolution was revolutionary because it produced changes far beyond those required to implement the new production techniques. The institution of work itself was changed in several important respects. Several interrelated features of this revolution make it stand out as one of the most important turning points in how we do work and how we think about it.

1. *Mechanical power.* In 1784, James Watt patented the modern steam engine for practical commercial use (see Mantoux 1961). For the first time in history it became possible to replace the relatively feeble power of people and animals and the often capricious power of wind and water with a strong, constant source of energy. The harnessing of steam meant that people could then accomplish feats formerly not within their grasp.
2. *Large-scale organization.* In order to utilize the power of steam efficiently, it became necessary to build large engines to drive the industrial machinery. Only in this way was mechanical power more cost-effective than human power. Large factories were built in order to achieve economies of scale, or greater volumes of output at a reduced cost per *unit* of output. This

marked the beginning of modern bureaucratization and the preponderance of wage- and salary-earners, as opposed to self-employed people in the labour force. (Recall the discussion in Chapter 10 on this topic.)
3. *Market production.* Mechanical power and large-scale organization were responsible for the widespread change from subsistence to market production. People produced goods no longer only for their own needs but for a larger, amorphous market of consumers. In order to take advantage of the increased capacity of mechanized production, industrial entrepreneurs had to create a demand for their great volume of goods. In this way, industrialization resulted in what we have come to call the marketplace. Various goods are produced according to the demand that exists for them. This is one of the essential bases of mass production.
4. *Improved transportation.* The need to obtain raw materials for manufacture and to get goods to market resulted in a great expansion and improvement in transportation. In fact, this was the second stage of the industrial revolution as the steam engine was applied directly to transport. Railways and steam ships fed the increased production, which required ever-increasing access to surrounding areas.
5. *Urbanization.* Because the first factories were large in order to achieve economies of scale and because they had to locate near available sources of energy (such as coal), the people in labouring classes had to go to and live near these factories. Industrialization thus was accompanied by urbanization as large industrial towns and cities sprang up in the vicinity of these factories. (The history of modern urbanization is presented more fully in Chapter 16.)
6. *Time metric.* The co-ordination of equipment and labour involved a scheduling problem previously unexperienced. Because steam is powerful only when it is contained under pressure and because that pressure is expensive to maintain, precise work schedules had to be established to accommodate the new industrial enterprise. Time, hitherto recorded as day and night, was now measured meticulously by the minute.
7. *Division of labour.* Work in the large, steam-powered factories came to be organized differ-

**The industrial revolution provided more efficient agricultural equipment, which made it possible to grow more food with less labour.**

ently than it had been. No longer was each individual worker responsible for the manufacture of a completed product. Instead, work was broken down into specialized tasks, so that a group of relatively unskilled workers could complete these tasks with a minimum of training. An integral part of the industrialization process was a division of labour on a scale never before witnessed.

8. *Labour market*. With the introduction of a division of labour came a demand for various categories of specialized labour. In order to match supply with demand, the idea of an industrial labour market was established. Consequently, two modes or sectors of production — the agricultural and the industrial — came to co-exist, each operated by different principles. The older agricultural sector was organized traditionally, with no clear demarcation between work and

other social activities; work there was primarily family-based and constituted one of the many functions in which families engaged. On the other hand, work in the industrial sector was strictly defined and was available only for those within the labour market. Individuals not in the labour market were economic liabilities in that they were not earning wages. The principles of an industrial labour market thus influenced the move toward smaller families and increased female labour-force participation.

9. *Ideology*. Because the changes that were introduced were so radical and occurred over a relatively short period, some justifying rationale or ideology was required to explain the new type of society that was emerging. One important legitimating ideology was Protestantism, in which work is held to be of service to God. Particularly in the view of Calvinists, work

— and more important, hard work — is a religious duty. According to the **Protestant work ethic**, how successful one is in this endeavour can be measured by how much money and property one acquires. Therefore, the early industrialists were gratified not only by their labour and the amount of capital they gained, but also by the knowledge that they were being employed in the service of God.

Another important set of beliefs that provided justification for the industrial revolution, a rationale that has become one of the most dominant political ideologies in the world today, came from the work of the Scottish moralist Adam Smith (1937, originally published in 1776). Smith, the father of modern capitalism, advocated "free enterprise." Unfettered by government intervention, the marketplace is governed by the law of supply and demand, which acts in the best interests of all. Industrialists and capitalists therefore felt justified in almost any activity in which they engaged.

All of these features transformed the societies in which they appeared — first in Britain and later in Germany, France, the United States, and Canada. One set of reactions to these changes resulted in the formation and consolidation of the discipline of sociology. Each of the three early theorists discussed in Chapter 1 — Durkheim, Weber, and Marx — wrote major works on what they believed to be the most important issues arising out of the industrial revolution.

## Theoretical Perspectives

Durkheim, Weber, and Marx each were concerned about the relationship of individuals to society and how this relationship had changed as a result of the industrial revolution. Some of these changes are outlined in Figure 15-1. The changing relationship was their major dependent variable, or what they were attempting to explain. However, the independent or causal variables that they chose differed, as did the theoretical perspectives they employed.

### Durkheim

In writing about the effects of the industrial revolution, Durkheim (1964a, originally published in 1893) argued that it was changes in the division

---

### Figure 15-1. The Great Dichotomy

---

From the time of Durkheim, Weber, and Marx to the present, sociologists have attempted to spell out the variety and types of social change that occurred as a result of the technological changes brought about by the industrial revolution. The list below is a simplified presentation; nevertheless, it shows that the effects of industrialization on the social structure are enormous in their impact.

---

| Social Dimension | Pre-industrial Society | Industrial Society |
|---|---|---|
| Economy | Agricultural Subsistence production Simple division of labour Barter exchange | Industrial Market production Complex division of labour Money exchange |
| Culture | Homogeneous standards Based on consensus | Heterogeneous standards Differentiation |
| Values | Traditional Sacred Ceremony and ritual | Innovative Secular Functional/ instrumental orientation |
| Social organization | Traditional Based on kinship | Rational-legal (bureaucratic) Based on merit |
| Social control | Informal moral pressure | Impersonal bureaucratic control mechanisms |
| Social relations | Informal Mechanical solidarity | Formal Organic solidarity |
| Mode of behaviour | Based on custom and tradition | Based on contract |

of labour that were primarily responsible for changing the individual's relation to society. In the pre-industrial era, there was a very simple division of labour. The occupational titles in the children's rhyme "Tinker, tailor, soldier, sailor" were virtually the only ones in existence, and because there was little occupational differentiation, individuals' relationships with one another and with social groups were characterized by free and open interaction.

A simple division of labour means that individual differences are minimized; the grounds for common interests are heightened. In this type of society — which is characteristic of pre-industrial agrarian societies — social relations are based on what Durkheim termed *mechanical solidarity*. This concept implies common values, beliefs, and attitudes such that the bases for interaction are extensive. Social relations occur primarily in the kinship system and through community networks. The family is the most important social institution in maintaining mechanical solidarity and also acts as the major agent of social control.

With the industrial revolution, the division of labour became more complex, and social relations changed. The basis for society, then, according to Durkheim, became *organic solidarity*. Specialized work introduces differentiation into the social system, causing people to relate to one another in a more compartmentalized fashion. In an occupationally diverse society, there is a corresponding need for co-ordination and control, which is satisfied through written procedures, contracts, and enacted laws. Interaction is more impersonal, and the family is no longer the bulwark of society. Instead, Durkheim thought that it should be replaced by some kind of fraternal occupational association. Because such an association would be an integral part of the occupational structure, it would more adequately reflect the needs of society and be a more appropriate institution for maintaining social relations.

From this brief presentation, it can be seen that Durkheim's analysis is both structural and functional and that its perspective involves consensus. It is structural because the independent variable, the division of labour, is a macrosociological concept. The division of labour is an objective part of the social structure that, when it changes, also incurs changes in people's behaviour and how

they relate to one another. The analysis is also functional because Durkheim was writing in terms of the needs of society. When one aspect of society changes, other changes occur to bring the system into equilibrium. Finally, the perspective is consensual in that Durkheim was attempting to chart the most adequate social adaptations that could be made in response to the technological changes that had already occurred.

## Weber

Weber also was interested in explaining the vast changes that he was witnessing. In his book *The Protestant Ethic and the Spirit of Capitalism* (1958, originally published in 1905), he selects changing religious values as the most important independent variable to account for the rise of industrial capitalism. Prior to the Reformation, work was regarded as the curse God placed on Adam and Eve when they were expelled from the Garden of Eden. However, the Protestant reformers reinterpreted work as a calling, that is, a duty and service to God. Consequently, in countries in which there is a large proportion of Protestants, a strong value is placed on work.

Weber stated that differences in religious values placed on work would produce different economic structures; more specifically, he asserted that the work ethic as espoused by Protestants would give rise to conditions under which capitalism would flourish. Table 15-1 provides data that substantiate Weber's thesis. It shows that average energy consumption, which is often used as a measure of industrialization, is considerably higher in predominantly Protestant countries, such as Britain and the United States, than it is in countries with other religious beliefs. Thus, there is empirical support for Weber's argument that Protestantism gave rise to industrial capitalism.

Weber's analytical perspective is social action — what today we call *symbolic interaction*. He is stating that individual perceptions of society or parts of society cause changes in how that society is structured. Changes in values (toward work) produce changes in behaviour (the ascendancy of industrial capitalism). His analysis is also consensual because he highlights those features responsible for the way different societies maintain themselves.

**Table 15-1. Median Energy Consumption for Groups of Nations Classified by Dominant Traditional Religion**

| Dominant Traditional Religion | Median Energy Consumption | Number of Nations |
|---|---|---|
| Protestant | 5141 | 10 |
| Eastern Orthodox | 3060 | 4 |
| Roman Catholic | 914 | 31 |
| Islam | 208 | 24 |
| Eastern religions (Buddhism, Hinduism, etc.) | 193 | 13 |
| Pre-literate tribal faiths | 70 | 25 |

NOTE: Consumption is based on kilograms of coal equivalent consumed per person per year in the median nation in each category.
SOURCE: Gerhard Lenski and J. Lenski, *Human Societies* (New York: McGraw-Hill, 1978), p. 270.

## Marx

The major independent variable that Marx (1965, originally published in three volumes 1867, 1885, and 1895) used to explain the changes occurring in society and in individuals' relationship to it was ownership of the means of production. As you read in Chapters 1 and 8, he saw industrialism as forming two antagonistic classes — those who own the means of production (the bourgeoisie) and those who do not and who therefore must sell their labour (the proletariat). The bourgeoisie do not engage directly in the production process but extract profits (*surplus value*) from it and, therefore, enjoy a privileged position in society. The proletariat, on the other hand, work at highly specialized tasks over which they have no control and in which they cannot produce entire products. The result is *alienation* or personal feelings of both powerlessness and meaninglessness. Thus, the introduction of industrial capitalism created two diametrically opposed classes. Eventually, according to Marx, the proletariat will revolt against the bourgeoisie and seize the means of production. In turn, this will lead to a classless society.

Marx's analytical perspective employed both structural and conflict theory. Ownership of the means of production, like the division of labour, is an objective part of reality. It is a social fact distinct from people's perceptions of this same reality. The analysis also involves a conflict perspective because Marx sought out those factors he believed produced conflict that would ultimately destroy the existing society.

## Industrialization in the World Today

In 1850, when industrialization was well underway in both Europe and North America, per capita income was 70 percent higher in the industrialized, developed nations than it was in the developing countries of the world (Murdoch 1980). A century later, in 1950, the difference in per capita income was 2242 percent, and by 1980, it had increased to 3838 percent. Per capita income in the developing nations in 1980 was U.S.$245, while in the rich industrialized countries it had soared to U.S.$9648 (Seligson 1984).

Industrialization has produced a disparity among the peoples of the world on a scale never before thought possible. This disparity is reflected in the figures describing health, education, welfare, and the general quality of life. Table 15-2 presents 33 countries throughout the world ranked by per capita energy consumption. By this measure, Canada is the most industrialized of the countries listed. (In terms of per capita energy consumption, this is true, but it is also true that all energy consumed does not drive industrial machinery. Canadians, as you well know, live in a cold climate and consume much energy just to keep warm. Also, Canada is a very large country, requiring high energy consumption for transportation. Consequently, Canada's position in the rank order of industrialization is inflated when per capita energy consumption is used as the empirical measure. No measure is perfect; we must always be attentive to flaws and anomalies.)

Table 15-2 also presents data on eight social variables often used to measure the quality of life. They are strongly related to this measure of industrialization. Generally, the more industrialized a country is, the greater is its per capita Gross National Product. Also note that by the standards of the least industrialized countries, those in the industrially advanced nations can expect to live almost two lifetimes. The average life expectancy

**Industrialization has widened the disparity between industrialized and developing nations, leaving much of the world in dire poverty.**

in Afghanistan is 39 years, while in Sweden and Japan it is 77 years.

Another indicator of the quality of life is the proportion of income one has to spend in order to buy food. The data are not complete for this variable, but in the countries for which information is available, it ranges from just over 10 percent in the United States to 65 percent in the Sudan. Quite clearly, if the bulk of one's income is spent on food, there is very little left for other essentials, not to mention luxuries. A related condition of life is estimated malnourishment, according to the United Nations Food and Agricultural Organization. Data for most of the industrialized countries are missing, probably because malnourishment does not constitute as much of a problem for them as it does for the developing countries. There, anywhere from one-quarter to almost half of the population is officially designated as receiving less than the critical minimum limit of nutrition required to be healthy.

A very surprising statistic is the proportion of the population with access to a safe water supply. Again, this does not constitute as much of a problem in the developed nations, but in some of the developing nations the figures are truly shocking. For example, in Indonesia — the fifth most populous country in the world (almost 175 million people) — only one-third of the populace has access to safe water. The figures for Afghanistan and Ethiopia are even lower, which explains in part why their death rates are among the highest in the world. Another indicator of the quality of life is access to medical treatment as measured by the number of people per physician. Here again, the figures reveal wide discrepancies. In the developed industrialized countries, one doctor averages a caseload of 300 to 600 patients, while in

## Table 15-2. Selected Countries Rank Ordered by Industrialization[a] and Measures of the Quality of Life in These Countries

| Selected Countries | Per Capita Energy Consumption | GNP per capita[c] | Life Expectancy at Birth[e] | Percentage of Income Spent on Food | Percentage Malnourished[c] | Percentage with Access to Safe Water | Population per Physician | Percentage Enrolled in Secondary School[g] Boys | Girls | Average Number of Persons per Room |
|---|---|---|---|---|---|---|---|---|---|---|
| Canada | 288 | $13 670 | 76 | 15 | — | — | 550 | 102 | 102 | 0.6 |
| United States | 280 | 16 400 | 75 | 13 | — | — | 500 | 95 | 95 | 0.6 |
| Australia | 180 | 10 840 | 76 | 17 | — | — | 500 | 92 | 95 | 0.7 |
| USSR | 176 | 7 400 | 69 | — | — | — | 270 | 77 | 82 | 1.3 |
| West Germany | 163 | 10 940 | 74 | 24 | — | — | 420 | 90 | 93 | 1.5 |
| Belgium | 145 | 8 450 | 73 | 19 | — | — | 370 | 85 | 87 | 0.6 |
| United Kingdom | 138 | 8 390 | 74 | 18 | — | — | 680 | 76 | 78 | 0.6 |
| Sweden | 137 | 11 890 | 77 | 19 | — | — | 410 | 79 | 88 | 0.7 |
| Poland | 133 | 2 120 | 71 | — | — | — | 550 | 75 | 80 | 1.4 |
| France | 114 | 9 550 | 75 | 19 | — | — | 460 | 84 | 96 | 1.3 |
| Hungary | 112 | 1 940 | 70 | — | — | — | 300 | 73 | 73 | 1.1 |
| Japan | 111 | 11 330 | 77 | 26 | — | — | 740 | 94 | 94 | 1.1 |
| Venezuela | 96 | 3 110 | 69 | 39 | 7 | — | 1 000 | 40 | 49 | 1.5 |
| Italy | 90 | 6 520 | 75 | 31 | — | — | 750 | 74 | 73 | 0.9 |
| Yugoslavia | 73 | 2 070 | 71 | — | — | — | 700 | 84 | 80 | 1.4 |
| Israel | 69 | 4 920 | 75 | 23 | — | — | 400 | 70 | 78 | 1.5 |
| Argentina | 50 | 2 130 | 70 | — | 2 | 63 | — | 62 | 69 | 1.4 |
| Mexico | 50 | 2 080 | 67 | — | 8 | 74 | 1 200 | 56 | 53 | 2.5 |
| South Korea | 44 | 2 180 | 67 | 44 | 4 | 62 | 1 390 | 94 | 88 | 2.3 |
| Malaysia | 26 | 2 050 | 67 | 37 | — | 80 | 3 920 | 53 | 53 | 2.6 |
| Turkey | 26 | 1 130 | 62 | — | 7 | 63 | 1 530 | 47 | 28 | 2.2 |
| Brazil | 19 | 1 640 | 65 | — | 13 | 76 | 1 300 | — | — | 1.1 |
| Egypt | 19 | 680 | 59 | — | 8 | 75 | 760 | 70 | 46 | 1.8 |
| China | 19 | 310 | 66 | — | — | — | 1 730 | 43 | 31 | — |
| Bolivia | 10 | 470 | 53 | — | 45 | 43 | 2 000 | 40 | 34 | — |
| Indonesia | 8 | 530 | 58 | — | 30 | 33 | 12 300 | 45 | 34 | 1.5 |
| India | 7 | 250 | 55 | 58 | 30 | 54 | 3 700 | 44 | 23 | 2.8 |
| Pakistan | 6 | 380 | 50 | — | 26 | 39 | 2 910 | 20 | 7 | 2.8 |
| Kenya | 3 | 290 | 54 | — | 30 | 28 | 10 140 | 22 | 16 | 2.5 |
| Sudan | 2 | 330 | 49 | 65 | 30 | 48 | 9 800 | 23 | 16 | 2.5 |
| Afghanistan | 2 | —[d] | 39 | — | 37 | 10 | — | 23 | 4 | — |
| Bangladesh | 2 | 150 | 50 | — | 38 | 42 | 9 700 | 26 | 11 | — |
| Ethiopia | —[b] | 110 | 41 | — | 38 | 6 | 88 120 | 14 | 8 | 2.7 |

[a] Measured by per capita energy consumption of 0.163 "U.N. standard" barrels of oil equivalent, 1984.
[b] Less than one.
[c] U.S. dollars, 1985. Gross National Product is the total value of goods and services produced within a country during one year.
[d] Data not available.
[e] Life expectancy is the average number of years a newborn baby can expect to live given that country's current mortality rate.
[f] Percentage of the population below the critical minimum limit of nutrition as determined by the U.N. Food and Agricultural Organization.
[g] Number enrolled in school as a percentage of age group; number enrolled may be larger than total of "school-age" group due to older people enrolling as well.
SOURCES: World Bank, *World Development Report 1987* (New York: Oxford University Press, 1987); *1987 World Population Data Sheet* and *1982 World's Children Data Sheet* (Washington, DC: Population Reference Bureau).

Ethiopia there are 88 120 people for each doctor. Clearly, in that country the vast majority of the population never receive any medical treatment whatsoever.

A further disparity appears in education. In the most industrialized countries, virtually all the boys and girls of the relevant ages are enrolled in secondary schools. In the developing nations, however, the participation rate drops below one-quarter; moreover, boys in that age group are substantially more likely than girls to be in school. In the developed nations, the gender difference is negligible and, for the most part, reversed.

The final column in Table 15-2 reflects another aspect of the quality of life: housing. In the developed nations, the average person has almost two rooms at his or her disposal, whereas in the developing nations, the average person must share one room with two others.

All of these factors together provide documentation for the assertion that the growing gap between the industrialized rich countries and the developing poor ones constitutes one of the most pressing social problems in the world today. Two former Canadian prime ministers, Lester B. Pearson and Pierre Elliot Trudeau, spent much of their terms in office attempting to persuade a substantial number of countries to help redress this imbalance, but there are many complexities involved and their work failed to produce any concerted efforts.

The basis of the problem lies in the different patterns of growth and development in the rich and the poor nations. During the original industrial revolution in Europe, population growth was high, thereby reducing much of the productivity gain achieved through industrialization. One solution to this problem was emigration. During the period from 1840 to 1930, at least 52 million Europeans (double Canada's present population) emigrated (Davis 1974). This emigration was of two basic types (see Murdoch 1980). One involved permanent settlement in the temperate regions of the world (Canada, the United States, Australia, New Zealand, and southern South America and Africa) and was an important safety valve in the control of European population growth. The second type of emigration was to the tropical areas; its main purpose was not settlement but the acquisition of valuable raw materials (gold, silver, diamonds, and other goods not indigenous to Europe) that helped to finance the industrialization process in the home countries. Each of these migratory patterns contributed significantly to the development and modernization of the industrializing European nations.

Today, the problems are more complex, and it is not possible for industrialization in the developing nations to occur in the same fashion. For example, population growth in the poor, developing nations is now 2.1 percent per year (*1987 World Population Data Sheet*); the economies of these nations must grow annually by this amount just to stay even. Furthermore, even though the present world migration pattern has changed and there is now a general population movement from the poor to the rich nations, it is insufficient to absorb the excess growth. Given the present population of the underdeveloped areas of the world — almost 4 billion — and its annual rate of growth (2.1 percent), the developed nations would have to accept more than 80 million immigrants per year, or an annual increase of 6.8 percent. Thus, the escape valve of emigration that existed for the industrializing European countries cannot be used by the developing nations.

Another major obstacle is the financing of the very expensive industrialization process. As mentioned above, this was largely achieved in the European industrial revolution through the exploitation of countries in the tropical regions or, as one author puts it, the pillage of the Third World (Jalée 1968). Although some academics and politicians in the developed nations have suggested that it is now only fair for the industrialized countries to repay their debt to the developing nations and assist financially in their industrialization (Tinbergen 1976), generally this support has not been forthcoming in sufficient amounts to bring about the desired changes. Many of the developing nations currently are heavily in debt to the developed nations — close to $800 billion according to the most recent World Bank estimates (1987). Thus it is impossible for these countries to accumulate independently the capital necessary to achieve industrialization.

These differences in the growth and development patterns of the industrialized and the industrializing nations mean that the gap between the rich and the poor will probably continue to increase. It seems inevitable that at some point this gap will be perceived as intolerable by the rapidly growing populations of the developing nations. Already they are 76 percent of the world's population, and by the year 2000, given present growth rates, this figure will rise to 80 percent (*1987 World Population Data Sheet*). If the world's resources are not shared more equitably, it is likely that social unrest in all forms will increase dramatically. Already there are signs — mounting acts of terrorism and civil disobedience, massive illegal migration, rising crime rates, widespread famine, and internal disputes that escalate into international conflicts. Two decades ago, Lester Pearson noted: "Before long, in our affluent, industrial, computerized jet society, we shall feel the wrath of the wretched people of the world. There will be no peace" (quoted in Tinbergen 1976).

## Industrialization in Canada

Although Table 15-2 indicates that Canada is the most industrialized country in the world, many commentators have expressed concern about its recent industrial performance (Science Council of Canada 1984; Macdonald Commission 1985; Economic Council of Canada 1986, 1987). It is true that Canada is among the leading nations in per capita Gross National Product; the problem is that the "product" is largely natural resources, agricultural products, and semifinished manufactured goods such as lumber. According to another measure of industrialization — completely finished manufactures as a proportion of total exports — Canada lags behind such nations as Ireland, Mexico, Spain, Yugoslavia, and Portugal (Science Council of Canada 1977).

The Canadian manufacturing establishment is small, increasingly noncompetitive in the international marketplace, and largely foreign owned. In order to understand industrialization in Canada, it is necessary to realize how closely the country is bound to the American economy. The United States is by far Canada's largest trading partner, accounting for approximately three-quarters of both Canadian exports and imports (Macdonald Commission 1985). Canada exports mainly natural resources and primary products and imports finished manufactured goods. Traditionally, we have enjoyed favourable trade relations with the United States because of our lower production costs and comparable productivity levels. Within the last two decades, however, our competitive advantage relative to both the United States and Japan has eroded substantially (Kennedy 1986). In consequence, the Canadian dollar has fallen relative to American and Japanese currencies, permitting Canadian exports to remain competitive but at the price of manufactured imports' becoming very expensive.

Another characteristic of Canadian industry is foreign ownership and control. Canada has been described as a branch-plant economy in that our manufacturing, petroleum, and mining industries are almost half foreign controlled, mainly by American corporations (Macdonald Commission 1985). Because the foreign-controlled companies are subsidiary firms, they are often not complete manufacturing establishments in the sense of having all components of the production process, including vital research and development sections. In many cases, the subsidiaries are only assembly or warehousing operations.

Because most American exports to Canada are finished manufactured goods and because half of Canadian manufacturing firms are controlled by foreign — mainly American — interests, the development of a complete, self-sufficient, and technologically advanced industrial establishment in Canada is severely limited. As the Economic Council of Canada (1987) puts it, "Canada's industry continues to lag behind that of other countries in adopting the new technologies that are essential to its future prosperity." The presence of an industrial giant to the south has curtailed Canada's ability to industrialize in a fashion similar to that of other industrial nations. The traditional depiction of Canadians as hewers of wood and drawers of water contains more than a kernel of truth.

## Post-Industrialism

As can be witnessed in Table 15-2, industrialization is not an all-or-nothing proposition. It is a gradual process and can vary substantially from one country to another depending largely on when it is first introduced and on the indigenous human and natural resources. Figure 15-2 identifies the particular stages through which the now developed nations have evolved. The column labelled "Emergent Post-Industrial Age" indicates some fairly recent changes that have taken place within these advanced industrial countries.

## Occupational Structure

According to sociologists and other social scientists, the definitions of *industrialization* and *postindustrialism* are directly linked to what people do in the labour force. By convention, there are three

### Figure 15-2. Ages of Industrial Technology

| Important Determiners of Technology in Dominant Ages | Pre-industrial Age 1500– | Early Industrial Age 1785– | Mature Industrial Age 1870– | Emergent Post-industrial Age 1953– |
|---|---|---|---|---|
| Power | Muscle, wind, and water | Steam with the use of coal | Electricity and internal combustion machines with use of oil, gas, and coal | Atomic energy supplemented with solar, geothermal, and fusion energy |
| Tools | Hand | Machine | Automatic machine | Automatic factory |
| Work skills | All-round skilled craftspeople and unskilled manual workers | Skilled craftspeople replaced by machine (semiskilled) operatives as a result of subdividing manufacturing processes | Skilled inspectors, mechanics required as operations replace need for machine feeding or tending | Highly trained engineers as designers are required; skilled technicians required for monitoring controls and for maintenance of equipment |
| Materials | Wood, iron, bronze | Steel | Copper, alloyed steels, light alloys, aluminum | Plastic, superalloys, use of 32 new metals (notably magnesium and titanium) |
| Transportation | Walking, or use of animals, via dirt roads; sailboat over seaways | Steam train via steel rails; iron steamship via oceans | Automobile, diesel train, and prop airplane via paved highways, railways, and airways | Road and rail track; jet airplane, rocket, and helicopter; turbine and atomic train via railways, atomic ships via ocean surface and subsurface |
| Communication | Word of mouth, newspaper, messenger | Mail moved faster by rail and water; newspaper printed on steam press | Telephone, telegraph, AM and FM radio, movies, television, microfilm, magnetic tape | Television telephone, video cassette, talking book or newspaper, universal two-way radio-communication, high-speed computers, magnetic-tape photography, vocatypewriter, cable television |

SOURCE: Delbert C. Miller and W.H. Form, *Industrial Sociology* (New York: Harper and Row, 1980), pp. 40–41.

major sectors or divisions within the labour force; primary, secondary, and tertiary. People in the **primary sector** work in agriculture, logging, mining, fishing, hunting, or trapping — the vast majority are usually in agriculture. In each of these occupational groups, work involves some kind of extraction or harvesting; there is no transformation of raw materials into finished goods. If at least half of the workers in the labour force are in the primary sector, again by common agreement, the society is defined as **agricultural**.

**Industrialization** involves the movement of workers out of the primary and into the **secondary sector**, as work activity is concentrated on the manufacture of goods for market. Thus, by this definition, those engaged in the logging industry are working in the primary sector (that is, harvesting trees), but those working in sawmills are in the secondary sector (that is, transforming trees into lumber). The construction industry is also classified as secondary, in that it too involves transforming basic materials into a finished product. When fewer than half of the workers in the labour force are in the primary sector, we have an **industrial society**.

While the secondary sector involves the manufacture of finished and semifinished goods, people in the **tertiary sector** work to provide services. These include transportation, communication, the provision of public utilities, most professional work, and all occupations in commerce, finance, health, education, welfare, and recreation or leisure. When at least half the labour force works in the tertiary sector, that society is termed **post-industrial** (Bell 1967).

Table 15-3 reveals how the labour force has been distributed among these three sectors in Canada over the past 100 years. Until 1891, Canada was largely an agricultural society, with half its workers employed in the primary sector. At the turn of the century, Canada entered the industrial age, and by 1961, it had evolved into a post-industrial society: 54 percent of the labour force was working in the tertiary sector.

Today, the vast majority of those employed in Canada (70 percent) provide services rather than produce goods. The fact that fewer than one-third of all workers are in the goods-producing primary and secondary sectors is explained by the revolutionary mechanization of work. As an industrial

### Table 15-3. Canada's Occupational Structure, 1881–1987

| Year | Industrial Sector | | |
|------|---------|-----------|----------|
| | **Primary**[a] | **Secondary**[b] | **Tertiary**[c] |
| *Agricultural society* | | | |
| 1881 | 51% | 29% | 19% |
| 1891 | 50 | 26 | 24 |
| *Industrial society* | | | |
| 1901 | 44 | 28 | 28 |
| 1911 | 40 | 27 | 33 |
| 1921 | 37 | 27 | 37 |
| 1931 | 32 | 28 | 40 |
| 1941 | 31 | 28 | 41 |
| 1951 | 23 | 33 | 44 |
| *Post-industrial society* | | | |
| 1961 | 14 | 32 | 54 |
| 1971 | 9 | 28 | 63 |
| 1987 | 7 | 23 | 70 |

[a]Primary sector includes all those working in agriculture, mining, logging, fishing, hunting, and trapping.
[b]Secondary sector includes all those working in manufacturing and construction.
[c]Tertiary sector includes all those working in transportation, communication, trade, finance, and other services.
The difference between year percentage sums and 100 is a result of rounding.
SOURCES: Adapted from J. Smucker, *Industrialization in Canada* (Scarborough, Ont.: Prentice-Hall, 1980), p. 78; and Statistics Canada, *The Labour Force, October 1987* (Ottawa: Supply and Services, 1987), p. 20.

society matures, it changes from being *labour intensive* to being *capital intensive*. In the beginning stages of industrialization, human labour is cheaper than machines; as the standard of living improves with industrialization (see Table 15-2), labour becomes increasingly expensive. This phenomenon motivates owners and managers to substitute machines for labour. Thus, whereas early farms, mines, and factories swarmed with poorly paid unskilled and semiskilled workers, today these same places of work are notable for the relatively small number of workers used and for the presence of highly complex equipment and machinery.

The displacement of these workers from the primary and secondary sectors did not mean that they became unemployed, although at times there were serious dislocations. Rather, the whole occupational structure changed, as can be seen in Table 15-3. Occupations previously unknown came into being (for example, all the service jobs in the computer and microprocessing industries), while other occupational groups expanded enormously (for example, professional consulting in such fields as finance, housing, health, education, welfare, management, interior design, landscaping, fashion, and travel). The emphasis in society changed from production to consumption. It has been estimated by one expert that 90 percent of all new jobs created between 1969 and 1976 were in services (Ginzberg 1982).

Much of the work in the tertiary sector involves the manipulation of information, and this endeavour has been aided tremendously by the computer. The computer is revolutionizing the world of work today with about the same impact the steam engine had 200 years earlier. As an illustration of this electronic revolution in the tertiary sector, consider some of the ways computers are used currently in universities. For example, all student registrations and admissions are fed into the computer system, which monitors the number of classes offered at a specified time against the number of classrooms and seats available. If enrolment exceeds class size, the computer is programmed to search for other suitable rooms, including those in which enrolment is below the estimated target. Since some universities have 30 000 or more students, this task would take much longer to complete using traditional labour-intensive methods.

At the same time the computer is matching students with classrooms, it also accepts and processes student fees, which vary according to type of program and number of units taken. The computer continues to monitor students' progress through university by scheduling exams and recording marks on electronic transcripts. Meanwhile, the accounting department uses the computer to track and process the faculty and staff payroll, to devise financial statements that permit assessment of the university's present situation, and to project the institution's future development given variable revenue and cost parameters.

Various university departments besides the bursar's and accounting offices also make heavy use of computers. For example, the central purchasing and supplies department maintains inventory control by the computer, which automatically reorders when stocks decline below critical limits.

## Uses and Abuses of the Computer

*The text describes the many uses of computers in universities, while the following newspaper article indicates some of the abuses of these electronic marvels.*

University of Southern California officials are investigating allegations that phoney degrees, backed up by complete transcripts illegally placed in the university's computer system, were sold for up to $25,000 each.

The allegations, if substantiated, would represent the second instance of illegal tampering with the university's computer to surface since October. Thirty USC students are currently under investigation for allegedly paying to have unauthorized grade changes made on their transcripts.

"Our investigation has widened beyond grade changes," said USC Vice-Provost Sylvia Manning, who is coordinating the university's probe. "We are now investigating the possibility that someone may have created entire transcripts as well."

University officials have begun checking transcripts in search of the bogus degrees, Manning said, but said none have turned up yet.

When the university announced in October that it had initiated disciplinary proceedings against twenty-one students for allegedly paying to have their grades changed, officials said one employee in records and registration had admitted changing five grades for a payment of $1,500 and was fired in June.

University investigators have since discovered more transcripts with unauthorized grade changes, and nine additional students have been called in for questioning, said Robert Mannes, the university's dean of student life.

University officials believe they will be able to uncover any bogus degrees and any additional illegal grade changes by checking the transcripts against other records at the school, but they admit that it will be a slow, painstaking process

**Source:**

*Victoria Times-Colonist*, February 4, 1985.

Faculty also make extensive use of computers in their research. Many professors have personal computers or computer terminals, which they use for data and word processing, in their offices. These office computers may be connected to the central mainframe computer, which is often in turn linked to other computers throughout the country or even the world. Through this interlocking network, a professor can send and receive data to and from the secretary in the departmental office and colleagues across the campus or in a different university. Electronic messages are increasingly replacing the conventional letter and memo.

Finally, one of the largest and most rapidly growing program of studies in universities today is computer science. Students take courses in all aspects of computing, including programming, operations research, numerical and systems analysis, software engineering, data bases, and graphics. Even if students do not specialize in computer science, the acquisition of computing skills in today's work world is thought to be almost indispensable.

This brief description illustrates not only how necessary the computer has become but also how most of the work in post-industrial societies is involved with information and people processing. Because of gains achieved through the mechanization and rationalization of production, emphasis is now placed on consumption and the provision of services. This latter emphasis also explains in part the recent dramatic increases in female labour-force participation.

## Labour-Force Participation

As mentioned earlier, a consequence of industrialization is the creation of a labour market or labour force. Because work in an industrial society becomes a clearly defined activity, people must enter the labour force in order to secure employment. Through various public and private employment agencies, individual qualifications are matched against the requirements of job vacancies, and in this fashion the available labour supply is directed toward meeting current employment demand. Sometimes the available supply exceeds the demand or does not fulfill particular demand requirements; consequently, a portion of the labour force is unemployed.

Traditionally, labour-force participation has varied tremendously by gender and education. The demand for well-qualified males has always been great, and therefore the participation rate of this group is the highest of all (Statistics Canada 1984c). Recently, however, the labour-force participation of women has increased dramatically. This phenomenon involves several factors: (1) demographic changes, (2) families' desire for a better standard of living, and (3) shifts in the occupational structure. We will examine each of these factors in more detail.

The major demographic variable related to female labour-force participation is fertility. As you will have noted in Chapter 7, the fertility rate in Canada has never been lower than it is now. Because women are having fewer children and are spacing them more closely together, more of their time can be devoted to activities other than child-bearing and child-rearing. One option increasingly chosen is paid employment. Table 15-4 presents data on the labour force participation of Canadian women of various age groups over the past 35 years. Note that for all years the peak participation age is 20 to 24. Given that the mean age at first marriage for females during this 35-year period was between 22 and 23 (see Chapter 7), the majority of young women in this age group are either single or newly married.

Traditionally, just before the first child was born, many women dropped out of the labour force never to return. The figures for 1951 bear out this pattern. Forty-six percent of females aged 20 to 24 were in the labour force, but only 23 percent of the 25 to 34 age group. This represented a 50 percent decline, and there was continual additional erosion through the remaining years of the life cycle. Contrast these figures with those for 1987. Not only were three-quarters of women aged 20 to 24 in the labour force — an increase of 63 percent over 1951 — but also the participation rate for women in the next two age groups (25 through 44 years) remained constant. Clearly, women today are having children and working outside the home at the same time. This is explained in large part by the other two facts tied to increased female labour-force participation.

Economic as well as demographic variables are also important in accounting for why women are increasingly entering the labour force. Individuals

## Table 15-4. Canadian Female Labour-Force Participation by Age, 1951–1987

| | 15–19 Years | 20–24 Years | 25–34 Years | 35–44 Years | 45–54 Years | 55–64 Years | 65 Years + | Total Participation |
|---|---|---|---|---|---|---|---|---|
| 1951 | 36% | 46% | 23% | 19% | 18% | 12% | 4% | 25% |
| 1961 | 32 | 48 | 27 | 27 | 28 | 20 | 5 | 29 |
| 1971 | 37 | 63 | 41 | 41 | 41 | 18 | 4 | 36 |
| 1981 | 53 | 73 | 66 | 65 | 56 | 34 | 5 | 52 |
| 1987 | 52 | 75 | 74 | 75 | 65 | 35 | 4 | 56 |

SOURCE: Adapted from John D. Allingham, *Special Labour Force Studies, Series B, No. 1* (Ottawa: Dominion Bureau of Statistics, 1967), p. 11; Statistics Canada, *The Labour Force 1972* (Ottawa: Information Canada, 1973), and Statistics Canada, *The Labour Force, October 1987* (Ottawa: Supply and Services Canada, 1987), p. 26.

in a family who are not in the labour force constitute economic liabilities. Traditionally, this applied particularly to two categories of people: women and children. However, it applies less well today, in that there are now significantly fewer children per family, and more women than ever before are employed. Indeed, 40 percent of the Canadian labour force is comprised of women, of whom 62 percent are married (Statistics Canada 1984c).

Between 1951 and 1987, the overall labour-force participation rate for women increased from 25 to 56 percent (see Table 15-4). These figures compare with a relatively constant participation rate for men of 75 to 80 percent (Statistics Canada 1984c). Not only does the now-higher female participation decrease economic liability; it also substantially improves the standard of living of families with two wage-earners. Additionally, the increased economic independence of women resulting from their employment leads to greater marital satisfaction for both wives and husbands (Lupri and Frideres 1981).

The final factor explaining greater female labour-force participation is the general shift in the occupational structure presented in Table 15-3. In 1987, 70 percent of the labour force was employed in the tertiary sector, and this sector is the principal employer of women. Thus, there is a greater demand now by employers for female labour than ever before.

In order to understand how the shift in the occupational structure affects female participation, it is necessary to know that there are essentially two occupational structures — one for women and one for men (Oppenheimer 1973; Power 1975). For example, Hunter (1981) found that half of all Canadian working women were employed in 15 occupations; in 11 of these, at least two-thirds of all those employed were women (Hunter 1981). In other words, women, in comparison with men, are concentrated and segregated in the labour force in relatively few occupations. Furthermore, of these same 15 occupations, 13 are in the tertiary sector (for example, secretaries, sales clerks, bookkeepers, school teachers, waitresses, nurses, and tellers and cashiers).

Because of expanding employment in the tertiary sector and because of the occupational concentration and segregation of women, the traditional supply of female labour is insufficient to meet the growing demand. Whereas employers once typically preferred single young women, this source is now virtually exhausted (see Table 15-4), and employers increasingly are hiring older married women, many with children (see Hedley and Adams 1982).

Most of the work that women do in the labour force is simply an extension of what they have traditionally done in the home — being a helpmate to man (Armstrong and Armstrong 1984b). Secretarial and clerical work, cooking, waiting tables, hosting, teaching small children, nursing, cleaning, and sewing are all chores that women have done since time immemorial. The only difference between what most of them are doing now and what they traditionally did is that they are being paid directly for their labour.

The occupational concentration and segregation of women has one other important consequence. Because men and women for the most part are employed in different occupations, it is very difficult to make precise comparative assessments of the work that they do in relation to the income they receive. On average, however, women employed full-time in Canada earn only 60 percent of men's average earnings (Labour Canada 1987). Table 15-5 reports data for five industrialized nations with essentially the same income differential between the sexes. Although much of this difference in income can be explained as a function of different jobs, qualifications, experience, and length of time at work, nevertheless there is a substantial residual that cannot be explained away (Ferber and Lowry 1976; Stines, Quinn, and Shepard 1976). Women earn less than men.

Table 15-5 also reveals that income differentials are greater at the higher occupational levels. (See also Labour Canada 1987). There is a direct relation between age, labour-market experience, and qualifications on the one hand and income inequality on the other. These data appear to indicate that when a case for uniqueness of job or occupation can be made, income differentials between the sexes will be greatest. There is, as well, an unemployment differential between men and women; unemployment among women is generally higher than among men (Connelly 1978).

Certain demographic and economic variables, plus a shift toward greater tertiary-sector employment, have contributed to a great increase in female labour-force participation. However, the nature of this participation is very different for women than it is for men. Generally, women are concentrated in relatively few occupational groups in which they constitute the overwhelming majority. They continue to work in jobs that are associated with the traditional female role and for which they earn substantially less than men. However, as women become a more substantial and permanent proportion of the labour force, it

## Table 15-5. Women's Earnings as a Percentage of Men's at Various Occupational Levels in Selected Countries (1976–1979)

| Country | Women's Earnings as a Percentage of Men's | Occupational Level |
|---|---|---|
| Canada | 54% | Managerial |
| | 62 | Professional |
| | 67 | Clerical |
| West Germany | 74 | Skilled workers |
| | 77 | Semiskilled workers |
| | 83 | Unskilled workers |
| Switzerland | 65 | All white-collar workers |
| | 66 | Skilled workers |
| | 70 | Semiskilled and unskilled workers |
| Sweden | 69 | White-collar workers (mining and manufacturing) |
| | 87 | Blue-collar workers (mining and manufacturing) |
| Great Britain | 62 | Nonmanual workers |
| | 71 | Manual workers |

SOURCES: Adapted from Pat Armstrong and Hugh Armstrong, "The structure of women's labour force work: Everywhere and nowhere," in *Working Canadians*, Graham S. Lowe and H.J. Krahn, eds. (Toronto: Methuen, 1984), p. 136; and Michael Swafford, "Sex differences in Soviet earnings," *American Sociological Review* 43(1978): 670.

is likely that they will be able to make valid representations of their unequal treatment. One avenue through which these appeals can be made is human rights legislation and the Canadian Charter of Rights and Freedoms, which is now part of Canada's Constitution; another is through unionization.

## Labour Relations

Labour unions began to be formed before the industrial revolution, and the history of the labour union movement is one of power, struggle, and conflict. It is a history of attempts to distribute more equitably the material and symbolic rewards gained from work. By uniting together, workers constituted an emergent force to counteract the almost overwhelming power assumed by the early industrial capitalists.

The study and analysis of labour/management relations highlights most strongly the marked differences between consensus and conflict theorists (see Berg 1979). The consensus perspective asserts that management and labour have common goals, while the conflict perspective sees these same goals as essentially in opposition. With regard to the distribution of power, those with a consensus orientation argue that it is shared, while conflict theorists state that it is widely unequal. And finally, concerning the rewards received from work, the consensus advocates see the distribution as just and fair, reflecting differential contributions made, while conflict theorists argue that this distribution is grossly unjust. Consequently, since the sociological perspective influences the results to a certain extent, readers should understand at the outset what orientation is being presented.

In Canada today there are more than 800 unions made up of more than 3.7 million members and representing 38 percent of the nonagricultural work force (*Worklife Report* 1987; Chaison and Rose 1989). Sixteen of these unions have memberships in excess of 50 000, accounting for just over half of all union members. Table 15-6 presents the ten largest of these unions.

There are three basic types of unions — public, industrial, and craft — each of which emerged at a particular historical period in the unionization of the labour force. Generally, unionism in Canada began with skilled blue-collar workers, spread to the semiskilled and unskilled, and within the last few decades has made significant inroads among lower-echelon white-collar workers and professionals.

**1.** *Craft unions.* The earliest type of union was a **craft** (or trade) **union**, in which workers organized on the basis of the specialized working skills they had in common. In Britain, for example, the first unions, consisting of workers in the building and printing trades, actually pre-dated the industrial revolution (Reynolds 1959). These people formed the aristocracy of labour; because they possessed unique skills in high demand, they were able to organize to protect their own interests.

**Table 15-6. The Ten Largest Unions in Canada by Type of Union and Percentage Share of Total Union Membership, 1987**

| Union | Number of Members | Percentage of Total Union Membership | Type of Union |
|---|---|---|---|
| Canadian Union of Public Employees | 330 000 | 8.7% | Public-sector |
| National Union of Provincial Government Employees | 278 500 | 7.4 | Public-sector |
| Public Service Alliance of Canada | 179 900 | 4.8 | Public-sector |
| United Steelworkers of America | 160 000 | 4.2 | Industrial |
| United Food and Commercial Workers | 160 000 | 4.2 | Industrial |
| Canadian Automobile Workers | 143 000 | 3.8 | Industrial |
| Social Affairs Federation | 93 000 | 2.5 | Public-sector |
| International Brotherhood of Teamsters, Chauffeurs, Warehousemen and Helpers | 91 500 | 2.4 | Industrial |
| School Board Teachers' Commission | 75 000 | 2.0 | Public-sector |
| Service Employees International Union | 70 000 | 1.9 | Public-sector |
| TOTAL | 1 580 900 | 41.9% | |

SOURCE: Adapted from *Worklife Report* 5(5), 1987:16–17.

2. *Industrial unions.* With industrialization and increasing divisions of labour, semiskilled machine operatives became the majority of the working class. Unlike craft workers, these workers had no highly specialized skills and therefore could not organize in the same way. Joining together in **industrial unions**, however, they constituted a powerful force that could challenge the hitherto unassailable prerogatives of management.

This period in the labour union movement represented the most bloody and acrimonious in its history. Workers, attempting to organize on an industry-wide basis, for the first time posed a direct threat to the exclusive right of management to dictate the terms and conditions of work. Although craft workers had organized before industrial workers, they did not constitute the same problem. Numerically a very small proportion of the labour force, craft workers did not threaten the status quo; rather they wished to ensure their position within it. However, the unionization of the labouring masses posed quite a different set of conditions. Management resisted extensively and often violently the attempts by workers to form industrial unions. The history of unions in the mining, textiles, steel, and railway industries is replete with bloody confrontation as the industrial workers of the world attempted to establish and finally succeeded in establishing a new social, economic, and political contract (see Flanders 1965).

3. *Public-sector unions.* From the industrial revolution until the middle of this century, the labour union movement increased both its membership and its acceptance within society. Basically, it was a movement of male blue-collar workers in the industrial labour force. In 1958 in Canada, its membership peaked at slightly more than one-third of nonagricultural workers (Chaison and Rose 1989) as the traditional recruiting ground of the labour movement became saturated. Membership then remained constant and even declined somewhat, largely as a result of decreasing semiskilled jobs and increasing employment in the tertiary sector (see Table 15-3).

In 1972, there was a resurgence in union membership, but this time among nonmanual white-collar and professional workers. The

Labour leaders Bob White (Canadian Auto Workers), Jack Munro (International Woodworkers), and Ken Georgetti (B.C. Federation of Labour) continue a united labour tradition.

movement was particularly strong within the various levels of government, where workers formed **public-sector unions**. Today, although public-sector workers are almost one-third of the labour force, they constitute well over 40 percent of all union members in Canada (Ponak and Thompson 1989). Table 15-6 reveals that the three largest Canadian unions are public-sector unions; furthermore, they constitute half of the top ten. Another interesting point with regard to these ten largest Canadian unions is that seven of them represent workers in the tertiary sector, a sector traditionally not associated with the labour movement. Finally, 36 percent of all Canadian union members are female (Chaison and Rose 1989). This figure recently has risen dramatically and will continue to grow as a function of increasing tertiary-sector representation.

It is interesting to ask why at this particular time unionization has been successfully introduced in the tertiary sector in general and in public employment in particular. Most of those employed in the tertiary sector are nonmanual white-collar workers. Traditionally, this group largely rejected the notion that unionism could be relevant for its purposes. It espoused the values and goals of management, and attempted to emulate the lifestyle of the managerial class. However, with the increasing mechanization and rationalization of work, the distinction between nonmanual white-collar and manual blue-collar labour has become blurred. Working conditions throughout the labour force are becoming more and more similar.

Another important factor is the financial gains that unionized blue-collar workers have made relative to their nonunionized white-collar counterparts. Many blue-collar workers now earn wages far in excess of white-collar salaries. Also, a few white-collar unions that were in existence prior to the surge in tertiary-sector unionism demonstrated that they could achieve not only economic benefits but also a stronger voice in their own self-determination (Ponak and Thompson 1989).

These recent developments have several very important implications for the labour union movement throughout the industrialized world. The whole strategy of unionism is built on the premise that if workers organize, they will be in an effective and powerful bargaining position vis-à-vis the employer. If the employer does not accede to the proposals put forward by the workers, then their ultimate option is to withdraw their labour, to strike. This is an effective weapon against a *private* employer because, without labour, the employer cannot produce goods or provide services and therefore loses the opportunity to make a profit. However, this strategy becomes questionable when used against a *public* employer. In this case, the employer is the citizens of the municipality, province, or country, and if workers strike, it is these same citizens, not industrial capitalists, who suffer. As a matter of fact, a strike can work to the economic advantage of government by saving labour costs (which it does not have to pay during a strike). The costs of a strike to government are not economic but political.

Two related alternatives to the strike that are used in the public sector are conciliation and arbitration. When labour and management cannot reach a negotiated settlement, then, upon prior agreement, the case is referred either to an independent conciliation or arbitration board. A **conciliation** board examines all of the evidence and claims of both parties and then makes recommendations as to what would constitute a satisfactory compromise. However, these recommendations are not binding on either labour or management. In contrast, an **arbitration** board engages in the same process, but its judgment is final and becomes the new collective agreement between labour and management. Conciliation does not necessarily eliminate the possibility of a legal strike, but arbitration does. Although both conciliation and arbitration have been resorted to in the public as well as the private sector, neither is seen as an ideal solution. Labour and management together have traditionally objected to outside interference in reaching a collective agreement. Each jealously guards the right to determine its own destiny.

The history of labour relations may be seen as one of increased recognition that both management *and* labour have rights in setting the conditions of work and the rewards to be gained from it. Although management rights have never seriously been questioned, labour rights have. Today, the rights of labour have largely become recognized in law, as has the collective agreement on which ultimately both management and labour are in accord.

## Cultural Convergence

This section on post-industrialism has highlighted three important interrelated features common to mature industrialized societies. The first is a redistribution of the occupational structure as the provision of services takes precedence over the production of goods. The mechanization and rationalization of production permits more people to be employed in the tertiary sector than in both the goods-producing primary and secondary sectors. Another feature of post-industrial societies is increased labour-force participation, which results in a lower dependency ratio (see Chapter 7). This is achieved through lower fertility rates and the entrance into the labour force of increased numbers of women. The final feature we examined was labour-management relations. We found that, as industrial societies mature, workers have a greater voice in their own determination. Also, the relationship between labour and management becomes increasingly formalized as bureaucratically organized unions enter collective agreements with corporate enterprises.

These features and others have prompted some sociologists to claim that industrialization is producing **cultural convergence**, or what may be described as a common world culture (see Form 1979). In other words, the cultural diversity that existed among nations prior to industrialization is being inexorably eroded as nation after nation enters a process that hardly varies from one country to another. In turn, it is contended that the common structural features produced by industrialization also produce similar changes in people's values and behaviour. Industrialization, no matter where in the world it is introduced, produces a "modern" person (see Inkeles and Smith 1974). Some of the characteristics of this modern industrial person are an openness to new experiences, acceptance of change, interest in community and national affairs, a belief that individuals control their own destinies, an increased capacity for independent thought, greater social tolerance, and a high value placed on education. Although there is empirical support for the convergence thesis, nevertheless differences among workers also exist (Hedley 1980).

## Work Values

Much of the research on workers in industrial societies has been on how satisfied they are with their jobs, what they actually do at work. From the first landmark study (Hoppock 1935) to those most recently conducted, the results have been consistent over time and from one country to another. Overall, workers are largely satisfied with their jobs (see Table 15-7). Anywhere from two-thirds to three-quarters of the workers register satisfaction, while approximately 10 to 15 percent state that they are dissatisfied. These results may be interpreted to mean that, for most people, work is a necessary as opposed to a voluntary activity, there being little choice as to whether or not they engage in it. Because people learn this very early

### Table 15-7. Job Satisfaction of Industrial Workers in Britain, the United States, Australia, and Canada (1969–1979)

| Job Satisfaction | Britain 1969 | U.S.A. 1974 | Australia 1977 | Canada 1979 |
|---|---|---|---|---|
| Very satisfied | 14% | 17% | 19% | 15% |
| Satisfied | 62 | 51 | 55 | 59 |
| Indifferent | 14 | 15 | 14 | 13 |
| Dissatisfied | 6 | 11 | 8 | 10 |
| Very dissatisfied | 3 | 6 | 4 | 3 |
| Total | 99 | 100 | 100 | 100 |
| Number of workers | 3098 | 649 | 1359 | 363 |

SOURCE: R. Alan Hedley, "Attachments to work: A cross-national examination," *Comparative Research* 9, 1(1981):12.

in life, most approach work both instrumentally as a means to other ends and with resigned acceptance (Hedley 1984a).

Whereas general orientations to work are similar, specific attachments to it vary. These variations may be explained with recourse to three broad sets of factors — work-related, sociodemographic, and cultural. As an illustration of the impact of these factors on work attachments, let us look at some of the results from one cross-national questionnaire survey of industrial factory workers in Britain, the United States, Australia, and Canada (Dubin, Hedley, and Taveggia 1976; Hedley, Dubin, and Taveggia 1980).

### Work-Related Factors

Of the many work-related variables explaining differing perceptions of work, occupational skill is especially important. Generally, those with higher skill place greater emphasis on intrinsic job features or the actual performance characteristic of work than do less-skilled workers. The former value such features as the particular type of work they do (challenge, interest, variety, and responsibility), as well as the tools and equipment they work with. On the other hand, less-skilled workers focus more on features extrinsic to work performance than do those with greater skill. The actual hours they work, raises and bonuses, and holidays and vacations are valued more by less-skilled workers; so is getting along with both co-workers and supervisors.

Another important work-related variable is length of service or the number of years spent with one's employer. Long-service workers are concerned with the length of their employment and what this means in terms of their job security, company benefits, and being familiar with their jobs. As well, they attach greater importance to how the company is managed and how much profit it makes than do workers who have just begun working for the company. Those in the latter group are more interested in social relations on the job and the opportunities existing within the company. They value the chance to meet new people, being able to talk to others while working, and the relationship they have with their supervisor. They also are attracted to opportunities for advancement and promotion and to being able to learn more than one job.

## Sociodemographic Factors

Gender and age also produce differences with regard to how people perceive work. For example, women are attached to social relations at work. Not only do they value meeting new people, talking to them at work, and getting together with them after work, but they also want to get along with these same people (including supervisors) and are concerned with how the company judges them. In addition, they have an instrumental attachment. They place importance on the hours they work, how far they have to travel to work, knowing in advance what they will do each day, and holidays and vacations.

Men are also instrumentally attached to their work. They value job security, employee benefits including retirement plans, and their chances for advancement and promotion. Also, they tend to be more intrinsically attached to their work than are female workers. They place greater importance on the type of work they do, creating new methods to do their jobs, the quality of their equipment and tools, and the chance to learn new things.

Older workers value having a job as a way of life, their length of service with the firm, being familiar with their job, and knowing in advance what they will do each day. They also are interested in the amount of physical work they do, controlling the number of things they do, and the attention they have to pay to their work. Younger workers have a set of quite different priorities. They too are attached to their work, but through the challenge, interest, and variety of their jobs, creating new methods to do their job better, the usefulness of the company's products to society, knowing what goes on in the firm, teaching new employees, and their chances for advancement and promotion. Also, they are attached to social relations on and off the job.

## Cultural Factors

Comparisons of factory workers from Britain, the United States, Australia, and Canada reveal some interesting constellations of work attachments. British workers emphasize control over their work and the type of working conditions more than their co-workers in the other three countries. With regard to control, British workers value doing their job in their own way, being left alone by the people they work with, the control they jointly exercise over how the work is done, and time for personal needs. Also, they are concerned about the number of supervisors, knowing enough to get by, knowing tasks in advance each day, how hard they have to work, and the attention they must pay. Their priorities regarding working conditions involve the cleanliness of the work area, how well the facilities are kept, and how modern the firm is.

These work attachments contrast sharply with those specified by American workers. First and foremost, Americans are distinguished by their emphasis on the opportunity that work provides. Although most workers from the other countries do not value at all highly their chances for advancement and promotion, Americans by and large attribute great importance to this aspect of work. Two related features are getting respect from family and friends because of their job and how the company judges them. Apparently the American dream is still alive and well in the United States.

Another area of work attachments for Americans is intrinsic features of work, including the kinds of products produced. Challenge, interest, variety, and a chance to learn new things at work are emphasized, as are the value and usefulness of the products. Finally, Americans also are attached to the conditions of work, but in a manner quite different from the British; American workers stress the convenience of their work area, the quality of their equipment, and how well their equipment works compared to others'.

Australian workers present yet another picture of work attachments. They value social relations at work and extrinsic factors. Getting along with people at work (including supervisors), a chance to help work-mates, getting respect from people at work, and how the company judges them are all attachments highlighting the importance of social relations on the job. Concerning extrinsic work features, they value holidays and vacations, the hours they work, job security, and raises and bonuses.

Finally, Canadian workers also have distinct work attachments that set them apart. Intrinsically attached to their work, they rate as important the sense of accomplishment they receive from it, challenging and interesting work, and the particular tasks they perform. In addition, Canadians appear to be concerned about their own personal responsibility at work. They rate highly the amount of responsibility they have in their jobs, as well as how the company judges them.

Work-related, sociodemographic, and cultural factors all serve to produce differences in how people perceive the world of work. It is also important to note, however, that the foregoing analysis was based on revealing such differences, if indeed they existed. Industrial workers of all types — skilled and unskilled, women and men, Americans and Canadians — also have a *common* core of work attachments, which they perceive to be the most important of all. Generally, workers tend to be very instrumentally attached to their jobs and to their employer. Although they are concerned with achieving a sense of purpose in their work, they are attached to the economic security that will allow them to live their lives outside the workplace. In addition, they are attached to the obvious and immediate conditions and social relations at work that will permit them to perform their tasks with minimal personal cost. The reasons for this lie in the mandatory nature of employment, which produces an overriding instrumental orientation to work, and the similarity with which modern industrial bureaucratic enterprises are organized. Although diverse values and attitudes toward work can and do exist, one is nevertheless impressed by the constancy that is produced in individual assessments of the meaning of work.

# Work in a Changing Society

While it is important to ascertain the value people place on work, it is also interesting to determine what influence, if any, workers' employment has on their values and behaviour *outside* the workplace. Ever since Wilensky (1960, 1961) formalized some of the problems in this area of research, there have been many studies on the relationship between work and other activities. Generally, the results indicate that what people do for a living does exert influence on what they think and how they behave when they are not at work.

In this section, we will examine the substance of these findings and also explore the changing nature of work. If work does have an effect on non-work activities and if it can be demonstrated that the whole institution of work is in the throes of change, then it will be interesting at least to speculate upon what these changes will mean for our non-work values and behaviour in the future.

## Work and Non-work

There are two models of the relationship between work and non-work. According to the **holistic model**, there is no essential division between work and non-work. We think and act in basically the same manner in both spheres of activity, and therefore work spills over into non-work time. According to the **segmental perspective**, on the other hand, there is a sharp line between these two activities. Mentally, we partition our lives so that work does not interfere with non-work. The research to date supports both models. Generally, the holistic model applies better in studies of upper white-collar professional and managerial workers, while the segmental model is better suited to blue-collar workers. The nature of the work performed in these two cases explains the different relationships (Katz 1967).

In upper white-collar jobs, workers are given discretion to organize and execute work in their own way. Because of their prior professional socialization and training, they have a strong commitment to work and to perform well. Consequently, it is unnecessary to supervise these workers closely. Also, again because of extensive socialization and training, the occupational roles of these upper white-collar workers figure more prominently in how they define themselves than is true of blue-collar workers. These factors together explain why white-collar workers take their work roles outside of work. One early study, *The Organization Man* (Whyte 1956), documents how all-encompassing the spillover of work into non-work can be as the work role is infused into literally all aspects of existence. For example, Whyte found that the management hierarchy at work extended into executives' non-work lives, dictating such things as the appropriate type of neighbourhood to live in, the model of car to drive, and whom they should associate with as friends.

Blue-collar jobs, on the other hand, are more specifically defined. Explicit job descriptions inform workers precisely what they are to do in each task, how they will perform it, and the time it will take them to complete it. They exercise little discretion within their work role. Because they have relatively little specialized training and because it is assumed they have only limited organization loyalty, they are supervised closely. Also, because the corporate enterprise is alien to their blue-collar culture, they make a sharp distinction between work and non-work (Hedley 1982). As Dubin (1968) has noted in this regard, "Workers in modern industrial society do not make a living; they make money and buy a living." Regardless of the distinction made between work and non-work, however, work does impinge upon people's lives away from work (see Meissner 1971).

One excellent study that spells out more fully the distinction between blue-collar and white-collar workers was conducted by Pearlin and Kohn (1966). They asked Italian and American mothers and fathers from both the middle and the working classes to choose three of seventeen values that they considered most important for a boy or girl of their child's age. Then they analyzed whether culture, gender, or class explained most of the variation in the ranking of values produced. Overwhelmingly, they found that class, as measured by occupation, was the single most important independent or causal variable. For example, working-class parents from both countries selected "obedience to parents" far more often than did middle-class parents, while the latter group chose "self-control" more frequently than did working-class parents.

Pearlin and Kohn explain this finding by stating that obedience and self-control are two aspects of one dimension — control by others (obedience) and control by self. Because much blue-collar work involves obeying others, this becomes a value for blue-collar workers, and they then transmit it to their children. Similarly, because self-control and self-direction characterize white-collar occupations, these values become internalized by white-collar workers. This study suggests that, regardless of holistic or segmental orientations, the influence of one's work on values and behaviour is pervasive.

## Work in a New Era

All the developments presented thus far in this chapter have contributed to vast structural changes in society. In turn, these changes affect both how we perceive work and what we actually do at work. In fact, very recent developments may cause us to rethink and redefine what work is. Some experts declare that we are currently experiencing a work revolution just as profound and with just as many far-reaching implications as in the original industrial revolution.

Industrialization, when it first occurred in Britain 200 years ago, caused us to redefine the concept of work. Work became an explicit set of contractual obligations physically separated from private life in both time and space. Traditional work did not involve such a contract or such a separation. It took place within the context of the family as and when the need dictated. With the industrial revolution, however, work became a specifically defined activity that occurred at the

# New Work Trends

*The following newspaper article presents some of the ways in which traditional work is changing. Because of structural pressures and individual worker demand, it is likely that we will have to redefine what it means to have a job.*

Virtually everyone working at home, or at the home of a friend? Four-hour or even two-hour workdays? This new concept of work is steadily gaining ground. Does it represent progress? No one knows for sure.

You share your job with a neighbor. He alternates short assignments with periods of idleness. Another edits manuscripts on the family word processor in the morning and sells sweaters in the afternoon. All are new-era workers, with dreams of autonomy and self-improvement in an increasingly unstable world.

Work is not what it used to be. Not only are jobs difficult to find and to keep, but also the concept of full employment has gone out of fashion.

The current economic situation and increasing unemployment are reshaping the classical model of employment, which once was based on a full day's work and on lifetime employment with a single company, from training to retirement. The concept of total employment has been replaced by one of floating, uncertain work. In the past few years new and atypical forms of employment have flourished: temporary jobs, substitutions, piecework, subcontracting, shared workplaces, short workdays, tailored hours.

The number of active workers who are content with this permanent precariousness is growing. Part-time employment, for example, has been gaining ground in all the industrial countries. Since 1974 half of the new jobs in Europe have been part-time.

In most industrial countries there is a nearly inexhaustible reserve of labor. It includes the unemployed, young people seeking their first jobs, housewives and mothers eager to resume working, and retirees who find it difficult not to work. This labor reserve creates a new situation that favors innovations.

Flexibility has become the byword in both the private and public sector lately, as a means of reducing unemployment. And for many people flexibility means freedom. Who, especially among the younger generation, does not dream of throwing off the yoke of work restrictions?

New life-styles and new values lead more and more people to doubt the sacrosanct value of work. Studies in France underscore this profound change. During the 1950s, nine out of every ten French workers were motivated by a need for economic security. In 1982, that ratio had fallen to three out of ten, and the "need for personal expression" had become of paramount importance for half of the country's potential workforce.

**Source:**

Michel Herteaux, "Taking work home: A comeback for cottage industry," *World Press Review* 32 (January 1985): 38. (Originally published in *Le Monde*.)

---

workplace of the employer according to some prearranged set schedule.

Today, as a result of the electronic revolution, it is no longer necessary to perform much of what we do within explicitly defined space and time limits. Although a worker is still contractually responsible for achieving organizational goals, much more flexibility has been introduced into the system. Because most work today involves the manipulation of information rather than materials, former time/space constraints become redundant. Instead, workers are linked to each other in a freefloating electronic network. The portable computer is "the workplace." Where and, within certain limits, when workers perform their duties is largely irrelevant.

It is important to ask what changes this new work arrangement will produce and how it will modify our existing attitudes toward work. One potentially far-reaching consequence is that work loses the pre-eminence it once held. It becomes instead just one of many activities that can be fitted into a personal time schedule. Although work still must be done, it can be done at the discretion of the individual worker. Very likely this will result in a diminution of the value attributed to work in that it will increasingly have to compete with other important individual activities. No longer will work occupy its own separate space/time domain.

Another important implication of the electronic revolution is the reconstitution of the labour force. Because work is increasingly becoming an individualized activity, the former solidarity of the physically united labour force will be eroded. Labour/management relations enter a new era, and the strength of unions to organize the labour force and to represent its interests is placed in jeopardy. To the extent that unions also adapt to the new conditions, they can maintain their function, but in a radically different form. Union "meetings" will occur electronically rather than physically. (Since attendance at union meetings has traditionally been very low, this could actually increase membership involvement.) One cannot deny, however, the tremendous strain that will be placed on unions under the new work arrangement.

Finally, we should ask how extensive these changes we have been discussing will be. What proportion of the labour force will be affected? Farmers must still sow seeds; construction workers still have to work at the building site; and surgeons still have to appear in the operating room. It is impossible at this stage to make an accurate estimate, but technologically it is now feasible for a large proportion of conventionally employed workers in offices to switch to the new work arrangement. As with so many other revolutionary events, the technology changes before our norms and values do (Ogburn 1922) Although it is now possible for many workers to do their jobs not bound by traditional time and space considerations, there is a resistance on the part of most, management and labour alike, to enter into a radically changed work structure. Nevertheless change is occurring, and for you students about to enter the labour force, your experience with work and your reaction to it will likely be very different from those of the generation that preceded you.

## SUMMARY

1. The industrial revolution, occurring at the end of the eighteenth century, radically altered the organization of work. The development of the steam engine by James Watt introduced the factory system of production with goods being manufactured for large consumer markets.
2. Industrialization changed people's relationship to society. For Durkheim, the principal factor responsible for this change was the increased division of labour. For Weber, it was a change in the value people placed on work, while for Marx, it was the ownership of the means of production by the bourgeoisie that brought about these changes.
3. Industrialization has produced great disparity among the nations of the world, and the gap between the rich developed and the poor developing nations is increasing enormously. The industrialized nations enjoy a substantially higher per capita income and standard of living than do the developing countries.
4. Although Canada has one of the highest per capita Gross National Products in the world, it is not as industrially developed as the United States, Japan, or some European nations. This is explained in part by Canada's special and unique relationship with the United States.
5. Post-industrial societies are those in which at least half the labour force is engaged in the service-producing tertiary sector. By this definition, Canada is post-industrial. Post-industrialism is accompanied by a transformation of the occupational structure, increased labour-force participation (particularly by women), and more formal participation by workers in determining the contractual conditions of work. Some sociologists have asserted that there is a direct relationship between industrialization and cultural convergence.
6. Generally, workers are largely satisfied with their jobs, although they are instrumentally attached to them because of the necessity of work for survival. Work-related, sociodemographic, and cultural factors all produce variations in how people are attached to their work.
7. The kind of work people do affects what they value and how they behave outside the workplace. Some people attempt to maintain a sharp distinction between work and non-work (segmentalism), but others do not (holism). Generally, the higher occupational levels have a holistic perspective, while lower blue-collar workers have a segmental orientation.
8. The electronic revolution is changing popular conceptions of work. Work no longer need be confined in space and time. Rather, workers can be linked to their employment through interlocking electronic networks.

# GLOSSARY

**Agricultural society.** Society in which at least half the labour force is engaged in the primary sector.

**Arbitration.** Process whereby a third party intervenes between management and labour and passes binding judgment on the new collective agreement.

**Conciliation.** Process whereby a third party intervenes between management and labour and makes recommendations regarding a new collective agreement.

**Craft union.** Formal organization of workers based on their specialized skills. (Also called a trade union.)

**Cultural convergence.** Thesis that advocates that the process of industrialization will produce a common world culture.

**Holistic model.** Perspective asserting that there is no essential division between work and non-work.

**Industrialization.** The movement of workers out of the primary sector into the secondary (manufacturing) sector.

**Industrial revolution.** A series of technological and organizational changes in the process of manufacturing that occurred in Britain during the latter part of the eighteenth century; essential features included machine production, the factory system of manufacturing, and mechanical motive power.

**Industrial society.** Society in which less than half the labour force is engaged in the primary sector.

**Industrial union.** Formal organization of non-craft workers based on the private-sector industry in which they work.

**Post-industrial society.** Society in which at least half the labour force is engaged in the tertiary sector.

**Primary sector.** Division of the occupational structure in which employment involves either harvesting or extraction of goods (e.g., agriculture, logging, mining, fishing, hunting, and trapping.).

**Protestant work ethic.** Ideology that states (1) work is service to God; (2) one's duty is to work hard; and (3) success in work is measured by money and property.

**Public-sector union.** Formal organization of workers employed in some type of government enterprise.

**Secondary sector.** Division of the occupational structure in which employment involves the transformation of raw materials into semifinished or finished manufactured goods. The secondary sector includes all manufacturing and construction industries.

**Segmental model.** A perspective asserting that there is an essential division between work and non-work.

**Tertiary sector.** Division of the occupational structure in which employment involves the provision of services.

**Work.** Activity that permits one a livelihood. Work includes conventional paid employment, illegal employment, and homemaking.

# FURTHER READING

**Anderson, John, Morley Gunderson, and Allen Ponak (eds.).** *Union-Management Relations in Canada.* Don Mills, ON: Addison-Wesley, 1989. A collection of 18 articles on all aspects of labour/management relations in Canada, including comparative data.

**Chen, Mervin Y.T., and Thomas G. Regan.** *Work in the Changing Canadian Context.* Toronto: Butterworths, 1985. A recent industrial sociology textbook containing much data and many statistics.

**Krahn, Harvey J., and Graham S. Lowe.** *Work, Industry, and Canadian Society.* Scarborough, ON: Nelson, 1988. An industrial text that covers in much greater detail the issues raised in this chapter.

**Lenski, Gerhard, and Jean Lenski.** *Human Societies: An Introduction to Macrosociology.* New York: McGraw-Hill, 1982. An examination of how societies have evolved over time. Includes particularly good chapters on industrialization and the industrial revolution.

**Miller, Delbert C., and William H. Form.** *Industrial Sociology: Work in Organizational Life.* New York: Harper and Row, 1980. A basic industrial sociology text now in its third edition, and written by noted experts in the field.

**Murdoch, William W.** *The Poverty of Nations: The Political Economy of Hunger and Population.* Baltimore: Johns Hopkins University Press, 1980. An excellent treatment of the history and development of industrialization throughout the world, and an analysis of the reasons for the inequities that exist among nations.

**Smucker, Joseph.** *Industrialization in Canada.* Scarborough, ON: Prentice-Hall, 1980. A good treatment of industrialization and the labour union movement in Canada.

# CHAPTER 16

# Urbanization and Urbanism

A. R. GILLIS

Many urban sociologists would argue that their subfield of sociology is unique, with a distinct subject, a special way of looking at social life, and a discrete body of knowledge. Like other subfields, urban sociology includes both structural-functional and conflict viewpoints, as well as historical and contemporary approaches. Symbolic interaction has not been popular with urban sociologists (which probably means that urban sociology is not popular with symbolic interactionists). Also, students of cities often include the physical environment and the size of populations as important variables in their research. Because of their concern with "place," urban sociologists are continually faced with the question of whether particular environments cause people to behave in different ways, or whether different people are attracted to different types of places. This focus not only distinguishes urban sociology from other areas, but also forms the basis for a link with "applied" fields such as social policy, planning, and architecture. This side of urban sociology pleases utilitarians and bothers purists. In any case, a concern with the physical as well as the social environment often distinguishes sociologists who study cities from other sociologists.

It is hard to define the word "city" in a way that will please everyone. Architects, planners, and civil engineers, for example, are mainly interested in planning, design, and physical factors; the way they view and define the term "city" reflects these interests. Since social scientists are concerned with social life, their view of the city and what they regard as its distinct features leads them to a somewhat different definition.

# What is an Urban Area?

Current definitions of the word "urban" vary widely from one country to another. In Greece, for example, municipalities and communities containing fewer than 10 000 people are not classified as urban; but in neighbouring Albania, any towns with 400 or more are.

In Canada the minimum population necessary for a locality to be classified as urban (a "census urban area" or CUA) is 1000, while in the United States the figure is 2500. These different definitions of "urban" make international comparisons difficult. Statistics Canada tells us that approximately 75 percent of the Canadian population lives in urban areas, and the United States census reports roughly the same figure for that country. But it is important to realize that the level of urbanization in the United States is, from the Canadian standpoint, understated. In fact, the proportion of the American population living in towns of 1000 or more is much greater than 75 percent.

Here is another definitional problem: classifying a village containing 1000 people (or for that matter 2500 people) as an urban area has little intuitive appeal. For most of us, the word "urban" brings to mind places like Tokyo, New York, Montreal, or Toronto rather than Gimli, Manitoba, or Gibson's Landing, B.C., both of which are classified as urban areas in Canada. In view of this incongruity, in 1931, Statistics Canada (then the Dominion Bureau of Statistics) developed the concept of "census metropolitan area" (CMA) in the hope of offering a more satisfactory description of the number of Canadians who were living under urban *conditions*, not just in urban *areas*.

A CMA was defined as a principal city with at least 50 000 inhabitants; an urbanized core with a population density of at least 1000 people per square mile (2.6 km²); or an area outside the central city that either has a labour force of which at least 70 percent are engaged in nonagricultural activities, or has a total population of at least 100 000. This definition was more coincident with the spirit of the term "urban" as embodied in most of the early theories about urban life (nonagricultural) and the minimum size of a city (large). Unfortunately, the definition did not take into account what has recently become an essential element of the modern metropolis: living in one community and commuting to work in another. Most likely in response to this, in 1981 Statistics Canada redefined the CMA as

*the main labour market area of an urbanized core (or continuously built up area) having 100 000 or more population. . . . CMAs consists of (1) municipalities completely or partly inside the urbanized core; and (2) other municipalities if (1) at least 40% of the employed labour force living in the municipality works in the urbanized core, or (b) at least 25% of the employed labour force working in the municipality lives in the urbanized core. (Statistics Canada 1982)*

The United Nations (*Demographic Handbook for Africa* 1968) uses the following classification scheme:

*Big City*: a locality with 500 000 or more inhabitants.
*City*: a locality with 100 000 or more inhabitants.
*Rural Locality*: a locality with fewer than 20 000 inhabitants.

Canada's definition of a CMA is roughly equivalent to the United Nations' "city" classification. There are now 25 CMAs in Canada, all of which have been growing at a faster rate than the total population, indicating that the country is not just urbanizing, but "metropolitanizing." This is particularly apparent in Southern Ontario, which seems destined to become one very large metropolitan area (Gillis 1987).

So how urban *are* Canadians? The fact that Canada is 75 percent urban does not mean that each of us is three-quarters urban and one-quarter rural in orientation. A sociologist would say that this sort of reasoning is an example of an *ecological fallacy*. The characteristics of an aggregation are not necessarily displayed in the same proportions in each of the members that make it up. Urban sociologists, who examine collectivities such as cities or neighbourhoods and draw conclusions about the individuals who live in them, must be particularly careful to avoid these pitfalls of aggregation and disaggregation.

What the statistic actually means is that three out of four Canadians live in urban areas, and one does not. Moreover, in 1986 six out of ten lived in a CMA, one out of two lived in a "big city" (a metropolitan area of 500 000 or more), and three out of ten could be found in metropolitan areas of one million or more (Montreal, Toronto, or Vancouver). This suggests that Canada is an urban society. And it is. However, as Lucas (1971) points out, "many people in Canada live nowhere." Because of Canada's position in the world economy as a supplier of resources, many urban Canadians live in small, single-industry towns: Lucas counted 636, few of which were larger than 10 000 in population. When we call Canada an urban society, then, we should keep in mind that a substantial proportion of the population still lives in rural areas and small towns, and that life in these areas is very different than in larger urban centres (Lucas 1971; see also Marsh 1970).

**Sources:**

*Demographic Handbook for Africa* (Addis Ababa: United Nations Economic Commission for Africa, 1968); A.R. Gillis, *CMAs, Submetro Areas, and Megalopolis: An Examination of Montreal, Toronto, and Vancouver* (unpublished report to Statistics Canada, 1987); Rex, Lucas. *Minetown, Milltown, Railtown: Life in Canadian Communities of Single Industry* (Toronto: University of Toronto Press, 1971); Leonard Marsh, *Communities in Canada* (Toronto: McClelland and Stewart, 1970); Statistics Canada, *1981 Census Dictionary* (Ottawa: Supply and Services, 1982).

Sociologists define a **city** as "a large concentration of people who work in a wide range of specialized and interdependent occupations that, for the most part, do not involve the primary production of food." It is important to note that this definition does not ignore the physical characteristics of cities. The phrase "large concentration of people" implies that the number and density of people are noteworthy urban characteristics. In fact, many urban sociologists suspect that population density and other environmental factors have major effects on social life in cities.

The sociological view of cities is useful because it points to variables that allow us to explain where, when, and why the first cities were built, how cities grow and spread, and how and why people who live in them differ from people who do not. These are important questions for sociologists, especially in view of the recent and continuing rural-to-urban shift of the world's population.

## The Origin of Cities

Until recently, social scientists thought that the first permanent settlement with enough people in it to be called a city was built about 5000 years ago in the Middle East. However, recent archaeological evidence suggests that the first walled city may have been built 8000 to 10 000 years ago. (In fact, one of the first cities may have been Jericho, a city far more famous for its destruction than for its construction.) In any case, since *Homo sapiens* has existed for at least 250 000 years, it is clear that the natural history of humanity has taken place almost exclusively in wilderness and rural environments.

The relatively short period that people have lived in cities suggests to some scholars that pastoral living is our natural or preferred way of life. This may be true, but for the most part our ancestors' life in the wilderness was probably less indicative of preference than of necessity. Until about 8000 B.C. people were simply unable to sustain urban populations.

### Agricultural Surplus

According to our definition, a city is a large number of people living in a relatively concentrated area. To feed these people, a great amount of food must either be produced in and around the area or be brought into it from farther away. Moving large amounts of food long distances requires relatively sophisticated technology, and growing a great amount of food in a concentrated area requires high-yield agriculture. Neither of these requirements comes easily to people with primitive skills. To make matters worse, a large proportion of the urban population does not contribute to the production of food, so the rural residents who are growing food must supply not only themselves, but others as well.

Even if early humans had been inclined to live in cities, they would not then have been released from primary food production to become urbanites. As people advanced technically — developing the plow, domesticating draft animals, discovering high-yield grains, and inventing more efficient systems of transportation — larger **agricultural surpluses** could be taken from a wider range of environments. But these and other important innovations did not emerge until rather recently in the natural history of humans.

In view of this, it is not surprising that the first cities were built in the rich alluvial valleys of the Tigris, Nile, and Indus rivers, and, somewhat later on, in similar environments in Central America. These sites allowed people with simple technology to grow a surplus of food in a relatively concentrated area, and to feed a relatively large number of people who were not themselves contributing to the production of food.

Sociologists point to several factors that may have caused people to produce a surplus of food and to construct cities. Two major types of factors can be distinguished: limiting factors and motivating factors. **Limiting factors** include the natural environment and the technical ability of people to alter it. These factors determined where cities could *not* be built. **Motivating factors** include cultural values and social structure as forces that may have encouraged people to build the first cities.

### Limiting Factors

**The Natural Environment.** According to Bronowski (1973), the first cities resulted indirectly from the emergence of a new relationship between people and a specific part of their physical environment: wheat. Modern bread wheat resulted from

**Cities became possible only when agricultural surpluses could be accumulated.**

the accidental cross-fertilization of several kinds of wild grasses. The seeds of the new plant had a low chaff content, and the chaff separated easily from the kernel. This impaired their dispersal by the wind, which might have caused the extinction of the new hybrid. Because the chaff contains cellulose, it cannot be used for energy by humans, but the kernel is an efficient source of energy. The new hybrid was therefore a good food source for humans, who saw its value and replaced the wind as its principal means of dispersal. In this way people and wheat became involved in a mutually beneficial or *symbiotic* relationship. The plant provided people with a concentration of calories; in return, people refrained from consuming the whole harvest, saving some portion of it for planting next season's crop, thus ensuring the hybrid's survival.

This symbiotic relationship was the basis for the development of agriculture, which provided an important and desirable alternative to the hunting/gathering and herding economies that had previously characterized human societies.

The discovery and domestication of wheat — and of rice in Asia, and maize in Central America — allowed both plants and people to settle in mutually advantageous locations, such as the Mesopotamian basin. Settlement and the ease of storing wheat greatly helped people to create a surplus of food. The head of a family could support more

household members and would need to devote less time and energy to producing food for survival.

Some family heads, in fact, were released entirely from food production, while others continued to work at full capacity to feed themselves, their families, and all those not engaged in food production. In this way, the presence of ideal growing conditions and a high-yield grain set the stage for the emergence of agriculture, the production of a food surplus, settlement, and the division of labour. People were released from the pressures of the seasonal nomadism of hunting/gathering and herding societies, and the economic base of urban life was established.

**Technology.** Ideas and technology have helped humans to construct environments favourable to the production of an agricultural surplus, and to build the physical artifacts that contain urban populations. Natural environments, in contrast, often forced people to be nomadic. When game or edible plants disappeared from one region because of overhunting, overgrazing, or the changing seasons, people had to move on to where game and edible plants were more abundant. People who lived under such conditions were hardly in a position to settle down and construct cities. Agricultural technology gave people more control over their natural environment and allowed them to settle down.

The application of human ideas has frequently changed the natural environment, making it a more productive and less aversive place to live. People have discovered and even developed a wide variety of high-yield crops (such as wheat), learning how to care for them by improving their natural environments with various devices ranging from fertilizer to irrigation. Technology has vastly improved people's capacity to extract surplus food from the physical environment, and greatly extended the range of environments that will tolerate large numbers of people and cities.

City walls, as well as private and public buildings, represent alterations of the natural environment to suit certain human needs. Walls protect those they enclose from external threats, and buildings and cities themselves provide protection from extremes in climate. But concentrating large numbers of people in cities poses numerous challenges involving shelter, transportation, sewage disposal, and so forth. These challenges cannot be met with the methods used in rural areas, where the scale is small and the population is dispersed. New technological solutions must therefore be developed and applied. Thus, a city can be seen as a technical device that alters or controls the effects of the natural environment by substituting for it a *built environment*.

So we can see that humans applied technology to the natural environment in two ways important for the origin of cities: the production of surplus food and the construction of built environments. This combination not only protected people from natural threats but also solved many of the problems associated with large numbers of people living in close quarters. Technology thus made people less vulnerable to the limitations and variability of the natural environment. In an agreeable natural environment, simple technology may suffice to allow the survival of persons or plants. But complex technology enables a disagreeable natural environment to be improved. The absence of a minimal combination of natural environment and technology means that a city cannot be built.

## Images of the City

The word "city" brings different images to the minds of different people. And different cities, because of their traits, physical symbols, and nicknames, elicit different images — New York, world status; Washington, politics; Chicago, virility; and San Francisco, elegance.

Cities' traits tend to be emphasized or exaggerated by nicknames, which are particularly popular in the United States. Here in Canada, we have "the Cradle of Confederation" (Charlottetown), "the Forest City" (London), "the Stampede City" (Calgary), and "the Gateway to the North" (Edmonton). Montreal competes both with San Francisco and with Paris, Ontario, to be known as "the Paris of North America." Nicknames are generally positive, often reflecting boosterism, but as with other stereotypes, this need not always be the case: one of Toronto's nicknames is "Hogtown."

Some cities also have physical symbols, which may or may not be useful. The Golden Gate Bridge symbolizes San Francisco, while also allowing access to Sausalito; but the St. Louis Arch has no use but to symbolize St. Louis as "the Gateway to the West." A unique natural silhouette, like Montreal's Mount Royal, can also symbolize a city, as can a constructed silhouette, like the New York skyline.

The most distinctive city monument in Canada is probably the CN Tower in Toronto. The tower serves as a communications centre, and is gradually gaining worldwide recognition as the symbol for the city. However, it is not at all clear what meaning we should attach to this monument. Suggestions range from an exclamation point through more Freudian phallic interpretations.

Specific cities vary in the nature of their overall ambience or image. In comparing popular images of New York, Paris, and London, Milgram (1970) found that New York was distinguished primarily on the basis of architecture and "the pace of life." In contrast, London elicited images of its citizens and social quality, while Paris brought to mind both physical and social characteristics equally. As with the concept of "city" itself, then, both physical and social characteristics seem to be important in describing the character of specific cities, with some more physical and others more social (Lynch 1960).

**Sources:**

Selected references to Kevin Lynch, *The Image of the City* (Cambridge, MA: MIT Press, 1960); and Stanley Milgram, "The experience of living in cities," *Science* 167(1970): 1461–68.

We can conclude that certain environmental conditions, whether natural or altered, are necessary for the origin of cities.

The first cities emerged in natural settings that were hospitable to plants and people — necessarily so, because of the low level of technical development 10 000 years ago. After all, the plow was not even invented until the fourth century B.C. (Palen 1987). Later, as people extended their knowledge of and skills for environmental improvement, cities were constructed on a wider range of sites.

## Motivating Factors

Although an agreeable environment, whether natural or improved, is *necessary* for the origin of cities, it is not *sufficient*. The fact that people are able to stockpile a surplus of food does not guarantee that they will do so. For example, Tuan (1974) notes that some areas of New Guinea provide inhabitants with more food than they can eat. Yet they have not stockpiled a surplus that would allow a division of labour between food producers and others. As a result, urbanization has not occurred. This example demonstrates that the part played by the environment in the origin of cities is one of limiter, not motivator.

New Guinea natives have had little or no experience with cities, so it is hard to argue that their failure to stockpile food and to urbanize reflects a preference for rural living. Instead, sociologists suggest that either certain structural or certain cultural factors, or both, are necessary before a population can urbanize. These characteristics are absent in the New Guinea population. Before there can be cities, people must be organized at the very least into producers of food and nonproducers of food. Sociologists have several explanations for the development of this division of labour.

**Culture.** Social scientists who favour a functionalist model of society (for example, Davis 1955) observe that general and widespread economic benefits accrue from large-scale operations and a division of labour. They therefore argue that the first cities arose because the original inhabitants somehow recognized these economic benefits and wanted to realize them.

Others believe that the origin of the first cities had less to do with economics than with religion. According to Adams (1960) and Childe (1950), the first public buildings were temples, which often doubled as granaries. Priests may have been the first nonagricultural workers, forming the nucleus of urban society. They gave spiritual sustenance, supported and disseminated a hierarchy of values, and supervised the collection and storage of the agricultural surplus.

This argument is generally consistent with a structural-functional view of the relationship between culture and social structure; social organization is seen as a manifestation of culture. These views emphasize co-operation, consensus, and the importance of values and ideas as the motivation for developing cities. But it is also possible (and, according to many sociologists, more likely) that conflict and dissensus were the social forces that generated the initial division of the populace into producers and nonproducers of food — the division of labour that resulted in the first cities.

**Social Structure.** From a conflict perspective, the division of labour into producers and nonproducers of food resulted from victimization of the former by the latter. In other words, nonproducers took food from farmers, who were then forced to extract still more nourishment from the environment in order to survive and to plant a crop in the next growing season. From this viewpoint, the creation of surplus food accompanied or followed, rather than preceded, the division of labour and the first cities.

The nonproducers were a ruling elite of warriors who ensconced themselves behind walls — first, of castles, and later, of cities. They created an agricultural surplus by forcing farmers to produce more food to avoid starvation, or at least to increase their standard of living. This situation also motivated farmers to invent more labour-saving agricultural technology (Polanyi 1957; Sjoberg 1960).

Sociologists vary in their opinion of how much force had to be used to get farmers to give their food to the ruling elite. Outright pillaging, institutionalized taxation, and exchanging food for protection and other services each involve different degrees of open coercion, with the last involving less force than fraud (and not even that if the exchange can be deemed fair by some absolute standard). It is at this point that the conflict argument shades off into a consensus view of the relationship between a city and its **hinterland** (the surrounding area from which a city draws its food and other raw materials).

In any event, culture, social structure, or both in combination (Mumford 1961) can be seen as necessary motivating factors in the development of the first cities. Like the natural environment and technology, however, culture and/or structure are not by themselves sufficient to account for the first cities. Unless a surplus is possible — and the natural environment and technology may or may not permit this — the motivation to produce surplus food will be fruitless and will disappear, along with many of the people. So both limiting factors and motivating factors are necessary, but neither by themselves are sufficient to produce a city. Not

until these factors are considered together does one have a satisfactory explanation for the origin of the first city, in Mesopotamia, about 10 000 years ago. For more general discussions of this approach, see Schnore (1958), Duncan (1959), Duncan and Schnore (1959), and Tilly (1974).

## Urbanization

**Urbanization** refers to an increase in the proportion of a given population living in areas defined as urban. Increases have most often occurred as people migrate from rural to urban areas, and in recent years, from other countries. But urbanization can also occur as a result of differences in fertility and mortality rates, which sometimes give a relative advantage to urban populations. But fertility and mortality differentials have been more important in affecting **deurbanization** — a *decrease* in the proportion of a given population inhabiting urban areas. Historically, the higher rates of fertility that are typical in rural areas have on occasion combined with higher rates of urban mortality (especially during plagues) to create a deurbanizing effect on a population (Tilly 1976a).

### Urbanization: The Ancient Period

Ancient cities were small by today's standards and contained only a tiny proportion of the world's population. Athens, the foremost city of classical Greece, peaked with a population of 120 000 to 180 000. Both limiting and motivating factors kept its population low; poor soil and simple agricultural technology combined with a cultural preference for limited growth to keep cities small (Davis 1955; Palen 1987).

The other great city of the ancient period was Rome. A more generous natural environment, technical advances (especially in the areas of agriculture and the transportation of people, produce, and water), a more complex division of labour, and a cultural interest in expansion combined to push Rome far beyond the size of Athens. Estimates of the size of ancient Rome, whose population peaked just before the birth of Christ, range between 250 000 and 1.6 million (Palen 1987).

**Figure 16-1. The Origin of the First Cities**

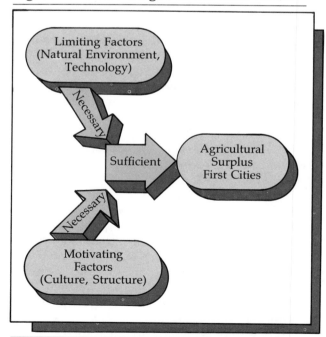

NOTE: Necessity is the state or level that one variable must reach before another can change. Sufficiency is the state or level reached by one variable that *always* produces a change in another.

## Deurbanization: The Middle Ages

Rome was the largest and most powerful city the world had ever seen, but when the Roman Empire fell (around the fifth century A.D.), neither the city nor its population could be maintained. When the Vandals cut the city off from its grain-producing areas in Africa, Rome was dealt a serious blow, and its population ultimately dwindled to less than 25 000 (Palen 1987).

The demise of the Roman Empire, like the decline of Greece before it, resulted in the disintegration of an extensive social network with a city at its centre. All roads had indeed led to Rome. They carried raw materials, food, traders, and labourers to the city, and armies from it to collect taxes, maintain order in the provinces, and extend the Empire's frontiers. The fall of Rome heralded a period of deurbanization and the return of Europe to rural life. The vast network developed by Rome withered, and outlying localities were forced once again into isolation and self-sufficiency. During urban growth, people flowed into the city on all the roads that led to Rome. In decline, the same roads took those people away. Their return to the land, and to local rather than imperial domination, marked the beginning of a 600-year period of economic and cultural stagnation (Pirenne 1939) during which few European cities surpassed 100 000 in population.

## Cities and Culture

For both Athens and Rome, dramatic developments in the arts, the sciences, and other dimensions of culture coincided with the rise of the city and its empire. Their decline was followed by an extended period of cultural inertia known as the Middle Ages or the Dark Ages. After the fall of Rome, Europe did not again begin to urbanize until the eleventh century, when innovations in abstract and material culture began once again (Huizinga 1924; Pirenne 1939).

This pattern suggests that there is an important relationship between cities and culture. We already saw that cultural factors affected the origin of cities, but it seems that cities also affected culture and civilization. (Both "civic" and "civilization" are words derived from *civis*, the Latin word for "citizen.") Athens and Rome are exemplary in

this respect, having developed and disseminated the classical traditions and served as the bases for Western civilization itself.

One way to understand the cultural contributions of Athens, Rome, and other great cities is by viewing the city as a mechanism for controlling time (Innis 1951) as well as space. Because they did not have to feed themselves and because of the efficiency of a more complex social organization, citizens of cities like Athens and Rome may have had more leisure time than did their rural counterparts (Herskowitz 1952). Inadequate leisure time can be seen as a limiting factor that prevents innovation and experimentation. Pushing back the amount of time spent on agricultural work freed people to do other things. This, combined with the fact that settlement allowed for a greater accumulation of cultural artifacts (few nomads carry libraries), released people from the tyranny of tradition and set the stage for cumulative cultural change. (See also Mumford 1963, Landis 1983, and Rifkin 1987 on the importance of time and its measurement.)

In addition, cities attracted and sustained creative people from a wide range of rural regions and different sociocultural backgrounds. (The same factors that caused individuals to break away from traditional ties and migrate to cities may also have inclined them to be innovative in other ways.) The concentration and social interaction of creative people with different cultural backgrounds proved to be fertile ground for the growth of new ideas and cultural change. (In fact, "a large concentration of creative people from different cultural backgrounds who do not have their time consumed in food-producing activities" is a good description of a university as well as of a city.)

The motivating factor for many cultural advances may have been the need felt by the urban elite to keep records concerning the taxation of the hinterland and the administration of the empire. Primitive accounting may have led to the development of writing, mathematics, and related fields. Advances in the sciences may have resulted from pressure to improve agricultural technology (Childe 1950).

Athens and Rome illustrate that the causal arrow between urbanization and the development of culture can go both ways. That is, cities are not only the products of people's ideas and values, but also the agents of innovation and cultural change.

## Reurbanization: The Renaissance

In the eleventh century, Europeans began to return to the cities. Again, these were small by today's standards. According to Weber (1958a, originally published 1921), each city had the following features:

1. a fortification;
2. a market;
3. a court of its own and at least partly autonomous law;
4. a related form of association (guilds, professional associations); and
5. at least partial political and administrative autonomy.

Weber thought that cities like this were characteristic of Europe and had an important effect on the economy. (See also Chirot 1985.)

By the fourteenth century, the economy of Renaissance Europe was becoming a city-centred, trade-oriented version of capitalism. The feudal self-sufficiency of the medieval period was in decline. Cities promised farm workers a place to live, greater freedom, and a better occupational deal than did the feudal manor. As a result, serfs increasingly fled the farms for the cities. If they were able to persuade the city fathers and the guilds that their particular skills were in demand, they would be admitted. If they could then avoid capture for a year, they were considered to be free. In this way, urbanization in Europe contributed to the destruction of the feudal economy and promoted the concentration of capital in cities (Marx 1965, originally published 1867–95). In this sense, then, the city affected the structure, as well as the culture, of Western societies.

The development of cities in Europe during the Renaissance was associated with important changes in culture (such as the Protestant Reformation) as well as in the economy (such as the rise of modern capitalism). The major effects on cities during this period were the forces of urbanization, discussed above, and the countervailing force of deurbanization caused by the bubonic plague. In a three-year period the plague killed about a quarter of the population of Europe. By 1400, a third of Europe's population was dead from the Black Death, and over half the residents of cities had died (Zinsser 1965; Langer 1973; McNeil 1976). The mortality rate from bubonic plague was higher in the cities than in the rural areas, reflecting the inadequate garbage and sewage disposal in most cities, as well as the greater ease with which communicable diseases spread in high-density settings, where rats, fleas, and people were in close contact (see Walter 1988).

In the short run, then, the plague had a deurbanizing effect on the European population. But in the long run, the Black Death dealt the final blow to feudalism and actually stimulated urbanization. The death of so many peasants, by totally depleting the already weakened supply of rural farm workers, accelerated the collapse of the feudal economy. Survivors left for the cities, where the plague had created severe labour shortages and capital had become increasingly concentrated through inheritance (McEvedy 1988). By the fifteenth century, the forces of urbanization had countered the forces of deurbanization, labour and capital began to concentrate, and European cities grew once again.

Plagues continued into the seventeenth century, but never again affected the size or distribution of the population the way they did in the latter part of the fourteenth century. The descendants of the survivors of the fourteenth-century plague were probably more resistant to the Black Death, according to McEvedy (1988). Still, the mortality rate from all causes continued to be higher in cities than in the countryside until the end of the nineteenth century. This mortality rate, combined with the typically lower rate of urban fertility, meant that heavy migration to the cities was required for urbanization to continue.

## The Modern Era: Industrialization

The urbanization of Europe proceeded slowly until late in the eighteenth century, when the entire population began to grow quickly, apparently because of a sudden drop in mortality rates. This drop probably resulted from Jenner's invention of the smallpox vaccine in 1792 and from a general improvement in health attributable to a significant increase in the amount and availability of food,

# How many farmers would it take . . . ?

In the first cities, between fifty and ninety farmers were required to produce enough food to sustain themselves and one other person. This tiny surplus kept the population of the earliest cities small. As technology improved, the number of farmers required to sustain one urbanite decreased. By the beginning of the nineteenth century the number of farms required to sustain an urban family had been reduced to nine, and the second largest city in the world was London, with a population of 900 000 (Davis 1955). (The largest was Edo [Tokyo], at one million [Rozman 1975].) Industrialization further decreased the number of farmers required to sustain an urbanite and increased the potential size of cities.

Today, in the United States, for example, one farmer can sustain himself or herself and approximately 45 other people. Less than 5 percent of the employed population is engaged in agricultural occupations, and the largest metropolitan area in the country is New York, with almost 18 million people (Palen 1981; Gist and Fava 1974).

**Source:**

Kingsley Davis, "The origin and growth of urbanization in the world," *American Journal of Sociology* 60(March 1955):430; Noel P. Gist and Sylvia F. Fava, *Urban Society*, 6th edition (New York: Thomas Y. Crowell, 1974); G. Rozman, "Edo's importance in the changing Tokugawa society," *Journal of Japanese Studies* 1(1975):91–112; John Palen, *The Urban World* (New York: McGraw-Hill, 1981).

---

which was in turn made possible by an extended period of good weather and by several important advances in agricultural and transportation technology (McKeown 1976). Extra food not only allowed a larger population to be better nourished, but released more people from agricultural occupations and rural areas. Many migrated to the cities; for the first time in history, close to 10 percent of the human population inhabited urban localities.

Apart from the natural environment, the most important factor limiting the expansion of cities is a lack of technology. Over the centuries, people have used many different kinds of techniques to extract larger and larger food surpluses from an increasingly wide range of natural environments. Because of this, technologically advanced nations have been able to take labourers from agricultural occupations and reallocate them to other tasks in urban centres. The most important technical advance in this respect, as noted in Chapter 15, was industrialization.

Industrialization replaced animate sources of energy (humans, horses, oxen) with inanimate sources of energy (mainly fossil fuels). This involved substituting machines for tools as energy converters. For example, the horse collar and harness are tools that convert horse power into pulling power, but the tractor is a machine that transforms inanimate energy into pulling power. Industrialization began in rural cottage industries in nineteenth-century England. Under the control of ascetic Protestants like the potter Josiah Wedgwood, this early industrialization ("protoindustrialization") was used to mass-produce consumer goods for wide distribution. In contrast, the mechanization of France and Switzerland, for example, involved the production of watches and toys for the elites. So new technology and the Protestant religion combined to make England the centre of the "industrial revolution" and one of the most industrialized nations in the world (Bronowski 1973).

Industrialization had at least three major effects on the city:

1. The application of its principles to agriculture greatly increased the efficiency of agricultural workers and the size of the surplus they could produce. This change probably released many workers from farming, creating a pool of labourers for work elsewhere (McQuillan 1980).
2. The application of its principles to transportation greatly extended the territory on which an urban area could draw. This increased the incoming amount of food and raw materials, and reduced the danger of starvation due to crop failure in a specific region. Such territorial extension had special implications for Canada, because it allowed England to draw on the colony as a supplier of wheat even more than it had done previously.
3. The industrialization of factories resulted in a new type of city — the manufacturing city.

Ironically, as industrialization replaced human labour in some sectors, especially in agriculture, it also produced a demand for labour in other sectors (for example, a growth in demand for factory workers). So the industrial revolution was also a social revolution that saw the emergence of new relationships between people and machines, and the development of highly specialized jobs and complex hierarchies. People and capital, which had been dispersed throughout rural areas, became concentrated in factories, which were themselves concentrated in industrial cities. It is noteworthy that by today's standards both the housing and working conditions of these industrial cities were horrific. Yet at the time they probably represented a clear improvement over rural poverty. (This may also be the case today, especially in developing countries.)

These effects combined to greatly expand the potential for the proliferation and growth of cities. Increased agricultural productivity meant that more food could be sent to cities. More efficient transportation technology meant that greater amounts of food could be sent faster and farther than before, and the urban promise of consumer goods and employment attracted millions of rural migrants.

Interestingly, although technology allows people to extract larger food surpluses from deserts, barren land, and the floor of the sea, some environments still deny surplus food to people. For example, we have not yet learned to control the central African tsetse fly, which carries sleeping sickness. Indigenous wildlife seem immune to the disease, but these animals are valuable neither as sources of food nor as draft animals; on the other hand, high-yield domestic beef, dairy, and draft animals are susceptible to sleeping sickness. As a result, we remain unable to convert vast expanses of prime grazing land into a food surplus because we still lack the necessary technology to control this insect, an important element of the central African environment.

Although technological advances cannot overcome all environmental limitations, human technology has enabled people to live in urban areas such as Yellowknife in northern Canada, where surplus food cannot be produced. Instead, a surplus is produced far to the south and transported to the city. Only modern technology allows the rapid transportation of massive amounts of material over such long distances.

## Urban Futures and Post-Industrial Economies

The last two centuries have seen a flood of people moving from rural to urban areas around the world. Urbanization has been most intense in industrialized countries, for the reasons outlined above. For example, England was one of the first countries to industrialize and also one of the first countries to experience a massive movement of people to the cities. As a result, England is now one of the most urbanized countries in the world, with 80 percent of its population living in urban areas (about 70 percent of the population live in large cities).

The rate of urbanization of the world's population is shown in Table 16-1. Between 1800 and 1950, the urban population of the world doubled every 50 years. After 1950, however, the urban population began to increase at a rate that would see it tripling every 50 years.

Projections indicate that, by the year 2000, 61 percent of the world's population will be living in urban areas, with some two-thirds of these living in cities with populations greater than 100 000. As with all projections, this one assumes that current trends will continue. However, there are signs

**Table 16-1. Percentage of World Population Living in Urban Areas, Actual and Projected, 1800–2000**

|  | Urban (over 200 000) | Large Cities (over 100 000) |
|---|---|---|
| 1800 | 2% | 2% |
| 1850 | 4 | 2 |
| 1900 | 9 | 6 |
| 1950 | 21 | 13 |
| 1975 | 42 | 26 |
| 2000 | 61 | 42 |

NOTE: Percentages are rounded.
SOURCE: Kingsley Davis, "The origin and growth of urbanization in the world," *American Journal of Sociology* 60(March 1955):430; Kingsley Davis, *World Urbanization 1950–1970*, Vol. 2 (Berkeley, CA: Institute of International Studies, 1972), pp. 126–127.

that the rate of urbanization in some industrialized countries, including Canada, is starting to decline and may even reverse (Bourne 1978).

Modern industrial countries are already heavily urbanized. Between 70 and 80 percent of the inhabitants of industrialized countries now live in urban areas, and it is unclear whether a much greater proportion of these populations will be able to do so in the future. Even now some adjacent cities in industrialized countries have spread so much that their boundaries are beginning to merge. The result of this process is called a **megalopolis** or *conurbation*. North American examples of this phenomenon include the urban belt that extends from Massachusetts to Virginia along the east coast of the United States, and the "Golden Horseshoe," which stretches from Oshawa to Buffalo around the west shore of Lake Ontario (see Gillis 1987a).

It is unclear whether nonindustrialized developing countries will industrialize and urbanize as have Western countries. Some social thinkers believe that capitalist countries overurbanized and contain too many residents who are not productively employed (see, for example, Szelenyi 1981). Further, industrial growth depends on the consumption of fossil fuels, particularly oil and gas (see Figure 16-2). Whether this consumption can continue indefinitely is uncertain. In fact, if urbanized, industrialized countries do not ultimately develop more energy-efficient machines and make greater use of other energy sources, deurbanization and deindustrialization will eventually begin in Western societies. The natural environment limits the degree to which we can urbanize, and we have developed the technology to extend the limits greatly by converting fossil fuels to energy. In fact, oil, gas, and coal — as part of the natural environment — may well become limiting factors through total depletion.

Deurbanization may occur as a result of motivating as well as of limiting factors. For example, some social thinkers (for example, Toffler 1970, 1982) believe that a third major technological innovation has arrived (the first was the invention of agriculture; the second, industrialization) that is beginning to have a profound effect on working life and the nature of cities in post-industrial societies. Toffler's "third wave" is the current explosion of information services associated with

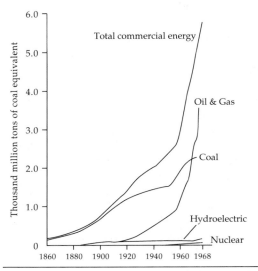

## Figure 16-2. World Use of Energy Sources

NOTE: World use of coal, oil, and gas has boomed in a single century. The substitution of inanimate sources of energy for the work energy of humans and animals is one of the hallmarks of industrialization. Used to propel machines, these new sources of energy have enormously increased productivity. (*Population Bulletin*, April 1971, p. 10. Based on data from Political and Economic Planning, *World Population and Resources*, London: George Allen and Unwin, 1964; and United Nations, *World Energy Supplies*, 1958 (#1), 1960 (#3), and 1970 (#13)).
SOURCE: Noel P. Gist and Sylvia F. Fava, *Urban Society*, 6th edition (New York: Thomas Y. Crowell, 1974), p. 30.

technological innovations such as transistors, fibre optics, and microchips. Satellite dishes, televisions, modems, computers, and the like are increasing our capacity to communicate to such an extent that proximity is becoming less and less important for the co-ordination of people with specialized tasks. So conference calls increasingly replace conferences, and people are able to live farther from their workplace, especially in information-service industries. As such industries and work patterns expand, populations may become less concentrated, and urbanization will decline in post-industrial societies.

Although many current projections have suggested that the world will be highly urbanized in the future, deurbanization is a definite possibility. It happened in ancient Rome and again in recent times when the atavistic Khmer Rouge intentionally executed educated citizens and specialists and moved other people out of the major cities of

Cambodia (Kampuchea), a move that was dramatically depicted in the 1984 movie *The Killing Fields* (Ngor and Warner 1988). Deurbanization may now be gradually happening in certain nonindustrialized countries (Szelenyi 1981), as well as in some major centres in North America because of technical change and economic relocation (Frey, 1987). So the urban future is not clear.

## Urbanization in Canada

Urbanization began in what is now Canada some time after French colonization in the seventeenth century. In the mid-1600s, the outposts of Quebec City, Montreal, and Trois-Rivières each contained fewer than 1000 people; by 1765, Quebec City and Montreal had grown into towns of more than 5000. It is noteworthy that at this time, New France was about 25 percent urban, while less than 10 percent of the population of the 13 English colonies to the south lived in urban areas. This difference may reflect the fact that, because it was based on the fur trade, New France was more of a commercial centre than its southern neighbour, which was primarily an agricultural colony. It may also reflect a greater antipathy on the part of the English for urban living (Gillis, Richard, and Hagan 1986).

By 1825, Fort York (later Toronto) was a garrison of about 2000 people, while Quebec City and Montreal had each passed 20 000. By the mid-1800s, Montreal was a city of more than 50 000 and both Quebec City and Toronto had populations of more than 30 000. In the Maritimes, Saint John and Halifax competed for regional dominance, each containing more than 20 000 people. In 1850, about seven percent of the populations of the Maritimes, Lower Canada (Quebec), and Upper Canada (Ontario) lived in cities of 20 000 or more, compared with a world figure of five percent (Stone 1967). So by world standards, Canada was an urbanized country at its birth in 1867.

Stone (1967) notes that "Canadian urban development probably had its 'take-off' toward high levels of urbanization in the 10 to 15 years following Confederation in 1867." In this respect, Canada followed the pattern of urban growth found in northwest Europe and in the United States. In the twentieth century, the urbanization of Canada continued, lagging slightly behind that of the colonial powers of the industrialized Western world,

but remaining far ahead of most other colonies and former colonies.

Canada's pattern of urbanization, like that of the United States, moved from east to west. Limiting factors causing this pattern included the physical environment, transportation technology, and the harsh climate of the North. Motivating factors were also important, including increasing population pressure in eastern Canada and the attraction of the natural resources (initially furs, later wheat and fossil fuels) that could be found in the central regions of the continent.

**Limiting Factors.** The first Europeans landed on the east coast of North America. Given the level of European technology, they found the forests virtually impenetrable. But native technology, in the form of the canoe, allowed rapid movement along rivers and lakes. So during the exploration of the continent, water was the principal means of transportation.

As the Europeans pushed their frontier westward, taming the wilderness, towns and cities sprang up behind them as forts and service centres. Most of those on the east coast began as ports: cities such as St. John's, Halifax, Saint John, and Charlottetown were built on natural harbours that gave ships protection from the sea. Quebec City, Montreal, and Trois-Rivières were situated on the St. Lawrence River in key natural locations favouring defence and transportation. Montreal, for example, was built at the point where the St. Lawrence narrows; there, people and goods were transferred from ocean-going ships to vessels that could proceed westward on the St. Lawrence and Ottawa rivers, while furs and other raw materials travelled eastward on the St. Lawrence.

Generally, the largest cities in Canada and the United States were eastern ports for ocean-going ships. In the United States, such places as Boston, New York, and Philadelphia were and still are among the largest and most influential cities in the country. In Canada, however, the St. Lawrence allowed the penetration of ocean-going vessels farther west. As a result, the east coast of Canada was partly bypassed, curtailing the development of its cities. For general discussions of the importance of the St. Lawrence in Canada's development, see Creighton (1956) and Lower (1939).

The westward movement of settlers in Canada was hampered to the north by climate, muskeg, and blackflies, and to the south by the political boundary with the United States. As a result, settlement was largely confined to a westward expansion along the southern border. Because of these and other limiting factors, then, most Canadian cities are located on waterways and relatively near the United States border. In the twentieth century, and especially the last half, new technology has reduced our dependence on waterways as transportation routes. So some newer cities, such as Regina, have been built on railway lines instead of rivers. And the lure of oil and other raw materials in the north has produced increased movement away from the American border.

Because Canada was colonized from its coastal regions inward, and chiefly from east to west, Canadian cities differ greatly in age. As a result, a city like Quebec contains a wider range of old and new buildings than does a city like Calgary. This — along with the tendency for newer cities to be built on grids, with numbered rather than named streets, and with a car rather than a pedestrian orientation — gives a very different character to eastern and western cities. Eastern cities are more picturesque, established, and European in atmosphere than the newer western cities, which are more modern, efficient, and American. (British Columbia's coastal cities are older than the western cities of the Prairies.) For these reasons, there is more variability among North American cities than among cities in other new countries, such as Australia, where most cities were founded at the same time, around the coast of the continent. (See Clark 1968; Kerr 1968; Bourne 1975; Hiller 1976 for discussions of the development of the Canadian urban system.)

**Motivating Factors.** By 1867, most of the arable land in the eastern provinces was occupied (Stone 1967), so migration flowed west. The scarcity of eastern land and the lure of assorted natural resources probably provided most of the motivation for the drive to the west.

The discovery and settlement of Canada by Europeans was part of a widespread pattern of colonialism, particularly on the part of Britain and France. Like other colonies, Canada specialized as a supplier of staples and raw materials to European countries. Because of this, European colonial powers were able to divert the energy they would otherwise have spent on primary production (the production of food and other raw materials) to manufacturing and other urban industrial activities (Innis 1930, 1940).

With the decline of the British Empire, Canada became less attached to England and more closely tied to the United States, where we now send more than three-quarters of our exports (still largely raw materials) in exchange for manufactured goods and services.

## Models of Development and Dependency

**Development.** Social scientists note that the nature of the relationships between countries is often the same as that between a **metropolis** (a large urban area and its suburbs) and its hinterland. Countries, metropolitan regions, or cities send manufactured items, ideas, and technology to nondeveloped and rural areas in exchange for labour and raw materials. The effects of such relationships on the hinterland are a source of continuing debate among social scientists. Sociologists who emphasize culture, consensus, and functional models point to the benefits of the division of labour to both parties and the system as a whole — for example, the great advances in medical care and general standard of living that association with the United States has brought to developing countries. Just as Athens and Rome developed and disseminated advances in arts, science, and technology to their hinterlands, the United States is seen by functionalists as doing the same for its hinterland, which includes Canada as well as less developed areas of the world.

**Dependency.** Conflict theorists are less persuaded of the mutual benefits and focus more on the political and economic nature of the relationship between metropolitan areas and their hinterlands. They argue that the benefits to the hinterland from this association go largely to a small, local, *indigenous elite* and to the *comprador elite*, the representatives of the metropolis who live in the hinterland and manage the economy. Further, the relationship puts pressure on the economy of the hinterland to become heavily specialized in the production of raw materials needed by the metropolis. Narrow economic diversification, particularly in the manufacturing sector, increases the strength of the relationship between metropolis and hinterland. This increases the dependency of the hinterland on the metropolis for goods and services that might otherwise have been produced locally. Conflict theorists see such economic dependence as leading to political powerlessness, retarded or even reversed industrial development, and the erosion of indigenous culture and its replacement with a mass culture that either justifies or obscures the whole arrangement. The needs of the metropolis, not the interests of the hinterland, prevail. Ultimately, if the resources of the hinterland are nonrenewable (for example, oil), the area risks not only underdevelopment but also abandonment by the metropolis when the resources become depleted or obsolete. For detailed discussions see Innis (1930, 1940), Frank (1969), and Bell and Tepperman (1979).

In Canada this model — known as the **dependency theory** — is most often applied by Toronto-based nationalists to the relationship between this country and the United States (see, for example, Laxer 1973; Warnock 1974). However, it is noteworthy that on the international level "Canada is in the 'semi-periphery' of the world economy" (Beaujot and McQuillan 1982). Some parts of the country, notably Southern Ontario and west Montreal, are considerably less peripheral than others. So the relationship between the urban industrial region of Canada and the rest of the nation can also be viewed from the metropolis/hinterland perspective (Davis 1971; House 1985). For example, some historians believe that the Maritimes would have been better off if they had not become a satellite of Upper Canada, thus losing their potential for local industrialization, urbanization, economic and political independence, and cultural integrity (Acheson 1977). Central Canadians protected their own manufacturing interests by imposing tariffs on competing items imported from the United States. So Maritimers had to pay more for manufactured goods than they would have paid if they had remained independent (see also Marsden and Harvey 1979).

From this viewpoint, the development and dissemination of Canadian nationalism reflects the struggle between central Canada and the United States for dominion over the Canadian hinterland (Berger 1969, 1970). Like continentalist perspectives, which overlook differences between Canada and the United States, nationalist arguments may trivialize or ignore regional differences and disparities within Canada. In fact, Clark (1966) suggested that anti-Americanism in Canada has often been used to divert attention from regional disparity within the country by focusing discontent on an external threat. Unlike the continentalist argument, however, the nationalist argument implies that U.S. ties foster regionalism and that people in the hinterland would be better off if they were less dependent on the United States.

This may or may not be true. Since dependency theory argues that metropolitan areas benefit more than do their hinterlands from the association, such benefits wind up disproportionately either in the cities of central Canada or in the metropolitan regions of the United States. So in either case, without greater industrial decentralization, the Canadian hinterland will remain relatively deprived.

At present, the links between urban centres in Canada are often weaker than the north–south links between Canadian centres and U.S. cities (Lithwick and Paquet 1968; Caves and Reuber 1969; Bourne 1975). This suggests that, insofar as the Canadian hinterland is indeed dominated by metropolitan regions, these areas are located disproportionately in the United States. (See Garreau 1981 for an interesting elaboration of this theme.)

Dependency theory can be applied on a world level to assess relationships between countries, on a national level to describe the relationship between regions within countries, or, as it was originally developed, on a regional level to characterize the relationship between cities and hinterlands. Whether one's locale is best seen as a metropolis or a hinterland typically depends on whether one looks upward to the exploiters or downward to the victims. For example, many Canadians outside Toronto may feel that "Hogtown" is too dominant within the country. But many Torontonians feel threatened by New York or by the U.S. in general. This suggests that a hierarchical exchange network may be more appropriate than the dependency model for characterizing the relationship between locales (see, for example, Wallerstein 1974).

**A Tale of Two Cities.** The drift from the British to the American economic sphere had important effects on the urban structure of Canada. Although the rise of the western cities may yet change things, "Canada's metropolitan development has been a tale of two cities: Montreal and Toronto" (Laxer 1975). Partly because of its location on the St. Lawrence, Montreal was the dominant metropolis during the early years, under the British. As Canada's ties to the United States grew, Toronto's links to New York — through the Great Lakes, the Erie Canal, and the railway system — gave the Ontario capital an edge over Montreal as an exporter. This link, along with the richness of Southern Ontario farmland, broke the commercial dominance of Montreal in the middle of the nineteenth century, and the ascendancy of Toronto began (Spelt 1955). Montreal's banks, with their links to London, continued to have a strong national influence well into the twentieth century. But after the Depression, the construction of American auto plants in Southern Ontario greatly extended the economic power of Toronto. By the end of World War II, Montreal's banks and head offices had begun moving to Toronto (Spelt 1973). This trend continued until, in 1976, Metropolitan Toronto's population finally surpassed Montreal's by 554 people. Between 1976 and 1981, Metro Toronto's population grew another 7 percent, crowding 3 million. At the same time, Montreal's metropolitan population grew only 0.9 per cent, to 2 828 349. By 1986 the Toronto metropolitan population was larger than Montreal's by half a million (see Table 16-2).

Although it is tempting for English Canadians to attribute the relative decline of Montreal to Quebec separatism, the latter may be more of a consequence than a cause. Toronto's dominance as *the* Canadian metropolis is probably a much less recent phenomenon than current growth rates would imply. Unlike Montreal, Toronto is part of a megalopolis that includes large industrial centres such as Hamilton (Jacobs 1982). This megalopolis, which extends from Oshawa to Buffalo, is known as the "Golden Horseshoe" or the "Mississauga Conurbation" (Baine and McMurray 1984) and has probably been the commercial centre of Canada for years. The recent relocation of head offices from both Quebec and the Atlantic provinces to the Golden Horseshoe and beyond is more likely a continuation of long-run economic trends than

a consequence of short-run politics (cf. Jacobs 1982).

Although the population of a metropolitan area gives an indication of its economic power and regional dominance, its position will be understated if it is part of a megalopolis (Gillis 1987a).

## World Networks and Modern Cities

Cities are concentrations of people who participate in and maintain local institutions, but modern urbanites are affected in a very real way by circumstances far beyond the boundaries of their immediate community. The world economy affects the nature of North American cities, the interconnections between them, and the lives of their inhabitants. For example, a worldwide energy crisis in the 1970s produced shock waves that devastated some industries and the cities that depended on them, while at the same time creating an economic boom in others. Increasing oil prices and competition from the European and Japanese auto industries combined to stagger the U.S. auto industry as well as its principal city, Detroit. Meanwhile, other cities such as Houston and Dallas, flush with accumulating oil revenues, were able to grow rapidly and diversify their economies by getting involved in the emerging computer industry. At the same time in Canada, the two fastest growing census metropolitan areas (CMAs) were Calgary and Edmonton, which underwent population increases of 25.7 and 18.1 percent, respectively, between 1976 and 1981. During this period Canada's "Motor City," Windsor, was one of the only CMAs in the country to lose population (the other was Sudbury, which was suffering from a sagging nickel market). The fall of oil prices ended the boom, and the growth rates of the two Alberta cities dropped sharply in the early 1980s. Those CMAs with more diversified economies have shown more stable rates of growth (see Table 16-2); they are like balanced stock portfolios, in that declines in one sector of the economy can be offset by increases in another.

The nature of a city and the lives of its residents, then, depend in part on its *raison d'être* and its position in local, national, and world economies. Some cities — for example, Hamilton and Sudbury in Ontario — are highly specialized indus-

## Table 16-2. 1986 Population of Census Metropolitan Areas and Percentage Change, 1971–1986

| Rank 1986 | Census Metropolitan Area | Population 1986 | Percentage Change[a] | | |
|---|---|---|---|---|---|
| | | | 1971–1976 | 1976–1981 | 1981–1986 |
| 1 | Toronto | 3 427 168 | 7.7% | 7.0% | 9.5% |
| 2 | Montreal | 2 921 375[b] | 2.7 | 0.9 | 2.1 |
| 3 | Vancouver | 1 380 729 | 7.8 | 8.7 | 8.9 |
| 4 | Ottawa-Hull | 819 263 | 11.8 | 3.6 | 10.1 |
| 5 | Edmonton | 785 465[b] | 11.7 | 18.1 | 6.0 |
| 6 | Calgary | 671 326[b] | 16.5 | 25.7 | 7.2 |
| 7 | Winnipeg | 625 304 | 5.2 | 1.1 | 5.6 |
| 8 | Quebec | 603 267 | 8.1 | 6.3 | 3.3 |
| 9 | Hamilton | 557 029 | 5.2 | 2.4 | 2.8 |
| 10 | St. Catharines-Niagara | 343 258 | 5.6 | 0.8 | 0.2 |
| 11 | London | 342 302 | 6.9 | 4.9 | 4.7 |
| 12 | Kitchener | 311 195 | 14.1 | 5.7 | 8.1 |
| 13 | Halifax | 295 990 | 7.0 | 3.6 | 6.6 |
| 14 | Victoria | 255 547[b] | 11.5 | 7.0 | 5.8 |
| 15 | Windsor | 253 988 | −0.5 | −0.6 | 1.2 |
| 16 | Oshawa | 203 543 | 12.4 | 14.1 | 9.2 |
| 17 | Saskatoon | 200 665 | 5.8 | 15.3 | 14.6 |
| 18 | Regina | 186 521 | 7.4 | 8.7 | 7.7 |
| 19 | St. John's | 161 901 | 8.8 | 6.5 | 4.6 |
| 20 | Chicoutimi-Jonquière | 158 468 | 1.8 | 5.1 | 0.2 |
| 21 | Sudbury | 148 877 | −0.4 | −4.5 | −4.6 |
| 22 | Sherbrooke | 129 960 | 1.8 | 6.1 | 3.8 |
| 23 | Trois-Rivières | 128 888 | 0.6 | 5.1 | 2.8 |
| 24 | Thunder Bay | 122 217 | 4.0 | 1.8 | 0.2 |
| 25 | Saint John | 121 265 | 5.8 | 0.9 | 0.2 |

[a]For each period, percentage change is calculated using the boundaries at the end of the period.
[b]Excludes population of one or more incompletely enumerated Indian reserves or Indian settlements.
SOURCE: Statistics Canada, Census of Canada.

trial centres, containing a large proportion of blue-collar workers, wide fluctuations in times of employment and prosperity, and periods of intense labour/management conflict. Other cities — such as the provincial capitals and Ottawa — are to a large extent administrative centres, with a large proportion of white-collar workers; historic government buildings, parks, monuments, museums, theatres, and other symbols of high culture; and relative socioeconomic stability.

Another way that the world economy has affected the nature of Canadian cities is through migration. Cities depend largely on in-migration and immigration for their growth, and at different times various parts of the world have contributed to the latter. Wars, famines, and other less dra-matic events have pushed waves of immigrants to North America, where they hope to find better economic and social circumstances. Many arrive after relatives or friends have established beach-heads in the new world: such *chain migration* has helped concentrate people with particular ethnic backgrounds in particular cities at particular times. For example, in the early nineteenth century, the Highland Clearances depopulated Scotland and sent tens of thousands of families to various centres in North America; a little later, the Irish potato famine drove tens of thousands more families to cities in the northeastern United States and what is now Atlantic Canada. As a result, cities such as Boston, Halifax, and others received a strong infusion of Celtic culture, which combined with

English institutions to give these cities a distinctive character that each still exhibits. Other centres — for example, Quebec City, Montreal, and New Orleans — reflect architecturally, linguistically, and in many other respects the cultural heritage of their French founders. Onion-shaped domes on Eastern Orthodox churches attest to the arrival of sizable Ukrainian populations in the newer cities of the Canadian west. The nature of some North American cities is shaped by the fact that one particular ethnic group has dominated social and cultural institutions — as in the case of Victoria and Quebec City, which are predominantly English- and French-Canadian cities, respectively. In others, such as New York, Montreal, Toronto, and Vancouver, a number of ethnic groups coexist, providing a range of institutions and giving the cities a more cosmopolitan character. It is interesting to note that the ethnic combinations in some of these cities (for example, New Orleans) make them unique, while in others the combinations can produce an element of similarity. San Francisco, Vancouver, and Toronto, for instance, were all basically English at first, but expanded later with waves of Chinese and Italian immigration.

## Urban Ecology

Social scientists have several explanations for the ways in which individual cities grow. The most influential of these was developed by Ernest W. Burgess (1925) at the University of Chicago. His general orientation (developed by Burgess and two of his colleagues, Robert E. Park and Roderick D. McKenzie) is known as **human ecology**. This term refers to the application of ideas from plant and animal ecology to the study of the relationship between humans and their physical habitat (Park, Burgess, and McKenzie 1925; McKenzie 1968).

**The Concentric Zone Model.** Burgess constructed a model of **concentric zones** for cities (see Figure 16-3) and applied to this model the following concepts from natural ecology: segregation, competition, invasion, succession, and natural areas.

**Segregation** refers to a tendency for certain activity patterns (such as commercial or residential

### Figure 16-3. Burgess's Concentric Zone Model Applied to Chicago

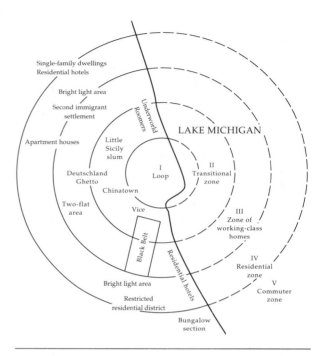

SOURCE: Redrawn from Ernest W. Burgess, "The growth of the city: An introduction to a research project," in *Studies in Human Ecology*, George A. Theodorson, ed. (Evanston, IL: Row, Peterson, 1961), p. 41.

activities) or certain groups of people (such as income or ethnic groups) to cluster and try to segregate themselves by excluding other activities or groups from "their" territory. To the extent that they are successful they form a *natural area* (a neighbourhood that is relatively homogeneous).

**Competition** occurs when one activity or group attempts to invade the territory of another. To the extent that such an *invasion* is successful and the incumbent activity or group is eliminated or driven out, *succession* has occurred. Some people and activities can share the same physical environment by operating at different times. Areas that are commercial by day are often recreational at night. See Tilly (1974) and Melbin's fascinating 1987 account of "night as frontier" for general discussions of this phenomenon.

Burgess used the city of Chicago as the basis for his model of concentric zones. To be appreciated, the model must be seen as dynamic rather than static. The concentric zones are not very good descriptions of the actual form of a city. Few cities actually look like a bull's-eye, and when the model is applied to Chicago itself, almost half of each zone falls into Lake Michigan, as Figure 16-3 illustrates. Instead, the concentric zones describe different patterns of urban activities and their tendency to concentrate, segregate, and create natural areas. The competition among activities for scarce space (more intense at the centre than at the periphery) and the territorial invasion and succession of activities and people represent the growth pattern of urban areas.

Burgess' zones radiate from the centre of the city:

I. the central business district (CBD), known in Chicago as "the Loop";
II. the zone of transition;
III. the zone of working-class houses;
IV. the middle-class residential zone; and
V. the commuter zone.

These five zones form the basis of the Burgess model, although two additional zones have sometimes been included: peripheral agricultural areas and the hinterland (Wilson and Shulz 1978).

Zone I is the central business district (CBD), the commercial as well as the geographic centre of the city. Retail shopping areas, entertainment centres (nightclubs, restaurants, theatres, art galleries, museums, hotels, and the like), and office buildings abound in the inner core of the CBD. The edge of this zone includes wholesale businesses, markets, and warehouses. Because of its centrality, the land in Zone I is the most valuable in the city. In fact, this land is so expensive that only commercial enterprises usually have the combination of motivation and means necessary to buy it. In the competition for the scarce space near the centre of the city, then, commercial activities typically "win" over residential activities.

Zone II — the zone of transition — is where the real action is. As the name suggests, this region is the battle zone: the main arena for competition between residential and commercial activities, with the latter usually destined to drive out the former. That is, the commercial activities in the CBD expand into a sector that formerly contained houses and related residential activities (child-rearing, house-related work, leisure activities, sleeping, and the like). One important effect of this invasion is the deterioration and devaluation of these areas as residential environments. As homes decline in value, they become a source of cheap rental housing. Speculators hold them for the potential commercial value of the land on which they are situated. In the interest of minimizing the costs of holding such property, they spend little or no money to maintain the buildings, while at the same time attempting to maximize the number of renters they contain. The result is the crowded, deteriorating housing known as slums.

It is likely but not certain that the invasion of commercial activities will result in succession, segregation, and a natural commercial area. Slums endure when the expected commercial expansion fails to occur.

The inexpensive housing in the transitional zone lets people with low incomes live in the city: the poor and unemployed, immigrants with little money, the physically and mentally disabled, and marginal people who survive through illegal commercial activities (mugging, theft, and the sale of such illicit commodities and services as drugs and prostitution). Because of this, the transitional zone has been declared "disorganized" by some sociologists.

As immigrants arrive in the city, they often locate in the cheap housing of the transitional zone. The arrival of members of alien ethnic groups amounts to the invasion of an area, prompting the incumbents to move out in order to maintain the integrity of their own ethnic group. When the members of ethnic groups become able to afford better housing, the pull of purely residential zones combines with the push from invading groups to bring them out of Zone II. Just as commercial activities invade, compete with, and succeed residential activities, so do some ethnic groups invade the territories of others and succeed the original inhabitants of those neighbourhoods.

Zone III contains inexpensive houses often inhabited by the upwardly mobile children of immigrants from the transitional zone. In Chicago these houses are typically semidetached houses.

# Suburbanization

**Suburbanization** refers to an increase in the proportion of urban residents who live on the periphery of central cities. Suburbanization in the United States took off with the "baby boom" in the period following World War II. By 1970, about one-third of the urban population lived in incorporated or unincorporated areas on the edge of cities. The suburbanization of the United States has occurred largely as a result of migration from the cities. In addition to the absolute growth in the suburban population, many of the largest central cities have been declining in population since the 1960s as fertility rates have fallen below population-replacement levels. This decline, of course, helps to account for the dramatic increase in the proportion of urbanites living in suburban areas.

Crime, racial violence, air pollution, and other urban problems have been important *push factors* motivating suburbanization, while the promise of less expensive housing and even employment in industrial suburbs have been *pull factors* for millions of those who have migrated to the suburbs in the United States.

Although Canadian cities are relatively free from the problems that plague the inner cities of the United States, great numbers of Canadians have also been moving to the suburbs in recent years. In fact, by 1976 over half (50.8 percent) of the population of Canada's metropolitan areas lived in the suburbs. (For details on the suburbanization of the Canadian population see Kalbach and McVey 1979.)

It is important to realize that the suburban population of a given metropolitan area cannot always be calculated by subtracting the city population from the metropolitan population. For example, in 1981 the population of metropolitan Calgary was 599 743. So was the population of the city itself. This does not mean that Calgary has no outer fringe. It simply means that the political jurisdiction of the city extends well beyond the edge of the city as a physical entity. In cases like this you will often see a sign in the middle of nowhere welcoming you to a particular city, which may or may not be visible in the distance. This most often happens with newer cities in the west.

In contrast to Calgary, there is metropolitan Toronto, which had a

---

The upwardly mobile children of the residents of Zone III would in turn try to move farther out into the suburbs — that is, the commuter zone.

Zone IV is the zone of better residences, where middle-class people live. Zone V is the commuter zone, where people with cars live in middle-, upper-middle-, and upper-class suburbs. Most of the residences in Zones IV and V are single, detached houses.

Like all ideal types, the concentric zone model reflects reality in some times and places better than it does in others. Nevertheless, this model provides some important general insights into the processes and form of urban growth.

For example, Burgess is generally accurate in his observation that activities and groups tend to concentrate within specific areas of North American cities. In fact, recent studies show that over the last few decades socioeconomic and ethnic residential segregation has increased in the cities of both the United States and Canada, especially in the larger ones (Marston and Darroch 1971; Richmond 1972, Balakrishnan 1976, 1979; Kalbach 1980; cf. Herberg 1988). Also, Burgess was generally accurate in noting that the socioeconomic status of urbanites increases directly with the dis-

tance of their residence from the city centre. In the United States, higher-status people have been more inclined to live farther from the centre of cities than have people in lower socioeconomic strata.

Although these observations seem accurate for many North American cities, it must be emphasized that Canada and the United States are industrial countries containing relatively new cities. In countries where the development of cities preceded industrialization or where industrialization has not occurred, the patterns observed by Burgess are not always found. For example, in pre-industrial cities, slums are more likely to be situated on the outskirts of the city, with the residences of the wealthy located downtown. The general tendency for commercial and residential activities to be segregated, with commerce at the centre of the city, seems also to be a modern industrial phenomenon. In pre-industrial cities, many shopkeepers live in the same building in which they conduct commercial activities (Sjoberg 1960, 1973).

The concentric zone model should be applied with care even within North America. Both cultural constraints and the physical environment

population of 2 998 947 in 1981. But the population of the city in that year was only 599 217, almost exactly the same as Calgary's. This suggests that the Toronto metropolitan area resembles a doughnut and is about 80 percent suburbs. However, it also reflects Toronto's unusual system of metropolitan government. Old suburbs such as Etobicoke and York have not been annexed by the city of Toronto, even though after years of urban expansion they are no longer on the fringe of the metropolitan area. They remain self-governing municipalities.

Types of suburbs can be distinguished on the basis of their developmental history. For example, some suburbs began as villages and may have grown into small autonomous towns before being annexed or engulfed by the expanding city. Other suburbs gradually emerged on the periphery of cities, while still

others were created by developers as "instant communities" on previously unoccupied land. (Like modern cemeteries, the latter are typically given names that promise meadows, trees, streams, and other symbols of rural nostalgia. But names such as Meadowvale, Parkdale, and Mount Pleasant are more likely to represent wishful thinking than an accurate description of past, present, or even future topography.)

These three types of suburb differ in their patterns of social life as well as in their developmental histories. For example, the sudden creation of the "instant" suburb usually results in a relatively homogeneous area with respect to age, life cycle, income, and, of course, length of residence in the area. On the other hand, the annexed village contains both longtime residents of the village and newcomers from the city; these residents differ not

only in the length of time they have lived in the suburb, but also in age, life cycle, income, education, and other important variables. This results in the presence of different, and often competing, interest groups in the area (Fischer 1984). (For an interesting description of the community divisions and conflict arising from such heterogeneity in engulfed suburbs, see Westhues and Sinclair, 1974.)

**Sources:**

References are to Claude S. Fischer, *The Urban Experience*, 2nd edition (New York: Harcourt, Brace, Jovanovich, 1984); W.E. Kalbach and Wayne W. McVey, *The Demographic Bases of Canadian Society*, 2nd edition (Toronto: McGraw-Hill, 1979); and Kenneth Westhues and Peter R. Sinclair, *Village in Crisis* (Toronto: Holt, Rinehart and Winston, 1974).

have occasionally produced incongruities between the Burgess model and urban realities. For example, cultural constraints in the form of zoning laws have often kept commercial activities from pushing into residential areas. Also, in a number of North American cities, there have recently been successful attempts by young urban professionals ("yuppies") to reclaim deteriorated sections of both commercial and transitional areas for residential purposes — a process known as *gentrification*. Toronto's "Cabbagetown" area is exemplary in this respect. (See Whyte's 1988 study of social life in the centre of cities.) So commerce need not always invade and succeed residential areas.

In other instances the physical environment may prevent the operation of the forces Burgess observed in Chicago. Vancouver, for example, bounded on one side by mountains and on the other by the sea, has developed an outer ring containing both commercial and residential sections. These areas are connected and many of their residents do not work "in town" (Hardwick 1971).

Although the concentric zone model was developed in Chicago in the 1920s, it continues to be relevant. The patterns of segregation,

competition, invasion, and succession Burgess described can still be observed in many North American cities. However, as we have seen, application of the model is restricted. It does not fit pre-industrial cities or smaller cities and towns. Moreover, topographic factors and cultural values can produce important deviations from the Burgess model, even in large industrial cities. The concentric zone model should be seen as an ideal type that illustrates the general operation of certain ecological principles in large cities in industrial capitalist societies — in particular, the United States. Seen this way, the model has value (Guest 1969).

**The Sector Model.** Social scientists have produced other models of city growth in an attempt to improve on the idea of concentric zones. Hoyt (1939) proposed a **sector model** of urban expansion, which emphasizes transportation arteries rather than concentric rings. Like Burgess, Hoyt believed that activities and groups are segregated into natural areas and that cities expand outward. But Hoyt argued that the commercial and residential areas and different ethnic and income groups expanded from the centre of cities in wedge-

## Figure 16-4. Sector Model Applied to Calgary, 1961

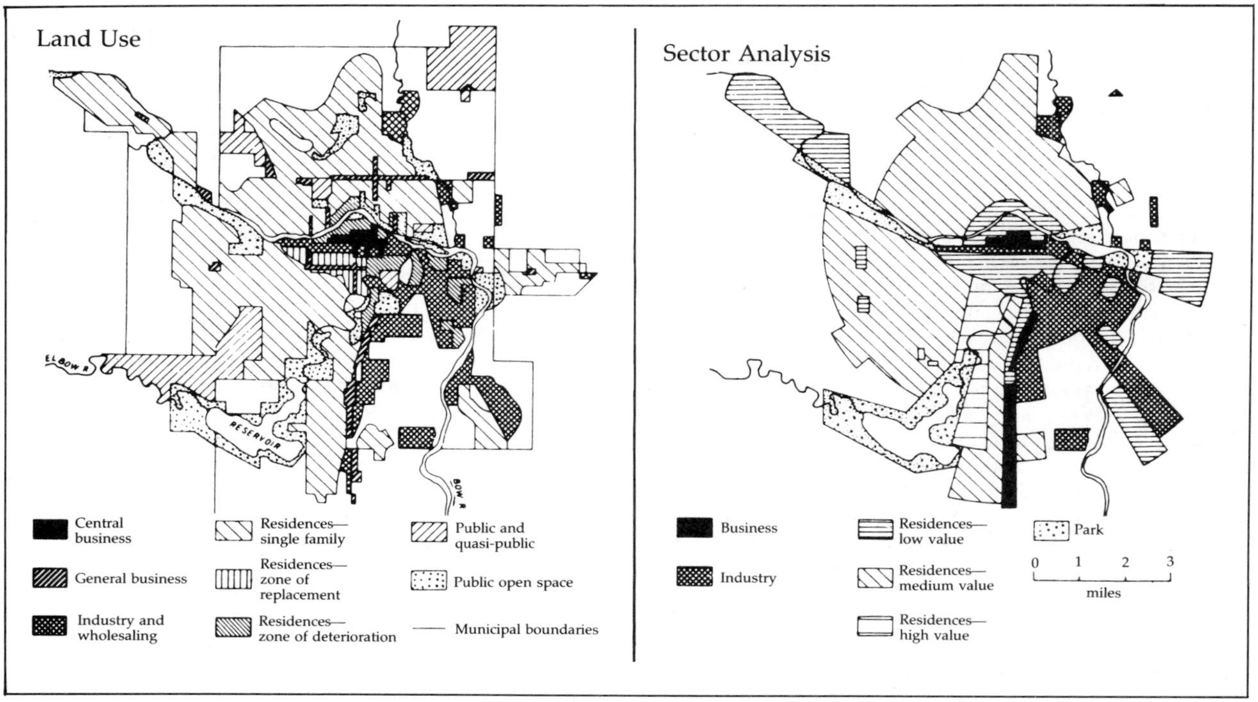

Land Use

Sector Analysis

| | | |
|---|---|---|
| ■ Central business | Residences— single family | Public and quasi-public |
| General business | Residences— zone of replacement | Public open space |
| Industry and wholesaling | Residences— zone of deterioration | Municipal boundaries |

| | | |
|---|---|---|
| ■ Business | Residences— low value | Park |
| Industry | Residences— medium value | 0  1  2  3 miles |
| | Residences— high value | |

SOURCE: P.J. Smith, "Calgary: a study in urban pattern," *Economic Geography* 38 (1962): 318–328.

shaped sections, along natural boundaries and transportation arteries. Figure 16-4 shows the sector model applied to Calgary in the early 1960s.

The sector model accounts for the existence of high-rent residential areas near the centre of cities (such as Forest Hill in Toronto and Westmount in Montreal) and acknowledges the importance of traffic arteries. In this way the sector model is an improvement over the concentric zone model, which was developed at a time when traffic arteries, especially highways, had less impact.

**The Multiple-Nuclei Model.** Like Burgess and Hoyt, Harris and Ullman (1945) believed that activities and groups were segregated within areas of cities. But Harris and Ullman rejected the idea that these natural areas radiated from the centre of the city in either concentric rings or wedge-shaped sectors. Instead, they saw the city as a series of centres, or *nuclei*, that attract similar activity patterns or social groups and repel others.

For example, both the University of Western Ontario in northwest London and the University of Alberta in south-central Edmonton act as nuclei for several smaller colleges and schools, a number of research institutes, a university hospital (related to the medical school), and a variety of student-related service centres (such as bookstores, recreational facilities, pubs, and taverns), as well as both faculty and student housing. Other nuclei emerge around mutually supporting (or symbiotic) commercial activities (such as law firms, insurance companies, and real estate offices, around industrial activities, and around residences.

The **multiple-nuclei model**, illustrated in Figure 16-5, is the most recently developed of the three models of urban expansion. Perhaps that is why it seems most applicable to those cities that have developed with the automobile as a major means of transportation; cars have allowed a much greater degree of decentralization of facilities and city sectors.

## Figure 16-5. Multiple-Nuclei Model of a City

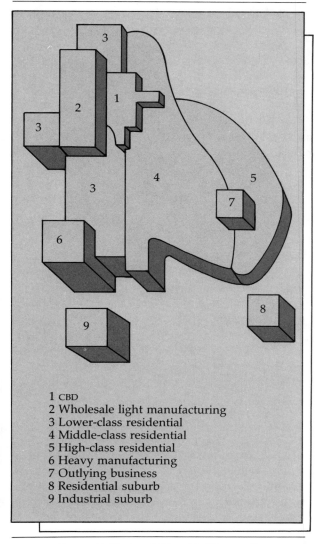

1 CBD
2 Wholesale light manufacturing
3 Lower-class residential
4 Middle-class residential
5 High-class residential
6 Heavy manufacturing
7 Outlying business
8 Residential suburb
9 Industrial suburb

SOURCE: Chauncy D. Harris and Edward L. Ullman, "The nature of cities," *Annals of the American Academy of Political and Social Science*, 242(Nov. 1945):7–17.

The concentric zone model, the sector model, and the multiple-nuclei model are three ideal types. Each stresses different aspects of city growth. They are alike in portraying competition, segregation, and natural areas as characteristic of urban areas. All three were developed from observations of relatively new cities in industrial capitalist societies. The models differ in the extent to which they emphasize the invasion and succession of economic activities in residential areas and the relation of the different areas to one another. No single model perfectly fits any specific city. However, all three models emphasize factors that to varying degrees affect the expansion of all cities, especially in the United States.

**Canadian and U.S. Cities.** Because general rather than specific statements are a goal of social science, sociologists typically generalize from their observations. But urban sociologists must be aware that most of the published observations concern U.S. rather than Canadian cities. Certainly the similarities between the two countries are great — probably much greater than the differences. But there are differences, and some of these affect the nature of Canadian and U.S. cities.

Canadian and U.S. cities differ in several important ways. First, Canadian cities are higher in density, since the U.S. contains a much higher proportion of single, detached houses. Probably because of tax breaks on mortgage interest, a higher proportion of people in the U.S. live in their own single, detached houses (Goldberg and Mercer 1986). So cities in the United States are troubled by urban sprawl to a much greater degree than are those in Canada, where cities tend to be more compact.

Second, like their U.S. counterparts, Canadian cities have lost population from their core areas in recent years, as both jobs and people have moved to industrial and residential suburbs. However, the growth of Canadian suburbs has not involved the widespread exodus of inner-city employers and residents that has drained the cores of so many U.S. cities, leaving in its wake a narrowed range of occupations, a drastically reduced tax base, and entire blocks of abandoned residential housing. As a result, the centres of Canadian urban areas have stayed economically, physically, and socially viable. In fact, the core areas of Canadian cities typically contain some of the most desirable (and expensive) housing. In contrast, the core areas of many U.S. cities contain a visible underclass, who cannot leave because they are either unemployed or poorly paid. The overall rate of violent crime is six times greater in the U.S. than in Canada, and much of the criminal activity occurs in inner-city areas. This situation

**The core areas of many U.S. cities have lost population in recent years, leaving behind those who cannot afford to move.**

shows no sign of improving, and may even be becoming worse (Massey and Denton 1987; Wilson 1987; Lichter 1988). For their part, Canadian cities are relatively safe and are perceived as such by their residents (Bourne 1975). So the differences between the suburbs and cities with respect to socioeconomic factors and crime are much greater in the U.S. than in Canada.

Third, Canadian city-dwellers use public transit much more often than do U.S. urbanites. The lower rate of crime and the compact form of Canadian cities probably has a lot to do with this. But U.S. society has also been accused of being "based on the religion of the motor car" (Mumford 1968). There are more cars — and, accordingly, more highways — in and around cities in the U.S. than in Canada. Thickets of federally funded freeways are another distinctive feature

of U.S. urban areas (Goldberg and Mercer 1986). It is unclear whether this orientation toward the automobile represents a reflection of actual cultural differences or whether it is simply another manifestation of the higher standard of living in the U.S.

These differences indicate that the three models of city growth, which were all developed in the U.S., probably fit cities in that country better than they do those in Canada. This is not to say that these models are irrelevant for Canadian cities; it merely means that they should be applied with care and modified for the Canadian context. Even within Canada, cities differ dramatically in form, so a particular model fits some better than others. Montreal, for example, constrained by its island site, is a compact city of apartments and renters (Linteau and Robert 1977). In contrast, Toronto is a sprawling city of single, detached, owner-occupied houses in distinct neighbourhoods connected by highways.

## Urbanism

Besides trying to explain the origin, growth, and proliferation of cities at the macro level, urban sociologists have given a great deal of attention to the micro level. Studies of individuals and small groups involve more social-psychological than purely sociological orientations. However, the same variables (environment, technology, structure, and culture) used at the macro level can be used as limiting and motivating factors to explain situations at the micro level.

**Urbanism** refers to the attitudes, beliefs, and behaviours or lifestyles of people who live in cities. Many sociologists think that there is a great difference in the lifestyles of people who live in urban as opposed to rural environments. Furthermore, the changes required of people who move from one environment to the other are said to produce a variety of social and psychological problems. Some social scientists believe that urbanism itself, rather than the change from a rural lifestyle to city living, causes social disorganization and psychological disorders among urban-dwellers.

### Community Organization

In 1885, the German sociologist Ferdinand Tönnies produced one of the first analyses of rural/urban differences. He argued that rural social organization involves small populations; close, personal relationships among people, most of whom share common values; a collective orientation or sense of identity; informal social control; strong kinship ties to extended families; and a strong respect for tradition as the basis for these patterns and social obligations (1957, originally 1887). Tönnies referred to such systems as **gemeinschaft** ("community") organizations. On the other hand, urban systems contain many people with different values and more individualistic attitudes. Interpersonal relationships tend to be temporary, impersonal, and specifically focused. Nuclear rather than extended family orientations predominate; social control is formal, with laws, courts, and police. Tönnies called this type of organization *gesellschaft* ("association") in its orientation.

In rural areas and small towns, people are likely to know one another in a variety of contexts and statuses. Social network analysts use the term *multiplexity* to describe such an arrangement. For example, your dentist may also be a client or customer of yours, belong to the same clubs or friendship groups as you do, live in the same neighbourhood, and be married to your cousin. So when you go to the dentist, your relationship is more than just that between dentist and patient. You have a number of common interests and lots to talk about. In large cities, on the other hand, your semi-annual visit is likely to be the only time you see your dentist in a six-month period. You are unlikely to know each other in other contexts; thus, apart from the weather and, say, sports, you probably have little to talk about. Harris (1981) suggests that this fact may mean you get better service in rural settings, where people are more likely to care: a botched extraction or filling may deprive a dentist of a golfing partner as well as a patient.

Cities are highly specialized organizations; as we have seen, this specialization has a physical manifestation, especially in larger cities. The extreme segregation of different types of activities from each other can give individuals a grossly distorted view of the nature of the community and of life itself. For example, people who live in rural areas in pre-industrial societies are likely to be familiar with all stages of the life cycle, including death. Meat-eaters not only may have seen their most recent roast on the hoof, but may have assisted in its birth, its raising, its slaughter, and its preparation for the table. In contrast, urban carnivores who order a Big Mac are unlikely to have been near, let alone inside, the slaughterhouse that provided the meat they intend to consume. Giddens (1982) and others refer to this removal of essential aspects of life from the industrial world as *sequestration*. Sequestration preserves the "flow of everyday life" for most urbanites. It may also produce differences between rural and urban people in their orientation to nonhuman animals. In rural areas, animals are

**According to Simmel, urbanites cope with high levels of stimulation by developing filtering techniques.**

seen more instrumentally — as sources of food, clothing, and energy — while in urban areas attitudes are more expressive and animals are largely viewed as pets or zoo curiosities.

Tönnies's work was the basis for a number of similar rural/urban analyses. Durkheim's "mechanical" and "organic" solidarity (see Chapter 10), Miner's "folk-urban continuum," and Parsons's pre-industrial and industrial "pattern variables" all parallel Tönnies's views of the differences between rural and urban life. However, the most important intellectual offspring of Tönnies's work is probably Louis Wirth's article "Urbanism as a Way of Life" (1938).

## "Urbanism as a Way of Life"

Wirth drew heavily on the ideas of Georg Simmel (1950), as well as those of Tönnies, in developing his viewpoint. Simmel argued that urban envi-

ronments produce a continuous and intense bombardment of stimuli. The sounds, sights, and smells of the city combine with the press of large numbers of people to assault the nervous systems of its residents. According to Simmel, urbanites cope with such high levels of stimulation by developing techniques to filter the onslaught of noise and unnecessary information. People in cities learn to ignore what is irrelevant to them as they engage in routine work and leisure activities. Urbanites can sleep with the sounds of traffic in the background, can ignore intimate conversations occurring between other people within listening distance, and can treat most of those they encounter with a minimum of interpersonal involvement.

As noted before, cities contain large numbers of people in specialized and interrelated roles. According to Simmel, co-ordination and planning are necessary to bring the right people together

# City Size and Social Life

Just as groups are more than the sum of their parts, "big cities are not just bigger versions of smaller ones, but different things" (Simmons and Simmons 1974).

The size of urban populations is directly related to a variety of socially relevant factors, some rewarding and some punishing. Large cities can supply specialized goods and services that smaller cities and towns cannot. For example, if only one out of every 500 people is interested in paying for a massage, and 200 clients are required to sustain a massage parlour, cities of fewer than 100 000 (the "threshold population" for massage parlours) will in most cases be unable to support such a service. People in smaller communities, then, must travel to larger cities for a massage. Fischer

(1984) points out that the same principle holds for the formation of special interest groups. That is, individuals with relatively unusual interests, such as spouse-swapping, body-building, or Zen Buddhism, are more likely to find people with similar interests in large rather than small cities. As a result, voluntary associations catering to these activities are rarely found in small communities; larger cities are more likely to attract and contain visible clusters of people with atypical, bizarre, or deviant preferences.

The optimum size of cities has been debated for centuries by philosophers, planners, and social scientists. Estimates range from Plato's 5040 to Le Corbusier's 3 million. Unfortunately, the ideal size for

optimizing one factor is not necessarily the most appropriate for optimizing another. For example, fear of crime is greater in a city of 1 million than in a city of 100 000, but a city of 1 million is also more likely to contain a university, highly specialized medical care, a museum, a symphony, or a zoo. Whether these facilities are worth a greater fear of crime involves a value judgment.

In the 1930s, the Soviets concluded that the ideal population size for most cities was between 50 000 and 60 000. However, they were unable to prevent cities from growing larger. Accordingly, "ideal" was redefined at a higher value. By the mid-1950s, "ideal" had grown to between 150 000 and 200 000, and by the 1960s it had risen to between 200 000 and 300 000 (Bater 1980). Praxis makes perfect.

In the United States, migration patterns suggest that many people find economy and climate more important attractions than city size, since so many Americans are moving to the "sunbelt" cities: Dallas, Houston, and the like. Recent polls support this conclusion, indicating that the U.S. city with the worst image is Detroit — which, though large, has an often-troubled economy and a less-than-perfect climate) (*Detroit Free Press* 1984). In Canada, as the list below indicates, the most satisfied citizens seem to live in cities of medium or small size: Victoria, St. Catharines, Ottawa-Hull, London, Saskatoon, Kitchener, Charlottetown, and Quebec are the eight most popular places to live, at least according to their residents. However, it is important to recognize that the differences in level of satisfaction between the most and least popular cities are small. Even the people in the least popular metropolitan area (Saint John) are reasonably pleased with their city. In view of this, and remembering the importance of self-selection, there is no guarantee that if the citizens of the New Brunswick city were all moved to Victoria (the most popular city) they would prefer living there; the young ones in particular might be less happy,

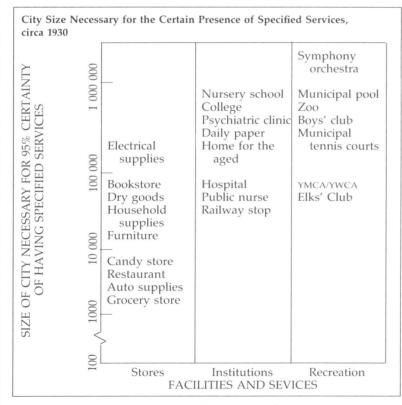

**City Size Necessary for the Certain Presence of Specified Services, circa 1930**

SIZE OF CITY NECESSARY FOR 95% CERTAINTY OF HAVING SPECIFIED SERVICES

| | Stores | Institutions | Recreation |
|---|---|---|---|
| 1 000 000 | | | Symphony orchestra |
| 100 000 | Electrical supplies | Nursery school / College / Psychiatric clinic / Daily paper / Home for the aged | Municipal pool / Zoo / Boys' club / Municipal tennis courts |
| 10 000 | Bookstore / Dry goods / Household supplies / Furniture | Hospital / Public nurse / Railway stop | YMCA/YWCA / Elks' Club |
| 1000 | Candy store / Restaurant / Auto supplies / Grocery store | | |
| 100 | | | |

FACILITIES AND SEVICES

SOURCE: F. Keyes, "The correlation of social phenomena with community size," *Social Forces* 36(1958):311–315.

since Victoria contains a high proportion of older people. (In fact, Victoria's high rating with its residents may actually be a direct reflection of its high proportion of older people. Perhaps older people in general are more satisfied with their surroundings than younger people are.)

According to *The Financial Post*, this was the ranking of Canadian cities by satisfaction of residents in 1979:

1. Victoria
2. St. Catharines
3. Ottawa-Hull
4. London
5. Saskatoon
6. Kitchener
7. Charlottetown
8. Quebec City
9. Toronto
10. Halifax
11. Vancouver
12. St. John's
13. Chicoutimi
14. Calgary
15. Thunder Bay
16. Winnipeg
17. Edmonton
18. Sudbury
19. Hamilton
20. Montreal
21. Windsor
22. Regina
23. Saint John

**Sources:**

James H. Bater, *The Soviet City* (London: Edward Arnold, 1980); *Detroit Free Press*, November 25, 1984; *The Financial Post*, August 4, 1979; Claude S. Fischer, *The Urban Experience*, 2nd edition (New York: Harcourt, Brace, Jovanovich, 1984); James Simmons and Robert Simmons, *Urban Canada*, 2nd edition (Toronto: Copp Clark, 1974), p. 32.

in a particular place at a specific time. For example, the removal of your tonsils usually requires the co-ordinated efforts of at least one physician, an anesthetist, several nurses, and many other technicians and workers to prepare the equipment, the patient, and the room for the event at a specific time. Such co-ordination of specialists and locations produces pressure on urbanites to be punctual: "the clock is not merely a means of keeping track of the hours, but of synchronizing the actions of men" (Mumford 1963; see also Rifkin 1987). Because of this concern, the residents of urban areas are more often in a hurry than are their country cousins.

If city folks invested emotion and time in every person they met, noticed every sound they heard, and paid attention to every new or different sight they encountered, they would always be behind schedule. Both individuals and social systems would break down. So people in cities move and think quickly. They learn to act on little information and avoid becoming bogged down with details. Life in the city is thus sometimes seen as a "rat race," especially by rural people.,

According to Simmel, then, the more relaxed, personal, and spontaneous way of living that is possible in rural societies simply would not allow anyone to cope effectively with the demands of the city. People in urban areas think differently and engage in different lifestyles, and those who migrate from rural to urban areas must learn to do so too. (For an updated elaboration of Simmel's argument, see Milgram 1970.)

Wirth (1938) extended Simmel's argument and focused more on the social than on the psychological side of urban life. He thought that the elements of the urban environment with the greatest impact on social life in cities are the size, density, and social heterogeneity of the urban population. Wirth's model of the city is based on these three variables. He argued that extensive exposure to large numbers of socially different people causes urbanites to withdraw psychologically and reduce the *intensity* of social interaction. This leads to superficial, impersonal, and "segmented" social relationships; increased individualism, self-interest, and anomie (normlessness); low morale; and reduced community integration. Wirth's picture of life in the city, then, is largely negative (cf. Sennet 1970; Gillis and Hagan 1990).

## Selection

The views of Simmel and Wirth are examples of *environmental determinism* (the idea that the physical environment can affect or determine people's attitudes, behaviours, or conditions). The urban environment is seen as causing people who live in it to be different from their rural counterparts. This is not, however, the only way sociologists explain rural/urban differences in lifestyle. Other sociologists believe that differences between people in one environment and those in another reflect cultural or structural factors and "selection," rather than the impact of either environment on inhabitants.

**Selection theory** holds that while situations or behaviours and places may be related, the physical environment need not be the *cause* of the situations or behaviours. Instead, they argue, people with particular characteristics may choose to live in some areas of the city and may avoid other areas. Additionally, certain people are given access to some areas but denied access to others. This denial may take the form of direct discrimination, but in industrial capitalist societies, the mechanism is usually more indirect, though equally persuasive: income.

Earlier we saw that some areas of the city — for instance, the transitional zone in the Burgess model — contain cheap, high-density housing, and socially heterogeneous populations. Most people who live in such areas are poor and are plagued with a variety of poverty-related troubles. Few of them would choose to live in these physical or social circumstances, but low income prevents them from moving elsewhere. In contrast, the suburbs are typically homogeneous, low in density, and contain middle- or upper-income populations who face few of the income-related troubles of slum-dwellers. Consequently, density and heterogeneity are correlated with such problems. But in this example, income determines both residence (through selection) and problems. If this is true, the conclusion that density or heterogeneity is causing the problems would be a spurious interpretation. From a selection standpoint, then, the physical environment is merely a place where action occurs; it is not important as a cause (see Figure 16-7).

The selection argument can also be used to explain rural/urban differences in behaviour. According to Simmel (1950) and Wirth (1938) the urban environment causes people to behave in particular ways. A selection argument denies the causal impact of the environment. Instead, demographic, cultural, and socioeconomic variables cause people to behave in specific ways and also determine whether they live in rural areas or migrate to cities.

# Population Density and Social Pathology

In 1962, John Calhoun found that when rats are exposed to high population densities for long periods of time they change their behaviours. They engage in aberrant activities: rape, agression, asexuality, careless mothering, infanticide, and cannibalism, among others. Calhoun attributed these behaviours, which he considered symptoms of "social pathology," to excessive population density.

It seems obvious that extremely high population densities *can* cause all sorts of unpleasant experiences — including death — in rats, humans, and other animals. So the relevant question is not *whether* population density causes discomfort, but *what level* of population density produces symptoms of crowding, what these symptoms are, and what can be done about it.

Most research on humans has produced conflicting results, but the general absence of extreme social pathology in areas of the world with relatively high densities (such as Hong Kong and Calcutta) suggests that even higher densities are probably required before people begin to behave like Calhoun's rats (Gillis 1979b).

Unlike rats, people invent techniques enabling them to overcome many unpleasant aspects of their physical environment. Urbanites have developed a variety of ways of "cocooning" — protecting themselves from stimulus overload (Altman 1975). For example, watching television may be a way of psychologically withdrawing from potentially unpleasant surroundings such as those with high population densities (Gillis 1979a).

Population density probably does affect people, and it may affect some more than others (Gillis, Richard, and Hagan 1986). But the types and levels of density in the Calhoun experiment have little relevance for understanding what effects density may have on people or why such effects occur. In any case, Canadians apparently need not worry too much about becoming cannibals, at least not because of excessively high population density.

---

**Sources:**

Irwin Altman, *The Environment and Social Behavior* (Monterey, CA: Brooks/Cole, 1975); John B. Calhoun, "Population density and social pathology," *Scientific American* 206 (1962):139–48; A.R. Gillis, "Coping with crowding: Television, patterns of activity, and adaptation to high-density environments," *The Sociological Quarterly* 20(1979a):267–277; A.R. Gillis "Household density and human crowding: Unravelling a non-linear relationship," *Journal of Population* 2(1979b):104–117; A.R. Gillis, M. Richard, and J. Hagan, "Ethnic susceptibility to crowding: An empirical analysis," *Environment and Behavior* 18(1986):683–706.

## Figure 16-6. Wirth's Model and the Selection Model

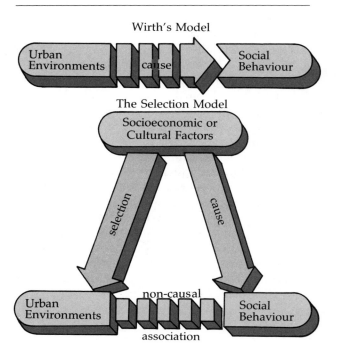

To the extent that this selective migration occurs, then, we would expect to find differences between rural and urban areas in rates of crime as well as other forms of deviance. But it is selection and composition, not differences in the nature of the rural and urban environments that cause the association (see Gordon 1975, 1976; Romanos 1979; Butterworth and Chance 1981; Laub 1983; Fischer 1984).

These, then, are the major questions social scientists have about the effects of the urban environment on people. Some, like Simmel, Wirth, and Milgram, argue that elements of the urban environment actually shape and determine human attitudes and behaviours. Others, like Gans, argue that social and cultural factors, rather than the environment, affect the lives of people.

## Environmental Opportunities and Constraints

Michelson (1976) has developed a viewpoint that falls between the environmental determinist and social selection perspectives. He argues that persons with particular lifestyles are attracted to some environments and repelled by others. Because particular places discourage or inhibit certain kinds of behaviours, people who want to engage in these behaviours will try to avoid these environments. For example, few highrise buildings provide either adequate soundproofing or the space that workshop activities require. As a result, people committed to puttering in a workshop will feel pressure to select residences more appropriate to the pursuit of their hobby.

Similarly, the suburban housing environment is often seen as conducive to home-centred, child-oriented lifestyles. Couples with young children typically prefer to live in single, detached houses in the suburbs rather than in other types of housing in the city. In fact, Clark (1966) discovered that it is more the desire for an affordable single, detached house than the desire to live in the suburban environment that attracts young married people to the suburbs. On the other hand, people with fewer or older children are often less child-oriented and are more likely to enjoy the facilities of a downtown environment as a place to live. (For discussions of the relationship between life cycle and housing environment, see Clark 1966

Most people who migrate from rural to urban areas do so for economic reasons (Fischer 1984). This includes people with highly specialized skills, who are *pulled* to the more lucrative markets in urban areas. It also includes people with low skill levels, who are surplus labour in rural areas. These people are *pushed* out, and gravitate to urban areas, where they also find little demand for their limited skills. Clark (1978) calls the latter category the "new urban poor." (See, for example, Don Shebib's classic Canadian film, *Goin' Down the Road*.)

Because urban areas tend to attract migrants from the top and the bottom of the range of marketable skills, rural areas lose a portion of their most talented and ambitious young people. At the same time, rural areas lose a portion of those who are most likely to experience "instability and deviance" (Fischer 1984). This migration pattern has the effect of stabilizing the skill levels, as well as lowering the proportion of young people and misfits, in rural populations. Urban areas, on the other hand, wind up containing younger populations who have highly specialized skills, and a higher proportion of unemployables and deviants.

and Michelson 1976, 1977.)

This view of the relationship between environment and behaviour on the micro level is the same as the macro-level view we took earlier when we looked at the origin of cities. That is, the physical environment can act as a limiter, preventing people from doing things. This is the case both for building cities and for workshop activities in the home. The physical environment does not so much motivate human behaviour, as Wirth (1938) suggested, as inhibit some activities and allow others. Some environments are necessary (if not sufficient) for the occurrence of certain behaviours. Warm climates or flat topography prevent the possibility of alpine skiing, and highrise apartments discourage or inhibit boat-building as a hobby. Because of this, significant statistical associations can be found between specific environments and specific behaviours. From this perspective, then, the physical environment is neither irrelevant, as the selection argument suggests, nor a determinant, as Simmel and Wirth described it. Instead, the physical environment plays an important and complex part in affecting urban life in a variety of ways apart from direct determinism (see, for example, Gillis 1979a, 1979b).

## City Life and Social Networks

Although social scientists have several explanations for rural/urban differences in attitudes, behaviours, and conditions, it remains unclear exactly what actual differences exist between rural and urban lifestyles. For example, the social isolation, psychological withdrawal, and anomie that Wirth (1938) attributed to urbanites is also found in rural populations (Leighton 1959). It is not at all clear that psychological withdrawal or other disorders are more prevalent among urban than among rural populations (Webb and Collette 1977, 1979; Crothers 1979). This probably means that, like life in the city, life in rural areas is also no bed of roses for many people. The strain of the factory assembly line and the rush-hour traffic may be more than matched by the physical and mental strain associated with farming, fishing, and the limited facilities available in rural areas. The belief that life is somehow better in the countryside may reflect only romantic nostalgia for a rural past, an increasing ignorance of many of the harsher aspects of rural life, and a tendency to take for granted many urban conveniences, such as high pay and access to specialized medical care, dental care, and education.

If characterizations of rural life have been too favourable, most descriptions of urban life have been too unfavourable (White and White 1962). Urban life is much less atomized or anomic than Wirth and his colleagues (in what has come to be called "the Chicago school") believed. Gans (1962a, 1962b, 1967), Jacobs (1961), Reiss (1959), Wellman (1979), and others argue that city folks have friends, too, and are involved in important social networks that are analogous to communities. These networks may, like Gans's "urban villages," have discrete physical settings. But even when these networks are not physically identifiable in the same way as neighbourhoods, small towns, and villages are, they nevertheless may exist as social entities. Social networks flourish in urban areas as "communities without propinquity" (Webber 1963; Gillis and Whitehead 1970). Extended families with frequent and intense interaction are often maintained in cities, although residences may be physically distant (Young and Willmot 1957; Pineo 1971). People in cities may indeed be less likely to be friends with their next-door neighbours. But the reason for this unneighbourly behaviour may have less to do with the size, density, and social heterogeneity of the urban population than it has to do with the fact that city people frequently change residence (Sorokin and Zimmerman 1929). This results in friends and relations being widely dispersed and also reduces people's time or inclination for getting to know their neighbours. In small rural communities intimate contacts are more likely to live nearby because people move less often. In any case, people in cities seem to draw their friends more from their place of work or their voluntary associations (recreational clubs) than from their neighbourhoods.

City-dwellers are not as friendly or helpful to strangers as rural residents are (Franck 1980; Fischer 1981). This, along with the fact that urbanites are not very friendly with their neighbours, could lead one to think of the city as socially cold. But it is not. Urbanites draw a sharper distinction between friends and strangers, and have a larger proportion of friends who do not live close to them. But these represent important differences

## Planning and Progress

When social change is agreeable we call it "progress"; when it is intentional we call it "planning." Urban or town planning involves attempts to improve life by intentionally changing the structure or management of urban environments: it is a concrete expression of social policy.

Social scientists contribute to planning on both conceptual and methodological levels. Sociological concepts and research motivate, guide, and justify changes in both the design and management of urban areas. For the most part, however, it is probably in the critical evaluation of planning efforts that sociology makes its most important — albeit not its most appreciated — contribution to the field (Gans 1970; Smith 1979).

Whether a specific plan or design represents progress is not always easy to determine. What seems useful or beautiful to some people may not appeal to others. Planners, architects, and developers may consider a project a success for a variety of aesthetic, technical, and economic reasons. But they are rarely affected by the projects they produce, and may have little in common with the people who are. Planners, architects, and developers are usually highly educated, middle-class, cosmopolitan, and male. As such, they are not always representative of the majority of urban residents, especially those who live in low-income areas or slums.

Since differences in social class, lifestyle, and gender affect the way people "fit" with the urban environment (Michelson 1976, 1977; Gillis, 1977, 1979), declaring a project successful (or defining a change as progress) on the basis of professionals' reports may be premature. User evaluation studies should be conducted to see how the consumers themselves react.

For example, many attempts to clear slums and relocate residents in modern, efficient, and socially integrated public housing projects have been apparent successes. That is, planners, architects, and other professionals have assumed that slum-dwellers would prefer newer housing to older buildings and disorganized neighbourhoods. While this may be true, professionals often overlook the importance of the informal organizations that flourish in physically deteriorating neighbourhoods (Whyte 1943; Jacobs 1961; Gans 1962). Even when professionals recognize the value of informal social networks, they are often too optimistic in expecting such organizations to emerge immediately in new, socially integrated developments. To residents who value friends and neighbours over modern housing, such developments may be worse to live in than the slums they left behind.

From the viewpoint of nonresidents, clearing slums is aesthetically pleasing, and placing former residents in integrated housing projects may be seen as socially valuable. So some

---

in the *form* of rural and urban friendship ties, rather than differences in their number or strength.

Differences in individual and group life in rural and urban areas may have been more dramatic when Wirth published "Urbanism as a Way of Life" in 1938. At that time, many of the residents of Chicago had been raised in rural areas; the "urbanism" Wirth described may have been their way of adapting to what was, for them, an unfamiliar environment. Most North Americans are now considerably more familiar with urban environments, both from firsthand and secondhand experience. The mass media, especially television and satellite dishes, bring urban values, beliefs, and behaviours to rural regions. Just as many urbanites are now fans of "country" music, many rural residents may adopt urban lifestyles without actually spending much time in cities. As a result, rural and urban belief systems and styles of life may have converged over the last few decades.

Finally, there is evidence that North American cities have changed in theoretically important ways since Wirth's time. More and more people have moved to smaller, socially homogeneous suburbs, and until the last few years the centres of cities were declining in population size and density. The reduction in the size, density, and heterogeneity of urban (and suburban) populations may have all but eliminated the social and psychological impact of these population variables (Guterman 1969). However, for some city-dwellers, density and heterogeneity may still cause malaise. For example, people who have little money and few housing alternatives often have to live in areas where density and heterogeneity are high. When this happens they are more likely to suffer from psychological strain (Gillis 1983). So the combination of Wirth's factors and an inability to escape may produce in more limited areas the effects he observed in Chicago on a more widespread basis.

people will define a change as progress, while others will not. It is noteworthy that when such differences of opinion develop, those who are most directly affected by a change do not necessarily win. Instead, professional policymakers and planners are more likely to prevail, especially if the opposition is not socially powerful. Clairmont and Magill (1974) showed this clearly in their account of the destruction of Africville, a community of blacks in the north end of Halifax.

The poet Robert Frost once wrote, "Home is the place where, when you have to go there, they have to take you in." Frost's words emphasize the fact that, unlike "house," "home" implies a set of social relationships, obligations, and expectations. It means much, much more than the physical structure that houses people. In this way the meaning of "community" is similar to that of "home," while "neighbourhood" means something similar to "house."

Sociologists and other social scientists contribute to both people and planning by conducting evaluative research on the effects of planned change. Although the results of such studies often place policymakers, planners, and their products in a bad light, and although evaluative research may not provide solutions to the problems it uncovers, such research is nevertheless important. Politically, it provides a voice for people who might otherwise be unheard. It also alerts sincere but misguided meliorists to inadequacies in their plans. Without this information, mistakes would continue to be made, and more progressive solutions (should they exist) could remain undiscovered.

---

**Sources:**

Donald Clairmont and Dennis Magill, *Africville: The Life and Death of a Canadian Black Community* (Toronto: McClelland and Stewart, 1974); Robert Frost, "The death of the hired man," in *The Poetry of Robert Frost*, Edward Connery Lathem, ed. (New York: Random House, 1979); Herbert Gans, *The Urban Villagers* (New York: Free Press, 1962); Herbert Gans, "Social planning: A new role for sociology," in *Neighborhood, City and Metropolis*, Robert Gutman and David Popenoe, eds. (New York: Random House, 1970); A.R. Gillis, "High-rise housing and psychological strain," *Journal of Health and Social Behavior* 18(1977):418–31; A.R. Gillis, "Coping with crowding: Television, patterns of activity, and adaptation to high-density environments," *The Sociological Quarterly* 20:(1979):267–277; Jane Jacobs, *The Death and Life of Great American Cities* (New York: Random House, 1961); William Michelson, *Man and His Urban Environment*, 2nd edition (Reading, MA: Addison-Wesley, 1976); William Michelson, *Environment Choice, Human Behavior, and Residential Satisfaction* (New York: Oxford University Press, 1977); Michael Smith, *The City and Social Theory* (New York: St. Martins, 1979); William F. Whyte, *Street-Corner Society: The Social Structure of an Italian Slum* (Chicago: University of Chicago Press, 1943);

## Urban Deviance

There are several reasons for the proliferation and distribution of urban crime. One viewpoint, drawn from the arguments of Simmel and Wirth, centres on the freedom and anonymity found on city streets. Urbanites are more tolerant of differences and nonconformity (Stephan and McMullin 1982; Wilson 1985; Tuch 1987). They also draw a sharper distinction between friends and strangers, and are much more likely to treat the latter with indifference. This attitude shows up in the phenomenon of "bystander apathy," which not only allows deviants to get away with their behaviours, but may even *provoke* deviance. Many of the city's strange sights and activities may in fact be expressions of individualism and attempts to gain recognition, to be a "somebody" (Rainwater 1966). Because it is hard to make any impression at all on an audience of blasé urbanites, some efforts go beyond the bizarre and wind up damaging property and shocking or injuring passers-by.

This view suggests that both creativity and expressive crime can come from the same source. In fact, creativity and deviance can be hard to distinguish. The graffiti covering New York City subway cars can be seen as an artistic and stylized form of vandalism. Street musicians often break local laws when they perform, and the once-shocking affectations of punk rockers were in some ways the precursors of current fashions. Even the Hell's Angels can be seen as a sometimes dangerous manifestation of this "Hey, look at me!" phenomenon, falling somewhere between a loose-knit pack of demented thugs and a band of modern knights, cultural symbols that represent individualism, freedom, and romance (Thompson 1968).

If anonymity increases with the size of localities, then the expression argument accounts not

**The high tolerance urbanites have for non-conformity may encourage artistic deviance.**

only for differences between rural and urban areas, but also for differences between small and large cities. Moreover, once areas become known as centres of expressive deviance, they may attract colourful characters and repel more conservative people. On a broad scale, California can be seen as something of a magnet for both bizarre and creative people. On a more specific level, San Francisco and New York probably attract nonconformists for this reason, and on an even more confined level, particular areas within cities do the same. Greenwich Village in New York has attracted unusual people for many years. In the 1960s, San Francisco's Haight-Ashbury district drew hippies and flower children from all over the continent. The Yorkville area in Toronto attracted beatniks in the 1950s and hippies in the 1960s. The 1970s and 1980s, however, saw Yorkville transformed into the chic domain of yuppies, while the Yonge Street strip has become Toronto's main deviance service centre. Anonymity may combine with selection to produce some of the deviance we see in urban areas: the adventurous go where the action is. In so doing, they deprive their home area of their creativity, eccentricities, and criminality, which are added to what Tilly (1976b) calls the "chaos of the living city." Ad-

venturous people may also commit crimes when they visit cities, driving up the crime rates in urban areas (Gibbs and Erickson 1976).

Although Thrasher (1927) argued that deviance can be expressive and even fun, most of his colleagues in the Chicago school believed that urban deviance was the result of the breakdown of social order. In 1972 Newman produced an interesting variant of this argument. He suggested that some types of urban architecture inhibit or prevent surveillance and control in neighbourhoods, even within apartment buildings. High walls, underground parking areas, long corridors, and hidden spaces such as stairwells discourage residents from taking responsibility for what happens in these places. Criminals can lurk behind walls or in stairwells; they can loiter in hallways, where they are bothered by neither the police nor the residents. Because of these design factors, which are typically associated with high-density housing, some areas of the city have higher rates of crime than others have (Gillis 1974).

Newman's view of the effect of the physical environment is similar to Michelson's and to Bronowski's (both discussed earlier). That is, the physical environment — in this case, urban architecture — prevents or permits action, rather than motivating it. Law-abiding people are not driven to thoughts of mayhem by the sight of a stairwell. But someone with mugging or sexual assault in mind may be deterred by the absence of such a secluded space. It is when residents are either unable or unwilling to provide informal surveillance that urban spaces can become attractive crime sites (see also Gillis and Hagan 1983). This situation may be aggravated by the routine activity patterns of urbanites, which frequently leave houses empty, lowering surveillance and providing more appealing targets for thieves (Cohen and Felson 1979; Felson and Cohen 1980).

Although Newman's view accounts for differences in crime rates among different buildings, neighbourhoods, and areas of the city, other explanations also fit the data. One of these is drawn from the symbolic-interaction tradition. By definition areas of the city with high-density housing contain a lot of people. Consequently, the police pay more attention to these locations as likely trouble spots. It makes little organizational sense to deploy many police in low-density areas, since there are neither as many potential victims nor as many potential offenders in these locations. So high-density areas tend to be overpatrolled, while lower-density areas are underpatrolled. As a result, incidents that take place in high-density areas are more likely to be detected and processed as criminal offences than are those that happen in low-density areas. This outcome occurs independently of the socioeconomic status of the populations involved. So the principle of "seek, and ye shall find" — rather than actual differences in rates of criminal behaviour — is the reason that some areas have higher rates of crime than others have (Hagan, Gillis, and Chan 1978).

A similar argument can be used to explain differences between rural and urban crime rates. In rural or smaller urban areas, the police are more informal, and less likely to process minor offences as crimes. Because larger cities have modern, more bureaucratic police forces, minor offences are more likely to be processed "by the book" — that is, as crimes (Wilson 1968). It is interesting to see that both viewpoints — the one suggesting that higher crime rates are the result of "undercontrol" (inadequate surveillance by residents), and the one attributing higher crime rates to "overcontrol" by the police — produce logical explanations of these differences in crime rates. In fact, recent studies show that both views may be empirically accurate, depending on the nature of the offence (Gillis and Hagan 1982).

At present it is hard to determine the precise relationship between urbanization and crime. If one focuses on rates of serious crime (such as homicide, sexual assault, and aggravated assault) and long-run trends, there is little doubt that urbanization is related to crime. But the relationship is *negative*. Historical analyses show that in Western countries rates of serious crime have been in decline over the last several centuries (Lane 1980; Gurr 1981; Archer and Gartner 1984; Gillis 1984, 1987b, 1989). At the same time, the urbanization of these countries has increased. Moreover, some cross-sectional analyses of serious crimes show that rural areas continue to be more dangerous than urban areas. In some parts of rural Mexico, for example, residents are more likely to be murdered than wartime Londoners were likely to die from the Blitz. In Canada, rates of expressive violence continue to be somewhat higher in rural than

**Figure 16-7. Canadian Crime Rates by City Size Expressed as Ratio of Small-Town Rates, 1978**

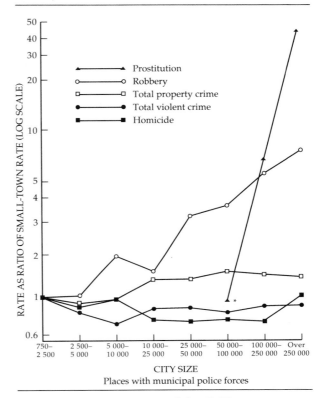

*Too few prostitution crimes in cities below 50 000
SOURCE: Claude Fischer, *The Urban Experience*, 2nd edition (New York: Harcourt, Brace Jovanovich, 1984), p. 106.

urban areas (Nettler 1982; Wilkinson 1984). However, as Figure 16-7 shows, rates of more rational crime (for example, robbery) and vice (for example, prostitution) are directly related to the size of Canadian communities (Fischer 1984).

Before deciding that urbanization does not cause crime and rejecting all the theories outlined earlier, we should note two points. First, overall rates of *minor* crimes have been increasing dramatically over the last five centuries, and urbanization may indeed be a causal factor in this shift (Gillis 1984, 1989). The second point concerns very recent trends in violent crime. Historically, serious crimes against persons have most often involved family members and friends. For example, women had more to fear from their husbands and male friends than from anyone else; only a minority of homicides, sexual assaults, and aggravated assaults involved strangers. This continues to be the case in Canada and other Western countries. But recent trends suggest that important changes may be taking place. Over the last several decades, homicide rates have stopped declining and have begun to increase. This change is due largely to an increased incidence of people killing strangers — that is, people with whom they have had no previous contact (Gillis 1985). Since this shift has only been going on for a few decades, it is hard to decide whether the pattern represents a new trend or only a short-term fluctuation or drift. Brown's (1984) observations of his native Harlem over a 20-year period have led him to believe that social life in cities is deteriorating. Many of the young residents of large cities are frustrated and feel like nobodies. They place little value on themselves or others. Therefore, according to Brown, the act of killing someone, especially a stranger, is simply not as repugnant to these young people as it would have been to their counterparts 20 years ago. And even if the killer is caught, the notoriety conferred by peers and the press may be better than no attention at all (Brown 1984).

Several of the theories of urban crime fit with Brown's description of the situation in Harlem. But Harlem is not representative of all urban centres, so whether the patterns described by Brown will be observed elsewhere remains to be seen. However, post-war *suburbanization* — the movement of upwardly mobile urbanites toward the suburbs — probably depleted the core areas of many U.S. cities of their most law-abiding citizens as well as of their principal taxpayers. The departure of the former would increase the proportion of criminals in the remaining population of core areas, which would increase the crime rate in cities. The departure of the latter would decrease the money available for social services, including policing, which would further aggravate the situation. This shows that the relationship between social disorganization and crime may go both ways. That is, higher crime may promote out-migration, which results in further disorganization. Since suburbanization has been occurring in both Canada and the United States since World War II, Harlem may simply be an extreme case of a phenomenon that is widespread, particularly in

the U.S. If this is true, suburbanization may be the cause of the recent reversal of the five-century decline in serious crime that urbanization brought to Western nations. In the meantime, public fear of urban crime continues to grow (Fischer 1984; Sacco 1985), and people continue to move to the suburbs to avoid crime (Fuguitt and Zuiches 1983), a process that depletes the populations of the major cities in the U.S. and Canada. However, there are signs that this out-migration is subsiding — and, with gentrification, may even be reversing. So reports of the death of the great North American cities may be premature (see Whyte 1988).

## New Urban Sociology

Dependency theory and a Marxian conflict orientation are the bases of what has been called the **new urban sociology** (Zukin 1980). For adherents of this view, the term "urbanization" refers not only to the proportion of a given population who live in areas defined as urban, but also — and more importantly — to the localization of labour, the concentration of capital, and the integration of hinterlands into the capitalist world system (see, for example, Harvey 1975, 1976; Castells 1976, 1977, 1983). For the new urban sociologists, "urbanism" refers to "the culture of industrial capitalism" (Zukin 1980).

Historically, the relationship between industrialization and urbanization is strong. Some non-industrialized countries contain cities, but few industrialized countries are not highly urbanized. The new urban sociologists recognize this and argue that patterns of urbanization reflect not only industrialization but the forces of capitalism as well. From their viewpoint, urban sociology has traditionally focused on at least irrelevant and at most intervening variables, rather than the ultimate political/economic causes of urbanization. Structural functionalists are seen as missing the point, because their views do not take account of the industrial capitalist context in which they make their observations.

For example, Lorimer (1978) argues that the proliferation of highrises in Canadian cities occurred because this type of housing gave devel-

**The high price of housing in large cities has produced the phenomenon of homelessness.**

opers the biggest payoff. Lower-density housing is actually cheaper to build on a per-unit basis and is also more popular with planners. The majority of consumers still hope to live in low-density housing, viewing it as an important component of their ideal family life. Research in Calgary and Edmonton has even shown that living in highrises is related to psychological strain in women with children at home — and that the higher up they live, the worse the strain gets (Gillis 1977).

According to the new urban sociologists, the combination of industrial technology and the pursuit of profit — rather than construction costs, the preferences of planners, or consumer demand — has structured the physical and social character of urban Canada. Furthermore, because housing demand has outstripped supply, urban residents must now either pay a much higher proportion of their incomes to own a house in the city or leave for the suburbs. The dream of owning a house has pulled many to the suburbs, while others have abandoned the dream and now try to make their lifestyle conform to the available high-density downtown housing.

Rex (1968) argues that this competition among consumers for residences is the most salient manifestation of urban inequality, and that social mobility occurs between "housing classes." Most of the conflict occurs at the borders of these classes, as higher-income earners compete with one another for mortgages and entry into the relatively exclusive home-owner class, while lower-income urbanites compete with one another for access to public housing (Rex 1968; cf. Szelenyi 1972).

The new urban sociologists also suggest that the traditional viewpoints serve the state by de-

# Territoriality, Community, and Ideology

*"Peace! You never know what peace is until you walk on the shores or in the fields or along the winding red roads of Abegweit on a summer twilight when the dew is falling and the old, old stars are peeping out and the sea keeps its nightly tryst with the little land it loves. You find your soul then . . . you realize that youth is not a vanished thing but something that dwells forever in the heart. And you look around on the dimming landscape of haunted hill and long white sandbeach and murmuring ocean, on homestead lights and old fields tilled by dead and gone generations who loved them . . . [and] you will say, 'why . . . I have come home!' "*

— LUCY MAUD MONTGOMERY

Many ethologists — scientists who study the behaviour of nonhuman animals — are convinced that people have an innate willingness to defend their home area and the people in it. They call this tendency "territoriality." Whether it is innate or learned, a form of territoriality does seem to exist in humans. For example, the closer to home they are, the more likely they are to protect the person and property of others (Gillis and Hagan 1983).

Sociologists disagree about the importance of the physical environment as a determinant of **community**. Some, such as Reiss (1959), have placed great emphasis on a territorial factor; others, such as Martindale (1964), have ignored the importance of territory and focused exclusively on the ideas of social interaction, shared values, and group consciousness. Because a specific territory may contain several distinct, and even competing, groups, most sociologists seem now to regard territory as a nonessential component of urban or rural communities. However, Westhues and Sinclair (1974) note that "while the physical setting is not the only important factor that leads to community formation, it is a basic and important one. Physical boundaries may create an isolated group, hence limiting the social interaction which is necessary for community formation." Westhues and Sinclair also note that the physical environment can help symbolize a community for its members: "When there are real physical boundaries, like mountains or rivers, that delimit a particular geographic area, the people in that area are more likely to develop a sense of social cohesion. When the

village limits encompass distinctive scenery, that scenery can come to symbolize in an important way the distinctiveness of the social life that goes on there" (1974).

Applying these principles on a broader scale helps us understand how the residents of a place like Prince Edward Island are able to maintain a well-defined collective identity in spite of its small size (about 126 645 people in 1986) and despite strong political and economic pressures to merge with one or more of the other Atlantic provinces. The 14 km of water in the Northumberland Strait symbolically, as well as physically, separate the province and its residents from the mainland, which is probably why many Islanders voted against being joined to the mainland with a "fixed link." Moreover, the outstanding beaches and unusual soil colour of PEI have been used as symbols for the uniqueness of Islanders and their style of life. (For example, listen to Nancy White's song "Red is the Soil.")

Whether people in specific communities have a distinctive lifestyle — and if it is distinct, whether it is better than life elsewhere — is difficult to determine. However, as Westhues and Sinclair point out, the accuracy of this idea may be far less important than its effects. They call such notions "community ideology," which they define as "a set of beliefs distinctive to the community which serves to justify its existence, to give residents a sense of pride in living there, and to unify the residents as a result of that pride" (1974). Community ideology is based on historical and geographical individuality, and may be an important

component of community survival — particularly in the case of small towns (or provinces), whose young people constantly face economic and other enticements to migrate to larger centres.

Community ideology helps small localities resist total depletion through migration by offering intangible rewards to people who stay. "The basic item in community ideology is simply that living in the village is better than living elsewhere" (Westhues and Sinclair 1974). Community ideology and a local history also give meaning and a sense of belonging to a location. "To inhabit a place physically, but to remain unaware of what it means or how it feels, is a deprivation more profound than deafness at a concert or blindness in an art gallery. Humans in this condition belong *nowhere*" (Walter 1988).

---

**Sources:**

References are to A.R. Gillis and J. Hagan, "Bystander apathy and the territorial imperative," *Sociological Inquiry* 53(1983):448–460; D.A. Martindale, "The formation and destruction of communities," in *Explorations in Social Change*, G.K. Zollschaun and W. Hirsch, eds. (London: Routledge and Kegan Paul, 1964); Albert J. Reiss, Jr., "The sociological study of communities," *Rural Sociology* 24(1959):118–130; E.V. Walter, *Placeways: A Theory of the Human Environment* (Chapel Hill: University of North Carolina Press, 1988); Kenneth Westhues and Peter R. Sinclair, *Village in Crisis* (Toronto: Holt, Rinehart and Winston, 1974).

The quote at the beginning of this insert is from Lucy Maud Montgomery, "Prince Edward Island," in *The Spirit of Canada* (1939), as quoted in Francis W.P. Bolger, Wayne Barrett, and Anne Mackay, *Spirit of Place: Lucy Maud Montgomery and Prince Edward Island* (Toronto: Oxford University Press, 1982).

fining urban social movements as deviance or disorganization and by blaming the urban environment for producing violence and misery. These perspectives, they suggest, deflect attention from the idea that urban social movements — even those that find expression in violence — represent the attempts of exploited people to challenge an oppressive elite. For example, in their study of the effects of urbanization on collective violence, Lodhi and Tilly (1973) found that collective disorders such as riots vary independently of other types of crime. This is not surprising since, unlike other crimes, many "contentious gatherings" seem to be politically motivated (Lupsha 1976; Tilly 1976a). The new urban sociologists contend that classifying these activities together as urban violence, disorganization, or deviance not only obscures important differences in their origins, but justifies their repression by the state (Castells 1977).

In some respects the new urban sociology is neither new nor urban sociology. It is based on Marxian conflict theory and the dependency model, and neither of these is new. It resembles the study of social movements that happen to occur in urban areas (see, for example, Castells 1983). Chapter 17 discusses social movements in more detail. A concern with the physical environment has traditionally characterized urban sociology, yet the new urban sociology either ignores physical factors altogether or reduces their importance from a leading to a supporting role. In spite of these differences, though, the new urban sociology contributes to the subfield, drawing it more into the mainstream of sociology, and pointing out new directions for students of cities. However, followers should not go too far. The specific emphasis on capitalism and industrialization is of no benefit to sociologists who focus on the origin and growth of cities in nonindustrial, noncapitalist settings. The motivation for constructing the first cities may indeed have been the exploitation of one group by another, but this extends far beyond capitalism. The new urban sociologists' fixation on advanced capitalism is unnecessarily narrow.

Also, "just as the early urban sociologists treated some urban social groups as maladjusted, so some of the new urban sociologists view these groups as heroic resisters or embryonic revolutionaries — rebels in an urban paradise, an anti-capitalist

conscience. To put it mildly, this may be a mistaken appraisal" (Zukin 1980). Lodhi and Tilly (1973) suggest that not all those who engage in urban violence can be seen as politically motivated. Similarly, just as traditional scholars may have overstated the impact of the physical environment, the new urban sociologists may be too inclined to disregard it. Defining urban areas solely in terms of labour, capital, and social structure facilitates and extends Marxian views of social life. But for students of cities the definition is less satisfactory. "Cities are, above all, places whose analysis requires a sense of spatial and physical structure" (Tilly 1981).

It is hard to rely solely on argument to sort out the conflicting claims of the two perspectives. Each side is equally deficient. One ignores the political/economic context of the urban environment, and the other makes excessive and strident claims on its behalf. So far, the data are not very helpful in resolving the issue.

Cross-sectional and longitudinal analyses of the impact of urbanization, industrialization, and capitalism are hampered by the fact that the three variables are too entangled to enable researchers to sort out their independent effects (Gillis 1984). This situation — where conceptually independent variables are in fact highly correlated with each other — is known as *multicollinearity*, and efforts to estimate such variables' correlations with dependent variables are usually unreliable.

One of the ways of improving this situation is to get more information on urbanization and its correlates and on patterns of city growth in countries with a range of political and economic systems. By so doing we can determine to what extent the findings of the Chicago school can be generalized beyond capitalist countries. So far, information is scarce, but what we have supports both sides. For example, cities in the Soviet Union are not as highly segregated with respect to the social status of residents as those in both industrial and pre-industrial capitalist countries. However, instead of living in working-class areas of the city, many urban labourers in eastern-bloc countries live outside the cities and commute to work. Also, despite the absence of profit-seeking developers, highrises have still managed to proliferate in the industrial eastern bloc. Finally, although neighbourhoods within cities differ little from one an-

504   U N I T   V   *Social Change*

other in socioeconomic status, housing is clearly allocated — in terms of both quantity and quality — on the basis of power and privilege (Bater 1980).

As usual in the social sciences, the available information indicates that it would be worthwhile to get more information. There may indeed be universal patterns and consequences of urbanization, but their expression may be greatly affected by the political system, economic structure, level of industrialization, and historical experience of different nations. Rather than replacing traditional perspectives, the new urban sociology provokes new debate in an old subfield and provides exciting new directions for research.

## SUMMARY

1. Sociologists define a city as a large concentration of people engaged in a wide range of interdependent occupations that, for the most part, do not involve the primary production of food.

2. The shift of the world's human population from rural to urban areas has been associated with technical, organizational, and cultural developments that have allowed the development of large agricultural surpluses. Industrialization seems to have had the largest effect on urbanization.

3. The urbanization of Canada temporarily followed the patterns in industrial Europe and the United States, proceeding generally from east to west.

4. At present about three-quarters of the Canadian population live in urban areas. In recent years, the most obvious change in the Canadian urban population has been within cities; many have stopped growing or are even declining in population, while their suburbs have grown dramatically.

5. One of the most important explanations of the relationship between metropolitan areas and their hinterlands is the dependency theory. This perspective has also been used to explain the relationships among countries and among regions within countries. It is one of the bases for the new urban sociology.

6. Several perspectives have been developed that incorporate ecological principles to explain the growth of an individual city. The concentric zone, sector, and multiple-nuclei models are three of

these. All have some applicability within the large cities of industrial North America, but more so in the United States than in Canada.

7. Social scientists have developed various explanations for the existence of a distinct urban way of life — that is, urbanism. The most important of these theories is Wirth's. He focused on the size, density, and social heterogeneity of urban populations and argued that these factors cause segmented social relationships, social isolation, and psychological withdrawal. But recent evidence suggests that the impact of these variables may no longer be as great as in the past.

8. A number of arguments have been developed to explain urban deviance. However, except for recent trends, the overall relationship between urbanization and serious crimes is negative. In Canada, people are still safer in the cities than in rural areas.

## GLOSSARY

**Agricultural surplus.** Quantity of food greater than that required to meet the needs of its producers.

**City.** Large concentration of people engaged in a wide range of specialized and interdependent occupations that, for the most part, do not involve the primary production of food.

**Community.** Identifiable self-conscious group with shared common interests. Communities may or may not have a territorial base, and they vary in their level of self-sufficiency.

**Competition.** Action of two or more groups or activities that attempt to occupy the same area.

**Concentric zone model.** Model of the city in which economic and residential activity patterns and social groups are segregated in concentric zones, with economic activities located at the centre of the city and residential activities located toward the periphery.

**Dependency theory.** Theory that the economies of hinterland areas become so specialized in primary industries (such as farming, fishing, or the extraction of raw materials) that trade with metropolitan areas for manufactured goods and services is necessary for the hinterland population to maintain a given standard of living. This places the hinterland in a politically disadvantageous position.

**Deurbanization.** A decrease in the proportion of a given population inhabiting urban areas.

**Gemeinschaft.** Tönnies's term for relatively small organizations characterized by a commitment to tradition, informal social control, intimate interpersonal contact, a collective orientation, and group consciousness.

**Gesellschaft.** Tönnies's term for relatively large organizations characterized by formal social control, impersonal contact, an orientation to individualism, and little commitment to tradition.

**Hinterland.** Rural or nonindustrialized region from which a city or metropolitan area extracts labour, food, and other raw materials.

**Human ecology.** Application of such ecological principles as competition, invasion, and succession to the scientific study of human behaviour.

**Limiting factors.** Variables that can prevent or inhibit change in other variables.

**Megalopolis.** Greek term for the most powerful of several cities in a given country or region. The term is now used to describe an unbroken urban region created when the borders of two or more metropolitan areas expand into one another (also known as *conurbation*).

**Metropolis.** Relatively large urban area containing a city and its surrounding suburbs. The term has also been used to refer to an industrial region or society that transforms raw materials extracted from its hinterland.

**Motivating factors.** Variables that can produce or encourage changes in other variables.

**Multiple-nuclei model.** Model of a city as several specialized areas located along and connected by major traffic arteries, such as highways. Unlike the concentric zone and the sector models, the multiple-nuclei model does not suggest that zones radiate from the centre of the city.

**New urban sociology.** This perspective, which is based on Marxian conflict theory and the dependency model, emphasizes the impact of industrial capitalism on the form of urban areas and the lives of the people they contain.

**Sector model.** Model of a city as a series of wedge-shaped sectors radiating from the centre of the city, each containing different activities or land uses and separated from each other by major traffic arteries or natural boundaries.

**Segregation.** Tendency for specific activities or groups to cluster and exclude other activities or groups from occupying a region or neighbourhood at the same time.

**Selection theory.** Viewpoint that relationships between the physical environment and behaviour reflect the migration or movement of people with particular characteristics to particular places.

**Suburbanization.** Increase in the proportion of a given population living on the outer limits of a metropolitan area.

**Urbanism.** Set of attitudes, beliefs, and behaviours that are thought to be characteristic of city-dwellers.

**Urbanization.** An increase in the proportion of a given population inhabiting areas designated as urban.

# FURTHER READING

**Baldassare, Mark (ed.).** *Cities in Urban Living*. New York: Columbia University Press, 1983. A good collection of articles on topics in urban sociology that have appeared in sociology journals.

**Bronowski, Jacob.** *The Ascent of Man*. London: British Broadcasting Corporation, 1976. Chapter 2, "The Harvest of the Seasons"; Chapter 3, "The Grain in the Stone"; and Chapter 8, "The Drive for Power" are particularly relevant to the study of cities. (*The Ascent of Man* is also available on film.)

**Clairmont, Donald, and Dennis Magill.** *Africville: The Life and Death of a Canadian Black Community*. Toronto: McClelland and Stewart, 1974. A detailed account of the destruction of Africville (a settlement of blacks in the north end of Halifax) and the motivations behind this "urban renewal."

**Clark, S.D.** *The Suburban Society*. Toronto: University of Toronto Press, 1966. This monograph discusses the forces affecting the suburbanization of Toronto.

**Fischer, Claude.** *The Urban Experience*. 2nd edition. New York: Harcourt, Brace, Jovanovitch, 1984. A good review of current work in American urban sociology. The author presents his own views on the importance of city size, subcultures, and social networks. This is one of the best-written and most interesting texts in urban sociology.

**Goldberg, Michael A., and John Mercer.** *The Myth of the North American City: Continentalism Challenged*. Vancouver: University of British Columbia Press, 1986. An analysis of cities in North America that highlights differences between Canada and the United States.

**Kennedy, Leslie W.** *The Urban Kaleidoscope*. Toronto: McGraw-Hill Ryerson, 1982. An examination of most of the models and theories developed by urban sociologists, with special attention given to Canada.

**Lucas, Rex A.** *Minetown, Milltown, Railtown: Life in Canadian Communities of Single Industry*. Toronto: University of Toronto Press, 1971. A detailed account of the impact of small, single-industry towns on the institutions and lives of their inhabitants. A classic in the study of Canadian communities.

**Lyon, Larry.** *The Community in Urban Society*. Chicago: Dorsey, 1987. An excellent urban sociology text that focuses on the community and on different approaches to analyzing it.

**McGahan, Peter.** *Urban Sociology in Canada*. 2nd edition. Toronto: Butterworths, 1986. Another good examination of urban sociology in the Canadian context.

**Melbin, Murray.** *Night as Frontier: Colonizing the World After Dark*. New York: Free Press, 1987. An excellent and readable account of the social implications of the "civilization" of the night in cities.

**Palen, John J.** *The Urban World*. 3rd edition. New York: McGraw-Hill, 1987. A good general text in urban sociology. Includes sections on urbanization in the Third World.

**Westhues, Kenneth, and Peter R. Sinclair.** *Village in Crisis*. Toronto: Holt, Rinehart and Winston, 1974. An interesting study of community life and change in a small Ontario town (Elora) on the fringe of larger urban centres.

**Whyte, William H.** *City: Rediscovering the Center*. New York: Doubleday, 1988. An interesting micro-level analysis of the behaviour of people in urban spaces, by a student of cities who likes them. (See also Whyte's film *The Social Life of Small Urban Spaces*.)

# CHAPTER 17

# Social Movements and Social Change

PATRICIA FITZSIMMONS-LECAVALIER
GUY LECAVALIER

Defiant Anti-Abortion Campaigners
Vow to Put Pressure on Government
*Globe and Mail*
January 19, 1988

Students at [University of Toronto] Sit-In to
Protest School's Holdings in South Africa
*Toronto Star*
March 5, 1987

120,000 [Petitioners] Want Non-Profit Day Care
*Globe and Mail*
June 16, 1987

34 Arrested as Crowd Hits Military Ties
*Vancouver Sun*
April 6, 1987

Many people think that the era of social protest died with the 1960s. As the above headlines suggest, this popular view falls short of reality. The marches, demonstrations, sit-ins, and other protest tactics associated with the 1960s have since been adopted by social movements advocating a wide range of social changes. A diversity of peace, environmental, women's rights, minority rights, and gay rights movements, as well as anti-seal-hunt, anti-pornography, anti-cutbacks, anti-smoking, pro- and anti-abortion, and other single-issue movements have engaged in organized shows of discontent. Protest may no longer be the focus of campus and media attention, and a number of the 1960s movements may have disintegrated, but the use of protest has spilled over to many contemporary causes.

# Refuse the Cruise

*In 1983, a set of diverse organizations united in mass marches to protest the testing of the cruise nuclear missile in Canada. When this strategy failed, participation in demonstrations fell off dramatically. The peace and anti-nuclear movements were left searching for new pressure tactics that did not require large turnouts of protesters.*

## 1983

They came in the thousands to Toronto's downtown, bringing their message of "Refuse the Cruise" and making their demonstration the largest anti-nuclear protest in the city to date.

Organizers put their numbers at 30,000; the police estimated 18,000. Other observers settled on 25,000. The march stretched for about one kilometre and took 35 minutes to pass a given point.

Across Canada, roughly 50,000 demonstrators in at least forty cities and towns from coast to coast took to the streets to protest against the imminent deployment of cruise and Pershing 2 missiles in Europe.

From St. John's to Vancouver, marchers focused on Canada's agreement to allow the testing of the cruise missile in Alberta, but their number appeared to be down by one-third or more compared with the number that protested last April against the cruise testing.

In Montreal, between 10,000 and 15,000 people, in two separate demonstrations, attempted to link hands between the city's American and Soviet consulates.

In Ottawa, about 4,000 people rallied on Parliament Hill, some parading across the river from Hull. Roughly 8,000 congregated in Vancouver's Vanier Park, compared with a crowd of 60,000 in April.

Three thousand people took part in a rally in Saskatoon and 1,500 in a Winnipeg demonstration, according to reports.

Planners of the Montreal protest had expected only 3,000 people to join their demonstration, but sunny skies produced a turnout about four times that.

At Cold Lake, Alberta, where the program to test the cruise missile should begin early next year, a confrontation between 50 protesters and the military was avoided when the marchers agreed to a private meeting between two organizers and the base commander.

In Toronto, Saturday's show of anti-cruise strength passed off peacefully in a carnival atmosphere of music and general good humour encouraged by sunny skies.

The familiar anti-cruise contingents — supplemented by ethnic groups; church lobbies; high school supporters, women's movement representatives; human rights organizations; performing artists; political parties; and separate lawyers', physicians' and psychologists' sections — were chaperoned by Metro Toronto Police motorcycle outriders, as the march snaked its way from its University Avenue rallying point through the city centre to Queen's Park.

The only anxious moment in the protest came as marchers passed by about 500 counter-demonstrators lined up on the northwest corner of College Street and Queen's Park.

The counter-demonstrators' shouts were easily drowned out by the loudspeakers used for the main demonstration, and most of the

# What Are Social Movements?

## Change-Seekers, Change-Resisters

What are these social movements that are still so much a part of contemporary life? **Social movements** are collective attempts to promote, maintain, or resist social change (Wood and Jackson 1982). Social movements are often associated with demands for a change in the status quo to improve the material circumstances of a disadvantaged group. The changes pursued may also relate to improvements in the social, ideological, or political status of groups dissatisfied with the established order. Peace activists demand that efforts to avert a nuclear disaster be made a priority in government policy-making. Gay rights groups ask that their lifestyles be treated as a legitimate alternative, not as a deviant or illegal activity. Religious sects seek the same freedom as established churches to recruit converts to their ideals. Whether the goals involve changes in the class, social, or political status quo, all such groups constitute social movements.

The movement demands just listed would be described as **reformist**. Movements are said to be reformist when they seek adjustments in society's way of doing things to include new interests, while maintaining the overall existing system. But change-seekers do not always have such limited goals; a discontented group may also aim to replace established elites, institutions, or values with arrangements that would make the movement's

smaller group contented themselves with holding up placards and banners. "All we are saying is give freedom a chance," "Soviets Promise Peace of the Graveyard," and "Test the Cruise" were among the messages.

### 1987

Peace groups across Canada will begin using sophisticated lobbying tactics before the next federal election to try to make Canada end cruise missile testing and revamp its current defence policy.

"We've asked people to walk for peace (in rallies) before. Now we're asking people to vote for peace," said Sheena Lambert, national campaign co-ordinator of the Canadian Peace Pledge Campaign.

Ms Lambert said the peace movement is better prepared than ever to give voters the knowledge and tools to try to force the federal Government to reverse [the position put forward in] its white paper on defence.

The paper, released by Defence Minister Perrin Beatty in June, advocates increased spending on military equipment, including buying 10 to 12 nuclear-powered submarines at a cost of about $7.5-billion. . . .

"The peace movement has clear backing from the labor movement, church groups and a strong network of peace groups across the country," said David Thompson, a Newfoundland representative of the peace pledge drive.

"We've also got lawyers, academics, health-care workers and teachers. We've become professional."

Ms Lambert said members of the peace movement have made a "tactical decision" to lobby politicians and candidates in the next federal election to make Canada a nuclear weapons free zone.

The movement wants to put a stop to cruise missile testing and the entry into Canadian waters of nuclear-armed ships. . . .

Showering Canadians with "vote for peace pledge cards" will be a crucial part of the campaign, Ms Lambert said.

The cards, each containing a pledge of support for politicians who will speak out against Canada's support for the arms race, will be used to persuade politicians that voters take the peace issue seriously, she said.

Jane Mackey, the Victoria co-ordinator of the peace campaign, said at least 2,000 pledge cards have been signed in Victoria so far. "The response has been really good. I haven't been able to keep up with all the people who want to volunteer to help."

Mr. Thompson said his group in St. John's will set up booths outside churches, theatres and shopping malls.

Daniel Prima, a spokesman for Nuclear Free North, said winning native support is an important part of the northern peace campaign.

"It's a fairly exotic place up here with its musk ox, caribou and wolves. But it's a little unsettling when huge planes, some carrying plutonium, others flying low to test their nuclear-war fighting powers, disrupt this way of life."

This weekend, anti-nuclear rallies were held in Montreal and Toronto.

Organizers estimated that about 4,000 people gathered at the Ontario Legislature on Saturday. . . .

In Montreal, a peace activist said about 1,500 people marched on Saturday to protest against the federal government's position on defence.

**Sources:**
Michael McDowell, *The Globe and Mail*, October 24, 1983; Alexandra Radkewycz, *The Globe and Mail*, November 2, 1987.

---

interests the predominant ones in society. Movements pursuing such a displacement of the established order would be described as **radical**. They may focus on any social sector or relationship. A workers' movement to replace a capitalist economic system with a socialist one constitutes a radical movement. The many independence movements attempting to overthrow colonial rule qualify as radical political movements. Less obviously, a religious movement that seeks to have its spiritual values dictate society's social and political behaviour also qualifies as a movement for radical social transformation.

In practice, social movements tend to be rated on a reformist-to-radical scale according to the degree and speed of change they advocate in the status quo. Groups seeking more moderate changes or step-by-step solutions are generally regarded as reformist. Those groups devoted to more extensive or immediate changes are generally regarded as radical.

Social movements are not necessarily change-seekers. They may also be change-resisters. In the 1960s, social movements became strongly identified with demands for liberalizing changes, for greater lifestyle freedom and greater government intervention to promote social and economic equality (Freeman 1983). Certain concessions were gained; in response, new movements arose in the 1970s and 1980s to resist further change, or to reverse some of the changes made and return to a more traditional social order. These efforts to resist or reverse change brought about by social movements are called **counter-movements**.

This movement and counter-movement phenomenon is a prominent feature of the debate over Canada's abortion laws. Protesters favouring abortion on demand (the pro-choice movement) are opposed by protesters favouring restricted access to abortion (the pro-life movement). The pro-choice movement aims to liberalize abortion laws and access, while the counter-movement aims to roll back the liberalized legislation. There is also a counter-movement for a return to capital punishment, which was abolished in the 1970s after much agitation by prisoners' rights groups. In reaction, police associations mobilized a protest to restore the death penalty and swung public opinion to their side. When Parliament was forced to reconsider the situation in 1987 it again supported the abolition of the death penalty, and the restoration counter-movement was left to regroup. The current blend of movements to advocate change, to maintain recent change, or to resist and reverse change clearly illustrates the diversity of outlooks that social movements may have, even though they are all change-related.

As for change-seekers, change-resisters may also be rated on a moderate-to-radical scale, depending on how far their goals vary from the status quo.

## Nonroutine Group Action

At a time when society is bombarded with social changes of many sorts, what distinguishes social movements from other change-related activities? Social movements imply some degree of group action and shared goals. Change brought about through isolated individual acts does not constitute a social movement. For instance, there might be many parents who object to violent television programs and, as a matter of personal conscience, restrict their own children's television viewing to nonviolent shows. Such separate, unrelated acts would not constitute a movement against television violence. However, if some objectors grouped together to raise general awareness of the problem, and to promote a boycott of violent programs as a means of changing network practices, this shared commitment to change would take on the characteristics of a social movement. While shifts in individual attitudes and tastes often contribute to social change, those favourable to

**The movement and counter-movement phenomenon is a prominent feature of the debate over Canada's abortion laws.**

change constitute a social movement only when they consciously support a shared cause.

Another distinguishing feature of a social movement is that it is a **noninstitutionalized activity**. Social movements are said to be noninstitutionalized because their interests are not already met by the routine operation of society's established institutions and conventions. They do not have ready access to authority or to legitimacy in the social sphere that concerns them. Since they do not have routine influence in decision-making, social movements explore channels of influence that are out of the ordinary to advance their goals. Social movement action is essentially nonroutine action to promote interests that are not met by society's established institutions and conventions (Tilly 1978; Jenkins 1981; Wood and Jackson 1982).

That social movement activity is noninstitutionalized does not necessarily mean that it is not organized. Some social movements have a high level of formal organization with a distinct hierarchy of authority, well-defined operating procedures, and clear-cut membership criteria. A movement organization such as the National Action Committee on the Status of Women fits such a formally structured model. Other movements may be loosely organized — for example, consciousness-raising groups. Riots sparked by a particular incident of discrimination are likely to be even more loosely organized. Thus, in terms of their internal organization, social movements may range from the highly to the loosely structured. However, it is in terms of their external relations with the larger society that social movements are defined as noninstitutionalized, because movement goals are not routinely treated as rights by society's established institutions. For instance until recently, Canadians' right to smoke was taken for granted, and nonsmokers' rights were not institutionally backed. In the past few years, many localities and workplaces have responded to protesters' demands for limits on smoking, and the federal government has introduced legislation to ban all tobacco advertising by 1989. All such moves make the anti-smoking movement's goals more institutionalized than they were at the time of its formation in the 1970s. But the movement still has a long way to go to institutionalize its main goal of a smoke-free society.

## Success and Institutionalization

All social movements begin with noninstitutionalized interests; success for a movement involves having its interests institutionalized to some degree. There are several dimensions to **movement success**. A movement attains partial success when society recognizes and accepts its representatives as the defenders of a legitimate set of concerns. A movement may also attain partial success when it achieves certain of its stated goals (Gamson 1975). But a movement gains full success only when its interests are fully institutionalized, that is, when society routinely recognizes and enforces the movement's goals as rights.

So many movements achieve partial success that it is often difficult to decide where social movements stop and mainstream interest groups or political parties begin. The Parti Québécois (PQ) provides a good example of the problems partial success can cause a social movement. This political party sprang from a coalition of social movements for Quebec independence in the 1960s. The PQ's twin goals of getting its representatives elected and of gaining Quebec independence were clearly noninstitutionalized at its foundation, but the party

gained some success in the provincial elections of 1970 and 1973, gaining only a handful of seats but 23 and 30 percent, respectively, of the popular vote.

During the next campaign, the party modified its stance to separate its twin goals in response to low voter support for outright independence. It announced that independence was not an issue in that election, that a vote for the PQ would be taken solely as a vote for good government. The party promised to seek the voters' support for sovereignty association (a form of political independence that would retain an economic association with the rest of Canada) in a later referendum. This strategy led to electoral success; in November 1976 the PQ formed the Quebec government. But the referendum on sovereignty association, which was held in May 1980, was defeated: almost 60 percent of those who voted rejected it. In campaigning for the provincial election the following year, the PQ again downplayed and delayed the decision on independence, and won again with an even larger majority.

Thus, the PQ gained electoral success for a number of years, but it failed to institutionalize its original main goal of independence. This contradiction created obvious conflicts for many of the party's activists, who had devoted time, money, and expertise to the PQ because they were committed to the independence cause. While it was in office, the party retained a strong social-movement character that frequently conflicted with its more routine, vote-seeking character. The tensions inherent in this dual character eventually led to a split just before the 1985 election. When René Lévesque responded to low voter support by persuading the party to again drop independence from its election platform, many of the strongly pro-independence activists — the orthodox wing of the party — left the PQ. In the resulting struggle to define the true nature of the PQ, Lévesque himself had to resign as leader, and the even more moderate electoralist Pierre-Marc Johnson took over.

These changes did nothing to improve the PQ's performance, and the Liberal Party swept to power, stripping the PQ of even the partial success it had achieved by having the movement's representatives form the government. Ever since, there has been a struggle for control of the party between the electoralist and the orthodox/independentist wings of the movement. This struggle surfaced dramatically in 1987, in the wake of the renewed focus on Quebec independence precipitated by ex-leader Lévesque's death. This time, Johnson resigned and the hard-core independentist Jacques Parizeau took the lead in the race to replace him. At that point the social-movement side of the party seemed to have won out. But Parizeau's pragmatic, vote-getting moves indicate that the search is on for a new formula to reconcile the dual social-movement/mainstream-party character of the PQ.

In a similar vein the American anti-pollution movement achieved great success in influencing government experts and policies in the 1970s (Freeman 1983). With the election of the Reagan government, this apparent institutionalization vanished and the movement returned to a distinct protest position (for example, in its efforts against acid rain). Since the gains made by social movements are often shaky, they cannot be considered to be institutionalized until the movement's goals are routinely fulfilled by society's institutions.

## Traditional Approaches

### Classical Theories

Social movements are not a central preoccupation of the classical sociological theories. Traditionally, they have fallen into the domain of symbolic interactionists, who treat them as exceptional events of collective behaviour.

**Structural Functionalism and Breakdown Theory.** For structural functionalists, the discontent that spawns social movements is caused by a disequilibrium in the social system that results when society changes too quickly. The source of change most frequently cited is too-rapid economic development, but other major dislocations (such as serious economic depression, massive rural/urban migration, or rapid bureaucratization), might also provoke conflict. In this view, not all parts of the social system adapt to change immediately: some lag behind. These lags lead to disorganization since social structures are no longer con-

sistent with the social values that legitimize them. Established social values no longer make sense of the individual's everyday reality. This inconsistency loosens society's hold over the individual's behaviour and encourages unrealistic hopes or fears, and beliefs in utopian solutions for the new social problems. It is a breakdown in the social system that generates the disorganization and unrealistic beliefs that foster social movements, according to this view.

For structural functionalists, social movements are only transitory phenomena. They disappear once the social system has made a realistic adaptation to change by co-ordinating its social structures with its legitimizing values. Such transitory conflict is not a major concern for functionalists. When social movements do receive analytical attention in this tradition, they are attributed to the temporary disorientation and disorganization provoked by changing times, an approach called **breakdown theory**.

**Marxism.** Classical Marxism does focus on conflict and social change, but concentrates on a very limited range of workers' protests and revolutionary movements. Marx argued that the working class, in capitalist societies, had an inherent interest in revolution because capitalist development led inevitably to the deterioration of the workers' economic position and to the gradual destruction of the independent middle class. Thus society became polarized into two clearly opposed classes of workers and owners. By concentrating the working class in cities and factories, the capitalist system also promoted consciousness of common class interests and working-class solidarity against oppressive conditions. In this approach, it is not the disorganization but the solidarity of the discontented that leads to movements for revolutionary change. Marxian analysts concentrate mainly on the degree and clarity of class exploitation to explain revolutionary movements, or on sources of "false consciousness" that mask the underlying class conflict to explain the absence of revolutionary action.

**Smelser's Synthesis.** Smelser (1963) made an effort to overcome the limitations of the structural-functional and Marxist approaches in order to develop a comprehensive theory of social movements. Borrowing from a wide range of research and analytical concepts, Smelser attempted a synthesis of the major findings on social movements. He argued that discontent alone is not a sufficient cause of social movements. Before grievances can be translated into a social movement, the discontent must be filtered through other social conditions that encourage a belief in collective solutions and facilitate the organization of collective action and resistance to social control. Because it combines a functional analysis of discontent and generalized beliefs with a Marxian emphasis on the need for shared consciousness and solidarity in the face of repression, Smelser's highly abstract theory has sparked more debate than theoretical application. However, Smelser's accounting scheme, stripped of its theoretical underpinnings, has been used by researchers to indicate the list of social conditions to be studied in analyzing social movements (Pinard 1971; Oberschall 1973; Wood and Jackson 1982).

## Collective Behaviour Theories

The most widespread traditional approach to the study of social movements treats them as part of collective behaviour, which includes phenomena as diverse as panics, crazes, fads, fashion, and crowds of all sorts. In the collective behaviour tradition, social movements are associated with all group outbursts, whether change-related or not. What such collective behaviour is supposed to have in common is its distinctive difference from everyday behaviour. Unlike everyday behaviour, collective behaviour is not seen as having a rational base. In this tradition, a group action that is unconventional is also seen as somewhat irrational.

**LeBon's Theory.** The collective behaviour tradition was deeply influenced by the work of nineteenth century French analyst, Gustave LeBon (1960, originally published in 1895). LeBon was appalled by the intensity of the riots and the erosion of aristocratic authority during the century encompassing the French Revolution and the subsequent industrial revolution. LeBon branded this era "The Age of the Crowd," as it seemed to him that unruly mobs and the masses had taken over the power to direct society. LeBon attributed to

crowds a distinct psychological state, a uniform group mind, a kind of herd instinct that suppresses individual differences and moral judgments. In crowds, he believed, individuals lost their critical faculties. Therefore, people in crowds were suggestible, ideas were spread by contagion, and behaviour was easily manipulated by leaders who played on the crowd's emotions. LeBon argued that crowds were amoral and dangerous because they acted in unison directed by this highly contagious group mind. It is worth nothing that LeBon not only attributed a crowd psychology to rioting groups but also to juries, parliaments, and other types of groups where decision-making was not controlled by traditional elites. Although LeBon's bias against democratic institutions was dropped by later theorists, his notion that people massed in crowds catch an irrational common psychology became widely applied in sociological research.

**Blumer's Theory.** LeBon's influence is most clearly visible in the work of Herbert Blumer (1951). Blumer thought that collective behaviour was distinct from normal everyday behaviour because the usual process of symbolic interaction was suspended in crowds. Rather than interpreting one another's actions and responding on the basis of rational thought, people in crowds bypass interpretations and directly copy one another's reactions, in a state of **circular reaction**. Like LeBon's idea of psychological contagion, Blumer's postulated circular reaction rapidly stimulates passions and builds up a common mood of social unrest. As the crowd shifts its focus from one target to another, disorderly episodes of collective action ensue. In Blumer's approach, social movements are the somewhat more organized forms that emerge from this epidemic of social unrest.

**Criticisms of Collective Behaviour Theories.** While the collective behaviour approach to social movements was widely accepted for many years, there is little compelling evidence to support its view of collective irrationality (Berk 1974; Jenkins 1981). Collective action is at times violent or disorderly, but that does not mean it is irrational, or that a special psychological state must be proposed to explain crowd dynamics. It is true that everyday rules of behaviour are often inadequate guides in exceptional circumstances, such as a spontaneous protest. However, there is a great deal of evidence to support the alternative **emergent norm** thesis, positing that new norms tend to be generated to guide and contain behaviour in such exceptional circumstances (Turner and Killian 1972). Research about even highly disorderly episodes of collective action, such as riots, has frequently uncovered orderly guidelines controlling behaviour (Rudé 1967; Oberschall 1968). Individuals in a disorderly setting may have difficulty getting the information needed to assess their personal situation fully, but people do the best they can to make rational choices with the information available, just as they do in other aspects of life (Berk 1974).

Much of the initial research challenging the collective irrationality thesis sprang from observation of the race riots that swept through several American cities in the 1960s. The rioters' goals and the targets of these riots were neither chosen at random nor strictly on impulse. The riots focussed on longstanding grievances that community representatives had been articulating through more conventional channels for years, with little success. For instance, after persistent community complaints about police practices, one Los Angeles riot was sparked by the perception that police used undue force in arresting a black youth (Oberschall 1968). The targets of most personal attacks during the rioting were Los Angeles police officers — those directly linked to the grievance — not the other law-enforcement officers attempting to control the riot scene. Nor were targets for burning and looting chosen at random: residences, government and social service agencies, and black-owned businesses were spared, while white-owned businesses were more likely to be attacked. By far the majority of ghetto residents did not take part in the rioting, contrary to the "swept away" concept of collective behaviour involvement. Most residents did what they could to control the situation and help bystanders caught in the disorder. Even in such an extraordinarily disorderly bout of collective action, then, there was much evidence of strategic thinking and individual rationality.

Further research findings give little support to the irrational crowd psychology concept. Crowd bystanders are not automatically swept into par-

ticipation in protest action. Among those who do participate in collective protest, not all play the same role — most people do not engage in acts they disapprove of and scatter if the action threatens their wellbeing. Even when the use of violence is planned as a pressure tactic, it does not always get crowd support. For instance, the disruption planned by Quebec's pro-independence RIN (Rassemblement pour l'Indépendance Nationale) at the 1968 Saint-Jean-Baptiste Day parade in Montreal did not drag in large numbers of crowd members. Although the parade was a traditional celebration of national pride, the parade-goers resisted involvement in the RIN's tactics, which were widely considered to be risky and illegitimate (Frank 1984).

Although collective behaviour theorists maintain that social movements evolve from bouts of collective unrest, the evidence shows the opposite. Protest action usually springs from already existing social movements. Most demonstrations are planned by and recruit participants who are already members of organizations directly or indirectly linked with the cause immediately at issue. For instance, the 1970 Toronto demonstrations against the war in Vietnam and the Kent State killings attracted members from 50 associations with pacifist leanings, ranging from middle-class citizen groups to "yippies" and Maoists. Demonstrations that lack the means of co-ordinating the actions of such diverse groups are more likely to be marked by disorder, as was this particular demonstration (Frank 1984). But most demonstrations do have organizational means of guiding their participants' actions. As an example, most of the demonstrators involved in the Toronto experience were veterans of other peace and quality-of-life protests that were dramatic enough to attract media attention but seldom disorderly. Protest action generally attracts people who already have personal or organizational links or a common outlook on a social problem: it does not often recruit converts at random off the streets.

There is a certain factor in large crowds, often called **safety in numbers**, that can promote disorderly acts because it makes them appear to be cost-free. The larger the number of people involved in an action, the less the blame for that action can be attributed to any one individual. The fact that individuals can at times get away with behaviour that would be punished in another setting can encourage disorder, especially in spontaneous collective action like riots where there are few official leaders to be held responsible for the group. Taking disorderly action that has no personal cost cannot as such be branded irrational, since it could result from an individual's rigorous analysis of the potential payoffs and penalties. In any case, the evidence shows that most collective action is not disorderly, despite the temptation that the safety-in-numbers factor would seem to offer (Berk 1974). This is so because most protesters are already socially linked to other protesters and therefore not anonymous, or because most suspect that violent protest would hurt their cause.

There is no compelling research evidence to indicate a fundamentally irrational basis to collective action. Once this common thread of irrationality is broken, there is also little reason to group the study of social movements with other kinds of unconventional group behaviour. The change-related dimension distinguishes social movements as much as the collective dimension. Current research approaches regard groups with change-related goals — that is, social movements — as a distinct category for analysis.

## Sources of Discontent

Current approaches treat social movements as normal outgrowths of conflicting interests concerning the distribution of rewards in society's various institutions. Current approaches also treat social movements as rational activities, in which the calculation of group and individual interests is neither more nor less rational than in any other social activity. The range of conflicts that may generate social movements is extremely wide. The most frequently cited conflicts are those that follow the lines of the major status and income inequalities in complex societies, such as inequalities based on occupation, ethnicity, race, gender, region, and age (Lenski 1966; see also Chapter 8 of this book). These are the most frequently cited sources of discontent; other conflicts may relate to access to political power or to decision-making

Current sociological approaches treat social movements as normal outgrowths of conflicting interests concerning the distribution of rewards in society's various institutions.

in any of society's institutions. The situation of being a ratepayer and subject to decisions or services that do not meet one's interests could be a source of conflict and discontent. For another example, student governments are at times monopolized by a clique from one department or one region; inside information and privileges attached to the institution go mainly to these insiders. There could then be an inherent conflict between insiders and outsiders — the rest of the students who have no choice but to pay fees to support student government. Issues such as the slant of the student newspaper or the spending of the student government budget for travel and other insider "perks" might lead to protest. In a similar vein, clients' rights groups and taxpayers' revolts often emerge to combat the powerlessness that citizens feel in trying to influence government and bureaucratic practices that benefit mainly the leaders of these institutions.

A number of self-help movements, such as single-parents' or battered-wives' groups, have also emerged to support those who share problems not recognized or not adequately treated by existing institutions. A cause of this type is the parent-finders' movement among adopted children who want the right to know their birth parents. Any institutional practice or policy that excludes the interests of a social group may be a source of the kind of conflict and discontent that gives rise to a social movement.

Analysts who focus on underlying conflicts of interest to explain social movements ask the research questions: Why are these people dissatisfied? What makes them believe that change is needed or must be prevented? Not all analysts agree on the nature or the level of grievances most likely to foster social movements.

## Absolute Deprivation

Many analysts seek the source of social movements in the structures of disadvantage built into society. Among the most common structural sources of discontent they find are economic and occupational inequalities. Even movements that do not have an explicit class character are often rooted in economic deprivation. For instance, the movement to improve the status of women concentrates heavily on the barriers to income equality that women face.

But structural grievances need not be only economic. Scott and El-Assal (1969) have attributed the rise of student unrest in the 1960s to the rapid growth of the multi-university — large, heterogeneous, impersonal universities resembling knowledge factories. They maintain that in these new structures, students had little direct contact with or influence on professors and the university bureaucracy. These blockages produced educational grievances that erupted in protests for student rights and representation in decision-making. Indeed, their research shows that student protest action was much more likely to occur on large multi-university campuses than on smaller campuses. Disadvantages that are structurally inherent in any of society's institutions can be possible sources of discontent.

Among the most studied protest groups in Canada are the prairie farmers' movements that surfaced during the 1920s and 1930s. Prominent explanations for the emergence of the Farmers' Union, the Progressives, the Social Credit League,

and the Co-operative Commonwealth Federation (the CCF — the forerunner of today's New Democratic Party) point to economic and political discontent that originated in the structure of the farm economy. All of these agrarian protest movements appeared during depressed economic times (MacPherson 1953; Irving 1959; Lipset 1968; Skogstad 1980). The problems of hard times were compounded by the farmers' heavy financial dependence on banks and other commercial institutions:

*That relationship was one of subordination and dependence, and of extreme vulnerability to the vicissitudes of the market. Dependent on monopolistic banks for credit, subordinate to the railways, elevator companies and the Grain Exchange for the marketing and prices of their farm products, and at the mercy of eastern manufacturing interests for the costs of their agricultural supplies, farmers were almost completely unable to control the prices and sale of their products. (Skogstad 1980)*

Given this structure of dependence, western farmers had developed an entrenched distrust of eastern banks, railways, and other commercial institutions, which they felt were exploiting them (Morton 1950). This distrust was transferred to the federal political parties, which seemed to support the eastern interests (Smith 1967; Skogstad 1980). When falling prices for their product forced a drop in farm incomes, the sum of the farmers' grievances incited them to launch local protest parties.

In such an interpretation, social movements are considered to be a direct response to declining material conditions. History is full of revolts, rebellions, and political protests that fit this model. In eighteenth-century France, recurrent food riots were sparked by sharp increases in food prices and growing hunger among the urban poor (Rudé 1967). In nineteenth-century Europe, artisans organized attacks on the factory machines that had eliminated their jobs (Jenkins 1981). More recently, citizens' groups emerged in the 1960s to defend downtown Canadian neighbourhoods from the freeway, highrise, and commercial development that was destroying the quality of life in these residential areas (Magnusson 1983).

While many movements are related to a severe decline in a group's economic or political position, many others are not. For example, the women's movement surfaced in the 1960s even though women had made educational gains that were beginning to bring them status and income gains. Although their economic conditions were not deteriorating, women's situation was still far from equal to that of men (see Chapter 4). Whatever the gains they had made, women were deprived of equal opportunities for job advancement and equal returns on their education (see Chapter 8). We might say that women suffered from limited opportunities or blocked mobility; that is, they faced major barriers to achieving full equality with men whatever their education. Rather than being based on deteriorating conditions, the grievances underlying the women's movement appear to have been based on structurally restricted opportunities. This type of discontent, based on inequality rather than on deteriorating conditions, is also the source of many ethnic and racial movements.

Structural disadvantages rooted in either deteriorating life conditions or unequal opportunities are known as **absolute deprivations**. Analysts who rely on absolute deprivation to explain social movements hold that the greater the actual disadvantage a group faces, the greater the likelihood that a social movement will be formed. Absolute deprivations are concrete and generated by the social structure, in contrast to relative deprivations, which depend heavily on subjective feelings.

## Relative Deprivation

The notion of relative deprivation adds a social-psychological dimension to discontent. Some theorists stress that being disadvantaged is not alone sufficient to stir discontent strong enough to incite social movements. They maintain that to provoke protest a disadvantage must be perceived to be unfair or unjust, and that this perception depends on individual experiences and beliefs. People feel deprived relative to their expectation of fair treatment. It is feelings of relative deprivation, not absolute deprivation, that are thought to stir discontent.

**Relative deprivation** occurs when there is a gap between what people think they should get and what they do get or seem likely to get — to their disadvantage (Gurr 1970). When achievements are low, relative to expectations — when people do not get the rewards they feel entitled to — they are likely to rebel. In this **frustration/aggression approach**, frustrated expectations lead directly to aggressive behaviour. The greater the gap between what people expect and what they get, the more intense the frustration and ensuing conflict.

The relative deprivation approach to the study of social movements was proposed by Davies (1962) to explain the outbreak of revolutions and rebellions. He maintained that revolutions are most likely to occur when a prolonged period of economic growth and wellbeing is followed by a period of sharp decline like a sudden depression or a serious stock market crash. This rise-and-drop pattern, he said, generates a sense of relative deprivation, because the period of improving fortunes heightens expectations that are then dashed when a depression, war, or some other crisis brings a sudden downturn in the economy. In contrast, a steady downward drift of economic conditions would not generate conflict because people's expectations would have had time to deflate gradually. According to Davies, the sharper the gap between the original economic success and the later failure, the greater the relative deprivation and the more violent the ensuing political conflict.

Gurr (1970) expanded on the original rise-and-drop definition of relative deprivation to include any social conditions that raise expectations without increasing satisfaction, or any conditions that reduce satisfaction without bringing down expectations. People's expectations might rise because they are exposed to new beliefs about the rewards they are entitled to, or to new information about the gains that other groups have made. Even if their situation remains stable or is improving, people may feel deprived if other comparable groups begin to pull ahead of them. Any events that raise the standards of justice or of fair treatment in a group can provoke feelings of relative deprivation. In this view, the greater the gap between these new expectations and the lagging achievements, the greater the frustration and the more intense the rebellion.

The concept of relative deprivation is central to an approach that emphasizes perceived institutional deficiencies as the source of social-movement discontent (Clark, Grayson, and Grayson 1975). In this approach, a large gap between the way people expect to be treated and the way they really are treated provokes dissatisfaction because it exposes the gaps between ideal and real institutional practices in society. When institutions fail to measure up to people's expectations and standards of fairness, the resulting dissatisfaction provokes feelings of restlessness and the urge to do something to change the offending situation. For instance, the discontent behind the youth movement of the 1960s has been attributed to the clash between young people's new expectations of personal freedom rooted in liberalized child-rearing practices, and the personal restrictions that young people faced in increasingly bureaucratized universities and work settings (Clark, Grayson, and Grayson 1975; Westhues 1975). The frustration of holding do-your-own-thing ideals in live-by-the-book institutions sparked a sense of relative deprivation, and hence the youth revolt. Whether the frustrating gap results from a sudden deterioration of treatment or the growth of new expectations, or both, the greater the gap between ideal and real institutional practices, the greater the perceived unfairness and the likelihood of a social movement.

## Absolute versus Relative Deprivation

The debate over the relative or absolute nature of the deprivations most likely to spark social movements has raged on in the research literature for years.

While the concept of relative deprivation is based on social-psychological principles, attempts to measure it have focused on group rather than individual characteristics and on objective rather than subjective measures of treatment. Gurr (1970) uses such indicators as employment rates, drops in production, increased taxes, and loss of income status to approximate subjective evaluations of expectations and achievements. A case could be made for absolute deprivation as much as for relative deprivation in many of the situations studied. For instance, relative deprivation theory has commonly been used to explain the emergence of the civil rights movement and of race riots in the United States (Morgan and Clark 1973). Can we say that the source of racial discontent was relative deprivation because blacks' expectations of equality with whites grew much faster than the actual improvements in their life conditions in the

1960s? Or can we say that the racial discontent was based on real incidences of discrimination and absolute, structurally based inequalities? Data on educational and income levels, housing conditions, and residential segregation have been used to argue both sides of this case (Marx and Wood 1975).

Much of the choice of interpretation depends on whether the analyst sees protest action as a means of releasing pent-up frustrations — the relative deprivation perspective — or as a means of combating real conflicts of interest and structural disadvantages — the absolute deprivation perspective. The tendency among social movement analysts has been to adopt the absolute deprivation interpretation, especially when serious inequalities are involved (Marx and Wood 1975). Many analysts reserve the notion of relative deprivation for the unfulfilled ideals that give rise to social movements not based on obvious material disadvantages — for example, certain lifestyle movements such as the "Moonies" and other religious cults. Whether the interpretation stresses the absolute or relative aspect of discontent, research findings offer little support for the direct frustration/aggression link that the relative deprivation approach has advanced (Marx and Wood 1975). Currently, those who retain the relative deprivation concept use it to pinpoint sources of dissatisfaction but not to fully explain the appearance or intensity of rebellions (Clark, Grayson, and Grayson 1975).

# Resource Mobilization

## Commonplace Conflicts

The currently dominant approach to the study of social movements does not concentrate on absolute, relative, or any other kind of deprivation to explain collective action. Instead, it focuses on the ways in which personal, organizational, and political resources encourage people to take group action for social change. This is not because conflicts over the good things in life are not considered central to society. Rather, conflicts and discontent are thought to be so common to so-

**Highly integrated groups may generate social movements because they so thoroughly blend their members' individual and group interests.**

ciety's institutions that knowing why people are dissatisfied cannot tell us what, if anything, they are going to do about it. How can a severe disadvantage directly explain why one group unites to protest for social change, when other equally disadvantaged or dissatisfied groups suffer in silence? As Oberschall (1973) explains,

*At any given moment, there exists a certain distribution of scarce resources and of rewards — the good things desired and sought after by most, such as wealth, power, and prestige — among the individuals, groups, and classes in a society. Some are better off, and others are worse off. Those who are favored have a vested interest in conserving and consolidating their existing share; those who are negatively privileged seek to increase theirs, either individually or collectively.*

Not only are serious disadvantages not enough to explain the appearance of social movements, they are not even necessary. The dissatisfaction behind social movements is based on any group's desire to keep or to get more of the good things in life, whether they are privileged or underprivileged. Dissatisfaction is widespread in society because of the conflicts over rewards that drive social life. Since as Oberschall (1973) says, the good things in life are in short supply, those who have wealth, prestige, and the power to control their life circumstances want to keep those advantages and get more, while the disadvantaged want a greater share. When the privileged fail to get what they want through the well-institutionalized means that usually work for them, they are likely to be dissatisfied and desire a social change that would benefit them. Although the truly disadvantaged

## Selling Spiritual Revival

*Not only Christian fundamentalist movements have become big business in our affluent society. Other spiritual movements have successfully commercialized their ideals, to the benefit of their celebrity-status leaders. The New Age phenomenon is one example of successful movement-marketing to highly educated, upwardly mobile North Americans.*

Shirley MacLaine, the actress who has become the high priestess of the paranormal, is said to be flying to Lake Baikal in the Soviet Union this weekend to greet the dawning of a "new age on earth."

This is good news for the world weary who may well think that a new age is way overdue. But for those who do not share Ms MacLaine's formidable past — she claims to have been a brothel madam in San Fransisco, a citizen of the late continent of Atlantis and her own daughter's daughter, all in previous lives — this country's new spiritualism takes some keeping up with.

Despite skepticism, however, thousands of believers will be heading for various "power spots" around the world this weekend to ring out the old age and ring in the new. This mystical pilgrimage is particularly popular in the West, where the occult is big enough business to have enriched its advocates. Ms MacLaine has made a fortune from her bestselling books on her occult adventures, and a five-hour television series earlier this year in which she joined the space age in an

"out of body experience," or OBE, for what appeared to be a trip to the moon.

The excitement is to peak on Sunday, the day of "harmonic convergence" when the earth changes its "time beam" and enters the last 25 years of a 5,000-year cycle. New Age devotees claim this is a long-held belief of Mayan, Aztec and Hopi Indians, who believe the sun and earth have been passing through a galactic beam that has formed human history. When the end of the beam is reached in 2012, there will be a great "moment of transformation," according to *The Mayan Factor*, a popular book by Jose Arguelles, of Boulder, Colo.

Mr. Arguelles — who has popularized the New Age but has yet to make as much money from it as Ms MacLaine — forecasts that as the New Age approaches, "sensitive" people

are in a position to have a chronic and wide-ranging desire for social change, they are not the only dissatisfied people in society. In an affluent, "have-it-all" society such as ours, any want can become a need, and difficulties in fulfilling that need can be defined as a social problem. The current spate of upper-income movements to achieve the perfect body or the New Age of psychic harmony show that the potential for dissatisfaction is almost infinite, whether based on deprivations or on high aspirations.

Although dissatisfaction is commonplace in society, discontented people are likely to form social movements only when it seems likely that they can improve their situation by acting together. Discontent is common, yet social movements come and go, many grievances are never aired, and the social movements that do surface do not always arise when dissatisfaction is at its worst. If there were a direct link between discontent and social movement formation, wouldn't we have seen a major youth movement in the early 1980s, when expectations for affluence were still high but job

opportunities were rapidly shrinking due to the economic recession? It is not likely that young people felt less frustrated or worried about their future in the 1980s than in the 1960s. Rather, it seems likely that it was much more risky for young people to challenge the established order in the setting of the 1980s with its limited opportunities than in the setting of the 1960s with its growing wealth and job opportunities.

Even many severely disadvantaged groups do not rebel, because they feel powerless to change their situation through collective action (Tilly 1978). Poverty-stricken peasants may endure the most demeaning living conditions until leaders emerge who can afford the costs of organizing their cause, until outside sympathizers pour resources into their cause, or until some event weakens the authorities' ability to punish them for rebellion. Discontented groups are sensitive to the costs and probable benefits of collective action. If the group does not have the organizational resources needed to mount a collective challenge for change, or if such a challenge stands little chance of success,

may feel disoriented and have "déjà vu" experiences. They will also see flying saucers and notice strange coincidences.

Through popular works such as the MacLaine books, what was an esoteric cult has become a mass following. A recent survey published in the scientific magazine American Health reported that belief in reincarnation, clairvoyance and OBES is a fast-growing phenomenon, especially among educated people.

Fully 42 percent of Americans believe they have had contact with someone already dead, according to Father Andrew Greeley, a sociologist and priest who conducted another survey at the University of Chicago. "If these experiences were signs of a mental illness," he says, "our numbers would show that the USA is going nuts."

Various theories abound for the mounting interest in the supernatural. Most popular is the approaching millenium, a portentous date at which people believe something *must* happen beyond just a change in the calendar. Others philosophize about dissatisfaction with material prosperity and unease with encroaching technology. Unmitigated cynics say it's just easy money.

Despite the scorn of skeptics, and satire from popular Doonesbury cartoonist Garry Trudeau, an estimated tens of thousands will converge in California at such "power spots" as Mount Shasta (4,200 metres high) and Mount Tamalpais near San Fransisco. Other sites are in New Mexico, Arizona, the Black Hills of Dakota, Haleakala volcano in Hawaii, the Great Pyramid in Egypt and the Aztec ruins of Machu Picchu in Peru.

In the small town of Mount Shasta, every motel room has been booked for weeks and nearby campgrounds are full. Local people are slightly nervous about the influx of super-spiritualists and hope they will not levitate too much and frighten the horses.

Jeff Daly, a California lawyer, is promoting the festivities through a group called Global Family, and says he has been receiving 200 telephone inquiries daily. But he has assurance for those with no bookings: "All you have to do is sit on Mother Earth and open your heart. You can do it any place."

Meanwhile, at the tribal offices of the Hopi in Arizona, no "convergence" ceremony is planned. "It's nothing to do with us," said a weary Hopi official. "They've got it all wrong."

**Source:**
Christopher Reed, *The Globe and Mail*, August 14, 1987.

no social movement is likely to appear — whatever the level of discontent. When collective action is too costly or hopeless a pursuit, individuals look for personal means of coping or escaping; they look for individual rather than collective solutions to their problems.

According to the currently dominant resource-based approach, it is not frustration or the absence of dissatisfaction but the high cost of organizing an effective response to problems that is most likely to inhibit social movement formation.

## Discontent or Resources?

There is considerable research evidence to support the thesis of an indirect link between discontent and social movement involvement. Pinard (1971) found that although the poor were the most discontented Quebecers, they were the least likely of all dissatisfied groups to support Quebec's Social Credit movement. As in many other protest movements, the poor were late joiners, giving support only after the backing of better-off farmers and workers had made the party a viable political force. Likewise, Lipset (1968) found that Saskatchewan's CCF movement was not built on the support of the poorest farmers, even though they were the most exposed to the economic reversals of the 1930s depression. The protest action was initiated by the farmers with the highest incomes and status; the poorest joined in large numbers only after the depression had passed. A review of research findings shows that it is frequently not the most discontented, but those among the discontented who can best afford the risks of collective action who tend to launch protest movements (Jenkins 1981). Peasants who have independent land rights are more likely to rebel in defence of their interests than are peasants who are highly dependent on the favour of large landlords (Wolf 1969). Ghetto residents with jobs and strong neighbourhood links were more likely than the unemployed and socially isolated to take part in the riots of the 1960s (Feagin and Hahn 1973). These are only part of a long list of cases in which it was the dissatisfied having the highest level of resources — not those having the highest degree of absolute or relative deprivation — who initiated collective action.

An even less direct link between discontent and social movement formation has been found in other studies. Examining the characteristics of cities that did and those that did not experience race riots in the 1960s, Spilerman (1976) found no relationship between levels of black deprivation, either absolute or relative, and the incidence or severity of rioting. The cities with high black unemployment rates, dilapidated housing conditions, and large gaps between black and white income levels were not more likely to have had outbreaks of rioting than others. Two factors were highly related to rioting: the riot cities were most likely to be those with the largest black populations and those located outside the South. It was in cities where the black population was large enough to have some political impact that riots to end discriminatory practices were most evident. In the southern United States rioting was discouraged by the severe punishment that usually met black dissidence — a reflection of blacks' severe lack of political resources. Riots emerged mainly in those cities where disorderly tactics could work — where riots stood a chance of getting results other than all-out repression.

While the American riot studies show the central importance of political resources, other studies have shown the importance of organizational resources for social movements. A review of industrial violence over a 130-year period in France found that growing social ties and organizational links among industrial workers were much more directly related to protest action than were economic downturns or income losses (Snyder and Tilly 1972).

There is, then, much evidence that changing levels of discontent are too indirectly related to episodes of collective action to explain movement formation. Even so, most analysts who find that conflicting interests and dissatisfaction are so pervasive that they cannot be the decisive factors do give discontent at least a secondary role in social movement formation. Many hold that social movements are more likely to be sparked by direct threats to a group's interests than simply by aspirations for a greater share of society's rewards (Oberschall 1973; Tilly 1978). Events such as changes in policies or practices that threaten a loss of rewards, that create obvious barriers to achievement, or that directly confront ideals frequently — but not necessarily — give rise to social movements. Other analysts maintain that no widespread sense of grievance or threat need precede a social movement at all (McCarthy and Zald 1973). Rather, the feeling of discontent is often spread by the movement itself, initiated by only a handful of leaders. This has been found to be the case of the environmental movement, which started with a few natural scientists and policy researchers who used the media to spread awareness and a sense that pollution is a social problem (Wood 1982). Until then, pollution had been only of vague concern to the general public, not a matter of widespread discontent.

Those who downplay the role of discontent stress that sharing an interest in social change is no guarantee that people will act together to bring about change. Wanting social change is not enough. Taking collective action requires a lot of resources. It requires time, money, expertise, leadership, and a host of other resources to mount the kind of challenge that can compel society to accept change. Before an assortment of concerned people can act together, they have to put a lot of effort into getting enough resources under the group's control to challenge their opponents. This process of attracting, co-ordinating, and applying resources toward a common goal is called **resource mobilization**. In the resource mobilization approach, a group's capacity to act together and its chances of making gains through group action are seen as the most decisive factors in social movement formation. If group action for change seems likely to provoke more costs than benefits, no social movement will emerge. This focus on organizational and political resources affects the choice of research questions that are considered important. Rather than ask why people are dissatisfied, the resource mobilization analyst asks: What chance do these people have of organizing a collective demand for change? What makes them think that a collective challenge can overcome the opposition to change? The answers lie in the group's access to resources that could lower the costs of organizing an effective solution to problems.

**Social movements are said to be noninstitutionalized because their interests are not met through the routine operation of society's institutions and conventions.**

## The Obstacles to Mobilization

The very nature of their desire for social change poses a mobilization dilemma for social movements. Demands for change in any of society's institutions are likely to be resisted by those individuals or groups who benefit from existing arrangements. Groups advocating change start with few established means of influence, but they face opponents who have low-cost, institutionalized means of defending their position. Demands for change challenge the position of groups whose interests are recognized as legitimate, who have ready access to decision-makers, and whose rights are enforced by society. For instance, when anti-nuclear activists picket a nuclear plant, the owners and the members of the population who fa-

vour nuclear power do not have to come out in force to prevent a blockade. Their rights are protected by law, law enforcement agencies bear the cost of keeping the demonstration under control, and the state bears the cost of prosecuting disorderly protesters. But the movement has to directly bear the costs of its ongoing organization, the demonstration, and its activists' legal defence. Since its goals are not institutionally protected as rights, the anti-nuclear movement has to meet the full costs of pursuing its goals. Moreover, the pro-nuclear interests are recognized by governments and large segments of the population as the legitimate ones. Movement demands that seem illegitimate risk hardening opposition and alienating public opinion, rather than raising the awareness and sympathy needed to build support for the cause. Since movements do not have routine recognition or support, they face serious obstacles to meeting the full cost of pursuing change. However, their opponents' resources to resist change are usually formidable and well-institutionalized.

It is not only the high costs imposed by external opponents that create a mobilization dilemma for social movements. Movements also face an internal mobilization dilemma, stemming from the collective nature of the good that a movement pursues. Unlike a private good, which exclusively benefits a particular person, a **collective good** benefits all members of a group or social category, whether or not they contribute to gaining it (Olson 1965). If an anti-pollution movement wins an end to acid rain, everyone benefits from the resulting clean environment, not only the people who took part in the movement.

It is difficult to mobilize support for a collective good because it is not always in a person's immediate individual interest to invest in such a group interest. Investing in a social movement entails opportunity costs — committing resources to social change means giving up leisure, career, or other personal opportunities to which the resources could have been devoted. Social move-

---

## Converting Free Riders

*To overcome the free-rider syndrome, social movements often stress that only a low-cost personal contribution is needed to combat a shared problem that individuals cannot afford to solve on their own, as in this Pollution Probe fund-raising ad.*

Pollution Probe
12 Madison Avenue,
Toronto, Ontario
M5R 2S1

To date, more than 250,000 Canadians have been proven to have had dioxin-tainted tap water in their homes.

Dear Fellow Canadian,

Water — *fresh water* — is one of Canada's most precious resources.

Canada is blessed with at least one-fifth of the world's supply of fresh water. We're the envy of other countries where fresh water is scarce . . . where safe, clean water supplies don't exist.

So Canadians are going to look very foolish when we let our fresh water become so poisoned we can't even drink it. And that day isn't far off. In the past few years:

- A major spill of highly hazardous PCBs threatened Regina's water.
- In Windsor and Sarnia, a form of dioxin was found in the tap water.
- High levels of dozens of cancer-causing chemicals were found in Edmonton's drinking water.
- 34 wells supplying 200 families in the community of Fairvale, New Brunswick, were condemned when high concentrations of illegally dumped tetrachloroethylene (a dry cleaning fluid) were found in them.
- In Fredericton, New Brunswick, a municipal well was closed in 1986 when percholoroethylene (a dry-cleaning solvent) was found to be above safe levels.

*We are drinking chemical stew.*

You don't just have to swallow all of this and wait to see what happens. You can help Pollution Probe fight for safer drinking water. A Safe Drinking Water Act for Canada is badly needed. There are no laws setting drinking-water standards in Canada. We have guidelines . . . but they ignore most chemical pollutants . . . governments are not required to meet them . . . and the public has no legal rights.

It is not practical for every Canadian to test their own drinking water or install their own home water treatment units. The most practical and cost-effective solution is for Canada to follow the lead of other nations and install more effective water treatment equipment. Only action by informed citizens like yourself and outspoken and knowledgeable groups like *Pollution Probe* can improve the quality of our drinking water. Please send your donation to *Pollution Probe* today!

Add your voice to the thousands of Canadians who are demanding a Safe Drinking Water Act. And, to help Pollution Probe confront polluters and lax government and carry on the fight for clean water, send your donation in the postage-paid envelope [we've] enclosed.

Pollution Probe's record of success in environmental research and advocacy is based upon the expertise of its internationally acclaimed professional staff. . . plus the advice and guidance of eminent scientific advisors.

Thousands of individual Canadians and hundreds of Canadian corporations make annual financial contributions to support the Pollution Probe team.

*Your tax-deductible donation of $25, $35 or even $50 will allow us to carry on this important work.*

**Source:**

Direct-mail materials circulated by Pollution Probe in the autumn of 1987.

ments also entail direct participation costs — for example, the time involved in attending numerous meetings, and the risk of arrest or of being branded a troublemaker — that few people are anxious to bear. Since the benefits of social change will be shared by everyone anyway, individuals have an interest in letting others take on the major costs of procuring that change. For instance, the socially concerned student who spends three years getting a degree and a job benefits as much from a clean environment as the dropout who spends most of that time successfully agitating for the clean-up of a hazardous-waste dump. Those who benefit from a collective good without contributing to it are called **free riders**. Free riders get the best of both worlds. Others pay to improve their group position, while they pour all of their own resources into personal advancement. This tension between a person's individual and collective interests leads to the familiar cry, "Why doesn't somebody do something about it? (But don't look at me — I'm too busy)".

The tension between individual and group interests has another dimension. An individual has no reason to make sacrifices for a collective cause, if that person's efforts do not seem to make a noticeable difference to advancing the cause. In a classic example involving economics, Olson (1965) argued that an individual would not be likely to cut personal spending to bring down inflation, since one such effort would not appear to have much impact on the overall economic situation. Still less would an individual be expected to volunteer for a pay cut to fight inflation, for the good of all. People ask, "Why should I be the one to pay? What harm could my little raise do anyway?"

This logic also applies to social movements. Few people have an interest in increasing the level of lead pollution in the environment. But individuals have difficulty seeing how their own switch to lead-free gasoline would improve the overall pollution problem. They themselves would pay more for gas, and that one gesture is not going to end pollution. Their single contribution seems to be an insignificant drop in the bucket. An individual's sacrifice is even less likely to seem worthwhile if people have no reason to expect that enough others would make a similar sacrifice to solve their shared problem. Why should one person pay the cost of pursuing change, if others

who would benefit are not going to do likewise? Since one individual cannot possibly pay the full cost of a collective good, a personal contribution may easily seem to be insignificant or useless.

With the combined effects of the free-rider syndrome, the individuals' tendency to downplay their impact on group problems, and the high costs imposed by opponents, it is not surprising that many deprived groups never overcome mobilization obstacles to form social movements. People can be expected to invest in collective action only when the personal costs involved are lower than the value of the benefits that collective action is likely to bring them. This cost/benefit reasoning explains why the better-off members of dissatisfied groups are frequently the ones who launch social movements; an investment in collective action is less of a sacrifice for them than for the deprived (Fitzsimmons-LeCavalier 1983). Individuals who have lots of resources — money, free time, organizational experience, and respectability — can afford to take risks for potential gains. The very deprived, on the other hand, have few resources that are not devoted to survival needs. They are not only powerless but nearly resourceless; for them, the costs of collective action are enormous. Benefits have to be tangible and almost assured before the deprived can afford to take risks to gain them.

## Selective Incentives

Simply having a lot of resources does not guarantee that a person will invest in collective action. The better off people are, the more they can afford individual solutions to their problems, or individual escape. Well-off people are not likely to be more inclined than anyone else to bear the costs of pursuing a collective good when their own personal share of the good may be slight. They are as likely as anyone else to engage in free-ride behaviour and to downplay their personal responsibility for group problems.

Highly institutionalized groups that pursue a collective good have found a solution to attracting such individuals' resources. They provide **selective incentives**, personal rewards that are only available to people who contribute to the collective cause, not to free riders (Olson 1965; McCarthy and Zald 1973; Oberschall 1973).

For instance, professional associations that lobby for the interests of a whole occupational group provide such personal benefits as professional journals, conventions at reduced travel rates, certification, and other career enhancements only to those who pay their membership dues. All scientists benefit from their professional association's lobbying, but only paid-up members get to present their research findings at the association's meetings, an important step in career advancement. Political parties hold out the promise of patronage appointments and other political plums to those who contribute heavily to building and maintaining the party, particularly to those who remain loyal in the party's years out of power. Providing such separate, personal incentives is one of the chief means that organizations use to assure that individuals contribute to group efforts. If only a few people are going to pay for the whole group's benefit, they will probably ask "What's in in for me?" The more personal resources they put into the group, the more personal payoffs they will need in return.

While some organizations offer personal inducements for participation, others offer selective sanctions for nonparticipation, that is, penalties only for those individuals who do not contribute to the collective cause. Governments do not rely on the population's interest in collective goods, such as top-quality hospitals, to inspire voluntary tax payments. Governments use compulsory taxation. They apply fines and penalties to individuals who do not contribute their assigned share to collective goals. Discontented groups may have to do the same thing to build a social movement.

Social movements can solve their mobilization problems by giving activists selective incentives. But they are seldom in a position to hand out the kind of material inducements or punishments that institutionalized groups use to assure participation. Their very nature — nonroutine and unconventional — means that movements would have to mobilize a lot of voluntary resources before they could hope to maintain support through material payoffs or coercion. At the same time, their mobilization costs are higher than those of other voluntary groups, because of the opposition provoked by the movements' challenge to the status quo. Luckily for social movements, there are social conditions that can help overcome these serious obstacles to mobilization.

## Organizational Resources

Social movements escape heavy mobilization costs if they can avoid building their organizations from scratch. In fact, discontented groups that manage to mobilize something more than sporadic, short-term protests are usually built on resources transferred from established organizations. Recruiting support for a challenging group on an individual-to-individual basis is extremely costly and forbidding. But **bloc recruitment**, the attraction of groups of people who have already existing links and means of co-ordinating their actions, makes collective action much more affordable. If people experiencing a new problem already have ways of pooling their resources, there is a strong chance that they will pursue a collective solution to that problem.

Pre-established links reduce the costs of collective action in several ways. If the people facing a threat have a long-lasting shared identity, the individuals involved are more likely to feel that the group problem is their problem and contribute accordingly. Thus a television show that is seen as an insult to a distinct ethnic community is more likely to elicit strong protest than is a show that insults the random set of viewers opposed to the recreational use of drugs like marijuana. Anonymous viewers have little basis for developing a sense that they share a problem with the random collection of others who are also offended by a program. In many longstanding ethnic communities, however, a person's fate is habitually identified with the group's fate. When people share such a strong group identity, individuals are more inclined to act in a group-oriented way.

People are even more likely to act in a group-oriented way, if they are tied together by shared networks of communication and friendship (Tilly 1978). When individuals are already linked by shared beliefs and information networks, these channels of communication offer an easy means of spreading the consciousness of new threats. In addition, when people are already linked by friendship networks of exchanged favours and duties, these channels of co-operation offer a low-cost means of pulling individuals into the fight for group goals. Building on existing channels of communication and co-operation is one of the main means social movements use to overcome the obstacles to mobilization.

Numerous studies have shown the mobilizing effect of established information and friendship networks. Pinard (1971) found that in Quebec, the discontented farmers and workers who met other similarly discontented individuals socially, were highly likely to know about and support the Social Credit movement. The most socially active discontented were early joiners and strong supporters of the cause, while the socially isolated gave little support. In Alberta, Social Credit support rapidly spread through the rural areas among the religious followers of William Aberhart; Aberhart's Calgary-based radio sermons were enormously popular in the 1920s, having an estimated 200 000 to 300 000 prairie listeners. When he used his radio show to spread the Social Credit solution to economic problems during the depression, Aberhart's religious followers gave their strong support to his political cause (Irving 1959). In both the Alberta and Quebec cases, the new political movement spread along the lines of established social networks — clear instances of bloc recruitment.

But the strongest incentive to collective action comes when a threatened group has existing formal organizational links. If there are already a large number of associations within a group facing a new social problem, there will also be a ready supply of leaders having both the experience and organizational backing needed to defend the group. The presence of community, voluntary, political, and occupational associations means there are also likely to be a lot of individuals whose personal resources are already openly committed to the group (Obershall 1973). These associations offer more powerful channels for pooling and applying a diversity of group resources than informal friendship networks do. When pre-established leaders, participants, and associations throw their support behind efforts for social change, a movement's mobilization costs are dramatically reduced. Recruiting five associations with leaders, staff, offices, and 1000 members each can mobilize a social movement much more rapidly than spending the same amount of time recruiting five individuals.

Pinard (1971) found that membership in farmers' groups or labour unions had an even stronger effect than involvement in friendship networks had on support for Quebec's Social Credit movement. While socially active, discontented individuals were more likely to support the movement, participants in farm and labour associations gave strong support to the movement, whether they personally felt discontented or not. The leaders of the local farm and labour associations had adopted the Social Credit solutions to the widespread economic problems in rural Quebec. In turn, the participants in these committed associations backed and voted for the movement even if they themselves did not suffer from the economic problems, another obvious case of bloc recruitment.

Likewise, Lipset's (1968) study of Saskatchewan shows that the first major backers of the CCF's protest platform were the already established leaders of the province's many consumer and marketing co-operatives. These co-operatives had been set up in order to eliminate farmers' dependence on brokers and on unstable prices. It has been estimated, that on the average, each Saskatchewan farmer was a member of as many as four or five such co-operatives. In addition, the rural areas had a dense network of voluntary associations offering the social, health, and other community services otherwise only available in distant cities. The active participants in these co-operatives and community associations gave early and strong backing to their leaders' sponsorship of CCF protest. The membership, meeting places, and other physical and social facilities controlled by the associations were turned to building the protest party. The movement's rapid and extensive mobilization depended heavily on the support these existing organizations made available.

Indeed, Brym (1978) argues that the absence of a similar agrarian protest movement among the equally discontented New Brunswick farmers is a direct result of the lack of pre-established organizational links. In New Brunswick, subsistence rather than commercial farming predominated. Farmers therefore remained socially isolated, having little reason to associate in co-operatives, since they were not involved in outside markets. Attempts to mount protest parties in economic hard times were never very successful. The cost of mobilizing such a socially isolated set of individuals was too high to be sustained, and farmers' protest efforts in that province quickly died out.

## Social Incentives

Established networks and associations are such strong mobilizers because they are in a good position to apply **social incentives** — including social pressure, the threat of lost career contacts, the social pleasure of shared activities with friends — to ensure that individuals recognize their personal interest in supporting the group. In fact, Oberschall (1973) maintains that highly integrated groups, whether held together by informal or associational links, frequently generate social movements because they so thoroughly blend their members' individual group interests. In a highly integrated collectivity, an individual is not free to pursue purely personal interests with no concern for the group.

Leaders of such groups usually have their personal power and status so closely tied to the group's position that they have built-in selective incentives for group defence. Leaders stand to lose more than others if the group's interests suffer, and to gain more than others if the group's position improves. For instance, being the leader of an ethnic community that is losing rights, members, and social standing is not a very rewarding position, either financially or socially. Being the leader of an ethnic community that stands to gain in wealth, membership, or social and political strength is a distinctly rewarding position. The leaders' personal standing is so tied to the group's standing that they can seldom afford to act like free riders and hope that someone else defends the group against new problems.

Once a group's leaders have thrown their personal and associational resources behind a cause, it is not always easy for the members of a cohesive group — a *solidary* group — to ignore that cause. In a highly integrated social structure, a good part of a person's social life, or even livelihood, may depend on maintaining good relations with other group members. Earning approval in the group

means doing your share for group goals — pulling your weight. There can be powerful social pressures for conformity to group ends, as well as sanctions for nonconformity. It is hard to be a free rider when your close friends and colleagues twist your arm to participate in a movement and treat you as disloyal if you do not. For instance, professionals whose clients come mainly from their own ethnic group can feel obliged to donate their skills to that group's causes to avoid a loss of business. But cohesive groups do not only apply such sanctions. They also have strong social incentives to reward participation. It can be a lot of fun to work for a cause you believe in with people you know and like. The social pleasure of shared activities with friends can also be used by cohesive groups, along with the threat of lost social and career contacts, to assure that individuals recognize a personal interest in supporting group interests. The ready supply of resources that already established groups can deliver to a social movement gives such solidary groups a strong mobilization advantage.

## Social Segmentation

Every social movement has to have some kind of organizational base. If it can borrow that base from already existing structures, the movement's mobilization costs will be significantly reduced. But knowing the kind of organization that exists within a group does not tell us how easily that organization can be transferred to dissent and protest. The existence of solidary networks can work either for or against movement formation (Pinard 1971). If group leaders oppose a movement, the same social incentives and sanctions that are frequently used to encourage movement support can be used to suppress it. There is little incentive in speaking out for a movement you personally believe in, if a group you are closely tied to actively resists that cause. To know how available a group's organizations will be for protest, it is important for analysts to know about the group's external links with those opponents who will be challenged by the protest. The more ties that bind a group's leaders and active participants to potential opponents, the less likely it is that the group's organizational base will be made available for challenging action.

For a group to throw resources behind demands for social change, its leaders and associations must be more alienated from than tied to the movement's potential opponents. Studies of the American civil rights movement illustrate this point (Von Eschen, Kirk, and Pinard 1971). While active participants in other social movements and dissident political groups were likely to get involved in the civil rights cause as well, participants in mainstream political parties were not likely to get involved. Active members of established political parties were linked to the reward-and-approval structures of institutions that were threatened by the movement's demands, making the risks of open protest unacceptable to them.

Weak ties between a group and any specific institutional elite may encourage a challenge to that institution. But strong social movements are most likely to be sustained when an aggrieved group has few links and little interaction with any outside group or institutions — when the group's social and economic life is almost totally limited to its own members. A society is said to have high levels of **social segmentation** when there is great social distance and few ties of interdependence between at least two of its groups (Oberschall 1973). The level of social segmentation indicates how tied to or cut off from one another groups are. Under conditions of extreme segmentation, social groups may be so segregated that they constitute almost complete mini-societies, each with control of a wide range of institutions, linked only by a few overreaching political and economic structures. The more segmented a social group is, the more cut off its leaders and active participants will be from outside opponents' reward-and-approval structures. Consequently, highly segmented social arrangements encourage a sense of alienation from outside groups and make affordable the risks involved in challenging the interests of a powerful outside opponent.

## External Breaks, Internal Bonds

It is possible to get a fairly accurate idea of the groups most likely to engage in ongoing protest by examining the nature of the social breaks between groups and the social bonds within them. In Canada, provinces have only weak links to one another and a great deal of independent control over their own institutions. The food- and resource-producing regions — such as Alberta and Saskatchewan — have few direct co-operative links with the more industrialized regions. Quebec is even more segmented than other provinces and regions. Its extensive set of francophone social networks and institutions add language barriers to the already weak links between provinces. This combination of weak external ties and extensive internal organization gives the provinces, regions, and francophone Quebec a high capacity to mobilize against threats to their separate interests (Clark, Grayson, and Grayson 1975). Not surprisingly, matters of provincial control, regional development, and Quebec autonomy have been the central and recurrent themes of Canada's major political protest movements.

Other groups also have weak ties to outsiders; for instance, Canada's native peoples are highly segmented from non-natives. However, the native peoples are divided internally by language, by different band identities, and by cultures. In addition, they have little independent control over the valuable organizational resources needed to mobilize a social movement since their funding is so dependent on the federal government, which is also their chief adversary. Consequently, native peoples do not have readily available, low-cost means of maintaining a movement organization. Because of this organizational difficulty, native protest throughout the 1960s and 1970s was sporadic, even though native grievances have been serious and chronic (Ponting and Gibbins 1980). In the 1980s, native protesters have turned their modest resources to gaining media coverage, a move that has raised their profile but not, to any great extent, their payoffs (Ponting 1986b). It is only when a group's independence from opponents is combined with extensive internal organization that the capacity to act collectively for social change is high.

Driedger's (1986) study of a Saskatchewan Mennonite community's successful movement to block the building of an Eldorado Nuclear Ltd. plant shows that another structural factor can further heighten a segmented group's mobilization potential. This community's leaders had a high level of segmentation, since they were both independent from their pro-nuclear opponents and central to their own group's strong network of traditional ties. But in addition, these leaders had developed an extensive network of ties to outside sympathizers such as politicians, academics, and other religious and pacifist group leaders, whose resources could be counted on to defend the Mennonite's cause. When deep external breaks with opponents and strong internal bonds are coupled with such established links to powerful potential allies, the chances that a discontented group will form a social movement are extremely high.

Breton (1978) maintains that the pattern of links between and within ethnic groups not only affects their capacity to act collectively, it also affects the kind of issues that will generate ethnic conflict. When ethnic groups are tightly organized internally and independent from one another, this segmented situation will raise conflict over collective rights, group representation, and the defence of each group's own set of institutions. On the other hand, when ethnic groups already share a lot of social links and common institutions, conflict will revolve around individual civil rights and equal opportunities for ethnic individuals' advancement in an integrated society. This prediction quite accurately reflects the emphasis on demands for individual rights and equal integration made by most of Canada's ethnic groups, and the demands for collective rights and further institutional autonomy made by the independence movement in highly segmented Quebec (Morris and Lanphier 1977).

The Quebec independence movement provides an interesting example of how segmentation affects support for a cause. Francophone Quebec is segmented from anglophone Canada, but it is not completely segmented. There are still enough ties between the two segments that most Quebecers have to balance two often conflicting interests: their interest in increased cultural autonomy to protect their French-speaking society against their interest in a profitable economic link with Canada. The concern for French-language protection and promotion is widespread in Quebec but, for most Quebecers, it leads to support for milder reforms than full-fledged independence because of their economic concerns. It has been noted that only the very highly segmented — those whose economic and cultural interests both stand to benefit from greater Quebec autonomy — tend to fully support the independence option. Guindon (1975) first attributed independence support to the francophone new middle class, the growing group of white-collar, salaried workers who emerged in the 1960s, as distinct from the traditionally self-employed middle class. Given the barriers against francophone advancement in the anglophone companies that dominated the private sector, he concluded that the interests of this new salaried middle class lay in expanding the job opportunities in Quebec's francophone public sector, a major thrust of the independence movement. According to the new-middle-class thesis, the chief independence supporters would be the white-collar employees of Quebec's state bureaucracies, because they stood to profit more than any other Quebecers from the state's increased power and resources (McRoberts and Posgate 1980).

Research results give some support to the new-middle-class thesis, although it is only now in the process of being tested. Cuneo and Curtis (1974) found that in 1968, support for independence was not high in any occupational group, but it was highest among professionals — that part of the francophone middle class least likely to have links with anglophone institutions. However, many of these professionals were in the private sector or were self-employed and therefore cannot be considered state bureaucrats. Turning to the 1980 referendum, the data concern the softer sovereignty-association option, which involves Quebec's political independence combined with an unspecified economic link to Canada. Prereferendum polls showed that while 45 percent of francophones intended to vote "yes" in favour of giving the Quebec government a mandate to negotiate sovereignty association, only 25 percent did so out of support for sovereignty association as such. The others aimed to vote a tactical "yes," hoping to strengthen Quebec's bargaining position in order to gain moderate reforms from the federal government. Like the majority of voters, they favoured the compromise option of renewed federalism, which decentralized more cultural and social powers to Quebec but left existing political and economic arrangements largely intact (Pinard and Hamilton 1984).

Strong support for sovereignty association came not from the francophone middle class as a whole but from the intellectuals — professors, teachers, scientists, artists, journalists, writers, and others whose jobs are concerned with the creation or transmission of knowledge and culture. Almost half the francophone intellectuals supported the sovereignty option, while just over one-third of other professionals, technicians, and clerical workers did. But only one-fifth of francophone managers and owners supported sovereignty. These managers, the largest section of the middle class, were no more likely than blue-collar workers or farmers to be in favour of sovereignty association (Pinard and Hamilton 1984). The large gaps between the intellectuals', professionals', and managers' support for sovereignty suggest that something more complex than simply state versus private employment has an influence on the sovereignist leanings of the middle class.

There is strong evidence for a more specific type of segmentation effect on independence outlooks. Most francophone Quebecers' cultural concerns did lead them to favour changes in the federal system, as illustrated by the poll finding that only 12 percent wanted the maintenance of the federal status quo. However, most also found sovereignty association too risky and instead opted for more moderate reforms to strengthen Quebec's autonomy. It was the francophone intellectuals, the elite of Quebec's cultural institutions — those whose economic interests were most closely tied to Quebec's separate francophone institutions and most cut off from anglophone control — who were the strongest supporters of the sovereignty option. This strong support is further demonstrated by the fact that, while the Parti Québécois was in power, over half of its elected representatives and two-thirds of its cabinet ministers were intellectuals (Pinard and Hamilton 1984). As segmentation theory suggests, those who had the weakest ties to outside opponents and the strongest ties to the group's own organizations were the most heavily involved in the challenging action.

## Opportunities for Success

As we have noted, the resource mobilization approach holds that social movements will emerge when the costs of pursuing challenging action are lower than the gains to be made through that action. No matter what kind of organizational base it has, a group is not likely to push collective demands for change if those demands provoke nothing but heavy losses. It is important, then, that groups seeking social change have reason to believe that their opponents are vulnerable to col-

lective action. Since the state is the main target and mediator for such demands, this usually means that the polity must be vulnerable to the movement's pressure tactics (Tilly 1978). Before engaging in collective action, people ask "What good will it do?" In that sense, social movements are directly dependent on expectations, but not the expectations that relative deprivation theorists think would increase frustration and discontent. Rather, it is the expectation that the movement will be a success — that it really will make a difference in overcoming their problems — that incites group leaders and members to participate in a social movement.

Much of the expectation of success depends on past political and movement experiences. Through their own experiences and those of others who have challenged the system, people build up a repertoire of social change tactics that worked or were acceptable in the past. Social movement success breeds other social movements. Social movement failure breeds hopelessness and demobilization. But expectations of success also depend on the existing balance of power between challengers and their opponents. Social movements have to pursue change through nonroutine tactics precisely because their concerns are not being taken seriously by decison-makers in crucial institutions. Movements have to find innovative means of exerting pressure because they do not have easy access to the conventional channels that influence the decisions made by institutional leaders.

Since a movement's demands for social change are likely to be opposed by groups who do have institutionalized power, there is no guarantee that authorities will always be vulnerable to pressure tactics that worked in the past or that worked elsewhere. For instance, a government slipping in popularity could be very vulnerable to movement efforts to gain public support for social change. A newly elected government with a strong majority would be much less vulnerable to such appeals. In times of fiscal restraint and government cutbacks, a social agency would be less likely to give in to protesters' demands than in times of expanding social programs when there is money available to experiment with solutions. The expectancy of success then, is shaped by the response that social movement action seems likely to draw from the targeted authorities.

Turner and Killian (1972) maintain that there are essentially three types of collective tactics a social movement can adopt: persuasive, bargaining, and coercive. *Persuasive tactics* rely on the authorities holding certain values that can be activated in favour of the movement's goals. Any group whose demands for social change represent a major challenge to established interests is not likely to achieve success by persuasion alone. *Bargaining tactics* rely on having something valuable to trade with authorities, such as votes or a potential impact on their reputations. Bargaining can depend on getting broad public support, or at least the support of some powerful sector that is important to authorities.

**Coercive tactics** depend on the symbolic or actual disruption of institutional life in order to bring compliance with group demands. Most coercive tactics, such as marches, demonstrations, or sit-ins, are designed to cause only minor, nonviolent upsets to routine. They are aimed at gaining public attention and sympathy, or at showing the movement's already considerable support in order to build bargaining power. Other coercive tactics are more directly disruptive: for instance, Greenpeace attempted to stop, rather than merely protest, the seal hunt by chasing seal herds away from the hunt site or by putting coloured marks on baby seals to reduce the value of their fur. Highly coercive tactics, such as threatened violence, rioting, or terrorist tactics, depend on directly inflicting damage in order to force a response from authorities. Highly coercive tactics are extremely risky, in terms of both the repression and the backlash they can provoke. In many circumstances, violence raises the risks of movement participation without increasing the likelihood of success; violent protest is not often adopted by social movements. But, as the many hijackings, hostage-takings and terrorist bombings show, if violent or illegal acts promise to get results with few risks for those involved, they may become attractive means of dissent.

Even though most movements purposely avoid violent protest, most do use some kind of coercive strategy in their efforts to overcome the opposition to their demands. In Western democracies, a protocol of protest has evolved that tolerates the orderly, disciplined expression of discontent (Oberschall 1973; Tilly 1978). Demonstrations that follow this protocol inflict mainly symbolic disruption. But the officially tolerated protest tactics are not cheap — they call for a high level of organizational resources, negotiating skills, and "showbiz" skills if the media are to be interested in transmitting the movement message. And even standard protest action can turn to violence, making movement activity much more risky and costly.

We can illustrate that protest is a dynamic process — and one that depends as much on the authorities' as on the movement's actions — from a study of four Canadian protest efforts that ended in violence: a Ukrainian-Canadian demonstration against the USSR (Toronto, 1971), an anti–Vietnam war demonstration (Toronto, 1970), the Saint-Jean-Baptiste Day demonstration (Montreal, 1968), and a Yorkville sit-in (Toronto, 1967) by hippies who wanted traffic blocked and youth hostels subsidized to preserve Yorkville as Canada's anti-materialistic, counter-cultural mecca. Frank (1984) showed that in each of these four cases, violence was a police response to protest action that the law-enforcement authorities considered deviant. These protests that became violent had three points in common. First, the activities did not follow standard protest protocol; the action was either disorganized, chaotic, or spontaneous (as in the Yorkville sit-in) and police found the behaviour unpredictable and difficult to control. Second, the protesters were judged by police to be of low, marginal, or counter-cultural status, not "respectable." Third, police officers resorted to beating and other violent acts to break up what they considered to be illegitimate protest. In three of the four cases, the movement lost credibility and bargaining power because of the violent outcome. The Ukrainian-Canadian protesters, however, gained sympathy because of what a later inquiry termed the "police riot" — the obvious loss of police officer's control over their own actions.

Many analysts have found that police perceptions of respectability play an important role in their reaction to protesters (Frank and Kelly 1979; Torrance 1986). Middle-class protesters, who are considered respectable by authorities, are allowed a lot of leeway for letting off steam during protest activities. The irony is that disadvantaged and marginal groups, who often do not have the organizational resources for anything but spontaneous protest, are the very ones whose protest activities are least likely to be met with a favourable response. The difficulty involved in finding protest strategies that are affordable and effective has a strong demobilizing effect on social movements.

## Affordable Effective Action

In deciding what kinds of tactics are most likely to bring results, movements are tightly constrained by their own resource base, as well as by their opponents' and the public's likely reactions. Ponting and Gibbins (1981) have shown that Canadian native Indians engaged in a wide range of persuasive, bargaining, and coercive protest tactics in the 1960s and 1970s — yet these were largely ignored by most Canadians. Even the confrontational and violent tactics that many feared would cause backlash against the native cause remained irrelevant to the Canadian public. It is not that Canadians feel indifferent to violent protest; the findings in this study show that the majority of Canadians found persuasive and bargaining tactics as well as protest marches acceptable, but found more coercive tactics — in particular, the threatening of violence — unacceptable. Indian protests were ignored because they were so sporadic and regionally isolated that both the protests and the Indians' problems had not really registered with the non-native population. In their choice of strategies, Indians faced a dilemma. They did not have the organizational base to sustain the persuasive and bargaining tactics that most Canadians approve of, while the more coercive tactics for which they could mobilize resources were not acceptable and threatened to provoke backlash if they even attracted attention at all. This tactical dilemma is very common to resource-poor groups and severely hampers their chances of gaining support for their demands.

Even among groups with many resources, the difficulty of finding effective collective action tactics can inhibit the formation of social movements. A good illustration of this phenomenon comes from Quebec, where the nonfrancophone minority has adopted mainly individual, rather than collective, solutions to language grievances. At first glance, Quebec's nonfrancophones would seem to have textbook-perfect conditions for mounting a collective challenge. The various measures taken by the Quebec government to remove English as an official language, culminating in the mid-1970s in Bill 101, presented open targets for discontent. Furthermore, this minority is divided from the francophone majority by language, separate social networks, and a set of separate minority institutions — the kind of segmented social arrangements that we have seen tend to encourage the mobilization of a collective stand.

But a close look shows that these conditions were not as well structured to promote collective action as they first appeared to be (Fitzsimmons-LeCavalier and LeCavalier 1981, 1984). For one thing, the nonfrancophone population is a collection of socially diverse groups, divided internally by ethnic, racial, linguistic, and religious differences. Furthermore, the nonfrancophone community associations and service institutions are also divided along these many lines, and most are dependent on the Quebec government for funding and continued survival. A survey of nonfrancophone leaders' opinions showed that the difficulties involved in getting the diverse minority representatives and organizational resources united in a common cause was a major barrier to collective action (Fitzsimmons-LeCavalier and LeCavalier 1984).

These heavy organizational costs were magnified by the leaders' belief that making collective demands would not improve the minority situation. When language tensions were very high in Quebec, the defence of nonfrancophone language, ethnic, or racial rights could have been interpreted as a rejection of francophones' rights, themselves a threatened minority in the Canadian context. Confronting the Quebec government on language issues could have meant political suicide for the leaders of the government-funded minority institutions. The limited opportunities for success available through collective action encouraged nonfrancophones to adopt individual solutions to overcome their minority situation. The main individual solution was to master the French language — in 1981, nearly two-thirds of the nonfrancophone labour force was bilingual. Another individual solution was to escape the minority situation — almost 15 percent of nonfrancophones left Quebec between 1971 and 1981.

As the position of the French language strengthened in Quebec, francophones' language grievances eased and a greater openness to minority problems emerged. In response to this greater political openness, nonfrancophones started taking co-ordinated stands to press for changes in the conditions of minority life in the 1980s. As in many other cases, it was at a time of increasing political opportunities that the mobilization of a movement for social change surfaced, not at the time of greatest crisis and discontent.

## Overcoming the Obstacles to Mobilization

Currently, the most widespread approach to the study of social movements focuses on the ways discontented groups overcome the obstacles to mobilization. Discontent, frustration, and unfulfilled ideals are all considered too widespread to explain the appearance of a protest group, when so many other groups continue to suffer in silence. Making collective demands for social change requires a lot of resources, co-ordination, and persistence in the face of opposition. In this resource mobilization approach, social movements are considered most likely to emerge when the people facing a new problem already form a solidary group. The more a discontented group has **solidary traits** — pre-established leaders, shared outlooks, friendship networks, formal organizations, and other mechanisms for encouraging commitment to group ends — the more likely the individual members are to support collective solutions to their problems. Of course, discontented groups seldom have a perfect, pre-established solidary base. But there are often many distinct, well-organized groups within the larger collection of people who share a social problem. Movements frequently mobilize by recruiting the most central leaders and most active participants from these various organizations. Movements overcome high mobilization costs by building a coalition of the most solidary subgroups in the larger discontented group. These groups' already assembled resources are then transferred to backing the new cause.

But building on solidarity is not the only solution movements can use to overcome their high organizational costs. Not all dissatisfied groups rely solely on their own members' donations to sustain the fight for social change. Some build social movements on the donations of outside sympathizers — better-off people or organizations that support the cause as a matter of conscience. In prosperous times, when many individuals and organizations have free time and money at their disposal, causes that defend important social ideals may attract considerable backing from outside allies. At times, movements get enough outside financial support for leaders and organizers to make a full-time career of pursuing social change (McCarthy and Zald 1973). Such movements maintained by a small, full-time core of activists dependent on the financial backing of outside sympathizers are called **professional social movements**. Pollution Probe is one example of a movement that has been highly subsidized by outside agencies. These movements can be built with very little support from the discontented base itself, thus avoiding heavy mobilization costs. However, professional social movements are vulnerable to changing economic conditions and to the shifting priorities of well-off sympathizers. A cause may be "in" one year and "out" the next, and the leaders' salaries may disappear with the changing trendiness of social problems.

A full-time leadership core is more likely to be sustained by "conscience money" when there are a large number of well-off people who are part of the dissatisfied group itself. In fact in very affluent groups, a movement may be maintained by a small core of unpaid activists who donate their leadership resources out of ideological commitment to the cause (Fitzsimmons-LeCavalier 1983). People who have a high level of organizational skills, leisure time, and money are resource-full and, unlike resource-poor groups, can often afford to pursue their ideals. Still, highly committed people who work only for the pleasure of doing what they believe in tend to suffer burnout if the challenging action is too risky, time-consuming or long drawn out. Movements led by people who get only ideological rewards are also prone to splitting into warring ideological **factions**, splinter groups whose ideals of social change are incompatible. With everyone working for different ide-

# The Cost of Dissent

*The 1988 Supreme Court decision to strike down the federal abortion law left the pro-choice movement jubilant and the pro-life movement defiant. This ongoing struggle means that abortion on demand is far from a fully institutionalized reality. Here is an account of the high costs such a struggle for social change can entail.*

## 1984

To the man whose name is synonymous with abortion in Canada — Dr. Henry Morgentaler — his Toronto abortion trial was "a fight between light and darkness, democracy and totalitarianism."

To Joseph Borowski of Winnipeg, the country's best known anti-abortionist, it was "a charade, a perversion of justice, a waste of money."

But if there is anything the two symbols agree on, it is that the emotion-laden abortion issue is not about to go away just because Dr. Morgentaler and two associates were acquitted in Ontario of a charge of conspiring to commit a miscarriage.

The future of his crusade to open clinics across the country is as clouded as it ever was. Worn out and $250,000 poorer, Dr. Morgentaler faces the distinct possibility of more criminal charges, more expenses and an increasingly hostile anti-abortion lobby.

"Probably the anti-abortion people will step up their attacks," he said in an interview during the trial. "They're pretty desperate — they have lost the battle. In desperation they might do what they did in the United States: commit violence against clinics and slander me even more than they have."

Mr. Borowski agrees: "If that man walks away free, the Government of Canada will be sowing the seeds of violence." he said last week. "There are extremists everywhere.

Morgentaler was saying it is justified to break the law in order to change the law. Well, what's sauce for the goose is sauce for the gander."

As the legal scorecard stands now, Dr. Morgentaler has won three acquittals in Quebec and one in Toronto. He faces trial in Winnipeg, and says he plans to challenge the law in other provinces whenever he gets enough money to open clinics there.

The court battles "are like an absurd piece of theatre each time — a doctor being prosecuted for helping people," Dr. Morgentaler said.

In each of his legal battles, he has sought out prosecution, and then during the trial he virtually admits guilt, but appeals to the social conscience of the jury. The challenges have written a new page in Canadian legal history.

Dr. Morgentaler, who needed seven years to pay the legal debts incurred during his three jury trials in Quebec in the mid-1970s, now acknowledges his forays into Toronto and Winnipeg may have been premature. He is in financial trouble. "I did overextend myself. From a business point of view, this is sheer madness."

And worse for his cause is the fact that Dr. Morgentaler's supporters have not donated enough money to pay for his recent cases, let alone the ones to come.

## 1985

Dr. Henry Morgentaler has launched a personal appeal to the public for donations to meet legal and security costs in the fight to keep his Toronto abortion clinic open.

In an advertisement which appeared on Saturday in *The Gazette* in Montreal, Dr. Morgentaler said he cannot personnally afford to pay for his legal battles and the high cost of extra security at the Harbord Street clinic in Toronto.

No such advertisement appeared in Toronto newspapers. However, an advertisement asking for donations to the Pro-Choice Defence Fund appeared in *The Globe and Mail* on December 20, the day after Dr.

Morgentaler's associate, Dr. Robert Scott was arrested and charged with conspiring to procure a miscarriage at the clinic. The same charge was laid against Dr. Morgentaler on December 20.

Readers were also asked to send a coupon to Ontario Attorney General Roy McMurtry demanding an end to prosecutions against Dr. Morgentaler.

Dr. Morgentaler also plans to go on a five-day tour of Calgary, Edmonton, and Winnipeg later this month to drum up support and raise funds.

Anti-abortionists in Calgary say they will demonstrate against Dr. Morgentaler's announced intention to open at least one abortion clinic in Alberta within the next year.

Judy Rebick, spokesperson for the Ontario Coalition for Abortion Clinics, said that a personal appeal from Dr. Morgentaler is the "most effective vehicle" to deal with the "ongoing problem" of financing his defence fund. The target is $150,000 "over the next month or so."

Ms. Rebick said publicly solicited money goes into the "war chest" to cover legal fees and not to operate the clinic, which is financed by Dr. Morgentaler and his backers. The fund has managed to raise about $150,000 so far, she said.

"If they continue the legal harassment and continue with charges in Winnipeg," Ms. Rebick said, legal costs could reach $500,000. Although most of the costs for past court battles have been paid, she said lawyers in Toronto are still owed $50,000 and $20,000 is still outstanding for the defence against abortion-related charges at Dr. Morgentaler's Winnipeg clinic.

Meanwhile, the Calgary Coalition for Life promised to hold protests similar to those held in Toronto against Dr. Morgentaler when he visits Calgary on Jan. 15.

---

**Sources:**

Kirk Makin, *The Globe and Mail*, November 9, 1984; Bernard Marotte, *The Globe and Mail* January 7, 1985.

ological rewards, the movement disintegrates long before the battle for social change has been won.

Although there are many ways to mobilize for collective action, social movements built on a solidary organizational base are more likely to endure through the highs and lows of a major challenge for social change.

## SUMMARY

1. Social movements are collective attempts to promote, maintain, or resist social change. The changes may be related to the material, social, ideological, or political status of a dissatisfied group.
2. Change-seekers and change-resisters can only be considered to form a social movement when the individuals involved consciously support a shared cause. Social change brought about by a series of unrelated individual decisions does not constitute a social movement.
3. Social movement action is essentially nonroutine, noninstitutionalized action to promote interests that are not met through society's established institutions or conventions.
4. In the traditional collective behaviour approach, social movements are seen as part of a wide range of unconventional crowd behaviour that has an irrational base.
5. Current approaches treat social movements as normal outgrowths of conflicts of interest regarding the distribution of rewards in society.
6. In the resource mobilization approach — the currently dominant perspective — discontent, frustration, and unfulfilled ideals are all considered too widespread to directly explain the appearance of a social movement.
7. Making collective demands for social change requires lots of resources: time, money, leadership, co-ordination, and persistence in the face of opposition. Groups advocating social change have heavy mobilization costs, since they start with few established resources or means of influence but face opponents who have low-cost, institutionalized means of defending the status quo.
8. Dissatisfied groups are most likely to overcome the high costs of mobilizing a social movement if they have a long-standing shared identity, established leadership, friendship networks, and organizational links, along with weak ties to opponents. Such a solidary organizational base offers built-in incentives for individuals to support group action.
9. Movements may also overcome the obstacles to mobilization by relying on well-off individuals and agencies to donate enough resources out of sympathy to the cause to sustain full-time leadership. Such movements are vulnerable to the shifting priorities of their well-off backers, however, and are not as likely as those built on a solidary institutional base to maintain a long-term challenge.
10. No matter what kind of organizational base it has, a social movement is not likely to push collective demands for social change if those demands provoke nothing but heavy losses. Social movements are sensitive to the opportunities for success and adapt their action according to the authorities' and their opponents' expected responses.

## GLOSSARY

**Absolute deprivation.** Structured disadvantages rooted in concrete inequalities of wealth, status, or power.
**Bloc recruitment.** The attraction of sets of supporters already linked by friendship or organizational ties.
**Breakdown theory.** An approach that attributes social movement formation to disorganization and disorientation caused by rapid social change.
**Circular reaction.** A process through which individuals in crowds directly copy one another's excited moods and actions leading to disorderly, irrational behaviour.
**Coercive tactics.** The symbolic or actual disruption of institutional routines in order to attract support or exert pressure for movement demands.
**Collective good.** A benefit available to all members of a group, whether or not they contribute to the cost of gaining it.
**Counter-movements.** Collective attempts to resist or reverse change or the demands for change made by some other social movement.
**Emergent norms.** Norms that are generated in exceptional circumstances to guide and contain group behaviour.
**Factions.** Splinter organizations within a movement holding conflicting views on the degree, nature, or tactics of social change to be pursued.
**Free riders.** Individuals who benefit from a collective good without contributing to the costs of acquiring it.

**Frustration/aggression approach.** An approach that makes a direct link between the level of dissatisfaction and the intensity of rebellion it will provoke.

**Movement success.** The process of institutionalization through which the movement's goals become recognized and routinely enforced by society as rights.

**Noninstitutionalized activity.** Nonroutine action taken to promote interests that are not met by society's established institutions and conventions.

**Professional social movements.** Movements maintained by a small, full-time core of activists dependent on the financial donations of unrelated sympathizers or outside agencies.

**Radical movement.** A social movement that seeks to overturn and replace the established social order.

**Reformist movement.** A social movement that seeks some adjustment in society while maintaining the overall system.

**Relative deprivation.** A feeling of unfairness provoked by a gap between the rewards that people expect to receive and those they actually do receive.

**Resource mobilization.** The process of attracting, coordinating, and applying resources toward a collective goal.

**Safety in numbers.** A factor, operative in large gatherings, whereby the larger the crowd, the less the blame for disorder is likely to be attached to any one person, allowing a potentially rational base for disorder.

**Selective incentives.** Personal rewards that are available only to individuals who contribute to a collective cause, not to free riders.

**Social incentives.** The built-in rewards and penalties solidary groups have available to assure that individual members act in a group-oriented way.

**Social movements.** Collective attempts with varying degrees of formal organization to promote, maintain, or resist social change.

**Social segmentation.** A deep break between social groups, in which there are few co-operative ties to bind the groups and separate sets of social institutions to maintain the divisions between them.

**Solidary traits.** Social arrangements that integrate individuals to cohesive groups; examples include a long-standing shared identity, friendship networks, and formal organizations.

# FURTHER READING

**Clark, Sam, J. Paul Grayson, and L.M. Grayson (eds.).** *Prophecy and Protest: Social Movements in Twentieth-Century Canada*. Toronto: Gage, 1975. A collection of articles covering a wide range of such Canadian social movements as the "social gospel," the CCF, the union, and western protest movements in English Canada, as well as Quebec's nationalist and Social Credit movements.

**Freeman, Jo (ed.).** *Social Movements of the Sixties and Seventies*. New York: Longman, 1983. A reader that presents analyses of typical 1960s and 1970s movements — such as the women's, environmental, anti-war, civil rights, disabled, and counter-cultural movements — from a resource mobilization perspective.

**Oberschall, Anthony.** *Social Conflict and Social Movements*. Englewood Cliffs, NJ: Prentice-Hall, 1973. The first major theoretical outline of the resource mobilization perspective, this study documents the way in which prior social organization and the dynamics of conflicts with opponents affect the identity and course of social movements.

**Pinard, Maurice.** *The Rise of a Third Party*. Englewood Cliffs, NJ: Prentice-Hall, 1971. A study of the emergence of the Social Credit party in Quebec. This work draws on a wide range of data to show how the grievances, available organizational base, and political opportunities came together to shape a specific movement.

**Ponting, J. Rick (ed.).** *Arduous Journey: Canadian Indians and Decolonization*. Toronto: McClelland and Stewart, 1986. A collection of readings that offers much data on the current situation and social movements among Canadian Indians; includes articles by social scientists as well as by movement activists and legislators.

**Torrance, Judy M.** *Public Violence in Canada*. Montreal: McGill-Queen's, 1986. A review of the major incidents of social-movement action that have turned to violence in Canada; incorporates a wide range of collective behaviour as well as resource mobilization approaches.

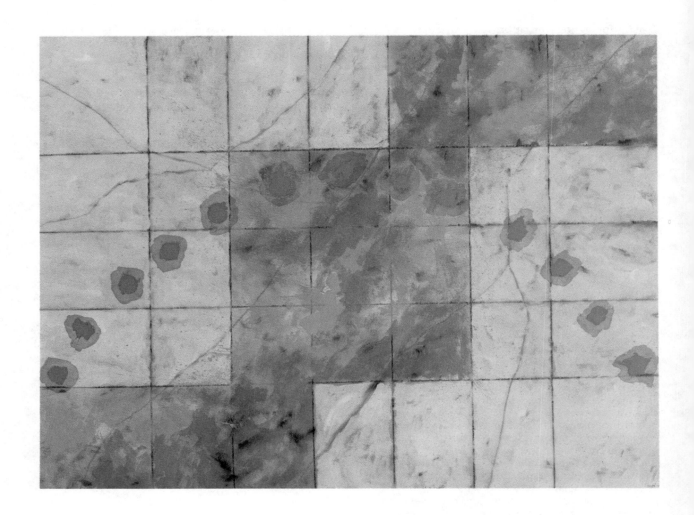

# UNIT VI

# Research Methods

*Throughout this book you have read about surveys, participant observation, interviews, rates, averages, standard deviations, correlations, and significant findings. This final section is concerned with what these terms mean.*

*Chapter 18 describes how sociologists conduct their research. The approach here is to see the reader as a consumer of information. Divorce rates, crime rates, life expectancy, percentage employed, average income — such statistics are the stuff of life, the content of the daily news. The impact of oil pipelines on the environment, the effect of television violence on children, the legalization of marijuana — our response to such issues determines our future. When presented with research findings, we need to ask several questions. How was this research done? Is it good research? What do all these averages, rates, and percentages mean? Are the findings rational? Are they relevant? Are they true?*

*The intention in Chapter 18 is to help you evaluate for yourself the vast amounts of information concerning society that are reported in the news media — and in this book.*

# CHAPTER 18

# Social Research

ROBERT HAGEDORN
R. ALAN HEDLEY

Sociologists writing a chapter or book on social research methods realize full well that few students approach the subject with wide-eyed enthusiasm. However, these same sociologists are not dissuaded from their venture, because they know that a sound knowledge of how research should be carried out leads to more valid results and more appropriate interpretations of them.

An understanding of the process of social research is necessary if you plan to become a professional researcher, and extremely useful even if you do not. You are constantly being called upon to evaluate the results of research. Reading your daily newspaper, purchasing a car, writing or evaluating reports at work, even buying a bottle of vitamins: all these things require you to arrive at some interpretation or conclusion. A knowledgeable appreciation of how facts come about or are arrived at — that is, of the research process — is essential to a sound interpretation of what they mean.

It is the purpose of this chapter to provide you with enough information to begin to evaluate critically not only the results of scientific research found in the library but also the mass of information with which you are bombarded daily. Academics are not the only people who do social research. Whenever questions are posed, observations made, and conclusions drawn, research is done. In our daily lives, we are constantly involved in the research process. The rest of this chapter describes the various stages of the research process and some of the obstacles we must avoid in order to arrive at clear answers to the questions we address.

# Planning and Doing Research

Robert Burns observed that the best-laid schemes of mice and men often go astray. His observation applies with particular force to social research: we should plan and design our research as carefully as possible, but when we come to carrying it out, we should realize that there will *inevitably* be problems — some we may have expected and some not. There is no such thing as an absolutely perfect piece of research that answers once and for all the particular questions posed. Competing alternative explanations will always be possible for two reasons. First, snags, difficulties, and obstacles are inherent in the research process. Second, even if it were possible to anticipate and thus avoid these snags, it is impossible to design one piece of research to produce findings that simultaneously are unambiguous, have general applicability, and pertain directly to the real world.

It is extremely important to realize these inherent limitations at the outset, and we will address them throughout the chapter. Because of them, every single research result can be accepted only tentatively. We can never know with absolute certainty. However, if we are careful in designing and conducting research and if the same result is obtained on several occasions, we can have confidence in that result.

## The Scientist and the Citizen

*Whether or not you do research, the results of research will affect you.*

It has been a common refrain in recent years that the Canadian public has a very limited knowledge of science and technology, despite the fact that developments in these areas have brought and will continue to bring about countless changes in the fabric of daily life. Many of today's developments hold tremendous potential both to improve the quality of human life and to put it at serious risk, but Canadians are largely unaware of their implications.

Treatment of science-related issues by the media has led many people to believe that scientists are the only people who can understand the subject matter of science and that it would be best to leave science to the scientists. But the applications of the products of science are too important to leave the subject to scientists alone.

Many important decisions to be made by our politicians in the near future deal with the products of science. The CANDU reactor, the dangers of asbestos, mercury and arsenic, communications satellites and a tar sands development are all examples of science-related matters that will have a profound effect on the lives of Canadians. Yet the legislators who are making the decisions have a very limited knowledge of science. Of the 264 Members of Parliament, 61 are businessmen, 60 are lawyers, while 7 are engineers and technologists and 5 are university teachers and researchers by profession. A survey carried out during lobbying efforts by the CAUT and the CFBS during December 1976 and April 1977 indicated that the level of comprehension of science-related issues and scientific research was lowest among those MPs surveyed who were businessmen prior to their election. Lawyers were rated second to last in their comprehension of the situation.

One overriding theme that emerged from the lobbying efforts was the need to generate public interest in science in order to influence government decisions. Without public input into science-related decisions, the horrors resulting from the effects of past applications will continue. Incidents such as the dumping of poisonous wastes into the Love Canal in the United States, an action which led to the contamination of entire neighbourhoods more than 20 years later, will become an all too familiar story. But effective public response to such decisions cannot take place until people have made informed choices about them, based on reputable sources of information. The source of that information should be those who know whereof they speak — the scientists. . . .

While important steps have already been taken, much remains to be done to accomplish the long-term goals of those engaged in "bringing science to the people." Popularization of science will rely to a great extent on the cooperation of Canada's scientists, and it will be their responsibility to ensure the accuracy of statements made in the media concerning developments in their areas of research. It will also be necessary to encourage journalists and students of journalism to consider science writing as a specialty and to encourage a concern for accurate science writing. The final responsibility, however, rests with the members of the general public to become knowledgeable and involved in matters which could ultimately have a profound effect on their daily lives.

**Source:**

From Catherine Simpson, "Science in the public eye," *Canadian Association of University Teachers Bulletin* 26(May 1979):15. Catherine Simpson was Project Assistant with the Task Force on Public Awareness of Science in Canada.

The research process by its very nature involves uncertainty. We can't get around this, but we can suggest ways to reduce the uncertainty and thus increase our confidence in the results (see Figure 18-1). Think of the research process as an obstacle course and a series of decision points. Researchers have learned a great deal about these obstacles and the kinds of decisions possible. Furthermore, they can estimate the kinds of difficulties you will confront or the uncertainty you will face should you not make or not be able to make the appropriate decision. This is the kind of information you will need when you come to assess the overall results of research, whether it involves social problems or what kind of breakfast cereal you are going to eat.

## The Research Problem

You are reading a newspaper article on juvenile delinquency. A police officer is quoted as saying that most of the delinquents arrested come from the predominantly poor areas of your city. You might conclude on the basis of this casual observation that there is something about being poor that causes delinquency. However, you want to test this proposition systematically before you are convinced. If you pursue your hunch — for at this stage that is all it is — you will then be engaged in genuine social research. What do you do? How do you go about it?

First, you should become familiar with previous research on delinquency. Are there any studies on delinquency? Have other researchers noted the relationship between poverty or lower-class status and delinquency? Is it a well-established relationship, repeated in many studies? Depending on the answers to these questions, you may or may not decide to proceed with your own research. In all serious research undertakings, a review of the research literature relevant to the problem is a necessary first step. Because science is a cumulative process, you first want to know how your own research compares to other studies in the same area.

Next, you need to write down the relationship you expect to find among the variables in which you are interested. A **variable** is a factor that can

### Figure 18-1. The Stages of Social Research

1. Select the problem.
2. Review previous research on the problem.
3. State the hypothesis (predict what you will find).
4. Construct indicators for all variables in the hypotheses (operational definitions).
5. Set up the research design.
6. Select appropriate sample or population.
7. Decide on data collection method(s).
8. Collect the data.
9. Analyze the data.
10. Interpret the data (write the research report).

differ or vary from one situation to another or from one individual or group to another. Delinquency is a variable in that some people are more or less delinquent than others (some may not be delinquent at all). Similarly, social class is a variable. People may be upper, middle, or lower class. In your statement of relationship, you may propose that the lower the social class, the greater the likelihood of delinquency. This is a **hypothesis**, a prediction of what you expect to find in your research.

The variable that you are attempting to explain — delinquency — is the **dependent variable**; that is, the variation in this factor depends on or is caused by some other factor — in this case, social class. The causal factor — social class — is called the **independent variable**. In other words, you are saying that depending on what social class an adolescent is from, there is a greater or lesser chance of delinquency. If young people are upper class, the chances of delinquency are slight; if they are lower class, the chances are relatively greater. This is your hypothesis.

After you state your hypothesis, it is necessary to find out if the hypothesized relationship actually exists. This involves measurement, but how do you measure social class and delinquency? How do you differentiate between upper and middle class? How do you know whether a person is delinquent? At this stage, it is necessary to construct measuring instruments of your variables.

Remember your original observation in the newspaper. How did you first measure social class and delinquency? In this case, your measure or indicator of social class was residential area. Your indicator of delinquency was the arrests of juve-

# Figure 18-2. Operational Definition of Delinquency Checklist

How often have you done each of these things?

| Offences | Never | Once or Twice | Several Times | Quite Often | Very Often |
|---|---|---|---|---|---|
| 1. Driven a car without a driver's licence | | | | | |
| 2. Taken little things that did not belong to you | | | | | |
| 3. Skipped school without a legitimate excuse | | | | | |
| 4. Driven beyond the speed limit | | | | | |
| 5. Participated in drag races along the highway with your friends | | | | | |
| 6. Engaged in a fist fight | | | | | |
| 7. Been feeling "high" from drinking beer, wine, or liquor | | | | | |
| 8. Gambled for money at cards, dice, or some other game | | | | | |
| 9. Remained out all night without parents' permission | | | | | |
| 10. Taken a car without owner's knowledge | | | | | |
| 11. Been placed on school probation or expelled from school | | | | | |
| 12. Destroyed or damaged public or private property of any kind | | | | | |
| 13. Taken little things of value between $2 and $50 that did not belong to you | | | | | |
| 14. Tried to be intimate with a member of the opposite sex | | | | | |
| 15. Broken into or tried to break into and enter a building with the intention of stealing | | | | | |
| 16. Sold, used, or tried to use drugs of some kind | | | | | |
| 17. Bought or tried to buy beer, wine, or liquor from a store or adult | | | | | |
| 18. Taken money of any amount from someone or place that did not belong to you | | | | | |
| 19. Taken a glass of beer, wine, or liquor at a party or elsewhere with your friends | | | | | |

SOURCE: Adapted from E.W. Vaz, "Middle-class adolescents: Self-reported delinquency and youth culture activities," *Canadian Review of Sociology and Anthropology* 2(1965):52–70.

niles reported by the police. **Indicators** are measures of variables in the same way that a thermometer is a measure of temperature. For any one variable, there are potentially a variety of indicators to measure it.

The construction or selection of appropriate indicators of variables is crucial to the research process. The indicators you choose can influence your results dramatically and cause you to draw wrong conclusions. For example, does arrest necessarily imply guilt? No, you decide, but conviction does. But if you choose to use official conviction records instead of lists of arrests as your indicator of delinquency, other problems arise. In some cases, for instance, delinquents are handled informally by the courts and no official record is maintained. Furthermore, conviction records give you a list of only those *found* guilty. What about those who committed indictable offences but were neither arrested nor convicted?

By now you will appreciate that achieving correspondence between variables and indicators is a difficult process. The process is called the *operationalization* of variables, and the measures or indicators adopted constitute your **operational definitions**. Depending on what operational definition you use for delinquency, your results will differ, and it is important to realize that this difference will be produced by the measurement process itself — not by changes in the actual incidence of delinquency. This is why it is necessary, when evaluating research results, to judge the appropriateness of what is actually being used to measure what.

Edmund Vaz (1965), a sociologist interested in delinquency, devised an interesting operational definition of this variable, a checklist of 19 activities that constituted violations of the law for juveniles (see Figure 18-2). Adolescents were asked to respond to this checklist by indicating how often, if ever, they had engaged in each activity. Although there are difficulties with Vaz's operational definition (will people tell the truth about their illegal behaviour?), it does avoid the problem of recording only those who have been caught for their offences. You will also note that if one researcher used official records to measure delinquency while another used self-reported behaviour, any discrepancy produced could be a result of the different operational definitions and not a reflection of differences in the incidence of actual delinquency.

Vaz's measure of social class involved two indicators: the father's occupation and his highest level of education attained. (Because juveniles assume the social class of their parents, it becomes necessary to measure class by this means.) The two indicators were then combined to form an index or overall operational definition of social class. Figure 18-3 outlines the progress of our research problem to this point.

The hypothesized relationship between social class and delinquency can be tested in a variety

**Figure 18-3. The Research Problem: Variables, Hypotheses, and Operational Definitions**

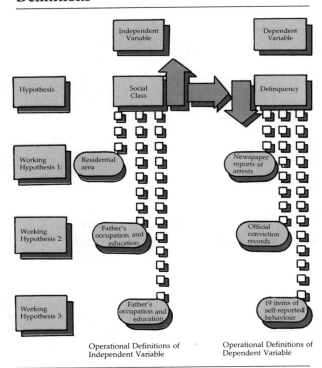

Operational Definitions of Independent Variable

Operational Definitions of Dependent Variable

NOTE: The hypothesis — the predicted relationship between social class and delinquency — is presented in the top part of the diagram. The arrows refer to the direction and type of the expected relationship: in this case, that social class, the independent variable, influences or causes differential rates of delinquency, the dependent variable. The higher the social class (arrow pointing up), the lower the delinquency rate (arrow pointing down). The circled areas represent the indicators of the independent and dependent variables.

of ways. Unfortunately, we may obtain a variety of answers, depending on what operational definitions are used. In fact, as you saw in Chapter 6, just such a discrepancy is obtained in the strength of the relationship between social class and delinquency, depending on whether official records or self-reported behaviour is used to measure delinquency. Obviously, if we encounter these kinds of difficulties in systematic, rigorous research, we should certainly be wary of accepting casual observations at face value.

## Problems in Measurement

So far, we have indicated some of the difficulties involved in the measurement of variables and the testing of hypotheses. We now address this issue directly, because measurement is the weakest part of the research process. As any chain is only as strong as its weakest link, so too are research results only as good as the measurements used to produce them.

Achieving valid results is a major goal of all research. **Validity** is the result of having measured what you intended to measure. This sounds simple enough, but it is one of the most elusive goals in research because we can never be certain that we are indeed measuring what we want. Earlier, for example, we considered the process of constructing operational definitions for variables. We can never know with absolute certainty whether we have achieved valid measurement of variables, but there are indirect ways of estimating validity and at the same time increasing our confidence in research findings. It is to these strategies we now turn.

---

## "They rushed tumultuously to the cathedral."

*What are the dangers of drawing conclusions from limited observations? The following humorous description demonstrates some of the dangers.*

I constructed four miniature houses of worship — a Mohammedan mosque, a Hindu temple, a Jewish synagogue, a Christian cathedral — and placed them in a row. I then marked 15 ants with red paint and turned them loose. They made several trips to and fro, glancing in at the places of worship, but not entering.

I then turned loose 15 more painted blue; they acted just as the red ones had done. I now gilded 15 and turned them loose. No change in the result; the 45 traveled back and forth in a hurry persistently and continuously visiting each fane, but never entering. This satisfied me that these ants were without religious prejudices — just what I wished; for under no other conditions would my next and greater experiment be valuable. I now placed a small square of white paper within the door of each fane; and upon the mosque paper I put a pinch of putty, upon the temple paper a dab of tar, upon the synagogue paper a trifle of turpentine, and upon the cathedral paper a small cube of sugar.

First I liberated the red ants. They examined and rejected the putty, the tar and the turpentine, and then took to the sugar with zeal and apparent sincere conviction. I next liberated the blue ants, and they did exactly as the red ones had done. The gilded ants followed. The preceding results were precisely repeated. This seemed to prove that ants destitute of religious prejudice will always prefer Christianity to any other creed.

However, to make sure, I removed the ants and put putty in the cathedral and sugar in the mosque. I now liberated the ants in a body, and they rushed tumultuously to the cathedral. I was very much touched and gratified, and went back in the room to write down the event; but when I came back the ants had all apostatized and had gone over to the Mohammedan communion.

I saw that I had been too hasty in my conclusions, and naturally felt rebuked and humbled. With diminished confidence I went on with the test to the finish. I placed the sugar first in one house of worship, then in another, till I had tried them all.

With this result: whatever Church I put the sugar in, that was the one the ants straightaway joined. This was true beyond a shadow of a doubt, that in religious matters the ant is the opposite of man, for man cares for but one thing: to find the only true Church; whereas the ant hunts for the one with the sugar in it.

---

**Source:**

Mark Twain, "On experimental design," reprinted in *Readings in Organizational Behavior and Human Performance*, L.L. Cummings and W.E. Scott, Jr., eds. (Homewood, IL: Irwin and Dorsey, 1969).

## Reliability

**Reliability** is the stability of results over time using the same measuring instrument, or the equivalence of results at one time when more than one investigator uses the same instrument. The argument for reliability is that if we can achieve a consistent result over time or with several investigators, we are measuring what we want, and therefore we probably have valid operational definitions. The argument is weak, however, because it is possible to measure a variable reliably but invalidly.

Early research on the measurement of intelligence is a good case in point. Although researchers could consistently produce the same result with their IQ tests (reliability), it was later discovered, as you saw in Chapter 14, that the tests contained a cultural and class bias and were thus not measuring exactly what was intended (invalidity). White, native anglophone, middle- and upper-class individuals averaged higher on IQ tests than did nonwhite, non-native-English-speaking, or lower-class individuals — not because the former were more intelligent but because use of written English (paper and pencil tests) was a more central, and therefore more familiar, feature of their lives.

Consequently, although reliable measures constitute an important aspect of social research, because reliability is an essential prerequisite for validity, a reliable measurement is not necessarily a valid measurement.

## Replication

**Replication,** the systematically repeated measurement of a given relationship, is one of the bywords of science, and it suggests that any single finding by itself is or should be unconvincing. Only with repeated corroboration and confirmation should researchers express confidence in the validity of their findings.

In his classic study, *Suicide* (1964b, originally published 1897), Emile Durkheim employed two types of replication. His hypothesis was that the more integrated individuals are into their society, the less likely they are to kill themselves. He argued that being married is an indicator of social integration, a bond that links individuals to the larger society. Therefore, married people should have a lower suicide rate than single people.

First, Durkheim tested his hypothesis in all the provinces of his native France for which he could obtain relevant data (official statistics) on the marital status of suicide victims. Each province therefore constituted a separate, independent test of his hypothesis, and its repeated confirmation lent considerably more credence to the hypothesis than it would have had if it had been upheld only once. Second, Durkheim reasoned that individuals are linked to society through all the various social institutions that constitute it. The family is but one social institution; religion and work are others. He constructed separate operational definitions for each of these institutions in an attempt to test the applicability of his general hypothesis that individual social integration is related inversely to suicide. With the confirmation of his hypothesis for each of the several operational definitions he employed, he became more confident that he was indeed measuring what he intended.

By now, many of you will appreciate that there are two common themes in the measurement strategies presented above: variation and repetition. The key to validity is varied and repeated measurement. The use of several indicators measured by a variety of methods upon several occasions should produce a common core of findings.

# Research Design

If your professor claimed that the lecture method of instruction was superior to the discussion method in producing greater overall student achievement, how would you go about testing this claim or establishing its truth? After a research problem has been selected, previous studies examined, hypotheses formulated, and operational definitions constructed, it becomes necessary to plan systematically how the research will be undertaken. This is called research design, and it is the next stage of social research.

We must draw up a deliberate plan or design prior to the actual research in order to eliminate competing alternative explanations for the results we obtain. If the lecture method is employed and class achievement is extremely high, can we say that this achievement results directly from the lecture method? Depending on how the research is designed, we can be more or less confident in answering yes or no. Research design forces us to anticipate systematically the difficulties we will confront, the decisions we will have to make, and the explanations possible for the results we will achieve.

## Classical Experimental Design

In science, the ideal type of research design has for many years been the **classical experimental design**. It allows researchers to obtain relatively clear, unequivocal results that are largely attributable to the design's following features:

1. Two equivalent groups are selected. Equivalence is judged in terms of the dependent variable — in the example used, student achievement. If the two groups are not similar in achievement before the experiment, any difference found could be due to the initial difference between the groups, not the result of the independent variable — the lecture method. Equivalence may be obtained either by randomly assigning individuals to one or the other group or by matching individuals with respect to the dependent variable and then assigning, again randomly, one member of each matched pair to one group and the other member to the other group. (Random assignment is explained in the following section, "Sampling.")

2. One group, called the **experimental group**, is subjected to the independent variable, in this case, the lecture method of instruction. The other group, the **control group**, is treated identically to the experimental group, except it is not subjected to the independent variable. It could receive its instruction via the discussion method, for example.

3. Both the experimental and control groups are measured on the dependent variable twice. The first measurement (Time 1) occurs *before* the introduction of the independent variable to the experimental group. The second measurement (Time 2) takes place *after* the experimental group has received the effects of the independent variable. In our example, one section of an intro-

ductory sociology class could be given a test at the beginning of the course to determine the students' current level of sociological knowledge. They would then receive instruction by lecture. An equivalent introductory section would be administered the identical test, but this group would then receive instruction via the discussion method. Both sections would be given the same or an equivalent test at the conclusion of the course.

4. The difference between Time 1 and Time 2 for each group is computed (Time 2 minus Time 1). Then any difference in outcome between the experimental and control groups can be attributed directly to the effect of the independent variable. Provided that the groups are equivalent at the outset and that they are treated identically in every respect except for the introduction of the independent variable to the experimental group, any difference in result between the two groups can only be a result of the independent variable. All of these features of the classical experimental design are presented in diagram form in Figure 18-4.

For decades, the classical experimental design has been the norm against which social scientists have judged the adequacy of their research designs. However, it is not perfect. Two problems can arise in generalizing from experimental results. One is that people in an experiment may be *sensitized* and therefore respond differently from people not in the experiment. For example, people who see a violent movie in an experimental situation may be aware of the fact that they are in an experiment and therefore respond differently to the dependent variable — for example, aggressive behaviour — from similar people who see the same movie on a Friday night.

The second problem is that in the social sciences experimental subjects are usually volunteers and often students. They are not a representative sample of the general population and, consequently, the results of the experiment may be quite biased.

Furthermore, in many research situations it is simply impossible to design research ideally with equivalent experimental and control groups. In these cases, it is necessary to use deviations from the classical design while recognizing the limitations inherent in them.

## Figure 18-4. Classical Experimental Design

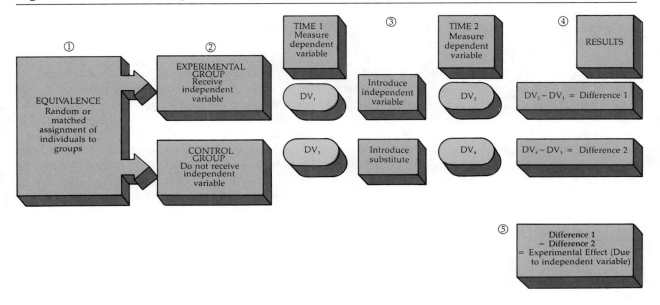

Perhaps the most used design in sociological research is the **cross-sectional design**. Two or more groups with varying degrees of an independent variable are measured at one time to determine how they compare with respect to a dependent variable. For example, much research has been undertaken on the effects of university education (independent variable) on the values of students (dependent variable). Common to all these studies is a comparison of representative groups of students from each year of university. To the extent that year groups vary in the predicted direction (regarding, for example, values such as conservatism), it is concluded that university education is primarily responsible.

In order for this conclusion to be the appropriate one, however, it must be assumed that each year group was equivalent at the beginning of its university education. The assumption cannot be validated with this type of design, and thus competing explanations must be considered as possible alternatives. For example, changes in student values could be because of the aging process of the students and not due to university education. Is the hypothesis necessarily wrong? No. The point is that circumstances frequently force us to go

with a less than ideal design. This does not mean, however, that we can learn nothing, or that what we learn is wrong. Provided that we are careful in designing our study and realize fully the alternative explanations possible, we can still do good research and make modest contributions to scientific knowledge in spite of deviations from the classical experimental design.

It is also important to recognize that in sociology we are often faced with *after* situations for which it is difficult or impossible to set up control groups. Independent variables, such as the changing of school boundaries, the closing of a plant, or the occurrence of a tornado, happen without sociologists' advance knowledge. We may wish to study the effects of such events on individuals, but it is impossible to know what the people in question were like or how they felt *before* the events occurred. Also, we have no way of knowing whether the groups we are comparing were equivalent prior to the occurrence of these independent variables.

Furthermore, we cannot say to the graduating class of a local high school that this half will go to university (experimental group) and this half will not (control group). Instead, the graduates themselves determine the groups. Sociologists, quite rightly, exert little control over people's lives, but this lack of control does make their job more difficult. Some researchers have taken to the laboratories in an attempt to recreate social reality on a small scale. Their findings are, however, often criticized as artificial and negligibly applicable.

To sum up: most researchers keep the classical experimental design in mind when planning their studies. Though it is often impossible to apply this ideal design, knowledge of the particular discrepancies between researchers' own designs and the ideal allows them to anticipate difficulties.

# Sampling

At the same time the research design is being planned, thought must be given to the appropriate sample or population of groups, individuals, or behaviours on which to test the hypothesis. A **population** (or universe) is that body of individuals (or other social units) in which you are interested and to which you will generalize your findings. A **sample** is a smaller representation of this whole, the group that is actually studied. Providing that the sample has been carefully selected, according to well-defined sampling procedures, reliable and valid inferences can be drawn about the larger population.

Taking a sample is not something we do independently of the research we are undertaking. It is an integral part of the research process, and how we do it can greatly influence the kinds of results we achieve. For example, 30 or 40 years ago many hypotheses concerning general social behaviour were tested on samples of university students. The researchers were university professors, and their students were convenient guinea pigs. University students, however, are not typically representative of society, and consequently the findings could not properly be generalized to the larger population. University students are on the average younger, more educated, of a higher social class, and more homogeneous in their values than the larger society of which they are a part. Any or all these characteristics could sys-

tematically affect the results, and therefore they would be specific to this particular group and not appropriate to society in general.

Consider the popular advertising ploy "Four out of five doctors surveyed recommend. . . ." At first glance, this statement appears to suggest that 80 percent of all doctors solidly support Brand X. In order to interpret it accurately, however, we must ascertain the sampling process involved. Were the surveyed doctors a representative sample of the Canadian Medical Association? Were they employees of the company selling Brand X? Quite obviously, a "yes" to either of these questions would evoke different levels of confidence in Brand X. Consequently, as with the other stages of research we have discussed, it is necessary to know the method used — here, how individuals or groups were selected — in order to assess the findings properly.

## Why We Sample

You might think that taking a sample is not as good as making a complete enumeration of the entire population. In many cases, however, it is better, and here is why:

1. *Destruction of the universe*. This ominous phrase is intended simply to suggest that absolute certainty can be too dearly bought. For example, suppose your doctor asks, "What is your blood type?" Would you prefer the doctor to take a sample of your blood or to test the entire population — that is, to take *all* of your blood? This example is not unique. In some cases, it is necessary to take a sample, rather than a complete enumeration, because to do otherwise would destroy the entire universe.

   Consider the claim by a light bulb company that its product burns an average of $x$ hours. What is the factual basis of this claim? Sampling is necessary. If the company tested its entire population of products, it would have no light bulbs to sell. That is, it would have destroyed the entire universe. We have heard that a foolproof method of distinguishing real pearls from fakes is to immerse all specimens of both categories in vinegar. But those that dissolve will be the genuine pearls — a costly way to achieve certainty.

2. *Cost.* In most research, cost considerations are extremely important. Obviously, if we can obtain essentially the same information at a lower cost, we will do so. Sampling allows just such savings, and provided that it is done according to accepted procedures, the data obtained are no less accurate than those from a complete enumeration.

3. *Accessibility to all elements within the universe.* In very large populations, such as Canadian society, it is difficult, costly, and time-consuming simply to locate all the people. Criminals actively avoid being located, many indigents have no fixed address, and occupationally mobile people are constantly relocating. An estimated 1.93 percent of the Canadian population was not counted during the 1971 census, and Kalbach and McVey (1979) argue that this group is different in particular, significant ways from those people who were counted:

*The census tended to miss more persons in British Columbia (2.89 percent) than elsewhere, more divorced persons (5.47 percent) than those of other marital statuses, those who rented (2.82 percent) rather than those who owned their own homes, and those who lived in mobile homes (12.03 percent), etc. In other words, the more socially and economically mobile persons, i.e., young adult males, recent immigrants, and those not related to the head of their households, are more difficult to locate in a census operation.*

Because of these differences, the census itself is not a completely accurate representation of the Canadian people, even though the attempt is made to count everyone. Thus, we see that a sample can actually be a more accurate representation of a population than attempts at a complete enumeration because more time and money *per unit* can be spent in locating relatively inaccessible cases. Consequently, inferences drawn from a sample to a population can be more valid than those drawn from an enumeration — again, provided that proper sampling procedure is observed.

## Types of Samples

First and foremost, a sample should be *representative* of the particular population or universe from which it is drawn. There are many dimensions along which a sample may be representative; the researcher, whenever possible, should attempt to represent those characteristics that pertain directly to the problem being studied. In the social class/delinquency problem discussed earlier, the sample should mirror the distribution of social class within the target population. Because the actual incidence of delinquency is not known and is not easily discernible, it would be impractical to attempt to fill the sample with the same proportion of delinquents and nondelinquents as are found in the universe. But because gender is related to delinquency — the rate is higher for boys than for girls, although as noted in Chapter 6, the gap is narrowing — some attempt should be made to match the gender distribution of the sample to the target population. Otherwise, the results could be misleading and may be misinterpreted.

To the extent that the population is relatively *homogeneous* — that is, to the extent to which each element of the universe is similar with respect to the problem being studied — sampling is much easier, and any sample is likely to be representative. For example, whether your doctor samples your blood from your finger or your toe is unlikely to make a difference. If the population is *heterogeneous*, however, great care must be taken in selecting a sample that reflects this heterogeneity. For this reason, samples of heterogeneous populations should generally be larger than those drawn from homogeneous universes.

There are two main categories of samples. **Random samples** (also known as *probability samples*) are designed to be representative, and the degree to which they are can be estimated very accurately. **Non-random samples** (sometimes known as *non-probability samples*) are also drawn to be representative, but the extent of representativeness cannot be determined. Non-random samples are, however, easier and less costly to take. The defining characteristic of a simple random sample is that each element within the universe has an equal chance (probability) of being selected into the sample. There are many varieties of random samples, but this feature is central to all of them. Because of it, random samples are likely to be representative of the populations from which they are drawn.

**Random Samples.** An essential aspect of random samples is that the population must be explicitly defined or identified. In order for each element to have an equal probability of selection, all elements must be listed. Suppose that you wish to take a random sample of your class, your university, or your town. It is first necessary to make a list of all the people who make up these populations. In many cases, lists already exist (class lists, student directories, registrar records, enumeration lists, city directories, telephone books, tax records). But you must ensure that these lists correspond to your target population, that is, to the population on which you want to make generalizations. Enumeration lists contain only adult citizens; telephone books contain only those people with listed telephones and so probably exclude the very poor, the highly mobile, and those who desire privacy.

Once a list of the particular population is in hand, a random sample is relatively easy to draw. You can literally draw names out of a hat or, if the list is very long, number the people (elements) on the list and then consult a table of random numbers to determine which elements to select. (Tables of random numbers are generated by a computer in such a way that no pattern exists within the numbers; they are randomly listed.) Table 18-1 provides an example of a random sample drawn in this fashion from a numbered population of 80 elements.

Somewhat easier to select is a systematic sample, which combines features of both random and non-random sampling. For **systematic sampling**, the first element is selected at random, and then every fourth, twelfth, or fifteenth name thereafter, depending on what numerical proportion of your population you wish your sample to be. Systematic samples are among the most popular type of sample because they are easy to select and because they generally produce samples similar to random samples (Sudman 1976). Care must be exercised in taking systematic samples, however, in that lists generated for some other purpose may be biased. For example, if you wish to make a

**Table 18-1. A Simple Random Sample of 20 Elements, Selected from a Table of Random Numbers Out of a Population of 80**

| | | | | | |
|----|----|----|----|----|----|
| 34 | 14 | 17 | 68 | 26 | 75 |
| 45 | 39 | (17) | 26 | (95) | |
| 02 | 06 | 77 | (85) | 67 | |
| 05 | (86) | 66 | 11 | (97) | |
| 03 | (87) | 14 | 16 | 73 | |

NOTE: Circled numbers are deleted from the sample either because they have already been included in the sample, or because they do not represent numbers in their population.

survey of a newly constructed housing tract and use a list of addresses provided by the city, you could conceivably have in your sample only those people who live on corner lots. Enough housing studies have been conducted over the years to show that people living on corner lots are significantly different from other residents (for example, people usually pay more for corner lots than for other lots). Consequently, your systematic sample would not be representative of all people living in the suburb.

Another popular random sample is the **stratified random sample**. This type of sample takes into consideration the characteristics that may be relevant to the study and represents them in the sample in proportion to their representation in the population. To return to the social class/delinquency problem, you could take with relative ease a random sample stratified by gender of all secondary school students in your city. Essentially, this would involve taking two simple random samples or two systematic random samples — one of all boys and the other of all girls. The stratified random sample does not leave to chance the appearance of relevant variables in the sample. Thus, if these variables are known before the study, a stratified random sample is to be preferred over simple or systematic random ones.

It is possible to stratify on more than one variable at a time. For example, if the list of secondary school students also contained addresses and if it was possible to approximate social class with neighbourhood, then six simple random samples could be drawn — upper-, middle-, and lower-class boys and upper-, middle-, and lower-class girls. This example should suggest that the more variables chosen on which to stratify (and the more categories within these variables), the more difficult and tedious the sampling becomes. Thus, stratified random samples are seldom stratified on more than two or three variables, even though many more might be directly relevant to the problem at hand.

A more complex type of random sample is termed **multistage**. Generally used with very large populations, it consists of descending stages of random samples toward a level where the use of lists of individuals is practical. Continuing with the social class/delinquency problem, you might want to study this relationship among all secondary school students in Canada. Even if you could secure lists for every high school in the country, the chore of taking a simple, systematic, or stratified sample at this stage would be immense. Instead, it would be much more feasible to take a random sample of school districts, perhaps stratified by province. From this sample, it would then be possible to draw a random sample of schools. Finally, at the third stage, you could take a stratified random sample of students by gender from your sample of schools. In this fashion, a multistage random sample eliminates the tedium and near impossibility of the task and avoids the problem of sampling a population for which no lists exist. This example illustrates that the type of sample drawn is very much related to the kind of problem you have and the population on which you want to generalize.

**Non-random Samples.** The major argument for all random samples is that they are representative of the populations from which they were drawn. Although this point is extremely important to any researcher, there are other factors to consider. Sometimes a case can be made for non-random sampling.

Non-random samples are usually considerably cheaper than random ones. In a random sample, it is necessary to locate specifically selected respondents, who may not always be immediately accessible. Because of this feature, costs increase. People randomly selected who are not at home must be recontacted at a later date. In a non-random sample, by contrast, particular individuals are not chosen. If someone does not answer the door, the next-door neighbour can be substituted. Respondents randomly chosen may not all live in the same geographical area. Consequently, greater expense is involved in reaching these individuals than in non-random samples, which are usually geographically clustered in order to cut costs. Thus, although random samples may be more representative than non-random ones, they are also more costly.

Another argument for non-random sampling is the difficulty encountered in obtaining a random sample. Suppose that you are interested in determining the factors responsible for the apathy regarding student affairs on your campus. In order to get a representative cross-section, you decide to take a random sample stratified by year level. Questionnaires are mailed out, and you obtain a mere 30 percent return, perhaps because of the apathy you are trying to study. How representative is your sample now, particularly in relation to the problem being studied? The point is that there are often serious and sizable discrepancies between the sampling *plan* and its actual *execution*. The greater these discrepancies, the less preferred is the random over the non-random sample.

In some cases, it is simply impossible to take a random sample, and if knowledge is to be gained, a non-random sample must be used. For example, in a well-known study comparing the job satisfaction of people from various countries, Soviet refugees were used to form the sample for the USSR. For a variety of reasons, refugees cannot be considered representative of the Soviet labour force. No other sampling options existed, however, if Soviets were to be included in the comparisons. Similarly, if a researcher is interested in various aspects of crime and deviance, it is impossible to take a random sample of criminals and deviants. The population is not known, so a non-random sample is the only alternative.

The most common type of non-random sample is a **quota sample**. A quota sample is the non-random equivalent of a stratified random sample. The researcher determines which characteristics of the population are important to the study (for example, gender, age, education, occupation, residential area) and then selects a sample with the same proportions of these characteristics as are found in the population. However, because the population is not explicitly defined (that is, listed), each individual does not have an equal chance of being selected, and therefore the sample is not random. In fact, it may be biased in several important ways. Interviewers, in order to fill their quotas, will tend to select those individuals who are most immediately available, and these people could significantly differ from others who are less accessible. Quota sampling has, however, been found to be relatively inexpensive and relatively representative. It is used considerably in market research and public opinion polls.

One important final note on sampling should be made. We are often engaged in sampling without being aware of it. For instance, the time (of the day, week, month, or year) that we choose to do our research can bear on the results. Time for most people is extremely patterned. Most work during the day, engage in more leisure activities during the weekend, get paid at certain times during the month, and are apt to take holidays at regular times of the year. Because we are so time-bound, this should be taken into consideration in the overall research plan and some attempt made to reduce its impact.

Also, the context in which we conduct our research can affect the results. For example, most people are consistently different at work than at home. Researchers have also found that individuals respond differently when alone than when in groups, and the constitution of various groups themselves often affects response.

## Data Collection

Once you decide what problem you are interested in, the basic research design you plan to use, and the sample or population you plan to study, you then gather the data needed to solve your problem. Actually, these decisions are not made sequentially, so you will already have thought of how to gather the data. It is a fact of life that your decision will likely be a compromise between the best way to collect data and what time and money will allow.

There are two general ways of gathering data: asking people for the information you want, and observing their behaviour or the products (**physical trace evidence**) of their behaviour. To illustrate these ways: if you are interested in the drinking patterns of a community, you could ask a sample of the residents how much and how often they drink; you could attempt to learn their actual drinking behaviour by observing them in bars, homes, and liquor stores; or you could gather physical trace evidence by counting bottles in their garbage cans.

Let us consider the first of our data-gathering methods — asking questions. There are two ways of asking people for information: by questionnaire and by interview. The questions can be highly structured, with fixed response categories, or they can be open-ended, allowing more flexibility of response.

## Questionnaires

A questionnaire is a series of questions to be answered by the *respondent*. It may be handed out at work or school or mailed directly to a person's home. If you sample the general population of an area, the respondents are spread out over a fairly large geographical area, so considerations of time and money may make a mail questionnaire your only choice. The questionnaire includes a letter informing the person of the purpose of the questionnaire, how she or he was chosen, reasons encouraging the person to respond, and, usually, assurance of anonymity. A stamped, addressed return envelope is included, and followup letters may also be sent out to increase the rate of response.

The importance of constructing a good questionnaire cannot be overemphasized. Following is the preferred procedure for making a structured questionnaire. You first formulate the questions (indicators) that you believe measure the variables of interest. Once you have constructed the items composing the measures of your concepts and the response categories, you pre-test them. Ideally, this involves sampling a group similar to the group you intend to survey. You then analyze the results of the pre-test, to see if they make sense, and interview the pre-test subjects, to see if the questions mean the same thing to them as they do to you. You can also partly determine if any of the items, as well as the whole set of items, is biasing the results. That is, are the questions worded in such a way that they are forcing or indicating to the respondents how they should answer? For example, you ask, "How old are you?" Suppose a person answers, "20." And you ask, "Are you really 20 right now?" and the reply is, "No, I'm 19 now, but I'm closer to 20 than 19." Consequently, you rephrase your question and ask, "How old are you, to your nearest birthday?"

## Interviews

The procedures used for constructing questionnaires are essentially the same as those used for constructing interview schedules. Since interviewing involves human interaction, however, the potential for problems is greater than with questionnaires, mainly because personal characteristics of researchers and respondents must be considered. Research using face-to-face interviews must be designed so that the results of the study are not the consequence of the interviewer's characteristics. Age, gender, race, behaviour (a raised eyebrow, a vocal inflection), dress, and general appearance — all can influence the respondents' answers. The chances of this occurring are so great that many books have been written about the interviewing process and techniques for minimizing such influence.

The interview itself may vary from a brief, structured session to a lengthy, complicated, unstructured one lasting several hours. The structured interview uses a schedule, which is essentially a questionnaire that is read to the respondents in a specified order. A schedule that specifies only some questions is called semistructured; a schedule that simply indicates the general area to be explored is called unstructured.

There are advantages and disadvantages to structured, as opposed to unstructured, interviews. The structured interview is easy to score, reduces interviewer bias, is more easily replicated, and is more reliable than an unstructured interview. The major advantage of the unstructured interview over the structured one is that the interviewer can explore the respondents' an-

Research using face-to-face interviews must be designed so that the results of the study are not the consequences of the interviewer's characteristics.

swers. The success of this type of interview, however, depends on the skill of the researcher in winning the respondent's confidence and in asking the appropriate questions. It presents serious problems of interpretation; it is also low in reliability and difficult to replicate. Consequently, the tendency is to use structured interviews. However, if the problem being researched is very sensitive (for example, human sexual behaviour), or if little is known about the topic being researched, an unstructured interview may be the best technique to use.

Interviews have several advantages over questionnaires:

1. Interviews generally can be longer.
2. The populations are less restricted, because the respondents need not be able to read or write; they merely have to understand the language of the interviewer.
3. The response rate is usually higher.

4. The identity of the respondents is known, which is very useful in determining differences between respondents and nonrespondents.

But interviews have some major disadvantages compared to questionnaires:

1. Interviews can be expensive to conduct. This problem is becoming so severe that large interview surveys are mainly being undertaken now only by large public and private research institutes (for example, Gallup and Roper), and structured telephone interviewing is becoming increasingly popular as a means of avoiding some of the expense involved in face-to-face interviews.
2. Interview data can be, to varying degrees, affected by characteristics of the interviewer.

## Observation

Both questionnaires and interviews measure opinions, attitudes, and perceived behaviour. But they do not measure actual behaviour, and actual behaviour may be crucial for certain problems. Because of this drawback — nonmeasurement of actual behaviour — and because of the problems associated with questionnaires and interviews, some studies employ various types of observation. *Observation* is the term applied to methods of gathering data without direct questioning. There are basically two different types of observational techniques. One is highly structured and is called nonparticipant observation or, simply, observation. The second type is participant observation.

**Nonparticipant Observation.** Like other structured techniques, **nonparticipant observation** is based on developing explicit categories in order to increase reliability and replicability and to reduce observer bias. This is much easier said than done. It is extremely difficult to obtain accurate and objective observations. If, for example, several of us observed aggression among children in a particular playground and we did not carefully arrive at a common definition of aggression, our observations would be quite different. Some of us might see very little aggression; others would witness a great deal, depending on our subjective

understanding of the term. If a child picks up a toy and looks as if she is going to throw it at another child, some would record this as an aggressive act; others would not. So in order to ensure that we observe the same things in the same way, careful operational definitions of categories are required.

An example of the problems involved in constructing good operational definitions is provided in an observational study of military leadership (Davis and Hagedorn 1954). The researchers were interested in "ways of giving orders," seen as varying on a democratic–authoritarian continuum. Originally, they assumed they would simply record whether or not an order was democratic or authoritarian. They soon discovered, however, that in many instances they could not even be sure whether an order had been given. For example, a sergeant in a car pool says, "Is there a wrench?" and a private stops what he is doing and brings the sergeant a wrench. Was an order given? The researchers solved the problem by writing down anything that a noncommissioned officer said that could in any way be interpreted as an order; then three people classified the notations into "orders" and "non-orders." Where at least two out of three coders agreed that the statement was an order, it was included in the analysis.

**Participant Observation.** Systematic nonparticipant observation, using two or more observers to study the same interaction with predefined categories, has not been widely used in sociological research, probably because of the time and expense involved. **Participant observation**, on the other hand, has been widely used and has resulted in some of the classics of sociological research.

Participant observers are part of the social setting in which they observe events. There is wide variation in the degree of participation by the observer. In an extreme form, the observer is a member of the group being observed, and the group is unaware of the observer's role.

A less intense form of participant observation occurs when the researcher stays with a particular small group or lives in a community. In this case, the researcher usually participates in some of the group's activities while observing them. The members of the group or community are aware that they are being observed. This technique was used by Whyte (1943) in his classic study of a street-corner gang in an Italian slum in the Boston area. Whyte lived in Cornerville for three and a half years and participated in most of the group's activities. They knew he was engaged in research, but presumably they did not care.

The third type of participant observation involves the least participation of the researcher in the activities of the group. In this type of observation, the researcher takes on the role of the objective, neutral observer. The group members know they are being observed, and the observer does not usually participate in the group's activities while observing the group. A person observing a classroom, for example, might spend several hours a day for several weeks recording the various behaviours of the class members; a sociologist might observe a work group over a similarly long period of time. There are two basic differences between this type of participant observation and nonparticipant observation. First, the observers do not have preconceived categories for scoring their observations, and second, they tend to spend a much longer time in the field.

There are several advantages to participant observation:

1. The observations take place in a natural setting. An observational study of workers at their place of work, as opposed to an experimental study of students in a laboratory doing the same kind of work, is more natural and for this reason may be more easily generalized. That is, the findings are more likely to be true of workers in general than only of the experimental subjects.
2. By observing over a long period of time, the researcher gathers a great deal of information on many variables. Also, the dynamics of changes that occur in the situation can be explored. Other methods are rarely this adaptable.
3. The observer can record the context, including the emotional reactions of the subjects, in which the behaviour occurs.
4. Firsthand experience enables the observer to acquire some sense of the subjective meanings that events have for the subjects.
5. An observer who has established good relations (rapport) with the people being observed

may be able to ask sensitive questions that would otherwise not be allowed.

There are, however, at least five major problems associated with participant observation:

1. There is a lack of reliability, which stems from the selective perception of the lone observer. (In this type of research there is nearly always just one observer.) The observer has a particular theoretical orientation, interest, and training — all of which are likely to affect the perception, recording, memory, and interpretation of the events observed.
2. Observers who are not complete participants may sensitize their subjects by their presence. **Sensitization** concerns the alteration of subject behaviour because of the presence of the observer. If, when children are being observed, their behaviour in a classroom is different from their normal behaviour, the observer is not getting a true picture of children's classroom behaviour.
3. If an observer is a member of the group, his or her role in the group greatly restricts the observations that can be made. For example, one participant observer, who took the role of a machine operator, could not observe other work groups, his foreman, or other superiors. He was restricted to one room in one building with one group (Roy 1959).
4. It is difficult to participate in any continuing group without becoming involved in it. If involvement occurs, loss of objectivity results, and the possibility of bias increases. Also, even if the other members of the group are not sensitized by the observer, the behaviour of the group itself changes as a result of the observer's participation.
5. Most observers must wait for occurrences of the behaviour in which they are interested (for example, playground aggression); it is possible that this behaviour may not occur during their time of observation.

Furthermore, with the exception of complete participant observation, all these data-gathering methods — questionnaires, interviews, and observation — have one disadvantage in common: the people being researched know they are being studied, and there is the possibility that they will therefore behave differently from the way they otherwise would. This in turn means the results may be biased.

**Unobtrusive Data-Gathering.** The disadvantage of subjects' being aware that they are being studied is not inevitable; there are unobtrusive data-gathering methods. Any type of research procedure conducted in such a way that the subjects do not know they are being studied is called unobtrusive. Such measures are rarely reactive — that is they do not sensitize subjects (or, to put it another way, subjects do not react to being studied). One type of widely discussed unobtrusive measure is the use of physical trace evidence (Webb et al. 1981), which can be classified as either erosion or accretion. *Erosion measurements* include any type of data occurring from human behaviour that results in the wearing away of some physical object. Examples of erosion indicators are the wearing away of tiles at an art or museum exhibit (popularity), the wear on library books (use), and the wear on children's shoes (activity). *Accretion measurements* include any type of data resulting from human behaviour that leaves some physical trace. Examples of accretion indicators include garbage, archaeological evidence such as pottery and tools, and graffiti. Although seldom used as a major basis of social research, unobtrusive measures can be extremely important for ascertaining the degree to which the other techniques may have sensitized subjects, as well as being used as direct and indirect measures in their own right.

## Content Analysis

The last data collection technique we discuss is **content analysis**, which is "any technique for making inferences by objectively and systematically identifying specified characteristics of messages" (Holsti 1969) — examining the speeches of political candidates, for example, or searching newspaper ads for sexist bias. Content analysis is, then, a systematic procedure for examining the content of recorded information. It renders objective the usually casual and superficial judgments we make of communication content.

There are special problems with content analysis. First is the problem of coding the data or determining the categories. For example, if you want to study changes in gender-role presentation in women's magazines, what categories do you count, what characteristics of women's roles do you look at, and how can you construct exhaustive and reliable categories? You might count the number of fictional heroines who are single as opposed to the number married, the number who work, the types of jobs they hold, and the number with and without children. It should be pointed out, however, that even determining who is a heroine is sometimes difficult.

The second special problem is selecting a sample. In the above example, which magazines do you look at and what time periods do you choose? Virtually any content analysis of mass media involves both a sample of the media (specific books, television shows, or newspapers) and a sample of time. For instance, you might look at a random sample of two women's magazines for a ten-year period. The following example of a content analysis will clarify the problems.

As part of a general study to determine sociologists' ability to make valid social generalizations based on their research, Hedley (1984b) did a content analysis of major sociology journals. His first problem was to decide which of the many journals to choose. After seriously considering all the alternatives, he chose the official journals of the national sociological associations in the United States, Canada, and Great Britain. Because he was concerned with the discipline of sociology as a whole, he wished to avoid selecting journals in only one country. Although it would have been ideal to examine official journals from other countries as well, the time-consuming aspect of content analysis simply prohibited this course.

The next problem was selecting a time period. Hedley hypothesized that the methods of recent sociological research are superior to those of the past and, because of this improvement, sociologists can now make more valid social generalizations. He decided to do a content analysis of journals at a ten-year interval, which would constitute a rigorous test of the hypothesis. This decision resulted in his reading close to 7000 pages of sociological research.

The next task was to operationalize the particular methodological features in which he was interested. With regard to research design, Hedley decided that data collected on at least two separate occasions (*longitudinal designs*) are to be preferred over cross-sectional designs, in that measurement over time tends to reduce the impact of unique historical and social events that can by themselves affect the sociological relationships being studied. He also examined sampling procedures and concluded that representative national or cross-national samples permit greater generalizability than do non-random samples and samples of particular groups or regions. Finally, concerning data collection methods, he noted sociologists' very heavy reliance on interviews and questionnaires. To the extent that researchers use other data sources (for example, nonparticipant and participant observation, physical trace evidence, and already available data from the census, newspapers, or institutional records), there is a balance, and thus less likelihood of attributing social generalizations to a particular method of data collection.

Table 18-2 presents part of the results of this content analysis, showing the changes occurring from the beginning to the end of the ten-year period. Hedley's hypothesis is substantiated in the United States and Canada but rejected in Great Britain. At least in North America then, sociologists' ability to produce valid social generalizations has definitely improved, according to these criteria.

If this example illustrates well the difficulties in doing content analysis, it also demonstrates the advantages of such research:

1. The data are accessible and inexpensive.
2. The data cover a long time period; this makes content analysis very useful for studying trends.
3. The data are gathered unobtrusively; that is, the data collection methods are not reactive.
4. Content analysis can be used to study the larger society or macrosociological problems.

Content analysis also has several main disadvantages. First, almost all the material used is screened or processed and the researcher does not know what selection processes have occurred. It

### Table 18-2. Percentage Change in Selected Methodological Features of Journal Articles, 1968–1978

| Percentage Change in Articles Reporting | Countries in Which Journals Appear | | |
| --- | --- | --- | --- |
| | United States | Canada | Great Britain |
| Longitudinal designs | +21% | +9% | −7% |
| Representative national and foreign samples | +13 | +6 | −6 |
| Data collection methods other than interviews and questionnaires | +15 | +4 | −5 |
| Total number of research articles examined | (143) | (61) | (79) |

SOURCE: Adapted from R. Alan Hedley, "Social generalizations: Biases and solutions," *International Journal of Comparative Sociology* 25(1984):168.

is obvious that a government-censored newspaper is not a very good source of unbiased data. But to some extent all material used in content analysis has been selected by someone for some purpose, and therefore an objective picture may not be possible. Second, content analysis is a very laborious and time-consuming process; this may be one of the reasons it is not used more frequently.

The third disadvantage is that it is very difficult to avoid a great deal of judgment and subjectivity in the coding process and in making inferences. This, of course, introduces bias. The amount of bias can be reduced, but for many types of content analysis it probably cannot be eliminated. The fourth and final disadvantage is that content analysis has historically been mostly used for descriptive and comparative purposes and not for the study of relationships or causal analysis, although there seems to be no inherent reason why it cannot be used for the latter kinds of studies.

## Which Is Best?

This brings to an end our discussion of the main ways in which social scientists collect their data, and the advantages and disadvantages of each method. It is important to remember that there is no reason to consider any particular method as better than or in competition with the others. Social reality should look the same no matter what technique is used to observe it. Sample surveys using questionnaire or interview schedules are the most common method employed by sociologists to collect data. This reliance on one method implies the disadvantages of that method, as previously discussed. The best approach is probably to use as many different techniques as you can. Then, if the same relationship is observed with a variety of methods, relatively more confidence can be placed in the validity of the findings.

## Data Analysis

Analysis of data is a complicated and difficult process. Our concern here is not that you learn how to analyze data; rather, we want to stress the interpretation of the major statistics used in sociological analysis. We hope to make you more competent as consumers of social research. To accomplish this, we will briefly discuss first the processing of data and second the statistics used to describe those data. Because most data in sociology are still gathered by questionnaires or interview-surveys, we will restrict our description to this form of data collection.

### Processing the Data

If you do an honours thesis based on a 30-item questionnaire given to 200 students, you end up with 6000 pieces of information — a relatively small number. Even so, it is impossible to analyze the data by flipping through the pages of the questionnaires. Most questionnaire results are analyzed by computers. The first step in this process is to code the data. This involves making up a code book in which each variable is assigned a column number(s). A *column number* refers to one of a given number of columns on a computer file. For example, gender may be recorded in column 3 with row 1 equalling male, row 2 equalling female, and row 3 equalling all other responses in-

cluding nonresponses. When this has been done, the next step is usually to go through each questionnaire and transfer the data to a code sheet. Alternatively, one can transfer the precoded responses directly into the computer.

**Coding**, then, is reducing the information to a standardized form and always involves a loss of data. For example, in coding census occupations, thousands of occupations must be lumped together. Sociologists, for example, are pooled with people in several other occupations, including penologists and social ecologists. Demographers are coded with statisticians and actuaries. This basic coding is irreversible; you cannot, after the fact, combine demographers with sociologists (Pineo et al. 1977). In the coding process, therefore, you have to be concerned with validity and reliability. A code is valid if it puts similar phenomena in the same category or assigns the same values to similar phenomena. A code is reliable if different coders obtain identical or similar results when coding the same data. Both of these should be checked carefully.

After the data are transferred to code sheets, the common procedure is to have them keyed into a computer for analysis. An increasingly popular technique is to use for questionnaires answer sheets like those students use for taking objective tests. These data can be read by machine and entered directly into a computer. If you decide to do the analysis by hand using a calculator, however, you will still find it more convenient to put the data on code sheets and work from them.

### Quantitative Data Analysis

The enormous amount of information usually gathered in survey research is incomprehensible in raw form. The data are useful only when reduced to some relevant statistic. **Statistics** has two basic definitions. First, statistics mean numbers — that is, the actual data gathered. When someone says, "Statistics show the Tories will win," he or she is using the word in this sense. Average age at marriage, average income, percentage Liberal, and so on are examples of statistics defined as numbers. Second, statistics refer to the theories and techniques that have been developed to manipulate data. Percentages, rates, averages, and measures of relation are statistics in this sense. In

**The rapid development of computer technology has dramatically increased the size of the data sets sociologists analyze.**

either sense, statistics concern the manipulation of numbers.

Some of the first statistics you might use to make sense out of your data are percentages, rates, and ratios. For most problems there is little sense in comparing, for example, the provinces of Ontario and Manitoba on the total number of births, deaths, suicides, or crimes. Obviously, Ontario is going to have more of all of these because of its larger population. Even if Ontario has a low crime rate and Manitoba a high one, Ontario will have more crimes. If we want to compare these two or any two units that differ greatly in size, we must control for this factor. This can be done by computing percentages, ratios, or rates.

Instead of computing births, deaths, suicides, and crimes, we compute birth rates, death rates, suicide rates, and crime rates. For example, the crude birth rate, as you saw in Chapter 7, is the number of births divided by the population of a given community and multiplied by 1000. This mathematical operation eliminates population size as a factor and thus makes possible meaningful comparisons between groups of different sizes. Percentages provide the same kind of control. The point is that it is not meaningful to compare groups without knowing the size of both groups. For example, 50 people in group A are alcoholics and 100 people in group B are alcoholics, but there are 100 people in group A and 400 in group B. Then 50 percent of group A are alcoholics, compared to 25 percent for group B.

Such statistics are usually easy to compute, are necessary for comparing groups of different sizes,

# Which Headline Is Correct?

1. "White Incomes Increase More Than Black!"
2. "Black Incomes Increase More Than White!"
3. "Little Change Between White and Black Incomes!"

Many statistics in the mass media — and certainly income statistics should be included — are too important to be handled or read carelessly. The consumer of these statistics needs knowledge to interpret them correctly.

In 1969, white per capita income in the United States was $6522; by 1979 it was $7808, for an increase of $1286. Black per capita income was $3566 in 1969 and $4545 in 1979, an increase of only $979. On the basis of the dollar amounts or the raw numbers, Headline 1 is an accurate statement.

For whites, the increase of $1286 represents 19.7 percent over their 1969 income; for blacks, their increase $979 is 27.5 percent of the 1969 figure. On the basis of percentage change in per capita incomes, Headline 2 is also accurate.

Now, look at black income as a proportion of white income for the two periods: in 1969 it is 3566/6522, or 0.55; in 1979 it is 4545/7808, or 0.58. On the basis of proportions or ratios, Headline 3 is accurate as well.

Based on the same data, we have three very different conclusions. All are correct, depending on how you analyze the data. Just as you prefer one of these conclusions over the others, so too may the person presenting these data. This suggests that we should add another question to our list of aids in interpreting statistics: what possible biases may the author have?

Which headline is correct?

**Source:**

Adapted from John G. Keane, "Questionable statistics," *Population Today* 13(December 1985):9.

---

and are easy to interpret. Nevertheless, there are certain questions that can be asked to help interpret these statistics:

1. What is (are) the operational definition(s) of the variables?
2. What is the sample or population?
3. What can the specific statistic be compared with?
4. What is the reverse conclusion?

The following example deals with each of these four questions. Consider the following newspaper headline:

30% Failures in Forces' Fitness Test
(*Victoria Colonist*)

The size of the headline alone suggests that the Canadian armed forces are falling apart.

1. What is the operational definition or measure of fitness? In this case, fitness meant that a male under 30 years had to be able to run 2400 metres in less than 14 minutes.
2. What is the sample or population? In this case it was 67 000 military personnel. There was no statement as to what the population was, how this sample of 67 000 was drawn, or what pro- portion of the population it represented. This lack of information made it very difficult to interpret what the 30 percent failure rate meant. If all 67 000 were combat troops, who presumably should be in good physical condition, a 30 percent failure would seem to be more serious than if the group included deskbound officers and enlisted men. Also, since the fitness test was defined in terms of males, one might presume that none of the 67 000 was female. But this is only a presumption.
3. What can we compare this 30 percent failure with? No data were given as to the failure rate for the general population, but a major was quoted as saying, "I would suggest the fitness level is slightly above that of the general population but not a great deal better." No evidence was given to support that statement. The article did point out that five years previously, 50 percent had failed. If the tests were comparable, this would suggest considerable improvement in fitness of military personnel. So is the military falling apart or upgrading itself?
4. What is the reverse conclusion? If the headline had said "70% Pass Forces' Fitness Test," would you have interpreted the statement differently? The meaning behind headlines is often elusive.

The next time you read that one in four marriages ends in divorce, remember that three out of four do not.

## Measures of Central Tendency

It is frequently necessary to use summary statistics that describe group characteristics. One of the most common of these are measures of **averages**. An average is an important measure because it reduces the data to one meaningful value that is readily understood and easily communicated. We often refer to averages — the average person, average weight, average height, average income, average grade point — and the typical person on the street.

Briefly, there are three types of averages — the mode, median, and mean. The **mode** is the most frequently occurring score or category in a distribution. The **median** is the category or point above and below which half the total frequency lies (it is the middle category that divides the frequency in half). The **mean** is what we usually think of when we use the word *average*. It is the value obtained by adding all values in the distribution and dividing by the number in the distribution. Another way of thinking of the mean is that it is the amount of something that everyone would have if each person had the same. In a group of five people, if two have $1, one has $3, one has $5, and one has $40 dollars, the mode is $1 — the most common category. The median is $3; it divides the frequency in half, two persons having more than $3 and two less than $3. The mean is $10; add up the five amounts and divide by the total number of persons ($50 ÷ 5 = $10).

In describing the central tendency or typical value of the group, the researcher must select the average that best reflects this typical value. The mode is very unstable. In our example, if one member who had $1 finds $4 more, the mode is now $5. Should that member be lucky enough to find $39, the mode would be $40. So one score can drastically change the mode.

The mean is by far the most widely used measure, because it is used to compute many other statistics, and because it is relatively stable across samples. Its major disadvantage is that it is unduly affected by extreme scores. This should be clear from the example, where the mean of $10 is not very descriptive of the typical value of the group, because of the one person with $40 and the two with only $1 each. If the distribution had been two with $5, one with $10, and two with $15, the mean would still be $10, but it would be a more accurate description of the average amount of money in this group.

The median is not as useful as the mean for computing other statistics and can itself be difficult to compute. If the data are only rank ordered, or if there are extreme scores, however, the median will likely be the most accurate description. Consequently, if you have reason to believe that there are extreme scores or values, usually true of income data, be wary of the mean, and tend to prefer the median.

It is probably obvious at this point that you can have distributions that look very different, but have the same mean. This fact suggests that to interpret an average, to know how accurately it describes the population, you need to know what the distribution is like. More specifically, you need to know how far group members depart from the mean. Another way of saying the same thing is that you need to know how the scores are dispersed, or spread, around the mean. In the previous example of five people, if each has $10, there is no dispersion, and the mean tells you exactly what each member has. In the case where four people have $1 and one has $46, however, there is great dispersion around the mean, and it is therefore an inaccurate description of the typical value of the group. It simply does not contain much meaningful information. Averages can be misleading and uninformative, and that is why an accompanying dispersion measure can be helpful.

In order to inform readers of the accuracy of the average, a measure of **dispersion** is usually given. Almost all the dispersion measures you will encounter are based on deviations from average scores, either the median or the mean. The statistic you will most frequently encounter is called the **standard deviation** (SD). The larger the SD, the greater the spread of values around the mean or the less the group members are alike. In our example, the SD for the first distribution where all five have $10 is 0 and for the second distribution is 18. (Eighteen is obtained by subtracting the mean from each score, squaring the results, and summing the squares, then dividing the sum of the squares by the number of people and taking the square root of the result.) A measure of dispersion, then, helps you determine the degree to which an average is an accurate description of the typical values of the group. If you ever go swimming in a strange lake and are told the average depth is 7 metres, find out the standard deviation *before* you dive in.

## Measures of Association

The measures we have been discussing are used to describe a single variable, such as income, births, or crime. Sociologists are seldom interested, however, in collecting facts for the sake of facts. Usually they want to know how these facts are related to one another. If they calculate a crime rate, it is to see if it is related to some other variable, such as gender or income. It is relationships that sociologists try to explain. This means that they must determine the degree to which the variables they are interested in are related.

There are many ways to measure **association** and each one may be interpreted in ways different from the others. However, some general comments will aid you in interpreting these measures. The measures most often used in sociology are *gamma, tau, rho, lambda,* and *r* (the Pearson correlation coefficient). Most measures of association, including all of the ones just mentioned, have values between zero and one. Values close to zero indicate a low relationship; those near one indicate a high relationship. In other words, the higher the value, the greater the relationship between any two variables.

The direction of the relationship is also included in these statistics: positive or negative. A **positive (direct) relation** occurs when one variable increases as the other variable increases, or when one decreases as the other decreases. The two variables move or change in the same direction. For example, many students attend university because of a belief in a positive relationship between education and income. That is, as education increases, income increases. A perfect positive relationship equals $+1.00$. On the other hand, a **negative (inverse) relation** occurs when one variable increases as the other decreases. For example, as age increases, athletic prowess decreases. A perfect negative relationship equals $-1.00$.

As we stated previously, there is no one simple interpretation for the various statistics. However, for the most commonly used measure, $r$, the simplest interpretation is in terms of $r^2$, which is the variance explained. If our $r = 0.70$, $r^2 = 0.49$, which is the proportion of the variance explained by one variable on the other. In the education-income example, 49 percent of the variance in income is explained by education. This also means that 51 percent of the variance in income is not accounted for by education. With other measures of association, it is necessary to rely on the magnitude of the relationship in order to interpret it; the closer to 1 the particular measure is, the greater the relationship between them.

In order to interpret these measures (percentages, rates, and measures of association), sociologists frequently report a "P value." Generally, at the bottom of a table you will see an equation such as $P = 0.05$ (or some other value), or a statement such as "Correlation significant at 0.05 level." This statistic is telling you that the correlation is not a result of chance. To put the point another way, if the study was done again, you would find approximately the same correlation.

In the social sciences, if a relation occurs at the 0.05 level, or 0.01, or 0.001, it is considered statistically significant. To say that the finding is statistically significant is only to say that the finding is very unlikely to be a result of chance. To say that a finding is not a chance finding, however, is not to say what it is. And it should not be confused with saying something is theoretically or practically significant. It does mean, however, that whatever was found is likely what is there; that is, if you do the study again, you will likely find the same thing.

We hope that this brief review of data analysis will give you a sense of how data are processed and analyzed. Furthermore, we hope that the discussion of the major statistics used in the analysis of data will enable you to read with heightened understanding the tables and charts in this book and to some extent interpret the statistics for yourself.

# The Value of Research Methods

Knowledge and understanding of what is involved in the research process enables consumers of research findings to assess the results independently and to arrive at their own conclusions. Depending on how the research was undertaken, what kind of design was used, the sample taken, and the data collection methods employed, the results may be more or less valid. The informed consumer can evaluate results in light of these considerations.

As a fruitful exercise in critical evaluation, you can use what is contained in this chapter to assess the research reported in other chapters of this book. Questions that should constantly come to mind include: how do you know? what are the operational definitions? can any other factors explain this result? under what conditions does this assertion hold? To the extent that you develop this critical appreciation of research, you will not be obliged to accept the claims of others on faith. Even if you never undertake a single piece of research in your lifetime, it is essential to have knowledge of what is involved in social research.

## SUMMARY

1. Hunches, personal problems, observations, conversations, and theory are all sources of research problems. Whatever the source, the steps in researching a problem are familiarizing yourself with previous research and writing on the problem, stating the relationship you expect to find between your independent and dependent variables, and constructing operational definitions of the variables.

2. The basic problem in measurement is achieving validity — measuring what you intend to measure. Reliability checks and replication are ways of solving the problem of validity. The key to validity is varied and repeated measurement.

3. The purpose of a research design is to eliminate alternative explanations for the results. The ideal, although not perfect, design is the classical experimental design. A much-used deviation from the classical design is the cross-sectional design.

4. In sociology, most research involves a sample rather than the total population. The major concern in sampling is attempting to make the sample representative of the population. To achieve a representative sample, random sampling procedures are usually employed. Types of random samples are simple random, systematic, stratified random, and multistage. Sometimes it is impossible or too costly to use random sampling procedures. In these cases, non-random samples, such as quota samples, are used.

5. All data collection is based on asking or observing; it can be structured or unstructured. The most commonly used techniques in sociology are structured questionnaires, structured interviews, and participant observation. A particularly useful method for already recorded information is content analysis. All these techniques have advantages and disadvantages that determine their usefulness for a particular research problem.

6. After quantitative data have been collected, they are submitted to analysis. This frequently involves coding the data and keying them into a computer for analysis. Various statistics are used to describe the data and to tell how important findings and relationships are. The emphasis in this section is on how to interpret the major statistics used in sociological research.

## GLOSSARY

**Association.** Statistical relation between two or more variables. The most common measures of association are *gamma, tau, rho, lambda,* and *r.*

**Average.** A measure that reduces a set of data to one meaningful value: for example, **the mean**, the **median**, or **the mode**.

**Classical experimental design.** Research design that involves the comparison of two equivalent groups at two points in time to determine the effects of an independent variable on a dependent variable.

**Coding.** Process of transforming answers in a questionnaire into usable data.

**Content analysis.** Any systematic procedure for examining the content of recorded information; usually applied to the mass media.

**Control group.** The comparison group that is denied the effects of the independent variable in the classical experimental design.

**Cross-sectional design.** Research design in which two or more groups with varying degrees of an independent variable are measured at one point in time to determine how they compare with respect to a dependent variable.

**Dependent variable.** The variable that research attempts to explain according to how it is affected by some other variable(s).

**Dispersion.** Statistics that describe the spread in the scores of a distribution.

**Experimental group.** The comparison group that is subjected to the independent variable in the classical experimental design.

**Hypothesis.** Prediction of what you expect to find as a result of research; a statement of the relation between two or more variables.

**Independent variable.** Causal or explanatory variable.

**Indicator.** Empirical measure of a variable.

**Mean.** Sum of all of the scores divided by the number of scores; the score each case would have if the variable were distributed equally.

**Median.** Score that divides a distribution into two equal parts.

**Mode.** Score that occurs most frequently in a distribution.

**Multistage random sample.** Combination of random samples through several stages.

**Negative (inverse) relation.** Relation in which two or more variables change in opposite directions; as one increases the other decreases.

**Nonparticipant observation.** Systematic, objective observation of social behaviour using explicit predefined categories.

**Non-random sample.** Sample in which the probability of elements within the population being chosen cannot be known; easier and less costly than a random sample.

**Operational definition.** Precise set of instructions enabling a researcher to measure indicators that correspond to variables; operational definitions enable different researchers to get the same results when measuring the same phenomena.

**Participant observation.** Situation in which the researchers take an active part, in varying degrees, in the situation they are directly observing.

**Physical trace evidence.** Observational data based on accretion or erosion.

**Population.** Largest number of individuals or units of interest to the researcher.

**Positive (direct) relation.** Relation in which two or more variables change in the same direction; as one increases the other increases, or as one decreases the other decreases.

**Quota sample.** Sample with the same proportion of certain characteristics as found in the population; the non-random equivalent of a stratified random sample.

**Random sample.** Sample in which each element within the population has an equal chance of appearing; also called *probability sample*.

**Reliability.** Consistency of results over time or with several investigators.

**Replication.** Systematic repeated measurement of a given relationship.

**Sample.** Smaller representation of a population or universe; properties of the sample are studied to gain information about the whole.

**Sensitization.** Process by which subjects become aware that they are being studied.

**Standard deviation (SD).** Measure of dispersion based on deviations from the mean.

**Statistics.** Actual numbers; and the theories and techniques used to manipulate data.

**Stratified random sample.** Series of random samples designed to represent some population characteristic.

**Systematic sample.** Sample in which the first element from a population is selected at random followed by every succeeding $n$th element.

**Validity.** Property of measurement whereby what is measured is what is intended to be measured.

**Variable.** Factor that can differ or vary from one situation to another, or from one individual or group to another; a concept that has more than one value.

## FURTHER READING

**Hammond, Phillip E. (ed.).** *Sociologists At Work.* New York: Basic Books, 1964. A collection of essays by sociologists on how they conducted their own research projects and the problems they encountered.

**Kaplan, Abraham.** *The Conduct of Inquiry.* San Francisco: Chandler, 1964. An exploration of how we know something is true and how we explain the social world in a clear way.

**Labovitz, S., and R. Hagedorn.** *Introduction to Social Research.* 3rd edition. New York: McGraw-Hill, 1981. A small, highly readable book that treats in slightly more detail the issues raised in this chapter.

**Smith, H.W..** *Strategies of Social Research.* 2nd edition Englewood Cliffs, NJ: Prentice-Hall, 1981. Chapter 5 is a very complete description of structured observational techniques.

**Sudman, Seymour.** *Applied Sampling.* New York: Academic Press, 1976. A readable and well-written text covering all aspects of sampling.

# Glossary

**Absolute deprivation.** Structured disadvantages rooted in concrete inequalities of wealth, status, or power.

**Activities of daily living (ADL).** Everyday activities, such as rising and going to bed, personal hygiene, and shopping.

**Activity theory.** A theory that emphasizes that continuing activity through social roles is required in order to attain high life satisfaction in the later years.

**Adult socialization.** Socialization that takes place after childhood to prepare people for adult roles (for example, husband, mother, computer technician).

**Age-specific birth rate.** Incidence of births in a given year per 1000 women of a given age group. The rates are calculated for five-year age groups. For example, the age-specific birth rate for women aged 20 to 24 would be calculated as follows:

$$\text{Age-specific birth rate} = \frac{\begin{array}{c}\text{Number of births to}\\\text{women aged 20 to 24}\\\text{in a given year}\end{array}}{\begin{array}{c}\text{Mid-year population of}\\\text{women aged 20 to 24}\end{array}} \times 1000$$

**Age strata.** Socially recognized divisions ordered over the life course, with which are associated rights, responsibilities, obligations, and access to rewards.

**Age-stratification perspective.** A theoretical approach that focuses on the progression of birth cohorts through the age strata of a society and, in addition, views the age-stratification system as changing in response to cohort characteristics and other social phenomena.

**Age structure.** When pertaining to population, the proportion of people in each age category.

**Agricultural society.** Society in which at least half the labour force is engaged in the primary sector.

**Agricultural surplus.** Quantity of food greater than that required to meet the needs of its producers.

**Alienation.** Individuals' feelings that, as workers, they are small, meaningless parts of an insensitive production system over which they have little control.

**Altercasting.** Casting the other person in a role we choose for him or her in order to manipulate the situation.

**Amalgamation.** Process by which groups are blended into a melting pot where none remains distinctive.

**American Civil Religion.** Tendency for nationalistic emphases in the United States to have many characteristics similar to religions; established Judeo-Christian tradition is drawn upon selectively.

**Androgyny.** Presence of both masculine and feminine characteristics within individuals of both sexes.

**Anomie.** Term originally used by Durkheim to refer to an absence of social regulation, or normlessness. Merton revived the concept to refer to the consequences of a faulty relationship between goals and the legitimate means of attaining them.

**Anticipatory socialization.** Role-learning that occurs in advance of the actual playing of roles.

**Arbitration.** Process whereby a third party intervenes between management and labour and passes binding judgment on the new collective agreement.

**Arranged marriage.** Marriage in which the spouses are chosen by parents or other family elders.

**Assimilation.** Process by which a group becomes like the dominant group, and no longer remains distinctive. Also referred to in North America as "Anglo-conformity."

**Association.** Statistical relation between two or more variables. The most common measures of association are *gamma, tau, rho, lambda,* and *r*.

**Average.** A measure that reduces a set of data to one meaningful value: for example, **the mean**, the **median**, or **the mode**.

**Biosociology.** The branch of sociology that studies the interaction and mutual influences between the social order and the biological makeup of its members.

**Blended family.** Type of nuclear family that is based on remarriage and includes children from previous marriages; also known as a *reconstituted* family.

**Bloc recruitment.** The attraction of sets of supporters already linked by friendship or organizational ties.

**Bourgeois democracy.** The view held by Marxists that government policies in a capitalist society necessarily favour the bourgeoisie — that is, the capitalist class. This is so even in polities with universal voting rights.

**Breakdown theory.** An approach that attributes social movement formation to disorganization and disorientation caused by rapid social change.

**Bureaucracy.** A formal organization based on the application of legal-rational principles.

**Care orientation.** Gilligan's feminine orientation to morality, which emphasizes concern for and connectedness with others.

**Centralized structure.** Structure of an organization in which authority and decision-making are concentrated in a few people at senior levels.

**Charismatic authority.** Authority that is based on the belief that the individual leader is special and possesses some exceptional ability or magic, which inspires loyalty in the followers.

**Charter groups.** The two original European migration groups (British and French) whose legalized claims for such historically established privileges as the perpetuation of their separate languages and cultures are enshrined in the Canadian Constitution.

**Church–sect typology.** Framework, dating back to Weber and historian Ernst Troeltsch (1931), that examines religious organizations in terms of ideal-type, church, and sect characteristics.

**Circular reaction.** A process through which individuals in crowds directly copy one another's excited moods and actions leading to disorderly, irrational behaviour.

**City.** Large concentration of people engaged in a wide range of specialized and interdependent occupations that, for the most part, do not involve the primary production of food.

**Class conflict.** Antagonism between social classes, especially between the class that owns the means of production and the classes that do not.

**Classical conditioning.** Type of learning that involves the near-simultaneous presentation of an unconditioned stimulus (UCS) and a conditioned stimulus (CS) to an organism in a drive state (that is, a state during which needs such as hunger or thirst require satisfaction). After several trials, the previously neutral stimulus (CS) alone produces the response normally associated with the UCS.

**Classical experimental design.** Research design that involves the comparison of two equivalent groups at two points in time to determine the effects of an independent variable on a dependent variable.

**Closed system.** Theoretical perspective of organizations as relatively self-contained units in which particular structural arrangements and individual behaviour patterns can be accounted for by factors internal to the organization.

**Coding.** Process of transforming answers in a questionnaire into usable data.

**Coercive tactics.** The symbolic or actual disruption of institutional routines in order to attract support or exert pressure for movement demands.

**Cohesiveness.** Conditions whereby individuals identify themselves as members of the group, members want the group to remain together, and group members have a high regard for each other.

**Cohort.** Group of people in a population sharing a common demographic event (for example, year of birth, or year of marriage).

**Cohort (birth).** A set of individuals born at approximately the same time, who move through the life course together.

**Cohort measures.** Measures of the frequency of a given event characteristic of a cohort.

**Collective conscience.** Durkheim's term for the awareness that the group is more than the sum of its individual members; norms, for example, appear to exist on a level beyond the consciences of individual group members.

**Collective good.** A benefit available to all members of a group, whether or not they contribute to the cost of gaining it.

**Collective religiosity.** Religious commitment as manifested in and through religious groups; key to the creation and sustenance of personal religiosity.

**Commodity production.** Goods and services created for exchange in the marketplace.

**Community.** Identifiable self-conscious group with shared common interests. Communities may or may not have a territorial base, and they vary in their level of self-sufficiency.

**Competition.** Action of two or more groups or activities that attempt to occupy the same area.

**Concentric zone model.** Model of the city in which economic and residential activity patterns and social groups are segregated in concentric zones, with economic activities located at the centre of the city and residential activities located toward the periphery.

**Conciliation.** Process whereby a third party intervenes between management and labour and makes recommendations regarding a new collective agreement.

**Conflict crimes.** Acts that are defined by law as criminal and are often severely punished, but are usually regarded as only marginally harmful; typically they are subjects of conflict and debate.

**Conflict perspective.** A macrosociological view emphasizing that conflict, power, and change are permanent features of society.

**Conflict subculture.** Illegal group activity that is prone to violence and is common in settings (for example, "disorganized slums") where legitimate and illegitimate spheres are not integrated.

**Conflict theories of deviance.** Theories that focus particularly on the way dominant societal groups impose their legal controls on members of subordinate societal groups.

**Conjugal family.** Type of nuclear family pattern characterized by an emphasis on the husband/wife tie and a relative de-emphasis on the wider kin network.

**Consensus crimes.** Acts defined by law as criminal that are widely regarded as extremely harmful, are severely punished, and are consensually identified as deviant.

**Consensus perspective.** A macrosociological perspective that stresses the integration of society through shared values and norms.

**Conservative perspective on social inequality.** Normative theory holding that inequality is necessary, inevitable, and basically just.

**Content analysis.** Any systematic procedure for examining the content of recorded information; usually applied to the mass media.

**Contest mobility.** Open competition for elite status.

**Continuity theory.** A loosely defined theoretical approach that argues that life satisfaction in the later years is enhanced by a continuation of lifelong patterns of activity and role involvement, whether high or low.

**Control group.** The comparison group that is denied the effects of the independent variable in the classical experimental design.

**Corporate elite.** Those who sit on the boards of directors of the largest corporations and financial institutions.

**Corporation.** Legal entity created for purposes of conducting business; it has an existence separate from that of its members while providing them with limited liability.

**Counter-ideologies.** Reformist and radical ideologies that call for changes in the status quo.

**Counter-movements.** Collective attempts to resist or reverse change or the demands for change made by some other social movement.

**Craft union.** Formal organization of workers based on their specialized skills. (Also called a trade union.)

**Crime control model.** Model of law enforcement that places heavy emphasis on the repression of criminal conduct, because ensuring order is seen as the only way to guarantee individual freedom.

**Cross-sectional design.** Research design in which two or more groups with varying degrees of an independent variable are measured at one point in time to determine how they compare with respect to a dependent variable.

**Crude rate.** Frequency of an event per unit of the total population, usually 1000. Applied especially to deaths and births.

**Cultural convergence.** Thesis that advocates that the process of industrialization will produce a common world culture.

**Cultural diffusion.** The process whereby cultural elements are borrowed by one society from another (as opposed to independent development of these elements in each society).

**Cultural infrastructure.** Specialized groups with an interest, often economic, in the production and preservation of cultural symbols and the supporting ground rules.

**Cultural relativism.** The view that all cultures are equally valid and valuable and that each culture must be judged by its own standards.

**Cultural universals.** Behaviour patterns found in many cultures.

**Culture.** Shared set of symbols and their definitions or meanings prevailing in a society.

**Decentralized structure.** Structure of an organization in which authority and decision-making are widely distributed among people at various levels.

**Definition of the situation.** Beliefs and norms about an interaction setting.

**Delinquent subculture.** Collective response of working-class adolescents to their failure to satisfy middle-class expectations; the result is an inversion of middle-class values.

**Democratic citizenship training.** Preparation for political participation in the affairs of a democratic society.

**Democratic elitism.** Idea that the most important function of mass participation in politics is the formation of a political elite, the members of which compete for the votes of a largely passive electorate.

**Demographic momentum.** Tendency for future population growth due to a concentration of people in the young ages.

**Demographic transition theory.** Description and explanation of the three-stage transition or "shift" from high birth and death rates to low birth and death rates as societies become industrialized and urbanized.

**Demography.** Scientific study of population.

**Denominationalism.** Tendency for a wide variety of Protestant religious groups to come into being, seemingly reflecting variations not only in theology but also — and perhaps primarily — in social characteristics.

**Dependency ratio.** Ratio of the economically dependent population (under 15, 65 and over) to the productive population (15 to 64). Calculated as follows:

$$\text{Dependency ratio} = \frac{\text{population under 15} + \text{Population aged 65 and over}}{\text{Population aged 15 to 64}} \times 100$$

**Dependency theory.** Theory that the economies of hinterland areas become so specialized in primary industries (such as farming, fishing, or the extraction of raw materials) that trade with metropolitan areas for manufactured goods and services is necessary for the hinterland population to maintain a given standard of living. This places the hinterland in a politically disadvantageous position.

**Dependent variable.** The variable that research attempts to explain according to how it is affected by some other variable(s).

**Descriptive beliefs.** Statements or claims about what is, was, or will be, including ideas about cause and effect.

**Deurbanization.** A decrease in the proportion of a given population inhabiting urban areas.

**Deviance.** Variation from a norm, made socially significant through the reaction of others.

**Differential association.** Process by which criminal behaviour is learned in conjunction with people who define such behaviour favourably and in isolation from those who define it unfavourably.

**Dimensions of religiosity.** Various facets of religious commitment; Glock and Stark, for example, identify four — belief, experience, practice, and knowledge.

**Discrimination.** Process by which a person is deprived of equal access to privileges and opportunities available to others.

**Disengagement theory.** A theory that argues that successful aging involves a mutual withdrawal of the aging individual and society. This is seen as functional for the society and beneficial for the individual. Such disengagement is viewed as normal and, ideally, voluntary on the part of the individual.

**Dispersion.** Statistics that describe the spread in the scores of a distribution.

**Division of labour.** Process whereby general tasks and roles become increasingly specialized.

**Dominant ideologies.** Ruling ideologies that explain and justify the existing ways of doing things.

**Doubling time.** Number of years it would take for a population to double its present size, given the current rate of population growth. Calculated as follows:

$$\text{Doubling time} = \frac{693}{\text{Annual rate of growth}}$$

**Due process model.** Model of law enforcement that emphasizes procedural safeguards thought useful in protecting accused persons from unjust applications of criminal penalties.

**Dynamic equilibrium.** Parsons's term for the orderly change that constantly occurs among the interrelated parts of a social system.

**Dysfunctional.** Adjective applied to parts of a social system that disrupt or are harmful to the system.

**Education.** Deliberate, organized transmission of values, knowledge, and skills.

**Egalitarian families.** Families in which the spouses share equally in power and authority.

**Ego.** The director of the Freudian personality. The Ego attempts to mediate among the demands of the Id, the Super-ego, and the external world. The Ego, which encompasses the cognitive functions and the defence mechanisms, is governed by the reality principle.

**Elaborated language code.** Form of communication that makes meanings explicit and universal.

**Elite.** A relatively small number of persons who occupy the key decision-making positions in an institutional sphere.

**Elite preparatory.** Stage of educational development in a society: the majority of students do not finish high school, and the function of the high school is restricted to preparing a select group of students for university education.

**Emergent norms.** Norms that are generated in exceptional circumstances to guide and contain group behaviour.

**Empty box view of education.** View that schools are passive transmitters for outside influences, with no life of their own.

**Endogamy.** Marriage rule stipulating that marriages must occur within a defined social group.

**Entrance group.** Ethnic group that is not a founder of the country and whose members enter as immigrants after the national framework has been established.

**Equality of access.** Removal of external barriers to educational participation.

**Equality of nurture.** Removal of barriers to educational performance.

**Equilibrium.** In consensus theory, or structural functionalism, the overall balance that exists among the elements in a system.

**Ethnic group.** Group of individuals with a shared sense of peoplehood based on presumed shared sociocultural experiences and/or similar characteristics. They perceive themselves as alike by virtue of their common ancestry.

**Ethnic identity.** Attitude of being united in spirit, outlook, or principle with an ethnic heritage. An attachment and positive orientation toward a group with whom individuals believe they have a common ancestry and interest.

**Ethnic stratification.** Order in which ethnic groups form a hierarchy of dominance and socioeconomic status in a society.

**Ethnocentrism.** Tendency to use one's own group or culture as the only valid standard for evaluating other cultures, societies, and peoples.

**Ethnomethodology.** Sociological perspective concerned with the methods people use to carry out their everyday activities; language and meaning; and the implicit norms that govern behaviour.

**Exchange theory.** A view of social interaction as an exchange of rewards. Individuals are assumed to seek to maximize rewards and minimize costs.

**Exogamy.** Marriage rule stipulating that marriages must occur outside a defined social group. This rule may be seen as an extension of the incest taboo.

**Experimental group.** The comparison group that is subjected to the independent variable in the classical experimental design.

**Extended family.** Family type consisting of two or more nuclear families joined through blood ties — that is, through a parent/child relationship.

**Factions.** Splinter organizations within a movement holding conflicting views on the degree, nature, or tactics of social change to be pursued.

**Family time.** Changes that occur within a family as it develops over time.

**Fecundity.** Physiological capacity of a woman or group of women to produce children.

**Federal system.** Political system in which entrenched powers are divided between a central government and subcentral governments. In Canada, the latter are called provinces.

**Fertility.** Actual child-bearing performance of a woman or group of women; an important component of population change.

**Folkways.** Traditional rules about customary ways of behaving that are informally enforced and of mild concern to society members.

**Forces of production.** A Marxist term for the resources, both natural and human, and for the technology typical of a particular economic system.

**Formal organization.** Relatively enduring or continuing social collectivity in which roles and resources are co-ordinated through a division of labour in the use of a technology to achieve a goal or goals. Co-ordination, control, and problem-solving are facilitated through communication, leadership, and varying degrees of written rules and procedures.

**Formalization.** Process by which the informality of relationships is gradually replaced by varying degrees of rules, codes of conduct, laws, and other means of regulation.

**Free riders.** Individuals who benefit from a collective good without contributing to the costs of acquiring it.

**Frustration/aggression approach.** An approach that

makes a direct link between the level of dissatisfaction and the intensity of rebellion it will provoke.

**Functional.** Adjective applied to parts of a social system that contribute to the overall stability of the system.

**Gemeinschaft.** Tönnies's term for relatively small organizations characterized by a commitment to tradition, informal social control, intimate interpersonal contact, a collective orientation, and group consciousness.

**Gender.** Societal definition of appropriate female and male traits and behaviours.

**Gender assignment.** The designation of a person as female or male.

**Gender identity.** The individual's conviction of being male or female.

**Gender script.** The details of a society's ideas about masculinity and femininity contained, for example, in gender stereotypes and gender attitudes.

**Gender socialization.** The lifelong processes through which people learn to be feminine or masculine according to the expectations current in their society.

**Gender transcendence.** Ideal socialization goal in which masculinity and femininity are superseded as ways of labelling and experiencing psychological traits. Boy/girl and male/female would then refer exclusively to biological distinctions.

**General fertility rate.** The incidence of births in a given year per 1000 women between the ages of 15 and 49. Calculated as follows:

$$\text{GFR} = \frac{\text{Number of births in a given year}}{\substack{\text{Mid-year population of} \\ \text{women aged 15 to 49}}} \times 1000$$

**Generalized other.** Mead's "organized community or social group [that] gives to the individual his unity of self." Although the equivalence of terms is not exact, "reference group" is the more modern way of referring to this notion of the organized attitudes of social groups.

**Generation.** When used in other than the kinship or family sense, the term refers to a cohort, large proportions of whose members have experienced significant socio-historical experiences. Such generational experiences frequently lead to the development of shared generational consciousness.

**Gesellschaft.** Tönnies's term for relatively large organizations characterized by formal social control, impersonal contact, an orientation to individualism, and little commitment to tradition.

**Group marriage.** The marriage of more than one man and more than one woman.

**Growth rate.** Number of people added to or subtracted from a population in a given period for every 100 or 1000 total population.

**Hinterland.** Rural or nonindustrialized region from which a city or metropolitan area extracts labour, food, and other raw materials.

**Holistic model.** Perspective asserting that there is no essential division between work and non-work.

**Homogamy.** Persons with similar characteristics choosing one another for marriage partners. Occurs along two dimensions: personal and social.

**Human capital theory.** Economic theory holding that the skill level of the labour force is the prime determinant of economic growth.

**Human ecology.** Application of such ecological principles as competition, invasion, and succession to the scientific study of human behaviour.

**Humanist perspectives.** Systems of meaning used to interpret the world without a supernatural referent (for example, communism, scientism).

**Hypothesis.** Prediction of what you expect to find as a result of research; a statement of the relation between two or more variables.

**I.** The dimension of Mead's notion of self that is active, spontaneous, creative, and unpredictable. The "I" is a component of a process, not a concrete entity.

**Id.** The reservoir of inborn, biological propensities in the Freudian personality structure. The selfish, impulsive Id operates according to the pleasure principle.

**Ideologies.** Emotionally charged sets of descriptive and normative beliefs and values that either explain and justify the status quo or, in the case of counter-ideologies, call for and justify alternative arrangements.

**Incest taboo.** Rule that prohibits close relatives from marrying and/or having intimate sexual relations.

**Independent variable.** Causal or explanatory variable.

**Indicator.** Empirical measure of a variable.

**Industrial capitalism.** Economic system in which productive property (for example, factories) is privately owned and goods and services are produced for profit.

**Industrial revolution.** A series of technological and organizational changes in the process of manufacturing that occurred in Britain during the latter part of the eighteenth century; essential features included machine production, the factory system of manufacturing, and mechanical motive power.

**Industrial society.** Society in which less than half the labour force is engaged in the primary sector.

**Industrial union.** Formal organization of non-craft workers based on the private-sector industry in which they work.

**Industrial world-view.** Outlook associated with industrialization and characterized by empiricism (the limiting of reality to what can be known through the senses) and materialism (the commitment of one's life to the pursuit of empirical reality).

**Industrialization.** The movement of workers out of the primary sector into the secondary (manufacturing) sector.

**Inequality of condition.** Inequality in the overall distribution of rewards (for example, money or prestige) in a society.

**Inequality of opportunity.** Inequality in the chances available to various members of a society for obtaining resources such as money, prestige, or power.

**Infant mortality rate.** Incidence of death among children under the age of one in a population.

$$\text{IMR} = \frac{\substack{\text{Number of deaths of children} \\ \text{under the age of 1 in a given year}}}{\text{Number of live births in a given year}} \times 1000$$

**Infecund.** Term applied to people incapable of producing children.

**Interests.** A basis for individual or group profit, benefit, or advancement.

**Justice orientation.** Gilligan's masculine orientation to morality, which emphasizes preserving rights and upholding principles.

**Lateralization.** Functional specialization of left and right hemispheres of the brain.

**Laws.** Norms that have been formally promulgated by a legislative body and are enforced by an executive body of government.

**Legal-rational authority.** Authority based on belief in the legality of formally specified rules and relationships.

**Life expectancy at birth.** Statistic indicating the average number of years that newborn babies can expect to live.

**Life table.** Mathematical model used to estimate the average number of years that people of a given age and a given sex can expect to live.

**Limiting factors.** Variables that can prevent or inhibit change in other variables.

**Lobbying.** Activities by special interest groups aimed at influencing government legislation.

**Looking-glass self.** Cooley's formulation of the self as the interpreted reflection of others' attitudes. It consists of "the imagination of our appearance to the other person, the imagination of his judgment of that appearance, and some sort of self-feeling, such as pride or mortification."

**Macrosociology.** Study of large-scale structures and processes of society.

**Marital power arrangements.** Varying arrangements of power between the husband and wife in a marriage. These arrangements include *owner/property* (the husband is legally and in practice the owner of his wife); *head/complement* (the husband is the decision-maker); *senior-partner/junior-partner* (the husband and wife are unequal partners with the husband having more power); and *equal-partner/equal partner* (husband and wife contribute equally to income and tasks).

**Marriage.** A commitment or exchange, recognized either legally, contractually, or socially, in which reciprocal rights and obligations (both instrumental and expressive) are carried out.

**Marxism.** A conflict theory that emphasizes the economic basis of social inequality.

**Mass terminal.** Stage of educational development in a society: secondary education has become universal, but post-secondary education is pursued by a minority only.

**Material culture.** Physical artifacts or products of a society embodying cultural meanings.

**Matriarchal families.** Families in which power (authority) is vested in females.

**Me.** The dimension of Mead's notion of self that represents internalized societal attitudes and expectations. The "Me" is an aspect of a process, not a concrete entity.

**Mean.** Sum of all of the scores divided by the number of scores; the score each case would have if the variable were distributed equally.

**Mechanical solidarity.** Feeling of people in primitive societies that they are held together by kinship, neighbourliness, and friendliness.

**Mechanistic management.** Management style in which duties and responsibilities are precisely defined, communication is filtered upward through a formalized hierarchy of authority, and control is maintained at the top.

**Median.** Score that divides a distribution into two equal parts.

**Megalopolis.** Greek term for the most powerful of several cities in a given country or region. The term is now used to describe an unbroken urban region created when the borders of two or more metropolitan areas expand into one another (also known as *conurbation*).

**Melting pot.** Situation in which the amalgamation and blending of groups have left none distinctive.

**Meritocracy.** Society in which merit constitutes the basis for social stratification and in which all people have an equal chance to display their talents and to be evaluated fairly.

**Metropolis.** Relatively large urban area containing a city and its surrounding suburbs. The term has also been used to refer to an industrial region or society that transforms raw materials extracted from its hinterland.

**Microsociology.** Study of small-scale structures and processes of society.

**Migration.** Movement of people from one geographic locale to another; can be either internal or international.

**Ministerial responsibility.** Principle that cabinet ministers in a parliamentary system are held accountable for the actions of civil service officials in the departments over which the ministers preside.

**Minority group.** Ethnic group that is subordinate to another group.

**Mode.** Score that occurs most frequently in a distribution.

**Modernization thesis.** An argument that maintains that as societies modernize, aspects of modernization — such as industrialization, urbanization, increased emphasis on technology, and improved health and longevity — contribute to a decline in the social status of the aged.

**Modified pluralism.** Glazer's and Moynihan's modification of pluralism theory, describing a situation in which numerous groups maintain distinctly different cultures, ideologies, or interests; although they will be changed and modified somewhat, they will not be transformed entirely.

**Monogamous marriage.** The marriage of one man and one woman.

**Moral autonomy.** Piaget's later stage of moral thought, in which children over age eight judge wrongdoing in terms of intentions and extenuating circumstances, as well as consequences, and view rules as social conventions that can be changed.

**Moral realism.** Piaget's early stage of moral development, in which children from four to seven years old judge wrongdoing strictly in terms of its consequences, and believe all rules are immutable absolutes.

**Morbidity.** Occurrence of illness in a population.

**Mores.** Traditional rules about how the individual must or must not behave, invested with strong feelings and informally enforced.

**Mortality.** Occurrence of deaths in a population; an important component of population change.

**Motivating factors.** Variables that can produce or encourage changes in other variables.

**Movement success.** The process of institutionalization through which the movement's goals become recognized and routinely enforced by society as rights.

**Multicultural.** Relating to or designed for a combination of several distinct cultures.

**Multiple-nuclei model.** Model of a city as several specialized areas located along and connected by major traffic arteries, such as highways. Unlike the concentric zone and the sector models, the multiple-nuclei model does not suggest that zones radiate from the centre of the city.

**Multistage random sample.** Combination of random samples through several stages.

**Multivariate assimilation.** Gordon's modification of assimilation theory, which maintains that assimilation is not a single social process but a number of cultural, structural, marital, identificational, attitudinal, behavioural, and civic subprocesses.

**Natural fertility.** Fertility that is lower than the biological maximum level and results from behaviour not aimed deliberately at reducing child-bearing.

**Natural increase.** Excess of births over deaths in a population in a given time period.

**Naturalist position.** View that the scientific method, as used in the physical sciences, can be used to study social phenomena. Facts are established by reliable and verifiable observation.

**Negative (inverse) relation.** Relation in which two or more variables change in opposite directions; as one increases the other decreases.

**Net migration.** Difference between the number of in-migrants and the number of out-migrants.

**Neutralization techniques.** Linguistic expressions that, through a subtle process of justification, allow individuals to drift into deviant lifestyles.

**''New left'' movement.** A largely student-centred movement in many Western societies in the 1960s and early 1970s that emphasized participatory democracy (in contrast to the state-centred views of what adherents called the ''old left''). In both cases, a socialist society was the goal.

**New urban sociology.** This perspective, which is based on Marxian conflict theory and the dependency model, emphasizes the impact of industrial capitalism on the form of urban areas and the lives of the people they contain.

**Noninstitutionalized activity.** Nonroutine action taken to promote interests that are not met by society's established institutions and conventions.

**Nonparticipant observation.** Systematic, objective observation of social behaviour using explicit predefined categories.

**Non-random sample.** Sample in which the probability of elements within the population being chosen cannot be known; easier and less costly than a random sample.

**Normative beliefs.** Ideas about what should or should not be, referring especially to goodness, virtuousness, or propriety.

**Normative theory.** Any theory concerned mainly with moral evaluation and the question of justice. Can be contrasted with scientific theory.

**Norms.** Formal or informal rules stating how categories of people are expected to act in particular situations, violations of which are subject to sanction.

**Nuclear family.** Family type consisting of a married couple and their unmarried children who live apart from other relatives.

**Objectivity.** Ability to observe and interpret reality in such a way that subjective judgments and biases are eliminated.

**Observational learning.** No reinforcement or reward is required for the initial learning to occur. However, reinforcements do influence where and when learned responses that are in the individual's repertoire (for example, swearing) will be performed.

**Occupational segregation.** The concentration of one sex in a relatively few occupations in which they greatly outnumber the other sex.

**Occupational sex-typing.** The societal view that certain occupations are more appropriate work for one sex than the other.

**Occupational socialization.** Preparation for entering the job market.

**Open system.** Theoretical perspective of organizations whereby particular structural arrangements and individual behaviour patterns can be accounted for by a combination of factors internal to the organization and its external environment.

**Operant conditioning.** Type of learning whereby the organism gives a number of trial-and-error responses. Those responses followed by reward (positive reinforcement) tend to be repeated on future occasions. Those responses followed by negative reinforcement, or by no reinforcement, tend to be extinguished.

**Operational definition.** Precise set of instructions enabling a researcher to measure indicators that correspond to variables; operational definitions enable different researchers to get the same results when measuring the same phenomena.

**Organic management.** Management style in which decisions are based on knowledgeable suggestions, communication patterns tend to be lateral as well as horizontal, duties and responsibilities are not rigidly defined, and status differentials are of minor importance.

**Organic solidarity.** Dependencies among people in developed societies created as a result of a more specific division of labour.

**Organization.** A collectivity in which people and resources are co-ordinated through a division of labour in the use of a technology to achieve a goal. Co-ordination, control, and problem-solving are facilitated through communication and leadership.

**Organizational structure.** Patterns of relationships among organization statuses.

**Participant observation.** Situation in which the researchers take an active part, in varying degrees, in the situation they are directly observing.

**Partnership.** Joint business venture in which normally all partners experience unlimited liability equally.

**Patriarchal families.** Families in which power (authority) resides with males and is meted out autocratically.

**Patriarchy.** A society oriented toward and dominated by males.

**Period measures.** Measures of the frequency of a given event at one point in time.

**Persistence argument.** Assertion that religion will continue to have a significant place in the modern world, arguing either that it has never actually declined, or that people can absorb only so much rationality and materialism.

**Personal religiosity.** Religious commitment at the level of the individual.

**Physical trace evidence.** Observational data based on accretion or erosion.

**Plural elites.** Situation in which the elites in each of the major institutional spheres remain sufficiently autonomous to enable them to check each other's power and compete for additional power resources.

**Pluralism.** Social situation in which numerous ethnic, racial, religious, and/or social groups maintain distinctly different cultures, ideologies, or interests.

**Polyandry.** The marriage of one woman and two or more men.

**Polygamous families.** Occur when nuclear families are joined together through marriage ties.

**Polygyny.** The marriage of one man and two or more women.

**Population.** Largest number of individuals or units of interest to the researcher.

**Population composition.** The characteristics of people within a population, particularly age and sex. Also included are marital status, religion, ethnicity, and other characteristics.

**Population distribution.** The geographic location of people within a population.

**Population pyramid.** Graphic representation of the age and sex composition of a population.

**Population size.** The number of people in a given area.

**Positive (direct) relation.** Relation in which two or more variables change in the same direction; as one increases the other increases, or as one decreases the other decreases.

**Post-industrial society.** Society in which at least half the labour force is engaged in the tertiary sector.

**Prejudice.** A feeling (usually negative) toward a person, group, or thing prior to, or not based on, actual experience. Prejudging others without sufficient warrant.

**Primary deviance.** Deviant behaviours that precede a societal or legal response and have little impact on the individual's self-concept.

**Primary sector.** Division of the occupational structure in which employment involves either harvesting or extraction of goods (e.g., agriculture, logging, mining, fishing, hunting, and trapping.).

**Primary socialization.** Socialization that occurs during childhood.

**Privatization.** Parsons's term for people's alleged tendency to work out their own religious beliefs and associations in an individualistic, autonomous manner.

**Production of use-values.** Goods and services produced in the home.

**Profane and the sacred.** Two categories into which Durkheim claimed all things are classified by human beings; the sacred represents those things viewed as warranting profound respect, the profane encompasses everything else.

**Professional social movements.** Movements maintained by a small, full-time core of activists dependent on the financial donations of unrelated sympathizers or outside agencies.

**Proportional representation.** Electoral system in which each party is allotted seats according to the percentage of the popular vote it receives.

**Protestant Ethic.** Term (associated with Weber) that refers to the emphasis placed by Calvin, Luther, and other leaders of the Protestant Reformation on the importance of work performed well as an indication of living one's life "to the glory of God"; key characteristics include diligence, frugality, and rational use of time.

**Protestant work ethic.** Ideology that states (1) work is service to God; (2) one's duty is to work hard; and (3) success in work is measured by money and property.

**Public-sector union.** Formal organization of workers employed in some type of government enterprise.

**Quota sample.** Sample with the same proportion of certain characteristics as found in the population; the non-random equivalent of a stratified random sample.

**Race.** Arbitrary biological grouping of people on the basis of physical traits.

**Radical movement.** A social movement that seeks to overturn and replace the established social order.

**Radical perspective on social inequality.** Normative theory holding that inequality is unnecessary and unjust.

**Random sample.** Sample in which each element within the population has an equal chance of appearing; also called *probability sample*.

**Refined rate.** Frequency of an event per unit of population, usually 1000, that are exposed to the risk of experiencing that event.

**Reformist movement.** A social movement that seeks some adjustment in society while maintaining the overall system.

**Regional mosaic.** Distinctive ethnic patterns formed by the various regions of a country that have different combinations of linguistic and cultural groups.

**Relative deprivation.** A feeling of unfairness provoked by a gap between the rewards that people expect to receive and those they actually do receive.

**Reliability.** Consistency of results over time or with several investigators.

**Religions.** Systems of meaning used to interpret the

world that have a supernatural referent (for example, Christianity, Hinduism, astrology).

**Replication.** Systematic repeated measurement of a given relationship.

**Reserve army of labour.** According to conflict theorists, women constitute a flexible labour supply, drawn into the labour market when needed, and sent home when the need is past.

**Residual rule-breaking.** Category conventionally called "mental illness" that includes forms of rule-breaking for which society has no specific labels.

**Resocialization.** Replacement of established attitudes and behaviour patterns.

**Resource mobilization.** The process of attracting, coordinating, and applying resources toward a collective goal.

**Restricted language code.** Form of communication that leaves meanings implicit.

**Retreatist subculture.** Group-supported forms of escapist behaviour, particularly drug abuse, that result from failure in both legitimate and illegitimate spheres of activity.

**Role-taking.** Process of imaginatively putting yourself in the role of another and seeing the world from that person's perspective.

**Ruling class concept.** Idea that the economically dominant class has the overriding influence on government policies; a central tenet of Marxist theory.

**Safety in numbers.** A factor, operative in large gatherings, whereby the larger the crowd, the less the blame for disorder is likely to be attached to any one person, allowing a potentially rational base for disorder.

**Sample.** Smaller representation of a population or universe; properties of the sample are studied to gain information about the whole.

**Science.** Systematic methods by which reliable, empirical knowledge is obtained. Also refers to the actual body of knowledge obtained by these methods. See also **naturalist position**.

**Scientific beliefs.** Thoughts about what actually exists (or could exist) that are felt to be consistent with what is known about empirical reality. Can be contrasted with value judgments and normative theories.

**Scientific law.** A hypothesis that has been repeatedly supported by empirical tests.

**Scientific management.** Taylor's term for achieving perfection in productivity by finding the one best way to do each and every task.

**Secondary deviance.** Deviant behaviours that follow a societal or legal response and involve a transformation of the individual's self-concept.

**Secondary sector.** Division of the occupational structure in which employment involves the transformation of raw materials into semifinished or finished manufactured goods. The secondary sector includes all manufacturing and construction industries.

**Sector model.** Model of a city as a series of wedge-shaped sectors radiating from the centre of the city, each containing different activities or land uses and separated from each other by major traffic arteries or natural boundaries.

**Secularization argument.** Assertion that religion as it has been traditionally known is declining continuously and irreversibly.

**Segmental model.** A perspective asserting that there is an essential division between work and non-work.

**Segregation.** Separation or isolation of a race, class, or ethnic group by forced or voluntary residence.

**Selection theory.** Viewpoint that relationships between the physical environment and behaviour reflect the migration or movement of people with particular characteristics to particular places.

**Selective incentives.** Personal rewards that are available only to individuals who contribute to a collective cause, not to free riders.

**Self-report survey.** Paper-and-pencil questionnaires used with adolescents and adults to obtain first-person accounts of amounts and types of deviant behaviour.

**Self-selected marriage.** Marriage in which individuals choose for themselves who they will marry.

**Sensitization.** Process by which subjects become aware that they are being studied.

**Sex.** The physiological differences between females and males.

**Sex ratio.** Number of males per 100 females in a population.

**Significant other.** The particular individuals whose standpoint the child adopts in responding to himself or herself during Mead's play stage.

**Single-member plurality system.** Electoral system in which the candidate with the most votes wins the seat in each constituency, and the number of seats won by each political party is determined on a constituency-by-constituency basis.

**Social action.** Occurs between two individuals when each person takes into account the other's actions.

**Social clock.** Socially shared expectations about the normal or appropriate timing and sequence of events over the life course. For example, people may see themselves as making slow or rapid career progress compared to general expectations, or they may see themselves as "delaying" marriage or parenthood.

**Social democracy.** Normative theory of inequality holding that ownership consists of a divisible bundle of rights and that satisfactory progress toward equality can be achieved through nonviolent, gradual reform within the political institutions of democratic capitalist societies.

**Social deviation.** Noncriminal variation from social norms that is nonetheless subject to frequent official control.

**Social distance.** In contrast to social nearness, Simmel defines social distance as ecological, emotional, and social detachment from others.

**Social diversion.** Variations of lifestyle, including fads and fashions of appearance and behaviour.

**Social-exchange perspective.** Set of propositions that relates people's interactions to the level of satisfying outcomes they experience and that specifies the consequences of these outcomes.

**Social facts.** Durkheim's term to indicate things that are external to, and constraining upon, the individual.

**Social incentives.** The built-in rewards and penalties solidary groups have available to assure that individual members act in a group-oriented way.

**Social inequality.** Situation in which various members of a society have unequal amounts of socially valued resources (for example, money or power) and unequal opportunities to obtain them.

**Socialization.** Complex learning process through which individuals develop selfhood and acquire the knowledge, skills, and motivations required to participate in social life.

**Social mobility.** Upward or downward movement of individuals or groups into different positions in the social hierarchy.

**Social movements.** Collective attempts with varying degrees of formal organization to promote, maintain, or resist social change.

**Social segmentation.** A deep break between social groups, in which there are few co-operative ties to bind the groups and separate sets of social institutions to maintain the divisions between them.

**Social structure.** Factors that are persistent over time, are external to the individual, and are assumed to influence behaviour and thought.

**Social system.** Within the consensus, or structural-functionalist, perspective, a series of interrelated parts in a state of equilibrium, with each part contributing to the maintenance of other parts.

**Social time.** Changes occurring in the wider society that have an influence on the family life course.

**Sociological perspective.** Point of view about society and social behaviour that provides an overall orientation for examining sociological problems.

**Sociology.** The description and explanation of social behaviour, social structures, and social interaction in terms of these social structures, and/or in terms of people's perceptions of the social environment.

**Sole proprietorship.** Simplest manner in which to establish a business; the sole owner experiences unlimited liability.

**Solidary traits.** Social arrangements that integrate individuals to cohesive groups; examples include a long-standing shared identity, friendship networks, and formal organizations.

**Sponsored mobility.** Competition for elite status on the basis of criteria set by the existing elite.

**Spontaneous organization.** Temporary co-ordination of individuals and resources that disbands when its task or mission has been completed.

**Stable criminal subculture.** Illegal group enterprises made more persistent by the protection they receive from persons in legitimate social roles (for example, politicians and police).

**Standard deviation (SD).** Measure of dispersion based on deviations from the mean.

**Statistics.** Actual numbers; and the theories and techniques used to manipulate data.

**Status.** Culturally defined position in society, consisting of ideas about rights and obligations.

**Status quo.** The existing state of affairs.

**Status socialization.** Process of teaching people to accept their position in the social stratification system. Includes two components: *ambition regulation* and *legitimation.*

**Stem family.** A three-generational family in which one son, upon marriage, remains in the parental home, along with his wife and children.

**Stereotype.** Folk beliefs about the attributes characterizing a social category (the genders, ethnic groups) on which there is substantial agreement.

**Stratified random sample.** Series of random samples designed to represent some population characteristic.

**Structural-functional perspective.** A perspective that stresses what parts of the system do for the system. This perspective is usually classified with the consensus perspective.

**Subcultures.** More or less distinctive beliefs, norms, symbols, values, and ideologies shared by groups within a larger population.

**Subfecund.** Term applied to people who are biologically able to produce children but, even without using birth-control measures, have difficulty doing so.

**Suburbanization.** Increase in the proportion of a given population living on the outer limits of a metropolitan area.

**Super-ego.** The Freudian conscience, or internalization of societal values and behavioural standards.

**Symbol.** Anything that can stand for or represent something else, such as a word or gesture.

**Symbolic interaction.** A macrosociological perspective that emphasizes the interactions between people that take place through symbols, especially language.

**Synthesis.** A theoretical approach to the study of social inequality that attempts to use insights from both the radical and the conservative perspectives and attempts to be scientific in its methodology.

**Systematic sample.** Sample in which the first element from a population is selected at random followed by every succeeding *n*th element.

**Task environment.** Those elements in an organization's environment that are relevant or potentially relevant to setting goals and attaining them.

**Technological functionalism.** A perspective that sees rising educational requirements as a reflection of the increased complexity of the occupational structure.

**Technology.** Application of a body of knowledge through the use of tools and processes in the production of goods and/or services.

**Tertiary sector.** Division of the occupational structure in which employment involves the provision of services.

**Third parties.** In Canada, any party contesting an election other than one of the two major parties that have formed the government and the official opposition, changing places from time to time, since Confederation.

**Totalitarian society.** A one-party state that exercises control over all institutional spheres and mobilizes mass participation in the building of a new social order.

**Traditional authority.** Authority that is based on followers' belief that the monarch has a divine right to rule that is transferred down through eligible descendants.

**Treaty status.** Certain privileges and obligations passed on to native Indians from their ancestors, who signed treaties with the Canadian government.

**Urbanism.** Set of attitudes, beliefs, and behaviours that are thought to be characteristic of city-dwellers.

**Urbanization.** An increase in the proportion of a given population inhabiting areas designated as urban.

**Validity.** Property of measurement whereby what is measured is what was intended to be measured.

**Value-free sociology.** The position, held by naturalists, that personal judgments and biases can and should be excluded from social observations and interpretations.

**Value judgments.** Moral or ethical opinions about what is right or wrong, good or bad, desirable or undesirable. Can be contrasted with scientific judgments about what actually exists or could exist.

**Values.** Cultural conceptions about what are desirable goals and what are appropriate standards for judging actions.

**Variable.** Factor that can differ or vary from one situation to another, or from one individual or group to another; a concept that has more than one value.

**Verifiability.** Characteristic of a conclusion or factual statement by which it can be subjected to more than one observation or test.

**Verstehen.** Weber's term for the subjective interpretation of social behaviour and intentions, usually based on empathy (in German, literally "to understand").

**Weimar constitution.** Document drawn up in Germany following World War I that abolished the monarchy and established in its place a republic with a popularly elected president and a two-chamber parliament.

**Work.** Activity that permits one a livelihood. Work includes conventional paid employment, illegal employment, and homemaking.

# Works Cited

**Abercrombie, Nicholas, Stephen Hill, and Bryan S. Turner. 1980.** *The Dominant Ideology Thesis.* London: George Allen and Irwin.

**Aberle, D., and K. Naegele. 1952.** "Middle-class fathers' occupational roles and attitudes towards children." *American Journal of Orthopsychiatry* 22:366–378.

**Abu-Laban, Sharon McIrvin. 1980.** "Social supports in older age: The need for new research directions." *Essence* 4:195–210.

**Abu-Laban, Sharon McIrvin. 1981.** "Woman and aging: A futurist perspective." *Psychology of Women Quarterly* 6(1):85–98.

**Abu-Laban, Sharon McIrvin, and Abu-Laban, Baha. 1980.** "Women and the aged as minority groups: A critique." In *Aging in Canada: Social Perspectives.* Victor W. Marshall, ed. Toronto: Fitzhenry and Whiteside.

**Acheson, T.W. 1977.** "The maritimes and Empire Canada." In *Canada and the Burden of Unity.* D.J. Bercuson, ed. Toronto: Macmillan.

**Acock, Alan C. 1984.** "Parents and their children: The study of intergenerational influence." *Sociology and Social Research* 68:151–171.

**Adams, Bert N. 1980.** *The Family: A Sociological Interpretation.* 3rd edition. Chicago: Rand McNally.

**Adams, O.B., and L.A. Lefevre. 1980.** *Retirement and Mortality: An Examination of Mortality in a Group of Retired Canadians.* Ottawa: Statistics Canada, Health Division, Catalogue No. 83-521e, occasional.

**Adams, Robert M. 1960.** "The origin of cities." *Scientific American* 203(Sept.):153–172.

**Adler, Freda. 1975.** *Sisters in Crime.* New York: McGraw-Hill.

**Adler-Karlsson, G. 1970.** *Reclaiming the Canadian Economy.* Toronto: Anansi.

**Aird, John S. 1978.** "Fertility decline and birth control in the People's Republic of China." *Population and Development Review* 4:225–253.

**Alcock, J.E., D.W. Carment, and S.W. Sadava. 1988.** *A Textbook of Social Psychology.* Scarborough, ON: Prentice-Hall.

**Alford, Robert R. 1963.** *Party and Society: The Anglo-American Domocracies.* Chicago: Rand McNally.

**Al-Issa, Ihsan. 1982.** *Gender and Psychopathology.* New York: Academic.

**Allen, Richard. 1971.** *The Social Passion: Religion and Social Reform in Canada, 1914–28.* Toronto: University of Toronto Press.

**Allport, Gordon W. 1954.** *The Nature of Prejudice.* New York: Doubleday.

**Almond, Gabriel, and James S. Coleman (eds.). 1960.** *The Politics of Developing Areas.* Princeton, NJ: Princeton University Press.

**Almy, Fredric. 1902.** "Juvenile courts in Buffalo." *Annals of the American Academy of Political and Social Science* 20:279–285.

**Ambert, Anne-Marie. 1976.** *Sex Structure.* 2nd edition. Don Mills, ON: Longman Canada.

**Ambert, Anne-Marie. 1980.** *Divorce in Canada.* Don Mills, ON: Academic.

**Ambert, Anne-Marie. 1985.** "Custodial parents: Review and a longitudinal study." In *The One-Parent Family in the 1980s.* Benjamin Schlesinger, ed. Toronto: University of Toronto Press.

**Ambert, Anne-Marie, and Maureen Baker. 1984.** "Marriage dissolution: Structural and ideological changes." In *The Family: Changing Trends in Canada.* Maureen Baker, ed. Toronto: McGraw-Hill Ryerson.

**Amirault Ernest, and Maurice Archer. 1976.** *Canadian Business Law.* Toronto: Methuen.

**Anderson, C.A. 1944.** "Sociological elements in economic restrictionism." *American Sociological Review* 9(Aug.):345–358.

**Anderson, Grace M., and J.M. Alleyne. 1979.** "Ethnicity, food preferences and habits of consumption as factors in social interaction." *Canadian Ethnic Studies* 11:83–87.

**Anderson, Michael. 1971.** *Family Structure in Nineteenth Century Lancashire.* Cambridge: Cambridge University Press.

**Archer, Dane, and Rosemary Gartner. 1984.** *Violence and Crime in Cross-National Perspective.* New Haven: Yale University Press.

**Archer, John. 1976.** "Biological explanations of psychological sex differences." *Exploring Sex Differences.* Barbara Lloyd and John Archer, eds. New York: Academic.

**Armstrong, D. 1970.** *Education and Economic Achieve-*

*ment.* Ottawa: Information Canada.

**Armstrong, Pat. 1987.** "Women's work: Women's wages." In *Women and Men: Interdisciplinary Readings on Gender.* Greta Hofmann Nemiroff, ed. Toronto: Fitzhenry and Whiteside.

**Armstrong, Pat, and Hugh Armstrong. 1978.** *The Double Ghetto: Canadian Women and Their Segregated Work.* Toronto: McClelland and Stewart.

**Armstrong, Pat, and Hugh Armstrong. 1983.** A *Working Majority: What Women Must Do For Pay.* Ottawa: Canadian Advisory Council on the Status of Women.

**Armstrong, Pat, and Hugh Armstrong. 1984a.** *The Double Ghetto: Canadian Women and Their Segregated Work.* Revised edition. Toronto: McClelland and Stewart.

**Armstrong, Pat, and Hugh Armstrong. 1984b.** "The structure of women's labour force work: Everywhere and nowhere." In *Working Canadians: Readings in the Sociology of Work and Industry.* Graham S. Lowe and H.J. Krahn, eds. Toronto: Methuen.

**Armstrong, Pat, and Hugh Armstrong. 1987.** "The conflicting demands of 'work' and 'home.' " In *Family Matters: Sociology and Contemporary Canadian Families.* Karen L. Anderson et al., eds. Toronto: Methuen.

**Aronoff, Joel, and William D. Crano. 1975.** "A re-examination of the cross-cultural principles of task segregation and sex role differentiation in the family." *American Sociological Review* 40:12–20.

**Aronson, Jane. 1985.** "Family care of the elderly: Underlying assumptions and their consequences." *Canadian Journal on Aging* 4(3):115–125.

**Aronson, Jane, Victor W. Marshall, and Joanne Sulman. 1987.** "Patients awaiting discharge from hospital." In *Aging in Canada: Social Perspectives.* Victor W. Marshall, ed. 2nd edition. Toronto: Fitzhenry and Whiteside.

**Ascah, Louis. 1984.** "Recent pension reports in Canada: A survey." *Canadian Public Policy* 10(4):415–428.

**Atchley, R.C. 1971.** "Disengagement among professors." *Journal of Gerontology* 26(4):476–480.

**Atchley, R.C. 1977.** *The Social Forces in Later Life.* Belmont, CA: Wadsworth.

**Atwood, Margaret. 1972.** *Survival: A Thematic Guide to Canadian Literature.* Toronto: Anansi.

**Auer, L. 1987.** *Canadian Hospital Costs and Productivity.* Ottawa: Economic Council of Canada.

**Bachrach, Peter. 1967.** *Democratic Elitism.* Boston: Little, Brown.

**Baer, Douglas E., and James E. Curtis. 1984.** "French-Canadian–English-Canadian differences in values: National survey findings." *Canadian Journal of Sociology* 10(4):405–427.

**Baer, Douglas E., and Ronald D. Lambert. 1982.** "Education and support for dominant ideology." *Canadian Review of Sociology and Anthropology* 19(2):173–195.

**Bailey, M.B., B.W. Haberman, and H. Alksne. 1965.** "The epidemiology of alcoholism in an urban residential area." *Quarterly Journal of Studies on Alcohol* 26:19–40.

**Bainbridge, William Sims, and Rodney Stark. 1982.** "Church and cult in Canada." *Canadian Journal of Sociology* 7:351–366.

**Baine, Richard, and A. Lynn McMurray. 1984.** *Toronto: An Urban Study.* 3rd edition. Toronto: Irwin.

**Baker, Maureen. 1985.** *"What Will Tomorrow Bring? . . ."*: A *A Study of the Aspirations of Adolescent Women.* Ottawa: Canadian Advisory Council on the Status of Women.

**Baker, Maureen, and J.I. Hans Bakker. 1980.** "The double-bind of the middle-class male: Men's liberation and the male sex role." *Journal of Comparative Family Studies* 11:547–561.

**Baker, Maureen, and Mary-Anne Robeson. 1986.** "Trade union reactions to women workers and their concerns." In *Work in the Canadian Context.* Katherina L.P. Lundy and Barbara Warme, eds. 2nd edition. Toronto: Butterworths.

**Balakrishnan, T.R. 1976.** "Ethnic residential segregation in the metropolitan areas of Canada." *Canadian Journal of Sociology* 1(1):481–498.

**Balakrishnan, T.R. 1979.** "Changing patterns of residential segregation in the metropolitan areas of Canada." *Canadian Review of Sociology and Anthropology.*

**Balakrishnan, T.R., K. Vaninadha Rao, Evelyne Lapierre-Adamcyk, and Karol J. Krotki. 1987.** "A hazard model analysis of the covariates of marriage dissolution in Canada." *Demography* 24(3):395–406.

**Bandura, A., and R.H. Walters. 1963.** *Social Learning and Personality Development.* New York: Holt, Rinehart and Winston.

**Bank, Stephen P., and Michael D. Kahn. 1982.** *The Sibling Bond,* New York: Basic.

**Bardwick, Judith M., and Elizabeth Douvan. 1971.** "Ambivalence: The socialization of women." In *Women in Sexist Society.* Vivian Gornick and Barbara K. Moran, eds. New York: Signet.

**Barfield, Ashton. 1976.** "Biological influences on sex differences in behaviour." In *Sex Differences: Social and Biological Perspectives.* Michael S. Teitelbaum, ed. Garden City, NY Anchor.

**Barnard, Chester. 1938.** *The Functions of the Executive.* Cambridge, MA: Harvard University Press.

**Barnes, Rosemary. 1985.** "Women and self-injury." *International Journal of Women's Studies* 8:465–474.

**Barrett, Michele. 1980.** *Women's Oppression Today.* London: Verso.

**Barter, James T., George Mizner, and Paul Werme. 1970.** "Patterns of drug use among college students: An epidemiological and demographic survey of student attitudes and practices." Department of Psychiatry, University of Colorado Medical School. Unpublished.

**Basavarajappa, K.G. 1979.** "Incidence of divorce and the relative importance of death and divorce in the dissolution of marriage in Canada, 1921–1976." Paper presented at the annual meeting of the Canadian Population Society.

**Basow, Susan A. 1986.** *Gender Stereotypes: Traditions and Alternatives.* 2nd edition. Monterey. CA: Brooks/Cole.

**Bater, James H. 1980.** *The Soviet City.* London: Edward Arnold.

**Beaujot, Roderic P. 1978.** "Canada's population: Growth and dualism," *Population Bulletin* 33(2). Washington, DC: Population Reference Bureau.

**Beaujot, Roderic 1982.** "The family." In *Introduction to*

*Sociology: A Canadian Focus.* James J. Teevan, ed. Scarborough, ON: Prentice-Hall.

**Beaujot, Roderic P., and Kevin McQuillan. 1982.** *Growth and Dualism: The Demographic Development of Canadian Society.* Toronto: Gage.

**Becker, Howard. 1963.** *Outsiders: Studies in the Sociology of Deviance.* New York: Free Press.

**Becker, Howard. 1964.** *The Other Side: Perspectives on Deviance.* New York: Free Press.

**Becker, Howard, Blanche Greer, and Everett Hughes. 1960.** *Making the Grade.* New York: Wiley.

**Beetham, David. 1974.** *Max Weber and the Theory of Modern Politics.* London: George Allen and Unwin.

**Béland, François. 1987.** "Living arrangement preferences among elderly people." *Gerontologist* 10(6):797–803.

**Bell, D.V.J., and Lorne Tepperman. 1979.** *The Roots of Disunity.* Toronto: McClelland and Stewart.

**Bell, Daniel. 1953.** "Crime as an American way of life." *Antioch Review* 13:1–154.

**Bell, Daniel. 1967.** "The post-industrial society: A speculative view." In *Scientific Progress and Human Values.* Elizabeth Hutchings, ed. New York: Elsevier.

**Bell, Daniel. 1977.** "The return of the sacred: The argument on the future of religion." *British Journal of Sociology* 28:419–449.

**Bellah, Robert. 1967.** "Civil religion in America." *Daedalus* 96:1–21.

**Bem, Sandra L. 1976.** "Probing the promise of androgyny." In *Beyond Sex-Role Stereotypes: Readings toward a Psychology of Androgyny.* Alexander G. Kaplan and Joan P. Bean, eds. Boston: Little, Brown.

**Bem, Sandra L. 1981.** "Gender schema theory: A cognitive account of sex typing." *Psychological Review* 88:354–364.

**Bem, Sandra L. 1983.** "Gender schema theory and its implications for child development: Raising gender-aschematic children in a gender-schematic society." *Signs* 8:598–616.

**Bem, Sandra, and Daryl J. Bem. 1971.** "Training the woman to know her place: The power of a nonconscious ideology." In *Roles Women Play: Readings toward Women's Liberation.* Michele Hoffnung Garskof, ed. Belmont, CA: Brooks/Cole.

**Bendix, Reinhard. 1962.** *Max Weber: An Intellectual Portrait.* New York: Doubleday.

**Bengtson, Vern L., and J.A. Kuypers. 1971.** "Generational differences and the developmental stake." *Aging and Human Development* 2(4):249–260.

**Benston, Margaret. 1969.** "The political economy of women's liberation." *Monthly Review* 21:13–27.

**Berardo, Felix M. 1970.** "Survivorship and social isolation: The case of the aged widower." *Family Coordinator* 1(Jan.):11–25.

**Berg, D.F. 1970.** "The non-medical use of dangerous drugs in the United States: A comprehensive view." *International Journal of Addictions* 5(4):777–834.

**Berg, Ivar. 1970.** *Education and Jobs: The Great Training Robbery.* New York: Beacon.

**Berg, Ivar. 1979.** *Industrial Sociology.* Englewood Cliffs, NJ: Prentice-Hall.

**Berger, Brigitte, and Peter L. Berger. 1984.** *The War Over the Family: Capturing the Middle Ground.* Garden City, NY: Doubleday Anchor.

**Berger, Carl. 1969.** *Imperialism and Nationalism 1884–1914: A Conflict in Canadian Thought.* Toronto: Copp Clark.

**Berger, Carl. 1970.** *The Sense of Power: Studies in the Ideas of Canadian Imperialism, 1867–1914.* Toronto: University of Toronto Press.

**Berger, Peter. 1961.** *The Noise of Solemn Assemblies.* New York: Doubleday.

**Berk, Richard. 1974.** *Collective Behavior.* Dubuque, IA: Wm. C. Brown.

**Bernard, Jessie. 1971.** "The paradox of the happy marriage." In *Women in Sexist Society.* Vivian Gornick and Barbara K. Moran, eds. New York: Mentor.

**Bernard, Jessie. 1973a.** *The Future of Marriage.* New York: Bantam.

**Bernard, Jessie. 1973b.** "My four revolutions: An autobiographical history of the USA." *American Journal of Sociology* 78:773–791.

**Bernard, Jessie. 1975.** *Women, Wives, Mothers: Values and Options.* Chicago: Aldine.

**Bernard, Jessie. 1981.** *The Female World.* New York: Free Press.

**Bernstein, Basil. 1970.** "Education cannot compensate for society." *New Society* 26 (Feb.):345.

**Bernstein, Basil. 1971.** "On the classification and framing of educational knowledge." In *Knowledge and Control: New Directions for the Sociology of Education.* M. Young, ed. London: Collier-Macmillan.

**Bernstein, Basil. 1973, 1974, 1976.** *Class, Codes and Control.* (3 vols.). London: Routledge and Kegan Paul.

**Berry, John W., Rudolf Kalin, and Donald M. Taylor. 1977.** *Multiculturalism and Ethnic Attitudes in Canada.* Ottawa: Supply and Services.

**Best, Raphaela. 1983.** *We've All Got Scars: What Boys and Girls Learn in Elementary School.* Bloomington, IN: Indiana University Press.

**Beynon, Erdmann D. 1938.** "The voodoo cult among Negro migrants to Detroit." *American Journal of Sociology* 43(May): 894–907.

**Bibby, Reginald W. 1976.** "Project Canada: A story of deviance, diversity, and devotion in Canada." Codebook. Lethbridge, AB: University of Lethbridge.

**Bibby, Reginald W. 1979.** "Consequences of religious commitment: The Canadian case." Paper presented to the Society for the Scientific Study of Religion.

**Bibby, Reginald W. 1980.** "Sources of religious commitment: The Canadian case." Paper presented to the Society for the Scientific Study of Religion.

**Bibby, Reginald W. 1983.** "Religionless Christianity." *Social Indicators Research* 13:1–16.

**Bibby, Reginald W. 1985.** "Religious encasement in Canada: An argument for Protestant and Catholic entrenchment." *Social Compass.* (forthcoming).

**Bibby, Reginald W. 1987.** *Fragmented Gods: The Poverty and Potential of Religion in Canada.* Toronto: Irwin.

**Bibby, Reginald W., and Merlin B. Brinkerhoff. 1973.** "The circulation of the saints: A study of people who join conservative churches." *Journal for the Scientific Study of Religion* 12:273–283.

**Bibby, Reginald W., and Merlin B. Brinkerhoff. 1983.** "Circulation of the saints revisited: A longitudinal look at conservative church growth." *Journal for the Scientific Study of Religion* 22:253–262.

**Bibby, Reginald W., and Armand Mauss. 1974.** "Skidders and their servants: Variable goals and functions of the skid road rescue mission." *Journal for the Scientific Study of Religion* 13:421–436.

**Bibby, Reginald W., and Donald C. Posterski. 1985.** *The Emerging Generation: An Inside Look at Canada's Teenagers.* Toronto: Irwin.

**Bibby, Reginald W., and Harold R. Weaver. 1985.** "Cult consumption in Canada: A Critique of Stark and Bainbridge. *Sociological Analysis.* (forthcoming)

**Bienvenue, Rita M., and Betty Havens. 1986.** "Structural inequalities, informal networks: A comparison of native and non-native elderly." *Canadian Journal on Aging* 5(4):241–248.

**Bird, Frederick, and Bill Reimer. 1982.** "Participation rates in new religious movements and para-religious movements." *Journal for the Scientific Study of Religion* 21:1–14.

**Black, Donald J., and Albert J. Reiss, Jr. 1970.** "Police control of juveniles." *American Sociological Review* 35 (Feb.):63–77.

**Blau, Peter M., and Richard A. Schoenherr. 1971.** *The Structure of Organizations.* New York: Basic Books.

**Blauner, Robert. 1964.** *Alienation and Freedom.* Chicago, IL: University of Chicago Press.

**Blishen, Bernard R. 1967.** "A socio-economic index for occupations in Canada." *Canadian Review of Sociology and Anthropology* 4:41–53.

**Blount, Roy, Jr. 1984.** "Erma Bombeck gets the dirt out." *Esquire* 101(June):208–210.

**Blumberg, Abraham S. 1967.** "The practice of law as a confidence game." *Law and Society Review* 1(Jan.): 15–39.

**Blumberg, Paul. 1968.** *Industrial Democracy.* London: Constable.

**Blumberg, Rae L. 1978.** *Stratification: Socioeconomic and Sexual Inequality.* Dubuque, IA: Wm. C. Brown.

**Blumer, Herbert. 1951.** "Collective behavior." In *New Outline of the Principles of Sociology.* Alfred McLung Lee, ed. New York: Barnes and Noble.

**Blumer, Herbert. 1962.** "Society as symbolic interaction." In *Human Behavior and Social Processes: An Interactionist Approach.* Arnold Rose, ed. Boston: Houghton Mifflin.

**Bogardus, Emory S. 1959.** *Social Distance.* Los Angeles: Antioch.

**Bogatz, G.A., and S. Ball. 1972.** *The Second Year of Sesame Street: A Continuing Evaluation.* Princeton, NJ: Educational Testing Service.

**Bogue, Donald J. 1969.** *Principles of Demography.* New York: Wiley.

**Boisen, B. 1939.** "Economic distress and religious experience." *Psychiatry*(May).

**Bonger, Willem Adrian. 1916.** *Criminality and Economic Conditions.* Boston: Little, Brown.

**Bonnie, Richard J., and Charles H. Whitebread.**

**1974.** *The Marihuana Connection.* Charlottesville, VA: University of Virginia Press.

**Boocock, Sarane. 1972.** *An Introduction to the Sociology of Learning.* Boston: Houghton Mifflin.

**Bottomore, T.B. 1964.** *Karl Marx: Selected Writings in Sociology and Social Philosophy.* New York: McGraw-Hill.

**Bottomore, T.B., and Maximilian Rubel (eds.). 1956.** *Selected Writings in Sociology and Social Philosophy.* New York: McGraw-Hill.

**Bottomore, T.B., and Maximilian Rubel. 1963.** *Karl Marx.* Middlesex, UK: Pelican.

**Boulet, J.A., et al. 1983.** *L'évolution des disparités linguistiques de revenu de travail au Canada de 1970 à 1980.* Ottawa: Economic Council of Canada: Document no. 245.

**Bouma, Gary D. 1970.** "Assessing the impact of religion: A critical review." *Sociological Analysis* 31:172–179.

**Bourdieu, P. 1974.** "The school as a conservative force: Scholastic and cultural inequalities." In *Contemporary Research in the Sociology of Education.* J. Eggleston, ed. London: Methuen.

**Bourne, L.S. 1975.** *Urban Systems: Strategies for Regulation.* London: Oxford University Press.

**Bourne, L.S. 1978.** "Emergent realities of urbanization in Canada: Some parameters and implications of declining growth." Research paper 96. Toronto: University of Toronto, Centre for Urban and Community Studies.

**Bowles, Samuel, and Herbert Gintis. 1976.** *Schooling in Capitalist America: Educational Reform and the Contradictions of Economic Life.* New York: Basic.

**Boyd, Monica. 1975.** "English-Canadian and French-Canadian attitudes toward women: Results of the Canadian Gallup Polls." *Journal of Comparative Family Studies* 6:153–169.

**Boyd, Monica. 1977.** "The forgotten minority: The socioeconomic status of divorced and separated women," In *The Working Sexes.* Patricia Marchak, ed. Vancouver: University of British Columbia.

**Boyd, Monica. 1984.** *Canadian Attitudes Toward Women: Thirty Years of Change.* Ottawa: Women's Bureau, Labour Canada.

**Boyd, Monica. 1985.** "Immigration and occupational attainment in Canada." In *Ascription and Achievement.* M. Boyd et al., eds. Ottawa: Carleton University Press.

**Boyd, Monica, et al 1985a.** *Ascription and Achievement: Studies in Mobility and Status Attainment in Canada.* Ottawa: Carleton University Press.

**Boyd, Monica, et al 1985b.** "Summary and concluding comments." In *Ascription and Achievement.* M. Boyd et al., eds. Ottawa: Carleton University Press.

**Braithwaite, John. 1981.** "The myth of social class and criminality reconsidered." *American Sociological Review* 46:36–57.

**Brannon, Robert. 1971.** "Organizational vulnerability in modern religious organizations." *Journal for the Scientific Study of Religion* 10:27–32.

**Breton, Raymond. 1964.** "Institutional completeness of ethnic communities and personal relations to immigrants." *American Journal of Sociology* 70:193–205.

**Breton, Raymond. 1972.** *Social and Academic Factors in the Career Decisions of Canadian Youth.* Ottawa: Information Canada.

**Breton, Raymond. 1978.** ''Stratification and conflict between ethnolinguistic communities with different social structures.'' *Canadian Review of Sociology and Anthropology* 15(2):148–157.

**Breton, Raymond, Jeffrey G. Reitz, and Victor Valentine. 1980.** *Cultural Boundaries and the Cohesion of Canada.* Montreal: Institute for Research on Public Policy.

**Brill, A.A. (ed. and transl.). 1938.** *The Basic Writings of Sigmund Freud.* New York: Modern Library.

**Brim, Orville G., Jr. 1966.** ''Socialization through the life cycle.'' In O.G. Brim, Jr. and Staunton Wheeler, *Socialization After Childhood: Two Essays.* New York: Wiley.

**Brim, Orville G., Jr., and Jerome Kagan. 1980.** ''Constancy and change: A view of the issues.'' In *Constancy and Change in Human Development.* O.G. Brim, Jr., and J. Kagan, eds. Cambridge, MA: Harvard University Press.

**Brinkerhoff, Merlin B., and Eugen Lupri. 1978.** ''Theoretical and methodological issues in the use of decision-making as an indicator of conjugal power.'' *Canadian Journal of Sociology* 3(1):1–20.

**Brinkerhoff, Merlin B., and Marlene Mackie. 1985.** ''Religion and gender: A comparison of American and Canadian student attitudes.'' *Journal of Marriage and the Family.* (forthcoming)

**Britton, John N.H., and James M. Gilmour. 1978.** *The Weakest Link: A Technological Perspective on Canadian Industrial Underdevelopment.* Background study 43. Ottawa: Science Council of Canada.

**Brody, Elaine M. 1978.** ''The aging and the family.'' *Annals of the American Academy of Political and Social Science* 438:13–27.

**Brody, Elaine M. 1981.** ''Women in the middle and family help to older people.'' *Gerontologist* 21(5): 471–480.

**Brodzinsky, David M., Karen Burnet, and John R. Aiello. 1981.** ''Sex of subject and gender identity as factors in humor appreciation.'' *Sex Roles* 7:561–573.

**Bronowski, J. 1973.** *The Ascent of Man.* London: British Broadcasting Corporation.

**Brophy, J.E., and T.L. Good. 1974.** *Teacher-Student Relationship.* New York: Holt, Rinehart and Winston.

**Broverman, I.K., et al. 1972.** ''Sex-role stereotypes: A current appraisal.'' *Journal of Social Issues* 28:59–78.

**Brown, Claude. 1984.** ''Manchild in Harlem.'' *The New York Times Magazine* (Sept. 16):36–44, 54, 76–78.

**Brown, L., and L. Brown. 1973.** *An Unauthorized History of the R.C.M.P.* Toronto: Lewis and Samuel.

**Bruce, Christopher J. 1978.** ''The effect of young children on female labour force participation rates: An exploratory study.'' *Canadian Journal of Sociology* 3:431–439.

**Bryden, M.P. 1979.** ''Evidence of sex-related differences in cerebral organization.'' In *Sex-Related Differences in Cognitive Functioning: Developmental Issues.* M.A. Wittig and A.C. Peterson, eds. New York: Academic.

**Brym, Robert J. 1978.** ''Regional social structure and agrarian radicalism in Canada: Alberta, Saskatchewan and New Brunswick.'' *Canadian Review of Sociology and Anthropology* 15(3):339–351.

**Brym, Robert J. 1986.** ''Trend report: Anglo-Canadian sociology.'' *Current Sociology* 34:1–152.

**Bullock, Henry A. 1961.** ''Significance of the racial factor in the length of prison sentences.'' *Journal of Criminal Law, Criminology, and Police Science* 52:411–417.

**Burch, Thomas K. 1985.** *Family History Survey: Preliminary Findings.* Ottawa: Statistics Canada, Catalogue No. 99–955.

**Burgess, Ernest W. 1925.** ''The growth of the city.'' In *The City.* Robert E. Park, E.W. Burgess, and Roderick D. McKenzie, eds. Chicago: University of Chicago Press.

**Burgess, Ernest W. 1960.** ''Aging in western culture.'' In *Aging in Western Societies.* E.W. Burgess, ed. Chicago: University of Chicago Press.

**Burke, Mary Anne. 1986.** ''The growth of part-time work.'' *Canadian Social Trends* Autumn:9–14.

**Burnet, Jean. 1978.** ''The policy of multiculturalism within a bilingual framework: A stocktaking.'' *Canadian Ethnic Studies* 10:107–113.

**Burns, Tom, and G.M. Stalker. 1961.** *The Management of Innovation.* London: Tavistock Institute.

**Burstein, M., et al. 1984.** ''Canadian work values.'' In *Working Canadians.* Graham S. Lowe and Harvey J. Krahn, eds. Toronto: Methuen.

**Bush, Diane Mitsch, and Roberta G. Simmons. 1981.** ''Socialization processes over the life course.'' In *Social Psychology: Sociological Perspectives.* Morris Rosenberg and Ralph H. Turner, eds. New York: Basic.

**Butterworth, D., and J.K. Chance. 1981.** *Latin American Urbanization.* New York: Cambridge University Press.

**Cahalan, Don. 1970.** *Problem Drinkers.* San Francisco: Jossey-Bass.

**Cahill, Spencer E. 1980.** ''Directions for an interactionist study of gender development.'' *Symbolic Interaction* 3:123–138.

**Cahill, Spencer E. 1987.** ''Children and civility: Ceremonial deviance and the acquisition of ritual competence.'' *Social Psychology Quarterly* 50:312–321.

**Cairns, Alan. 1977.** ''The governments and societies of Canadian federalism.'' *Canadian Journal of Political Science* 10(4):695–726.

**Campbell, C., and G. Szablowski, 1979.** *The Superbureaucrats.* Toronto: Macmillan.

**Campbell, Ernest Q. 1975.** *Socialization: Culture and Personality.* Dubuque, IA: Wm. C. Brown.

**Canadian Radio-television and Telecommunications Commission. 1982.** *Images of Women: Report of the Task Force on Sex-Role Stereotyping in the Broadcast Media.* Ottawa: Supply and Services.

**Cape, Elizabeth. 1987.** ''Aging women in rural settings.'' In *Aging in Canada: Social Perspectives.* Victor W. Marshall, ed. 2nd edition. Toronto: Fitzhenry and Whiteside.

**Cape, Ronald D.T., and Philip J. Henschke. 1980.** ''Perspective of health in old age.'' *Journal of the American Geriatrics Society* 28(7):295–299.

**Caplow, Theodore. 1971.** *Elementary Sociology.* Englewood Cliffs, NJ: Prentice-Hall.

**Cardinal, Harold. 1969.** *The Unjust Society: The Tragedy of Canada's Indians.* Edmonton: Hurtig.

**Carnoy, Martin, and Henry M. Levin. 1976.** *The Limits of Educational Reform.* New York: David McKay.

**Carrigan, Tim, Bob Connell, and John Lee. 1985.** "Towards a new sociology of masculinity." *Theory and Society* 14:551–604.

**Carrigan, Tim, Bob Connell, and John Lee. 1987.** "Hard and heavy: Toward a new sociology of masculinity." In *Beyond Patriarchy: Essays by Men on Pleasure, Power, and Change.* Michael Kaufman, ed. Toronto: Oxford University Press.

**Carroll, Lewis. 1896.** *Through the Looking-Glass.* New York: Random House.

**Carroll, William K. 1986.** *Corporate Power and Canadian Capitalism.* Vancouver: University of British Columbia Press.

**Castells, Manuel. 1976.** "Theory and ideology in urban sociology." In *Urban Sociology: Critical Essays.* C.G. Pickvance, ed. London: Tavistock.

**Castells, Manuel. 1977.** *The Urban Question.* London: Edward Arnold.

**Castells, Manuel. 1983.** *The City and the Grassroots: A Cross-Cultural Theory of Urban Social Movements.* Berkeley: University of California Press.

**Caves, R.E., and G.L. Reuber. 1969.** *Canadian Economic Policy and the Impact of International Monetary Flows.* Toronto: University of Toronto Press.

**Chaison, Gary N., and Joseph B. Rose. 1989.** "Unions: Growth, structure, and internal dynamics." In *Union-Management Relations in Canada.* John C. Anderson, Morley Gunderson, and Allen Ponak, eds. 2nd edition. Don Mills, ON: Addison-Wesley.

**Chalfant, Paul H., Robert E. Beckley, and C.E. Palmer. 1986.** *Religion in Contemporary Society.* 2nd edition. Palo Alto, CA: Mayfield.

**Chambliss, William, and Robert Seidman. 1971.** *Law, Order and Power.* Reading, MA: Addison-Wesley.

**Chappell, Neena L. 1983.** "Informal support networks among the elderly." *Research on Aging* 5(1):77–99.

**Chappell, Neena L., and Nina Lee Colwill. 1981.** "Medical schools as agents of professional socialization." *Canadian Review of Sociology and Anthropology* 18:67–81.

**Chappell, Neena L., and Betty Havens. 1980.** "Old and female: Testing the double jeopardy hypothesis." *Sociological Quarterly* 21(Spring):157–171.

**Chappell, Neena L., Laurel A. Strain, and Audrey A. Blandford. 1986.** *Aging and Health Care: A Social Perspective.* Toronto: Holt, Rinehart and Winston.

**Charon, Joel M. 1979.** *Symbolic Interactionism.* Englewood Cliffs, NJ: Prentice-Hall.

**Cheal, David J. 1983.** "Intergenerational family transfers." *Journal of Marriage and the Family* 45(4):805–813.

**Childe, J. Gordon. 1950.** "The urban revolution." *Town Planning Reviews* 21:4–7.

**Chiricos, Theodore, and Gordon Waldo. 1975.** "Socioeconomic status and criminal sentencing: An empirical assessment of a conflict proposition." *American Sociological Review* 40:753–772.

**Chirikos, Thomas N., and Gilbert Nestel. 1981.** "Impairment and labor market outcomes: A cross-sectional and longitudinal analysis." In *Work and Retirement.* Herbert S. Parnes, ed. Cambridge, MA: MIT Press.

**Chirot, D. 1985.** "The rise of the west." *American Sociological Review* 50(2):181–195.

**Clark, Burton R. 1956.** *Adult Education in Transition.* Berkeley, CA: University of California Press.

**Clark, Burton R. 1960.** "The 'cooling-out' function in higher education." *American Journal of Sociology* 65(May):569–576.

**Clark, Burton R. 1962.** *Educating the Expert Society.* San Francisco: Chandler.

**Clark, Lorenne, and Debra Lewis. 1977.** *Rape: The Price of Coercive Sexuality.* Toronto: Canadian Women's Educational Press.

**Clark, S.D. 1948.** *Church and Sect in Canada.* Toronto: University of Toronto Press.

**Clark, S.D. 1966.** *The Suburban Society.* Toronto: University of Toronto Press.

**Clark, S.D. 1968.** *The Developing Canadian Community.* 2nd edition. Toronto: University of Toronto Press.

**Clark, S.D. 1976.** *Canadian Society in Historical Perspective.* Toronto: McGraw-Hill Ryerson.

**Clark, S.D. 1978.** *The New Urban Poor.* Toronto: McGraw-Hill Ryerson.

**Clark, Samuel, J.P. Grayson, and L.M. Grayson, eds. 1975.** *Prophecy and Protest: Social Movements in the Twentieth Century.* Toronto: Gage.

**Clark, Susan, and Andrew S. Harvey. 1976.** "The sexual division of labour: The use of time." *Atlantis* 2(1): 44–66.

**Clark, Warren, Margaret Laing, and Edith Rechnitzer. 1986.** *The Class of 82: Summary Report on the Findings of the 1984 National Survey of the Graduates of 1982.* Ottawa: Supply and Services.

**Clausen, John A. 1968.** "Perspectives on childhood socialization." In *Socialization and Society.* J.A. Clausen, ed. Boston: Little, Brown.

**Clement, Wallace. 1975.** *The Canadian Corporate Elite.* Toronto: McClelland and Stewart.

**Clement, Wallace. 1977.** *Continental Corporate Power.* Toronto: McClelland and Stewart.

**Cloward, Richard, and Lloyd Ohlin. 1960.** *Delinquency and Opportunity: A Theory of Delinquent Gangs.* New York: Free Press.

**Coale, Ansley. 1973.** "The demographic transition reconsidered." *International Population Conference.* Liege, Belgium: International Union for the Scientific Study of Population.

**Coale, Ansley. 1974.** "The history of population." *Scientific American* 231:41–51.

**Coale, Ansley, and Edgar M. Hoover. 1958.** *Population Growth and Economic Development in Low Income Countries.* Princeton, NJ: Princeton University Press.

**Cogley, John. 1968.** *Religion in a Secular Age.* New York: New American Library.

**Cohen, Albert. 1955.** *Delinquent Boys.* New York: Free Press.

Cohen, Lawrence E., and Marcus Felson. 1979. "Social change and crime rate trends: A routine activities approach." *American Sociological Review* 44:588–607.

Collins, K. 1978. *Women and Pensions*. Ottawa: Canadian Council on Social Development.

Collins, Randall. 1968. "A comparative approach to political sociology." In *State and Society*. Reinhard Bendix, ed. Boston: Little, Brown.

Collins, Randall. 1971. "Functional and conflict theories of educational stratification." *American Sociological Review* 36(Dec.):1002–1019.

Collins, Randall. 1975. *Conflict Sociology*. New York: Academic.

Collins, Randall. 1979. *The Credential Society: An Historical Sociology of Education and Stratification*. New York: Academic.

Collins, Randall. 1985. *Three Sociological Traditions*. New York: Oxford University Press.

Colwill, Nina L. 1982. *The New Partnership: Women and Men in Organizations*. Palo Alto, CA: Mayfield Publishing.

Condry, John C., and Douglas Keith. 1983. "Educational and recreational uses of computer technology." *Youth and Society* 15:87–112.

Connelly, M. Patricia. 1978. *Last Hired, First Fired: Women and the Canadian Work Force*. Toronto: Women's Press.

Connelly, Patricia, and Linda Christiansen-Ruffman. 1977. "Women's problems: Private troubles or public issues?" *Canadian Journal of Sociology* 2:167–178.

Connidis, Ingrid. 1982. "Women and retirement: The effect of multiple careers on retirement adjustment." *Canadian Journal on Aging* 1(3–4):17–27.

Connidis, Ingrid. 1983. "Living arrangement choices of older residents: Assessing quantitative results with qualitative data." *Canadian Journal of Sociology* 8(4):359–375.

Connidis, Ingrid, and Judith Rempel. 1983. "The living arrangements of older residents: The role of gender, marital status, age, and family size." *Canadian Journal on Aging* 2(3):91–105.

Connor, W. 1979. *Socialism, Politics and Equality*. New York: Columbia University Press.

Cook, Shirley, 1969. "Canadian narcotics legislation, 1908–1923: A conflict model interpretation." *Canadian Review of Sociology and Anthropology* 6(1):36–46.

Cook, T.D., et al. 1975. *Sesame Street Revisited*. New York: Russell Sage.

Cooley, Charles H. 1902. *Human Nature and the Social Order*. New York: Scribner's.

Corin, Ellen. 1987. "The relationship between formal and informal social support networks in rural and urban contexts." In *Aging in Canada: Social Perspectives*. Victor W. Marshall, ed. 2nd edition. Toronto: Fitzhenry and Whiteside.

Coser, Rose Laub. 1974. *The Family: Its Structure and Functions*. 2nd edition. New York: St. Martin's.

Coser, Rose Laub, and Gerald Rokoff. 1971. "Women in the occupational world: Social disruption and conflict." *Social Problems* 18:535–554.

Cousineau, D.F., and J.E. Veevers. 1972. "Juvenile justice: An analysis of the Canadian Young Offenders Act." In *Deviant Behaviour and Societal Reaction*. C. Boydell et al., eds. Toronto: Holt, Rinehart and Winston.

Cowan, Ruth Schwartz. 1986. "Twentieth century changes in household technology." In *Family in Transition*. A.S. Skolnick and J.H. Skolnick, eds. 5th edition. Boston: Little, Brown.

Cowgill, Donald O. 1986. *Aging Around the World*. Belmont, CA: Wadsworth.

Cowgill, Donald O., and Lowell D. Holmes. 1972. *Aging and Modernization*. New York: Appleton-Century-Crofts.

Coyne, D. 1988. "Corporate concentration and policy." In *Social Inequality in Canada*. J. Curtis et al., eds. Scarborough, ON: Prentice-Hall.

Crawford, Craig, and James E. Curtis. 1979. "English-Canadian–American differences in value orientations: Survey comparisons bearing on Lipset's thesis." *Studies in Comparative International Development* 14(Fall-Winter):23–44.

Crean, Susan M. 1976. *Who's Afraid of Canadian Culture?* Don Mills, ON: General Publishing.

Crean, Susan M., and Marcel Rioux. 1983. *Two Nations*. Toronto: James Lorimer.

Creighton, Donald. 1956. *The Commercial Empire of the St. Lawrence*. Toronto: Macmillan.

Cressey, Donald. 1971; 1953. *Other People's Money: A Study of the Social Psychology of Embezzlement*. Glencoe, IL: Free Press.

Crothers, Charles. 1979. "On the myth of rural tranquillity: Comment on Webb and Collette." *American Journal of Sociology* 84(6):1441–1445.

Crysdale, Stewart. 1961. *The Industrial Struggle and Protestant Ethics in Canada*. Toronto: Ryerson Press.

Cumming, Elaine, and William H. Henry. 1961. *Growing Old: The Process of Disengagement*. New York: Basic.

Cuneo, Carl J., and James E. Curtis. 1974. "Quebec separatism: An analysis of determinants within social class levels." *Canadian Review of Sociology and Anthropology* 11(1):1–29.

Cuneo, Carl J., and James E. Curtis. 1975. "Social ascription in the educational and occupational status attainment of urban Canadians." *Canadian Review of Sociology and Anthropology* 12:6–24.

Currie, Ray, Rick Linden, and Leo Driedger. 1980. "Properties of norms as predictors of alcohol use among Mennonites." *Journal of Drug Issues* (Winter): 93–107.

Curtis, James E., and Ronald D. Lambert. 1975. "Status dissatisfaction and out-group rejection: Cross-cultural comparisons within Canada." *Canadian Review of Sociology and Anthropology* 12(2):178–192.

Curtis, James E., and Ronald D. Lambert. 1976. "Educational status and reactions to social and political heterogeneity." *Canadian Review of Sociology and Anthropology* 13(2):189–203.

Cutler, Neal E. 1981. "Political characteristics of elderly cohorts in the twenty-first century." In *Aging: Social Change*. Sara B. Kiesler, James N. Morgan, and Valerie Kincade Oppenheimer, eds. New York: Academic.

Dahl, Roald. 1961. *Who Governs?* New Haven: Yale University Press.

**Dahrendorf, Rolf. 1959.** *Class and Class Conflict in Industrial Society.* Palo Alto, CA: Stanford University Press.

**Daniels, Arlene Kaplan. 1975.** "Feminist perspective in sociological research." In *Another Voice: Feminist Perspectives on Social Life and Social Science.* Marcia Millman and Rosabeth Moss Kanter, eds. Garden City, NY: Doubleday Anchor.

**Dannefer, Dale. 1984.** "Adult development and social theory: A paradigmatic reappraisal." *American Sociological Review* 49(Feb.):100–116.

**D'Arcy, Carl. 1980.** "The manufacture and obsolescence of madness: Age, social policy and psychiatric morbidity in a prairie province." In *Aging in Canada: Social Perspectives.* V.W. Marshall, ed. 1st edition. Don Mills, ON: Fitzhenry and Whiteside.

**Darroch, A. Gordon. 1979; 1980.** "Another look at ethnicity, stratification and social mobility in Canada." *Canadian Journal of Sociology* 4:1–25; also in *Ethnicity and Ethnic Relations in Canada.* J. Goldstein and R. Bienvenue, eds. Toronto: Butterworths.

**Dashefsky, Arnold. 1976.** *Ethnic Identity in Society.* Chicago: Rand McNally.

**David, Deborah S., and Robert Brannon. 1976.** *The Forty-Nine Percent Majority: The Male Sex Role.* Reading, MA: Addison-Wesley.

**Davies, James C. 1962.** "Toward a theory of revolution." *American Sociological Review* 27:5–19.

**Davies, Mark, and Denise B. Kandel. 1981.** "Parental and peer influences on adolescents' educational plans: Some further evidence." *American Journal of Sociology* 87:363–387.

**Davis, A.K. 1971.** "Canadian society and history as hinterland versus metropolis." In *Canadian Society: Pluralism, Change and Conflict.* R.J. Ossenberg, ed. Scarborough, ON: Prentice-Hall.

**Davis, F. James, and Robert Hagedorn. 1954.** "Testing the reliability of systematic field observations." *American Sociological Review* 19(3):345–348.

**Davis, Kingsley. 1940.** "Extreme social isolation of a child." *American Journal of Sociology* 45:554–564.

**Davis, Kingsley. 1947.** "Final note on a case of extreme isolation." *American Journal of Sociology* 52:432–437.

**Davis, Kingsley. 1949.** *Human Society.* New York: Macmillan.

**Davis, Kingsley. 1955.** "The origin and growth of urbanization in the world." *American Journal of Sociology* 60:429–437.

**Davis, Kingsley. 1974.** "The migration of human populations." *The Human Population.* San Francisco: W.H. Freeman.

**Davis, Kingsley, and Pietronella van den Oever. 1982.** "Demographic foundations of new sex roles." *Population and Development Review* 8:495–511.

**Day, Lincoln H. 1972.** "The social consequences of a zero population growth rate in the United States." In *United States Commission on Population and the American Future: Demographic and Social Aspects of Population Growth.* Charles F. Westoff and Robert Parke, Jr., eds. Washington, DC: U.S. Government Printing Office.

**Deaux, Kay. 1984.** "From individual differences to social categories: Analysis of a decade's research on gender." *American Psychologist* 39:105–116.

**Deaux, Kay. 1985.** "Sex and gender." *Annual Review of Psychology* 36:49–81.

**Decore, John V. 1964.** "Criminal sentencing: The role of the Canadian courts of appeal and the concept of uniformity." *Criminal Law Quarterly* 6(Feb.):324–380.

**DeFleur, Melvin L., and Lois B. DeFleur. 1967.** "The relative contribution of television as a learning source for children's occupational knowledge." *American Sociological Review* 32:777–789.

**DeMaris, Alfred, and Gerald Leslie. 1984.** "Cohabitation with the future spouse: Its influence upon marital satisfaction and communication." *Journal of Marriage and the Family* 46:77–84.

**Demerath, N.J., III. 1965.** *Social Class in American Protestantism.* Chicago: Rand McNally.

**Demerath, N.J., III, and Phillip E. Hammond. 1969.** *Religion in Social Context.* New York: Random House.

**Demos, John. 1986.** *Past, Present and Personal: The Family and Life Course in American History.* New York: Oxford University Press.

**Denton, Frank T., Christine H. Feaver, and Byron G. Spencer. 1987.** "The Canadian population and labour force: Retrospect and prospect." In *Aging in Canada: Social Perspectives.* Victor W. Marshall, ed. 2nd edition. Toronto: Fitzhenry and Whiteside.

**Denton, Frank T., S. Neno Li, and Byron G. Spencer. 1987.** "How will population aging affect the future costs of maintaining health-care standards?" In *Aging in Canada: Social Perspectives.* Victor W. Marshall, ed. 2nd edition. Toronto: Fitzhenry and Whiteside.

**Deutsch, Morton, and Robert M. Krauss. 1965.** *Theories in Social Psychology.* New York: Basic.

**de Vaus, David, and Ian McAllister. 1987.** "Gender differences in religion: A test of the structural location theory." *American Sociological Review* 52:472–481.

**deVries, John, and Frank G. Vallee. 1980.** *Language Use in Canada.* Ottawa: Supply and Services.

**Dill, William R. 1958.** "Environment as an influence on managerial autonomy." *Administrative Science Quarterly* 2(Mar.):409–443.

**Dion, K., and E. Berscheid. 1972.** "Physical attractiveness and social perception of peers in preschool children." Mimeographed research report.

**Disman, Milada. 1983.** "Immigrants and other grieving people: Insights for counselling practices and policy issues." *Canadian Ethnic Studies* 15:106–118.

**Dohrenwend, Bruce P., and Barbara S. Dohrenwend. 1975.** *Social Status and Psychological Disorder.* New York: John Wiley and Sons.

**Dowd, James J. 1980.** *Stratification among the Aged.* Monterey, CA: Brooks/Cole.

**Dowd, James. 1986.** "The old person as stranger." In *Later Life: The Social Psychology of Aging.* Victor W. Marshall, ed. Beverly Hills, CA: Sage.

**Downs, A. 1957.** *An Economic Theory of Democracy.* New

York: Harper.

**Doyle, James A. 1983.** *The Male Experience.* Dubuque, IA: Wm C. Brown.

**Doyle, James A. 1985.** *Sex and Gender.* Dubuque, IA: Wm. C. Brown.

**Drakich, Janice, and Connie Guberman. 1987.** "Violence in the family." In *Family Matters: Sociology and Contemporary Canadian Families.* Karen L. Anderson et al., eds. Toronto: Methuen.

**Driedger, Leo. 1974.** "Doctrinal belief: A major factor in the differential perception of social issues." *Sociological Quarterly* (Winter):66–80.

**Driedger, Leo. 1975.** "In search of cultural identity factors: A comparison of ethnic students." *Canadian Review of Sociology and Anthropology* 12:150–162.

**Driedger, Leo. 1976.** "Ethnic self-identity: A comparison of ingroup evaluations." *Sociology* 39:131–141.

**Driedger, Leo. 1986.** "Community conflict: The Eldorado invasion of Warman." *Canadian Review of Sociology and Anthropology* 23(2):247–269.

**Driedger, Leo, and Neena L. Chappell. 1987.** *Aging and Ethnicity: Toward an Interface.* Toronto: Butterworths.

**Driedger, Leo, and Glen Church. 1974.** "Residential segregation and institutional completeness: A comparison of ethnic minorities." *Canadian Review of Sociology and Anthropology* 11:30–52.

**Driedger, Leo, Raymond Currie, and Rick Linden. 1982.** "Traditional and rational views of God and the world." *Review of Religious Research.* (forthcoming)

**Driedger, Leo, and Richard Mezoff. 1980.** "Ethnic prejudice and discrimination in Winnipeg high schools." *Canadian Journal of Sociology* 6:1–17.

**Dubin, Robert. 1968.** "Workers." *International Encyclopedia of the Social Sciences.* New York: Macmillan and Free Press.

**Dubin, Robert, R. Alan Hedley, and T.C. Taveggia. 1976.** "Attachment to work." In *Handbook of Work, Organization, and Society.* R. Dubin, ed. Chicago: Rand McNally.

**Duffy, Ann. 1986.** "Reformulating power for women." *Canadian Review of Sociology and Anthropology* 23:22–46.

**Dumas, Jean. 1987.** *Current Demographic Analysis: Report on the Demographic Situation in Canada 1986.* Ottawa: Supply and Services.

**Duncan, Otis Dudley. 1959.** "Human ecology and population studies." In *The Study of Population.* Philip M. Hauser and O.D. Duncan, eds. Chicago: University of Chicago Press.

**Duncan, Otis Dudley, and Leo F. Schnore. 1959.** "Cultural, behavioral, and ecological perspectives in the study of social organization." *American Journal of Sociology* 65:132–146.

**Durdin-Smith, Jo, and Diane DeSimone. 1983.** *Sex and the Brain.* New York: Arbor House.

**Durkheim, Emile. 1938; 1895.** *The Rules of Sociological Method.* Sarah A. Solway and John H. Mueller, transl. George E.G. Catlin, ed. Glencoe, IL: Free Press.

**Durkheim, Emile. 1951; 1897.** *Suicide.* John A. Spaulding and George Simpson, transl. Glencoe, IL: Free Press.

**Durkheim, Emile. 1964a; 1893.** *The Division of Labor in Society.* George Simpson, transl. Glencoe, IL: Free Press.

**Durkheim, Emile. 1964b; 1897.** *Suicide.* John A. Spaulding and George Simpson, transl. Glencoe, IL: Free Press.

**Durkheim, Emile. 1965; 1912.** *The Elementary Forms of the Religious Life.* New York: Free Press.

**Durkin, Kevin. 1986.** "Sex roles and the mass media." In *The Psychology of Sex Roles.* David J. Hargreaves and Ann M. Colley, eds. New York: Harper and Row.

**Duster, Troy. 1970.** *The Legislation of Morality: Law, Drugs and Moral Judgment.* New York: Free Press.

**Eagly, Alice H., and L.L. Carli. 1981.** "Sex of researchers and sex-typed communications as determinants of sex differences in influenceability: A meta-analysis of social influence studies." *Psychological Bulletin* 90:1–20.

**Eagly, Alice H., and Valerie J. Steffen. 1984.** "Gender stereotypes stem from the distribution of women and men into social roles." *Journal of Personality and Social Psychology* 46:735–754.

**Eakins, Barbara Westbrook, and R. Gene Eakins. 1978.** *Sex Differences in Human Communication.* Boston: Houghton Mifflin.

**Economic Council of Canada. 1964.** *First Annual Review.* Ottawa: Supply and Services.

**Economic Council of Canada. 1965.** *Second Annual Review.* Ottawa: Supply and Services.

**Economic Council of Canada. 1986.** *Changing Times: Twenty-Third Annual Review.* Ottawa: Supply and Services.

**Economic Council of Canada. 1987.** *Innovation and Jobs in Canada.* Ottawa: Supply and Services.

**Eder, Donna, and Maureen T. Hallinan. 1978.** "Sex differences in children's friendships." *American Sociological Review* 43:237–250.

**Edwards, John N. 1969.** "Families' behavior as social exchange." *Journal of Marriage and the Family* 31:518–526.

**Eichler, Margrit. 1978.** "Women's unpaid labour." *Atlantis* 3(2):52–62.

**Eichler, Margrit. 1983.** *Families in Canada Today: Recent Changes and Their Policy Implications.* Toronto: Gage.

**Eichler, Margrit. 1987.** "Family change and social policies." In *Family Matters: Sociology and Contemporary Canadian Families.* Karen L. Anderson et al., eds. Toronto: Methuen.

**Ekeh, Peter. 1974.** *Social Exchange Theory.* London: Heinemann.

**Ekstedt, John W., and Curt T. Griffiths. 1984.** *Corrections in Canada: Policy and Practice.* Toronto: Butterworths.

**Elder, Glen H., Jr. 1974.** *Children of the Great Depression.* Chicago: University of Chicago Press.

**Elder, Glen H., Jr. 1978.** "Approaches to social change and the family." *American Journal of Sociology* 84:S1–S38.

**Elkin, Frederick. 1983.** "Family, socialization, and ethnic identity." In *The Canadian Family.* K. Ishwaran, ed. Toronto: Gage.

**Ellis, Godfrey J. 1983.** "Youth in the electronic environment: An introduction." *Youth and Society* 15:3–12.

**Emerson, Richard M. 1981.** "Social exchange theory." In *Social Psychology.* Morris Rosenberg and Ralph H.

Turner, eds. New York: Basic.

**Employment and Immigration Canada. 1984.** *Background Paper on Future Immigration Levels.* Ottawa: Supply and Services.

**Engels, Friedrich. 1942; 1884.** *The Origin of the Family, Private Property and the State.* New York: International Publishers.

**Ericson, Richard V. 1982.** *Reproducing Order: A Study of Police Patrol Work.* Toronto: University of Toronto Press.

**Erikson, Erik. 1963.** *Childhood and Society.* 2nd edition. New York: Norton.

**Erikson, Erik. 1968.** *Identity: Youth and Crisis.* New York: Norton.

**Espenshade, Thomas J. 1978.** "Zero population growth and the economies of developed nations." *Population and Development Review* 4:645–680.

**Estes, Carroll L. 1979.** *The Aging Enterprise.* San Francisco: Jossey-Bass.

**Ewen, Robert B. 1980.** *An Introduction to Theories of Personality.* New York: Academic.

***Fact Book on Aging.* 1983.** Document prepared for the Second Canadian Conference on Aging. Ottawa: Supply and Services.

**Fallding, Harold. 1978.** "Mainline Protestantism in Canada and the United States: An overview." *Canadian Journal of Sociology* 2:141–160.

**Fallo-Mitchell, Linda, and Carol D. Ryff. 1982.** "Preferred timing of female life events: Cohort differences." *Research on Aging* 4(2):249–267.

**Feagin, J.R., and H. Hahn. 1973.** *Ghetto Revolts.* New York: Macmillan.

**Felson, Marcus, and Lawrence E. Cohen. 1980.** "Human ecology and crime: A routine activity approach." *Human Ecology* 8:389–406.

**Ferber, Marianne A., and H.M. Lowry. 1976.** "The sex differential in earnings: A reappraisal." *Industrial and Labor Relations Review* 29(3):377–387.

**Ferree, Myra Marx, and Beth B. Hess. 1987.** "Introduction." In *Analyzing Gender: A Handbook of Social Science Research.* Beth B. Hess and Myra Marx Ferree, eds. Newbury Park, CA: Sage.

**Fine, Gary Alan. 1986.** "The dirty play of little boys." *Society* 24(Nov./Dec.):63–67.

**Fink, Arlene, and Jacqueline Kosecoff. 1977.** "Girls' and boys' changing attitudes toward school." *Psychology of Women Quarterly* 2:44–49.

**Finkelhor, David. 1983.** "Common features of family abuse." In *The Dark Side of Families: Current Family Violence Research.* David Finkelhor et al., eds. Beverly Hills, CA: Sage.

**Firestone, Melvin M. 1978.** "Socialization and interaction in a Newfoundland outport." *Urban Life* 7(Apr.): 19–110.

**Fischer, Claude S. 1981.** "The public and private worlds of city life." *American Sociological Review* 46(3):306–316.

**Fischer, Claude S. 1984.** *The Urban Experience.* 2nd edition. New York: Harcourt Brace Jovanovich.

**Fitzsimmons-LeCavalier, Patricia. 1983.** "Resourceful movements: The mobilization of citizens for neighbourhood planning control." Doctoral dissertation. Montreal: McGill University.

**Fitzsimmons-LeCavalier, Patricia, and Guy LeCavalier. 1981.** "Becoming a minority: Quebec's nonfrancophones and the sovereignty question." Paper presented to the American Sociological Association.

**Fitzsimmons-LeCavalier, Patricia, and Guy LeCavalier. 1984.** "Individual versus collective action: The minority response of Quebec's nonfrancophones." Paper presented to the Canadian Sociology and Anthropology Association.

**Flacks, Richard. 1979.** "Growing up confused." In *Socialization and the Life Cycle.* Peter I. Rose, ed. New York: St. Martin's.

**Flanders, Allan. 1965.** *Trade Unions.* London: Hutchinson University Library.

**Foner, Anne. 1974.** "Age stratification and age conflict in political life." *American Sociological Review* 39 (Apr.):187–196.

**Foner, Anne, and David Kertzer. 1978.** "Transitions over the life course: Lessons from age-set societies." *American Journal of Sociology* 83(5):1081–1104.

**Foner, Anne, and Karen Schwab. 1981.** *Aging and Retirement.* Monterey, CA: Brooks/Cole.

**Foot, David K. 1982.** *Canada's Population Outlook: Demographic Futures and Economic Challenges.* Toronto: James Lorimer.

**Forcese, D. 1980.** *The Canadian Class Structure.* 2nd edition. Toronto: McGraw-Hill Ryerson.

**Ford, Catherine. 1983.** "Leave-me-alone group tunes out." *Calgary Herald* (July 23).

**Form, William. 1979.** "Comparative industrial sociology and the convergence hypothesis." *Annual Review of Sociology* 5:1–25.

**Fouts, Gregory T. 1980.** "Parents as censors of TV content for their children." *Journal of the Canadian Association for Young Children* 6:20–31.

**Fox, Bonnie (ed.). 1982.** *Hidden in the Household: Women's Domestic Labour Under Capitalism.* Toronto: Women's Press.

**Franck, K.A. 1980.** "Friends and strangers: The social experience of living in urban and non-urban settings." *Journal of Social Issues* 36(3):52–71.

**Frank, André Gunder. 1969.** *Capitalism and Underdevelopment in Latin America.* New York: Monthly Review.

**Frank, J.A. 1984.** "La dynamique des manifestations violentes." *Canadian Journal of Political Science* 17(2): 325–350.

**Frank, J.A., and M. Kelly. 1979.** "Street politics in Canada: An examination of mediating factors." *American Journal of Political Science* 23:593–614.

**Fraser, Sylvia. 1987.** *My Father's House: A Memoir of Incest and of Healing.* Toronto: Doubleday.

**Frazier, E. Franklin. 1964.** *The Negro Church in America.* New York: Schocken Books.

**Freeman, Jo. (ed.). 1983.** *Social Movements of the Sixties and Seventies.* New York: Longman.

**Freeman, Richard B. 1976.** *The Overeducated American.* New York: Academic.

**Freud, Sigmund. 1962; 1928.** *The Future of an Illusion.* New York: Doubleday.

**Frey, W.H. 1987.** "Migration and depopulation of the metropolis: Regional restructuring or rural renaissance?" *American Sociological Review* 52(2):240–57.

**Frideres, James S. 1974.** *Canada's Indians: Contemporary Conflict.* Scarborough, ON: Prentice-Hall.

**Friedan, Betty. 1963.** *The Feminine Mystique.* Harmondsworth, UK: Penguin.

**Friedl, Ernestine. 1975.** *Women and Men: An Anthropologist's View.* New York: Holt, Rinehart and Winston.

**Friedl, Ernestine. 1978.** "Society and sex roles." *Human Nature* (Apr.):70.

**Friedland, Martin. 1981.** "Gun control in Canada: Politics and impact." Paper presented to Seminar on Canadian–U.S. Relations, Harvard Center for International Affairs, University Consortium for Research on North America.

**Frieze, Irene H., et al. 1978.** *Women and Sex Roles: A Social Psychological Perspective.* New York: W.W. Norton.

**Fry, Christine L. 1976.** "The ages of adulthood: A question of numbers." *Journal of Gerontology* 31(2):170–177.

**Fuguitt, Glen, and James Zuiches. 1975.** "Residential preferences and population distribution." *Demography* 12(3):167–80.

**Fullan, Michael. 1970.** "Industrial technology and worker integration in the organization." *American Sociological Review* 35(Dec.):1028–1039.

**Fuller, Mary. 1978.** "Sex-role stereotyping and social science." In *The Sex Role System: Psychological and Sociological Perspectives.* Jane Chetwynd and Oonagh Hartnett, eds. London: Routledge and Kegan Paul.

**Gaffield, Chad M. 1979.** "Canadian families in cultural context: Hypotheses from the mid-nineteenth century." *Historical Papers* Canadian Historical Association:48–61.

**Gamson, William. 1975.** *The Strategy of Social Protest.* Homewood, IL: Dorsey.

**Gans, Herbert. 1962a.** "Urbanism and suburbanism as ways of life." In *Human Behavior and Social Processes.* Arnold M. Rose, ed. Boston: Houghton Mifflin.

**Gans, Herbert. 1962b.** *The Urban Villagers.* New York: Free Press.

**Gans, Herbert. 1967.** *The Levittowners: Way of Life and Politics in a New Suburban Community.* New York: Pantheon.

**Gans, Herbert. 1972.** "The positive functions of poverty." *American Journal of Sociology* 78:275–289.

**Garn, Stanley M. 1966.** "Body size and its implications." In *Review of Child Development Research* 2. Lois W. Hoffman and Martin L. Hoffman, eds. New York: Sage.

**Garnets, Linda, and Joseph H. Pleck. 1979.** "Sex role identity, androgyny, and sex role transcendence: A sex role strain analysis." *Psychology of Women Quarterly* 3:270–283.

**Garreau, Joel. 1981.** *The Nine Nations of North America.* New York: Avon.

**Garrison, Howard H. 1979.** "Gender differences in the career aspirations of recent cohorts of high school seniors." *Social Problems* 27:170–185.

**Gecas, Viktor. 1976.** "The socialization and child care roles." In *Role Structure and Analysis of the Family.* F. Ivan Nye, ed. Beverly Hills, CA: Sage.

**Gecas, Viktor. 1981.** "Contexts of socialization." In *Social Psychology: Sociological Perspectives.* Morris Rosenberg and Ralph H. Turner, eds. New York: Basic.

**Gee, Ellen M. Thomas. 1980.** "Female marriage patterns in Canada: Changes and differentials." *Journal of Comparative Family Studies* 11:457–473.

**Gee, Ellen M. 1986.** "The life course of Canadian women: An historical and demographic analysis." *Social Indicators Research* 18:263–283.

**Gee, Ellen M. 1987.** "Historical change in the family life course of men and women." In *Aging in Canada: Social Perspectives.* Victor W. Marshall, ed. 2nd edition. Toronto: Fitzhenry and Whiteside.

**Gee, Ellen M., and Meredith M. Kimball. 1987.** *Women and Aging.* Toronto: Butterworths.

**Geertz, Clifford. 1968.** "Religion as a cultural system." In *The Religious Situation.* Donald Cutler, ed. Boston: Beacon.

**Gerbner, George, and Larry Gross. 1976.** "The scary world of TV's heavy viewer." *Psychology Today* 9(Apr.):41–45, 89.

**Gergen, K.J., and S. Worchel (eds.). 1980.** *Social Exchange: Advances in Theory and Research.* New York: Plenum.

**Gerlach, Luther P., and Virginia H. Hine. 1968.** "Five factors crucial to the growth and spread of a modern religious movement." *Journal for the Scientific Study of Religion* 7:23–40.

**Gerth, H., and C. Wright Mills (eds.). 1958.** *From Max Weber: Essays in Sociology.* New York: Oxford University Press.

**Gibbs, Jack P., and Maynard Erickson. 1976.** "Crime rates of American cities in an ecological context." *American Journal of Sociology* 82:605–620.

**Giddens, A. 1973.** *The Class Structure of the Advanced Societies.* London: Hutchinson.

**Giddens, Anthony. 1982.** *Sociology.* New York: Harcourt Brace Jovanovich.

**Giddens, Anthony. 1987.** *Sociology.* 2nd edition. New York: Harcourt Brace Jovanovich.

**Giffen, P.J. 1966.** "The revolving door: a functional interpretation." *Canadian Review of Sociology and Anthropology* 3(3):154–166.

**Gillie, Oliver. 1979.** "The great IQ fraud." *Atlas* (Feb.):26–28.

**Gilligan, Carol. 1982.** *In a Different Voice.* Cambridge, MA: Harvard University Press.

**Gillis, A.R. 1974.** "Population density and social pathology: The case of building type, social allowance, and juvenile delinquency." *Social Forces* 53(2):306–314.

**Gillis, A.R. 1977.** "High-rise housing and psychological strain." *Journal of Health and Social Behavior* 18(4):418–431.

**Gillis, A.R. 1979a.** "Coping with crowding: Television, patterns of activity, and adaptation to high-density environments." *Sociological Quarterly* 20:267–277.

**Gillis, A.R. 1979b.** "Household density and human crowding: Unravelling a non-linear relationship." *Journal of Population* 2(2):104–117.

**Gillis, A.R. 1983.** "Strangers next door: An analysis of density, diversity and scale in public housing projects." *Canadian Journal of Sociology* 8(1):1–20.

**Gillis, A.R. 1984.** "Violent crime, policing, and urbanization in nineteenth century France: An analysis of trends." Paper presented to the Social Science and History Association.

**Gillis, A.R. 1985.** "Domesticity, divorce, and deadly quarrels: A macro analysis." In *Critique and Explanation: Essays in Honor of Gwynne Nettler*. Timothy F. Hartnagel and Robert A. Silverman, eds. New Brunswick, NJ: Transaction.

**Gillis, A.R. 1987a.** "CMAS, submetro areas, and megalopolis: An examination of Montreal, Toronto, and Vancouver." Report submitted to Statistics Canada.

**Gillis, A.R. 1987b.** "Crime, punishment, and historical perspectives." *Sociological Forum* 2(3):602–609.

**Gillis, A.R. 1989.** "Crime and state surveillance in nineteenth-century France." *American Journal of Sociology* 95(2):259–278.

**Gillis, A.R., and John Hagan. 1982.** "Density, delinquency and design: Formal and informal control and the residential environment." *Criminology* 19(4):514–529.

**Gillis, A.R., and John Hagan. 1983.** "Bystander apathy and the territorial imperative." *Sociological Inquiry* 53(4):448–460.

**Gillis, A.R., and John Hagan. 1990.** "Delinquent Samaritans: A study of group conflict, subcultural sentiment, and the willingness to intervene." *Journal of Research on Crime and Delinquency* (forthcoming).

**Gillis, A.R., and Paul C. Whitehead. 1970.** "The Halifax Jews: A community within a community." In *Minority Canadians: Immigrant Groups*. Jean Leonard Elliott, ed. Scarborough, ON: Prentice-Hall.

**Gillis, A.R., Madeline A. Richard, and John Hagan. 1986.** "Ethnic susceptibility to crowding: An empirical analysis." *Environment and Behavior* 18(6):683–706.

**Ginzberg, Eli. 1982.** "The mechanization of work." *Scientific American* 247(3):67–75.

**Glaser, Barry G., and Anselm L. Strauss. 1971.** *Status Passage*. Chicago: Aldine Atherton.

**Glazer, Nathan, and Daniel P. Moynihan. 1963.** *Beyond the Melting Pot*. Cambridge, MA: MIT Press.

**Glazer, Nona. 1977.** "Introduction to part two." In *Women in a Man-Made World*. N. Glazer and Helen Youngelson Waehrer, eds. 2nd edition. Chicago: Rand McNally.

**Glickman, Yaacov, and Alan Bardikoff. 1982.** *The Treatment of the Holocaust in Canadian History and Social Science Textbooks*. Downsview, ON: B'nai Brith Canada.

**Glock, Charles, Benjamin Ringer, and Earl Babbie. 1967.** *To Comfort and to Challenge*. Berkeley, CA: University of California Press.

**Goffman, Erving. 1959.** *The Presentation of Self in Everyday Life*. Garden City, NY: Doubleday Anchor.

**Goffman, Erving. 1963a.** *Behavior in Public Places*. New York: Free Press.

**Goffman, Erving. 1963b.** *Stigma: Notes on the Management of Spoiled Identity*. Englewood Cliffs, NJ: Prentice-Hall.

**Goffman, Erving. 1977.** "The arrangement between the sexes." *Theory and Society* 4:301–331.

**Gold, Deborah T. 1987.** "Siblings in old age: Something special." *Canadian Journal on Aging* 6(3):199–215.

**Gold, Gerald L. 1975.** *St. Pascal*. Montreal: Holt, Rinehart and Winston.

**Goldberg, Herb. 1976.** *The Hazards of Being Male: Surviving the Myth of Masculine Privilege*. New York: Signet.

**Goldberg, Michael A., and John Mercer. 1986.** *The Myth of the North American City: Continentalism Challenged*. Vancouver: University of British Columbia Press.

**Goldsen, Rose K. 1979.** Book review of Marie Winn, *The Plug-in Drug: Television, Children and the Family*. In *American Journal of Sociology* 84:1054–1056.

**Goldstein, Jay. 1981.** "Has the popularity of Anglo-conformity waned?: A study of school naming events in Winnipeg, 1881–1979." *Canadian Ethnic Studies* 13:52–60.

**Goleman, Daniel. 1978.** "Special abilities of the sexes: Do they begin in the brain?" *Psychology Today* (Nov.): 48–49, 51, 54–56, 58–59, 120.

**Goode, William J. 1970 (3rd edition); 1963 (1st edition).** *World Revolution and Family Patterns*. New York: Free Press.

**Gordon, Milton M. 1964.** *Assimilation in American Life*. New York: Oxford University Press.

**Gordon, R.A. 1976.** "Prevalence: The rare datum in delinquency measurement and its implications for the theory of delinquency." In *The Juvenile Justice System*. Malcolm Klein, ed. Beverly Hills, CA: Sage.

**Gorsuch, Richard, and Daniel Aleshire. 1974.** "Christian faith and ethnic prejudice: A review and interpretation of research." *Journal for the Scientific Study of Religion* 13:281–307.

**Gould, Meredith, and Rochelle Kern-Daniels. 1977.** "Toward a sociological theory of gender and sex." *American Sociologist* 12:182–189.

**Gove, Walter. 1975.** "Labelling and mental illness: A critique." In *The Labelling of Deviance: Evaluating a Perspective*. Walter Gove, ed. New York: Halsted.

**Gove, Walter, and Jeanette Tudor. 1973.** "Adult sex roles and mental illness." *American Journal of Sociology* 78:812–835.

**Gove, Walter R., Michael Hughes, and Omer R. Galle. 1979.** "Overcrowding in the home: An empirical investigation of its possible consequences." *American Sociological Review* 44:59–80.

**Goyder, John C. 1983.** "Ethnicity and class identity: The case of French- and English-speaking Canadians." *Ethnic and Racial Studies* 6:72–89.

**Goyder, John C., and James E. Curtis. 1979.** "Occupational mobility in Canada over four generations." In *Social Stratification: Canada*. J. Curtis and W. Scott, eds. 2nd edition. Scarborough, ON: Prentice-Hall.

**Goyder, John C., and Peter C. Pineo. 1979.** "Social class self-identification." In *Social Stratification: Canada*. J. Curtis and W. Scott, eds. 2nd edition. Scarborough, ON: Prentice-Hall.

**Graff, Harvey J. 1975.** "Towards a meaning of literacy: Literacy and social structure in Hamilton, Ontario, 1861."

In *Education and Social Change: Themes from Ontario's Past.* Michael B. Katz and Paul H. Mattingly, eds. New York: New York University Press.

**Gray Report. 1972.** *Foreign Direct Investment in Canada.* Ottawa: Supply and Services.

**Grayson, J.P., and L.M. Grayson. 1978.** "The Canadian literary elite: A socio-historical perspective." *Canadian Journal of Sociology* 3(3):291–308.

**Greeley, Andrew. 1972.** *The Denominational Society.* Glenview, IL: Scott, Foresman.

**Green, Edward. 1961.** *Judicial Attitudes in Sentencing.* London: Macmillan.

**Green, Richard. 1974.** *Sexual Identity Conflict in Children and Adults.* Baltimore: Penguin.

**Greenberg, David. 1981.** *Crime and Capitalism.* Palo Alto, CA: Mayfield.

**Greenfield, Patricia Marks. 1984.** *Mind and Media: The Effects of Television, Video Games, and Computers.* Cambridge, MA: Harvard University Press.

**Greenglass, Esther R. 1982.** *A World of Difference: Gender Roles in Perspective.* Toronto: Wiley.

**Greenglass, Esther R. 1985.** "A social-psychological view of marriage for women." *International Journal of Women's Studies* 8:24–31.

**Grindstaff, Carl F. 1975.** "The baby bust: Changes in fertility patterns in Canada." *Canadian Studies in Population* 2:15–22.

**Grossman, Brian A. 1969.** *The Prosecutor.* Toronto: University of Toronto Press.

**Guberman, Connie, and Margie Wolfe (eds.). 1985.** *No Safe Place: Violence Against Women and Children.* Toronto: Women's Press.

**Guest, A. 1969.** "The applicability of the Burgess Zonal Hypothesis to urban Canada." *Demography* 6:271–277.

**Guillemard, Anne-Marie. 1977.** "The call to activity among the old: Rehabilitation or regimentation?" In *Canadian Gerontological Collection* (Vol. I). Blossom T. Wigdor, ed. Winnipeg: Canadian Association on Gerontology.

**Guillemard, Anne-Marie. 1980.** *La vieillesse et l'Etat.* Paris: Presses Universitaires de France.

**Guindon, Hubert. 1975.** "Social unrest, social class and Quebec's bureaucratic revolution." In *Prophecy and Protest.* S.D. Clark et al., eds. Toronto: Gage.

**Gunderson, Morley. 1976.** "Work patterns." In *Opportunity for Choice: A Goal for Women in Canada.* Gail C.A. Cook, ed. Ottawa: Information Canada.

**Gunderson, Morley 1983.** *Economics of Poverty and Income Distribution.* Toronto: Butterworths.

**Guppy, Neil. 1984.** "Access to higher education in Canada." *Canadian Journal of Higher Education* 14:79–93.

**Guppy, Neil, Doug Balson, and Susan Vellutini. 1987.** "Women and higher education in Canadian society." In *Women and Education: A Canadian Perspective.* Jane Gaskell and Arlene McLaren, eds. Calgary, AB: Detselig.

**Guppy, Neil, Paulina D. Mikicich, and Ravi Pendakur. 1984.** "Changing patterns of educational inequality in Canada." *Canadian Journal of Sociology* 9:319–331.

**Gurr, Ted. 1970.** *Why Men Rebel.* Princeton: Princeton University Press.

**Gurr, Ted Robert. 1981.** "Historical trends in violent crime: A critical review of the evidence." In *Crime and Justice: An Annual Review of Research.* N. Morris and M. Tonry, eds. Chicago: University of Chicago Press.

**Gusfield, Joseph R. 1963.** *Symbolic Crusade: Status Politics and the American Temperance Movement.* Urbana, IL: University of Illinois Press.

**Guterman, S.S. 1969.** "In defence of Wirth." *American Journal of Sociology* 74(5):492–499.

**Gutman, Gloria M. 1980.** "The elderly at home and in retirement housing: A comparative study of health problems, functional difficulties, and support service needs." In *Aging in Canada: Social Perspectives.* Victor W. Marshall, ed. Toronto: Fitzhenry and Whiteside.

**Haas, Jack, Victor Marshall, and William Shaffir. 1981.** "Initiation into medicine: Neophyte uncertainty and the ritual ordeal of professionalization." In *Work in the Canadian Context.* Katherina L.P. Lundy and Barbara D. Warne, eds. Toronto: Butterworths.

**Hacker, Helen Mayer. 1951.** "Women as a minority group." *Social Factors* 30:60–69.

**Hagan, John. 1974a.** "Extra-legal attributes and criminal sentencing: An assessment of sociological viewpoints." *Law and Society Review* 8(3):357–383.

**Hagan, John. 1974b.** "Criminal justice and native people: A study of incarceration in a Canadian province." *Canadian Review of Sociology and Anthropology* (Aug): 220–236.

**Hagan, John. 1975.** "Parameters of criminal prosecution: An application of path analysis to a problem of criminal justice." *Journal of Criminal Law, Criminology, and Police Science* 65(4):536–544.

**Hagan, John. 1977.** "Finding discrimination: A question of meaning." *Ethnicity* 4:167–176.

**Hagan, John. 1982.** "The corporate advantage: The involvement of individual and organizational victims in the criminal justice process." *Social Forces* 60(4):993–1022.

**Hagan, John. 1984.** *The Disreputable Pleasures: Crime and Deviance in Canada.* 2nd edition. Toronto: McGraw-Hill Ryerson.

**Hagan, John. 1985.** "Toward a structural theory of crime, race and gender: The Canadian case." *Crime and Delinquency* 31:129–146.

**Hagan, John, and Celesta Albonetti. 1982.** "Race, class and the perception of criminal injustice in America." *American Journal of Sociology* 88:329–355.

**Hagan, John, and Kirsten Bumiller. 1983.** "Making sense of sentencing: A review and critique of sentencing research." In *Research on Sentencing: The Search for Reform.* Alfred Blumstein et al., eds. Washington, DC: National Academy Press.

**Hagan, John, and Jeffrey Leon. 1977.** "Rediscovering delinquency: Social history, political ideology and the sociology of law." *American Sociological Review* 42:587.

**Hagan, John, and Patricia Parker. 1985.** "White collar crime and punishment: The class structure and legal sanctioning of securities violations." *American Sociologi-*

*cal Review* 50:302–316.

**Hagan, John, A.R. Gillis, and J. Chan. 1978.** "Explaining official delinquency: A spatial study of class, conflict, and control." *Sociological Quarterly* 19:386–398.

**Hagan, John, A.R. Gillis, and John Simpson. 1985.** "The class structure of gender and delinquency: Toward a power-control theory of common delinquent behavior." *American Journal of Sociology* 90:1151–1178.

**Hagan, John, A.R. Gillis, and John Simpson. 1987.** "Class in the household: A power-control theory of gender and delinquency." *American Journal of Sociology* 92:788–816.

**Hagan, John, Ilene Nagel, and Celesta Albonetti. 1980.** "The differential sentencing of white-collar offenders in ten federal district courts." *American Sociological Review* 45:802–820.

**Hagestad, Gunhild O. 1982.** "Life-phase analysis." In *Research Instruments in Social Gerontology: Clinical and Social Psychology* (Vol. 1). David J. Mangen and Warren A. Peterson, eds. Minneapolis: University of Minnesota Press.

**Hagestad, Gunhild O., and Bernice L. Neugarten. 1985.** "Age and the life course." In *Handbook of Aging and the Social Sciences*. Robert H. Binstock et al., eds. 2nd edition. New York: Van Nostrand Reinhold.

**Hajnal, John. 1965.** "European marriage patterns in historical perspective." In *Population in History: Essays in Historical Demography*. D.V. Glass and D.E.C. Eversley, eds. London: Edward Arnold.

**Hall, Edward T. 1962.** "Our silent language." *Americas* 14(Feb.):6.

**Hall, Peter M. 1972.** "A symbolic interactionist analysis of politics." In *Perspectives in Political Sociology*. Andrew Effrat, ed. Indianapolis, IN: Babbs-Merrill.

**Haller, A., and D. Bills. 1979.** "Occupational prestige hierarchies: Theory and evidence." *Contemporary Sociology* 8:721–734.

**Haller, Mark. 1970.** "Urban crime and criminal justice: The Chicago case." *Journal of American History* 57:619–635.

**Hamilton, Richard F. 1982.** *Who Voted for Hitler?* Princeton, NJ: Princeton University Press.

**Hammer, Muriel. 1963–64.** "Influence of small social networks on factors of mental hospital admission." *Human Organization* 22(Winter):243–251.

**Hardin, Herschel. 1974.** *A Nation Unaware: The Canadian Ecomonic Culture.* Vancouver: J.J. Douglas.

**Harding, Deborah, and Emily Nett. 1984.** "Women and rock music." *Atlantis* 10:60–76.

**Hardwick, W.G. 1971.** "Vancouver: The emergence of a 'core-ring' urban pattern." In *Geographical Approaches to Canadian Problems*. R.L. Gentilcore, ed. Scarborough, ON: Prentice-Hall.

**Hareven, Tamara K. 1978.** *Transitions: The Family and the Life Course in Historical Perspective.* New York: Academic.

**Hareven, Tamara K. 1987.** "Family history at the crossroads." *Journal of Family History* 12:iv–xxiii.

**Hargreaves, D.H. 1967.** *Social Relations in a Secondary School.* London: Routledge and Kegan Paul.

**Harlow, Harry F. 1959.** "Love in infant monkeys." *Sci-*

*entific American* 200(June):68–74.

**Harlow, Harry F., and Margaret Harlow. 1962.** "Social deprivation in monkeys." *Scientific American* 207(Nov.):136–146.

**Harrington, M. 1972.** *Socialism.* New York: Saturday Review.

**Harris, Chauncy D., and Edward L. Ullman. 1945.** "The nature of cities." *Annals of the American Academy of Political and Social Science* 242(Nov.):7–17.

**Harris, Louis, et al. 1975.** *The Myth and Reality of Aging in America.* Washington, DC: National Council on the Aging.

**Harris, Marvin. 1981.** *America Now: Why Nothing Works.* New York: Simon and Schuster.

**Harrison, Paul. 1959.** *Authority and Power in the Free Church Tradition: A Social Case Study of the American Baptist Convention.* Princeton, NJ: Princeton University Press.

**Hartley, Ruth E. 1959.** "Sex-role pressures in the socialization of the male child." *Psychological Reports* 5:457–468.

**Hartz, Louis. 1964.** *The Founding of New Societies.* New York: Harcourt, Brace and World.

**Harvey, David. 1975.** "The political economy of urbanization in advanced capitalist societies: The case of the United States." In *The Social Economy of Cities*. Gary Geppert and Harold M. Rose, eds. Beverly Hills, CA: Sage.

**Harvey, David. 1976.** "Labor, capital, and class struggle around the built environment in advanced capitalist societies." *Politics and Society*: 265–295.

**Harvey, Edward. 1974.** *Educational Systems and the Labour Market.* Toronto: Longman.

**Harvey, Edward, and Jos. Lennards. 1973.** *Key Issues in Higher Education.* Toronto: Ontario Institute for Studies in Education.

**Hawthorne, H.B., et al. 1967.** *A Survey of Contemporary Indians of Canada* 1 & 2. Ottawa: Indian Affairs.

**Hayford, Alison. 1987.** "Outlines of the family." In *Family Matters: Sociology and Contemporary Canadian Families*. Karen L. Anderson et al., eds. Toronto: Methuen.

**Heald, Tim. 1982.** "A job well done." *Today* (Feb. 6): 7–11.

**Hedley, R. Alan. 1980.** "Work values: A test of the conveyance and cultural diversity theses." *International Journal of Comparative Sociology* 21(1–2):100–109.

**Hedley, R. Alan. 1982.** "Work, life, and the pursuit of happiness: A study of Australian industrial workers." *Journal of Industrial Relations* 23(3):397–404.

**Hedley, R. Alan. 1984a.** "Work–nonwork contexts and orientations to work: A crucial test." *Work and Occupations* 11(3):353–376.

**Hedley, R. Alan. 1984b.** "Social generalizations: Biases and solutions." *International Journal of Comparative Sociology* 25:159–172.

**Hedley, R. Alan, and Susan M. Adams. 1982.** "Mom in the labor force—Verdict: not guilty!" *Perception* 6(1): 28–29.

**Hedley, R. Alan, R. Dubin, and T.C. Taveggia. 1980.** "The quality of working life, gender, and occupational status: A cross-national comparison." In *The Quality of Life*. A. Szalai and F.M. Andrews, eds. Beverly Hills,

CA: Sage.

Hendricks, Jon. 1981. "The elderly in society: Beyond modernization." Paper presented to the Gerontological Society of America and the Canadian Association on Gerontology.

Henley, Nancy M. 1975. "Power, sex, and nonverbal communication." In *Language and Sex: Difference and Dominance*. Barrie Thorne and N. Henley, eds. Rowley, MA: Newbury House.

Henry, F., and E. Ginzberg. 1988. "Racial discrimination in employment." In *Social Inequality in Canada*. J. Curtis et al., eds. Scarborough, ON: Prentice-Hall.

Henry, Louis. 1961. "Some data on natural fertility." *Eugenics Quarterly* 8:81–91.

Henschel (Ambert), Anne-Marie. 1973. *Sex Structure*. Don Mills, ON: Longman.

Herberg, Edward N. 1988. *Ethnic Groups in Canada: Adaptations and Transitions*. Toronto: Nelson.

Herberg, Will. 1955. *Protestant, Catholic, Jew*. New York: Doubleday.

Herberg, Will. 1960. *Protestant, Catholic, Jew*. Revised edition. New York: Doubleday.

Herskowitz, M. 1952. "Population size, economic surplus, and social leisure." In *Economic Anthropology*. Melville Herskowitz, ed. New York: Alfred A. Knopf.

Hetherington, E. Mavis, and Ross D. Parke. 1979. *Child Psychology: A Contemporary Viewpoint*. 2nd edition. New York: McGraw-Hill.

Hewitt, C. 1977. "The effect of political democracy on equality in industrial societies: A cross-national comparison." *American Sociological Review* 42:450–464.

Hexham, Irving, Raymond Currie, and Joan Townsend. 1985. "The new religions." *New Canadian Encyclopedia*. Edmonton, AB: Hurtig.

Hill, Clifford. 1971. "From church to sect: West Indian religious sect development in Britain." *Journal for the Scientific Study of Religion* 10:114–123.

Hiller, Harry H. 1976. "The sociology of religion in the Canadian context." In *Introduction to Canadian Society*. G.N. Ramu and Stuart D. Johnson, eds. Toronto: Macmillan.

Hiller, Harry H. 1986. *Canadian Society*. Scarborough, ON: Prentice-Hall.

Hindelang, M.J. 1978. "Race and involvement in common law personal crimes." *American Sociological Review* 43:93–109.

Hindelang, M.J. 1979. "Sex differences in criminal activity." *Social Problems* 27(2):143–156.

Hindelang, Michael, Travis Hirschi, and Joseph Weis. 1981. *Measuring Delinquency*. Beverly Hills, CA: Sage.

Hirschi, Travis. 1969. *Causes of Delinquency*. Berkeley, CA: University of California Press.

Hobart, Charles. 1979. "Courtship process: Premarital sex." In *The Canadian Family*. G.N. Ramu, ed. Toronto: Holt, Rinehart and Winston.

Hobart, Charles. 1983. "Marriage or cohabitation." In *Marriage and Divorce in Canada*. K. Ishwaran, ed. Toronto: Methuen.

Hobart, Charles, and C. Brant. 1966. "Eskimo education Danish and Canadian: A comparison." *Canadian Review of Sociology and Anthropology* 3:47–66.

Hochschild, Arlie Russell. 1973. *The Unexpected Community*. Englewood Cliffs, NJ: Prentice-Hall.

Hochschild, Arlie Russell. 1975. "Disengagement theory: A critique and proposal." *American Sociological Review* 40(5):553–569.

Hogan, Dennis P. 1981. *Transitions and Social Change: The Early Lives of American Men*. New York: Academic.

Hogarth, John. 1971. *Sentencing as a Human Process*. Toronto: University of Toronto Press.

Holsti, Ole R. 1969. *Content Analysis for the Social Sciences and Humanities*. Reading, MA: Addison-Wesley.

Holt, John B. 1940. "Holiness religion: Cultural shock and social reorganization." *American Sociological Review* 5(Oct.):740–747.

Hoppock, Robert. 1935. *Job Satisfaction*. New York: Harper and Brothers.

Horowitz, Gad. 1968. "Conservatism, liberalism, and socialism in Canada: An interpretation." In his *Canadian Labour in Politics*. Toronto: University of Toronto Press.

Horton, Paul B., and Chester L. Hunt. 1972. *Sociology*. 3rd edition. New York: McGraw-Hill.

Hostetler, John A., and Gertrude Enders Huntington. 1967. *The Hutterites in North America*. New York: Holt, Rinehart and Winston.

Houghland, James G., and James R. Wood. 1979. "Inner circles in local churches." *Sociological Analysis* 40:226–239.

House, J.D. 1985. "The Don Quixote of Canadian politics?: Power in and power over Newfoundland society." *Canadian Journal of Sociology* 10(2):171–188.

Houston, Barbara. 1987. "Should public education be gender-free?" In *Women and Men: Interdisciplinary Readings on Gender*. Greta Hofmann Nemiroff, ed. Toronto: Fitzhenry and Whiteside.

Howe, Florence. 1974. "Sexual stereotypes and the public schools." In *Women and Success: The Anatomy of Achievement*. Ruth B. Kundsin, ed. New York: William Morrow.

Hoyt, Homer. 1939. *The Structure and Growth of Residential Neighborhoods in American Cities*. Washington, DC: Federal Housing Authority.

Huber, Joan. 1976. "Toward a socio-technological theory of the women's movement." *Social Problems* 23:371–388.

Hughes, David R., and Evelyn Kallen. 1974. *The Anatomy of Racism: Canadian Dimensions*. Montreal: Harvest House.

Hughes, Everett C. 1943. *French Canada in Transition*. Chicago: University of Chicago Press.

Hughes, Everett C. 1971. *The Sociological Eye: Selected Papers*. Chicago: Aldine Atherton.

Hughes, Everett C., et al. (eds.). 1950. *Race and Culture: Vol. 1, The Collected Papers of Robert Ezra Park*. Glencoe, IL: Free Press.

Huizinga, Joan. 1924. *The Waning of the Middle Ages*. New York: St. Martin's.

Hunsberger, Bruce. 1980. "A reexamination of the antecedents of apostasy." *Review of Religious Research* 21:158–170.

Hunsberger, Bruce. 1984. "Religious socialization, apostasy, and the impact of family background." *Journal for the Scientific Study of Religion* 23:239–251.

**Hunter, Alfred A. 1981.** *Class Tells: On Social Inequality in Canada.* 2nd edition. Toronto: Butterworths.

**Hyde, Janet. 1979.** *Understanding Human Sexuality.* New York: McGraw-Hill.

**Inciardi, James. 1975.** *Careers in Crime.* Chicago: Rand McNally.

**Inglehart, Ronald. 1977.** *The Silent Revolution: Changing Values and Political Styles Among Western Publics.* Princeton, NJ: Princeton University Press.

**Inglehart, Ronald. 1981.** "Post-materialism in an environment of insecurity." *American Political Science Review* 74(4):880–900.

**Inglis, J., and J. Lawson. 1981.** "Sex differences in the effects of unilateral brain damage on intelligence." *Science* 212:693–695.

**Inkeles, A., and D.H. Smith. 1974.** *Becoming Modern: Individual Change in Six Developing Countries.* Cambridge, MA: Harvard University Press.

**Innis, Harold A. 1930.** *The Fur Trade in Canada: An Introduction to Canadian Economic History.* Toronto: Oxford University Press.

**Innis, Harold A. 1940.** *The Cod Fisheries: The History of an International Economy.* New Haven, CT: Yale University Press.

**Innis, Harold A. 1951.** *The Bias of Communication.* Toronto: University of Toronto Press.

**Irving, John. 1959.** *The Social Credit Movement in Alberta.* Toronto: University of Toronto Press.

**Ishwaran, K. (ed.). 1976.** *The Canadian Family.* Revised edition. Toronto: Holt, Rinehart and Winston.

**Ishwaran, K. (ed.). 1980.** *Canadian Families: Ethnic Variations.* Toronto: McGraw-Hill Ryerson.

**Jackman, R. 1975.** *Politics and Social Equality.* New York: Wiley.

**Jackson, John D. 1975.** *Community and Conflict: A Study of French–English Relations in Ontario.* Montreal: Holt, Rinehart and Winston.

**Jacobs, Jane. 1961.** *The Death and Life of Great American Cities.* New York: Random House.

**Jacobs, Jane. 1980.** *The Question of Separatism.* New York: Random House.

**Jacobs, Jane. 1982.** *Canadian Cities and Sovereignty Association.* Toronto: Canadian Broadcasting Corporation.

**Jalée, P. 1968.** *The Pillage of the Third World.* New York: Monthly Review.

**Jenkins, J. Craig. 1981.** "Sociopolitical movements." In *The Handbook of Political Behavior.* Samuel L. Long, ed. New York: Plenum.

**Jensen, G.F., J.H. Strauss, and V.W. Harris. 1977.** "Crime, delinquency and the American Indian." *Human Organization* 36:252–257.

**Johnson, Harry M. 1960.** *Sociology: A Systematic Introduction.* New York: Harcourt, Brace and World.

**Jourard, Sidney M. 1964.** *The Transparent Self.* New York: Van Nostrand Reinhold.

**Joy, Richard J. 1972.** *Languages in Conflict.* Toronto: McClelland and Stewart.

**Kagan, Jerome. 1984.** *The Nature of the Child.* New York: Basic.

**Kahn, Robert L. 1975.** "In search of the Hawthorne effect." In *Man and Work in Society.* E.L. Cass and F.G. Zimmer, eds. Toronto: Van Nostrand Reinhold.

**Kalbach, Warren E. 1980.** "Historical and generational perspectives of ethnic residential segregation in Toronto, Canada: 1851–1971." Research paper 118. Toronto: University of Toronto, Centre for Urban and Community Studies.

**Kalbach, Warren E., and Wayne W. McVey. 1979.** *The Demographic Bases of Canadian Society.* 2nd edition. Toronto: McGraw-Hill Ryerson.

**Kalish, Richard A. 1982.** *Late Adulthood: Perspectives on Human Development.* Monterey, CA: Brooks/Cole.

**Kallen, Horace M. 1924.** *Culture and Democracy in the United States.* New York: Liverright.

**Kandel, Denise B. 1978.** "Homophily, selection, and socialization in adolescent friendships." *American Journal of Sociology* 84:427–436.

**Katz, Fred E. 1967.** "Explaining informal work groups in complex organizations: The case for autonomy." In *Readings in Industrial Sociology.* W.A. Faunce, ed. New York: Appleton-Century-Crofts.

**Katz, Michael. 1975.** *The People of Hamilton West: Family and Class in a Mid-Nineteenth Century City.* Cambridge, MA: Harvard University Press.

**Keating, Norah C., and Priscilla Cole. 1980.** "What do I do with him 24 hours a day?: Changes in the housewife role after retirement." *Gerontologist* 20(1):84–89.

**Keating, Norah C., and Judith Marshall. 1980.** "The process of retirement: The rural self employed." *Gerontologist* 20(4):437–443.

**Keith, Jennie. 1982.** *Old People as People.* Toronto: Little, Brown.

**Kelly, W., and N. Kelly. 1976.** *Policing in Canada.* Toronto: Macmillan.

**Kelner, M. 1970.** "Ethnic penetration into Toronto's elite structure." *Canadian Review of Sociology and Anthropology* 7:128–137.

**Kendig, Hal L. 1986.** "Intergenerational exchange." In *Ageing and Families: A Social Networks Perspective.* Hal L. Kendig, ed. Boston: Allen and Unwin.

**Kennedy, Michael. 1986.** "Measuring Canada's international competitiveness." *Quarterly Economic Review* (Dec.):37–45.

**Kernaghan, Kenneth. 1982.** "Politics, administration, and Canada's aging population." *Canadian Public Policy* 8(1):66–79.

**Kerr, Donald. 1968.** "Metropolitan dominance in Canada." In *Canada: A Sociological Profile.* W.E. Mann, ed. Toronto: Copp Clark.

**Kessler, Suzanne J., and Wendy McKenna. 1978.** *Gender: An Ethnomethodological Approach.* New York: John Wiley.

**Kimmel, Michael S. (ed.). 1987.** *Changing Men: New Directions in Research on Men and Masculinity.* Newbury Park, CA: Sage.

**Kingston, Anne. 1989.** "When marital status is a dubious asset." *Financial Times* (Feb. 13):35.

**Kirkpatrick, Clifford. 1949.** "Religion and humanitarianism: A study of institutional implications." *Psychological Monographs* 63, 9.

**Knipscheer, Kees, and Anton Bevers. 1985.** "Older parents and their middle-aged children: Symmetry or asymmetry in their relationship." *Canadian Journal on Aging* 4(3):145–159.

**Kohlberg, Lawrence. 1976.** "Moral stages and moralization: The cognitive-developmental approach." In *Moral Development and Behavior*. T. Lickona, ed. New York: Holt, Rinehart and Winston.

**Kohn, Melvin L. 1977.** *Class and Conformity.* 2nd edition. Homewood, IL: Dorsey.

**Komarovsky, Mirra. 1946.** "Cultural contradictions and sex roles." *American Journal of Sociology* 52:184–189.

**Kome, Penney. 1982.** *Somebody Has To Do It: Whose Work is Housework?* Toronto: McClelland and Stewart.

**Koyl, L.F. 1977.** "The aging Canadian." In *Canadian Gerontological Collection* (Vol. I). Blossom T. Wigdon, ed. Winnipeg: Canadian Association on Gerontology.

**Kunkel, John H. 1977.** "Sociobiology vs biosociology." *American Sociologist* 12:69–73.

**Kuypers, Joseph A., and Vern L. Bengtson. 1973.** "Competence and social breakdown: A social-psychological view of aging." *Human Development* 16(2):37–49.

**Labour Canada. 1986.** *When I Grow Up: Career Expectations and Aspirations of Canadian Schoolchildren.* Ottawa: Women's Bureau.

**Labour Canada. 1987.** *Women in the Labour Force.* Ottawa: Supply and Services.

**LaFree, Gary. 1980.** "The effect of sexual stratification by race on official reactions to rape." *American Sociological Review* 45:842–854.

**Lamb, Theodore A. 1981.** "Nonverbal and paraverbal control in dyads and triads: Sex or power differences?" *Social Psychology Quarterly* 44:49–53.

**Lambert, Ronald D. 1971.** *Sex Role Imagery in Children: Social Origins of Mind.* Study 6. Royal Commission on the Status of Women in Canada. Ottawa: Information Canada.

**Lambert, Ronald D. 1981.** *The Sociology of Contemporary Quebec Nationalism: An Annotated Bibliography and Review.* New York: Garland.

**Lambert, Ronald D., and James E. Curtis. 1979.** "Education, economic dissatisfaction, and nonconfidence in Canadian social institutions." *Canadian Review of Sociology and Anthropology* 16(1):47–59.

**Lambert, Ronald D., and James E. Curtis. 1982.** "The French- and English-Canadian language communities and multicultural attitudes." *Canadian Ethnic Studies* 14(2):43–58.

**Lambert, Ronald D., and James E. Curtis. 1983.** "Opposition to multiculturalism among Québécois and English-Canadians." *Canadian Review of Sociology and Anthropology* 20(2):193–207.

**Lambert, Ronald, et al. 1986.** "Effects of identification with governing parties on feelings of political trust and efficacy." *Canadian Journal of Political Science* 19(4):705–728.

**Lancaster, Jane Beckman. 1976.** "Sex roles in primate societies." In *Sex Differences: Social and Biological Perspectives*. Michael S. Teitelbaum, ed. Garden City, NY:

Doubleday Anchor.

**Landis, David S. 1983.** *Revolution in Time: Clocks and the Making of the Modern World.* Cambridge, MA: Harvard University Press (Belknap).

**Landsberg, Michele. 1982.** *Women and Children First.* Markham, ON: Penguin.

**Lane, Roger. 1980.** "Urban homicide in the nineteenth century: Some lessons for the twentieth." In *History and Crime: Implications for Criminal Justice Policy.* J. Inciardi and C. Faupel, eds. Beverly Hills, CA: Sage.

**Langer, William. 1973.** "The black death." In *Cities: Their Origin, Growth and Human Impact. (Scientific American.)* San Francisco: W.H. Freeman.

**Large, Mary-Jane. 1981.** "Services for the elderly." *Ontario Medical Review* (Jan.):38–41.

**Larson, Reed, and Robert Kubey. 1983.** "Television and music: Contrasting media in adolescent life." *Youth and Society* 15:13–31.

**Lasch, Christopher. 1977.** *Haven in a Heartless World: The Family Besieged.* New York: Basic.

**Laslett, Barbara. 1972.** "The family as a public and private institution: A historical perspective." *Journal of Marriage and the Family* 35:480–492.

**Laslett, Peter. 1976.** "Societal development and aging." In *Handbook of Aging and the Social Sciences*. Robert Binstock and Ethel Shanas, eds. New York: Van Nostrand Reinhold.

**Laslett, Peter. 1977.** "The history of aging and the aged." *Family Life and Illicit Love in Earlier Generations.* Cambridge: Cambridge University Press.

**Laslett, Peter. 1983.** *The World We Have Lost.* 3rd edition. New York: Scribner.

**Laslett, Peter, and Richard Wall. 1972.** *Household and Family in Past Time.* Cambridge: Cambridge University Press.

**Laub, John H. 1983.** "Urbanism, race, and crime." *Journal of Research on Crime and Delinquency* (July):183–198.

**Lauer, Robert H., and Warren B. Handel. 1977.** *Social Psychology: The Theory and Application of Symbolic Interactionism.* Boston: Houghton Mifflin.

**Lautard, E. Hugh, and D.J. Loree. 1984.** "Ethnic stratification in Canada, 1931–1971." *Canadian Journal of Sociology* 9(3):333–343.

**Lawrence, Paul R., and Jay W. Lorsch. 1967.** *Organization and Environment: Managing Differentiation and Integration.* Cambridge, MA: Harvard University Press.

**Laws, Judith Long. 1979.** *The Second X: Sex Role and Social Role.* New York: Elsevier, North Holland.

**Laxer, Gordon. 1975.** "American and British influences on metropolitan development in Canada, 1878–1913." Paper presented to the Canadian Sociology and Anthropology Association.

**Laxer, Robert (ed.). 1973.** *Canada Ltd.: The Political Economy of Dependency.* Toronto: McClelland and Stewart.

**Lazarsfeld, P.F., and R.K. Merton. 1954.** "Friendship as a social process." In *Freedom and Control in Modern Society.* M. Berger, T. Abel, and C.H. Page, eds. Princeton, NJ: Van Nostrand.

**Leacock, Eleanor B. 1982.** *Myths of Male Dominance.* New York: Monthly Review.

**LeBon, Gustave. 1960; 1895.** *The Crowd.* New York: Viking.

**Lee, Dennis. 1974.** *Alligator Pie.* Toronto: Macmillan.

**Lee, Gary, and Robert Clyde. 1974.** "Religion, socioeconomic status and anomie." *Journal for the Scientific Study of Religion* 13:35–47.

**Leighton, Alexander. 1959.** *My Name is Legion.* New York: Basic.

**LeMasters, E.E. 1977.** *Parents in Modern America.* 3rd edition. Homewood, IL: Dorsey.

**Lemert, Edwin. 1967.** *Human Deviance, Social Problems and Social Control.* Englewood Cliffs, NJ: Prentice-Hall.

**Lemon, B.W., Vern L. Bengtson, and J.A. Peterson. 1972.** "An exploration of the activity theory of aging: Activity types and life satisfaction among in-movers to a retirement community." *Journal of Gerontology* 27:511–523.

**Lenski, Gerhard. 1961.** *The Religious Factor.* New York: Doubleday.

**Lenski, Gerhard. 1966.** *Power and Privilege.* New York: McGraw-Hill.

**Lenski, Gerhard, and Jean Lenski. 1982.** *Human Societies: An Introduction to Macrosociology.* 4th edition. New York: McGraw-Hill.

**Lever, Janet. 1978.** "Sex differences in the complexity of children's play." *American Sociological Review* 43:471–483.

**Levine, Donald N., Ellwood B. Carter, and Eleanor Miller Gorman. 1976.** "Simmel's influence on American sociology." *American Journal of Sociology* 81:813–845.

**LeVine, Robert A., and Donald T. Campbell. 1972.** *Ethnocentrism: Theories of Conflict, Ethnic Attitudes, Group Behavior.* New York: Wiley.

**Levine, Saul V. 1979.** "Role of psychiatry in the phenomenon of cults." *Canadian Journal of Psychiatry* 24:593–603.

**Levinson, Daniel J., et al. 1978.** *The Seasons of a Man's Life.* New York: Knopf.

**Levitt, Cyril. 1984.** *Children of Privilege: Student Revolt in the Sixties.* Toronto: University of Toronto Press.

**Levitt, K. 1970.** *Silent Surrender.* Toronto: Macmillan.

**Levy, J. 1976.** "Cerebral lateralization and spatial ability." *Behavior Genetics* 6:71–78.

**Levy, Marion J. 1965.** "Aspects of the analysis of family structure." In *Aspects of the Analysis of Family Structure.* A.J. Coale et al., eds. Princeton, NJ: Princeton University Press.

**Lewin, Kurt. 1948.** *Resolving Social Conflicts.* New York: Harper.

**Lewis, Michael. 1972.** "Culture and gender roles: There's no unisex in the nursery." *Psychology Today* 5(May): 54–57.

**Lewis, Oscar. 1966.** "The culture of poverty." In *Structural Inequality in Canada.* John Harp and John R. Hofley, eds. Scarborough, ON: Prentice-Hall.

**Li, Peter S., and B. Singh Bolaria (eds.). 1983.** *Racial Minorities in Multicultural Canada.* Toronto: Garamond.

**Lichter, D.T. 1988.** "Racial differences in underemployment in American cities." *American Journal of Sociology* 93(4):771–792.

**Liebert, Robert M., and Joyce Sprafkin. 1988.** *The Early Window: Effects of Television on Children and Youth.* 3rd edition. New York: Pergamon.

**Liebert, Robert M., Joyce N. Sprafkin, and Emily S. Davidson. 1982.** *The Early Window: Effects of Television on Children and Youth.* 2nd edition. New York: Pergamon.

**Liebowitz, Lila. 1983.** "Origins of the sexual division of labor." In *Woman's Nature: Rationalizations of Inequality.* Marian Lowe and Ruth Hubbard, eds. New York: Pergamon.

**Lindblom, Charles E. 1977.** *Politics and Markets.* New York: Basic.

**Lindenthal, Jacob, et al. 1970.** "Mental status and religious behavior." *Journal for the Scientific Study of Religion* 9:143–149.

**Lindesmith, Alfred. 1947.** *Opiate Addiction.* Bloomington, IN: Principia.

**Lindesmith, Alfred R., Anselm L. Strauss, and Norman K. Denzin. 1977.** *Social Psychology.* 5th edition. New York: Holt, Rinehart and Winston.

**Lindsay, Colin, and Craig McKie. 1986.** "Annual review of labour force trends." *Canadian Social Trends* Autumn:2–7.

**Linteau, P., and J. Robert. 1977.** "Land ownership and society in Montreal: An hypothesis." In *The Canadian City: Essays in Urban History.* Gilbert A. Stelter and Alan F.J. Artibise, eds. Toronto: McClelland and Stewart.

**Lipman-Blumen, Jean. 1984.** *Gender Roles and Power.* Englewood Cliffs, NJ: Prentice-Hall.

**Lipman-Blumen, Jean, and Ann R. Tickamyer. 1975.** "Sex roles in transition: A ten-year perspective." *Annual Review of Sociology* 1:297–337.

**Lippmann, Walter. 1922.** *Public Opinion.* New York: Harcourt and Brace.

**Lipset, S.M. 1960.** *Political Man.* Garden City, NY: Doubleday.

**Lipset, S.M. 1961.** "Introduction." In *Political Parties* (by Robert Michels). New York: Collier-Macmillan.

**Lipset, Seymour Martin. 1965.** "Revolution and counter-revolution: Canada and the United States." In *The Revolutionary Theme in Contemporary America.* Thomas Ford, ed. Lexington, KY: University of Kentucky Press.

**Lipset, Seymour Martin. 1968.** *Agrarian Socialism.* New York: Doubleday Anchor.

**Lipset, Seymour Martin. 1985.** "Canada and the United States: The cultural dimension." In *Canada and the United States.* Charles F. Doran and John H. Sigler, eds. Englewood Cliffs, NJ: Prentice-Hall.

**Lithwick, N.H.G., and G. Paquet. 1968.** "Urban growth and regional contagion." In *Urban Studies: A Canadian Perspective.* N.H.G. Lithwick and G. Paquet, eds. Toronto: Methuen.

**Litwak, Eugene. 1965.** "Extended kin relations in an industrial democratic society." In *Social Structure and the Family.* Ethel Shanas and Gordon F. Streib, eds. Englewood Cliffs, NJ: Prentice-Hall.

**Lodhi, A.Q., and Charles Tilly. 1973.** "Urbanization, crime and collective violence in nineteenth century France." *American Journal of Sociology* 79(2):296–318.

**Lofland, Lyn H. 1975.** "The 'thereness' of women: A

selective review of urban sociology." In *Another Voice: Feminist Perspectives on Social Life and Social Science.* Marcia Millman and Rosabeth Moss Kanter, eds. Garden City, NY: Doubleday Anchor.

**Lopata, Helena Z. 1979.** *Women as Widows: Support Systems.* New York: Elsevier.

**Lorimer, James. 1978.** *The Developers.* Toronto: James Lorimer.

**Lott, Bernice. 1981.** "A feminist critique of androgyny: Toward the elimination of gender attributions for learned behavior." In *Gender and Nonverbal Behavior.* Clara Mayo and Nancy M. Henley, eds. New York: Springer-Verlag.

**Lowe, George D., and H. Eugene Hodges. 1972.** "Race and treatment of alcoholism in a southern state." *Social Problems* (Fall):240–252.

**Lowe, Graham S. 1980.** "Women, work and the office: The feminization of clerical occupations in Canada, 1901–1931." *Canadian Journal of Sociology* 5:361–381.

**Lowe, Graham S., and Harvey J. Krahn. 1984.** "Working women: Editors' introduction." In *Working Canadians: Readings in the Sociology of Work and Industry.* Graham S. Lowe and Harvey J. Krahn, eds. Toronto: Methuen.

**Lowe, Marian. 1983.** "The dialectic of biology and culture." In *Woman's Nature: Rationalizations of Inequality.* Marian Lowe and Ruth Hubbard, eds. New York: Pergamon.

**Lower, A.R.M. 1939.** "Geographical determinants in Canadian history." In *Essays in Canadian History.* Ralf Flenley, ed. Toronto: Macmillan.

**Lucas, Rex A. 1971.** *Minetown, Milltown, Railtown: Life in Canadian Communities of Single Industry.* Toronto: University of Toronto Press.

**Luckmann, Thomas. 1967.** *The Invisible Religion.* New York: Macmillan.

**Lupri, Eugen, and J. Frideres. 1981.** "The quality of marriage and the passage of time: Marital satisfaction over the family life cycle." *Canadian Journal of Sociology* 6(3):283–305.

**Lupri, Eugen, and Donald L. Mills. 1987.** "The household division of labour in young dual-earner couples: The case of Canada." *International Review of Sociology* 23.

**Lupri, Eugen, and Gladys L. Symons. 1982.** "The emerging symmetrical family: Fact or fiction?" *International Journal of Comparative Sociology* 23:166–189.

**Lupsha, P.A. 1976.** "On theories of urban violence." In *Urbanism, Urbanization, and Change.* P. Meadows and E. Mizruchi, eds. 2nd edition. Reading, MA: Addison-Wesley.

**Luxton, Meg. 1980.** *More Than a Labour of Love: Three Generations of Women's Work in the Home.* Toronto: Women's Press.

**Luxton, Meg. 1981.** "Taking on the double day." *Atlantis* 7(1):15–16.

**Luxton, Meg. 1987.** "Thinking about the future." In *Family Matters: Sociology and Contemporary Canadian Families.* Karen L. Anderson et al., eds. Toronto: Methuen.

**Lynn, David B. 1959.** "A note on sex differences in the development of masculine and feminine identification." *Psychological Review* 66:126–135.

**Lynn, David B. 1969.** *Parental and Sex-Role Identification: A Theoretical Formulation.* Berkeley, CA: McCutchan.

**Maccoby, Eleanor Emmons. 1980.** *Social Development: Psychological Growth and the Parent-Child Relationship.* New York: Harcourt Brace Jovanovich.

**Maccoby, Eleanor Emmons, and Carol Nagy Jacklin. 1974.** *The Psychology of Sex Differences.* Stanford, CA: Stanford University Press.

**Maccoby, Eleanor Emmons, and Carol Nagy Jacklin. 1980.** "Sex differences in aggression: A rejoinder and reprise." *Child Development* 51:964–980.

**Macdonald Commission. 1985.** See *Royal Commission on the Economic Union and Development Prospects for Canada.*

**Mackie, Marlene. 1973.** "Arriving at 'truth' by definition: The case of stereotype inaccuracy." *Social Problems* 20:431–447.

**Mackie, Marlene. 1974.** "Ethnic stereotypes and prejudice: Alberta Indians, Hutterites and Ukrainians." *Canadian Ethnic Studies* 6:39–52.

**Mackie, Marlene. 1975.** "Defection from Hutterite colonies." In *Socialization and Values in Canadian Society* (Vol. 2). Robert M. Pike and Elia Zureik, eds. Toronto: McClelland and Stewart.

**Mackie, Marlene. 1987.** *Constructing Women and Men: Gender Socialization.* Toronto: Holt, Rinehart and Winston.

**MacLeod, Linda. 1987.** *Battered But Not Beaten: Preventing Wife Battering in Canada.* Ottawa: Canadian Advisory Council on the Status of Women.

**MacLeod, R.C. 1976.** *The North-West Mounted Police and Law Enforcement, 1873–1905.* Toronto: University of Toronto Press.

**MacPherson, C.B. 1953.** *Democracy in Alberta.* Toronto: University of Toronto Press.

**Maddox, George L. 1970.** "Themes and issues in sociological theories of human aging." *Human Development* 13:17–27.

**Magnusson, Warren E. 1983.** "The development of Canadian urban government." In *City Politics in Canada.* W.E. Magnusson and A. Sancton, eds. Toronto: University of Toronto Press.

**Manheimer, Dean I., Glen D. Millinger, and Mitchell B. Balter. 1969.** "Use of marijuana among the urban cross-section of adults." Unpublished manuscript.

**Mann, Michael. 1970.** "The social cohesion of liberal democracy." *American Sociological Review* 35(3):423–439.

**Mann, W.E. 1962.** *Sect, Cult, and Church in Alberta.* Toronto: University of Toronto Press.

**Mannheim, Karl. 1936.** *Ideology and Utopia.* New York: Harcourt, Brace and World.

**Mannheim, Karl. 1953; 1952.** "The sociological problem of generations." In *Essays on the Sociology of Knowledge.* P. Kecskemeti, ed. London: Routledge and Kegan Paul/New York: Oxford University Press.

**Mantoux, Paul. 1961; 1928.** *The Industrial Revolution in the Eighteenth Century.* New York: Harper and Row.

**Manzer, R. 1974.** *Canada: A Socio-Political Report.* Toronto: McGraw-Hill Ryerson.

**Marchak, Patricia. 1975.** *Ideological Perspectives on Canada.* Toronto: McGraw-Hill Ryerson.

**Marchak, Patricia. 1979.** *Whose Interests: An Essay on*

*Multinational Corporations in a Canadian Context.* Toronto: McClelland and Stewart.

**Marini, Margaret Mooney, and Ellen Greenberger. 1978.** "Sex differences in occupational aspirations and expectations." *Sociology of Work and Occupations* 5:147–175.

**Marsden, Lorna R., and Edward R. Harvey. 1979.** *Fragile Federation: Social Change in Canada.* Toronto: McGraw-Hill Ryerson.

**Marshall, Victor W. 1975a.** "Socialization for impending death in a retirement village." *American Journal of Sociology* 80(5):1124–1144.

**Marshall, Victor W. 1975b.** "Organizational features of terminal status passage in residential facilities for the aged." *Urban Life* 4:349–358.

**Marshall, Victor W. 1980a.** *Last Chapters: A Sociology of Aging and Dying.* Monterey, CA: Brooks/Cole.

**Marshall, Victor W. 1980b.** "No exit: An interpretive perspective on aging." In *Aging in Canada: Social Perspectives.* Victor W. Marshall, ed. Toronto: Fitzhenry and Whiteside.

**Marshall, Victor W. 1981.** "State of the art lecture: The sociology of aging." In *Canadian Gerontological Collection* (Vol. III). John Crawford, ed. Winnipeg: Canadian Association on Gerontology.

**Marshall, Victor W. 1983.** "Generations, age groups and cohorts: Conceptual distinctions." *Canadian Journal on Aging* 2(2):51–61.

**Marshall, Victor W. 1986a.** "Dominant and emerging paradigms in the social psychology of aging." In *Later Life: The Social Psychology of Aging.* Victor W. Marshall, ed. Beverly Hills, CA: Sage.

**Marshall, Victor W. 1986b.** "A sociological perspective on aging and dying." In *Later Life: The Social Psychology of Aging.* Victor W. Marshall, ed. Beverly Hills, CA: Sage.

**Marshall, Victor W. 1987a.** "The health of very old people as a concern of their children." In *Aging in Canada: Social Perspectives.* Victor W. Marshall, ed. 2nd edition. Toronto: Fitzhenry and Whiteside.

**Marshall, Victor W. 1987b.** "Older patients in the acute hospital setting." In *Health in Aging: Sociological Issues and Policy Directions.* Russell Ward and Sheldon Tobin, eds. New York: Springer.

**Marshall, Victor W. 1987c.** "Social perspectives on aging: Theoretical notes." In *Aging in Canada: Social Perspectives.* Victor W. Marshall, ed. 2nd edition. Toronto: Fitzhenry and Whiteside.

**Marshall, Victor W., and Vern L. Bengtson. 1983.** "Generations: Cooperation and conflict." In *Gerontology in the Eighties: Highlights of the Twelfth International Conference on Gerontology.* M. Bergener et al., eds. New York: Springer.

**Marshall, Victor W., and Carolyn J. Rosenthal. 1982.** "Parental death: A life course marker." *Generations* 7(2):30–39.

**Marshall, Victor W., Carolyn J. Rosenthal, and Joanne Daciuk. 1987.** "Older parents' expectations for filial support." *Social Justice Review* 1(4):405–425.

**Marshall, Victor W., Carolyn J. Rosenthal, and Janet Synge. 1983.** "Concerns about parental health." In *Women and Aging.* Elizabeth W. Markson, ed. Lexington, MA: Lexington.

**Marston, W.G., and A.G. Darrock. 1971.** "The social class of ethnic residential segregation: The Canadian case." *American Journal of Sociology* 77(3):491–510.

**Martin, M. Kay, and Barbara Voorhies. 1975.** *Female of the Species.* Toronto: Methuen.

**Martin, Wilfred B.W., and Allan J. Macdonell. 1978.** *Canadian Education: A Sociological Analysis.* Scarborough, ON: Prentice-Hall.

**Martin Matthews, Anne. 1982.** "Canadian research on women as widows: A comparative analysis of the state of the art." *Resources for Feminist Research.* Toronto: Ontario Institute for Studies in Education.

**Martin Matthews, Anne. 1987.** "Widowhood as an expectable life event." In *Aging in Canada: Social Perspectives.* Victor W. Marshall, ed. 2nd edition. Don Mills, ON: Fitzhenry and Whiteside.

**Martin Matthews, Anne, and Ralph Matthews. 1986.** "Infertility and involuntary childlessness: The transition to non-parenthood." *Journal of Marriage and the Family* 48:641–649.

**Martin Matthews, Anne, et al. 1982.** "A crisis assessment technique for the evaluation of life events." *Canadian Journal on Aging* 1(3–4):28–39.

**Martyna, Wendy. 1980.** "Beyond the 'he/man' approach: The case of nonsexist language." *Signs* 5:482–493.

**Maruyama, G., and N. Miller. 1975.** *Physical Attractiveness and Classroom Acceptance.* Social Science Research Institute Report 75-2. Los Angeles: University of Southern California.

**Marx, Gary, and James L. Wood. 1975.** "Strands of theory and research in collective behavior." *Annual Review of Sociology* 1:363–428.

**Marx, Karl. 1965; 1867–1895.** *Capital: A Critical Analysis of Capitalist Production* (Vol. 1). New York: International.

**Marx, Karl. 1970; 1843.** *Critique of Hegel's 'Philosophy of Right.'* Annette Jolin and Joseph O'Malley, transl. Cambridge, MA: Harvard University Press.

**Marx, Karl. 1974.** *The First International and After.* David Fernbach, ed. New York: Random House.

**Marx, Karl. 1978.** *Karl Marx: Selected Writings.* D. McLellan, ed. Oxford: Oxford University Press.

**Maslow, Abraham A. 1970.** *Motivation and Personality.* 2nd edition. New York: Harper and Row.

**Massey, D.S., and N.A. Denton. 1987.** "Trends in the residential segregation of blacks, Hispanics, and Asians: 1970–1980." *American Sociological Review* 52(6):802–825.

**Massey Report. 1951.** See *Royal Commission on National Development in the Arts, Letters and Sciences.*

**Mathewson, S.B. 1931.** *Restriction of Output among Unorganized Workers.* New York: Viking.

**Matras, J. 1980.** "Comparative Social Mobility." *Annual Review of Sociology* 6:401–431.

**Matthews, Sarah H. 1979.** *The Social World of Old Women: Management of Self-Identity.* Beverly Hills, CA: Sage.

**Matthews, Sarah H. 1986.** *Friendships Through the Life Course.* Beverly Hills, CA: Sage.

**Matthews, Victor. 1972.** *Social-Legal Statistics in Alberta: A Review of Their Availability and Significance.* Edmonton, AB: Human Resources Research Council.

**Mauss, Armand, and Milton Rokeach. 1977.** "Pollsters as prophets." *Humanist* (May-June):48–51.

**Maynard, Rona. 1984.** "Women and men: Is the difference brain-deep?" *Chatelaine* 57(Oct.):76, 86, 88, 90, 98.

**Mayo, Elton. 1945.** *The Social Problems of an Industrial Civilization.* Cambridge, MA: Harvard University Press.

**McCarthy, J.D., and M.N. Zald. 1973.** *The Trends of Social Movements in America: Professionalization and Resource Mobilization.* Morristown, NJ: General Learning.

**McDaniel, Susan A. 1986.** *Canada's Aging Population.* Toronto: Butterworths.

**McDaniel, Susan A. 1987.** "Demographic aging as a guiding paradigm in Canada's welfare state." *Canadian Public Policy* 13(3):330–336.

**McDavid, John W., and Herbert Harari. 1966.** "Stereotyping of names and popularity in grade-school children." *Child Development* 37:453–460.

**McDonald, L., and R.A. Wanner. 1982.** "Work past age 65 in Canada: A socioeconomic analysis." *Aging and Work* 5:169–179.

**McDonald, L., and R.A. Wanner. 1984.** "Socioeconomic determinants of early retirement in Canada." *Canadian Journal on Aging* 3(3):105–116.

**McDonald, Neil. 1978.** "Egerton Ryerson and the school as an agent of political socialization." In *Egerton Ryerson and His Times.* Neil McDonald and A. Chaiton, eds. Toronto: Macmillan.

**McEvedy, Colin. 1988.** "The bubonic plague." *Scientific American* 258(2):118–123.

**McFarlane, A.H., et al. 1980.** "A longitudinal study of influence of the psychosocial environment on health status: A preliminary report." *Journal of Health and Social Behavior* 21:124–133.

**McGlone, Jeannette. 1980.** "Sex differences in human brain asymmetry: A critical survey." *Behavioral and Brain Sciences* 3:215–227.

**McGlone, J., and A. Kertesz. 1973.** "Sex differences in cerebral processing of visual-spatial tasks." *Cortex* 9:313–320.

**McKenzie, Roderick D. 1968.** *On Human Ecology.* Chicago: University of Chicago Press.

**McKeown, Thomas. 1976.** *The Modern Rise of Population.* New York: Academic.

**McKie, D.C., B. Prentice, and P. Reed. 1983.** *Divorce: Law and the Family in Canada.* Ottawa: Statistics Canada, Catalogue No. 89–502E.

**McNaught, Kenneth. 1975.** "Political trials and the Canadian political tradition." In *Courts and Trials: A Multi-Discipline Approach.* M.L. Friedland, ed. Toronto: University of Toronto Press.

**McNeill, William H. 1976.** *Plagues and Peoples.* Garden City, NY: Doubleday.

**McPherson, Barry, and Neil Guppy. 1979.** "Pre-retirement life-style and the degree of planning for retirement." *Journal of Gerontology* 34(2):254–263.

**McQuillan, K. 1980.** "Economic factors and internal migration: The case of nineteenth-century England." *Social Science History* 4(4):479–499.

**McRoberts, H. 1985.** "Language and mobility: A comparison of three groups." In *Ascription and Achievement.* M. Boyd et al., eds. Ottawa: Carleton University Press.

**McRoberts, Hugh A., et al. 1976.** "Différences dans la mobilité professionnelle des francophones et des anglophones." *Sociologie et Sociétés* 8(2):61–79.

**McRoberts, K., and D. Posgate. 1980.** *Quebec: Social Change and Political Crisis.* Revised edition. Toronto: McCelland and Stewart.

**McTavish, Donald G. 1982.** "Perceptions of old people." In *Research Instruments in Social Gerontology* (Vol. 1): *Clinical and Social Psychology.* David J. Mangen and Warren A. Peterson, eds. Minneapolis: University of Minnesota Press.

**Mead, G.H. 1934.** *Mind, Self, and Society.* Chicago: University of Chicago Press.

**Mead, Margaret. 1950;1935.** *Sex and Temperament in Three Primitive Societies.* New York: Mentor.

**Meissner, Martin. 1971.** "The long arm of the job: A study of work and leisure." *Industrial Relations* 10(3):239–260.

**Meissner, Martin, et al. 1975.** "No exit for wives: Sexual division of labour and the cumulation of household demands." *Canadian Review of Sociology and Anthropology* 12(Part I):424–439.

**Melbin, Murray. 1987.** *Night as Frontier: Colonizing the World After Dark.* New York: Free Press.

**Meltzer, Bernard N. 1978.** "Mead's social psychology." In *Symbolic Interaction: A Reader in Social Psychology.* Jerome G. Manis and B.N. Meltzer, eds. 3rd edition. Boston: Allyn and Bacon.

**Menzies, Heather. 1984.** "Women and microtechnology." In *Working Canadians.* Graham S. Lowe and Harvey J. Krahn, eds. Toronto: Methuen.

**Merton, Robert. 1938.** "Social structure and anomie." *American Sociological Review* 3(Oct.):672–682.

**Merton, Robert. 1957.** *Social Theory and Social Structure.* Glencoe, IL: Free Press.

**Messinger, Hans, and Brian J. Powell. 1987.** "The implications of Canada's aging society on social expenditures." In *Aging in Canada: Social Perspectives.* Victor W. Marshall, ed. 2nd edition. Toronto: Fitzhenry and Whiteside.

**Metz, Donald. 1967.** *New Congregations: Security and Mission in Conflict.* Philadelphia: Westminster.

**Miall, Charlene. 1986.** "Self-labelling and the stigma of involuntary childlessness." *Social Problems* 33(4):268–282.

**Michelson, William. 1976.** *Man and His Urban Environment.* 2nd edition. Reading, MA: Addison-Wesley.

**Michelson, William. 1977.** *Environmental Choice, Human Behavior, and Residential Satisfaction.* New York: Oxford University Press.

**Michelson, William. 1985a.** *From Sun to Sun: Daily Obligations and Community Structure in the Lives of Employed Women and Their Families.* Totowa, NJ: Rowman and Allanheld.

**Michelson, William. 1985b.** "Divergent convergence: The daily routines of employed spouses as a public affairs agenda." *Public Affairs Report* 26(4):1–10.

**Milgram, S. 1970.** "The experience of living in cities." *Science* 167(3924):1461–1468.

**Miliband, Ralph. 1973; 1969.** *The State in Capitalist So-*

*ciety.* London: Quartet Books.

**Miller, Casey, and Kate Swift. 1977.** *Words and Women.* Garden City, NY: Doubleday Anchor.

**Millman, Marcia, and Rosabeth Moss Kanter (eds.). 1975.** *Another Voice: Feminist Perspectives on Social Life and Social Science.* Garden City, NY: Doubleday Anchor.

**Mills, C. Wright. 1951.** *White Collar.* New York: Oxford University Press.

**Miner, Horace. 1939.** *St. Denis: A French-Canadian Parish.* Chicago: University of Chicago Press.

**Ministry of Education, Ontario. 1975.** *Education in the Primary and Junior Divisions.* Toronto: Queen's Printer.

**Mitchell, Robert. 1966.** "Polity, church attractiveness, and ministers' careers." *Journal for the Scientific Study of Religion* 5:241–258.

**Mommsen, Max. 1974.** *The Age of Bureaucracy.* New York: Harper and Row.

**Money, John, and A.A. Ehrhardt. 1972.** *Man and Woman, Boy and Girl: The Differentiation and Dimorphism of Gender Identity from Conception to Maturity.* Baltimore: Johns Hopkins University Press.

**Money, John, and Patricia Tucker. 1975.** *Sexual Signatures: On Being a Man or a Woman.* Boston: Little, Brown.

**Moore, Maureen. 1987.** "Women parenting alone." *Canadian Social Trends* Winter:31–36.

**Moore, Wilbert. 1966.** "Aging and the social system." In *Aging and Social Policy.* John C. McKinney and Frank T. de Vyver, eds. New York: Appleton-Century-Crofts.

**Morgan, W.R., and T.N. Clark. 1973.** "The causes of racial disorders." *American Sociological Review* 38:611–624.

**Morris, Cerise. 1980.** "Determination and thoroughness: The movement for a royal commission on the status of women in Canada." *Atlantis* 5:1–21.

**Morris, Raymond N., and C. Michael Lanphier. 1977.** *Three Scales of Inequality: Perspectives on French-English Relations.* Don Mills, ON: Longman.

**Mortimer, Jeylan T., and Roberta G. Simmons. 1978.** "Adult socialization." *Annual Review of Sociology* 4:421–454.

**Morton, Peggy. 1972.** "Women's work is never done." In *Women Unite!: An Anthology of the Canadian Women's Movement.* Toronto: Canadian Women's Educational Press.

**Morton, William L. 1950.** *The Progressive Party in Canada.* Toronto: University of Toronto Press.

**Mumford, Lewis. 1961.** *The City in History: Its Origin, Its Transformation, and Its Prospects.* New York: Harcourt, Brace and World.

**Mumford, Lewis. 1963.** *Technics and Civilization.* New York: Harcourt, Brace and World.

**Mumford, Lewis. 1968.** *The Urban Prospect.* New York: Harcourt, Brace and World.

**Murdoch, Peter. 1957.** "World ethnographic sample." *American Anthropologist* 59(4):664–687.

**Murdoch, William W. 1980.** *The Poverty of Nations.* Baltimore: Johns Hopkins University Press.

**Murdock, G.P. 1931.** "Ethnocentrism." In *Encyclopedia of the Social Sciences* 5. E.R.A. Seligman, ed. New York: Macmillan.

**Murphy, Emily F. 1920.** "The grave drug menace." *Maclean's* 33(3):1.

**Murphy, Emily F. 1922.** *The Black Candle.* Toronto: Thomas Allen.

**Murphy, Raymond. 1981.** "Teachers and the evolving structural context of economic and political attitudes in Quebec society." *Canadian Review of Sociology and Anthropology* 18:157–182.

**Musto, David. 1973.** *The American Disease: Origins of Narcotic Control.* New Haven, CT: Yale University Press.

**Mutran, Elizabeth, and Donald C. Reitzes. 1984.** "Intergenerational support activities and well-being among the elderly: A convergence of exchange and symbolic interaction perspectives." *American Sociological Review* 49:117–130.

**Muuss, Rolf E. 1988.** *Theories of Adolescence.* 5th edition. New York: Random House.

**Myles, John F. 1980.** "The aged, the state, and the structure of inequality." In *Structured Inequality in Canada.* John Harp and John Hofley, eds. Scarborough, ON: Prentice-Hall.

**Myles, John F. 1984.** *Old Age in the Welfare State: The Political Economy of Pensions.* Boston: Little, Brown.

**Nagel, Stuart. 1969.** *The Legal Process from a Behavioral Perspective.* Homewood, IL: Dorsey.

**Nagnur, Dhruva, and Owen Adams. 1987.** "Tying the knot: An overview of marriage rates in Canada." *Canadian Social Trends* Autumn:2–6.

**Nash, Dennison, and Peter L. Berger. 1962.** "The child, the family, and the 'religious revival' in suburbia." *Journal for the Scientific Study of Religion* 2:85–93.

**Nathanson, Constance. 1977.** "Sex, illness and medical care: A review of data, theory and method." *Social Science and Medicine* 111:13–25.

**Nelsen, Hart M., and Raymond H. Potvin. 1980.** "Toward disestablishment: New patterns of social class, denomination, and religiosity among youth?" *Review of Religious Research* 22:137–154.

**Nelson, L.D., and Russell Dynes. 1976.** "The impact of devotionalism and attendance on ordinary and emergency helping behavior." *Journal for the Scientific Study of Religion* 15:47–59.

**Nett, Emily. 1981.** "Canadian families in social-historical perspective." *Canadian Journal of Sociology* 6(3):239–260.

**Nettler, Gwynn. 1973.** "Embezzlement without problems." *British Journal of Criminology* 14(1):L70–L77.

**Nettler, Gwynn. 1978.** *Explaining Crime.* New York: McGraw-Hill.

**Nettler, Gwynn. 1982.** *Killing One Another.* Cincinnati, OH: Anderson.

**Neugarten, Bernice L. 1970.** "The old and the young in modern societies." *American Behavioral Scientist* 14(1):13–24.

**Neugarten, Bernice L., W. Crotty, and S. Tobin. 1964.** "Personality types in an aged population." In *Personality in Middle and Later Life: Empirical Studies.* New York: Atherton.

**Newman, Oscar. 1972.** *Defensible Space.* New York: Macmillan.

**Newman, P. 1982.** *The Acquisitors: The Canadian Establishment* (Vol. 2). Toronto: McClelland and Stewart.

**Newman, William M. 1973.** *American Pluralism.* New York: Harper and Row.

**Ngor, Haing, and Roger Warner. 1988.** *A Cambodian Odyssey.* New York: Macmillan.

**Nicholson, John. 1984.** *Men and Women: How Different Are They?* Oxford: Oxford University Press.

**Niebuhr, H. Richard. 1929.** *The Social Sources of Denominationalism.* New York: Holt.

**Nielsen, Joyce McCarl. 1978.** *Sex in Society: Perspectives on Stratification.* Belmont, CA: Wadsworth.

**1987 World Population Data Sheet. 1987.** Washington, DC: Population Reference Bureau.

**Niosi, J. 1981.** *Canadian Capitalism.* R. Chodos, transl. Toronto: Lorimer.

**Nishio, Harry K., and Heather Lank. 1987.** "Patterns of labour participation of older female workers." In *Aging in Canada: Social Perspectives.* Victor W. Marshall, ed. 2nd edition. Toronto: Fitzhenry and Whiteside.

**Norris, Joan E. 1980.** "The social adjustment of single and widowed older women." *Essence: Issues in the Study of Aging, Dying and Death* 4(3):135–144.

**Norris, Joan E. 1987.** "Psychological processes in the development of late-life social identity." In *Aging in Canada: Social Perspectives.* Victor W. Marshall, ed. 2nd edition. Toronto: Fitzhenry and Whiteside.

**Northcott, Herbert C. 1984.** "Widowhood and remarriage trends in Canada 1956–1981." *Canadian Journal on Aging* 3(1):63–77.

**Nye, F. Ivan. 1982.** *Family Relationships: Rewards and Costs.* Beverly Hills, CA: Sage.

**Oberschall, Anthony. 1968.** "The Los Angeles riot." *Social Problems* 15(Winter).

**Oberschall, Anthony. 1973.** *Social Conflict and Social Movements.* Englewood, NJ: Prentice-Hall.

**OECD. 1975.** *Education, Inequality and Life Chances* (2 vols.). Paris: OECD.

**OECD. 1976.** *Reviews of National Policies for Education: Canada.* Paris: OECD.

**Ogburn, William F. 1922.** *Social Change with Respect to Culture and Original Nature.* New York: B.W. Huebsch.

**Ogburn, William F. 1933.** "The family and its functions." In *Recent Social Trends in the U.S.* W.F. Ogburn, ed. New York: McGraw-Hill.

**Ogburn, William F., and Meyer F. Nimkoff. 1964.** "The social effects of innovation." In *Sociology.* W.F. Ogburn and M.F. Nimkoff, eds. 4th edition. Boston: Houghton Mifflin.

**Ogmundson, R. 1975.** "Party class images and the class vote in Canada." *American Sociological Review* 40:505–512.

**Ogmundson, R. 1976.** "Mass-elite linkages and class issues in Canada." *Canadian Review of Sociology and Anthropology* 13(1):1–12.

**Ogmundson, R. 1980a.** "Towards study of the endangered species known as the Anglophone Canadian." *Canadian Journal of Sociology* 5:1–12.

**Ogmundson, R. 1980b.** "Liberal ideology and the study of voting behaviour." *Canadian Review of Sociology and Anthropology* 17:45–54.

**Okediji, Francis O. 1974.** "Changes in individual reproductive behavior and cultural values." *Lecture Series on Population.* Bucharest, Rumania: International Union for the Scientific Study of Population.

**Olsen, Dennis. 1977.** "The state elites." In *The Canadian State: Political Economy and Political Power.* Leo Panitch, ed. Toronto: University of Toronto Press.

**Olsen, Dennis. 1980.** *The State Elite.* Toronto: McClelland and Stewart.

**Olson, Manur. 1965.** *The Logic of Collective Action.* Cambridge, MA: Harvard University Press.

**Ontario Council of Health. 1978.** *Health Care for the Aged.* Toronto: Ontario Council of Health.

**Oppenheimer, Valerie K. 1973.** "Demographic influence on female employment and the status of women." In *Changing Women in a Changing Society.* Joan Huber, ed. Chicago: University of Chicago Press.

**Orbach, Harold L. 1981.** "Mandatory retirement and the development of adequate retirement provisions for older persons." *Canadian Gerontological Collection* (Vol. II). George Gasek, ed. Winnipeg: Canadian Association on Gerontology.

**Ortner, Sherry B., and Harriet Whitehead. 1981.** *Sexual Meanings: The Cultural Construction of Gender and Sexuality.* Cambridge, UK: Cambridge University Press.

**Osberg, L. 1981.** *Economic Inequality in Canada.* Toronto: Butterworths.

**Ostry, Bernard. 1978.** *The Cultural Connection.* Toronto: McClelland and Stewart.

**O'Toole, James. 1981.** *Making America Work.* New York: Continuum.

**Ouchi, William. 1981.** *Theory Z.* Reading, MA: Addison-Wesley.

**Overbeek, Johannes. 1974.** *History of Population Theories.* Rotterdam, Netherlands: Rotterdam University Press.

**Packer, H. 1964.** "Two models of the criminal process." *University of Pennsylvania Law Review* 113:1–68.

**Palen, John. 1987.** *The Urban World.* 3rd edition. New York: McGraw-Hill.

**Palmore, Erdman. 1969.** "Sociological aspects of aging." In *Behaviour and Adaptation in Late Life.* Ewald W. Busse and Eric Pfeiffer, eds. Boston: Little, Brown.

**Palmore, Erdman, and Clark Luikart. 1972.** "Health and social factors related to life satisfaction." *Journal of Health and Social Behavior* 13(Mar.):68–80.

**Palmore, Erdman, and Kenneth Manton. 1974.** "Modernization and status of the aged: International comparisons." *Journal of Gerontology* 29:205–210.

**Pappert, Ann. 1983.** "The one and only." *Quest* (Dec.): 38–42.

**Park, Robert E., Ernest W. Burgess, and Roderick D. McKenzie. 1925.** *The City.* Chicago: University of Chicago Press.

**Parker, Graham. 1976.** "The Juvenile Court Movement." *University of Toronto Law Journal* 26:140–172.

**Parkes, C.M., B. Benjamin, and R.G. Fitzgerald. 1969.** "Broken heart: A statistical study of increased mortality among widowers." *British Medical Journal* 1:740.

**Parkin, F. 1979.** *Marxism and Class Theory.* New York: Columbia University Press.

**Parkin, Frank. 1972.** *Class Inequality and Political Order.* London: Paladin.

**Parsons, H.M. 1974.** "What happened at Hawthorne?" *Science* 8(Mar.):922–932.

**Parsons, Talcott. 1949.** "The kinship system of the contemporary United States." *Essays in Sociological Theory: Pure and Applied.* Glencoe, IL: Free Press.

**Parsons, Talcott. 1951.** *The Social System.* New York: Free Press.

**Parsons, Talcott. 1955.** "The American family: Its relation to personality and social structure." In *Family Socialization and Interaction Patterns.* T. Parsons and R.F. Bales, eds. New York: Free Press.

**Parsons, Talcott. 1959.** "The school as a social system." *Harvard Educational Review* 29:297–318.

**Parsons, Talcott. 1960.** *Structure and Process in Modern Societies.* New York: Free Press.

**Parsons, Talcott. 1964.** "Christianity and modern industrial society." In *Religion, Culture, and Society.* Louis Schneider, ed. New York: Wiley.

**Parsons, Talcott, and Robert F. Bales (eds.). 1955.** *Family Socialization and Interaction Process.* Glencoe, IL: Free Press.

**Parsons, Talcott, and Neil Smelser. 1956.** *Economy and Society.* London: Routledge and Kegan Paul.

**Patterson, E. Palmer, II. 1972.** *The Canadian Indian: A History Since 1500.* Toronto: Collier Macmillan.

**Pearlin, Leonard I., and Melvin L. Kohn. 1966.** "Social class, occupation, and parental values: A cross-national study." *American Sociological Review* 31(4):466–479.

**Peplau, Letitia Anne, and Steven L. Gordon. 1985.** "Women and men in love: Gender differences in close heterosexual relationships." In *Women, Gender, and Social Psychology.* Virginia E. O'Leary, Rhoda K. Unger, and Barbara S. Wallston, eds. Hillsdale, NJ: Lawrence Erlbaum Associates.

**Perry, Robert L. 1971.** *Galt, U.S.A.* Toronto: Maclean-Hunter.

**Peter, Karl. 1988.** Personal communication.

**Peters, John. 1982.** "Children as socialization agents through the parents' middle-years." Paper presented to the Canadian Sociology and Anthropology Association.

**Peters, John. 1984.** "Cultural variations in family structure." In *The Family: Changing Trends in Canada.* Maureen Baker, ed. Toronto: McGraw-Hill Ryerson.

**Peters, John F. 1987.** "Changing perspectives on divorce." In *Family Matters: Sociology and Contemporary Canadian Families.* Karen L. Anderson et al., eds. Toronto: Methuen.

**Peterson, Gary W., and David F. Peters. 1983.** "Adolescents' construction of social reality: The impact of television and peers." *Youth and Society* 15:67–85.

**Peterson, Richard A. 1979.** "Revitalizing the culture concept." *Annual Review of Sociology* 5.

**Pfeffer, Naomi, and Anne Woollett. 1983.** *The Experience of Infertility.* London: Virago.

**Phillips, Andrew, and Cindy Barrett. 1988.** "Defining identity." *Maclean's* (Jan.):44–45.

**Piaget, Jean. 1928.** *Judgment and Reasoning in the Child.* New York: Harcourt.

**Piaget, Jean. 1932.** *The Moral Judgment of the Child.* New York: Harcourt.

**Pike, Robert M. 1975.** "Introduction and overview." In *Socialization and Values in Canadian Society* (Vol. 2). R.M. Pike and Elia Zureik, eds. Toronto: McClelland and Stewart.

**Piliavin, Irving, and Scott Briar. 1964.** "Police encounters with juveniles." *American Journal of Sociology* 70 (Sept.):206–214.

**Pinard, Maurice. 1975; 1971.** *The Rise of a Third Party.* Montreal and Kingston: McGill-Queen's University Press (enlarged edition)/Englewood Cliffs, NJ: Prentice-Hall.

**Pinard, Maurice, and Richard Hamilton. 1984.** "The class bases of the Quebec independence movement: Conjectures and evidence." *Ethnic and Racial Studies* 7(1):19–54.

**Pineo, Peter C. 1971.** "The extended family in a working-class area of Hamilton." In *Canadian Society.* Bernard Blishen, ed. Toronto: Macmillan.

**Pineo, Peter C. 1976.** "Social mobility in Canada: The current picture." *Sociological Focus* 9(2):120.

**Pineo, Peter C. 1980.** "The social standing of ethnic and racial groupings." In *Ethnicity and Ethnic Relations in Canada.* J. Goldstein and R. Bienvenu, eds. Toronto: Butterworths.

**Pineo, Peter C. 1983.** "Stratification and social class." In *An Introduction to Sociology.* M.M. Rosenberg et al., eds. Toronto: Methuen.

**Pineo, Peter C., and Dianne Looker. 1983.** "Class conformity in the Canadian setting." *Canadian Journal of Sociology* 8:293–317.

**Pineo, Peter C., and John Porter. 1967.** "Occupational prestige in Canada." *Canadian Review of Sociology and Anthropology* 4:24–40.

**Pineo, Peter C., et al. 1977.** "The 1971 census and the socioeconomic classification of occupations." *Canadian Review of Sociology and Anthropology* 1:91–102.

**Pirenne, Henri. 1939.** *Medieval Cities.* Princeton, NJ: Princeton University Press.

**Platt, Anthony M. 1969.** *The Child Savers: The Invention of Delinquency.* Chicago: University of Chicago Press.

**Pleck, Joseph. 1981.** "Men's power with women, other men, and society: A men's movement analysis." In *Men in Difficult Times.* Robert A. Lewis, ed. Englewood Cliffs, NJ: Prentice-Hall.

**Polanyi, Karl. 1957.** In *Trade and Markets in the Early Empires.* C.M. Arsenberg and H.W. Pearson, eds. Glencoe, IL: Free Press.

**Ponak, Allen, and Mark Thompson. 1989.** "Public sector collective bargaining." In *Union-Management Relations in Canada.* John C. Anderson, Morley Gunderson, and Allen Ponak, eds. 2nd edition. Don Mills, ON: Addison-Wesley.

**Ponting, J. Rick. 1986a.** "Canadian gender-role attitudes." Unpublished.

**Ponting, J. Rick (ed.). 1986b.** *Arduous Journey: Canadian Indians and Decolonization.* Toronto: McClelland and Stewart.

**Ponting, J. Rick, and Roger Gibbins. 1980.** *Out of Irrelevance: A Socio-Political Introduction to Indian Affairs in Canada.* Toronto: Butterworths.

**Ponting, J. Rick, and Roger Gibbins. 1981.** "The reactions of English Canadians and French Québécois to native Indian protest." *Canadian Review of Sociology and Anthropology* 18(2):222–238.

**Porter, Elaine. 1987.** "Conceptual frameworks for studying families." In *Family Matters: Sociology and Contemporary Canadian Families.* Karen L. Anderson et al., eds. Toronto: Methuen.

**Porter, John. 1965.** *The Vertical Mosaic: An Analysis of Social Class and Power in Canada.* Toronto: University of Toronto Press.

**Porter, John. 1967.** *Canadian Social Structure: A Statistical Profile.* Toronto: McClelland and Stewart.

**Porter, John. 1970.** "Research biography on a macro-sociological study: *The Vertical Mosaic.*" In *Macrosociology: Research and Theory.* James S. Coleman, Amitai Etzioni, and John Porter, eds. Boston: Allyn and Bacon.

**Porter, John. 1979.** *The Measure of Canadian Society.* Toronto: Gage.

**Porter, John, Marion Porter, and Bernard Blishen. 1982.** *Stations and Callings: Making It Through the Ontario Schools.* Toronto: Methuen.

**Porter, Marion, John Porter, and Bernard Blishen. 1973.** *Does Money Matter?* Toronto: York University, Institute for Behavioural Research.

**Posner, Judith. 1980.** "Old and female: The double whammy." In *Aging in Canada: Social Perspectives.* Victor W. Marshall, ed. Toronto: Fitzhenry and Whiteside.

**Posner, Judith. 1987.** "The objectified male: The new male image in advertising." In *Women and Men: Interdisciplinary Readings on Gender.* Greta Hofmann Nemiroff, ed. Toronto: Fitzhenry and Whiteside.

**Postman, Neil. 1982.** *The Disappearance of Childhood.* New York: Penguin.

**Poulantzas, N. 1973.** *Political Power and Social Classes.* London: New Left.

**Powell, Brian J., and James K. Martin. 1980.** "Economic implications of Canada's aging society." In *Aging in Canada: Social Perspectives.* Victor W. Marshall, ed. Toronto: Fitzhenry and Whiteside.

**Power, Margaret. 1975.** "Women's work is never done—by men: A socio-economic model of sex-typing in occupations." *Journal of Industrial Relations* 17:225–239.

**Pratt, David. 1984.** "Bias in textbooks: Progress and problems." In *Multiculturalism in Canada: Social and Educational Perspectives.* Ronald J. Samuda, John W. Berry, and Michel Laferrière, eds. Toronto: Allyn and Bacon.

**Press, Andrea. 1985.** "The differential effects of liberal feminism on working-class and middle-class women." Paper presented to the Pacific Sociological Association.

**Putnam, R. 1976.** *The Comparative Study of Political Elites.* Englewood Cliffs, NJ: Prentice-Hall.

**Pyke, S.W. 1975.** "Children's literature: Conceptions of sex roles." In *Socialization and Values in Canadian Society* (Vol. 2). Robert M. Pike and Elia Zureik, eds. Toronto: McClelland and Stewart.

**Quadagno, Jill S. 1980.** "The modernization controversy: A socio-historical analysis of retirement in nineteenth century England." Paper presented to the American Sociological Association.

**Quinney, Richard. 1970.** *The Social Reality of Crime.* Boston: Little, Brown.

**Rainwater, Lee. 1966.** "Work and identity in the lower class." In *Planning for a Nation of Cities.* Sam Bass Warner, Jr., ed. Cambridge, MA: MIT Press.

**Ramcharan, Subhas. 1982.** *Racism: Nonwhites in Canada.* Toronto: Butterworths.

**Ray, Arthur J. 1974.** *Indians in the Fur Trade: Their Role as Hunters, Trappers and Middlemen in the Lands Southwest of Hudson Bay 1660–1870.* Toronto: University of Toronto Press.

**Reasons, Charles. 1974.** "The politics of drugs: An inquiry in the sociology of social problems." *Sociological Quarterly* 15(3):381–404.

**Reichard, S., F. Livson, and P.G. Petersen. 1962.** *Aging and Personality.* New York: Wiley.

**Reiss, Albert J., Jr. 1959.** "The sociological study of communities." *Rural Sociology* 24:118–130.

**Reiss, Albert. 1971.** *The Police and the Public.* New Haven, CT: Yale University Press.

**Rex, John. 1968.** "The sociology of a zone of transition." In *Readings in Urban Sociology.* R.E. Pohl, ed. Oxford: Pergamon.

**Reynolds, Lloyd G. 1959.** *Labor Economics and Labor Relations.* Englewood Cliffs, NJ: Prentice-Hall.

**Rheingold, Harriet L. 1966.** "The development of social behavior in the human infant." In *Concept of Development: A Report on a Conference in Commemoration of the 40th Anniversary of the Institute of Child Development.* H.W. Stevenson, ed. Monographs of the Society for Research in Development 31 (5, whole no. 107). Minneapolis: University of Minnesota.

**Rheingold, Harriet L. 1969.** "The social and socializing infant." In *Handbook of Socialization Theory and Research.* David A. Goslin, ed. Chicago: Rand McNally.

**Rich, H. 1976.** "The vertical mosaic revisited." *Journal of Canadian Studies* 11(1):14–31.

**Richardson, Laurel Walum. 1981.** *The Dynamics of Sex and Gender.* 2nd edition. Boston: Houghton Mifflin.

**Richer, Stephen. 1979.** "Sex-role socialization and early schooling." *Canadian Review of Sociology and Anthropology* 16:195–205.

**Richer, Stephen. 1983.** "Sex-role socialization: Agents, content, relationships, and outcomes." In *The Canadian Family.* K. Ishwaran, ed. Toronto: Gage.

**Richer, Stephen. 1984.** "Sexual inequality and children's play." *Canadian Review of Sociology and Anthropology* 21:166–180.

**Richling, Barnett. 1985.** " 'You'd never starve here': Return migration to rural Newfoundland." *Canadian Review of Sociology and Anthropology* 22:236–249.

**Richmond, Anthony H. 1972.** *Ethnic Residential Segre-*

*gation in Toronto.* Toronto: York University, Institute for Behavioural Research.

**Richmond, Anthony H., and Warren E. Kalbach. 1980.** *Factors in the Adjustment of Immigrants and Their Descendants.* Ottawa: Statistics Canada.

**Richmond-Abbott, Marie. 1983.** *Masculine and Feminine: Sex Roles over the Life Cycle.* Reading, MA: Addison-Wesley.

**Rifkin, Jeremy. 1987.** *Time Wars: The Primary Conflict in Human History.* New York: Henry Holt.

**Riley, Matilda White. 1976.** "Age strata in social systems." In *Handbook of Aging and the Social Sciences.* Robert Binstock and Ethel Shanas, eds. New York: Van Nostrand Reinhold.

**Riley, Matilda White. 1980.** "Age and aging: From theory generation to theory testing." In *Sociological Theory and Research: A Critical Approach.* Hubert M. Blalock, Jr., ed. New York: Free Press.

**Riley, Matilda White, Marilyn Johnson, and Anne Foner. 1972.** *Aging and Society: Vol. 2 A Sociology of Age Stratification.* New York: Sage.

**Riley, Matilda White, et al. 1969.** "Socialization for the middle and later years." In *Handbook of Socialization Theory and Research.* David Goslin, ed. Chicago: Rand McNally.

**Riley, Susan. 1985.** "Anti-feminist group incensed over lack of funding." *Calgary Herald* (July 2).

**Rinehart, James W. 1987.** *The Tyranny of Work.* 2nd edition. Toronto: Harcourt Brace Jovanovich.

**Rioux, Marcel. 1971.** *Quebec in Question.* Toronto: James, Lewis, and Samuel.

**Ritchie, Marguerite. 1975.** "Alice through the statutes." *McGill Law Journal* 21:702.

**Roberts, Donald F., and Nathan Maccoby. 1985.** "Effects of mass communication." In *The Handbook of Social Psychology* (Vol. 2). Gardner Lindzey and Elliot Aronson, eds. 3rd edition. New York: Random House.

**Roberts, Keith A. 1984.** *Religion in Sociological Perspective.* Homewood, IL: Dorsey.

**Robertson, Ian. 1977.** *Sociology.* New York: Worth.

**Robinson, Barrie W., and Wayne W. McVey, Jr. 1985.** "The relative contributions of death and divorce to marital dissolution in Canada and the United States." *Journal of Comparative Family Studies* 16(1):93–109.

**Rock, Ronald, Marcus Jacobson, and Richard Janopaul. 1968.** *Hospitalization and Discharge of the Mentally Ill.* Chicago: University of Chicago Press.

**Roethlisberger, F.J., and W.J. Dickson. 1947.** *Management and the Worker.* Cambridge, MA: Harvard University Press.

**Rohner, Ronald P., and Evelyn C. Rohner. 1970.** *The Kwakiutl: Indians of British Columbia.* New York: Holt, Rinehart and Winston.

**Rokeach, Milton. 1965.** "Paradoxes of religious belief." *Information Service.* National Council of Churches (Feb. 13):1–2.

**Rokeach, Milton. 1969.** "Religious values and social compassion." *Review of Religious Research* 11:3–23.

**Rokeach, Milton. 1974.** "Some reflections about the place of values in Canadian social science." In *Perspectives on the Social Sciences in Canada.* T.N. Guinsberg and G.L. Reuber, eds. Toronto: University of Toronto Press.

**Romanos, M.C. 1979.** "Forsaken farms: The village-to-city movement in Europe." In *Western European Cities in Crisis.* M.C. Romanos, ed. Lexington, KY: Lexington Press.

**Roof, Wade Clark, and Dean R. Hoge. 1980.** "Church involvement in America: Social factors affecting membership and participation." *Review of Religious Research* 21:405–426.

**Rosaldo, Michelle Zimbalist. 1974.** "Woman, culture, and society: A theoretical overview." In *Woman, Culture and Society.* M.Z. Rosaldo and Louise Lamphere, eds. Stanford, CA: Stanford University Press.

**Rosaldo, Michelle Zimbalist. 1980.** "The use and abuse of anthropology: Reflections on feminism and cross-cultural understanding." *Signs* 5:389–417.

**Rosaldo, Michelle Zimbalist, and Louise Lamphere, eds. 1974.** *Woman, Culture and Society.* Stanford, CA: Stanford University Press.

**Rose, Arnold L. 1965.** "The subculture of the aging: A framework of social gerontology." In *Older People and Their Social World.* Arnold M. Rose and Warren A. Peterson, eds. Philadelphia: F.A. Davis.

**Rosen, B.C. 1965.** *Adolescence and Religion.* Cambridge, MA: Schenkman.

**Rosenberg, Miriam. 1976.** "The biological basis for sex role stereotypes." In *Beyond Sex-Role Stereotypes: Readings toward a Psychology of Androgyny.* Alexandra G. Kaplan and Joan P. Bean, eds. Boston: Little, Brown.

**Rosenberg, M. Michael, and Morton Weinfeld. 1983.** "Ethnicity." In *An Introduction to Sociology.* M.M. Rosenberg et al., eds. Toronto: Methuen.

**Rosenfeld, Rachel A. 1979.** "Women's occupational careers: Individual and structural explanations." *Sociology of Work and Occupations* 6:283–311.

**Rosenhan, D.L. 1973.** "On being sane in insane places." *Science* 179(Jan. 19):250–258.

**Rosenmayr, Leopold. 1977.** "The family: A source of hope for the elderly." In *Family, Bureaucracy and the Elderly.* Ethel Shanas and Marvin B. Sussman, eds. Durham, NC: Duke University Press.

**Rosenthal, Carolyn J. 1982.** "Family responsibilities and concerns: A perspective on the lives of middle-aged women." *Resources for Feminist Research* (Winter).

**Rosenthal, Carolyn J. 1985.** "Kinkeeping in the familial division of labor." *Journal of Marriage and the Family* 47(4):965–974.

**Rosenthal, Carolyn J. 1986.** "The differentiation of multigenerational households." *Canadian Journal on Aging* 5(1):27–42.

**Rosenthal, Carolyn J. 1987a.** "Aging and intergenerational relations in Canada." In *Aging in Canada: Social Perspectives.* Victor W. Marshall, ed. 2nd edition. Toronto: Fitzhenry and Whiteside.

**Rosenthal, Carolyn J. 1987b.** "Generational succession: The passing on of family headship." *Journal of Comparative Family Studies* 18:61–77.

**Rosenthal, Carolyn J. 1987c.** "The comforter: Providing personal advice and emotional support to generations in the family." *Canadian Journal on Aging* 6(3): 228–240.

**Rosenthal, Carolyn J., and Victor W. Marshall. 1986.** "The head of the family: Social meaning and structural variability." *Canadian Journal of Sociology* 11(2):183–198.

**Rosenthal, R., and L. Jacobson. 1968.** *Pygmalion in the Classroom*. New York: Holt, Rinehart and Winston.

**Rosow, Irving. 1967.** *Social Integration of the Aged*. New York: Free Press.

**Rosow, Irving. 1973.** "The social context of the aging self." *Gerontologist* 13(Spring):82.

**Rosow, Irving. 1974.** *Socialization to Old Age*. Berkeley, CA: University of California Press.

**Rosow, Irving. 1976.** "Status and role change through the life span." In *Handbook of Aging and the Social Sciences*. Robert H. Binstock and Ethel Shanas, eds. New York: Van Nostrand Reinhold.

**Rossi, Alice S. 1980.** "Life-span theories and women's lives." *Signs* 6:4–32.

**Roy, Donald. 1952.** "Quota restriction and goldbricking in a machine shop." *American Journal of Sociology* 57: 427–442.

**Roy, Donald. 1954.** "Efficiency and 'the fix': Informal intergroup relations in a piecework machine shop." *American Journal of Sociology* 60:255–266.

**Roy, Donald. 1959.** "Banana time: Job satisfaction and informal interaction." *Human Organization* 18(4):158–168.

**Royal Commission on Bilingualism and Biculturalism. 1965.** *Report*. Ottawa: Queen's Printer.

**Royal Commission on the Economic Union and Development Prospects for Canada. (Macdonald Commission.) 1985.** *Report* (Vols. 1–3). Ottawa: Supply and Services.

**Royal Commission on National Development in the Arts, Letters and Sciences. (Massey Report.) 1951.** Ottawa: Supply and Services.

**Royal Commission on the Status of Women in Canada. 1970.** *Report*. Ottawa: Information Canada.

**Rubin, J.Z., F.J. Provenzano, and Z. Luria. 1974.** "The eye of the beholder: Parents' views on sex of newborns." *American Journal of Orthopsychiatry* 44:512–519.

**Rubin, Lillian B. 1979.** *Women of a Certain Age: The Midlife Search for Self*. New York: Harper and Row.

**Rudé, George. 1967.** *The Crowd in the French Revolution*. New York: Oxford University Press.

**Ruether, Rosemary R. (ed.). 1974.** *Religion and Sexism: Images of Woman in the Jewish and Christian Traditions*. New York: Simon and Schuster.

**Rusche, George, and Otto Kirchmeimer. 1939.** *Punishment and Social Structure*. New York: Columbia University Press.

**Rushby, William, and John Thrush. 1973.** "Mennonites and social compassion." *Review of Religious Research* 15: 16–28.

**Russell, Peter. 1975.** "The political role of the Supreme Court of Canada in its first century." *Canadian Bar Review* 53(3):576–596.

**Ryan, William. 1971.** *Blaming the Victim*. New York: Pantheon.

**Ryder, Norman B. 1965.** "The cohort as a concept in the study of social change." *American Sociological Review* 30(6):834–861.

**Ryff, Carol D. 1986.** "The subjective construction of self and society: An agenda for life-span research." In *Later Life: The Social Psychology of Aging*. Victor W. Marshall, ed. Beverly Hills, CA: Sage.

**Sacco, V.F. 1985.** "City size and perceptions of crime." *Canadian Journal of Sociology* 10(3):277–293.

**Sanday, P.R. 1981.** *Female Power and Male Dominance: On the Origins of Sexual Inequality*. Cambridge, UK: Cambridge University Press.

**Sayers, Janet. 1982.** *Biological Politics: Feminist and Anti-Feminist Perspectives*. London: Tavistock.

**Scanzoni, John. 1982.** *Sexual Bargaining: Power Politics in the American Marriage*. 2nd edition. Chicago: University of Chicago Press.

**Scheff, Thomas. 1966.** *Being Mentally Ill: A Sociological Theory*. Chicago: Aldine.

**Schellenberg, James A. 1974.** *An Introduction to Social Psychology*. 2nd edition. New York: Random House.

**Schellenberg, James A. 1978.** *Masters of Social Psychology: Freud, Mead, Lewin, and Skinner*. New York: Oxford University Press.

**Schelsky, K. 1961.** "Family and school in modern society." In *Education, Economy, and Society*. A.H. Halsey et al., eds. Glencoe, IL: Free Press.

**Schlesinger, Benjamin. 1978.** *Remarriage in Canada*. Toronto: University of Toronto Press.

**Schlesinger, Benjamin. 1983.** "Living in one-parent families: The children's perspective." In *The Canadian Family*. K. Ishwaran, ed. Toronto: Gage.

**Schlossman, Steven. 1977.** *Love and the American Delinquent*. Chicago: University of Chicago Press.

**Schmidt, Wolfgang, Reginald Smart, and Marie Moss. 1968.** *Social Class and the Treatment of Alcoholism*. Monograph No. 7. Toronto: University of Toronto/Addiction Research Foundation.

**Schnaiberg, Allan, and Shelley Goldenberg. 1986.** "From empty nest to crowded nest: Some contradictions in the returning young-adult syndrome." Paper presented to the American Sociological Association.

**Schneider, Frank W., and Larry M. Coutts. 1979.** "Teacher orientations towards masculine and feminine: Role of sex of teacher and sex composition of school." *Canadian Journal of Behavioural Science* 11: 99–111.

**Schnore, Leo F. 1958.** "Social morphology and human ecology." *American Journal of Sociology* 63:620–634.

**Schreiber, E. 1980.** "Class awareness and class voting in Canada." *Canadian Review of Sociology and Anthropology* 17:37–44.

**Schulz, David A. 1984.** *Human Sexuality*. 2nd edition. Englewood Cliffs, NJ: Prentice-Hall.

**Schwenger, C.W., and M.J. Gross. 1980.** "Institutional care and institutionalization of the elderly in Canada." In *Aging in Canada: Social Perspectives*. Victor W. Marshall, ed. Toronto: Fitzhenry and Whiteside.

**Science Council of Canada. 1977.** *Uncertain Prospects: Canadian Manufacturing Industry, 1971–1977*. Ottawa: Supply and Services.

**Science Council of Canada. 1984.** *Canadian Industrial Development: Some Policy Directions.* Ottawa: Supply and Services.

**Scott, Joseph W., and M. El-Assal. 1969.** "Multiuniversity, university size, university quality and student protest: An empirical study." *American Sociological Review* 34:702–709.

**Scott, W. Richard. 1987.** *Organizations.* 2nd edition. Englewood Cliffs, NJ: Prentice-Hall.

**Scull, Andrew. 1977.** *Decarceration: Community Treatment and the Deviant—A Radical View.* Englewood Cliffs, NJ: Prentice-Hall.

**Seashore, Stanley E. 1954.** *Group Cohesiveness in the Industrial Work Group.* Ann Arbor, MI: University of Michigan, Survey Research Center.

**Seligson, Mitchell A. 1984.** "The dual gaps: An overview of theory and research." In *The Gap Between Rich and Poor.* M.A. Seligson, ed. Boulder, CO: Westview.

**Selznick, Philip. 1949.** *TVA and the Grass Roots.* Berkeley, CA: University of California Press.

**Sennet, Richard. 1970.** *The Uses of Disorder: Personal Identity and City Life.* New York: Vintage.

**Shanas, Ethel, with the assistance of Gloria Heinemann. 1982.** *National Survey of the Aged.* Publication No. OHDS 83–20425. Washington, DC: U.S. Department of Health and Human Services, Administration on Aging.

**Shanas, Ethel, et al. 1968.** *Old People in Three Industrial Societies.* New York: Atherton.

**Shapiro, Evelyn, and N.P. Roos. 1987.** "Predictors, patterns and consequences of nursing-home use in one Canadian province." In *Aging in Canada: Social Perspectives.* Victor W. Marshall, ed. 2nd edition. Toronto: Fitzhenry and Whiteside.

**Shaw, Marvin E., and Philip R. Costanzo. 1970.** *Theories of Social Psychology.* New York: McGraw-Hill.

**Sheehy, Gail. 1976; 1974.** *Passages: Predictable Crises in Adult Life.* Toronto: Clarke Irwin/New York: Dutton.

**Shibutani, Tamotsu, and Kian M. Kwan. 1965.** *Ethnic Stratification: A Comparative Approach.* New York: Macmillan.

**Sigelman, Lee. 1977.** "Multi-nation surveys of religious beliefs." *Journal for the Scientific Study of Religion* 16:289–294.

**Silberman, Charles. 1970.** *Crisis in the Classroom.* New York: Random House.

**Simmel, Georg. 1950a.** *The Sociology of Georg Simmel.* Kurt Wolff, ed. Glencoe, IL: Free Press.

**Simmel, Georg. 1950b.** "The metropolis and mental life." In *Neighborhood, City, and Metropolis.* Robert Gutman and David Popenoe, eds. New York: Random House.

**Simon, Julian L. 1981.** *The Ultimate Resource.* Princeton, NJ: Princeton University Press.

**Singer, Benjamin D. 1986.** *Advertising and Society.* Don Mills, ON: Addison-Wesley.

**Singer, J.L., and D.G. Singer. 1988.** "Some hazards of growing up in a television environment: Children's aggression and restlessness." In *Television as a Social Issue.* Stuart Oskamp, ed. Newbury Park, CA: Sage.

**Sjoberg, Gideon. 1960.** *The Preindustrial City.* Glencoe, IL: Free Press.

**Sjoberg, Gideon. 1973.** "The origin and evolution of cities." In *Cities: Their Origin, Growth and Human Impact.* (*Scientific American.*) San Francisco: W.H. Freeman.

**Skinner, B.F. 1953.** *Science and Human Behavior.* New York: Macmillan.

**Skogstad, Grace. 1980.** "Agrarian protest in Alberta." *Canadian Review of Sociology and Anthropology* 17(1):55–73.

**Smelser, Neil J. 1963.** *Theory of Collective Behavior.* New York: Free Press.

**Smith, Adam. 1937; 1776.** *The Wealth of Nations.* New York: Modern Library.

**Smith, C.W. 1985.** "Uncle dad." *Esquire* 103(Mar.):73–85.

**Smith, Denis. 1967.** "Prairie revolt, federalism and the party system." In *Party Politics in Canada.* H.G. Thorburn, ed. Scarborough, ON: Prentice-Hall.

**Smith, Dorothy E. 1974.** "Women's perspective as a radical critique of sociology." *Sociological Inquiry* 44:7–13.

**Smith, Dorothy E. 1975.** "An analysis of ideological structures and how women are excluded: Considerations for academic women." *Canadian Review of Sociology and Anthropology* 12(1):353–369.

**Smith, Dorothy E. 1977.** *Feminism and Marxism: A Place to Begin, A Way to Go.* Vancouver: New Star.

**Smith, Dorothy E. 1983.** "Women, the family and the productive process." In *Introduction to Sociology.* J. Paul Grayson, ed. Toronto: Gage.

**Smith, Douglas. 1982.** "Street level justice: Situational determinants of police arrest decisions." *Social Problems* 29:167–177.

**Smith, Douglas, and Christy Visher. 1980.** "Sex and involvement in deviance crime: A quantitative review of the empirical literature." *American Sociological Review* 45(4):691–701.

**Smith, Drake S. 1985.** "Wife employment and marital adjustment: A cumulation of results." *Family Relations* 34:483–490.

**Smith, Kathleen, Muriel Pumphrey, and Julian Hall. 1963.** "The 'last straw': The decisive incident resulting in the request for hospitalization in 100 schizophrenic patients." *American Journal of Psychiatry* 120(Sept.):228–232.

**Smith, Michael D. 1975.** "The legitimation of violence: Hockey players' perceptions of their reference groups' sanctions for assault." *Canadian Review of Sociology and Anthropology* 12(1):72–80.

**Smith, Michael D. 1979.** "Towards an explanation of hockey violence: A reference other approach." *Canadian Journal of Sociology* 4:105–124.

**Smith, Robert Paul. 1979.** "Kids, clubs, and special places." In *Socialization and the Life Cycle.* Peter I. Rose, ed. New York: St. Martin's.

**Smyth, J.E., and D.A. Soberman. 1976.** *The Law and Business Administration.* Scarborough, ON: Prentice-Hall.

**Snyder, David, and Charles Tilly. 1972.** "Hardship and

collective violence, 1830–1960." *American Sociological Review* 37:520–532.

**Sorokin, Pitirim. 1927.** *Social and Cultural Mobility.* New York: Free Press.

**Sorokin, Pitirim, and C.C. Zimmerman. 1929.** *Principles of Rural-Urban Sociology.* New York: Holt, Rinehart and Winston.

**Southard, Samuel. 1961.** *Pastoral Evangelism.* New York: Abingdon.

**Spanier, Graham B., and Frank F. Furstenberg, Jr. 1987.** "Remarriage and reconstituted families." In *Handbook of Marriage and the Family.* Marvin B. Sussman and Suzanne K. Steinmetz, eds. New York: Plenum.

**Spelt, Jacob. 1955.** *Urban Development in South-Central Ontario.* Toronto: Collier-Macmillan.

**Spelt, Jacob. 1973.** *Toronto.* Toronto: Collier-Macmillan.

**Spender, Dale. 1985.** *Man Made Language.* 2nd edition. London: Routledge and Kegan Paul.

**Spilerman, Seymour. 1976.** "Structural characteristics of cities and severity of racial disorders." *American Sociological Review* 41:771–793.

**Spitzer, Steven. 1975.** "Toward a Marxian theory of deviance." *Social Problems* 22:638–651.

**Srole, Leo. 1956.** "Social integration and certain corollaries." *American Sociological Review* 21:709–716.

**Stack, S. 1980.** "The political economy of income inequality: A comparative analysis." *Canadian Journal of Political Science* 13:273–286.

**Stanley, George F.G. 1960.** *The Birth of Western Canada: A History of the Riel Rebellion.* Toronto: University of Toronto Press.

**Stark, Rodney. 1971.** "Psychopathology and religious commitment." *Review of Religious Research* 12:165–176.

**Stark, Rodney, and William Sims Bainbridge. 1985.** *The Future of Religion.* Berkeley, CA: University of California Press.

**Stark, Rodney, and Charles Glock. 1968.** *American Piety.* Berkeley, CA: University of California Press.

**Statistics Canada. 1973.** *Education in Canada 1973: A Statistical Review for the Period 1960–1961 to 1970–1971.* Ottawa: Supply and Services.

**Statistics Canada. 1978.** *Historical Compendium of Education Statistics: From Confederation to 1975.* Ottawa: Supply and Services.

**Statistics Canada. 1981.** *Education in Canada 1980.* Ottawa: Supply and Services.

**Statistics Canada. 1984.** *Labour Force Annual Averages, 1975–1983.* Ottawa: Supply and Services.

**Statistics Canada. 1985a.** *Language in Canada.* Ottawa: Supply and Services.

**Statistics Canada. 1985b.** *Women in Canada: A Statistical Report.* Ottawa: Statistics Canada Catalogue No. 64–202.

**Statistics Canada. 1986.** *Education in Canada 1985.* Ottawa: Supply and Services.

**Statistics Canada. 1987.** "Report on the demographic situation in Canada, 1986." *Current Demographic Analysis* (Vol. 2). Ottawa: Supply and Services.

**Stebbins, Robert A. 1967.** "A theory of the definition of the situation." *Canadian Review of Sociology and Anthropology* 4:148–164.

**Steffensmeier, D. 1978.** "Crime and the contemporary woman: An analysis of changing levels of female property crime, 1969–75." *Social Forces* 57:566–584.

**Stephan, G.E., and D.R. McMullin. 1982.** "Tolerance of sexual nonconformity: City size as a situational and early learning determinant." *American Sociological Review* 47:411–415.

**Stephens, William. 1963.** *The Family in Cross-Cultural Perspective.* New York: Holt, Rinehart and Winston.

**Stephenson, Marylee (ed.). 1973.** *Women in Canada.* Toronto: New Press.

**Stines, Graham L., R.P. Quinn, and L.J. Shepard. 1976.** "Trends in occupational sex discrimination: 1969–1973." *Industrial Relations* 15(1):88–98.

**Stolnitz, George J. 1964.** "The demographic transition: From high to low birth rates and death rates." In *Population: The Vital Revolution.* Ronald Freeman, ed. New York: Anchor.

**Stone, Leroy O. 1967.** *Urban Development in Canada.* Ottawa: Dominion Bureau of Statistics.

**Stone, Leroy O., and Susan Fletcher. 1987.** "The hypothesis of age patterns in living arrangement passages." In *Aging in Canada: Social Perspectives.* Victor W. Marshall, ed. 2nd edition. Toronto: Fitzhenry and Whiteside.

**Storm, Christine, Thomas Storm, and Janet Strike-Schurman. 1985.** "Obligations for care: Beliefs in a small Canadian town." *Canadian Journal on Aging* 4(2):75–85.

**Stryckman, Judith. 1981.** "The decision to remarry: The choice and its outcomes." Paper presented to the Gerontological Society of America and the Canadian Association on Gerontology.

**Stryckman, Judith. 1987.** "Work sharing and the older worker in a unionized setting." In *Aging in Canada: Social Perspectives.* Victor W. Marshall, ed. 2nd edition. Toronto: Fitzhenry and Whiteside.

**Suchman, Edward. 1968.** "The hang-loose ethic and the spirit of drug use." *Journal of Health and Social Behavior* 9:146–155.

**Sudman, Seymour. 1976.** *Applied Sampling.* New York: Academic.

**Sudnow, David. 1965.** "Normal crimes: Sociological features of the penal code in a public defender office." *Social Problems* (Winter):255–276.

**Sullivan, Teresa A. 1983.** "Family morality and family mortality: Speculation on the demographic transition." In *Families and Religions.* William. V. D'Antonio and Joan Aldous, eds. Beverly Hills, CA: Sage.

**Sumner, William G. 1960; 1906.** *Folkways.* New York: Ginn.

**Supreme Court of Canada. 1981.** *The Supreme Court Decisons on the Canadian Constitution.* Toronto: James Lorimer.

**Surtees, R.J. 1969.** "The development of an Indian reserve policy in Canada." *Ontario History* 61:87–98.

**Sutherland, Edwin. 1924.** *Criminology.* Philadelphia: J.B. Lippincott.

**Sutherland, Edwin. 1949.** *White Collar Crime.* New York:

Dryden.

**Sykes, Gresham, and David Matza. 1957.** "Techniques of neutralization: A theory of delinquency." *American Sociological Review* 22:664–670.

**Symons, G.L. 1986.** "Careers and self-concepts: Managerial women in French and English Canada." In *Work in the Canadian Context.* Katherina L.P. Lundy and Barbara Warme, eds. 2nd edition. Toronto: Butterworths.

**Synge, Janet. 1977.** "The sex factor in social selection processes in Canadian education." In *Education, Change and Society.* Richard Carlton et al., eds. Toronto: Gage.

**Synge, Janet. 1980.** "Work and family support patterns of the aged in the early twentieth century." In *Aging in Canada: Social Perspectives.* Victor W. Marshall, ed. Toronto: Fitzhenry and Whiteside.

**Szelenyi, Ivan. 1972.** *Social Structure and the Housing System. (Tarsadalm: Struktura es Lakastrendszer.)* Budapest: Kandidatusi eretekezes.

**Szelenyi, Ivan. 1981.** "Structural changes and alternatives to capitalist development in the contemporary urban and regional system."

**Tannenbaum, Frank. 1938.** *Crime and the Community.* Boston: Ginn.

**Task Force on Canadian Unity. 1978.** *Report.* Ottawa: Information Canada.

**Tavris, Carol. 1988.** "Beyond cartoon killings: Comments on two overlooked effects of television." In *Television as a Social Issue.* Stuart Oskamp, ed. Newbury Park, CA: Sage.

**Tavris, Carol, and Carole Wade. 1984.** *The Longest War.* 2nd edition. San Diego, CA: Harcourt Brace Jovanovich.

**Taylor, Frederick W. 1947; 1911.** *Scientific Management.* New York: Harper and Row.

**Taylor, Ian, Paul Walton, and Jock Young. 1973.** *The New Criminology: For a Social Theory of Deviance.* London: Routledge and Kegan Paul.

**Taylor, Ian, Paul Walton, and Jock Young (eds.). 1975.** *Critical Criminology.* London: Routledge and Kegan Paul.

**Taylor, Norman W. 1964.** "The French-Canadian industrial entrepreneur and his social environment." In *French-Canadian Society* (Vol. 1). M. Rioux and Y. Martin, eds. Toronto: McClelland and Stewart.

**Tepperman, Lorne. 1975.** *Social Mobility in Canada.* Toronto: McGraw-Hill Ryerson.

**Terry, C., and M. Pellens. 1970.** *The Opium Problem.* Montclair, NJ: Patterson Smith.

**Theberge, Nancy. 1989.** "Women's athletics and the myth of female frailty." In *Women: A Feminist Perspective.* Jo Freeman, ed. 4th edition. Mountain View, CA: Mayfield.

**Thomas, Kauser, and Andrew Wister. 1984.** "Living arrangements of older women: The ethnic dimension." *Journal of Marriage and the Family* 46:301–311.

**Thomas, W.I. 1928.** *The Child in America.* New York: Knopf.

**Thomlinson, Ralph. 1965.** *Population Dynamics: Causes and Consequences of World Demographic Change.* New York: Random House.

**Thompson, Hunter. 1968.** *Hell's Angels.* New York:

Ballantine.

**Thompson, James D. 1967.** *Organization in Action.* New York: McGraw-Hill.

**Thompson, Warren, and David Lewis. 1965.** *Population Problems.* 5th edition. New York: McGraw-Hill.

**Thorndike, E.L. 1898.** *Animal Intelligence.* New York: Macmillan.

**Thorndike, E.L. 1913.** *The Psychology of Learning.* New York: Columbia University.

**Thorne, Barrie. 1983.** "An analysis of gender and social groupings." In *Feminist Frontiers: Rethinking Sex, Gender, and Society.* Laurel Richardson and Verta Taylor, eds. Reading, MA: Addison-Wesley.

**Thrasher, Frederic. 1927.** *The Gang.* Chicago: University of Chicago Press.

**Tienhaara, Nancy. 1974.** *Canadian Views on Immigration and Population: An Analysis of Post-War Gallup Polls.* Ottawa: Manpower and Immigration.

**Tillich, Paul. 1966.** *On the Boundary.* New York: Scribner's.

**Tilly, Charles. 1974.** "Ecological triangle." In *An Urban World.* C. Tilly, ed. Boston: Little, Brown.

**Tilly, Charles. 1976a.** *Sociology, history and the origins of the European proletariat.* Working paper 148. Ann Arbor, MI: University of Michigan, Center for Research on Social Organization.

**Tilly, Charles. 1976b.** "A travers le chaos des vivantes cités." In *Urbanism, Urbanization and Change.* P. Meadows and E. Mizurchi, eds. 2nd edition. Reading, MA: Addison-Wesley.

**Tilly, Charles. 1978.** *From Mobilization to Revolution.* Reading, MA: Addison-Wesley.

**Tilly, Charles. 1981.** *The Urban Historian's Dilemma: Faceless Cities or Cities Without Hinterlands?* Working paper 248. Ann Arbor, MI: University of Michigan, Center for Research on Social Organization.

**Tilquin, C., et al. 1980.** "The physical, emotional, and social condition of an aged population in Quebec." In *Aging in Canada: Social Perspectives.* Victor W. Marshall, ed. Toronto: Fitzhenry and Whiteside.

**Timberlake, James. 1963.** *Prohibition and the Progressive Movement: 1900–1920.* Cambridge, MA: Harvard.

**Tinbergen, Jan. 1976.** *Reshaping the International Order.* New York: Dutton.

**Tindale, Joseph A. 1980.** "Identity maintenance processes of old poor men." In *Aging in Canada: Social Perspectives.* Victor W. Marshall, ed. Toronto: Fitzhenry and Whiteside.

**Tindale, Joseph A. 1987.** "Age, seniority, and class patterns of job strain." In *Aging in Canada: Social Perspectives.* Victor W. Marshall, ed. 2nd edition. Toronto: Fitzhenry and Whiteside.

**Tindale, Joseph A., and Victor W. Marshall. 1980.** "A general conflict perspective for gerontology." In *Aging in Canada: Social Perspectives.* Victor W. Marshall, ed. Toronto: Fitzhenry and Whiteside.

**Tittle, C.R., W.J. Villemez, and D. Smith. 1978.** "The myth of social class and criminality: An empirical assessment of the empirical evidence." *American Sociolog-*

ical Review 43:643–656.

Tobin, Sheldon S., and Regina Kulys. 1980. "The family and services." In Annual Review of Gerontology and Geriatrics (Vol. 1). Carl Eisdorfer, ed. New York: Springer.

Toby, Jackson. 1974. "The socialization and control of deviant motivation." In Handbook of Criminology. Daniel Glaser, ed. Chicago: Rand McNally.

Toffler, Alvin. 1970. Future Shock. New York: Random House.

Toffler, Alvin. 1982. The Third Wave. New York: Bantam.

Tönnies, Ferdinand. 1957; 1887. Community and Society. (Gemeinschaft und gesellschaft.) New York: Harper Torch.

Torrance, Judy M. 1986. Public Violence in Canada, 1867–1982. Kingston and Montreal: McGill-Queen's University Press.

Treiman, D. 1978. Occupational Prestige in Comparative Perspective. New York: Academic.

Tresemer, Davis. 1975. "Assumptions made about gender roles." In Another Voice: Feminist Perspectives on Social Life and Social Sciences. Marcia Millman and Rosabeth Moss Kanter, eds. Garden City, NY: Doubleday Anchor.

Trigger, Bruce G. 1969. The Huron: Farmers of the North. New York: Holt, Rinehart and Winston.

Trist, E.L., and K.W. Bamforth. 1951. "Some social and psychological consequences of the Longwall method of coal getting." Human Relations 4:3–38.

Troeltsch, Ernest. 1931. The Social Teaching of the Christian Churches (2 vols.). New York: Macmillan.

Trow, Martin. 1961. "The second transformation of American secondary education." International Journal of Comparative Sociology 2:144–165.

Tsui, Amy Ong, and Donald J. Bogue. 1978. "Declining world fertility: Trends, causes, implications." Population Bulletin 33(4). Washington, DC: The Population Reference Bureau.

Tuan, Yi-Fu. 1974. Topophilia: A Study of Environmental Perception Attitudes and Values. Englewood Cliffs, NJ: Prentice-Hall.

Tuchman, Gaye. 1978. "Introduction: The symbolic annihilation of women by the mass media." In Hearth and Home: Images of Women in the Mass Media. G. Tuchman, Arlene Kaplan Daniels, and James Benet, eds. New York: Oxford University Press.

Tuchman, Gaye. 1979. "Women's depiction in the mass media." Signs 4:528–542.

Tumin, M. 1967. School Stratification: The Form and Functions of Inequality. Englewood Cliffs, NJ: Prentice-Hall.

Turk, Austin. 1969. Criminality and the Legal Order. Chicago: Rand McNally.

Turner, Ralph H. 1961. "Modes of social ascent through education: Sponsored and contest mobility." In Education, Economy, and Society. A.H. Halsey, ed. Glencoe, IL: Free Press.

Turner, Ralph H. 1962. "Role-taking: Process versus conformity." In Human Behavior and Social Processes: An Interactionist Approach. Arnold M. Rose, ed. Boston: Houghton Mifflin.

Turner, Ralph H., and Lewis M. Killian. 1972. Collective Behavior. Englewood Cliffs, NJ: Prentice-Hall.

Turrittin, Anton H., Paul Anisef, and Neil J. MacKinnon. 1983. "Gender differences in educational achievement: A study of social inequality." Canadian Journal of Sociology 8:395–419.

Tyree, A., et al. 1979. "Gaps and glissandos: Inequality, economic development, and social mobility." American Sociological Review 44:410–424.

Uhlenberg, Peter. 1980. "Death and the family." Journal of Family History 5:313–320.

Ujimoto, K. Victor. 1987. "The ethnic dimension of aging in Canada." In Aging in Canada: Social Perspectives. Victor W. Marshall, ed. 2nd edition. Toronto: Fitzhenry and Whiteside.

United Nations. 1984. The World Population Situation in 1983. Population Studies No. 85. New York: U.N., Department of International Economic and Social Affairs.

Vachon, M.L.S. 1979. "Identity change over the first two years of bereavement: Social relationships and social supports." Doctoral dissertation. Toronto: York University, Department of Sociology.

Vachon, M.L.S., et al. 1976. "Stress reactions to bereavement." Essence 1(1):23–33.

Valentine, V. 1980. "Native peoples and Canadians: A profile of issues and trends." In Cultural Boundaries and the Cohesion of Canada (Part 2). R. Breton et al., eds. Montreal: Institute for Research on Public Policy.

Vallee, Frank G., and John deVries. 1975. Data Book for the Conference on the Individual Language and Society. Ottawa: Canada Council.

Van den Berghe, Pierre. 1974. "Bringing beasts back in." American Sociological Review 39(6):777–788.

Van Stolk, Mary. 1983. "A harder look at the battered and abused child." In The Canadian Family. K. Ishwaran, ed. Toronto: Gage.

Vaz, E.W. 1965. "Middle-class adolescents: Self-reported delinquency and youth culture activities." Canadian Review of Sociology and Anthropology 2:52–70.

Veevers, Jean E. 1980. Childless by Choice. Toronto: Butterworths.

Verdon, Michel. 1980. "The Quebec stem family revisited." In Canadian Families: Ethnic Variations. K. Ishwaran, ed. Toronto: McGraw-Hill Ryerson.

Von Eschen, Donald, J. Kirk, and Maurice Pinard. 1971. "The organizational substructure of disorderly politics." Social Forces 49:529–544.

Wagley, Charles, and Marvin Harris. 1958. Minorities in the New World. New York: Columbia University Press.

Wakil, S. Parvez, C.M. Siddique, and F.A. Wakil. 1981. "Between two cultures: A study in socialization of children of immigrants." Journal of Marriage and the Family 43:929–940.

Waller, Irvin. 1974. Men Released from Prison. Toronto: University of Toronto Press.

Waller, Irvin, and Janet Chan. 1975. "Prison use: A Canadian and international comparison." Criminal Law Quarterly 47–71.

Wallerstein, Immanuel. 1974. The Modern World System. New York: Academic.

Wallis, Roy, and Steve Bruce. 1984. "The Stark-

Bainbridge theory of religion: A critical analysis and counter proposals." *Sociological Analysis* 45:11–28.

**Walter, E.V.** 1988. *Placeways: A Theory of the Urban Environment.* Chapel Hill, NC: University of North Carolina Press.

**Ward, Dawn, and Jack Balswick.** 1978. "Strong men and virtuous women: A content analysis of sex role stereotypes." *Pacific Sociological Review* 21:45–53.

**Waring, Joan.** 1976. "Social replenishment and social change." In *Age in Society.* Ann Foner, ed. Beverly Hills, CA: Sage.

**Warnock, John W.** 1970. *Partner to Behemoth.* Toronto: New Press.

**Warnock, John W.** 1974. "Metropolis/hinterland: The lost theme in Canadian letters." *Canadian Dimension* 10(2):42–46.

**Waters, H.F.** 1977. "What TV does to kids." *Newsweek* (Feb. 21):62–70.

**Watkins, M.** 1973. "The trade union movement in Canada." In *Canada Ltd.* R. Laxer, ed. Toronto: McClelland and Stewart.

**Webb, Eugene J., et al.** 1981. *Nonreactive Measures in the Social Sciences.* Boston: Houghton Mifflin.

**Webb, Stephen D., and John Collette.** 1977. "Rural-urban differences in the use of stress-alleviative drugs." *American Journal of Sociology* 83:700–707.

**Webb, Stephen D., and John Collette.** 1979. "Rural-urban stress: New data and new conclusions." *American Journal of Sociology* 84(6):446–452.

**Webber, Melvin.** 1963. "Order in diversity: Community without propinquity." In *Cities and Space: The Future Use of Urban Land.* L. Wingo, Jr., ed. Baltimore, MD: Johns Hopkins University Press.

**Weber, Max.** 1947. *The Theory of Social and Economic Organization.* A.M. Henderson and Talcott Parsons, transl. New York: Free Press.

**Weber, Max.** 1958a; 1921. *The City.* D. Martindale and G. Neuwirth, transl. New York: Free Press.

**Weber, Max.** 1958b; 1930. *The Protestant Ethic and the Spirit of Capitalism.* New York: Scribner's.

**Weber, Max.** 1963. *Sociology of Religion.* Boston: Beacon.

**Weber, Max.** 1968. *Economy and Society.* 2 vols. Guenther Roth and Claus Wittich, eds. Berkeley, CA: University of California Press.

**Weber, Max.** 1969. "Class, status, party." In *Structured Social Inequality.* C. Heller, ed. New York: Macmillan.

**Weinstein, Eugene A.** 1969. "The development of interpersonal competence." In *Handbook of Socialization Theory and Research.* David A. Goslin, ed. Chicago: Rand McNally.

**Weisstein, Naomi.** 1971. "Psychology constructs the female, or the fantasy life of the male psychologist." In *Roles Women Play: Readings toward Women's Liberation.* Michele Hoffnung Garskof, ed. Belmont, CA: Brooks/Cole.

**Wellman, Barry.** 1979. "The community question: The intimate networks of East Yorkers." *American Journal of Sociology* 84(5):201–231.

**Wellman, Barry, and Alan Hall.** 1987. "Social networks and social support: Implications for later life." In *Aging*

in Canada: Social Perspectives. Victor W. Marshall, ed. 2nd edition. Beverly Hills, CA: Sage.

**Wernick, Andrew.** 1987. "From voyeur to narcissist: Imaging men in contemporary advertising." In *Beyond Patriarchy.* Michael Kaufman, ed. Toronto: Oxford University Press.

**Westhues, Kenneth.** 1973. "The established church as an agent of change." *Sociological Analysis* 34:106–123.

**Westhues, Kenneth.** 1975. "Inter-generational conflict in the sixties." In *Prophecy and Protest.* Samuel D. Clark et al., eds. Toronto: Gage.

**Westhues, Kenneth.** 1978. "Stars and stripes, the maple leaf, and the papal coat of arms." *Canadian Journal of Sociology* 3:245–261.

**Westley, Frances.** 1978. "The cult of man: Durkeim's predictions and new religious movements." *Sociological Analysis* 2:135–145.

**White, James M.** 1987. "Premarital cohabitation and marital stability in Canada." *Journal of Marriage and the Family* 49:641–647.

**White, Morton, and Lucinda White.** 1962. *The Intellectual versus the City.* Cambridge: Harvard University Press.

**White, Terrence H.** 1977. *Organization Size as a Factor Influencing Labour Relations.* Ottawa: Royal Commission on Corporate Concentration.

**White, Terrence H.** 1978. *Power or Pawns: Boards of Directors in Canadian Corporations.* Toronto: Commerce Clearing House.

**Whitehurst, Robert N.** 1984. "The future of marriage and the nuclear family." In *The Family: Changing Trends in Canada.* Maureen Baker, ed. Toronto: McGraw-Hill Ryerson.

**Whyte, Donald.** 1966. "Religion and the rural church." In *Rural Canada in Transition.* M.A. Tremblay and W.J. Anderson, eds. Ottawa: Agricultural Economics Research Council of Canada.

**Whyte, William Foote.** 1943. *Street-Corner Society: The Social Structure of an Italian Slum.* Chicago: University of Chicago Press.

**Whyte, William Foote.** 1982. "Social inventions for solving human problems." *American Sociological Review* 47(1):1–13.

**Whyte, William H., Jr.** 1956. *The Organization Man.* New York: Simon and Schuster.

**Wilensky, Harold L.** 1960. "Work, careers, and social integration." *International Social Science Journal* 12:543–560.

**Wilensky, Harold L.** 1961. "Orderly careers and social participation: The impact of work history on social integration in the middle class." *American Sociological Review* 26:521–539.

**Wiley, N.** 1967. "America's unique class politics: The interplay of the labor, credit, and commodity markets." *American Sociological Review* 32:529–541.

**Willhoite, F.** 1976. "Primates and political authority." *American Political Science Review* 70(4):1110–1126.

**Williams, John E., and Deborah L. Best.** 1982. *Measuring Sex Stereotypes: A Thirty-Nation Study.* Beverly Hills, CA: Sage.

**Williams, Tannis MacBeth (ed.).** 1986. *The Impact of*

*Television: A Natural Experiment in Three Communities.* Orlando, FL: Academic.

**Williams, Thomas Rhys. 1983.** *Socialization.* Englewood Cliffs, NJ: Prentice-Hall.

**Williamson, Nancy E. 1976.** "Sex preferences, sex control, and the status of women." *Signs* 1:847–862.

**Wilson, Alan B. 1959.** "Residential segregation of social classes and aspirations of high school boys." *American Sociological Review* 24:836–845.

**Wilson, Bryan. 1975.** "The secularization debate." *Encounter* 45:77–83.

**Wilson, James Q. 1968.** "The police and the delinquent in two cities." In *Controlling Delinquents.* Stanton Wheeler, ed. New York: John Wiley.

**Wilson, Robert A., and David A. Shulz. 1978.** *Urban Sociology.* Englewood Cliffs, NJ: Prentice-Hall.

**Wilson, T.C. 1985.** "Urbanism and tolerance: A test of some hypotheses drawn from Wirth and Stouffer." *American Sociological Review* 50(1):117–123.

**Wilson, William J. 1987.** *The Truly Disadvantaged: The Inner City, The Underclass, and Public Policy.* Chicago: University of Chicago Press.

**Wimberley, Ronald C. 1971.** "Mobility in ministerial career patterns: Exploration." *Journal for the Scientific Study of Religion* 10:249–253.

**Winn, C. 1988.** "The socio-economic attainment of visible minorities: Facts and policy implications." In *Social Inequality in Canada.* J. Curtis et al., eds. Scarborough, ON: Prentice-Hall.

**Winn, Marie. 1977.** *The Plug-in Drug: Television, Children and the Family.* New York: Viking.

**Winn, Marie. 1983.** *Children without Childhood.* New York: Pantheon.

**Wirth, Louis. 1938.** "Urbanism as a way of life." *American Journal of Sociology* 44:3–24.

**Wister, Andrew V. 1985.** "Living arrangement choices among the elderly." *Canadian Journal on Aging* 4(3):127–144.

**Wister, Andrew V., and Laurel Strain. 1986.** "Social support and well-being: A comparison of older widows and widowers." *Canadian Journal on Aging* 5(3):205–220.

**Wolf, E. 1969.** *Peasant Wars of the Twentieth Century.* New York: Harper and Row.

**Wolf, Wendy C., and Neil D. Eligstein. 1979.** "Sex and authority in the workplace: The causes of sexual inequality." *American Sociological Review* 44:235–252.

**Wolfgang, Marvin, and Marc Riedel. 1973.** "Race, judicial discretion, and the death penalty." *Annals of the American Academy of Political and Social Science* 407 (May):119–133.

**Wood, James L., and Maurice Jackson (eds.). 1982.** *Social Movements: Development, Participation and Dynamics.* Belmont, CA: Wadsworth.

**Wood, Patricia. 1982.** "The environmental movement: Its crystallization, development and impact." In *Social Movements: Development, Participation and Dynamics.* J.L. Wood and M. Jackson, eds. Belmont, CA: Wadsworth.

**Worklife Report. 1987.** 5(5).

**Wright, Erik Olin. 1978.** *Class, Crisis and the State.* London: New Left.

**Wright, James D., and Sonia R. Wright. 1976.** "Social class and parental values for children: A partial replication and extension of the Kohn thesis." *American Sociological Review* 41:527–537.

**Wrong, D.H. 1961.** "The oversocialized concept of man in modern sociology." *American Sociological Review* 26(Apr.):183–193.

**Wuthnow, Robert. 1973.** "Religious commitment and conservatism: In search of an elusive relationship." In *Religion in Sociological Perspective.* Charles Glock, ed. Belmont, CA: Wadsworth.

**Wynne, Derek, and Tim Hartnagel. 1975a.** "Plea negotiation in Canada." *Canadian Journal of Criminology and Corrections* 17(1):45–56.

**Wynne, Derek, and Tim Hartnagel. 1975b.** "Race and plea negotiation: An analysis of some Canadian data." *Canadian Journal of Sociology* 1(2):147–155.

**Yinger, J. Milton. 1971.** *The Scientific Study of Religion.* New York: Macmillan.

**Yoels, William C., and David A. Karp. 1978.** "A social psychological critique of 'over-socialization': Dennis Wrong revisited." *Sociological Symposium* 24:27–39.

**Young, M., and P. Willmot. 1957.** *Family and Kinship in East London.* London: Routledge and Kegan Paul.

**Yussen, Steven R., and John W. Santrock. 1978.** *Child Development.* Dubuque, IA: Wm. C. Brown.

**Zerubavel, Eviatar. 1977.** "The French Republican calendar: A case study in the sociology of time." *American Sociological Review* 42(Dec. 6):870.

**Zerubavel, Eviatar. 1981.** *Hidden Rhythms: Schedules and Calendars in Social Life.* Chicago: University of Chicago Press.

**Zinsser, Hans. 1965; 1935.** *Rats, Lice, and History.* New York: Bantam.

**Zukin, Sharon. 1980.** "A decade of the new urban sociology." *Theory and Society* 9:539–574.

**Zureik, Elia T., and Robert M. Pike (eds.). 1975.** *Socialization and Values in Canadian Society* (Vol. 1). Toronto: McClelland and Stewart.

**Zusman, J. 1966.** "Some explanations of the changing occurrence of psychotic patients: Antecedents of the social breakdown syndrome concept." *Milbank Memorial Fund Quarterly* 64(1):1–2.

# Credits

## PHOTO CREDITS

Christina Andersen   47, 498
Bettman Archives   6, 8
Canapress   5, 10, 91, 132, 139, 217, 245, 257, 260, 349, 352, 380, 391, 393, 423, 439, 443, 454, 488, 501, 510, 515, 519, 523
   Wide World Photos   99
CHIN   34
*Globe and Mail*   378
Dick Hemingway   2, 30, 96, 158, 194, 250, 280, 342, 398, 506
Mary Lucier   60
Darren Macartney   133, 270
Masterfile   289, 329, 436
   Nick Boothman   150
   Dennis Hallinan   122
   Al Harvey   246
   Walter Hodges   318
   Roy Marsch   168
   Diana Obson Rasche   221, 283
   Joe Standart   237
   Mark Tomalty   490, 540
Barbara Mighton   80, 162
Miller Comstock   43, 109, 134, 248
   H. Armstrong Roberts   346
   M. Beedell   253
   D. Brereragen   561
   R. Chambers   468
   Robert Houser   290, 409
   Russ Kinne   555
   Michael Saunders   430
S.S.C. Photo Centre A.S.C.   203
   Pierre St-Jacques   165, 287, 331
   R. Vroom   394
Kirsten Taylor   83, 85, 228
Angie Vetere   464

## ART CREDITS

*COVER and UNIT I*
William Ronald   (Canadian b. 1926)
*Lake Placid Revue-A*, 1973
oil on cotton
121.9 × 121.9 cm.
Art Gallery of Ontario, Toronto

*UNIT II*
Alina Megami Matsumoto
*Sculptures*, 1987
painted plaster
Ontario College of Art, Toronto

*UNIT III*
André Lapine   (Canadian 1866-1952)
*Street Extension*
watercolour on paper
48.9 × 35.1 cm. (sight)
Art Gallery of Ontario, Toronto

*UNIT IV*
Alexandra Pennycook
acrylic on canvas
Ontario College of Art, Toronto

*UNIT V*
Mike Coscia
acrylic on canvas
Ontario College of Art, Toronto

*UNIT VI*
Claude Breeze   (Canadian b. 1938)
*Spacing #12*, 1975
acrylic on canvas with china marker
121.9 × 160 cm.
Art Gallery of Ontario, Toronto

# Index

## NAME INDEX

# SUBJECT INDEX